WHO'S WHO IN CHRISTIAN HISTORY

J. D. Douglas and Philip W. Comfort,
Editors

Donald Mitchell, Associate Editor

 Tyndale House Publishers, Inc.
WHEATON, ILLINOIS

Front cover and endsheet photo credits:
Catherine Booth: Courtesy of The Salvation Army Museum, Chicago, Illinois
Martin Luther: Courtesy of The Billy Graham Center Museum, Wheaton, Illinois
Jonathan Edwards: Courtesy of The Billy Graham Center Museum, Wheaton, Illinois
Mother Teresa: Religious News Service, New York
St. Francis of Assisi: The Crosiers, Minneapolis
Joan of Arc: The Crosiers, Minneapolis
Billy Sunday: Courtesy of The Billy Graham Center Archives, Wheaton, Illinois
Billy Graham: Courtesy of The Billy Graham Center Archives, Wheaton, Illinois
Dante's *The Divine Comedy:* Historical Pictures/Stock Montage

Unless otherwise noted, Scripture quotations are from the *Holy Bible*, King James Version.

Scripture quotations marked RSV are from the *Holy Bible*, Revised Standard Version, copyright © 1946, 1952, 1971 by Division of Christian Education of the National Council of Churches in the United States of America. All rights reserved.

Scripture quotations marked NIV are from the *Holy Bible*, New International Version®. Copyright © 1973, 1978, 1984 by International Bible Society. Used by permission of Zondervan Publishing House. The *"NIV"* and *"New International Version"* trademarks are registered in the United States Patent and Trademark Office by International Bible Society.

Scripture verses marked TLB are taken from *The Living Bible*, copyright © 1971 owned by assignment by KNT Charitable Trust. All rights reserved.

Scripture quotations marked NKJV are from the New King James Version. Copyright © 1979, 1980, 1982, Thomas Nelson Inc., Publishers.

Scripture quotations marked NRSV are from the New Revised Standard Version of the Bible, copyrighted, 1989 by the Division of Christian Education of the National Council of the Churches of Christ in the United States of America, and are used by permission. All rights reserved.

Library of Congress Cataloging-in-Publication Data

Who's who in Christian history / J.D. Douglas and Philip W. Comfort,
    editors ; Donald Mitchell, associate editor.
        p.   cm.
    ISBN 0-8423-1014-2
    1. Christian biography—Dictionaries.   I. Douglas, J. D. (James
Dixon)   II. Comfort, Philip Wesley.   III. Mitchell, Donald (Donald R.)
BR1700.2.W47   1992
270'.092'2—dc20
    [B]   92-8040

Printed in the United States of America

98 97 96 95 94 93 92
10 9   8   7   6   5   4   3   2

WHO'S WHO
·IN·
CHRISTIAN
HISTORY

CONTRIBUTORS

David Adeney
Dr. John N. Akers
Rev. C. F. Allison
Rev. Dan P. Amsler
Dr. Marvin Anderson
Dr. Brian G. Armstrong
Dr. Glen F. Arnold
Dr. Saphir P. Athyal
Dr. Paul M. Bassett
Dr. E. Beatrice Batson
Dr. Pierce Beaver
Dr. Paul M. Bechtel
Dr. Harold M. Best
Derrick C. Blanchette
Dr. J. Ronald Blue
Dr. Ian Breward
Dr. Geoffrey Bromiley
Dr. Colin Brown
Kenneth J. Bryer
Dr. Allen Cabaniss
Georgia A. Comfort
Dr. Philip W. Comfort
Richard W. Comfort
David Cornell
Dr. Jack R. Crawford
Dr. D. S. Cushman
Dr. Wayne A. Detzler
Paul E. Dorman
Dr. J. D. Douglas
Rev. Heinrich Eiler
Dr. Walter Elwell
Dr. C. Stephen Evans
Dr. Robert P. Evans
Dr. Mark Fackler
Dr. Hobert K. Farrell
Dr. Charles L. Feinberg
Dr. Tom Firak
Kenneth Foreman
Charles W. Forman, Jr.
Albert H. Freundt, Jr.
Dr. W. Robert Godfrey
Dr. Louis Goldberg

Dr. John A. Gratian
Dr. Donald Guthrie
Dr. Donald A. Hagner
Dr. Alan L. Hayes
Dr. Deborah Hayes
Dr. Walter Hearn
Carl Wayne Hensley
Ronald Hesselgrave
Cadmus Hicks
Rev. Norman Hillyer
Kenneth Hoglund
Dr. Donald Hoke
Dr. Edwin A. Hollatz
Dr. Arthur F. Holmes
Dr. Norman V. Hope
H. Wayne House
Dr. Dave M. Howard
Dr. David Huttar
Dr. Herbert Jacobsen
Dr. James E. Jennings
Dr. Lloyd A. Kalland
Dr. Herbert Kane
Hans Kasdorf
Dr. Thomas O. Kay
Dr. Clyde Kilby
Dr. William J. Kornfield
Dr. Donald M. Lake
Kathy Leid
Lucille Leonard
Dr. David E. Maas
John L. McKenzie
Dr. J. B. MacMillan
Norris Magnuson
Dr. George M. Marsden
Dr. D. C. Masters
George Mindeman
Dr. Chris Mitchell
Dr. Donald R. Mitchell
Dr. Samuel H. Moffett
Dr. Leon Morris
Virginia J. Muir
Donald Munson

Dr. Ronald Nash
Dr. John Newton
Dr. Mark A. Noll
Mark R. Norton
Dr. Wilbert Norton
Dr. Grant R. Osborne
Daniel Partner
Gladys J. Peterson
Dr. William Phemister
Dr. Richard V. Pierard
Dr. Austin H. Potts
Dr. W. Stanford Reid
George Riser
Joanne Riser
Doris Roethlesberger
Rev. Errol G. Rohr
Garth M. Rosell
Robert D. Shuster
Dr. Thomas H. Spence
Dr. Alva Steffler
Dr. Alan R. Tippett
Dr. Peter Toon
Edvard P. Torjesen
Dr. Richard L. Troutman
Dr. Susumu Uda
Dr. Peter Veltman
Rev. Robert Vonderlack
Dr. Arvin Vos
Dr. Howard F. Vos
Dr. Victor Walter
Dr. Robert E. Webber
Dr. David F. Wells
Carla Whitacre
Milton Winter

*Special thanks to the
following people for
their labor on this book:*
Lynne Bensinger
Jeremy P. Comfort
Timothy Olson
Margaret Partner
Kathy Stinnette

87399

INTRODUCTION

"The history of the world," wrote Thomas Carlyle, "is but the biography of great men."

We all owe much to pioneers—not only those who opened up the New World, but also the veterans of the faith throughout the centuries. Theirs is a story just as exciting, and those who dismiss history as boring have obviously never tried to come at it through biography.

We are the inheritors of a tremendous legacy that has been ill-acknowledged. By this neglect we deprive ourselves of a rich benefit. Here are thrilling accounts of courage, adventure, and endurance—tales of those early believers who stood up for their faith against kings who had no allegiance to the One Great King and believers who battled also against heretics seeking to undermine the true faith. Many of those heretics and rulers also find mention in this volume because they too loomed large on the stage of church history. So also did other figures who made contributions through music, philosophy, literature, painting, and other arts.

It is impossible to cover two thousand years of Christian biography adequately in one volume or to offer complete background information on each entry. Inevitably we are vulnerable to criticism about why some individual has been omitted when some lesser luminary finds place. We are mindful that one of Cicero's laws for a historian stipulates that "there should be no suspicion of partiality in his writing or of malice." We hope that the wide range of material presented here and the manner in which we have handled it will acquit us on both counts. The selection we have made is intended primarily to represent those men and women who made a lasting impact on Christian faith and experience. They followed "Jesus, the author and finisher of faith"—and yet "they, without us, are not complete." May their inspiring stories encourage us and our generation to run the race as they have run.

J. D. Douglas
Philip W. Comfort

ABBO (c. 945–1004)

Benedictine monk who as abbot of Fleury (France) reformed the monastery and learning there

Abbo began his monastic career at Fleury, but from 985 to 987 was in charge of a monastery at Ramsey in England. The next year he was chosen abbot of Fleury despite the preference of King Hugh Capet (reigned 987–996) for another candidate. After his installation, Abbo started reforms such as those taking place at the Benedictine monastery at Cluny.

An authority on philosophy, astronomy, and mathematics, Abbo is thought to have written a commentary on Aristotle's *Categories*. The earliest manuscript of Aristotle's *Analytics* was written about the same time at Fleury. Other writings by Abbo included a letter to two kings of France, Hugh Capet and his son Robert II (reigned 996–1031), that warned of the dangers of greed and heresy; a collection of canon laws; and brief *Lives* of ninety-one popes. Abbo was killed while arbitrating a dispute between monks in Gascony. C. HICKS

ABBOT, GEORGE (1562–1633)

Archbishop of Canterbury, 1611–1633

Born in Kent, Abbot graduated from Ox-ford and was master of University College, Oxford (1597–1609), dean of Winchester Cathedral (1600–1609), bishop of Lichfield, and bishop of London before moving to Canterbury in 1611. He served on the New Testament committee for production of the King James Version of the Bible. He was sympathetic to various Puritan demands for further reform in the national church, but preferred bishops to presbyters. Abbot's Calvinist sympathies were evident in his insistence that England have representatives at the Synod of Dort in 1618. His eventual fall from royal favor was related both to his theology and to an unfortunate accident. While out hunting in 1621 he accidentally shot a gamekeeper and so became a "man of blood," some said, and thereby disqualified himself from spiritual office. A commission of bishops was divided over the issue. King James I (reigned 1603–1625) supported Abbot. After Charles I had been crowned king in 1625, Abbot's influence was gradually eclipsed by a rising bishop, William Laud, who eventually succeeded him as archbishop of Canterbury. Among Abbot's writings is an *Exposition of the Prophet Daniel* (1600). P. TOON

ABELARD (ABAILARD), PETER
(1079–1142)

Medieval French philosopher, teacher, and theologian

Born in Brittany, Abelard studied with several of the great teachers of his day—including Roscelin (a rebel nominalist), William of Champeaux (an orthodox realist), and Anselm of Laon—at several locations in northern France, including Paris. Abelard first taught at Melun and Corbeil, and later at Paris. A bold and original thinker, he attracted large numbers to his lectures and counted many of the great minds of the twelfth century as his students, including Peter Lombard, John of Salisbury, and Otto of Freising. Many future leaders of Christendom were in attendance: several popes, twenty cardinals, and about fifty bishops.

While in Paris, Abelard lived at the house of Fulbert, who was the canon at Notre Dame. He fell in love with Fulbert's niece, Heloise, and a son was born to her. Abelard offered to marry her, but she thought it better to enter a convent since marrying would hamper Abelard's career in the church. Fulbert in retaliation ordered the castration of Abelard, who then retired to the monastery of St. Denis. The lifelong correspondence of Abelard and Heloise, known especially through her published Letters, has made the two of them classic figures among the world's lovers.

In 1121 Abelard was condemned by the Council of Soissons for heresy and was forced to seek refuge. He found asylum in the remote monastery of St. Gildas in Brittany, where he stayed for ten years and was abbot until the monks forced him to leave. Returning to Paris, he remained popular with students. New charges of heresy from Norbert of Premontre and Bernard of Clairvaux resulted in Abelard's condemnation by the church at the Council of Sens (1141) and the order to be silent. After a brief stay in a monastery, he began a journey to Rome to appeal his case. He stopped at Cluny where the abbot, Peter the Venerable, regarded Abelard's case as hopeless and advised him not to continue. Abelard died shortly thereafter and was buried at Troyes; eventually Heloise was buried beside him.

Abelard's training brought him into contact with two traditions of early scholastic thought, realism and nominalism. Abelard had difficulties with both and suggested an alternative, conceptualism—a meaningful "halfway house" to some, a heretical compromise to others. For Abelard there was reality both in the particular object and in the idea or universal (concept), although for Abelard the concept had reality only in the mind. His idea of reality caused his view of the Trinity to be regarded as heresy.

Further, Abelard had difficulty with church leaders because of his high regard for reason and its critical use in the study of theology and philosophy. Abelard, however, was not the forerunner of modern nationalism and atheism as some have judged. His own words attest that he was truly a Christian: "I do not want to be a philosopher if it means resisting St. Paul; I do not wish to be Aristotle if it must separate me from Christ." Abelard sought to evaluate and understand his faith in the light of reason. His motto, "I understand so that I might believe," reversed the order of Augustine of Hippo and Anselm of Canterbury. Abelard stressed the importance of reasoned experience. He also maintained that all persons should be able to read the Scripture and arrive at valid conclusions on their own.

Abelard's most important contribution was the establishment of a critical methodology for theology. In reaction against the unreasoning pietism of some of his fellow monks, he stressed the value of a more analytical approach to theology, having been pointed in that direction by Anselm of Laon. Abelard lined up conflicting authorities on both sides of 158 theological problems in his controversial work of 1123 entitled *Sic et Non (Yes and No)*. In an approach less dogmatic than Anselm's rationalism, Abelard cited contrasting texts from both the Bible and the church fathers without harmonizing them. His collection of alternative views, however, was prefaced with rules for resolving such problems by distinguishing various senses of the words used.

Abelard's disciple, Peter Lombard, continued that procedure in his *Sentences,* which became a standard textbook. For the next two hundred years, Abelard's approach influenced the scholastic method of debating alternative positions and citing conflicting arguments, as seen, for example, in the writings of Thomas Aquinas.

Abelard published a more thorough presentation of his theology as *Theologica Christiana* in 1123 and 1124. He also wrote an autobiography, *The Story of My Misfortunes,* as well as other theological and philosophical works. T. O. KAY & A. F. HOLMES

ABERDEEN DOCTORS

A group of six theologians in northeast Scotland who spoke out against the National Covenant of 1638

Three of the Aberdeen Doctors (John Forbes, Robert Baron, and William Leslie) were theological professors, and the other three (James Sibbald, Alexander Scroggie, and Alexander Ross) were ministers in the city. The group was so named because each of them had earned Aberdeen University's doctorate in divinity. They held that the National Covenant had not been published by the king or by any recognized authority, and that it distanced itself from "the practice of the ancient Church and much Reformed opinion." Their manifesto, *Generall Demands Concerning the Late Covenant,* pointed out that the Covenant was a very different thing from the Negative Confession of 1581 on which it claimed to be based, and was unnecessary because King Charles I had withdrawn the "innovations in religion" which had sparked off the protest.

The Aberdeen Doctors were men of learning and moderation, but this was an age of extremes. However courageous and reasonable an objection, it was unfashionable, even dangerous, to go against the tide in that time of turmoil and intense patriotism, and temperate men suffered accordingly. Chief spokesman of the Dissenters, professor of divinity John Forbes was made the main target because he opposed the Covenanters, whose aim was to overthrow epis-

copacy in Scotland. Forbes was deposed from his university chair and evicted from his residence which, formerly his own, he had given to the university. Later, when pressure was put on him to sign the complementary Solemn League and Covenant (1644), he felt compelled to leave for Holland where he spent two years. When he died, two years after his return to Scotland, his opponents even disallowed his last request that he be buried beside his wife and father. J. D. DOUGLAS

ABERHART, WILLIAM (1878–1943)
Canadian schoolteacher, radio evangelist, and politician

Born in Huron county, Ontario, Aberhart taught in Ontario (1898–1910) and in Calgary, Alberta (1910–1935). He was a 1906 graduate of Queen's University in Kingston, Ontario. Aberhart's career as a Bible teacher began in Calgary Protestant churches. He was instrumental in building the Prophetic Bible Institute in Calgary, a combination of Baptist church and Bible school. His radio Bible broadcasts, begun in 1925, eventually reached an estimated audience of 350,000.

During the depression of the early 1930s, Aberhart adopted the economic ideas of British engineer C. H. Douglas. Douglas thought the economy would recover if governments issued "social credit" to increase the purchasing power of the people. In 1932 Aberhart began including social credit ideas in his religious broadcasts, helping to found the Social Credit Party which came to power in the province of Alberta in 1935.

Elected premier of Alberta, Aberhart provided honest and efficient government, but was unable to apply his social credit theories because they were beyond the constitutional power of the Alberta provincial government.

Although his Social Credit Party was far from being a religious party, Aberhart himself was a significant example of an evangelical Christian in politics. He and such evangelical colleagues as E. C. Manning stressed the doctrine of sinners saved by grace, but they were also political activists. Aberhart and his colleagues were neoconservative opponents of socialism who advocated social reform within the framework of the free-enterprise system. D. C. MASTERS

ABRAHAM, BISHOP (1880–1947)
Church leader in India and bishop for thirty years in the Mar Thoma (St. Thomas) Church

Bishop Abraham was suffragan (second highest office) for twenty-six years and then metropolitan (main bishop) from 1943 to 1947. He was also called Abraham Mar Thoma. The Christian community in southwest India traditionally traces its origin to the work of the apostle Thomas in South India dating back to A.D. 52.

Abraham was born in Kallooppara in central Kerala, India's southernmost state. He committed himself to the Lord's service at the age of thirteen and was ordained at thirty. After theological training in Wycliffe College, Toronto, Canada (1911–1914), and a period of parish work, he was consecrated as bishop in 1917. He was an ardent missionary and evangelist who encouraged lay leadership in the church. He founded both the Voluntary Evangelists Association of lay people who volunteered to do systematic evangelistic work, and Sevika Sangam (Women Workers' Association) for evangelistic and social work. Besides recruiting many educated young men for the ministry, he was constantly engaged in conducting refresher courses for clergy and summer institutes for youth.

For twenty years Bishop Abraham served as president of the Mar Thoma Evangelistic Association (founded in 1888). He recruited national missionaries for pioneer work in most of the Indian states and in neighboring countries. In the Christian "ashrams" he helped establish, evangelists witnessed through simplicity of life, indigenous lifestyle, and identification with non-Christians. The Mar Thoma Church and its missionary program have always been supported entirely through indigenous funds. In place of fees levied by the church, Bishop Abraham encouraged tithing and the giving of offerings and firstfruits. S. P. ATHYAL

ACTON, JOHN EMERICH EDWARD DALBERG (1834–1902)
English historian and philosopher; chiefly remembered as the author of a frequently quoted aphorism: "Power tends to corrupt and absolute power corrupts absolutely."

Born in Naples (Italy), Acton was the son of an English baronet who died when the boy was only three. His German mother then married the future Lord Granville, who became British foreign secretary, a connection that introduced the stepson into a world of political liberalism. Since he was Roman Catholic and therefore barred from attending Cambridge University, Acton studied at Paris and at Munich (Germany). At Munich, under J. J. I. Von Döllinger, Acton learned the new German methods of historical research.

Acton traveled in many countries, including the United States, and then in 1859 entered parliament as a Liberal. In that year also he succeeded J. H. Newman as editor of the *Rambler* (later called the *Home and Foreign Review*), a Roman Catholic monthly. But he disagreed with Pope Pius IX over the relation of historical studies to theological doctrine and, convinced that limitations were being placed on journalistic independence, resigned his editorship in 1864. His parliamentary career was also brief, but because of his personal friendship with Prime Minister Gladstone, he continued to have influence on British politics. Gladstone made him a peer in 1869. In that year Acton went to Rome to organize resistance at Vatican Council I to the projected definition of papal infallibility. Unlike his friend Von Döllinger, he remained in the Roman Catholic Church when the dogma was promulgated.

Turning his attention to modern history, in 1886 Acton helped found the *English Historical Review*. Always interested in human liberty, he claimed that his liberalism was based firmly on Christianity. "I fully admit," he said, "that political rights proceed directly from religious duties." The dictates of conscience were to be regarded as above those of the state. One of his most significant statements, still relevant today, was that a country's freedom was to be judged by minorities. In 1895 he was appointed regius professor of history at Cambridge, where discriminations against Roman Catholics had finally been repealed. He was the key figure in the planning of *The Cambridge Modern History* (1901–1911), a project that broke his health and forced his retirement to family property in Germany, where he died. Lord Acton summed up his life thus: "The story of a man who started in life believing himself a sincere Catholic and a sincere Liberal; who therefore renounced everything in Catholicism which was not compatible with Liberty and everything in Politics not compatible with Catholicism." J. D. DOUGLAS

ADAM OF ST. VICTOR (c. 1110–c. 1180)

Latin hymn writer and poet of the Middle Ages

Very little is known of Adam's life, although he was probably born in Brittany (France). About 1130 he entered the monastery of St. Victor near Paris, the inhabitants of which were noted for their mysticism, austerity, and piety. Evidently he spent his entire life at St. Victor's.

Adam wrote at least fifty hymns, though scholars have suggested that more than one hundred can be identified as his. In addition he composed much of his own music. Adam's poetic ability was evidenced by extensive and skillful use of double and occasionally triple rhyme. Most of his hymns were written to instruct the faithful in piety through the examples of the lives of saints. Best known are those written for the services of Easter and St. Stephen; most of the others honor other saints. Adam's work has been criticized for being too concerned with form as well as for exaggeration and the use of difficult allusions. He made frequent references to Scripture, however, and he could say much in a few words. His poetry was not widely read in the post-Reformation era, but renewed interest in it developed in the late nineteenth century. T. O. KAY

ADDISON, JOSEPH (1672–1719)

English statesman, essayist, and hymn writer

Addison attended Queen's College and Magdalen College, Oxford, and won the attention of leaders in the Whig party, particularly the Earl of Halifax. In spite of the Whigs' changing fortunes, Addison eventually became secretary of state.

Addison is best remembered as an essayist in *The Spectator,* a periodical published daily from March 1 to December 6, 1711, and revived from June 18 to December 20, 1714. Addison contributed the majority of the 555 essays.

The tenth issue of *The Spectator* stated the aim of the editors: "to enliven morality with wit, and to temper wit with morality." To keep readers alert, Addison added, "I have resolved to refresh their memories from day to day until I have recovered them out of that desperate state of vice and folly into which the age is fallen." Banteringly but effectively, he held up to ridicule the prevailing manners and morals, such as those of individuals who collected books for show, theatergoers who indulged in catcalling, upper-class gentlemen who paraded their drunkenness, rakes and atheists who sneered at moral standards and Christian beliefs.

His essays showed no antagonism between good breeding and true religion ("Devotion," Nos. 201, 207; "Prayer," No. 391; "Faith," No. 465; "Temporal and Eternal Happiness," No. 575). In No. 494, Addison railed at long-faced, sour-looking Christians who mistook solemnity as the identifying mark of a believer. Number 267 was the first of a series of Saturday *Spectator* papers on Milton's *Paradise Lost* published over many weeks. Addison wanted to give the general public an intelligent understanding of Milton's masterpiece. Probably best known of Addison's hymns was "The Spacious Firmament on High," written in 1712. E. B. BATSON

ADOLPHUS, GUSTAVUS VASA II (1594–1632)

King of Sweden, 1611–1632

Born in Stockholm, the son of King Charles IX, Gustavus was educated as a Lutheran. When he became king at the age of seventeen, he first had to establish his right to the Swedish throne against a rival contender, his cousin Sigismund of Poland. After protracted wars and negotiations, Sigismund renounced his claim—though not that of his family—to the Swedish throne (treaty of Altmark, 1629). Gustavus then sought to consolidate and extend the territory over which he ruled. Under the Treaty of Stolbava made with Russia in 1617, more lands were ceded to Sweden, and Russia was excluded from the Baltic Sea and its trade. In 1630 Gustavus decided to intervene in the Thirty Years' War (1618–1648), the last and longest of the post-Reformation religious wars in Europe. His decision was motivated partly by his sincere concern for the Protestant cause and for the German Lutherans, then in danger of complete defeat by the Catholic forces of the Holy Roman emperor under the impetus of the Counter-Reformation. Gustavus also wanted to repel the imperialist advance which threatened Sweden's position on the Baltic. Landing in Germany, he sought to unite the Protestant princes of Brandenburg and Saxony behind him. The sacking of the city of Magdeburg in 1631 by Tilly, the Catholic emperor's veteran general, pointed up to those princes the dangers of neutrality. With John George of Saxony, Gustavus defeated Tilly at the battle of Breitenfeld. In 1632 Gustavus's army, by then Europe's most formidable military force, defeated the Catholic forces (under the mercenary general Wallenstein) at Lutzen. In the course of the battle Gustavus was killed, and the Swedish-Protestant cause lost direction and cohesion.

Gustavus was both a successful military commander and an enlightened king who improved educational and economic conditions in Sweden. N. V. HOPE

ADRIAN I (died 795)
Pope, 772–795

A Roman noble by birth, Adrian ruled longer than any other ancient or medieval Pope. He was a friendly partner with Charlemagne, both in creating the Carolingian Empire and in developing the papacy's temporal rule in northern Italy. Adrian and Charles's earliest joint effort was their greatest: complete defeat of the forces of Desiderius, King of the Lombards, in 774. This not only initiated the papacy's many centuries of Italian political rule, but also established the Western European–papal alliance that henceforth transcended any Eastern Church or Roman Empire connections.

Adrian had Charlemagne's explicit support against heresy, especially Adoptionism, a western Christological error. Most importantly, Charles also helped enforce Adrian's installation of the Gregorian Sacramentary, and other efforts toward uniformity in western Church liturgy and law. But Adrian and Charlemagne did conflict at times. The great king often failed to support his promises in the Donation of Pepin, the official entitlement of the papacy's Italian political authority. Probably due to a misunderstanding, Adrian also could not gain Charles's agreement to the anti-iconoclast decrees of the Council of Nicea, 787. Overall, Adrian appears to have been an upright leader who cultivated local church life along with his political interests. At least there was improvement in church buildings and other material provisions. Adrian died a much-respected figure. In a supreme compliment, Charles commissioned Alcuin to write Adrian's epitaph as the king's own personal expression. Most of the information on Adrian I comes from his various letters to Charlemagne. K. J. BRYER

ADRIAN IV (died 1159)
Pope, 1154–1159

Born Nicholas Breakspear, Adrian was the only Englishman to serve as bishop of Rome. He began life in or around St. Albans, but in his youth left England for study in France. After several years in Paris and Arles, Adrian entered St. Rufus, an Augustinian monastery near Avignon. He became abbot of St. Rufus in 1137, but soon Pope Eugenius II summoned him to the papal court.

Adrian's consecration as cardinal bishop of Albano (near Rome) occurred sometime before 1150. Needing an able reformer, Eugenius commissioned him as legate to the Scandinavian Church. Adrian's talents brought quick improvements in Norway and Sweden. The archbishopric he established at Troudheim, Norway, was an especially effective move. For all of Scandinavia, Adrian made reforms that proved to be valuable and enduring. Much acclaimed for his Scandinavian achievements, Adrian was elected to the papacy soon after his return to Rome. Yet his five years as pope were thorny ones, especially in the realm of political relations.

Immediately upon assuming office, Adrian faced Arnold of Brescia's insurrection in the city of Rome. The new pope placed Rome under an interdict. Soon the city leaders forced Arnold to surrender, and Adrian began actions to restore peace. Next he confronted opposition to William I of Sicily and his conquest of papal lands in southern Italy. Despite losing several battles, Adrian obtained a treaty in which William agreed to possess Naples, Salerno, and other cities under fealty to the pope and to make tribute payments to him. His relations with Frederick I (Barbarossa), the Holy Roman Emperor, were the most critical of Adrian's political conflicts. At their famous meeting at Sutri (north of Rome) in 1155, the pope forced Frederick to pay him homage and receive his crown as a papal benefice. The resentful Frederick refused to aid Adrian over Lombardian invasions or to support the pope's agreements with William I. And there were further repercussions a few years later. It was partly Frederick's smoldering anger toward Adrian that ignited the emperor's long, open break with Alexander III in the late 1100s.

Boso's biography, *Vita Adrianum*, and statements by John of Salisbury in *Policraticus* are the best sources of original information on Adrian IV. Other important sources are works by Matthew Paris, Gerald of Wales, William of Newburgh, and Otto of Freising. K. J. BRYER

AGGREY, JAMES (1875–1927)
Educator in Africa and the United States

Born in Anamabu in Ghana (then called Gold Coast), Aggrey came from a politically influential family in the Fanti Confederation. Heir to dignity, wisdom, and eloquence, he used these gifts to interpret one race to another on both sides of the world. He has been called an "apostle of cooperation," an indication of the significance of his career.

From childhood Aggrey had an intense hunger for education that never lessened. He became a schoolteacher in charge of his own school at age fifteen and the following year was permitted to preach. In 1898 he sailed to America where he studied at Livingstone College (North Carolina). After graduating with honors he became a professor at that college in addition to pastoring two nearby churches. He sought to ameliorate the economic difficulties of poor blacks in the rural south by establishing credit unions and introducing agricultural improvements.

Aggrey served on an Education Commission in Africa, then moved back to Ghana with his wife in 1924 to become vice principal of Achimota College. Three years later he returned to the U.S.; he died while working on a doctoral dissertation at Columbia University. J. A. GRATION

AGRICOLA, JOHANN SCHNEIDER (1494–1566)
German theologian and reformer

Born in Eisleben, Johann Schneider later took the name of Agricola. He studied under Martin Luther at Wittenberg, serving as his secretary at the Leipzig Disputation (1519). He adopted Luther's reformational views and became a Protestant minister, in time becoming a pastor and head of the school in Eisleben.

Agricola emphasized Luther's principle that Christians are under the gospel rather than under law, and as early as 1527 he was in controversy with Philip Melanchthon (Luther's colleague) about the place of the ten commandments in Christian experience— Agricola found no place for them. Agricola was taking some of Luther's earlier unguarded sayings and making a theology of them, to Luther's embarrassment. Luther called Agricola's position "antinomianism," that is, denial of any role of law in Christian living. By 1540 Agricola modified his views and became a court preacher and superintendent of churches in Brandenburg. He is of interest to literary historians as the first collector of German proverbs, which he published in 1528, 1529, and 1548. P. TOON

AGRICOLA, MIKAEL (c. 1510–1557)
Lutheran pastor, theologian, and educator; principal reformer of Finland

Probably the greatest name in the Finnish Lutheran Church, Agricola is not improperly called the "Finnish Luther." His contributions to Finnish religion and culture compare with those of Luther to German religion and culture.

Finland in the sixteenth century was under the control of Sweden. The coming of the Reformation to Finland was a part of the story of Sweden's break with the Roman Church. The strong, authoritarian Swedish King, Gustav I of the house of Vasa (1523–1560), broke with the church to gain political and economic control over his lands. But the break with Catholicism also had deep religious causes.

Lutheran preachers such as Olaus Petri proclaimed the Protestant message of God's grace in both Sweden and Finland. In Finland the king appointed a Lutheran sympathizer, Martinus Skytte, to the bishopric of Turku (Abo in Swedish), the highest office in the Finnish church. Skytte sent aspiring ministerial students to study under Luther at Wittenberg, and Agricola was among them. He had received his early education at Viipuri (Vyborg in Swedish) and Turku. Agricola's stay at Wittenberg made him a firm Lutheran. He began his ecclesiastical career as rector of the cathedral school in Turku and eventually became bishop of Turku, from which position he firmly secured the Lutheran Reformation in Finland. His were the first works published in the Finnish language, making him the father of Finnish as a literary medium. His writings included an introductory grammar (1542), devotional literature, and a translation of the New Testament (1548). Agricola's reforms were carried out with unusual moderation. The lasting success of his endeavors seems to testify to the wisdom of his methods. B. G. ARMSTRONG

AIDAN (died 651)
Celtic monk; first bishop of Lindisfarne

When King Oswald of Northumbria requested from the monastery at Iona a teacher of the Christian faith, the abbot sent a monk called Corman. He soon abandoned his mission, complaining it was impossible to evangelize "so rude a people." Aidan, a fellow monk who had joined the community about 630, suggested that Corman had expected too much and had forgotten Paul's teaching about "milk for babes." Aidan was appointed to fill the gap, was consecrated bishop in 635, and made his base on the island of Lindisfarne, just off the coast of England. Simple, humble, and gentle, he soon won the confidence of king and people. Initially he could not preach in the Saxon language, and the king sometimes accompanied him on many journeys on the mainland and acted as his interpreter to the crowds who flocked to hear him. He founded not only a monastic community, but a school for twelve English boys who would continue his work. The Venerable Bede was so impressed with Aidan's accomplishments that he put him ahead of Augustine of Canterbury as "the true apostle of England." J. D. DOUGLAS

AILRED (or AELRED) (1109–1167)
Anglo-Saxon abbot who expressed his faith in God through a poetic mysticism

Best known as a devotional writer in the tradition of Bernard of Clairvaux (France), Ailred wrote his first work, *Speculum Caritatis* (the Mirror of Love) at the request of Bernard. Because of the spiritual depth of his writings, he came to be called the "Bernard of the North" (that is, of northern England).

In his meditations Ailred was particularly concerned with Jesus Christ the suffering Savior, and thus in his writings he often dwelt on the suffering humanity of Jesus the

Man. He adapted the *De Amicitia* (On Friendship) by the Roman writer Cicero to Christian usage by relating friendship to the love of Christ. Also, after attending the canonization of King Edward the Confessor in Westminster Abbey, London, Ailred wrote a biography of him in 1161.

Apart from his literary career, Ailred also held high office in the Cistercian order. He entered the Cistercian abbey at Rievaulx in Yorkshire (England) when he was about twenty-four years old. He became master of the novices at Rievaulx and then became abbot at Revesby, Lincolnshire, from 1143 to 1147, at which date he was recalled to Rievaulx as abbot. Most of the details of his life come from a biography written by his pupil, Walter Daniel. P. TOON

AINSLIE, PETER (1867–1934)
American ecumenist

Ainslie, a minister of the Christian Church (Disciples of Christ), pastored a large church in Baltimore, Maryland, for most of his life, but was better known for his labors on behalf of Christian unity. Ainslie's life spanned the period of the Restoration (or "Christian") Movement, out of which came the more open Disciples of Christ. Alexander Campbell (1788–1866), an early leader of the Restoration Movement, had proposed a unity of all believers around what he saw as simple New Testament Christianity. Ainslie led the way in applying that idea in the modern ecumenical movement. He edited the *Christian Union Quarterly* for many years and was president of the Association for the Promotion of Christian Unity from 1910 to 1925. His many books arguing for cooperation among believers included *The Message of the Disciples for the Union of the Church* (1913). Said Ainslie, "Henceforth let no man glory in his denomination; that is sectarianism; but let men glory in Christ and practice brotherhood; that is Christianity." M. A. NOLL

AINSWORTH, HENRY (1571–1622)
English Old Testament scholar; church reformer

Educated at Caius College, Cambridge, Ainsworth believed that the church should be separated from the state. That conviction, both rare and heretical in Elizabethan England, forced him to escape persecution by fleeing to Holland, a more tolerant country, where several English "separatist" congregations were to be found. In Amsterdam Ainsworth served as teacher for a congregation pastored by Francis Johnson, since they held that each congregation should have both a teacher and a pastor (see Eph. 4:11, KJV). The church was congregationally governed until Johnson came to believe that it should be ruled by elders. In 1610 Ainsworth reluctantly led about thirty members away to form a new congregation. As an exiled separatist, Ainsworth attacked the principles not only of the Church of Rome but also of the Church of England, which for him was insufficiently reformed. As a biblical scholar he established a European reputation by his *Annotations* on the books of Moses, Psalms, and Song of Solomon. Though a separatist and an early teacher of congregationalist principles, Ainsworth was neither an Anabaptist nor a Puritan. He opposed Baptist principles and disagreed with Puritans over the idea of a national church. P. TOON

AKIBA (AQIBA, AKIVA), RABBI
Jewish leader, fl. 110–135

Akiba came from a humble background and began his scholarly training at the age of forty. Having attained recognition in rabbinical study, he taught at his own school in Bene Berak, near Jaffa. During the Jewish uprising against the Romans in A.D. 132 to 135, Akiba was arrested for teaching the Jewish laws and willingly suffered a martyr's death. He had strongly supported the revolutionary leader Bar Kochba, believing him to be the long-awaited Messiah. Akiba's rabbinical activities fall into three categories.

1. Canon of the Old Testament. Akiba was at Jabneh (Jamnia) when discussions were being held there (c. A.D. 90) concerning books to be included in the Old Testament

and those to be left out. The discussions were less concerned with admitting new books than with reaffirming the canonical status of books that had come into question, especially Ecclesiastes and the Song of Solomon. Concerning the Song of Solomon, whose literal interpretation some may have regarded as too sensual for Scripture, Akiba said, "All the writings are holy, but the Song is Holy of Holies."

2. Oral law. Following a plan worked out by others, Akiba began collecting and systematizing the confusing mass of oral law. Oral law had been developed by the rabbis as a means of applying the written law of the Old Testament to life-situations not dealt with in the Old Testament itself. The materials were organized into six main books (orders), each further divided into tractates. This arrangement of the oral law was completed in the early part of the third century A.D. by Rabbi Judah Nasi, and it became the basis of the Mishna and later of the Talmud, the standard body of Jewish law (which still did not contain all legal opinions.)

3. Principles of Biblical Interpretation. Rabbi Ishmael held that the language of Scripture was to be treated as ordinary human language (that is, it followed the same grammar, word meanings, etc.). In contrast, Akiba insisted that Scripture was to be interpreted in a way that was not applicable to ordinary language. Ordinary language might allow different spellings of the same word with no difference in meaning, for example; but if such a thing happened in Scripture, to Akiba there had to be some reason. Other schools of interpretation accused him of twisting the language of Scripture to force his own interpretations on Scripture. Akiba encouraged a scholar named Aquila to make a translation of the Old Testament into Greek which would embody his principles of interpretation. Aquila's translation was therefore over-literal; because it disregarded standard principles of grammar, it cannot be said to be real Greek. D. HUTTAR

ALACOQUE, MARGUERITE MARIE (1647–1690)

French nun of the Visitandine Order who promoted popular devotion to the "Sacred Heart" of Jesus and influenced Catholic devotional practices

Alacoque was born at Lauthecourt as the fifth child of a royal notary and had little formal education. After the death of her father, she suffered from illness and from difficulties with relatives. In 1671, at the age of twenty-four, she entered the Visitandine Convent at Pary-le-Monial. Her experience of a series of revelations over the next four years convinced her that she had been commissioned by Christ to encourage devotion to his Sacred Heart. This devotion was to be expressed by the regular observance of the Holy Hour (an hour of prayer and meditation on Jesus' sufferings), the partaking of the Communion of Reparation on the first Friday of each month, and by celebration of a special feast day in honor of the Sacred Heart. Considerable controversy centered around Alacoque's activities, but devotion to the Sacred Heart was eventually recognized and spread widely among Roman Catholics. Marguerite was beatified by Pope Pius IX in 1864 and canonized by Benedict XV in 1920. D. R. MITCHELL

ALAIN (ALAN) OF LILLE (1125–c. 1203)

French Roman Catholic philosopher and theologian

Alain attended the University of Paris, continued there as a scholar, and later became a Cistercian monk living at Citeaux, France, until his death. His theological writings were a positive assertion of Christian thought to counter the challenge of heretical and Muslim thought of his day. Alain maintained that reason must be used to convince unbelievers, since they would not be convinced by the authority of Scripture.

The *Art of Catholic Faith* and *Catholic Faith Against the Heretics* were his main efforts to construct a deductive theology following certain rules of method which were almost mathematical in character. Alain hoped that unbelievers would be defeated by the "art of faith" rather than the "art of war." His arguments prefigured in concept and form the work of Raymond Lull a century later. *Anti-Claudian*, a refutation of paganism, and *The Lament of Nature* were masterful, poetic allegories setting forth the medieval view of nature. The former has been compared with similar works of Dante and Milton. Alain viewed nature as subordinate to God, knowable through the human intellect. Being above nature, God can be known only through faith. Alain's encyclopedic mind led to his being called "Universal Doctor." T. O. KAY

ALBERT OF BRANDENBURG
(1490–1545)
Member of the important Hohenzollern family of North Germany

The Hohenzollerns had their power base in Brandenburg and were contesting with Saxony for dominance in the area. In 1513, Albert, youngest brother of elector Joachim of Brandenburg and first cousin of Albert of Prussia, began accumulating even greater power for the Hohenzollerns. He was appointed bishop of Halberstadt as well as archbishop of Magdeburg, the latter a position previously held by Saxons. Even more important, the following year he was made archbishop of Mainz. In that position he was an elector of the so-called Holy Roman Empire—that is, he was one of seven princes of Germany who had the privilege of electing the political leader of the country, the Holy Roman emperor. With the electoral votes of Brandenburg and Mainz, the Hohenzollerns were becoming a dominant power.

Albert, however, was technically not eligible for these high offices because of his age. Also, church law forbade multiple occupation of high ecclesiastical offices by one person. But the pope agreed to overlook the legal problems if Albert would pay him a huge sum of money. Albert borrowed the money from the wealthy and powerful Fugger banking house of Augsburg. Then, to enable Albert to raise money to pay his debts, and to raise money to build the new St. Peter's Church in Rome, Pope Leo X authorized an "indulgence" which Albert was permitted to have preached and sold in his dioceses. (An indulgence was an official church provision by which a penitent sinner could purchase from the pope a remission of the punishment for temporal sins—sins that would otherwise have to be atoned for in purgatory. Indulgence benefits were even extended to departed souls supposedly already in purgatory.)

Albert commissioned a Dominican monk, John Tetzel, as the indulgence preacher. Tetzel's crassly mercenary sermons were successful in filling church coffers but aroused the anger of conscientious people. Among those offended was an Augustinian monk, Martin Luther, who drew up his Ninety-five Theses in opposition in 1517. Thus began the protest that led to the Protestant Reformation.

It is somewhat ironic that Albert was a key figure in causing the Reformation, for he was a "Renaissance man," a lover and patron of the arts and learning. Initially he seemed to support Luther's reform ideas, but his position changed as the Reformation increasingly progressed in his lands and thereby reduced his power. Eventually he allied with the Reformation's most inveterate opponents in North Germany—his brother Joachim, elector of Brandenburg, and Duke George of Saxony. But the progress of the Reformation continued, and Albert lost both influence and fortune. The Hohenzollern family's push for ascendancy was temporarily frustrated. Albert of Brandenburg's main legacy remained the sumptuous Renaissance buildings he had constructed in Mainz and Halle.
B. G. ARMSTRONG

ALBERT OF PRUSSIA (1490–1568)
German political figure of the Reformation period

In 1526, Albert established the new Lutheran Church as the official religion of East Prussia. He was of the house of Hohenzollern, a powerful noble family of North Germany destined to play an important role later in German history.

Albert became sovereign of East Prussia in 1511 when he was elected Grand Master of the Teutonic Knights. The Knights were a religious order created for military activity during the period of the Crusades. After serving in the Crusades, the Knights were given the task in the thirteenth century of converting by the sword the heathen tribes on the shores of the Baltic. Their success led the Holy Roman Emperor to make the order's Grand Master a prince of the empire, and, by implication, ruler of their lands of conquest. Defeated by Poland in the fifteenth century, the Grand Master lost all territory except East Prussia, which had to be recognized as a Polish fiefdom.

As Grand Master, Albert attempted to gain independence from Poland, but failed. Seeking allies against Poland, he attended the Diet of Nurnberg (1522) where he heard the sermons of a Lutheran reformer, Andreas Osiander, and was converted. After consulting with Luther, Albert abolished the religious function of the Teutonic Knights and made himself duke of their now secular holdings (East Prussia). East Prussia became a Lutheran territory with Albert as bishop. To support the new church, Albert founded the University of Königsberg in 1544 and called Osiander there as theology professor. Osiander's theological views caused a great deal of turmoil, but nevertheless Albert's secularized state grew in power and influence. When the other branch of the Hohenzollern family in Brandenburg also adopted Lutheranism, the Brandenburg-Prussia axis became an important element of Protestant strength in North Germany.
B. G. ARMSTRONG

ALBERTUS MAGNUS (1193–1280)
German theologian and thinker who earned for himself the title "Doctor of the Church"

Born in Bavaria, Albertus entered the newly founded Dominican order in Padua (Italy) in 1223. He taught in a number of Dominican schools in Germany (1228–1245), then at Paris (1245–1248) and Cologne (1248–1255), where he had Thomas Aquinas as his student. One of his last efforts was to defend Aquinas's theology in Paris in 1277 after the death of Aquinas in 1274.

Albertus mastered Aristotle's thought, which had a profound effect on the church through Aquinas. He also read the Jewish thinkers Gabirol and Maimonides, as well as Arab philosophers (Averroes, Avicenna, and Algazel) who brought Aristotelian philosophy in Arabic to Europe through Spain, where it was later translated into Latin. Albertus, though, did not accept certain ideas in Averroes's thought which could not be adopted in a Christian framework (for example, that God was separated from the world except for intelligences emanating from God; and that matter is eternal).

Albertus's writings laid the groundwork for future generations of scholars. He wrote twenty-one volumes, primarily commentaries on Aristotelian philosophy and the beginnings of a theological system based on Aristotle. He also wrote commentaries on the *Sentences* of Peter Lombard and on a number of biblical books. A careful student of nature, he wrote a treatise based on Aristotle's prescientific works on nature; some of his ideas were brilliant and were later substantiated by scientific inquiry. Because he studied nature, Albertus was often accused of neglecting theological pursuits. Because he sought to be exhaustive in his writings, his thought often digressed and was not presented in a logical manner. But he was careful to distinguish what was ascertained by revelations, pointing to the limitations of rational thought. He regarded revelation as primary in testing any thought (for example, philosophy cannot explain the triunity of God), although he did engage in speculative discussion. He adopted the same approach toward the existence of God. By drawing upon Aristotle and attempting to synthesize a philosophy and theology, Albertus Magnus insisted that human knowledge could be used to discover divine mysteries. L. GOLDBERG

ALBRIGHT, JACOB (1759–1808)
Founder of the Evangelical Association, one of several forerunners of what is today the United Methodist Church

Born to German Lutheran immigrant parents in Pennsylvania, by the age of thirty Albright had fought in the last years of the American Revolution and had earned a local reputation as a successful farmer and honest tile-maker. His religious life had been uneventful. For most Americans the early years after the revolution were spiritually barren. Albright, however, was brought to an active commitment to Christ through a severe shock in his personal life. In 1791 several of his children died suddenly. The sermon at the funeral of one of his children aroused his conscience. Shortly thereafter, Albright came in contact with a "class" of local Methodists and developed an intense concern for the gospel. He was soon licensed as a lay preacher, but held back from active preaching because he lacked confidence in his educational preparation.

Finally in 1796 Albright's burden for Pennsylvania's large German population overcame his reluctance, and he began to preach widely. By 1800 enough Germans had responded to Albright's preaching to form three small "classes." In 1803 the "Albright People," as they were called, formally ordained their leader, and in 1807 the group's first conference was held. At that time these "German Methodists" (another of their nicknames) had five traveling ministers, three ministers in towns, and a total membership of two hundred. Albright was named the group's bishop. The official name chosen was "The Newly Formed Methodist Conference." The name was appropriate because the new group held views very similar to the Methodists. It took steps, in fact, to join the Methodist Episcopal Church. Albright and Francis Asbury, the early leader of America's Methodists, were on friendly terms, but Albright's denomination did not join the Methodists in his lifetime. The Methodists were unwilling to have a German-speaking body permanently in their midst. After that rebuff, Albright's group called themselves "The Evangelical Association."

By 1808 Albright had worn himself out with constant traveling and died of tuberculosis. His association (later called the Evangelical Church), was organized into classes and conferences. It preached a doctrine of salvation along lines laid down by John Wesley and Francis Asbury, providing strong evangelical preaching and warm spiritual fellowship for many German-speaking Americans. Years later, in 1968, a merger with the Methodists finally occurred when the Evangelical United Brethren Church (from a 1946 merger of the Evangelical Church with the United Brethren Church) joined with the Methodist Church to form the United Methodist Church. M. A. NOLL

ALBRIGHT, WILLIAM FOXWELL
(1891–1971)
American pioneer in biblical archaeology

Known as the "dean" of Palestinian archaeologists, Albright had unparalleled influence on biblical studies in America and abroad. Under his directorship the American School of Oriental Research (ASOR) in Jerusalem became a universally recognized center of research and learning. After studying under Paul Haupt at the Johns Hopkins University, Albright later taught there for thirty years as the W. W. Spence Professor of Semitic Languages.

Albright was born to Methodist missionary parents in Coquimbom, Chile. After receiving his A.B. from Upper Iowa University in 1912 and spending one year as a high school principal in Menno, South Dakota, he began graduate work. In 1916 he was awarded the Ph.D. in Semitic languages from Johns Hopkins University. In 1919, after a short stint in the army, he became a Thayer Fellow at ASOR. He served as acting director (1920), then as director (1921–1929) of the school (now named the Albright Institute of Archaeological Research). In 1929 he became a professor at Johns Hopkins and from 1933 to 1936 served both at Johns Hopkins and at ASOR. He conducted four campaigns of excavation at Tell Beit Mirsim (1925–1933), still a model of excellence in excavation. He was editor of ASOR's *Bulletin* from 1931 to 1968 and vice-president and trustee for over thirty years. Albright married Ruth Norton (Ph.D. in Sanskrit from Johns Hopkins) in

Jerusalem in 1921. After retiring from Johns Hopkins in 1958, he served as a visiting professor at numerous institutions.

Albright's bibliography contains over a thousand titles, including more than a dozen books of his own and still others on which he collaborated. His many doctoral students found his range of personal and scholarly interests remarkable. He insisted on accuracy of data and logical reasoning. His work blended the natural sciences and the humanities, chiefly Hebrew religion and Greek philosophy. Albright moved from an initially skeptical attitude toward the accuracy of the Old Testament to an insistence on the substantial historicity of the Mosaic record and the antiquity of Israelite monotheism. He is considered one of the originators of Near Eastern pottery chronology.

Albright maintained close contact with scholars throughout the world. Among his close friends were the archaeologist Père L. H. Vincent in Jerusalem and Cardinal Bea, the pope's confessor, in Rome—Albright himself was a Protestant. He was a loyal friend of the state of Israel from 1948 until his death. Many of his students are in prominent academic positions and are sometimes called the "Albright School." Albright received many honors, including twenty-eight doctorates from schools in America, Europe, and the Near East—Protestant, Catholic, and Jewish. In 1969 he was accorded Israel's highest honor, the title "Nobleman of Jerusalem." C. L. FEINBERG

ALCUIN OF YORK (c. 732–804)

English scholar who became adviser to Charlemagne

Alcuin preferred to be called by his Latin name, Albinus. Born at York (England), he was educated at the cathedral school there and was taught by Aelbert, later archbishop of York. Alcuin succeeded him in 766 as head of the school, remaining for about four years. Then Charlemagne, king of the Franks, whom Alcuin met while visiting Parma in 781, persuaded him to leave England and come to his court. Alcuin was made head of the abbeys of Ferrieres and

Saint-Loup. Alcuin's major duty, as Charlemagne saw it, was to make the monks of his kingdom familiar with the Latin language, culture, and theology which had been lost over the previous century. Alcuin did his task so well that he is regarded as the most prominent figure in the Carolingian renaissance (the revival of classical learning under Charlemagne).

After a brief return to England, Alcuin was called back by Charlemagne to overcome the attractive but heretical teaching of Felix of Urgel, who held the erroneous view of the sonship of Jesus Christ known as Adoptionism. (Felix was eventually condemned at the Council of Frankfurt in 794 and the Synod of Aachen in 799). Two years later, Charlemagne, by then Holy Roman emperor, made Alcuin abbot of the Abbey of St. Martin of Tours, where he remained until his death. The remodeled abbey school began to attract many students.

Alcuin developed a handwriting known as Caroline Minuscule to copy manuscripts. He wrote on educational matters, theology, the Bible, the eucharist, and liturgy in general. In England a society known as the Alcuin Club is named after him; its general purpose is to promote the study of liturgy (the worship of God by the church). P. TOON

ALEANDER, GIROLAMO (1480–1542)

Diplomat of the Roman Catholic Church during its struggle with Luther

Born in the Venetian Republic (Italy) into a well-to-do burgher family, Aleander was schooled in theology and medicine at Padua and Venice. In early life he was associated with a brilliant circle of humanists congregated around the printing press of Aldus Manutius at Venice. There in 1506 and 1507, Erasmus, the Dutch humanist scholar, was his roommate. Aleander, renowned for his skill in Latin, Hebrew, and Greek, taught those languages for many years at the University of Paris. In 1519 Pope Leo X appointed him director of the Vatican Library. A year later he became one of two special envoys from the pope to Holy

Roman Emperor Charles V to help put an end to Martin Luther.

Aleander was totally dedicated to the cause of the Roman Church and was unprincipled in his efforts to secure the destruction of Luther (and perhaps of Erasmus as well). Aleander's dispatches from Germany, now in the Vatican library, present a lively account of the intense popular support for Luther. According to those letters, Aleander pressed Charles V for action by bribing, threatening, and cajoling, and finally persuaded him to issue an edict in his lands that Luther's books be burned. Luther was called before the political assembly (diet) of the empire to be condemned. At that diet, held at Worms (1521), Luther won the hearts of the Germans. Aleander, however, drew up an edict declaring Luther an outlaw and calling for his arrest and execution. Although Luther himself escaped, Aleander was responsible for the execution of two Lutherans in Brussels, two of the first Protestant martyrs. Aleander was later rewarded for his services by being made an archbishop and a cardinal. He eventually retired to Venice, where he died. B. G. ARMSTRONG

ALESIUS, ALEXANDER (1500–1565)
Scottish Lutheran reformer

Born Alexander Alane in Edinburgh, Alesius graduated in arts from St. Andrews in 1515 and subsequently became a canon in the priory there. He won ecclesiastical approval by a stout defense of the old faith against the views of Martin Luther, and in 1528 he was chosen to reclaim the young Patrick Hamilton who had become infected with Lutheran views. Alesius, however, also became influenced, for the aristocrat's faithful testimony so moved him that he felt as if "the morning star were rising in his heart." After Hamilton was executed (the first martyr of the Reformation in Scotland), Alesius found his own position untenable because of his superior's opposition and immorality. Alesius was imprisoned for almost a year, then fled to Germany where he became an intimate friend of Luther and Melanchthon (who gave him the name Alesius).

Armed with a letter of recommendation from Melanchthon, Alesius visited England about 1535. He was warmly welcomed by the English reformers and by Henry VIII who obtained for him a teaching post at Cambridge University. (He may have been the first to give lectures on the Hebrew Scriptures there). But when the king again veered toward Roman Catholic opinions, Alesius felt in 1540 that the time had come for him to return to Germany. A sound and persuasive scholar, he taught first at Frankfurt-on-the-Oder (in what was later Prussia), then at Leipzig University where the last twenty-one years of his life were fruitfully spent. He published many theological treatises and was continually active in the Reformation cause. He accompanied Melanchthon to the colloquies of Worms (1540–1541) and Ratisbon (1541), and it seems likely that he was the first Scot to meet John Calvin, the European reformer who was to have profound influence on Scotland. The Reformation in Scotland was achieved five years before Alesius died, but because of his age or the fact that his old St. Andrews enemies were still active, he never again visited his native land. Alesius's contribution to the Reformed cause in Scotland has not been fully appreciated.
J. D. DOUGLAS

ALEXANDER (died 328)
Bishop of Alexandria in Egypt, 313–328

Two major conflicts of the early church began in Alexandria and were underway when Alexander was bishop. The first was a threat by Melitius of Lycopolis to Alexander's authority over the churches of Egypt and Libya. During the persecution under the Roman emperor Diocletian (245–305), Peter, then bishop of Alexandria, had been lenient with those who denied the faith. Melitius had formed a split-off church in reaction, and his schismatic group continued to give problems to later bishops. The second conflict began with Arius, a presbyter in Alexandria, who taught that Christ was not eternal but was created by the Father. Arius was condemned by Alexander at a council in Alexandria (about 321), but Arius's views continued to spread rapidly in the eastern church because several prominent bishops there held the same view.

The major surviving works of Alexander are seventy letters recorded by several eastern church historians. The letters are directed against the teaching of Arius; they lack the clarity of Arian writings, however. Alexander taught that the Father and Son are inseparable realities and that they are not different. The Son is begotten, and he is the only begotten God. Alexander did not speculate on the divinity of Christ; he affirmed it as a matter of faith.

The Roman emperor Constantine called the council of Nicea (325) to settle the Melitian and Arian issues and to bring unity to the church. Before the council met, Alexander had already won to his position the court bishop Hosius of Cordova (Spain). Constantine, whose views were guided by Hosius, took part in the debate and his will prevailed. The creedal outline of Alexander and his followers was adopted, and Arius was condemned. Although 318 bishops out of 320 signed the creed, peace and unity were not achieved because of ambiguity in the bishops' understanding of the creed. In 335, the emperor ordered Alexander's successor, Athanasius, to restore Arius to his former position because he had eventually signed the creed (with a few private additions). However, Arius died before that order could be carried out. J. NEWTON

ALEXANDER II (died 1073)
Pope, 1061–1073

Named Anselm, Alexander was born of noble Italian parentage in Baggio (near Milan). He studied under Lanfranc at Bec, and at ordination he already was a vocal advocate of Church reform. Sent to the court of Holy Roman Emperor Henry III, Alexander used his position to spread reform ideas in Germany. In 1057 his obvious gifts brought him appointment as bishop of Lucca (northern Italy). In this capacity, he spent much time with Peter Damian and Hildebrand, the era's two most outspoken Church reformers.

Soon, in 1061, the College of Cardinals' reformist wing obtained his election as pope. This choice immediately provoked deep conflict with Roman nobles and the Holy Roman Empire, the latter being ruled by Agnes, regent for her minor son, Henry IV. Holding out for imperial authority over papal elections, these forces installed Honorius II as pope and tried to depose Alexander. Honorius, however, could not attract support, and eventually, his death in 1072 ended his opposition.

During Alexander's twelve-year reign, he pursued his Church-renewal aims vigorously. He had four main objectives: eradication of simony, enforcement of clerical celibacy, rejection of royal investiture, and imposition of strict marriage rules. Occupied constantly with legations and synods, Alexander's actions on these matters were very firm. Recalcitrant Church leaders, even prominent archbishops, were summoned to Rome for discussions. After varied warnings, the archbishop of Milan was deposed for his opposition. Alexander's program had the respect, if not full submission, of Philip I of France and William I of England. In return, the pope supported William's conquest of England and also Roger of Normandy's subjugation of Sicily. It was Alexander who blessed the selection of Lanfranc, his former mentor, as archbishop of Canterbury. After 1066, however, when Henry IV assumed control, the empire's conflicts with the papacy greatly increased. In 1069, Alexander did stop Henry from divorcing his wife, Bertha, through Peter Damian's intervention. But, at Alexander's death, the basic dispute over investing Milan's bishopric was still intense. This discord epitomized the Church conditions and chief reform issue that Alexander left his successor, the great Hildebrand, Gregory VII. His papacy also opposed the mistreatment of Spanish Jews and promoted military action against Islamic forces. K. J. BRYER

ALEXANDER III (died 1181)
Pope, 1159-1181

Born to a Siena, Italy, family, Alexander's

name was Orlando Bandinelli. He showed much brilliance as a student. Fulfilling this promise, Alexander achieved eminence as a University of Bologna specialist in Canon law. Eventually he published two works: *Summa magistri Rolandi,* a commentary on Gratian's *Decretum,* and *Sententiae Rolandi,* a theological work following Abelard's views. In 1150, Pope Eugenius III brought Alexander to Rome and the papal court. Rising quickly, he became a cardinal deacon, cardinal priest, and finally papal chancellor. From 1154 to 1159, Alexander was Pope Adrian IV's closest advisor. He supported Adrian's insistence that Frederick I, the Holy Roman emperor, held his office as a papal benefice. In response, Frederick was adamant that the emperor must have independent authority. Fueled by this disagreement, the emperor's enmity with Adrian and then Alexander continued for years. The conflict affected most of Alexander's remaining days.

The cardinals unhesitantly elected Alexander pope on Adrian's death. But just as quickly, Frederick made efforts to obtain a papacy favorable to his policy. The emperor was able to gather churchmen at Pavia, Italy, for another election. Responding forcefully, Alexander declared such proceedings usurpacious, excommunicated the emperor, and removed the papacy from Rome and Frederick's troops. Unabashed, Frederick had his man, Victor IV, installed as pope. The subsequent papal-imperial rift was a protracted seventeen-year schism. Throughout this time, Alexander kept out of Frederick's range—mainly by moving around in France. He was forced also to contend with four antipopes; nonetheless, Alexander had the Church's respect as a whole. Military reversals forced Frederick's reconciliation with Alexander in the Treaty of Venice, 1177. Though escaping a general pledge of fealty, Frederick now agreed to honor Alexander as pope and respect his general Church sovereignty. Alexander was able to reside in Rome his last four years.

Remarkably, despite exile-like conditions, Alexander's twenty-two-year reign saw immense amounts of Church business being conducted. Yet very largely, this was ines-

capable due to the Church courts' increasingly broad role in western European life. Alexander's wisdom in countless cases— many highly complex, some needing new law—made his papacy truly extraordinary. Nonetheless, the dispute in England between Henry II and Archbishop Becket sorely tested his judicial ability. As the dispute proceeded, the pope refused both Becket's full vindication and most of Henry's jurisdictional claims. In 1170, the two finally consented to a reconciliation. A sound compromise might have ensued had Becket's murder not occurred.

Alexander presided over Lateran Council III, which formalized the two-thirds rule for papal elections by the cardinals, ordered that every Cathedral establish a school for clergy, and condemned the Catharist heresy prevalent among the Albigensians. Alexander gave the Waldensians respectful treatment and encouraged their poverty vows. But he also prohibited public preaching by the group. Not long thereafter, the Waldensians also were adjudged heretics.

While his papacy saw much drama, Alexander's great mark on Church history had other grounds. This came through his common tasks as the Church's chief jurist. Unmistakably, it was his day-by-day decisions—his judgments on political, economic, and social cases by the hundreds— that became Alexander's most historic labor. First, his insight into complex human problems, particularly as to social structures, was exceptional. For handling knotty ethical dilemmas, no pope in history had superior gifts. Alexander came at a critical time, years when moral and social custom, after decades of flux, were crying for establishment. Moreover, western Europe's respect for Christian moral doctrine, and adjunct social norms, was now at a peak. From betrothal custom to slave possession, from loan practices to indigent aid, many of Western society's crucial issues had Alexander's attention. Alexander's decisions became critically important due to their prominence in the Canon law.

Many of Alexander III's letters are reproduced in Migne's *Patrologia Latina.* Edited

by Duchesne, a contemporary biography by Boson exists in the *Liber Pontificalis*.
K. J. BRYER

ALEXANDER, ARCHIBALD (1772–1851)
American Presbyterian minister and educator

Born near Lexington, Virginia, of Scots-Irish parentage, Alexander studied at Liberty Hall (now Washington and Lee University) and pursued theological studies under William Graham, its principal. Licensed in 1791 and ordained in 1794, he served as a traveling minister in the Ohio-Virginia frontier area, then was elected president of Hampden-Sydney College in 1796. In 1807 he became minister of the large Third Presbyterian Church (also called Pine Street Church) in Philadelphia. That same year he was elected moderator of the Presbyterian General Assembly. In his retiring address from the moderator's chair in 1808 he suggested the establishment of a theological seminary "for the single purpose of educating youth for the ministry." The General Assembly of 1809 appointed a committee to consider the idea and present it to the presbyteries. The majority favored establishment of a single school centrally located. Accordingly, the General Assembly of 1811 voted to establish what was called "The Theological Seminary of the Presbyterian Church in the U.S.A." at Princeton, New Jersey. Alexander was the first professor in the new theological school, later to be joined by Samuel Miller and Charles Hodge. Combining in an unusual degree both personal piety and sound scholarship, he gave Princeton Seminary an excellent start as a Presbyterian school of quality and influence.
N. V. HOPE

ALEXANDER OF HALES (c. 1170–1245)
First Franciscan professor of theology at the University of Paris

Alexander was born in Hales in western England, studied in Paris, and became known as the "greatest master in theology and philosophy" because of the breadth and profundity of his work. A major contribu-

tion of his was helping to open the way for Franciscan participation (notably by the Italian theologian Bonaventure) in the Scholastic renaissance that occurred around the middle of the thirteenth century.

Alexander brought the Christian theology of earlier thinkers such as Augustine, Anselm, and John of Damascus together with the philosophy of Aristotle. Alexander recognized the tensions between Christian and pagan thought, but also the constructive contributions that rational inquiry could make to Christianity. In fact, anti-intellectual hostility to technical theological study he ascribed to Satan, who did not want Christians to have cultivated minds. More specifically, philosophical reasoning could demonstrate the existence of God from the contingency of created things and could discover something of his power and wisdom. But while analogies existed, for example, between the triune nature of God and his creatures, God was unique in being indivisibly one. For doctrines such as that of the Trinity, then, the Christian must depend on revelation.

Most of Alexander's writings consisted of summary notes on the views, questions, and arguments discussed in his teaching. A more systematic *Summa of Brother Alexander* used to be attributed to him, but is now believed to be a later compilation of his work plus that of various other members of the Franciscan order. It has value, however, as a presentation of the Augustinian tradition underlying thirteenth century Franciscan theology. To his religious order, Alexander of Hales contributed not only a lifetime of Christian scholarship but also a thoughtful voice of leadership. He coauthored, for example, an exposition of the famous *Rule of St. Francis* by which the Franciscans were governed. A. F. HOLMES

ALFORD, HENRY (1810–1871)
Church of England minister; New Testament scholar

Born into a long line of Anglican clergymen, Alford lived with his widowed father in Wiltshire. Having shown remarkable talent in classical languages and in history, at the age of eighteen he entered Trinity College, Cambridge. Following a brilliant undergraduate career, he was ordained in 1833 as assistant to his father. Two years later he married and became vicar of Wymeswold in Leicestershire, where, along with his pastoral concerns, he continued scholarly research and even produced several books of poetry: *The School of the Heart* (1835) and *The Abbot of Muchelnaye* (1841). Alford returned to Cambridge in 1841–1842 as a visiting lecturer, giving the prestigious Hulsean Lectures on the doctrines of redemption. Moving from his rural isolation in 1853, he became minister of the fashionable Quebec Chapel in London and four years later became dean of Canterbury. He stayed at Canterbury until his death, executing moderate reforms at the cathedral.

Alford translated the *Odyssey* (an ancient Greek epic poem) into blank verse, edited a literary journal called *The Contemporary Review* (1866–1870), wrote music for piano and organ, and composed a number of hymns, including "Come, Ye Thankful People, Come" and "Ten Thousand Times Ten Thousand."

He is best known for his four-volume commentary on the New Testament in Greek (1849–1861). Placing before English readers the latest continental research on the meanings of Greek words, he led the way from the traditional homiletical commentary toward a more exegetical approach. Although weak in spots, Alford's careful commentary on the Greek text of the New Testament was often reprinted and is still useful. P. TOON

ALFRED THE GREAT (849–899)
Early English king

Ruler of Wessex, Alfred faced two major challenges during his career: invasions by the Danes and the ignorance of his people. The wars with the Danes came in three cycles. The first began in 865 when Halfdan and Ivar led an invasion of England and ended in 878 with Alfred's victory over the Danes at Eddington. As a consequence, Guthrum, the Danish leader in the south, agreed to be baptized a Christian and to lead his forces out of Wessex. A second phase began when the Danes besieged the town of Rochester in 884 and 885. Alfred broke the siege and went on to retake London in 886. After that event England was formally divided between the Danes and the English, with the Danes holding Northumbria, East Anglia, Eastern Mercia, and Essex. The final phase of the Danish wars lasted from 893 to 896. During that period the Danes three times marched westward across England and three times were compelled by Alfred's forces to retreat to their own territory. For the last three years of his reign Alfred enjoyed relative peace. By that time, he had laid the foundations for the English army and navy.

Desiring to revive learning in England, Alfred gathered scholars around himself and learned how to translate the writings of great Christian thinkers into the language of the common people. The most notable scholars were Asser, who taught Alfred Latin and wrote his *Life*; Plegmund, who became archbishop of Canterbury; Werferth, who translated the *Dialogues* of Pope Gregory the Great (540–604) into Anglo-Saxon; Grimbald; and John from Europe. The works that Alfred is personally credited with translating are *Pastoral Care* by Gregory the Great, a manual for the training of priests; Orosius's *History Against the Pagans*; Boethius's *The Consolation of Philosophy,* a work that was not explicitly Christian but became so in Alfred's translation; and the *Soliloquies* of Augustine of Hippo.

In addition to the translation work, Alfred encouraged learning by setting up a palace school in which the sons of noblemen were trained. He also founded two monasteries. Alfred's Christian piety was deep. Twice during his youth he had gone to Rome to see the pope. As an adult he endeavored to devote half his time and money to religious purposes. C. HICKS

ALLEN, RICHARD (1760–1831)
Founder of the African Methodist Episcopal Church, which became one of America's most vigorous black denominations

Born a slave, Allen was converted at the age of seventeen under Methodist preaching. He immediately began to preach the gospel himself, first to his family, then to his master (who was converted), and finally to blacks and whites throughout America. Allen taught himself to read and write, and then after much hard work was able to purchase his freedom.

After working at several trades, all the time preaching as a layman, he arrived in Philadelphia at the age of twenty-six. With several other blacks he worshiped regularly at St. George's Methodist Church. One Sunday in 1787 a distressing incident drove the blacks from that congregation. While Allen's friend, Absalom Jones, was praying publicly, white trustees of the church forced him to his seat in an effort to keep him quiet. In response, Jones, Allen, and the other blacks left the church. Shortly thereafter, Allen and Jones founded the Free African Society, America's first organization established by blacks for blacks. The nonsectarian society provided mutual aid and spiritual encouragement to Philadelphia's black community. Four years later Jones and Allen left the Society, and Jones eventually became the founder of the Negro Episcopal Church. In 1793 Jones and Allen led other blacks in providing aid to the entire population of Philadelphia during a severe epidemic of yellow fever. Also in 1793 Allen established Bethel Church (Philadelphia) for Negro Methodists. He himself was ordained a Methodist minister in 1799. Because of uneasiness in the predominantly white Methodist church, Allen's congregation and other black Methodist churches organized their own denomination, the African Methodist Episcopal Church, and Richard Allen became its first bishop in 1816. He served this growing body of black Methodists as its widely respected leader until his death in 1831. M. A. NOLL

ALLEN, ROLAND (1868–1947)

Modern missionary strategist

Allen's books published in the early part of the twentieth century continue to have great impact and to be reprinted along with the most current missionary works. As an Anglican clergyman, Allen served as a missionary in China from 1895 to 1903 with the Society for the Propagation of the Gospel. Thereafter he served as a voluntary clergyman in England and from time to time abroad.

Allen's main thesis was that national churches should be self-supporting, self-governing, and self-propagating. He believed that lengthy dependence on foreign missionaries was counterproductive, stifling the people's own genius. If the world were ever to be reached with the gospel, he believed, it would be done through a multiplying national church that had taken root and grown in its own cultural soil. Allen perceived that foreign missionaries and subordinate national workers could never complete the evangelistic task.

Allen's most significant writings included *Missionary Methods: St. Paul's or Ours?* (1912, 1927), *The Spontaneous Expansion of the Church and the Causes which Hinder It* (1927), and *The Case for Voluntary Clergy* (1930). W. J. KORNFIELD

ALLINE, HENRY (1748–1784)

Nova Scotian evangelist

Born at Newport, Rhode Island, of Congregational parents, Alline went to Falmouth, Nova Scotia in 1760. After a conversion experience in 1775 he began a preaching career that lasted until his death. His central message was the need for salvation through the new birth. He was the principal instigator of the New Light Movement in the Canadian maritime colonies, which led to the decline of the Congregational Church in the Maritimes and to great strength for the Baptists. Alline gave tremendous impetus to evangelical Christianity in the Maritimes. D. C. MASTERS

ALLIS, OSWALD THOMPSON (1880–1973)

American Old Testament scholar who strongly defended the authority and integrity of the Old Testament

Allis was born in Wallingford, Pennsylvania, graduated from the University of Pennsylvania (1901), Princeton Theological Seminary (1905), and Princeton University (1907), and received a Ph.D. from the University of Berlin (1913). Allis was on the faculty of Princeton Theological Seminary (department of Semitic philology) from 1910 until 1929. He edited the *Princeton Theological Review* from 1918 to 1929.

In 1929, concerned about liberal trends in the Presbyterian Church, U.S.A., Allis joined with J. Gresham Machen and others in founding Westminster Theological Seminary, although he remained a member of the Presbyterian Church in the U.S.A. (later the United Presbyterian Church in the U.S.A.) until his death. He was professor of Old Testament at Westminster Seminary until 1936. Allis was noted especially in evangelical circles for his writings, including *The Five Books of Moses* (1943), *The Unity of Isaiah* (1950), and *The Old Testament: Its Claims and Its Critics* (1972). Most of his writings were directed against the assertions of liberal scholars, although *Prophecy and the Church* (1945) challenged the dispensationalist understanding of Old Testament prophetic passages. J. N. AKERS

ALTHAUS, PAUL (1888–1966)

German Lutheran theologian; best known for his attempts to reinterpret Luther for contemporary readers

Althaus was born near Hanover. His father (also Paul Althaus, 1861–1925) was a theological professor at Erlangen and Göttingen. The younger Althaus became professor of dogmatics at Rostock in 1920, and in 1925 was appointed professor of theology at Erlangen. His attempt to make Luther relevant led him to emphasize the reformer's eschatology. He believed that Luther tried to identify a contemporary antichrist because biblical teaching about the "last things" also refers to the present time.

Althaus defined two types of eschatology. What he called the axiological, or vertical, confronted the present with the eternal. On the other hand, teleological, or horizontal, eschatology was to be fulfilled in the future.

At first Althaus believed that the future was fulfilled in the present, but later he embraced the teleological outlook. In this understanding he found a positive meaning for history. Although all human history would come under judgment, it also had revelational value in the present.

Althaus's horizontal hypothesis for history brought him into conflict with Rudolf Bultmann's existentialist eschatology. Althaus also opposed Karl Barth's view that God's revelation is confined to Christ's redemption. Althaus believed that man's experience in time also discloses God's intentions.

German interpretations of eschatology have generally embraced present and future elements without much difficulty. Thus Paul Althaus is considered as contributing to one side of a continuing discussion. He had many theological interests and wrote extensively on such matters as church-state relationships, the Synoptic problem, law and the gospel, Christian ethics, and the Lutheran doctrine of the sacraments. R. P. EVANS

AMBROSE (c. 339–397)

Bishop of Milan (northern Italy)

Born into the aristocratic Roman family of Aurelius at Trier, the imperial residence in Gaul, Ambrose was the first Latin church father from a Christian family. He was trained in rhetoric and law, with thorough preparation in the Greek language. He moved up rapidly in the Roman government to become governor of the northern provinces in Italy by the age of thirty.

As governor, Ambrose came to the church in Milan to resolve the conflicts between Catholics and Arians after the death of the Arian bishop Auxentius. Both parties in Milan acclaimed Ambrose as bishop, but only after a period of resistance did he accept election. He was an orthodox Christian, although he had not yet received baptism.

Ambrose was a champion of orthodoxy,

affirming the creed of Nicea. He wrote several works against the Arians in support of the orthodox position. They include *On the Faith, The Mystery of the Lord's Incarnation,* and *On the Holy Spirit.* In them his knowledge of Greek helped him evaluate the eastern writers and move beyond them. His writing on the Holy Spirit is regarded as a significant theological contribution.

As bishop, Ambrose brought new life to the church. By introducing the allegorical interpretation of Scripture into the West, he became an effective century preacher. He also introduced congregational singing, and his hymns gave a strong spiritual expression to the Latin church. His primary writing was a work to instruct the clergy of Milan—*On the Duties of the Church's Servants*—the first book on Christian ethics.

Ambrose's greatest impact was on the relationship of church and state. Through his influence the Roman emperor brought an end to official paganism, even though the Roman senate had a large pagan majority. Ambrose was able to win a long struggle against the Arian emperors by the use of passive resistance involving his entire congregation in Milan. As a result he developed a strong position of the church independent from the state. The Latin bishops did not become the servants of the emperor as was true in the East. In his relationship with the orthodox emperor Theodosius, Ambrose was able to bring the emperor under the moral authority of the church. When Theodosius executed several thousand people in Thessalonica as punishment against the city for a riot, Ambrose as his pastor threatened to bar him from communion unless he did public penance for his sin. Theodosius submitted to public penance in the church of Milan, and in the eyes of the Christians he was a "son of the church," according to Ambrose's own description of a Christian emperor. Ambrose exercised his authority in such matters as the bishop of Milan without reference to the bishop of Rome. In his work *On the Incarnation,* he gave primacy to the church of Rome in the area of faith but not in the area of order.

Although Ambrose drew much from classical morals and philosophy, his writings show a biblical understanding of salvation in Christ. In his commentary on Luke, he spoke of Christ living within the Christian and of personal salvation. Ambrose was the first Latin church father to break away from a strong legalism, but it was Augustine, who was baptized by Ambrose, who made the grace of the gospel the theme of Western theology. J. NEWTON

AMSDORF, NICHOLAS VON (1483–1565)

German reformer, professor, and pastor; close friend of Martin Luther

As a student at Wittenberg in 1502, Amsdorf came under the influence of Luther. After serving as professor at Wittenberg from 1511, he went with Luther to the "disputation of Leipzig" in 1519 and to the Diet of Worms in 1521. Amsdorf initiated the Lutheran reform at Magdeburg (1524) and helped to introduce it in Goslar (1531) and Einbeck (1534). He was generally a strong defender of Luther, but in 1539 disagreed with his friend's opinion on the bigamous marriage of Philip of Hesse, a German prince. Upon Luther's recommendation Amsdorf was made bishop of Naumburg-Zeitz in 1542. After 1547 he was counselor to the nobles at Eisenach, living there until his death.

A quick-tempered and intense partisan, Amsdorf attacked the anabaptist Melchior Hoffman and the followers of Zwingli. He also disputed with Martin Bucer and Philip Melanchthon, believing that Melanchthon's view on the place of good works in salvation tended toward compromise with Roman Catholicism. During the "Synergist controversy" Amsdorf attacked Johann Pfeffinger's position that man partly cooperated with God's grace in salvation. He maintained instead that man's will was not free, being enslaved by sin. Against Georg Major he contended that good works were not only useless but actually harmful. That extreme statement was contradicted in the Formula of Concord (1577). Amsdorf's support of Luther pushed him to found the Lutheran University of Jena in 1558. There he installed Matthias Flacius to teach and to help him complete the Jena edition of Luther's works.

Luther probably needed Amsdorf's stormy but stalwart friendship. Amsdorf helped Luther with his translation of the German Bible at Wartburg Castle. Luther's "Letter to the Christian Nobility" was dedicated to Amsdorf. Probably Amsdorf and Flacius were the most important leaders of classic, "right-wing" Lutheranism against Melanchthon and his followers, the Philippists. Amsdorf's dispute with Melanchthon arose in 1548 during a period known as the Leipzig Interim. The emperor Charles had allowed Moritz of Saxony to reintroduce certain Catholic practices into his territory. Melanchthon had consented, calling the practices *adiaphora* or "nonessential matters." Amsdorf bitterly denounced what he viewed as compromise and told Luther that he was harboring a snake in his bosom in the person of Melanchthon. R. P. EVANS

ANDERSON, SIR ROBERT (1841–1918)

Irish-born lawyer, police chief, and Bible teacher

Born in Dublin and educated at Trinity College there, Anderson became a barrister specializing in political crime and was adviser to the British Home Office (1868–1888). Then as assistant commissioner he headed the criminal investigation department at Scotland Yard (1888–1901). A Presbyterian layman, he spoke and wrote widely on Bible teaching, with prophecy as one of his major concerns. He retired in 1901, in which year he was knighted, but remained active in the religious field. Among his numerous published works, which achieved a remarkable popularity, were *The Gospel and Its Ministries* (1876), *The Coming Prince* (1882), *The Silence of God* (1897), *The Bible and Modern Criticism* (1902), *The Lord from Heaven* (1910), and *Misunderstood Texts of the New Testament* (1916). J. D. DOUGLAS

ANDREWES, LANCELOT (1555–1626)

Famous English preacher and church administrator

Andrewes attended Pembroke Hall, Cambridge, and became a fellow of the college in 1576 and was ordained in 1580. In 1589 he became master of his college, a post held until 1605. He was appointed chaplain-in-ordinary to Queen Elizabeth and then dean of Westminster in 1601. His career as a churchman began to develop with the same steadiness as his academic career.

His public life was that of a powerful court prelate. He was among the clergymen at the Hampton Court Conference (1604) and one of the translators of the Authorized King James Version of the Bible. In 1605 he became bishop of Chichester, in 1609 bishop of Ely, and in 1619 bishop of Winchester. He was also a privy councillor and the dean of the King's Chapel.

Andrewes, a learned clergyman, was also a theological statesman, continuing the work of men like Richard Hooker in formulating the intellectual and historical position of the Church of England. Against Rome he defended the Anglican or "true catholic" church, and against the Calvinists in Geneva he justified its rites and ceremonies. He saw the church as sum and symbol of God's design on earth, the very "abridgement of the world."

From 1605 through most of his remaining years Andrewes was court preacher. His sermons, particularly on Easter, Christmas, and Whitsunday, drew on the writings of the church fathers, with all their indebtedness to the traditions of classical oratory, and on his thorough training in the Scripture. He frequently used farfetched comparisons and breathtaking antitheses, and labored at meticulous definition in his sermons. Each sermon was learned, analytical, and closely argued.

Andrewes's aim was never to display his learning or rhetorical power, but to cause people to think about the Scripture and to awaken them to a new life. "And sure it is," he said, "on whom a sermon works aught, it leaves him not leisure to say much, to use many words, but makes him rather full of thoughts." His sermons were ultimately addressed to the inner meaning of the spiritual life: "Go we then to the kernel, and let the husk lie: let go the dead letter, and take we to us the spiritual meaning that hath some life in it." Andrewes's contemplation of the Word of God and his desire to arouse his audience both to reflection and to personal application gave warmth to his most exhaustive analyses.

Andrewes's personal life was one of devotion and sanctity. Published after his death, his *Private Devotions* shows evidence of his inner life of meditation and prayer. Recording the death of Lancelot Andrewes, Archbishop Laud referred to him in his diary as "the great light of the Christian world." E. B. BATSON

ANERIO, GIOVANNI FRANCESCO (c. 1567–1630)
Italian composer

The musical contributions of Anerio came at a peak of Roman influence upon European styles in sacred music, and are vital in the first formations of the Oratorio. Anerio was Music Director at the Lateran Church (1600–1603), and later joined the Polish Court of Sigismund III (Cracow, 1607). Prior to directorship of the Royal Chapel at Warsaw (1623–1628), Anerio also was choirmaster at Verona Cathedral (1609) and prefect at the Roman Seminary (1611–1612) and at the Jesuit Church of St. Maria dei Monte in Rome (1613–1620). His musical style is related to the late sixteenth century "Pure Roman" or a capella style exemplified in works of Palestrina and Victoria.

The oratorio takes its name from the Roman Congregation of the Oratory, a general prayer-hall used by laymen, and in which devotional songs known as *laude* were sung. As an indoctrination the lauda had important relations to the Counter-Reformation, and Anerio composed various laude in a dialogue format—and importantly, with a narrator (actually sung in parts). Such a format is close in type to the oratorio, which was based on biblical subjects, though not always liturgical in structure. Anerio's *Teatro Armonico Spirituale* (1619) is a collection of laude foreshadowing the oratorio in form and intent. D. S. CUSHMAN

ANGELA MERICI (1474–1540)
Italian founder of the Ursulines, the first women's teaching order in the Roman Catholic Church

Angela Merici was born at Desenzano, twenty miles west of Verona, Italy, in the Republic of Venice. In her early years she was a tertiary (lay associate) of the Franciscan order, devoting herself to the education of young girls and the care of sick women. In 1516 she accepted an invitation to go to Brescia as a counselor and helper of a family that had lost two sons. There she began to instruct young girls in the Christian faith, and in 1531 she organized a group of twelve young women to help her in that work. By 1535, with the group grown to twenty-eight, Angela Merici formed them into the Company of Saint Ursula. In 1537 she was elected First Superior of the group. Members continued to live in their own homes, constituting a secular educational and relief agency. In 1572 the group was organized into a regular conventual religious order, largely under the influence of Charles Borromeo. Angela died at Brescia in 1540 and was canonized in 1807. N. V. HOPE

ANGELICO, FRA (c. 1400–1455)
Italian monk and painter

Angelico was born Guido di Pietro da Mugello in Vicchio, Italy. At the age of twenty he entered a Dominican monastery at Fiesole where he was known as Fra Giovanni (Fra is short for the Italian *frate,* "brother"). After his death he became known as Fra Angelico. His early training in painting is unknown, but documents refer to him as a painter by 1430. His first works were dominated by the earlier international Gothic style with slight figures, garish colors, and elaborate decoration. By 1433 his work began to show the influence of the new technical discoveries of the Renaissance, namely linear perspective and realistic settings. After numerous works for churches and monasteries, in 1437 Angelico began his most famous series of frescoes in the San Marco Monastery of Florence. In those scenes from the life of Christ, he reduced his compositions to a simple beauty and naturalism. In 1447 he was called to Rome to decorate a chapel at the Vatican for Pope Nicholas V. He was in constant demand as a painter of religious subjects for the eight years before his death in Rome.

Angelico's work expressed his concern for spiritual content. His early biographers referred to holiness, simplicity, and modesty as hallmarks of his character. By combining traditional techniques with Renaissance innovations, he forced the viewer to confront the spiritual significance of the scenes depicted. His use of color was in accord with earlier traditions where color denoted a spiritual state and not a realistic portrayal. Yet he placed his figures in realistic poses with a naturalistic gracefulness unique to his work. Some art historians see this mixture of style as a deliberate rejection of those elements of Renaissance techniques which Angelico perceived as incompatible with his strong Christian faith. K. HOGLUND

ANNE (1665–1714)
British queen, 1702–1714

The younger daughter of King James II, Anne was brought up as an Anglican and was married in 1683 to Prince George of Denmark, a Lutheran. In 1702 she succeeded her brother-in-law William III of Orange on the English throne.

In domestic matters Anne's reign was important for the parliamentary union of England and Scotland in 1707 to form the United Kingdom. In foreign affairs a major event was the long and costly War of the Spanish Succession, which did not end until 1715.

Anne was a devoted Anglican churchwoman. In 1704 she donated to the Church of England for "augmentation of poorer livings" (that is, for larger stipends to poor clergy), the "first fruits and tithes" which Henry VIII had annexed to the Crown, amounting to sixteen thousand pounds annually. These funds became known as Queen Anne's Bounty. Anne favored the High Church party and made appointments accordingly. That party was strongly opposed to Dissenters (evangelical Christians such as Presbyterians, Baptists, Congregationalists, and Quakers) who could not conscientiously join the Church of England. The Tories, political allies of the High Church party, came to power in 1710, and passed the Occasional Conformity Act. That law restrained Dissenters from receiving Holy Communion in the Church of England in order to qualify for government positions. In 1714 the Schism Act was passed to forbid Dissenters from conducting schools and engaging in teaching. Both of those Acts were repealed under Anne's successor, George I. N. V. HOPE

ANSELM OF CANTERBURY
(1033–1109)
Archbishop of Canterbury; sometimes described as the founder of Scholasticism

Born in Aosta (northwest Italy) of noble family, Anselm was educated at the abbey of St. Leger, where the classical curriculum trained him for the clarity of expression later characteristic of his writings. Anselm's father intended him for a political career and opposed his son's decision to become a monk. In 1057 Anselm left home and traveled in Burgundy (France) and Normandy for two years before settling in a Benedictine monastery at Bec, Normandy, to study under the renowned theologian Lanfranc. Anselm took monastic vows and succeeded his teacher as prior in 1063, a tribute to his intellect and piety. He later became abbot of Bec (1078–1093). Under Anselm's leadership the monastery and its school became a prominent center of learning. Once when a neighboring abbot complained that he could not improve his boys no matter how much he beat them, Anselm gently responded with what sounds like a twentieth-century question: "Have you tried not beating them?"

Although he could be scathing in condemnation of monks who laid up treasure on earth, he showed compassion for ordinary human weakness. His humble faith produced the prayer, "Grant that I may taste by love what I apprehend by knowledge, that I may feel in my heart what I touch through the Spirit."

After the Norman conquest of England in 1066, English lands were granted by William I ("The Conqueror") to the monastery of Bec. Because of that property, Anselm paid three visits to England, where he made a favorable impression on the clergy during a period of reorganization in their church. When the archbishopric of Canterbury became vacant on Lanfranc's death in 1089, the English clergy urged that the abbot of Bec should succeed him. For the gentle monk it was not an inviting prospect. William II ("Rufus"), who had come to the English throne in 1087, was notably disinclined to appoint someone with strong views about the rights and independence of the church. Indeed, the king was reluctant to appoint anyone at all. A four-year vacancy ensued, much to Rufus's satisfaction, for the revenues of any vacant diocese went to the Crown. No help came from Rome, since at the time an unseemly squabble was going on between two rival claimants for the papacy.

Then the dilemma was unexpectedly resolved. Anselm, in England on monastic business, was called to hear the confession of the king who had become seriously ill. The apprehensive Rufus, it is related, forced the pastoral staff into Anselm's clenched hands. The abbot protested, "You have yoked an old sheep with an untamed bull to the plough of the church, which ought to be drawn by two strong oxen." Anselm refused to be consecrated until Rufus restored certain lands to Canterbury, recognized the archbishop as his spiritual father, and acknowledged Urban II as the rightful pope (a choice forced upon Anselm because of his Norman connections). Rufus agreed, but he recovered and was never one for keeping his promises. The yokefellows did indeed prove incompatible. Again and again Rufus, one of the most evil and rapacious of English sovereigns, thwarted Anselm's administration of the church and his concern for the spiritual welfare of the nation. The king would not even permit the archbishop to go on a visit to Rome. Anselm would not dilute his Christian principles to satisfy a royal tyrant, but his position gradually became so untenable that he left the country in 1097. He returned only after Rufus had died in mysterious circumstances and his brother Henry I had sent an invitation to the exiled primate (1100).

By that time the Investiture Controversy was at its height, and in keeping with a papal decree of 1099 Anselm declined to pay the expected homage to the new king or to consecrate bishops who had done so. Six unhappy years passed before a compromise was reached. Anselm was never at his best in political affairs, so his early rejection of a career in politics proved to be a wise decision. Only the last two years of his primacy were spent in peace. The papacy made some amends for the halfhearted support given him in England by canonizing him a little less than a half century after his death.

As a scholar, Anselm reintroduced the spirit of Augustine into theology. Much of Anselm's writing was done during the placid decades at Bec—notably *Monologion, De veritate,* and *Proslogion.* Anselm sought to demonstrate the existence and attributes of God by an appeal to reason alone. He spoke of an absolute norm above time and space that could be comprehended by the mind of man. That norm was God, the ultimate standard of perfection. Anselm's so-called Ontological Argument was that the existence of the idea of God necessarily implied the objective existence of God. He always insisted, however, that faith must precede reason: "I do not seek to understand in order that I may believe, but I believe in order to understand."

To him is attributed what became known as the "satisfaction theory" of the atonement, which sees God as the offended party and man as the offender. That view was elaborated in a famous work *Cur Deus homo? (Why Did God Become Man?),* which Anselm completed in 1098 in Italy. He rejected the view of the Atonement that saw it as the settlement of a lawsuit between God and the devil. Anselm's hypothesis was that all human beings had sinned in and with Adam. God's honor demanded that every creature should subject itself to him so that his eternal purposes should be completed. Since finite man could never make satisfaction to the infinite God, "no one but one who is God-man can make the satisfaction by which man is saved." The voluntary death of the sinless Christ on the cross was the only way and the only acceptable satisfaction.

Acknowledged as the greatest scholar between Augustine and Aquinas, Anselm's distinctive characteristic was his resort to intellectual reasoning rather than to biblical tests and traditional writings—while still upholding the prime place of faith. His theology has had profound influence on many modern theologians, including Karl Barth.
J. D. DOUGLAS

ANSELM OF LAON (died 1117)

Theologian, scholar, and "teacher of teachers" who laid the foundations for the great intellectual awakening known as the twelfth-century Renaissance

This Anselm, a student of the well-known Anselm of Canterbury, in 1076 was teaching at Paris where one of his students was William of Champeaux. Before 1100 he went to Laon, about eighty miles northeast of Paris, with his brother Ralph (Raoul), a noted mathematician. There Anselm taught Abelard and others whose work became part of the mainstream of academic inquiry over the next several decades. Under Anselm's direction the small cathedral school of Laon became a great twelfth-century center for the study of Scripture and theology.

Anselm wrote what became the standard "gloss" or commentary on the Bible during the high Middle Ages. He also prepared the first book of *Sentences* (a manual of systematic theology), which established a style used by many theologians of the scholastic tradition over the next two centuries. Anselm set forth all the conflicting statements of earlier authorities on basic theo-

logical propositions. The same format was used by Abelard (*Sic et Non*), Peter Lombard (*Sentences*), and Thomas Aquinas (*Summa Theologiae*). In organizing the *Sentences* Anselm followed the outline used by John Scotus Erigena, starting with the Creation, the fall of the angels and man, the necessity of redemption, and redemption and the sacraments. He was particularly attracted to the problems of creation, original sin, and the definition of the soul.

Anselm was a philosophical realist in the tradition of Anselm of Canterbury. That position brought him into conflict with his former student Abelard, who frequently attacked him. Abelard described Anselm of Laon as the "fig tree of the Gospel," who "while covered with leaves remained fruitless," and as "smoke without flame." Anselm's work, however, was not without fruit. Seldom can so much influence be traced to one person as to Anselm of Laon.
T. O. KAY

ANSKAR (801–865)

First archbishop of Hamburg; known as the "Apostle of the North"

Anskar was born of Saxon stock in northwestern France and was educated at the monastery of Corbie, not far from his home. About 823 Anskar was sent to found a new abbey called New Corbie on the Weser River in Westphalia. In 826 he was asked to accompany the Danish king Harold back to his homeland. Harold had sought the help of the Frankish king, Louis the Pious, to reconquer Denmark and gain the throne. Meanwhile Ebo, archbishop of Rheims, had been designated legate to the north countries by Pope Eugenius II. With Ebo's permission, Anskar accompanied Harold, but the attempt to win the throne of Denmark was aborted.

About a year later a delegation from the king of Sweden informed Louis that their sovereign desired Christian missionaries. Anskar was asked to fulfill the mission. On their way north he and his assistant were robbed by Vikings. The king of Sweden received them in a friendly way and they were allowed to make converts. After the leader of

Birka (an island in Lake Malar) was baptized, others also asked for baptism. The first church in Scandinavia was built at Birka, near present-day Stockholm, in 830.

In 831 Louis had Anskar consecrated as archbishop of the new see (area of jurisdiction) of Hamburg. With Ebo, he was also given jurisdiction over future churches in Scandinavia by Pope Gregory IV. At first he ruled only three congregations in Holstein and one in Sweden. Anskar brought Danish boys to Germany for training for the evangelization of Denmark. He suffered from lack of funds and the destruction of Hamburg by the Danes in 845. Meanwhile Ebo and Anskar appointed Gauzbert bishop of Sweden, but he was driven out for a period of seven years. In 854 Anskar returned to Denmark, and Erik, king of Jutland, was converted. The first two Danish churches were built at Slesvig and Ribe. Two Danes, Ansfred and Rimbert, succeeded Anskar as archbishop. It is not known how long the churches founded under Anskar's leadership continued, nor what link existed between them and the eventual total conversion of the Scandinavian countries. For more than a generation after his death, pagan reaction persisted, but the following century saw a momentum of evangelization. R. P. EVANS

ANTONY OF EGYPT (c. 251–356)

Early Egyptian hermit; generally regarded as the founder of Christian monasticism

Antony was born in Comus (Egypt) and died in the Egyptian desert. He was the son of well-to-do parents who died when he was about twenty and left him all their possessions. Shortly thereafter, on hearing the words of the gospel, "If you want to be perfect, go and sell everything you have and give the money to the poor" (Matt. 19:21), he gave away all his worldly goods and devoted himself exclusively to religious exercises.

At first Antony pursued the normal practices of fasting, prayer, and works of piety. He visited various ascetics and attempted to learn from them by imitating the virtue in which each excelled. He lived in a tomb near his native village, where, according to his

biography by Athanasius, he fought off demons and wild beasts. After fifteen years, when he was about thirty-five, Antony withdrew into absolute solitude. He crossed the Nile River to a mountain (then called Pispir, now known as Der el Memun) to live in an old fort without seeing another person for twenty years. Gradually a number of disciples established themselves nearby in caves and huts on the mountain.

That community of ascetics, desiring to be discipled by Antony, persuaded him to break his solitude and give them spiritual leadership. When he came forth, they were surprised to find him vigorous in mind and body. He began to instruct his followers, who called themselves Antonians, paying special attention to means of overcoming temptation as well as to the gift of discernment of good and evil spirits. He organized his followers into a great body of monks. Then he spent the last forty-five years of his life with them in an inner desert between the Nile and the Red Sea. Less secluded than before, he saw those who came to him and crossed the desert frequently.

Antony once broke his pattern of solitude and became involved in the lives of the needy. He offered himself as a martyr during the persecution of Maximin, but was not martyred. Instead, he was able to give counsel to the Christians in prison, helping them in both spiritual and material ways. He also crossed the desert toward the close of his life to preach against the Arians.

Antony died at the age of 105. In death as in life he was courageous and simple. Knowing the end was near, he took two companions with him into the desert. There, after his death, they buried him without a marker so no one would make his body an object of reverence. His life and teachings were made famous by *The Life of Antony*, a biography written by the fourth-century theologian Athanasius. R. E. WEBBER

ANTONY OF PADUA (1195–1231)

Influential, first-generation Franciscan; usually regarded as the first commissioned teacher of the Franciscan order

Born of a noble family in Lisbon (Portugal), Antony first joined the Augustinian Canons in 1210 and gained a reputation for excellent preaching and scholarship. After associating with the Franciscan order, he went to Africa as a missionary, but returned because of illness after only a brief stay. Following a period of withdrawal for study and contemplation, Antony was prevailed upon by Francis of Assisi to come out into the world again and take up a teaching ministry. As a result, he taught theology at Bologna, Montpellier, Toulouse, and Padua over the next ten years. Antony is usually regarded as the person responsible for directing Franciscan theology toward an Augustinian emphasis. During his teaching years he also served the order in administrative capacities in France and Italy.

Antony continued to be a popular preacher. His sermons were directed at some of the major heretical groups of his day. His enthusiasm won him the title "Maleus hereticorum" ("Hammer of the heretics"). Crowds of up to thirty thousand people were reported to have heard him, and many people responded to his evangelistic appeals. His concern for those who sought to follow more closely the teachings of Christ led to the organization of the "Brotherhood of the Penitents" for new converts.

Antony's preaching and teaching were based upon Augustine's theology, plus much medieval mysticism and the medieval allegorical tradition of biblical interpretation. Antony emphasized repentance and contempt for the world. His life was exemplary, and within a year of his death he was canonized. He is regarded as the patron saint of the poor in both Portugal and Padua. Antony's life has often been overshadowed by the popularity of his contemporary, Francis of Assisi. T. O. KAY

APOLLINARIUS (c. 310–390)

Syrian theologian responsible for a major christological heresy known as Apollinarianism

Apollinarius was born in Laodicea (Syria). Because his father was a grammarian and priest, Apollinarius received a good education in both secular and religious studies. He served as a lector in the church of Laodicea and also taught rhetoric. At one point in his somewhat tempestuous career he was excommunicated for participating in a pagan ceremony, but he was later readmitted to the church. He was an ardent supporter of Athanasius's view of the Trinity and was excommunicated a second time for showing Athanasius hospitality during one of his banishments. However, sixteen years later (c. 361) Apollinarius became bishop of Laodicea. In 374 he lectured in Antioch, where Jerome was one of his auditors.

Apollinarius is best known for his view of Christology which was rejected by the church as heretical. Within the church a Trinitarian controversy had raged between 325 and 381. If the second person of the Trinity was indeed fully God, a view which Apollinarius espoused, how could Jesus' human form be explained? Apollinarius rejected the view that the Incarnation represented the bringing together of a complete divinity with a complete humanity. For him, such a compounding smacked too much of the monsters of mythology. Instead, Apollinarius advocated a literal interpretation of John 1:14 ("the Word became flesh"). For him, the Word had not assumed flesh; rather it was made into flesh. There was, he argued, an absolute union between the Godhead and flesh so that Christ could be spoken of as "flesh-bearing God."

The special feature of his theory that made it questionable was Apollinarius's view of the human spirit in Jesus. For him, the spirit was the seat of sin. Christ, he argued, could not have had a human spirit or else he would have been liable to sin and therefore could not have been the Redeemer. His view was based on a Platonic understanding of human nature as body, soul, and spirit. According to Apollinarius's anthropology, man was spirit united with flesh. Thus in the God-man, the preexistent Word fulfilled the role of the Spirit and the mind. Elimination of a human mind and flesh insured the Savior's sinlessness, excluded the possibility of two wills and two intelligences, and emphasized the oneness of the nature of Christ. Apollinarius was well aware that his theory made Jesus different from other human beings. But he insisted that scriptural phrases like "found as a man" and "in the likeness of man" supported his view. Also, he thought that he could give a better explanation of the Virgin Birth. The spermatic matter that ordinarily produces human life was not needed for the birth of Jesus. Instead, the divine spirit entered Mary's womb and was born as flesh.

Other church fathers argued against Apollinarius on three grounds. First, it was insisted that Scripture taught that the Word assumed all that is human, yet without sin. It was not necessary to reject the spirit to preserve the sinlessness of Christ. It was sufficient to accept the biblical teaching. Second, it was argued that Christ without a rational soul would not be human. As the Trinitarian controversy had centered around full identification of the Word with the Father, so the Christological controversy centered around full identification of the Word with man. Christ had to be fully God and fully man. Third, the fullness of Christ's manhood was insisted upon because it was argued that any part of human nature that Christ had not assumed, he had not healed. The third reason, to which the other two pointed, was the crucial issue. It concerned the "soteriological dimension" of the person of Christ, central to both the Trinitarian and Christological controversies. That soteriological dimension is the teaching of the church that only God can save his creation, but to do so, he chose to enter into it and fully identify with it. Only that with which he identifies is fully saved. Thus, to deny the human spirit and rational soul in Christ, as Apollinarius did, is to deny the fullness of redemption.

The view of Apollinarius was condemned in several church councils, first in the Council of Alexandria (362) without mention of his name. His view was condemned again in Rome (376). Between 376 and 381 when Apollinarius was condemned for the final time, a state of open theological conflict existed between the more orthodox church fathers and Apollinarius and his followers.

In the Council of Constantinople (381), which settled the Trinitarian controversy by affirming the full identity of the Word with the Father, Apollinarianism was condemned in the seventh anathema: "We pronounce anathema against those who say that the Word of God is in the human flesh in lieu and place of the human rational and intellective souls. For, the Word of God is the Son Himself. Neither did he come in the flesh to replace, but rather to assume and preserve from sin and save the rational and intellective soul of man."

In the Council of Chalcedon (451), the church finally and officially affirmed the full humanity of Christ. Rejecting the notion that Christ did not have a rational soul, the Chalcedonian statement affirmed that Christ is "consubstantial with us in manhood, like us in all things except sin."

Apollinarius died still affirming his heretical view. His following, which at one time was quite large throughout Constantinople, Syria, and Phoenicia, barely survived him. Within a few years of his death they either returned to the mother church or drifted off into Monophysitism, a view which insisted that there was only one nature in Christ.

The works of Apollinarius have not survived except in fragment form in the writings of the church fathers who discussed his views. R. E. WEBBER

AQUINAS, THOMAS (1225–1274)
Distinguished medieval theologian and philosopher

Born in the town of Aquino (Italy), about eighty miles southeast of Rome, Aquinas had a large physique which earned him the nickname "dumb ox." His combination of theological learning and Christian devotion, however, later earned him the label "angelic doctor." Educated at the Universities of Naples, Paris, and Cologne, he belonged to the Dominican order of preachers. He taught in Paris, Rome, and elsewhere, and provided the Dominicans with both theological and organizational leadership. The traditional theologians of his day so distrusted his use of Aristotelian philosophy that some of his teachings were condemned by the church for about fifty years. But his cause soon became that of the whole Dominican order, with the result that they adopted his theology (known as "Thomism"), whereas the Franciscans followed instead the teachings of Bonaventure and Duns Scotus.

In 1879 an encyclical of Pope Leo XIII, *Aeterni Patris,* precipitated a major revival of Thomistic influence in the Roman church by calling for a return to Aquinas's teaching to combat the modernism and agnosticism of that day. Thus, various Thomistic schools grew up, dominating Roman Catholic theology and philosophy until the 1960s, when Aquinas's authority was moderated by the influence of phenomenology and of European biblical theology. Although Thomism is not the official Catholic position, Aquinas is held in the highest respect, is diligently studied, and has had a profoundly stabilizing effect on Catholic thought through the centuries.

Protestant appraisals vary. Some Protestants are themselves Thomists. Lutheran and Reformed theologians tend in other directions—Lutherans being closer to William of Ockham's nominalism and Reformed thinkers to John Calvin. Aquinas is criticized because he attempted a synthesis of Aristotelian philosophy and biblical theology which, in the judgment of some, compromised such doctrines as the sovereignty of God and the total depravity of man.

Central in Protestant discontent is Aquinas's perception of the relation between philosophy and theology, and of the role of reason in each. Philosophy, he maintained, is the servant of theology, which is taken as the "queen of the sciences." Philosophy establishes what theology assumes, the existence of God and the immortality of the soul. But the philosophical attitude is religiously neutral in that its premises are universally accessible truths about nature, such as Aristotelian science provided, and its method is strictly logical and argumentative, rather than depending on biblical revelation. The "autonomy of natural reason" is what some scholars regard as unbiblical, and

it is associated with other doctrinal problems.

In the first place, Aquinas assumed that human reason remains fully operative despite the Fall. Aquinas could hold that position in view of his separation of will and intellect (sin diverts will, not intellect, from its proper end), and of his distinction between the image and likeness of God in humanity. The "image" of God is human reason, without which men and women would not be human but merely animals. The "likeness" is moral, for human beings were created good. Sin therefore corrupts their moral likeness to God and perverts their will, but it does not destroy their essential identity as rational beings. Reformed theology, on the other hand, tends to regard the image and likeness as synonymous, so that sin affects both, depravity extends to all a person is, and reason is no longer religiously neutral—nor was it ever so.

In the second place, Aquinas's confidence in philosophy rested on his adoption of Aristotelian realism, the view that the order observable in nature is due to universal and objectively real forms that determine an unchanging nature of things. That being so, the nature of things is equally accessible to all rational minds, rather than just to those enlightened by God's grace. Understandably, the Lutheran thinker who follows Ockham and Luther in rejecting the realistic theory of universals is likely to lack Aquinas's confidence that natural reason can gain universal truth.

On "Natural Theology" Aquinas's position remains controversial, but his work is of such lasting significance that it still receives attention from many who are not Thomists. He is held in high regard as a philosopher both within and outside a Christian context. The reason is evident from a perusal of his prolific works. In addition to commentaries on Aristotle, commentaries on the Bible, theological and philosophical essays, and scripts of various public debates in which he engaged, he left two major works: the *Summa Thelogica* and *Summa Contra Gentiles.*

The *Summa Theologica* was prepared to

instruct undergraduates in theology and is an encyclopedic statement of his teachings, meticulously developed and defended with replies to objections, real and hypothetical, of both Christian and non-Christian authorities. Written between 1265 and 1273, it provides a systematic compendium on all the theological, philosophical, and ethical topics debated in medieval universities, including what have become classical statements on such things as the relation of theology to philosophy, the arguments for God's existence, the doctrine of creation, natural law, ethics, etc. Its organization reflects the Scholastic method: each question is divided into several sub-questions known as "articles." Each article is introduced with objections to a standard position, following which Aquinas presents his own argument beginning "I answer that . . ." and then his replies to each initial objection. In the process he not only argues from Scripture but also considers the opinions of various Christian and non-Christian authorities—this in accordance with his view of the supplementary roles of reason and revelation. He divides theology into three major areas: God (including his relation to creation), Man (including his relation to God's law and to grace), and Christ (including his person and work, his sacraments, and his church).

The *Summa Contra Gentiles,* equally exhaustive, is a reasoned account of the Christian faith addressed to the Islamic mind. Although an apologetic, it treated many of the same topics as the earlier treatise but with different purpose and emphasis. Both works had a profound effect on theology (Roman Catholic and otherwise) and on philosophy. They continue to attract scholarly attention.

Among Aquinas's distinctive contributions are his natural theology and natural law ethic. Building on suggestions made by some of his predecessors, Aquinas formulated "five ways" of proving the existence of God. He rejected the famous ontological argument formulated by Anselm of Canterbury and did not regard the existence of God as self-evident to human beings, who do not initially know enough about God to know

the necessity for his existence. His five ways, therefore, argued from universal truths about nature to nature's cause and creator, God.

First, Aquinas observed that every natural process of change actualizes some potential. Firewood is potentially hot, but it becomes actually hot when it burns; yet it is not both potentially and actually hot at the same time. Nor can it both burn and be the cause of its own burning and of the changes that burning entails. The universal truth here is that whatever is changed or moved must be changed or moved by another. But an infinite chain of movers is impossible, for without a "first mover" there could be no first movement or change. Hence a first mover, itself moved by nothing else, must exist— namely an unchanging God.

Second, Aquinas observed in nature a seemingly endless array of cause-effect relations, "efficient causes" in his Aristotelian terminology. But that array is not actually endless, for nothing can be its own cause, as the whole causal order would be if it were actually endless. Therefore a first efficient cause of the whole array of causes must be admitted, namely God.

Third, nature exhibits a large variety of possibilities, things that are created and destroyed and therefore do not have to be. But if all that exists could possibly not exist, then at one point in an endless time past nothing at all could have existed, and consequently nothing would now exist. There must therefore exist some being whose existence is not merely possible but necessary by virtue of his very nature. That necessary being is God.

The first three "ways" argue from the dependent or contingent existence of finite things to the independent existence of God and are varieties of the so-called "cosmological argument." Aquinas's remaining two ways begin with order and purpose in nature and are variations of the "teleological argument," as it was later called. The fourth way observes varying degrees of goodness, beauty, truth, and so forth in different things, each according to the form of its own species. This hierarchy of being and goodness implies that something must exist that is best, most beautiful, truest, most real. That something is in fact the God who is perfect in all his attributes.

The fifth and final way starts from the fact that even unthinking things follow natural and preestablished tendencies, as if they are deliberately pursuing some good end. But things do not pursue ends unless they are intelligent, or else are guided by an intelligent being. Therefore some intelligent being exists who draws all things to those ends, namely the God who works his purposes in and through the things he made.

The God whose existence these arguments purport to prove is a self-existent, all-powerful, all-good, intelligent creator. Human beings do not know from nature that he acts redemptively in history, but his "power and Godhead" are nonetheless attested by the creation (as Paul indicated in Rom. 1:20). "Natural theology," as this kind of discussion is labeled, says less about God than does biblical theology, but it says enough to underscore all people's responsibility to God and to prepare them for the fuller revelation in Scripture.

Aquinas's natural theology also included arguments for human immortality, a topic much debated at that time because of the difficulty Aristotelians had in proving individual survival. Aquinas held that the human soul is actually a rational, intellectual being whose intellectual potential comes to be a reality in this life. Intellectual things are immaterial and so cannot be destroyed. Hence the soul, an intellectual thing, is indestructible and immortal. Another argument he offered depends on the idea that a final cause, or natural purpose, inheres in everything. In human beings it is revealed in a natural desire to live forever, not just through their descendants but as individuals. If this tendency inheres in human beings by nature, and nature does not lie, then they indeed are immortal. The first of these two arguments for human immortality was adapted from analogous attempts at such reasoning by Plato and Augustine. The second was more original with Aquinas. Both of the arguments are characteristic of the

"proofs of immortality" employed in Christian apologetics ever since.

Running through Aquinas's arguments for God's existence and for immortality is the conviction that all nature has ends or "final causes" implanted by God. Evidence of those ends constitutes a natural revelation of God's purposes for his creation. Aquinas accordingly developed a "natural law ethic" based on human knowledge of those ends, parallel to his natural theology.

With respect to "Ethics," Aquinas distinguished (1) eternal law, (2) divine law, (3) natural law, and (4) human law. The eternal law is God's unchanging wisdom and counsel, his eternal decree in accordance with which he created everything he made. The eternal law is revealed in two ways: divine law in the Scriptures entrusted to the church, and natural law, the nature of the creation itself. The theory of final causes means that the nature of every species of created things is such that it naturally tends to actualize its essential God-given possibilities, or in other words, it seeks its natural end or good. As rational beings, humans are so created as to seek a rationally ordered society, and they are created to know God. These are therefore ends they ought to pursue. But men and women are rational animals and share with other animals the natural ends of reproduction and the rearing of their young. They share with every "thing" the goal of self-preservation. The natural law then speaks of the preservation of life, including self-preservation; of sex and the family; of the social and political order and of religion. As natural theology affords less than biblical theology, so a natural law ethic affords less than biblical ethics. But the natural law enables human beings to identify universal and unchanging moral obligations which they face in all areas of life, obligations for which all are held accountable (as Paul pointed out in Romans 1 and 2). The fourth kind of law Aquinas discussed is human law, which is derived from natural law. Some human laws are universal because they are simply deduced from natural law—for example, laws against murder or theft. Others are more variable applications to specific situations, such as penal codes that assess ranges of punishment for particular crimes. But in both cases the natural law provides a moral yardstick for use in evaluating and formulating legislation. Aquinas accordingly talked about what makes a law unjust and what to do in that case. Questions of civil disobedience and conscientious objection are not new in our day; in fact, the contemporary debate draws heavily on Aquinas.

Natural law is universally the same, even though some human laws vary. So Aquinas provided a basis for international agreements about law. Some later Thomists developed that line of thought, asserting the need for a rule of law among the nations, a rule now called "international law." They applied it to the legitimacy of going to war and to the conduct of war, developing in detail some of Aquinas's tentative proposals. Aquinas had simply outlined a "just war theory," bringing wars under the judgment of "just laws" rooted in natural law.

The influence of Thomas Aquinas even today is profound and widespread: it is seen in theology, philosophy, ethics, and in major issues facing government and other branches of society. A Christian of such deep, broad, and lasting impact is the kind of thinker with the kind of vision that the church needs in every age. A. F. HOLMES

ARISTIDES (second century)
Christian philosopher who lived at Athens and addressed an Apology *to a Roman emperor, most probably Antoninus Pius (ruled 138–161)*

The *Apology* of Aristides was popular among Christians in the fourth century. In the late nineteenth century, Armenian and Syriac versions of it were discovered. It was then seen that the *Apology* had been included in the *Lives of Barlaam and Josaphat,* an eighth-century Christian apology supposedly written by John Damascene. This latter work, actually coming from Buddhist sources, had been changed into a Christian story which was widely known during the Middle Ages.

In his *Apology* Aristides argued that non-

Christians had an inadequate view of God. The barbarians went astray because they worshiped the changeable elements of nature. The mistake of the Greeks was that they pictured the gods with human weaknesses. The Jews were close to the truth since they worshiped one God but they were misled by their emphasis on rituals. Though generally Aristides did not rely on philosophical subtleties, he did show that he was familiar with pagan philosophers. Thus in demonstrating the existence of God, he included an argument from Aristotle's principle of motion. C. HICKS

ARISTO OF PELLA (second century)
Christian apologist to the Jews

In Aristo's *Dialogue between Jason and Papiscus concerning the Christ,* Jason, a Jewish Christian, persuaded Papiscus, a fellow Jew, to become a Christian. He argued that passages in the Jewish Scriptures concerning the Christ have to do with Jesus.

Aristo's *Dialogue* was known to Celsus, Jerome, Tertullian, Maximus the Confessor, Clement of Alexandria, and Origen. Celsus disliked it because he thought it contained absurdities. From the *Dialogue* an early church historian, Eusebius, learned that Roman emperor Hadrian (who ruled 117–138) excluded all Jews from Jerusalem following the Bar Kochba Revolt (132–135). By that time Pella, one of the ten cities of the Decapolis east of the Jordan, had already become a haven for Christians escaping Roman military activity. The exact nature of Aristo's relation with the city is, however, unknown. The text of the *Dialogue* no longer exists, except for a fragment recorded by Jerome. C. HICKS

ARISTOTLE (384–322 B.C.)
Greek philosopher

Born in the small town of Stagita, Greece, Aristotle attended the Academy of Plato in Athens for twenty years until Plato's death. After teaching and tutoring for a few years, he established a school in Athens known as the Lyceum. His aim was to establish a

program of investigation and teaching in almost every branch of knowledge. He taught while walking or strolling with his students (hence, the word "peripatetic"), and believed that this was the most effective method in learning the "truths." It was known as the *Peripatetic Philosophy*. His philosophy consisted in his contributions to the sciences and his reflections on their interrelations. With the exception of Plato, his teacher, he is considered to be the most influential philosopher in the history of western thought.

Though a disciple of Plato, Aristotle's philosophical position was very different. In fact, by the end of his life Aristotle rejected most of Plato's metaphysical philosophy, replacing it with empirical science. Aristotle believed that philosophic wisdom must be intuitive reason combined with scientific knowledge, and that practical wisdom is concerned with things "human."

Aristotle believed that the relations between man and God are so different because man has imperfections and hindrances that do not exist in the perfect God. God, according to Aristotle, goes through no processes as man does. He is pure mind, which can contemplate in a single instant. He is the one full and perfect being. God does not go out to the world, but the world cannot help going out to him. He is the necessary goal of perfection, and he moves as the object of desire. According to Aristotle, "God is the Unmoved Mover." The "dunamis," or urge of nature, propels man to grow to maturity and seek to be like the excellent, virtuous God. Aristotle believed that virtue in man is a "state of character." A man is virtuous both in word and life because his character is such. Virtue is in our own power, also vice. For where it is in our power to act, it is also our power not to act. Men make themselves responsible for being unjust or self-indulgent, therefore creating a character that reflects God.

Aristotle supervised the education of Alexander (son of Philip II of Macedon, later know as Alexander the Great). After several years in Athens, Aristotle was charged by the Athenians with "impiety"—a lack of reverence for the gods. He fled to Chalcis, since he had not forgotten the fate of Socrates, condemned to death on a similar charge. He died in Chalcis one year later.

In the early centuries of the Christian church, Aristotle's philosophy was regarded with suspicion because many people thought that his teachings led to a materialistic view of the world. However, after firsthand acquaintance with Aristotle had disappeared for some centuries, knowledge of his teachings was recovered from Arabic translations made by Jews and Muslims. His writings were translated into Latin and after some suspicion, were actually incorporated into use by Christian philosophers such as St. Albertus Magnus and St. Thomas Aquinas. To these leading scholars, his writings seemed to contain the sum total of human knowledge, and his thoughts were comparable to those of the Christian philosophers. The systems of these philosophers were built on an avowedly Aristotelian basis. This basis has been accepted by philosophical theology in the West ever since.

J. Riser

ARIUS (died 336)
Presbyter of Alexandria; founder of the heresy known as Arianism

Arius had been trained at Antioch, with which city Alexandria had long been in dispute, notably about the way Scripture should be handled. About 318 Arius accused Bishop Alexander of Alexandria of subscribing to Sabellianism (the view that Father, Son, and Holy Spirit were merely roles or modes assumed in turn by God). Though Alexander had probably been guilty of no more than an incautious use of language, Arius was concerned to emphasize the oneness of God.

Unhappily, he went to the other extreme. If the Father was absolutely one, where did the Son come in? Arius explained it thus: "The Father existed before the Son. There was a time when the Son did not exist. Therefore, the Son was created by the Father. Therefore, although the Son was the highest of all creatures, he was not of the essence of God."

This was no mere exercise in semantics, but an attack on the doctrine of God and a challenge to the very foundation of Christianity, which holds that Jesus is really and truly God. Alexander, who until then had had a high regard for Arius as an expert logician, brought him to meet with some of the diocesan clergy. Alexander himself chaired the discussion. Arius defended his position, but the others (joined belatedly by Alexander) contended that the Son is consubstantial and coeternal with the Father. The bishop commanded Arius to receive this doctrine and to reject his former opinions.

Arius was not prepared to do so, and in 319 he was officially anathematized, as were all others who made "shameless avowal of these heresies." There the matter might have rested, but Arius was cunning and persuasive. The emperor Constantine had been at first inclined to dismiss the theological differences as "of a truly insignificant character," but he was less concerned about the unity of God (which he imperfectly understood) than about the unity of his empire. The churchmen persisted, however, and Constantine convened the first ecumenical council of the Church, held at Nicea in A.D. 325.

Almost three hundred bishops were present, predominantly from the East. Arianism was the major item on the agenda. Arius and his supporters were given every opportunity to make their case and seemed confident of success. To their dismay, both Arianism and a compromise viewpoint were rejected, and the council produced a creed that upheld the orthodox position. Its crucial point was its insistence on Christ's being of the same essence with the Father, rather than of similar essence (a view the Arians would have accepted). The difference in Greek centered around the presence or absence of the letter Greek letter iota (i)—i.e., whether it should be *homoousios* (of the same essence) or *homoiousios* (of similar essence). The orthodox at Nicea, notably the young Athanasius who was an invaluable aide to Bishop Alex-

ander, rightly saw that this was not merely a battle over a letter, but that true Christian doctrine was at stake.

At the end of the council Arius was excommunicated, but within two years he deceived Constantine into thinking he was orthodox at heart. Athanasius, who became bishop of Alexandria in 328, would not have Arius back in the city, and this became a source of unrest, fully exploited by Athanasius's enemies. Even when the exasperated Constantine sent Athanasius into exile, Arius was refused Communion in the diocese and returned to Constantinople, where he soon died. Arianism was not dead, however, but persisted (often among the highly placed) until its final condemnation at the Council of Constantinople in 381.

J. D. DOUGLAS

ARMINIUS, JACOBUS (1559–1609)
Dutch theologian; founder of an
anti-Calvinist Reformed theology

Arminius was born in the Netherlands during the Spanish occupation, at Oudewater near Utrecht. His father, an armorer or smith, died around the time of the boy's birth, so Arminius was educated under the direction and at the expense of family friends who recognized his abilities as a student. He had just entered Marburg University (Germany) when news came of the infamous Oudewater massacre by the Spanish. Arminius returned home to learn that his mother and several of his brothers and sisters had been among the victims.

When the new University of Leiden opened nearby in 1576, Arminius was the twelfth student enrolled. That seems to have been the first public recording of his Latinized name (Jacobus Arminius; he had been born Jacob Harmenszoon). At Leiden he adopted the controversial theology of the French scholar Peter Ramus (1515–1572), and later went on to study at the Geneva Academy (1582), which was then headed by Theodore Beza, Calvin's successor. Because Arminius's defense of Ramus angered the Genevan authorities, he left briefly for Basel (1583). There he was offered a doctorate but declined, convinced he would not bring honor to the title.

After returning to Geneva, Arminius must have been more prudent, for in 1585 Beza wrote to the Amsterdam city rulers (who were sponsoring the young man's education), commending his ability and diligence highly and encouraging a continuance of their "kindness and liberality." Perhaps significantly, Beza made no mention of Arminius's theology. After a short visit to Italy, Arminius returned home, was ordained, and in 1588 became one of the ministers of Amsterdam. His 1590 marriage to a merchant's daughter gave him influential links.

From the outset Arminius's sermons on Romans 7 drew the fire of "high" Calvinists who disliked his views on grace and predestination. (Grace is the unmerited favor God shows toward sinners. Predestination is the biblical doctrine that God determines beforehand who will be saved.) High Calvinists held that although God's saving grace is completely unmerited, he extends it only to those whom he predestines to salvation. Arminius disagreed. In 1592 a colleague formally accused him of Pelagianism (an emphasis on free will, among other things, that took form in the fifth century), overdependence on the early church fathers, deviation from the Belgic Confession and the Heidelberg Catechism (two early Calvinist standards), and erroneous views on predestination. When challenged, however, his critics proved reluctant to substantiate the charges—and the city authorities were on his side. The question of predestination was not systematically raised until Arminius became professor of theology at Leiden (1603–1609), where he spent the last six years of his life in controversy.

In his 1606 rectorial address "On Reconciling Religious Dissensions among Christians," Arminius argued that such dissension damages people intellectually and emotionally and creates doubt about religion that leads to despair, atheism, and Epicureanism (hedonistic withdrawal from responsibility). He proposed as remedy the calling of a national synod, "an orderly and free convention of the parties that differ from each other." Further, Arminius believed that the natural arbiter between feuding churchmen was the "godly magistrate," a view called Erastianism. The dispute with Arminius, led by Franciscus Gomarus at Leiden, centered around the Calvinist interpretation of the divine decree about election and reprobation. When a synod finally met at Dort (1618) to resolve the dispute, Arminius had been dead nine years.

In his attempt to give the human will a more active role in salvation than orthodox Calvinism conceded, Arminius came to teach a conditional election in which a person's free will might or might not affect the divine offer of salvation. Nevertheless, it is important to distinguish between Arminius's teaching and what later became known as Arminianism, which was more liberal in its view of free will and of related doctrines than was its founder. Arminius's views were never systematically worked out until the year after his death, when his followers issued a declaration called the Remonstrance (1610), which dissented in several points from orthodox Calvinism. It held, among other things, that God's predestination was conditioned by human choice, that the gospel could be freely accepted or rejected, and that a person who had become a Christian could "fall from grace" or lose salvation.

A mild-tempered man, Arminius nonetheless spoke his mind in controversy and characteristically defended his position from Scripture. His friend Peter Bertius paid tribute to the oft-misunderstood scholar when he declared at his funeral that those who truly knew Arminius could not sufficiently esteem him. J. D. DOUGLAS

ARNAUD, HENRI (1641–1721)
Pastor and leader among the Waldensians, founded by Peter Waldo

Arnaud was born near Grenoble (France) and studied for the Waldensian ministry at Basel and Geneva (Switzerland). He served two pastorates in France before King Louis XIV revoked the Edict of Nantes in 1685, an event that threatened all Protestants. Shortly thereafter Arnaud fled to Piedmont (a region now in northwest Italy), where he became pastor at La Tour, the chief Waldensian village in the area. When Duke Amadeus of Savoy began to persecute Waldensians, Arnaud led a thousand of his people to seek refuge in religiously tolerant Switzerland. By 1689 conditions had improved in Piedmont, and Arnaud was able to return with nine hundred of the exiles. In 1698 renewed persecution again forced him and three thousand others into exile. He then took up residence in Württemberg (Germany) as pastor of the Waldensians who had settled in that area, and remained there until his death. N. V. HOPE

ARNAULD, ANTOINE (1612–1694)

Jansenist theologian and controversialist, called "The Great Arnauld"

Born in Paris, Arnauld entered the Sorbonne where in 1635 he presented a thesis on the doctrine of grace. In 1638 he came under the strong influence of the Abbe de Saint-Cyran, leading exponent of Jansenism, a movement of Catholic renewal through personal holiness that centered in France. At Saint-Cyran's urging, Arnauld studied for the priesthood, to which he was ordained in 1641. In 1643, the year of Saint-Cyran's death, Arnauld obtained his doctorate at the Sorbonne and published a controversial book, *De la Frequente Communion,* which provoked a strong reaction from the Jesuits. From then on regarded as leader of the Jansenists, Arnauld was expelled in 1656 from his professorship of theology at the Sorbonne and went into semi-retirement. In 1669 after Pope Clement IX had put a temporary end to the Jesuit-Jansenist strife, Arnauld was reinstated at the Sorbonne. Turning his argumentative guns on the Calvinistic Protestants, Arnauld published the most learned of his controversial books, *La Perpetuite de la Foi Catholique Touchant l'Eucharistie* (1669–1674). When the Jesuit controversy broke out again in 1679, Arnauld left France for self-imposed exile in the Netherlands and Belgium. From Brussels he continued to attack the Jesuits (especially their morals), and died there in

1694. His extensive writings are now available in over forty volumes. N. V. HOPE

ARNAULD, JACQUELINE MARIE ANGELIQUE (1591–1661)

French monastic reformer; sister of Antoine Arnauld

Abbess of Port Royal convent near Versailles (1602–1630), she was converted to a more serious and disciplined life-style in 1608 by the preaching of a Capuchin friar. Thereupon, though only seventeen, she instituted a series of basic reforms in her monastery (community of goods, uniform dress for all nuns, observance of prescribed canonical services, periods of silence, etc.) and sought to extend these new regulations to other monastic foundations. In 1630 she was replaced as abbess of Port Royal by her sister Agnes but continued to influence policy, particularly in having the Abbe de Saint-Cyran, leader of the Jansenist movement, appointed as spiritual counselor. When Jacqueline Arnauld again became abbess (1642–1655), she disseminated Jansenist ideas through refugees who sought shelter at her convent. Historians agree that the Port Royal, which attracted mathematician-philosopher Blaise Pascal, was largely her creation. N. V. HOPE

ARNDT, WILLIAM FREDERICK (1880–1957)

American Lutheran biblical scholar and apologist

Born in Mayville, Wisconsin, Arndt was educated at Concordia College (1894–1900) and Concordia Seminary (1900–1903). He later studied at the University of Chicago and earned a Ph.D. at Washington University in St. Louis (1935). From 1902 to 1912 Arndt served Lutheran (Missouri Synod) parishes in Tennessee, Missouri, and Brooklyn, New York. In 1912 he became professor of ancient languages at St. Paul's College, Concordia, Missouri, and in 1921 accepted the chair of New Testament literature and exegesis at Concordia Seminary, St. Louis, where he served for over thirty years.

Arndt wrote *Does the Bible Contradict Itself?* (1926) and *Gospel According to St. Luke* (1956). He also translated and edited, along with F. W. Gingrich, Walter Bauer's *Greek-English Lexicon of the New Testament and Other Early Christian Literature* (1957).

N. V. HOPE

ARNOLD, GOTTFRIED (1666–1714)
German Pietist pastor and historian

Born at Annaberg in Silesia, Arnold studied theology at Wittenberg and taught at Dresden and Giessen. He was heavily influenced by Gottfried Wilhelm Leibnitz (1646–1716) and even more so by Philipp Jacob Spener (1635–1705), founder of Pietism. While a teacher at Quedlinburg, Arnold joined a group of mystical and separatistic Pietists and for a time broke with the Lutheran church. Among his beliefs at that time was rejection of marriage. In 1669 he wrote a book called *The First Love,* eulogizing the primitive church and condemning the later accretions of doctrines and ceremonies.

Probably Arnold's greatest claim to fame was his *Impartial History of the Church and Heresy* (published in 1699–1700). In it Arnold tried to view heretics through their own writings rather than those of their opponents. He professed to see more truth in some of the skeptics than among the orthodox. His attacks on the Lutherans of his time were especially severe. In 1701 Arnold retreated from some of his mysticism, married, and accepted a parish in Saxe-Weimar. After becoming more reconciled with the establishment, he became church inspector at Perleberg on the river Elbe, where he lived until his death.

Arnold appreciated Luther's emphasis on justification by faith. Yet he criticized what he considered the reformer's grossness, coarseness, and indecently immodest utterances. He also deplored Luther's dependence on rulers to govern the churches. "Civic authority," Arnold wrote, "took them over, place after place, and took with the parish the right to appoint the preacher."

Arnold did not feel that Luther should be idolized nor his teaching regarded as universal and normative. Arnold's views were popular among the Pietists of his time, who both valued Luther and reacted against him.

R. P. EVANS

ARNOLD, MATTHEW (1822–1888)
English scholar, poet, and critic of religion

The oldest son of Thomas Arnold, headmaster of Rugby, Arnold distinguished himself there in classics and later attended Balliol college, Oxford, where he graduated with second-class honors. Convinced that the times were chaotic, he set about with a kind of aloof austerity to turn anarchy back into order. In 1857 he was appointed professor of poetry at Oxford, retaining the chair for the customary ten years.

Arnold's poetry reveals the conflicts of mid-Victorian mentality: empathy with the past yet discontent with its perception of God and of reality. "Dover Beach," his most famous poem, ends in joyless, pitiless struggle and in isolation from a faith and a world both in disarray.

Culture and Anarchy (1869) gave Arnold's diagnosis of his age: anarchy due to worship of "machinery." His prescription was "to learn and propagate the best that is known and has been thought in the world." One chapter compared the Greek and Hebrew attitudes of mind.

In 1870 Arnold turned to writing books on religion. *St. Paul and Protestantism* (1870) set forth his belief, contrary to that of his famous father, that a new age should depart from "old foundations" of biblical theology. The book dealt chiefly with dissent in regard to the Church of England and endeavored to correct the "mistakes" of Nonconformity. *Friendship's Garland* (1871) fought against weaknesses in society, politics, education, and religion. Two years later Arnold published *Literature and Dogma* (1873), which was followed by *God and the Bible* (1875), a review of the objections to *Literature and Dogma.* He also wrote *Last Essays on Church and Religion* (1877), *Isaiah of Jerusalem* (1883), and *A Friend of God* (1887).

As national inspector of schools (1851–1886), Arnold was active in the advancement of public schools in England. He demanded secondary as well as elementary schools operated by the government; in 1879 he wrote to his sister that he regarded the establishment of public secondary schools as "the first practicable of those great democratic reforms to which we must one day come." If the middle and lower classes were to rule England, it was essential that they be educated.

Discourses in America (1885) contained lectures Arnold gave in the winter of 1883–1884 on a tour of the United States. In "Literature and Science," his most popular lecture, he upheld education in the literary classics. E. B. BATSON

ARNOLD OF BRESCIA (c. 1100–1155)

Italian church reformer

Arnold joined the Canons Regular at an early age and rose to a position of leadership. He joined a revolt against the bishop of Brescia to establish an independent city government or commune.

Arnold was a popular preacher, able to sway the masses. He blamed the vices of priests and monks upon their possessions, primarily land. Such possessions, he maintained, produced a church built upon wealth and power and whose sacraments were thereby invalidated. Application of his viewpoints led to a strong anticlerical position. Instead of confessing their sins to a priest, Arnold maintained, people should confess to one another and provide mutual spiritual support. Such ideas provided a theological basis for Arnold's active support of popular revolution.

Arnold was condemned by the second Lateran Council in 1139 and exiled from Brescia. He had studied under Abelard, a Scholastic philosopher, and stood with him at the Council of Sens in 1140. Both were condemned and banished to separate French monasteries where they continued to teach, in spite of warnings to the contrary. Arnold was then exiled from France and went to Zurich and Bohemia, proclaiming

his radical doctrines. In 1145 he returned to Rome and made his peace with the pope.

However, Arnold again became involved in revolution. He joined a revolt in Rome, gaining a dominant influence in the revolutionary government that centered in the Senate. He was excommunicated again in 1148 by Eugenius III (pope from 1145–1153), a spiritual disciple of Bernard of Clairvaux. Arnold competed for control of the city for nearly a decade so that Adrian IV (pope from 1154–1159) was not able to reside in Rome at first. Since Arnold was a threat to both empire and church, the pope and emperor, usually at odds, joined to drive the revolutionaries out of the city. Betrayed by some of his former supporters, Arnold was arrested and turned over to the emperor, Frederick Barbarossa, for execution. He was hanged, his body burned, and his ashes spread on the Tiber River. Throughout the years of turmoil Bernard of Clairvaux was Arnold's active antagonist and frequently served to rally opposition against him.

Arnold had followers who continued some of his emphasis into the following decades. They taught a life of poverty and opposed the hierarchy of the church. They maintained that the sacraments were invalid when administered by clergy who possessed material goods. The "Arnoldists" were condemned by the Council of Verona in 1184. T. O. KAY

ARNOLD, THOMAS (1795–1842)

Clergyman and historian; headmaster at Rugby, a famous English boys' school

Arnold attended Oxford, where his industry and piety gave him a conspicuous place among his fellow students. His distinguished student career terminated with an Oriel College fellowship.

Arnold married young and settled in the country as a private tutor, but he found time to deliver a series of sermons in the parish church and to begin writing a history of the church for young people. At thirty-three he became headmaster at Rugby. His primary objective as headmaster was to "make the school a place of really Christian education." He introduced the prefectorial system which handed over the life of the school to an oligarchy of seventeen-year-old young men, responsible to the headmaster alone for its internal management. In the earlier years Arnold faced much opposition. His broad religious views were often unappreciated and sometimes strongly contested. In time, hostility waned.

Arnold introduced reforms in the actual sphere of teaching. He brought modern history, modern languages, and mathematics into the school curriculum where the core was still Greek and Latin. Arnold was convinced that not knowledge itself, but how to acquire it was the chief goal of education. He provided his students with "formulae" for studying, especially for reading both ancient and modern history: "what to look for in it, how to judge it," and "how to apply it." His historical insight caused him to argue continually against laissez-faire morality in the state and against outmoded sectarianism in the church. His vision of God's purposes for England included the establishment of a democratic, unified Christian community.

The focal point of the Rugby curriculum was the chapel service. The headmaster sang, read the Psalms, and quoted or chanted the Nicene Creed with the young men. He also administered the elements of communion and delivered the sermon. Arnold's powerful sermons were collected into five volumes and read by an audience far wider than the students at Rugby—including Queen Victoria.

In spite of his responsibilities as headmaster, Arnold participated verbally and in print in the controversial issues of his day. He was critical of the rising Oxford Movement in the Church of England, though its leaders were from his own Oriel College. In 1831 he started a short-lived weekly newspaper, *The Englishman's Register,* the goal being "to improve its readers morally." Arnold's commentary on the New Testament and a book on the church and state were never finished. His later efforts in the study of philology and in historical composition were rewarded in 1841 with a professorship of modern history at Oxford.

At Arnold's death, his published works, composed during such intervals as he could spare from his headmastership of Rugby, included seventeen volumes and a large number of pamphlets and articles. E. B. BATSON

ARNOT, FREDERICK STANLEY (1858–1914)
Scottish Plymouth Brethren missionary to central Africa

Born in Glasgow and converted in early life, Arnot planned to follow in the footsteps of David Livingstone, whose work had greatly impressed him and whose family he knew. In 1881 Arnot went to South Africa and made his way up the Zambezi River, the first of nine journeys of exploration he made into the hinterland. He preached the gospel to the Barotse chief Lewanika and was favorably received. He prepared the way for the French Mission in that area. He also persuaded Lewanika to reject the proposal of Lobengula, opportunistic chief of the Matabele, that the two tribes should ally themselves against white people. Arnot advised Lewanika rather to seek the friendship of the Christian king Khama.

Arnot began work in Benguela (Angola), then in 1885 set out for the Belgian Congo on the invitation of Mushidi, king of Garenganze. In 1886 the Garenganze Mission of the Plymouth Brethren was established. In many respects Arnot was like Livingstone. He was a "loner" of independent mind and great enterprise. He was criticized by many who were dubious about missionaries doubling as explorers or functioning without formal links to any well-known missionary society. On his journeys he endured incredible hardships from hostile natives, wild animals, and poisonous snakes. He suffered from disease, lack of food and water, and physical exhaustion. Yet he persevered in the work to which he believed God had called him and established many mission stations. Secular explorers recognized his achievements, and he was named a fellow of London's Royal Geographical Society. As with Livingstone, Arnot directed attention to Africa. Among those he brought to the Dark Continent was another Scotsman Daniel Crawford, who later made his own contribution to the annals of missions and exploration.

J. D. DOUGLAS

ASBURY, FRANCIS (1745–1816)
Father of American Methodism

Born in Handsworth, Staffordshire, four miles from Birmingham (England) of poor parents who had been among the early converts of Methodism's founder, John Wesley, Asbury was converted at the age of fourteen. He began lay preaching when only sixteen and was apprenticed as a blacksmith. In 1771 when John Wesley asked for volunteers to go to America as missionaries, Asbury eagerly responded. On board ship he recorded in his journal why he was making the dangerous journey: "I am going to live to God, and to bring others so to do."

Arriving in the colonies Asbury assumed leadership among the four Methodist missionaries then in America. His colleagues favored a "settled" or stationary clergy, but Asbury was convinced that preachers should be out and about wherever they could spread the gospel. Asbury's example set the style for the itinerating (traveling) Methodist minister in early America: "Go into every kitchen and shop; address all, aged and young, on the salvation of their souls." Asbury's dedication to a traveling ministry lasted throughout his life and through some 270,000 miles, mostly on horseback. He crossed the Allegheny Mountains more than sixty times; he saw more of the American countryside than any other person of his generation; and he may have been the best-known man in North America.

Methodist growth was hindered by the American war for independence from Great Britain. When violence erupted, all Methodist missionaries except Asbury returned to England. Lack of leadership hurt the young movement, as did their relationship to the Church of England. The Methodists, as a branch of Anglicanism, were suspected of disloyalty. Asbury was forced to retire into Delaware when he was banished from Maryland for not signing a loyalty oath to the new government. He was once shot at by American patriots. Nor did John Wesley make things easier for American Methodists by speaking out against American independence. For some years after the war the good citizenship of Wesley's American followers was still being questioned.

In a move in 1784 that marked a break with the Church of England, Wesley ordained clergymen for service in America. He also appointed Asbury "general superintendent" of the Methodists in the United States. In December 1784 at a Christmas conference in Baltimore, the Methodist Episcopal Church in America was officially organized, with Asbury as its guiding force. From that time the church grew rapidly. Along with the Baptists, with whom Asbury cooperated amicably, Methodism spread throughout the new nation. Asbury's traditional Christian message had special Wesleyan emphasis: God's free grace, mankind's freedom to accept or reject that grace, and the Christian's need to strive for an end to willful sin after conversion. The Methodist pattern of organization—local classes, preaching circuits, and general conferences—was also used effectively by Asbury.

Throughout his life Asbury set an example of devoted labor for God: "My present mode of conduct is . . . to read about one hundred pages a day; usually to pray in public five times a day; to preach in the open air every other day; and to lecture in prayer meeting every evening." His journeys were often difficult: "The water froze as it ran from the horse's nostrils . . . I have suffered a little by lodging in open houses in this cold weather; but this is a very small thing when compared to what the dear Redeemer suffered for the salvation of precious souls." Asbury's health was bad for many years.

When Asbury came to America in 1771 there were four ministers and about three hundred Methodists. When he began his work, Methodists were found only on the Atlantic seaboard. At the close of his career, the movement had spread into every state as far as the Mississippi River, then the nation's western boundary. Asbury ordained more than four thousand preachers. At the time of his death (1816) there were over 214,000 Methodists in the United States. He had worked to establish educational institutions and willed his modest estate to the Methodist "Book Concern." He took interest in practical areas of life, being among the first Americans to argue against slavery and for abstinence from hard liquor. M. A. NOLL

ATHANASIUS (c. 295–373)
Bishop of Alexandria (Egypt)

Athanasius did more than anyone else to bring about the triumph of the orthodox Nicene faith over Arianism, a struggle to which he devoted forty-five years and for which he was exiled five times.

Athanasius was born in Alexandria and was trained there as a theologian. He moved up rapidly as reader, deacon, and theological adviser for Bishop Alexander, accompanying him in 325 to the Council of Nicaea (near Constantinople, now Istanbul in modern Turkey). Athanasius succeeded Alexander as bishop upon Alexander's death in 328.

The conflicts which necessitated the Council of Nicaea began in Alexandria. They existed when Alexander was bishop and continued throughout the life of Athanasius. The first came from a challenge by Melitius of Lycopolis to the authority which the bishop of Alexandria exercised over the whole church of Egypt. Melitius formed a schismatic church in reaction to the lenient treatment Alexander's predecessor gave to those who had denied the faith during the persecution of Christians by the Roman emperor Diocletian. A greater conflict soon to engulf the whole church began when Arius, and Alexandrian presbyter, advocated the view that Christ was not eternal but was created by the Father. Arius was condemned by Alexander in 319 at a synod in his city; but Arian views spread rapidly in the East, where prominent bishops held similar views. The Council of Nicaea was called in 325 by the Roman emperor Constantine to settle the Melitian and Arian issues and to

bring unity to the church and civic peace to the area.

Condemnation of Arius by the council and even the adoption of the Nicene Creed did not bring the peace and unity which Constantine desired. There was ambiguity in the way the bishops understood the creed they had signed. As a result, Arius eventually signed the creed himself (with a few private additions). The emperor then ordered Athanasius, now bishop of Alexandria, to restore Arius. When the order arrived, Athanasius refused to readmit Arius—whereupon false charges were brought against Athanasius at the synod of Tyre (335), and Constantine exiled him.

The sanction of Arian views by the emperor threatened to turn Christianity into a philosophy mixed with pagan thought. Arians believed in a single supreme God who made contact with the world through lower creatures such as the Son and the Spirit. The Son was a suffering divine hero who was to be worshiped, very much like the hero gods of the Greeks. Since that view was so similar to paganism, Arianism made the monotheism of Christianity acceptable to many who were adopting the religion of the emperor. Athanasius recognized the danger and frequently called the Arians heathens.

As Arianism's greatest opponent, Athanasius emphasized redemption and the necessity of the Incarnation of the Word (Christ) for man's salvation (*Oration on the Incarnation of the Word*). He taught that it was necessary for the Word to be as eternal as God if he was to form the divine image in man. This was also the emphasis of his primary theological work, *The Three Orations against the Arians* (335 or later). In *Three Orations* Athanasius taught that since the Scripture describes the Son as "begotten" of the Father, he must be of the same nature as the Father, not a creature of the Father. Christ was generated spiritually, not created. In the second oration Athanasius rejected the Arians' baptism because they did not baptize in the name of the Trinity as understood in Scripture.

Athanasius's periods of exile spanned the

rule of four emperors: Constantine, Constantius, Julian (a pagan who tried to restore the old gods), and Valens (who exiled Athanasius for only four months). His first exile lasted until Constantine's death in 337. He returned to Alexandria only to be deposed the same year by a synod of Antioch. From 346, there was relative peace until he was again deposed in 355. The years 361 and 362 saw him back in his bishopric, but emperor Julian exiled him in the fall of the second year. He went back to Alexandria in 363, was deposed in 365, and recalled in 366. Through these trying times Athanasius struggled for the faith without yielding. He made it difficult for emperors to deal with him. At times he would delay appearing before their court, or would escape to appear before the emperor at another time and place—to the surprise of everyone. Throughout the struggles the majority of Christians in Alexandria remained devoted to him. One major benefit resulted from his two exiles in the West: the Latin church came under his influence.

There were, however, many bishops in the East who were not Arians and had no sympathy with the Arian bishops who controlled the Eastern church during the rule of Constantius. At the same time, they did not completely agree with the wording of the Nicene Creed: "the Son of God . . . of one substance with the Father." The majority of those bishops held that the essence of the Son is "like" that of the Father. For them the creedal phrase did not make a clear distinction between Father and Son. In 359 Athanasius made a great step toward reconciliation with that majority in his *Letter Concerning the Synods*. He apologized to Basil of Ancyra and said that those who accepted the Nicene Creed but questioned the term "of one substance" should be treated as brothers. Athanasius went further toward reconciliation by calling a synod in Alexandria (362) during his brief return while Julian was emperor. The final step in the triumph of orthodoxy came after the death of Athanasius under the emperor Theodosius at the Council of Constantinople in 381.

In addition to contributing to the defeat of Arianism, Athanasius helped shape the Christian ideal of monasticism. He brought monasticism out of isolation in Egypt with his book, *The Life of Antony*. Athanasius knew the desert hermit monk personally and through his writing made the pattern of Antony's life the ideal in the East. *The Life of Antony* also had an impact on many in the West. J. NEWTON

ATHANASIUS THE ATHONITE
(c. 920–1003)
Monk who founded the first monasteries of the Orthodox Church on Mount Athos (Greece)

Born to an upper class family on the southeast coast of the Black Sea and originally named Abraham, he became a monk early in life and changed his name to Athansius. Traveling with an elder monk, he visited Constantinople and during his second stay there was introduced to Nicephorus Phocas, a successful general who later became Byzantine emperor (ruled 963–969). Athanasius left the capital to avoid the honors and activity there, but even in self-imposed exile he was visited by Nicephorus. When he came to Mount Athos, which was already inhabited by ascetic monks not yet formed into a community, Athanasius took the name Barnabas so that he would not be recognized. He was discovered and summoned to Crete by Nicephorus to pray for the general's upcoming expedition against Saran pirates. At the urging of the other monks Athansius eventually went to Crete, where he found that Nicephorus had already won his victory. The elated general offered the monk aid to build the "Lavra," the first monastery on Athos, which Athanasius began in 961.

Two years later Nicephorus became emperor and continued to support Athanasius's authority on Athos. But when Nicephorus was assassinated and replaced by Tzimisces (ruled 969–976), the original Athonite monks resisted Athanasius's leadership and forced him to flee. He was, however, restored to power by the new emperor and by the time of his death was abbot-general of all fifty-eight communities on the peninsula. He died while trying to place the keystone on a new building.

Although this tenth-century monk was less famous than the third-century Athansius, a number of legends grew up about him—one that he broke his ankle while wrestling with devils, another that he spoke to the Virgin Mary. C. HICKS

ATHENAGORAS (second century)

Christian philosopher from Athens who allegedly became a Christian while reading the Scriptures in order to argue against them

Athenagoras's familiarity with pagan philosophy is evident in his works. Athenagoras wrote an *Apology* (177) defending Christians to the Roman emperors Marcus Aurelius (ruled 161–180) and Commodus (ruled 180–192). In it he refuted three charges brought against Christians: that Christians were atheists, that they practiced incestuous immorality, and that they ate human flesh as part of their ritual. Athenagoras argued that Christians, like the philosophers, recognized only one God who is uncreated, immaterial, and known to the understanding alone. As for the false gods, he wrote, the pagans did not even agree on who they were and, further, they described them as doing immoral deeds. The wonders which the false gods were thought to perform were really done by demons. Christians could not be called immoral since they believed that it was wrong to sin even in one's thoughts and since they believed that sins would be punished eternally. Finally, Athenagoras argued, no people would engage in cannibalism who refused to watch combats in the circus, who did not expose infants to die, and who thought abortion was wrong.

Athenagoras also wrote a pamphlet, *On the Resurrection of the Body*. His first argument for bodily resurrection was that if one believed God created all that is, then there was no reason to think that God could not reunite body and soul. His second argument was that God created man, body and soul, for a purpose; that purpose could be fulfilled only if body and soul were made to exist together after death. Thus, even as the body shared pleasures and pains with the soul in this life, so should it share rewards and punishments in the next. C. HICKS

ATTILA THE HUN (died 453)

Leader for nearly two decades of the Huns, a warlike Mongoloid people who terrorized eastern and central Europe in the fifth century

Known to Christian writers as the "Scourge of God," Attila began to rule a confederacy of nomadic tribes with his brother Bleda around 434. The two quickly doubled the tribute which the Romans had been paying since 424 and in 440 invaded the Balkans. In 447, having killed Bleda, Attila invaded the eastern Roman empire a second time and won a costly victory. Attila's attention turned farther westward in 450 when Honoria, sister of the western Roman emperor, asked Attila to rescue her from a marriage which had been forced upon her. When he invaded what is now France, Attila was defeated in 451 by an alliance of Romans, Visigoths, and Franks led by the Roman Aetius.

The next year Attila entered Italy but pestilence and the presence of eastern troops convinced him to yield to the entreaties of Leo I (pope, 440–461) and leave Italy. Attila died within a year and thereafter the Huns ceased to be a threat to the empire. Despite the terror which he inspired, Attila himself was not excessively brutal for his time and was capable of patient diplomacy. C. HICKS

AUGUSTINE OF CANTERBURY (died c. 604)

Missionary who brought Christianity back to southern England and founded the metropolitan bishopric of Canterbury, now the mother church of the Anglican Communion

An earlier Christian presence in southern England had been driven north by invading Angles, Saxons, and Jutes. Augustine brought the worship of Jesus Christ to the Anglo-Saxons, who had worshiped Thor and Woden. With their new religion came contact with Greco-Roman civilization.

Augustine and the forty monks who accompanied him to England in 596 were all trained in Pope Gregory's monastery in Rome. Augustine was not a common baptismal name, so it is possible that the name was taken (or given) when he entered the monastery. It served to indicate that he was a young man of promise who might emulate the great Augustine of Hippo. By 596 Augustine was assistant to the abbot and was an expert in theology, monastic rules, counseling, and the management of monastic lands. He was ready to do Gregory's bidding.

How Augustine came to be sent to England is associated with a well-known incident told by Bede the historian. Pope Gregory saw some Anglo-Saxon boys being sold as slaves in Rome and on inquiring who they were was told that they were "Angles." To him they looked like "angels" because of their fair complexion. So he determined to send Augustine and other monks to the land of those pagan Angles to convert them to Christ. They began their journey by visiting the bishop of Aix-en-Provence and the island monastery of Lerins. From there Augustine was sent by his colleagues back to Rome to be consecrated abbot and to get letters of papal commendation to the bishops and princes they expected to meet.

On Augustine's return the party traveled north on an old Roman road through Sens and Paris to the coast. With interpreters they crossed the channel and landed in the mouth of the river Stour on the isle of Thanet. From there they sent a message of good will to the king, Ethelbert, who resided at the ruined city of Durovernum Cantiacorum (Canterbury). The king came to meet the missionaries and offered them a place of residence in his capital. He knew of Christianity through his wife, Bertha, a Christian princess from the kingdom of the Franks, but he and the Anglo-Saxon people were pagans. Augustine and the monks worshiped in the queen's church, St. Martin's, the only church still standing from earlier days. Having made a permanent settlement, Augustine returned to the continent of Eu-

rope to be consecrated bishop. Conversion of the Anglo-Saxons proceeded and eventually Ethelbert himself was baptized in 601. The event marked the beginning of profound influence of Mediterranean civilization on the tribal though not primitive Germanic (Saxon) society.

With the conversion of the king who was also the bretwalda (senior king among the Anglo-Saxons of England), the time was ripe to extend the mission to all of England. Augustine sent to Rome for further helpers, for ecclesiastical vessels and vestments, and for advice for what became known as the second mission to England. Able men including Mellitus, "the abbot from the Gauls," with letters from Gregory to the king, queen, and Augustine arrived in 601. The letter to Augustine was the foundation document for creation of the archepiscopal provinces of Canterbury and York. In it the pope instructed Augustine on future development of the church throughout England, but before his death Augustine was able to consecrate only two bishops, Mellitus to London and Justus to Rochester.

In 596 Christians in Rome and Canterbury knew little of the Celtic Christianity in northern England, Wales, Ireland, and Scotland. Since Celtic Christians were suspicious of the Anglo-Saxons (whom they regarded as foreign invaders), it was extremely difficult for Augustine, the friend of Ethelbert, to have meaningful negotiations with them or their bishops. Yet Augustine did meet some of the bishops and according to Bede actually healed a blind man to prove to them that he was a true servant of Christ. But the meetings achieved little, and it was not until archbishop Theodore arrived in Canterbury from Rome in 668 that the Celtic churches were brought into communion with Canterbury and Rome.

In Canterbury Augustine supervised the building of the Church of the Savior for general use. He also received land from Ethelbert to build a monastery for the monks who had arrived in 596 and 601, but who had not become engaged in teaching and evangelism. The church of the monastery was dedicated to St. Peter and St. Paul because the pope had sent relics of the two apostles. That church or "minster" was the first of many in England which became important teaching centers for the Anglo-Saxon church. Augustine was buried in 604 near the incomplete monastery in Canterbury. On his tomb was written: "Here rests ... Augustine. ... Supported by God's help by the working of miracles, he led Ethelbert ... and his people from the worship of idols to faith in Christ." P. TOON

AUGUSTINE OF HIPPO (354–430)
Greatest of the Latin church fathers

Augustine was bishop of Hippo Regius, a town on the North African coast in the Roman province of Numidia. His impact is still felt both in western churches and in western culture.

More is known about Augustine than any other figure in the early church because of his *Confessions* (397–401) and *Retractions* (426–427). He was born in the small town of Tagaste in Numidia, the son of a pagan father, Patricius, and a Christian mother, Monica. With great personal sacrifice both parents sought the best Roman education for their gifted son as a key to his advancement from their small African town. Augustine studied first at Madaura and then received training in rhetoric at Carthage (375) which prepared him to "dress his words in style." At Carthage Augustine abandoned the faith of his mother and followed the immoral practices of his fellow students. In 372 he took a mistress who remained with him for about thirteen years and bore him a son, Adeodatus (who died around 390).

AUGUSTINE'S QUEST FOR TRUTH
Reading Cicero's *Hortensius* (now lost), Augustine was stirred to a religious quest for wisdom through philosophy. His quest took him to the Manichaean sect with which he remained as a "hearer" for nine years. The Manichaeans taught a radical dualism: an absolute evil power or substance (a "Kingdom of Darkness"), and the opposite, a good power or substance (a "Kingdom of Light").

According to that sect, the god of the Old Testament was an evil demon and the god of Christianity a good god. As a hearer, Augustine adopted their views of the Old Testament and of personal evil, excusing his own conduct by saying "It was not I who was sinning, but some other nature within me." He abandoned the Manichaeans when their expert, Faustus, was unable to resolve basic problems that Augustine had with their views. The disappointed teacher of rhetoric moved to Rome to start his own school.

During Augustine's brief stay in Rome he turned to the writings of the Skeptics (Academics) who said that knowledge was not possible. Withdrawal of his students from the school before paying their bills added to his despair. Through a Manichaean contact with the pagan senator, Symmachus, Augustine was appointed professor of rhetoric in Milan (384), then the residence of the Roman emperor. As part of his appointment Augustine was to give the public oration honoring the emperor (Valentinian II).

Augustine attended the preaching of Bishop Ambrose in order to hear his eloquence, and Ambrose's allegorical preaching began to remove the problems raised by the Manichaeans. Although Augustine could not bring himself to converse with the busy Ambrose, he sought out Christian intellectuals in Milan who instructed him and gave him Latin translations of the Neoplatonist writers Plotinus and Porphyry. Those pagan writers corrected the Manichaean errors but did not present the truth about Christ; in fact, the work of Porphyry encouraged Augustine to attempt moral "self-purification" of his soul by practicing what Porphyry called the "purifying virtues." At that time Augustine was in the midst of a moral struggle: he had sent his mistress back to Africa and was waiting for his mother to arrange a proper marriage into a wealthy family. Porphyry's method failed to rid Augustine of desire for worldly honor or for sexual gratification. But reading Romans 13:14 brought Christ as a moral authority to give him a "new will." In a sudden moral conversion he abandoned his teaching position and all desire for an advantageous marriage. Augustine withdrew with some close friends, relatives, and his mother, to a friend's villa at Cassiciacum to pursue truth.

With confidence that a purified soul was able to arrive at clear truth, Augustine engaged the group at Cassiciacum in Socratic dialogue, a method in which a teacher directs questions to individuals in a group and leads them in the discussion, yet often without conclusion. The dialogues, recorded by a scribe and later supplemented by Augustine, were the basis of three of his writings. He later said of those early works that he had too high a regard for the teachings of the Platonists at the time and was still influenced by their school of pride. Augustine received baptism from Ambrose on Easter of 387, and in 388 he returned to North Africa after the death of his mother, Monica.

AUGUSTINE AS A BISHOP

For a two-year period at Tagaste (389–391), Augustine supervised and instructed a group of baptized laymen called "servants of God." Writing at that time against the Manichaeans his views moved closer to a biblical position, especially in understanding pride and humility (*On True Religion*). The North African church was then struggling against the Manichaeans and also against the split-off Donatist church. Many congregations were without the guidance of a bishop. On a visit to Hippo, Augustine was compelled by the congregation to become their priest because their old Greek bishop spoke Latin with difficulty. After further study of the Bible, Augustine served as priest and in 396 became bishop of Hippo, where he remained until his death.

From Augustine's ordination to the time he began his *Confessions*, there was a marked development of his biblical thought: he recognized pride as the beginning of all sin (*The Lord's Sermon on the Mount*, 393) and Christ's humility as the way to life for mankind fallen through pride (*Discourses on the Psalms*, 391, and *On the Free Will*, 388–395). Augustine as a mature biblical theologian appears in the *Confessions*, the best known of his writings. The first section of the book moves from Augustine's birth to his rebirth

with a new will in Christ, ending with the death of Monica (her goal of her son's conversion fulfilled). The last section is an examination of the inner world and the outer world, with a perceptive study of memory and time. The book follows the pattern of Augustine's life. After his conversion he sought to understand all of God's creation with his new will. His book *Confessions* describes his self-examination as a Christian and reflects a clear biblical understanding of man (which was missing in most of the church fathers). Augustine elevated the grace of the gospel and found God's grace acting in his own life. He criticized the Neoplatonists for their pride: they missed the "way to God" by not yielding to the humility of the incarnation; it is the humble Jesus who lifts up those who cast themselves upon him.

In his major theological work, *On the Trinity* (399–419), Augustine brought the Western treatment of the Trinitarian doctrine to completion. He approached the doctrine from the nature of God in his unity and then treated the Persons of the Trinity, avoiding a historical development of Father, Son, and Holy Spirit. The Eastern church had difficulty with the doctrine, because in trying to understand the Trinity's existence in historical sequence they were often forced to give priority to the Father. In his book *On the Trinity*, which Augustine considered the most difficult of his writings, he drew upon Neoplatonic models to state the nature of God: God is simple, undivided by persons or by attributes. A major section is devoted to analogies of the Trinity found in creation. In those he moved beyond his philosophical models in a Christian direction: within the individual spiritual soul there is a memory of God, an understanding of God, and the love of God.

With the same philosophical models Augustine wrote *Epistle 137*, one of several letters written to a pagan intellectual who questioned him about the Incarnation. In that letter Augustine anticipated the Council of Chalcedon (451) on the doctrine of the Person of Christ: one person in two natures, divine and human, without confusion of the natures. Leo the Great (pope 440–461), who had an impact upon the council and its statements, was influenced by Augustine's letter and his other writings.

AUGUSTINE VERSUS THE DONATISTS

When Augustine became bishop at Hippo, the Donatist church was the dominant church in the province of Numidia, and Catholics were in the minority even in Hippo itself. The Donatists traced their doctrines to Cyprian (died 258), a martyred African bishop who held that the sacraments performed by an unholy bishop were invalid. The Donatist church was formed (311) when eighty Numidian bishops applied that teaching to the consecration of a new bishop of Carthage. They believed that he and others had denied the faith during the last Roman persecution. Their newly formed "pure" church became known as the followers of Donatus, their second leading bishop. Augustine sought every possible means to draw the Donatists into the Catholic church with at least eleven writings (including a popular song).

In his anti-Donatist writings, Augustine dealt with the nature of the sacraments and the church. He taught that the validity of baptism and the other sacraments did not depend upon the moral character of man, the agent, but upon God who gave the sacrament. The word of the gospel is good in spite of the minister who delivers it. For Augustine there was only one church in Christ, and the Donatists were outside that unity and outside the place of salvation. The one church was not pure, but in it the "wheat and tares" would grow together until the day of judgment. Augustine failed in his effort to bring the Donatists into the Catholic church, although a few came as a result of his debates. The Donatists were finally forced into the church by two edicts of Emperor Honorius (405, 411). Augustine had opposed the use of force by the state but changed his mind when he saw the peace and happiness that came to Hippo after the forced unity. The Catholic church adopted Augustine's position and moved beyond it, encouraging the use of force by the state

against all schismatics. When the strong Donatist church disappeared after 411, African Christianity began to wane.

AUGUSTINE VERSUS
ROMAN PAGANISM

On August 28, A.D. 410, troops of the barbarian King Alaric entered and sacked Rome, the "eternal city," sending a shock wave through the empire that shook both pagan and Christian. The pagans blamed the fall of the city on the Christians who had deserted the old gods. The Christians had no reply because they had claimed that God would protect the empire of the Christian emperors. Refugees reaching North Africa demanded an answer from Augustine. His answer was the *City of God*. Although the complete work (twenty-two books) took twenty-two years to complete, the crisis in Rome made early circulation of the first three books necessary. The plan which Augustine set forth at the beginning of that "great and arduous work" was carried through to the end.

In the first book Augustine treated the crisis in Rome by showing the pagans that Alaric had recognized Christian churches as sanctuaries and that those who fled there were spared, a clemency never practiced by pagan Rome. He also recalled calamities that had come to the Romans during the Punic wars in the pre-Christian period when only the pagan gods were protecting them. Finally, Christians suffered along with pagans in the city of Rome in order to teach them not to love the present world but to lay hold of eternal life. Actually Augustine devoted only a small part of the *City of God* to the crisis in Rome. From the opening page he launched a massive attack on paganism as being at the root of man's evil, his pride. At its core Rome was "ruled by the lust to rule"; what the Roman writer Virgil gave as the virtue of rulers, "to put down the proud," was the prerogative only of God (Ps. 94).

Right through Book 10 Augustine carried the attack into every area: religion, philosophy, history. He concentrated on the ancient form of Roman religion because educated pagans of the fifth century were living in their classical literary past. Their gods were formerly famous men, demons, or the projection of human sinful desires; and even a pagan writer of the past, Varro, had seen something of those errors.

With respect to philosophy, Augustine directed his attention to the most recent and most influential pagans, the Neoplatonists, whose teachings had become a religious philosophy. The *City of God* expanded the attack made in the *Confessions* by naming Porphyry and centering upon him as the most learned philosopher and the Christians' bitterest enemy. Augustine showed the contradictory elements in Porphyry's thought. That philosopher approved the magical control of the demons, yet followed the way of philosophy. He considered the coming of God in flesh as unbelievable yet believed that the stars were divine, a belief far more incredible. Augustine argued that followers of Porphyry were seeking redemption in a "superior knowledge" which served only to blind them by pride to the humility of the Incarnation. It is the humility of God in flesh that becomes a "medicine" to heal human pride. The Neoplatonist sought God in the "beyond" through intermediaries, but God has come down to man. The followers of Porphyry had no rational basis for rejecting Christ; they did so only because Christ is humble and they were proud.

Augustine dealt with Roman history from the time of Romulus, the founder, until the Christian period. In what many considered an unpatriotic attack, he criticized the greatest Roman historian, Sallust, who in the days after the assassination of Julius Caesar saw the decline of Rome in the loss of primitive Roman virtues. Rather than praising the early Romans, Augustine used the writings of both historians and poets to lay bare the true motives of even the most virtuous pagan Romans. What he found at the root of their great virtue was a desire for the praise of men. They would give away their life and wealth for such "glory."

In the last half of the *City of God* (Books 11–22) Augustine traced the history of two cities, the city of earth and the city of God, from their origin to their destiny at the final judgment. In that history he attempted a theological answer to every possible question that could be raised by both pagan and Christian. The city of earth, which at its root is the city of pride, had its origin in the pride and evil will of Satan, not in an evil substance. It began in the heart of man when Adam, in his pride, desired to be as God. The origin of the city of God is found in God himself, and the only way to that city is Jesus Christ, the God-man. Beginning with Cain and Abel, Augustine used historical parallels and "types" to point forward to Christ as the fulfillment of events as well as the fulfillment of prophecy. With historical parallels he illustrated the two cities in all periods of time.

The *City of God* is a biblical approach to history: God began the events in creation, controls them by his will, and at the second coming of Christ will bring the events to an end. In contrast, pagan histories viewed events as part of some great cycle or as structured about "man" himself. Augustine did not develop the idea of a "Christian state" as did an Eastern church historian, Eusebius of Caesarea (died c. 339). Even when Augustine wrote about the Christian emperor Theodosius (ruled 379–395), he merely praised him for his Christian deeds and piety. Augustine said that God gives the possession of empires to good and bad alike according to his will, as he sends the blessings of light and air.

If the Christian empire of Theodosius was not the city of God, did Augustine consider the institutional church to be the city of God? The organized church had been stressed in his anti-Donatist writings, but in the *City of God* it appears only as the body of believers whose citizenship is in heaven, the wheat among the tares on earth. Augustine himself was not thinking of the Roman Catholic structure of the church as it dominated the Middle Ages. Rulers and church leaders of the Middle Ages, however, later misused the *City of God* to support the Roman church as the powerful city of God on earth.

AUGUSTINE VERSUS PELAGIANISM

Among the refugees who came to Africa from the crisis in Rome were some who stirred a controversy in the church over the grace of God and the freedom of man. The leading figure was Pelagius, an ascetic layman from Britain who drew followers in Rome to his monastic ideal. Pelagius taught that human nature was capable of perfection and that the demands of God could be carried out by man, who had no original sin passed along from Adam. Pelagius was an activist who had a goal of reforming society through the young noblemen converted to his ideal. He also criticized Augustine's dependence upon "grace" in the *Confessions* as an encouragement to laziness. Pelagius moved from Africa to Jerusalem without seeing Augustine; but Pelagius's outspoken pupil, Celestius, remained in Africa to apply for the office of priest. Through the efforts of Augustine, the Council of Carthage (411) condemned Celestius as a heretic for views which included the following: (1) Adam died because he was mortal and not because of his sin; (2) there is no original sin; (3) infants are without sin, as Adam was before his fall; and (4) man can live without sin through his own effort.

Against the Pelagians, Augustine wrote thirteen works and letters from 412 until the end of his life. Even at the end he was writing a work against Julian, the bishop of Eclanum in southern Italy, who had become an effective spokesman and writer for the Pelagian movement. Augustine died before finishing that final work. In his anti-Pelagian works, Augustine affirmed that (1) Adam had immortality before his fall; (2) original sin is transmitted from Adam to all his descendants; (3) infants need baptism and remission of sins; (4) the grace of God is sovereign, and the will of man does not overcome the will of God; (5) every good work of man is the gift of the grace of God; and (6) perfection is not reached in this life—even the saints must confess their sins (1 John 1:8).

When the anti-Pelagian writings appeared, some monks in southern France and North Africa reacted against them but did not move to the radical position of Pelagius. They constituted a group known later as the Semi-Pelagians, who taught that the beginning step in salvation is made by the will of man and that perseverance in faith is also an act of man. Augustine was mild in his treatment of those monks; he even received several of them in Hippo to answer their questions. To correct their views he wrote five works and letters. In those writings he used themes already presented in his anti-Pelagian works but emphasized predestination and perseverance. According to Augustine predestination is the act of God from beginning to end. It is his act in his will and not based on foreknowledge of later merit in the elect. He has chosen the elect beforehand and the number of the elect is fixed. The perseverance of the elect in Christ to the end of their life comes not by their power but as a gift from God.

Augustine led the Western church through the Pelagian controversy to a peak in theology where the grace of God was the central theme. The Eastern church had not had such a clear view of sin and the grace of God; most Latin church fathers before Augustine (except Ambrose) treated the gospel only as a new law to be observed. Augustine moved the church to a more biblical position and delivered it from teachers like Pelagius and the Pelagian bishop, Julian of Eclanum, who represented the Old Roman culture with its elevation of man. Several church councils condemned the Pelagians, and the Council of Orange (529) condemned the Semi-Pelagians. In spite of those actions the later Roman Catholic Church did not follow Augustine in all points on grace, the will of man, and predestination. From the thirteenth century Roman Catholics followed Thomas Aquinas, who modified the Augustinian position.

AUGUSTINE'S FINAL WORK

Four years before his death Augustine began to reread his works. He recognized the impact his thought was having on the church and what his critics were saying. At that point he did what few writers have done: he wrote the *Retractions,* a book that examined all his previous writings (except letters and sermons) in chronological order. It is more than an index of his writings; it is an evaluation of his written thought at the end of his life.

During the last months of Augustine's life the Vandals held the fortified town of Hippo under siege by land and sea. They had destroyed Roman North Africa and the outward evidence of Latin Christianity. Hippo was filled with refugees, including bishops and priests. Augustine preached to a congregation filled with refugees and had the golden vessels of the church melted down to give aid to the many who came. Augustine's letters acknowledged that Africa was ripe for God's judgment at the hands of the barbarians. In that final crisis Augustine contracted a fatal disease. With the penitential psalms hanging on the walls of his room, the seventy-five-year-old bishop who had cultivated so many friendships ordered that he be left alone to prepare himself for death.

The measure of Augustine's importance goes beyond the rare title, "Doctor of the Church," given to him in the Middle Ages. He was the first to give a self-examination before God in the form of his *Confessions* and thus give the church a biblical understanding of a man's life under the grace of God. He was the first to give a biblical view of history, time, and the state in his *City of God.* He established the doctrine of the church in his anti-Donatist writings, a view that prevailed in the church for centuries. He gave the Western church a clear statement concerning the person of Christ, which was later established as doctrine by Leo. He made the grace of God in the gospel the theme of theology in the West.

J. NEWTON

AVVAKUM (1620–1682)
Russian archpriest and author

In 1652 Nikon, patriarch of the Russian church, attempted to accomplish reform by bringing the church's practices into closer conformity with those of the Greek Ortho-

dox Church. Nikon instituted "corrections" of the old Russian rituals by adapting them to contemporary Greek forms. He did the same with the texts of the sacred books. All this was done, however, without proper philological training on the part of the correctors.

Avvakum belonged to another group of reformers who restored ancient rules of prayer, fasting, and personal morality, as well as preaching and confession. For them Nikon's "reforms" were not reforms but apostasy, introducing theological errors into the rites and sacred texts. Consequently, the church divided into "old believers" and "new believers," with Avvakum as a principal figure in the old believers' camp. Opposition of the old believers to Nikon's reforms resulted in severe repressions. The old believers were excommunicated by the Council of 1666–1667. Severe measures were taken to stamp them out. Many died at the gallows or the stake. During Avvakum's fifteen years in prison at Pustozersk he wrote his autobiography. Ten years later, in 1682, he was burned at the stake. Avvakum has been remembered not only because of his martyrdom, but because the spirituality recorded in his writings reached great heights as a result of his sufferings and persecution.

R. E. WEBBER

AYLWARD, GLADYS (1902–1970)
Missionary to China

Born near London, daughter of a postman, Aylward was converted at eighteen while in domestic service. She determined to be a missionary in China, but lack of educational qualifications led to her rejection by the China Inland Mission. Nothing daunted, she saved money from her small salary and in 1832 embarked on an incredible journey by train through Siberia. Further hampered by the Russian-Chinese war, she finally went through Japan to join missionary Jeannie Lawson in isolated Yangcheng. They opened an inn and attracted listeners by telling Bible stories. Not only did Aylward adopt a Chinese life-style, but she also became a naturalized Chinese citizen in 1936.

After Miss Lawson's death Aylward continued and extended the work. When the Japanese invaded China in 1940 she led nearly a hundred Chinese children on a historic and hazardous journey to safety, a feat that inspired the film *The Inn of the Sixth Happiness*. After a serious illness she returned to England in 1947, then went back to the Orient to open an orphanage in 1955, serving there until her death. Biographies of her were written by Alan Burgess (*The Small Woman*, 1957) and Phyllis Thompson (*London Sparrow*, 1971).

J. D. DOUGLAS

AZARIAH, VEDANAYAKAM SAMUEL (1874–1945)

First Indian bishop in the Anglican Church

Azariah was born at Vellalanvillai, Tinnevelly District, South India. His father, a convert from low-caste Hinduism, was a village pastor. His mother was a deeply devoted woman with a fervent love for the Word of God. In 1895 Azariah went into YMCA student work and in 1898 married Anbu Mariammal.

Keenly interested in evangelism, Azariah founded the Indian Missionary Society of Tinnevelly in 1903 and was one of the founders of the National Missionary Society (1905), whose objective was the evangelization of India with "Indian men, Indian money, and under Indian direction." As secretary of the Tinnevelly Society he helped begin pioneer missionary work in Dornakal, the Telegu language area. That work proved so challenging that Azariah resigned from the YMCA, was ordained in 1909, and went to serve the depressed classes in that area. A great mass movement to Christ took place, with the church in his area growing from 50,000 in 1912 to 235,000 in 1945. In 1912 Azariah was consecrated bishop of Dornakal. Henry Whitefield, bishop of Madras, fervently supported him.

Azariah was as much an evangelist as a bishop. He taught that Indian evangelists should serve as equal partners with missionaries from other countries. He adamantly opposed caste or color distinctions within the church. He supported indigenous movements in church work and missions and gave a provocative address on that subject at the Edinburgh Missionary Conference (1910). He was a key leader at the World Missionary Conference at Tambaram (India) in 1938 and represented "the younger churches" in several international conferences. He served as chairman of the National Christian Council of India, Burma, and Ceylon (Sri Lanka) (1929–1945). In 1920 Cambridge University conferred upon him the honorary LL.D. degree.

Beginning with the Tranquebar (South India) Conference (1919), Bishop Azariah gave leadership to South India church union efforts, hoping to form a united front for the task of evangelization. He did not live to see the birth of the Church of South India in 1947. S. P. ATHYAL

B

BACH, JOHANN SEBASTIAN
(1685–1750)

German organist and composer; one of the most illustrious figures in music history

Bach's contributions united many details of German, French, and Italian musical styles during the closing years of the Baroque period. His importance in the history of organ literature, the chorale, the cantata, and oratorio has had significant relation to the Lutheran liturgy, and his works are recognized for their large quantity together with high craftsmanship.

The Bach family was active musically for nearly two centuries. With twenty known musicians in its lineage it had aspects of a musical dynasty. Johann Sebastian, with his sons Karl Philipp Emanuel, Johann Christian, and Wilhelm Friedemann, form the best-known group, coming relatively late in the history. Karl Philipp Emanuel (1714–1788) was J. S. Bach's second surviving son, known for his experiments with the emerging Classic Era sonata. Johann Christian (1735–1782), the eleventh surviving son, was known as the "London" Bach, and wrote symphonies, concertos, and vocal and chamber music. Wilhelm Friedemann, known as the "Halle" Bach, was the eldest son, and wrote a sinfonia, piano works, and dance pieces.

J. S. Bach's early studies included the violin and the organ. In 1703 he was attached to the orchestra of the brother of the Duke of Saxe-Weimar. His posts as organist began at the new church in Arnstadt (1704) and at St. Blasius', Muhlhausen. After his marriage to Maria Barbara Bach (a cousin), Johann Sebastian went to Weimar, first as court organist and chamber musician (from 1708) and later as concertmaster. Bach's "Weimar Period" (until 1717) was an important stage in his early career as a composer. From 1717 to 1723 Bach served as Chapel-director and overseer of chamber music to Prince Leopold of Anhalt, at Cothen. This "Cothen Period" is generally known for the rich legacy in orchestral and chamber works. On the other hand, research has indicated that many of Bach's cantatas probably originated at this time, as well as earlier, at Weimar. It was also during this period that Bach's wife died (1720). Subsequent remarriage to Anna Magdalena Wulken was also important musically. Anna copied numerous parts of the cantatas and possessed two books that included entries in her own hand, in addition to entries of her husband.

From 1723 until his death, Bach held the post of cantor at St. Thomas's School, Leipzig, where he was also organist and kapell meister at St. Thomas Church and Nicholai

Church. Bach's Leipzig period of twenty-seven years was a period marked, compositionally, by deep intensification within a rather limited number of works. One important example of the later works, the *Musical Offering,* was constructed from a theme of Frederick II of Prussia, acquired by Bach during a visit to Potsdam (1747), where he performed before the king. Although earlier scholars believed that nearly 200 cantatas were written during the Leipzig years, recent findings indicate that these years were marked by borrowing from works written at Cothen and/or Weimar. New works were, to a great extent, resettings (including texts) of earlier works. Such settings are known as *contrafacta.* In the Leipzig years the contrafacta occur perhaps fifty to sixty times, owing to the pressures of daily routines and administrations. The genuine late works are profound experiments in technical resources and are marked by harmonic colors and by tensions of texture that stand somewhat apart from the earlier years.

INSTRUMENTAL WORKS

Bach's interest in order and relationship within his compositions was an important part of Late Baroque aesthetics. Many of his works are united by principles of (a) liturgical meaning, (b) chorale uses (see also *Chorale Church Music*), (c) overarching structures of key, or (d) special technical devices such as prelude/fugue pairings, dance patterns, and canon or variation cycles. Many works are grouped into educational or other didactic arrangements such as suites or liturgically ordered series.

1. Works intended as a cycle in the church year include the *Little Organ Book* (begun in Weimar, finished in Cothen). Although this work was designed to contain 164 chorale preludes, it has 45 pieces, arranged according to the Lutheran church year. The pieces are condensed in scope, featuring abstract textures or pictorially expressed materials in relation to the chorale tunes.

2. The *Keyboard Practice* (*Clavierubung*) dates from 1731 onward and is a monumental collection in four parts. It has bearing on

Bach's contribution to the Lutheran liturgy as well as to his secular output.

3. Chorale preludes are also represented in the organ literature by the *Eighteen Great Preludes* and the *Six Schubler Chorales* (the latter being transcribed cantata movements). Bach also made numerous congregational-style settings of chorales in four voices, including a collection of 371 harmonizations and a group of 69 melodies with figured bass.

4. A very important contribution is the numerous organ preludes and fugues, including the "Great" ones in C major, E minor, B minor, G minor, and E-flat major. Some pieces are modeled on concerto principles, while the prelude from the G Minor is a fantasy, and its fugue is based on a seventeenth-century folk song, the "Rolandston." The *Prelude and Fugue in A Major* has dance characteristics and pastoral implications in its texture and rhythm.

5. Among other instrumental works should be included orchestral suites, concertos, solo and accompanied sonatas, and keyboard partitas and suites.

VOCAL WORKS

J. S. Bach wrote four short masses consisting largely of retexted music drawn from the cantatas. For example, the *Mass in F* uses the Lutheran Litany chorale: "Christ, Thou Lamb of God" in the "Kyrie," while the "Gloria" borrows material from Cantatas 102 and 210. The remaining masses in A major, G minor, and G major also employ similar borrowings.

The *Mass in B Minor* is one of the most famous works of choral literature. A Catholic work, it is known for its five-voice choral texture and its great, integrative sections of recurring material. To a great extent this work is also the product of borrowing from Bach's cantatas, but significant sections are also original. Cantatas represented include Nos. 1, 46, 12, 171, among others. Gregorian quotation also occurs.

The Passions are another type of large-scale choral work and are similar in scope to the B-minor mass. These works are known as Oratori-Passions, owing to their relationship to unstaged operatic-style influences and the presence of a narrator (or evangelist). Two works exist: the *St. John Passion* (1724) and the *St. Matthew Passion* (about 1729). A third passion, the *St. Mark's Passion* (1731) has been lost, except for seven borrowed sections identifiable from the original settings (especially *Cantata 198*). Double chorus and orchestra exist in the *St. Matthew Passion*, where the chorale "O Sacred Head" is also used five times as an integrating agent. The chorus varies in its function: Chorus I functions as the twelve disciples, Chorus II represents other followers. Combined forces are employed for crowd scenes or for Christians in general.

The *Christmas Oratorio* is a special work (not related to the Passions) consisting of six parts, each in the format of a cantata, featuring an opening chorus (or "Symphony") and a closing chorale, and infilled with recitatives, choruses, chorales, duos, and trios. Different cantatas were to be sung at the six services between Christmas and Epiphany.

Bach wrote approximately two hundred cantatas, intended for integration into the Lutheran church year. The cantatas are generally limited in individual performing lengths to about a half hour. Many of Bach's most effective writing techniques are used in these works, and structural relations to other musical types such as the concerto or the trio sonata are evident. Features include (1) high middle parts, which add intensity to the texture; (2) uses of the tenor part in parallel motion with the soprano; (3) areas of imitation and antiphonal effects; (4) uses of descriptive or "imitative" tone-painting in relation to textual meaning. (5) The arias often contain an ongoing solo instrument that interlocks with the voice (obbligato). This effect, when added to the bass line, is that of a trio sonata.

There are cantatas for solo voice and for more than one voice. Some cantatas are called *Choral Cantatas* because the melody of a chorale is integrated (together with its text) into the texture of all—or nearly all—movements of a given work. In these works a change in textual verse is accompanied by a change in musical material, worked out imitatively.

The *Free Cantatas* are works having little or no chorale association. Often they are written in the style of instrumental concertos. There are at least thirty-two examples of this kind.

The cantatas as a whole express many of the best examples of Bach's synthesis of style and medium. Even though history does not show Bach to have been an innovator, his ability to assimilate varied materials into structures of highest technical craftsmanship and imagination—and the expressive power and consistency that result—have remained virtually unequalled.

D. S. CUSHMAN

BACON, FRANCIS (1561–1626)
English philosopher of science

Born into a prominent family, Bacon studied at Trinity College, Cambridge, and later at Gray's Inn of Court, London. He became a member of Parliament in the reign of Queen Elizabeth I, but not until the time of James I were his gifts given public recognition. In 1607 he became solicitor-general, in 1613 lord keeper, and in 1618 lord chancellor. In 1621 he had to retire from public life because of a bribery scandal.

During his busy life Bacon pursued scientific inquiry. His *Proficiency and Advancement of Learning* (1605) looked at the content of human knowledge and man's power to control nature. In *Novum Organum* (1620) he developed his ideas on the use of the inductive method in scientific inquiry, showing that by induction from the facts of human experience could come the discovery of God's laws of nature. In *New Atlantis,* published after his death, he described the ideal state on earth as one in which the new science/philosophy would serve the whole population.

He was a loyal though discriminating member of the Church of England. As a scientist he worked from a belief in the creation and preservation of the world by God. Some of his theological ideas are found in his *Essays* (1597, 1612, 1613). P. TOON

BACON, ROGER (1214–1292)
Christian philosopher

Bacon was born in England, but the details of his life are lacking. He evidently began his studies at Oxford under Robert Grosseteste. Before 1245 he was at Paris studying theology and teaching. He never gained a degree in theology and his other teachers are not known. He returned to Oxford for ten years and concentrated on scientific experimentation and writing. After becoming a Franciscan monk in 1257 he returned to Paris. His ideas about science gained a certain popularity during the papacy of his old friend Clement IV (pope, 1265–1268). But Bacon also made some enemies. After Clement's death, they condemned some of his teachings; as a result, Bacon was imprisoned about 1277 in Paris. He was released in 1292, but died shortly thereafter.

Bacon's most important writings are *Opus Maior, Opus Minor,* and *Opus Tertium.* He had proposed an additional work of encyclopedic nature. Bacon's significance rests in his attacks on the scholastic method of his day. He called for a greater application of mathematics in science, use of the experimental method, and studies in foreign languages, especially Hebrew, Greek, and Arabic, so that the sources of philosophy and theology might be read in the original language. He believed that science would someday produce powered ships, vehicles, and aircraft, along with other technological wonders.

His overriding concern was the integration of Christian wisdom and secular knowledge. Scripture was the ultimate source of truth as interpreted by canon law and philosophy. He was loyal to the authority of the church and believed that faith in God was basic to all other knowledge.
T. O. KAY

BAEDEKER, FRIEDRICH WILHELM (1823–1906)
Evangelist to the Russians

Baedeker's family moved to England from Germany while he was a child. At the age of sixteen he left school to form his own business, and five years later entered the army for a two-year tour of duty. He lived on the Continent, studied at several universities, and obtained a doctorate from Bonn. He returned to England and married in 1851, and his wife tragically died three months later. In 1862 he married again. British evangelist Lord Radstock held a series of meetings in 1866, during which time Baedeker heard Radstock and was converted. He spent the next ten years in Bible study and preaching across England. After that he made extensive trips to the Continent, mostly to Russia and Germany, holding evangelistic meetings and distributing Scriptures. His efforts in Russia met with warm approval from the czarist government, including official permission to preach in prison camps in Russia, a ministry of particular concern to Baedeker. He died of pneumonia at age eighty-three. K. HOGLUND

BAILLIE, DONALD MACPHERSON (1877–1954)
Scottish theologian, preacher, and ecumenist; elder brother of John Baillie

Born at Ross-shire, Baillie was educated at Edinburgh, Marburg, and Heidelberg universities. For sixteen years he served three Scottish parishes (Inverbervie, Cupar, and Kilmacolm) as minister. From 1935 until his death he was professor of systematic theology at St. Andrews University. His best-known work, *God Was in Christ* (1947), has been described as "one of the most original treatments of Christology in modern theology." He also produced a series of lectures, *The Theology of the Sacraments,* posthumously published (1957).

Like his brother, Baillie was deeply interested in the Faith and Order branch of the ecumenical movement. He attended the Edinburgh conference of 1937 and the Lund conference of 1952; as chairman of the Theological Commission of that movement he coedited (along with John Marsh) an important volume, *Inter-Communion* (1952).
N. V. HOPE

BAILLIE, JOHN (1886–1960)
Scottish theologian, educator, and ecumenical leader; younger brother of Donald MacPherson Baillie

John was educated at Edinburgh, Jena, and Marburg universities. After serving with the YMCA in World War I he became professor of theology at Auburn Seminary, New York, (1919–1927); Emmanuel College, Toronto (1927–1930); Union Seminary, New York (1930–1934); and finally Edinburgh University, where he occupied the chair of divinity until his retirement in 1956. During World War II he served the Church of Scotland as chairman of a commission appointed "for the interpretation of the will of God in the present crisis," presenting influential reports from 1941 to 1945. In 1943 he was moderator of the Church of Scotland General Assembly. Baillie was keenly interested in the ecumenical movement, particularly its Faith and Order branch, as was his brother. He was present at the first assembly of the World Council of Churches in Amsterdam in 1948 and was elected a member of its central committee. In 1954 he was appointed one of its six world presidents. Baillie wrote on many aspects of the Christian faith. His best-known works are the devotional classic *A Diary of Private Prayer* (1936), *And the Life Everlasting* (1934), and *The Sense of the Presence of God* (1962). N. V. HOPE

BAILLIE, ROBERT (1599–1662)
Scottish church leader

After graduating from Glasgow University, Baillie was ordained in 1622, served as regent of philosophy at Glasgow, and then became minister at Kilwinning in Ayrshire. In 1642 he became professor of divinity at Glasgow; in 1643 he was a Scottish representative at the Westminster Assembly. In 1649 Baillie, a man of moderation and diplomacy, was sent to Holland to invite the exiled Charles II (son of the executed King Charles I) to sign the National Covenant and accept the crown of Scotland. Baillie was successful in that but later regretted it. Baillie's *Letters and Journals* are among the most important historical documents of seventeenth-century Scotland.
J. D. DOUGLAS

BAKER, HENRY WILLIAMS (1821–1877)
Hymn writer and Anglican clergyman

Baker spent the mature years of his life as vicar of Monkland, near Leominster (England). He studied at Trinity College, Cambridge (1841–1843) and became a member of the Tractarian (Anglo-Catholic) Movement, a group that held to the need for celibate clergy and taught that prayer to the Virgin Mary was proper. Baker is known primarily as a writer of hymns (for example, the harvest hymn, "Praise, O Praise Our God and King"; "The King of Love My Shepherd Is"; and "Lord, Thy Word Abideth"), and as originator and editor of a famous Anglican hymnbook, *Hymns Ancient and Modern* (1861). P. TOON

BALLARD, GUY (1878–1939)
Kansas mining engineer who founded the I AM movement

The I AM movement's basic doctrines were supposed to have been communicated to Ballard by St. Germain, a sixth-century bishop of Paris, who appeared to him repeatedly on Mount Shasta, California, in 1930. Using the pseudonym Godfre Ray King, Guy described his experiences in the books *Unveiled Mysteries* and *The Magic Presence*. He also published books attributed to the Ascended Masters and to the Great Cosmic Beings.

The I AM group believed in the reincarnation of souls and that Ballard would ascend to heaven without dying. When he died, membership decreased. His wife, Edna, tried to continue the movement, but in 1941 was convicted of mail fraud. The movement had a strong nationalistic bias, believing that St. Germain had a special interest in America and had encouraged the writers of the Declaration of Independence. C. HICKS

BANEZ, DOMINGO (1528–1604)
Spanish Thomist theologian

Banez studied at Salamanca and in 1547 was ordained in the Dominican Order. He was a professor in the Spanish Universities of Avila and Valladolid. Returning to Salamanca in 1577, he taught theology until he was elected to the chief chair in 1580. He held this post for some twenty years. Banez was an advocate of Scholastic theology, usually following Thomas Aquinas and Augustine. He influenced Teresa of Avila as confessor and spiritual director, defending her when she was persecuted for her work. Later he recommended her canonization. Banez engaged in theological disputes with the Jesuits over Christ's meritorious death, God's predestination, and how a person is justified. His work demonstrates a mastery of logic, metaphysics, and theology.
L. GOLDBERG

BARCLAY, JOHN (1734–1798)
Scottish minister and founder of the Bereans

Born in Muthill, Barclay graduated with an M.A. from St. Andrews University, where he distinguished himself as a classical scholar. In 1759 he became assistant minister at Errol, but after four years was dismissed "for teaching obnoxious doctrines." But the alleged heresy hardly finds support in Barclay's *Rejoice Evermore*. For nine years he assisted the elderly minister of Fettercairn, with people crowding the church to hear him preach. When his senior colleague died, the parishioners of Fettercairn almost unanimously sought Barclay's appointment to the vacancy, but the presbytery blocked it (1772). Joined by many of his former members, he formed a congregation nearby which continued even after Barclay himself became pastor of another congregation of sympathizers in Edinburgh. His followers began to call themselves Bereans after certain disciples mentioned in the New Testament (Acts 17:10-12).

Barclay was as yet not ordained, but that problem was solved in 1773 through the action of a presbytery of five members in Newcastle (northeast England). A Berean church was founded in London in 1776, and during its first two years Barclay ministered there before returning to Edinburgh. For Barclay, who experienced great financial hardship after separating from the national (Presbyterian) church, faith was the acceptance of biblical revelation through the action of the Holy Spirit. He encouraged the various Berean assemblies by his visits and by his writings, which detailed the doctrinal distinctives of his generally Calvinist position. J. D. DOUGLAS

BARCLAY, ROBERT (1648–1690)
Scottish Quaker theologian

Son of an army colonel, Barclay was educated in Paris where his uncle was rector of the (Roman Catholic) Scots College. On returning to Scotland, however, he followed his father into the Society of Friends (1667) having found "a secret power among them, which touched my heart."

In an age not conspicuous for religious toleration, he often suffered arrest and imprisonment. With his friend William Penn, Barclay visited Holland and Germany (1676), explaining the Society's principles. Barclay found an unlikely friend in the Roman Catholic duke of York, later James II, a link that helped to open prison doors for many of his colleagues. That friendship also led to the patent (grant of land) for a Quaker settlement in East New Jersey (1682) of which Barclay was nominal governor for its first six years (he never visited America).

Barclay became the only systematic apologist among the early Quakers, producing particularly *A Catechism and Confession of Faith* (1673) and *An Apology for the True Christian Divinity* (Latin version 1676, English 1678), both of which became standard statements of Quaker doctrine—a religion of the "inner light" and pacifism. Barclay believed that the work of the Holy Spirit in the believer took precedence over church and Scripture. He rebuked Roman Catholics and Protestants for making philosophy the handmaid of divinity, and wished for clergy of all sorts "unfeigned repentance, unto the acknowledgment of the truth." He warned Charles II that his condemnation would be great if he did not turn from oppression, lust, and vanity. The *Apology,* which has been reprinted many times, was termed by even the humanist Voltaire "as good as a book of its kind could possibly be."

J. D. DOUGLAS

BARCLAY, WILLIAM (1907–1978)
Scottish biblical scholar

Born in Wick, son of an evangelical lay preacher, Barclay graduated in arts and divinity from Glasgow University (1932) and studied a further year at Marburg (Germany). In 1933 he became minister of Trinity Church, Renfrew, a congregation whose connections were almost entirely with the Clydeside shipyards and factories. In that pulpit he learned to speak in language intelligible to ordinary people. Yet he also learned not to underestimate his audience, a point he later urged upon his students.

In 1946 he was appointed lecturer in New Testament at Glasgow, and in 1964 professor of New Testament. He retired from that post in 1974, but his services were imaginatively enlisted by Strathclyde, a technical university, as visiting professor of professional ethics. A prestigious accolade came when the Queen made him a Commander of the Most Excellent Order of the British Empire (CBE).

Barclay is chiefly remembered for his writings and broadcasts. He began producing *Daily Study Bible* readings as a stopgap measure in 1954—"until we get someone decent to do them for us," as the Church of Scotland's publications manager put it. No one else was found, Barclay continued the work, and the original edition sold more than five million copies in English. It was translated into many other languages and in 1975 and 1976 a new edition of the New Testament series was published. By that time Barclay had begun work on the Old Testament.

In that project and in all the other books he authored (more than 50), he disclaimed any originality, insisting that he merely explained and expounded other thinkers' ideas. "I have an essentially second-class mind," he said. Barclay attributed his success as a communicator to several factors: a classical education, a good memory, a capacity for disciplined work (he never wrote a sermon after Thursday), a facility with words, an ability to work to order, and the knack of thinking in pictures rather than in theological abstractions. Thus equipped and untroubled by "original ideas struggling to be expressed," he felt that he could "at least be the pipeline which brought the living springs to others." He was firmly convinced that one who would write for ordinary people must have some experience of speaking to them. So he cultivated friendships among people of a wide variety of walks of life and social positions. He shunned church committees, and once declined nomination as moderator of the Church of Scotland's general assembly.

On other matters he was likewise reticent. His autobiography, *Testament of Faith* (1975), says nothing about how he came to enter the ministry and nothing about his attitude toward the inspiration and authority of Scripture. Theologically he called himself a "liberal evangelical," but he once uncharacteristically claimed that he was the only member of his divinity faculty who believed that Matthew, Luke, and John wrote the Gospels attributed to them. Barclay was a universalist (one who believes that all people ultimately will be saved). He criticized many evangelicals who held to substitutionary atonement as being "too authoritative" and expressed dislike of closed minds more than anything else. He, nevertheless, displayed none of the intolerance shown by some liberals, and was always courteous and helpful to evangelical students and friends. He deplored the virtual disappearance of church discipline and advocated two-tier church membership: one kind for those who were "deeply attracted to Jesus Christ and the Christian way," and another kind for "the many fewer . . . prepared to make a total commitment to Jesus Christ."

Despite his exposure to millions via television, Barclay continually pointed out that the ministry of print could reach where the ministry of the voice could not. The written word, he said, was "the true ecumenical movement." J. D. DOUGLAS

BARING-GOULD, SABINE (1834–1924)
English historian, hymn writer, novelist, and amateur geographer

After his education at Clare College, Cambridge, Baring-Gould taught at two Anglo-Catholic institutions: the choir school of St. Barnabas and Hurstpoint College. After ordination in the Church of England, he served as vicar of Dalton, Yorkshire (1866–1871); East Mersea, Essex (1871–1881); and Lew Trenchard, Devon (1881–1924). He published over 150 books of which *The Lives of the Saints* (sixteen volumes, 1897–1898) and *The Lives of the British Saints* (1908) are well known. But other books also were very popular: his studies on the natural history of the English West Country—such as, *A Book of Dartmoor* (1900); his biography—such as, *A Life of Robert S. Hawker* (1876); and his novels—such as, *Mehalah* (1880). As a hymn writer, Baring-Gould is best known for his hymn, "Onward, Christian Soldiers." P. TOON

BARNARDO, THOMAS JOHN (1845–1905)
British social reformer

Born in Dublin (Ireland), Barnardo was converted in 1862 and went to London to train as a medical missionary under the China Inland Mission. He was so moved by the plight of homeless children in England, however, that he dedicated his life to their welfare. In 1867 he founded the East End Juvenile Mission, which rapidly expanded into an immense organization called "Dr. Barnardo's Homes." (He obtained medical degrees at the Edinburgh College of Surgeons in 1876 and 1879.)

Barnardo's motto was No Destitute Child Ever Refused Admission. Besides providing homes for children, his program included social and evangelistic centers for working men, a boarding-out system, and an emigra-

tion plan under which boys and girls were sent to Canada for training and settlement. Barnardo rescued and trained almost 60,000 children and otherwise assisted about 250,000. N. V. HOPE

BARNBY, SIR JOSEPH (1838–1896)
English composer, conductor, and organist

Barnby's posts as organist included the churches of St. Michael's, St. James the Less, St. Andrew's, and St. Anne's—all in London. He was also organist of the Sacred Harmonic Society. His contribution to the English choral movement began in 1864 with his founding of Barnby's Choir, which performed oratorios in London for five years. He was also a director of the Royal Albert Hall Choral Society. He conducted at the Cardiff Festivals of 1892 and 1895 and the South Wales Festival. At St. Anne's, Barnby initiated annual performances of Bach's *Passions*. Like Mendelssohn, Barnby helped revive Bach performances and reintroduce them into the Romantic era. In 1874 he began a daily concert series at Albert Hall. His conductorship of the London Music Society (1876–1886) included the English premiere of Dvorak's *Stabat Mater.* Barnby served as precentor and music director at Eton (from 1875), and in 1892 became principal of Guild Hall School of Music. He was knighted in 1892.

Barnby's musical works include an oratorio (*Rebekah*), a *Service in Three Parts* (*Morning, Noon, Evening*), a Magnificat and *Nunc Dimittis,* and a motet ("King All Glorious"). He wrote 45 anthems and 246 hymn tunes (published in a complete collection, 1897). Barnby also edited several hymnals, including *The Hymnary* (1872), his major editorial contribution. His instrumental works include many organ and piano pieces. D. S. CUSHMAN

BARNES, ALBERT (1798–1870)
Presbyterian preacher and writer; central figure in the split of the Presbyterian Church in the United States of America in 1837

Born of Methodist parents in Rome, New York, Barnes came under the influence of the writings of Thomas Chalmers, a Scottish Presbyterian writer, while studying for a legal career at Hamilton College. He became a Presbyterian, and in 1820 entered Princeton Theological Seminary. In 1825 he became pastor of the Presbyterian Church at Morristown, New Jersey.

In 1830 Barnes was called to the First Presbyterian Church of Philadelphia, but his call was challenged by the conservative, or "old-school," Presbyterians. They claimed that statements he made in a printed sermon, "The Way of Salvation," were out of accord with Presbyterian doctrine, especially on the imputation of Adam's sin and the nature of human will. Barnes's case reached the Presbyterian General Assembly in 1831, and for the first time sharp disputes arose between "old-school" and "new-school" Presbyterians in the Assembly. The Assembly, firmly in control of new-school men, acquitted him of the heresy charges. The publication of his book *Notes Explanatory and Practical, on the Epistle to the Romans* (1835) led to a renewed doctrinal controversy. Sympathetic to the new-school position, the 1836 General Assembly exonerated him, but the action stimulated old-school efforts to rid the denomination of new-school tendencies. The 1837 General Assembly, under the control of the old school, exscinded the new school.

Barnes was an advocate of numerous social causes, including temperance and the abolition of slavery. A prolific writer, he produced many books, best known of which were his biblical commentaries. Barnes's commentaries sold an estimated one million copies during his lifetime and are still in print. J. N. AKERS

BARNES, ROBERT (1495–1540)
English theologian who became a Protestant martyr

Barnes began his career as an Augustinian friar in Cambridge; then, influenced by Erasmus and by Lutheran ideas, he adopted views critical of the late medieval system of religion current in England. He was examined in London first by Cardinal Wolsey and then by four bishops concerning twenty-five points on which it was asserted he held erroneous views. He confessed to teaching unorthodox views and was forced to do public penance in St. Paul's Cathedral, London, in 1526. After further imprisonment Barnes escaped to Antwerp (Belgium) and from there went to Germany. There he was able to meet Luther and other Protestants and began to write in defense of Protestant ideas. He was recalled to England by Thomas Cromwell to help serve Henry VIII in his negotiations with the pope over Henry's divorce. After fulfilling various duties, Barnes allied himself with Protestant interests at court and was condemned to the stake as a heretic. P. TOON

BARNHOUSE, DONALD GREY (1895–1960)
American minister, editor, and radio Bible teacher

Born in Watsonville, California, Barnhouse was educated at the Bible School of Los Angeles (1913–1915), Princeton Theological Seminary (1915–1917), and Eastern Baptist Theological Seminary (1926–1927). Ordained by the Presbytery of Monmouth, New Jersey (Presbyterian Church in the United States of America), in 1918, he worked as a Protestant evangelist and teacher in Belgium and France between 1919 and 1926. In 1927 he became pastor of the Tenth Presbyterian Church in Philadelphia, Pennsylvania, serving there for the rest of his life. He received an honorary doctorate in divinity from the Evangelical Theological College of Dallas in 1923 and in theology from the Faculte Libre de Theologie Protestante of Aix-en-Provence (France) in 1951. From 1931 to 1949 he edited *Revelation* magazine, and from 1950 to 1960 *Eternity* magazine. Barnhouse was considered an effective Bible teacher and dynamic preacher, both over the radio and in many places besides his home church. He concentrated particularly on Paul's Epistle to the Romans and published a number of books of biblical exposition. N. V. HOPE

BARROW, HENRY (c. 1550–1593)

English Separatist who believed that the established church was corrupt and thus had to be forsaken in order to create a pure church

After his graduation from Clare Hall, Cambridge, in 1570 he became a lawyer in Gray's Inn, London, where he lived "without reference to God's law." After a dramatic conversion, he began to take great interest in the Bible and theology. He associated with Separatists, of which there were only several hundred in England at the time, and read the writings of Robert Browne (died 1633), who had been a Separatist, and John Greenwood, pastor of a Separatist group. While visiting Greenwood in prison in 1586, Barrow was arrested on orders from Archbishop Whitgift. He was in and out of prison and examined and reexamined by authorities of the Church of England over the next few years. He was charged with being the author or distributor of certain seditious books (books which sought to undermine the Church of England) and was finally executed with Greenwood. His books were printed in Holland and smuggled into England. They included studies of the "true form of church government" and of the corruptions of the Church of England. It is wrong, however, to see Barrows as a founding father of the Congregationalists, who came later. P. TOON

BARROW, ISSAC (1630–1677)

Anglican theologian, classicist, and mathematician

After his education at Trinity College, Cambridge, Barrow became a fellow there in 1649. A royalist, he found it expedient to travel in Europe and the Middle East from 1655 to 1660 while England was ruled by Oliver Cromwell. At the restoration of the monarchy in 1660 he returned to Cambridge where he became professor of Greek, and later (1663) professor of mathematics. He resigned in order to allow his famous pupil, Isaac Newton, to take his place. In 1673, King Charles II made Barrow master of Trinity College. His theological works, collected in four volumes by his admirer,

John Tillotson, were published from 1683 to 1687. Barrow was Arminian in theology and Episcopalian in church polity. P. TOON

BARTH, KARL (1886–1968)

Swiss theologian; one of the most influential Protestant leaders of the twentieth century

Barth was born in Basel and was the son of Fritz and Anna Sartorius Barth. His father was a pastor and professor of New Testament and church history in a school related to the Swiss Reformed Church. Karl Barth's brother Peter edited a critical edition of John Calvin's Reformation works; another brother, Heinrich, taught philosophy at the University of Basel. In 1913 Barth married Nelly Hoffmann, and they eventually had five sons, one of whom, Markus, became internationally known for biblical and theological scholarship.

Barth received his early schooling in Bern, where he showed an interest in military affairs, history, and drama. Following European custom, he studied at several universities: Bern, Berlin, Tübingen, and Marburg. At Bern he was introduced to Immanuel Kant's philosophy and Friedrich Schleiermacher's theology and, in time, went on to study with the leading neo-Kantian theologian, Wilhelm Herrmann of Marburg. Barth first studied at Berlin, however, where he was influenced by church historian Adolf von Harnack. To honor his father's wishes, Barth then went to Tübingen to study with a conservative New Testament theologian, Adolf Schlatter. Finally, in 1908, Barth went to Marburg. He later considered Herrmann's teaching the greatest single influence of his student days.

Barth's training was typical of early twentieth-century German theology. Its anthropocentric philosophy of religion emphasized human understanding of God, human history as the outworking of God's purposes, and human capacity to develop a society in which God's purposes and human intelligence collaborated in ever-increasing progress.

Barth was ordained in the Swiss Reformed Church in 1909. He served one pastorate for two years in Geneva, and a second for ten years in the small town of Safenwil (canton Aargau).

In Safenwil, Barth renewed acquaintance with a fellow student from Marburg, Eduard Thurneysen, who had become pastor of another small church nearby. Together they struggled throughout the years of World War I to teach their congregations how to apply the Bible's message in complex modern life. Initially they rejected a conservative emphasis on personal salvation in favor of a liberal stress on social change. Barth went so far in that emphasis that, contrary to ministerial custom, he joined a socialist political party.

In August 1914 the Western world was on the edge of total war, with Barth's respected teachers supporting their nation's military aims. Barth saw this is as a failure of German liberal theology to answer crucial modern questions. Turning to a fresh study of the Bible, Barth and Thurneysen found a whole new world. That new world was the "word of God" within the Bible that explains how God, solely in grace, seeks to redeem humankind. In 1917 the two published a book of sermons titled *Seek God and You Shall Live*.

Barth studied the apostle Paul's letters, preparing manuscripts on Romans, Ephesians, and 2 Corinthians. In 1918 Barth's commentary on Romans was published in an edition of one thousand copies. That early commentary marked the beginning of Barth's departure from his liberal theological training. With a completely revised second edition of the commentary in 1921, his break with liberalism was complete. He then challenged contemporary theology by emphasizing God's utter difference from humanity (that is, God's transcendence). Because of that transcendence, Barth maintained, people need a revelation from God if he is to be known and obeyed. Barth was awesomely impressed by the fact that God has spoken his "word" to people, which became a fundamental idea in his theology.

Barth gradually refined his thought, developing a total theological system. In it he emphasized God's holiness, his incomprehensibility to the human mind, and his sovereign grace. Barth's early expressions of his "new orthodoxy" were strongly influenced by Danish philosopher Søren Kierkegaard (1813–1855) and Russian novelist Fyodor Dostoyevski (1821–1881), as well as by a rediscovery of the Reformation emphasis on God's grace.

Barth and Thurneysen were joined in their theological explorations by a number of other young theologians, including Emil Brunner, Rudolf Bultmann, and Friedrich Gogarten. Barth eventually differed with his early companions on various issues, but their "new beginning" completely reshaped twentieth-century biblical interpretation. Barth spent over forty years teaching his new theology at several European universities: Göttingen (1921–1925), Münster (1925–1930), Bonn (1930–1935), and Basel (1935–1962).

When Adolf Hitler and National Socialism (Nazism) came to power in Germany in 1933, Barth and Thurneysen published a series of pamphlets entitled *Theological Existence Today* to oppose Hitler's cultural perversion of the Christian faith. By 1934 Barth was a leader in the German movement known as the Confessing Church. He was the major framer of its statement of faith, the Barmen Declaration. Such activities forced him to flee in 1935 to Basel where, in addition to his new teaching responsibilities, he served in the Swiss army as a border guard. At the war's end, Barth advocated Allied openness to helping the German people, a seeming turnaround that brought him sharp criticism from some of his colleagues.

The majority of Barth's life was spent teaching and writing, with some public lecturing and preaching. His major writings include the commentary on Romans, *Church Dogmatics* (a multi-volume systematic theology of nearly seventy-five hundred pages, 1932–1967), *The Word of God and the Word of Man* (1928), *Evangelical Theology* (1963), and *The Humanity of God* (1960). In 1937 he gave the Gifford Lectures at Aberdeen (Scotland), and in 1962 he lectured in America at Princeton Theological Seminary and the University of Chicago. During the decade before his retirement in 1962, Barth often preached to inmates in Basel's prison.

Barth's devotion to the gospel was shown by the topic he chose for his final lecture at Basel: divine love seeking humankind in Jesus Christ. For Barth, theology was a "particularly beautiful science" and a joyful task. He had a probing intellect, a sense of humor, and a humble spirit. Like Martin Luther, with whom he is often compared, Barth enjoyed music. He especially appreciated the work of Wolfgang Amadeus Mozart, whose portrait hung near that of John Calvin in Barth's study.

Barth's greatest influence was theological, with his emphasis on God's sovereignty placing him firmly in the Reformed (Calvinistic) tradition. He differed radically from the mainstream of continental European theology, rejecting both its subjective emphasis on religious experience and the prevalent idea that Christian doctrine is subject to, or limited by, its historical origins. By reaffirming what Kierkegaard had called an "infinite qualitative difference" between God and humankind, Barth rescued theology from captivity to anthropology—that is, he reasserted God's reality and sovereignty over human knowledge or imagination.

Three major themes characterize Barthian theology. First, Barth saw no justification for the idea of "natural theology." In a crucial debate with his friend Emil Brunner (published in 1934), he contended that all human efforts to define God by means of natural observation end in idolatry. Against Brunner's attempts to defend theology based on God's revelation in nature, Barth stressed the crippling effect of sin on human reason. To Barth, people are innately sinful and unable to receive or comprehend God's message apart from his redeeming grace. People will come to God only through faith in God's self-revelation.

A second focus of Barth's theology was the way God makes his revelation known. Human knowledge of God comes only as he discloses himself in his Word—manifested in Jesus Christ, in the Bible, and in Christian preaching.

Because Barth accepted certain higher critical views of Scripture, he refused to equate the words of the Bible and God's inspired Word. Inspiration, for Barth, had more to do with the Bible reader than with either the Bible itself or its writers. The words of the Bible convey the Word of God as the Holy Spirit speaks through them to the reader. Perhaps more than any other aspect of Barth's theology, his doctrine of Scripture created serious misgivings among many evangelical theologians.

Third, following Calvin, Barth insisted that true knowledge of God comes in obedience to God. Barth's approach to theology was Christ centered. Jesus' devotion to doing God's will and his call to discipleship provided the model of obedient service.

Barth's neoorthodox theology strengthened many Christian leaders in Europe, giving them a basis for standing against persecution. But its lack of objective criteria for judgment in theological matters created severe problems for its adherents. Some of the "death of God" theologians in the 1960s began as followers of Barth. Near the end of his career, Barth considered the "humanity of God" a corrective balance to his earlier radical stress on God's transcendence. For all the shifts of emphasis in his later theology, however, he continued to defend the earlier position as being appropriate to the crisis in which it first appeared.

H. JACOBSEN

BASIL THE GREAT (c. 330–379)
Early church father

Basil was born into one of the remarkable families of Christian history. His grandmother, Macrina, his father, Basil, his mother, Emilia, his sister, Macrina, and his two younger brothers, Gregory of Nyssa and Peter, bishop of Sebaste, were all venerated as saints by the church. This wealthy landowning family, probably of senatorial rank, had a history of stalwart witness in spite of persecutions, and a reputation for ascetic piety and Christian charity. It offered Basil every advantage.

Basil's development included the teaching by his saintly grandmother on a secluded estate, literary training in Caesarea, and schooling in Constantinople and the great school at Athens. There he associated with Gregory Nazianzus (whose father was bishop of Nazianzus, 363–374, Gregory later becoming bishop of Constantinople, 380–381) and Julian (final pagan Roman emperor, 361–363). Gregory became Basil's friend and together with Basil's brother, Gregory of Nyssa, the three are known to church history as the Cappadocian fathers.

Basil returned to Caesarea from Athens about 357, serving briefly as a teacher of rhetoric. Increasingly he turned toward asceticism under the influence of his sister, Macrina, who had founded a monastery on family property at Annessi. Basil traveled to visit ascetics of Syria, Palestine, and Egypt, and then founded his own monastery in Annessi around 358. For the monks there he drew up his moderate and famed *Asceticon* (often called Longer and Shorter Rules) consisting of 55 Great Rules (i.e., monastic regulations) and 313 Little Rules which were largely practical answers to questions.

Around 364 Basil was ordained a presbyter at Caesarea by Bishop Eusebius. Basil devoted himself to four lifetime tasks: winning recognition for monasticism as a regular part of the church; healing the Antioch schism in the eastern church; doing works of charity in Caesarea; and above all else defending Nicene Trinitarian orthodoxy. When he succeeded Eusebius as bishop of Caesarea in 370, support by the common people—as well as his position, training, ability, and ecclesiastical office—made Basil a man of immense influence. Even at the height of conflict with the Arian emperor Valens (364–378), Basil so impressed the emperor that he was never exiled.

Basil died in Caesarea, worn out by labors, asceticism, and a liver ailment, just before his life's work bore fruit. Antioch's schism began to be resolved (Synod of Antioch, 375) and Nicene orthodoxy was reaffirmed by the Council of Constantinople (381) along lines of the East-West understanding Basil had advocated. His brother Gregory (who became bishop of Nyssa in 371 and succeeded Basil as metropolitan in Caesarea

in 380) and his friend Gregory Nazianzus eulogized him formally. They also continued to develop the Cappadocian blend of modified Origenism and reaffirmed Nicene Trinitarianism for which they and Basil the Great are renowned. V. WALTER

BAUER, BRUNO (1809–1882)
German biblical critic of the nineteenth century who held radical views about Jesus and the New Testament

During his early years, Bauer was basically a conservative Hegelian theologian. In 1839 he changed teaching positions, moving from Berlin to Bonn; the change in geography seemed to signal a change in his theology. Within three years Bauer's views had become so radical that he was removed from his teaching post. His lack of an established teaching position caused his work to be neglected by most of the scholars of his day. Bauer was no doubt influenced by the radical views of David Friedrich Strauss (1808–1874), who claimed that Jesus and the entire gospel story were inventions of the early Christian community. Bauer moved even further to claim that a single individual living in the second century had invented Jesus. Even the apostle Paul's epistles, he maintained, were not written by a first-century Jew, but were also composed by someone living in the second century. After his dismissal, Bauer devoted himself to writing and political activity. Bruno Bauer was equally radical in his hatred of the Jews. D. M. LAKE

BAUR, FERDINAND CHRISTIAN (1792–1860)
German Protestant theologian

Born in southern Germany, Baur studied and later taught at the University of Tübingen. In his early years he was greatly influenced by Friedrich Schleiermacher (1768–1834). Later, however, the philosophy of Hegel (1770–1831) became a more pronounced influence in his theology. Baur was one of the first to apply the Hegelian idea of dialectical tension to New Testament studies. Hegel's idea that truth develops out of the tension between an idea and its opposite was used by Baur to explore differences between the apostolic writings of Peter and Paul. He viewed Peter as being more Jewish and Paul as advocating a more Gentile form of Christianity; out of conflict between those two schools of Christianity, he saw development of the compromised form of Roman Catholicism.

Baur's major work after becoming professor of theology at Tübingen in 1826 was an investigation into the New Testament pastoral epistles. In 1845 he published a book called *Paul the Apostle of Jesus Christ* that denied Paul's authorship of Ephesians, Philippians, Colossians, 1 and 2 Thessalonians, 1 and 2 Timothy, Titus, and Philemon.

Baur was one of the first theologians to stress the historical rather than the systematic method in theological study—another example of Hegelian influence. At the time of his death, he had prepared and published studies on the Atonement, the Trinity, the Canon, and the church, as well as a textbook on the history of Christian theology. Because of the importance of the topics with which he dealt and because of the important influence that the Tübingen school exerted on Continental theology during the nineteenth century, Baur's influence has been felt well into the twentieth century. Only in recent years have biblical studies overcome the negative influence of Baur and his school.
D. M. LAKE

BAVINCK, HERMANN (1854–1921)
Dutch systematic theologian of the Calvinist school

Born at Hoogeveen (the Netherlands), Bavinck received his theological training at the Kampen theological seminary and the University of Leiden (D.D., 1880). After a short pastorate in Franeker and a professorship at Kampen (1882–1903), he became professor of systematic theology at the Free University of Amsterdam. Most of Bavinck's books have not been translated into English. Thus he is not well known in Britain and America except among Christian Reformed

and other Dutch groups. Part of *Gereformeerde Dogmatiek* (four volumes, 1895–1901) has been translated by W. Hendriksen as *The Doctrine of God* (1977). Other books include *Christelijke Wetenschap* and *Christelijke Wereldbeschouwing*. L. Berkhof's *Systematic Theology* is indebted to Bavinck, as is the theology of G. C. Berkouwer, who was also systematics professor in Amsterdam (see Berkouwer's *A Half Century of Theology*, 1977). P. TOON

BAVINCK, JOHAN HERMAN (1895–1964)
Dutch missionary and missiologist

Educated at the Free University of Amsterdam, Bavinck received his doctorate at Erlangen University (1919). A minister of the Gereformeerde Kerken (Reformed Church), he was pastor of Dutch-speaking churches in Medan (Sumatra) and Bandung (Java) in what is now Indonesia (1919–1926). Because of his interest in mysticism, he studied psychology at Leiden (the Netherlands) while pastor at Heemstede (1927–1929). Bavinck spent several years at Solokarta (Sviakarto) in mid-Java in youth ministry, studying Javanese mysticism, and writing (1930–1933), followed by a professorship in the Theological School at Jogjakarta (1935–1939). Bavinck was the Netherlands' first professor of missiology, teaching at the Free University and the Theological School at Kampen (1939–1964). A person of great influence in Europe and America, he wrote many books including *Jesus Christ and Oriental Mysticism, An Introduction to the Science of Missions*, and *The Church Between Temple and Mosque*.
P. BEAVER

BAXTER, RICHARD (1615–1691)
English author, hymn writer, and preacher; known as one of the foremost spokesmen of the Puritan party within the Church of England

We know of Baxter's life chiefly through his memoirs, which appeared five years after his death as *Reliquiae Baxterianae*, written in a disorderly, loose style by a friend, Matthew Sylvester. In 1702 Edmund Calamy, another friend of Baxter's and a Puritan minister, published an *Abridgement* of the memoirs. They finally became available in readable form in 1925 when J. M. Lloyd Thomas published them as the *Autobiography of Richard Baxter* (Everyman Library).

The first section of the *Autobiography*, covering the years 1615 to 1660, deals with Baxter's childhood and education, his brief period at Court, ordination as a deacon, years in the ministry (which were interrupted by the Civil War), and his pastoral charge at Kidderminster. Interwoven with his personal story is the history of England immediately before and during the Civil War and the Protectorate.

Part II shows Baxter pleading the cause of primitive episcopacy against the prelatists. Meanwhile, he was offered the bishopric of Hereford, but he refused it rather than compromise his beliefs or betray the convictions of Puritan ministers who refused to submit to the demands of the High Church party. What Baxter desired was a mediation between the extremists in English religious life, but he received only distrust from both sides. Part III of his *Autobiography* describes the Great Fire, the havoc within London, the imprisonments, illnesses, and persecutions.

In 1681 Baxter published, on the death of his wife, a *Breviate of the Life of Margaret . . . Wife of Baxter,* a beautiful tribute to her memory containing a number of her private expressions of religious faith. In the same year he published *Poetical Fragments,* an autobiography in verse. Although he knew his poetic gifts were slight, Baxter was fond of poetry and church music. As a hymn writer Baxter earned limited poetical fame. "Ye Holy Angels Bright" is from one of his poems, as is "Lord, It Belongs Not to My Care," from a poem revealing his wife's "covenant" at her conversion.

Baxter's *The Saints' Everlasting Rest* was among the most widely read books of the seventeenth century. He used as its focal point, "There remaineth therefore a rest to the people of God" (Heb. 4:9, KJV). The primary concerns of the book are: the neces-

sary signs of the candidate for the "rest," helps and hindrances toward a life fitting one for the "rest," and the need to help others to become candidates. Particular individuals, such as those who possess learning and those who have a gift for expressing thought effectively, have special responsibilities to aid others in becoming candidates for "rest," but no regenerate person is without responsibility.

Those who would lead a "heavenly life upon earth" are cautioned against living in known sin, sharing the company of the ungodly, disputing over peripheral matters in Christian doctrine and behavior, or possessing a proud and slothful spirit.

Baxter also gives positive guidelines for the "heavenly life." He exhorts believers to engage in frequent conversation on the subject of "rest," to develop habits of praising God, and to meditate on God's infinite love for the world. Meditation and prayer should frequently occur at particular times and places. The Lord's Day affords numerous opportunities for reflection on Christian matters. Affliction, disappointment, and bereavement should also be accepted as platforms on which God gives abundant grace and necessary strength for growth toward the "everlasting rest." The book closes with a prayer that the author might not be a stranger to those privileges, responsibilities, and joys which he depicts for others.

Typical of many seventeenth-century writers, Baxter was fond of complex and terse epigrams: "eternity is a piece of infiniteness" and "truth loseth more by loose friends than by sharpest enemies."

Believing that all should employ their time and energy fully with a view to God's glory, Richard Baxter was active in public affairs, was one of England's most renowned preachers, and was the author of more than 160 works. E. B. BATSON

BAYLE, PIERRE (1647–1706)

French teacher and scholar who laid the rational groundwork for the French Enlightenment and the Age of Reason

The son of a Reformed pastor, Bayle was

raised and educated a Calvinist, was converted to Catholicism, and after returning to Calvinism, gradually drifted into skepticism. Bayle taught in Protestant schools in Sedan (France) and Rotterdam (Holland), where he spent most of his life. He lived during the persecutions of Louis XIV, culminating in the revocation of the Edict of Nantes (1685).

Bayle's principal ideas are expressed in his *Dictionnaire historique et critique* (1695–1697, revised 1702), an encyclopedia specializing in radical views. He was a skeptic opposed alike by Roman Catholics and Protestants. For Bayle, morality was enshrined in conscience, which was independent of Christian revelation. He argued that atheists could be moral and Christians immoral. Faith, as he conceived it, was not especially personal or Christ-directed, and the basic intent of the *Dictionary* seemed to be an attempt to undermine faith, rather than build it up. R. P. EVANS

BAYLY, LEWIS (1565–1631)
Welsh bishop

Bayly was best known to later generations as the author of a much-used devotional handbook, *The Practice of Piety*. He was an exceptional man in his own day, a bishop of the Church of England in Wales who actually preached in the Welsh language. Educated at Exeter College, Oxford, he received a B.D. degree in 1611 and D.D. in 1613. He was ordained and became known as a gifted preacher. Henry, Prince of Wales, made him his chaplain, and Bayly dedicated *The Practice of Piety* to the prince. Although Bayly's sympathies were toward Puritanism, King James showed him favor by making him a royal chaplain in 1616 and later that year bishop of Bangor. As Puritanism was popular in North Wales, Bayly encouraged and made use of it. In so doing he was refusing to implement the laws of the church, so he was often in trouble with ecclesiastical authorities in London. He remained bishop until his death and was buried in his native Wales at Bangor. P. TOON

BEATON, DAVID (1494–1546)
Scottish cardinal; archbishop of St. Andrews

Beaton was educated at St. Andrews and Glasgow and at the University of Paris. In 1528 he was made Lord Privy Seal of Scotland. Employed in diplomatic services abroad by King James V, he was also honored by the pope by being made a cardinal; two years later he succeeded his uncle James Beaton in the archdiocese of St. Andrews. In charge of James V's foreign policy, Beaton was instrumental in obtaining two French princesses in succession as James's queens. When James died in 1542, leaving a week-old daughter, Mary, as his successor, Beaton sought to become regent. That position was taken by the Earl of Arran, so as compensation Beaton was made chancellor (1543). As chancellor Beaton used his great political power in conjunction with his ecclesiastical authority to persecute Protestants. His attacks culminated in the martyrdom of George Wishart (1545). Partly because of this, Beaton was murdered in his castle at St. Andrews in May 1546. Beaton, who had a number of illegitimate children, was noted for his love of political power, his accumulation of wealth, and his support of the French party in Scotland. W. S. REID

BECKET, SAINT THOMAS (c. 1118–1170)
Archbishop of Canterbury who clashed with King Henry II of England

Born to a London merchant family, Becket received a good education for his day and moved into the court of Archbishop Theobald in 1141. He served as an archdeacon and was sent to the University of Bologna for study in church law. In 1154 he became chancellor to King Henry II (ruled 1154–1189). Becket was highly regarded by his contemporaries and seemed to be in agreement with the king on most matters. His legal training and administrative experience were put to good advantage on behalf of the ambitious young king.

When the archbishop of Canterbury died in 1162, Henry, anxious to strengthen ties between church and state and bring the church under his closer supervision, nominated his chancellor, Becket, for the position. In one day Becket moved from priest to archbishop and assumed the responsibilities of the primate of England.

To his surprise, Henry had not chosen a compliant underling. When Becket donned the archbishop's robes he underwent a radical change. With his allegiance transferred to the church and its interests, he maintained a highly disciplined, sober, and pious pattern of living. His seriousness was shown in his resignation from all responsibilities not related to his new position, an act of devotion not required in the twelfth century.

The king, to advance his administrative interests and centralize the authority of the Crown, issued the Constitutions of Clarendon in 1164. Some provisions dealt with clergy charged with criminal behavior. Although custom had relegated them to church courts, Henry wanted them under state jurisdiction, which would mean more income and power for the king. Becket at first agreed to those demands but then changed his mind. Although most of the bishops were willing to submit to the king's demands, the archbishop held back.

As a result of continuing antagonisms with Henry, Becket went into exile in France. After they seemed to reach some understanding with each other, he returned to Canterbury—and proceeded to excommunicate his enemies. The angered king, visiting in France, indicated a desire to be rid of such an annoyance. Some of his knights who overheard his statement took it literally. They returned to England and violently murdered Becket before an altar in the cathedral at Canterbury. Popular reaction forced the king to retract his position on the clergy and in 1178 to do penance for his defiance of ecclesiastical authority.

Becket achieved more as a martyr than as an archbishop. He was made a saint in 1173. His firm resistance to the king on this issue of ecclesiastical authority and his loyalty to the church were a source of inspiration for many medieval men and women, lay and cleric. His devoted service and his relations with the secular power became a model for later Christians who had to wrestle with the problems of church and state. A modern drama by T. S. Eliot, *Murder in the Cathedral* (1935) was based on the life of Becket.

T. O. KAY

BEDE (c. 673–735)
Father of English history; known as "the Venerable Bede"

Born in what is now Durham and was then the Anglo-Saxon kingdom of Northumbria, Bede entered the monastery at Wearmouth when he was seven years old. Soon afterward the whole community transferred to Jarrow where Bede spent the rest of his life. Incredibly, in that isolated spot he became one of the most learned men of Europe. As a youth he devoted himself to the study of Scripture, learning Hebrew, Greek, and Latin; after his ordination he taught in the monastery. His earliest writings were textbooks for students. Bede used his scholarship to defend the ecclesiastical settlement of the Synod of Whitby (664), showing how the date for Easter according to Roman usage (which had replaced Celtic usage) was to be calculated. He wrote expositions on Scripture much prized both in and after his time. In his writings on Mark, Luke, Acts, and Revelation, Bede made use of commentaries by Augustine, Ambrose, Jerome, and Gregory.

In modern times Bede is best known for his historical writings. These include biographies of various abbots in his history of the monastery, and a life of Cuthbert Lindisfarne. In 731 he completed his *Historia Ecclesiastica Gentis Anglorum* (*Ecclesiastical History of the English People*), a primary source for early English history. Bede took great care to collect and transcribe documents that are now lost. His history is written in a pleasing style, setting the life of the church in the life of the nation. Less than a century after his death he was given the title of "the Venerable," and his bones were moved to Durham where a commemorative stone in the cathedral reminds worshipers and visitors of him. Bede's student Egbert founded the school at York at which Aluin, famous English theologian and scholar, became a student in 745. P. TOON

BEECHER, HENRY WARD (1813–1887)
Congregational clergyman

Beecher was born at Litchfield, Connecticut, and was educated at Amherst College and at Lane Theological Seminary, Cincinnati, where his father, Lyman Beecher, was president. After two "new-school" Presbyterian pastorates in Indiana, he was called in 1847 to the Plymouth Congregational Church, Brooklyn, where he served until his death. He became one of the most popular and widely known preachers and lecturers in America. He was a colorful figure with great oratorical skills and audience rapport. Crowds flocked to hear him.

As a moderate reformer and political activist, Beecher addressed moral and social issues, advocating such causes as antislavery, industrial reform, and women's suffrage. In theology he rejected historic Calvinism and interpreted the Bible in moralistic terms, emphasizing the love of God. He became more and more liberal, accepting the theory of evolution and rejecting the doctrines of eternal punishment and verbal inspiration. To avoid controversy he led his congregation out of the Congregational Association in 1882.

Beecher edited *The Independent* (1861–1863) and *The Christian Union* (1870–1882) and wrote for *The New York Ledger.* After 1859 his sermons were published in several volumes of *The Plymouth Pulpit.* Other important books include *Seven Lectures to Young Men* (1844), *Lecture-Room Talks* (1870), *Life of Jesus the Christ* (1871), *Yale Lectures on Preaching* (1872–1874), and *Evolution and Religion* (1885).

Henry Ward Beecher was the brother of author Harriet Beecher Stowe.
A. H. FREUNDT, JR.

BEECHER, LYMAN (1775–1863)
American evangelical leader during the first half of the nineteenth century

Born in New Haven, Connecticut, Beecher entered Yale University in 1793.

Yale's new president, Timothy Dwight, inspired him to become a revivalist. In 1799 Beecher was ordained into the Presbyterian ministry and for the next thirty-three years he served churches in New York, Connecticut, and Massachusetts. During this period he became well known from his revivalistic efforts and his attacks on dueling, intemperance, Unitarianism, and Roman Catholicism. He also helped to found the American Bible Society.

In 1832 Beecher moved westward to become the first president of the newly founded Lane Theological Seminary near Cincinnati. His early years as president were stormy. Hard feelings resulting from the antislavery movement and charges of heresy brought against Beecher by fellow Presbyterians plunged him into prolonged controversy. In 1852 Beecher resigned his presidency and spent the last years of his life in Brooklyn, New York, in the home of his son, the famous preacher, Henry Ward Beecher. The dominating idea in Beecher's life was "the promotion of revivals of religion." When asked as an old man what he considered the greatest thing in life, he replied, "It is not theology, it is not controversy, but it is to save souls." Among his children were Henry Ward Beecher and Harriet Beecher Stowe. R. L. TROUTMAN

BEETHOVEN, LUDWIG VAN (1770–1827)
German composer

Born in Bonn, Beethoven lived at a time of great upheaval, culminating in the French Revolution. In spirit, he was as much a revolutionary as any of his artistic compatriots. His works *Egmont, Fidelio,* and the *Ninth Symphony* especially reflect his liberal idealism. Both his father and grandfather were musicians in the employ of the elector of Cologne at Bonn. Beethoven studied violin, viola, harpsichord, and organ; he studied counterpoint with Johann Georg Albrechtsberger and with Franz Joseph Haydn, whose teaching he disliked.

Beethoven's personal life was full of tragedy. He became totally deaf, so that the major portion of his creative life was spent with that agonizing handicap. Later in life he was obliged to become the guardian of a nephew, Karl, a strained and sorry relationship which brought him much pain.

As a composer, Beethoven worked tirelessly in spite of his difficulties. He was sharply self-critical, reworking and revising extensively until he was satisfied. In a given composition many more pages might be devoted to preliminary sketches or versions than to the final product. Even so, his total output was large, considering his performing and teaching obligations as well as his personal tragedies.

Beethoven, still regarded as among the most original of all composers, had enormous influence on nineteenth-century secular music; yet he did not influence church music significantly. With the exception of the hymn, "Joyful, Joyful We Adore Thee," adapted from the *Ninth ("Choral") Symphony,* and "The Glory of God in Nature," adapted for choir from one of six sacred songs (Opus 48), or an occasional transcription for organ of one of his slow melodies, his music is rarely used in worship services. His two sacred choral works, the *Mass in C Major* (Opus 86) and the *Missa Solemnis* (Opus 123), along with an infrequently heard oratorio, *Christ on the Mount of Olives,* are performed almost exclusively in concert halls. Yet these works bring to culmination a quality inherent in most of his music: a generic human religiosity. In that sense, Beethoven's music speaks to all who, whatever their religion, are openly aware of and responsive to an ultimate force which must be taken into solemn account. With great spiritual capacity and immense musical imagination, Beethoven created a body of music which for sheer power and other-worldliness is almost without equal in western music. H. M. BEST

BELL, GEORGE KENNEDY ALLEN (1883–1958)

Bishop of Chichester (England); a founder of the World Council of Churches

The son of a clergyman, Bell was educated at Christ Church, Oxford, where he excelled academically and gained a reputation as a poet. After ordination he served first in the industrial city of Leeds and there developed an interest in the social implications of Christian faith. Returning to Oxford as a tutor, he met and became friendly with William Temple (later archbishop). In 1914 when war came, Bell went to be a domestic chaplain to Archbishop Davidson and became known as an organizer.

In 1919 Bell heard Archbishop Soderblom describe his dream of a permanent ecumenical movement, a vision that deeply affected Bell. From 1924 to 1929 he was dean of Canterbury Cathedral, where he initiated administrative reforms and also commissioned plays to be performed in the cathedral (for example, T. S. Eliot's *Murder in the Cathedral*). From 1929 until shortly before his death, Bell was bishop of Chichester, where he again used the performing and visual arts in evangelism and worship. In the world church he was a leader of the Life and Work Movement and a supporter of the Confessing Church in Germany before and during World War II. He was chairman of the central committee of the World Council of Churches from 1948 until 1958. He wrote a detailed biography of Archbishop R. Davidson and edited *Documents on Christian Unity* (1924–1958). Bell's own biography has been written by R. C. D. Jasper.
P. TOON

BELL, L. NELSON (1894–1973)

American missionary, surgeon, writer, and Presbyterian leader

Nelson Bell was born of devout Presbyterian parents in western Virginia. He set out to be a lawyer, but shortly after enrolling at Washington and Lee University in 1911 he felt strongly called to be a missionary doctor. Shortly after graduation from the Medical College of Virginia he married Virginia Leftwich. He was invited to go to China by the mission board of the Presbyterian Church in the United States. The Bells arrived in China in late 1916 and joined the staff of a Presbyterian mission hospital in

Tsingkiangpu, in the province of North Kiangsu. A few years later Bell was made superintendent of the hospital. He actively sought contributions in the United States for the work, and by the mid-1930s the hospital was the largest Presbyterian hospital in the world. Because of his innovative surgical and medical techniques (especially in connection with a dreaded tropical disease, kala-azar or black fever), Bell was made a fellow of the American College of Surgeons in 1934.

During much of Bell's missionary career, China was torn by civil disorder, so the mission's work was often carried on under extreme difficulties. Finally, in May 1941, the Bells were forced to leave China because of Japanese occupation.

Returning to the United States, Bell settled in Montreat, North Carolina, and established a surgical practice in nearby Asheville. He soon became concerned over liberal theological trends in the Presbyterian Church in the United States, and was largely responsible for founding the *Southern Presbyterian Journal* to defend a conservative biblical position within the denomination. He strongly opposed a proposal for union between the Presbyterian Church in the United States ("Southern Presbyterians") and the Presbyterian Church in the United States of America ("Northern Presbyterians"), largely because of theological liberalism in the northern church. The proposal was defeated in 1950, with Nelson Bell unquestionably a major factor in the defeat.

Bell's concern for biblical Christianity led him, along with his evangelist son-in-law Billy Graham and Carl F. H. Henry, to establish *Christianity Today* magazine in 1956. He retired from his medical practice and devoted full time to the magazine as its executive editor. He also contributed numerous articles to the magazine, especially through a regular column, "A Layman and His Faith."

Although a series of heart attacks caused him to relinquish some duties with *Christianity Today,* Bell continued a wide ministry of writing and speaking. In 1972 he was elected the moderator of the Presbyterian Church in the United States, the highest elected office in the denomination. Although opposed to liberal trends within the denomination, Bell urged fellow conservatives not to withdraw from the denomination. His biography, *A Foreign Devil in China,* was written by John Pollock in 1971.

J. N. AKERS

BELLARMINE, ROBERT (1542–1621)

Catholic theologian, cardinal, and saint of the Jesuit order; regarded by many as the greatest and fairest Catholic critic of Protestantism in the late Reformation period

Born in Tuscany (Italy) into an important and devout Catholic family, Bellarmine's entire life was an example of the combination of devotion and scholarship.

Joining the Jesuits by the age of seventeen, Bellarmine received the best training the Catholic Church had to offer. Sent in 1569 to Louvain University in Belgium to expose the "errors of Protestantism," he read the Protestant theologians with great care and respect. Thus his lifetime work of trying to refute Protestant ideas was both informed and equitable. He established a new standard for Protestant-Catholic debates, which had often been carried on in bad faith. Moving to Rome in 1577, he became the most respected Catholic theologian and personal theologian to the pope. He brought many needed reforms to the church.

B. G. ARMSTRONG

BENDER, CARL JACOB (1869–1935)

Missionary to the Cameroons

Born in Germany, Bender came to the United States at the age of twelve. Following his graduation from German Baptist Theological Seminary in Rochester, New York, Bender went to the Cameroons in 1899 under the Berlin-based German Baptist Missionary Society (now the European Baptist Missionary Society). The German flag was raised over the Cameroons in 1887, and the mission entered in 1891. Bender was supported, however, by German churches in the United States. His first station was Douala.

74

In 1909 he moved to Soppo on Mount Cameroon. Bender established at that station a school and a rest house for missionaries, and founded numerous outstations. When British forces defeated the German troops in the region in World War I, all Germans were interned or deported. Bender alone of the missionaries of German societies was permitted to remain throughout the war, because he was an American citizen. He retired from active service in 1919. Because of the pressing need, however, he returned to Sappo in 1929, where he stayed for the remainder of his life. P. BEAVER

BENEDICT VII (died 983)
Pope, 974–983

Benedict VII is remembered for suppressing simony (the selling of sacred offices or objects for profit) and for promoting monasticism. He also granted many privileges to the churches and monasteries of Germany and worked for the conversion of the Slavs. P. TOON

BENEDICT VIII (died 1024)
Pope, 1012–1024

Benedict VIII was first of the Tusculan Popes (a series of popes from Tusculum, Italy, most of whom were feudal barons). He was consecrated bishop of Rome as a layman without having to work his way through the ranks of ordination. He crowned Henry II, a German, as Holy Roman emperor in 1014 and was one of the few popes of that period who was strong both at home and abroad. He also worked for the moral reform of the church. P. TOON

BENEDICT XII (1285–1342)
Pope, 1334–1342

Born Jacques Fournier, he received a doctorate in theology from Paris, became bishop of Pamiers (1317) and of Mirepoix (1327). Made a cardinal in 1327, he was unexpectedly elected pope in 1334, being the third of the Avignon popes (reigning from Avignon, France, in order to escape political pressures in Rome). He was a zealous reformer, especially of the religious orders, but he had little success in European politics. His bull, *Benedictus Deus* (1336), taught that just souls see God (the Beatific Vision) before the resurrection of the dead. P. TOON

BENEDICT XIII
This title was claimed by two popes: Pedro de Luna (c. 1328–1423) and Pierfrancesco Orsini (1649–1730)

Orsini was accepted by Roman Catholics as a true pope. Pedro de Luna reigned from Avignon as an antipope (1394–1423), refusing to recognize the papal succession that had reestablished itself in Rome. Orsini was made cardinal in 1672 and archbishop of Benevento in 1686. As pope (1724–1730), he attempted to enforce clerical discipline, especially through the rules formulated by the provincial Lateran Council of 1725. By placing too much confidence in the guidance of an unscrupulous cardinal, Nicolo Coscia, he damaged the papacy's effectiveness. P. TOON

BENEDICT XIV (1675–1758)
Pope, 1740–1758

Born Prospero Lorenzo Lambertini, he worked in the Vatican before being made a cardinal in 1728 and archbishop of Bologna in 1731. After a conclave of six months he was elected pope. An excellent administrator and ecclesiastical statesman, he did much to strengthen the papacy's moral influence in Europe. He wrote several authoritative books based on his study and experience while a Vatican administrator. His study of the processes of beatification and canonization (1734–1738) and his study of local church synods (1748) were noteworthy. P. TOON

BENEDICT XV (1854–1922)
Pope, 1914–1922

Born Giacomo della Chiesa, he served as secretary to the papal nuncio in Madrid

(Spain). After returning to Rome he was appointed archbishop of Bologna in 1907. Soon after the outbreak of World War I he was elected pope. During the hostilities he attempted to maintain the neutrality of the papacy, believing that papal authority stood above political conflicts; nonetheless, he gave help to those ravaged by war. He also fought "modernism," worked for the advancement of missions, and increased the Vatican's diplomatic relations with secular states. P. TOON

BENEDICT OF ANIANE (c. 750–821)
French monastic reformer

Benedict began his career as a military officer under Pepin (715–768) and Pepin's son Charlemagne (742–814), but in 733 became a monk. Six years later he founded a monastery on his lands at Aniane. The "Monastic Chapter," drawn up according to Benedict's wishes in 817 by a meeting of abbots, required that all French monasteries follow the Benedictine Rule drawn up by Benedict of Nursia (died about 547). Louis supported the code by sending around inspectors to see that it was followed. He was an adviser on church affairs to Charlemagne's son, the Holy Roman emperor, Louis I the Pious (who ruled from 814–840).

Benedict also joined Alcuin (a British scholar then serving in the imperial court) in writing against the adoptionist heresy. That heresy taught that Jesus was not originally divine but was "adopted" by God to become his son. C. HICKS

BENEDICT OF NURSIA (c. 480–c. 547)
Italian monk; author of the Benedictine Rule, which established the pattern for European monastic life from the early Middle Ages

Benedict was educated in rhetoric and law at Rome, but was so repelled by the immorality there that before finishing his studies he went off to live in a cave near Subiaco. Twice while living in that area he became the abbot for groups of monks. The first time he had to leave because the monks resented his strictness. The second time he was forced

out by a jealous priest. About 520 he established a monastery at Monte Cassino, where he stayed until his death and where he drew up his Rule.

Although there is no evidence that Benedict intended to found an order, he did conceive of his Rule being followed in widely distant regions. Thus, for example, when speaking of the monk's clothing he makes allowances for differences in climate. His Rule is characterized by moderation, sensibility, and humanity. Benedict was opposed to the extreme ascetic practices of some monks; instead, he sought to create an environment where ordinary men could pursue the service of God and their own spiritual improvement through a balanced life of manual labor, reading, prayer, and worship. In 1965 Benedict was proclaimed the patron saint of Europe by Pope Paul VI. C. HICKS

BENGEL, JOHANN ALBRECHT (1687–1752)
German biblical scholar

A pastor's son, born at Winnenden, Württemberg, Bengel entered the University of Tübingen in 1703. He devoted himself to study of the Scriptures, though he was also interested in philosophy, especially Spinoza's. He entered the Lutheran ministry (1707) as vicar at Metzingen, after which he became a professor at the seminary of Denkendorf (1713–1741). Then he became superintendent of Herbrechtingen (1741) and Alpirsbach (1749), remaining there until his retirement and death in Stuttgart.

Bengel's early work was in classical literature and the writings of the early church fathers (patristic literature), but his most important contributions were in New Testament textual criticism and exposition. As a student he had been confused about variant readings in the Greek manuscripts of the New Testament, so he began to study that subject. His famous rule for determining a textual variant was "The more difficult reading is to be preferred," because it was more likely that a scribe would change a more difficult reading to an easier one than vice versa. His most important work for textual criticism was a critical edition of the New Testament (1734), which was the beginning of modern textual criticism. Following that critical work came an exegetical one, *Gnomon Novi Testamenti* (1742), a commentary giving a detailed analysis of the Greek text. That work had considerable influence on biblical exegesis in Germany, was favored by John Wesley, and is valuable to scholars even today. H. W. HOUSE

BENSON, CLARENCE H. (1879–1954)
American Christian educator and publisher

Benson received his theological education at Princeton Theological Seminary (Presbyterian) and served several pastorates in the United States and one in Japan. In 1922 Moody Bible Institute in Chicago employed him to train students to teach in Sunday schools. In 1924 Benson expanded the Sunday school course into a religious education course that eventually became the Christian education department, which Benson headed until 1942. In 1927 a teaching training course was developed, and in 1931 a combined Christian education/music major was offered. In 1930 Benson, with President Gray of Moody and representatives of key Bible institutes, organized the International Bible Institute Council of Christian Education which eventually developed an evangelical standard educational course. From that framework came the Evangelical Teacher Training Association, to train teachers adequately in Bible, personal evangelism, and missions. Benson served as its first executive secretary. He worked with students at Moody Bible Institute from 1925 to 1933 to develop the All Bible Graded series of Sunday school curriculum materials. Benson and Victory Cory then teamed up to found Scripture Press to publish the new materials. Other writing projects included the development of the Uniform Bible Lesson series, *A Popular History of Christian Education, The Sunday School in Action, Introduction to Child Study,* and others. Benson founded and served as first editor of the *Church School Promoter,* which became *Christian Life* magazine. L. GOLDBERG

BENSON, EDWARD WHITE (1829–1896)
Church of England educator; archbishop of Canterbury

Born in Birmingham, Benson attended King Edward's School there before going to Trinity College, Cambridge. After ordination he became headmaster of Wellington School, where he showed abilities as an educator and organizer. In 1872 he became chancellor of Lincoln Cathedral, and there he set in motion various schemes of theological education and diocesan evangelism. In 1877 he was consecrated the first bishop of Truro, in Cornwall. He delighted in the Cornish people and set up the administration for an efficient diocese. He was the first bishop to employ a full-time diocesan evangelist and spent much time planning the cathedral and several schools. His fame spread and he became archbishop of Canterbury in 1882. He had a busy archiepiscopate, his main concerns being education and the church in Wales. The most important single event of his primacy was the trial set before him of Edward King, bishop of Lincoln, on charges of illegal ritualism. His decision in favor of the bishop and against the Protestants who brought the charge was epoch-making in the Church of England. Throughout his life Benson set before himself the example of Cyprian, early bishop of Carthage; after Benson's death his own study of Cyprian was published (1897). P. TOON

BERDYAEV, NIKOLAI (1874–1948)
Russian thinker; Christian existentialist

Arrested for criticizing the synod of his Russian Orthodox Church, Berdyaev, a thorough individualist, escaped sentence only because the revolution erupted. Attracted to Marxism as a student and exiled to northern Russia for three years on that account, he was given a professorship at the University of Moscow after the revolution. Two years later he was exiled for rejecting the materialistic basis and collectivist form of Marxist socialism. He worked in Berlin with the YMCA, then settled in Paris.

Independence of mind was consistent

with his religious and philosophical views. As an existentialist his interest focused on the dehumanization of man and the individual's loss of meaning in life. According to Berdyaev, the loss of meaning comes from debasement and denial of human creativity. Both in capitalism and in a collectivist society, persons are in bondage to things as well as to fictitious economic and political ideals. Such ideals are given a scientific aura, as if they represented objective laws that govern social processes, and thereby they stifle the free creativity of the human spirit. Hope lies in a revival of the human spirit by creative acts extending into all areas of life.

Berdyaev regarded knowledge not as a mental accumulation of impersonal and objective information but as a creative attempt to give meaning and value to things. He saw art and religion as expressions of a free spirit creating meaning, and he advocated a personalistic kind of socialism that would encourage the creative growth of individuals.

But since human creativity is spontaneous and could create chaos, whereas existence is not in reality chaotic, there must be another free spirit, God, whose creative activity in the course of history makes possible what meaning and value we do give to life. Berdyaev combined his religiously grounded existential hope with a mystical experience of the divine and an almost pantheistic theology that left unresolved problems about the transcendence of God. Berdyaev wrote with the spontaneous outspokenness of a prophet rather than as an objective thinker who weighed every suggestion and implication in what he said. His style fits his message. A. F. HOLMES

BERENGAR OF TOURS (c. 1000–1088)
Medieval French scholar

A pupil of Fulbert of Chartres, and from 1029 a student and later head of the school at Tours, Berengar was also an archdeacon at Angers. He appeared as a leading thinker at a time when many questions were being raised about the authority and traditions of the early medieval church. Berengar was concerned to bring all the mysteries of faith

under the scrutiny of reason or, as it was then called, the dialectic. Reason, not simply unquestioned tradition, was Berengar's final judge of truth. Since it was in reasoning that human beings most resembled their Maker, reason was not opposed to God but was the completion of faith. To Berengar all knowledge could be attained by reason, which was more trustworthy than mere custom or tradition. Berengar, an early representative of Scholasticism, was critical of ancient authorities like Boethius, Priscian, and Donatus. His was the new learning of the day.

Berengar's rational approach led him to oppose the developing notions of transubstantiation (the medieval doctrine of the Eucharist). The controversy sharpened the theological and philosophical positions. Berengar's views were condemned by Pope Leo IX at the Synod of Paris in 1051. Berengar first was ready to remain a heretic, but later agreed to a statement supporting the prevailing doctrine of transubstantiation. T. O. KAY

BERGGRAV, EIVIND (1884–1959)
Norwegian Lutheran bishop, writer,
anti-Nazi churchman, and ecumenical leader

Berggrav was ordained in 1908. After serving as a pastor and prison chaplain, he became bishop of Tromso (1928–1937), bishop of Oslo, and primate of the Church of Norway (1937–1950). In 1909 he founded and edited the periodical *Kirke og Kultur,* which attempted to link the church with cultural life. He also wrote thirty books in various fields. Although liberally oriented, he took no part in such theological debates, and won the respect of the majority of Norway's Lutherans.

Berggrav became internationally famous through his moral leadership in resisting the Nazi occupation of Norway. He wrote strong declarations and pastoral letters while under house arrest from 1942 to 1945, when he also wrote *Man and State* (English translation, 1951). After World War II Berggrav retired from his bishopric (1950) and took part in ecumenical efforts. He was one of the copresidents of the World Council of Churches (1950–1954). R. P. Evans

BERGSON, HENRI (1859–1941)
French philosopher and Nobel Prize winner

Bergson criticized mechanistic interpretations of life, including Darwin's theory of natural selection, and offered instead a teleological account in which a living force drives all living things to achieve certain ends. Coming from a Jewish background, Bergson may have noted the Old Testament's emphasis on the process of time and history in which God achieves his ends. But his reasons were scientific and philosophical rather than religious.

Since the Renaissance, modern science has gradually extended its causal explanations to one phenomenon after another, psychological and biological as well as the purely physical, accounting even for life and consciousness in purely physical or chemical terms. Creative novelty, human purpose, and freedom have often been disregarded. Bergson claimed that such reductionist science fails to explain (1) how an organism or animal can function as a unified whole if it is a product of random variations, and (2) why the process of natural selection would produce more and more complex things when simple organisms are already well adjusted to their environments. The survival of the fittest would surely favor simplicity. Rather, he concluded, the evolutionary process must be driven by some creative force to produce higher and more complex levels of life, and ultimately man himself. The freedom of the human spirit is the culmination of the whole historical development.

Applying his conception of creative evolution to ethics and religion, Bergson objected to fixed moral laws that inhibit spontaneity, and to ritualistic or dogmatic religions whose intellectualized or conventional forms prevent fresh mystical experience. Toward the end of his life he gained more sympathy for Roman Catholicism, but his thought tended throughout in a pantheistic rather than a theistic direction. Bergson was a forerunner of the process theologies that have arisen since World War II.
A. F. Holmes

BERKELEY, GEORGE (1685–1753)
Irish-born philosopher and Anglican bishop

As a young man Berkeley built upon the empiricist views of John Locke, developing an idealist philosophy that denied any objective reality to matter and the material world. His philosophical ideas are recorded in *Essay toward a New Theory of Vision* (1709), *A Treatise concerning the Principles of Human Knowledge* (1710), and *Three Dialogues between Hylas and Philonous* (1713).

Berkeley wrote in criticism of the mechanistic science of his day, with its emphasis on material particles, natural forces, and absolute space and time. Various thinkers, supposing such scientific ideas to imply that the material world is self-sufficient, had adopted materialism and deism as worldviews. Berkeley set out to show the lack of any empirical basis for abstract ideas of matter, force, space, and time—a fatal consideration for Lockean empiricists. Instead of sense impressions being caused by actual things and forces in a world of time and space, Berkeley proposed that God is their direct cause. Thus, for Berkeley, the orderly laws and processes of the world of experience are mental phenomena produced by an actual Creator rather than by an independently operating material reality.

Berkeley was zealous to spread Protestantism in the American colonies. He spent three years in Rhode Island, and he intended to establish a college in Bermuda for training missionaries to counteract Roman Catholic influence among blacks and Indians. When financing for the school failed, Berkeley returned to Ireland, where in 1734 he was consecrated Anglican bishop of Cloyne. During his eighteen years as bishop, he centered his attention on the quality of religious life in England and Ireland. Berkeley also continued to oppose philosophical materialism and spoke out against deism.
K. Leid & A. F. Holmes

BERKHOF, LOUIS (1873–1957)
American Calvinist theologian

Transplanted as a child from his native Netherlands, Berkhof had a lifelong affiliation with the Christian Reformed Church. For the major part of his professional life he served its Calvin Seminary in Grand Rapids, Michigan, as professor and president.

Berkhof's influence in propagating Calvinist theology, however, extended far beyond the seminary. There he taught Old Testament and New Testament, as well as systematic theology—his particular specialty. Through his seminary students who took varied church assignments, through his own preaching ministry, and through his writings for seminarians, for the lay public, and even for high school and catechism students, his impact was significant.

Berkhof championed and popularized the ideas of two other Dutch Calvinist theologians, Abraham Kuyper (1837–1920) and Hermann Bavinck (1854–1921). Bavinck's *Reformed Dogmatics* (in Dutch) especially seems to have made a permanent impression on Berkhof's work. More than simply articulating Reformed doctrine, Berkhof also traced historical-cultural movements related to it and contrasted it with other philosophical and theological positions. Berkhof's works, some of which have been translated into foreign languages, include his own three-volume *Reformed Dogmatics* (1932)—entitled *Systematic Theology* after 1939, *A Summary of Christian Doctrine* (1938), *The History of Christian Doctrines* (1949), *Principles of Biblical Interpretation* (1950), and *The Second Coming of Christ* (1953). P. VELTMAN

BERLIOZ, LOUIS-HECTOR (1803–1869)
French composer of symphonies, sacred music, operatic and solo vocal pieces

Born in La Côte-St. André, Berlioz originally undertook a classical musical education at the Paris Conservatory, but became part of the developing Romantic aesthetic of his day. Many of his works have a large-scale, dramatic format and brilliant (often delicate) orchestrations and choral scorings.

Programmatic intent was important to him. His use of the "fixed idea" (a theme representing a specific person important to Berlioz) superimposed symbolic material onto classically conceived texture and form. His tendency to interject rather than to integrate such symbolic material left his music with certain stylistic problems.

Sacred works composed by Berlioz include a *Solemn Mass* (1825); an enormous *Requiem* (1837) with antiphonal brass effects; a sacred trilogy (*L'Enfance du Christ*, 1854); and *Te Deum* employing tenor solo, triple chorus, antiphonal organ, and orchestra. Berlioz, a successful music critic, contributed to the Paris *Journal of Debates* and the *Musical Gazette*. His *Treatise of Modern Instrumentation and Orchestration* remains an authoritative work on the subject. D. S. CUSHMAN

BERNADETTE (surnamed SOUBIROUS) (1844–1879)
French peasant girl from Lourdes; famous for her visions of the Virgin Mary

The oldest of six children in the family of a poor miller, Bernadette grew up in great poverty and received very little religious education. On February 11, 1858, at the age of fourteen, she saw a vision of the Virgin Mary at Massabielle Rock near Lourdes. In the course of appearances, which ended July 16, 1858, Mary announced her presence by causing a spring to begin miraculously, and requested that a chapel be built on the site. After the young girl told others about her vision, she was doubted and questioned by the curious until the parish priest took her to the Sisters of Notre Dame at Nevers. Bernadette joined that religious group in 1866 and remained there until her death. She was canonized in 1933. Lourdes has since become a famous and much-publicized Roman Catholic shrine for people seeking healing. C. HICKS

BERNARD OF CLAIRVAUX (1090–1153)
Leader and spokesman of medieval Christianity

Both Protestants and Catholics still appreciate Bernard for his hymns, his exemplary life, and his mystical piety. His motto has been adopted by others throughout the ages: To Know Jesus and Jesus Crucified.

Bernard entered the abbey of Citeaux (France) in 1113 and two years later chose a more remote location to found a new monastery apart from the world. He spent much of the rest of his life at Clairvaux ("bright valley"), experiencing continual tension between a life of ascetic retirement and a life of Christian involvement in the world.

Bernard challenged popes and princes about the quality of their Christian practice and called all Christendom to lives of mystical devotion. Such a life was pictured as a separation of soul and body, an emptying of worldly desire, and a final union of the soul with God. A concord of the divine and human wills was sought which would not confuse the distinction between God and man. The procedure for gaining such harmony was outlined in Bernard's *Twelve Steps to Humility*. His view that the highest truth, that of God, could be known through mystical contemplation brought Bernard into conflict with the university men of his day, most of whom were approaching the problem of truth more philosophically. One of his antagonists was Abelard, upon whom Bernard did not waste any charitable thoughts. He challenged Abelard and other scholars throughout his lifetime because of their reliance upon the worldly learning of the mind.

Bernard supported the second Crusade in 1149 with great fervor and convinced kings Louis VII and Conrad II to "take up the cross" in that rather unsuccessful enterprise. Bernard also launched an evangelistic mission to university students in Paris, as well as in the south of France, hoping to limit heresy in those areas.

Highly respected in his own day for his saintliness, austerity, and personal charm, Bernard of Clairvaux has continued to influence the church through his writings. He has been called the "greatest master of language in the Middle Ages." His hymns included "Jesus, the Very Thought of Thee"

and "O Sacred Head Now Wounded." He also wrote many sermons, devotional treatises, and commentaries. His mysticism, well-stated and positive, was based solely on the love of God. Although other Christian mystics had already said many of the same things, Bernard's way of saying them continued to be influential.

Bernard's zeal produced a certain bluntness of communication and an often seemingly uncharitable attitude, but his commitment to God and the church was unquestioned. T. O. KAY

BERNARD OF CLUNY
(mid twelfth century)
Monk who was a renowned poet

Born in either Brittany or England, Bernard spent most of his adult life as a Benedictine monk at the famous monastery of Cluny under its great abbot, Peter the Venerable. Bernard was an extraordinary and prolific poet. In addition, he made compilations of earlier monastic customs that became the basis of the Cluniac reform.

Bernard's best-known poem is *De Contemptu Mundi* (*In Contempt of the World*), a three-thousand-line satire directed at the clergy of his day, full of apocalyptic utterances and Dantesque descriptions of the afterworld. Portions of the work are known in John Neale's translations: "Brief Life Is Here Our Portion"; "For Thee, O Dear, Dear Country"; and "Jerusalem the Golden." Bernard also composed many sermons and rhythmic praises of the Blessed Virgin. A. CABANISS

BERNINI, GIAN LORENZO
(1598–1680)
Italian sculptor and architect

Born in Naples as a sculptor's son, Bernini moved with his family to Rome in 1605, where he labored for the rest of his life. His earliest works show close acquaintance with the art of the Roman Empire. His early sculpted busts are marked by their realism and psychological insight.

Bernini's reputation as one of the greatest

artists of his time was launched by a series of life-size sculptures (1618–1624) done for Cardinal Scipione Borghese. Filled with vigor and movement, those sculptures achieved a realism in marked contrast to other sculpture of Bernini's time. After completion of that group, Bernini was commissioned by Pope Urban VIII (1568–1644) to work on several ecclesiastical projects which culminated in his being appointed architect of St. Peter's in 1629. His architectural achievements include the colonnade of St. Peter's Square (1656–1667), seen as an expression of the church's duty to enfold her faithful. His entrance to the Scala Regia (1663–1666) was a masterpiece of shaping space and light. That same concern was shown in his famous "Ecstasy of St. Theresa" (1645–1652), a work combining sculpture, painting, and architecture in an attempt to portray Theresa's mystical vision. Throughout his work, Bernini strove to express his deep faith in "the church triumphant" and in the unity of faith and reason in life and art, under the rule of the Roman Catholic Church. K. HOGLUND

BESANT, ANNIE (1847–1933)
Theosophical leader and Indian political figure

The only daughter of a London businessman, Annie was educated privately. She married Frank Besant in 1867. Her husband became vicar of Sibsey in Lincolnshire, but she lost her Anglican religious conviction and left her husband in 1873, taking their two children. In 1874 she joined the National Secular Society and soon became vice-president. After she authored a book entitled *Gospel of Atheism* (1877) and promoted a neo-Malthusian social order, the courts of England removed her daughter from her care. Mrs. Besant continued her social activism by joining the Fabian Society in 1885. She participated in the matchmakers' strike of 1888 and helped the match workers form a union. In 1888 she also reviewed theosophist leader Madame Blavatsky's book *The Secret Doctrine*. After meeting the author, Mrs. Besant visited India in 1893, and on her return to England claimed to have been re-incarnated in India many times. She became a leader in the Theosophical Society and was eventually elected president (1907). Mrs. Besant settled permanently in India in 1895 and became active in the political struggle for a free India. In 1899 she was instrumental in founding Central Hindu College. In 1916 she launched the Home Rule for India League, which had wide influence. She remained active in both theosophical circles and Indian politics until her death. K. HOGLUND

BEZA, THEODORE (1519–1605)
Calvin's successor at Geneva

Beza was born at Vezelay in Burgundy (France) and educated at Orleans and Bourges under Melchior Wolmar. Back at Orleans in 1534, he earned a law degree in 1537 and practiced law for some years in Paris. He continued his earlier literary interests, however, and published some Latin poems (*Juvenilia*) in 1548. He married Claudine Desnoz in 1544. Since he held two benefices and had thoughts of ordination, he kept the marriage secret until in 1548. But a severe illness brought about his acceptance of Reformation teaching.

Leaving Paris, Beza went to Geneva (Switzerland), where he married Claudine publicly, and then to Lausanne, where Pierre Viret secured for him the professorship of Greek. Here he quickly rose to prominence. In 1550 he wrote a tragedy on the sacrifice of Isaac; he defended Calvin's doctrine of predestination against the attack of Jerome Bolsec; in 1554 he wrote a tract vindicating the execution of Michael Servetus; and in 1556 he prepared a Latin version of the New Testament. In 1557 he went with William Farel to confer with the Waldensians. He also worked to achieve agreement between Reformation groups on the doctrine of the Lord's Supper.

Beza left Lausanne in 1558 to teach Greek in Geneva. He became first rector of the Genevan Academy when it was founded in 1559, continuing also to teach Greek and later theology. In 1560 he paid a visit to the rulers of Navarre at Nerac to discuss the Huguenot (French Protestant) situation. In 1561 he completed Clement Marot's metrical translation of the Psalms into French and went to France to represent the Reformed Church at the important Colloquy of Poissy. After the failure of the conference, he remained in France for two years as an adviser to the Huguenots.

Beza returned to Geneva in 1563. When Calvin died in 1564, Beza followed him as moderator of the company of pastors, of which Beza remained until 1580. The office involved Beza in dealings with the city government and also made him a leading spokesperson for the Reformed faith. Until ill health forced him to retire in 1600 Beza did much to develop and defend the Reformation in six important areas:

1. Beza continued and consolidated Calvin's work in Geneva. He maintained the presbyterian order Calvin had established. He also maintained the discipline but succeeded in setting up better relations with the Little Council and therefore in relaxing many of the earlier tensions. Beza also set high standards at the academy so that it continued to be an international center of Reformed learning.

2. Beza defended Reformed teaching against significant deviations. Three developments in particular were targets of his polemical work. The first was the new logic of Peter Ramus, which ran contrary to the Aristotelianism Beza favored. The second was the teaching of Arminius, which questioned the rigid predestinarianism Arminius had heard from Beza himself when a student in Geneva. The third was a lingering understanding of the Lord's Supper as simply a commemoration of Christ's death.

3. Beza worked constructively as well as critically for the Reformed cause. With other Reformed churches he endorsed Bullinger's Second Helvetic Confession (1566) as a common doctrinal statement. He later helped to prepare a *Harmony of Reformed Confessions* designed to emphasize points of agreement in the statements considered. Through his many contacts in Geneva he was able to assist reformers in Holland and

also to make inroads into the empire, even though Calvinism was not recognized under the Peace of Augsburg of 1555.

4. Beza continued to have a special interest in France. After returning to Geneva in 1563 he continued to advise the Huguenots. In 1571 he presided at the Reformed Synod of La Rochelle and resisted the Congregationalism proposed by Ramus. After the 1572 massacre (St. Bartholomew's Day) he championed the view that lesser government officers might legitimately resist a tyrannical ruler and thus provided theological backing for the military action of the Huguenots, which finally won them toleration by the Edict of Nantes (1598).

5. Beza made a considerable contribution by his various writings. Though he can hardly be compared with Calvin in this area, his works exerted no little influence. His doctrinal works were published in the *Theological Treatises* (1582), which included a "Confession of the Christian Faith" that summarized his teaching. He also wrote a *Life of Calvin* and edited Calvin's letters (1575). In 1580 he wrote a *History of the French Reformed Churches*. Beza also devoted himself to textual work. He published a further edition of the New Testament text in 1582 in which he made limited use of the codex named after him (the Codex Bezae which was found at Lyons and which he donated to Cambridge University) and also the Codex Claromontanus (now at Paris). His texts were used in the Geneva Bible and the King James Version.

6. Beza did a great deal to forge the link between Calvin and the classical Calvinism of the following century. In three areas in particular this was an achievement of doubtful value: With his strong Aristotelianism he gave theology a more intellectual and rationalist character than one finds in Calvin's own writings. In his statement and defense of the doctrine of predestination he strengthened the emphasis on double predestination (election to both salvation and perdition), preparing the way for the rigid formulation of the doctrine at the Synod of Dort (1519). In his understanding of church order Beza developed the dogmatic Presbyterianism

which replaced Calvin's more open and tolerant position and which hardened the English Puritans in their opposition to the Anglican settlement. Nevertheless, Beza also had a strong positive influence, for with his stress on excellence in scholarship and his personal example, he laid the foundation for the outstanding dogmatic work that was a mark of the Reformed churches throughout the seventeenth century. G. BROMILEY

BILNEY, THOMAS (c. 1495–1532)

English church reformer and martyr

Bilney was born in Norfolk and educated at Trinity Hall, Cambridge. After graduating he found spiritual comfort in an edition of the New Testament produced by Erasmus. He became a friend of Hugh Latimer, who later became a Protestant martyr. As a preacher from 1525 in the diocese of Ely, Bilney zealously denounced the worship of saints and the attendant ceremonials and pilgrimages (to Walsingham and Canterbury). Although he held to traditional medieval doctrines of the authority of the pope and the miracle of the Mass ("transubstantiation"), he evidently disturbed Cardinal Wolsey, who arrested him in 1527. While in prison in London, Bilney eventually recanted his Erasmian/Lutheran views and was released. Returning to Cambridge he felt guilty about his apostasy in London and began once more to preach Reformation doctrines, this time in the fields. He was arrested, tried, sentenced, and burned at the stake. P. TOON

BINGHAM, HIRAM (1789–1869)

Pioneer Congregational missionary to Hawaii

Born in Bennington, Vermont, educated at Middlebury College and Andover Seminary (ordained 1819), Bingham was sent by the American Board of Commissioners for Foreign Missions as one of their first missionaries to Hawaii, then called the Sandwich Islands. He helped establish the first mission stations in Honolulu and Lahaina, conducted preaching tours accompanied by the Hawaiian queen (who urged Christian-

ity upon her subjects), and advised the king and chiefs in their relations with foreigners. Bingham created a written language for the people, established schools, and translated Scripture and other literature into Hawaiian. The entire Bible was completed in 1839 with the help of colleagues and was printed with financial aid from the American Tract Society. In 1841 he returned to New England with his ill wife. He wrote *A Residence of Twenty-one Years in the Sandwich Islands* (1847). At intervals until 1863 he served as pastor of a black church in New Haven, Connecticut. A. H. FREUNDT, JR.

BINNEY, THOMAS (1798–1874)

English Congregational clergyman and Nonconformist leader

Born at Newcastle-on-Tyne and trained in the academy at Wymondley, Hertfordshire, Binney became minister at the prestigious Weigh House Chapel in London. His congregation was so large that a new chapel was built in 1834. Binney was friendly to Anglicans, but greatly opposed to the "state church" principle. He is best remembered as a pioneer of liturgical worship in the Nonconformist churches, as reflected in his service book, *The Service of Song in the House of the Lord*. He composed the hymn "Eternal Light! Eternal Light!" Aberdeen University conferred the LL.D. degree on Binney in 1852, and he was twice chairman of the Congregational Union. P. TOON

BLAKE, WILLIAM (1757–1827)

English Christian mystic, engraver, artist, and poet

Blake was born in London of a family of Dissenters who ran a hosiery shop. He had little formal schooling, but studied the Bible, Milton, Shakespeare, and Dante. Barely earning a living at the age of twenty-five, Blake married an illiterate girl whom he taught to write and draw.

A vivid imagination manifested itself early in his life: at the age of four he was sure he saw God looking in at his window. Later a dead brother appeared in a vision. Just before Blake himself died, a deathbed observer reported that "his eyes brightened and he burst out singing of the things he saw in heaven."

Developing a new method of printing from etched copper plates, Blake illustrated and sometimes engraved his own works. He also illustrated Gray's *Poems*, Chaucer's *Canterbury Tales*, *The Book of Job*, and Dante's *Divine Comedy*.

Blake's early writings were among his best. *Poetical Sketches* departed from poetic modes of the day; *Songs of Innocence* included "The Little Black Boy," a poem setting forth the equality of black and white before God, and "A Cradle Song," depicting a mother watching over the Eternal Child. *Songs of Experience* contained "The Little Boy Lost" and "London," a poem about the corrupting influence of reason upon life. In 1818 Blake published *The Everlasting Gospel*, a poem that has been called his confession of faith.

The Book of Thel (1789), earliest of Blake's elaborately symbolic "prophetic books," was a "song of the Ante-world." A diffuse, revolutionary attitude toward authority was the theme of a projected seven-book poem *The French Revolution*, finished and set in type in 1791 but never published.

In 1793 Blake engraved and illustrated three more prophetic books: *Visions of the Daughters of Albion,* an attack on conventional morality, and *America: A Prophecy,* spanning the period of the Christian era from the birth of Christ until the time of Blake, and *The Book of Urizen,* a highly symbolic work dealing with the creation of man. *The Four Zoas* (1796) depicted a revolutionary Christianity bringing the redemption and regeneration of man through Christ.

A less symbolic but highly controversial work, *The Marriage of heaven and hell* (1790), was an attack on various opposites pervading the language of Christianity, such as heaven and hell, God and Satan, and other dichotomous features. Blake's *Milton* (1815) depicted an imaginary return to earth by the author of *Paradise Lost*. Another long poem was *Jerusalem, the Emanation of the Giant Albion* (1804–1820). E. B. BATSON

BLANCHARD, CHARLES (1848–1925)
President of Wheaton College, 1882–1925

Born at Galesburg, Illinois, Charles was the son of Jonathan Blanchard, then president of Knox College. In 1860, the family moved to Wheaton, Illinois. This resulted from the father's new duties as Wheaton College's first president. Graduating from Wheaton in 1870, Blanchard soon embarked on his lifelong career in education. He returned to Wheaton College in 1874 as professor of English language and literature. But in 1878, Blanchard was appointed the college's vice-president. That same year, he also secured ordination as a Congregationalist minister. Subsequently, for a few years he was a pastor as well as college administrator. From 1878 to 1883, Blanchard was pastor of College Church of Christ (later College Church in Wheaton). He also served as interim pastor for Chicago Avenue Church (later Moody Memorial Church) from 1883 to 1885.

Wheaton College chose Blanchard to succeed his father as president in 1882. During his long tenure, the College attained its position as one of midwest America's most reputable liberal arts colleges. This came through diligent attention to general standards of academic excellence. At the same time, Blanchard's leadership made Wheaton College an important center of conservative Christianity. Throughout this time, Blanchard was one of American fundamentalism's major spokesmen. For years he was an officer in the National Fundamentalist Association. In well-defined fashion, Blanchard also led Wheaton College into an interdenominational stance over doctrine and organization.

A number of interests outside the College also attracted Blanchard. Like his father before him, he was a vocal opponent of American secret societies. Many of his writings concern this matter. In his later years Blanchard was president of the Chicago Hebrew Mission. He was also a strong supporter of overseas missions.
K. J. BRYER

BLANCHE OF CASTILE (1188–1252)
Mother of Louis IX of France

Daughter of Alfonso VIII of Castile and Eleanor, daughter of Henry II of England, Blanche became the wife of Louis, who ascended the French throne as Louis VIII in 1223. It was in their son, Louis IX (born 1224), that France saw the life and reign of its greatest monarch. Her nurture of and influence on Louis was Blanche's supreme work. Blanche herself actually ruled France—first, during the time of Louis's adolescence (1226–1234) and second, during the years of Louis's first (Europe's seventh) Crusade (1248–1252).

Blanche was remarkable for her exemplary Christian conduct, a woman not only of deep piety but exceptional energy and judiciousness. Her political acuity had practical display on many occasions. Two memorable events were her firm handling of recalcitrant French nobles in 1226, and her repulsion of a large-scale English attack in 1230. For Blanche, though, nothing transcended her role as mother of Louis IX—one of history's few truly godly rulers and a figure whose character and achievement still evoke respect. Incontrovertibly, Blanche's was the largest of human influences on Louis, even after her death in 1252. But Louis did not always heed his mother's sound counsel. In 1248, it was only reluctantly that Blanche assumed France's rule while Louis began his military efforts against Islam. The wisdom of her opposition to Louis's action became plain in the abortive results of the great king's two Crusades.
K. J. BRYER

BLAND, SALEM (1859–1950)
Canadian Methodist minister and college professor

In 1903 Bland was appointed to the faculty of Wesley College, Winnipeg, which was a Methodist liberal arts college and theological school. He was a strong exponent of the social implications of the Christian gospel and was on friendly terms with Winnipeg trade unionists. He was dismissed from his post in 1917 for reasons of econ-

omy or because of his politics. He became pastor of Broadway Methodist Tabernacle in Toronto in 1919 and constituted a main link between the Methodist Church and former Methodist ministers like J. S. Woodsworth and William Ivens, who had entered Canadian political life. Bland was influential in the formation of the Canadian Progressive party, a farmer's party, in 1918–1920. In 1920 he published *The New Christianity, or the Religion of the New Age.*
D. C. MASTERS

BLISS, PHILIP PAUL (1838–1876)
American hymn writer and gospel singer

Born in Pennsylvania, Bliss entered the Normal Academy of Music (New York City) in 1860. At the urging of Dwight L. Moody, Bliss put his musical talents to work in evangelism. A Baptist, he participated in the revival campaigns of D. W. Whittle as song leader and children's worker. Many of his songs became standard gospel hymns in evangelistic meetings throughout the United States. His songs speak of the individual's desire for God and express deep personal commitment. Bliss published four collections of his works from 1871 to 1874. His most popular songs include "Let the Lower Lights Be Burning," "Hallelujah! What a Savior!" "Almost Persuaded," and "Wonderful Words of Life." At age thirty-eight Bliss was killed with his wife in a train wreck. K. LEID

BODELSCHWINGH, FRIEDRICH (1831–1910)
German Lutheran pastor of Pietistic tendencies; founder of an institution for epileptics known as Bethel

Bodelschwingh's decision to become a missionary was made in 1854 as a result of a revival then strong in Germany. After theological studies in Basel, Erlangen, and Berlin, he ministered to Germans in Paris. In 1864 he was a pastor in Dellwig, where he lost four of his children in 1869 within two weeks. Deeply moved by that tragedy, he responded in 1872 to a call of the Inner

Mission of the Rhenish-Westphalian Lutherans to direct a colony of epileptics and the deaconess home Sarepta in Bielefeld. His first building, erected in 1873, took the name Bethel. In 1877 a school for deacons, called Nazareth, was begun. By 1888 a dormitory for theological candidates was opened, which led to the addition of a theological school in 1905. One of Bodelschwingh's activities, the German East Africa Mission, was also moved to Bethel in 1905. Five miles south, a home for itinerant workmen was built in 1882. Eventually other homes were founded in Berlin and elsewhere. In 1903 Bodelschwingh was elected to the Prussian diet. R. P. EVANS

BOEHM, MARTIN (1725–1812)

American revivalist; cofounder of the Church of the United Brethren in Christ (now subsumed under the United Methodist Church)

Boehm was born in Conestoga, Pennsylvania, into a Mennonite family. Chosen in 1753 as preacher of a local Mennonite congregation, he was plagued by the feeling that he had little to offer his hearers. Seeking greater spiritual depth, he experienced a conversion in 1758. Immediately he began testifying to the work of God's grace in his life, proclaiming repentance and salvation by faith.

On a visit to Virginia in 1761 Boehm's contact with followers of revivalist George Whitefield (1714–1770) spurred his desire to preach the doctrine of immediate salvation. In 1768 Boehm spoke at a "Great Meeting" held in Conestoga Valley. During the meeting Philip William Otterbein (1726–1813) heard him and was moved to "fellowship" with him. The two men enjoyed a long association, forming the roots of what was to become the United Brethren Church. In 1777, because of his revivalist activities and communion with non-Mennonites, the Mennonite Conference of Lancaster County excommunicated him. Thereafter, Boehm functioned as an itinerant revivalist among German settlers in Pennsylvania, Maryland, and Virginia. During that time he was closely associated with Methodism and was a friend of Francis Asbury (1745–1816). In 1800 Boehm and Otterbein were elected bishops of the United Brethren. A funeral tribute to Boehm's nearly fifty years of evangelistic work was given by Bishop Asbury. K. HOGLUND

BOEHME, JACOB (1575–1624)

Influential German Lutheran mystic

Born in Altseidenberg near Goerlitz into a well-to-do farming family, Boehme became a shoemaker and established a business in Goerlitz in 1599. Goerlitz was a center for religious and philosophical activity. Followers of the mystics Schwenckfeld and Weigel, as well as the alchemist Paracelsus, were active in the city. These groups all had an influence on Boehme's work. A Lutheran pastor, Martin Moller, came to Goerlitz in 1600 and organized a "conventicle of God's real servants" which Boehme joined. The conventicle was part of a greater movement that was opposing the so-called Protestant orthodoxy, whose theological dogma was viewed as a lifeless defense of its own views. A contemporary of Boehme, a Lutheran pastor, Johann Arndt, very much influenced this movement, which stressed personal spiritual experience and growth. Although influenced by those about him, Boehme stressed that what he wrote was formulated primarily by divine revelation and spiritual experience.

The beginning of Boehme's revelations occurred while he was gazing at a reflection in a dish. This experience unlocked the mystery of the coexistence of a just, loving God and evil. He recorded his insights and their developments after twelve years (in 1612). This work was called *Aurora* and may have been meant only for his close associates to read, but it was copied by a nobleman in the neighborhood and distributed. By 1613 Moller had been succeeded by Gregory Richter as the primary Lutheran minister in Goerlitz. Richter defended the Lutheran Orthodoxy and was not fond of Boehme. When a copy of *Aurora* came into his hands, Richter pushed the town council to banish Boehme and charge him to write nothing further. The banishment was revoked, but Boehme wrote nothing more for nearly seven years.

In 1619 Boehme put out *The Three Principles of the Divine Essence,* which is probably the easiest of all his books to read. He then wrote a companion volume, *The Threefold Life of Man,* a book that focused on spiritual regeneration. The book that earned him the reputation of the "Teutonic Philosopher" was *The Forty Questions.* This work began when the knowledge-seeking Balthazar Walter compiled a list of the most debated questions in theology and philosophy among the leading universities in Germany. The questions were sent to Boehme, who responded within three months. Boehme wrote numerous treatises between 1619 and 1624 covering esoteric cosmological questions (such as *Concerning the Birth and Designation of All Being*) as well as themes closer to traditional Christian theology (such as *On Election to Grace, On Christ's Testaments,* and *A Treatise on Baptism and the Lord's Supper*). He also wrote an allegorical commentary on the book of Genesis, named *Mysterium Magnum.* The village authorities were unaware of these writings because many of them were not published for circulation until after his death.

In 1624 Boehme published *The Way to Christ* on New Years Day. This work was specifically meant for the serious seeker of God and is somewhat biographical. It is devotional in nature and meant to lead the reader step-by-step through repentance and confession on a path that will result in harmony with God. The publication of this compilation of treatises, along with the enthusiasm of Boehme's disciples in Goerlitz, enraged Richter who this time convinced the village council to send Boehme elsewhere. Boehme spent a short time in Dresden, then in Silesia. He returned home in 1624, Richter being dead by this time. Boehme developed a severe and sudden illness and died shortly after his return to Goerlitz.

Boehme's work involved difficult and very often nontraditional concepts and language. Boehme himself put out a "key" to his principal points and expressions used in his writings. He covered a broad spectrum of theological and philosophical topics, such as the person of God, the divine nature, the Fall, sin and death, time and space, and much more. At the center of his complex theology God is seen symbolically as a fire that is either a light to illumine those who resign their will to God or the flames of wrath toward those who are self-willed. The light of love is revealed in Christ, the Word of God.

Boehme's views postdated Luther's by more than fifty years. Though he was a Lutheran himself, his theology diverged significantly from Luther's into areas of speculative mysticism, which Luther for the most part downplayed. Faith, to Luther, was first and foremost, bringing all God's grace to the believer at the moment of justification. Boehme felt that faith was the entrance into a progressive experience of God's grace. Both agreed that union with God is the goal of salvation. A life of repentance, prayer, and praise lifts fallen humans into an increasingly Christlike life which culminates, by virtue of union with God, in deliverance from the fallen will into spiritual joy.

Boehme's influence reached beyond Germany. William Law greatly revered his works. John Milton and Isaac Newton both bear some mark of Boehme's thought in their writings. The Philadelphian Society in London was established by followers of Boehme. The German philosopher Hegel said German philosophy began with Boehme. The Pietist movement also bore his influence. John Sparrow in England translated Boehme's work into English by 1661. *The Way to Christ* is available to readers today, and it would acquaint one with Boehme's thought and life in its most mature form.

T. FIRAK

BOETHIUS, ANICIUS MANLIUS TORQUATUS SEVERINUS
(c. 480–c. 524)

Roman Christian thinker of late antiquity who helped set the tone for the intellectual life of the Middle Ages

Boethius was from a noble family, his father having been a Roman consul in 487. Boethius entered the service of Theodoric, the Ostrogoth king who became master of Italy in 493. Theodoric, who wanted to take advantage of Roman culture, employed Boethius as an adviser, making him consul in 510 and giving him in 523 the position of master of offices, one of the most influential posts in the kingdom. Suddenly Boethius fell from favor; he was imprisoned the next year on charges of treason and sentenced to die. He and some other nobles were supposed to have been engaged in intrigue with the Byzantine emperor, though the real reason for the arrests may have been religious differences between Theodoric, an Arian, and his orthodox officials.

During the year or so before his execution, Boethius wrote his best-known book, *The Consolation of Philosophy.* In it, Philosophy, in the form of a woman, visits Boethius in his cell and explains why he, an innocent man, must suffer. In the process she discusses the nature of evil and of good, divine providence, and free will. The *Consolation* makes no mention of Christ or the Bible, but argues solely on the basis of natural reason as found in the Greek philosophers, especially Plato. Boethius originally intended to translate all the writings of Plato and Aristotle into Latin and to reconcile their systems of thought. He never had time to finish that ambitious project but did manage to translate and comment on Aristotle's logical works. Boethius also wrote works on logic and music, a commentary on Victorinus Afer's translation of Porphyry's *Isagoge,* and some treatises on Christian theology.
C. HICKS

BOLEYN, ANNE (c. 1507–1536)
English queen whose marriage to King Henry VIII played a role in the separation of the Anglican Church from Roman Catholicism

Henry wanted a male heir, so he decided to end his eighteen-year marriage with Catherine of Aragon, whose sons had all died in infancy, and marry Anne, grand-daughter of the second duke of Norfolk. Reluctance of Pope Clement VII to grant an annulment (largely for political rather than religious reasons) infuriated the king. Henry persuaded Parliament to declare the English church independent of Rome and obtained his divorce from the new archbishop of Canterbury, Thomas Crammer. In 1533 Anne Boleyn became the second of Henry's six wives and that same year bore him a daughter, the future Queen Elizabeth I. In 1536, Anne gave birth to a dead son. Henry's affections faded thereafter, and rumors arose concerning unfaithfulness on her part. In May, she was accused of adultery and beheaded. W. HEARN

BOMPAS, WILLIAM CARPENTER (1834–1906)
Pioneer Anglican missionary bishop in Canada

Born in London (England), Bompas was converted in early youth by a Baptist group. He was later attracted to an evangelical Anglican group, was ordained to the Anglican ministry, and volunteered for missionary service in North America. Arriving at Fort Simpson on the Mackenzie River in 1865, he began a long career of service among the Indians and Eskimos in northwestern Canada. In 1874 he was consecrated bishop of Athabaska. His diocese was twice subdivided and on each occasion he chose the more northerly and more difficult part. A man of devotion and courage, he carried on his ministry in the face of many hardships. He was a prodigious traveler, sometimes on foot. He published several books including *Northern Lights on the Bible* (London, 1893) and *A Cree Primer* (London, 1899). He retired in 1905 and died at Caribou Crossing in the Yukon. D. C. MASTERS

BONAR, ANDREW ALEXANDER (1810–1892)
Scottish minister

Son of a solicitor, Bonar was educated in Edinburgh and ordained minister of Collace, Perthshire, in 1838. Like most of his evangelical colleagues he left the Church of Scotland at the Disruption of 1843 when the Free Church was formed. In 1856 he left Collace for Finnieston, Glasgow, where he ministered until his death. During college days in Edinburgh he and his brother Horatius Bonar were briefly influenced by the meteoric Edward Irving; they remained keen premillennialists (those who believe that Christ will come again before the millennium). Bonar visited Palestine in 1839 and wrote about the condition of the Jews; he also came to America in 1881 at the invitation of the evangelist Dwight L. Moody. Author of many scholarly works, Bonar excelled in devotional literature. Apart from his own *Diary*, he is remembered most for the *Memoirs* of his friend, Robert Murray McCheyne, and for the definitive edition of Samuel Rutherford's *Letters*. J. D. DOUGLAS

BONAR, HORATIUS (1808–1889)
Scottish minister and hymn writer

Educated at Edinburgh in arts and divinity, Bonar was ordained in 1837 on appointment as minister of the North Church, Kelso. His ministry there continued after he had joined the Free Church of Scotland at the Disruption of 1843, until he was called to Chalmers Memorial Church, Edinburgh, in 1866. Like his brother Andrew Bonar, he wrote a great deal, making significant contributions in the biographical field. He also edited several religious journals. As a hymn writer his name is known throughout the English-speaking world. Ira D. Sankey, musical associate of Dwight L. Moody, among others, acknowledged a debt of gratitude to him. Bonar published several volumes of hymns, many of which are still widely sung. They include "I Heard the Voice of Jesus Say" and "Here, O My Lord, I See Thee Face to Face." J. D. DOUGLAS

BONAVENTURA (1221–1274)
Philosopher, theologian, and mystic

Born Giovanni Fidanza of Bagnorea in Tuscany, Bonaventura possessed one of the

outstanding minds of the Middle Ages. He has been called the second founder of the Franciscan order, which he joined about 1238. He studied under Alexander of Hales at Paris, and from 1248 to 1255 he taught theology there. He then became the general or head of the Franciscans. Bonaventura regarded theology as the basis for understanding what was believed. Faith and reason were brought together and made compatible by love. Like Augustine and Anselm he said, "I believe in order to understand." For Bonaventura reason or nature alone could not lead one to God, although they displayed God's glory. Human knowledge was dependent on divine knowledge and truth, which were gifts of God's grace.

An important aspect of Bonaventura's mysticism was the primacy of the will. Purification of the will preceded salvation, after which one could go on to enlarge upon personal Christian experience. Bonaventura's mysticism has been described as more joyful, less doctrinal, and less cloistered than that of many other mystics of the past.

In addition to his theological achievements and his reputation as a man of piety, Bonaventura demonstrated considerable administrative ability. He helped to develop his order's constitution through his commentary on the rule of St. Francis and his biography of the founder. He tried to bring together diverse elements that had arisen among the Franciscans.

As head of the order and with a different approach to knowing spiritual truth, Bonaventura became an opponent of Thomas Aquinas, the most influential thinker during the Middle Ages. Later theologians tended to appeal to Bonaventura, whose ideas were more akin to those of Augustine and the Protestant reformers. Bonaventura became known as the "seraphic doctor." His most significant writings include a commentary on the *Sentences* of Peter Abelard and *The Journey of the Soul unto God*. T. O. KAY

BONHOEFFER, DIETRICH (1906–1945)
German theologian and modern Christian martyr

Born in Breslau (now Wroclaus in Poland), Dietrich and his twin sister, Sabine, were the children of Karl and Paula Bonhoeffer. Karl Bonhoeffer was the foremost neurologist and psychiatrist teaching at the University of Berlin; his wife was the granddaughter of Karl von Hase, a nineteenth-century church historian. At the age of seventeen Dietrich began theological studies at Tübingen. He also matriculated at the University of Berlin where he took additional theological studies under Adolf von Harnack. He qualified for the Licentiate under Reinhold Seeberg with a work entitled *The Communion of Saints*. That creative study brought the structures of society (sociology) under the judgment of Scripture, providing an identification and interpretation of the personal community: the church in society. At the age of twenty-four Bonhoeffer qualified for teaching at the University of Berlin with the presentation of his work, *Act and Being*. Building on his first work, Bonhoeffer spoke of God being found in the Word and realized in real-life situations, and of the reality of Christ living in his community of believers. Bonhoeffer's two philosophical/theological books provide the structure for his later books, which are basically biblical, ethical, and personal in character.

His two most widely read (but not always correctly interpreted) books are *The Cost of Discipleship* and *Letters and Papers from Prison*. Within the depth of thought and breadth of ideas disclosed in these and in his other writings, the key idea is Bonhoeffer's interpretation of Christ and of his "body," the church on earth.

The maturation of this theology moved from Jesus Christ, the reality of revelation in the church, to Jesus Christ as Lord over the body, the church (where Jesus calls his people to costly obedience), to Jesus Christ in relation to the whole world. The core of Bonhoeffer's theology is given a practical turn in his *Ethics,* where he states that God in Christ manifests himself in the sphere of revelation through concrete (particular) moral decisions in the secular world.

While studying at Union Theological Seminary in New York City (1930–1931), Bonhoeffer team-taught a Sunday school class in a black church in Harlem. That experience proved to be a powerful lesson on how "enslaved" people could endure dehumanizing oppression by exercising childlike, biblical faith, particularly in praise and worship. Unquestionably, that exposure strengthened Bonhoeffer in his struggle against Nazi power in Germany.

When many pastors yielded to Hitler's interference in church affairs, Bonhoeffer refused to go along and shared in creating the Confessing Church in Germany. In 1935 he began and led an "illegal" seminary in Finkenwalde. Bonhoeffer early identified himself with the resistance movement against Adolf Hitler, who in 1933 had become the dictator of Germany. The November 9, 1938 Krystalnacht, which saw the destruction of six hundred German synagogues, the looting of seventy-five hundred shops, and the arrest of thirty-five thousand Jews, led Bonhoeffer and other conspirators to intensify their efforts against Hitler. Bonhoeffer was arrested in April 1943 and hung in 1944, shortly after the plot to kill Hitler failed.

The life, times, and thoughts of Dietrich Bonhoeffer continue to be researched, especially by members of the several Bonhoeffer societies. L. A. KALLAND

BONIFACE (680–754)
English monk; missionary to Germany

Known as the "apostle of Germany," Boniface's real name was Wynfrith; he was an Anglo-Saxon, born in Devonshire. Boniface became a monk and excelled as a scholar and preacher. In 716 he attempted a mission to Germany, but war and opposition caused his return. Still intent on evangelizing in Frisia, he went to Rome where Pope Gregory II commissioned him to evangelize Germany and to bring all the churches there into submission to Rome. From 719 to 722 he labored successfully in Frisia, Hesse, and Thuringia, and then once more went to Rome where he was consecrated a bishop.

He returned to Germany to evangelize but

also to suppress heresy. Making use of devoted monks from England, his evangelism turned out to be a systematic crusade against Saxon paganism: destroying idols, baptizing the heathen, establishing churches and monasteries. In 732 Boniface became archbishop. He organized the church in Bavaria into four bishoprics (Regensburg, Freising, Salzburg, and Passau). Then with the help of the civil powers he attempted to reform the whole Frankish church. He divided the east Frankish church into four dioceses (Erfurt, Wurzburg, Buraburg, and Eichstadt), making his own trusted helpers the new bishops. Then he called a council of the church in 742 and presided at it. He founded the great abbey of Fulda which became the center of German monastic culture. As Boniface saw it, the task of suppressing heresy included doing battle with Virgil, the Celtic bishop of Salzburg who insisted that there were other worlds than this one, and also with Adalbert, a Frankish bishop who claimed to have received relics of the saints directly from angels.

In 747 a synod of Frankish bishops sent to Rome a statement of their submission to the papacy. That and the creation of the bishopric of Mainz as preeminent in Germany may be seen as further triumphs for Boniface. Instead of remaining in the comfort of Mainz, he decided in 754 to take up once more his desire to evangelize in Frisia, where he and his helpers were soon martyred.

An organizational genius, Boniface left his mark on the church well into later centuries. In bringing under control the missionary movements previously led by independent Irish monks, he did significant service to Rome and perhaps to the church as a whole. Boniface is regarded as a saint in the Roman Catholic church. P. TOON

BONIFACE VIII (c. 1234–1303)
Pope, 1294–1303

Born Benedict Gaetani, Boniface came from a noble Italian family. His early years were spent studying at Todi, Spoleto, Rome, and Paris. In 1276, with a doctorate of canon law, Boniface joined the papal court. He eventually became a cardinal priest with successes as a papal diplomat. In 1294, his actions secured the abdication of the saintly but incompetent Pope Celestine V. This event prompted much disapproval since Boniface himself soon was elected pope. But ignoring his critics, Boniface proceeded with his far-reaching aims for the Church. These embraced two main efforts: subjection of western European governments to papal authority, and liberation of the Holy Land from Muslim domination. Yet in both spheres, despite exhaustive efforts, Boniface's papacy experienced grave difficulties and losses. The period saw Church structures and western European life undergo many wide-ranging changes.

Boniface's attempts to mediate between Genoa and Venice, then Aragon and Naples, symbolized his papacy's troubles. In both cases, he lacked sufficient respect to prevent war or obtain a peace. The pope's desire for a Holy Land Crusade also generated no interest. Little besides indifference came from Europe's rulers. But above all, Boniface wished to intervene between France's Philip IV and England's Edward I. And it was here, plainly, that his papacy had its greatest breakdown. English and French forces were at war over England's rights in Gascony. To halt the war, Boniface's plan was to curtail the combatants' finances, mainly clerical taxation revenues. In 1299, Boniface did persuade the two kings to sign a marriage treaty. All the same, however, both rulers developed an acute enmity with the pope. This came in reaction to Boniface's three most famous letters. The first, *Clericos laicos,* forbade any collection of clerical taxes without express papal consent. The other two, *Ausculta fili* (1301) and *Unam sanctum* (1302) reaffirmed the papacy's general sovereignty over governments and peoples. With much vehemence, both monarchs rejected such claims, and Philip became very belligerent toward the pope. In his initial action, Philip simply shut down all transfer of French funds to Rome. Boniface then saw he lacked effective means to counteract the French king. Very soon, his consent to Philip's control of French clerical taxes became unavoidable.

As a kind of interlude to his problems, Boniface did celebrate the Jubilee of 1300. Although no important monarchs attended, the ceremony was impressive and effective. But simultaneously, other woes surfaced. In 1298, Boniface had defeated the Colonna family insurrectionists. Yet this proved to be another loss. The Colonna had begun to join with the French. Then quickly, in 1301, Philip continued hostilities by mistreating legates from the pope. He even declared he would put Boniface on trial. In 1303, some forces representing Philip actually took Boniface prisoner. After three days, the harried pope was released by Italian troops. But he returned to Rome only to die a month later.

In assessing Boniface VIII's papacy, it appears his concept of supremacy did not exceed similar claims by important predecessors. Declarations by Innocent III and other thirteenth-century popes were just as wide-reaching. Thus neither unprecedented demands nor his provocativeness were a chief cause of Boniface's troubles. Primarily, the pope's situation came from a rising nationalism and respect for national rulers, newly characterizing Europe's political mentality. Western Europe's kings obviously understood this social current far better than the papal court did. Consequently, it was Boniface who faced the first large-scale rejection of papal authority in western European affairs. As to the Holy Land, it was of course the western monarchs' apathy or fear that allowed continuing Muslim dominance. Hence, the pope encountered large forces that were usually beyond his control.

But finally, Boniface's papacy did see some accomplishments in certain areas. In the era which began Italy's (and Europe's) Renaissance, the pope's patronage of fine art was quite important. This is true however much Dante's *Divine Comedy* excoriated him. Morever, it was Boniface who promulgated the *Liber sextus decretalium*, a basic addition to the canon law. Many Roman church buildings also owe extensive improvement to Boniface. And he was founder of the Sapienza, the University of Rome.

Les Registres de Boniface VIII, edited by Digard, Faucon, Thomas, and Fawtie, is the major collection of Boniface VIII's works.

K. J. BRYER

BOOTH, BALLINGTON (1857–1940)

Founder of the Volunteers of America, a religious social-welfare organization

Booth was born at Brighouse, Yorkshire (England), and educated at Taunton Collegiate Institute and Nottingham Seminary. He was also trained by his father, William Booth, founder (along with his wife, Catherine) of the Salvation Army, to work with the Salvation Army. His activity with that organization began when he was seventeen. He was commander of the Salvation Army in Australia (1885–1887) and the United States (1887–1896). After a disagreement with his father over policies, he broke his connection with the Salvation Army, was ordained a nondenominational evangelist, and founded the Volunteers of America, a group less authoritarian than the Salvation Army. He served the Volunteers of America as general and commander-in-chief until his death. Booth was a gifted musician, an impressive speaker on evangelical and social topics, and the author of *The Salvation War* (1885), *From Ocean to Ocean*, and *The Prayer that Prevails* (1920).

A. H. FREUNDT, JR.

BOOTH, CATHERINE MUMFORD (1829–1890)

English "mother of the Salvation Army"

Born at Ashbourne, Derbyshire, Catherine Mumford moved with her family to London in 1844. In that year she was converted and joined the Methodist Church in Brixton. Later expelled from that congregation, she helped to found the Reformers Chapel, where in 1851 she met William Booth, whom she married in 1855. Together they left the Methodist New Connexion to start the movement later known as the Salvation Army. Catherine Booth became an influential

preacher in her own right and conducted many evangelistic missions with marked success. Besides preaching under the Salvation Army's auspices, she persuaded William Booth to give women a place of great importance in its organization and work. She exerted herself to improve the position of women and children in the Great Britain of her day, before her death from cancer.
N. V. HOPE

BOOTH, EVANGELINE CORY
(1865–1950)
English Salvation Army leader

Daughter of William and Catherine Mumford Booth, founders of the Salvation Army, Evangeline Booth spent her whole life in the Salvation Army's service. She became a sergeant at age fifteen and at twenty-three was made principal of the Salvation Army's International Training College at Clapton, London. In 1896 she was appointed field commissioner for Canada and in 1904 became commander of operations in the United States. In 1934 she was elected fourth general, the first woman to hold the position. She retired in 1938 to the United States, of which she had become a citizen. She received many public honors, among them a Distinguished Service Medal conferred by President Woodrow Wilson in 1919. N. V. HOPE

BOOTH, WILLIAM (1829–1912)
English evangelist; founder and first general of the Salvation Army

Booth was born in Nottingham and was converted in 1844. He became a minister of the Methodist New Connexion Church, but resigned from it in 1861 after being refused permission to become an itinerant evangelist not restricted to a local circuit.

Moved by compassion for the churchless slum-dwellers of London, in 1865 Booth and his wife, Catherine, began a mission in Whitechapel. In 1878 it was named the Salvation Army, with Booth as its first general. Realizing that unconventional tactics would be necessary to reach slum-dwellers, Booth

held open-air meetings accompanied by a band playing lively music, visited taverns and jails, and preached in theaters, factories, and other unchurchly places.

Booth realized that in order to win his constituents' souls he would have to relieve their physical wretchedness—their hunger, poverty, intemperance, and unemployment. Hence, with the assistance of his son Bramwell, he built up a network of agencies of social relief and rehabilitation, supported by funds Booth was able to raise. In 1890 the book *In Darkest England and the Way Out* was published by journalist W. T. Stead, but it bore Booth's name and embodied his ideas. It vividly depicted the miserable life of the "submerged tenth" of the population. Among its suggestions to improve their lot were "farm colonies" to train city dwellers as agricultural laborers and "overseas colonies" in countries like Canada, Australia, and South Africa to which Britain's surplus population could be sent and gainfully employed.

Booth's methods were autocratic. His organization was run on military lines, his subordinates being expected to give him unquestioning obedience. His authoritarianism caused problems; three of his children rebelled and left the Salvation Army. But the Salvation Army, after encountering initial opposition, won widespread acceptance for its success in reclaiming the drunkard, the depraved, and the irreligious. It has been described as one of the most successful religious revivals of modern times. N. V. HOPE

BORIS (died 907)
Khan (ruler) of Bulgaria, 852–889

Under pressure from Constantinople, Boris accepted baptism circa 864 at the hands of Greek clergy sent by the patriarch Photius. Boris also encouraged widespread acceptance of Christianity in Bulgaria, where there had been missionaries two centuries earlier. Alarmed at this encroachment from the East, the Western church also sent emissaries, but Boris wished to have his own church free from Rome and Constantinople. Boris played them—one against the other—

to get the most favorable terms. Eastern and Western clergy clashed over matters such as celibacy, confirmation, the question of fasting, and the Filioque clause in the Nicene Creed (whether the Spirit proceeds from the Father, or from both the Father and the Son). Boris inclined at first toward the West despite a hostile aristocracy that resented the introduction of Western civilization—a factor that tended to consolidate the ruler's power. Boris put down the rebellion, but the battle between West and East continued, with both sides reluctant to accept the concept of an independent Bulgarian church. In 870, however, the patriarch Ignatius consecrated a Bulgar as archbishop and sent him with ten bishops back to his homeland.

In 889 Boris abdicated and retired to a monastery in favor of his son Vladimir who promptly led a pagan reaction against Boris's innovations. Boris came back from retirement in 893, had Vladimir deposed and confined, appointed another son—Simeon—as successor, and retired again to the monastic life. Boris was a warm supporter of indigenous literature, and he substituted Slavonic for Greek as the language of the Bulgarian church. J. D. DOUGLAS

BORROMEO, CHARLES (1538–1584)
Italian cardinal; archbishop of Milan; prominent Catholic reformer

Of noble birth, Borromeo received his first office at the age of twelve, and then studied for a doctorate in law at the University of Pavia. His uncle became Pope Pius IV in 1559, providing Borromeo opportunity for a brilliant career in the church.

Borromeo held a number of offices in the Roman Curia. Appointed cardinal in 1560, he served as protector of Portugal, the Netherlands, the Catholic cantons in Switzerland, and a number of religious orders. His services were particularly valuable during the third period of the Council of Trent (1562–1563). After the loss of an elder brother, he became very austere in his manner of living.

Through both his pastoral and literary work he brought reform to the College of

Cardinals and revised the missal, breviary, and an edition of the writings of the church fathers. From 1556 Borromeo exerted considerable influence in the archdiocese of Milan. He had a strong sense of social concern for the poor, and he expected his priests to have personal knowledge of the people under their care. His work of reform and education through six new seminaries became a model for pastoral care in religious renewal, preaching, the sacraments, the keeping of the feasts, and right deportment of the priest. During the plague of 1576, when city officials had fled, he was tireless in caring for the sick. Civil authorities were uneasy about his exercise of power; his disciplinary demands on clergy likewise made him enemies. Twice his life was endangered in assassination attempts.

Borromeo also tried to institute reform movements in areas outside his diocese, fighting against ignorance and Protestantism. He died of a fever contracted on his journeys and subsequently was canonized by Pope Paul V in 1610. His work is still influential in the Roman Catholic Church.
L. GOLDBERG

BORROW, GEORGE HENRY
(1803–1881)
English linguist; agent for the London Bible Society; minor novelist

Born the son of an army captain at East Dereham, Norfolk, Borrow spent his childhood at army posts throughout the British Isles and became fascinated with gypsies. In addition to learning their language, he learned some thirty others. He published translations of Danish ballads, Russian poems, and "Turkish humor." As an agent of the Bible Society he traveled in Russia, Spain, Portugal, and North Africa.

Borrow's writings reveal some familiarity with a few authors like Defoe, Bunyan, Smollett, and Sterne. One of his best-known works is *The Bible in Spain* (1843), with a lengthy, prepossessing subtitle, "The Journeys, Adventures, and Imprisonment of an Englishman in an Attempt to Circulate the Scriptures in the Peninsula." Rarely have so many adventures been overcrowded into one book: encounters with gypsies, bull fighters, quaint and strange characters of every kind, all combined with the wanderings of a Bible Society agent. Publication of *The Bible in Spain* made Borrow famous for a time in many parts of the world.

At the age of forty-eight he brought out *Lavengro* after working on it intermittently for ten years. Both *Lavengro* and its sequel, *The Romany Rye* (1857), adhere rather closely to the experiences of Borrow's career; if the two are considered a unit, they fall within the English novel tradition. Undoubtedly he planned *Lavengro* as an autobiography. But as an admirer of Defoe, he wanted his own work to be "in the Robinson Crusoe style." Less of an impartial recorder than Defoe, he perpetually digressed into diatribes against Roman Catholics and other groups and individuals whom he considered radical. His actual material included accounts of people he had known, some of them no doubt libelous; yet he stated that he wished to encourage charity and free genial manners.

Borrow wrote and translated other works, many of which went either unpublished or unpraised. He died an obscure man whose works were all but forgotten. His greatest literary work, *Lavengro,* has been reprinted posthumously with introductions by able literary critics; notable essayists have at times proclaimed Borrow's worth.
E. B. BATSON

BORTHWICK, JANE LAURIE (1813–1897)
Scottish translator of hymns

Born in Edinburgh, Miss Borthwick was the daughter of an insurance manager and was an active member of the Free Church of Scotland. With her younger sister Sarah (Mrs. Eric Findlater), she published a series of *Hymns from the Land of Luther* (1854–1862). Like the work of many other nineteenth-century women, that series originally appeared under a pseudonym. The Borthwick sisters used the initials, "H. L. L." Best known of Jane Borthwick's many trans-

lations is Katharina von Schlegel's hymn, "Be still, my soul: the Lord is on thy side." She was a supporter of many missionary and humanitarian projects, both in her own denomination and in others. She and her sister composed hymns themselves, but none of them has lasted as long as their translations of German hymns. J. D. DOUGLAS

BOSCO, JOHN (1815–1888)
Roman Catholic educator and founder of the Salesian Order

Bosco was born Giovanni Melchior Bosco at Becchi (Italy) near Turin. He was left fatherless at an early age. Encouraged by his mother and parish priest, he studied for the priesthood, entered seminary in 1835, and was ordained in 1841. He began in 1842 to devote his life to the welfare of underprivileged boys, especially orphans. In 1846 he opened his own hospice (or shelter) in the Valdocco section of Turin; within ten years 150 boys were in residence. He educated them by methods of kindness and trust rather than force, by love rather than fear. With Turin rapidly becoming industrialized, he sought to train boys for gainful employment.

In 1859, along with seventeen other priests who were his coworkers, he founded the Salesian Order. Its patron saint was St. Francis of Sales, a noted seventeeth-century bishop of Geneva. In 1868 the new order won papal approval. It spread so quickly that by the time of Bosco's death it had 1,039 members in fifty-seven houses and was operating in Italy, Spain, France, England, Argentina, Uruguay, and Brazil. In 1872, with Sister Marie Mazzarello, Bosco founded the Salesian Sisters. He was canonized in 1934.
N. V. HOPE

BOSSUET, JACQUES BENIGNE (1627–1704)
French preacher, theologian, and controversialist

Born in Dijon (France), Bossuet started his education at the Jesuit school there, continuing it at the College de Navarre in Paris.

Ordained to the priesthood and earning his doctorate in 1652, he became canon and archdeacon at Metz, where he began to achieve fame as a preacher. In 1669 he was made bishop of Condom in Tuscany, but resigned after being appointed tutor to the Dauphin in 1670. In 1681, his tutorial duties over, he became bishop of Meaux and served until his death.

In an age of great French Catholic preachers, Bossuet was one of the most outstanding. He was especially famous for his funeral orations, which were masterpieces of rhetorical skill. His writings were mainly apologetic and controversial in character. In 1681 he published his *Discourse on Universal History,* a philosophy of history that saw the fate of nations as controlled by God in relation to a single event, the incarnation of Jesus Christ. Against Protestants Bossuet published his *History of the Variations of the Protestant Churches* (1688). In it he pointed to a multiplicity of standards and organizations in early Protestantism as proofs of the whole movement's inherent perversity.

Bossuet hoped for a rapprochement between Roman Catholicism and Protestantism. With that in view he engaged in correspondence with the Protestant philosopher G. W. Leibnitz between 1691 and 1702. When there was no meeting of minds, the correspondence was broken off. Though a convinced Catholic, Bossuet was no ardent papist. He presided at the assembly of the French clergy summoned by King Louis XIV in 1682 to defend the liberties of the French church against papal claims to domination. There he won acceptance for the Four Articles he had drawn up that sought to set limits to papal authority in France. Those Articles, however, were soft-pedaled in the compromise that was finally worked out between king and pope in 1693. N. V. HOPE

BOSTON, THOMAS (1676–1732)
Scottish theologian

Born in Berwickshire, Boston graduated at Edinburgh in 1694 and thereafter taught school while he studied theology. He became minister of Ettrick in 1707. About

1700 he had discovered an old Puritan work entitled *The Marrow of Modern Divinity,* originally published by Edward Fisher in 1645. Quoting lengthy extracts from Reformed and Puritan writers (including Luther, Calvin, Beza, Goodwin, and Sibbes), the book made a great impression on Boston and on his preaching. Reprinted in 1718 with a preface by James Hogg of Carnock, it was condemned by the General Assembly of the Church of Scotland because of its Arminian statements. For opposing that decision, Boston and eleven other "Marrow-Men" were formally admonished and rebuked, but no further action was taken against them. The controversy died down and did not revive even when Boston's new edition of *The Marrow* with copious and learned notes was published in 1726, the outcome of four years' work in the Ettrick manse. For Boston *The Marrow* cleared away certain problems that until then, he said, had prevented his offering the gospel freely and fully.

He was a faithful and conscientious pastor in his rural parishes as well as being a notable scholar. Thomas Boston's other works included his *Memoirs, Human Nature in Its Fourfold Estate* (1720), and *A View of the Covenant of Grace* (1734). J. D. DOUGLAS

BOTHWELL, EARL OF (c. 1535–1587)
Title of James Hepburn, the fourth earl, who succeeded to the earldom in 1556

Although Hepburn claimed to be a Protestant, his religious identification seems to have been purely nominal. He supported Mary of Guise, the Catholic regent of Scotland, in her conflicts with the Protestant lords of the Congregation. On the return of Mary, Queen of Scots, to Scotland as a young widow in 1561, Hepburn became a member of her privy council. Shortly afterward he was accused by the Earl of Arran of plotting to kidnap the queen and was imprisoned in Edinburgh Castle. He escaped to France in 1564. The following year Mary recalled him to assist her in overcoming the rebellion of her half brother James, earl of Moray, over her marriage to Henry Darnley. As one of her chief advisers, Hepburn also gave her loyal support when in 1566 David Rizzio, her secretary and suspected lover, was murdered by a group of nobles led by Darnley, her husband.

About that time, it seems, Mary and Bothwell fell in love, with the result that they were both implicated in the subsequent murder of Darnley (1567). In the popular mind, Bothwell was held to be the actual perpetrator of the murder, and Mary an accomplice. Bothwell was acquitted in a rigged trial and, after divorcing his wife, married Mary in 1567. That action brought both Protestant and Roman Catholic nobles together against the couple. The opposing forces faced each other at Carberry Hill, Lothian, where Mary's forces refused to fight. She then agreed to surrender to the lords if Bothwell could escape. He thereupon fled to Orkney, Shetland, and finally Denmark. There, at the request of the Earl of Moray, now regent, he was arrested by Frederick II and imprisoned. In 1573, when Mary's party collapsed in Scotland with the capture of Edinburgh Castle, Bothwell was imprisoned in solitary confinement in Dragsholm Castle in Zeeland where he died insane. Mary had had their marriage annulled in 1570. Her involvement, however, ultimately lost her the throne of Scotland. W. S. REID

BOTTICELLI, SANDRO (c. 1445–1510)

Italian Renaissance painter

Born in Florence, Botticelli was initially apprenticed to a goldsmith, then later came to study under the painter Fra Filippo Lippi (1406–1469). Early in his career Botticelli earned the patronage of some of Florence's leading noble families, including the Medici. His early paintings demonstrate a technical mastery of line, which many think has not been equaled since, plus a richness and opulence in subject matter abandoned in his later works. His painting *St. Sebastian* (1474) combined the lyrical beauty, aristocratic melancholy, and simplicity of line that have become Botticelli's identifying characteristics. His art also has an intellectual sophistication that rewards a viewer's patient, analytical inspection.

Except for a brief period during which he was summoned to Rome by Pope Sixtus IV to help fresco the Sistine Chapel (1481–1482), Botticelli lived and worked in Florence. There he was in the circle of artists and scholars gathered about a wealthy, powerful patron, Lorenzo de' Medici (the magnificent). Much of Botticelli's work, including his two most famous paintings, *Primavera* (*Spring*) and *The Birth of Venus,* with their classical subject matter and Neoplatonic allegory, shows the influence of Florentine humanism. Nonetheless, many of his works were religious, the most famous being his *Adoration of the Magi* (1481–1482). He also produced a long series of woodcuts for Dante's *Divine Comedy,* nineteen of which were painted in 1481.

After Lorenzo's death in 1492, Botticelli came under the influence of the fiery Italian priest and reformer, Savonarola. Reportedly, the artist burned some of his classical paintings and sketches, considering them pagan "vanities." In his later works—virtually all religious allegories (such as *The Calumny of Appelles*) or devotional scenes—he set aside his earlier sensuous abandon in favor of a more abstract and formal treatment. K. HOGLUND

BOUNDS, EDWARD MCKENDREE (1835–1913)

American Methodist Episcopal minister

Bounds's early education was in law, but after a brief period of legal practice he left the legal profession for the ministry. His years as pastor were spent in Alabama, Tennessee, and Missouri. He served during the American Civil War as a captain in the Confederate Army. And for nine years Bounds served as editor of the *St. Louis Christian Advocate.* He is probably best known for his devotional classic *Power Through Prayer.* D. M. LAKE

BOURGEOIS, LOUIS (c. 1510–1561)

French composer who arranged many of the hymn tunes for the Genevan Psalter

Little is known of Bourgeois's life. Presumably he came to the haven of Geneva as a refugee about the time the reformer John Calvin returned in 1541 from a brief exile. Calvin gave Bourgeois the task of revising the tunes of the metrical psalms which Calvin had by then assembled for the use of his congregation. By 1551 the collection of tunes had grown to eighty-three, all of which were to some degree edited, adapted, or composed by Bourgeois. They were designed for unison singing without supporting harmonies. Bourgeois used only two note values (corresponding to our whole and half notes), but with ingenious variety.

A number of the Genevan tunes have been taken into the Lutheran repertory, and a few found their way into the English and Scottish Psalters. Most widely known is the tune of the Genevan Psalm 134, which, with a slightly simplified rhythm, is "Old Hundredth" and is used today for the well-known Doxology.

Bourgeois had poor relations with the Genevan authorities. He was once briefly imprisoned for altering some tunes without authorization. Calvin seems to have obtained Bourgeois's speedy release and to have supported his complaints about inadequate remuneration. Bourgeois left Geneva in disgust circa 1557. It is still uncertain who provided tunes for the remaining psalms, although Calvin's successor, Theodore Beza, ultimately completed the Genevan Psalter. J. B. MACMILLAN

BOURNE, HUGH (1772–1852)
English leader of Primitive Methodism

Born in Stoke-on-Trent, Bourne had a dramatic conversion through the study of evangelical literature. After some hesitance he joined the local Methodist society in 1802. A carpenter by trade, his work as an evangelist began through his speaking freely to a cousin, Daniel Shubotham, about his experience of Christ. A converted collier, William Clowes, came to join forces with Bourne in the work of evangelizing the tough working-class areas of Staffordshire. They followed the American pattern of camp meetings and saw spiritual revivals. Mow Cop, a "bleak and frowning hill" in Staffordshire, became a center for prayer and preaching, and the local Methodist circuits felt the power of renewal. But the enthusiasm was not liked by all. Bourne (and later Clowes) was removed from membership. Their evangelistic work led to the creation of new societies. Since they were not accepted by the older Methodist body, inevitably a new type of Methodist, a "Camp Meeting" Methodist, was created. Later, to emphasize that they wished to capture the original thrust of Methodism, they were known as Primitive Methodists. They had their first conference in 1820. At the time of Bourne's death there were nine districts, each with several circuits. P. TOON

BOWEN, GEORGE (1816–1888)
American missionary to India

A graduate of Union Theological Seminary in New York in 1847, Bowen went immediately to Bombay, where he remained all his life. He tried to identify with the common people by living as near their economic level as possible, much to the dislike and even fury of Europeans and Americans. He also did street preaching. He was known as "the white saint of India" because he approximated the life-style of Indian holy men as few western missionaries had done.

Bowen edited and published the *Bombay Guardian* from 1851 until 1888 and also edited the Marathi language publications of the Bombay Book and Tract Society. He lived on the premises of the Tract Society after he became its agent. When an American Methodist, William Taylor, undertook work for the neglected and repressed Anglo-Indians, Bowen joined him in 1871 and became a Methodist. His *Daily Mediations, The Amens of Christ,* and *Love Revealed* were widely used books of devotion. P. BEAVER

BOWRING, SIR JOHN (1792–1872)
English author, public servant, and hymn writer

Born in Exeter, Bowring became editor of the *Westminster Review* at the age of thirty-three. He served twice as a radical member of Parliament, where he made notable contributions to prison and other social reforms. As a servant of the British government, he was counselor to France and finally governor of Hong Kong; for his public service he was knighted in 1854. Though Bowring was a Unitarian in formal church affiliation, his hymns—"Watchman, Tell Us of the Night" and "God Is Love, His Mercy Brightens"—have strongly appealed to Christians of all denominations and have been included in many hymnbooks.

N. V. HOPE

BOYLE, ROBERT (1627–1691)

English scientist; one of the forerunners of modern chemistry; an earnest Christian

Having inherited private wealth, Boyle funded his own experiments and in 1654 established a laboratory at Oxford. There he constructed one of the first air pumps, which enabled him to study the properties of air and gases and to formulate Boyle's Law, for which he is still famous. His studies of the compressibility of gases helped to establish the existence of atoms.

Although an empiricist, Boyle was conscious of the limitations of science, particularly of its theories and axioms. He followed Francis Bacon in insisting on observations and experiments in the formulation and revision of theories. He held that mechanistic theories (that is, explanations based on physical forces moving particles of matter) cannot explain the functions of living organisms, let alone the interaction of man with nature. For such explanations we have to move beyond science to a consideration of "final causes": the ends and purposes for which things are created.

Boyle's *The Sceptical Chymist* (1661) marked a transition from ancient alchemy to the beginnings of chemistry as a science. His experimental approach did much to introduce new scientific methods and to bring speculation about nature under control. Although Boyle's limited support of mechanistic science has been blamed for encouraging the rise of materialism and atheism, his intention was entirely contrary. From his early

twenties he was deeply devoted to the Christian faith. He learned Hebrew, Greek, and Aramaic in order to study the Scriptures more effectively; he wrote theological treatises and a religious novel, *The Martyrdom of Theodora and Didymus*; and he financially supported the distribution of the Bible in foreign lands. In his will he endowed lectures for the defense of Christianity against its pagan and atheistic opponents, "without descending to any controversies among Christians." The Boyle Lectures helped develop an extensive apologetic literature against deism, materialism, and related views. A. F. HOLMES

BRADFORD, JOHN (c. 1510–1555)

English Protestant martyr

Born in Manchester, Bradford began his career as a secretary to Sir John Harrington. Then in 1547 he went to the Inner Temple Court of Law in London to study. Finding theology preferable to law, he went to St. Catherine's Hall, Cambridge, in 1548. So diligently did he study that he was allowed to take his M.A. degree after one year. After a brief period as a fellow of Pembroke Hall, he went to London to be chaplain to the young king, Edward VI, and thus became one of the important preachers in the kingdom. The Scottish reformer John Knox had a high opinion of Bradford's ability and Christian stance. When Queen Mary came to the throne in 1553 Bradford was arrested and imprisoned for eighteen months. In prison he kept busy writing letters of encouragement to others. Eventually brought to trial, he refused to retract his Protestant principles and was sentenced to burn at the stake. His works were reprinted by the Parker Society in 1848. P. TOON

BRADFORD, WILLIAM (c. 1589–1657)

Governor of the Plymouth plantation in the New World during that colony's first quarter century

Born on a farm in Austerfield, Yorkshire (England), Bradford as a child developed a deep religious interest. At twelve he was an avid reader of the Bible, and as a teenager he withdrew from the Anglican Church. When his relatives were disturbed over his joining the Puritan congregation at Scrooby, he explained: "To keep a good conscience, and walk in such a way as God has prescribed in his Word, is a thing which I must prefer before you all, and above life itself." Bradford followed the separatists to the Netherlands and after a brief imprisonment sailed on the Mayflower in 1620 to establish the Plymouth Colony. He was a strong leader, described by a fellow Puritan as possessing a "holy, prayerful, watchful, and fruitful walk with God, wherein he was very exemplary." Bradford was Calvinist in theology, Congregationalist in church polity, and a perennial governor from 1621 until 1656. During those formative years of the colony, Bradford wrote a 528 page *History of Plymouth Plantation,* still the best primary source on the Pilgrims. D. E. MAAS

BRAHMS, JOHANNES (1833–1897)
German pianist and composer

Brahms's father was a double-bass player in Hamburg theaters. Johannes Brahms's early life was spent in training under a local musician and playing in cafes and dancing halls. Through a concert tour he came to the attention of both Hungarian pianist and composer Franz Liszt and the great violinist Joachim. Joachim eventually introduced him to composer and critic Robert Schumann, who declared Brahms's genius to the world in an 1853 article in the *Neue Zeitschrift für Musik.*

In 1857 Brahms moved to Detmold where he taught Princess Friederike. From 1860 to 1863 he lived in Hamburg and turned increasingly to composing, though his great reputation as a pianist continued. In 1863 he moved to Vienna, which became his home for the rest of his life.

Brahms's compositional genius ranged through every important musical genre except the opera and oratorio. His four symphonies, two piano concerti, a violin concerto, a double concerto for violin and cello, and his many songs, solo sonatas, and works of chamber music are consistently of the highest quality. His fusion of lyricism and musical intellect, though at first unrecognized, is now universally admired.

Brahms was a musical conservative in the best sense of that word. He found new ways to restate and further the traditional. Yet in so doing, along with Richard Wagner, he helped to open the way for the innovations of the twentieth century.

Brahms, intensely religious, knew theology and the Scriptures well. He himself compiled the biblical texts for his choral work *A German Requiem* (opus 45). Although he was not employed in an ecclesiastical position, he wrote significantly for the church. The *Requiem* (composed in memory of his mother), with its great expanses of beauty, craft, and energy, is his largest sacred work. The eleven *Chorale Preludes* for organ, his last compositions, are models of succinctness and warmth. Between them and the *Requiem,* he wrote a significant body of religious music, including motets for choir, works for female voices, and the masterful *Four Serious Songs,* based on passages from Ecclesiastes, Ecclesiasticus, and 1 Corinthians. H. M. BEST

BRAINERD, DAVID (1718–1747)
Pioneer American missionary to the American Indians

Born at Haddam, Connecticut, Brainerd was converted in 1739 and later that year entered Yale College to prepare for the ministry. Because he had made critical remarks concerning a college tutor and had attended a revival meeting forbidden by the rector, Brainerd was expelled from Yale in 1742 without graduating, though he stood first in his class. In November of 1742, under the auspices of the "Society in Scotland for the Propagation of Christian Knowledge," founded in 1709, Brainerd was appointed missionary to the Indians and began his work near Stockbridge, Massachusetts. He pursued his missionary labors in Massachusetts, Pennsylvania, and finally New Jersey, where in June 1744 he was ordained by the Presbytery of Newark. In New Jersey, during the last two years of his ministry, he achieved considerable success in the conversion of Indians, but in April 1747 tuberculosis compelled him to abandon his work. In July he went to the home of Puritan theologian Jonathan Edwards, to whose daughter Jerusah he was engaged to be married, and died there in October. Soon after Brainerd's death Edwards published an account of his life together with his diary. The book exerted a deep influence in promoting the cause of Christian missions. Missionaries such as William Carey, Henry Martyn, and Thomas Coke were profoundly influenced by Brainerd. N. V. HOPE

BRANT, JOSEPH (1742–1807)
Mohawk Indian chief who helped establish Anglicanism in Ontario

Born along the Ohio River, Brant became a protégé of Sir William Johnson, colonial superintendent of Indian affairs, and at Johnson's instigation attended a school for Indian boys at Lenanon, Connecticut, from 1761 to 1763. At the outset of the American revolutionary war he rallied the Iroquois Indians to support the British and served throughout the war as a leader of Indian troops. After the war, Brant secured a grant of land for the Mohawks along the Grand River in Upper Canada. During the latter part of his life he was an honored though controversial figure in Canada among the English and the Indians. Brant was a strong supporter of the Church of England. Under his auspices, John Stuart, an Anglican missionary, visited the Grand River Indian settlement in 1784. In the following year the Mohawks built the first Protestant church in Upper Canada. Brant translated Mark's Gospel and the Anglican prayer book into the Mohawk language (1787). He died at Burlington in what is now Ontario. D. C. MASTERS

BRAY, THOMAS (1656–1730)
English founding father of two Anglican missionary and educational societies

Born in Shropshire, Bray was educated at All Souls' College, Oxford, and afterward became a country parson. At that time he wrote (but published later) his four-volume *Catechetical Lectures* (1696), which made him famous. In 1696 he was appointed commissary to Maryland by the bishop of London, Henry Compton, to organize the work of the Anglican church there. Bray was in the American colony in 1699 and 1700. On his return to England, realizing the need to organize home support for missions, he became founder of the Society for the Propagation of the Gospel (1701). Before that, he worked to provide parochial (church) libraries both for the colonies and for parishes in England and Wales. Out of that educational project came what was called the Society for the Propagation of Christian Knowledge (1698). Bray became rector of St. Botolph-Without-Aldgate, London, and was engaged in philanthropic and literary pursuits until his death. P. TOON

BRAY, WILLIAM (1794–1864)
Evangelist of the Bible Christians, a branch of English Methodism

Bray was born near Truro in Cornwall and as a drunken miner was impressed by reading John Bunyan's *Visions*. He had a powerful conversion experience: "They said I was a madman but they meant I was a gladman." For forty years Bray's nimble figure moved about Cornwall, singing, praying, shouting, preaching—not only the Good News but also abstinence (drunkenness was a terrible social problem in the mines). Unaffected by poverty or other difficulties, he declared that as he lifted one foot it seemed to say "Glory" and the other replied "Amen." His doings and sayings enriched early Methodist literature. Over half a million copies of Bray's biography, *The King's Son; or a Memoir of "Billy" Bray* (1871) by F. W. Bourne, have been sold in the last hundred years. P. TOON

BREASTED, JAMES HENRY (1865–1935)
American archaeologist

Born in Rockford, Illinois, Breasted studied at Chicago Theological Seminary, Yale

University, and received his Ph.D. at the University of Berlin (Germany). Appointed professor of Egyptology and Oriental history at the University of Chicago in 1905, he became chairman of the department of Oriental language and literature in 1915. He founded the Oriental Institute at that university (1919). Under Breasted's leadership the Institute, with funding by John D. Rockefeller, Jr., became one of the world's outstanding agencies for rediscovery of the ancient Near East. Breasted led several archaeological expeditions to the Near East and persuaded Rockefeller to build the Palestine Archaeological Museum in Jerusalem. Significant among his writings were *History of Egypt* (1905), *Conquest of Civilization* (1926), *Dawn of Conscience* (1933), and *Ancient Records of Egypt* (five volumes, 1906–1907). H. F. VOS

BRENT, CHARLES HENRY (1862–1929)
First Protestant Episcopal bishop of the Philippines; chief founder of the Faith and Order movement

Born at Newcastle, Ontario (Canada), and ordained in 1887, Brent served parishes in Buffalo and Boston. He was consecrated bishop of the Missionary District of the Philippines in 1901 soon after the United States acquired them by treaty following the war with Spain. Considering the Filipinos to be Christians, the Episcopal Church limited its work to Chinese, British, Americans, and tribal people. In the Philippines, he was active in the fight against the opium trade and was later the American representative on the League of Nations Advisory Committee on Narcotics (1923).

Because of ill health Brent left the Philippines in 1917 and became bishop of western New York. He was chief of chaplains of the American Expeditionary Force in Europe during World War I.

As a delegate to the World Missionary Conference at Edinburgh in 1910, Brent saw a vision of the unity of the church and believed that an "Edinburgh-type" conference could be used to further that cause. That became the great passion of his remaining years. He was a leader in planning and convening the Universal Conference on Life and Work at Stockholm in 1925, and was involved in all three branches of the ecumenical movement that developed from the Edinburgh Conference. The crowning event of his career was the First World Conference on Faith and Order at Lausanne in 1927, which formally launched the Faith and Order movement. Brent was certain that dialogue between churches and confessional bodies would bring recognition of the unity found in Christ. P. BEAVER

BRIDGES, ROBERT SEYMOUR (1844–1930)
English classical scholar and poet laureate

Born on the coast of Kent, young Bridges enjoyed lying on the cliffs, his daydreams as his comrades, watching the restless sea below. He attended Eton and Oxford, where he made the second class in the Final School of Litterae Humaniores and excelled at cricket and rowing. At Oxford he formed a close friendship with Gerard Manley Hopkins, whose poetry he gave to the world about fifty years later. Following his graduation Bridges traveled in Europe and the Orient for several years. Upon his return he studied medicine at St. Bartholomew's Hospital, settled in London as a physician, and practiced there for fifteen years. Restive in the hurry of the city and desiring a quieter life, he retired in 1882 to a suburban residence, abandoned the practice of medicine, married in 1884, and devoted his professional life to poetry. His wide-ranging interests included cricket, hymnology (he collaborated in editing a hymnal), the encouragement of fellow poets (Hopkins, for example), Greek and Shakespearean plays, and music, especially music for the harpsichord.

Bridges was a scholarly poet, sometimes called a poet's poet. Some of his poems, however, such as "O Weary Pilgrim" (from *The Growth of Love*), "On a Dead Child," "A Passer-By," and "I Will Not Let Thee Go," found a more general audience. Many elements enter into his poems: delicate observation, delight in art, ethical seriousness, justice, reason, courage, meditation, solitude, and piety.

Appointed poet laureate to succeed Alfred Austin in 1913, he wrote odes of courage during World War I and a song of victory at its close. His most outstanding achievement in the postwar period was publication in his eighty-fifth year of *The Testament of Beauty* (1929). Intellectually the most ambitious of his poems, it presents a blending of Christian theology, modern science, and Platonic doctrine. The poem contains some passages of a conversational quality and has been criticized for long proselike sections. Yet it also has passages of great beauty and stirring imagination.

Both admirers and critics of the poetry of Bridges agree that as a craftsman he was one of the masters of English verse; some regard him as the greatest of the post-Victorian traditional poets. E. B. BATSON

BRIDGET OF SWEDEN (c. 1303–1373)
Roman Catholic saint

Bridget was married at about the age of fourteen to a Swedish nobleman. Eight children were born of that union, one of whom, Catherine, followed her mother in canonized sainthood, becoming St. Catherine of Sweden. Bridget was a lady in waiting to the Swedish queen. After her husband's death she devoted herself to a life of charity and penance. She is credited with frequent visions and revelations, which she duly recorded.

In 1346 Bridget gathered a following and established the Order of the Most Holy Savior, commonly called Brigittines. The order was made up of dual monasteries, that is, communities of men and women ruled by abbesses. It was not granted official approval until 1370. In 1349 Bridget went to live in Rome, where she remained until her death—except for some pilgrimages, one of which she made to the Holy Land shortly before she died.

Bridget's life encompassed the papacy's time at Avignon. She urged the pope to return to Rome and is recognized as a major influence in bringing that to pass. Her can-

onization of 1391 was confirmed in 1415. Bridget's life of piety and service touched the whole church. A. CABANISS

BRIDGMAN, ELIJAH COLEMAN (1801–1861)
First missionary sent to China by the American Board of Commissioners for Foreign Missions

Bridgman joined Robert Morrison, a Scot, in the foreign factory district of Canton in 1830, before the land was officially open to foreign residence. Bridgman and Morrison founded the Christian Union for the diffusion of Christian knowledge. He operated a school and in May 1832 began editing and publishing the renowned *Chinese Repository,* which he continued for twenty years. Twice he served as secretary and translator to American ambassadors making treaties with China. Bridgman had but one brief furlough in 1852. He transferred to Shanghai where he edited the *Repository,* headed the Union Bible Translation Committee, taught a famous Bible class, and was pastor of a small church. A noted sinologue (student of Chinese culture), he was president of the Shanghai Literary and Scientific Society and an officer of the North China Branch of the Royal Asiatic Society. P. BEAVER

BRIGGS, CHARLES AUGUSTUS (1841–1913)
Biblical scholar and theologian

Born in New York City, Briggs was educated at the University of Virginia, Union Theological Seminary in New York, and the University of Berlin. Ordained a Presbyterian minister, he served a church in Roselle, New Jersey (1870–1874), and spent the rest of his life as a member of the Union Seminary faculty (1874–1913). As professor of Hebrew and cognate languages, he gained recognition as a leading Old Testament scholar and greatly enhanced the reputation of the institution (1874–1891).

As editor of the *Presbyterian Review* (1880–1890), Briggs espoused application of the methods of literary and historical criticism to the study of the Bible and rejected the doctrines of the inerrancy and verbal inspiration of Scripture. In 1890 his inaugural address upon his appointment to a new chair of biblical theology brought charges of heresy from conservatives and led to his trial and acquittal by his presbytery; upon appeal to the higher church courts, the General Assembly of the Presbyterian Church, U.S.A., suspended him from the ministry (1893). Union Seminary, however, retained Briggs and severed its relations with the Assembly. Briggs was eventually ordained to the ministry of the Protestant Episcopal Church (1899). From 1904 he held the chair of Theological Encyclopedia and Symbolics and gave himself to the promotion of Christian unity. In his later years he was critical of radical theology.

Briggs was one of the editors of the *International Critical Commentary* and the *Hebrew and English Lexicon of the Old Testament* (1906). He wrote dozens of scholarly books, from *Biblical Study* (1883) to the posthumously published *History of the Study of Theology* (1916). A. H. FREUNT, JR.

BRITTEN, EDWARD BENJAMIN (1913–1977)

Prominent English composer

Born in Lowestoft, Britten showed great talent for composition from his early youth. Although his instrumental works are generally acknowledged to be of the first order, his greater strength lay in his vocal and choral works, large and small, sacred and secular.

Through his deftness in word setting (that is, matching particular words and texts to complementary musical settings), his attention to children's voices, the clarity and inventiveness of his vocal lines and textures, and his enthusiasm for sacred as well as secular works, Britten brought back to English music an indigenous sense it had lacked since the seventeenth century. His most important work is an opera, *Peter Grimes* (1945). Notable among his religious compositions are *A Boy Was Born, The Prodigal Son, Noye's Fludde, A Ceremony of Carols, Rejoice in the Lamb,* and the *War Requiem.* H. M. BEST

BROOKS, PHILLIPS (1835–1893)

American Episcopal minister; bishop of Massachusetts

Brooks was born in Boston, the son of a merchant. His family joined the Protestant Episcopal Church when he was twelve, in reaction to growing Unitarianism in Congregational circles. Their rector was A. N. Vinton, a strongly evangelical preacher and a trusted adviser. In 1856, one year after graduating from Harvard and a short period of teaching in a preparatory school, on Vinton's advice Brooks entered an Episcopal seminary in Virginia. There he encountered slavery and became an abolitionist.

In 1859 Brooks was installed as deacon at the Church of the Advent in Philadelphia, where his preaching drew wide attention. He soon became rector of the socially prominent parish of Holy Trinity in Philadelphia, a position he held from 1862 to 1869. From the pulpit, Brooks gained national prominence for his preaching ability. He was also a practical minister, promoting the education of children in the parish, various outreach ministries to Philadelphia's poor, and foreign missions. During the Civil War he strongly supported the Union cause.

Brooks accepted a call to Boston's Holy Trinity Church in 1869. His ministry there ranged from Sunday services attended by wealthy Bostonians to missions among the city's laborers. He spent much time with Harvard students, seeking to strengthen their Christian beliefs. He substituted for evangelist D. L. Moody during Moody's Boston revival services in 1877. That same year, Brooks delivered a series of influential lectures on preaching at Yale Divinity School.

Frequently working himself to exhaustion, Brooks was refreshed by long vacations used for travel. On his travels to England, he was greatly influenced by theologians F. D. Maurice, A. P. Stanley, and F. W. Farrar. Brooks studied in Germany in 1882. On a trip to the Near East he wrote the words to the Christmas carol "O Little Town of Bethlehem." In 1891 he became bishop of Massachusetts, a ministry that he undertook with great vigor. As bishop he traveled extensively throughout the state, preaching an average of twelve times a week until his death. K. HOGLUND

BROTHER LAWRENCE (1611–1691)
Christian mystic

Born in Lorraine (France), Brother Lawrence was originally named Nicholas Herman. His life almost spanned the seventeenth century, and he may be considered a representative of what A. N. Whitehead has called "the century of genius." After an obscure boyhood he entered the army, in which he spent an undistinguished eighteen-year period. Thereafter he served in Paris as aide to the treasurer of France. In Paris, where he eventually died, Lawrence became enamored with the life of the severe order of Discalced Carmelites. Ultimately he made his profession there and continued in it for the remainder of his life. He never sought advancement beyond the humble status of lay brother, serving his community "of the Resurrection" as a cook for thirty years. He was released from his duties because of blindness, and he died few years later.

As one might expect, he left no major writings, only a few spiritual notes and a few edifying letters. But within a short time after his death, his simple writings were assembled and, together with some verbal maxims, published in 1691. Two years later a shorter version was published. Some of the passages in those publications have been translated, edited, and published as *The Practice of the Presence of God,* on which book his fame now rests. His quasi-mystical spirituality, although orthodox, gained considerable influence among, or was at least used by, Quietists and Jansenists. As a result, he has never had such popularity in the Roman Catholic Church as he has among Protestants. A. CABANISS

BROWN, JOHN (OF HADDINGTON) (1722–1787)
Scottish theologian, preacher, and author

Born of impoverished parents at Carpow, Perthshire (Scotland), and orphaned at twelve years of age, Brown found employment as a herdboy. Although he suffered severe illness during his childhood and had little formal education, he quickly learned Latin, Hebrew, and Greek, teaching himself Greek without the use of a grammar by guessing what the Greek should be from his knowledge of Latin. His brilliance, even as a teenager, amazed the professors at St. Andrews University. After serving as a soldier in 1745, he became a schoolmaster at Gairney Bridge and then at Penicuik, near Edinburgh, in 1747. In 1751, he became the pastor of a church in Haddington, where he labored until his death.

A moderate and gentle man, Brown was an earnest preacher with a simple, direct style. As a pastor he tried to make biblical truth available for the common people of his day and directed his literary efforts to that end. Author of numerous books, Brown was best known for compiling earlier materials into a "self-interpreting Bible" published in 1778. He did it "in a manner that might best comport with the ability and leisure of the poorer and laboring part of mankind, and especially to render the oracles of God their own interpreter." The book was so popular that Scottish poet Robert Burns made mention of it in a poem.

Brown's steady labors ruined his health; he was buried in the Haddington churchyard, where a monument was erected to his memory. W. ELWELL

BROWN, WILLIAM ADAMS (1865–1943)
Liberal Presbyterian theologian; ecumenical leader

Born in New York City, Brown studied at Yale University and Union Theological Seminary in New York City. He did graduate work at the University of Berlin under German liberal theologian Adolf Harnack (1890–1892). From 1898 to 1930 he was

Roosevelt professor of systematic theology at Union Seminary, and from 1930 until retirement in 1936 was research professor of applied theology.

To Brown, Christian theology was a study not of dogmas but of God as he is experienced by Christian believers. In that experience Jesus Christ is central: he is "the vitalizing principle of theology." Brown's major systematic work was *Christian Theology in Outline* (1906). He also published many other theological books including *The Christian Hope* (1912) and *The Church Catholic and Protestant* (1935). In his later years Brown played an active part in both the Faith and Order and the Life and Work branches of the ecumenical movement, and was a member of a committee that in 1938 drafted a constitution for the proposed World Council of Churches. N. V. HOPE

BROWNE, ROBERT (c. 1550–1633)
English separatist preacher and author

A 1572 graduate of Corpus Christi College, Cambridge, Browne was deeply influenced by the Puritan movement. After teaching school for awhile, he began to preach around Cambridge but refused an episcopal license. After a confrontation with church authorities, he and Robert Harrison helped found a separatist congregation in Norwich, which migrated to Middelburg in the Netherlands in 1582 to escape persecution.

There in Norwich Browne wrote *A Treatise of Reformation without Tarrying for Anie*, setting out his views on the relation of church and state, and insisting that the authority of the magistrate did not extend to the worship and discipline of the church. The true church, Browne argued, was ruled by the risen Christ through his Word and Spirit. It was composed of true believers who covenanted together to demonstrate the reformation of life and worship commanded by Scripture—practices that were largely ignored by the Elizabethan Church of England.

Browne's views on church organization did not always stand the test of reality. After

bitter divisions in Middelburg, Browne returned to England and submitted to Archbishop Whitgift in 1585. Browne continued to exert influence among those who were dissatisfied with the Presbyterian group of Puritans, but by 1591 he had resolved his own conscientious scruples about the Church of England sufficiently to become rector of Thorpe-cum-Achurch. The remainder of his life was spent in relative obscurity. He died in prison after attacking a policeman.

Although Browne was a pioneer writer on separatism (those following him were known as "Brownists"), he was not so original or influential in the development of independent churches as was once thought. Yet his concept of a church independent of the state and obedient to Christ did have an effect on church history in England and North America. I. BREWARD

BROWNE, SIR THOMAS (1605–1682)
English physician and author; especially known for his book Religio Medici

Born in London and educated at Westminster and Oxford, Browne studied medicine on the continent. In 1637 he settled in Norwich (England), where he spent the rest of his life. His writings have been admired by many literary figures, including C. S. Lewis.

Browne's *Religio Medici (Religion of a Doctor)* appeared in 1642 after having circulated for several years in manuscript. Some readers accused Browne of being a Roman Catholic in disguise; others accused him of being an atheist. Yet some admiring Puritan editors suspected him of being a "sound Puritan," and one Quaker leader was so impressed that he invited Browne to join the Society of Friends.

Browne's book dealt with a wide range of religious and philosophical topics such as the relation between faith and reason, with emphasis on the mystery and wonder of believing. His famous phrase, "I love to lose myself in a mystery, to pursue my reason to an *O Altitudo*," is typical of its spirit.

Delighting in a faith that accepted

miracles, Browne cautioned against believing in the so-called miracles of some religionists. He was glad not to have been an Israelite who passed through the Red Sea, or one of Christ's "patients" on whom he performed a healing. Had he seen those miracles, Browne wrote, his faith would have been "thrust upon him." Acknowledging his doubts, he refused to dwell on questions he could not answer. He chose instead to live with the reality of answers he could not escape.

Browne also wrote *Hydriotaphia*, which began with scientific speculation on burial customs and concluded with what has been called the most eloquent contemplation of death in English. Another work, *The Garden*, studied patterns that might explain a principle of formal structure in the world and ended with "a dream of Paradise itself." In these two books Browne balanced death and life, mortality and immortality, body and form, time and timelessness. He pleaded for religion in an age dominated by the rise of science, and he frequently expressed concern that the new science was a portent of the decay of the world. He was knighted by Charles II in 1671.   E. B. BATSON

BRUCE, ALEXANDER BALMAIN
(1831–1899)
Scottish theologian

Son of a Perthshire farmer who had left the Church of Scotland and joined the Free Church, Bruce was educated at the university and the Free Church Divinity College in Edinburgh. He ministered at Cardross (1859–1868) and Broughty Ferry (1868–1875), then was appointed professor of apologetics and New Testament exegesis in the Free Church College, Glasgow (1875–1899). A good teacher and scholar of independent mind, Bruce was "in sympathy with modern religious thought, while maintaining solidarity with all that is best in the theology of the past; in favor of freedom in critical inquiries on the basis of evangelical faith, and of a simplified and more comprehensive creed." He maintained that viewpoint in his books, among which were *The*

Training of the Twelve (1871), *The Humiliation of Christ* (1876), *The Kingdom of God* (1889), and *St. Paul's Conception of Christianity* (1894). A complaint about the critical content of Bruce's biblical teaching was made to the Free Church's General Assembly of 1890, but was dismissed by that body. J. D. DOUGLAS

BRUCE, F. F. (FREDERICK FYVIE)
(1910–1990)
Scottish biblical scholar

Born at Elgin, son of a well-known Plymouth Brethren speaker, Bruce studied at Aberdeen, Cambridge, and Vienna, and taught at Edinburgh, Leeds, and Sheffield (1935–1959) before appointment to the historic Rylands Chair of Biblical Criticism and Exegesis at Manchester (1959–1978). The foremost figure in the post–World War II resurgence of evangelical scholarship in Britain, he was a man of total integrity who would never accept long-entrenched views without fresh examination. His loyalty to the Brethren was lifelong and unquestionable, yet he believed in the full participation of women in the Church's ministry. He did not like the prefixing of "evangelical" with "conservative" and was generally impatient with partisan labels. Highly acclaimed also by nonevangelicals, he was president of both the Society for Old Testament Studies and its New Testament counterpart (he also had a D.D. from Aberdeen and was a fellow of the British Academy).

In a busy life he took time to encourage younger writers in habits of meticulous research and presentation of material. Only after his death did his wife learn from numerous letters something of his unobtrusive help to individuals both pastorally and academically. In addition, he edited the *Evangelical Quarterly* (1949–1980) and *Palestine Exploration Quarterly* (1957–1971), and published commentaries that covered most of the New Testament. Among his many other works are *The Books and the Parchments* (1950), *Second Thoughts on the Dead Sea Scrolls* (1956), *The Spreading Flame* (1958), *Israel and the Nations* (1963), *New*

Testament History (1969), The Message of the New Testament (1972), Paul and Jesus (1974), Paul: The Apostle of the Free Spirit (1977), History of the Bible in English (1979), the autobiographical In Retrospect (1980), The Real Jesus (1985), The Pauline Circle (1985), and The Canon of Scripture (1988).
J. D. DOUGLAS

BRUCE, ROBERT (1554–1631)

Scottish Presbyterian minister and theologian

Born in Stirlingshire, Bruce entered St. Andrews and graduated with an M.A. in 1572. Thereafter he studied law at the University of Louvain (Belgium), and on his return to Scotland he practiced law. After his conversion in 1581 he began theological study at St. Mary's college, St. Andrews, and in 1587 accepted a call to be minister of St. Giles' Church, Edinburgh. Bruce was moderator of the General Assembly in 1588 and 1592. In 1598, when King James VI left Scotland to woo Princess Anne of Denmark, Bruce was virtually regent of the realm during the king's absence. When Anne came to Scotland, Bruce anointed her at her coronation. Because he opposed the king's attempt to control and manipulate the Church of Scotland, however, Bruce was suspended from his Edinburgh pulpit in 1600. In 1606 he was banished to Inverness in the Highlands until 1613 and again from 1622 to 1625.

Bruce's major theological contribution lay in his masterly exposition of the Calvinist doctrine of Jesus Christ's real spiritual presence in the sacrament of the Lord's Supper, first given as five sermons from his Edinburgh pulpit. Those sermons, along with eleven others, were published in The True Peace and Rest (1617). N. V. HOPE

BRUCKNER, ANTON (1824–1896)

Austrian composer and organist

Bruckner's chief renown lies in his nine symphonies (the last unfinished), which, despite their length and formal sameness, reflect a large and sincere vision. Born in Ansfelden, Bruckner was trained as a choris-

ter, after which he became a schoolmaster. In 1855 he became organist at Linz Cathedral, a position that enabled him to travel to Vienna for his first studies in composition. In 1868 he was employed to teach organ and counterpoint at the Vienna Conservatory.

Influenced by Richard Wagner, Bruckner's works have been described as "romantic in style and characterized by a mixture of homely simplicity and Catholic mysticism." Although his compositions for the church are not numerous, they include three masses, a setting of Psalm 150, and the powerful Te Deum, upon which his reputation as a church composer most firmly rests.
H. M. BEST

BRUNNER, HEINRICH EMIL (1889–1966)

Swiss Reformed theologian; often considered with Karl Barth as a leader of the movement known as "neoorthodoxy" or "dialectical theology"

Brunner was reared in the Reformed tradition by devout parents. In his youth he encountered the religious socialist movement, which gave him one set of roots for a dialectical method in theology. Trained in liberal theology in the Universities of Zurich and Berlin, Brunner was ordained in 1912. After an eight-year pastorate in Obstalden (Switzerland), interrupted by a year of study at New York's Union Theological Seminary and a term of teaching in England, he taught systematic and practical theology at the University of Zurich (1924–1953). From 1953 to 1955, Brunner was visiting professor at the International Christian University of Tokyo. During his long career he lectured frequently in America. He was father of four sons, two of whom died during his lifetime.

DIALECTICAL THEOLOGY
In the 1920s Brunner's thinking paralleled that of a small but influential group of theologians including Karl Barth (1886–1968), Friedrich Gogarten (1887–1967), and Rudolf Bultmann (1884–1976). Their reevaluation of nineteenth-century liberal theology led them to develop a dialectical form of

doctrine. Brunner was particularly influenced by the Christian existentialism of Søren Kierkegaard (1813–1855) and the Jewish religious philosophy of Martin Buber (1878–1965). For Brunner, theology was the task of interpreting the "personal correspondence" between God and humankind revealed in the Bible. His writings display great sensitivity to both the simple message of the New Testament and the complex demands of the twentieth century.

Brunner's theological emphasis on personality was shaped by early experience with the Oxford Group (later Moral Rearmament) as well as by Buber's "I-Thou" concept of personal communication. From Buber he developed a focus on God as the divine subject who acts in revelation and redemption, thus shifting from liberal Protestantism's optimism about human ability to find God by reason or religion. The Oxford Group's practical methods (public testimonials, confession, prayer) impressed on Brunner the role of personal encounter in religion. His own theology incorporated such insights in a paradoxical way to rethink traditional concepts about God and the world.

To Brunner, human beings are responsible creatures. Although made by God to respond to him in faith and love, they actually rebel against God because of sin. In revelation God personally makes himself known to his creation. What distinguishes the Christian, according to Brunner, is not mere knowledge of God (making God an object instead of the subject of revelation) nor absorption into union with God, but *communion* with God. Brunner saw the sixteenth-century Reformation as a temporary recovery of that insight, but thought it had been lost again when the medieval doctrine of an infallible church was displaced by belief in an infallible Bible.

NATURAL THEOLOGY

Brunner agreed with Barth that one's knowledge of God depends on God's sovereign choice to disclose himself. But he differed with Barth in a 1934 publication (translated in 1946 as *Natural Theology*) about the way that God's revelation and human reason connect. Barth argued that the two cannot possibly be united because of sin's effects on human nature. Brunner maintained that certain factors in the way God created and governs the world make the natural creation a valid means of divine revelation. Human beings, though rebels against God, remain the image of God. Human history and every person's conscience contain evidence of God's revelation. The continuing existence of people and things is manifestly a gift of God. And God has created specific "orders" by which the natural world runs: family, work, culture, church, and state. Human nature's personal character makes people able to hear God's Word in nature as well as in the Bible. Finally, Brunner argued that God's grace does not abolish anything, but perfects redeemed believers. Conversion is the Holy Spirit's work of deepening a person's self-consciousness rather than creating it, in continuity with all that has preceded one's faith in Christ. Christians are thus restored personalities, not wholly new creatures, and non-Christians are capable of receiving revelation apart from redemption.

THEOLOGICAL WRITINGS

Brunner's many books reveal his theological breadth and express his personality-oriented approach to doctrine. *The Mediator* (1927), in expounding the person and work of Christ, rejected the Virgin Birth as an unfounded idea and unnecessary for faith in Jesus' deity. Brunner did affirm in that book an ambiguous doctrine of the Resurrection. His basic view on the "orders of creation" was set forth in *The Divine Imperative* (1932). *Man in Revolt* (1937) stressed Brunner's break from liberal theology's optimistic view of human nature, and attempted to develop a new doctrine of sin. In *The Divine-Human Encounter* (1938) his existentialist idea of God's dealings with people was evident. *Revelation and Reason* (1941) served as an introduction to his three-part systematic theology, published between 1946 and 1960.

Brunner's Gifford lectures (on natural theology) at the University of St. Andrews

(Scotland) were published as *Christianity and Civilization* (1947–1948). Two works that were especially important to him were *Our Faith* (1935), a small compendium of theology intended as studies for lay people, and *Eternal Hope* (1953), an eschatological study written in response to his second son's tragic death.

Although Brunner was never as popular a theologian a Karl Barth, his writings were actually better known. His writing style was clearer than Barth's, and his views were generally thought to be more moderate. Many of Brunner's treatises, especially his three-volume systematic theology, *Dogmatics* (1946–1960), have been used as seminary textbooks.

PRACTICAL CONCERN
Brunner's theology emphasized personal values. His actions expressed the beliefs he taught. Along with his Oxford Group activity already mentioned, he worked for the international YMCA. Although he later withdrew from the ecumenical movement because of his doctrine of the church being primarily a fellowship rather than an organization, Brunner labored in the 1930s for both the Faith and Order and the Life and Work forerunners of the World Council of Churches. His commitment to a "missionary theology" led him to travel often as a teacher and adviser in his later years. He also preached frequently in Protestant churches. D. M. LAKE & H. JACOBSEN

BRUNO THE CARTHUSIAN
(c. 1030–1101)
Founder of the Carthusian Order

Bruno, born at Cologne (Germany), became master of the cathedral school at Rheims (1056) where he taught both the arts and theology. Although he had some problems with the archbishop and other associates, he refused an appointment to become a bishop on two occasions and became chancellor of the archdiocese in 1075.

After 1080 Bruno began to turn away from the cares and distractions of the world. In 1084 he became a hermit and took up residence at Chartreuse near Grenoble (southeast France), a desolate location. The severe "rule" he adopted combined aspects of both the communal and solitary style of monastic life. It restricted manual labor to the lay brothers. Bruno died at a hermitage in southern Italy which he had founded, and he received sainthood from Pope Leo X, though some authorities believe he was never formally canonized. In 1130 Bruno's rules were written down by one of his associates in the order.

The name *Carthusian* was Latin for Chartreuse, the location of the order's foundation. The order, which had only limited growth, never encountered the problems of corruption or administrative complexity that plagued many Roman Catholic orders. Its rule, followed strictly, called for great discipline yet achieved a balance between a life of self-denial and the daily needs of practical living. The order has boasted that it never required reform since it never became deformed.

Bruno's surviving writings include two letters discussing asceticism and some biblical commentaries on the Psalms and the letters of the apostle Paul. T. O. KAY

BRYAN, WILLIAM JENNINGS
(1860–1925)
Best-known fundamentalist in American public life from the Civil War to the Great Depression

Although born in Salem, Illinois, Bryan gained national recognition as a newspaper editor (Omaha's *World Herald*) and congressman from Nebraska. His oration at the 1896 national Democratic Convention ("you shall not crucify mankind upon a cross of gold") was an eloquent plea for the "little man" in American life. It also catapulted him into the nomination for president. Bryan lost the 1896 election to William McKinley and later lost in two other presidential campaigns (1900; 1908). When Woodrow Wilson was elected president in 1912, he named Bryan secretary of state. Bryan worked ardently for peace. He was responsible for more than thirty international agreements designed to solve problems between nations by submitting disputes to impartial arbitration and then delaying hostilities for a full year while negotiation was in progress. When the Wilson administration refused to apply this principle to Germany in 1915, Bryan resigned from the cabinet rather than compromise his principles.

Bryan's retirement from politics was far from quiet. He traveled extensively throughout the country and made known his views. He supported better conditions for workers, popular election of senators, women's suffrage, international peace, and the League of Nations. He opposed the liquor trade. He argued long and hard for the authority of the Bible. His opposition to the teaching of evolution in the schools led him to Dayton, Tennessee, to participate in the Scopes trial of 1925, where he defended the reliability of the Bible against the attacks of Clarence Darrow. Although he was unprepared to deal with scientific questions, Bryan supported the Bible reasonably and coherently. But he was attacked by some fundamentalists for not taking a hard enough line because he allowed the possibility that the "days" of Genesis 1 and 2 were not literal twenty-four-hour periods of time. The trial became something of a circus and the national press pictured Bryan as a redneck buffoon embarrassing himself and all orthodox Christians before the cultured and "scientific" Darrow. While the jury's decision was technically in Bryan's favor, public opinion was strongly against him. Bryan died only a few days after the trial.

It is one of the great injustices of American history that Bryan should be remembered mainly for the Scopes trial. His entire life—as social reformer, dedicated Presbyterian layman, and thoroughly Christian politician—offers a worthy model to modern evangelicals for Christian involvement in public life. M. A. NOLL

BUBER, MARTIN (1878–1965)
Jewish religious existentialist writer

Born in Vienna (Austria), Buber fled from Germany after Hitler's rise to power and taught religious and social philosophy at the Hebrew University in Jerusalem until shortly before his death.

His central theme was the difference between the "I-It" and "I-Thou" methods of relating, a concept he introduced into the currency of the West that has profoundly influenced theology and other disciplines. An "I-It" relation treats another as a thing—an impersonal object—whether it is actually a thing or a person; when we treat persons as things, we use them, talk "about" them, depersonalize them, regard them as just a part of the scenery. On the other hand, in "I-Thou" relations we respect persons as persons: we address them, dialog with them, trust them, and share ourselves with them. Reciprocally, we sometimes treat things as "Thou," relating to animals and plants and scenery in personalized ways. I-It relations dehumanize. I-Thou relations, marked by communication, dialogue, and love, give personal meaning to life. Inevitably we live in relationships of some sort, but it takes I-Thou relationships to humanize us.

Buber applied this insight to education, to psychotherapy, and to the idea of a community—something he envisioned for the Israeli kibbutz. He also applied it to religion, maintaining that biblical religion deals with our I-Thou relation with God and that the biblical covenant brings the kingship of God into all areas of community life. On the other hand, Buber said that under the influence of Greek philosophy, New Testament writers such as Paul make God an object of thought rather than a subject who speaks. They talk *about* him and tie faith to a content of knowledge. The prophets, on the other hand, along with Jesus in the synoptic Gospels, regard faith as trust. They treat God as the Eternal Thou, a subject who addresses us as we address him. True religion becomes a dialogue between a human being and God. The purported disagreement between Paul and the Old Testament conception of religion was characteristic of liberal Christian theology, but Buber's "I-Thou" is also picked up by more recent existential theology. A. F. HOLMES

BUCER, MARTIN (1491–1551)
Early Protestant Reformer

Bucer is not well known today, partly because no church group bears his name and partly because Reformation histories usually focus on Martin Luther and John Calvin. Nevertheless, Bucer's impact on his own age was enormous. He was the leading Reformer in the strategic German city of Strassburg, capital of the territory of Alsace. At many meetings attempting to bring about unity among various Protestant groups, and even with the Roman Catholics, Bucer was spokesman and negotiator for Protestantism. He had a lifelong dedication to union and cooperation among the Christian churches. His organizational ability was shown in his development of an effective Protestant structure of church government, a structure used by Calvinist churches throughout the world. Finally, Bucer produced an influential type of biblical commentary and helped to establish many basic Protestant theological positions. His talents were remarkably diverse.

Bucer was born in Alsace near Strassburg. Although his family was poor, he received an excellent early education in a local Latin school. There he was trained in the new ideals and advances of Renaissance humanism. At the age of fifteen he joined the Dominican order of the Roman Catholic Church, where he was trained in the Scholastic theology of Thomas Aquinas. Bucer quickly mastered complex Thomist theology and was named professor of theology among the Dominicans. But being attracted to the practical program of the Renaissance, he became a follower of Erasmus, a reform-minded, Dutch humanist scholar and theologian. From Erasmus, Bucer moved on to the then-startling teachings being developed by Martin Luther.

In 1518 while serving in the Dominican cloister at Heidelberg, Bucer heard Luther explain his new teachings before officials of the Augustinian order. He was converted to Luther's belief in "salvation by faith alone" and withdrew from his order in 1521. Soon thereafter he married, becoming one of the first Protestant ministers to take such a rad-ical step. Excommunicated, he sought refuge in Strassburg in 1523. For the next twenty-five years he labored as chief pastor of that city, developing a tolerant but carefully nurtured Protestant church. Bucer's teachings on the Holy Spirit, on discipline as a vital part of church polity, and on the need for lay participation in church affairs all became an integral part of the Calvinist message. Calvin learned much from Bucer during a three-year (1538–1541) stay in Strassburg. Bucer's last three years were spent at Cambridge University in England, where his ideas had a powerful impact on the developing Church of England, influencing the revision of the 1549 *Book of Common Prayer*. B. G. ARMSTRONG

BUCHANAN, GEORGE (1506–1582)
Scottish classical scholar and humanist; a devastating critic of the Roman Catholic Church

Born in Killearn, Stirlingshire, and educated at the University of Paris (1520–1522) and St. Andrews University (1525), Buchanan taught first at College Ste. Barbe in Paris (1528). In 1535 he returned to Scotland, but because of his attacks on Franciscan friars in two plays, *Somnium* and *Franciscanus*, he thought it prudent to return to France (1539). He then taught at the College de Guyenne in Bordeaux, where one of his pupils was Montaigne, later famous as an essayist.

In 1547 Buchanan taught at the University of Coimbra (Portugal), where he held the position of regent. Nonetheless, he was accused of heresy by the Inquisition and was confined to a monastery for reeducation. During that time of enforced quiet he wrote a Latin paraphrase of the Psalms that was later used in Scotland for instruction in Latin. In 1552 he was released. He returned to France, tutored for a while, but spent much of his time in poetic composition. In 1561 he returned to Scotland and gave his support to Queen Mary, whom he may have met in France. He wrote a poem on her marriage to Francis, the French crown prince, later Francis II. However, after her involvement in the murder of her second husband, Henry Darnley, Buchanan turned against her and helped to prepare the case against her presented to Queen Elizabeth of England. In 1566 Buchanan was made principal of St. Leonard's College at St. Andrews, and in 1570 he became the tutor of the young King James VI. While in that position he wrote *De Jure Regni apud Scotos* (1579), in which he set forth a Calvinistic theory of limited monarchy; he stated that the Scots could legally remove an oppressive monarch. The book was publicly burned on a number of occasions by royalists. Buchanan was working on a history of Scotland, *Rerum Scoticarum Historie*, at the time of his death. W. S. REID

BUCHMAN, FRANK NATHAN DANIEL (1878–1961)
Founder and leading figure of the Oxford Group movement, which was later renamed Moral Rearmament

An American, Buchman was born into a Lutheran family and was educated at Muhlenberg College and Mount Airy Seminary in Philadelphia. He entered the Lutheran ministry and took a parish in Philadelphia. Later he tried ministering among poor young men but became disillusioned, resigning in 1908. He went to England, where he came into contact with the teachings of the Keswick Conference and experienced a conversion. On a suggestion from John R. Mott, Buchman returned to the United States to undertake evangelistic work among students at Pennsylvania State College.

After World War I, a series of visits by Buchman to Oxford University in England launched the Oxford Group movement. Meeting informally with groups of students, he challenged them to experience an individual change which included a determination to live with "absolute love, absolute honesty, absolute purity, and absolute unselfishness." In 1938, under the growing menace of World War II, Buchman launched the Moral Rearmament movement, a more socially oriented application of the Oxford

Group principles. That phase of his work achieved great popularity immediately after the war. Buchman saw himself as leading a lifelong campaign for moral and spiritual awakening, though many critics denounced his movement for lack of emphasis on Christ's atonement. K. HOGLUND

BUCK, DUDLEY (1839–1909)
American organist, composer, and teacher

Buck's training took place in America (Trinity College, Hartford, Connecticut) and Europe (Leipzig, Dresden, and Paris). His training was solid: piano, organ, composition, and instrumentation. Returning to America, he held organ posts in Hartford, Chicago, Boston, and Brooklyn. He became known as a conductor and also wrote several books, including *Illustrations in Choir Accompaniment*. Buck's music is seldom performed today (except perhaps his *Festival Te Deum*), but he was one of the first American-born church musicians to gain recognition for both sacred and secular works. H. M. BEST

BUDGE, E. A. WALLIS (1857–1934)
Cambridge scholar in Assyrian and Hebrew who became keeper of Egyptian and Assyrian antiquities at the British Museum, 1893–1924

Budge directed excavations at Nineveh, Aswan, Meroe (capital of ancient Ethiopia), and along the banks of the Nile in Sudan when the first Aswan Dam threatened to cover antiquities at the beginning of the century. His better-known writings include *The Gods of Egypt, The Nile, Literature of the Ancient Egyptians, By Nile and Tigris,* and an edition of the ancient Egyptian *Book of the Dead.* He was knighted by the king of England. H. F. VOS

BUGENHAGEN, JOHANN (1485–1558)
Early German Reformer

Born near Stettin in Pomerania, Bugenhagen was ordained a priest and became a pastor at Treptow in 1504 after completing studies at the University of Greifswald. Appointed lecturer at the abbey school at Belbuk in 1517, he was influenced by the writings of Erasmus, a Dutch humanist scholar, to see a need for reform in the Roman Catholic Church. Won over to the Reformation in 1520, he went to Wittenberg in 1521. There he formed close friendships with Martin Luther and Philip Melanchthon and held the pastorate of the collegiate church from 1523 until his death.

A distinguished scholar, Bugenhagen helped Luther translate the Old Testament into High German and published his own translation of the Bible in Low German in 1533. He was the author of numerous works, perhaps the best of which was *Interpretation of the Book of Psalms* (1523). He is chiefly remembered as the able organizer of the Reformation in northern Germany and Denmark. He is credited with preparing the church constitutions for the Lutheran establishment in Brunswick, Hamburg, Lubeck, Pomerania, and Schleswig-Holstein. Called to Denmark by King Christian II in 1537, Bugenhagen spent five years organizing the church and schools there along Lutheran lines. H. F. Vos

BULLINGER, JOHANN HEINRICH (1504–1575)
Successor to the Protestant Reformation leader, Ulrich Zwingli, in Zurich (Switzerland)

Born in the little Swiss village of Bremgarten, the illegitimate offspring of the parish priest, young Bullinger received a good education arranged for by his father. While attending the University of Cologne in Germany, he was converted to Protestantism. From 1523 to 1529 he taught Bible and ancient languages at a Cistercian monastery in the Swiss village of Kappel, although in 1527 under his influence the monastery dissolved and formed a Protestant church. In 1529 he succeeded his father at Bremgarten, by then a Protestant parish, and in 1531 he succeeded Zwingli at Zurich.

Zwingli's death on the battlefield in 1531 had caused serious problems for the Refor-

mation. The Swiss-German Protestants were shocked over the loss of their great leader and a number of challenges immediately faced Bullinger: (1) Zwingli had had less than ten years to set the pattern for the Swiss-German reform movement, and Bullinger had had only cursory contact with the Zurich situation. (2) Although the Protestant Reformation had been established in other parts of Switzerland, each area had adopted the reform cause under a local and independent impulse. Hence no real unity existed. (3) Zwingli's attempts to unite the tiny Swiss Reformation with other Protestant groups had not been successful. (4) Oecolampadius of Basel (1482–1531), the greatest Swiss reform leader after Zwingli and the person looked to for stability and direction at that crucial moment, suddenly took ill and died only seven weeks after Zwingli. (5) Although Zwingli had written brilliant theological works, no mature statement of faith existed for the movement.

Bullinger was able to overcome all of those problems. He served the Zurich church for forty-four years with great success and was the leading voice in the Swiss-German Reformation. An outstanding preacher, Bullinger was probably the greatest Reformed pastor of his age. Fifty of his sermons, published as his *Decades,* express the core of his theology. He was beloved for his self-giving service to people in all kinds of difficult circumstances. His hospitality was legendary.

Many English Protestants who fled the persecution of Mary Tudor's England between 1553 and 1558 sought refuge in Zurich. Through them Bullinger exercised considerable influence on the English church. Bullinger was a prolific letter writer and corresponded with Henry VIII and Edward VI in addition to many of the English reformers. Queen Elizabeth I allied herself with Bullinger against the rigidly Calvinistic Puritans. She also asked Bullinger to prepare her reply to Pope Pius V after her excommunication in 1570.

It is hard to imagine the survival of Swiss Protestantism without the work of Bullinger, counselor and confidant of so many Protestant leaders, promoter of education, historian of the Reformation, and accomplished theologian. Bullinger's personal statement of faith, the Second Helvetic (Swiss) Confession (1566), became the most widely used confession of the Reformation. B. G. ARMSTRONG

BULTMANN, RUDOLF (1884–1976)

Prominent twentieth-century German
theologian and New Testament scholar;
known primarily for his theological method
of "demythologizing" the New Testament

Bultmann was born in Wiefelstede and educated at Tübingen, Berlin, and Marburg universities. He taught at Marburg (1912–1916), Breslau (1916–1920), and Giessen (1920–1921), and then returned to Marburg (1921–1951). In 1951 he was appointed professor emeritus at Marburg and thereafter made several lecture tours to Scandinavia, Holland, and the United States. He delivered the Shaffer lectures at Yale University (1951), which became his book *Jesus Christ and Mythology* (1958). His 1955 Gifford lectures at Edinburgh University (Scotland) were published as *The Presence of Eternity* (1957).

Bultmann's theological thinking stemmed partly from his family heritage. His father, born to missionary parents in Sierra Leone (Africa), was a clergyman in the Evangelical Lutheran Church; his maternal grandfather was also a minister. The political events of twentieth-century Europe also contributed to his thought. One of his brothers was killed in World War I, the other in a concentration camp in World War II. Bultmann was a supporter of the German "Confessing Church" in the 1930s and a signer of the Barmen Declaration, that movement's statement of opposition to Nazism's growing control over church affairs.

Theological debate in the universities helped to shape Bultmann's systematic thought. Various German theologians and biblical scholars (among them Hermann Gunkel, Adolf Harnack, Johannes Weiss, and Adolf Julicher) influenced the young Bultmann. He was also impressed by the teachings of Friedrich Schleiermacher (1768–1834), often called the "father of liberalism." Two contemporaries, Karl Barth and Friedrich Gogarten, both shared with Bultmann an existentialist outlook on life, although Barth eventually renounced his early philosophical zeal. Especially influential was Bultmann's Marburg colleague, existentialist philosopher Martin Heidegger (1889–1976). Such influences and Bultmann's own originality created a unique modern theology of New Testament interpretation.

Bultmann's first book, *The History of the Synoptic Tradition* (1921), was based on an interpretative method known as "form criticism." The material of the Gospels supposedly existed first as an oral tradition in various "forms" conditioned by different circumstances. Bultmann contended that the forms of New Testament tradition were rarely intended as historical reports, but were shaped by preaching and teaching. Thus he concluded that the Gospels were not reliable sources for a history of the life of Jesus; they were theological, but not factual.

Bultmann's later thought further developed a division between theological truth and historical fact. His 1941 essay "The New Testament and Mythology" set forth his own ideas and laid the foundation for a significant symposium on biblical interpretation published in English as *Kerygma and Myth* (1953). He understood the historical elements of the New Testament to reflect a "myth" or worldview that is unacceptable to a modern scientific outlook. Hence that old worldview must be reinterpreted (demythologized) in order for the truth contained in the Gospels to become clear to the modern mind.

Building on Heidegger's existentialism, Bultmann closely associated theological truth and present human experience. For Bultmann, the truth of the Gospels can be grasped only through an act of decision in response to the "proclaimed Word of God" (*kerygma* in Greek). Such decision is not based on reasonable historical evidence (Bultmann denied that possibility), but on an experience of Christ's eternal presence.

According to Bultmann, the New Testament authors were not trying to write facts about God and the world. Rather, they were expressing in inadequate human terms their encounter with the kerygmatic Christ. God had acted and spoken in Jesus, but humans wrote the Bible as their reaction to God's Word. Bultmann rejected the Bible's three-storied universe (heaven, earth, and hell) and its view of history as spiritually controlled; he believed those concepts were derived from Jewish apocalypticism (prophetic, visionary writing) or gnostic redemption stories. He also disqualified such doctrines as the Virgin Birth, the Atonement, and the Resurrection. The modern worldview and sense of morality, said Bultmann, prohibit blind acceptance of such material as factual stories. For Bultmann, a loss of belief in Jesus' historicity is a benefit for true faith; to locate Jesus in a world of facts and "objectivity" would miss the present meaning of Christ, the object of faith.

However, the inadequacy of biblical language and doctrine does not mean that nothing significant happened in biblical history. In Jesus, God confronted the Bible's writers; today he confronts the readers of the Bible. The "myths" are not to be dismissed but interpreted, or demythologized, for clear communication of their meaning for faith. By demythologizing the New Testament, Bultmann believed he was recovering Christianity's essence and making it accessible to the modern mind.

The basic focus of interpretation for Bultmann's theology was human existence as a complex of anxieties and decisions. He saw authentic life as full of risks, offering a person no guarantees. For Bultmann, Christian faith is similar to other human choices, resting on unseen realities expressed in the story of Jesus Christ rather than on factual certainties. Theology, to Bultmann, must also lack easy guarantees and be dialectical in character. Christian theology proclaims that God has acted for people's good in Christ. Such a faith replaces anxiety and guilt with love and confidence toward God, who makes life's risks worthwhile.

Bultmann's views provoked a debate that has not ended. Some critics have objected to his selective use of an existentialist philosophy in his theological work; theologians and philosophers alike suspect that he inadequately united the two disciplines. His views of history have also been challenged as a threat to faith rather than a help. Demythologizing could logically lead to belief that Jesus never lived and that factual history has no bearing at all on the content of faith. Bultmann's use of the term *myth* has also been criticized; all kinds of symbolic or analogical language might be included in his definition, leaving no possibility for any way to speak about God. His theology thus could lead to a godless worldview, or at least one in which nothing about God could be known.

In addition to works already mentioned, Bultmann's important writings include *Jesus and the Word* (1926), *The Gospel of John* (1941), *Essays, Philosophical and Theological* (1954), and a three-volume *Theology of the New Testament* (1948, 1951, 1953).
H. JACOBSEN

BUNYAN, JOHN (1628–1688)

English tinker and preacher; author of more than sixty books, among them the famous Pilgrim's Progress.

Born at Elstow, Bedfordshire, Bunyan went either to the newly founded grammar school at Bedford or to the more humble one at Elstow. He married when he was twenty-one. His wife brought to their new home two religious books belonging to her godly parents. Reading those books awakened a sense of religion in Bunyan and produced changes in his habits. The insufficiency of outward change became clear to him when he overheard the spiritual conversation of some poor women while pursuing his tinker craft; he was a complete stranger to the "inner experience" of which the women spoke. The conversation was the beginning of the conflict later described by him in *Grace Abounding to the Chief of Sinners* (1666).

In 1653 Bunyan settled in Bedford, joining an independent congregation there. When he began preaching in 1657, news that the once-blaspheming tinker had turned preacher drew crowds "from all parts" to hear him.

In 1656 Bunyan had published his first written work, a pamphlet against the Quakers called *Some Gospel Truths Opened*. Answered by Edward Burroughs, an ardent Quaker, Bunyan replied the following year with *A Vindication of Some Gospel Truths Opened*. His third work was a book on the parable of the rich man and Lazarus, *Sighs from Hell, or the Groans of a Damned Soul* (1658).

Bunyan's first wife and the mother of their four children died in 1658 (her name is unknown). He married a second wife, Elizabeth, in 1659. In 1660 old acts against Nonconformists were revived. Meeting houses were closed; all persons were required under severe penalties to attend their parish church; it became illegal to conduct worship services except in accordance with Anglican ritual. Bunyan continued to preach in barns, in private homes, under the trees, or in a church if an invitation came. He was arrested in November 1660 on his way to conduct a religious service about twelve miles from Bedford. In 1661 his wife Elizabeth made a moving plea for him before the judge in Bedford.

The circumstances of Bunyan's imprisonment were less severe than some have maintained. There was no prohibition on visitors, and his good behavior and the regular appearance of his publications increased his reputation. In the early days of his imprisonment he attended Bedford Church, but after October 1661 his name was not again on the attendance record until October 1668; evidently his confinement became stricter. After 1668 he began to have times of parole, although his formal pardon did not come until 1672.

While in prison Bunyan wrote *Grace Abounding to the Chief of Sinners*, the greatest Puritan spiritual autobiography. It was patterned on the Christian account of human history with its two chief climaxes, the fall of man through the original sin of Adam, and the redemption of man through the sacrifice of Christ. Bunyan also revealed the

doubts, struggles, temptations, fears, and hopes in his own growth from lostness to salvation.

Bunyan's *Christian Behavior* (1663) was one of many Puritan manuals dealing with proper relations between fathers and families, masters and servants. *The Holy City* (1665) interpreted the symbolism of the heavenly city described in Revelation. Bunyan published his famous allegory *Pilgrim's Progress* in 1678. Early in the Christian tradition, pilgrimage had come to represent the journey through life or the progress of human life to a state of blessedness. (In *Pilgrim's Progress* the pilgrim is a seeker after a state of grace and the pilgrimage is the progress of a human soul in quest of peace with God.)

Pilgrim's Progress was followed by two books in which Bunyan again used the allegorical method. *The Life and Death of Mr. Badman* (1680) was a realistic dialogue between Wiseman and his disciple Attentive, who together considered the wicked life and quiet death of their neighbor, Mr. Badman. *The Holy War* (1682) was an elaborate depiction of the war between King Shaddai and Diabolus for the town of Mansoul. In 1684 Bunyan published a sequel to Christian's pilgrimage in a *Second Part to the Pilgrim's Progress*, which showed how Christiana and her children, accompanied by Mercy, followed the same route and at length crossed the river to enter the Holy City.

Bunyan authored many lesser-known books, but his *Pilgrim's Progress* has been translated into hundreds of dialects and languages. His archetypal figures—the pilgrim, the burden, the monsters, the road with its sloughs and bypaths, the guides true and false, the resting places, and the final goal of the heavenly city—seem to call forth response from people of all ages in all countries.

On one of his preaching journeys to London in August 1688 Bunyan went out of his way to Reading to help settle a quarrel between a father and son. After riding through heavy rain he arrived at the home of a London friend. He preached the following Sunday but in a few days developed a violent fever and died. He was buried in Bunhill Fields, London. E. B. BATSON

BURCHARD (c. 965–1025)
Bishop of Worms; canonist

Born to a Hessian noble family, Burchard had his education at Coblenz and elsewhere in Germany. He began his life of church service as a deacon under Mainz's Archbishop Willigis. Soon recognized for his exceptional discernment, Burchard was appointed by Willigis as Mainz's principal judge. This position brought him the special notice of Emperor Otto III. Within a few years, Burchard advanced to the offices of priest and bishop, and in 1000, Otto III assigned him to Worms and its region. Burchard continued as this bishopric's main figure for the remainder of his life.

Burchard was one of the church's ablest leaders during his twenty-five years at Worms. Both in spiritual and secular matters, his integrity and creativity became known and respected throughout western Europe. Under Burchard's direction, reconstructive work on the Worms Cathedral was completed and many monasteries and church buildings came into existence— among them were facilities for a women's order headed by Burchard's sister, Mathilda. Burchard also devoted much energy to the educational efforts that centered in the Worms Cathedral School. From all over Europe, questions came to him about difficult theological and moral issues. As relevant both to clergy and laity, Burchard's many visitations and synods gave moral reform especially large attention. His concerns extended much beyond internal church matters. Under his supervision, Worms rebuilt its city walls, and Emperor Henry II gave him permission to demolish a nearby refuge for criminals. All Holy Roman Emperors of his time held Burchard in esteem. Drawing on his considerable legal talents, Burchard also assembled a body of impartial secular laws for his region.

Along with local duties, Burchard became deeply involved with moral reform in the church at large. His compilations of moral and social teachings became the leading canon law collection in the early 1000s. Originally a manual for young churchmen, Burchard's main work was the twenty books of the *Collectarium canonum,* called *Decretum* for short. Its great value lay in its inclusion of basic statements by early and later Fathers, decrees by Councils and popes, directives in penitential books and other moral writings. Other than Ivo of Chartres' even larger work, Burchard's was the most important of canon law compilations prior to *Concordia Discordantium,* Gratian's monumental work issued in 1140. It is difficult to overstate the critical role played by canon law collections of the 1000s and 1100s, both for subsequent Christian moral and social practice and for European law and custom in general. On most issues, Burchard's *Decretum* restated long-standing, orthodox Christian positions, many of which Gratian included in his compilation. One noticeable liberal deviation from mainstream Christianity was Burchard's marital teaching, most pointedly his allowance of remarriage by divorced believers.
K. J. BRYER

BURKITT, FRANCIS CRAWFORD (1864–1935)
British scholar who made many original contributions to New Testament critical studies

Burkitt was educated at Trinity College, Cambridge. Free from financial concerns because of his father's business success, Burkitt was able to pursue his education and research with single-minded devotion. He mastered several ancient languages and became an expert in Syriac. Burkitt was one of the scholars who transcribed a manuscript containing the four Gospels in Syriac found in Saint Catherine's Monastery on Mount Sinai. In 1904 he published a valuable edition of the Syriac Gospels.

In his book *The Gospel History and its Transmission* (1906), Burkitt asserted that the book of Mark has essentially the same form it had when Matthew and Luke used it in writing their Gospels. Burkitt also studied the Jewish background of Christianity, recording his lectures on the subject in *Jewish and Christian Apocalypses* (1914). He recognized the importance of Albert Schweitzer's work in refuting liberal interpretations of Jesus' life and was instrumental in having Schweitzer's *Quest of the Historical Jesus* translated into English (1910). Burkitt wrote voluminously on many subjects. A list of his writings occupies ten pages in the *Journal of Theological Studies* (October 1925). K. LEID

BURNS, WILLIAM CHALMERS
(1815–1868)
Pioneer missionary to China

Born at Duns, Scotland, Burns was accepted in 1839 as a missionary of the Church of Scotland to India. However, before he left, a mighty revival began under his preaching in his father's parish, so he instead became an itinerant preacher during the spiritual awakening in Scotland, Ireland, England, and Canada.

In 1846 the English Presbyterians recruited him for China, where he engaged in itinerant evangelism after six years' resident ministry in the Amoy region. He left to others of the mission the gathering of converts into churches and the nurturing of congregations. He began the Presbyterian mission at Swatow and visited other newly opened ports. It is said that Burns deeply influenced J. Hudson Taylor, founder of the China Inland Mission. Among Burns's literary works was a Chinese translation of *Pilgrim's Progress*. Burns was drawn to the virgin territory of Manchuria and began evangelistic work at Newchwang in 1867. He died less than a year later, but his appeal to the Irish Presbyterian church brought successors to build on his foundation. P. BEAVER

BUSHNELL, HORACE (1802–1876)
American religious writer who became an important link between the orthodox Christianity of the Puritans and the liberal Christianity of twentieth-century modernism

Bushnell, a Connecticut resident all his life, attended Yale College and studied law before a conversion experience led him to enter Yale Divinity School. He accepted the pastorate of the North Congregational church in Hartford in 1833, where he remained until ill health forced him to retire in 1859. Bushnell was well liked by his church members, who left their local "consociation" when it began to question their pastor's orthodoxy.

Bushnell's place in American theological history is marked out by his four most controversial books. *Christian Nurture* (1847) took a backhanded slap at revivalism by arguing for long-range education as the surest foundation for Christian experience. His "Dissertation on Language" (prefaced to *God in Christ*, 1849) contended that language about God and salvation can at best be only an approximate and symbolic representation of reality. *Nature and the Supernatural* (1858) suggested that all things, natural and supernatural, shared a common spiritual character. *Vicarious Sacrifice* (1866) suggested that Christ's death was intended primarily as an example for religious people to imitate. Bushnell's guides in theology were the German theologian Friedrich Schleiermacher and the English poet Samuel Taylor Coleridge, both of whom inspired him to take a more "romantic" view of God, man, and the world. Bushnell's extensive moderation of traditional Calvinism met the desires of many of his contemporaries for a new religious orientation. They were optimistic about the benefits of American democracy, skeptical about the "vulgarity" of revivalism, anxious for a more refined life, and eager to be intellectually respectable in the eyes of Europeans. Bushnell did not completely forsake his theological heritage, but he made the way easier for others who later would.
M. A. NOLL

BUTLER, JOSEPH (1692–1752)
English philospher and Anglican bishop

Born at Wantage in Berkshire and intended by his father for the Presbyterian ministry, Butler attended a Dissenting Academy at Tewkesbury, Gloucestershire, run by Samuel Jones. He decided to become a member of the Church of England and went to Oriel College, Oxford, in 1715, after which he was ordained. Through the help of friends he was able to gain preferment (advancement in ecclesiastical rank—at that time usually open only to the aristocracy). In 1726 he published his *Fifteen Sermons Preached at the Rolls Chapel.* The *Sermons* were hardly noticed at first but later became known as one of the best introductions to moral philosophy.

In 1736 Butler published his *Analogy of Religion,* a work that not only established his reputation among his contemporaries but has given him a respected place among English theologians. The *Analogy* is one of the masterpieces of Christian apologetics notable for its comprehensive non-polemical review of the principal arguments in defense of Christian belief. Its arguments are aimed particularly against the deism prevalent in the eighteenth century. Butler's *Fifteen Sermons* and *Analogy* are still read by twentieth-century students of philosophy and the history of Western thought.

In 1738 Butler was appointed to the bishopric of Bristol and, because those were days when a person could hold more than one church appointment, he was made dean of St. Paul's, London, in 1740. In 1750 he was appointed bishop of Durham. The most notable event during the short tenure of his Durham bishopric was publication of his *Charge on the Use and Importance of External Religion* to the clergy of the diocese. The *Charge* reflects a true concern for spiritual religion. P. TOON

BUXTEHUDE, DIETRICH (1637–1707)
Danish composer and organist

Next to Johann Sebastian Bach, Buxtehude was perhaps the most imaginative church musician of the baroque era. Born in Helsingborg, he was the son of a church organist, with whom he did his early

study. Few other facts are known of his formative years.

In 1668 Buxtehude became the organist at St. Mary's Church in Lubeck (Germany), a prestigious and lucrative position. The quality of his playing attracted much attention. There is even a story that the young J. S. Bach walked two hundred miles to hear him play the organ.

Buxtehude's talents took him beyond his regular duties at Lubeck. He put together large-scale musical performances that were called *Abendmusiken,* or "evening music" concerts. They took place annually on the five Sundays preceding Christmas between four and five o'clock, after the afternoon church service. These concerts, which combined organ performances with choral works accompanied by orchestra, added to Buxtehude's already considerable influence throughout northern Europe. St. Mary's attracted many musicians who sought the master's advice and insight.

Although Buxtehude's music is not difficult to perform, it is richly individual and full of variety, surprise, and vigor. His organ works consist primarily of preludes, toccatas, and chorale preludes. The preludes and toccatas are cast in several contrasting sections and generally end with a fugue. Other than that, the sections follow no set pattern and vary in length. Exhibiting Buxtehude's ranging imagination, they are pleasantly unpredictable, less systematic than the works of his contemporaries. Buxtehude's often-angular harmonies, free, fantasialike passage work, and rhythmic subtleties make his music some of the most delightful organ literature. His chorale preludes, likewise, although simpler and generally less extroverted than the preludes and toccatas, exhibit the same freedom. The chorale tune may be subject to several treatments in the same composition; the accompanying texture may be strict, then free; full, then sparse.

Buxtehude's vocal works consist primarily of church cantatas. Over a hundred are still in existence, and certainly many more were composed. They are simple and less prone to experiment than his organ works.

The texts are derived from the Bible, the hymnbook, or sacred verse. The musical settings are of three types: for solo voice, for choir with or without accompaniment, and for choir and soloists. They are models of brevity and excellent for use in worship.

Both the cantatas and the organ works continue to be popular. The organ compositions form part of every trained organist's repertoire and are equally at home in concert or worship. Even churches with relatively modest choral resources are capable of performing many of Buxtehude's cantatas. H. M. BEST

BYRD, WILLIAM (1543–1623)

English composer; often regarded as the greatest composer of the Elizabethan era

Byrd's boyhood days were spent under the musical tutorship of Thomas Tallis, also an exceptional musician. Byrd's professional duties began in 1563 when he was appointed organist of Lincoln Cathedral. In 1572 he moved to London to take a position in the Chapel Royal where he shared duties with Thomas Tallis. In 1575 Elizabeth I granted Byrd and Tallis a joint monopoly for the printing, publishing, and sale of music for all of England.

Byrd was a Catholic whose loyalty to the government never wavered. The character of Reformation England was such that, during the years between Edward VI and Elizabeth I, musicians were in a position to compose for both the Roman and Anglican rites. Byrd thus composed five *Services* and nearly sixty anthems for Anglican use, plus three settings of the Mass as well as two books of *Gradualia*. He composed works for virtually every musical medium then in use. His vocal music, however, was of greatest importance to the church.

In such compositions as *Ego sum panis vivus* (I am the living bread), *Ave verum* (Christ rising again), and *Non vos relinquam* (I will not leave you comfortless), one sees what Byrd meant in his dedication of the *Gradualia*: "I have found there is such a power hidden away and stored up in those words [of Scripture] that—I know not how—to one who meditates on divine things, pondering them with detailed concentration, all the most fitting melodies come as it were of themselves, and freely present themselves when the mind is alert and eager." H. M. BEST

CABLE, MILDRED (1877–1952)

Missionary in central Asia; with Evangeline and Francesca French, coauthor of several books related to their missionary work and to spiritual growth

Mildred Cable was born in Surrey (England) and qualified as a chemist before going to China as a worker with the China Inland Mission. She arrived there just after the missionary who had influenced her toward that work was murdered in the Boxer Rebellion of 1900. Cable joined Eva French, who had been with CIM since 1893. Then for almost twenty-two years she also worked with Francesca French, who arrived in 1909. At Hwochou the three women developed a model girls' school graded from kindergarten to a teachers' training department.

In 1923 the women set out to be pioneer missionaries among the polyglot peoples of central Asia. They located in the region of the Gobi Desert (Mongolia), a largely unknown territory which they crossed no fewer than five times. For fifteen years they led "a free, untrammeled missionary life," itinerating among the Gobi oases, "gossiping the gospel," observing the customs of the area, studying its languages, and making observations later incorporated into two books, *Through Jade Gate and Central Asia*

(with Eva French, 1927) and *The Gobi Desert* (1942).

Cable's work with the China Inland Mission ended in 1936 when the women were forced to leave the Gobi because of worsening political conditions. In England, Cable continued to write extensively, producing with Francesca French such books as *The Book that Demands a Verdict, The Story of Topsy, Something Happened, The Making of a Pioneer, Towards Spiritual Maturity,* and *Ambassadors for Christ.* Cable worked energetically for the British and Foreign Bible Society, and her brief account of that Society's work (*Why Not for the World?*) was published posthumously in 1952.

D. R. MITCHELL

CABRINI, FRANCES-XAVIER (1850–1917)

Founder of the Missionary Sisters of the Sacred Heart; the first American citizen to be canonized

Born in Lombardy, Italy, Cabrini became a teacher, but her aim was to be a missionary in China. This was ruled out because of her poor health, and in 1880, three years after taking vows, she founded her own women's missionary society with the motto, "I can do all things through Christ who strengthens me" (Phil. 4:13). In 1889 Pope Leo XIII directed her not east, but west, to work among the neglected immigrants who were pouring into New York. Concerned with nursing, child care, education and other welfare work, she traveled widely and established sixty-seven houses—one for every year of her life. Mother Cabrini was canonized in 1946 (an unusually speedy process) and is regarded as the patron saint of emigrants and the displaced. J. D. DOUGLAS

CADBURY, HENRY JOEL (1883–1974)
American New Testament scholar and educator

A "birthright" Quaker (that is, recognized as a Quaker because his father was), Cadbury was born in Philadelphia and educated at Haverford College and Harvard University. In 1910 he became professor of biblical history at Haverford. In 1919 he was made professor of biblical literature at Harvard, and from 1926 to 1934 he taught at Bryn Mawr College (Philadelphia). He returned to Harvard in 1934 as Hollis professor of divinity, where he remained until his retirement in 1954.

Cadbury's principal area of New Testament research centered in Luke's Gospel and the book of Acts. He published *The Making of Luke-Acts* in 1928 and *The Book of Acts in History* in 1955. He was a member of the committee which produced the Revised Standard Version of the New Testament in 1946.

Cadbury was one of the founders of the American Friends Service Committee in 1917. He served as its chairman for two periods (1928–1934 and 1944–1960). In 1947, during his second term of office, the American committee shared the Nobel peace prize with its British counterpart. N. V. HOPE

CAECILIAN (died c. 340)
Bishop of Carthage from c. 311 until his death

Although Caecilian had been chosen bishop by the populace and clergy of Car-

thage, he was opposed by two men who had wanted the post themselves and by a woman whom he had rebuked for venerating false relics. The three persuaded Bishop Secundus of Tigisi to hold a meeting at which Caecilian was deposed on the grounds that he had been consecrated by Felix of Aptunga, a "traditor" (a bishop who had allegedly "betrayed the Scriptures" during the recent Roman persecution). Emperor Constantine I, when asked to decide the case, had the bishop of Rome hold an inquiry, which in 313 declared in favor of Caecilian. The same decision was reached in an investigation held the next year at Arles, and in one held in Constantine's presence at Milan in 315–316. Those who had opposed Caecilian formed a separatist group and elected their own bishop, Majorinas. His successor was Donatus. The Donatist church spread rapidly, especially in Africa.

Caecilian was the only African bishop at the council of Nicaea in 325, and a Latin version of the Nicene Creed goes under his name. C. HICKS

CAEDMON (died c. 678)
Earliest known Christian Anglo-Saxon poet

Caedmon was an illiterate herdsman who, after an evening of revelry, had a vision in which he was commanded to write verse. In the vision, he recited "verses which he had never heard." To his surprise he found that on the next day he could repeat the verses, and to them he added others. His employer, upon hearing of this, introduced him to Hilda, the local abbess of Whitby, who tested his gift by reading aloud a portion of the Bible which he was then asked to put into verse. He did so by the following morning. As a result he was employed in the abbey and continued until his death to render biblical stories and events of the life of Christ into poetry.

Our knowledge of Caedmon is gained from the *Ecclesiastical History* of Bede, an early English historian. Of all his poetry, only what is commonly called "Caedmon's Hymn" survives. It is written in a four-stressed alliterative meter and is similar in style to other Anglo-Saxon poetry. Bede wrote a moving account of Caedmon's death after interviewing others in the monastery where Caedmon served. P. TOON

CAIRD, JOHN (1820–1898)
Scottish theologian and philosopher

John Caird was born in industrial Greenock, graduated from Glasgow University, and became a leading advocate of the philosophical school that revived the teachings of German philosopher Hegel (1770–1831). Caird was ordained in the Church of Scotland; served parishes in Ayrshire, Edinburgh, Perthshire, and Glasgow (1845–1862); was an eloquent preacher; and published sermons which had a wide circulation. In 1862 he became professor of divinity at Glasgow and in 1873 was appointed principal (head) of the university. He believed that the existence of Infinite Thought (God), which is the reality of all things, is confirmed by the limitations of finite thought. Among Caird's chief writings were *An Introduction to the Philosophy of Religion* (1880) and *The Fundamental Ideas of Christianity* (2 volumes, 1899). J. D. DOUGLAS

CAJETAN, TOMMASO DE VIO
(c. 1469–1534)
High-ranking Italian official of the Roman Catholic Church during the Reformation era

As the pope's legate (special envoy), Cajetan was the most powerful church official in Germany. He was also a cardinal and vicar general of the influential Dominican order.

Cajetan is known as the most learned of the Roman Catholic dignitaries sent to silence Martin Luther in the early days of the young monk's protest. Cajetan's credentials and theological expertise qualified him to confront Luther. In 1518 Cajetan summoned Luther to the southern German city of Augsburg and ordered him to recant his heresies. Despite Cajetan's persuasive arguments and threats of imprisonment (or worse), Luther refused. Luther had become such a national hero that it would have been politically dangerous for Cajetan to take punitive action.

Cajetan was born at Gaeta (from which the word Cajetan is derived), a small Italian town some fifty miles north of Naples. His name at birth was Giacomo de Vio, but he changed it to Tommaso (Thomas) de Vio in honor of his hero, Thomas Aquinas. Cajetan is recognized as one of the most competent interpreters of Aquinas. He published more than one hundred works, most of them expounding Thomistic theology. Cajetan was also the inspiration and architect of the Dominican missionary effort in America.
B. G. ARMSTRONG

CAJETAN OF THIENE (1480–1547)
Italian church reformer

Born near Vicenza into a noble family, Cajetan studied law in Padua and in 1505 became a protonotary apostolic (papal clerk) to Pope Julius II. Cajetan was ordained in 1516 and joined the Oratory of Divine Love in Rome. Concerned about piety and charity, he founded a hospital for incurables (1522). With three companions (one was Pietra Caraffa, who later became Pope Paul IV), Cajetan founded in Rome a group later called the Theatine order. Its members were priests who took religious vows but lived in the secular world and worked for a Christian reform of society. The Theatines were important in the Counter-Reformation. In 1533 Cajetan was made superior of a new foundation in Naples. He opposed the teachings of Juan Valdez and Bernardino Ochino. Cajetan was beatified in 1629 by Pope Urban VIII and canonized in 1671 by Pope Clement X.
L. GOLDBERG

CALLISTUS I (150–c. 222)
Bishop of Rome, 217–222

According to Hippolytus, Callistus was a slave in early life. Hippolytus also depicted Callistus's early years as a series of escapes after serious wrongdoing. But in 198, Zephyrinus, when he became bishop of Rome, thought enough of Callistus to make him a responsible archdeacon. And Callistus was himself elected bishop of Rome on Zephyrinus's death in 217.

Callistus's five years as pontiff were filled with controversy and criticism. First, much trouble came from varied schisms, two of the largest led by Tertullian and Hippolytus, the early Church's most famous separatists. Callistus opposed the schismatics vigorously. And since works by Tertullian and Hippolytus provide the main early information, Callistus's actions on many matters cannot be judged precisely. There were basic complaints that Callistus indulged the modalist heresy. But since he condemned Sabellius, a prominent modalist, this charge seems worthless. Lax discipline toward erring clergy and laity was also a frequent accusation. Three outstanding complaints here were: refusal by Callistus to depose some bishops confessing to mortal sin; failure to demand public penance from converted heretics; and acceptance of excommunicants upon return from a schismatic sect. Yet Callistus's orthodoxy appears little marred by such actions since later all were viewed as not inappropriate.

Many complaints concerned decisions by Callistus on marriage or sexual wrongdoing. Much criticism arose around his reinstatement of repentant adulterers and fornicators to church membership. There were objections also to his consent to marriage among lower clergy, and his agreement that widowed clergy, even bishops, could remain in office after a second marriage. But probably the greatest stir came on a more basic issue: Callistus's consent to church marriage which crossed the empire's class boundaries. In late ancient times, Roman law distinguished between six forms of wedlock, these aligned largely with long-established social divisions. Any marriage violating these divisions was at least socially offensive if not legally punishable. In Callistus's view, many of these barriers were indefensible within the church. Particularly upsetting was Callistus's agreement that Roman noblewomen might marry below their class, even including former slaves. Yet finally, in subsequent centuries, the church's efforts to establish unique

Christian marital practices were very successful, both among believers and in western Europe at large. These customs included Callistus's innovation that consenting, unimpedimented couples might enter Christian wedlock, however mixed in class.

Nothing of Callistus's own writings still exists, except some probably unauthentic statements on penance. The bulk of early information about Callistus comes from works by Tertullian and Hippolytus.

K. J. Bryer

CALLISTUS II (died 1124)
Pope, 1119–1124

Son of William of Burgundy, Callistus's family name was Guido of Burgundy. Nothing is known about his life before his appointment as archbishop of Vienne, France, in 1088. During the years 1106 to 1118, he was Paschal II's legate in France and strongly opposed the concessions Henry IV, Holy Roman Emperor, forced on Pope Paschal regarding investiture rights.

Callistus's election as pope took place at Cluny, France, because Henry IV had installed his own bishop in Rome. There was hope that Callistus, related to most of Europe's royal houses, could bring Henry to a settlement on the investiture discord. But seeing nothing conciliatory in Henry, Callistus excommunicated the emperor at the Synod of Reims. Callistus then made his way to Rome, where, with some Italian nobles' help, he quickly evicted Gregory VIII, Henry's false pope. Realizing Callistus's resoluteness, the German princes began to press Henry for an agreement with the papacy, whereupon the emperor consented to a meeting with Callistus at Worms. This concluded in the Concordat of Worms, 1122, which did give the Church mainly favorable terms on investiture, as well as on other issues. Callistus immediately convoked Lateran Council I (1123), the very first held in western Christendom. Amid decrees on numerous disciplinary matters, Lateran I's pronouncements confirmed the investiture decisions of the Concordat of Worms and formed the main turning point on the centuries of division. Monarchial election of bishops declined in Europe after the council. Lateran I's other disciplinary canons strove to capture the era's burgeoning Church reform ideas.

Callistus's last years were occupied with maintaining political order in Rome and papal territories and effecting reform and settling disputes, especially in France. Callistus's sagacity and strength make him one of the medieval papacy's most admirable figures, despite the fact that he was seemingly inundated by monumental disputes. Callistus gave weighty support to England's archbishopric of York and its independence, to beautification of the city of Rome, and to protecting Rome's community of Jews.

Some of the "Saints' Lives" written by Callistus II, with many of the great pope's letters, are reproduced in Migne's *Patrologia Latina*. K. J. BRYER

CALLISTUS III (1378–1458)
Pope, 1455–1458

Born Alfonso de Borgia, Callistus began life as son of a prominent Valencian family. His early years centered in studies and teaching at the University of Lerida, Spain, where his piety and legal acumen stood out. In 1429, on helping Alfonso V, king of Aragon, reconcile with Pope Eugenius IV, Callistus was appointed bishop of Valencia. That same year he was influential also in persuading the Great Schism's last antipope, Clement VIII, to submit to Martin V, the now accepted bishop of Rome. This aided the ascendancy of decisions by the Council of Constance (1417). In 1444 Callistus received a cardinal's hat, and as an elderly compromise choice, he became pope in 1455.

Callistus's three years as pope were spent relieving Constantinople from its capture by the Turks. Still the heart of Eastern Christianity, Constantinople became a deep concern for Western churchmen after its fall to Islam in 1453. Callistus contacted many rulers, but, in short, Europe's Western monarchs were too preoccupied with local conflicts to campaign effectively in the East. In 1456 Western forces did lift the siege of

Belgrade, and the Turkish fleet also suffered defeat at Metelino in 1457. But military designs for recapturing Eastern Christian territories had little realistic prospect. Callistus even sometimes added to the West's troubles. Among other such incidents, he claimed Naples for the papacy, thus rejecting Ferdinand, son of Alfonso V, the port city's longstanding ruler.

Despite general competence, Callistus's papacy involved itself in wide-scale nepotism, even for his appointments. Various complaints about avarice seemed justified when the papacy revealed a large sum of money on hand. Nonetheless, it was Callistus who corrected one of the Church hierarchy's most famous errors. Thus, twenty-five years after her death at the stake, the papacy annulled all charges against Joan of Arc and declared her innocence. Callistus's concentration on the Turks also deterred his tenure from much involvement with his era's literary and intellectual revivals. On the other hand, he did acquire numerous art objects and other valuable items for the Vatican Library and other repositories.

Original materials about Callistus III are listed in Pastor's *History of the Popes*. K. J. BRYER

CALVERT, CECILIUS (c. 1605–1675)
Second Lord Baltimore; son of George Calvert

Following the death of his father in 1632, Cecilius Calvert inherited the charter rights to more than 10 million acres along the shores of the northern half of Chesapeake Bay. The colony that resulted was named Maryland for Charles I's Catholic queen, Mary Henrietta of France.

Cecilius Calvert wanted to use this land grant to provide a haven for English Catholics and to increase the family fortune through rents of the proprietary lands. In spite of Calvert's Catholicism, however, many Protestants were included among the original settlers. There are several reasons for this. English Catholics were reluctant to leave England at a time when Charles I was looking more favorably on their religion. Cecilius Calvert also wanted to reassure

Protestants in England that Maryland would not become a hostile Catholic enclave. After the arrival of the first settlers in 1634, Catholic missionaries began work among the native Indians. Most of the other settlers turned to the raising of tobacco. In 1649 Calvert issued the famous "Act Concerning Religion" for Maryland. It provided freedom of belief for all who called themselves Christian, whether Catholic, Anglican, or Puritan. It was an advanced step for that day. Yet it was proposed more to protect Catholic interests against Puritan parliament in England than out of theoretical commitment to freedom of religion. In 1691, after the death of Cecilius Calvert, the original Maryland charter was stripped from the Calvert family, only to be returned in 1715 when the fourth Lord Baltimore entered the Church of England. Maryland remained a proprietary possession of the Calverts until the American Revolution. M. A. NOLL

CALVERT, GEORGE (c. 1580–1632)
Bearer of the title "Lord Baltimore";
Secretary of State under James I of the
United Kingdom

Upon the accession of Charles I in 1625, Calvert was forced to resign his post. He had converted to Catholicism earlier the same year and was unable to swear allegiance to the Protestant Church of England. Charles I was, however, eager to repay George Calvert for the loyal service that he had rendered to his father and to himself. He fulfilled this desire by giving the family a large proprietary grant in Newfoundland. Because of the climate, George Calvert's business ventures failed, so he appealed to Charles I for land farther south. The king granted him the proprietorship of Maryland in 1632, but Calvert died before the charter was signed, so it was issued to his son Cecilius. M. A. NOLL

CALVERT, JAMES (1813–1892)
English Wesleyan missionary in the Fiji
Islands and South Africa

Trained at Hoxton Theological Institution, Calvert married Mary Fowler (1838) and served in Fiji at Lakemba and Viwa (1838–1855). He trained Fijian converts in printing and bookbinding. In England he supervised publication of Hazelwood's Fijian Old Testament, revised the New Testament translation, edited John Hunt's *Letters on Entire Sanctification*, and wrote the mission history volume of *Fiji and the Fijians* (1860). Having earned a reputation as an administrator and arbitrator with chiefs and cannibals by the 1850s, Calvert was reappointed to Fiji (at Levuka). He revised the Old Testament translation, was retired in 1865, and then worked for the British and Foreign Bible Society and updated his mission history (1870). He came back from retirement for service (1872–1881) in Transvaal and Natal (South Africa). After returning to England, Calvert revised the Fijian New Testament again (1885).
A. R. TIPPETT

CALVIN, JOHN (1509–1564)
French Protestant reformer; generally
regarded as second in importance only to
Martin Luther as a key figure in the
Protestant Reformation

Calvin's *Institutes of the Christian Religion*, regarded by historian Will Durant as among the world's ten most influential works, gave birth to a distinctive "Reformed" theology, sometimes named after Calvin himself.

Calvin has also been called "the organizer of Protestantism" because in his pastoral work of organizing evangelical churches in Strassburg and Geneva, he developed an adaptable model of church government. The cultural impact of that "presbyterian" model has extended beyond church polity to influence modern democratic political theory. In the sixteenth century new social institutions emerged to replace the deteriorating ones that had once held medieval civilization together; many of the new institutions were influenced by Calvin's model.

EARLY LIFE
Calvin was born in northwestern France, twenty-five years after the birth of Martin Luther. His actual name, Jean Cauvin, became

"Calvin" years later when as a scholar he adopted the Latin form (Calvinus). His birthplace, Noyon, was an old and important center of the Roman Catholic Church in northern Europe. A bishop resided there; and the economic, political, and social life of the city revolved largely around the cathedral. From a middle-class status Calvin's father, Gerard, after serving the church in various offices including notary public, had risen to become the bishop's secretary. As a result, young Calvin was closely tied to church affairs from the beginning. He was brought up with children of the aristocracy, a background that made him a much more refined reformer than the notoriously earthy Luther.

To enable his son to advance to a position of ecclesiastical importance, Calvin's father saw to it that he received the best possible education. At age fourteen Calvin was enrolled in the University of Paris, the intellectual center of western Europe. There he eventually attended the College de Montaigu, the same institution Erasmus had attended (and hated) some thirty years earlier. Although Calvin pursued a similar career in theology, for several reasons his life took an unexpected turn. First, the new learning of the Renaissance (humanism) was waging a successful battle against scholasticism, the old Catholic theology of the late Middle Ages. Calvin encountered the new learning among the students and was powerfully attracted to it. Second, a strong movement for reform in the church, led by Jacques Lefevre d'Etaples (1455–1536), had been flourishing in Paris not far from the university. Calvin became a close friend of some of Lefevre's disciples. Third, Luther's writings and ideas had circulated in Paris for some time, causing a moderate stir; Calvin undoubtedly became familiar with them during his student years. Finally, Calvin's father had a falling-out with the church officials in Noyon, including the bishop. Thus in 1528, just as Calvin had completed his master of arts degree, his father sent word for him to leave theology and study law. Dutifully, the son migrated to Orleans, where France's best law faculty was located.

Calvin threw himself into his law studies, winning acclaim for his mastery of the material. He often taught classes for absent professors. After about three years of study at Orleans, Bourges, and Paris, he had earned a doctorate in law and his law license. Along the way he had learned Greek and had immersed himself in the classical studies, which were of great interest to the contemporary humanists. He associated closely with a group of students at odds with the teachings and practices of Roman Catholicism. When his father's death in 1531 left Calvin free to choose the career he favored, he did not hesitate. Excited and challenged by the new learning, he moved to Paris to pursue a scholarly life. Had he not been converted to Protestantism, he would undoubtedly have lived out his days in Paris as a leading Renaissance scholar.

Little is known about Calvin's conversion except that it occurred between 1532 and early 1534, when his first religious work was published. When Nicholas Cop was elected rector of the University of Paris in 1533, his rectoral address strongly advocated reform along Lutheran lines. Whether Calvin actually contributed to the address, as is often supposed, is impossible to prove. His association was close enough, however, that when the rector was accused of heresy, they both fled the city.

Calvin returned shortly afterward, but only briefly, spending the next three years traveling widely in other parts of France, in Switzerland, and in Italy. In the spring of 1534 he returned to Noyon to resign his ecclesiastical benefices (regular income the church had granted him which had supported him during his studies). No longer able to draw on that stipend with a clear conscience, Calvin burned his bridges to Roman Catholicism permanently behind him with his resignation.

When the French king, Francis I (reigned 1515–1547), decided that persecution was the solution to the Protestant problem, Calvin realized it was no longer safe to live in Paris or anywhere else in France. For the rest of his life, therefore, he was a refugee.

HIS CAREER AS REFORMER

In Basel (Switzerland) early in 1536 Calvin published the first edition of his *Institutes of the Christian Religion*. When he learned that Francis I's objection to Protestants was on the basis that they rejected all civil authority, as some Anabaptist groups in fact did, Calvin rushed the *Institutes* to press with a dedication and preface to the king, acknowledging the king's authority and laying out the articles of Reformed faith in clear fashion. The work, which underwent several revisions before its final exhaustive edition in 1559, was without question one of the most influential handbooks on theology ever written. Its publication marked Calvin as a leading mind of Protestantism and kept him from pursuing the quiet scholarly life he had hoped for. As he described it, "God thrust me into the fray."

Traveling to Strassburg (a free city between northern France and Germany) in 1536, Calvin stopped for the night in Geneva, a small city at the eastern end of the Alps. With the help of its Swiss neighbors, Geneva had recently declared its political independence from the Holy Roman Empire. Only two months earlier under the prodding of fiery reformer William Farel (1489–1565), it had declared allegiance to Protestantism. Farel, who had been working in Geneva for nearly three years, somehow learned of Calvin's presence in the city and asked him to join in the task of leading the Genevan church. Calvin declined, explaining that he desired only to find a quiet refuge for study. But Farel, with characteristic zeal, thundered that Calvin's refusal to help in Geneva would bring God's condemnation down upon his head. Obviously shaken, Calvin accepted Farel's invitation as God's call. He was twenty-eight at the time. The rest of his life was given mostly to the work of reform in Geneva.

Calvin immediately set to work reorganizing the church and its worship. Under Catholicism the Genevan church had observed Communion only two or three times a year; Calvin, who favored a weekly celebration, recommended a monthly observance as an interim compromise. Calvin's emphasis on church discipline grew directly out of his high regard for the Lord's Supper. To oversee that the sacrament was taken worthily Calvin instituted a church board (the Genevan Consistory) which insured that all communicants (those participating in Communion) truly belonged to the "body of Christ" and also were practicing what they professed. Calvin also introduced congregational singing into the church—"to incite the people to prayer and to praise God."

Calvin spent the following three years (1538–1541) in Strassburg, enjoying his long-sought period of peaceful study. There he associated closely with Martin Bucer (1491–1551), whose ideas, particularly on predestination, the Lord's Supper, and church organization, markedly influenced Calvin's own. In Strassburg Calvin also pastored a congregation of Protestant refugees from France, organizing its church government after what he believed to be the New Testament pattern and compiling a liturgy and popular psalm book. He also participated as a representative of Strassburg in the religious colloquies at Worms and Regensberg (both in Germany) between Roman Catholics and Evangelicals (Protestants). He succeeded, in fact, in converting to the Reformed faith at least two Anabaptist observers. One of them, Jean Stordeur of Liege, died in 1539, and Calvin, who had been urged by his colleagues to find a wife, married Stordeur's widow, Idelette de Bure. She brought him much consolation and happiness. "During her life she was the faithful helper of my ministry," Calvin wrote at her death ten years later. "Truly mine is no common grief. I have been bereaved of the best friend of my life."

In the meantime, the Roman Catholic Church, mindful of Calvin and Farel's expulsion from Geneva, judged that with some diplomatic care the city might be persuaded to return to Catholicism. Early in 1539 the city council received a letter urging such a move from Cardinal Jacopo Sadoleto, an Italian archbishop with a reputation for favoring moderate reform. The council was at a loss to find anyone in Geneva sufficiently competent to respond to the letter. They forwarded it to Calvin in Strassburg, whose reply to the cardinal still stands as a brilliant explanation and justification of the Protestant Reformation.

Through a remarkable series of coincidences, the four principal Genevan leaders who had secured Calvin's exile were disgraced—all in unrelated incidents—and in 1541 the city implored him to return. The prospect horrified Calvin, who regarded Geneva as "that cross on which I had to perish daily a thousand times over." Nevertheless, at Farel's insistence, he reluctantly returned.

The city council, now much more attentive to Calvin's proposals, approved his reforms with few emendations. He began a long, unbroken tenure as Geneva's principal pastor. Though constantly embroiled in controversy and bitterly opposed by strong political factions, Calvin pursued his tasks of pastoring and reform with determination.

In addition to traditional areas of Christian works, such as arranging for the care of the elderly and poor, many of Calvin's reforms reached into new areas: foreign affairs, law, economics, trade, and public policy. Calvin exemplified his own emphasis that in a Christian commonwealth every aspect of culture must be brought under Christ's lordship and treated as an area of Christian stewardship. Calvin worked on the recodification of Geneva's constitution and law, mollifying the severity of many of the city's statutes and making them more humane. In addition, he helped negotiate treaties, was largely responsible for establishing the city's prosperous trade in cloth and velvet, and even proposed sanitary regulations and a sewage system that made Geneva one of the cleanest cities in Europe. Although the legal code, much of it adopted upon Calvin's recommendations, seems strict by modern standards, nonetheless it was impartially applied to small and great alike and was approved by the majority of Geneva's citizens. As a result, Geneva became a "Christian republic," which the Scottish reformer John Knox called "the most perfect school of Christ . . . since the days of the apostles." Church and state served as "separate but equal" partners.

At the outset of his return to Geneva, Calvin confessed his own past impatience and severity and his intention to correct those faults. His openness undoubtedly helped to regain for him the city's respect and admiration. When he died twenty-three years later, all Geneva turned out to honor him.

Calvin's reputation and esteem always seemed greatest among the population of Protestant refugees who flocked to the city, making Geneva the uncontested center of the Protestant movement. Missionaries fanned out from Geneva to the surrounding countries. The "Reformed Church" thus became the only Protestant group with a universal program.

CALVIN'S TEACHING AND INFLUENCE ON THEOLOGY

The Huguenot scholar Joseph Scaliger in the generation after Calvin described him as "alone among the theologians." Clearly he was the greatest theologian of his age. Yet he consistently tried to make the Scriptures, as interpreted by the Holy Spirit and experience, the source of his ideas. "Let us not," Calvin admonished, "take it into our heads either to seek out God anywhere else than in his Sacred Word, or to think anything about him that is not prompted by his Word, or to speak anything that is not taken from that Word."

In the past some have said that the sovereignty of God was Calvin's central teaching. Today many Calvin scholars argue that he made no attempt to reduce the biblical message to any one central idea, but rather appreciated and retained the biblical teachings in their complexity, affirming, for example, both human responsibility and God's sovereign control, as well as other teachings that seem inconsistent when paired.

Calvin's system does possess unity. Behind everything that he wrote is the idea suggested earlier by Augustine of Hippo (345–430) that God created human beings for fellowship with himself. Lacking that fellowship, they are miserable and disoriented. Thus Calvin began his *Institutes* by stressing that all wisdom comes from a knowledge of God and of ourselves. The God-man relationship was so basic for Calvin that he argued that in knowing God we learn of ourselves, and vice versa.

Knowledge meant much more to Calvin than intellectual exercise. Rather, theological knowledge requires a moral response by the whole human personality. The whole person, including mind and body, is engaged in the spiritual relationship. The one goal of that "knowing" experience is the worship of God in obedience and gratitude.

Calvin also emphasized that what we know about God is strictly limited to what God has revealed. He has revealed in Scripture only what is profitable for human beings to know for a covenant relationship with him. Consequently, Calvin taught that Christians should not engage primarily in theological speculation but in moral edification. Knowledge that does not lead to piety is off course. Calvin followed his own advice in explaining the biblical doctrine of predestination, giving no priority to the rules of logic or philosophic discourse. The "why" of God's actions has not been revealed but remains a secret bound up in his inscrutable counsel. The Christian must simply affirm with the Bible that God is intimately connected with the universe and that he "accomplishes all things according to the counsel of his will" (Eph. 1:11, RSV).

Calvin hoped that his main contribution would be guidance for the Christian's spiritual pilgrimage. His theology was intended to be a worship aid. Yet he was also convinced that the worship of God must properly penetrate every aspect of societal life. To do that effectively the church must commit itself to a maximum use of the gifts God has given it for service in every area of life.

CALVIN'S TEACHING AND INFLUENCE ON EDUCATION AND GOVERNMENT

In addition to theology, two areas in which Calvin made major contributions are education and church government. The excellence of his own educational training is attested by the fact that his writings have had a lasting effect on the French language. He is considered one of the creators of mod-

ern French prose. Perhaps more important, he encouraged the development of universal education. Calvin was convinced that for every person to be adequately equipped to "rightly divide" God's Word, he or she had to be educated in language and the humanities. To that end he founded an academy for Geneva's children, believing that all education must be fundamentally religious. The city's university grew out of the academy, linked to evangelical preaching and offering an education comparable to the finest in Europe. Some have called the University of Geneva Calvin's "crowning achievement."

Calvin's ideas on church government, which have had a powerful effect on political theory in the West, are regarded by other scholars as his greatest contribution. The representative form of government he developed was organized so that basic decisions are made at the local level, monitored through a system of ascending representative bodies, culminating in a national "general assembly" with final authority. At each level, power is shared with the laity, not controlled exclusively by the clergy or administrative officials. In emergencies the local church can function without meetings of the upper-level bodies; in the midst of a hostile culture the church cannot be destroyed by silencing the minister. As a result, the Calvinist church was able to survive, even flourish, under adverse conditions. It experienced severe persecution in Holland under Spanish occupation, in France (except during brief periods of toleration), in England under Queen Mary, in Scotland, in Hungary, and elsewhere.

CALVIN AND THE HISTORIANS

In spite of his powerful influence on European affairs, Calvin has rarely been treated sympathetically by historians. Except among his followers, he has been portrayed as a cold, unfeeling, and calculating man, who imposed his stern will on a helpless or cowed people. He is seen as the proponent of an austere and joyless religion of fear and constraint, and of a vengeful and arbitrary omnipotent God who treats human beings as puppets, demanding of them servile obedience, yet severely punishing the slightest deviation from his strict moral code. Such a legalistic and negativistic religion, popularly attributed to Calvin, is a ridiculous caricature that recent scholarship has only begun to correct.

Calvin regarded himself as primarily a pastor and theologian. Spending almost all of his productive years as a refugee and a foreigner in the Genevan republic, he was accorded citizenship only five years before his death, and then only after he appeared to be dying. Because his opinions were highly regarded, his political views were influential, but he never held political office. His cultural impact was not that of an autocrat, but of a persuasive thinker who sought to apply biblical principles to every area of life.

Far from ruling as a religious despot, Calvin was continually frustrated by the Genevan city council's unwillingness to implement many of the social reforms he advocated. The city, in fact, was remarkably heterogeneous, by no means unanimously Protestant in partisanship. Before Calvin arrived, Geneva had the reputation of being one of Europe's most immoral communities; throughout his career a strong libertine and antinomian faction in the city resisted his reform efforts.

In 1553, at a point in his career when that resistance was at its keenest, events occurring in connection with a certain Michael Servetus seem to have secured for Calvin a permanent bad reputation. Throughout the intellectual centers of Europe, Servetus, a Spanish physician and theologian, was infamous for his anti-Trinitarian polemics. A Catholic, he had already been condemned by the Catholic Inquisition but had escaped. When Servetus appeared in Geneva, he was recognized, arrested at Calvin's instigation, found guilty, and burned at the stake with the unanimous approval of the other Protestant Swiss cities. Despite the fact that religious toleration did not become a popular conviction until at least two hundred years later, and that what was done in Geneva was done virtually everywhere else in Europe on a much grander scale, Calvin's part in that execution has evidently served to confirm his image as an intolerant authoritarian.

Calvin was never a popular hero, even locally, nor did he act the hero's customary part. Lacking the charm of Luther's blustering Germanic confidence and humor, Calvin held an intensely serious view of life. Sensing a divine call to the work of God's kingdom, he approached his task with great zeal and expected the same of others. Few light-hearted moments or intimate glimpses of Calvin were recorded. He would not, even momentarily, set aside his deep conviction that, as God's creation, he was put on earth to glorify God. He deliberately avoided the limelight and the sensational in order that nothing might detract from the message of God's grace in Christ. Humility and self-denial were his principal Christian virtues. He lived modestly, had few possessions, lived in borrowed quarters, and stubbornly refused salary increases. In theology, he was completely awed by the concept that sinful human beings had been "reckoned righteous" in Christ and accounted worthy to serve the incomprehensibly holy and sovereign God of the universe. In contrast to the caricature, then, there is probably more truth to the conviction of the nineteenth-century French historian Joseph Renan (who was no Reformed enthusiast) that Calvin was "the most Christian man of his time."

B. G. ARMSTRONG

CAMERON, JOHN (c. 1579–1625)
Controversial Scottish Calvinist minister and theologian

Cameron was born and educated at Glasgow. Through the work of Scottish reformer Andrew Melville (1545–1622), Glasgow University had adopted the new learning of the Renaissance, stressing Latin and Greek and a historical approach to knowledge, in opposition to the heavy reliance on philosophy that had characterized the old approach.

Looking at biblical study and theology from the new perspective, Cameron came to believe that Protestant teaching was governed too much by philosophy and too little by the Bible. He feared that theology had become so complex that only professional theologians could understand it, and that preaching was becoming ineffectual. Therefore, first as a minister for ten years in Bordeaux (France) and then as a theology professor at the University of Saumur (1618–1620), Cameron sought to reform Calvinism further through his teachings on faith, predestination, and the extent of efficacy of Jesus' death. His most famous student was French theologian Moise Amyraut (1596–1664). Except for one year as principal of Glasgow University (1622), Cameron continued to live and write in France, where he died. B. G. ARMSTRONG

CAMERON, RICHARD (c. 1648–1680)

Leader of the Scottish Covenantors; called "the Lion of the Covenant"

Born in Falkland, Fife, Cameron first became schoolmaster and precentor (one who led the singing) under the Episcopal curate there. Upon converting to Presbyterianism he went to study theology in Holland, where he was ordained to the ministry in the Scots Kirk of Rotterdam in 1679. Later that year he returned to Scotland and gathered a group strongly opposed to King Charles II's episcopalizing of the Church of Scotland.

In 1680 Cameron and some of his followers, who became known as "Cameronians," published "The Declaration and Testimony of the True Presbyterian, Anti-prelatic, and Anti-Erastian, Persecuted Party in Scotland." That document, sometimes called the Sanquhar Declaration after its place of publication, disowned the English king and declared open warfare on him because he was "a tyrant and usurper." The next month Cameron was killed by government forces. In 1743 his movement organized itself independently of the established Church of Scotland, calling itself the Reformed Presbyterian Church. Never large in numbers, the church now (1991) has very few members in Scotland itself, but its principles are still maintained by sister churches in Northern Ireland and North America.

N. V. HOPE

CAMPBELL, ALEXANDER (1788–1866)

One of the founders of the Disciples of Christ and the Church of Christ

Born in Ballymena (Ireland), the son of Thomas Campbell, Alexander was a minister in the Secessionist church (a group separated from the Church of Scotland). The elder Campbell immigrated to Pennsylvania in 1807; delayed by smallpox, his son followed in 1809, meanwhile studying at Glasgow University. On his arrival in America, Alexander Campbell joined his father's Christian Association of Washington County, Pennsylvania, and two years later became pastor of the Brush Run church. About the same time, his father moved to Ohio.

After Alexander Campbell married, he and his wife decided to withhold "covenant baptism" from their child (believing that baptism is appropriate only upon personal profession of faith by the one being baptized); they themselves were rebaptized by immersion. Their congregation joined a Baptist association—a relationship that was terminated when Campbell appeared to be getting "soft" on Calvinistic doctrine.

A vigorous preacher and writer, Campbell wrote or edited more than sixty volumes and spread his views during preaching tours of Kentucky, Ohio, Indiana, West Virginia, Tennessee, Virginia, Canada, and Europe. His publishing efforts, which included a hymn book (1828), were so prolific that the federal government established a post office in his town and appointed him postmaster, a position he held for thirty years.

When Campbell's alliance with Regular Baptists ended in 1830, emergence of a new denomination seemed imminent. Although the Campbells were opposed to sectarianism, their emphasis on Christian unity around the twofold requirements of confession of Christ as Lord and baptism by immersion spawned a unique identity on the American religious scene. The Campbell group (called "Campbellites") joined others of like convictions, most notably the followers of Kentucky preacher Barton W. Stone. From that merger came the Disciples of

Christ, a body from which the Churches of Christ later broke away.

Campbell founded Bethany College in West Virginia in 1840. As founding editor of the *Christian Baptist* magazine (changed to the *Millennial Harbinger* in 1830), he opposed missionary societies, Sunday schools, the clergy as a special class, emotional revivalism, speculative theology, and secret societies. Alexander Campbell was tolerant of slavery and desired a return to a simpler theology, which he identified with the apostolic church. M. FACKLER

CAMPBELL, JOHN MCLEOD
(1800–1872)
Scottish theologian famous for his interpretation of the Atonement

Educated at Glasgow and Edinburgh universities, Campbell became a minister of the Church of Scotland and in 1825 took the parish of Row on the Gareloch, west of Glasgow. His views of the assurance of salvation led him eventually to propose that Christ died not merely for the elect (which was official Church of Scotland teaching), but for the whole world. That led to a heresy charge against him, a trial by the General Assembly, and his removal from the parish ministry in 1831. After a time as an itinerant minister, he became minister of a large chapel specially built for him in Glasgow. It was never his desire to found a sect.

In 1856 Campbell published *The Nature of the Atonement,* in which he attempted to view Christ's atonement in the light of the Incarnation instead of viewing it against the background of the eternal purposes of God. Campbell's book is regarded as an important contribution to studies of the Atonement. Retiring in 1859, Campbell was given the D.D. by Glasgow University (1869) and continued to write until his death. P. TOON

CAMPBELL, REGINALD JOHN
(1867–1956)
Congregational, then Anglican, clergyman

Raised in Northern Ireland, Campbell attended Christ Church, Oxford, where he was impressed with the spirituality of the Anglo-Catholic circle around Charles Gore, then at Pusey House. Campbell, however, decided to enter the Congregational ministry and in 1895 became pastor of Union Street Chapel in Brighton. In 1903 he succeeded Joseph Parker at City Temple, London. Campbell took an active part in politics, speaking for the Nonconformist interest, and became known as a public figure in London. Suspected of theological liberalism, in self-defense he wrote his *New Theology* (1907), a work that elicited many replies.

Several years later, Campbell was again attracted to Anglo-Catholicism and in 1915 resigned his charge to become an Anglican layman. After serving in World War I, Campbell was ordained and served the church of England for the rest of his life. P. TOON

CAMPBELL, THOMAS (1763–1854)
Senior founder of the Disciples of Christ

As a minister in the Secession Church, which had broken off from the Church of Scotland, Campbell tried without success to unify that movement. Then, for health reasons, he sailed in 1807 to the United States and settled in western Pennsylvania. Differences with Presbyterians and Baptists forced his group, called Disciples, to develop their own identity. His "Declaration and Address" became the basis of the Christian Association of Washington County, Pennsylvania. That group became the Disciples of Christ and flourished under the leadership of Campbell's son, Alexander. Thomas Campbell was a popular itinerant preacher who sought to unite all Christians around a simple confession of Christ as Lord and baptism by immersion. M. FACKLER

CAMPEGGIO, LORENZO (1474–1539)
Presiding judge at the court called to annul the marriage of Henry VIII and his first wife, Catherine of Aragon

Campeggio was born of a well-known family and became professor of law at the

University of Bologna. Although married and a father, he joined the ranks of the church after his wife's death. He became very influential, serving as bishop of Feltre in 1512 and nuncio to Emperor Maximilian I in 1511 and 1513. When Pope Leo X tried to stop the Turks in eastern Europe, Campeggio was sent to the court of Henry VIII to secure English support, which was not forthcoming. Nevertheless, Henry VIII highly honored Campeggio, who in 1523 became archbishop of Bologna. In 1524 he was made protector of England in the Roman Curia, and he became bishop of Salisbury in England.

In 1528 Henry VIII petitioned for the annulment of his marriage to Catherine, and Campeggio conveniently delayed his arrival in England, thinking that Henry's interest in Anne Boleyn, a maid of honor to Catherine, would disappear. Subsequently, the prelate was able neither to reconcile the royal couple nor to persuade Queen Catherine to retire to a convent. After a number of sessions, Campeggio adjourned the court, resulting in a loss of favor with Henry VIII and, in 1535, loss of his bishopric in Salisbury. Although representing Roman Catholicism at the diets of Regensburg (1524) and Augsburg (1530), Campeggio felt that any meetings with Protestants were fruitless. After representing Pope Paul III in 1538 at a council in Vincenza, Campeggio died on his return to Rome and was buried in Bologna. He had become a cardinal in 1537.

L. GOLDBERG

CAMPION, EDMUND (1540–1581)

English Jesuit theologian and missionary

A native of London, Campion studied at Oxford and became a fellow of St. John's College there in 1557. He excelled as an orator and gave the speech of welcome to Queen Elizabeth in 1566. When his religious convictions began moving away from Anglican Protestantism toward Roman Catholicism, he went via Dublin to France. In Dovai, he joined the Roman Catholic Church (1571) and was ordained as a dea-

con. He moved to Rome and in 1573 joined the Jesuit order.

After further work and travel in Europe, in 1580 Campion became a member of the Jesuit mission to England. In England he lived the life of an itinerant preacher and priest, always only a step ahead of pursuing government officials. Following publication of his pamphlet, "Decem Rationes," which contained arguments against Anglicanism (four hundred copies of which were found in Oxford), Campion was arrested. He was imprisoned in the Tower of London, examined before Queen Elizabeth, tortured in an attempt to get him to recant, and finally executed for allegedly conspiring against the Crown. He was beatified in 1886 by Pope Leo XIII and canonized in 1970 with thirty-nine others by Pope Paul VI.

P. TOON

CANDLISH, ROBERT SMITH (1806–1873)

Scottish church leader

Born in Edinburgh, Candlish received an M.A. from Glasgow University and attended Divinity Hall (1823–1826). Licensed in 1828, he became assistant minister at St. Andrew's Church, Glasgow, and later at Bonhill, Dunbartonshire. In 1834 he became minister of the prestigious St. George's Church, Edinburgh. In 1839 he joined the evangelicals in the Church of Scotland, led by Thomas Chalmers, whom he supported on the patronage issue. Eventually Candlish took part in the formation of the Free Church of Scotland (1843).

A man of great ability, Candlish maintained a position of leadership despite a rather abrupt manner. When Chalmers died in 1847 Candlish could have succeeded him as professor of divinity at New College, but he preferred to stay in St. George's Church. In 1861 he gave the Cunningham Lectures, in which he attacked F. D. Maurice's view of the fatherhood of God, thereby stirring up a controversy. The following year he became principal of New College. Candlish helped to organize the Free Church school system (later absorbed by the national system), was one of the founders of the Evangelical Alliance (1845), and wrote prolifically in the field of theology and its application. Among his better-known works are *The Atonement: Its Reality, Completeness and Extent* (1861); *The Fatherhood of God* (1865); and *The First Epistle of John Expounded in a Series of Lectures* (1866). W. S. REID

CANISIUS, PETER (1521–1597)
Roman Catholic educator and writer

Canisius was born in Nijmegen (Netherlands) to a prominent local family. He studied at Cologne and Louvain, where he was greatly influenced by Roman Catholic proponents of church reform. In 1543 Canisius became one of the first members of the Society of Jesus, the order founded by Ignatius Loyola. After serving at the Council of Trent for a short time and teaching at Messina (Sicily), he was assigned to Germany. The Catholic church in that land had been greatly weakened by the Reformation and the corruption of the clergy. Through Canisius's efforts during the next five decades, the German Catholic church was strengthened and renewed.

An important contribution of Canisius to the Roman Catholic Counter-Reformation was his composition of catechisms that simply and clearly explained the beliefs of the Roman Catholic Church. His catechisms went through hundreds of editions and were in use until the nineteenth century. Canisius was also important as an administrator (he was the first head of the Jesuits in Germany from 1556 to 1559), reformer, evangelist, educator (he founded many schools), and writer. He often took advantage of dissensions among Protestants to strengthen the Catholic position. Disagreement with other Jesuits over such issues as the propriety of charging interest on loans resulted in his being transferred to Switzerland during his last years, where he died in Freiburg. Canisius was canonized in 1925.

R. D. SHUSTER

CAPITO, WOLFGANG FABRICIUS (1478–1541)
Protestant reformer and theologian

Born in Hagenau in Alsace, the son of a blacksmith, Capito obtained degrees in medicine, law, and theology. He knew Hebrew well; he published a Hebrew grammar and a translation of the Psalms. He was professor of theology and preacher at the cathedral of Basel (1515–1520). While there he corresponded with reformers Luther and Zwingli and had numerous contacts with Dutch humanist Erasmus. Capito was then made chaplain and chancellor to the archbishop of Mainz (1519–1523). In 1523 when he moved to Strassburg, he took up reform through Matthew Zell's influence. That interest in reform caused him to be dismissed by the Roman Catholics, whereupon he became pastor of New St. Peter's.

Capito had many contacts with the Anabaptists, feeling optimistic about peaceful discussions between them and other church leaders. He was disturbed by formal rituals and espoused a piety that emphasized a believer's inward devotion. He continued with his studies, producing commentaries in Latin on the Old Testament books of Habakkuk and Hosea, also using this material in his pulpit. For a time he was influenced by such radicals as Schwenkfeld, Sattler, and Cellarius, but eventually aligned himself with Martin Bucer and his reforms. Capito spelled out church orders for conferences held at Berne (1532), Frankfurt (1535), and Worms (1540). His later writing espoused a stronger system of control of churches in fellowship. L. GOLDBERG

CAREY, WILLIAM (1761–1834)
Pioneer missionary to India; linguist and agriculturist

Although Protestant missionary activity began one hundred years before William Carey, he is called the "father of modern missions." Prior missionary movements had been concerned with home country or colonial territories; Carey's vision was to take the gospel to the entire world. Born near Northampton (England), he apprenticed to a shoemaker at age fourteen. Converted at eighteen, Carey directed his vigorous intellect to mastering Latin, Greek, Hebrew, Italian, and Dutch. He was ordained by the Particular Baptists in 1787 and began to urge that worldwide missions be undertaken. In 1792 Carey preached a sermon based on Isaiah 45:2-3, coining the now familiar aphorism: "Expect great things from God. Attempt great things for God." That message took hold, aided by Carey's eloquent missionary appeal, *An Enquiry into the Obligations of Christians to Use Means for the Conversion of the Heathen* (1792). The same year, the Particular Baptist Society for Propagating the Gospel Among the Heathen (later called the Baptist Missionary Society) was formed. Members paid dues to support the society. Carey sailed to India the following year as part of the society's first overseas contingent.

Carey was joined by William Ward and Joshua Marshman in 1799, and the three became known as the Serampore Trio. They founded 26 churches and 126 schools (total enrollment ten thousand), translated Scripture into 44 languages, produced grammars and dictionaries, and organized India's first medical mission, savings bank, seminary, Indian girls' school, and vernacular newspaper (in Bengali). In addition, Carey campaigned for the eradication of suttee (burning a widow on her husband's funeral pyre) and conducted extensive agricultural experiments. He was instrumental in founding the Agricultural and Horticultural Society of India in 1820. Carey was responsible for India's first organized printing operation, paper mill, and steam engine. He initiated the first English translation of the great Sanskrit epics the *Ramayana* and *Mahabharata*. The translation of the Bible into Sanskrit was his work, as was the baptism in 1800 of the first Hindu Protestant convert.

Carey's efforts inspired the founding of other mission boards, among them the London Missionary Society in 1795, the Netherlands Missionary Society in 1797, the American Board in 1810, and the American Baptist Missionary Union in 1814. Carey's work sparked the entire Christian world to carry out the Great Commission. His tombstone reads: "A wretched, poor, and helpless worm/On thy kind arms I fall."
M. FACKLER

CARLILE, WILSON (1847–1942)
Anglican minister; founder of the Church Army (Episcopal equivalent of the Salvation Army)

Born in Brixton, London (England), and son of a merchant, Carlile took over the family business but suffered financial ruin in an economic slump in 1873. After a serious illness his thoughts turned to religion and he was converted to Christ. On one occasion he assisted Dwight L. Moody and Ira Sankey as their organist. Carlile studied at St. John's College, Highbury, before being ordained.

In 1882 Carlile founded the Church Army to work in the slums and new industrial areas of the cities and became known as "the archbishop of the gutter." For the rest of his life his chief interest was the promotion of the Church Army. He visited labor colonies in Europe to expand his knowledge; he described them in *The Continental Outcast* (1906). Carlile composed a simple choral setting for Holy Communion which was widely used in working-class areas. In 1915 he was given an honorary doctor of divinity degree by Oxford University, followed in 1922 by another from the University of Toronto. P. TOON

CARLSTADT, ANDREAS BODENSTEIN VON (c. 1477–1541)
German Protestant reformer

Born in Karlstadt, Bavaria, Carlstadt studied at the Universities of Erfurt and Cologne. In 1504 he moved to the University of Wittenberg, where he became a teacher of philosophy and a strong supporter of the scholasticism of Roman Catholic theologian Thomas Aquinas. Carlstadt became a canon (that is, a member of the clergy living according to the canon, or rule, of a religious group) and later archdeacon of Wittenberg. In 1515, he went to Rome to study law, hoping in vain to become the first bishop of the newly created diocese of Wittenberg.

In Rome Carlstadt became disenchanted with the Church because of the immorality and venality of the papal court. He also began to read the writings of Augustine of Hippo and gradually came to accept Augustine's doctrines of grace, perhaps even before the Protestant reformer Martin Luther had done so. Carlstadt's first published work, a reply to Roman Catholic apologist John Eck's attack on Luther's Ninety-five Theses, indicated his change of view. In that work Carlstadt also indicated his acceptance of the absolute authority of the Bible. In 1519, in a disputation with Eck in Leipzig, Carlstadt voiced his opposition to the Roman Church's doctrine of justification, but without convincing Eck.

In 1521 Carlstadt tried to bring about a Lutheran reform in the church of Denmark, but was driven out by the nobles and bishops. At that time he began to develop his own ideas about two types of biblical interpretation, literal and spiritual. While Luther was in protective custody in the Wartburg Castle after the Diet of Worms (1521), Carlstadt, still a professor at Wittenberg, took over leadership of the reform movement in Wittenberg. With the support of the city council he instituted many radical reforms, abolishing Communion "in one kind" (serving the communicants only the consecrated bread), auricular confession (that is, to a priest), elevation of the host (bread or wafer) in the Mass, and pictures and statues in the church. In 1522 he married.

Although he did not favor the three radical reformers known as the "Zwickau prophets" when they came to Wittenberg, his own drastic moves toward reform disturbed many citizens of Wittenberg and their ruler, the elector Frederick. Luther, who believed that reforms should be introduced slowly to avoid disturbing people, left Wartburg Castle for Wittenberg and forced Carlstadt to stop (1522). Since most Christians were illiterate, Luther feared that too many changes made too rapidly might totally undermine people's faith.

Deprived of his influence, Carlstadt remained a professor. Carrying his views about the interpretation of Scripture to their logical conclusion, he rejected both the Roman Catholic and the Lutheran doctrines concerning Holy Communion, as well as clerical orders. Because of his radical views he left Wittenberg to preach in Orlamunde. Both Luther and the radical reformers such as Thomas Munzer tried in vain to gain Carlstadt's support. After wandering through Europe, Carlstadt spent the last years of his life as a professor in Basel (Switzerland). W. S. REID

CARLYLE, THOMAS (1795–1881)
Literary figure in nineteenth-century England: biographer, social and philosophical essayist, historian, and critic

Carlyle was born into poverty in Dumfriesshire, Scotland. His father was a stonemason and a Calvinist with a high regard for education. He made certain that his son received the best—first at Annan Grammar School and later at the University of Edinburgh. His parents wanted him to study divinity and become a minister in the Scottish church, but he abandoned the idea, leaving Edinburgh in 1814 without a degree. He earned a bare living at hack writing.

In 1826 Carlyle married Jane Walsh and began to write his more enduring works at her farm in Craigenputtock. There he wrote a famous essay on Robert Burns, as well as a work often referred to as his "spiritual autobiography," *Sartor Resartus* (1833–1834). The title means "The Tailor Retailored." The first part sets forth the idea that the universe is to be considered as "a large suit of clothes which invests everything"; part two shows Carlyle's own spiritual struggles, including an episode about his denial of kinship with the Devil (the Everlasting No), his theory of the Center of Indifference, and his Everlasting Yes.

In 1834 the Carlyles took up residence in Chelsea, London, where he lived and wrote for the remainder of his long life, becoming known as the "Sage of Chelsea." The first in a long series of works produced there was his *History of the French Revolution* (1837), a prose-poem warning England of impending dangers unless social reforms were initiated. The work brought him fame but little income. As a result of his comparative poverty, he decided to give a series of public lectures, the most famous of which were *On Heroes and Hero Worship* and *The Heroic in History,* delivered in 1840 and published in 1841. In them his central ideological concern was to demonstrate that the history of the world was basically the work of an intellectual and political elite. His essays on *Chartism* (1839), *Past and Present* (1843), and the *Latter Day Pamphlets* (1850) present his economic and industrial theories. He returned to biography with the *Letters and Speeches of Oliver Cromwell* (1845), *The Life of John Sterling*, and the *History of Frederick II of Prussia called Frederick the Great* (1858).

Carlyle asserted the superiority of the outstanding individual over the masses of humanity, and the right of the strong man to lead, rather than the average or mediocre. He insisted on the ascendance of spiritual values over material, although spirituality to him was indistinguishable from personal idealism. He constantly emphasized that principles are more excellent than rules, that love of labor is preferable to love of pleasure, and that responsibility, not indulgence, gives purpose to living. The style of his writings has been called "an echo of the utterances of the Old Testament Prophets," and Carlyle himself has been referred to as "the vitriolic Jeremiah." E. B. BATSON

CARMAN, ALBERT (1833–1917)
Canadian Methodist clergyman and educator

Carman was born at Iroquois, Upper Canada, and entered Victoria College, Cobourg, Ontario, in 1852. After his conversion there at a revival, Carman was ordained to the ministry of the Methodist Episcopal Church (1859) and was a bishop from 1874 to 1883. As principal of Albert College, Belleville, Ontario (1858–1868), he exercised strong leadership. He had courage, perseverance, and enterprise, plus great gifts as a public speaker. After entry of the Methodist Epis-

copal Church into the Methodist Church, Carman served as general superintendent (1884–1915).

In the long struggle in the Methodist Church over the higher criticism of the Bible, Carman was a strong advocate of the conservative position. A contemporary described him as "positive, assertive, dogmatic." In 1909 he engaged in a famous controversy with George Jackson, a Methodist minister in Toronto, over a lecture by Jackson on the book of Genesis. D. C. MASTERS

CARMICHAEL, AMY WILSON (1867–1951)
Missionary to India; founder of the Dohnavur Fellowship, a society devoted to saving neglected and ill-treated children

Amy Carmichael was born into a strong Presbyterian home in northern Ireland. The oldest of seven children, she was thrust into early maturity by the death of her father. She was adopted and tutored by Robert Wilson, cofounder of the Keswick Convention, and through his influence she became the first missionary supported by the Keswick Missions Committee. After fifteen months in Japan, Amy Carmichael arrived in India in 1895 under the Church of England Zenana Missionary Society. She served in India for fifty-six years without a furlough. The children of India, especially those who were to be dedicated as temple prostitutes, became the focus of her efforts. From it arose in 1901 the Dohnavur Fellowship, with more than one thousand children in three homes, a hospital, and evangelistic work. Because of her devotion to these children, Amy was known as "Amma" ("mother" in the Tamil language).

Carmichael was a prolific writer, producing thirty-five published books including *His Thoughts Said . . . His Father Said* (1951), *If* (1953), and *Edges of His Ways* (1955). Best known, perhaps, is an early historical account, *Things as They Are: Mission Work in Southern India* (1903). The book's frankness stunned a Christian public accustomed to "victory stories" from missionaries. In 1931

Miss Carmichael was badly injured in a fall, which left her bedridden much of the time until her death. She remained in India, however, and continued to write devotional books and poetry. M. FACKLER

CARNELL, EDWARD JOHN (1919–1967)
American evangelical theologian

Carnell was born at Antigo, Wisconsin, studied at Wheaton College and Westminster Theological Seminary, and did doctoral work at Harvard and Boston. He taught first at Gordon College and Seminary (1945–1948), then moved to Fuller Theological Seminary, founded by Charles E. Fuller. As professor of philosophy of religion and ethics, he gained a reputation as a solid and stimulating teacher. He also served as president of Fuller from 1954 to 1959, being forced to resign through administrative pressures and ill health, which also hampered him in his academic work.

In addition to his work as professor and president, Carnell authored many significant books. He began with one of his best writings, the *Introduction to Christian Apologetics* (1948). In 1951 he then put out a fair but critical examination of American neo-orthodoxy in *Reinhold Niebuhr*. His *Philosophy of the Christian Religion* followed in 1952. In later works, *Christian Commitment* in 1957, *The Kingdom of Love and the Pride of Life* in 1960, and *The Burden of Søren Kierkegaard* in 1965, he turned to the more ethical and personal elements in Christian thought and life. His most provocative work, and the one that brought the fiercest opposition, was his *Case for Orthodox Theology* (1959), in which he criticized what he regarded as the "cultic" aspects of the fundamentalism in which he had been reared.

With Harold J. Ockenga and Carl F. H. Henry, Carnell initiated a powerful movement for better theology and greater social concern in the evangelical world. In spite of suspicions roused by the term "Neo or New Evangelicalism," he remained true to his original doctrinal orthodoxy, but looked for new ways by which to increase its theologi-

cal and practical effectiveness. In so doing he contributed in part to the great evangelical resurgence of the closing decades of the twentieth century. G. BROMILEY

CARROLL, JOHN (1735–1815)
First Roman Catholic bishop in America; first archbishop of Baltimore

Carroll was born in Upper Marlborough, Maryland, was educated at St. Omer's College in Flanders, completed training in the Society of Jesus at Watten, Leige, and Bruges (Belguim), and was ordained a priest in 1769. He became a professor of philosophy and theology at Jesuit colleges in Liege and Bruges. A suppression of the Jesuits by a papal brief in 1773 forced his escape to England, and in 1774 he returned home to Maryland. Here he became a protector of Jesuit holdings until the Society was restored in 1814. In 1776 the Continental Congress appointed him to be part of a delegation, along with Benjamin Franklin, Samuel Chase, and Charles Carroll (his cousin and a signer of the Declaration of Independence), to win either aid or neutrality from Quebec during the Revolution. They were not successful.

In 1784 he was appointed prefect apostolic for the United States by Pope Pius VI. In 1786 he was instrumental in establishing a Catholic academy, which became Georgetown University. He was consecrated bishop of Baltimore in 1790.

In 1791 he founded the Sulpician seminary, St. Mary's, in Baltimore, and the Baltimore Library, which he served as president until 1815. In 1805 he was made administrator apostolic of Louisiana and the Floridas, and when his see was made an archdiocese in 1808 with the erection of sees in Boston, New York, Philadelphia, and Bardstown, Kentucky, Bishop Carroll became archbishop, receiving the pallium in 1811.

Carroll was determined to keep the American Catholic church free from foreign entanglements, except for the spiritual union with the church in Rome. With George Washington's help he secured federal funds for Catholic missionaries to the Indians in the American West. He was a patron of religious and secular schools and assisted in the founding of religious orders, notably the Sisters of Charity, established by Elizabeth B. Seton. L. LEONARD

CARTWRIGHT, THOMAS (1535–1603)
Puritan church leader in England

A graduate of Cambridge, Cartwright was forced to leave his post at St. John's College on the accession of Mary Tudor (1553). The Puritans, with Thomas Cartwright as one of their leading figures, wanted to remain within the Anglican church but remove certain practices from that church. Even under the Protestant Queen Elizabeth, Cartwright (by then a divinity professor) incurred official disfavor at Cambridge. He delivered a series of lectures criticizing the Church of England for deviating from certain New Testament church practices. He was dismissed from his teaching position and forced to leave England temporarily. For a time he lived in Geneva (Switzerland), where he met Theodore Beza, the Protestant leader who succeeded John Calvin.

Back in England, in 1573 Cartwright was again compelled to leave the country for supporting a written attack on church officials called *Admonition to the Parliament* (1572). While abroad he published Walter Travers's translation of *Ecclesiastical Discipline* (1574), an explanation of Puritan theories of church government. In 1590 Cartwright was accused of helping to write the Marprelate Tracts, which exposed the inefficiency of the Anglican bishops and advocated reforms in church organization. He was soon arrested in England and was not released until 1592.

Cartwright's personal ideal for church government was a Presbyterian type in which local autonomous churches joined freely together to form a synod or assembly. Churches in the synod would be equals, with each church governed by a local board of elders rather than a synod leader. Cartwright helped other Puritan leaders write petitions seeking support for the Puritan

cause from leading government officials. He was preparing to address the royal court when he died. K. LEID

CARVER, WILLIAM OWEN
(1868–1954)
Southern Baptist theologian and professor of missions

Educated at Richmond College, Virginia, and Southern Baptist Theological Seminary in Louisville, Kentucky, Carver taught philosophy and ancient languages for three years at Boscobel College in Tennessee. In 1896 he became professor of New Testament, homiletics, and theology at Southern Baptist Theological Seminary. He was head of the missions department from 1900 until his retirement in 1943. He visited mission fields around the world and became an authority on missions.

Carver founded the Women's Missionary Union Training School (1907) and was one of its professors for many years. When he died, the school became the Carver School of Missions and Social Work. He was a member of several Baptist historical societies, including the Southern Baptist Historical Society, of which he was a charter member and president, and the historical commission of the Southern Baptist Convention, of which he was a founder.

The author of nineteen books, seven of them relating to missions, Carver also edited the *Review and Expositor* for twenty-two years. He was a contributing editor to *The Commission* and wrote frequently for other periodicals. H. KANE

CASE, SHIRLEY JACKSON (1872–1947)
Male educator and church historian

Born at Hatfield Point, New Brunswick, Case was educated at Acadia, Yale, and Marburg universities. After teaching at Bates College (Lewiston, Maine) from 1906 to 1908, he joined the faculty of the University of Chicago Divinity School, becoming a full professor of New Testament in 1815 and, two years later, of early church history. In addition he served as dean of the school

from 1933 until his retirement in 1938. In 1940 he became professor of religion at Florida Southern College and dean of the Florida School of Religion at Lakeland, where he remained until his death. The liberal "Chicago School" of theological thought, of which Case was a prominent member, laid much stress on the total environment in which any historical event occurred, and viewed historical events as evolutionary in character, usually denying anything supernatural or miraculous. Case published many books, including *Jesus: A New Biography* (1927) and *The Social Triumph of the Ancient Church* (1933).
N. V. HOPE

CASSIAN, JOHN (c. 360–c. 435)
Monastic theologian

Cassian was born probably in what is now Romania. As a young man he journeyed to Bethlehem and joined a monastery there. He left four years later, traveling to Egypt, where he spent thirteen years studying ascetic life, especially that of bishop Paphnutius of Scete. In 399 Cassian went to Constantinople, where he met the eloquent preacher and reformer John Chrysostom, who befriended him and ordained him as a deacon. When Chrysostom was banished in 404, Cassian went to Rome to persuade Pope Innocent I to come to the aid of his friend. Thereafter Cassian became a priest, and a decade later he founded a monastery and a convent in Marseilles.

All of Cassian's books have been preserved and were very influential in transmitting Eastern monastic patterns to the Western church. The book *The Institutes* describes both the external and spiritual life of a monk, emphasizing the vices that must be overcome. *The Collations* deals in greater detail with the spiritual life. Because of portions of that work, Cassian has been identified with Semi-Pelagianism (the belief that although all of Adam's descendants are tainted with original sin, they can still, on their own, desire goodness and thereby receive from God the grace for justification). Cassian, wanting to offer an incentive for undertaking rigorous monastic life, may have felt that a doctrine of total depravity and overemphasis on the grace of God undermined that incentive. His third work, *Against Nestorius on the Incarnation of the Lord*, refutes Nestorianism (the heretical belief that Christ was two distinct persons, one human and one divine) and contains much praise for Chrysostom.

After his death, Cassian was considered a saint by the Eastern church and is also venerated in Marseilles. R. D. SHUSTER

CASSIODORUS, FLAVIUS MAGNUS AURELIUS (c. 490–c. 585)
Roman statesman, author, and scholar

Cassiodorus was born in Scyllacius, Calabria (southern Italy), and received a good classical education. He served a series of Ostrogothic kings, first as quaestor (official in charge of public finances) and secretary and then counsel to Theodoric the Great, Ostrogothic king of Italy (493–526). Later as prime minister, Cassiodorus tried to reconcile the conquered Romans and the Goths. He became praetorian prefect under Athalaric and patrician under Vitiges. When Byzantine military action in northern Italy crumbled the Ostrogothic rule, Cassiodorus retired to his home at Vivarium in Calabria (about 540) to found a monastery where monks could study and copy sacred and secular books.

Cassiodorus, never ordained as a priest, wrote widely about government, politics, and history. He wrote a history of the nomadic Gothic peoples (based on tribal legends and oral traditions), which is no longer in existence but is referred to by other writers. His *Chronica* is a world history in which the achievements of the Goths are predominant. His *Variae* was a collection of twelve books containing his official letters from the days when he was in government service. He also produced several Bible commentaries, on, for example, the Psalms, Paul's letters, and Acts. In his last work, revealing Augustinian influence, he spoke of the problems of the knowledge of the soul—from its origin to its destination in immortality.

Cassiodorus's most important work, *Institutiones diuinarum et saecularium litterarum* (550–560), appeared in two books. The first provided a record of theological works that monks were to read in order to understand Scripture and to know the church's teachings. The second provided a list of works that discuss the seven liberal arts. Cassiodorus was intent on preserving the culture of the church, and his work had influence on the scholarship of the Middle Ages. When he died, the library at Vivarium was destroyed, although most of the manuscripts were preserved and transferred to the papal library in the Lateran. The Benedictine order continued the intellectual interests of Cassiodorus. L. GOLDBERG

CASTELLIO, SEBASTIAN (1515–1563)
Protestant theologian and champion of religious liberty

Born in Savoy, Castellio became a Protestant after meeting Calvin in 1540, was forced to leave France, and was rector in the college in Geneva. He left that city because he disagreed with Calvin on various points: how to interpret the descent of Christ into hell; the inspiration of the Song of Solomon; and, most prominently, predestination. Castellio went to Basel and supported himself by manual labor until he brought out highly commended translations of the Bible in classical Latin and colloquial French. Accompanying them were eloquent pleas for religious liberty. Because of these works he was appointed professor of Greek at Basel University in 1553. That same year, he denounced the execution of Servetus (one of the few to do so publicly), and under a pseudonym, published a work which argued that heretics ought not to be punished by the civil authority. Thereafter he was inhibited from publishing anything but classical works. He was of the Erasmian school of thought. He held that in the eyes of God creeds are less important than deeds, and that creeds should be assessed in terms of the individuals they produced. He made a distinction between essential and nonessential elements of salvation, holding that the essential must be capable of being understood by all. J. D. DOUGLAS

CASWALL, EDWARD (1814–1878)
Anglican minister, poet, and hymn writer who converted to Roman Catholicism in 1847

In 1850, as a widower, Caswall retired into a semimonastic life (with the Oratory of St. Philip Neri, a religious society of secular priests directed by John Henry Cardinal Newman). Caswall translated French, German, Italian, and Latin hymns into English and composed original scores used in both Anglican and Roman Catholic worship services. Two of the familiar hymns he translated are "Jesus, the Very Thought of Thee" and "When morning gilds the skies." He also wrote the *Lyra Catholica* (1849), which contains all the hymns in the breviary and missal. In addition to poetry, Caswall wrote devotional essays. K. LEID

CATESBY, ROBERT (1573–1605)
English Roman Catholic; famous as a conspirator against the Protestant Crown

Catesby was a prime promoter of the Gunpowder Plot, an attempt to blow up the houses of Parliament in 1604. Born into a prominent Roman Catholic family, he remained fanatically committed to Roman Catholicism and used a great part of his wealth to promote its cause. He seems to have been a headstrong man of action rather than of foresight. After discovery of the Gunpowder Plot, Catesby fled with other conspirators but was eventually found and, apparently resisting arrest, was killed. P. TOON

CATHERINE DE' MEDICI (1519–1589)
Italian noblewoman and, by marriage, queen of France

Catherine de' Medici was the daughter of Lorenzo de' Medici of Florence. In 1533 her uncle, Pope Clement VII, arranged her marriage to Henry, duke of Orleans, who became king of France as Henry II in 1547. Well educated for her day and a clever queen, Catherine was highly esteemed in the French court. She personally supervised her children's education.

Henry died in 1559, leaving Catherine as queen mother and young Francis II (whose wife was Mary, queen of Scots) on the throne. Catherine allied herself with the powerful, staunchly Roman Catholic Guise family, and they jointly ruled France in the vacuum of power caused by Francis's weak and inexperienced rule. Catholic political hegemony under Catherine's reign fostered dissatisfaction among the French nobility, spearheaded by the Bourbon princes—many of whom were Protestant Huguenots. Catherine's role in the ensuing "wars of religion" vacillated. At times she mediated between the Protestant and Roman Catholic nobility; at other times she encouraged the Guises' persecution of the Huguenots.

After Francis's death in 1560, Catherine acted as regent for his younger brother, Charles IX. In 1562, she issued an edict granting Protestants limited religious rights. The queen's policy of toleration, however, did not end the violent conflict. Protestant influence at court grew as Gaspard de Coligny, a Huguenot admiral, undercut Catherine's influence over the young king. Catherine's plotting with the Guise princes to assassinate Coligny resulted in the murder of most of the Huguenot leaders in the infamous St. Bartholomew's Day Massacre of 1572. The country remained badly divided and filled Catherine's dying days with renewed bloodshed. K. HOGLUND

CATHERINE OF GENOA (1447–1510)
Italian noblewoman, mystic, and
humanitarian

Catherine was born Caterinetta Fieschi of a noble family named Guelph. In 1463 her brother, for diplomatic purposes, arranged for her marriage to Guiliano Adorni. Guiliano, of the noble family of Ghibelline, proved a wayward and self-indulgent husband. Catherine was converted in 1473, and at the same time her husband's financial reverses brought about his conversion.

Guiliano became affiliated with the Third Order of the Franciscans. Catherine worked with the Ladies of Mercy in St. Lazarus hospital in Genoa, caring for the sick and poor of that district; she was the administrative director of the hospital from 1490–1496. She fasted often, withdrawing many times from human contact in mystical devotion with God. Her spiritual thoughts were expressed in her *Treatise on Purgatory* and *Spiritual Dialogues*. In later life she depended much on a priest, Cattaneo Maraboto, in her ministry at the hospital and in training disciples. She was canonized in 1737.
L. GOLDBERG

CATHERINE OF SIENA (c. 1347–1380)
Italian mystic; member of the Sisters of
Penance (a Dominican lay order)

Born in Florence, Catherine chose her religious vocation at age sixteen and, as a Dominican lay sister, led a strict ascetic life in her own home. Later, Catherine embarked upon an active public life of menial service, ecclesiastical reform, and political diplomacy. Although almost illiterate, she influenced many through her dictated letters and in Siena exercised great authority over her followers.

In 1376 Catherine visited Pope Gregory XI in exile in Avignon (France), hoping to persuade him to return to Rome. After Gregory's death in 1378, she worked tirelessly for reconciliation among rival factions in the Catholic Church, giving full support to Pope Urban VI. Her efforts to unite the church brought on an illness which led to her death.

Catherine's book *The Dialogue* was her spiritual testament. Ranking high among the church's mystics, she was canonized in 1461 and declared a patron saint of Italy in 1939. L. GOLDBERG

CAVEN, WILLIAM (1830–1904)
Canadian Presbyterian minister and educator

Born in Scotland, Caven migrated to Ontario in 1847 and was ordained to the Presbyterian ministry in 1852. In 1866 he joined the staff of Knox College, Toronto, becoming its principal (head) in 1873, a position he held until his death. Caven was an influential teacher, said to have had the traditional respect of a "true Scot" for education. As moderator of the Presbyterian Church of Canada, he helped to bring about the general union of the Presbyterian churches in Canada in 1875. As president of the Pan-Presbyterian Alliance (1900–1904), he furthered the ecumenical cause. Conservative in theology, he wrote an article on Christ's testimony to the Old Testament which was published posthumously in the fourth volume of *The Fundamentals* (1910-1915). Caven endeavored to show in the article that Jesus regarded the entire Old Testament as "divine, authoritative, infallible." D. C. MASTERS

CAXTON, WILLIAM (c. 1422–1491)
First English printer

As a young man, Caxton was sent by his employer to Bruges (Belgium), the center of the European wool trade, and in the next thirty years became a prominent member of the English trading community there. In 1453 he was admitted to the Mercers' Company, and ten years later he took the duties of "Governor of the English Nation of Merchant Adventurers." In 1470 he entered the service of Margaret, Duchess of Burgundy.

Although employed as a merchant, Caxton retained an interest in books. In 1469 he began translating the manuscript *Recuyell of the Histories of Troye* by Rauol le Fevre. He was persuaded by the duchess to complete the translation while in Cologne in 1471. There Caxton mastered the art of printing. When he returned to Bruges he printed the work by le Fevre in 1475, the first book printed in English.

Toward the end of 1476 Caxton set up his printing press at Westminster, intending to print works of general interest to English readers. His first book printed in England was *Dictes and Sayenges of the Phylosophers*, dated November 18, 1477. Caxton printed nearly all the works of English literature available to him, including Chaucer's *Canterbury Tales* about 1478. Caxton's printing press not only prepared the way for the printing of the Bible, but also helped spread

the humanism of that day to a large reading audience. R. VONDERLACK

CELESTINE I (died 432)
Pope, 422–432

Besides his birth in Rome, almost nothing is known about Celestine before his election as pope. It is certain that he was once a deacon, since a letter so addressed exists among Augustine of Hippo's works. As bishop of Rome, Celestine's main problems, like those of other fifth-century holders of his office, were church schism and heresy, and the empire's political disintegration. And like his fellow bishops Innocent I and Leo I, Celestine upheld a high view of Rome's supremacy in the church.

Celestine's papal authority ran into early trouble in his decision on Apiarius, a deposed African priest. In 424, repudiating the legate Faustinius, African bishops at the Council of Carthage rejected Celestine's reinstatement of Apiarius, protesting that he unwisely countermanded local authority in the matter. Nevertheless, a basic deference to Celestine seems to have developed in the church at large. Augustine of Hippo, who held Celestine in much esteem, asked for his help in settling a dispute with Antonius, bishop of Fessula (Africa). Later, after Augustine's death, Gaulish church leaders heeded Celestine's admonition against attacks on the great African's person and doctrine. Bishops in England and Gaul concurred with Celestine's opposition both to Pelagius's ideas and to John Cassian's semi-Pelagian compromises. Still further, when he criticized certain Gaulish practices—inappropriate dress and improper lay leadership—no objections resulted.

During its last four years, Celestine's papacy was taken up primarily with the Nestorian controversy. In 428, Celstine had commended Nestorius at his installation as bishop of Constantinople. However, on hearing reports that Nestorius's teaching included serious heresy, he commissioned Cyril, bishop of Alexandria, to investigate. Cyril wrote that Nestorius was indeed openly propagating a heterodox view of

Christ, a doctrine ascribing to Christ two distinct personalities. Backed by the Synod of Rome, in 430 Celestine ordered Cyril to excommunicate Nestorius unless he retracted his teaching within ten days. Nestorius rejected this order and also refused to leave his office as bishop. Nonetheless, at the Council of Ephesus (431), Celestine's demand received overwhelming support. Nestorius, still obdurate, was removed from the church. Also in 431, Celestine showed his concern for church extension by sending Palladius as bishop for the Irish. A little later Patrick left on his mission to Ireland, perhaps at Celestine's instigation. Throughout his time in office, Celestine was much involved with restoration of Church buildings and local Church life in general.

Celestine I's sixteen extant letters have been reproduced by Migne's *Patrologia Latina*. With them is an apparently authentic fragment of Celestine's statement on Nestorius at the Synod of Rome.
K. J. BRYER

CELESTINE III (c. 1106–1198)
Pope, 1191–1198

Born Giacinto Bobo-Orsini into a noble Roman family, he studied under Abelard as a youth, and later he was one of Abelard's defenders. He was also an intimate counselor of Thomas Becket. About 1144, Celestine joined the papal court as a cardinal deacon. He remained forty-seven years in this role, serving the papacy on many special missions, mainly in Germany, Spain, and Portugal. At the age of eighty-five, Celestine became the cardinals' choice for pope. His judiciousness was needed for the papacy's rift with Henry VI, who in 1190 succeeded his father, Frederick I, as Holy Roman Emperor. A patient conciliator throughout Frederick's long rule, Celestine approached the violent, unstable son similarly. More significantly, from 1192 to 1194, he did not act against Henry's odious ransoming of England's Richard I.

Henry VI's aggression in Italy, however, drove Celestine to stronger opposition.

Celestine refused to be bribed by Henry's offer of German church revenues, and he sought military help to remove Henry from Italy. Finally, however, Henry's deceitful promise to lead a Crusade mollified the pope. Celestine confronted other European monarchs more effectively. This was true on one of the era's most critical issues: consolidation of the Church's marital principles. Among other actions, Celestine forced Alfonso IX of Leon to abandon plans to marry outside Church rules. It was also his firm stand that began the Middle Ages' preeminent divorce dispute, the case of France's Philip II and Ingeborg. Uncompromisingly, Celestine repulsed the French bishops who allowed Philip not only to divorce Ingeborg, but also to replace her officially with Agnes. This matter reached its climax under Innocent III, Celestine's successor.

His call for a Crusade (Europe's Third Crusade) was Celestine's greatest interest. Toward this end he encouraged the Knights Templar and the Hospitallers and also created the Teutonic Knights. Many of Celestine III's letters appear in Migne's *Patrologia Latina*. The famous *Liber Censum,* a survey of Roman property, was also compiled in his reign. K. J. BRYER

CELSUS (second century)
Pagan philosopher who attacked Christianity in his book The True Word

Celsus's thought is known only through a treatise called *Against Celsus* (c. 250) by Origen, a third-century Christian scholar. Celsus did not trust Christians because they met secretly and did not support the Roman state. The doctrine of the Incarnation (which taught that Jesus as the Son of God took on a human form and nature) was offensive to him. He was annoyed that some Christians answered his objections by saying that one must "simply believe" and not investigate spiritual truths so closely. Celsus appreciated the Christians' standard of morality and their worship of one supreme, immaterial God, but he claimed that those ideas had already been formulated by pagan philosophers. C. HICKS

CERINTHUS (died c. 100)

Gnostic heretic

Probably born in Egypt and reared a Jew, Cerinthus was leader of a group of Christians who had Gnostic tendencies. He apparently believed that the world was created not by God, but by a lesser being (called the Demiurge) or by angels, one of whom gave the Law to the Jews. Cerinthus also taught that Jesus was an ordinary man, upon whom "the Christ" descended at his baptism. This divine power revealed the transcendent and unknown God. This "Christ" abandoned Jesus before his crucifixion.

The church father Eusebius (c. 260–340) quotes a story from Irenaeus (who lived in the late second century), who heard it from Polycarp (a disciple of the apostle John). The story says that John heard that Cerinthus had come into an Ephesian bathhouse where he (John) was. John immediately rushed out of the bathhouse shouting, "The building will collapse because the enemy of truth is inside!" Some scholars believe that certain passages in John's writings may have been directed against Cerinthus (see John 1:1-3, 14; 1 John 4:1-3).

C. HICKS & M. WINTER

CERULARIUS, MICHAEL (c. 1000–1058)

Patriarch of Constantinople

Born of a distinguished family of the Byzantine Empire and trained for civil service, Cerularius became embroiled in the unstable politics of that realm. In 1040 he was suspected of complicity in a plot against Emperor Michael IV. In consequence he entered monastic life. Although he was never really conversant with theological and ecclesiastical matters, he was appointed by Emperor Constantine IX as successor to the patriarchate of Constantinople in 1043. He quickly developed a very high concept of his position, fighting on all fronts for his dignity as patriarch. Against the civil authority Cerularius advanced the supremacy of ecclesiastical authority. Against the Roman pontiffs he advanced the supremacy of Constantinople. In 1054 he broke with Rome and emissaries of both bishops mutually ex-communicated each other. (The result was the Great Schism, which separated the churches in the east and west.) In the empire Cerularius became arrogant in his assertions of power, but the result was exile in 1058, during which he died the following year.

A. CABANISS

CHAFER, LEWIS SPERRY (1871–1952)

Founder and president of Dallas Theological Seminary

Chafer was born in Rock Creek, Ohio. His father, a Congregational minister, died of tuberculosis when Chafer was eleven years old. The youngster worked to support the family, then resumed his schooling, completing studies in music composition and conducting at Oberlin College. Chafer became a gospel singer. In 1900 he was ordained to the congregational ministry.

In 1903 Chafer joined the faculty of Dwight L. Moody's Mount Hermon School for Boys in East Northfield, Massachusetts. He changed his membership to the Presbyterian Church, within which he stayed for the rest of his life. Chafer left Mount Hermon to join the faculty at the Philadelphia School of Bible in 1914. Nine years later he became pastor of Scofield Memorial Church in Dallas, Texas, and general secretary of the Central American Mission. A year after that he was named president of the new seminary in Dallas.

Chafer wrote eight popular books. His first, *Satan,* was published in 1909. The best-known of his popular works was *He That Is Spiritual* (1918). Chafer's enduring legacy is his eight-volume *Systematic Theology,* which he began in 1937 and finished in 1948. He approached evangelical theology from the dispensationalist and premillennial viewpoint he learned from C. I. Scofield, with whom he had traveled for some years. In 1940 Chafer was named editor of *Bibliotheca Sacra,* Dallas Seminary's theological journal. He retained the editorship until his death. Chafer traveled extensively as a preacher and theological educator.

M. FACKLER

CHALLONER, RICHARD (1691–1781)

Roman Catholic bishop, scholar, and Bible translator

Born in Lewes, Sussex (England), Challoner was reared a Roman Catholic by his widowed mother. His gifts were early recognized, and he was sent to the English College at Douai (France), where he studied for the priesthood. After graduating he stayed on as professor of philosophy and theology, becoming the vice-president in 1720. In 1727 he received a doctor of divinity degree from Douai. He went to London as a missionary in 1730, where he worked and wrote in defense of Roman Catholicism. After the publication of *The Catholic Christian Instructed in the Sacraments, Sacrifice, Ceremonies, and Observances of the Church* (1737), he judiciously returned to Douai. In 1741 he was consecrated bishop of Debra, a jurisdiction that included the London District, becoming Vicar Apostolic in 1758. Challoner returned to London and spent the rest of his life ably overseeing his charge (including the American colonies) in the interests of the Roman Catholic Church. He successfully weathered persecutions, political upheaval, internal problems, and riots. At his death, his friend Dr. Talbot remarked, "we have lost one who manifestly led the life of an angel."

Challoner is probably best remembered for his revision of the Douai-Reims Bible. It had been published in 1582–1610 and even then was virtually incomprehensible in places. It was the original translator's principle to create Latinized English words where no English equivalent could be found. This produced such curiosities as Romans 1:30, where the Vulgate "Deo odibiles" becomes "odible to God," and Philippians 2:7, where "semet ipsum exinanivit" becomes "he exinanited himself." The passage of time made understanding even more difficult. Acutely aware of this, Challoner revised the Douai-Reims text by comparing it with the Clementine Vulgate, correcting whatever needed simplification by referring to the King James Version. The New Testament appeared in 1749, and the Old Testament in 1750. That his translation has shortcomings is well known, but the measure of its success has been its use by English-speaking Roman Catholics until this day. Challoner also wrote numerous books on doctrinal and polemical topics, including *The Garden of the Soul* (1740).

W. ELWELL

CHALMERS, JAMES (1841–1901)

Scottish pioneer missionary and explorer in the South Pacific islands

Son of an Argyllshire stonemason, Chalmers was converted in his teens, worked for two years with Glasgow City Mission, then went in 1862 to Cheshunt College, Cambridge. He was ordained a Congregational minister in 1865, trained further under the auspices of the London Missionary Society, and in 1867 began work at Raratonga, in the Cook Islands, where there was already a substantial Christian presence. In 1877 he went on to unevangelized areas of New Guinea. When part of that territory became British in 1888, the changes made were more acceptable because Chalmers had won the trust of the people.

Like fellow Scot David Livingstone, Chalmers was an avid explorer, a warm supporter of indigenous churches, and a critic of misguided attempts to westernize native customs. He established a training college and a line of mission posts through which whole areas were reached with the gospel. In the process he brought together much new geographical information in *Adventures in New Guinea* (1885) and *Pioneering in New Guinea* (1887). It was while venturing into new territory that he, with fellow missionary Oliver Tomkins and a band of native Christians, was killed by hostile tribesmen on Goaribari Island. J. D. DOUGLAS

CHALMERS, THOMAS (1780–1847)

Foremost minister and leader of the evangelical party in the Church of Scotland during the first half of the nineteenth century

Chalmers became a principal organizer of the Free Church of Scotland. Through ministering to a dying brother and through the gentle persuasion of evangelicals, Chalmers adopted a fervent evangelical ministry and theology while in his first parish.

Called to Tron Church, Glasgow, in 1815, his concern became evangelization of the urban poor who were swelling Scotland's industrial cities. He advocated an intensive program of education and social help, coupled with evangelical teaching and visitation. That meant teaching families about the Bible and Christian life, removing them from dependence upon public charity, and motivating and training them for responsible citizenship. In 1819 he accepted the new parish of St. John (organized by the town council at his urging) in the poorest, most densely populated area of Glasgow. Thus Chalmers became an important contributor to modern social work.

To promote his parish system more widely, in 1823 Chalmers accepted a professorship at St. Andrews University and in 1828 became professor of theology at Edinburgh. His talent for popular preaching and lecturing and his warm, cheerful personality helped to popularize his methods of evangelism and social relief throughout Scotland and parts of England. Chalmers believed that the state had a God-given duty to support the Church of Scotland, but when the British Parliament failed to grant additional endowments he led a massive program of church extension beginning in 1834. In five years, 201 new churches were built with the money raised by Chalmers's church extension committee.

When Parliament refused either to recognize the legality of the new churches or to make other concessions, the evangelical party formed the Free Church of Scotland. Chalmers prepared the way by careful organization, including a system for financing the new church. He gained pledged endorsements from ministers, elders, and ministerial candidates in advance. Close to 40 percent of the ministers and elders of the Church of Scotland seceded in 1843, electing Chalmers first moderator of the new denomination. His *Institutes of Theology* (1849) was published posthumously. D. MUNSON

CHAMBERS, OSWALD (1874–1917)

Lecturer, missionary, and preacher of the "deeper life"

Born in Aberdeen, Scotland, the fourth son of a Baptist preacher, Chambers was converted under the preaching of Charles Spurgeon. At age twenty-seven he underwent a second spiritual crisis which he described as baptism in the Holy Spirit. Chambers studied art in London and Edinburgh but abandoned a promising career to train at Dunoon College for the Baptist ministry.

Most of the public ministry of Oswald Chambers was with the Pentecostal League of Prayer, especially after the League's founder, Howard Hooker, died in 1909. Chambers visited "Holiness" camps in the United States and Japan before becoming principal of the Bible Training College, Clapham Common, London (1911–1915). With his wife (Gertrude Hobbs) and daughter, he ministered to British troops in Egypt, where a sudden illness ended his life. More than forty titles of Chambers's works have been published posthumously. The most popular, *My Utmost for His Highest,* is a compilation of talks Chambers delivered at the Bible Training College and at YMCA huts in Egypt. M. FACKLER

CHAMPOLLION, JEAN-FRANÇOIS (1790–1832)

French scholar; especially known for decoding Egyptian hieroglyphics (from the Rosetta Stone) in 1822

Champollion founded the Egyptian museum of the Louvre in Paris, conducted a scientific expedition to Egypt to copy inscriptions and obtain antiquities (1828–1829), and in 1831 was appointed to the chair (professorship) of Egyptology at the College of France. To establish scholarly study of the Egyptian language, he wrote an Egyptian grammar and an Egyptian dictionary, both published posthumously. Champollion is generally acclaimed as the founder of Egyptology. H. F. VOS

CHANNING, WILLIAM ELLERY
(1780–1842)
Best-known American Unitarian in the first half of the nineteenth century

Channing grew up in Rhode Island under the preaching of Samuel Hopkins, a strict Calvinist, and had a conversion experience as a Harvard undergraduate. In spite of his later beliefs, he never regretted his early religious experiences. In 1803 he became minister of Boston's Federal Street Congregational Church and remained there for the rest of his life. His presence, plus that of the liberal Harvard College, made Boston a Unitarian stronghold.

It was not in Boston, however, but in Baltimore that Channing in 1819 preached a sermon setting out the basic outlines of his Unitarian beliefs. In it he denied the Trinity, the deity of Christ, the total depravity of man, and the substitutionary atonement. Nonetheless he affirmed the reality of the Resurrection, other New Testament miracles, and the moral perfection of Christ, along with the perfectibility of man and the fatherhood of God. He believed that the Bible recorded inspiration, but was not itself inspired. Later in life he criticized other American thinkers, such as Ralph Waldo Emerson, who took further steps away from traditional Christianity. Channing's moderate and temperate personality did much to spread his views. He also took strong stands against slavery and the use of liquor.
M. A. NOLL

CHAPMAN, JOHN WILBUR
(1859–1918)
American clergyman and evangelist

Born in Richmond, Indiana, Chapman was educated at Oberlin College, Lake Forest University, and Lane Seminary (Cincinnati). Ordained to the Presbyterian ministry in 1882, for twenty years he served Presbyterian and Reformed churches in Ohio, Indiana, New York, and Pennsylvania. In 1903 he became a full-time evangelist for the Presbyterian Church in the U.S.A. In association with the gospel singer Charles M. Alexander, he conducted evangelistic campaigns in the United States and abroad (for example, Australia in 1909 and 1912; Great Britain in 1910 and 1914). Chapman was one of the founders of the Winona Lake (Indiana) Bible Conference in 1885, and helped to promote similar summer conferences elsewhere, as at Montreat, North Carolina. In 1917 he was moderator of the General Assembly of the Presbyterian Church in the U.S.A.
N. V. HOPE

CHARLEMAGNE (742–814)
Greatest of the Carolingian rulers of western Europe

Charlemagne reigned from 768 to 814 over what is now France, the low countries (Netherlands and Belgium), and western Germany, and added other areas during his lifetime. His name means "Charles the Great." His brother, Carloman, reigned briefly with him from 768 to 771. When Charlemagne became sole monarch, he set up an effective administration and began a steady pattern of territorial conquest. His most important acquisitions were Saxony (a region in Germany) and northern Italy. He also fought the Avars and other tribes in central Europe and the Muslims in northern Spain. In all areas he established frontier zones important to the future expansion of Christian Europe.

Charlemagne's administrative system was the key to the well-being of his kingdoms and empire. He divided the realm into districts called counties, supervised by appointed officials (counts). Border areas were administered by military leaders of operation. Regions recently acquired were called marks or marches and a "count of the march" (margrave or marquis) was essentially autonomous. The counts were overseen by two itinerant officials (*missi*), one a layman and one a cleric, who did not repeat the same circuit every year.

Perhaps the pinnacle of Charlemagne's career was his coronation as emperor (on Christmas Day, 800, by Pope Leo III). The significance of that event is much debated, but it did represent an attempt to renew the idea of the Roman Empire in the West.

Although Charlemagne owed nothing to the pope or church for his power, the act had symbolic significance for the relationship of church and state. There were interruptions in the use of the imperial title over the next few centuries. What came to be known as the Holy Roman Empire, however, continued as the focal point of western European political authority throughout the Middle Ages.

Charlemagne regarded himself as a loyal son of the church. He did much to foster Christian virtues for himself, his court, and his realm. Yet he was a child of his times and his morals were not always in accord with biblical standards. In contrast to his father, Pepin (reigned 751–768), and grandfather, Charles Martel (reigned 719–741), he gave more freedom to ecclesiastical personnel and institutions. He sponsored reform councils and measures that were basic for medieval Christianity, and he defended the traditions of the Western church. He turned to ecclesiastical leaders for advice, the most notable being Benedict of Aniane. Charlemagne did use the church for his own interests politically and culturally, but without the same ill effects as his predecessors. The Carolingian church was the core of the reforms of the next two hundred years.

During Charlemagne's reign, feudalism reached many of its distinctive medieval characteristics. The decentralized political administration and economy, the need for local law and order, and the shifting economic and social alignments were contributing factors. The arrangements between Charlemagne and his subjects, as well as the administration of his own estates, were models for the rest of his realm. Charlemagne was the motivating influence for the Carolingian renaissance. His personal guidance and direction sustained the intellectual vigor of his age. His renaissance was not a revival of classical learning (as was the Italian Renaissance of the fourteenth and fifteenth centuries) but a desire to perpetuate intellectual traditions through education, manuscript copying, and libraries. Charlemagne brought to the palace school at Aachen some of the leading scholars of his

day, chief of whom was Alcuin of York. Others were Peter of Pisa, Paul the Deacon, and Einhard, biographer of Charlemagne. They studied, wrote, taught, and inspired others who in turn taught at the monastic and cathedral schools. The preservation of manuscripts was of great importance; but beyond the production of copies, the movement fostered the development of libraries and the use of a legible handwriting which is now called Carolingian miniscule. The value of Charlemagne's work and inspiration in this regard cannot be overestimated. Many ancient writings are known only by their Carolingian copies. The Carolingian schools were the roots of medieval education.

Charlemagne has been regarded as the founder of Europe. His political, economic, social, religious, and intellectual contributions were critical to the well-being of his kingdom, both in his own time and in the tumultuous years that followed his death. T. O. KAY

CHARLES I (1600–1649)
King of Great Britain and Ireland, 1625–1649

Younger son of King James I, Charles succeeded to the throne on his father's death in 1625. In the same year he married the French Roman Catholic princess Henrietta Maria. Brought up by his father to believe in the "divine right of kings," Charles soon clashed with Parliament, ruling without it between 1629 and 1640. In churchmanship he was a devout Anglican, favoring the High Church party, whose theology was Arminian, and whose leader, William Laud, Charles made bishop of London in 1628 and archbishop of Canterbury in 1633. Laud's heavy-handed measures, designed to make Puritan clergy and laity conform strictly to Prayer Book practices, caused many to emigrate to America and left a lasting resentment among those who remained in England.

The same policy was advanced in Scotland. In 1636 Charles issued a Book of Canons, which among other things proclaimed the king to be head of the Church of Scotland. In 1637 he sought to impose on Scotland a Prayer Book whose sacramental teaching seemed more Roman Catholic than that of the English *Book of Common Prayer.* The Scots responded with the National Covenant of 1638, which required Presbyterianism in the Scottish church, and with a successful revolt against Charles in 1639. Needing funds to fight the Scots, Charles summoned the English Parliament in 1640. A confrontation took place between king and Parliament, however, and civil war broke out in 1642. Parliamentary forces, led by Oliver Cromwell and supported by the Scots, defeated Charles's army and compelled him to surrender to the Scots in 1646. By making concessions Charles won the Scots to his side, but they were defeated by Cromwell at Preston in 1648. Charles was executed by Cromwell and his supporters following an abortive attempt to form a secret alliance with the Scots. His dignified bearing in death and the subsequent publication of *Eikon Basilike* (*The Royal Image*), allegedly his autobiography, helped to win Charles recognition in some circles as a martyr. N. V. HOPE

CHARLES II (1630–1685)

King of Great Britain and Ireland, in exile 1649–1660, on the throne 1660–1685

Proclaimed king on the execution of his father in 1649, Charles in 1650 accepted Scottish Presbyterianism in order to obtain Scotland's help in winning possession of the throne. When Oliver Cromwell defeated the royal forces at Worcester in 1651, Charles returned to Anglicanism. He remained in exile on the Continent until 1660, when he was invited by Parliament to return to Britain as king. Before his return he issued the Declaration of Breda, in which he promised "liberty to tender consciences." When he sought to implement it in 1662 by issuing a Declaration of Indulgence, he was overridden by a strongly Anglican Parliament. They not only reestablished the Church of England but, by the Clarendon Code (1662),

denied dissenters any place in it and forbade all religious gatherings other than Anglican.

To repay a monetary debt, Charles signed the Treaty of Dover in 1670 with the French king, Louis XIV, in which he promised to promote Roman Catholicism in England. To implement that treaty he issued another Declaration of Indulgence in 1672. Parliament responded with the Test Act of 1673, which forbade anyone who would not take Communion according to the Anglican rites from holding civil or military office under the Crown. Charles was unable to save thirty-five Roman Catholics who were put to death between 1678 and 1681 following disclosure by Titus Oates of a so-called "Popish Plot." Nevertheless, he prevented Parliament from excluding his Roman Catholic younger brother James from the British throne in 1680. A secret Roman Catholic, Charles II avowed his faith publicly only on his deathbed. N. V. HOPE

CHARLES V (1500–1558)

Holy Roman Emperor; ruler of the Hapsburg family's Spanish and Austrian territories

Charles was the most powerful ruler in Europe. The eldest son of Philip of Burgundy and grandson of Ferdinand and Isabella of Spain, he was heir to Spain, Austria, and the Netherlands. When he became Holy Roman Emperor in 1519 at the death of his grandfather Maximilian, the major religious conflict of his reign—the Protestant revolt of Martin Luther—was already two years in progress. Charles, a staunch Catholic, wanted to suppress the Lutheran movement. At the Diet of Worms in 1521 he had Luther condemned and put under the ban of the Holy Roman Empire.

Charles was unable to concentrate on solving the German religious problem, however. First, he was engaged in dynastic wars until 1544 with Francis I, king of France, over conflicting territorial claims in Italy and Flanders. That kept him out of Germany during the years when Lutheranism was gaining a strong foothold there. Second, the Muslim Turks were menacing Charles's Austrian dominions: in 1529 they besieged

Vienna, and in 1541 they conquered most of Hungary. Charles was forced to compromise on the religious issue in Germany in order to win support against the Turks from the Protestant princes and cities, organized after 1531 in the Schmalkaldic League.

Only after 1544 was Charles able to concentrate on the German religious problem. In 1547 he defeated the Protestant forces and broke up the Schmalkaldic League at the battle of Muhlberg. Thereafter he sought to impose on all Germany the Augsburg Interim, which, though it made a few weak concessions to Protestantism, retained the basic Roman Catholic doctrines. Then Charles's chief henchman, Maurice of Saxony, turned against him. The Protestants made a pact with the new French king, Henry II, which virtually nullified the Interim and renewed the conflict. Charles finally realized that Protestantism could not be suppressed, and under the treaty of Augsburg (1555) Lutheranism was granted official status and toleration. Charles abdicated in despair and died two years later in retirement at the monastery of San Yuste in Estremadura (Spain). N.V. HOPE

CHARLES, ROBERT HENRY (1855–1931)
British biblical scholar

Born in Cookstown, County Tyrone (Ireland), Charles was educated at Queen's College, Belfast, and Trinity College, Dublin. Between 1884 and 1893 he served as curate (assistant to the parish priest) in several Anglican parishes in London. He also taught at Dublin and Oxford. After an illness he settled in Oxford in 1891, where he studied the necessary ancient languages and relevant literary materials to become an authority on Apocryphal literature of the intertestamental period. He became professor of Biblical Greek at Dublin in 1898. From 1906 to 1913 he served at Oxford, and in 1913 he was appointed canon (clergyman serving in a cathedral) of Westminster and in 1919 archdeacon, a position he held until his death. Charles edited *The Apocrypha and Pseudepigrapha of the Old Testament in En-*

glish (2 volumes, 1913), and he wrote *A Critical and Exegetical Commentary on Revelation* (2 volumes, 1920) and *A Critical and Exegetical Commentary on Daniel* (1929)— all regarded as models of exacting scholarship. N. V. HOPE

CHARLES, THOMAS (1755–1814)
Welsh Methodist preacher, writer, and leader

As a schoolboy, Charles joined the Methodist society at Carmarthen and in 1773 experienced a "full awakening" to the gospel through a sermon by Daniel Rowland. In 1775 Charles went to Jesus College, Oxford, where he came to know the evangelical leaders John Newton and William Romaine. Ordained a minister of the Church of England, Charles served in Somerset until opposition to his enthusiasm for the gospel led him to return to Wales. There, in 1784, he joined the Methodist society in Bala.

Charles remained in Wales for the rest of his life, exerting a profound influence on Welsh religion and culture. His wife managed a drapery business, which freed him from financial worries and enabled him to travel extensively in north Wales. In 1785 he organized a system of portable schools, which moved from village to village teaching children to read the Bible in Welsh. His Welsh catechism and Bible dictionary were widely used by families in Wales.

Shocked by the unavailability of Welsh Bibles, Charles set in motion activities that contributed to the founding of the British and Foreign Bible Society. He was also instrumental in leading the Methodist societies of Wales to break with the Church of England (and Wales), in whose parishes they had been organized, in order to form the Calvinistic Methodist Church of Wales. P. TOON

CHARLES MARTEL (c. 688–741)
Charlemagne's grandfather who at the Battle of Tours (732) led the Franks in repelling the Muslim advance into western Europe

Charles, known as Martel ("the hammer") for his repeated attacks against the

Saracens (Muslims), was an illegitimate son of a Merovingian ruler, Pepin of Heristal. (The Merovingians were the first Frankish dynasty.) At Pepin's death, Charles seized his father's office with its near-kingly power and forced the two legitimate heirs into a monastery. Under the title "mayor of the palace" (prime minister), he administered his office well, acting as a king. He was independent in his relations with Frankish nobility, foreign royalty, and clerics and popes. He refused to aid the pope when requested. Frequently seizing for his personal use lands and possessions belonging to the church, Charles built up Charlemagne's eventual inheritance.

Although the Battle of Tours (near Poitiers) was indecisive, it served to bolster the morale of the Franks, who were encouraged by it to halt further Muslim encroachment and to take the offensive. Although Muslim attacks continued, they were less forceful than in the past, largely because of Muslim internal dissension and complacency.

When Charles Martel died, he left his lands and office to his two sons, Pepin and Carloman. Within a few years Pepin was ruling alone, which prevented the splintering of the Carolingian dynasty. T. O. KAY

CHARNOCK, STEPHEN (1628–1680)
English Puritan theologian and preacher

Charnock, a London solicitor's son, accepted the Puritan position while a student at Emmanuel College, Cambridge. Shortly after graduating he went to Oxford, in 1654 becoming proctor of New College during the chancellorship of Oliver Cromwell, leader of the Puritan party. In 1655 Charnock went to Ireland as chaplain to the lord deputy, Henry Cromwell. After the lord deputy's death, Charnock returned to London, devoting himself to study and occasional preaching. In 1675, along with another Puritan, Thomas Watson, he was appointed joint pastor of a large Presbyterian congregation in London.

Charnock was recognized during his lifetime as a preacher having deep conviction, practical insight, and great learning. Shortly after his death a number of his writings were edited by Messrs. Adams and Veal and published over a period of years. They included *A Discourse on Divine Providence; Discourses on Christ Crucified;* and *Discourses on Regeneration, the Lord's Supper, and Other Subjects.* His fame as a theologian, however, rests principally on his *Discourses Upon the Existence and Attributes of God* (1682). A massive work that ran to some thirteen hundred pages in the first American printing, it demonstrated both Charnock's thorough scholarship and his practical concern. It remains one of the most exhaustive treatments of the doctrine of God in the English language, having been reprinted many times. A complete edition of his works was published in nine volumes in 1815. J. N. AKERS

CHATEAUBRIAND, VICOMTE FRANÇOIS-AUGUSTE-RENÉ DE (1768–1848)
French Roman Catholic apologist and writer of the French Romantic period

Born at St. Malo, Chateaubriand enlisted in 1786 as a second lieutenant in the regiment of Navarre. In 1791 he visited America but returned to France on hearing the news of the arrest of King Louis XVI in June of that year. He was wounded at the siege of Thionville while serving in the royal army. Between 1793 and 1800 he lived as a poverty-haunted exile in England. In 1800 news of the death of his mother and sister helped to bring about his conversion to Christianity, which he defended throughout the rest of his life. Returning to Paris, he outlived the Napoleonic regime, and after Louis XVIII's accession to the French throne served as his country's ambassador to Prussia (1820), Great Britain (1822), and Rome (1828). (In England an elegant steak dish was invented and named for Chateaubriand.) After Louis Philippe became king of France at the revolution of 1830, Chateaubriand lived in virtual retirement until his death in Paris.

Chateaubriand's major apologetic work, *The Spirit of Christianity or the Beauty of the Christian Religion* (1802), reflects his Romantic thinking in that it avoids rational argument, emphasizing instead an aesthetic, intuitional, and moral defense. Chateaubriand asserted that Christianity is not only the most moral of all the religions, but also the most poetic and most conducive to liberty and the arts. At the time when skepticism concerning Christianity was prevalent, Chateaubriand's book commended the Christian faith to the literary and artistic world. An English literary critic, John Morley, described it as "the most superb rainbow that ever rose in a storm-beaten sky."

N. V. HOPE

CHAUCER, GEOFFREY (c. 1340–1400)
English poet of the Middle Ages

Born to a well-to-do middle-class family, Chaucer early entered military service and was sent to France, captured, and later ransomed. He held various positions at court in the king's service and in 1372 was sent to Italy, where it is believed he met the Florentine poets Boccaccio and Petrarch. Thereafter he held various civil responsibilities in London. At his death he was buried in Westminster Abbey, where a monument to him was erected in 1555.

Among Chaucer's best-known works are *The Book of the Duchess, Troilus and Creseyde, The Legend of Good Women,* and one of the enduring classics of English literature, *The Canterbury Tales. Canterbury Tales* is a collection of twenty-four stories, all but one in verse, told by a group of travelers to amuse themselves during a pilgrimage from London to the shrine of Thomas à Becket at Canterbury. The vivid *Prologue* to the *Canterbury Tales* offers a memorable picture of contemporary life in its description of thirty-one pilgrims. Especially striking are the knight and squire; the prioress, friar, and parson; the clerk of Oxford; and the wife of Bath. Each tale is known by the name of the character who tells it, and the best known are the knight's, the wife of Bath's, the pardoner's, the miller's, the prioress's, and the nun's priest's. The elaborate work was probably designed around 1387 but was left unfinished at the poet's death.

It is not known whether Chaucer was a Christian. Although his stories evidence a strong sense of justice and moral responsibility, they are often related in a heavily ambiguous and ironic tone that seems to border on skepticism. Through his skillful use of narration, humor, and satire in portraying the Canterbury pilgrims, Chaucer severely criticized, among other things, abuses practiced by the church and clergy of his day. By so doing, he contributed to the spirit of the times which eventually demanded reformation in England.

P. M. BECHTEL

CHAUNCY, CHARLES (1705–1787)
Boston clergyman and leader of New England "liberals"

Chauncy, great-grandson of Harvard's second president, was born in Boston. He graduated from Harvard in 1721 and became pastor of Boston's First Church (Congregational) in 1727, a position he held for sixty years.

Chauncy is noted for his articulate opposition to three religious movements of the 1700s: the Great Awakening, the attempt to create an Episcopal hierarchy in the American colonies, and the resurgence of Calvinistic theology—especially as preached by Jonathan Edwards.

An intellectual man, Chauncy distrusted the emotions as a perversion of the mind. He accused the Great Awakening's revivalists, principally Edwards and George Whitefield, of excessive emotion and antinomianism (neglect of the moral law). In *Seasonable Thoughts on the State of Religion in New England* (1743), he defended a more rational approach to religion.

A second controversy arose over the question of appointing an Anglican bishop for Massachusetts. The original charter of the colony of Massachusetts had been revoked in 1684, making it a royal province. Most of the governors appointed by the English monarchs wanted to make the Anglican (Episcopal) church the official religion, regarding it as the proper religion for all of Britian's territories and the only divinely ordained form of church government. For nine years Chauncy argued against importation of England's established church, a position that culminated in his *Complete View of Episcopacy* (1771).

Chauncy also opposed the popular revival (through the Great Awakening) of the Calvinistic doctrines of grace and divine judgment. To counter Jonathan Edwards's influence in New England, he wrote *Salvation for All Men Illustrated and Vindicated as a Scripture Doctrine* (1782) and *The Benevolence of the Deity* (1784).

Chauncy, who was married three times, died while still pastor at First Church in Boston. M. FACKLER

CHEMNITZ, MARTIN (1522–1586)
Lutheran theologian

Born in poor circumstances at Treuenbrietzen (Germany) near Berlin, Chemnitz overcame considerable economic difficulty to attend school in Magdeburg, studying then at the Universities of Frankfurt an der Oder and Wittenberg, where he was primarily interested in mathematics and astrology. At Wittenberg he met the Lutheran reformer and theologian Philip Melanchthon (1497–1560), who eventually persuaded him to turn to theology. The Schmalkaldic War (1546–1547) forced Chemnitz to leave Wittenberg for Konigsberg, where he taught briefly. A conflict with another German reformer, Andreas Osiander (1498–1565), over theories of grace drove Chemnitz back to Wittenberg, where he was briefly a philosophy professor. In 1554 he moved to Brunswick as vice-superintendent of the church, becoming superintendent fourteen years later and remaining in that office until 1584. There he was active in founding and organizing Lutheran churches in Prussia, Brunswick, Wolfenbuttel, and Luneberg, drawing up a number of doctrinal statements for their guidance. He was also a cofounder of the University of Helstedt (1576).

Not a great preacher, Chemnitz was nonetheless a diligent pastor and a voluminous writer. Active in efforts to keep the Lutheran churches united, he helped prepare the Formula of Concord (1577). Yet he was constantly engaged in controversy. He wrote against the followers of Melanchthon who adhered to the Leipzig Interim (1548–1552) and carried on a running battle with them and the Zwinglians over the doctrine of the "presence of Christ" in the Lord's Supper.

Chemnitz wrote two important works against the Roman Catholic Church. In 1572 he replied to a Jesuit attack on Luther's catechism in *Theologiae Jesuitarum Praecipua Capita,* and from 1565 to 1573 he produced a thorough analysis and refutation of the doctrines of the Council of Trent (1545–1563) in the four-volume *Examen Concilii Tridentini.* In the fierce Lutheran controversies that broke out after Luther's death, Chemnitz usually took a middle, conciliatory position. Through his conservative and practical outlook, Chemnitz exerted considerable influence on the Lutheran church in the second half of the sixteenth century. W. S. REID

CHESTERTON, G. K. (GILBERT KEITH) (1874–1936)
English author and journalist; known as a defender of the Christian faith

Few writers have been more prolific than Chesterton. Born and educated in London, he wrote a hundred books and made innumerable contributions to periodicals: short stories, poetry, novels, biographies, essays, and the well-known detective stories about Father Brown. For some years he had his own magazine, *G.K.'s Weekly.* Not all his work has lived, but his best writings seem destined for permanence.

Chesterton had a way of expressing an opponent's views better than that person could and then demolishing them. He is known for his use of paradox, and his style is marked by brilliance, wit, inventiveness, and originality. He described his book *Orthodox* as "my elephantine adventures in pursuit of the obvious" (that is, old-fashioned Christianity). In it he upheld the freedom offered by belief in Christ over materialistic and other current philosophies.

Chesterton was among the first to point

out clearly that science is greatly limited in its method and is therefore forbidden to ask philosophic questions or to consider anything ultimate. In *The Everlasting Man* (1925) Chesterton insisted that the caveman was not a brutal creature wrapped in an animal skin and carrying a big club; rather, he was an artist and poet of no small talent, and possibly more reasonable than modern man. Chesterton saw humanity not as rising up out of brutality and senselessness but degenerating from a high origin. He also pointed out that many thinkers who try to "explain religion" simply explain it away.
C. KILBY

CHILLINGWORTH, WILLIAM
(1602–1644)
Anglican theologian; best known for his statement, "The Bible, the Bible alone . . . is the religion of Protestants"

Educated at Trinity College, Oxford, Chillingworth became a fellow there. Later, influenced by a Jesuit priest, he went to study at the Jesuit College at Douai (France). However, on the advice of his godfather, William Laud, archbishop of Canterbury, he began an "impartial" study of the competing claims of Anglicanism and Roman Catholicism. In the end, on the grounds of Scripture and reason, Chillingworth decided in favor of Protestantism. Yet he refused ordination at that stage because he felt unable to subscribe to the Church of England's doctrinal articles.

Chillingworth spent several years preparing his famous book *The Religion of Protestants a Safe Way to Salvation* (1638), which argued for the supremacy of Scripture over tradition and for the right of the individual to decide its meaning in spiritual matters. His book was aimed against another entitled *Mercy and Truth,* written by a Jesuit, E. Knott. By 1638, ordained and having sufficiently resolved his major questions about Anglicanism, Chillingworth joined the Church of England. He soon was appointed chancellor of the diocese of Salisbury. In the armed struggle between Parliament and king, Chillingworth took the side of the royalists, became a prisoner of the parliamentary armies, and died in captivity.
P. TOON

CHINIQUY, CHARLES P. T. (1809–1899)
Canadian clergyman and temperance advocate

Chiniquy was born at Kamouraska, Lower Canada, and was ordained a Roman Catholic priest in 1833. He became the rector of Kamouraska in 1842 and was a great advocate of temperance there and later in Montreal. From 1851 to 1856 he led a large group of French Canadian colonists who settled in the Kankakee region in Illinois.

Chiniquy, in repeated difficulties with the bishops in Quebec and Illinois on grounds of misconduct, eventually left the Roman Catholic Church in 1858 and became a Presbyterian minister. A considerable number of his parishioners in Illinois followed him into the Presbyterian church. He was admitted to the synod of the Canada Presbyterian Church in 1863 and later was transferred from Illinois to Montreal to superintend the work of French evangelization. He established some sixty French Canadian Presbyterian congregations in Quebec and died in Montreal. D. C. MASTERS

CHRISTINE DE PISAN (1364–1430)
French author and moralist

Born to Italian parents in Venice, Christine moved to Paris at age five, and because her father, Thomas de Pizzano, was a royal counselor, she was raised and educated at the court of Charles V. She married Etienne de Castel, a French nobleman, after whose unexpected death she made the extraordinary decision (for a medieval woman) to pursue writing as a career. In a short time, she demonstrated an unmistakable and variegated literary talent. Her short poems—balades, rondeaux, lais, complaintes—had an enthusiastic, remunerative readership. Less attractive are her long poems, which were allegorical commentaries on life. But overall, Christine's poetry is guided in its moral and spiritual ideals by Christian truths.

As her understanding evolved, Christine turned increasingly to prose writing for expression of her moral convictions. Her first important effort here was *Epistre d'Othea a Hector de Troye*, a story of the perfect knight immersed in much theological and ethical commentary. One or both of two themes infused Christine's later major writings: advocacy of unblemished ethics, and defense of women and their worth. Christian standards now appeared even more to inform Christine's views. Especially prominent in this regard are Christine's works on youth education and many instructive moral writings on a broad gamut of political, military, and social issues. But perhaps the best constructed, most enduring of Christine's prose works are *Cite des dames* and *Tresor de la cite des dames* (also called *Livre des trois virtus*). Produced with great care, both writings skillfully interweave ideas about women and morality. The first depicts an allegorical city of women and its occupants' special virtues, basic problems, and social merits. The second describes varied religious, moral, and social steps to greatness in the city of women. The two works seem intended for women at all social levels, and it is unquestionable that Christian devotion is central to the instruction set forth. The stream of writings continued even after Christine's retirement to a monastery in 1418. One of her last works, *Ditte de Jeanne d'Arc*, a celebration of Joan of Arc's early victories, perhaps gave her something of a triumph in old age.

A number of Christine's original manuscripts, some copied by her own hand, still exist in various places. Not only in her autobiography but also in many of Christine's poems and prose works there is information about her life. K. J. BRYER

CHRYSOSTOM, JOHN (c. 347–407)
Early church father

Born in Antioch into a moderately wealthy Christian family, Chrysostom studied philosophy, logic, and rhetoric in hopes of becoming a lawyer. Through the influence of another student he became interested in monasticism, but his own monastic ambitions were delayed by his responsibilities for his widowed mother. Even at home, however, he lived under a modified ascetic rule, finally retiring to the mountains about 373 for almost ten years of study and a hermit's existence. When his health broke under the physical hardship, he returned to Antioch and studied under the bishop Melitius, who ordained him deacon in 381. Five years later, he became a priest.

Chrysostom was a gifted and popular preacher, combining sound biblical exposition with practical application. His most famous series of sermons, *On the Statues*, was delivered in 387 after a tax revolt in the city climaxed with the desecration of certain statues of the emperor and his family. The people feared imperial retribution. Chrysostom's able preaching guided the city calmly through the crisis. During his ministry in Antioch he instructed the congregations in Christian doctrine and assumed responsibility for correcting local abuses of clerical office.

When the patriarch of Constantinople died in 397, Chrysostom was appointed to replace him. Unwilling to accept, Chrysostom was captured by the emperor's troops, taken to the imperial city, and consecrated bishop in 398. Dismayed by the laxity in clerical morality and discipline and by the materialistic greed of the laity, Chrysostom fearlessly attacked the vices of the congregation and even criticized the empress Eudoxia and the dissipation of the imperial court. She and the bishop of Alexandria, a frustrated ecclesiastical rival, joined together to remove Chrysostom from office by securing his conviction on twenty-nine charges, including Origenist heresy. (Origen was an Alexandrian theologian whose doctrines had become controversial.) Exiled in 403, Chrysostom was quickly recalled, but soon offended the empress again and was again banished. He died three years later in transit to a more remote place of exile.

Chrysostom's eloquence, which earned him in the sixth century the name

Chrysostomos ("golden-mouthed"), is evident in his extensive sermons and treatises, most of which survive, including commentaries on Genesis, Psalms, Matthew, and Romans, as well as writings on the priesthood and monastic life. Opposed to the allegorical interpretations of Scripture made fashionable by the Alexandrian church, Chrysostom followed the Antiochene method of biblical exegesis. He sought the exact, literal meaning of each verse from a close grammatical examination of the Greek text—a method revived by the Protestant reformers, who regarded Chrysostom as a church father second only to Augustine. K. LEID

CHURCH, RICHARD WILLIAM
(1815–1890)
Anglican scholar and preacher; dean of St. Paul's Cathedral, London

Born in Lisbon (Portugal), Church entered Oxford University in 1833, where he was deeply influenced by John Henry Newman, vicar of St. Mary's Church. In 1851 he became rector at Whatley in Somersetshire. In 1871, on the nomination of W. E. Gladstone, he was appointed dean of St. Paul's Cathedral in London, where he remained until his death. Church achieved distinction as a religious journalist, contributing over one thousand articles to *The Guardian*, an Anglican weekly religious newspaper founded in 1846 to publicize High Church principles. As historian and man of letters he wrote important monographs, including his *Life of St. Anselm* (1870) and a highly acclaimed history, *The Oxford Movement, Twelve Years, 1833 to 1845* (1891). Ten volumes of Church's sermons have been published, some of them described as "among the greatest in the English language."
N. V. HOPE

CLARKE, SAMUEL (1675–1729)
English philosophical theologian

While in Caius College, Cambridge, Clarke became convinced that the physical laws postulated by the scientist and mathematician Isaac Newton explained the facts of natural philosophy better than any other system. He became close friends with Newton and defended Newton's principles throughout his life, thus helping universities accept the validity of the new system of physics. Clarke became a chaplain to Queen Anne in 1706 and the rector of St. James's, Westminster, in 1709. He wrote several theological works but is best known for his Boyle Lectures, published as *A Demonstration of the Being and Attributes of God* (1705) and *A Discourse Concerning the Unchangeable Obligations of Natural Religion* (1706). In these lectures he argued, using mathematical concepts, for belief in God and in Christianity.

Although Clarke defended philosophical theism against empiricism (belief that experience is the only source of knowledge) and deism (belief in an impersonal God on the basis of reason rather than revelation), he sympathized with many empiricist and deist positions. In 1712 he provoked church leaders by writing *The Scripture Doctrine of the Trinity*, which had some Unitarian leanings. The Church of England sought to punish him for heresy, but when Clarke agreed to write no more on the subject, no action was taken. Later Clarke corresponded with the philosopher and mathematician Gottfried Wilhelm Leibnitz, debating such issues as the nature of free will. Clarke claimed that Newtonian principles supported Christian doctrine. Clarke's *Works* were published posthumously in four volumes (1738–1742). G. MINDEMAN

CLARKSON, THOMAS (1760–1846)
English antislavery reformer

Born at Wisbech, Cambridgeshire (England), Clarkson was educated at Cambridge University, where in 1785 he won a prize for a Latin essay on the subject, "Is it lawful to enslave others against their will?" Disturbed by the gross iniquities of slavery, Clarkson decided to devote his life to its abolition. Along with Granville Sharp and ten other Quakers and evangelical Anglicans, he formed a "brotherhood of Christian politicians" dedicated to ending slavery.

Clarkson's chief contribution to the campaign was his tireless diligence in gathering factual data showing the inequities and abuses of slavery, which he published in his *Summary View of the Slave Trade and the Probable Consequences of Its Abolition* (1787).

As a direct result of the agitation of this group, in 1807 importation of slaves was ended in the British empire and in 1833 the institution of slavery was abolished there. Eight hundred thousand slaves were freed and their owners were given 20 million pounds in compensation. Clarkson wrote several books on the history of slave trade, Quakerism, William Penn, and the origins of religion. N. V. HOPE

CLEMENT I (first century)
Pope, c. 88–c. 97

In ancient lists Clement is often placed as the third bishop after the apostle Peter. When Clement served the church of Rome, however, it is doubtful that that church was ruled by a single bishop. He is usually referred to as "Clement of Rome." An early letter to the Corinthian church is attributed to him. (See *Clement of Rome.*) P. TOON

CLEMENT II (died 1047)
Pope, 1046–1047

In 1046 there were three claimants to the papacy: the twenty-five-year-old "puppet pope," Benedict IX; his godfather, Gregory VI, who bought the pontificate from Benedict; and Sylvester II, bishop of Sabina (Italy), who was victim of his rivals' ambitions and ruled only several weeks. Henry III, king of Germany, removed them all and had Suidger, bishop of Bamberg, elected as Clement II in their place. The new pope called a synod in Rome in 1047 where simony (the selling of sacred offices), then a major evil, was condemned. While returning to Rome from a visit to Germany that same year, he died and was buried in the cathedral of Bamberg. P. TOON

CLEMENT III (died 1191)
Pope, 1187–1191

Paoli Scolari, a Roman by birth, was cardinal bishop of Palestrina (Italy) before he became pope. He was the primary organizer of the Third Crusade to the Holy Land. After a bitter quarrel with Henry VI about territorial claims in Italy, Clement died as the German emperor was marching in to annex Sicily. P. TOON

CLEMENT IV (died 1268)
Pope, 1265–1268

Guido Fulcodi was a layman of noble French birth who had two daughters. After his wife's death, he took holy orders and then rose rapidly in the church hierarchy. He was bishop of Le Puy (1257), archbishop of Narbonne (1259), and cardinal-bishop of Sabina (1261). The major preoccupation of his papal rule was a violent struggle between French and German rulers for control of Naples. Clement IV crowned Charles of Anjou king of Sicily in 1266 in gratitude for his victory over the armies of German emperor Manfred, which promised security for the papacy from further German invasion. P. TOON

CLEMENT V (1264–1314)
Pope, 1305–1314

Born at Villandraut in Gascony (France), Bertrand de Got belonged to a prominent French family. He became bishop of Cominges (1295) and archbishop of Bordeaux (1299). He was crowned pope in Lyon (France), and in 1309, by living at Avignon instead of Rome, he began what is called the "seventy years' captivity of the papacy." He allowed the French king, Philip IV, to dominate him, resulting in revision of former papal decisions and the condemnation of Boniface VIII. Clement V showed few scruples in political or church affairs. His positive achievements were in education; he founded the Universities of Orleans (1306) and Perugia (1308). P. TOON

CLEMENT VI (1291–1352)
Pope, 1342–1352

Born at Maumont, Correze (France), Pierre Roger became first a Benedictine monk and then a teacher at the University of Paris. After serving as abbot of Fecamp (1326), bishop of Arras (1328), archbishop of Sens (1329), and archbishop of Rouen (1330), he was elected pope at Avignon. His excessive concern for his relatives and for the interests of France made him a biased and unsuccessful mediator between France and England in the Hundred Years' War. A patron of the arts, he lived in pomp—although to pay for it, he took money from bishoprics throughout Europe, taxed heavily, and practiced simony. Positively, Clement VI showed great courage and charity at the time of the "Black Death" (plagues in Europe during the 1340s), defended the mendicant friars against their enemies, and protected the Jews living in papal states. His bull (papal decree) of 1343 entitled *Unigenitus* provided a "doctrine of indulgences" for the church. P. TOON

CLEMENT VII (1478–1534)
Pope, 1523–1534

Giulio was a cousin of Pope Leo X and a member of the prominent Italian family of Medici. He was elected pope at a time when many were calling for church reform. Though learned, clever, and industrious, he had little enterprise and less decision. His attempts to pursue a middle path in the conflict between Francis I of France and the German emperor Charles V made him appear irresolute and deceitful. His indecision concerning the divorce of Henry VIII from Catherine of Aragon increased tension between England and Rome. In the tradition of his family, however, Clement VII was a patron of the arts who commissioned work to Raphael and Michelangelo. P. TOON

CLEMENT VIII (1536–1605)
Pope, 1592–1605

Born into a distinguished Italian family, Ippolito Aldobrandini was elected pope after a stormy conclave (session of the college of Cardinals called to elect a new pope). He had a reputation for honesty and blamelessness, having been for many years under the spiritual direction of Philip Neri, the "apostle of Rome."

Clement VIII fulfilled the hopes of those who had elected him by reducing the influence of Spain over papal affairs and by helping to bring peace between France and Spain. He encouraged reform in the church and issued new editions of the Vulgate (Latin Bible), the breviary (book of daily services), the missal (book containing the Mass), and the pontifical (book of services used by a bishop). His "Jubilee Year" of 1600 attracted great numbers to Rome to see the renovated holy places. P. TOON

CLEMENT IX (1600–1669)
Pope, 1667–1669

Born Giulio Rospigliosi, Clement IX became a professor of philosophy before entering the service of Pope Urban VIII. Clement became a cardinal and was unanimously elected pope. He sought to identify with the citizens of Rome, visiting hospitals, giving alms, and hearing confessions in St. Peter's two days a week. His interventions in European politics were perceptive. He was instrumental in helping Crete battle Turkish invasions. P. TOON

CLEMENT X (1590–1676)
Pope, 1670–1676

Emilio Altieri, born at Rome, was in his eighties when he was finally elected pope. He had already served four popes in different administrative capacities. He is remembered for his additions to the architectural beauty of Rome: the two fountains adorning the Piazza of St. Peter's, the Palazza Altierei, and the decoration of the bridge of Sant' Angelo. In 1671 he canonized Rose of Lima (Peru) as the first Roman Catholic saint in the New World. P. TOON

CLEMENT XI (1649–1721)
Pope, 1700–1721

Giovanni Francesco Albani led an intellectually active but austere life. His entire career was connected with the papal court. In 1690 he became a cardinal and was only fifty-one years old when elected pope. Although he was very industrious and brought a high moral tone to the papacy, his efforts to influence European rulers met with little success. He failed in an attempt to organize an alliance of Christian princes to defend Venice against the Turks. In the theological sphere, Clement XI condemned Jansenism (a French philosophical movement that formulated a moral rigorism derived from Augustinian theology) in two papal bulls: *Vineam Domini Sabaoth* (1705) and *Unigenitus Dei Filius* (1713). He made the feast of the immaculate conception of the Blessed Virgin Mary compulsory for the Roman Catholic Church. P. TOON

CLEMENT XII (1652–1740)
Pope, 1730–1740

Lorenzo Corsini was born at Florence into a distinguished family. Before his election as pope, he held many important offices at the papal court. In his second papal year he became totally blind but continued with his plans. He initiated a large building program in Rome and the Vatican and attempted to facilitate union with Eastern churches. He issued the first papal decree against the Freemasons (secret trade and religious fraternity) in 1738 and continued the earlier policy of opposition to the Jansenists. P. TOON

CLEMENT XIII (1693–1769)
Pope, 1758–1769

Born in Venice, Carlo della Torre Rezzonico studied law at Padua where later he was appointed bishop. After his election as pope, he made defense of the Society of Jesus his major concern. The Jesuits suffered attacks by the outspoken French thinker François Voltaire and the "Encyclopedists" (French philosophers who authored a com-pendium on the arts and sciences). After the Jesuit order was banned in France, Clement XIII issued the bull *Apostolicum pascendi munus* (1765), which highlighted the merits of the Jesuits and their work. Clement died at a time when pressure on the papacy from Portugal, Spain, Naples, and Parma (now in northern Italy) to abolish the Society of Jesus became impossible to withstand. With respect to piety, he encouraged devotion to the "sacred heart of Jesus." P. TOON

CLEMENT XIV (1705–1774)
Pope, 1769–1774

Born near Rimini (Italy), Giovanni Vincenzo Antonio Ganganelli became a Franciscan at the age of eighteen and in 1759 was created a cardinal by Clement XIII. He was elected pope after a conclave noted for bitter political machinations. Clement XIV inherited the Jesuit controversy from his predecessor and decided, in order to improve relations with the major European powers, to suppress the Jesuits. The brief (papal letter) *Dominus ac Redemptor* (1773), however, did not ease political tension or impede the irreligion and atheism which were often promoted by European secular powers. Positively, Clement XIV is remembered as founder of the University of Munster (1773). Rumors spread that he was poisoned by a Jesuit, but in fact he died of natural causes. P. TOON

CLEMENT OF ALEXANDRIA (c. 155–c. 220)
First Christian writer to show extensive knowledge of pagan and Christian writings

Titus Flavius Clement was probably born in Athens of pagan parents and became a Christian through his study of philosophy. After traveling to the centers of learning in the Greek-speaking East, he joined Pantaenus's school in Alexandria. Pantaenus impressed Clement by his ability to interpret the Scripture. The school which began with Pantaenus in 180 later became the official church catechetical school of Alexandria under Origen. Clement succeeded Pantaenus as head of the school circa 190.

The nature of the school in that early period and the writing of Clement reflected the cultural mixture of Alexandria. It was a mixture in which an independent school operated by Clement could have pagans, Christians, and Jews seeking an education together. Thus an Alexandrian philosopher, Ammonius Saccas (c. 175–c. 242), could teach both the Greek philosopher Plotinus, founder of Neoplatonism, and Origen, influential Christian theologian and successor of Clement.

During his years as a teacher in Alexandria (190–202) Clement wrote most of his works. In them he followed Philo (c. 20 B.C.–A.D. 50), an Alexandrian Jewish writer who had used Greek philosophy to interpret the Old Testament. Clement adopted Philo's allegorical method of interpreting Scripture, often quoting Philo at length and using his thought. To pagans, Clement wrote *Exhortation to the Gentiles* with the same arguments employed by the Christian writers known as the Apologists, but with a more sophisticated style. Also, by using extensive quotes, he tried to show an ascending revelation upward through the poets, the philosophers, the Sybil prophetess, and the Hebrew prophets to the highest revelation, the "Divine Word," Christ. In the *Instructor* he covered almost every aspect of Christian conduct, including even a long section on "laughter." The pattern of conduct he recommended was one of moderation. The authority he quoted most often in the *Instructor* was Ecclesiasticus, a book from the Apocrypha. *Miscellanies* was Clement's major work. According to his explanation of it and its title, one must go through a "patchwork" of ideas to the truth, like winnowing wheat through sieves. In it he called philosophy the "schoolmaster" to bring the Hellenistic mind to Christ. He believed that God had used philosophy to lead the pre-Christian Greeks to a knowledge of the truth of Christ. Although the teaching of Christ was complete in itself, philosophy served Clement as the "wall of the vineyard" to defend the truth of Christianity. One of

Clement's sermons has survived (*Who is the Rich Man that shall be Saved?*), but only outlines and fragments of some eight other works. He also wrote many letters. Although the status of Clement as a church father was later called into question, he was the forerunner and teacher of Origen, who exerted a primary influence upon the theology of the East.

Clement fled Alexandria during the persecution under Roman emperor Septimius Severus about 202 and died in Asia Minor.
J. NEWTON

CLEMENT OF ROME (died c. 100)
Earliest of the apostolic fathers

Clement was a presbyter (priest) and bishop in Rome who wrote a letter to the church at Corinth (96), probably the earliest Christian writing outside the New Testament. Dionysius of Corinth (170) was the first to name Clement as the author of that letter. Origen, an Alexandrian theologian, and Eusebius, the first church historian, identified the writer as the "Clement" listed in the *Shepherd of Hermas,* a Christian writing from the mid-second century. There are problems, however, with all attempts to identify Clement.

Clement, in the letter to the Corinthians, wrote on behalf of the church in Rome, admonishing the Corinthian Christians to restore some older presbyters who had been ousted by younger members. Clement drew from the "noble examples" of the Old Testament and of the New Testament church to show the way of humility which yields to God's order. The order had been established in the presbyter-bishops and deacons appointed by the apostles. Clement followed a New Testament form of church government, but gave emphasis to the apostolic appointment of officers.

There is a marked departure from the New Testament in Clement's letter. In his use of "noble examples" and in his view of nature, Clement showed the influence of Stoic philosophy (a Greek school of thought stressing the development of virtue and the concept of natural law). He used the myth of the phoenix as an example from nature to illustrate the resurrection of Christ. In his quotation of the entire chapter of Isaiah 53, he made no attempt to teach the death of Christ for sins but, rather, used it only as an example of humility. Clement seemed to lack the New Testament's understanding of Christ's work.

Clement quoted extensively from the Old Testament as "Scripture" and from the words of Jesus, using sayings found in Matthew, Mark, and Luke. He also quoted Romans, 1 Corinthians, and Hebrews. Thus Clement provides important evidence that books which later became part of the New Testament canon were circulating among the churches by the end of the first century. Clement's letter also provides important evidence for the martyrdom of the apostles Peter and Paul, and for a mission of Paul to the "western boundary" (i.e., Spain).

J. NEWTON

CLERMONT-GANNEAU, CHARLES (1846–1923)

French consul in Jerusalem; Orientalist

Clermont-Ganneau gained scholarly recognition for his part in the recovery of the Moabite Stone (1869), now in the Louvre Museum in Paris. The text on the stone describes the wars of Mesha, a Moabite king, supplementing the account in 2 Kings 3:4-27. In 1871 Clermont-Ganneau found an inscribed stone from the Temple in Jerusalem forbidding Gentiles to enter the "court of the Jews" (see Acts 21:28-29). Subsequently (1873–1874), when the Palestine Exploration Fund put him in charge of an archaeological mission in Palestine, he identified the site of Gezer. In later years he directed expeditions to Syria (1881), to the Red Sea (1886), to Cyrenaica and Crete (1895), and to the island of Elephantine in Egypt (1906–1908). Clermont-Ganneau rose to a high position in the French consular service and later served as director of the School of Oriental Languages and professor at the College of France in Paris.

H. F. VOS

CLIFFORD, JOHN (1836–1923)

English Baptist minister and politician

Clifford as a teenager worked in a lace factory in Derbyshire until local Baptists (in 1855), seeing his talents, sent him to study at the General Baptist Academy in Leicester. In 1859 he was called to be the minister of a congregation that met in Praed Street Chapel, which in 1877 moved to Westbourne Park Chapel, London. While there he pursued his education, taking four degrees from the recently founded University of London. In 1883 Bates College in the United States awarded him the doctor of divinity degree. In 1888 and 1889 he was President of the Baptist Union for the first time and for some years was engaged in the "downgrade" controversy after the Union was accused of heresy by C. H. Spurgeon.

Politically, Clifford was closely associated with the radical wing of the Liberal party and led a movement for passive resistance against the Education Act of 1902, believing that the act was injurious to Nonconformists (English Protestants who were not members of the Church of England). That resistance contributed to the defeat of the Unionist government in 1906. From 1905 to 1911 Clifford was the first president of the Baptist World Alliance. Toward the end of his life he became more interested in personal evangelism than controversial issues. Theologically he was less conservative than many of his Baptist colleagues, but his participation in national life made him influential among Nonconformists. P. TOON

CLOUGH, JOHN EVERETT (1836–1910)

Baptist missionary in South India; often known as the "apostle to the Telugus"

Born in Frewsbury, New York, Clough lived a rugged youth in frontier Illinois and Iowa. He and his wife, Emma, began missionary service in the Ongole area of India in 1865. Through their efforts a mass movement began, especially among Madiga outcastes. During the famine of 1876 to 1878 Clough organized relief work that included building the Buckingham Canal, a government project. During a six-week period after the famine, about nine thousand people were baptized and joined the church.

Keenly aware of the social implications of the gospel, Clough fought adamantly against social evils. When he evangelized people, he respected the social and ethnic customs of the converts and built churches on indigenous principles. When Clough reluctantly left India in 1910, he left behind sixty thousand church members in a mission field that had been almost abandoned in discouragement before his coming. His wife compiled his biography. S. P. ATHYAL

CLOVIS (c. 466–511)

King of the Franks, 481–511; founded the Merovingian dynasty and led his people in accepting Christianity

Clovis first learned of Christianity when he married Clothilda of Burgundy. She continually tried to convert him, but he did not become a Christian until 496, when the danger of losing a battle against the Alemanni inspired him to seek the aid of his wife's God. After emerging victorious he consented to be baptized. Clovis then used his religious faith as an excuse to expand his political power, pushing the Visigoths, who were Arians and hence heretics, out of southern France. His apparent conversion did not diminish his willingness to use brutality and treachery against those who opposed him. Receiving church support, he appointed clergymen as envoys and governors and thereby secured wider territorial control. Thus Clovis established Frankish rule firmly in Gaul and created footholds for wider Roman Catholic influence in western Europe. C. HICKS

CLOWES, WILLIAM (1780–1851)

Founder, along with Hugh Bourne and James Steele, of the Primitive Methodist Church in Britain

Born in the working-class area of Staffordshire, where pottery was a major industry, Clowes became a potter. After a dramatic conversion in the revival of 1805 at Tunstall at a Methodist "love-feast" (based

on 1 Corinthians 11), he became an enthusiastic Methodist.

He felt called to preach and took part in the first American-style camp meeting at Mow Cop in 1807. His commitment to this type of evangelism led to his expulsion from his Methodist society in 1810. He and others then formed an independent society at Tunstall which in 1812 united with the "camp-meeting Methodists" (who also had been expelled by official Methodism) led by Hugh Bourne to form the Primitive Methodist Church. A person of lively imagination and fluent utterance, Clowes traveled widely as a preacher and organizer in the revival movement among the working classes. P. TOON

COCCEIUS, JOHANNES (1603–1669)

Reformed linguist and father of "federal theology"

A German by birth, Cocceius was educated at Hamburg and Franeker and taught at Bremen, Franeker, and Leyden. He denounced the scholastic tendencies within Calvinistic orthodoxy and emphasized the need to develop theology from the historical covenants of Scripture. He asserted that God related to mankind through two covenants, one made with Adam and the other with Moses. God's first covenant was a covenant of works, contingent on Adam's obedience. Cocceius's federal theology emphasized that Adam was the natural head of the human race and represented all mankind. The entire human race fell with Adam's disobedience, so God replaced this covenenant with a covenant of grace with Moses which offered salvation as the gift of God. This covenant was revealed through a succession of historical events, prefigured in the Old Testament and fully revealed in the New Testament through Jesus Christ. Jesus has become the federal head, or representative, of all believers under the covenant of grace. "As in Adam all die," wrote Paul, "even so in Christ shall all be made alive" (1 Cor. 15:22). Cocceius emphasized God's covenant of grace as opposed to the more austere Calvinistic emphasis on God's unilateral decrees. After his death, his followers were accused of unorthodoxy. He was a professor of Hebrew and displayed his considerable knowledge of oriental languages throughout his written works. His most important treatise was *Summa doctrinae de Foedere et Testament Dei.* C. WHITACRE

COCHLAEUS, JOHANNES (1479–1552)
Roman Catholic controversialist

Cochlaeus was born in Wendelstein, near Nuremberg (Germany), and he studied in Nuremburg under Heinrich Grieninger, a humanist; he also studied at the University of Cologne (1504), where he was associated with the reformer Ulrich von Hutten. After teaching in Nuremberg for five years, Cochlaeus went to Italy, where he received a Th.D. at Ferrara (1517).

At first in favor of Martin Luther, Cochlaeus later began writing violent pamphlets against him and the Reform movement. In 1525 he vigorously opposed the printing of Tyndale's New Testament in Cologne because of its Lutheran tendencies. Many of Cochlaeus's fellow Roman Catholics thought his writings too violent. After living in several places in western Germany, he finally settled in Dresden (1528) under the protection of Duke George of Saxony. While there he was chosen to serve on a Roman Catholic commission established to refute the Augsburg Confession. After George's death, Cochlaeus moved to Breslau. He attended a number of diets (formal assemblies), but because of his temperament he was usually not permitted to participate. He was not allowed to participate in the Council of Trent. Before his death, Cochlaeus wrote a history of Hussitism and attacks on Luther's doctrine of the sacraments. Cochlaeus's scurrilous account of Luther's activities later formed the basis of certain Roman Catholic anti-Lutheran polemics. W. S. REID

CODRINGTON, ROBERT HENRY (1830–1922)
English missionary anthropologist; fellow of Wadham College, Oxford

After becoming a clergyman of the Church of England in 1860, Codrington migrated to New Zealand and joined the Melanesian Mission. As a missionary he trained Melanesian evangelists at Norfolk Island (publishing the autobiography on one, Clement Marau) and traveled throughout Melanesia. After the murder of Bishop Patteson, Melanesia's first missionary bishop, Codrington headed up the mission (1871–1877), although he declined the bishopric.

Codrington researched the Torres, Loyalty, Banks, and eastern Solomon Islands languages, especially Mota, compiling a major linguistic volume. His greatest contribution to anthropology was investigating and interpreting the doctrine of *mana,* the dominant phenomenological concept of Melanesian religion. He analyzed much of Melanesian social structure and the functional role of secret societies.

After leaving Melanesia he served as vicar of Wadhurst (1888–1893) and bishop of Chichester (1894–1901) and published his Melanesian anthropology, a basic reference work for later missionaries. A. R. TIPPETT

COFFIN, HENRY SLOANE (1877–1954)
American Presbyterian clergyman and educator

Born in New York City, Coffin was educated at Yale University, New College (Edinburgh), and Union Theological Seminary (New York). In 1900 he founded the Bedford Park Presbyterian Church in the Bronx. In 1905 he became minister of the Madison Avenue Presbyterian Church in Manhattan, from which he was called in 1926 to be president of Union Seminary, a post he held until 1945. Coffin gave the seminary's program a new dimension by founding its School of Sacred Music in 1928. In 1943 he was elected moderator of the General Assembly of the Presbyterian Church in the U.S.A.

Coffin was an able and influential preacher and wrote two books on the subject: *What to Preach* (1926) and *Communion Through Preaching* (1951). He was many-sided in his ecclesiastical concerns. In 1910 he coedited a hymnbook entitled *Hymns of the Kingdom of God*. A convinced believer in the social gospel, he expounded his views on that question in his Lyman Beecher lectures at Yale in 1918, entitled *In a Day of Social Rebuilding*. A leader of the liberal wing of his denomination, Coffin worked actively in the ecumenical movement as an early participant in its Life and Work branch and at its Oxford Conference in 1937, where he was chairman of the section on Church, Community, and State in Relation to Education. Between 1940 and 1946 he took part in union negotiations between the Presbyterian Church in the U.S.A. and the Protestant Episcopal Church, which proved fruitless. N. V. HOPE

COGGAN, FREDERICK DONALD
(born 1909)

Archbishop of Canterbury, 1974–1980

Born in London, he graduated from Cambridge and taught Semitic studies at Manchester University (1931–1934) before training for the priesthood at Wycliffe Hall, Oxford. He was professor of New Testament at Wycliffe College, Toronto (1937–1944); principal of London College of Divinity (1944–1956); bishop of Bradford (1956–1961); and archbishop of York (1961–1974) before appointment as the 101st archbishop of Canterbury. The first mainline evangelical to hold the post this century, he was concerned about sound biblical scholarship and preaching. He was an early supporter of the Inter-Varsity Fellowship in England (he wrote its official history: *Christ and the Colleges*, 1974), and subsequently undertook leading roles in the United Bible Societies, in the preparation of the New English Bible, and in *Feed the Minds*, with its concern for Third World literature. He was an eager advocate also of home mission work. His many books include *The Ministry of the Word* (1946), *Stewards of Grace* (1958), *Christian Priorities* (1963), *On Preaching* (1978), and *Mission to the World* (1982). He was created a baron by Queen Elizabeth II on his retirement. J. D. DOUGLAS

COKE, THOMAS (1747–1814)

Methodist superintendent and bishop who served as John Wesley's emissary to America and did much to strengthen Methodist missions

Born in Brecon (Wales), Coke graduated from Oxford in 1768 and then returned home to take municipal posts. Four years later he became the Anglican curate of South Petherton, Somerset (England). A visit with Thomas Maxfield, one of Wesley's evangelists, led to Coke's conversion and inclined him toward Methodism. When in 1776 he was dismissed from his parish for being too "fervent" in his preaching, he joined the Methodist cause.

Appointed the Methodist superintendent for America, Coke came to the new nation in 1784 with instructions from Wesley to Francis Asbury, the only one among Wesley's appointees who had remained in America during the American Revolution. A "Christmas Conference" chaired by Coke was called in that year, leading to the formation in America of the Methodist Episcopal Church. Coke's influence on American Methodism soon waned, however, while Asbury's increased. Though the two leaders frequently disagreed, they were united in antislavery sentiments and together presented an antislavery petition to George Washington in 1785.

Coke traveled from England to the United States nine times. In 1791 he made an unsuccessful effort to unite Methodists and Episcopalians; the American movement begun by Wesley was following its own increasingly autonomous course. After Coke's last transAtlantic voyage in 1803, he turned his efforts to missionary ventures in the West Indies, Gibraltar, and Africa, becoming president of the first Methodist missionary organization, formed in England in 1804. Coke died at sea, en route to Ceylon (now Sri Lanka) with a group of missionaries. M. FACKLER

COLENSO, JOHN WILLIAM
(1814–1883)

Bishop of Natal (South Africa); biblical scholar

Colenso was born in Cornwall (England) and educated at St. John's College, Cambridge, where he was elected fellow in 1837 and tutor in 1842. He served as vicar in Norfolk, and in 1853 was appointed bishop of Natal. Colenso's initial concern as bishop was the problem of polygamous converts. Conservatives within the Anglican church insisted that they divorce all but one wife. Colenso was more lenient, allowing converts to retain their wives, a position for which he was harshly criticized by some fellow clergy.

In 1861 Colenso authored a commentary on the book of Romans in which he denied eternal punishment and rejected sacramental theology. Again his views placed him at the center of controversy. Then he wrote a series of works titled *The Pentateuch and the Book of Joshua Critically Examined* (published between 1862 and 1879), which challenged the Mosaic authorship of the Pentateuch and the historicity of the narratives. An uproar resulted in both England and South Africa. Colenso was deposed as bishop in 1863 but appealed the decision, which was reversed in 1865. He continued his work in Africa, enjoying the affection and support of his adopted people until his death. K. HOGLUND

COLERIDGE, SAMUEL TAYLOR
(1772–1834)

English poet, philosopher, and literary critic

Coleridge was the son of a village vicar who died when the boy was nine. Coleridge attended Christ's Hospital, one of the best schools in England, and in 1791 entered Cambridge, which he left, returned to, and left again without ever taking a degree. Briefly influenced by utopian socialist ideas during those years, he married Sarah Fricker, the daughter of a family that figured prominently in the utopian movement. The marriage was not a happy one.

Coleridge's real achievement began only after he met the English poet William Wordsworth in 1795. That association resulted in their collaborating to publish the *Lyrical Ballads* (1798), a landmark in liter-

ary history. Coleridge's most significant contribution to the volume was "The Rime of the Ancient Mariner," an eerie ballad of the supernatural that concludes with the ancient mariner destined to teach reverence for all things God made. In the same year Coleridge composed two poetic *fragments*: "Christabel," which captures the magical glamour of a medieval romance, and "Kubla Khan," an exotic and visually opulent product of an opium dream.

In 1798 Coleridge toured the European continent with William and Dorothy Wordsworth. The next year he attended the University of Göttingen (Germany), and, mastering the German language, he absorbed German Romanticism and the philosophy of Immanuel Kant. Coleridge's return to England coincided with the waning of his poetic powers. He became addicted to opium, with which he had earlier dabbled, and although he was able to diminish that addiction, his creative work was permanently hampered. In spite of the high quality of his poetry, his overall poetic output was disappointingly small. "Dejection: An Ode" (1802) and "Youth and Age" (1828–1832) depict the disillusionment brought by his realization of his impeded abilities.

Coleridge spent his remaining years working on a variety of literary and philosophical projects but writing only a few more poems. His *Biographia Literaria* (1817), probably the most important work of his later years, is a study of the Romantic ideals of art and life. It is heavily tinged with Neoplatonic ideas that, in Coleridge's treatment, border on pantheism. To some extent, the work is a spiritual autobiography.

Although Coleridge's reputation today is based chiefly on his poetry, he was also very active in philosophical and religious reflection. After being attracted to Unitarianism and to German mystical pantheism, he returned to the Christian faith. Thereafter one of his chief concerns was to reconcile philosophy (in which he opposed the rampant rationalism and materialism of his day) with the Christian beliefs he held. That concern produced several works, among them the

Lay Sermons (1816); Aids to Reflection (1825); On the constitution of Church and State (1830); and the posthumous Confessions of an Inquiring Spirit (1840), dealing primarily with the authority of Scripture. Coleridge's concern for the unity of Christendom expressed in some of his writings influenced the late-nineteenth-century broad-church movement in the Anglican church. E. B. BATSON

COLET, JOHN (c. 1466–1519)
Dean of St. Paul's Cathedral; educator

Son of Henry Colet, twice London's lord mayor, Colet was educated at Oxford. He also studied in France and Italy, where he added Greek to his existing knowledge of Latin. Ordained in 1497, Colet returned to Oxford to deliver his momentous lectures on Paul's letters, a five-year series. Based on Paul's life and traits, this featured Colet's original exegesis and his concern over the early church's character and example. From this point, his ministry emphasized corrupt practices in his era's church life and avenues for broad renewal.

Colet's reformist message elicited frequent charges of false teaching from other churchmen. But unmoved by thoughts of leaving the Roman Catholic Church, he had many supporters, including his fellow reformers, Desiderius Erasmus and Thomas More, both close friends. In 1504, Colet was made dean of London's St. Paul's Catheral, a post he retained until his death. Inheriting his father's fortune in 1505, he distributed this wealth to various worthy enterprises. A large part was used to found and endow his great achievement, St. Paul's School in London. This provided high-quality instruction for the best students irrespective of background. With its inclusion of Greek, the school also stressed humanist studies (the classics) together with Scripture and theology. All of Colet's important works have been preserved. His greatest writings, *Sacraments of the Church,* and *Commentaries on St. Paul's Letters,* have English translations and modern editions. Colet's life and work exemplified a very responsible yet penetrating type of church reform. K. J. BRYER

COLIGNY, GASPARD DE (1519–1572)
Hero of French Protestants during religious strife of the 1560s

Born into an important family, by the age of twenty-two Coligny was a favorite at the French court. During France's territorial conflicts, in 1544 he served in the Italian campaign, later becoming colonel general of infantry and in 1552 admiral of France. Captured by the Spaniards, he was held prisoner for two years, during which time he was evidently converted to Protestantism.

In 1555 Coligny planned to establish a colony for Huguenots (French Protestants) in Brazil, but failed. In 1560 he came out publicly on the side of the Huguenots, although he disdained the political power struggles between Catholic and Protestant factions in France. On the death of the prince of Conde in 1569, however, Coligny became chief of the Huguenot forces. Defeated at Montcontour in 1569, he raised another army and forced a favorable treaty from the young king Charles IX. Coligny soon became one of the king's favorites and sought to persuade him to raise a combined army of Huguenots and Catholics to fight the Spaniards. That proposal was unacceptable to the powerful queen mother, Catherine de' Medici, and her supporters, the Guises, the principal Catholic family. Together they persuaded Charles to order the massacre of Protestants gathered in Paris for Henry of Navarre's marriage to Catherine's daughter Margaret. In the resulting massacre of St. Bartholomew's Eve (1572), Coligny and thousands of other Protestants were killed. W. S. REID

COLUMBA (521–597)
Irish monk; missionary to Scotland

Born in Donegal, descended from royal blood on both sides, Columba was educated in monastic schools and soon acquired scholarly distinction, a saintly reputation, and growing fame as a miracle worker. After nearly twenty years in Ireland as an evangelist and a founder of churches and monasteries, he set out for Scotland with twelve companions and arrived on the island of Iona in 563. He overcame the Druids, secured the independence of the Scots from the Picts, brought civilization to lawless people, improved their agriculture, and gave them the Bread of Life.

From the monastery he established on Iona, his monks went out. Their influence was to play a key part in the evangelization also of England. Columba contributed greatly to the blending of pagan and Christian culture that was to mean so much in the re-Christianization of Europe, and in the revival of secular learning. He was responsible for introducing the written Gaelic language, spreading it with the gospel among the Picts, and so providing the medium for the Celtic literature of the Highlands. He was fresh and full of zest, which led to his being called the saint of the young. Like a true Celt he held that Christ had redeemed all creation and that to reject the loveliness of earth was to reject the kingship of Christ, Lord of all life. He died just after he was engaged in his much-loved occupation of copying the Scriptures. It was 597—the very year Augustine landed to initiate his great work in England. J. D. DOUGLAS

COLUMBANUS (c. 543–615)
Irish scholar; missionary to western Europe

Born into a Christian home in Leinster (east Ireland), Columbanus studied for some years under the Irish monk and educator Comgall in his famous monastic institution at Bangor. Columbanus wrote religious verse, became proficient in Hebrew and Greek (an unusual accomplishment for that time), and developed into a noted biblical expositor.

When he was past forty Columbanus went to Gaul (France), where in the kingdom of Burgundy he established monasteries at Anegray, Luxeuil, and Fontaines. Discipline was strict: Columbanus gave six strokes of the lash for failing to respond "Amen" when grace was said at table. In his own Celtic church, saints mortified the flesh by standing neck-deep in cold water to recite the psalms. His Celtic practices brought opposition from the French bishops and clergy, but the Irish abbot was uncompromising and thought nothing of disagreeing with Pope Gregory the Great (pope, 590–604).

Columbanus had a great ministry to nominal Christians. His counsel was sought even by bishops and clergy whose simony (the buying and selling of church offices) and immorality he rebuked. He set up a pattern of missionary outreach to pagans, which his successors followed. Expelled from Burgundy by its king in 610 for outspokenness against court irregularities, Columbanus resettled first at Bregenz on Lake Constance (Switzerland), then in 613 at Bobbio in northern Italy. At Bobbio the monastic house became a prominent center for learning and for the defense of orthodoxy. J. D. DOUGLAS

COMENIUS, JOHN AMOS (1592–1670)
Educator and bishop of the Bohemian Brethren (later called the Moravian Brethren)

Comenius was born in Moravia (now the central part of Czechoslovakia). He studied theology there and then at Heidelberg (Germany). From 1618 to 1621 he was a Brethren minister at Fulnek (Moravia). Moving away from the hostilities of the Thirty Years' War, he taught at Lissa (Poland). There he produced a major educational work, *The Great Didactic,* published in 1632. In it he presented a plan for a complete system of education for every province and country, from the home through elementary public and Latin schools to the university. In a world suffering from a bloody war, Comenius saw education as the medium to bring peace. From 1641 to 1648 he traveled to England, Sweden, and Germany, collecting materials for his continuing educational work.

Comenius returned to Lissa in 1648 and became a bishop of the Bohemian Brethren. From 1650 to 1654 he lived in Hungary, where he finished his last work, *Unum Necessorium*, not published until 1668.

Comenius's educational ideals were based upon his personal religious faith. In *Unum Necessorium* he hoped for a utopian church to unite all religions in Christian love through education. The goal of schooling was to mold students into the image of Christ. That is, Christian character, not just the absorption of facts, was the object of learning. Before Comenius, education had focused largely on learning languages, but he thought the acquisition of linguistic ability should be accompanied by the observation of one's physical environment, one's own body, and features in one's country. He believed in educating boys and girls equally and rejected physical punishment. In later centuries some of his writings were rediscovered and the Comenius Society was formed in 1890 to preserve his educational ideals. One seven-volume work by Comenius, of which only two volumes had been published in his lifetime, was lost in the eighteenth century, found in the 1930s, and published in 1966 in Czechoslovakia.

R. VONDERLACK

CONDE, LOUIS I DE BOURBON, PRINCE DE (1530–1569)

French Huguenot (Protestant) and opportunistic political leader

In 1560 Conde took part in the Amboise Conspiracy, an unsuccessful attempt to secure official recognition for Reformed Christianity in France and to end the influence of the Guise family in the government. Conde was arrested, but escaped execution when Francis II died. The new regime of Catherine de' Medici favored the Huguenots and gave Conde the position of governor of Picardy. In 1562, however, when the government changed back into the hands of the Guises, he left his post and ultimately joined the Huguenot army to fight for religious liberty. Conde's effectiveness as a religious leader was hampered considerably by his licentious way of life. He was executed following surrender at the battle of Jarnac.

G. MINDEMAN

CONSTANTINE THE GREAT
(c. 285–337)

First "Christian emperor" of the Roman Empire; ruled from 306–337

Constantine's parents were Constantius Chlorus, the Western coemperor of the Roman empire, and Helena, a concubine. When his father died in England in 306, Constantine was proclaimed emperor by the troops but grudgingly accepted by Galerius, the Eastern emperor. The government of the empire was thrown into turmoil, and within two years five men had claimed to be emperor.

Shortly before his death in 311, Galerius, the senior coemperor, issued an edict of toleration which ended the persecution of Christians. With Galerius gone, Constantine and Licinius (who had become his coemperor) allied themselves together against Maxentius and Maximin Daia. In 312 Constantine defeated and killed Maxentius in a battle at the Mulvian Bridge near Rome. Maximin Daia fell to Licinius in the next year. An uneasy peace between Constantine and Licinius was maintained until 323, when Constantine crossed into Licinius's territory while chasing out Gothic invaders. Battles at Adrianople and Chrysopolis in the next year decided the matter and left Constantine the sole emperor.

One of his most significant political moves was the founding of the city of Constantinople, dedicated in 330 on the site of Byzantium. Its location on the Strait of Bosporus was ideal from a military standpoint since it gave access to both the Rhine-Danube and Persian fronts. Constantine continued a reorganization of government started by Diocletian (reigned 284–305) and reformed the currency. He also allowed barbarians to settle within the empire in order to use them in the army.

Constantine is most remembered for his religious policies. The nature of his own religious beliefs has been disputed. From the first he was tolerant of Christians in his own realm. His preference for Christianity was demonstrated just before the battle at the Mulvian Bridge. According to one account, in a dream before the battle Constantine saw a vision of a monogram composed of the first two Greek letters of the name of "Christ." The next day he had his soldiers inscribe that monogram on their shields. Another story says that while marching one day he and his army saw the image of a cross appear before the sun with the words, "In this sign conquer." During the winter of 312 and 313, he wrote to an officer in North Africa instructing him to supply money to the bishop of Carthage in order to pay expenses of the clergy. When he and Licinius met in Milan in 313, they issued an edict granting all persons the freedom to follow whichever religion they wished. His Christian sentiments also resulted in laws allowing bishops to decide civil lawsuits, banning any branding on the face (because it marred the image of God), closing law courts and workshops on Sunday, and banning gladiatorial games. Though he favored Christianity, Constantine was also tolerant of paganism and, as late as 324, pagan themes were engraved on his coins. With Christians such a minority in the empire, Constantine felt he could not risk offending the pagan majority.

Constantine took an active role in church controversies. When Caecilian was challenged as bishop of Carthage (313) by the Donatists (separatists in the African church), Constantine instructed the bishops of Rome to summon a commission to hear the case. Since the Donatists were not content with the results of that commission, Constantine himself eventually heard the case, and in 316 he declared Caecilian to be the rightful bishop. Constantine also summoned the Council of Nicea in 325, which ruled against Arianism (a heresy that denied that Christ as the Son of God was coeternal with the Father). It was the emperor's edict which gave legal force to the Nicean decision.

One serious scandal marred Constantine's reign. In 326 he had his son Crispus and his own wife, Faustus, executed on charges of adultery. Constantine was succeeded by his three other sons (Constans, Constantius, Constantine II), after being baptized a Christian on his deathbed (according to legend). C. HICKS

CONTARINI, GASPAR (1483–1542)
Venetian cardinal concerned with reconciliation of Protestants and Roman Catholics in the early Reformation period

Contarini was born into an aristocratic family and was well educated. In 1521 he was Venetian ambassador to Emperor Charles V, and after the Spanish sack of Rome he helped to reconcile pope and emperor. In 1516, Contarini wrote a defense of the immortality of the soul directed against Pietro Pompnazzi. He also published a work against Martin Luther entitled *Confutatio Articulorum Seu Quaestionum Lutheri* (1530). In 1535 Pope Paul III appointed Contarini, although a lay person, to be a cardinal.

Although Contarini had evangelical leanings, he was not prepared to break with the Roman Catholic Church. He did not care for Luther or popular movements, believing that reform must come from within the church hierarchy. He was appointed to a commission for recommending reforms and prepared a statement about reconciling Protestants and Roman Catholics in Italy. Although that proposal was shelved, in 1541 Contarini was a delegate to the Colloquy of Ratisbon, where he strove to bring the Lutherans back into the Roman Catholic Church. At that time he wrote a treatise on justification which was opposed by Counter-Reformation leaders.

Contarini died while he was a papal legate at Bologna. Had he lived longer, he might have been forced by the Inquisition, the Roman Catholic tribunal then authorized to suppress heresy, to decide whether he would remain in the Church. His two most important writings were *De Magisratibus Republica Venetorum* (1543), in which he advocated republican principles, and *Epistola de Justificatione* (1541). In 1539 his *Concilium de Emendanda Ecclesia* (1537) was placed on the Index (the Roman Catholic list of officially banned books). W. S. REID

CONWELL, RUSSELL HERMAN (1843–1925)

Minister of what became the Baptist Temple in Philadelphia; best known for a lecture ("Acres of Diamonds") that he gave more than six thousand times across the United States

Born in Worthington, Massachusetts, Conwell was converted from atheism to Christianity after suffering severe wounds at the battle of Kennesaw Mountain during the Civil War, in which he served as a Union officer. He graduated from Albany University in 1866 and was ordained a Baptist minister in 1879. In Philadelphia Conwell started Temple College in 1888 (a night school for working people), which developed into Temple University. The Conwell School of Theology, originally part of the university, merged in 1969 with Gordon Divinity School (Massachusetts).

Exhorting his audiences—who paid for admission—Conwell, in his "Acres of Diamonds" address, said: "I say that you ought to get rich, and it is your duty to get rich . . . to make money honestly is to preach the gospel." While honoring the Bible as true, Conwell stressed his belief that hard, intelligent work and godliness yield material reward. D. MUNSON

COOK, DAVID CALEB (1850–1927)

Pioneer publisher of Sunday school materials; founder of the David C. Cook Publishing Company

Cook was born in a Methodist parsonage in East Worcester, New York. His parents moved to a farm near Wheaton, Illinois, and then to Wheaton, where Cook attended Wheaton College. When his father opened a small printing shop in Chicago, Cook learned to set type. This skill stood him in good stead when he became disappointed by the lack of suitable printed materials to help him teach his Sunday school classes of children gleaned from the streets of Chicago. He started writing his own lesson leaflets and printing them on a small press in his father's shop. Other teachers asked for copies, and what began as a spare-time occupation be-

came a full-time business. David C. Cook lived to see the company he founded in 1875 become the largest publisher of nondenominational Sunday school literature in the world. G. J. PETERSON

COPERNICUS, NICOLAS (1473–1543)

Polish astronomer and cleric; his theory of the operation of the solar system became the foundation of modern astronomy

Educated at the University of Kraków (Poland), Copernicus later went to Italy to study canon law in Bologna and to lecture on mathematics and astronomy in Rome. On his return in 1505, he began to formulate his ideas on the solar system.

Copernicus did not base his ideas primarily on his own observations of the heavens. Rather, he tried to straighten out the confusion experienced by other observers in predicting motions of the planets. Ptolemy (second century A.D.) had stated that the earth was the fixed center of the universe; around the earth all heavenly bodies moved in perfectly circular orbits. For almost fourteen hundred years the Ptolemaic system had been patched up by so many mathematical corrections that it was terribly complicated—but still didn't work very well. Instead of trying to patch it further, Copernicus abandoned the geocentric concept (of planets, sun, and moon revolving around the earth) for a heliocentric concept (of the earth and other planets orbiting around the sun). Others had made such a suggestion before Copernicus, but he proceeded to work it out mathematically.

The Copernican system still had some errors in it, such as the circular orbits retained from the Ptolemaic system and some "epicycles" necessary to adjust those cycles to fit the real planetary motions (which are in the form of ellipses). But it was far simpler than the old system and immediately explained several puzzles, including apparently backward (retrograde) motions of certain planets at times. At first Copernicus conceived his theory merely as an aid to calculation, not as a description of the true motions of the planets. The thought of the earth flying through space was too much for most people to grasp. Theologians feared it might destroy faith in God as Creator of an orderly and finite universe.

Toward the end of his life Copernicus was persuaded to publish the book *De Revolutionibus Orbium Coelestium* (*On Revolutions of the Heavenly Spheres*, 1543), in which he described his new system. He carefully dedicated it to Pope Paul III, and although Copernicus by then evidently thought he was describing real motions, someone else added a preface stating that the theory was not being put forward as a description of actual planetary motions. Nevertheless, both Martin Luther and the Roman Catholic hierarchy opposed the Copernican theory on theological grounds. *De Revolutionibus Orbium Coelestium* stayed on the Catholic Index of forbidden books until 1758. Later astronomers such as Giordano Bruno (1548–1600), Tycho Brahe (1546–1601), Johannes Kepler (1571–1630), and of course Galileo Galilei (1564–1642) validated and corrected the Copernican theory.

Although he laid the foundation of the scientific revolution brought to completion by Isaac Newton (1642–1727), Copernicus had other interests, including the church. Though never ordained as a priest, he served many years as a canon (member of the clergy) in the cathedral of Frauenburg (Poland), where his uncle was bishop. Having studied medicine, Copernicus also served as his uncle's private physician.
R. VONDERLACK

CORNELIUS (died 253)
Pope, 251–253

When Cornelius was elected pope, he excommunicated Novatian, a Roman presbyter who had received the minority vote for the office, and his followers. There was a conflict as to whether those who had sacrificed to the emperor's image during persecution of Christians by the Roman emperor Decius (249–251) should be allowed to return to the church. Bishop Cyprian of Carthage, one of Cornelius's supporters, favored

readmission, but Novatian's followers opposed it. Cyprian's position won out. Cornelius died in exile during Gallus's persecution of Christians (251–253) and is considered a martyr. C. HICKS

CORTÉS, HERNANDO (1484–1547)
One of the two most famous Spanish conquistadors, the other being Francisco Pizarro

Unlike Pizarro, who mercilessly conquered Peru, Cortés was deeply committed to the Roman Catholic faith and relatively benevolent. His conquest of Mexico was a remarkable military achievement. With scant supplies and fewer than six hundred soldiers, he set out from Cuba in February of 1519. Eighteen months later he had taken almost the entire peninsula of Mexico, had conquered the ancient and powerful Aztec capital of Tenochtitlan (Mexico City), and had won hundreds of thousands of new subjects for Charles V, king of Spain and Holy Roman Emperor. American historian W. H. Prescott called Cortés's achievement "too startling for the probabilities demanded by fiction and without parallel in the pages of history."

For a man of his times, Cortés could be considered a mild conqueror. Although ruthless in pursuit of his goals, he neither killed nor pillaged wantonly. Before battles he prayed and attended Mass. He generally attempted to enlist the Indians as his allies rather than attacking them first. After destroying Tenochtitlan, he immediately began rebuilding the city, which according to ancient testimony was magnificently restored within four or five months.

Several factors contributed to the success of Cortés's march on Mexico. He was able to get help from Indian tribes he conquered along the way. His mistress, Malintzin, a captured Indian princess who spoke Nahuatl, the Aztec language, served him faithfully as an interpreter. Further, the Aztecs believed that the fair-skinned Cortés was Quetzalcoatl, the god of ancient Aztec prophecy and rightful ruler of their kingdom.

Cortés is also remembered for his exploration of the lower California peninsula and Honduras in the 1530s.

Later in his life Cortés's many enemies in Spain gradually blunted his influence with the emperor. Cortés was forced to retire from court, spending the rest of his days on his estate near Seville. D. R. MITCHELL

COSIN, JOHN (1594–1672)
Bishop of Durham; writer

Son of a prominent Norwich family, Cosin was a graduate of Caius College, Cambridge. He was ordained in 1625, and for several years he held various offices in the Durham diocese. In these same years he became known for his Anglican partisanship and his closeness with Archbishop Laud and the royal family. Probably he compiled his famous work, *Collection of Private Devotions,* at Charles I's request. All this brought much disfavor with England's Presbyterians, soon to have supreme political power. Cosin was appointed master of Peterhouse, Cambridge, in 1635 and dean of Peterborough in 1640. But in 1641, after the Long Parliament's governmental takeover, his church offices were given to others. Hence he soon moved to Paris where he became chaplain to the exiled royal family and Anglican followers. Here he was known also for his friendship with Huguenots and disputes with Roman Catholics.

Puritan rule of England continued from 1649 to 1660. But at the restoration of Charles II, Cosin again assumed prominence in the English Church. In 1660, he was made bishop of Durham, a post he then held until his death. Ever a staunch Anglican, Cosin did make attempts to reconcile Presbyterianism with the Church of England, attending the Savoy Conference of 1661. Yet in Durham church worship, he compelled both Presbyterians and Roman Catholics to adhere strictly to Anglican forms. Cosin was a gifted writer of liturgy, and in 1662, some of his phrases were incorporated into the Book of Common Prayer's revision. Despite his conservatism, he stood for an allowance of divorce and remarriage within English Church discipline. This, of course, recapitulated early English Reformers' ideas. But like their sixteenth-century forebears, most seventeenth-century English churchmen rejected any and all remarriage after divorce. Provision for divorce with remarriage was not made by the English Church and Parliament until 1857.

Besides his devotional and liturgical writings, Cosin's works were mainly polemical pieces, largely refutations of Roman Catholic views. His works have been reprinted in the *Library of Anglo-Catholic Theology.* Cosin's translation of the enduring hymn "Veni Creator Spiritus" has been preserved in the Church of England's ordinal.
K. J. BRYER

COTTON, JOHN (1584–1652)
Leader of Congregationalism in the American colonies

A popular preacher sympathetic to the Puritan cause in his native England, Cotton left England in 1633 rather than defend himself against charges of Puritanism. He settled in Massachusetts, quickly distinguishing himself as an able teacher at Boston's First Church.

Cotton favored a theocratic form of government in which church and state are formally united. He modified the extreme separatist position of Rhode Island's Roger Williams, who refused to accept in Christian fellowship anyone who still participated in the Church of England. Cotton held that each individual must make a covenant with a particular church before receiving the sacraments. He insisted that salvation was not conditional on human action, but eternal. Church membership did not assure a person's entrance into the eternal, invisible kingdom of God. Each person must individually accept God's grace for salvation.

Cotton initially supported Anne Hutchinson, an articulate English woman whose strong criticism of Boston's rigid theocracy created widespread controversy. Although unruffled by accusations of Hutchinson's "antinomianism" (a term used more to disparage her views than to label their theological content), Cotton nevertheless yielded to political pressure during her trial in 1638 and withdrew his support.

Cotton set forth the Congregational form of government in two treatises: *The Keyes of the Kingdom of Heaven and the Power Thereof* (1644), and *The Way of the Churches of Christ in New-England* (1645). Cotton believed that each church was its own authority, having an obligation to choose its own leaders and to monitor its own discipline. K. LEID

COUPERIN, FRANÇOIS (1668–1733)
French keyboard composer of the eighteenth century

Couperin came from a long line of musicians whose activities spanned both the seventeenth and eighteenth centuries. Known as "Le Grand" ("the great") to distinguish him from an uncle who bore the same name, François received his earliest training from his father, then organist at Saint-Gervais Church, Paris. Upon his father's death, Couperin's education continued with his uncle. Meanwhile the organ post at Saint-Gervais was held over until 1685 or 1686 when the young François was able to fill it. That post he held until 1723. In addition he became organist of the royal Chapel in 1693. As the king's organist he took part in court concerts and was music master to the princes and princesses at Versailles.

In addition to his great ability in performance and composition, Couperin authored *L'Art de Toucher le Clavecin* (1717), a complete technical and stylistic method for harpsichord, which is still an outstanding reference for performance practices of the eighteenth century. Although he is not known for a great body of sacred music, he composed two organ masses (compositions in which the organ alone furnishes the music for the Mass). He designed one for parish use, the other for convents (religious houses); both have won their way into frequent liturgical and concert usage. H. M. BEST

COVERDALE, MILES (1488–1569)
English Bible translator

Coverdale was born in York and educated at Cambridge University, taking a degree in philosophy and theology. He was ordained to the priesthood in 1514, and soon afterward joined the Augustinian monastery in Cambridge. There he was strongly influenced by his prior, Robert Barnes (1495–1540), an early follower of Martin Luther's teachings. After Barnes's trial for heresy in 1526, Coverdale left the monastery to become a secular priest. His preaching against religious abuses of his day brought opposition that eventually forced him to leave England for the Continent.

In exile, he began Bible translation work, publishing a paraphrase of the psalms in 1534 and the first complete English Bible in 1535. (Tyndale had published the first English translation of the Greek New Testament in 1525.) This Bible, initially smuggled into England, achieved great popularity. Eventually it was published by English printers under the protection of Thomas Cromwell, a friend of Coverdale and vice-regent to the king. Cromwell convinced Henry VIII of the need for an official English Bible, so that in 1538 Coverdale was commissioned to revise his translation. The resulting "Great Bible" of 1539 was Coverdale's major achievement and a significant influence on the translators of the 1611 King James Version of the Bible.

Coverdale served briefly as bishop of Exeter; but with the crowning of Queen Mary (1553), his life was imperiled. He was rescued partly through the intervention of the king of Denmark. After living in Geneva and Germany, Coverdale returned to England to assist in consecrating Matthew Parker archbishop of Canterbury during the early part of Queen Elizabeth I's reign. Coverdale stayed in the London area the rest of his life, participating in the Puritan movement until his death. K. HOGLUND

COWPER, WILLIAM (1731–1800)
English hymn writer and poet

Cowper was the son of John Cowper, an Anglican rector, and Anne Donne, who belonged to the same family as John Donne, the seventeenth-century poet and preacher. Bullied and humiliated at a school in

Markyate, Hertfordshire, Cowper left it to enter the distinguished Westminster school, London, where he spent several years. He studied at Middle and Inner Temple and was called to the Bar in 1754. Cowper was nominated to two administrative posts in the House of Lords, but was so frightened by having to take an oral examination that he attempted suicide and emerged from the ordeal mentally unbalanced.

Cowper spent years searching for recovery from intermittent sieges of depression and insanity. *The Task*, Book III, refers to his mental problems: "I was a stricken deer that left the herd." In a private hospital he took up Bible reading and was converted to Christianity. At the age of thirty-four he settled in the town of Huntingdon, where he found help and comfort with the family of the Rev. Morley Unwin and his wife, Mary. He especially enjoyed the prayer time and reading by the fireside. When Mr. Unwin died (1767), Cowper, Mrs. Unwin, and her two children moved to Olney in Buckinghamshire. There he developed an earlier friendship with a strong spiritual adviser, John Newton, the evangelical preacher. Cowper lived happily in Olney for several years, but in 1773 suffered another mental unbalance and ultimately left Olney for rural retirement. Further attacks of insanity occurred in 1787 and after the death of Mrs. Unwin in 1796; from the latter he never recovered.

The evangelical *Olney Hymns,* written with John Newton "for the use of the plain people," appeared in 1779. Of the 348 in the collection, Cowper wrote about 68. Among his famous hymns are "O for a Closer Walk with God!" "There Is a Fountain Filled with Blood," "Hark, My Soul! It Is the Lord," "Jesus! Where'er Thy People Meet," and "God Moves in a Mysterious Way."

Cowper's *Poems* (1782) consists chiefly of delicate satire and didactic works. Titles in that volume include "Charity," which shows what humanity has made out of God's creation; "Truth," a sermon on grace; and "Expostulation," which exhorts the English to avoid the downfall that has overtaken God's "chosen people." Appearance of *The Task*

(1785) established Cowper's reputation as a poet. He was considered for the laureateship in 1788 but declined the honor. His other works include a translation of the *Iliad* and *Odyssey* in 1791. Cowper's *Letters* caused Southey to call him "the best of English letter writers." E. B. BATSON

CRABBE, GEORGE (1754–1832)
English poet and clergyman

Born at Aldeburgh, Suffolk, Crabbe received little formal education because his father was poor. He somehow managed to read the English poets, especially Shakespeare and Alexander Pope.

At the age of twenty-six, after numerous jobs, Crabbe left the little fishing town of Aldeburgh and went to London to seek his fortune as a writer. There he impressed the statesman Edmund Burke, who found a publisher for *The Library* (1781), a work which did nothing to establish Crabbe's reputation. Before its publication, he had failed with two others, *Inebrity* (1775), a satire on drink in the style of Alexander Pope, and *The Candidate* (1780), a string of couplets on the poet's desire for fame.

Discouraged in his writing career, Crabbe turned to the church. In 1781, after a brief period of study, he was ordained a deacon. The next year he assumed the duties of chaplain in the Duke of Rutland's household at Belvoir Castle in Leicestershire, where he remained until 1785. Meanwhile he had continued to write poetry and, with the publication of *The Village* (1783), he became a poet of some reputation. During the next twenty years, however, he devoted his energies largely to his parish work in Leicestershire. He had strong convictions and obvious prejudices, both of which he fearlessly expressed. With Methodism in the air, Crabbe rarely missed an opportunity to warn his congregation against what he called "that spiritual influenza."

As a rural preacher, Crabbe diversified his days by enjoying botany and writing verse. In 1807 he published *Poems*, including "The Parish Register," in which he reminisces over the official records of a year's baptisms, marriages, and burials in his rural parish. In 1810 *The Borough* appeared, twenty-four "letters" in verse to an imaginary correspondent describing the institutions and memorable people in his rural district. *Tales in Verse* (1812) contains twenty-one narratives in verse, followed by *Tales of the Hall* (two volumes, 1819). After Crabbe's wife died in 1813, he moved to Trowbridge, Wiltshire, where he stayed until his death. He was well received in his own day and Lord Byron later said of him, "Though Nature's sternest painter, yet the best." E. B. BATSON

CRANMER, THOMAS (1489–1556)

Archbishop of Canterbury; crucial figure in the separation of the Church of England from the jurisdiction of the bishop of Rome

A modest, even diffident person, Cranmer grew steadily in his understanding of Christianity. His fine theological judgment and sensitive ear for English are revealed in the classic liturgies and prayers he composed for the *Book of Common Prayer,* which have profoundly shaped English-speaking Christianity for over four centuries.

Born into a squire's family at Aslacton, Nottinghamshire, Cranmer survived a harsh schooling and proved himself an able student at Cambridge. After the death of his first wife, he was ordained a priest in 1523 and reelected a fellow of Jesus College. He soon gained a reputation as a biblical and patristic scholar, but was not a member of the small group of Cambridge scholars actively interested in Protestantism.

His academic career was interrupted by Henry VIII's welcome for his proposal that universities be canvassed for their opinion on Henry's marriage to Catherine of Aragon. Travels in Europe for this purpose brought him into personal contact with reformers like Andreas Osiander. Cranmer married Osiander's niece Margaret in 1532, an act of independence which indicated considerable departure from traditional Catholicism. Despite Cranmer's unwillingness to accept office as archbishop of Canterbury, Henry VIII was insistent. Cranmer was consecrated in 1533, after reading a carefully worded protestation against papal authority. His involvement in Henry's divorce of Catherine has often been taken to indicate undue subservience to Henry, but this is not supported by other aspects of Cranmer's role before Henry's death in 1547. He and his royal master disagreed at a number of points, but Cranmer was deeply convinced of the scripturalness of royal supremacy as a basis for much-needed reform in the Church of England, which itself was legally established by Parliament. Without Henry's support, Cranmer would not have survived the opposition of those who regarded him as a heretic, especially after the fall of Thomas Cromwell in 1540.

Cranmer was not a leader in the mold of Martin Luther or John Calvin. He had little influence on many of the major legal and administrative changes which took place under King Henry VIII. His concern for the removal of abuses and superstition by cautious doctrinal and liturgical change can be seen in his share in the *Bishop's Book* (1537), his resistance to the *Six Articles* (1539), and his sensitive *English Litany* (1544). In the long term, his support for making the Bible available in English (1534–1543) was very important in opening up new religious perspectives to the common people.

Cranmer's period of greatest influence came under King Edward VI (ruled 1547–1553), particularly in cooperation with the moderate policies of the Duke of Somerset. Both were deeply concerned for religious unity and sought to prevent popular unrest by checking extremist views. The Latin Mass remained for the early part of the new reign, but in 1548 important parts of the service, such as the prayers of general confession and absolution, were put into English. An English Bible and a copy of Erasmus's *Paraphrases* were to be provided in every parish, the cup was given to the laity, and Cranmer began the much more difficult task of revising the Mass itself. He drew on a wide variety of sources and had by the end of 1548 produced an English Prayer Book which showed him to be a masterly editor, translator, and composer of new prayers and formulae.

By this stage his convictions on justification and eucharistic theology had reached their final form. They were argued in a series of closely reasoned works which ably set out the main themes of Protestant sacramental theology. In more popular form, his contributions to the *Homilies* were influential among ordinary people and his *Forty-two Articles* (1533) provided the Church of England with an authoritative and balanced standard of evangelical and catholic belief. Cranmer's hopes for a reform of canon law were not realized, but some of the European scholars like Martin Bucer and Peter Martyr, whom he invited to assist in the task of reforming England, played an important part in widening horizons and persuading Cranmer to revise the *Book of Common Prayer.* The 1552 version went much further in a Protestant direction, but Cranmer's sense of the common Christian heritage and the need to avoid biblical legalism and sectarian error, led him to insist on the retention of customs like kneeling to receive the communion elements.

The seizure of power by Warwick (later Duke of Northumberland) pushed the process of reform ahead in a much more drastic and ill-judged manner—motivated more by desire for power and profit than by the truth of religion. Cranmer largely withdrew from the Council, devoting himself to administration and study. Very reluctantly he signed consent to Edward VI's will, granting the throne to Lady Jane Grey. His dilemma in reconciling conscience and obedience to the monarch was even more poignantly underlined after Mary Tudor's accession in 1553. His defense of Protestant sacramental theology led him to be charged with sedition, tried for treason, and sentenced to death. Though his life was spared, he was deprived of office. In April 1554, he defended his beliefs vigorously before a commission at Oxford, rejecting transubstantiation and emphasizing the completeness of Christ's death on the cross. A further trial in September 1555 led to his formal degradation and complete and humiliating recantations in February and March 1556, in which he unfeignedly accepted Roman Catholic teaching and anathematized the teachings of Martin Luther and Ulrich Zwingli. The strain of imprisonment, the psychological pressure used by his opponents, and his loyalty to the Crown all played a part in this collapse, which was a notable propaganda victory for the Roman Catholic cause.

Just before he was to be burned on March 21, 1556, and to the dismay of his persecutors, he recanted his recantation, abjured the pope's authority, and reasserted his former opinions. He died bravely, placing his right hand in the flames to show his regret at publishing what was contrary to the truth.

I. BREWARD

CRASHAW, RICHARD (c. 1613–1649)
English poet of the Counter-Reformation

Son of a clergyman especially noted for his negative attitude toward Roman Catholicism and the Jesuits, Crashaw moved in the opposite direction of his father throughout his life. His attraction to the devotional life of the Roman Catholic Church and his ultimate conversion to it were in some respects a natural expression of his temperament and religious affinities.

Educated first at Charterhouse and then at Pembroke College, Cambridge, a center of high-church Anglicanism, Crashaw became firmly attached to high-church ritual and to Roman Catholic art. At Pembroke and later at Peterhouse, another high-church college at Cambridge, he had some association with Nicholas Ferrar's Anglican religious community called Little Gidding. Little Gidding evidently supplied the subject for Crashaw's poem "Description of a Religious House and Condition of Life." By 1639, Crashaw was an Anglican priest, curate of Little St. Mary's, Cambridge, and lecturer at Peterhouse. In 1645, after fleeing the disruption of Cambridge caused by the civil war (1642–1646), Crashaw took up residence in Paris. There he became a Roman Catholic.

Steps to the Temple (1646), the title of Crashaw's first collection of sacred poems (published along with a collection entitled *The Delights of the Muses*), accurately suggests his dedication to sacred verse. He was influenced by the "emblem," a genre uniting picture (engraving) and poetry that spread throughout Catholic and Protestant Europe in the sixteenth and seventeeth centuries in the form of emblem books. Religious emblems frequently depicted personifications of states of the soul, then a short poem or a motto interpreted the picture. Crashaw included emblem engravings in his last collection of religious poems, *Carmen Deo Nostro* (1652).

Although associated with the seventeenth-century writers known as "metaphysical poets," Crashaw's poetry is almost in a class by itself. He sought to "focus the senses, imagination, and reflective powers on a religious emotion awakened by the enraptured consideration of great religious themes": the wounds and blood of the crucified Lord, the sorrows and sufferings of Mary, the tears of Magdalene, or the sufferings and joys of Teresa of Avila. Crashaw also wrote hymns, odes, and secular poems. E. B. BATSON

CRAWFORD, DANIEL (1870–1926)
Pioneer Scottish missionary with Christian Missions in Many Lands (a Plymouth Brethren missionary society)

Crawford served twenty-two years in northeastern Angola and southern Congo (now Zaire). Anticipating modern cultural anthropology, his book *Thinking Black* told how he was able to identify with the people he lived among and to adapt himself to their patterns of thinking. He had a gift for presenting the gospel convincingly to masses of people and for applying Christian truth to their customs and culture. Pioneering with Stanley Arnot, Charles Swan, and Walter Fisher, Crawford helped lay the foundation of a remarkable ministry of the Assemblies in Central Africa. He and his colleagues opened a chain of stations from the Atlantic Ocean across Angola and into southern Zaire. Each station became a center for further expansion of the gospel. Long before the modern emphasis of a holistic approach to the gospel, Crawford firmly believed that

he ought to meet the needs of the whole man—body, mind, and spirit. W. NORTON

CREED, JOHN MARTIN (1889–1940)
English theologian

Having graduated at Cambridge, he was ordained in 1913, and after serving a curacy in the Yorkshire city of Bradford, he returned to Cambridge as chaplain of Gonville and Caius College. In 1917, near the end of World War I, he went to France and for two years served as an army chaplain. From 1919 on, the rest of his life was spent in Cambridge as dean and lecturer in theology at St. John's College (1919–1926) and as Ely professor of divinity (1926–1940).

Creed's interests had originally been in the New Testament and early church history fields, but then he became interested in theological studies. In 1934 he gave the Hulsean lectures in the university, which emerged two years later under the title *The Divinity of Jesus Christ: A Study in the History of Christian Doctrine since Kant*. In 1935 he became one of the editors of the *Journal of Theological Studies*. The eighteenth and nineteenth centuries came to have a particular fascination for him, and this was reflected in part in *Religious Thought in the Eighteenth Century Illustrated from Writers of the Period* (1934), which Creed coauthored with J. S. Boys Smith. Creed was in many ways an Anglican of the old school, a great advocate of the place of the Church of England in the life of a nation. J. D. DOUGLAS

CREIGHTON, MANDELL (1843–1901)
Anglican bishop and historian

Born in Carlisle (England), Creighton graduated from Merton College, Oxford, in 1867. He was ordained to the priesthood in 1873 and then appointed vicar of Embleton in Northumberland (1875). In 1884 he became the first incumbent of the Dixie chair of ecclesiastical history at Cambridge University. In 1891 he was consecrated bishop of Peterborough, from which he was transferred to London in 1897. As bishop of London, Creighton was drawn into a controversy between ritualistic clergy (accused of Roman Catholic tendencies) and their protesting opponents. By his fairness, tact, and sense of humor he succeeded in moderating, though not settling, the controversy.

Always interested in history, Creighton wrote *The History of Rome* (1875), *The Age of Elizabeth* (1876), and *The Life of Simon de Montfort* (1876). He was editor of the *English Historical Review* from its establishment in 1886 until 1891. His fame as a historian rests on the unfinished *History of the Papacy from the Great Schism to the Council of Trent*. The five volumes of that work published between 1882 and 1894 were highly acclaimed for their skillful use of printed sources, their clear and interesting style, and their sound judgments.

N. V. HOPE

CRISP, TOBIAS (1600–1643)
Popular English preacher; champion of antinomianism

In 1627 Crisp became rector of Brinkworth in Wiltshire. He was sympathetic to the Puritan cause. Forced to leave Brinkworth in 1642 because of questionable teachings, he settled in London and began debating other ministers on the doctrine of "free grace." Crisp insisted that God's love was a gift, freely given and not earned. He had little respect for the legalism embedded in many religious practices; therefore, he became a champion of antinomianism (the belief that faith may be exercised apart from adherence to any moral law; hence, one's actions do not relate to salvation). After his death, several collections of his sermons and lectures were published by R. Lancaster under the general title of *Christ Alone Exalted*— the first two in 1643, a third in 1646, and a fourth in 1683. K. LEID

CROFT, WILLIAM (1678–1727)
English organist and composer of the late Baroque period

Born in Nether Ettington, Warwickshire, Croft was educated under John Blow at the Chapel Royal. Croft held several posts: cho-

rister of the Chapel Royal; organist at St. Anne's, Soho (1700–1712), Chapel Royal (beginning in 1707), and Westminster Abbey (beginning in 1708); and master of the children at Chapel Royal. Although his compositions covered a wide spectrum, Croft is remembered today mostly for his church music—anthems, hymn tunes, and settings of the Anglican service. His most familiar hymn tunes are St. Annes ("O God, Our Help in Ages Past") and Hanover ("O Worship the King"). H. M. BEST

CROMWELL, OLIVER (1599–1658)
Military leader in the English civil war; "Lord Protector" of England from 1653 to his death

Cromwell was born in Huntingdon (England) to Robert and Elizabeth Cromwell. He attended Sidney Sussex College, Cambridge, in 1616 and later studied law for a short period at the Inns of Court in London. In 1620 Cromwell married Elizabeth Bourchier, who exposed him further to the influence of Puritanism. His career in politics began when he was elected to the House of Commons in 1628.

Between 1642 and 1660 England experienced civil war and religious strife. Cromwell distinguished himself as a commander in the eastern part of England at the onset of the war and played a prominent part in Parliamentarian victories at Marston Moor (1644) and Naseby (1645).

As a Puritan, Cromwell shared the negative feelings of much of the army toward the rigid "Presbyterianism" of the Parliamentary majority and toward the old rule of the bishops. The Puritan standard for faith was the Bible, personal experience, and the freedom to follow one's own convictions. Thus the Puritans saw both "Presbyterian" and "Episcopal" forms of church structure as coming between the individual and God. The army's Puritan attitudes prevented the establishment of the Presbyterianism sanctioned by Parliament. Charles I (1600–1649) appealed to the Scots to invade England, leading them to believe he would support Presbyterianism. On August 20, 1648, the invading

Scottish army was scattered by Cromwell's forces near Preston. The latter army was now supreme in England. On December 6, in an action known as "Pride's Purge," Cromwell expelled the Presbyterian members from Parliament, leaving what was called the "Rump Parliament." Charles I was tried and condemned to death on January 30, 1649. Cromwell went on to subjugate Ireland (1649) and Scotland (1651) and finally drove Charles II into exile in 1651. When all opposition was put down (in 1653), Cromwell became Lord Protector of England, Scotland, and Ireland.

Cromwell made three significant contributions to English history. First, he established a period of peace in England, Scotland, and Ireland after ten years of civil strife. (In an English poet's words, "He fought to end our fighting.") Second, he made England into an acknowledged world power by opening up diplomatic relationships with various European countries and by strengthening the military and naval forces. Third, Cromwell established nonconformity (refusal to submit to the established church) as a way of life in England that has lasted to the present.

Cromwell believed in liberty of conscience for all, provided one did not violate the maintenance of law and order. Being an independent "Congregationalist," he held to the right of congregations to choose their own ministers and orderly manner of worship. He did not condone the extreme acts of the Society of Friends or of the Fifth Monarchy Men in breaking up church services and shouting down ministers during their sermons. Cromwell tried to persuade George Fox of the Society of Friends and John Rogers, a preacher of the Fifth Monarchy Men, to conduct themselves properly by promising them toleration if they would cease their disruptive activities. Similarly, he tried to induce John Lilburne, leader of a party of radicals called Levelers, to stop stirring up the army; in return Cromwell promised Lilburne the freedom to expound his ideas, however distasteful to the conservatives. Cromwell also took the first steps to allow the Jewish community to live openly in England. Cromwell's ideals of toleration, however, did not extend to Roman Catholicism and Anglicanism. The Irish were denied the right to celebrate the Mass. In England, Roman Catholics were allowed to celebrate Mass only in their homes.

Oliver Cromwell was succeeded by his son Richard. Richard had neither the force nor the stature of his father and ruled only two years (1658–1660) before his fall and the restoration of Charles II to the throne.
R. VONDERLACK

CROMWELL, THOMAS (c. 1485–1540)
Influential statesman concerned with English church reform

Born a commoner near London, Cromwell died as Earl of Essex after a career as one of the most powerful men in England. His early life is obscure, but he spent several years in Italy and the Netherlands before becoming a lawyer and a member of Parliament. His rapid climb to power and wealth began in the service of Cardinal Wolsey, where he gained a knowledge of the church unusual for a layman.

After Wolsey's fall, resulting from Henry VIII's desire for a divorce, Cromwell became one of the king's most important advisers. An outstanding administrator, Cromwell drafted many of the parliamentary laws that created a Church of England that was subject to the Crown and free of papal control. He believed that the power of the Crown and the powers of the church should be carefully separated in order to put an end to clerical privileges and to restore the laity to their rightful roles in church government.

As vicar-general from 1535, Cromwell organized the dissolution of the monasteries and worked closely with Archbishop Thomas Cranmer to encourage moderate reform of the Church of England. Though his religious convictions have not always been given due weight, his support for the publication of an English Bible led to a copy of the Bible being publicly placed in every parish. This in turn led to deep religious changes among the common people for the next century. In addition, Cromwell encouraged books defending the break with Rome. His injunctions of 1536 and 1538 made important administrative changes in English parishes, embodying new views about the role of the church in society. Shortly after becoming Earl of Essex in 1540, Cromwell attempted to secure an English alliance with the Protestant German princes by persuading Henry to marry Anne of Cleves. The marriage was not ultimately to Henry's liking and was annulled after six months. Henry blamed the whole episode on Cromwell and had him arrested and executed for treason.

Cromwell made a deep mark on the life of the Church of England by the skill with which he balanced the responsibilities of laity and clergy and provided a framework for a comprehensive national church that was reformed and yet retained much continuity with the medieval church. His convictions about the power of the Scriptures to bring lasting reform gave him detachment from doctrinal and liturgical disputes and a concern for unity, which became one of the Church of England's greatest strengths. I. BREWARD

CROSBY, FRANCES (FANNY) JANE (1820–1915)

American hymn writer

Born in Putnam county, New York, Fanny Crosby was blinded through a physician's negligence at the age of six weeks. She entered the New York City Institution for the Blind around 1835, completed training, and taught there from 1847 to 1858. In 1858 she married a musician, Alexander Van Alstyne, who was also blind. Under her own name, as well as under a curious assortment of initials and pen names, she wrote over two thousand hymns, including "Jesus, Keep Me Near the Cross," "Rescue the Perishing," "All the Way My Savior Leads Me," "I Am Thine, O Lord," "Sweet Hour of Prayer," and "To God Be the Glory."

There is hardly a hymnbook in the English language that does not contain at least one hymn by Fanny Crosby. Her poetic style is simple and earnest. The theological content, while unequivocally orthodox, is per-

sonal and experiential. Fanny Crosby was able to express both theological content and personal experience in her rhyming meters, speaking of the gospel of Jesus Christ in a way that has been meaningful to millions of people. H. M. BEST

CROWTHER, SAMUEL ADJAI (c. 1806–1891)

First African bishop of the Anglican Communion

Crowther was freed from a slave ship by the British Navy in 1822 and taken to Sierra Leone, where he became a Christian and was educated by missionaries of the Church Missionary Society. After being a tutor at Fourah Bay College and a member of the Niger Expedition of 1841, he was sent to England for further study. In 1843 he was ordained a priest and went to Yorubaland (Nigeria) as a missionary. There he located and baptized his mother. He established mission stations in Iboland in connection with the Niger Expeditions of 1854 and 1857. Crowther was consecrated bishop of the Niger Territories at Canterbury in 1864. A man of great vision and energy, he spent the rest of his life preaching the gospel and building up the Anglican Church in Nigeria, where he is remembered with great fondness to this day.

In his later years his ministry was greatly hampered by lack of administrative funds, scandals and schisms in his own diocese, and the opposition of white missionaries who resented being placed under an African bishop. P. BEAVER

CRUDEN, ALEXANDER (1699–1770)

Moral reformer; compiler of a Bible concordance

Cruden was born into a merchant's family in Aberdeen (Scotland). Raised in an atmosphere of rigid Presbyterianism, he received an A.M. degree from Marischal College sometime around 1720. After a romantic disappointment, Cruden developed mental problems and was placed in an asylum. He was released in 1722. About 1726 he left Scotland for London to work as a private tutor. Evidently he then served as a tutor on the Isle of Man.

Returning to London in 1732, Cruden opened a bookstore and in 1735 became official bookseller to the queen. In 1736 he began to compile his *Concordance,* an alphabetical listing of all important words found in the Bible. His thorough acquaintance with the Scriptures and his hobby of tracing words through the Bible helped him to complete the work in eighteen months and publish it in 1737. Discouragement over the lack of financial success of the first edition, however, led to another breakdown and confinement in 1738—although this time he was released ten weeks later.

Cruden took work as a proofreader for a publishing firm. Correcting proof seems to have given him the idea of correcting certain moral abuses in England, especially swearing and Sabbath-breaking. He launched a crusade for reform, taking upon himself the title "Alexander the Corrector." In 1753 Cruden was involved in a street brawl, after which his sister had him again committed to an asylum in Chelsea. He was released after seventeen days. In 1755, believing he had been divinely commissioned, Cruden petitioned Parliament to appoint him to the office of "Corrector." Ignored by Parliament, Cruden continued his campaign through numerous pamphlets. In 1769 he went back to Aberdeen to deliver public lectures about the need for moral reform and to complete his *Scripture Dictionary,* a work not published until after his death. Shortly after returning to London, Cruden died suddenly while praying. K. HOGLUND

CRUGER, JOHANNES (1598–1662)
German church musician

Born in Gross-Breese, Prussia, Cruger was for forty years cantor for St. Nicholas Church (Lutheran) in Berlin. Cruger's great interest in congregational singing was shown both in his published collections of chorales and in his own tunes. In 1644 he published *Praxis Pietatis Melica* (*Practice of Piety in Song*), an influential collection which passed through forty-four editions.

Cruger's tunes remain among the strongest and most musical in hymn and chorale literature. Hymnbooks generally include most or all of the following tunes: "Herzliebster Jesu" ("Ah, Holy Jesus"); "Jesu, Mein Freude" ("Jesus, Priceless Treasure"); "Nun Danket" ("Now Thank We All Our God"); "Schmucke Dich" ("Deck Thyself, My Soul, with Gladness"); "Zuversicht" ("Jesus Lives and So Shall I"); and "Cruger" ("Hail to the Lord's Anointed"). H. M. BEST

CUMMINS, GEORGE DAVID (1822–1875)
American churchman; founder of the Reformed Episcopal Church

Left fatherless at the age of four, Cummins was influenced by his mother's Methodism. He enrolled at Dickinson College (Carlisle, Pennsylvania), where he was converted and joined the Methodist Church. Cummins served as a Methodist circuit rider for several years with the intention of becoming a Methodist minister. A desire for a settled home and a more formal worship, however, led him to confirmation and ordination (1845) in the Episcopal Church. Energetic and successful in his career as a priest, Cummins served parishes in Norfolk, Richmond, Baltimore, Washington, and Chicago, ministering devotedly during a cholera epidemic in 1849.

In 1866 Cummins was elected assistant bishop of the Kentucky diocese, but his evangelical zeal found no sympathy for the Anglo-Catholic direction his church was following. Though he fought that trend and urged his fellow evangelicals not to abandon the church, after the General Convention of 1871 he considered his efforts to be futile. In 1873 he received considerable criticism for participating in an interdenominational communion service conducted by the Evangelical Alliance at New York's Fifth Avenue Presbyterian Church. Soon he relinquished his post to become presiding officer in the new Reformed Episcopal Church, organized in New York City in December of 1873. Cummins served the new church for only two years before his death. M. FACKLER

CUNNINGHAM, WILLIAM
(1805–1861)

Scottish pastor and theologian

Born in Hamilton and educated at Edinburgh, Cunningham ministered in Greenock and Edinburgh. He warmly supported Thomas Chalmers in events preceding the Disruption of 1843, when many evangelicals left the Church of Scotland and formed the Free Church of Scotland. Cunningham, an excellent scholar and pastor, put much time and energy into working for the church's independence from state control.

The Free Church appointed him to teach theology in "the New College" at Edinburgh as well as to visit America in its service, where he struck up a lasting friendship with Princeton theologian Charles Hodge. In 1847 Cunningham became principal of New College, a rather difficult task in a new church still feeling its way. He did not spare himself, least of all in his duties as church moderator (1859–1860). Considered one of Scotland's greatest theologians, Cunningham produced a two-volume work on *Historical Theology* (1862) that reflects his keenly analytical mind and his versatility; it is still regarded as a classic. J. D. DOUGLAS

CYPRIAN (THASCIUS CAECILIUS CYPRIANUS) (c. 200–258)

Early church father; bishop of Carthage, North Africa

Cyprian, the son of wealthy pagan parents in Carthage, was trained in rhetoric and probably in law. His conversion to Christianity, which came late in life (246), was described in his treatise *To Donatus*. Within two years of his conversion, he was elected bishop of Carthage, the largest church in Africa.

During a persecution by the Roman emperor Decian (250–251), Cyprian hid himself near the city and continued to conduct the affairs of the church. In the bishop's absence, however, those who had "lapsed" (i.e., made sacrifices to the pagan gods) during the persecution received easy readmission into the church from the "confessors," those steadfast survivors who had confessed Christ before the Roman officials, but without suffering martyrdom.

From exile Cyprian insisted that the lapsed Christians perform severe penance to atone for their apostasy, a hard-line position that bred division in the Carthaginian church. On his return after the Decian persecution, Cyprian convened two synods (church councils) of African bishops (in 251 and 252) that resolved the controversy in his favor. In the end, Cyprian's position steered a middle course between the lax discipline of the Carthaginian elders and those who viewed apostasy as a "sin unto death" (1 John 5:16 KJV). The threat of another persecution interrupted any further division and unified the African church in 252.

Cyprian next engaged in a rebaptism controversy with Stephen, the bishop of Rome. At issue was the validity of baptisms performed by the Novationists (a rival group of Christians who formed a string of separate churches in the wake of the Decian persecution and the readmission controversy). Stephen of Rome argued for acceptance, Cyprian against. For the first time, a bishop of Rome used his reputation as successor to the apostle Peter to claim authority over the other bishops.

Cyprian reacted to that claim through correspondence in his treatise *On the Unity of the Catholic Church*. Arguing for the equal authority of all bishops, he called attention to Peter's submission to the apostle Paul (Galatians 2) and to the lack of any claim by Peter to primacy. Stephen threatened to excommunicate Cyprian, but his martyrdom in 257 by the emperor Valerian brought a premature end to the conflict, at least in the third century. Cyprian was also arrested in Valerian's persecution, banished to the city of Curubis, recalled a year later, found guilty of sacrilege against the Roman gods, and beheaded. Stephen's position against rebaptism later prevailed when Augustine supported it against the Donatists (405–411), who had continued Cyprian's stricter views.

A strong spokesman for Latin Christianity, Cyprian stood in a continuity of prominent Carthaginian Christian writers, which included both Tertullian and Augustine of

Hippo. He is remembered for his strong position on church discipline. Cyprian also made a close identification of the church with "the visible church"—as his famous dictum states: "There is no salvation outside the church." J. NEWTON

CYRIL (826–869) AND METHODIUS (c. 815–885)

Two brothers who were "apostles to the Slavs"

At an early age Cyril accepted a call to scholarship and was trained at Constantinople by the patriarch Photius. Cyril was ordained, entered a monastery, and was asked to teach philosophy at Constantinople.

When he was sent on a mission to Crimea in southern Russia he took his brother, Methodius, with him. Although that mission resulted in some professions of Christianity, no long-term foundations were laid at that time. Later, Prince Ratislav of Moravia, in reaction to Western political, cultural, and religious infiltration, requested missionaries from Constantinople. Cyril and Methodius were sent.

Cyril created an alphabet, put the Slavonic language into writing for the first time, and then translated the Scriptures. His work thus involved both evangelization and instruction. As a result of conflict with the Western clergy, the missionaries were called to Rome. The pope, however, gave his approval to their work and made Cyril a bishop.

Cyril died shortly thereafter and was buried at Rome. The Prince of Pannonia (northern Yugoslavia) then sought the help of Methodius, who left Rome and became archbishop of Sirmium (near modern Belgrade). From there his work spread to other areas, including Bohemia, again with opposition from Western clergy—although his efforts were accepted by the pope and the people. Thus, Cyril and Methodius laid the foundations of the church in Slavic Europe. T. O. KAY

CYRIL OF ALEXANDRIA (370–444)

Early church leader whose stress on the unity of Christ's human and divine natures best represented the theological tradition of Alexandria (Egypt)

As a youth, Cyril lived with monks and worked his way through the church hierarchy until he succeeded his uncle Theophilus as patriarch (bishop) of Alexandria in 412. In church affairs Cyril always sought to maintain the superiority of Alexandria in the Eastern church against the rising power of Constantinople and the Christology of Antioch.

When Nestorius from Antioch became bishop of Constantinople in 428, he and Cyril soon clashed. Nestorius emphasized the humanity of Christ and refused to refer to Mary as "God-bearer," calling her "Christ-bearer" instead, on the grounds that she gave birth only to a man, who then became both an instrument and a vessel of divinity. In Christ, Nestorius taught, the human person (Jesus) and the divine person ("the Word" of John 1:1) were united by such a close and sympathetic association as to be virtually indistinguishable. Cyril, on the other hand, argued that although Christ had two completely separate natures, divine and human, they were united "hypostatically" (in a more intrinsic union).

Cyril accused Nestorius of dividing Christ's nature and called a synod in 430 to condemn him. Before the Antioch delegation arrived, Cyril deposed Nestorius, which provoked the Antiochenes to hold a council of their own in which they then deposed Cyril. A compromise was effected by Emperor Theodosius II, who banned both men from church affairs, although Cyril later regained his influence and had Nestorius imprisoned. Cyril achieved only partial success, however, because in 451 the Council of Chalcedon modified his Christology. Because Cyril's ambiguous wording failed to distinguish carefully between "nature" and "person," Chalcedon's clarification spoke of the two natures of Christ as united indivisibly and without confusion in one person.

Cyril's writings include several commentaries on various books of the Pentateuch, Isaiah, the Minor Prophets, Luke, and John. His commentaries stress the unity of the two Testaments. G. MINDEMAN

CYRIL OF JERUSALEM (c. 310–386)
Early church father; bishop of Jerusalem

When the emperor Constantine's Church of the Resurrection was dedicated in Jerusalem (335), Cyril was present as deacon to witness the event. That was only ten years after the Council of Nicaea had convened and formally condemned Arianism, the fourth-century heretical teaching that Christ was less than God. The Arian controversy continued even after Nicaea, and Cyril's career was caught up in both the theology and the politics of that dispute.

In 343 Cyril was ordained priest by Maximus, the aging bishop of Jerusalem, who had been persuaded earlier to join the Arian faction. Maximus later recanted his Arian views and supported the orthodox champion Athanasius, who insisted on Christ's full divinity. For unrelated reasons Cyril repudiated his ordination. The gesture temporarily won the favor of Acacius, the Arian metropolitan (ranking bishop) of Caesarea, who consecrated Cyril bishop of Jerusalem in 348, following Maximus's death.

During his early years as bishop, although he was orthodox in his views, Cyril lived in peace with the Arian bishops and emperors. Constantine was succeeded in 337 by his son Constantius, an Arian sympathizer. Cyril wrote a letter of praise to him, saying that just as God had recognized Constantine's piety by granting the discovery of the "true cross" and the "holy places" during his rule, now God had given even greater approval of Constantius by the appearance of a "bright cross" in the heaven over Golgotha on Pentecost (in 351), a sign that drove even pagans into the church.

A conflict developed with Acacius, however, over Cyril's moves toward greater independence for his own see (area of jurisdiction). Acacius charged Cyril with selling church property to feed the poor during a famine in Jerusalem. That conflict resulted in two exiles for Cyril (357 and 360) during Constantius's rule (337–361). The next emperor, Julian (called "the Apostate," who reigned 361–363), was a pagan who tried to restore worship of the old gods; he permitted exiles, including Cyril, to return to their positions. Shortly afterward, when Julian attempted to rebuild the Jewish temple in Jerusalem, in ruins since A.D. 70, Cyril opposed the project. Cyril was exiled for a third time (367–378), during the rule of another Arian emperor, Valens (reigned 364–378).

Cyril's theology can be established from his major work, the *Catechetical Lectures,* delivered before his ordination as bishop (348). Although he did not use the Nicene terminology "the Son of God . . . of one substance with the Father," he affirmed Christ as "very God" and "God of God" and attacked Arianism, using several phrases that had originated with Athanasius. Later Cyril was praised by the Synod of Jerusalem (381–382) as one "who fought a good fight" against the Arians. He placed emphasis on Christ's death and resurrection as the foundation of the Christian faith. Cyril also advocated the veneration of relics and the "holy places," and he was one of the first to teach that the bread and wine during Holy Communion changed into the actual "body and blood" of Christ (a doctrine called transubstantiation). J. NEWTON

D

DABNEY, ROBERT LOUIS (1820–1898)
American Presbyterian clergyman

Born in Virginia, Dabney graduated from Union Theological Seminary in Virginia in 1846. He was pastor in Tinkling Spring, Virginia (1847–1853), and a professor of theology at Union Theological Seminary (1853–1883). He was professor of philosophy at the University of Texas (1883–1894) and in 1870 was moderator of the general assembly of the Southern Presbyterian Church (the Presbyterian Church, U.S.). While at the University of Texas, he helped to found Austin Theological Seminary. During the Civil War Dabney served in the Confederate army, at first as chaplain and afterward as a combatant officer.

Dabney combined a position of theological conservatism with a fervent belief in the cause of the American South. He was an articulate exponent of his position in lectures, sermons, and published works, and in the deliberations of the Presbyterian Church. He believed that the Civil War was caused by the North and wanted "retributive Providence" to demolish the North and destroy the Union. He was a strong opponent of any reunion of his church with the northern branches of Presbyterianism.

Dabney, along with J. H. Thornwell, was a leading exponent of Southern conservative theology. Their views were adapted for southerners from those of Charles Hodge, a Princeton Seminary theologian. Dabney sought to bolster doctrinal orthodoxy in the face of attempts by James Woodrow of Columbia Seminary and others to revise it. In philosophy Dabney was a strong opponent of positivism and materialism. He died in Texas. His published works included *Defense of Virginia and the South* (1867) and *Syllabus and Notes of the Course of Systematic and Polemic Theology* (1871). D. C. MASTERS

D'AILLY, PIERRE (1350–1420)
French philosopher, theologian, and ecclesiastical diplomat

A diverse and prolific writer, Pierre d'Ailly treated not only theological and philosophical subjects but also scientific and astronomical themes. He was influenced by Franciscan scholar Roger Bacon and by scholastic theologian William of Ockham.

Born in Compiegne, d'Ailly entered the College of Navarre in Paris in 1363. In 1381 he received his doctorate in theology and delivered an important address before the French regent, the duke of Anjou. His purpose was to urge that the Great Schism, the papal controversy that had divided the

Roman Catholic Church since 1378, be settled through the efforts of a general council.

In 1384 he became rector of his college, and five years later, chancellor of the University of Paris. He remained closely associated with the French court, serving as confessor for Charles VI. He became archdeacon of Cambrai in 1391 and then bishop there in 1397.

In his concern for the healing of the Great Schism, d'Ailly participated in a council at Pisa (Italy) in 1409. That council ended, however, with three church leaders claiming to be pope. Of those, d'Ailly supported Alexander V. In 1411, courting d'Ailly's support, John XXIII (one of the claimants) made him cardinal.

In 1414 at the Council of Constance, d'Ailly sided against John XXIII. D'Ailly, head of that council's commission that tried the Bohemian reformer John Huss in 1415, concurred with the decree that Huss should die. In later council proceedings, d'Ailly took the position that the three synods which met in Pisa, Rome, and Constance were one body and had supremacy over the pope.

Near the end of the council's sessions, d'Ailly himself was considered for the office of pope. His failure to receive the position disappointed the French delegation, but Martin V, elected as the legitimate pope, appointed d'Ailly as legate at Avignon (France).

One of d'Ailly's published works, *Tractatus super reformatione Ecclesia*, the third part of a three-part treatise on general councils (1416), was popular in Germany and England. Many of his suggestions for reform were accepted by the Council of Trent.

D'Ailly, like William of Ockham, taught that there were no rational proofs for God; belief in God was possible only through faith. Further, he challenged the papacy's claim to preeminence and indispensability in the church. Such teachings were readily accepted by later Protestant reformers such as Martin Luther. L. GOLDBERG

DALE, ROBERT WILLIAM (1829–1895)
English Congregationalist minister; one of the great pulpiteers of his time

Famous as a preacher, lecturer, and author, Dale was invited to present the Lyman Beecher Lectures at Yale Divinity School in 1877.

From 1853 until his health failed in 1891, Dale drew large congregations to Carr's Lane Chapel in Birmingham (England). But he was concerned for the welfare of all Christians in England, especially those outside the Church of England.

After the first Keswick Convention, in 1874, Dale argued for its continuation, rejoicing in the convention's practical emphasis on prayer, Bible study, and personal growth in the Christian life. Because he sought equal opportunity for all Christians, he opposed the special privileges accorded the Church of England by the state and pressed for its disestablishment.

He supported the founding of new Congregational churches. At various stages in his ministry, he edited a paper (*The Congregationalist*), chaired the Congregational Union, and presided at the first International Council of Congregational Churches. A graduate of Spring Hill College, a Congregational institution in Birmingham, Dale led in its move to Oxford, where in 1886 it opened as Mansfield College.

Dale campaigned for a more fully developed Christian culture and society. He believed that such development would include education and progressive social reform, the latter based on individual response to the gospel, not on organized Christian political movements. Consequently he refused to attend the Free Church Congress in 1892 because he feared it was an effort to constitute a political party. He supported Joseph Chamberlain, the reforming mayor of Birmingham, and served on the school board there.

His best-known books are *The Atonement* (1875) and *Ephesians* (1882). D. MUNSON

DAMASUS I (c. 304–384)
Pope, 366–384

Damasus was a pivotal figure in the settlement of the Arianism controversy which had plagued the church for half a century.

(Arianism was a heresy that denied the Son's deity by asserting that he was created by God the Father.) Damasus was made a deacon by the man he eventually succeeded in the papacy, Liberius. Later, Damasus was elected pope by a majority, but a rival party elected Ursinus, and it took the Roman emperor Valentinian I's intervention to confirm Damasus's election.

Important bishops in the East, notably Basil of Caesarea, looked to Damasus for help in finally suppressing Arianism. Damasus's enormous influence helped turn the tide in favor of an orthodox settlement. He helped to end a schism in Antioch (caused by the Arian issue) and worked to suppress the Donatist schism in North Africa.

In 382 Damasus commissioned his secretary, Jerome, to prepare a new Latin text of the Bible. The result was the Vulgate Bible, which for centuries was the authoritative Bible in the Western church. P. TOON

DAMIAN, PETER (1007–1072)
Bishop and reformer in the Roman Catholic Church

Damian was born in Ravenna (Italy). In 1035 he entered a Benedictine hermitage at Fonte Avellana to pursue a life of solitary asceticism. He later joined a stricter order, the Camaldolese. Damian has been described as a "fierce ascetic." As abbot (head) of a monastery, he attacked clerical abuses, calling for prayer, humble service, and strict observance of celibacy and asceticism. In 1057 he reluctantly became cardinal bishop of Ostia.

A staunch defender of orthodoxy, Damian served on occasion as a papal legate in political and ecclesiastical affairs. Challenging all knowledge that came from reason and calling instead for complete trust in God, he opposed the early scholasticism of the eleventh century. He maintained that human knowledge was untrustworthy because God could not allow sinful humans by fallible reason to have any knowledge of truth. In spite of his distrust of reason, Damian firmly adhered to the Augustinian doctrine that

faith leads one to knowledge—that is, to "wisdom from above." He considered Scripture and the commentaries upon it as sufficient instruction for anybody.

Damian's writings indicate a great fear of God's judgment. He graphically described the torments of hell and the rewards of God's paradise. In his opinion there was little good to be found in this life; the present was only preparatory to the life hereafter. In 1828 Pope Leo XII declared Damian a "Doctor of the Church." T. O. KAY

DAMIEN, FATHER (JOSEPH DE VEUSTER) (1840–1889)
Roman Catholic priest and missionary

Damien was born in Tremelo (Belgium) of a peasant family. He received his higher education at Louvain and Paris from the Fathers of the Sacred Hearts of Jesus and Mary. In 1864 he was sent as a missionary to the Sandwich Islands (now Hawaii), where he served a number of years on the island of Hawaii. In 1873 he volunteered to go to a leper colony on the island of Molokai.

Between 1853 and 1866, leprosy had become such a problem in the Sandwich Islands that the government had decided to segregate all lepers on a separate island. Those contracting the disease were separated from their families, often forcibly, and sent to Molokai. There they had no permanent nurse, counselor, clergyman, or even grave digger. In time, Damien undertook all those functions. He disputed often with the Hawaiian board of health, partly because of a law (later relaxed) which imposed a strict quarantine on the island except for visitors willing to stay there permanently. Damien's work in creating an efficient and humane leprosarium became world renowned. In 1885 he contracted leprosy. After a stubborn battle of wills with his superiors, who wanted him to leave Molokai, he remained with his parishioners until his death at age forty-nine.

After Damien's death, a Congregational minister, Charles Hyde, accused him of being coarse and headstrong and of having played no part in improving Molokai. English writer

Robert Louis Stevenson came to the defense of Damien's character, as did the Roman Catholic Church. R. D. SHUSTER

DANTE ALIGHIERI (1265–1321)
Italian poet

Dante is one of the great figures of world literature and the most eminent of all Italian writers. Born in Florence of a rather noble family, he was educated under the supervision of members of the Dominican and Franciscan orders. As a young man, he was made one of the priors (chief magistrates) of the Florentine republic and entered into the political struggles that divided Florence into several hostile factions. While absent on a diplomatic mission in 1302, he was exiled. Some thirteen years afterward, he was invited to return to his native city if he would submit to certain humiliating conditions. Dante refused. He spent the rest of his life in exile in various Italian cities: Verona, Padua, Bologna. He died in Ravenna.

Dante's first significant work was *La Vita Nuova* (*The New Life*), written between 1292 and 1295. Composed partly in blank verse and partly in prose, the book tells of Dante's love for Beatrice and promises to treat the subject more worthily later, a promise kept in *The Divine Comedy*. Beatrice Portinari, object of the poet's idealized love, Dante hardly knew at all. He had met her only briefly when he was nine years old, and once again at eighteen.

De Monarchia (*On Monarchy*), written in exile about 1312, is a political treatise in which Dante defended the emperor's supremacy in temporal matters over the authority of the Church. Dante put forward the idea of one world government which would secure a universal peace, thus promoting the full realization of humanity's intellectual and cultural potential.

Dante's world fame rests on his great epic poem *The Divine Comedy*, begun early in his exile and completed shortly before his death. In many ways the poem is a summation of classical and medieval learning. In outline *The Divine Comedy* is a chronicle of a dream journey made by the poet at Easter

in the year 1300 through hell, purgatory, and paradise. The work is called a comedy because it ends happily, unlike a tragedy; further, it moves upward, both literally (from earth to heaven) and allegorically (from lostness to redemption). The adjective "divine" was added to the title later by admiring critics.

At the deepest level the poem is a theological, moral, and political allegory in which Dante represents humanity. As the Christian Everyman, he commits sin (at the outset of the poem he goes "astray from the straight road" and is lost in a dark wood); he is shown sin's punishment (hell), repents and is purified (purgatory), and is finally admitted to the company of the redeemed in paradise.

Virtually every aspect of medieval life and thought is represented in Dante's readable masterpiece, which has been called the greatest single work of imaginative literature in the Western world. Written in Florentine vernacular, it became the basis for a standardized Italian language. P. M. BECHTEL

DARBY, JOHN NELSON (1800–1882)
Distinguished leader among the Plymouth Brethren; Bible translator and commentator

Born into a prominent Anglo-Irish family, Darby received his early education at Westminster School in London. When he was fifteen his family moved to reside in an ancestral castle in Ireland. Darby then attended Trinity College, Dublin, where he graduated as a Classical Gold Medalist (1819). He then studied law and in 1822 was called to the Irish Chancery Bar.

Through ardent study of the Bible young Darby came to know Christ and felt that his legal career should be relinquished in order to fully devote himself to God's work. The main object of his service was the poor Catholics of Ireland. In 1825 he took Deacons' orders from Archbishop Magee and was made a priest the next year as a curate of the Church of Ireland. Assigned to a parish in the mountains of Wicklow, he lived in a peasants' cottage on a bog. He displayed great energy in pastoral service, rarely returning home from his visits before midnight. He remained in this post for two years and three months after which, being disturbed by the great discrepancy between the church of his day and what he saw in the Bible, he gave up his parochial position in 1827.

Darby felt the church was independent of the state and that ministry came from gifts given by the Holy Spirit, not by the ordination of man. Prophecy meetings were held at the mansion of Viscountess Powerscourt near Bray, and it was here that John Bellett introduced Darby to Anthony Groves and John Parnell (later Lord Congleton). These men, independent of one another, had all been exercised over the condition of the church. Their common desire to return to Scripture for details on church order and ministry was the catalyst for a revival of the functioning of believers as members of the body of Christ. Some principal others, such as Edward Cronin, Edward Wilson, Francis Hutchinson, and William Stokes, all played prominent roles in the beginning of this work.

The Brethren point to a meeting in Dublin in 1828 as the beginning of the movement. It was at Hutchinson's home where Darby met with a few other brothers on the Lord's day to break bread and to fellowship. The meeting was based on Matthew 18:20, which promises that if two or three are gathered in the Lord's name, the Lord is also present. To partake of the Lord's Supper one only had to be a Christian, not a member of a denomination. Additionally, a clergyman was not needed to administer the bread and wine since only One was their Teacher, Father, and Leader, and they were all brothers (Matt. 23:8-10)—hence the name "Brethren." The believers' gifts were to be practiced not according to human organization but according to the leading of the Spirit as in 1 Corinthians 14. In 1828, Darby put out a pamphlet entitled *The Nature and Unity of the Church of Christ* which embodied the beliefs and practices of this developing Christian community. This work spread rapidly and fueled similar movements outside of Ireland.

In 1830, Francis W. Neuman, brother of John H. (Cardinal) Neuman, persuaded Darby to visit Oxford where he introduced him to Benjamin W. Newton. Newton, a native of Plymouth, shared like affections with Darby and by 1832 a simple gathering of believers was formed in Plymouth. A publication called the *Christian Witness* began there to which Darby was a contributor. Darby made his first visit to the European continent in 1830 and supported the labors of F. P. Monod in France. Between the years of 1836 and 1879 Darby traveled extensively in western Europe, North America, Australia, and New Zealand. He loved the Bible and taught and wrote prolifically during these years. During 1837 and 1838 Darby visited French Switzerland where spiritual conditions seemed suitable for revival. Various groups stemming from the Methodists, Robert Haldane's reading groups, and the Anabaptists received Darby. He taught all believers, regardless of their church affiliations, on subjects such as the Lord's return, the position of the church, the believers' union with Christ, and the prophecies. Eventually all over Europe many believers began to separate from their original groups to meet along the lines prescribed by Darby. This trend was precipitated by Darby's fluency in French and German, as well as translations of his work into Dutch and Scandinavian tongues. Darby's brother, William, lived in Dusseldorf, Germany, and ministered with V. Prosek who later collaborated with John Darby to translate the entire Bible into German.

In 1845, Darby returned to Plymouth, which by that time had become a thriving center of the Brethren movement. Darby had heard that a sectarian spirit had developed around Benjamin Newton, a prominent teacher there, and that Newton had varied from views commonly held by the rest of the Brethren on prophecy and church order. When Darby arrived he found the situation as previously described. Shortly thereafter Darby separated himself from that assembly and began a new one with his sympathizers. This course of action was taken after several other avenues of resolve had been exhausted. Two years later some notes taken from Newton's messages were construed as heretical by Darby and his supporters. Newton admitted and repudiated error in several of his points, reaffirmed the orthodox views, and published a statement to correct the matter. But in the minds of Darbyites he was never absolved nor extricated from the errors; consequently, he and his group were excommunicated.

A more serious and complex development connected with the Newton affair occurred in 1848 at a Brethren meeting at the Bethesda chapel in Bristol, England. George Müller and Henry Craik, leaders at Bethesda, satisfied that two brothers from Newton's group in Plymouth held none of the errors attributed to Newton, welcomed them to the Lord's Table. Darby felt this action would undo the discipline applied at Plymouth and introduce evil into Bristol. Matters escalated, and Darby demanded that public refutation of Newton's teachings be a basis of admitting people to the Lord's Table in order that evil might not be given entrance. Darby was disturbed that Bethesda would not comply with his demands. Viewing their attitude as indifference to righteousness, he eventually would not receive those from Bethesda. A great division into the "Open" and "Exclusive" Brethren assemblies developed based upon how they viewed Bethesda's actions.

Darby was devoted to the Bible and advocated "thinking in Scripture." He engaged in the original exposition of the Bible all his adult life, writing as thoughts came to him on a subject. He viewed truth as a growing tree. He was at times weak in detail but always forceful on the moral aspect of biblical matters. His criticisms of what he considered error were forceful and enlightening yet at times extreme, perhaps closing otherwise open doors. Invited by Dwight Moody to give a series of Bible readings in Chicago, Darby differed with his host over the question of the freedom of will in believing. The controversy ended when Darby abruptly closed his Bible and refused to go on with the Bible readings. After this he condemned Moody's work, saying that it would bring worldliness into the church.

In 1866, Darby himself fell under attack by close friends, because he had developed certain views that appeared similar in nature to what Newton had retracted years before. Darby was an extreme dispensationalist and considered that the church was in a state of ruin due to human failure shortly after its inception. He felt that it was presumptuous and arrogant for anyone to attempt reconstruction of the church according to patterns seen in the early church since God had never previously revived a dispensation that had failed. All that was left for Christians to do, according to Darby, was to walk in faithfulness to the Lord, avoiding unrighteousness and awaiting his return while meeting together in the Lord's name in all simplicity. The Scriptures were to be the sole and sufficient guide for believers' faith and conduct.

Darby left a legacy of scholarly and devotional works. His *Synopsis of the Bible*, thirty-four volumes of *The Collected Works of J. N. Darby*, and three volumes of letters represent his theological views and personal labors. He translated the Bible from the original languages into English, French, and German. He wrote essays against the Oxford and modernist movements as well as spiritually rich hymns and poems that displayed his deep affection for Christ. Darby, along with many other Brethren teachers, laid a foundation that has proven to be the basis for theological thought in many fundamental and evangelical circles today. Although not generally recognized as originating from the Brethren, their teaching on topics such as Old Testament types, prophecies, the position of the church, the Lord's return, and assurance of salvation have been largely incorporated into today's churches.

Darby balanced his literary work with pastoral visitations and ministry tours. He traveled worldwide until his eightieth year—teaching the Bible, encouraging the priesthood of all believers, advocating the return of Christian worship and service to Scriptural simplicity. Darby died, never having married, in Bournemouth, England, remarking that Christ had been the object of his life. T. FIRAK

DARWIN, CHARLES ROBERT
(1809–1882)
English naturalist who purported the theory of natural evolution

Educated with a view to becoming a clergyman, Charles Darwin initially accepted both the Genesis creation account and the Aristotelian doctrine of the fixity of species. He became interested in the biological sciences toward the end of his years at Cambridge University. From 1831 to 1836 he sailed as "naturalist" on H.M.S. *Beagle's* exploratory voyage in the South Atlantic and Pacific, gathering a vast amount of data about the geology, flora, and fauna of the areas visited. He was particularly impressed by similarities he discovered in places separated by great distances.

Darwin made careful biological observations and searched for connections to explain them. From a thesis of economist T. R. Malthus (1766–1834) about the struggle for existence as an explanation of population changes, Darwin conceived a plausible explanation of the entire natural history of living things. In his famous book *On the Origin of Species by Means of Natural Selection, or the Preservation of Favoured Races in the Struggle for Life* (1859), usually known simply as *The Origin of Species,* Darwin developed his theory and argued for the transmutation of species. In "natural selection" he seemed to have found a unifying principle for all biology, which he supported with evidence from such areas as paleontology, comparative anatomy, and vestigial organs, as well as from the geographic distribution of varieties of life. In 1871 he applied the principle to human origins in *The Descent of Man.*

Not all scientists agreed with him, but Darwin received his strongest and most persistent criticism from religious thinkers, the more so as the evolutionary account was extended to human beings, to morality, and to religion, so that no unchanging realities appeared to remain. Darwin himself modestly and kindly took no part in such religious controversies. Instead T. H. Huxley championed evolution in debates with famous figures like Bishop Samuel Wilberforce and William Gladstone (later British prime minister). Huxley's own identification of evolution with religious agnosticism (a term Huxley coined) created the image of Darwin as an enemy of the church, the Bible, and the Christian faith.

Darwin himself was not active as an enemy of faith. At the time of *The Origin of Species* he held some kind of theistic belief, but by 1870 he admitted that his theology was a muddle. On the one hand, he was sure the universe had not resulted from blind chance. On the other hand, he found no evidence of beneficent design in its details; to him the struggle for existence seemed blundering, cruel, and wasteful. In later years he altogether abandoned Christian beliefs and became a reluctant agnostic.

Darwin's influence was greater than any other person's in creating widespread acceptance (in the Western world) of organic evolution. Analogous ideas can be traced to antiquity and variations of the theory have developed since, but it was Darwin who amassed the most persuasive evidence. Some Christian scholars, such as James McCosh of Princeton, granted the evidence and explained the evolutionary process as God's method of creation. Some insisted on "special acts of creation" at specific junctures in the evolutionary process. Some held out for a "special creation" of man. Other Christian scholars rejected the entire theory and questioned the evidence at every juncture.

Darwin's theory of evolution of plants and animals by natural selection has been widely accepted by scientists until this day. However, many Christians believe that Darwin's views (particularly on the origin of the human species) contradict the Bible. In particular, evangelical Christians are committed to believe (1) in God as the Creator and Ruler of all, (2) in the creation of human beings as those who have "God's image," and (3) in the authority and trustworthiness of the biblical record. A. F. HOLMES

D'AUBIGNÉ, JEAN HENRI MERLE
(1794–1872)
Protestant historian

D'Aubigné was born into a French family

in exile in Geneva. Although d'Aubigné's father was a citizen of Geneva, he was also a merchant in Marseilles and wanted his son to follow that calling. Young d'Aubigné, however, felt called to the ministry and entered the theological school in Geneva. While studying there, he came under the influence of Robert Haldane (1764–1842), the Scottish minister largely responsible for le Reveil ("the Awakening") in Switzerland. In July 1817 d'Aubigné was ordained as a minister and left shortly afterward for Germany, where he planned to devote his life to literary work. The celebration of the three-hundredth anniversary of the Reformation in October 1817 gave him the idea of researching and writing an exhaustive history of the Protestant Reformation.

D'Aubigné spent some time in Berlin, where he was influenced by church historian Johann Neander. In 1818 he became pastor of the Reformed Congregation in Hamburg, and in 1824, one of the court preachers in Brussels. Because of the Revolution of 1830, he returned to Geneva to become a professor for the Evangelical Society of Geneva and preacher in the Chapelle de L'Oratoire. He helped to found La Gazette Evangelique (1832) and was instrumental in separating his congregation from the state church.

He wrote voluminously on many topics. Some of his most important works set forth a case for the separation of church and state and advocated the presbyterial form of church government. Most important, however, was his thirteen-volume history of the Reformation, which appeared between 1835 and 1878. The first five volumes dealt with the Lutheran movement, Swiss reformers Ulrich Zwingli and Guillaume Farel, and the pre-Reformation movements in France and England. The last eight concentrated on the Genevan Reformation. Although d'Aubigné was not an objective historian (his work is quite emotional at times), his books are basic to most Protestant histories of the Reformation written since his day. W. S. REID

DAVENANT, JOHN (1572–1641)
Anglican bishop and theologian

Born in London, Davenant entered Queens College, Cambridge, in 1587, where he received his B.A. (1591), B.D. (1601), and D.D. (1609) degrees. He was made Lady Margaret professor of divinity in 1609 and in 1614 was unanimously elected sixteenth president of Queens College. He held both posts until his elevation to bishop in 1621, which required that he move his residence.

Davenant was chosen, along with George Carleton, Joseph Hall, and Samuel Ward (later joined by Thomas Goad) to represent the Anglican Church at the Synod of Dort (1618–1619). The English divines took a moderate position, and Davenant, along with Ward, went so far as to argue that Christ died for the whole world, not just the elect.

Davenant was elevated to bishop of Salisbury in 1621 by King James I. In 1629 he preached a Lenten sermon on Romans 6:23 before the new king, Charles I, which touched upon the proscribed subject of predestination. For this he was called to defend himself in counsel and escaped official censure, but the times were against him. Archbishop William Laud and his party were taking over, with the result that even moderate Calvinists lost favor with the court.

In 1631 Davenant wrote a treatise on justification, and in 1634 he produced a small work dealing with forty-nine disputed topics.

In the last year of his life Davenant wrote *Animadversions written by the Right Rev. Father in God, John, Lord Bishop of Salisbury, upon a Treatise intituled: God's Love to Mankind,* which was a reply to an earlier work by Samuel Hoard. Hoard had argued against the Calvinist doctrines of election and reprobation; and Davenant, finding his courage again, opposed him.

In 1650 a posthumous work on the extent of Christ's atonement appeared in which Davenant developed his theory of general redemption.

A portion of the inscription on Davenant's monument in Salisbury Cathedral admirably describes his life: "A living example of venerated antiquity, he discharged all the duties of a primitive bishop; and during his twenty years' oversight of this diocese he was honored by all good men, and even by his enemies." W. ELWELL

DAVID (died 589 or 601)

Patron saint of Wales; his Welsh name is "Dewi"

According to a legendary *Life,* written by Bishop Rhygyfarch, David was born at Henfynw in Cardigan, the son of a chieftain. David became a priest and monk and established twelve monasteries from Croyland to Pembrokeshire. Later he was abbot of a monastery at Menevia (now called St. David's) in Pembrokeshire, where he imposed strict rules of asceticism upon the community. Rhygyfarch claimed that David was consecrated bishop after a pilgrimage to Jerusalem. On his return to Wales, according to that legend, he took a principal part in church councils at Brefi in Cardigan (560) and at Caerleon. The Council of Brefi supposedly recognized him as senior bishop (primate) of all Wales.

Many ancient relics and places are associated with David in Wales, southwest England, and Brittany (France). David is also believed to have influenced Irish monastic development through students who came to him from Ireland. The association of leeks (as mentioned in Shakespeare's play *Henry V*) with March 1, St. David's Day, is longstanding, although its origin is not known. Roman Catholic veneration of St. David goes back to the twelfth century. P. TOON

DAVIDSON, ANDREW BRUCE (1831–1902)

Scottish Old Testament scholar

Davidson was born at Ellon (Aberdeenshire), the son of a farmer. After studying at the grammar school in Aberdeen, he attended the university in that city, receiving his M.A. in 1849. For three years he taught in a parish school, learning Hebrew in his spare time. In 1852 he entered New College,

Edinburgh (theological school of the Free Church of Scotland), where in 1858 he became assistant to John Duncan (1796–1870), professor of Hebrew. Davidson succeeded Duncan in 1863 and held the post until he died. A small, quiet man, he had a radiant personality which made a lasting impression on his students.

Davidson introduced into the Free Church a reverent approach to the higher criticism of the Old Testament, but one of his pupils, William Robertson Smith (1846–1894) was tried for heresy after taking the approach too far. Davidson wrote many articles for James Hastings's *Dictionary of the Bible.* His books include *An Introduction to Hebrew Grammar* (1874), *A Hebrew Syntax,* and commentaries on the books of Job (1884); Ezekiel (1892); and Nahum, Habakkuk, and Zephaniah (1896). He was honored by doctorates from Aberdeen and Edinburgh (both 1868) and from Cambridge (1900). P. TOON

DAVIDSON, RANDALL THOMAS (1848–1930)

Archbishop of Canterbury, 1903–1928

Born in Edinburgh, Davidson was educated at Harrow (a preparatory school) and Oxford University. Ordained an Anglican clergyman in 1875, he three years later became resident chaplain to A. C. Tait, archbishop of Canterbury, whose daughter Edith he married that same year. In 1883 he was appointed dean of Windsor; in 1891, bishop of Rochester; in 1895, bishop of Winchester; and in 1903, archbishop of Canterbury, an office he held until his resignation in 1928.

The twenty-five years of Davidson's primacy were eventful and critical for both state and church. For example, as a nation Great Britain fought World War I and in 1926 experienced a general strike. At the same time the Church of England was achieving self-government through the Enabling Act of 1919. The Church composed a new prayer book which, though rejected by the House of Commons in 1927 and 1928, did come into use in some dioceses of the Church. At the Lambeth Conference of

1920, over which Davidson presided, the Anglican Church made overtures of union to the English Free Churches, though subsequent negotiations proved fruitless. Between 1921 and 1925 it carried on similar, but informal conversations in Malines (Belgium) with representatives of the Roman Catholic Church, but they also led to no concrete results.

Davidson's leadership as the spokesman for the Church of England during those crucial years has been variously evaluated. Evangelicals note that only liberals were promoted and that in his ecumenical work Davidson seemed willing to compromise on important matters. Others, however, say that Davidson kept his Church united, always emphasizing its mission to the English people. Bishop Stephen C. Neill has characterized Davidson as "one of the outstanding ecclesiastical statesmen of this century."
N. V. HOPE

DAVIES, SAMUEL (1723–1761)
American Presbyterian clergyman

Born in New Castle County, Delaware, Davies was ordained in 1747 and was appointed at his own request to preach in Hanover County, Virginia. He was an important figure in the spread of evangelical Presbyterianism into Virginia, where he built on the work begun by William Robinson, Samuel Norris, and others. Davies was a preacher of great power. Strong in his sympathy for Christian revivals, he regarded personal declarations of faith as the center of the Christian life. For eleven years he conducted a highly successful ministry in Hanover County and furthered the organization of Presbyterianism in the region.

Davies was a great advocate of religious freedom. He opposed monopoly control in Virginia by the established Church of England. He argued that the Toleration Act of 1689 permitted religious freedom in the British colonies as well as in Great Britain. In 1753 and 1754, while in England and Scotland soliciting funds for the College of New Jersey (now Princeton University), he se-

cured a royal declaration that the Toleration Act extended to Virginia.

In 1758 Davies was chosen to succeed Jonathan Edwards as president of Princeton, where he raised standards for entrance and graduation, and held the position until his death. D. C. MASTERS

DAWSON, CHRISTOPHER (1889–1970)
Roman Catholic scholar and historian

The son of an army officer, Dawson grew up in Yorkshire, England. Graduating from Oxford in 1911, he pursued post-graduate studies for two years. He was drawn heavily to scholarly pursuits. In 1913, after much contemplation, Dawson converted from high Anglicanism to Roman Catholicism. Dawson's choice arose from his historical comparisons of Protestantism and Catholicism. Already a committed believer, Dawson's studies convinced him Luther and other Protestant leaders were actually not reformers but revolutionaries. As he saw it, the reformers broke not just with medieval corruption but with the essence of Christianity. For the rest of his life, an impetus to know a phenomenon's religious core, and its social and cultural effects, pervaded Dawson's endeavors.

Dawson pursued his work mainly as a private scholar. In 1916, after much sickness, he was diagnosed as unfit for regular work due to his frail condition. His wife and friends encouraged him toward independent scholarly writing. Dawson's father provided a stipend from the family estate. Through these unusual circumstances, a gifted mind was freed to produce some of the twentieth century's most extraordinary historical studies. After still more years of research, Dawson began significant writing in 1928. From this time until his death, he produced twenty major volumes and multiplied articles on the general history of civilization—primarily its Western European aspects. Dawson was a historian of ideas and their imprint on society and culture. Thus, his works examined custom, civilization, culture, and especially religion to analyze societal evolvements over long periods.

Among Dawson's conclusions, the most famous was his dictum "Religion is the key to history."

Some of Dawson's works sweep broadly over world cultures and their progress. His writings have been compared sometimes with Spengler's and Toynbee's. Even here the author's stress on religion is obvious. Primarily, Dawson's concern lay with the interconnections between Western European developments and Christian belief and life. Here his comprehensive grasp and potent anaylses reached their heights. In graphic, compelling detail, Dawson's works show the integral dependence of Western history on Christian ideas and practice. Christianity, in general overview, has been the "soul" of Western life. The author's works were also prominent for their warnings against modern secularism. In its ability to destroy civilization's religious axis, no threat to modern life is greater. Dawson has been criticized for being too religious, too philosophical, too irregular, and too anti-modern. Yet his first-rate scholarship has never been questioned. With captivating style and irenic spirit, his powerful works have consistently impressed even rank opponents.

Among Dawson's major writings, probably the best known are *Enquiries into Religion and Culture, Progress and Religion, The Making of Europe,* and *The Historic Reality of Christian Culture.* But the shorter works collected in *The Dynamics of World History* and *Medieval Essays* deserve mention also. As for honors, Dawson delivered the Gifford Lectures both in 1947 and 1948. These were published respectively as *Religion and Culture* and *Religion and the Rise of Western Culture.* At two times, Dawson took employment as a university instructor. From 1921 to 1933, he was a part-time lecturer at Exeter University. Then in 1958, he received his greatest accolade. Harvard University chose him that year as its first Stillman Professor of Roman Catholic Studies. His works *The Dividing of Christendom* and *The Formation of Christendom* derive from these lectures. Poor health forced Dawson's return to England after just four years in the United States. Before departing, Cardinal Cushing

called him one of those rare scholars who have "changed men's minds." K. J. BRYER

DECIUS (c. 201–251)
Roman emperor, 249–251; instituted a brief but severe persecution of Christians

After being proclaimed emperor by his Danubian troops, Decius defeated and killed Emperor Philip the Arabian (who ruled 244–249). Decius believed that Rome needed to return to its old traditions, so he revived the office of censor to supervise morals. To restore the Roman religion he required all citizens to offer sacrifices to pagan gods. Some Christians bought certificates (*libelli*) saying they had sacrificed. (Such ones were called *libellatici*.) Other Christians offered sacrifices, and their readmission to the church soon stirred a controversy. The issue was settled at the Council of Carthage (251), where it was decided that repentant libellatici should be restored to church membership, but those who actually sacrificed must do lifelong penance.

One of the first victims of the persecution was Fabian, bishop of Rome, who was killed in 250. His death left the see (bishop's jurisdiction) of Rome vacant for sixteen months. The bishops of Alexandria and Jerusalem were also killed. The theologians Origen and Cyprian, bishop of Carthage, suffered in Decius's persecution—but were not killed. When Decius was killed in a battle against the Goths, the persecution of Christians ended. C. HICKS

DELITZSCH, FRANZ JULIUS (1813–1890)
German Lutheran Old Testament scholar

Born and educated in Leipzig, he held professorships at Rostock (1846–1850) and Erlangen (1850–1867) before returning to teach at Leipzig until his death. Because of his Jewish ancestry, he was always concerned about anti-Semitism. He founded a school for training missionaries to work among the Jews, published a periodical for dialogue between Jews and Christians, and in 1877 completed his translation (still widely used) of the New Testament into Hebrew. His conservative theology is seen clearly in his many commentaries on the Old Testament. D. M. LAKE

DELITZSCH, FRIEDRICH (1850–1922)
German Assyriologist

Son of Franz Julius Delitzsch, Friedrich served as professor at Leipzig (1878–1893), Breslau (1893–1899), and Berlin from 1899 until he retired. Although his father was theologically conservative and Pietistic, Friedrich Delitzsch became hostile to orthodox Christianity. Some of his writings, numbering more than twenty, are direct attacks upon evangelical theology. In his most famous book, *Babel and Bible* (1902–1903), based on lectures given before Emperor Wilhelm II, Delitzsch claimed that Judaism possessed little that was unique, having developed out of Babylonian origins. He is thus remembered as a champion of the "pan-Babylonian" theory. D. M. LAKE

DE MAISTRE, JOSEPH MARIE (1754–1821)
Roman Catholic apologist

Born at Chambery in Savoy, de Maistre studied law with the Jesuits in Turin (Italy). He entered the Savoy civil service in 1774 and became a member of the senate in 1788. Driven from Savoy by the French Revolutionary armies in 1792, he moved to Sardinia (then in control of Savoy), and was Sardinian ambassador to Russia from 1802 until 1817. He then returned to Savoy, which Napoleon had briefly annexed to France before his fall in 1815.

De Maistre's major work was *Du Pape* (1819), in which he argued that the only sound basis for a worthwhile society is authority: the temporal sovereignty of political monarchy and papal lordship in the sphere of religion. Popes, he contended, were virtually infallible, since "no sovereign pontiff has ever made a mistake in speaking on matters of faith." His book, called the charter of "ultramontanism" (the doctrine of ab-

solute papal supremacy), was used to oppose Napoleon's control of the church in France. N. V. HOPE

DEMETRIUS, BISHOP (died c. 231)
Bishop of Alexandria (Egypt), 189–231

Eusebius of Caesarea, an early church historian, listed Demetrius as Alexandria's eleventh bishop. Demetrius supposedly appointed the theologian Origen as head of Alexandria's catechetical school around 203. When the emperor Caracalla began persecuting Christians in Alexandria in 215, Origen fled to Caesarea and later to Jerusalem. Because Origen was allowed to preach there even though he held no official church title, Demetrius called him back to Alexandria and rebuked him.

When Origen returned to Palestine around 228, he was ordained a presbyter by the bishops of Caesarea and Jerusalem without Demetrius's consent. Demetrius, however, ordered that Origen be deposed, on the grounds that he was a eunuch—which in Alexandrian tradition was a disqualification for church office.

Demetrius is said to have sent Pantaenus, a former head of the Alexandrian school, to preach in India. C. HICKS

DENCK, HANS (1495–1527)
Anabaptist leader; sometimes known as the "pope" of the Anabaptists

Born in Heybach, Bavaria (Germany), Denck was sent to the University of Ingolstadt (Germany), where by 1519 he had won a reputation as a humanist scholar (a master of the ancient languages and literature). For some time he associated with Christian humanists Desiderius Erasmus and John Oecolampadius in Basel (Switzerland). He also worked with the great humanist publishing ventures centered there. He probably joined the Protestant movement around 1523.

With the help of Oecolampadius, Denck secured a teaching post in the influential city of Nuremberg (Germany). There, influenced by the "spiritualist" views of Andreas

Carlstadt and Thomas Muntzer, he began to develop his idea that Christians should live in a free and spontaneous manner under the direct control of the Holy Spirit. He also became increasingly repulsed by institutional religion, hierarchial church structure, formal worship, and symbolic sacraments. Driven from the city by the Lutherans because of his views, he eventually arrived in Augsburg (Germany), where he joined the Anabaptists. A prolific writer, he became the most influential leader of south German Anabaptism. (Anabaptism was the largest group in the so-called "Radical Reformation," a name given to a variety of groups that wanted to push reform beyond the positions of Ulrich Zwingli and Martin Luther.) Believing that Christianity was above all a personal piety toward God, and being a gentle and peace-loving man, he left Augsburg when the authorities objected to the movement.

Rejected by authorities everywhere and forced to keep on the move, he came to believe that God was displeased with the divisiveness of Anabaptism. Returning to Basel in 1527, he was admitted to the Reformed church, thereby signaling his break with Anabaptism as a separate movement. Later that year he died of the plague.

In many ways Denck was a model of Christian behavior. His radical ideas, however, especially on the free work of the Holy Spirit, encouraged others of less moderate nature to excesses. B. G. ARMSTRONG

DENNEY, JAMES (1856–1917)
Scottish Biblical theologian and New Testament scholar

Born in Paisley, Denney was educated in arts at Glasgow University and in theology at the Free Church College in the same city. Ordained in 1886, he served for eleven years as minister of the East Free Church, Broughty Ferry, where his fervent evangelical preaching made a deep impression.

In 1897 Denney was elected professor of theology at his former college in Glasgow. Three years later he moved to the department of New Testament, continuing there

until his death. In 1915 he was elected principal of the Free Church College.

Denney wrote several New Testament commentaries, principally 1 and 2 Thessalonians (1892) and 2 Corinthians (1894) in the *Expositor's Bible*. In 1900 he published a massive work on Romans in the *Expositor's Greek Testament*. His major works in New Testament theology include *Jesus and the Gospel* (1908), which is "an exhaustive and luminous treatment of the historic basis of the Christian faith," and two works on the substitutionary atonement of Jesus Christ, *The Death of Christ* (1903) and *The Christian Doctrine of Reconciliation* (1917).

Denney also took part in the public life of his denomination. For example, he was a member of a committee to negotiate union with the Church of Scotland, and he served as convener of the Central Fund, to raise money for ministerial stipends. N. V. HOPE

DE NOBILI, ROBERT (1577–1656)
Jesuit missionary from Tuscany (now in Italy) who served for fifty-one years in India during the Portuguese colonial rule

With royal patronage of the Roman Catholic Church, many missionaries were trying to impose Portuguese customs and ways of life on Indian converts. De Nobili, however, rejected such practices and instead adopted certain Hindu customs, especially from the Brahmins (the priestly caste of orthodox Hinduism). He lived as a sanyasi (Hindu ascetic) and allowed his converts to continue living in their original cultural setting. Because of the rigid caste system (social class division) in India, he advocated separate evangelistic missions for each caste. De Nobili's views and methods were severely opposed by other missionaries and church leaders. A long dispute followed, and the pope finally approved de Nobili's approach but with certain cautions.

As a scholar and linguist, de Nobili was perhaps the first European to do serious firsthand studies of Sanskrit (the ancient Hindu language) and of the Vedas (sacred Hindu scriptures). He wrote over twenty books in the Sanskrit, Tamil, and Telugu

languages of India. It is estimated that nearly 100,000 people became Christians through De Nobili's efforts and influence. His greatest contribution to Christian missions was his attempt to free Christianity from Western cultural biases. De Nobili regarded biblical faith from India's indigenous perspective and tried to use the wisdom of that country to communicate the gospel.
S. P. ATHYAL

DESCARTES, RENÉ (1595–1650)
French philosopher, mathematician, and scientist

Born in Touraine (France) and schooled by Jesuit scholars, Descartes spent much of his adult life in Protestant Holland. Descartes developed a deductive system of thought modeled on mathematical methods. It included "proofs" (akin to those in geometry) for the existence of both the human soul and God. To Descartes the existence of the soul was an inevitable corollary of the act of thinking: "I think, therefore I exist"—as a "thinking thing," or soul. Although his famous statement (in Latin: *cogito, ergo sum*) may seem trivial, it countered the way mechanistic materialism was explaining everything merely as physical objects and forces. Descartes avoided reducing human beings to just matter. He introduced a dualistic theory in which the human body and soul are two separate and independent entities; the soul can therefore remain and is immortal.

From this starting point Descartes went on to a causal argument for the existence of God: if the soul exists, a finite thing, it must have a cause great enough to produce it. And one's idea of God, a perfect being, must likewise have a sufficient cause. No imperfect being is sufficient for that; therefore, a Perfect Being must exist. Descartes also developed what philosophers call an "ontological" argument, based on the logically necessary "properties" of a Supreme Being. Going back to geometry—as a triangle must have three angles equal to two right angles, so God, as Perfect Being, must necessarily

exist. To deny God's existence is logically self-contradictory.

Theologians and philosophers still debate the validity of such arguments. But the importance of Descartes goes beyond the arguments themselves to his "method." His optimism about logical proofs that were derived from undoubtable premises initiated a trend that has dominated segments of Western theology, philosophy, and science ever since. As such, Descartes has been called the "father of modern philosophy." Some Christian apologists have followed his method, but others have considered it antagonistic to biblical faith. A contemporary philosopher and mathematician, Blaise Pascal, considered Descartes a deist, willing to do without God except for "letting him give a tap to set the world in motion." Some scholars have suspected Descartes of being essentially atheistic—at a time when open avowal of atheism would bring persecution. But Descartes was careful to show his devotion to Roman Catholicism.

Descartes's contribution to mathematics was outstanding. By developing the system of "Cartesian coordinates" (named for him) he brought together algebra and geometry. Descartes thus paved the way for the calculus of Isaac Newton and the subsequent development of modern science. A. F. HOLMES

DES PREZ, JOSQUIN (c. 1450–1521)
Renaissance musical master

Josquin des Prez was associated with the Choir of Milan Cathedral (1459–1472), and was in the employment of the Sforza family of the same city. From 1486 to 1494 he was at the Papal Chapel, while after 1499 his patron was Hercules, Duke of Ferrara. General travels between Italy and France occurred from 1501 to 1515. It is probable that des Prez's attachment to the Chapel of Louis XII began around 1515. Most scholars agree on the enormous international reputation that grew up around the composer—in particular, des Prez's high status with Louis XII and Emperor Maximilian of Austria.

As a composer, des Prez wrote approximately twenty masses, and numerous motets of three to six voices. Generally, the motets are more innovative than the masses in the use of contemporary techniques. On the other hand, des Prez develops important tendencies to tie individual mass movements together by common thematic materials.

Textual clarity is essential to des Prez's style. Subtle, rhythmically intense lines interchange with simple note-against-note passages, for purposes of variety. Often voices are paired off in combinations of alternating duos. Overlapped entrances and/or releases are ongoing features, giving "seamless" effects to much of des Prez's music. Imitation, diversity of texture, syncopations, and an evolving sense of major/minor tonal reference characterize both the sacred and secular works. An unusual demonstration of des Prez's sense of instrumental color and a direct, aggressive rhythmic drive may be heard in his *Fanfare for Louis XII*.

The *Missa Pange Lingua* is particularly popular in this repertory, featuring a freely-spun, nonimitative counterpoint, along with passages of careful word-painting. The main material is based on the Hymn for Corpus Christi, the latter being derived from the Easter Hymn of the same title.

Josquin des Prez also wrote a Requiem, an Ave Verum, and several Magnificats. His *Collected Works* were first published under editorship of A. Smijers in 1925, in fifty-three volumes. Numerous valuable, critical studies in the form of articles and monographs have been written on Josquin des Prez's contributions, to the present day. D. S. CUSHMAN

DEVANANDAN, PAUL DAVID
(1901–1962)
Leading Christian theologian in India

Devanandan studied theology at the Pacific School of Religion in Berkeley, California, and received his Ph.D. from Yale. He taught at the United Theological College, Bangalore (India), lectured at Cambridge University (England), and was also a visiting professor at Union Theological Seminary in New York City. He was closely associated with the work of the British-based Student Christian Movement (SCM) and was literature secretary of the national council of the Young Men's Christian Association in India. He is well known in India for his many books and monographs.

Devanandan's major contribution was in developing a positive Christian attitude to Indian culture and religions. He advocated cooperation between people of all faiths, in pursuit of common spiritual values and a better society. He also called on the Christian church in India to participate fully in the task of building a free Indian nation.

Devanandan linked Christian theology, contemporary Hinduism, and secular society. He taught that Christians should help Hindus understand their own religion in light of secularism and changing patterns of life in modern India. Devanandan believed that the message of Christ's incarnation became relevant at the point of modern Hinduism's helplessness in reconciling its traditions with secularism. S. P. ATHYAL

DE VAUX, ROLAND GUERIN
(1903–1971)
Archaeologist and biblical scholar

Born in Paris, de Vaux received his doctorate in theology and was ordained to the priesthood of the Roman Catholic Church in 1929. Thereafter he became a member of the Dominican Order of Friars. In 1934 he was assigned to teach Old Testament at the École Biblique of Jerusalem; in 1945 he became the director of this school, a position he held for two decades. During his active years he became associated with studies in the patriarchal period of Israelite history and discoveries in the Judean desert, and he headed an international team of scholars working on the Dead Sea Scrolls. His archaeological expeditions included those at Tel-el-Farah (1946–1960), Qumran and the scroll caves (1949–1958), and the joint expedition in Jerusalem with the British School of Archaeology (1961–1963). Besides works on archaeology, such as *Archaeology and the Dead Sea Scrolls* (1961 and 1973), de Vaux published a skillful survey of Israel's life and institutions, which appeared in English in 1961 under the title *Ancient Israel*. In recognition of his fruitful researches, he was made a member of the French Academie des Inscriptions et Belles Lettres in 1941. N. V. HOPE

DE WETTE, WILHELM MARTIN LEBERECHT (1780–1849)
German theologian and biblical scholar

Born at Ulla, near Weimar (Germany), de Wette studied at Jena, where he obtained his doctorate and became a private docent (unsalaried lecturer) in 1805. He taught theology at Heidelberg from 1807 to 1810, then was called to be a professor in the newly founded University of Berlin. In 1819 he was dismissed from his professorship by King Frederick William III of Prussia for political reasons. After a stay in Weimar (in 1822) de Wette joined the theology faculty at Basel (Switzerland), where he remained until his death. At Basel he served as rector (head) five times.

De Wette was one of the most important pioneers in the field of historical criticism of the Bible. Beginning in 1806 he published several volumes on both the Old and New Testaments. From 1813 he wrote books on theological and related subjects, including a large work on Christian ethics.

Evidently under the influence of his Berlin colleague Friedrich Schleiermacher, de Wette came to emphasize the importance of religious experience rather than reason, thereby displeasing the rationalists. On the other hand, his methods of criticism led him to doubt the validity of biblical miracles, including the Resurrection. That view alienated the Pietists. Nevertheless, de Wette's influence helped shape much of later nineteenth-century theology. N. V. HOPE

DIBELIUS, MARTIN FRANZ (1883–1947)
German New Testament scholar, theologian, and ecumenist

Born in Dresden, Dibelius was educated in four universities, including Berlin, where he was an unsalaried lecturer from 1910 to

1915. He then succeeded Johannes Weiss as professor of New Testament exegesis at Heidelberg, a position he occupied until his death.

At first interested in Semitic studies, Dibelius later concentrated on New Testament interpretation. He pioneered in "form criticism," an attempt to investigate not only the literary character of New Testament books, but also their oral or preliterary formation. Dibelius examined the four Gospels and the book of Acts and identified in them several categories of expression, including sermon, paradigm, short story, exhortation, and myth. He looked for the life situation out of which various literary forms arose, in order to highlight the chief elements of the message on which New Testament Christianity was founded. The principal work in which Dibelius explained his views was *Die Formgeschichte des Evangeliums* (1919), translated into English as *From Tradition to Gospel* (1934).

Dibelius was interested in the ecumenical movement, particularly its theological foundation. He attended the World Conference on Faith and Order at Lausanne in 1927, and in 1928 became chairman of the theological committee of the Universal Christian Conference on Life and Work. N. V. HOPE

DIBELIUS, OTTO (1880–1967)
German Protestant bishop and ecumenist

Born in Berlin, Dibelius studied theology at Wittenberg and served as pastor at Crossen, on the Oder River, from 1906 until 1915. That year he was appointed to a pastorate in Berlin, where in 1925 he became general superintendent of the Kurmark (Brandenburg-Prussia). Because he opposed the Nazi government and its church administrator Hans Kerrl, Dibelius's public activities were curtailed between 1933 and 1945, and he was arrested three times.

In 1945 Dibelius became bishop of Berlin, and in 1949 president of the Council of the German Evangelical Church. Because part of his church constituency was located in communist East Germany, Dibelius worked with persistent courage to uphold religious freedom in the face of that government's militant atheism.

Dibelius was an ardent ecumenist. He attended the World Missionary Conference at Edinburgh in 1910, the Stockholm Life and Work Conference of 1925, and the World Conference on Faith and Order at Lausanne in 1927. From 1954 to 1961 he was one of the presidents of the World Council of Churches. N. V. HOPE

DICKINSON, CLARENCE (1873–1969)
American organist and composer

Dickinson was appointed organist at New York City's Brick Presbyterian Church in 1909. He and his wife, Helena Snyder Dickinson, organized a series of concerts at the church from 1920 to 1937 that featured various performers and attracted large audiences. Clarence Dickinson traveled throughout the United States and Europe as a successful concert performer. In 1912 he joined the faculty of Union Theological Seminary, New York; and in 1928, with his wife, Helena, he helped found the School of Sacred Music there. Dickinson taught organ, composition, and history of church music until his retirement in 1953. He published over five hundred compositions and arrangements, including *The Medicine Man; Sacred Choruses, Ancient and Modern; Book of Eighty Anthems;* and *Ninety Interludes for Organ.* K. LEID

DICKINSON, EMILY ELIZABETH (1830–1886)
American poet

The middle child of Edward Dickinson, a prominent lawyer, Emily attended Amherst Academy and spent one year at Mount Holyoke Female Seminary in nearby South Hadley. When asked about her education, Dickinson replied, "I went to school—but in your manner of phrase—had no education."

Not much is known about her personal life. Dickinson never married and rarely left her family home, the Homestead, in Amherst. She only left the small college town twice after her schooling, once to visit Washington, D.C., when her father served in the Congress, and the other time to go to Boston, where she was treated for an eye disorder. It was after the trip to Washington in 1855 that Dickinson withdrew to her upstairs bedroom and began to dress herself entirely in white.

The period from the late 1850s through the early 1860s was Dickinson's most productive. It was at this time that she began earnestly writing poems, often on scraps of paper. She did not follow the accepted poetic form of the day, choosing instead simple ballad or hymn verses. Dickinson varied poetic meters, feet, and rhyme patterns, using different kinds of rhyme patterns: exact, vowel, identical, suspended, imperfect, and visual. She creatively used punctuation, diction, and spelling to make her words come alive. It was this unorthodox style that kept Dickinson's poetry in obscurity during her lifetime. Dickinson chose Thomas Wentworth Higginson, a famous critic, to be her literary adviser, even though he thought the public would not accept her innovative works. Dickinson was fascinated by the subject of death, and naturally her poetry reflected this interest. Death, eternity, God, and the afterlife were all common topics in her writing.

By 1866, the majority of Dickinson's poems were complete. Only 7 of her 1,775 poems appeared in print while she was alive, and those that did were published anonymously. Dickinson died of Bright's disease in the home in which she was born.
D. C. BLANCHETTE

DICKINSON, HELENA (1875–1957)
Canadian-born educator and writer

Helena Adell Snyder married Clarence Dickinson in 1904. In 1928 they founded the School of Sacred Music at Union Theological Seminary in New York City, where she taught history of church music and liturgy. She collaborated with her husband on numerous lectures, books, and recitals. A concert series they began in 1920 at Brick Presbyterian Church in New York City was renowned and well attended, continuing for almost twenty years. Helena Dickinson's writings include translations of musical pieces and collections of hymns such as *The Coming of the Prince of Peace* (1919) and *A Treasury of Worship* (1926). K. LEID

DICKINSON, JONATHAN (1688–1747)
Colonial American pastor, educator, and theologian

Born in Massachusetts, Dickinson graduated from Yale and after further theological study pastored several Presbyterian churches in New Jersey. His influence in the middle colonies has been compared with that of Jonathan Edwards in New England. Although Dickinson wrote at least nineteen books, he is best known as a leader of the "New Light" faction of the Presbyterian Church and for his efforts in education.

Dickinson, a firm Calvinist, nonetheless opposed the rigid stance of those who wanted ministerial candidates to accept every detail of the Westminster confessional standards. He helped pass the Synod of Philadelphia's 1729 Adopting Act, which required candidates for ordination to subscribe to the Westminster standards yet allowed for minor differences of interpretation.

Dickinson supported the Great Awakening, which included the work of such men as George Whitefield and Gilbert Tennent and eventually divided the Presbyterian Church (1741). Dickinson tried at first to heal the schism, but later joined the revivalist "New Light" faction. With Gilbert Tennent, he helped found the College of New Jersey (later Princeton University) to train "New Light" ministers. The college opened in 1747 in Dickinson's home, with him as president, but he died only a few months later. J. N. AKERS

DIEULAFOY, MARCEL (1844–1920)
French archaeologist and road engineer in Persia

Dieulafoy and his wife, Jeanne, conducted extensive excavations at Susa (Shushan, Neh. 1:1; Esther 1:2, KJV) from 1884 to 1886,

clearing the way for later experts to continue the work. In Susa, hub of the ancient Persian empire, they investigated the palaces of Darius I (522–486 B.C.) and Artaxerxes I (464–424 B.C.) and took many artifacts to the Louvre museum in Paris. His most important writings are *The Art of Ancient Persia* (five volumes, 1884–1889) and *The Acropolis of Susa* (1890–1892). H. F. VOS

DIOCLETIAN (245–313)
Emperor of Rome, 284–305

Born to parents of humble means in Dalmatia (now part of Yugoslavia), Diocles changed his name to Diocletian when he became emperor. As a young man he joined the army and rose in rank, becoming commander of the imperial guard. When the emperor, Numerian, was murdered, Diocles's troops proclaimed him the new ruler. Numerian's brother, Carinus, was killed by his own troops when he sought the throne, and the way was clear for Diocles to assume control unopposed.

Diocletian, an able organizer and administrator, used his skills to enact many structural reforms in the Roman Empire, including the establishment of the tetrarchy (293), a new imperial system in which four rulers shared power. His other reforms affected military, administrative, and economic areas. As a result of such reorganization, Diocletian created an efficient bureaucracy. Nevertheless, Rome declined as a political power center and the senate was further subordinated to the tetrarchy.

A persecution of Christians began during Diocletian's reign in 303, which was aimed at destroying church buildings and copies of the New Testament Scriptures. Among the tetrarchs, Galerius was the most active in carrying out the persecution. Because persecution continued under Galerius after Diocletian's abdication, some scholars maintain that Diocletian was not responsible for the policy. Diocletian retired to a villa at Split in his native Dalmatia, avoiding public association with the new administration's superstitious and violent policies. G. MINDEMAN

DIODATI, GIOVANNI (1576–1649)
Calvinist theologian, Bible translator, and preacher

Born into an Italian Protestant family in Geneva (Switzerland), Diodati was educated at the Genevan Academy founded by John Calvin in 1559. At the age of twenty-one Diodati was selected by Theodore Beza, rector of the academy, to teach Hebrew there. Ordained to the ministry in 1608, he succeeded to Beza's chair as professor of theology the next year. As a delegate from Geneva to the Synod of Dort (1618–1619), he played an influential part in drawing up the synod's orthodox Calvinist doctrines.

Diodati was an able translator. His rendering of the Bible into Italian (1607) enjoyed a popular success comparable to that of Luther's German Bible. In 1644 Diodati published his revision of the French Bible translated in Geneva in 1588. Besides being a theologian and a translator, Diodati was such a noted preacher that he was known as the "Cato of Geneva." N. V. HOPE

DIONYSIUS THE GREAT (died c. 264)
Bishop of Alexandria

Known in his time as a great leader and theologian, Dionysius was head of the catechetical school in Alexandria before becoming bishop there in 247. He learned theology from Origen, perhaps the greatest original thinker of the early church. Dionysius used his training to develop a coherent, biblical doctrine of God against various contemporary heresies. Although his views may be judged as incomplete by later standards, for his own time they were adequate to withstand error.

When Roman persecution of Christians came in 250, Dionysius fled from Alexandria to the desert. When the troubles were over he had to make important decisions about how to treat church members who had betrayed Christianity (become apostate) in the persecution. He took a lenient position, readmitting them if they expressed sorrow. Another problem Dionysius faced was whether to rebaptize people who had been baptized by heretics or schismatics. Again

he took a moderate position and accepted as valid all baptisms done in the name of the Trinity.

None of his writings has been fully preserved; fragments appear in the works of Athanasius, a later bishop of Alexandria, and Eusebius, bishop of Caesarea. Although Dionysius died from old age rather than as a martyr, he is regarded as a saint in Roman Catholic and Eastern churches. P. TOON

DIXON, AMZI CLARENCE (1854–1925)
American leader in the cause of conservative theology; advocate for the fundamentalist movement

The son of a Baptist minister, Dixon was born in Shelby, North Carolina, where he graduated from Wake Forest College in 1873. After training at Southern Baptist Theological Seminary in Greenville, South Carolina, for six months, he served in several pastorates, the two most important being Chicago's Moody Memorial Church (1906–1911) and the Metropolitan Tabernacle of London (1911–1919). A zealous advocate of the League of Nations, Dixon also favored rigorous enforcement of national prohibition. Dixon participated in popular evangelistic, prophetic Bible conferences in both England and the U.S. He assisted in publishing a twelve-volume series entitled *The Fundamentals* (1910-1915) and was author of a number of other widely read publications. D. M. LAKE

DODD, CHARLES HAROLD (1884–1973)
Leading British New Testament scholar

Born in Wales, Dodd was educated in the classics and theology at Oxford University (England), was a pastor of the Congregational (or Independent) Church in Warwick, and was a respected professor and lecturer in many universities and seminaries in Britain, Europe, and the United States.

Dodd formulated a theological school of thought known as "realized eschatology." (In Greek, eschatology means doctrine of the "last things.") Generally the Bible is interpreted as teaching that history is headed toward a divinely ordained fulfillment and consummation. In *The Parables of the Kingdom* (1935), Dodd argued instead that Jesus' parables and the Gospel of John teach the fulfillment of the kingdom of God in Jesus' own generation, a present event rather than a future one.

Not all scholars agree with Dodd's interpretation, most arguing that the Scriptures teach that the kingdom of God both is present and is still coming. Some day there will be a fulfillment and consummation of what has already appeared in the Lord Jesus Christ.

Dodd is also known for his scholarship about the preaching and teaching of the early church (as in *The Apostolic Preaching and its Developments*, 1936). He believed that the early church's primary function was to preach the gospel. Its teaching was derivative, following the preaching as a means of strengthening and deepening faith. Other scholars believe that the early church's preaching and teaching were interchangeable. E. G. ROHR

DODDRIDGE, PHILIP (1702–1751)
English Nonconformist clergyman

One of twenty children, Doddridge was a person of strong religious convictions. He refused the offer of a university education, since it contained the condition that he conform to the established church. Instead, he attended a dissenting academy at Kibworth Beaucamp in Leicestershire run by John Jennings, a local minister. After a short pastorate at Kibworth he moved to Northampton in 1729, where he ministered for the rest of his life.

The academy, of which Doddridge then became principal, was also moved to Northampton and became a training center for many future Nonconformist leaders. In theology Doddridge steered a middle course between Calvinism and Arminianism. The warmth of the evangelical revival then beginning in England touched him and is reflected in his *On the Rise and Progress of Religion in the Soul* (1745) and in his hymns.

A friend of both Scottish and English religious leaders, Doddridge was given a D.D. degree by Aberdeen University in 1736. P. TOON

DOLLINGER, JOHANN JOSEPH IGNAZ VON (1799–1890)
Roman Catholic church historian and theologian

Born at Bamberg (Germany), Dollinger was ordained a priest in 1822. The next year he became professor of canon law and church history at Aschaffenburg; in 1826 he became professor of church history at Munich, a position he held until 1872. Dollinger authored several volumes on church history including *The Reformation* (1845–1848), *Christianity and Church* (1860), and *Papal Fables of the Middle Ages* (1863).

For the first three decades of his public career Dollinger was a conservative Catholic, highly critical of Martin Luther and the Protestant Reformation. In the 1850s, however, especially after a visit to Rome in 1857, he became a strong and vocal critic of papal policy. He disliked the dogma of the Immaculate Conception of the Virgin Mary, which Pope Pius IX promulgated in 1854, and he sharply attacked that pope's Syllabus of Errors, issued in 1864. When Vatican Council I was convened to announce the infallibility of the pope, Dollinger (under the pen name of Janus) wrote his most famous work, *The Pope and the Council* (1869). It has been called "the most vigorous historical indictment ever brought against ultramontanism" (the doctrine of papal supremacy). When papal infallibility was officially accepted in 1870, Dollinger said it was unacceptable to him "as a Christian, as a theologian, as a historian, and as a citizen." For that "open and formal heresy" he was excommunicated in 1872 by Archbishop Scherr of Munich. Dollinger then took part in organizing the Old Catholic Church. During the remainder of his life he participated in projects of Christian reunion such as the Bonn Conferences of 1874 and 1875. N. V. HOPE

DOMINIC (1170–1221)
*Founder of the Order of Preachers
(Dominicans)*

Dominic was born in Castile (Spain) to a noble family, who sent him at the age of fourteen to the University of Palencia. There he studied liberal arts for six years and then theology for four. A serious student, he nevertheless subordinated zeal for learning to compassion for the needy. In 1195 he was ordained a priest, becoming a prior in six years.

In 1203 Dominic accompanied Bishop Diego as chaplain on a mission to Denmark to arrange a marriage for the son of the king of Castile. Along the way they went through southern France, where they encountered the Albigensian heresy. Burdened by the need he saw there, Dominic returned to France and began a preaching ministry among the Albigensians. Their leaders were educated, well versed in Scripture, and persuasive preachers; yet they lived in poverty, a fact that profoundly influenced Dominic. To counter their influence he adopted a similar life-style, often preaching barefoot. He required that his disciples know the Scriptures well. In 1206 Dominic opened the first Dominican convent, a hostel at Prouille for women who had been converted from Albigensianism.

In 1208, Pope Innocent III called for a seven-year crusade against the Albigensians, during which time Dominic worked tirelessly to bring them back into the Roman Catholic Church. However, he encountered much resistance and had little apparent success.

In an effort to unify his assistants, Dominic presented his plan for an Order of Preachers to the Fourth Lateran Council in 1215. By adopting the rule of Saint Augustine for his order, Dominic surmounted a proposal that would have prohibited the formation of all new religious orders. Official sanction came in 1216 in a papal bull from Honorius III. Two general chapters (meetings of a religious order to determine policies), held in Bologna in 1220 and 1221, laid the foundation for the new order's organization.

During the last few years of his life, Dominic traveled throughout Europe preaching and winning converts. Although his fame and influence spread, he never lost his humble spirit—as evidenced by his refusal on three occasions to accept a bishopric. Shortly after the conclusion of the second general chapter, Dominic became seriously ill during a journey and returned to Bologna, where he died. He was canonized in 1234 by Gregory IX. G. MINDEMAN

DOMITILLA FLAVIA (died c. 100)
Roman matron of the imperial family who converted to Christianity

Domitilla's namesake grandmother and mother were the wife and daughter of the emperor Vespasian (70–79). She married Titus Flavius Clemens, a first cousin of the emperor Domitian (81–96). Such early historians as Suetonius have claimed that Domitilla's husband was a Christian; but whether or not this was so, she herself certainly was. Probably because of this, in 95 Clemens was put to death by the emperor, and Domitilla was banished to the island of Pandateria. The property of Domitilla on the Via Ardentina, outside Rome, was used as a place of Christian burial as early as the first century. N. V. HOPE

DONNE, JOHN (1572–1631)
English poet and preacher; dean of St. Paul's Cathedral in London

Born into a Roman Catholic family at a time when anti-Catholic feeling in England was high, Donne nevertheless was able to attend Oxford and Cambridge. He studied law at Lincoln's Inn, London, but never took a degree and never practiced law. Sometime during the 1590s, Donne abandoned his Roman Catholicism and became secretary to Thomas Egerton, the lord chancellor. His prospects for worldly success, however, were dashed in 1601, when he eloped with the lord chancellor's niece, Ann More. Egerton promptly dismissed him. A period of poverty and failure followed, which ended only in 1615 when Donne accepted the king's invitation to become an Anglican priest. Through rapid advancements, Donne became dean of St. Paul's in 1621.

Donne is considered the greatest of the seventeenth-century metaphysical poets, a group which includes George Herbert, Henry Vaughan, and Richard Crashaw. Donne's early poetry, represented best in his *Songs and Sonnets* and *Elegies,* is remarkable for its vivid language, startling and often exaggerated imagery, and frequent use of paradox. The *Divine Poems,* many of them splendid sonnets, are products of Donne's later years and reveal an intensity of feeling and depth of insight rarely equaled in English poetry.

Donne was also a great preacher. Brilliant in their fervor and rhetoric, Donne's sermons run to ten volumes in a modern edition. *Devotions Upon Emergent Occasions* (1624) contains the famous passage which begins, "No man is an island," and ends, "Ask not for whom the bell tolls; it tolls for thee." P. M. BECHTEL

DOOYEWEERD, HERMAN (1894–1977)
Dutch philosopher

Since Dooyeweerd spent most of his life in Amsterdam, his complicated philosophical system is frequently called the "Amsterdam philosophy." He received a doctoral degree in law from the Free University of Amsterdam in 1917. In 1926, he began a long and honored career as professor of legal philosophy at the same university. All of his publications were in Dutch, but several of his major books were translated into English in the 1950s and early 1960s. Best known are the four-volume *New Critique of Theoretical Thought* (1953–1958) and *In the Twilight of Western Thought* (1960).

Because Dooyeweerd's thought is too complex and difficult to cover adequately in any short article, only a few of his more basic theses can be summarized. One of the more important ones is his claim that the human heart is the religious root of every phase of human existence, including human thought. All non-Christian systems of thought believe that human reason is reli-

giously neutral, autonomous, and self-sufficient. Dooyeweerd disagreed, teaching that all theoretical thinking (including philosophy and the various sciences) is grounded in the heart. Because of the fall of man and the consequent separation of the unregenerated human heart from God, theoretical thinking begins with a religious tilt against the Creator. Man's heart is never neutral. It will either worship its Creator or else turn away from God and deify some aspect of the creation. One major task of a truly Christian philosophy is the unmasking of the idol of self-sufficient reason. Many Christian thinkers who are critical of other aspects of Dooyeweerd's system have expressed appreciation for his strong attack on what he called the "Dogma of the Autonomy of Theoretical Thought." Pure, unprejudiced, religiously neutral thought simply does not exist.

Dooyeweerd believed that God in his role as Sovereign Creator placed his entire creation under a cosmic law order that contains a multiplicity of laws established by God in a regular order. While God's entire creation exists under law, there are at least fifteen different kinds of law. For example, the laws of mathematics constitute a different "law sphere" than the laws of physics or those of biology. A juridical law is quite different from a law of logic. All the laws of a specific kind compose a law sphere. In addition to law spheres, Dooyeweerd also talked about meaning-aspects. The two terms are correlative. There are as many different aspects of meaning in the cosmos as there are law spheres. Thus, for example, when a person is interested in the price of a thing, he views it from a different aspect or angle (in this case, the economic aspect) than if he were merely interested in its beauty (the aesthetic aspect) or its age (historical aspect). The God-determined order of the law spheres or meaning-aspects can be discovered and studied by science and philosophy. In fact, each major science has its own law sphere to investigate. The law spheres are arranged according to complexity, the less complex coming first. Moving from the least to the most complex, the cosmic law order includes: number, space, movement, physics, life, sensation, logic (thought), history, language, social, economics, aesthetics, law, ethics, and faith. The law spheres must not be confused with individual things which function within the spheres. For example, an individual stone is subject to the laws of the various spheres and can be considered in any one of the many meaning-aspects. A related doctrine is Dooyeweerd's principle of sphere sovereignty. He believed that God has prescribed ordinances or limits for all the spheres of his creation. Since each sphere of reality is subject to its own God-given laws, no aspect of life has the right to infringe upon the domain of any other sphere. One important application of the principle is the sphere sovereignty of church, state, school, and family within their own proper areas. The state, for example, has no right to intrude on the sphere of the church or the family.

Dooyeweerd's system of Christian or Calvinistic philosophy has had only a modest influence in countries other than Holland, and then primarily among scholars of Dutch ancestry and Calvinistic convictions in the United States, Canada, and South Africa. The system has yet to have any impact on the broader philosophical community. Objections to Dooyeweerd's system are both philosophical and theological in nature but go beyond the scope of a short article. Recently, many theological critics within the Reformed movement (including several associated with Westminster Theological Seminary in Philadelphia) have accused the movement of heresy, especially with reference to its view of the Word of God. The outcome of this debate is still uncertain.
R. NASH

DOSTOYEVSKY, FYODOR (1821–1881)
Russian novelist

Born in Moscow's Foundling Hospital, where his father was a resident physician, Dostoyevsky grew up showing an early interest in literature. After serving a year in the Engineering Corps, he resigned to devote himself to writing. His first novel, *Poor Folk* (1846), was a tremendous success.

Soon afterward, Dostoyevsky and some others were arrested for participating in a study group that discussed, among other things, the writings of the utopian socialist Charles Fourier. They were led before a firing squad, then given a last-minute reprieve from the czar: four years' exile to Siberia to be followed by five years in the army. That incident left Dostoyevsky permanently scarred psychologically.

While imprisoned, Dostoyevsky was allowed to read only one book, the Bible, which had also played a significant part in his early education. He emerged from prison an ardent Russian nationalist and a Christian bound to the tenets of the Russian Orthodox Church. He gave a realistic account of his prison and exile experiences in *The House of the Dead* (1861).

Years of poverty followed his release, during which he published *Notes from Underground* (1864), the first of his novels, which maturely treats his principal themes: the eccentric and self-conscious protagonist; the bankruptcy of humanism, rationalism, materialism, and socialism; suffering and humiliation; and salvation in Christ (although the specifically Christian passages were cut by the czar's censors). Both his wife and his brother died during that time, leaving him with a large family to support. Not financially solvent until ten years before his death, Dostoyevsky fought a debilitating epilepsy and worked tirelessly at his novels, often dictating them at a feverish rate. In 1867 he married the young woman whom he had hired as a stenographer.

His two most famous novels, *Crime and Punishment* (1866) and *The Brothers Karamazov* (1880), are philosophical detective stories in which both the murderer and the meaning of life are simultaneously pursued. In *The Brothers Karamazov*, his last novel, Dostoyevsky portrayed the relationships of four brothers to their depraved and spiteful earthly father on the one hand, and to a mysterious, often ambivalent heavenly Father on the other. Throughout, Dostoyevsky was concerned with the justice of God and the idea that "if God does not exist, then everything is permitted." Dostoyevsky's novels anticipated later theories of the complexity and contradictions in human personality. He also wrote two other great novels, *The Idiot* (1868–1869) and *The Possessed* (1871–1872). E. B. BATSON

DOWIE, JOHN ALEXANDER
(1847–1907)
Faith healer and evangelist; founder of the Christian Catholic Church

Born in Edinburgh (Scotland) and reared in Australia, Dowie returned to Edinburgh in 1868 to study theology. Following his ordination as a Congregational minister, he served a pastorate in Sydney (Australia). A remarkable personal healing experience led him to develop a deep interest in spiritual healing, so that in 1878 he left the Congregational ministry and set up a tabernacle in Melbourne, founding the International Divine Healing Association.

In 1888 he moved to the United States, where he founded the Christian Catholic Church in 1896, with himself as "general overseer." In 1901, along with about five thousand followers, he established the city of Zion in northeastern Illinois and ran it as a Puritan theocracy. That same year he proclaimed himself "Elijah, the Restorer." In 1904 he took the title of "First Apostle," which he held until a year before his death, when he was replaced by Wilbur E. Voliva as the general overseer. N. V. HOPE

DRIVER, SAMUEL ROLLES (1846–1914)
Old Testament and Semitic languages scholar

Born at Southampton (England), Driver was educated at Winchester School and Oxford University, where he became a fellow of New College in 1870. In 1883 he succeeded E. B. Pusey in the Regius Chair of Hebrew at Oxford, which he occupied for the rest of his life. From 1876 until 1884 he was a member of the committee that produced the Revised Version of the Old Testament (1885).

Driver wrote commentaries on nearly half of the Old Testament, and his *Introduction to the Literature of the Old Testament* (1891) was a standard work for half a century. He adopted the literary critical view of the Old Testament pioneered by such German scholars as Julius Wellhausen but modified some of its excesses to suit British tastes. He was an effective propagandist for liberal views about the Old Testament and showed little sensitivity toward the fragmenting of both Scripture and faith that resulted. At the end of his life he became aware of the significance of archaeology for affirming the Bible, but his position on literary-critical matters remained unchanged. N. V. HOPE

DRUMMOND, HENRY (1786–1860)
British banker and politician; a founder of the Catholic Apostolic Church

Born at the Grange, Hampshire (England), Drummond was educated at Harrow School and Oxford University but did not graduate. From 1810 to 1813, and again between 1847 and 1860, he served in Parliament.

In 1817 Drummond came under strong religious influences and was on his way to the Holy Land when he stopped off at Geneva (Switzerland). There he met a Scotsman, Robert Haldane, with whom he worked to support the city's evangelical ministers in their struggle against Socinian (rationalist) opponents. In 1819 Drummond founded the Continental Society, which supported Protestant missionaries in France.

A conference on biblical prophecy, begun in Drummond's home in 1826, continued annually for five years. Out of those retreats came the Catholic Apostolic Church. Drummond was ordained as one of twelve "apostles" of that church in 1832, and two years later became its "angel" (bishop) for Scotland, continuing to preach until 1856. N. V. HOPE

DRUMMOND, HENRY (1851–1897)
Scottish writer and evangelist; whose career—a mixture of science, theology, and evangelism—influenced many young people

Born into a family that was deeply committed to the principles of the Free Church of Scotland, Drummond studied classics and English at Edinburgh University from 1866 but never received a degree. In 1870 he entered the theological college of the Free Church in Edinburgh and later spent one semester as a student at Tubingen University (Germany).

In the fall of 1873 Drummond assisted with Dwight L. Moody and Ira D. Sankey's first evangelistic meetings in Britain. When he followed up their work in 1874 and 1875, he became known as a gifted speaker in his own right. He wrote a meditation on 1 Corinthians 13 in 1874, *The Greatest Thing in the World*, which continues to be reprinted today. Returning to academic life in 1877, Drummond became a lecturer in natural science at the Free Church College in Glasgow. He assisted Moody once more in 1882. In 1883 Drummond published a book that made him famous, *Natural Law in the Spiritual World*. Although the work was extremely popular—within five years seventy thousand copies had been sold—it had some serious flaws as a scientific study.

In 1883 and 1884 Drummond was in southern Africa to make a geological survey and on his return produced an official report as well as another popular book, *Tropical Africa* (1888). In 1884 he was ordained and became professor of theology of the Free Church College in Glasgow. One of Drummond's later, significant books was *The Ascent of Man* (1894), based on lectures he gave in Boston, Massachusetts, in 1890.
P. TOON

DRYDEN, JOHN (1631–1700)
English critic, dramatist, and poet

Born in a vicarage in Northamptonshire and educated at Trinity College, Cambridge, Dryden was the most eminent literary figure in England during the last four decades of the seventeenth century. His life and work reflected most of the major trends fashionable in his time. In politics he was staunchly royalist; in religion, he was at first Anglican, later Roman Catholic; in philosophy he was cautiously rationalistic; in art, neoclassical. As is characteristic of English neoclassicism, his work, neither profound nor personal, was witty, intellectually playful, and pol-

ished. In 1668 Charles II created him poet laureate; consequently many of his poems were written for special occasions—a political crisis, a coronation, the death of a distinguished person.

In 1682 Dryden published *Religio Laici* (*A Layman's Faith*), a poem that examined his religious convictions and supported Anglicanism as the middle way between rationalism and Roman Catholicism. But when King Charles died in 1685 and was succeeded by his brother, James II, a Roman Catholic, Dryden and his two sons converted to Roman Catholicism. Many charged him with having made the change for political convenience. As a Roman Catholic, he wrote *The Hind and the Panther* in 1687, a long poem in which he defended his Church's doctrines and policies.

Of Dryden's many dramas, *All for Love* (1678), a version of the Antony and Cleopatra romance, is the best known. Through his critical works Dryden did much to establish a simple, clear, and natural prose. The eighteenth-century poet and critic Samuel Johnson called him "the father of English criticism." P. M. BECHTEL

DUFAY, GUILLAUME (c. 1400–1474)
Leading composer of church music of the Burgundian school of fifteenth-century France

Dufay is known for his departures from late medieval techniques and for the colorful and elegant textures of his three-voice songs, masses, and motets. His musical training began with his choral service at the cathedral of Chamrai (France), where he later became chapel master. In Italy, to which he made several trips, Dufay served in the papal chapels of Rome, Florence, and Bologna. As canon at the cathedrals of Cambrai and Mons (after 1445), he received a substantial income and had opportunity for his compositional work.

Dufay's contribution to sacred music is extensive. He made numerous efforts to unify mass settings through textural, harmonic, and melodic means. His melodies are flexible, often with sensuous tendencies in rhythm and phrase gesture. Harmonic development shows increasing use of thirds and sixths as consonant sounds, while Burgundian instrumentation shows subtleties of reedy colors in combination with the sounds of plucked and bowed strings. Vocal ranges tend to be high, suggesting tension and projections of personal feeling. Stylistic influences from the secular love song (chanson) come into Dufay's masses, while the architectural formality of his three-part settings show elements derived from chivalric poetry of the preceding century.

Dufay's compositions have been investigated carefully by many recent scholars. This task has been made easier by his frequent travels, which enabled libraries in Paris, Brussels, Bologna, Florence, and Trieste to obtain major holdings of his works. A collected edition of his works was published by De Van and Besseler (1947–1966).

Since people in the fifteenth century did not make marked distinctions between sacred and secular tunes, Dufay often employed secular tunes as foundational materials for his masses. As vehicles for worship, these quotations became abstracted and architecturally conceived, often with long-spun linear curves drawn out from the original melodic source. Dufay's masses include *Without a Name, St. James, Death of St. Gothard, If My Face Is Pale, Armed Man,* and *St. Anthony of Vienna.* D. S. CUSHMAN

DUFF, ALEXANDER (1806–1878)

First missionary to India from the Church of Scotland

Duff was born in Moulin, Perthshire, and studied at St. Andrews University. He and his wife arrived at Calcutta in May 1830 after two shipwrecks. There he founded an English-speaking college in which the Bible was a major textbook. Duff's aim, supported by the British governor general, was to train Indians to oppose Hinduism and superstition with Scripture and European culture. On a visit to Scotland in 1834 to gain support for his work, he addressed the members of the Church's General Assembly, holding them spellbound for three hours.

Soon after Duff returned to India he had to part company with the college he had founded, which belonged to the Church of Scotland, General Assembly, because he sided with the Free Church of Scotland (founded 1843) in its separation from the Church of Scotland. He then began other successful institutions. On a second trip home Duff crossed India by land to acquaint himself with the living conditions. He became moderator of the Free Church (1851) and used his authority and fame to impress the British Parliament with the need for more English schools and colleges in India. During a successful trip to America (1854), he received an honorary degree from New York University. A year after returning to India, Duff witnessed the Sepoy Rebellion (1857), the beginning of India's long struggle for independence from British rule. Afterwards he publicly condemned certain British government policies toward India. Duff had a major part in founding the University of Calcutta; had he not been recalled to Scotland he would have become its vice-chancellor. As a professor of theology at New College, Edinburgh (from 1867), Duff maintained his support for missions. P. TOON

DUNCAN, GEORGE SIMPSON (1884–1965)

New Testament scholar

Duncan was born in Scotland and attended Forfar Academy for boys. He then studied at Edinburgh, Cambridge, and St. Andrews universities, as well as at three continental universities. He was ordained a minister of the Church of Scotland in 1915 and served as chaplain to Field Marshal Earl Haig in World War I. From 1919 to 1954 Duncan was professor of biblical criticism at St. Andrews, and principal of St. Mary's College within that university from 1940 to 1954. In 1949 he was moderator of the general assembly of the Church of Scotland. Duncan served on the New Testament Translation panel for the New English Bible. His publications include *St. Paul's Ephesian Ministry* (1929), *The Epistle of Paul to the Galatians* (1934), and *Jesus, Son of Man* (1948). P. TOON

DUNS SCOTUS, JOHN (1266–1308)
Medieval scholastic theologian

By virtue of his Scottish birth, John Duns acquired the Latin nickname Scotus ("the Scot"), by which he is best known. Scotus was educated for the priesthood and became a member of the Franciscan order. Most of his career was spent lecturing at Oxford. He eventually taught at Paris and Cologne as well. On one occasion in 1303 he was thrown out of France for siding with the papacy in the famous clash between King Philip IV and Pope Boniface VIII over the church and state authority. He was allowed to return a year later.

Scotus's writings, based on his lectures, reflect the scholastic method of debating in great detail the alternative views propounded by earlier writers. Although generally in agreement with Thomas Aquinas, the scholastic theologian of a generation before, Scotus introduced significant changes into Thomas's philosophy and theology. Criticizing Aquinas's five proofs for the existence of God, Scotus maintained that many assertions in theology are not philosophically demonstrable or even probable. According to Scotus, God acts neither out of logical necessity nor out of the inner necessity of his own nature. If God does not act necessarily, then one cannot logically prove his necessity. God acts as he freely chooses.

In contrast to Aquinas's rationalism, Scotus put forward a "voluntarist" view, arguing that a choice by the will determines what a person does, with reason as merely an instrument to that end. Such an emphasis helped drive a wedge between faith and reason, which eventually led to scholasticism's decline.

Scotus also emphasized the uniqueness and importance of individuals. Aquinas taught that a human being consists of a body and a soul; the soul comprises the essence of human nature. Scotus insisted on a third ingredient, personal individuality. According to Scotus, God intentionally created individuals, not merely a universal human nature that heredity and environment have particularized. Each person, therefore, possesses an immortal individuality. Scotus thus placed great emphasis on each individual's God-given freedom and value.

Scotus maintained that Christ's incarnation would have occurred even if the Fall had not, again disagreeing with Aquinas. Scotus argued that since God willed from eternity for the Son of God to be both the beginning and the end of all creation, Christ would have come to provide humanity with an example of a life of dynamic and creative love. Scotus's theology has hence been described as Christocentric.

Scotus was the first major Catholic theologian to support the doctrine of the Immaculate Conception of the Virgin Mary. That doctrine teaches that the mother of Jesus, though herself born of two human parents, was conceived in holiness without the taint of original sin. That opinion had been set forward over a century earlier in France, where it immediately met with controversy. Scotus is said to have defended the view at a public debate in Paris, employing two hundred separate arguments for its support and thus winning the university there to his side. Although Aquinas (died 1274) had earlier rejected the opinion, Scotus's view won the day. In December 1854 Pope Pius IX, a Franciscan, declared the doctrine of the Immaculate Conception to be a divinely revealed fact and an official Catholic dogma.

Aquinas's reputation in philosophy and theology has otherwise eclipsed the Scot's, although Scotus's influence can be traced in a wide range of later thinkers, including the eighteenth-century German Protestant philosopher Gottfried Wilhelm Leibniz and the twentieth-century French Catholic theologian Pierre Teilhard de Chardin. With twentieth-century existentialism, Scotus's emphasis on will over reason has regained an ascendancy.

Scotus's argumentation, however, could hardly be considered a triumph of irrationalism over rationalism. Such intricacy characterized his analyses that he became known as "the subtle doctor." On the other hand, his reasoning tended so much toward obscurity that the word "dunce," coined from his name, is used to describe a muddle-minded person. A. F. HOLMES

DUNSTABLE, JOHN (c. 1385–1453)

English church musician and astronomer

Dunstable, who lived most of his life in France, introduced new chord intervals into church music and made skillful use of descant (a subordinate, higher melody). European music, especially the Burgundian school in northern France, was greatly influenced by him. Contrary to the claims of some of his contemporaries, he did not invent counterpoint.

Dunstable added musical unity to the mass by either beginning each section with a similar theme or using a single ending for all the sections. He wrote melodies for the soprano voice rather than the traditional tenor voice and is credited with being one of the first composers of church music to develop instrumental accompaniment for the vocal parts. Dunstable's other accomplishments include works on astronomy and on latitude and longitude. K. LEID

DUNSTAN (c. 909–988)

Archbishop of Canterbury, 960–988

Dunstan decided to become a monk and priest after recovering from a serious illness. As abbot of Glastonbury he made the abbey famous for discipline and learning. Dunstan served as adviser to King Edgar and was appointed bishop of Worcester and London before becoming archbishop. As archbishop he cooperated with the king in introducing reforms in church and state. Dunstan is particularly remembered for his restoration of monastic life and for founding monastic houses at Peterborough, Ely, and Thorney. He was also a brilliant musician and illuminator (decorative illustrator) of precious manuscripts. P. TOON

DUNSTER, HENRY (1609–1659)

First president of Harvard College

Dunster was born in Bury, Lancashire, England, and educated at Cambridge, Massachusetts (1634). After a period of teaching and then becoming a minister in Bury, he came to the United States to escape religious persecution (1640). Dunster had an excellent reputation for scholarship, especially in oriental languages. He was soon appointed president of Harvard, then a struggling new school. Harvard owed much to Dunster, who established the rules of admission and degree requirements and worked tirelessly to raise funds. Though his only salary was what tax revenue he himself could collect, Dunster donated one hundred acres to Harvard at a crisis in its affairs. The first printing press established in the United States (1639) was moved to Dunster's home and put under his direction.

In 1654 Dunster was obliged to resign his presidency because of his opposition to covenant (infant) baptism. He retired to Scituate, Massachusetts, where he served as a minister until his death. There he also produced a revised edition of the *Bay Psalm Book*. M. FACKLER

DUPLESSIS-MORNAY, PHILIPPE DE (1549–1623)

French Protestant statesman

Duplessis-Mornay belonged to Normandy and was educated at Paris. He came to reformed convictions early in life under his mother's influence. Surviving the St. Bartholomew's Day Massacre (1572), he moved to England. On his return he worked with the Reformed Church and became such an important adviser to Henry of Navarre that he was called "the Protestant pope." He is usually credited with the work *A Defense of Liberty against Tyrants* (1579), which defended taking up arms for religious freedom and argued that since kings are made by people and responsible to them, representatives of the people may lawfully resist tyrannical rulers. From 1578 to 1581 he served as Henry's ambassador in England and Holland. Supporting Henry's claim to the throne, Duplessis-Mornay was appointed governor of Saumur in the Loire valley in 1589 and played a big part in Henry's successful advance and his negotiations with the Catholic Holy League after the death of Henry III.

He disapproved, however, of what seemed to be the cynical conversion of Henry IV in 1593. Nevertheless he worked hard to secure favorable conditions for the Huguenots and achieved no little success with the Edict of Nantes (1598), which granted freedom of conscience, full civil rights, the right of public worship in Huguenot areas, and control of important fortresses as a guarantee. In 1598 he published a work on the eucharist in the early church which was severely criticized by Jacques Duperron, who in an ensuing disputation (1600) was thought to have proved some misquotations from the fathers. In 1599 Duplessis-Mornay played a big part in founding what would prove to be the very important Academy of Saumur. He also continued to participate in the direction of the French Reformed Church. In 1611 he published a controversial history of the popes as part of his substantial literary contribution to the advance and defense of reformed teaching. The assassination of Henry IV in 1610, however, weakened his position; and his opposition to the policies of Louis XIII cost him the governorship of Saumur in 1621, two years before his death. G. BROMILEY

DÜRER, ALBRECHT (1471–1528)
Painter, engraver, and designer of woodcuts

Born in Nuremberg, the son of an immigrant Hungarian goldsmith, Dürer studied art in several places—for example, Colmar, Basle, and Italy (particularly Venice), where he spent two formative years (1505–1507) absorbing the Renaissance spirit as well as Italian style. Settling in his native Nuremberg, he began to paint portraits as well as religious scenes, for example, "The Adoration of the Magi" (1504) and "The Feast of the Rose Garlands" (more properly "The Brotherhood of the Rosary") in 1506. Perhaps discouraged by the meager financial rewards of painting, Dürer turned increasingly to the more lucrative pursuits of engraving and woodcut designing, eventually transforming 100 of his drawings into engravings and 250 into woodcuts. In engraving he was creative as well as productive, introducing light and shade and thereby giving his work tone as well as pictorial quality. In this genre he produced such famous masterpieces as "Knight, Death, and the Devil" (1513), "Saint Jerome in His Study" (1513), and "Melancolia I" (1514). In woodcut designing Dürer was also innovative, creating such masterpieces in black and white as "The Triumphal Arch" (1515), composed of ninety-two wood blocks eleven feet two inches high.

Always a devout Christian, by 1519 Dürer was studying the works of Martin Luther, thereafter buying and reading whatever Luther wrote in the German language. His biographer, Erwin Panofsky, contends that Dürer converted to Protestantism and died a good Lutheran. This has been questioned; but there is no doubt that Dürer was greatly influenced by Luther, whom he described as "the Christian man who has helped me out of great anxieties." Thereafter he "practically abandoned secular subject matter except for scientific illustrations, travelers' records, and portraiture" (Panofsky), and produced such outstanding religious paintings as "The Four Apostles" (John, Peter, Paul, and Mark) between 1523 and 1526.

This painting, his gift to the city of Nuremberg in 1526, is his monument to the Reformation and his salute to Martin Luther. In his mind the apostles and their writings were the guardians of truth for Nuremberg's secular and ecclesiastical authority.

Dürer was an innovator. He brought the artistic discoveries of the Renaissance to the medieval north, infusing into it a spiritual vitality peculiarly German. N. V. HOPE

DVOŘÀK, ANTONÍN (1841–1905)
German romantic composer

Dvořàk was born in Mühlhausen (Germany) and received his early musical training at the Prague School of Organ, remaining prominent in church music as the organist of St. Adalbert's Church in Prague. He also played the violin and viola.

Dvořàk's important church compositions include: *Hymnus* for chorus and orchestra (1873) and *Stabat Mater* (1884), as well as *St. Ludmila* (an oratorio), *Mass in D, Psalm 149,* and his *Te Deum*. Most of these sacred works are concert pieces in their rich harmonies, dramatic texts, and large-scale organization. Johannes Brahms's influence, as well as Dvořàk's affinity for dance rhythms and folk music (including American), is apparent in his compositions.

Dvořák's fifth through ninth symphonies, cello concerto, chamber music, and songs still retain high international popularity.
D. S. CUSHMAN

DWIGHT, TIMOTHY (1752–1817)
American Congregational minister and educator

Dwight's career included farming, politics as a state legislator, and two years as a chaplain in the Continental Army, as well as theological writing, pastoral ministry, and higher education. He was born in Northampton, Massachusetts, a grandson of American theologian Jonathan Edwards. From early hard study, Dwight damaged his eyesight so badly that for most of his life he could not see well enough to read or write—yet he nonetheless published extensively.

Influenced strongly by Edwards's Calvinistic philosophy, Dwight was a leading conservative scholar in New England. His sober logical argumentation helped defeat French atheistic ideas that had begun flourishing in Connecticut, where he ministered at Greenfield, a parish of Fairfield, from 1783 to 1795. Dwight's practical theology and general scope of knowledge made him instrumental in a variety of social spheres. He reformed university education and encouraged coeducational schooling, he stimulated intellectual endeavor, and he participated in the Second Great Awakening's (1787–1825) opposition to deism and skepticism.

Dwight became president of Yale College (which he had attended) in 1795 and held that office until his death. During those years he helped found a theological school at Andover (Massachusetts), medical schools at Yale, the Missionary Society of Connecticut, the American Bible Society, and the American Board of Commissioners for Foreign Missions.

His posthumous works include *Theology Explained and Defended* (five volumes, 1818–1819); *Travels in New England and New York* (four volumes, 1821–1822); and *Sermons by Timothy Dwight* (two volumes, 1828).
K. FOREMAN

DYER, MARY (died 1660)
Quaker leader hanged for defying Puritan colonial rulers by preaching Quakerism in Massachusetts

Mary Dyer came to Boston from England in 1635 with her husband, William. They were influenced by Anne Hutchinson, a controversial woman who opposed the Calvinist doctrine of predestination and the Puritan hierarchy. Because of Hutchinson's banishment and the increasing hostility of colonial officials, the Dyers moved to Rhode Island and helped establish Portsmouth colony.

In England from 1650 to 1657, Mary Dyer was converted to Quakerism. Upon her return to Boston, authorities expelled and finally condemned her for preaching doctrines considered blasphemous and pernicious. Authorities offered clemency in exchange for her promise never to return, but she refused: "Nay, I cannot; for in obedience to the will of the Lord God I came, and in His will I abide faithful to the death."
M. FACKLER

DYKES, JOHN BACCHUS (1823–1876)
Anglican vicar and composer

Born at Kingston-on-Hull, Dykes entered St. Catherine's College, Cambridge (1843) and graduated in 1847. Ordained a deacon in the Church of England, he first served as a curate at Malton in Yorkshire. In 1849 he became a minor canon and then precentor (director of music) in the cathedral at Durham. In 1861 Durham University conferred on him a doctorate of music, and in 1862 he became vicar of St. Oswald's.

Dykes's church sympathies brought him into conflict with Charles Baring, the low-church bishop of the diocese. After a church court ruled against him (1874) he retired to Ticehurst in Surrey.

Though Dykes published sermons and writings on liturgics, his reputation rests primarily on his melodic hymn tunes, of which he wrote about three hundred. Some of his more noteworthy tunes are "Holy, Holy, Holy," "The King of Love My Shepherd Is," and "Lead, Kindly Light." N. V. HOPE

EADIE, JOHN (1810–1876)
Noted New Testament scholar

Born at Alva, Scotland, John Eadie was educated at Glasgow University. He was ordained into the ministry of the United Secession Church (which later became the United Presbyterian Church) and from 1843 was a professor in the denominational theological college.

In 1844 Eadie received his doctorate of law from Glasgow and in 1850 his doctorate of divinity from St. Andrews. Apart from writing for many journals, he published several encyclopedias and popular theological reference works. He also wrote scholarly commentaries on several Pauline letters. He was a member of the original committee of translators who produced the Revised Version of the King James Bible in 1885. In 1876 he published a scholarly history of the English Bible. P. TOON

EADMER (or EDMER) (c. 1055–1128)
British historian and theologian; traveling companion of Anselm, archbishop of Canterbury

Eadmer was educated in Christ Church Monastery, Canterbury (England), and learned to think deeply as a theologian from Anselm, who was also abbot of that monastery. Eadmer's books include a valuable biography of Anselm and a history of the political and ecclesiastical disputes of that period. He also produced a theological treatise on the doctrine of the Immaculate Conception of the Virgin Mary, a doctrine that became Roman Catholic dogma in 1854. Eadmer was offered bishopric of St. Andrews in Scotland in 1120, but was never able to take up the offer. P. TOON

ECK, JOHANN (1486–1543)
German Roman Catholic scholar; remembered chiefly for his opposition to Protestant reformer Martin Luther

Born as Johann Mayr (or Maier) at Eck (Egg) in Swabia, he studied at Heidelberg, Tübingen, and Freiburg. In 1510 he joined the faculty at Ingolstadt and in his later years served there as vice-chancellor.

Eck publicly defended charging five percent interest on loans—a practice consistently condemned by medieval church authorities. In 1514 that stance earned him favor with the Fuggers, a German banking house to whom the archbishop of Mainz was deeply in debt. Selling indulgences (pardons for sins—a practice attacked by Luther) was the means by which the archbishop could pay his debt.

When Luther issued his Ninety-five Theses (condemnations of abuses in the Roman Catholic Church) in 1517, Eck rebutted in a tract called *Obelisks* (1518), which evoked from Luther a response entitled *Asterisks*. A debate was then arranged in Leipzig (1519). Eck, with his fine scholarship and excellent memory, overwhelmed Luther's advocate Andreas Carlstadt. Eck pressed Luther hard, quoting extensively from Scripture and drawing from him the dangerous admission that some teachings of Jan Hus (a late-fourteenth-century reformer) "are most Christian and evangelical."

In 1520 Eck delivered a bull (papal edict) against Luther and thereby encountered considerable hostility among German princes sympathetic to Luther's cause. He continued, nevertheless, to campaign against Luther and defend papal authority as articulated in his work *On the Primacy of Peter* (1520). At the Diet of Augsburg in 1530, he presented a confutation of the Protestant Augsburg Confession.

Eck's works include a Roman Catholic translation of the Bible in German published in 1537, three years after Luther's edition. Eck's *Manual of Commonplaces against Luther* (1525), which contained scholarly arguments against reformers Philip Melanchthon and Ulrich Zwingli, went through forty-six editions by 1576.
G. BROMILEY

ECKHART, VON HOCHHEIM
(1260–c. 1327)
German mystic, pastor, and theologian

Little is known about the details of Eckhart's life. He probably studied at Cologne, where he was taught the Scholastic theology of Thomas Aquinas (1224–1274). He became a member of the Dominican order and within it held a number of responsible administrative posts, including vicar-general of Bohemia and prior (the rank below abbot) of Frankfort. He took his master's degree in theology at Paris in 1300 and served there briefly as lecturer. From about 1325 on, frequent accusations of heresy were leveled against him, particularly by Franciscans. In

1326 he was tried by the archbishop of Cologne and convicted. Eckhart nevertheless declared himself a loyal son of the Church and appealed to the pope in 1327. He probably died the same year. An official papal response came two years later in a bull issued by John XXII (pope, 1316–1334) which condemned twenty-eight of his specific teachings but defended Eckhart's Christian faith and claimed he had submitted to Rome.

Eckhart played an important part in shaping the German language. He wrote many of his works and preached in the vernacular instead of Latin, thereby showing that German could be used to express subtle and profound ideas. The vocabulary he created helped German become the language of philosophers, theologians, and historians.

Eckhart's fame, however, really comes from his mystical teachings in sermons, tracts, and sayings. He believed that the nature of God was unknowable and unknown even to itself. The Godhead of Christian belief was only a small part of the unfathomable and indescribable God. Every person, however, had in his or her soul a knowledge of God placed there by God. It was this inner, nonintellectual knowledge that made possible communion with God and participation in the divine nature. A person could reunite with God only by successfully renouncing individuality through discipline and practice. Eckhart's works combined these ideas with eloquent expressions of his love both for God and for his neighbors.

Eckhart's immediate disciples were Henry Suso (c. 1295–1365), John Tauler (c. 1300–1361), and Jan van Ruysbroeck (c. 1293–1381). In later generations Eckhart's writings have continued to influence the development of philosophy and mysticism.
R. D. SHUSTER

EDDY, CLARENCE (1851–1937)
Organist and teacher whose many concerts ultimately became a stimulus in the development of modern American organ playing

Born in Greenfield, Massachusetts, Eddy studied initially with Dudley Buck in New York. Following an educational trend of the late nineteenth century, he subsequently studied in Germany under Albert Loschhorn (1819–1905), known for his piano pedagogical studies, *School of Octaves*. Eddy made concert tours in Europe and the United States. In 1879 he performed one hundred organ recitals in Chicago, featuring a new program each time. Other engagements included the Vienna Exposition (1873), the Philadelphia Centennial (1876), and the Chicago Columbian Exposition (1893). Eddy published collections of organ pieces. Among his pupils were Edward Campion (pseudonym for James H. Rogers), composer of "The Ninety and Nine" and Cleveland organist. Another of his pupils, Harrison M. Wild, was one of the founders of the American Guild of Organists.

D. S. CUSHMAN

EDDY, MARY BAKER (1821–1910)
Founder of Christian Science

Born in Bow, New Hampshire, and raised a strict Congregationalist, Mary Baker had an interest in religious topics from an early age. Throughout her life she contended with emotional and physical illnesses. In 1843 she married George W. Glover, who died six months later. After ten years she married Daniel M. Patterson, a dentist. Patterson abandoned her because of her frequent illnesses, so she eventually divorced him for desertion.

In 1862 she sought out Phineas Quimby, a blacksmith in Portland, Maine, who practiced hypnotism. Quimby was fascinated with the therapeutic possibilities of hypnotism. He believed that sickness was the result of negative thoughts and could be cured with positive attitudes. Mary Glover (she resumed that name) adapted Quimby's ideas to her own experience, claiming to discover the divine law of life.

A crucial experience for her occurred in 1866; while meditating on Matthew 9:2, she experienced healing from injuries resulting from a fall. She soon began her own healing

ministry, based on the conviction that the "Eternal Mind" is the source of all being, matter is nonexistent, disease is caused by erroneous thoughts, and power is released through the teaching of "Christian Science."

In 1875 she formed a small band of followers into a society at Lynn, Massachusetts, and soon published her textbook of Christian Science, *Science and Health with Key to the Scriptures*. In 1877 she married Asa G. Eddy, one of her early followers, and together with other friends they established the Church of Christ, Scientist, in 1879. The movement prospered when it moved to Boston, where the Massachusetts Metaphysical College was established to train Christian Science practitioners. When she was eighty-seven, Mary Baker Eddy established the *Christian Science Monitor*, a daily newspaper that has sought to present news devoid of sensation and scandal. At the time of her death, the Christian Science movement numbered some 100,000 members.

R. VONDERLACK

EDDY, SHERWOOD (1871–1963)
Leader in the international Young Men's Christian Association (YMCA); evangelist for the "social gospel" movement

Born in Leavenworth, Kansas, Eddy studied at Yale University and Princeton Seminary. His worldwide work began in India in 1896, where he worked without salary as national secretary for the YMCA. He was appointed YMCA secretary for Asia in 1911 and under YMCA sponsorship worked among British and U.S. troops during World War I. Converted under Dwight L. Moody's preaching, Eddy was an evangelist himself in several campaigns in China in the early 1900s. The tragedy and hypocrisy he observed in World War I, however, convinced him of the need to present the gospel as socially redemptive. Eddy became the YMCA's major evangelist of the social gospel. A prolific writer and gifted orator, he produced thirty-seven books and conducted preaching tours around the world.

M. FACKLER

EDERSHEIM, ALFRED (1825–1889)
Biblical scholar

Edersheim was born in Vienna (Austria-Hungary) to Jewish parents and was converted to Christianity in Budapest through the ministry of a Scottish missionary, John Duncan. When Duncan was appointed professor of Hebrew in New College, Edinburgh (Scotland), in 1843, Edersheim accompanied him and enrolled as a student.

After studying at the University of Berlin, Edersheim became a minister—first Presbyterian, later Church of England. He served from 1846 to 1849 as a missionary to Jews in Romania. From 1849 to 1882 he was pastor of several churches in Great Britain.

Edersheim is best known for his writings on Bible history and the life of Christ. His ever-popular two-volume *Life and Times of Jesus the Messiah* (1883–1890) has been described as a "monument of learning, presented in eminently readable form." His research into the times of Jesus' life also led to publication of shorter books on the social life and worship of Jews in the first century A.D. N. V. HOPE

EDMAN, V. RAYMOND (1900–1967)
American missionary, educator, author, and college president

Born in Chicago Heights, Illinois, Edman served two years in the army in World War I before entering college. After studying at the University of Illinois and Nyack Missionary Training Institute, New York, he graduated from Boston University in 1923. He spent five years as a missionary to the Quechua Indians in Ecuador before returning home because of illness. While working on a Ph.D. at Clark University, Edman served as a pastor in Worcester, Massachusetts, from 1929 to 1935. From 1935 to 1940 he taught history and political science at Nyack (New York) and Wheaton College (Illinois).

In 1940 Edman began twenty-five years as president of Wheaton College. Under his leadership Wheaton increased its total assets from $6 million to $30 million and its endowment to $8 million, witnessed the construction of fourteen major buildings, and established branch campuses in the Black Hills of South Dakota and in northern Wisconsin. Despite such major undertakings, Edman found time to learn most Wheaton students' names, write over two hundred articles and twenty books, and edit the *Alliance Witness*. Evangelist Billy Graham once described him as "the most unforgettable Christian I ever met." D. E. MAAS

EDMUND OF ABINGDON (c. 1175–1240)
Archbishop of Canterbury, 1233–1240

Born at Abingdon, England (near Oxford), to a devout family, Edmund began a life of austere piety very early. He pledged himself at the age of twelve to celibacy and church service. Beginning his higher education in 1195, Edmund alternated between Paris and Oxford for several years. He became a dedicated scholar and a superb teacher of theology. Edmund also acquired a reputation as a preacher, and he was appointed by Gregory IX as England's preacher for the Sixth Crusade. While his interests lay with teaching and helping the needy, Edmund reluctantly became a treasurer of the Salisbury cathedral (in 1222) and subsequently archbishop of Canterbury, an appointment supported strongly by Gregory IX.

Edmund's time as archbishop was dominated by conflicts with King Henry III. Despite his gentle disposition, Edmund steeled himself to oppose Henry's encroachments on church prerogatives and resources. At one point, his efforts gained significant retreat and agreement from Henry on varied issues. But Edmund also faced opposition from some of England's monastic leaders. In 1237, through Otto, a newly arrived legate, even Gregory IX began to undermine Edmund's archepiscopal authority. Realizing his office's weak position, he left England for France. However, he grew ill on the journey and went only as far as Soissy, France, before he died.

While probably insufficiently prepared for the hierarchical disputes he faced, Edmund's upright character and genuine sanctity make him one of medieval England's most attractive figures. *Speculum Ecclesiae,* a treatise on Christian life in the church, was his most important writing. It exists in various modern printings. K. J. BRYER

EDWARD I (1239–1307)
King of England, 1272–1307

Eldest son of Henry III and Eleanor of Provence, Edward was permitted by his father, a sensitive but inept ruler, to take control of the English government (beginning in 1265). From 1270 to 1272, Edward participated in Europe's eighth and last important Crusade. Intending to join Louis IX in his campaign at Tunis, he went on to Acre (northern Palestine) at Louis's death in 1271. At Acre, Edward's prowess was proved in many battles and adventures, but none of this altered Islamic rule of the Holy Land. In 1272, as he proceeded back, the crusader became king of England on Henry's death. Quite easily, Edward might be pictured as England's most magnificent medieval monarch. Tall, handsome, intelligent, balanced, courageous, a brilliant warrior, Edward was also an affectionate family man and committed friend. He also possessed much creative ability in government and the administration of law and justice. He was one of Europe's most illustrious monarchs in the era sometimes called "the greatest of all centuries."

Edward's chief attainments were the consolidation of general law in England. He has been called the "English Justinian"—England's most eminent law-giver. His genius lay in redesigning a desultory statutory complex and giving it usable organization. Edward's actions mainly affected English common law, but his influence on canon law in England was important also. Concerning the common law, Edward's precise statutes were the glory of England in this time. These enactments brought simple, orderly definition to the densely layered rules of feudal government. Furthermore, it was Edward under whom meaningful English parliamentary meeting and action first developed. Numerous parliaments were called by Edward to assist his rule. Some of these even included representatives from England's lower social levels. Naturally, the king also used them to collect revenues he needed. Overall, these were some of England's first significant steps toward representative government.

Regarding the canon law, Edward's reign saw many important developments. Under Robert Kilwardby, John Peckham, and Robert Winchelsey, Edward's archbishops of Canterbury, Church law became a thoroughgoing reality in English life. Not only religious activities but much in social life came under the canon law in this era. The expectation that Church law might adjudicate and punish moral offenses now became well established in England. Edward's last decade saw many acrimonious conflicts with the Church. Yet on the whole, Edward was a benefactor of the Church, and many facilities were erected under his auspices.

Original materials on Edward I and his times are listed in appropriate sections of the *Cambridge Medieval History.* The pertinent bibliography in the *Oxford History of England* also discloses important sources. K. J. BRYER

EDWARD VI (1537–1553)
Boy king of England

The son of Henry VIII and his third wife, Jane Seymour, Edward was only ten years old on his accession to the throne. Henry had provided both Protestant and Roman Catholic counselors for him. The Protestants, however, under the leadership of the young king's uncle, the earl of Hertford and later duke of Somerset, soon gained control. The result was a move toward Edward's adoption of Protestant views.

The views were expressed in the Act of Uniformity of 1549, which authorized the new Prayer Book prepared by Archbishop Cranmer and others to be used in the vernacular and to set forth moderate Protestant teachings. This was the culmination of the first period of reform, which had already seen the repeal of laws against heresy and the granting of freedom to read the Bible.

The duke of Somerset was not popular in

certain circles, partially because of his ineffectual foreign policy and partially because of his sympathy with the lower classes. He was eventually ousted by the earl of Warwick, later duke of Northumberland, who took over, pushing the Reformation further with the formulation of the more radical Book of Common Prayer of 1552. His interests, however, were not so much religious as economic and political. In all this the sickly Edward, although a sincere Protestant, was largely a pawn. Much of the reform disappeared, therefore, when he died at the age of sixteen and was succeeded by his Roman Catholic half sister, Mary. W. S. REID

EDWARD THE CONFESSOR
(1003–1066)

King of England, 1042-1066; known more for his religious piety than for his political expertise

Son of Ethelred II and Norman noblewoman Emma, Edward was educated in Normandy. In 1045 he married Edith, the daughter of the powerful Earl Godwin (whose help in putting Edward on the throne masked his own ambitions).

Since Edward surrounded himself with Norman advisers, he was constantly criticized by the Saxon nobles, led by Godwin and his sons. Edward's appointment of a Norman, Robert of Jumieges, as archbishop of Canterbury almost precipitated civil war.

Edward is perhaps best remembered for building the great abbey of St. Peter at Westminster in London, which was consecrated in 1065 and thereafter the official coronation place of English monarchs. Because of his reputed holiness, Edward was canonized in 1161. P. TOON

EDWARDS, JONATHAN (1703–1758)

Colonial Congregational minister and theologian

Born at East Windsor, Connecticut, Edwards entered Yale College in 1716 at the age of thirteen, after receiving his early education under the tutelage of his father, who was a congregational minister. After gradu-

ating in 1720 he remained at the college to study for the ministry until August of 1722, when he went to serve as a minister to a Scottish Presbyterian church in New York. In 1723 he returned to Yale, passed the examination for an M.A. degree in September and assumed the office of tutor in May of 1724. He resigned two years later due to illness. In 1726 he accepted a call to become the colleague of his aging grandfather, the Reverend Solomon Stoddard, at Northampton, Massachusetts. He married Sarah Pierrepont the following year and assumed full ministerial duties when Stoddard died in 1729.

Under the influence of Edwards' preaching, Northampton and neighboring parishes experienced a powerful spiritual awakening in 1734–1735. Beginning in 1739, again under the influence of Edwards' preaching another more extensive religious revival occurred, known as the Great Awakening. During this time Edwards made the acquaintance of George Whitefield, who was instrumental in promoting Edwards abroad.

Controversy arose between Edwards and his congregation when he sought to restrict admission to Communion to only those who could give satisfactory evidence of conversion. In 1750 he was dismissed from his charge at Northampton and the following year resettled in Stockbridge, Massachusetts, where he led the small Stockbridge church and served as teacher and missionary to the Housatonnoc Indians who resided in the vicinity. In 1758 he reluctantly assumed duties as president of the College of New Jersey (later Princeton) but died a month later (March 22) of a smallpox inoculation.

Regarded as the leading theologian of his day and one of the greatest thinkers America has yet produced, Edwards' importance rests primarily upon his contributions in the areas of practical and theoretical religion and his championing of evangelical Calvinism. Two early sermons laid the groundwork. "God Glorified in Man's Dependence," delivered in Boston in 1731 and published a month later, attacked the liberal notions of sin and salvation, attributing them to the destructive developments of incipient Arminianism.

Edwards insisted that sin was inherent antagonism against God, and that salvation meant a radical change of the heart that was totally dependent upon the absolute sovereignty of God. It was a clarion call back to an unadulterated Calvinism. In the second sermon, "A Divine and Supernatural Light," preached in 1733 and later published in 1734, Edwards described the true nature of religious experience. Salvation does not involve simply a rational understanding of God and biblical truth, but rather, the impartation by God of a "true sense of the divine excellency of the things revealed in the word of God." It is essentially a regenerative experience that affects the heart, imparting a new "sense" of divine things that cannot be obtained by natural means. True religion, Edwards insisted, is essentially a matter of the heart, not the mind. These sermons set forth a theological platform from which Edwards never wavered.

His reputation and influence as a preacher and advocate of experiential religion grew quickly. In 1734 Edwards preached two sermons on the subject of justification, which caused a spiritual awakening among his and neighboring congregations. News of the revival spread as far as Britain and elicited from Edwards a written account of the events that was published in 1737 as *A Faithful Narrative of the Surprising Work of God*. In it Edwards interpreted the revival as a genuine work of God's redemptive grace among the people of New England. Three years later, during the first Great Awakening, Edwards wrote two influential works in defense of the revival that established him as the leading theologian of the movement. *The Distinguishing Marks of a Work of the Spirit of God* was published in 1741 and set forth a theological defense of the revival, explicating and defending it as authentic by distinguishing "true signs" of religious experience from "false signs." In 1743 this work was expanded and published as *Some Thoughts Concerning the Present Revival*. In addition to answering the critics of the revival, here Edwards also stressed the aberrant nature of religious experience in order to temper revival enthusiasts.

In addition to his writings, Edwards' preaching also was used to promote revivalism. While it is true that Whitefield's preaching more than anything else set the colonies ablaze with revival, the most famous sermon preached during the Great Awakening, and likely the most famous sermon in all American history, was Edwards' "Sinners in the Hands of an Angry God," delivered in Enfield in 1741.

Edwards' most mature analysis of religious experience, *A Treatise Concerning Religious Affections,* was published in 1746, several years after the revival was spent. The work is divided into three parts. The first defines the nature of religious experience as a matter primarily of the heart, stating that true religion is seated in the affections or inclinations. The second identifies and examines those manifestations that are not sure signs of true religion. The third, which takes up nearly three quarters of the Treatise, describes twelve marks that arise from a genuine religious conversion. True religion is essentially a changed heart that manifests itself in Christian practice. Edwards' position was attacked by Charles Chauncey, minister of the First Church of Boston, in his sermons "The Late Religious Commotions in New England Considered" and "Seasonable Thoughts on the State of Religion." These sum up the position taken by the critics of Edwards and the revival.

Edwards' emphasis on visible religion eventually placed him in conflict with his congregation at Northampton. By limiting church membership and participation in Communion to only those who professed their Christian faith as founded upon a definite religious experience, he reversed the position instituted by his grandfather, Solomon Stoddard, who had eliminated tests for Communion. In *A Humble Inquiry Concerning Qualifications for Communion,* published in 1749, Edwards set forth in characteristically explicit terms his position, which led to his dismissal in 1750.

In the summer of 1751 Edwards resettled in Stockbridge, Massachusetts, where he spent seven of the most productive years of his life. Although engaged in pastoral and missionary duties, he found time to write his most important theological and philosophical works. In *Freedom of the Will*, published in 1754, he defended the Calvinist position by arguing that prior to an individual's choosing or willing there is a more basic cause identified as motive. To will is to act according to the strongest motive prevailing within a person. Most important for Edwards were the implications for conversion. By God's regenerative act, a new motive or "sense of the heart" is implanted in the soul which necessarily directs the will to God. The unregenerate are devoid of this new "sense" which comes only through God's act of regeneration. They are not motivated by love for God but are rather given to self-love. Edwards defends this view of human nature in *The Great Christian Doctrine of Original Sin*, published in 1758. The subject of these two monumental works, themselves a development of the subject treated in *Religious Affection*, is carried on in the shorter but no less significant work *The Nature of True Virtue*, published posthumously in 1765.

The larger structure of Edwards' theological understanding is to be found in two works published after his death. Edwards placed his vision for personal salvation within a millennial design for history in a series of sermons preached during the spring and summer of 1739. This was first published in 1774 as *History of the Work of Redemption*. In *A Dissertation Concerning the End for Which God Created the World*, published in 1765, he set forth the belief that God's ultimate purpose in creation, and to which all history moves, is the revelation of his own glory.

Edwards' entire life and ministry were inextricably tied up with the investigation, identification, and promotion of a right understanding of religion. In his estimation the pursuit of true religion was the "greatest and most fundamental" duty of the Christian. The question of how to judge genuine from spurious piety was an interest so basic to Edwards that it has been suggested that "the whole of his thought might be viewed as one magnificent answer to the question, What is true religion?" This is the heart of

Edwards and the reason for the continued interest in his life and thought.

C. MITCHELL

EGEDE, HANS (1686–1758)
Pioneer Norwegian missionary to Greenland

A Pietist pastor, Egede took his family from northern Norway to Greenland in 1721. There, until 1736, he carried on the first evangelical missionary effort among the Eskimos. During a smallpox epidemic, Egede and his wife won the hearts of Greenland Eskimos as they ministered to the sick and buried the dead. His wife died in 1733.

Learning the Eskimo language was difficult for Egede. His sons, Paul and Hans, however, had grown up learning Eskimo in Greenland and were able to assist their father. Many Eskimos became Christians because of Paul Egede's preaching. After 1736, Hans Egede directed the mission work from Denmark while his sons carried on the work in Greenland.

Ultimately two Eskimo believers, baptized by Egede, were brought to Copenhagen (Denmark) and introduced to Count Ludwig von Zinzendorf, leader of the newly established Moravian church. Since the Pietist Greenland mission was about to close, Zinzendorf began the historic Moravian missionary effort by assuming responsibility to carry on Egede's work in Greenland.

W. NORTON

EICHHORN, JOHANN GOTTFRIED (1752–1827)
Biblical scholar and orientalist

Born in Dorrenzimmern, near Heilbronn, Germany, the son of a pastor, Eichhorn studied at the University of Göttingen from 1770 to 1774. In the latter year he became rector of a high school at Ordruff in the Duchy of Gotha, and in 1775 he was appointed professor of Oriental Languages at the University of Jena. In 1788 he went to Göttingen as professor in the philosophical faculty, a position which he held until his death.

Eichhorn published several books on the Bible, principally *Introduction to the Old*

Testament (three volumes, 1780–1783; with a fourth edition in five volumes, 1823–1826) and *Introduction to the New Testament* (two volumes, 1804–1812). Eichhorn was one of the pioneers of the historical-critical approach to the Bible, especially the Old Testament. Believing that "most writings of the Hebrews passed through several hands," in his analysis of the Pentateuch (the first five books of the Old Testament) he held that the earlier history is made up chiefly of two documents, the Jehovistic and the Elohistic, the former ending with the death of Joseph (Gen. 50:14) and the latter with the first public appearance of Moses (Ex. 3:25). His work has been criticized as lacking in thoroughness; but he has been called by T. K. Cheyne "the founder of Old Testament criticism." N. V. HOPE

ELEANOR OF AQUITAINE (1122–1204)
Wife of England's King Henry II

Oldest daughter of William I, Duke of Aquitaine, Eleanor inherited her father's vast holdings at his death in 1137. In 1138 she married Louis, who, as Louis VI's son, a month later at his father's death became Louis VII, king of France.

In 1146, Louis VII agreed to Eleanor's accompaniment on his Holy Land Crusade with Conrad III, Holy Roman Emperor. This was the ill-fated venture (Europe's Second Crusade) called for by Bernard of Clairvaux and Pope Eugenius III. While the crusaders did worship in Jerusalem, the expedition was disastrous, both for western Europe's military designs and for Louis and Eleanor's marriage. Probably for varied reasons—Eleanor's willfulness, her indiscretions, Louis's strictness, his ascetic piety—the two by 1148 were estranged severely. Plainly, Eleanor now showed herself to be a woman of restive independence as well as intelligence and force. On returning to France, Louis decided to seek annulment of the discordant union. Based on the Church's consanguinity rules, the only lawful basis, Eugenius III granted the request early in 1152.

Eleanor then married Henry, Duke of Normandy and Count of Anjou. Henry's lands covered even more territory than Eleanor's, and their marriage united the greater part of France under one family. Such power, despite fealty to the French crown, was unsettling in itself. But then, two years later, on the death of Stephen, Henry became the English throne's first choice. This situation fomented great jurisdictional disputes and wars, these lasting till the mid-1400s, when France finally expelled the last of English continental rule. Notably, in the final conflict, the Hundred Years' War, Eleanor's lands, mainly Aquitaine, formed England's last bastion in France.

After bearing their last child, Eleanor began distancing herself from Henry. She spent the years from 1168 to 1173 at Poitiers, France. With her sons and Louis VII, her former husband, Eleanor plotted to separate her lands from Henry II and the English crown. The intrigues all failed, and in 1173, after a particularly irksome revolt, Henry captured Eleanor and returned her to England. Off and on Henry then kept her confined until 1185, when she was permitted to govern Aquitaine from England. In 1194 Eleanor left England and returned to Poitiers and Aquitaine.

Eleanor was a capable administrator of various offices in England and France. But clearly, she was also incautiously passionate and restive. Thus over the centuries Eleanor's life has been something of an antitype to Christian wives and the faithful, submissive nature of their marital role. With only little solid evidence, many have even pictured Eleanor as a robust patron of the medieval phenomenon called "courtly love" with its romance, adultery, and varied anti-Christian values and ideas. Very probably, though, her reputation as a "courts of love" ruler in Poitiers and elsewhere represents a literary tradition, if it is true at all. Yet Eleanor's makeup did entail much recalcitrance, perhaps reflective partly of her first union's annulment. Thus a basic diffidence toward Christian marital teachings seems undeniable in her troubled relations with Louis VII and Henry II.

Most original sources pertinent to Eleanor of Aquitaine are listed in Kelly's *Eleanor of Aquitaine and the Four Kings.* Some other important materials are described also in *Eleanor of Aquitaine,* various articles edited by Kibler. K. J. BRYER

ELIAS, JOHN (1774–1841)
Welsh Calvinistic Methodist preacher

Born near Pwllheli in Caernarvonshire (Wales), Elias as a boy read all the Welsh literature he could find. After much religious searching, he joined a Methodist society when he was twenty. There his career as a preacher began. Following study of English and theology at a small academy in Caernarvon, he married Elizabeth Broadhead, a shopkeeper in Anglesey. She supported him while he worked as an itinerant preacher. Elias's major efforts were in Anglesey, but he was also known throughout Wales and to Welsh groups in Liverpool, Bristol, and London. People compared his preaching with that of George Whitefield, a well-known English evangelist of the eighteenth century.

In 1811, when the Methodists seceded from the Episcopal Church, Elias was ordained as a Methodist minister. A man of strong views, he was a Calvinist in theology, a Tory in politics, and an advocate of total abstinence from alcohol. His second wife was Lady Bulkeley, whose wealth freed him from worry over money and enabled him to give himself to preaching until the end of his life. Elias's popularity was so great that an estimated ten thousand people attended his funeral. P. TOON

ELIOT, JOHN (1604–1690)
Missionary to the Indians in
seventeenth-century Massachusetts

Born in Widford (England), Eliot emigrated to Massachusetts in 1631 when a group of Puritan friends urged him to accompany them as pastor. In 1632 he began his lifelong ministry to the Roxbury (Massachusetts) congregation.

One of the Indians captured in the Pequot War of 1637 was assigned to Eliot as a bond servant. Drawing on the linguistic training

he had received at Cambridge University, Eliot learned the Indian language and mastered the intricacies of its grammar. Within ten years he was preaching to the Indians in their language and working on a translation of the Bible. The result was the first Bible printed in North America (1661–1663).

Eliot believed that Indians themselves were best suited to carry the gospel to their people, so he carefully trained twenty-four Indians as preachers. Because of his tireless efforts among the Indians, Eliot was given the title "Apostle to the Indians."
R. L. TROUTMAN

ELIOT, T. S. (THOMAS STEARNS) (1888–1965)
American-born British poet, critic, and
dramatist

Although of old New England stock, Eliot was born in St. Louis, Missouri, where his grandfather had been one of the founders of Washington University. After graduation from Harvard, he studied philosophy and literature in France and Germany, and then Greek philosophy at Oxford. He taught school in London briefly, worked for a time in a bank, and finally began a long association with the London publisher Faber and Faber. His poetry began to appear shortly after he settled in London. He remained in England, married, and became a British citizen.

Eliot's first notable poem, "The Love Song of J. Alfred Prufrock," written in 1911, was not published until four years later at the urging of American poet Ezra Pound. "Prufrock" demonstrated the new poetic method Eliot was to use throughout most of his career. In it, meaning is suggested through a series of images rather than propositional statements. Unrelated images are placed side by side for ironic effect. Obscure literary allusions are introduced without reference to their source. J. Alfred Prufrock is seen as a cultivated but spiritless middle-aged man without courage or values. Eliot offers him as a symbol of an age morally adrift. More difficult to understand, *The Waste Land* (1922) offered a metaphor for the modern era that became widely used: we live in a morally desolate waste land. That work became a landmark in modern poetry.

In 1927 Eliot declared that he was a "classicist in literature, a Tory (that is, a conservative) in politics, and an Anglo-Catholic in religion." Evidence of Eliot's Christian convictions became clear first in "Journey of the Magi" (1930), which stresses the poet's spiritual pilgrimage. *Ash Wednesday* (1930) then emphasized the need for repentance. *Four Quartets* (1934–1943), the triumph of Eliot's poetic career, dealt with the relation between time and eternity.

Eliot also turned to drama, believing that he could reach more people through that popular form than through poetry. *Murder in the Cathedral* (1930) describes the psychological-spiritual events leading up to the assassination of archbishop Thomas à Becket in Canterbury Cathedral by the agents of the king. Becket was a strong defender of the primacy of the church over the state. *The Family Reunion* (1939) deals with the problems of guilt and redemption in a modern upper-class English family. *The Cocktail Party, The Confidential Clerk,* and *The Elder Statesman,* all appearing in the 1950s, employ serious religious themes in social comedy using conversational verse.

Eliot's wisdom as a critic is seen in works like *The Sacred Wood, Essays Ancient and Modern, The Idea of a Christian Society,* and *Notes Toward a Definition of Culture.* As a classicist he defended order and authority, drew heavily on Dante and Shakespeare, and revered the ancients. Eliot was elitist, not democratic, in his tastes. Awarded the Nobel Prize for literature in 1948, Eliot has been generally acclaimed as the most influential English writer in the twentieth century.
P. M. BECHTEL

ELIZABETH I (1533–1603)

Queen of England; creator of the Protestant national Church of England

The daughter of Henry VIII and his second wife, Anne Boleyn, Elizabeth had a turbulent childhood and youth. She ascended to the English throne in 1558. Her education under private tutors equipped her to understand the problems she faced as queen.

Her first major task was to settle the religious controversies raging as a result of her Catholic half sister Mary's bloody reign. Elizabeth's own religious feelings appear not to have been strong. Like her father she appreciated ritual, but unlike many of her subjects she favored neither Roman Catholicism nor Calvinism. She refused to let the pope rule her country, which won her papal excommunication in 1570. She also opposed the Calvinists' demanding the removal of bishops, which in practice challenged a hereditary monarchy ("no bishop, no king"). Lutheranism had some attractions for her, since by 1558 it was well established and was associated with monarchies and civil order. Elizabeth chose for her kingdom a religion that integrated Protestant and Catholic ritual and dogma but ultimately declared that the monarch was the supreme governor of the church and state. Thus episcopacy and dioceses were retained, and the Protestant Prayer Book of 1552 was reprinted. The settlement did not please devout Roman Catholics or many Protestants (especially the growing number of Puritans), but over the years it won the commitment of the majority of English people.

The other changes and innovations of Elizabeth's reign were many. The defeat of the Spanish Armada in its attempt to invade England in 1588 was interpreted as an act of divine intervention and it thus helped foster nationalism and the conviction that England was "an elect nation." With adventurers such as Sir Francis Drake and Sir Walter Raleigh, who took the English flag around the world, and the founding of the English East India Company, England embarked on a path of colonial expansion. Great writers such as William Shakespeare (1564–1616) and Edmund Spenser (c. 1552–1599) brought the English language to new literary heights. It was through Elizabeth's rule that England became the leading Protestant power in Europe. Historians have commented that no monarch since King Harold (eleventh century) had been so purely English in blood, and no sovereign was more superbly insular in character and policy. P. TOON

ELLICOTT, CHARLES JOHN
(1819–1905)

Bishop of Gloucester and Bristol, England

The son of an English clergyman, Charles Ellicott was educated at St. John's College, Cambridge, where he was ordained and became a fellow. After a period as professor at King's College, London, he became dean of Exeter in 1861, a post he held for two years, before beginning his forty-two-year episcopate.

As bishop, Ellicott improved the general efficiency of the clergy and raised money for the restoration of the cathedral in Bristol. Having agreed to a division of the dioceses in 1897, he continued as bishop of Gloucester. He took a major part in the administration of the Lambeth conferences of Anglican bishops in 1867, 1876, and 1888.

His series of New Testament commentaries was regarded as embodying the highest standards of English exegetical skill. Recognition in scholarly circles led him to direct the committee which produced the English Revised Version of the New Testament (1881). He also served on the committee revising the Apocrypha. P. TOON

ELLIOT, PHILIP JAMES (1927–1956)

Missionary to Ecuadorean Indians

Born into a godly family in Portland, Oregon, Elliot graduated in 1949 from Wheaton College (Illinois) with highest honor as a Greek major. He was intellectually gifted, with interests ranging over public speaking, music, art, and literature, especially poetry. He memorized hundreds of hymns. Taking up wrestling in college to develop his body for the glory of God, he became a wrestling champion.

In 1952 Elliot went to Ecuador, establishing a school and Bible-teaching ministry among the Quechua Indians. After a long and unorthodox courtship that began at Wheaton, he married Elisabeth Howard in 1953.

Elliot kept a journal, begun during college, in which he consistently recorded the growth of his soul. Some of his statements have become classics: "He is no fool who gives what he cannot keep to gain what he cannot lose."

"Wherever you are, be all there. Live to the hilt every situation you believe to be the will of God." His journals also reflected his sense of urgency: "I seek not a long life but a full one, like you, Lord Jesus." "Father, if thou wilt let me go to South America to labor with Thee and to die . . . let me go soon."

That vision was fulfilled when he and four companions began efforts to reach the Aucas, a primitive Indian tribe in eastern Ecuador. After three months of carefully planned weekly visits by air over a village, they landed on a beach of the Curaray River in Auca territory. They were encouraged by friendly contact with three Aucas, but two days later ten Aucas attacked and killed all five missionaries. Their deaths had repercussions around the world, including the subsequent conversion of many Aucas. The story of Jim Elliot's life and death is recorded in *Through Gates of Splendor* (1957) and *Shadow of the Almighty* (1958), both by Elisabeth Elliot. D. M. HOWARD

ELMO (1190–1246)

Spanish Dominican preacher and patron saint of sailors; his real name was Peter Gonzalez

Elmo was born into a noble Castilian family and appointed to a church canonry at an early age. He preferred a more austere life, however, and joined the Dominican order. He served as chaplain to Ferdinand III of Leon during the war against the Moors (Muslim invaders in Spain). Later he left the court and began his famous ministry among poor people and sailors living on the coasts of Spain. Sailors termed the phenomenon of an electrical discharge seen from a ship's masthead as "Elmo's fire" and viewed it as a sign of the saint's protection. G. MINDEMAN

EMBURY, PHILIP (1728–1773)

Early American Methodist preacher

Born in Ballingrane (Ireland) of German Lutheran stock, Embury was apprenticed as a carpenter. Converted on Christmas Day 1752 through Methodist influence, he soon became an active class leader and local preacher. In 1760 he emigrated to America. At first he joined Trinity Lutheran Church in New York City but later affiliated with St. Paul's Anglican Church.

In 1766, challenged by his cousin Barbara Heck, Embury resumed his ministry as a Methodist local preacher and began holding regular services in his home. He soon gathered a congregation, which in March 1768 purchased two lots. A church building, Wesley's Chapel, was erected, which Embury dedicated in October of that year. In 1770 Embury led several church families to Camden, east of Albany, New York, where on a tract of eight thousand acres they established a new center named Ashgrove. There Embury, while working as a carpenter and serving as a civil magistrate, organized a Methodist church, the first in America north of New York City. He died suddenly, evidently from overexertion while mowing under a hot sun. N. V. HOPE

EMERSON, RALPH WALDO (1803–1882)
American essayist and poet

Emerson was born in Boston, the son of a Unitarian minister. He was graduated from Harvard in 1821, taught briefly, studied at Harvard Divinity School, and in 1826 became a Unitarian minister. Shortly after his wife of two years died in 1831, Emerson resigned his pastorate because he could no longer administer the Lord's Supper in good conscience.

During the next two years he traveled in Europe, where he met the British literary giants William Wordsworth, Thomas Carlyle, and Samuel Taylor Coleridge, from whom he learned the rudiments of transcendentalism. Emerson elaborated these ideas in a series of essays which made him the chief interpreter and popularizer of American transcendentalism, a late Romantic philosophy. Transcendentalism taught that human beings possessed an intuitive faculty enabling them to know the truth without the aid of the senses, natural objects, or the exercise of reason.

Emerson's first major essay, *Nature*

(1836), is a tribute to nature as one of humanity's great teachers. Another essay, *The American Scholar* (1837), has been called an American declaration of literary independence because Emerson urged fellow writers to cease depending on European writers as their models. The widely influential and most popular of Emerson's essays was *Self-Reliance,* a strong defense of individualism, filled with familiar epigrams: "Trust thyself: every heart vibrates to that iron string"; "Society everywhere is in conspiracy against the manhood of every one of its members"; "A foolish consistency is the hobgoblin of little minds."

The Over-Soul (1841) describes the Supreme Mind, the great unifying force, as the basic precept of transcendentalism. Transcendentalism was not a religion but a philosophical position and was closely related to romanticism in American literature. Among Emerson's best-known poems are "Each and All," "Days," "Rhodora," "Concord Hymn," and "Brahma." P. M. BECHTEL

EMMONS, NATHANIEL (1745–1840)
Congregational minister

Born in East Haddam, Connecticut, Emmons secured his B.A. from Yale in 1767. He then studied theology under two Connecticut ministers, Nathan Strong of North Coventry and John Smalley of New Britain. In 1773 he was called to a rural church in Franklin, Massachusetts, which he served for fifty-four years.

Emmons was a gifted preacher and prolific writer. He trained some eighty-seven men for the Congregational ministry. He stood in the Calvinist tradition of Jonathan Edwards and Samuel Hopkins, but he adapted their Calvinism to nineteenth-century modes of expression.

Emmons was a firm believer in the autonomy of the local church. In 1803 he successfully resisted an attempt to form an association of Massachusetts Congregational churches. Emmons supported home missions within Massachusetts and was an editor of the *Massachusetts Missionary Magazine*. D. C. MASTERS

EMSER, HIERONYMUS (1477–1527)

German editor, polemicist, and papal defender

Hieronymus Emser pursued an active academic and political career before emerging as one of Martin Luther's sharpest critics. After studying Greek and law at Tübingen and Basel, he taught classics at Erfurt, claiming to have had Luther as a pupil.

Prior to 1519 he supported Luther's clerical reform. When he attended the Leipzig debates (between Luther and Roman Catholic authorities) as secretary to the duke of Saxony, he changed fronts and defended the papal primacy. In retaliation, in 1520, Luther burned Emser's writings and circulated his own vituperative tracts.

Emser also wrote polemical works against other reformers. Some of the more noteworthy works are *A Defense of the Canon of the Mass* and *Against Zwingli* (1523). That same year he translated *Defense of the Seven Sacraments*, John Fisher's treatise commissioned by Henry VIII against Lutheranism. In 1527 Emser renewed his attack on Luther by issuing a German New Testament in the same format (but with significant "corrections" and notes) as Luther's 1522 translation. Emser failed to arrest the course of the Reformation, but he did sway several German princes (particularly Duke George of Saxony), resulting in persecution of evangelical reformers throughout Germany.

G. BROMILEY

EPHRAEM THE SYRIAN (c. 306–373)

Deacon and teacher who labored to harmonize asceticism, culture, and Christianity

Ephraem was born in Nisibis (now Nusaybin, Turkey), probably into a pagan family. He was taught by ascetic bishop James of Nisibis, and legend claims he attended the Council of Nicea (325) with James. As a young man, Ephraem was baptized by James and shortly thereafter was ordained as deacon. Ephraem never became a priest, preferring to live in strict asceticism as a monk. At one time he supposedly pretended madness to avoid being made

bishop. He became famous as a teacher in Nisibis. When Emperor Jovian was forced to cede Nisibis to Persia in 363, Ephraem moved to Edessa where he taught and wrote, probably living there until his death.

Ephraem's hymns, commentaries, theological works, and homilies were so popular in Syria that he broke the influence of Bardesanes, a church leader who incorporated pagan philosophy and astrology into his Christian belief. Ephraem also helped suppress the heresies of Marcion and Manes in the East. He took a mediating position between Antiochene literalism and Alexandrian allegory. His forceful description of the last judgment inspired later writers such as Dante. He was a devotee of the Virgin Mary and believed in the immaculate conception. Pope Benedict XV made him a Doctor of the Church in 1920. V. WALTER

EPIPHANIUS (c. 315–403)

Metropolitan bishop of Salamis

Born near Eleutheropolis in Judea, Palestine, as a young man Epiphanius became a monk and about the year 335 founded a monastery near his home. He achieved such fame as a monkish ascetic that in 367 he was elected by the bishops of Cyprus to be the Metropolitan bishop of Salamis (Constantia). His episcopal career was marked not only by devotion to the monastic life but also by rigid adherence to Nicene orthodoxy and strong opposition to heresy and schism—for example, Melitianism and Apollinarianism. His best known work, the *Panarion* (374–376), described and attacked virtually every heresy that had emerged in Christian history. In 382 he joined St. Jerome in Rome in opposing Origenism, and in 394 he visited Jerome in Jerusalem to promote this campaign; but in the course of his visit he became embroiled in a controversy with Bishop John of Jerusalem. In 402 Epiphanius went to Constantinople at the instigation of Bishop Theophilus of Alexandria to arrange for the expulsion of certain Origenist monks. When he realized that he was being used as a pawn in the power struggle between Theophilus and Bishop

John Chrysostom of Constantinople, he embarked for home, but died at sea before he reached there. N. V. HOPE

EPISCOPIUS, SIMON (1583–1643)
Dutch Protestant theologian

Simon Episcopius studied under James Arminius, the Dutch theologian who sparked a movement to modify the more extreme sixteenth-century Calvinist doctrine of predestination.

Episcopius assumed a post as professor at Leiden at age twenty-one. After Arminius's death in 1609 Episcopius, along with his colleague Uytenbogaert, took over the leadership of the Arminian party identified by the revisionist document they issued known as the "Remonstrance." The remonstrants' outspokenness aggravated Arminian-Calvinist hostilities; general riots broke out and the country verged on civil war.

In 1618 the Dutch Church convened the Synod of Dort. The counter-remonstrant majority upheld Calvinism, and the Arminian party was denied official church status. Episcopius, forced out of his teaching position, traveled to Antwerp and later to Paris, where he continued to promote the Arminian cause. In 1625 he returned to Holland and taught at the remonstrant school in Amsterdam. From a theological perspective, he moved beyond Arminius. Episcopius stressed human moral ability, almost entirely denying predestination and election. His unorthodox views on the Trinity and Christ appalled strict Calvinists but were popular outside Holland among those with more liberal beliefs. D. M. LAKE

ERASMUS, DESIDERIUS (c. 1466–1536)
Dutch scholar; first editor of the Greek New Testament

Born a priest's son out of wedlock, Erasmus knew nothing of normal family life and was in that sense a deprived child. His schooling was largely at Deventer (Netherlands) under the auspices of the Brethren of the Common Life. Those followers of what was called the "Modern Devotion" move-ment sought a deepening of spiritual life. Under the Brethren, who produced some of the fifteenth century's best teachers, Erasmus acquired an enthusiasm for Bible study. In 1486, evidently under pressure from his guardians, he became an Augustinian canon at Steyn (Netherlands). In spite of his reluctance to enter the monastery, his six or seven years of study there produced in him a love for classical literature and thought.

About 1493 Erasmus was ordained and became Latin secretary to the bishop of Cambrai (France). The bishop's continuing interest allowed Erasmus in 1495 to pursue theological studies at Paris. Erasmus took a lasting dislike to the dogmatic theologians there, with their partisanship, intolerance, and hostility to new ways of thinking.

In 1496, after a brief visit to Steyn, Erasmus returned to Paris, reinforced in his resolve to leave the monastic life. He continued his theological studies but majored in the new biblical courses rather than in Scholastic theology. Meanwhile, he helped to support himself (and advanced his career) by tutoring the sons of leading European families. During that time he wrote his *Colloquies*, a series of imaginary dialogues. They originated as exercises for his students but were edited and supplemented over the years. Erasmus used a gallery of characters to critique the religious life of his day, in particular satirizing the forms of Scholasticism and monkish superstition he regarded as damaging to true piety and devotion. At times, however, the spirituality in his *Colloquies* is indistinguishable from Stoic morality.

In 1499 Erasmus paid his first visit to England. Prominent churchmen he met there included Bishop Warham of London (soon to be archbishop of Canterbury), John Fisher, William Latimer, John Colet, and Thomas More. The last two exercised a profound influence upon Erasmus.

In England Erasmus also found a battle in progress. Obscurantists were attempting to prevent the growth of Christian knowledge. Under the influence of the Italian Renaissance many Europeans had been rediscovering the classical learning of the Greeks and Romans. Erasmus wanted such learning to develop a truly Christian character instead of causing a return to pagan values. He found support for that wish in England, especially from people like John Colet, who encouraged Erasmus in the study of the New Testament.

In 1500 Erasmus left England, though his friends wanted him to stay. He went to Paris and then to Louvain (Belgium), where he declined a professorship. About that time he began to expose the ignorance and corruption of the age. In 1503 he published the *Handbook of the Christian Knight,* which purported to recall a nobleman to Christian faith and practice. "It has long been my cherished wish," he wrote in it, "to cleanse the Lord's temple of barbarous ignorance and to adorn it with treasures from afar, such as may kindle in generous hearts a warm love for the Scriptures." He advocated a middle course between extremes "so that we neither act too securely because we rely on divine grace, nor cast away our mind without arms because we are dispirited by the difficulties of war."

In 1505 and 1506 Erasmus revisited England, then went to Italy and received his doctorate at Turin (1506). He was in Italy three years without finding there the stimulus for which he had hoped. He did see much that was corrupt about the papacy. In 1508 the publication of *Adages,* in which he gathered more than three thousand proverbs from classical authors, confirmed his reputation as the foremost scholar in northern Europe.

In a wave of optimism that accompanied the accession of Henry VIII to the English throne, Erasmus went back to England in 1509 for five years. He stayed for a time with Thomas More, and that year wrote the *Encomium moriae,* later translated into English as *The Praise of Folly.* The book was a biting satire on monastic and ecclesiastical corruption, on the many supposed miracles wrought by images, on the scandal of indulgences, on useless rites, and on the papal hierarchy. That work significantly helped to prepare the way for the Reformation.

Erasmus criticized Scholasticism for its inordinate preoccupation with details and

its ignorance of true religion. He pointed to the early church and to the church fathers as his ideal of reform rather than to the complex argumentations of later Scholastics. He wrote, "He is truly a theologian who teaches not with syllogisms and contorted arguments, but with compassion in his eyes and his whole countenance, who teaches indeed by the examples of his own life that riches are to be despised, that the Christian man must not put his faith in the defenses of this world, but depend entirely upon heaven." The test of theology, Erasmus claimed, was whether it was reflected in Christian living.

From 1514 to 1529 Erasmus was often in Basel (Switzerland), where he went to collaborate with the publishing house of Froben. In 1514 he declined the call of the prior of Steyn to return to monastic life, defending his vocation of scholarship. In 1517 Leo X (pope, 1513–1521) granted two dispensations to permit Erasmus to live outside a monastery and to let him discard his order's dress.

For a return to first-century Christianity to occur, Erasmus thought, people must know what kind of Christianity that was. So in 1516 appeared the great work of his life: an edition of the Greek New Testament text. Beside it he placed his own elegant Latin version with critical notes, some as insightful as anything that came later from the Reformers. His Latin revealed mistakes in the Vulgate text (the Catholic church's official Latin Bible), though it was not itself free of errors. Nevertheless his pioneering work constituted a landmark from which successive generations of scholars took their bearings.

The book's prefatory essay itself was a masterly achievement, as Erasmus set down his aims and hopes. "I could wish," he declared in lines that became famous, "that every woman might read the Gospel and the Epistles of St. Paul. Would that these were translated into each and every language so that they might be read and understood not only by Scots and Irishmen, but also by Turks and Saracens . . . Would that the farmer might sing snatches of Scripture at his plough and that the weaver might hum phrases of Scripture to the tune of his shuttle, that the traveler might lighten with stories from Scripture the weariness of his journey."

Ironically, the work was dedicated to Pope Leo X (who gladly accepted the honor), and also was hailed with delight by Martin Luther. That was only one year before Luther defied the pope by posting his Ninety-five Theses on the church door in Wittenberg.

In 1516 Erasmus became a royal counselor in the Brussels (Belgium) court of the future Holy Roman Emperor Charles V. Between that year and 1518 Erasmus also published a nine-volume edition of the works of Jerome, Erasmus's favorite church father. Less ambitious editions of other fathers including Irenaeus, Augustine, Chrysostom, and Origen followed in the succeeding eighteen years.

From 1517 to 1521, the most critical period for the Reformation in Germany, Erasmus was at Louvain, a famous center of learning in the Low Countries. There he was a key figure among the humanists, maintaining an enormous correspondence. Although both sides of the Reformation solicited his help, Erasmus never met Martin Luther.

In 1521 Erasmus settled at Basel, a city he found most satisfying for his work. There, aided by his friend John Froben, he published many books and continued his "back-to-the-fathers" movement. Although friends in high places in a number of countries offered him various posts, Erasmus declined them all in order to maintain his literary freedom. Any limits on Erasmus were to a large extent self-imposed by his temperament. A scholar who could assail long-entrenched evils in the church, Erasmus nonetheless toned down his attack just when papal defenses were beginning to crumble. Despite appeals from both sides, he was reluctant to become embroiled in the controversy between Luther and the papacy. His neutrality worked to the benefit of the Reformation.

At last, however, in 1524 Erasmus yielded to pressure and attacked Luther in *Diatribe on Free Will*, to which Luther replied with *Bondage of the Will* (1526). Erasmus came back with *Hyperaspistes Diatribes*. Thus for the last

twelve years of his life he was associated with the conservative faction, remaining firmly if sometimes uneasily in the old church.

In 1529, after the Reformation under John Oecolampadius had come to Basel comparatively peacefully, Erasmus was among the humanists who left the city. He went to Freiburg, a German city with a young university. Six years later he returned to Basel, although ill, to supervise the printing of his edition of the works of Origen. Erasmus died in Basel the next year. No priest was present. "Most holy was his living," said one who was with him, "most holy his dying."

Erasmus was a man of moderation in an age of extremes; his reputation was therefore attacked by both sides of the Reformation controversy. He refused to be caught up in the turbulence of the times. So, despite the deft aim of his literary missiles, the shy, sensitive bachelor found his scholarly detachment misunderstood, sometimes by friend and foe alike. His words were taken out of context and made to serve undesired ends. His views were used to criticize the papacy, and in Henry VIII's England to liberalize divorce.

In that age, "bridge-building" was not an acceptable occupation. Many did not share Erasmus's enthusiasm for pagan literature nor even for the writings of the fathers. The range of his learning was enough to make him suspect; he knew classical antiquity (reading both Latin and Greek), the Bible, early church writings, and the philosophical and theological scholasticism of the Middle Ages.

None saw more keenly than Erasmus the need for reformation, but for him that need was bound up with the need for education. His edition of the Greek New Testament was evidence of his concern for scholarship. For Erasmus, the cause of reform required using the tools of scholarship to learn crucial lessons from the Christian past. Those lessons included humanity and piety.

Europe, having fallen out of the habit of scholarly studies, tended to allow the papacy to tell it what to do and think on religious matters. It seems paradoxical that Erasmus described himself as ceasing to be a skeptic where the church had defined things. The same Erasmus had compared

Julius II (pope, 1503–1513) unfavorably with Julius Caesar, though considering the analogy incomplete because it lacked another Brutus. Such language, however, was the common currency of his day. Erasmus basically wished to preserve the church's unity, and so urged the abolition of practices, such as giving indulgences, that nurtured superstition and gave offense (and ammunition) to the Reformers.

In Martin Luther, Erasmus saw some of the dogmatism that had repelled him in his early days, only now serving a different cause. Even if scandals had become inevitable, Erasmus was not the one to precipitate crises. Indulgences were indefensible, yet he never unconditionally condemned them. He detested compulsion in religion. Erasmus would have agreed with Archbishop Robert Leighton that persecution was like "scaling heaven with ladders fetched out of hell." Erasmus believed that faith persuades rather than compels. Yet even he agreed that "an extremely contumacious heretic might be burned."

Erasmus was a pacifist, but not an unqualified one. He doubted that the concept of the "just war" could be precisely defined. Like many pacifists, however, he was willing to wage "verbal warfare." Regarding himself as a cosmopolitan who belonged to no one country, Erasmus could embrace pacifism unimpeded by narrow nationalistic interest.

Critics have often said that Erasmus was little more than a "humanist with Christian overtones." They sometimes accuse him of neglecting the work of Christ as example and teacher. Yet Erasmus believed in salvation by grace. His work on the New Testament allowed the Word of God to speak for itself and so come alive for both simple people and scholars. A multitude of faults is more than offset by that kind of testimony. J. D. DOUGLAS

ERDMAN, CHARLES ROSENBURY (1866–1960)
American Presbyterian minister and teacher

Born at Fayetteville, New York, Erdman graduated from the College of New Jersey (later Princeton University) in 1886 and from Princeton Theological Seminary in 1891. After being ordained, he served two Presbyterian churches in Philadelphia: Overbook and First Presbyterian of Germantown. In 1906 Erdman was appointed professor of practical theology at Princeton Seminary, a position he held for thirty years.

From 1924 to 1934 Erdman also served concurrently as pastor of the First Presbyterian Church of Princeton. In 1925 he was elected moderator of the general assembly, and between 1928 and 1940 he was president of the Board of Foreign Missions. Erdman was much in demand as a preacher and Bible conference speaker. His thirty-five books, mostly of popular biblical commentary and exposition, enjoyed wide circulation. His New Testament commentaries and other writings were translated into other languages. Erdman retired from the seminary in 1936 and lived in Princeton until his death. N. V. HOPE

ERIGENA, JOHN SCOTUS (c. 810–877)
Known as "John the Scot"; an Irish monk

Erigena was a capable Greek scholar who attempted to show the rationality of Christian theology by reformulating it as a kind of neo-Platonic philosophy. He accordingly translated into Latin both the church father Gregory of Nyssa and the Christian neo-Platonist Pseudo-Dionysius. He prepared commentaries on both John's Gospel and the philosopher Boethius, and he wrote books on both predestination and *The Divisions of Nature*—the latter an essentially neo-Platonic theory of emanations. By trying to envision God and creation as a logically interconnected unity, Erigena followed Plotinus and Dionysius towards pantheism, failing to distinguish it from biblical theism as a rational explanation of Christianity. As a result, he lost sight of God's transcendence and was unable to ascribe freedom to God in creating the world and in redeeming man.

According to Erigena, everything is part of a necessary process in which things emanate from the being of God and return from whence they came. This eternal cycle of emanation and return proceeds in four stages:

from God the source of all (uncreated creator), through the divine logos and his eternal ideas (created creator), to the world of particular things (created non-creator), which eventually reunite in the eternal end of all things (God the uncreated non-creator). The practice of the Christian religion accordingly calls for the human soul's return to God in mystical union. Erigena believed this formulation to be the most rational interpretation of Scripture. All we know of God in any positive way is what is manifest in his creation, so the connection must be maintained. Yet we speak of God by "the way of negation," for he is beyond all the attributes his creatures possess. He is immutable, invisible, and the only wise God. So the distinction must be maintained. Yet by apparently discarding the doctrine of creation ex nihilo (out of nothing) which earlier theologians developed, he opened the door to pantheistic and mystical perversions of biblical Christianity. That influence was profound, not only in the Middle Ages but also in the Renaissance and modern thought. A. F. HOLMES

ERSKINE, EBENEZER (1680–1754)
Founder of the Secession Church in Scotland

Born in Dryburgh, Berwickshire, Ebenezer Erskine studied at Edinburgh University and served as chaplain and tutor to the family of the Earl of Rothes in Fife. In 1703 he was called to the parish of Portmoak in Kinross-shire. Due to his powerful preaching and diligent ministry, crowds of several thousands regularly came to his parish church.

Erskine was a highly controversial figure in the national church. First, he would not take the oath of abjuration concerning the son of Roman Catholic James VII (James II of England). Second, he opposed the right of parish patrons (or their heirs) to appoint a minister, especially against the expressed views of the congregation. Third, Erskine defended the Puritan book *A Marrow of Modern Divinity* against its condemnation in 1720 by the church's General Assembly.

In 1731 Erskine moved to a parish in Stirling and became moderator of the local synod. Once more he attacked the principle of patronage and was censured by his own synod and the General Assembly. In 1773 he, along with three others, was suspended. Those four protesting ministers then formed an "associate presbytery" at Gairney Bridge, Kinross, with Erskine as moderator. Though the national church's censure was removed in 1734, the breach remained unhealed and the Secession Church continued. Erskine, still preaching to his congregation in the open air, was formally deposed along with six others in 1740. His three-volume *Works*, mostly sermons, was published in 1799. Within about two centuries from his death most of the "seceders" had found their way back into the national church. P. TOON

ERSKINE, THOMAS (1788–1870)
Scottish progressive lay theologian

Born at Linlathen, Forfarshire, Thomas Erskine was educated at Edinburgh University in law. He entered the legal profession in 1810 but, upon inheriting his father's estates, he gave up his untried law practice and instead devoted himself to studying theology and literature.

Erskine's views were not readily accepted by the more conservative theologians in Scotland. He sympathized with J. McLeod Campbell, who was removed from the Church of Scotland ministry for his belief in a general atonement. Erskine also claimed that Calvinism was a sheep in wolf's clothing while Arminianism was a wolf in sheep's clothing. Among his friends were some of the leading Broad churchmen of England, such as F. D. Maurice and Dean Stanley. His books, which had a profound influence in theological discussion of his day, included *Remarks on the Internal Evidence for the Truth of Revealed Religion* (1820), *An Essay on Faith* (1822), *The Unconditional Freeness of the Gospel* (1828), and *The Doctrine of Election* (1837). P. TOON

ERSKINE OF DUN, SIR JOHN (1509–1591)
Scottish Protestant reformer

John Erskine came from noble lineage

and pursued his education in England and abroad. After traveling on the Continent he returned to Scotland in 1534, accompanied by a French professor who established the first Greek school in Montrose.

By 1540 Erskine had embraced Protestantism and given his support to other Scottish reformers, among them preacher George Wishart (martyred in 1546) and former Roman Catholic priest John Knox. In 1557 Erskine signed the first Protestant covenant establishing "The Congregation of Jesus Christ."

When Scottish Queen Regent Mary and the Protestant nobles were on the brink of war, Erskine sought unsuccessfully to bring about some accommodation. In 1560, after the Reformation party gained power in Parliament, he was appointed superintendent of Angus and Mearns. Ordained in 1561, he was elected moderator of the General Assembly of the Scottish reformed church four times.

A man of peaceful and moderate disposition, he sought to soften Knox's rebukes of Roman Catholic Queen Mary, who described Erskine as "a mild and sweet-natured man." He sat on the council of James VI (Mary's son) from 1579. He had strong Calvinist beliefs and diligently performed his supervisory duties. He helped compile the *Second Book of Discipline* (1578). P. TOON

ESTIENNE, ROBERT (1503–1559)
Scholar and printer

The son of a Parisian printer, Robert Estienne followed his father's trade. He began supervising the family business at age twenty-three. Shortly after, he married Perette Badius (daughter of scholar and fellow-printer J. Badius, who published Erasmus's early works).

Estienne published his *Thesaurus Linguae Latinae* (1532), a standard work in its field. In 1539 he was appointed printer to King Francis I of France. Estienne published several editions of the Latin Vulgate Bible of St. Jerome (in 1528, 1532, and 1540). He also produced editions of the Hebrew Old Testament in 1539 and in 1544 through 1546. He

published a small two-volume edition of the Greek New Testament in 1546. His 1550 large edition became a general source of the *Textus Receptus,* the primary "received text" of the Greek New Testament.

Estienne's 1550 revisions, which showed Protestant influences, incurred sharp criticism from theologians at the Sorbonne University in Paris, the center for Roman Catholic scholarship. The next year he left for Geneva and converted to Calvinism. In Geneva he started his own publishing house, producing a New Testament (1551) divided into verses, an arrangement which still persists. He published works by Protestant leaders, including many by reformer John Calvin. His work was continued by his son Henry, a scholar and poet influenced by his father's dedication to learning and evangelical theology. N. V. HOPE

EUGENIUS (POPES)
Four popes took this name: Eugenius I was pope 654–657; Eugenius II 824–827; Eugenius III 1145–1153; and Eugenius IV 1431–1447—it was the latter two who left a significant mark

Eugenius III, born Bernardo Pignatelli in Pisa, Italy, became a Cistercian monk in St. Bernard's abbey of Clairvaux in 1135. He became abbot of a house in Rome and in 1145 was elected pope. Most of his pontificate was spent outside of Rome because he refused to recognize the sovereignty of the Roman Senate, which in turn would not permit his presence in the city. He was consecrated at Farfa, some thirty miles northeast of Rome, and he eventually went to France. He organized the Second Crusade (1147), which was largely a failure. He held several synods that concerned themselves with matters of theology; the most notable (Reims, 1148) dealt with misunderstandings of the doctrine of the Trinity and with the prophetic vision of Hildegard. In 1153 he concluded the Treaty of Constance, which checked the power of Frederick (Barbarossa) and the Holy Roman Empire. The pope was deeply influenced by Bernard of Clairvaux (whose famous *De Consideratione* was written for him), and this led him to work for renewal in the moral and spiritual lives of clergy and monks. He died in Rome seven months after he was able to reenter the city.

Eugenius IV was born Gabriele Condulmaro, into a wealthy Venetian family. He entered an Augustinian monastery and in 1408 was made a cardinal by his uncle, Pope Gregory XII. He was elected pope in 1431. His pontificate was a turbulent one from the beginning. He clashed with bishops meeting at the Council of Basle who tried to limit papal authority. They stoutly resisted his protestations and in 1439 elected their own pope, Felix V (Amadeus VII, Duke of Savoy). In that same year, however, Eugenius effectively countered that ploy by presiding over a council in Florence which temporarily brought together the Greek and Roman Churches and greatly increased papal power. The pope was forced to flee Rome in 1434 for Florence in the wake of a popular insurrection. He was only able to return to Rome in 1443, but the following year met with a serious setback when Christian forces in the Crusade against the Turks were defeated. P. TOON

EUSEBIUS OF CAESAREA
(c. 260–c. 340)
Deemed the "father of church history"

Eusebius is important today because of his work, *Ecclesiastical History* (written in ten books). Eusebius began this project during the Great Persecution (303–313), finishing and revising it several times between Emperor Constantine's (306–337) Edict of Toleration (in 312) and his victory over Eastern Emperor Licinius (in 324). These ten books chart the heroic rise of primitive Christianity from obscurity; vouchsafe precious episcopal lists for major sees to all subsequent generations; catalog and quote copiously from the literature of the primary Christian centuries; illumine the church's internal struggles to understand the Trinity over against various heresies; and stand breathless on the threshold of Constantine's brave new world—one in which for the first time Christ can be envisioned as triumphant over Caesar.

However his own generation did not realize how famous a historian Eusebius would

become; instead, they knew him as friend of the scholarly Pamphilus, episcopal combatant in the Arian controversy, and imperially favored bishop of an important provincial capital.

Nobody, not even Eusebius himself, breathes a word of origins. He was apparently born in Palestine around 260. The first that is known of him is as pupil and assistant to Pamphilus at Caesarea. Pamphilus himself had come from Alexandria in Egypt and then had built at Caesarea one of the ancient world's greatest Christian libraries. Earlier Origen had labored in Caesarea from around 232 to 255 and his famed *Hexapla* (Bible with six comparative columns of text) was kept there. Thus the theological traditions and style of Alexandrian theology were mediated through Pamphilus to the earnest young Eusebius, who so revered his teacher that he called himself Eusebius Pamphili (son of Pamphilus). In the last throes of the Great Persecution Pamphilus was imprisoned (308) and finally martyred (310). However, his labors of love, the library and the pupil, both survived, the latter to write Pamphilus's *Life* in three books (now lost).

During this period Eusebius traveled to Egypt witnessing scenes of martyrdom. He may even have been a prisoner briefly, for years later in the emotionally charged atmosphere of the Council of Tyre (335) someone recklessly charged Eusebius with having treacherously compromised his way out of prison. This charge is belied by the fact that as the persecution closed Eusebius himself was elected bishop of Caesarea in 313 or 314. In Caesarea he wrote three of his largest works—a refutation of paganism in fifteen books called *Preparation*, an examination of the fulfillment of Old Testament prophecy in Christ in twenty books titled *Demonstration of the Gospel*, and his *Chronicle* of world history down to 303, which served as a prelude to the famed *Ecclesiastical History*.

In 318 the Arian controversy erupted and Eusebius chided Bishop Alexander with being too abrupt in his condemnation of Arius at Alexandria. As a result an anti-Arian synod held at Antioch in January of 325 provisionally excommunicated Eusebius.

He was forced to make his defense before the emperor at the Council of Nicea later in 325. The basis of his successful defense was the Caesarean baptismal formula; Eusebius was exonerated and that creed became the framework for the Nicene Creed. However, the council added to the more ambiguous Caesarean formula the sharp *homoousios* clauses describing Christ as of one substance with the Father. Eusebius signed this only under pressure from Constantine and never completely sympathized with it. Though he and Constantine apparently met only once (at the Council of Nicea) before the emperor's tricennalia (thirtieth anniversary of rule in 335) in Constantinople, Eusebius earned the respect of Constantine and was invited to give the congratulatory oration at that celebration. Eusebius participated in the stormy councils which deposed three Nicene bishops—Athanasius of Alexandria (Tyre 335), Marcellus of Ancyra (Ancyra c. 336), and Eustathius of Antioch (Antioch c. 337). His two books, *Against Marcellus* and *On the Theology of the Church,* written shortly before his death, show that Eusebius was no supporter of *homoousios,* though he had moved closer to the Nicene position. Eusebius also wrote a famous panegyric on Constantine at the emperor's death in 337. Eusebius's death followed shortly after, around 339 or 340. V. WALTER

EUSEBIUS OF NICOMEDIA
(died c. 342)
Bishop of Nicomedia

Eusebius, whose early life is unknown, was probably Syrian; he typified the ambitious, turbulent, determined, influential late Empire prelate who kept Christian controversy boiling. With Arius, Eusebius was a pupil of Lucian of Antioch (c. 240–312). Sometime thereafter he became bishop of Berytus (modern Beirut) and about 318 was promoted to Nicomedia (modern Izmit, Turkey), capital of Emperor Licinius. Influential, he survived Constantine's victory (in 324) through friendship with Constantia, Licinius's widow and Constantine's sister. From Nicomedia he supported Arius against

Athanasius of Alexandria and led the losing anti-*homoousios* (against saying Christ was consubstantial with God) group at Nicea (in 325). Constantine's pressure brought Eusebius to sign the Nicene canon, but three months later he recanted and was banished to Gaul, only to be recalled (in 328) as Constantine became more Arian. As restored bishop he used synods, exaggerated charges, and Sabellianism charges as weapons to topple a dozen Nicene bishops, the last being Athanasius himself (in 335). Before death Constantine was baptized by Eusebius in Nicomedia. Under Constantius II Eusebius became Patriarch of Constantinople (in 339). There he was briefly tutor to young Julian the Apostate. His last act was presiding over Antioch's Dedication Council (341), where it seemed the anti-Nicene forces triumphed and where he consecrated Ulfilas Bishop to the Goths, having confirmed him in Arianism. V. WALTER

EUTYCHES (c. 378–454)
Considered to be the father of Monophysitism, a heresy condemned at the Council of Chalcedon in 451

Eutyches was abbot of an important monastery just outside Constantinople during the reign of Theodosius II. The new patriarch of Constantinople in 427 was Nestorius, who carefully defined with greater precision than before the distinction between God and man in Christ. Traditional belief saw Christ as true God and true man. At Alexandria the Incarnate Logos was stressed as the divine nature of Jesus Christ. At Antioch Christ's manhood with all its limitations except sin was dwelt upon. Both positions were orthodox, yet Nestorius was a militant devotee of the Antioch position stressing distinction of the natures. Condemnation of Nestorianism at the Council of Ephesus (431) set the stage for another round of christological definitions. Cyril of Alexandria so bitterly opposed Nestorius that he issued twelve anathemas against his sermons. In 433 John of Antioch negotiated a withdrawal from Cyril of the anathemas. Eutyches supported Cyril's formula and recognized one nature in Christ. He tended in his sermons to assimilate the human side of Jesus to his divinity.

At the local council of bishops in 448 one member pointed out the dangers of this teaching. When summoned before the synod, Eutyches defended his position and was condemned by the bishops and deprived of his orders. Theodosius II, influenced by his favorite eunuch, Chrysophius, one of Eutyches's admirers, convoked another Ecumenical Council to vindicate Eutyches. The second synod of Ephesus, the Robber Council, met in August 449, during which all the old rivalries between Alexandria and Constantinople flared up. Flavianus, the patriarch of Constantinople, was manhandled by a crowd of monks and sailors whom Dioscorus brought from Alexandria. His death after three days led to the Council's exonerating Dioscorus, Cyril's successor at Alexandria.

The Council of Chalcedon endorsed the *Tome* of Pope Leo I, which spoke of Christ as one person having two natures—language repudiated by Dioscorus. Pope Leo I called Eutyches "an ignorant, imprudent old man" for holding that Christ's flesh was not consubstantial with ours. Even though the Robber Council rehabilitated Eutyches, he was exiled in 451 and nothing more is known of his life. M. ANDERSON

EVAGRIUS, SCHOLASTICUS (c. 536–600)
Byzantine lawyer and historian

Born at Epiphania, in Syria, after training as a grammarian and rhetorician Evagrius settled in Antioch, where he became a lawyer. About 594 he wrote a history of the church in six books, which continued Eusebius's *Ecclesiastical History*—that is, it begins with the Council of Ephesus in 431 and carries the story down to about 590, covering secular as well as ecclesiastical events. Though Evagrius was no great theologian and was unduly credulous with respect to legends, he was orthodox and reliable (except in chronology), and made use of good sources, incorporating extracts from them. His work is regarded as important and authoritative, particularly for the christological controversies which developed in the church during the fifth and sixth centuries. N. V. HOPE

EVANS, CHRISTMAS (1766–1838)
Welsh preacher

Born on Christmas day in Cardiganshire, as a youth Evans attended a Presbyterian chapel. Later, he joined a Baptist church. Ordained in 1789, he took pastoral charge of scattered Baptists in Caernarvonshire. There his experience of God gave a new dynamism to his preaching. In 1791 he moved to the island of Anglesey as minister to Baptist groups.

Each year Evans made long preaching tours throughout Wales, and his dramatic sermons always attracted large crowds. He was known as the "Welsh Bunyan" (a reference to John Bunyan, author of *Pilgrim's Progress*) and could make crowds first roar with laughter and then moments later break into tears.

Evans's autocratic style was a recurring problem in his ministry. In 1826 he left Anglesey and had two short pastorates. These moves resulted from his unwillingness to accept the democratic congregational form of church government. In 1832 Evans returned to Caernarvonshire, where he lived the rest of his life. He died on a journey to Swansea and is buried in the graveyard of a Baptist chapel there. Many of Evans's sermons, hymns, and tracts have been printed. P. TOON

EVANS, JAMES (1801–1846)
Methodist missionary to Canadian Indians

Born at Kingston-on-Hull (England), in 1828 Evans began teaching at the Canadian Methodist Indian school at Rice Lake in Upper Canada. There he developed a system of phonetic writing of Indian languages. After being ordained to the Methodist ministry in 1833, he worked among the Ojibwa Indians in the St. Clair River area.

In 1840, at the invitation of the Hudson's Bay Company, Evans went to Norway House at the outlet of Lake Winnipeg, where he became superintendent of the Indian mission. Within a year he moved the mission to a site called Rossville, two miles from Norway House, which soon became the Methodist mission center of the West. Evans adapted his syllabic alphabet to the Cree language, publishing a Cree hymnbook in 1841. For the next twenty years a translating team organized by Evans used this alphabet to translate the Bible into Cree. Disagreements with the Hudson's Bay Company in 1846 led to Evans's recall to England, where he died. D. C. MASTERS

EVELYN, JOHN (1620–1706)
English diarist

Born near Dorking, Surrey, he studied at Oxford for two years before taking to law at the Middle Temple in London. The years of 1643 though 1652 he spent largely in travel on the continent of Europe before he settled as a wealthy country gentleman at Sayed Court, on the southern edge of London. There during leisure time he tended his garden and wrote on a great variety of themes, including natural science, the history of art, and the deforestation of land (in which area he exerted great influence). He was a devout member of the Church of England and evinced royalist sympathies during the English civil war. When the monarchy was restored under Charles II in 1660, he began many years of faithful public service, though he disapproved of some aspects of the royal life-style. Evelyn remained at his post in London during the Great Plague of 1665 and had a prominent part in the rebuilding of St. Paul's Cathedral.

Living in an age of intense scientific inquiry, he saw no clash between his religious beliefs and his enthusiasm for scientific truth. That perspective led him to cofound the Royal Society, which he served for a time as secretary (he twice declined the presidency). His lifelong diary, written for himself alone and not published until 1818, is crammed with details about the seventeenth century. It makes numerous allusions to church doctrine, to religious controversy, and even to sermons he had

heard. While his more than thirty works were mainly concerned with scientific and cultural themes, he occasionally ventured into religious topics, notably in two volumes written against the Jesuits. P. M. BECHTEL & J. D. DOUGLAS

EWALD, GEORGE HEINRICH AUGUST VON (1803–1875)
German philologist and Old Testament scholar

Ewald studied under J.G. Eichorn at the University of Göttingen, and later taught there (1827–1837, 1848–1867) and at the University of Tübingen (1838–1848). A prolific writer, Ewald wrote Hebrew and Aramaic grammars, and studies in both Old and New Testaments. His *History of the Religion of Israel* (five volumes, 1843–1855) set the tone for subsequent histories on Israel. In his commentary on Genesis, he argued against the "fragmentary hypothesis," maintaining the book's unity on philological and other grounds.

Ewald's Hebrew grammar was a landmark in the philological study of the Old Testament. He accepted at first the "supplementary hypothesis" to the Pentateuch (the first five Old Testament books), the idea that there was one major document that was supplemented by the work of another author (which he called the "Jahvist"). He later changed to the "fragmentary hypothesis"—that there was material in the Pentateuch that did not go back to the J, E, or D sources.

In the area of the New Testament he defended Johannine authorship of the fourth Gospel, attacked the Tübingen school's approach to the New Testament, and opposed the "mythological" theory of Straus.

He was influenced by Schleimacher in his approach to the New Testament and by Hegel in his view of the development of religious ideas. Still he accepted the deity of Christ and a literal resurrection. He viewed Scripture as the supreme source of revelation for the church, yet not as the only avenue to ultimate truth. D. CORNELL

FABER, FREDERICK WILLIAM (1814–1863)

Anglican clergyman whose contributions as a hymn writer followed his turn to the Roman Catholic Church in 1846

Faber, educated at Balliol College, Oxford, was one of the earliest figures to be influenced by the Tractarian movement. He was involved in controversies over the appropriateness of Psalmody or Hymnody in the High Church contexts. Essentially, High Church authorities favored the apparent universality and objectivity of Psalm settings, while the more personal expressions found in hymns were favored by evangelicals. The outcome of Tractarian researches into early Catholic practices was the realization that hymn singing was a practice as old as the church. The realization gradually led to a change of attitude, and as a result numerous hymn translations and settings took place under the Anglo-Catholics. Frederick Faber became very active in his effort to motivate the movement toward Rome. Of his hymns, at least 150 are to be found in degrees of use at the present time. Well-known works of his include "There's a Wideness in God's Mercy," "Faith of Our Fathers," "All Hail, Dear Conqueror," "Hark, Hark My Soul!" and "Jesus My Lord, My God, My All." D. S. CUSHMAN

FABIAN (died 250)

Pope, 236–250; was martyred during the Roman emperor Decius's persecution

During his rule, Fabian divided Rome into seven church districts to be administered by deacons—an action Decius interpreted as usurping his authority. He also wrote against an African heretic named Privatus and compiled records of Christian martyrs. Fabian buried the bodies of the martyred pope Pontianus and the antipope Hippolytus in the catacombs of Rome. He was buried in the cemetery of San Callisto, though his body was later moved to the church of St. Sebastian. Fabian's death left the see of Rome empty for fourteen months. C. HICKS

FAIRBAIRN, PATRICK (1805–1874)

Biblical scholar in the Free Church of Scotland

Born in Berwickshire, Patrick Fairbairn was educated at Edinburgh University and ordained a minister in the Church of Scotland. At the Disruption of 1843 he joined the new Free Church serving as a parish minister in East Lothian. In 1853 Fairbairn became a professor of divinity in the Aberdeen Free Church College, moving in 1856 to its sister institution in Glasgow. Elected moderator of the Free Church general assembly in 1865, Fairbairn traveled to the United States two years later as a member of an official delegation to visit American Presbyterian churches.

Among Fairbairn's publications are: *The Typology of Scripture* (two volumes, 1845–1847), *The Interpretation of Prophecy* (1856), and *The Revelation of Law in Scripture* (1868). He edited several books, including the *Imperial Bible Dictionary,* and helped to translate into English several works by the German commentator E. W. Hengstenberg. Fairbairn was a convinced Calvinist.
P. TOON

FAIRBURN, ANDREW MARTIN
(1838–1912)
British Congregational theologian

Fairburn was born at Inverkeithing, Scotland. As a youth Fairburn joined the Evangelical Union in Scotland and in time became the minister of its church in Bathgate. He took time off to study in Germany where he listened to I. A. Dorner, E. W. Hengstenberg, and F. A. G. Tholuck, an experience that broadened his theological horizons. In 1872 Fairburn became minister of St. Paul's Congregational Church, Aberdeen, and while there published his *Studies in the Philosophy of Religion and History* (1876).

Fairburn's fame was now wide-spread, and in 1877 he became the principal of Airedale Congregational College in Bradford, Yorkshire (England). When a new Congregational college was opened in Oxford (Mansfield College), he became its first principal (1886). Fairburn's theological liberalism can be seen in his later books: *Christ in Modern Theology* (1893), *Catholicism, Roman and Anglican* (1899), and *The Philosophy of the Christian Religion* (1902). Educational questions deeply interested him and he served on various national commissions and enquiries. Fairburn was greatly respected by both churchmen and politicians, but he disappointed evangelicals with his freedom of thought. P. TOON

FAREL, WILLIAM (1489–1565)
French Protestant who played a decisive role in bringing the Reformation to French Switzerland

In 1509 William Farel left his home at Gap in Dauphine to study in Paris. Under the influence of evangelical scholars Jacques Lefevre (J. Faber Stapulensis) and Cornelius Hoehn, he adopted Protestant views. In 1520 Farel joined other Lefevre pupils in reform efforts at the Meaux diocese outside Paris. Although removed from the circle of Parisian Catholic orthodoxy, increasing pressure from church authorities forced him to leave France in 1523.

In 1524 Farel began reform work in Basel with J. Hussgen (Oecolampadius). Farel's impetuous championship of the evangelical cause provoked strong opposition. Chased from Basel in 1526, he undertook preaching tours in Switzerland. In 1528 he and Hussgen were successful in the Bern Disputation—a forum which decided that city's religion. Consequently, Bern sponsored Farel's work in the Vaud, in Neuchatel (1530), and in Geneva (1523).

In 1534 Farel and French scholar Pierre Viret began holding regular Protestant worship services in Geneva. By 1535 a theological debate won the sympathetic populace to their side. In 1536 Farel added Calvin to his staff by threatening him with divine judgment should he resist. At this point Geneva was in a state of social and religious turmoil; thus, Farel fully supported Calvin's new order and discipline. A series of confrontations with city magistrates led to ejection of the pastors in 1538. Unlike Calvin, Farel did not later return to Geneva but lived in Neuchatel. If he lacked the theological depth and consolidating powers of Calvin, Farel was nevertheless fervently dedicated to his evangelistic task.

Farel remained close friends with Calvin, officiating at the marriage of Calvin and Idelette de Bure (1540). Some tension developed when Farel at age sixty-nine married a young woman, a union Calvin strongly disapproved. The two were reconciled, however, before Calvin's death in 1564.
G. BROMILEY

FARRAR, FREDERICK WILLIAM
(1831–1903)
Anglican clergyman; dean of Canterbury

Born in India, Farrar was educated at King William's College on the Isle of Man and Trinity College, Cambridge. He was ordained in 1857 and, after holding several teaching positions, became a headmaster in 1871. In 1875 he was appointed canon of Westminster and rector of St. Margaret's Church. In 1895 Farrar was nominated dean of Canterbury, where he not only raised funds to restore the cathedral, but made it the center of spiritual life for the town and diocese.

Farrar's most popular religious works were *The Life of Christ* (1874) and *The Life of St. Paul* (1879). Combining accurate scholarship with a robust Christian faith, and written in a popular style, his works achieved wide circulation. In 1878 Farrar published *Eternal Hope*, a series of sermons that cast doubt upon the doctrine of eternal punishment. This book called forth numerous replies, notably from E. B. Pusey, and to some degree Farrar modified his position in his later volume *Mercy and Judgment* (1881).

Farrar was a diligent student of philology. It was in recognition of his work in that field that in 1866 he was elected a fellow of the Royal Society—on the recommendation of Charles Darwin. N. V. HOPE

FAURE, GABRIEL URBAIN (1845–1924)
French composer, organist, and teacher

Faure received his musical education under Camille Saint-Saens. He was organist of several churches including the Madeleine in Paris. Probably best known for his art songs and chamber music, Faure is also remembered as the composition teacher at the Paris Conservatory of such students as Maurice Ravel, Georges Enesco, Roger-Ducasse, and Nadia Boulanger. Among Faure's many religious works, his subtle and expressive *Requiem* (1877) is still popular. D. S. CUSHMAN

FAUSSET, ANDREW ROBERT
(1821–1910)
Anglican scholar

Fausset was of English descent, though born in Ireland. After studies at Trinity College, Dublin, he moved to England where he became rector of St. Cuthbert's in York. At a time when scholars tended toward more liberal views, he was a committed evangelical and held to a premillennial eschatology. With Robert Jamieson and David Brown, he wrote a famous commentary on the entire Bible. He was author of a number of other devotional and scholarly works. D. M. LAKE

FELLER, HENRIETTE (1800–1868)
Swiss missionary to the French Canadians

Born Henriette Odin at Montagny, Vaud (Switzerland), she married Louis Feller in 1822. Her husband died several years later and Feller, having an ardent Christian faith and a strong evangelical belief, left Switzerland in 1835 to do mission work in Canada.

Feller, accompanied by another Christian teacher, Louis Roussy, began teaching in 1836 in a log house on the Grande-Ligne road near the town of St. Johns, Quebec. From this beginning the two teachers, who encountered great hostility throughout the province, organized the Grande-Ligne school and mission center, which provided the basis for French Baptist work in Canada. As a result of her vigorous advocacy, the mission was generously supported by contributions from Switzerland and the United States. D. C. MASTERS

FÉNELON, FRANÇOIS DE SALIGNAC DE LA MOTHE (1651–1715)
French preacher and writer; Archbishop of Cambrai, 1695–1715

Educated at the seminary of St. Sulpice in Paris, François Fénelon was ordained to the priesthood in 1675. From 1678 to 1689 Fénelon supervised the Catholiques Nouvelles, a house for Protestant converts. During this time he wrote his *Traite de l'Education des Filles*, published in 1687. Between 1689 and 1697 he acted as tutor to King Louis XIV's grandson, the Duke of Burgundy, for whom he wrote his educational novel *Les Aventures de Telemaque,* completed and posthumously published in 1717.

In 1688 he became acquainted with Madame Jeanne Marie Guyon, whose Quietist practices he at first approved and defended. In 1696, however, he signed the Thirty-four Articles of Issy, which condemned Quietism. In 1697 he published his *Explications des Maximes des Saints,* a series of articles on mysticism, and was condemned by the pope in 1699. He made his submission in a statement that appeared to lack sincerity. In the Jansenist controversy Fénelon defended papal authority and the Bull Unigenitus (1713), which condemned Jansenists propositions. Appointed archbishop of Cambrai in 1695, Fénelon won a reputation in his diocese as a diligent and benevolent, though autocratic, administrator as well as an effective and influential preacher. N. V. HOPE

FERDINAND II (1452–1516)
King of Aragon, 1479–1516; also Ferdinand V of Castile, 1474–1504; his marriage in 1469 to his cousin Isabella, the ruler of Castile, united the two kingdoms and laid the foundations for modern Spain

Ferdinand did not exercise complete authority in Spain, since Isabella retained dominion over Castile. Nevertheless, under their joint rule, Spain became a major power. Ferdinand annexed Navarre, battled the French in Italy, and eventually gained control of Naples.

A militantly enthusiastic Catholic, Ferdinand used the church to consolidate his own power. In 1478 he began the tragic proceedings called the Spanish Inquisition in which many Spanish Jews lost their property and lives. In 1491 his forces captured Granada, the last defense of the Muslim Moors in Europe. Ferdinand then banished all Moors and Jews who refused to become Catholics. For this and the "success" of the Inquisition the pope gave Ferdinand and Isabella the title "Catholic Sovereigns." G. MINDEMAN

FERRAR, NICHOLAS (1592–1637)
Anglican leader of a Protestant Community at Little Gidding in Huntingdonshire (England)

The son of a rich London merchant, Ferrar studied at Cambridge and traveled in Europe before working in his father's business, the Virginia Company. He entered Parliament in 1624, but disputes between Puritans and Anglicans and the political upheaval following the death of James I in 1625 caused him to retire from public service.

In the manor house of Little Gidding, Ferrar brought together around his family a small community of people, who practiced the trade of bookbinding and gave themselves regularly to prayer. He became the district's parish vicar, and the Little Gidding community became the local spiritual and social center. There was a school for local children and many charitable works were done in the community. King Charles I visited the community in 1633 and was impressed. However, Puritan leaders attacked it in a pamphlet called *The Arminian Nunnery* (1641).

Though he was accused of being secretly Roman Catholic, Ferrar was in fact always a faithful Anglican. His community did follow monastic-like discipline, but did not require celibacy. The Little Gidding community continued after Ferrar's death but was destroyed by the Parliamentary army in the English civil war. The contemporary "community within the Christian church movement" has led to renewed interest in Ferrar's Little Gidding experiment. P. TOON

FIGGIS, JOHN NEVILLE (1866–1919)
Anglican theologian, historian, and Christian apologist

Born at Brighton (England) into an evangelical, Nonconformist home, Figgis studied mathematics and history at Cambridge University, where he won several university prizes and was strongly influenced by the political philosopher Frederic William Maitland and the theologian Mandell Creighton. His later books reflect their influences. After a short career as a Cambridge lecturer in history, Figgis attended Wells Theological College and was ordained as a Church of England minister. In 1896 he returned to Cambridge for six years as chaplain of Pembroke College. Then, after a period as a vicar in Dorset, during which he had a "middle age conversion," Figgis entered the Anglican Community of the Resurrection at Mirfield.

Figgis's books show his wide interests. *The Divine Right of Kings* (1892) and *From Gerson to Grotius* (1907) relate to the history of political thought. Other books reflect his commitment to Anglo-Catholic ideals and his opposition to the idea of an omnicompetent secular state. P. TOON

FILLMORE, CHARLES (1854–1948) and MYRTLE

Founders of the Unity School of Christianity

Charles was a real estate salesman, and Myrtle, a Methodist, was a New England schoolteacher who had been greatly influenced by the transcendental philosophy of Ralph Waldo Emerson (1803–1882).

After moving to Kansas City in 1884, Myrtle became a convert to Christian Science (1887), concluding that "I am a child of God, therefore I do not inherit sickness." It was the discovery of the power of positive thinking.

With this new power, the Fillmores began to advertise themselves as "healers" and "teachers." Gradually a small group of adherents formed, which they named the Society of Silent Help. In 1889 they launched a periodical, *Modern Thought,* to publicize their views. Later the Fillmores chose the name of "Unity" to express their central principle of the unity of life, spirit, soul, body, God, and all truth. They borrowed some of their teachings from spiritualism and Hinduism.

The Fillmores denied that they were starting a new religious sect, claiming their teaching was a practical philosophy to supplement the teachings of existing churches. To emphasize they were not calling people to break with the established churches, in 1903 they changed the name of the Society of Silent Unity to the Unity School of Practical Christianity. Together the Fillmores wrote *Unity* magazine, *Good Business, Wee Wisdom, Progress, Weekly Unity,* and *Daily Word.* R. VONDERLACK

FINNEY, CHARLES GRANDISON (1792–1875)

Father of modern revivalism

Charles Finney was born in Warren, Connecticut, the seventh child of farming parents. With land increasingly scarce and costly in Connecticut, in 1794 the Finneys joined with many other young families in the westward migrations of post-Revolutionary America. Charles first attended school in Hanover (now Kirkland), New York. At the Hamilton Oneida Academy in Clinton the bright, popular, six-foot-two student was introduced to classical education, singing, and the cello. In 1812 Finney returned to Connecticut to attend the Warren Academy. After teaching school for two years in New Jersey, he was forced by his mother's illness to return to New York. There in the town of Adams in 1818 he began to study law. Although never formally admitted to the bar, Finney did argue cases in the local justices' court.

Finney's religious conversion in 1821 dramatically changed the direction of his life. He left law, claiming he had been given "a retainer from the Lord Jesus Christ to plead his cause," and sought entry into the Presbyterian ministry. Taken under care by the St. Lawrence Presbytery in 1823, Finney studied theology with George Gale, his Princeton-trained pastor in Adams, later that year was licensed to preach, and was ordained in 1824. Hired by the Female Missionary Society of the Western District, Finney began working as a missionary to the settlers of upstate New York.

Under Finney's preaching, a series of revivals broke out in several villages in Jefferson and St. Lawrence counties. By 1825 his work had spread to the towns of Western, Troy, Utica, Rome, and Auburn. These so-called "Western Revivals" (centered in Oneida County), brought Finney national fame. In them he used such "new measures" as the "anxious seat" and protracted meetings (lasting several days or weeks). He also allowed women to pray in public.

Not all were pleased with his success. Yale-trained revival leaders like Lyman Beecher and Asahel Nettleton, troubled by false reports of alleged excesses, joined with other evangelical leaders from the northeast in 1827 to discuss their differences. At that meeting Finney emerged as the new leader of evangelical revivalism. Between 1827 and 1832 Finney's revivals swept cities like New York, Philadelphia, Boston, and Rochester. Although he continued to promote revivals throughout his life (including trips to England in 1849–1850 and 1859–1860), Finney's early years marked the height of his revival career.

Forced by tuberculosis in 1832 to curtail his travels, Finney became pastor of the Chatham Street Chapel (Second Free Presbyterian Church) in New York City. Subsequently he held pastorates at the Broadway Tabernacle of New York City and the First Congregational Church of Oberlin, Ohio—the latter for thirty-five years beginning in 1837. In 1835 he became professor of theology at the newly formed Oberlin Collegiate Institute in Ohio (now Oberlin College), which he also served as president (1851–1866).

Theologically, Finney was a "New School" Calvinist. His preaching and teaching stressed the moral government of God, the ability of people to repent and make themselves new hearts, the perfectibility of human nature and society, and the need for Christians to apply their faith to daily living. For Finney, this included investing one's time and energy in establishing the millennial kingdom of God on earth by winning converts and working for social reform (anti-slavery, temperance).

Finney wrote several books, sermon collections, and articles. Among them were his *Lectures on Revival* (1835), a kind of manual on how to lead revivals; his *Lectures on Systematic Theology* (1846, 1847), reflecting his brand of "arminianized Calvinism"; and his *Memoirs* (1876), recounting his part in the nineteenth-century revivals. G. M. ROSELL

FISHER, GEOFFREY FRANCIS (1887–1972)

Ninety-ninth archbishop of Canterbury

Born at Nuneaton, Warwickshire (England), Fisher was educated at Oxford University, and ordained as an Anglican clergyman in 1913. The following year he became headmaster of Repton School. In 1932 he was appointed bishop of London. He succeeded William Temple as archbishop of Canterbury in 1945. An able administrator, during his London years Fisher helped to reduce what has been described as the diocese's "undisciplined chaos"—financial and liturgical—to something like order.

While archbishop of Canterbury, Fisher led in the revision of the canon law endeavoring to improve the government of the Church of England, and did much to prepare the new canons that were finally authorized in 1969. He also encouraged missionary churches—especially in Africa—that had been under the jurisdiction of Canterbury to achieve ecclesiastical independence as self-governing provinces of the Anglican Communion.

Fisher also sought to foster better relations with other churches. In a 1946 Cambridge sermon, "A Step Forward in Church Relations," he recommended that the English free churches "take episcopacy into their systems"—thereby paving the way for greater interchurch cooperation and for union negotiations. His 1960 visit to Pope John XXIII in Rome (he was the first archbishop of Canterbury to call on a pope since 1397) opened a new era in Anglican–Roman Catholic relations. Always interested in the ecumenical movement, Fisher was elected one of the presidents of the newly formed World Council of Churches at Amsterdam in 1948. He retired as archbishop in 1961 and was made Lord Fisher of Lambeth. N. V. HOPE

FISHER, JOHN (1469–1535)

Bishop of Rochester, scholar, and patron of learning

John Fisher was born in Yorkshire (England) and studied at Michaelhouse, Cambridge. He became master of the college in 1497 and took the office of chancellor in 1504. Supported by the English countess Margaret Beaufort, Fisher promoted the new learning, made common cause with Erasmus, and helped add Greek to the university curriculum.

Although he advocated correcting abuses in the church, Fisher was unquestionably loyal to the Roman Catholic tradition. He regarded Protestant Martin Luther's theses as revolt rather than reform.

Fisher is thought by some to have aided in the *Assertion of the Seven Sacraments* (1521) published by Henry VIII in response to Luther's *Babylonian Captivity of the Church*. Fisher himself wrote on the Eucharist (Lord's Supper) in 1527. Henry's divorce suit against his first wife, Catherine of Aragon, brought a crisis for Fisher, who was the queen's confessor. When he spoke on her behalf he fell out of favor with Henry. Fisher's dilemma intensified as the king pursued anti-papal laws. Fisher refused to recognize the king as head of the English Church or to take the oath of succession that excluded Mary (Catherine's daughter) from the throne. For his resistance Fisher was charged with treason and imprisoned.

During his year in the Tower of London he wrote several treatises expressing his views on spiritual asceticism. Pope Paul III awarded him the cardinalate, but otherwise offered little aid. After his execution, however, Fisher was immediately hailed as a martyr by the Roman Church. Four hundred years later Pius IX canonized him with a contemporaneous English martyr, Sir Thomas More. G. BROMILEY

FISON, LORIMER (1832–1907)

Missionary anthropologist and journalist in Fiji

Born in Barningham (England), Lorimer Fison was converted on an Australian gold field. Thereafter he worked with the Wesleyan mission to Fiji over a twenty-year period in both precolonial (1864–1871) and colonial (1875–1883) times. The remainder of his ministry was in Australia.

As an anthropologist, Fison pioneered Pacific and Australian kinship studies, collected folklore, and studied comparative linguistics. He prepared several native testimonies for publication and published many anthropological articles, his aboriginal research establishing the methodology to be used by his successors. In recognition of his work the Australian Association for the Advancement of Science elected him president of its anthropology section. He was also honored by the British Association, his Fijian work winning him an imperial pension.

As a journalist, Fison served as Fiji special correspondent to several Australian newspapers and fought for native rights in Australia and Fiji. The anthropological depth and human compassion of his writing made him a powerful advocate for the oppressed. He saved Fijian native lands from alienation and exposed the Pacific "labor trade" as a kidnapping practice. In addition, he edited the Victorian *Spectator* (1888–1905), which covered the Pacific missions, through its greatest years, and compiled a history of Victorian Methodism.

As a missionary who spoke Fijian fluently and understood cross-cultural communication, Fison trained the native preachers, composed hymns, and wrote basic Fijian texts that served the pastors for sixty years. Further, he helped in the codification of Fijian law, called the government's attention to the extent of Fijian depopulation, and helped shape mission relations with the government. By the time of his death at Essendon he was understandably known as "an architect of the Fijian church." A. R. TIPPETT

FLACIUS, MATTHIAS ILLYRICUS (1520–1575)

Croatian biblical scholar and Lutheran leader

Usually called Illyricus from his birthplace in Albona Illyria (now Istia in Yugoslavia), Flacius's Croatian name was Matija Vlacic. While in Venice (1536–1539), his teacher Baptista Ignatius introduced him to humanist reformer Erasmus's writings. Originally planning a monastic career, Flacius instead studied at the centers of Reformation in Basel, Tübingen, and Wittenberg. By the time he became professor of Hebrew (1544), he had firmly espoused evangelicalism.

Flacius's opposition to the Augsburg Interim of 1548 (German emperor's temporary plan of religious syncretism) led to sharp disagreements with other Protestant leaders such as Philip Melanchthon's party, the more ecumenically-oriented Philippists. He criticized Melanchthon's synergistic concept of humanity's cooperation with God.

In 1551 Flacius moved to Magdeburg and began his thirteen-volume church history, *Magdeburg Centuries*. He later became professor of New Testament at Jena. Dismissed from that post, he spent his last years in constant movement throughout Germany. His works also include *Key to the Scriptures* (1567) and *Missa Illyrica* (1557), an order for the Catholic Mass. G. W. BROMILEY

FLAVEL, JOHN (c. 1630–1691)

Presbyterian minister and evangelical author

Born at Bromsgrove near Birmingham, England, Flavel was educated at University College, Oxford University. In 1650 he was ordained to the Presbyterian ministry at Diptford, a parish on the Avon in Devonshire, as assistant to a senior minister named Walplate, on whose death Flavel succeeded to the charge. In 1656 he removed to Dartmouth. On the passing of the Act of Uniformity in 1662, Flavel was ejected from his church as a Nonconformist, but he continued to preach until the passing of the Five Mile Act in 1665 forced him to cease from this ministry. Thereupon he moved to Slapton, five miles away, where he preached to all who desired to hear him. When the first Indulgence was proclaimed by King Charles II in 1672, Flavel returned to Dartmouth; but when this Indulgence was canceled next year, he went to London but soon returned to Dartmouth, where he conducted services in his own house. When King James II issued his Indulgence in 1687, a meeting house was erected for Flavel.

Flavel was a voluminous author of religious books of strongly evangelical character, a prime example being *The Method of Grace in the Gospel Redemption* (1680). His many practical writings have been reprinted as *The Works of John Flavel* (1968). N. V. HOPE

FLAVIAN (c. 320–404)

Bishop of Antioch, 381–404

Born, probably at Antioch, early in the fourth century, in 361 Flavian was ordained to the priesthood by the local bishop Melitius. When Melitius was banished from his see by the emperor Valens in 370, Flavian, along with Diodorus (afterwards bishop of Tarsus), remained to serve the churches of Antioch. There they are said to have introduced the practice of antiphonal psalm singing by the choir, a practice that subsequently became universal throughout the church. On the death of Valens in 378, Melitius was restored to his diocese, but his right to episcopal authority was contested by the Eustathian bishop Paulinus. In 381 Melitius was nominated by the emperor Theodosius to preside at the Council of Constantinople, to which he was accompanied by Flavian; and when Melitius died while the council was in session, Flavian was elected to succeed him. Paulinus, however, was still in residence in Antioch, claiming to be the rightful bishop. The Christian world was divided as to the claims of the two contenders, the Eastern bishops favoring Flavian while the Westerners supported Paulinus. After Paulinus's successor Evagrius died in 390, however, no successor was appointed; and Flavian was thereafter regarded as the legitimate bishop throughout all Christendom. At least two significant events marked his episcopate. In 386 he ordained John Chrysostom, the great preacher of Eastern Christianity, to the priesthood; and in 387 when the Antiochenes had pulled down a statue of Theodosius, Flavian journeyed to Constantinople and succeeded in appeasing the emperor's wrath. N. V. HOPE

FLETCHER, JOHN WILLIAM (1729–1785)

Leader in the Methodist Revival in England

Born in Geneva, John Fletcher wanted to be a professional soldier but, impressed by the preaching of the early Methodists, he decided to enter the ministry of the Church of England. In 1760 he took charge of the parish of Madeley in Shropshire and by faithful preaching and visiting over a twenty-five-year period made a powerful impact on that locality.

A friend of Selina Hastings, Countess of Huntingdon, Fletcher supervised her ministerial training college at Trevecca until a controversy between Calvinists and Arminians in the revival movement caused him to resign. His sympathies were with the Arminians, and his best-known work was *Checks to Antinomianism* (1771–1775), produced because of the fear of Calvinist excesses. In his journeys to promote and consolidate the revival, he was known as a wise and learned counselor. He married in later life, spending the last four years of life totally devoted to his parish, with his wife playing a notable part in that ministry.
P. TOON

FLEURY, CLAUDE (1640–1723)
French church historian

Born in Paris, the son of a prominent French lawyer, Fleury was educated at the Jesuit college at Clermont. Subsequently he studied law and qualified as an advocate in 1658. After the death of his father he took orders in the Roman Catholic Church, being influenced by such men as Bishop J. B. Bossuet; he was ordained a priest in 1669.

A firm adherent of the French monarchy under Louis XIV, Fleury secured a number of appointments from the king. In 1689 he became tutor to the king's grandsons, the dukes of Burgoyne, Anjou, and Berry; and in 1716 he was chosen confessor of Louis XV.

After the revocation of the Edict of Nantes in 1685, Fleury was associated with Bishop Fénelon in the attempt to win Huguenots back to the Roman Catholic Church. Fleury was not a great controversialist although he lived in the shadow of the controversies of his time over Quietism, Jansenism, and Gallicanism. He wrote extensively in the fields of education, law, and church history. His most important work was the *Histoire ecclésiastique*, a history of the church to 1414, which he began in 1691 and concluded in 1720. D. C. MASTERS

FLORENTIUS RADEWIJNS (1350–1400)
Cofounder and teacher of the Brothers and Sisters of the Common Life, a Catholic lay community at Deventer (the Netherlands)

Although little known, Florentius Radewijns played a significant role in church renewal through his work in the Common Life. After studying at Prague, he discovered the *devotio moderna* (modern devotion), Gerard Groote's practical spirituality advocating imitation of Christ through prayer and charitable works. Groote, having established one community of women then, with the help and counsel of Florentius, set up a second for men in Florentius's house. They later established a house of Augustinian canons at Windesheim.

When Groote died in 1384, Florentius took over the leadership of the Brethren. His organizing abilities brought rapid expansion. A new center was soon founded at Zwolle with associated houses in Holland and Germany.

Florentius forged a movement characterized by communal living, inner devotion, and an excellent education system that later helped promote the scholarly works of Desiderius Erasmus and Thomas à Kempis. In addition to his organizing work, Florentius wrote several devotional works on the inner spiritual life. G. BROMILEY

FLYNN, JOHN (1880–1951)
Australian Presbyterian minister and missions superintendent

Born at Moliagul, Victoria, John Flynn was successively a teacher, home missionary (1903), and Presbyterian minister (1911) at Beltana. Here his vision of ministry to the "outback" matured. After a skillful campaign by Flynn, the Presbyterian Church established the Australia Inland Mission in 1913. As missions superintendent Flynn established a network of hostels and saw the possibility of linking medical care with advances in aviation and broadcasting. Although his initial proposals for a Flying Doctor Service in 1917 were ignored, when Flynn persisted a service was begun (1928) and grew steadily. He also encouraged the development of a radio transceiver, which was a vital means of communication and, as such, saved many lives. Flynn was one of the few ministers in Australia with a national reputation. Inspired by a deep faith in Christ, he embodied the gospel in practical terms to the people of the outback.

I. BREWARD

FORMAN, CHARLES WILLIAM (1821–1894)
Educational missionary of the American Presbyterian Church in India

Forman came from a non-religious family but experienced conversion as a youth. His first work as a Christian was conducting a school for the slaves of his family and neighbors. He then went to Princeton Theological Seminary and from there to India in 1847. He was one of the first group of missionaries to enter Lahore, the capital of the Punjab. There he began a small school, which grew and developed a reputation for good education and strong character training. He immersed himself in the life of the city and was known and loved by large numbers of its people. He worked closely with his Indian colleagues in the school and came to an ever-greater appreciation for the life and culture of the country. He was one of the missionaries who supported a more indigenous type of Christianity and believed that the church should accept polygamists as members. His school, the Rang Mahal School, eventually became the base for a college, which was organized as a separate institution under his principalship in 1886. At the time of his death the college changed its name to Forman Christian College in his honor and over the years became one of the prime educational institutions of the Punjab. C. W. FORMAN, JR.

FORSYTH, PETER TAYLOR (1848–1921)
Congregationalist theologian

Born in Aberdeen (Scotland), the son of a postman, Forsyth became (in Emil Brunner's view) the greatest British theologian of his day. He studied at Aberdeen University and then went for a semester to Göttingen University in Germany, studying under Albrecht Ritschl. He prepared for the Congregational ministry at New College, London. During this period he was a liberal in the sense that he sought to accommodate Christianity to the modern mind, stressing evolution, not revelation, and minimizing sin. Over the next twenty-five years he held pastorates in Yorkshire, London, Manchester, Leicester, and Cambridge.

By 1896 Forsyth had turned his back on the liberalism of his younger days, and this he announced in a sermon entitled "The Holy Father," addressed to the Congregational Union. Although he did not become a conservative evangelical, he did put at the center of his theology the revelation and grace of God in Christ. In 1901 he began twenty years as principal of New College, London, and from there by word and example had great influence. Forsyth's five most important books were *Positive Preaching and the Modern Mind* (1907), *The Work of Christ* (1910), *The Principle of Authority* (1913), *The Justification of God* (1916), and *The Church and the Sacraments* (1917). Forsyth has erroneously been called a "Barthian" before Barth. Over the last two decades his books have been reprinted, and he is taken seriously by modern theologians. P. TOON

FOSDICK, HARRY EMERSON (1878–1979)
American Baptist preacher, teacher and author; champion of liberal Christianity

Fosdick was the center of the stormy conflicts in the church over liberalism during the mid-1920s. In college, Fosdick abandoned belief in biblical infallibility and traditional understanding of doctrines of historic Christianity. He emphasized human ability for moral and social progress. Throughout his ministry he encouraged interest in psychology, writing that "the genius of Christianity lies in reverence for personality." At times Fosdick saw preaching as group-counselling his congregation; at other times, speaking out on an issue.

In 1915 Fosdick moved from a popular

Baptist pastorate in Montclair, New Jersey, to Union Theological Seminary in New York City, where he became a professor of practical theology. He had been associated with Union since 1908, part time, as lecturer on Baptist principles and polity. In 1919 Fosdick enlarged his work by becoming guest preacher at the old First Presbyterian Church in New York City. There in 1922, he preached "Shall the Fundamentalists Win?" He argued against doctrinal belief as a requirement for church membership and advocated open admission, so that collectively, through the church, personal and social betterment might be pursued. That sermon and his defense of it brought forth repeated attacks by conservative Presbyterians and Baptists. Finally, in 1925, he resigned his pulpit.

He had won, however, the support of John D. Rockefeller, Jr., who obtained the pastorate of his own Park Avenue Baptist Church for Fosdick and soon built for him the new Riverside Church. The use in the decoration of that building of carvings of such people as Charles Darwin, Albert Einstein, John Wesley, David Livingstone, Moses, Confucius, Buddha, and Mohammed, alongside of Christ, illustrates Fosdick's broad religious inclusiveness.

At Riverside Church, Fosdick led a vast program of liberal teaching and service, which made him, by the time of his retirement in 1946, a national and even a worldwide figure who inspired others in their ministries. His writings include *The Modern Use of the Bible* (1924), *A Guide to Understanding the Bible* (1938), *The Manhood of the Master* (1913), *The Meaning of Prayer* (1915), and *On Being a Real Person* (1943). His autobiography, *The Living of These Days,* was published in 1956. D. MUNSON

FOX, GEORGE (1624–1691)
Founder of the Society of Friends (Quakers)

A Leicestershire weaver's son, Fox apparently had no formal education when he was apprenticed to a shoemaker. In 1643, the earnest youth left home and traveled in search of religious enlightenment. After painful experiences, he spoke of having found One who spoke to his condition, and he came in 1646 to rely on the "Inner Light of the Living Christ." Fox forsook church attendance, rejected outward sacraments and clergy, dismissed current religious disputes as trivial, and taught that truth is to be found primarily, not in Scripture or creed, but in God's voice speaking to the soul. So emerged the "Friends of Truth." Fox stressed the priesthood of all believers, and advocated a simple life-style to his colleagues, who later included William Penn.

For interrupting a Nottingham church service in order to uphold the authority of the Holy Spirit, Fox was jailed in 1649. At Derby in 1650 he was convicted of blasphemy, at which time the term "Quakers" originated in a judge's jibe, after Fox had urged the bench to "tremble at the word of the Lord."

Cromwell's regime temporarily made things easier for the movement, and Fox found a congenial base at Swarthmore Hall in England. He traveled much, not only in England, but in Ireland, Holland, the West Indies, and North America. He established local congregations; women preachers were as acceptable as men. Fox showed occasional meanness toward opponents, but he was a true pacifist and his use of group silence was a brake on impetuous conduct.

Eight times he saw the inside of prisons, from Carlisle to Worcester, serving terms that aggregated six years. This greatly impaired his health, but he was undeterred. From 1662 when the restored monarchy imposed severe legislation against the Quakers, the battle was doubly hard. Fox crusaded against prison conditions and other social evils. He moved to London, where he continued to fight for religious toleration, to promote schools, and to engage in other charitable works. One of the tragedies of the seventeenth century is that able men like Fox were forced to produce controversial pamphlets to defend their positions. Fox did however keep a famous journal, published three years after his death, which gives a comprehensive account of the origins of Quakerism. J. D. DOUGLAS

FOXE, JOHN (1516–1587)

English Protestant historian; author of
Foxe's Book of Martyrs

Educated at Brasenose College, and a fellow of Magdalen College, Oxford, Foxe later worked as a tutor to members of the nobility. He was ordained by Bishop Nicholas Ridley (c. 1500–1555) in 1550, with his earliest writings reflecting his strong commitment to Protestantism. The accession of Mary Tudor (1516–1558) to the English throne in 1553 and the restoration of Roman Catholicism caused Foxe and his wife to flee to Europe and take refuge first in Frankfurt and then in Basel.

The change of country did not diminish Foxe's determination, gained initially from Bishop John Bale (1495–1563), to write on English church history. At times in great poverty, he worked in Oporinus of Basel's printing shop in order to support his family. In 1559, after Elizabeth I (1533–1603) had become Queen of England, Foxe published—in 732 pages of Latin—his history of the Protestant martyrs. Soon after, he returned to England, then translated and extended the work, publishing it as *Actes and Monuments*. Four editions appeared in his lifetime (1563, 1570, 1576, 1583), published by his friend John Day.

Foxe was made a prebendary (clergy supported by income from cathedral lands) of both Salisbury and Durham cathedrals, but he tended to live in London, involved often in correspondence concerning his great book, *Foxe's Book of Martyrs,* which is a shortened version of his *Actes and Monuments of Matters Happening to the Church.* That treatise, which praised God for the fidelity of Protestants in England when persecuted, helped to give to England a sense of being, under God, an "elect Protestant nation." P. TOON

FRANCIS OF ASSISI (1182–1226)

Catholic preacher and mystic who began monastic communities for men and women devoted to poverty and service to the poor

Francis was born to Pietro Bernadone and Giovanna (di Pica) at Assisi (now northern Italy). Francis worked with his father, a wealthy cloth merchant, until the age of twenty when military adventures stole his attention. Taken prisoner for many months after a border dispute, he reflected on his life. It was not until 1204, however, that Francis became disenchanted with his reckless youth and materialistic values. He began to struggle inwardly in prayer and meditation.

This new spiritual sensitivity prepared him for two events which profoundly changed his life. The first was a pilgrimage to Rome, where he knelt beside a leper to give him alms and kiss his sores. The second event was the revelation Francis received at a little ruined church in San Damiano on the outskirts of Assisi. Here a voice from the crucifix ordered him to restore the building. Convinced that Francis was insane, his infuriated father denounced him, and Francis began his life as the *povercello,* the little poor man.

Francis did not intend to establish a religious order, nor did he anticipate disciples. A diverse group of men and women, however, sought him out. These people included Bernard of Quintravale, a wealthy merchant; Sylvester, a cleric; Giles of Assisi, a devout peasant; and Juniper, a slightly mad mystic. They were the early members of Friars Minor (or the Franciscans). In addition, Francis helped the sixteen-year-old Clare leave her wealthy family to become the first of an order of mendicant sisters. In his *Canticle of Brother Sun,* Francis and his early disciples musically expressed their faith and communion with God through nature. After another vision, in the church of Portiuncula in 1208, the Friars Minor began their mission of preaching repentance, singing, aiding the peasants in their work, and caring for lepers.

The heart of Francis's message was poverty. To renounce wealth was to find true freedom to serve God and needy people. The "first rule" issued in 1221 stated: "The Friars are to appropriate nothing for themselves, neither a house, nor a place, nor anything else . . . they beg alms trustingly."

Francis, faithful to the Catholic church, wrote that even "if they persecuted me, I should . . . turn to them for help." The Lateran council (1215) sought to curb the friars' "excessive enthusiasm" and to reorganize the brotherhood under existing monastic rules. Francis's friendship with the powerful cardinal Ugolino (later Pope Gregory IX) saved the order from dissolution and won them the right to subsist on begging. Since Francis lacked administrative skill, Ugolino increasingly dominated the order's policies. Francis occupied himself, instead, with missionary endeavors and spiritual guidance.

When the leadership passed to brother Elias of Cortona in 1232, the order went in many directions, displeasing Francis. New friars wanted a stronger emphasis on education, but Francis felt this would betray the simplicity of the gospel, create pride, and foster the keeping of possessions (such as books). In spite of Francis's pleadings, the friars eventually entered the political realm and the intellectual life of the universities.

With the direction of the order beyond his control, Francis retired to a semi-eremetic life, at which time he received the stigmata (wounds of Christ) on his body. Combined with the rigors of self-denial, this caused his health to weaken, and after extended illnesses he died in 1226. He was canonized two years later. R. VONDERLACK

FRANCIS OF PAOLA (1416–1507)
Roman Catholic saint and ascetic; founder of the monastic order of the Minims

Francis was born to a poor family, and before he turned twenty he left to spend a year with the Franciscans. He chose, however, the more austere life of a hermit. His spiritual self-discipline brought him many followers who took the official name of the Minims, considering themselves the least of all religious orders.

Francis's vigorous defense of the poor often brought him in conflict with the powerful. In Italy he incurred the displeasure of the king of Naples. The gravely ill Louis XI of France urged the friar to come to Paris to help him prepare for death. Francis went, only after urgings by the pope, Sixtus IV. After the king's death, Francis served as royal adviser to King Charles VIII and his successor Louis XII. He often influenced the French kings' handling of affairs of state. Francis was canonized in 1519 and declared the patron of seafarers in 1943.
R. D. SHUSTER

FRANCIS OF SALES (1567–1622)
Roman Catholic bishop, apologist, and writer

Francis was born in Savoy (France) to a large, aristocratic family of devout Roman Catholics. From childhood he had a deep, although secret, desire to be a priest. He studied first at the University of Paris and then at Padua, where he graduated with a doctorate of law. Despite parental objections, he was ordained in 1593.

The next year Francis was sent as a missionary to the Calvinist stronghold Chablais, a district of Geneva. By means of simple pamphlets explaining Roman Catholic beliefs, as well as public debates with Calvinist representatives, acts of charity, and a blameless life, Francis reclaimed thousands to the Roman Catholic Church. Through his influence over the region's ruler, Duke Charles Emmanuel, Francis initiated the restaffing of churches and Roman Catholic schools.

In 1599, at the Duke's suggestion, Francis became a coworker of the bishop of Geneva and became bishop himself in 1602. Francis continued his missionary endeavors and also worked diligently with several devout Catholic women on charitable projects. He was cofounder with Jeanne Frances de Chantal of the Visitation Order, dedicated to teaching and nursing the sick. In addition to his administrative and apologetic tasks, Francis wrote many pastoral letters and two popular works encouraging active lay spirituality: *Introduction to a Devout Life* and *Treatise on the Love of God*. In 1665 Francis of Sales was canonized, in 1877 made a doctor of the Church, and in 1923 declared "patron of the Catholic Press." R. D. SHUSTER

FRANCK, SEBASTIAN (1499–1542)
Humanist reformer, religious philosopher, and "apostle of inward religion"

Born at Donauworth, Bavaria, Sebastian Franck pursued the priesthood after having attended Ingolstadt and Heidelberg universities. In 1525 (one year after his ordination) he converted to Lutheranism, serving as a pastor at Gustenfelden near Nuremberg. In 1528 he married Ottilie Behaim, whose wide cultural contacts extended from painter Albrecht Dürer to Anabaptist leader Hans Denck.

Leaving the Lutheran ministry, in 1529 the Francks moved to Strassburg, establishing close ties with spiritualist theologian Caspar Schwenckfeld. In 1531 Sebastian Franck published *Chronica, Zeitbuch und Geschichtbibel*, recounting "the world's history from the earliest times to the present." In this book Franck chronicled various anti-Catholic heretical movements, rejected organized Protestantism, and aired his own humanist and mystic views. Expelled from Strassburg in 1531, he worked in Esslingen as a soapmaker, in Ulm as a writer and publisher, and finally in 1539 he settled in Basel.

Franck's religious viewpoint borrowed from several sources: Plato, medieval Catholic mysticism, and evangelical theology. Franck stressed the soul's capacity to hear, respond to, and live by the inner light of the word of God. The true church, according to Franck, was spiritual and invisible, independent of sacramental ceremonies or ecclesiastical organizations. N. V. HOPE

FRANCKE, AUGUST HERMANN (1663–1727)

German Pietist and educational reformer

About 1687, while a professor of Hebrew at Leipzig, August Francke came under the influence of Pietist preacher P. J. Spener. Francke began holding Bible study devotional meetings, sparking a revival at the institution. This unorthodox practice and his outspoken opinions on other issues led to conflict with the more conservative faculty members. Eventually he was forced to leave the school.

In 1692 Francke accepted a professorship at the new University of Halle and became a minister at a nearby church. He helped make Halle a center for Pietism and made impor-

tant contributions to the study of philology. Francke's educational reforms included founding an orphanage, grade school, high school, and a teacher-training school. To give his students practical job experience, he also opened a drugstore, bookstore, and publishing house. Prussian educational reform later incorporated many of his ideas. G. MINDEMAN

FRANSON, FREDRIK (1852–1908)

Swedish-American evangelist, biblical theologian, revivalist, and church and missions founder

Born in Sweden, Franson for financial reasons had to quit school at the end of his freshman year in high school. In 1869 the whole family emigrated to America. In 1872 he was converted through the patient prayer and counseling of his mother and submission to Romans 10:6-8. However, he gave no public testimony until 1874; but after that he never stopped.

Franson founded the first four local evangelical free churches in America in 1880. He formulated rigorous biblical positions on the church, baptism, and eschatology. These formulations significantly affected the later development of the Evangelical Free Church of America, giving that organization an essentially indigenous American character from its very birth.

In 1881 and 1882 Franson spearheaded the legal breakthrough on aggressive and interdenominational evangelism in Sweden. His 1883 campaigns in Norway led to revival in many cities and resulted in the organization of the Norwegian Mission Confederation in 1884. He stimulated viable spiritual movements in country after country, drawing out local leadership and respecting it. This work resulted in the founding of these other organizations as well: Danish Mission Confederation, Barmen Alliance Society and Alliance Mission—Barmen (Germany), Swiss Alliance Mission, The Evangelical Alliance Mission, Finnish Alliance Mission, Swedish Evangelical Mission in Japan, and Swedish Alliance Mission.

His work influenced other significant developments in each of the following organizations: Utah Presbyterian Church, Swedish Holiness Union, Finnish Free Church, China Inland Mission, Evangelical Free Church of Germany, The Christian and Missionary Alliance, German Fellowship Deaconry Union, Norwegian Missionary Alliance, and Orebro Mission of Sweden.

The Swedish Baptist Nebraska Conference elected him secretary in 1875. He began to study D. L. Moody's campaigns and, in February 1877, set out on his own full-time, aggressive, interdenominational evangelistic work. In 1878 he joined the independent, interdenominational Moody Church in Chicago. He organized seven new churches in Utah, Colorado, and Nebraska during 1880—and published the study, "Biblical Church Polity" (Swedish), setting forth the pattern of polity he had seen within and between the local churches in the New Testament. In 1881 he published in Danish *The Craftiness of Deception* to help Scandinavians disentangle themselves from Mormonism. That year he also cosponsored and prepared many of the papers for the Scandinavian Premillennial Conference in Chicago—the second premillennial conference on record in the United States.

He moved to Europe in 1881, pioneering aggressive evangelism in several countries. He developed lay evangelist courses as a major tool for local evangelism. He published the following German studies: *After-meetings in the Light of the Bible,* "Prophesying Daughter," and *The Precious Sons of Zion*—the latter as an aid to Jewish evangelism. He always promoted the any-moment expectation of Jesus' return.

From 1890 until his death in 1908, Franson concentrated on urgent worldwide missionary extension. He sent out missionaries, worked with them, studied, and engaged in missions around the world. Awakenings still resulted—New Zealand (1902), Japan and Korea (1903), China (1904), eastern Turkey (1906) and South Africa (1907). His lifelong revival motto was Constant, Conscious Communion with God. His last major writing, *Missionary Methods in Non-Christian Societies,* was published posthumously in Sweden.

E. P. TORJESEN

FREDERICK I (c.1122–1190)
Holy Roman Emperor, 1155–1190

Born to Frederick of Hohenstaufen, Frederick was a Guelph on his mother's side. In 1152, he was elected king of Germany with hopes he might resolve the longstanding Hohenstaufen-Guelph discord. Like his predecessor Otto I, Frederick sought an expanded Holy Roman Empire based on a closely united Germany. Toward these ends, he first satisfied the restive Guelphs by recognizing Henry the Lion's rule in Saxony, and also granting him Bavaria. At the same time, Frederick strengthened his internal base by renewed dominance of the German church, and an innovative government run by non-aristocratic agents. It was only two years before Frederick was ready to extend his empire's borders.

Frederick's first action outside Germany secured homage in 1153 from Sweyn III, the Danish king. Then in 1157, an expedition into Poland brought about Boleslav IV's submission. Having married Beatrice, daughter of Raynald II, ruler of Burgundy, in 1156, Frederick gained the Burgundian nobles' loyalty by 1157. (Frederick had his marriage to Adela annulled in 1155.) With these necessities achieved, Frederick's expansionism followed two main lines: military efforts to acquire Italian lands, and diplomatic efforts to quell opposing actions by the pope. Frederick's first incursion into Italy occurred in 1155. While it did subdue some northern Italian city-states, the campaign exactly reversed Frederick's aims for relations with Adrian IV. Frederick helped the pope defeat the insurrectionist Arnold of Brescia, but before crowning him in 1155, Adrian forced the new emperor to do homage to the papacy.

Beginning in 1158, Frederick pursued further military expeditions into Italy. On one hand, varied efforts to bring the empire's rule to northern Italy had general success. Frederick's relations with the papacy, on the other hand, degenerated into protracted conflict. The subjection exacted by Adrian, and the papacy's continued insistence on deference, were resented deeply by Frederick. In 1159, Alexander III, an exceptionally strong figure, was elected pope. Erecting continual harassments, Frederick openly opposed Alexander's papal authority for seventeen years (1159–1177). Among other indignities, the emperor put forth various anti-popes, forcing Alexander to move repeatedly and live mainly in France in this time. After 1166, however, though he did install Paschal, his false pope, Frederick lost his army to plague, and he had fewer successes in Italy. Finally in 1176, the Lombard League defeated him in the battle of Legnano, and Frederick soon began to sue for peace with his enemies. Most significantly, in 1177, the emperor concluded the Treaty of Venice with Alexander III. Without requiring homage to the papacy, this declared Frederick's allegiance to Alexander III as the Church's sovereign ruler. Then also, in 1183, peace between the empire and the Lombard League was concluded in the Treaty of Constance. In Germany, Frederick dealt with a newly rebellious Henry the Lion by removing all his holdings. The 1180s also saw peaceful relations between the empire and Henry II of England, Philip II of France, and Manuel, the Byzantine emperor. In his last year, 1190, Frederick consented to become one of the Third Crusade's leaders. He died crossing the Saleph River during the initial part of this expedition.

Otto of Freising's *Gesta Frederici imperatoris* is a contemporary account of Frederick I and his time. Most other original materials on the emperor have been printed by the *Monumenta Germaniae Historica.* K. J. BRYER

FREDERICK III (THE PIOUS)
(1515–1576)
Elector of the Palatinate (a dynastic state in the Holy Roman Empire) who tried to suppress Lutheranism in favor of Calvinism in his realm

Although educated as a Roman Catholic, Frederick's marriage in 1537 to the devout Lutheran, Maria of Brandenburg, brought

him under the influence of the Reformation and in 1546 he made his public profession as a Lutheran. In 1557 he succeeded his father as duke of Simmern and two years later became elector of the Palatinate.

Under Frederick's predecessor, the Palatinate had tolerated Lutheranism, Philippists (followers of Philip Melanchthon, a humanist Lutheran reformer), and Calvinists. In the summer of 1559 the strict Lutherans came into conflict with the Philippists over the doctrine of Communion. After studying the theological issues involved, Frederick gradually moved to a Calvinist position. He appointed Calvinist theologians such as Olivianus, Ursinus, and Tremellius as professors of the University of Heidelberg, and began removing any Lutheran influences. The Heidelberg Catechism prepared by Ursinus and Olivianus introduced a standard Calvinist doctrine for the electorate.

Although both Lutherans and Roman Catholics appealed to the Augsburg Confession (a conciliatory document between Lutherans and Catholics following the religious wars in Germany), Frederick refused to change his policy. He died in 1576 leaving as heir his son Louis, a convinced Lutheran who sought to undo his father's reforms. W. S. REID

FREDERICK III (THE WISE)
(1463–1525)
A German ruling prince who defended Luther

Born at Torgau and educated by Augustinian monks, Frederick succeeded his father Ernst as the influential elector of Saxony in 1486. With his Renaissance leanings, he became a generous patron of scholarship and the arts. He became president of the Council of Regency from 1500, and was nominated successor to Emperor Maximilian. In 1502 he founded the University of Wittenberg, whose theological faculty the Protestant reformer Martin Luther joined in 1511.

In 1517 at Wittenberg, Luther posted the Ninety-five Theses, challenging papal indulgences (the sale of the forgiveness of sins) and other ecclesiastical abuses. Although Frederick did not openly confess Luther's doctrine, he chose to protect the young Augustinian monk against papal repercussions. When Luther was summoned to Rome in 1518, Frederick demanded that the proceedings take place instead at Augsburg. Moved by his fair and judicious nature (hence his title "the Wise"), he then refused to carry out Pope Leo X's bull of excommunication (1520). One of the two dissenters at the Diet of Worms (1521) that outlawed Luther, Frederick sheltered him at the fortified castle at Wartburg. Later, he winked at Luther's return to Wittenberg in 1522. Oddly, he had no personal dealings with Luther and only communicated through his chaplain and Luther's friend, George Spalatin. The reformer Philip Melanchthon eulogized Frederick as having furthered the gospel. G. BROMILEY

FREE, JOSEPH PAUL (1911–1974)
Archaeologist and biblical scholar; widely known for his contributions in the areas of biblical criticism, Christian apologetics, and archaeological research

Born in Cleveland and educated at Stony Brook, Princeton, and the Oriental Institute of the University of Chicago, Free taught at Wheaton College (Illinois) from 1935 to 1965. He initiated that school's Archaeological Studies Program and its International Studies Program. He also founded the Near East School of Archaeology in Jerusalem, the Near East Archaeological Society, and the society's journal, the *Bulletin*. Free ranks as one of the pioneers in the development of twentieth-century Holy Land tourism. His major archaeological work was the excavation of the biblical city of Dothan in nine campaigns between 1953 and 1964. He authored *Archaeology and Bible History*, a popular textbook on biblical archaeology, as well as numerous professional publications. J. E. JENNINGS

FRELINGHUYSEN, THEODORE JACOBUS (1691–1748)
Dutch Reformed minister

Born in Germany in 1691, the son of a Reformed pastor, Frelinghuysen held two brief pastorates in the Dutch Reformed Church in Holland before coming to America. He was a minister in the Dutch Reformed Church in the Raritan Valley, New Jersey, from 1720 to about 1747. Frelinghuysen was a forerunner of the Great Awakening, a religious revival which occurred in the American colonies from about 1725 to 1760.

Like the key figures of the Great Awakening, Frelinghuysen stressed the importance of conversion, accompanied by conviction of sin, repentance, and reliance on the Holy Spirit. He insisted on evidence of conversion as a requirement for admission to Communion. Some members of his denomination resented his exercise of church discipline. Despite that unpopularity he made an important contribution to the organization of the Dutch Reformed Church in America. He helped form an assembly that the governing body of Amsterdam took under its jurisdiction in 1747.

Frelinghuysen exercised a widespread influence, which continued in the middle colonies for some time after his death. Among those he inspired was Gilbert Tennent, an important Presbyterian missionary in New Jersey. D. C. MASTERS

FRITH, JOHN (1503–1533)
English reformer, scholar, and martyr

Frith received his bachelor's degree from King's College, Cambridge in 1525. While serving as a canon of Cardinal (Christ's Church) College, he actively preached Protestant doctrines. After a brief imprisonment, he was forced to flee. He escaped to Marburg (Germany) where he met Protestant reformer William Tyndale, whom Frith helped to translate the Bible.

In 1529 he returned to England, where he was arrested under a warrant issued by Catholic chancellor Sir Thomas More. In the Tower of London Frith wrote extensively and formulated his views rejecting the Roman Catholic doctrine of transubstantiation of Christ through the sacrament of the Eucharist. Thomas More attacked Frith's statements in a pamphlet to which Frith replied.

Finally Henry VIII ordered him to be tried for heresy. Frith was condemned and sentenced by the bishop of London to death by burning. Refusing to refute his writings, he died at the stake. W. S. REID

FROBEN, JOHN (1460–1527)
Swiss printer and publisher

Born at Hammelburg, Bavaria, Froben studied at Basel (Switzerland), where he established his first printing press in 1491. At first he collaborated with J. Petri and later with John Amerbach, eventually acquiring seven presses. After 1513 he worked closely with humanist scholar and reformer Desiderius Erasmus, who entrusted Froben with most of his work. In 1516 Froben produced Erasmus's Greek New Testament, and subsequently his editions of the church fathers. A revised edition of Erasmus's popular *Colloquies* (colloquial Latin satires on historical and contemporaneous personages) was dedicated in 1522 to Froben's son, Erasmus's godchild.

In his books—about 250 in number—Froben is said to have revolutionized the art of printing. He popularized the Roman type, experimented with smaller and cheaper books, and employed German painter Hans Holbein (the younger) as illustrator. Under his son Hieronymus and his grandson Ambrosius, Froben's company continued in business until the end of the sixteenth century. N. V. HOPE

FROUDE, RICHARD HURRELL (1803–1836)
English Tractarian leader

Born at Dartington, Devonshire, the elder son of a Church of England clergyman, Froude entered Oxford University in 1821. There he made friends with John Keble, his tutor, and John Henry Newman, a fellow student. Shortly after being ordained as an Anglican clergyman (in 1829), Froude showed symptoms of the tuberculosis that led to his early death.

Along with Keble and Newman, Froude became a leader in the Tractarian (or Ox-ford) movement, which began in 1833 as an attempt to recall the Church of England to its Catholic heritage through apostolic succession. Froude wrote three of the ninety tracts that Newman issued between 1833 and 1841 in order to publicize the movement.

Keble and Newman published Froude's *Remains* posthumously in 1838 and 1839, extracts from his personal journal, letters and sayings, as well as selected sermons. They revealed a marked distaste for the Protestant Reformation (which Froude described as "a limb badly set") and a dislike of the reformers, whom he "hated more and more." The *Remains* reveal Froude's pro-Catholic leanings—for example, his praise of clerical celibacy and his devotion to the Virgin Mary. These volumes may have attracted some Tractarian sympathizers to the Roman church, but they deepened suspicion of the whole Oxford movement among many Anglicans, who were still predominately Protestant in sympathy and outlook. N. V. HOPE

FRY, ELIZABETH (1780–1845)
English Quaker who initiated many social reform ministries

Fry was born in Norwich (England), the daughter of John and Catherine Gurney, devout Quakers. At eighteen Elizabeth experienced a great spiritual awakening during a sermon by an American Quaker, William Savery. For a time she lost interest in the Quaker meeting, only to later devote herself again towards developing her spiritual life. She wrote in her diary, "I know not what the mountain is I have to climb. I am to be a Quaker."

In 1800 she married Joseph Fry, a prominent and wealthy Quaker merchant. Elizabeth Fry received strong support from her husband as she began ministering to the needs of others. She gave medicine and clothes to the needy, encouraged parents to send their children to school, advocated Bible reading, and organized libraries in more than five hundred coastguard stations around Britain. She also established the

"Nursing Sisters of Devonshire Square," a pioneer English institution for training nurses. Fry also found time to raise her eleven children.

Her burning desire, however, was to improve prison life. Fry subsequently traveled beyond London to visit the prisons of Scotland and northern England. She published notes of her tour and gave testimony in the House of Commons. Her travels to the prisons of France and northern Europe in 1838 awakened the need for reform there. Her influence reached into Italy, Denmark, and Russia. Some of her writings are contained in her *Memoirs,* a two-volume work published by her daughters in 1847.
R. VONDERLACK

FULBERT (c. 960–1028)
Bishop of Chartres; educator

Born to a noble Italian family, Fulbert spent his early life in Rome. He studied under Gerbert, the future Pope Sylvester II, at Reims and Chartres. Among other prominent figures, Robert, France's future king, was a fellow student. In 990, Odo, bishop of Chartres, made Fulbert head of the Chartres Cathedral school. Under his leadership, the Chartres school became France's greatest seat of learning. Fulbert's encyclopedic knowledge and dynamism drew students from all over Europe. His pupils called him "venerable Socrates." While covering all fields of knowledge, Fulbert strove consistently to keep Chartres's program centered on biblical teachings. He opposed any rationalistic tendencies. Chartres was a leading site for advanced studies for many decades.

Fulbert became bishop of Chartres in 1007. Though he continued to teach, his remaining years were occupied with general church business. Fulbert distinguished himself as a leader nearly as much as a teacher. Drawing on his friendship with Robert, now king, he gained many French nobles' confidence. He soon was known for his political sagacity. His actions did much to keep peace during the period. In 1020, the Chartres Cathedral burned down. But that very year, the bishop began the process of rebuilding,

with large beautification plans. Due to Chartres's reputation, King Canute of England, Duke William of Aquitaine, and other monarchs extended significant help. Fulbert died long before its completion, but the rebuilt Chartres eventually was one of Europe's most magnificent cathedrals. An advocate of clergy and monastic reform, Fulbert especially stood against his fellow bishops' corruptions. Quite a few of his writings have been preserved. These consist mainly of two treatises and many letters and sermons. Including the enduring "Chorus Novae Jerusalem," many of Fulbert's hymns are also extant. K. J. BRYER

FULLER, ANDREW (1754–1815)
Founding father of the English Baptist Missionary Society; an advocate of evangelistic Calvinism

Born in Wicken, Cambridgeshire, Fuller joined the Soham Baptist Church at the age of sixteen. Even though he had had no formal training in theology, he was called to be its minister five years later. In 1783 he became the minister of Kettering Baptist Church, where he remained until his death.

Among the Baptists of his circle there was a strong tendency toward hyper-Calvinism (the belief that there should not be any invitation to salvation in the proclamation of the gospel, since God would surely call his elect). After much careful study of both the Scriptures and such authors as Jonathan Edwards, Fuller concluded that hyper-Calvinism was a false and erroneous system. Thus in 1785 he published his *The Gospel Worthy of All Acceptation or the Obligation of Men Fully to Credit and Cordially to Approve Whatever God Makes Known,* a book that helped to create the evangelistic and missionary spirit among British "Free" churches. Some of Fuller's colleagues, however, did not like this, and so the terms "Fullerism" and "duty-faith" were coined to express their estimation of his evangelistic Calvinism. On the other hand, William Carey (1761–1834) was much impressed by it and, after the formation of the Baptist Missionary Society in 1792, Carey became its first missionary and Fuller its first home director.

Fuller also took a major part in the formation of the new Baptist Union in 1813. Americans recognized Fuller's contributions and gave him D.D. degrees at both Princeton and Yale. His complete works were published in 1838 and have been reprinted several times. Fuller's example and thought are a constant inspiration to Baptists today. P. TOON

FULLER, CHARLES E. (1887–1968)
American radio evangelist and cofounder of Fuller Theological Seminary

In 1910 Charles E. Fuller graduated from Pomona College and, until his conversion, worked in the orange orchards of Southern California. After his conversion he studied for three years at the Bible Institute of Los Angeles, where he came under the influence of R. A. Torrey. From 1925 to 1932 Fuller was pastor of Calvary Church in Placentia (California). Prior to the establishment of the "Old Fashioned Revival Hour" (which was aired for over thirty years), he conducted two other radio broadcasts: "The Pilgrim Hour" and "Heart to Heart Talks."

The "Old Fashioned Revival Hour" originated from the Municipal Auditorium in Long Beach (California), where thousands gathered each Sunday to hear Dr. Fuller's preaching, choir music, and the pianist Rudy Attwood. Thousands of tourists visited these services each year, with hundreds of Navy servicemen coming to know Christ through these meetings. Fuller was also cofounder of Fuller Theological Seminary, named for his father. D. M. LAKE

FYFE, ROBERT ALEXANDER (1816–1878)
Canadian Baptist minister and educator

Fyfe was born on the seigneury of Laprairie near Montreal. In 1835 he joined the Baptist church at Laprairie and resolved to enter the Baptist ministry. He studied at three colleges, graduating from Newton Theological Seminary near Boston in 1842. He was ordained in 1842 at Brookline, Massachusetts. Between 1842 and 1857 he was pastor of various Baptist churches in Perth in Upper Canada, Toronto, and the United States (1851–1855). In 1843 and 1844 he had temporary charge of the Baptist College in Montreal. During his ministry in Upper Canada he participated in political controversies in which the Baptist church had an interest. He led the way in attacking the clergy reserves and Anglican control of King's College. He used a Baptist paper, the Brantford *Christian Messenger* as the vehicle for his opinions. Fyfe and a friend purchased the *Messenger* in 1859, and Fyfe served as its editor until 1863.

By 1857 Fyfe had decided to concentrate on the role of the Canadian Baptist Church in education. In the 1850s he was influential in persuading the Baptists of Upper Canada to modify their previous coolness to the idea of Baptist participation in education, either at the school or the university level. In a notable article entitled "A Proposal," printed in the *Christian Messenger* in 1855, he urged the Baptists to establish a theological seminary and secondary school. As a result, the Canadian Literary Institute was established at Woodstock in 1860 with Fyfe as its first principal. Owing largely to his energy and zeal, the Institute was able to survive its early difficulties. Fyfe remained as principal until his death at Woodstock. He was not only a pioneer in education, but also very influential in the Baptist church, helping to unite various Baptist groups in Ontario and Quebec. D. C. MASTERS

G

GABRIELI, ANDREA (c. 1520–1586)
Organist, composer, and teacher

Pupil at St. Mark's Cathedral in Venice under the great Flemish composer Adrian Willaert, Gabrieli was the first Italian to wrest leadership in his art from the Netherlanders who had dominated musical creativity in Italy during the first half of the sixteenth century. He excelled in organ as well as sacred and secular choral music. His harmony was innovative for his time. Among his students were his nephew Giovanni and the great German organist Leo Hassler. J. B. MACMILLAN

GABRIELI, GIOVANNI (1557–1612)
Italian composer and organist; nephew and pupil of Andrea Gabrieli

Giovanni Gabrieli became organist of St. Mark's Cathedral in Venice at age twenty-seven. He was one of the first to write choral works with separate and contrasting parts for instruments. His instrumental works, composed for festal occasions in St. Mark's, are still favored by brass ensembles. Many of his motets are for double and even triple chorus, with as many as fifteen separate voice parts. Michael Praetorius and Heinrich Schuetz came from Germany to study under him. J. B. MACMILLAN

GAEBELEIN, ARNO CLEMENS (1861–1945)
Evangelist, author, and publisher; specialized in Jewish evangelism and prophecy

Gaebelein was born in Thuringia (Germany) and came to the United States in 1879 to avoid military conscription. His formal education stopped at the German "gymnasium" (secondary school), but he marshalled a vigorous intellect to learn Greek, Hebrew, Arabic, Syrian, Persian, and several spoken tongues. Converted at age twelve, shortly after his arrival in the United States he underwent a "commitment" experience.

When Gaebelein was diverted from a missionary career in Java due to his wife's ill health, he turned to the evangelization of Jews. Pastorates in Baltimore, Hoboken (New Jersey), and New York City followed his ordination by the Methodist Episcopal Church in 1886. He founded the Hope of Israel movement and a Hebrew language magazine, *Tigweth Israel* (*The Hope of Israel Monthly*), in 1893. Writing in Hebrew script, Gaebelein personally produced most of the copy. Circulation climbed to five thousand as the magazine reached into Russia and Eastern Europe as well as Jewish enclaves in the United States.

Through James Brookes, Gaebelein was

brought into the Niagara Bible Conference movement. "The professing church has ignored . . . the study of unfulfilled prophecy," he wrote in 1930, and to an alleviation of that vacuum he directed the second major part of his career. He was a coeditor of the *Scofield Reference Bible,* a vice-resident of Stony Brook School (which his son, Frank, founded), and a lecturer at Dallas Theological Seminary. Gaebelein considered his greatest published work to be the *Annotated Bible,* a nine-volume, three-thousand-page survey of Scripture that took ten years to complete. M. FACKLER

GAIRDNER, W. H. TEMPLE
(1873–1928)
Missionary with the (Anglican) Church
Missionary Society to Muslims in Egypt

Gairdner was born at Ardrossan, Ayrshire (Scotland), son of Sir William Gairdner, who was a professor of medicine at Glasgow and later president of the Royal College of Physicians at Edinburgh. Educated at St. Ninian's and Trinity College, Oxford, the younger Gairdner became active in evangelical associations and activities, including the Student Volunteer Movement (SVM). At a summer conference in 1894 he came under the influence of the SVM chairman, John R. Mott. After a year as traveling secretary of the British College Christian Union, he was accepted by the Church Missionary Society for Egypt in 1897. After his arrival there, Gairdner was ordained an Anglican priest at St. Mark's, Alexandria. In 1902 he was married to Margaret Dundas Mitchell at Nazareth (Palestine), where she served at a girls' hostel.

In Cairo, Gairdner and his intimate friend, Douglas Thornton, were assigned to minister to students and educated Muslims. That work required great competence in Arabic and led them into literary work. Gairdner developed special rapport with Arab businessmen and the sheiks of al-Azhar, the foremost Islamic university in the world. This led him to serious apologetics. In 1905 he and his friend Thornton (died 1907) began publishing *Orient and Occident,* an Ara-

bic and English Christian journal. Gairdner's first book, *The Reproach of Islam* (1909), revealed his thorough understanding of Islam and Arabic literature.

Mott encouraged Gairdner to take a leave of absence in 1910 and 1911 to participate in the Edinburgh Missionary Conference and to write its popular report, *Echoes from Edinburgh.* Then he studied Islamics in Germany and with A. C. Macdonald at Hartford, Connecticut. Returning to Cairo, Gairdner began a study center for orientation of new missionaries that eventually grew into the School of Oriental Studies of the American University at Cairo. He was active in local inter-mission cooperation, such as the Nile Mission Press, and in international conferences on work among Muslims. He devoted his last years to literary work and to pastoring the (Anglican) Church of the Savior at Boulac (Egypt). P. BEAVER

GALERIUS, VALERIUS MAXIMIANUS
(died 311)
Roman emperor of the East, 305–311

Galerius came from Illyria, a rugged province south of the Danube River. An uneducated man of peasant stock, he rose to prominence by service in the army. In 293 Galerius and Constantius Chlorus were appointed to be caesars (junior emperors) under Diocletian in the East and Maximian in the West. Galerius ruthlessly fought the tribes attacking the Danube frontier, defeated the invading Persians, and crushed a revolt in North Africa.

Diocletian, concerned with the empire's stability, pursued policies of economic consolidation and religious tolerance. The reactionary, superstitious Galerius, however, insisted on suppressing Christian worship. Diocletian, appalled by such fanaticism, resigned in 305, and Galerius succeeded him as "augustus." Constantius, then emperor of the West, died in the following year leaving a power struggle between his son Constantine, Maximian's son Maxentius, and Galerius's appointee Severus. Galerius's position in the East, nevertheless, remained unchallenged.

The four edicts that Diocletian had issued against the church, beginning in 303, are said to have been suggested by Galerius. As augustus, Galerius intensified the persecution until 311 when, as he was dying, he issued his edict of toleration. C. HICKS

GALILEO GALILEI (1564–1642)
Mathematician, physicist, and astronomer

A native of Pisa, Galileo was educated in the monastery of Vallombrosa near Florence, then at the University of Pisa, where in 1589 he became a lecturer in mathematics. His employment of the method of empirical observation rather than deduction from abstract principles enabled him to make discoveries in mathematics and dynamics but earned for him the strong opposition of Aristotelian philosophers. In 1591 he withdrew from Pisa and the next year was given a professorship at Padua where he remained until 1610.

In the latter year he was appointed philosopher and mathematician to the Duke of Tuscany, Cosimo the Great, at Florence. There he developed an interest in astronomy. By using his telescope to study the heavens, he became convinced of the truth that the sun, not the earth, was the center of the universe (technically known as the Copernican heliocentric theory of the universe). This was an astounding discovery that has earned Galileo the title "the father of modern European science."

In 1616 he was condemned by the Inquisition for this heresy, but in 1624 he obtained permission from Rome to discuss both Ptolemaic and Copernican conceptions noncommittally. The book he published in 1632, *Dialogue Concerning the Two Principal Systems of the Universe*, resulted however in his being hailed before the Inquisition in 1633, compelled to recant his unorthodox astronomical views, and sentenced to life imprisonment. This sentence was suspended, but he remained under house arrest at Arcetri near Florence until his death.

In religion Galileo considered himself a good Roman Catholic, to whom "the Holy Scriptures cannot err" whenever their true meaning is understood. But he maintained that the Bible cannot and should not always be interpreted literally, and he asserted that when Scripture seems to contradict the conclusions reached by scientific investigation of the universe, "it becomes the office of wise expounders to labor till they find how to make those passages of Holy Writ concordant with these conclusions." For this reason he has been regarded by some as contributing to the growth and development of religious rationalism. N. V. HOPE

GALLA, PLACIDIA (c. 390–450)
Roman empress of the West; daughter of Theodosius I and Galla

Galla was abducted from Rome by invading Goth tribes in 410. Her short marriage to Visigoth ruler Ataulf ended with his assassination in 415. Galla's brother Honorius, then emperor, arranged for her return to Rome and subsequent marriage to his general Constantius (417). Widowed again in 421 and alienated from Honorius, she retired to Constantinople with her children Honoria and Valentinian III. When Honorius died (423), eastern emperor Theodosius II recognized Galla's young son as Honorius's successor. Galla then left Constantinople to act as regent, residing at Ravenna.

During her rule, she battled Attila the Hun on Rome's northern borders and suppressed heretical sects within the empire. She opposed Arian factions, supporting Leo, bishop of Rome, at the Robber Synod of Ephesus (449). Galla built several churches at Ravenna and the mausoleum where she was buried. H. W. HOUSE

GALLUS, JAKOB (1550–1591)
Composer of church music

Also known by his German name, Handl, Gallus was born in Reifniz, in what later became part of Yugoslavia. He was educated under Jesuit influence and was associated with Counter-Reformation. Prague, at that time the capital of the Hapsburg Empire, was his chief place of activity. He wrote sixteen masses and motets for the whole church year, many of his works showing daring harmonic novelty. On the other hand, some of his shorter pieces were of simple beauty. J. B. MACMILLAN

GARDINER, ALLEN FRANCIS (1794–1851)
Missionary pioneer in South America

Born into a godly English home, Gardiner became a naval officer, reaching the rank of captain. After his wife's death in 1834, he determined to become a missionary pioneer; as a sailor he had seen the plight of Indians in South America.

Gardiner went first to South Africa, where he founded a mission station at Port Natal. After remarrying, he took his wife and children to South America where he made investigatory journeys into Chile and neighboring Patagonia (an area in southern Argentina and southern Chile) in order to determine the need for missions there. Returning to England he tried to persuade the Church Missionary Society to send missionaries to Patagonia, but they refused. So in 1844 Gardiner formed the Patagonian Missionary Society and with one companion set out to start work among Indians in Patagonia. Those efforts, however, failed.

Undeterred he made further dangerous, investigatory journeys into Bolivia and Tierra del Fuego. He then tried to interest the Moravians and the Church of Scotland in missions in South America, but was again unsuccessful. Consequently, he sought to revive the Patagonian Missionary Society and, with a gift of one thousand pounds sterling from a Cheltenham lady, was able to do so. Gardiner led a new party to Tierra del Fuego arriving there in 1850. But before long he and his companions had all died. When news of the calamity reached England, others there took up the work. In 1854 a schooner named Allen Gardiner sailed from Bristol carrying missionaries and supplies. The new society thus begun, known as the (Anglican) South American Missionary Society, had as its primary aim

the reaching of Indian tribes with the gospel. Gardiner had provided the vision and impetus; others then carried out the work. P. TOON

GARDINER, STEPHEN (c. 1490–1555)
Roman Catholic lord chancellor and church leader who was influential in the affairs of three English monarchs

A graduate of Cambridge, Gardiner was master of Trinity Hall from 1525 to 1549. As secretary to Henry VIII (reigned 1509–1547), he negotiated the king's arbitrary divorce from Catherine of Aragon. Later, Gardiner was a member of the court that invalidated that marriage (1533). His appointment as bishop of Winchester (1531) was followed by the anti-Protestant "Six Articles" (1539), which made noncompliance with the Church of England doctrines punishable by death.

During the Protestant reign of Edward VI (king, 1547–1553), Gardiner was confined to the Tower of London for more than five years. Under Catholic queen Mary (reigned 1553–1558), Gardiner regained his bishopric, reversing his previous statements on the illegitimacy of Mary, Catherine of Aragon's daughter. When appointed lord chancellor, Gardiner renewed persecution of Protestants and supported Mary's severe treatment of Elizabeth, her half sister and pretender to the throne. H. F. VOS

GARRISON, WILLIAM LLOYD (1805–1879)
Radical editor of the Liberator, *who called slavery a "heinous crime in the sight of God" and campaigned for its abolition for most of his adult life*

Garrison was born in Newburyport, Massachusetts, and as a youngster acquired a strong moral conscience. At age thirteen he was apprenticed to a printer and was writing pseudonymous essays for the Newburyport *Herald* by seventeen.

In the mid-1820s Garrison came under the influence of Quaker evangelist Benjamin Lundy. He adopted Lundy's zeal for the antislavery issue, becoming editor of the "Genius of Universal Emancipation" in Baltimore in 1829. Two years later, however, he split with Lundy, calling for an immediate end to slavery instead of Lundy's gradual approach.

The *Liberator*, considered the fiercest anti-slavery voice in the pre–Civil War years, was first published on January 1, 1831. It never rose above three thousand subscribers, but for thirty-five years its consistent weekly campaign did much to stir the conscience of the American public. Garrison strongly opposed the solution to slavery suggested by some churchmen that Negroes be exported to Liberia. He founded the first antislavery society in 1832; six years later more than one thousand such societies dotted the north and middle west. Garrison's immoderate career included seven months in jail on a libel conviction, abuse and near-death at the hands of a Boston mob in 1835, and rifling of his publication from southern mail sacks with the approval of the Postmaster General.

Garrison called the United States Constitution "a covenant with death and an agreement with hell" because of its tolerance of slavery. He denounced churches for the same reason. Once criticized for conduct unbecoming a "Christian gentleman," Garrison replied: "Caution . . . prudence . . . judiciousness . . . I have come to hate those words. Sir, slavery will not be overthrown without excitement—a most tremendous excitement." M. FACKLER

GARSTANG, JOHN (1876–1956)
Professor of archaeology at Liverpool and writer on the ancient Middle East

From 1900 to 1908 Garstang conducted excavations in Egypt, Nubia, Asia Minor, and N. Syria. He worked in the Holy Land from 1919 to 1926 as the first director of the British Department of Antiquities. From 1930 to 1936 he undertook his best known work—the excavation of Jericho. His writings are a mine of information even though chronological findings at Jericho and Hazor had to be revised. In 1947 he became direc-

tor of the British Institute of Archaeology in Turkey. His best books are *Hittite Empire* (1929) and *Joshua, Judges* (1931).
A. H. POTTS

GAVAZZI, ALESSANDRO (1809–1889)
Italian nationalist and religious reformer

Born in Bologna, Gavazzi at the age of sixteen joined the Barnabites, a Roman Catholic order founded in 1530 especially for education and mission work. In due course he was ordained to the priesthood. Early in life he became disenchanted with papal temporal sovereignty as an obstacle to Italian political unification. He objected to papal primacy in the church as having no valid scriptural or historical foundation and as constituting a religious tyranny.

After holding a teaching position in Naples, Gavazzi became a public preacher in Leghorn and Piedmont. Because of his antipapal stand he incurred the hostility of the Jesuits, who had him confined to a convent. When Pope Pius IX succeeded Gregory XVI in 1846, Gavazzi at first enjoyed the new pope's favor. In 1848 he was sent as chaplain to the papal volunteers who fought for Italian nationalism against Austria. When the pope turned reactionary and left Rome, a republic was set up in that city. In the siege that followed, Gavazzi helped in setting up hospitals to treat the wounded. After Rome surrendered and the pope again was ruler, Gavazzi was sought by the police. He was sheltered by the American consul, under whose protection he left for Britain and the United States where his antipapal lectures drew large audiences. After years abroad Gavazzi returned to Italy in 1859 to support Giuseppe Garibaldi in his fight for Italian independence. In 1863 he founded a Free Italian church for which he worked the rest of his life to raise money. N. V. HOPE

GEDDES, JENNY (died c. 1661)
Scottish vegetable seller

A persistent but unverifiable story features Geddes as the instigator of a riot that broke out in St. Giles's Church, Edinburgh, against an official attempt to impose Laud's Liturgy on the Church of Scotland in 1637. The doughty lady is said to have thrown her stool at an officiating prelate, indignant that he should dare "say mass" in her hearing. A more reliable account (which does not, however, disprove the earlier story) places her in the High Street of Edinburgh, celebrating the Restoration of King Charles II in 1660. The riot with which her name is always now associated sparked off a revolution that soon spread through the greater part of Scotland and led to the reestablishment of Presbyterianism—instead of Episcopacy—as the national church polity. J. D. DOUGLAS

GEDDIE, JOHN (1815–1872)

Presbyterian missionary to the New Hebrides Islands

Born in Banff (Scotland), Geddie was brought as an infant to Nova Scotia. After ordination he educated his first pastorate in "the idea of mission" and formed a "missionary Society" with an annual overseas project. Soon other Presbyterian congregations followed his example. As a result, Geddie has been called "the father of foreign missions in the Presbyterian Church of Canada."

Geddie next encouraged his denomination to establish its own mission, at that time an unprecedented step in Canada. Eventually a mission was planned to go to western Polynesia. In the absence of any other volunteer, in 1847 Geddie himself agreed to go. About the same time he published a pamphlet, "The Universal Diffusion of the Gospel."

A missionary pioneer on the island of Aneityum (New Hebrides), Geddie mastered the local language, did translation work, and printed devotional and instructional aids. His efforts remarkably transformed the people on Aneityum. The journals he kept of his work represent an important primary source for the study of mid-nineteenth-century missions. Geddie died in Geelong (Australia).

Geddie's work was subsequently expanded by Presbyterians to Australia and New Zealand. An Aneityumese dictionary, an expansion of Geddie's original word list, was published by his colleague John Inglis in 1882. A. R. TIPPETT

GELASIUS I (died 496)

Pope, 492–496

Gelasius, probably a Roman citizen in Africa, became a dominant figure in Rome during the reign of Pope Felix III and served as draftsman for that pope's letters. He is best known for his letters defending the apostolic authority of the Roman see. He admonished the Eastern church for denying Rome the right to excommunicate those who believed Christ had only one nature (Monophysites) and the secular authorities for attempting to meddle in religious disputes. Gelasius insisted that there are two powers, "the consecrated authority of the bishops and the royal power." His implicit statement that ecclesiastical authority is superior to civil authority set the theoretical ground rules for church-state relations in the Middle Ages. He was the first pope to be called the Vicar of Christ (495). He defended the right of the laity to receive the wine, as well as the bread, of the Eucharist. He also wrote on Arianism, Pelagianism, and Manichaeism. C. WHITACRE

GENNADIUS OF MARSEILLES

(died 496)

Theologian, historical biographer, and Christian apologist

Gennadius wrote a continuation of late-fourth-century theologian Jerome's *Concerning Famous Men.* Gennadius's addition, which contains 101 articles about fifth-century church writers (including himself), primarily documents the books of those men rather than their lives.

Although he labeled late-fourth-century Christian moralist Pelagius a "heresiarch" (leader of a heretical group), he chided Augustine, bishop of Hippo, Pelagius's forceful opponent. Gennadius praised the works of two Semi-Pelagians, indicating his desire to avoid both Pelagian and Augustinian extremist views.

Other works by Gennadius, which have been lost, include *All Heresies*; books against contemporaneous theologians Nestorius and Eutyches; and translations of Greek devotional literature. He may also have written a book on church dogmas. C. HICKS

GEORGE, MARGRAVE OF BRANDEN-BURG-ANSBACH (1484–1543)
German noble who actively promoted the Protestant Reformation in Germany

Born at Ansbach, George belonged to the Franconia Hohenzollern ruling house. Through his mother he was related to the king of Bohemia and Hungary, whom he served as a soldier. By a grant and through negotiation he obtained Jagerndorf and most of upper Silesia. In 1523 he inherited Ansbach and later succeeded to Franconia.

George became interested in Protestantism after reformer Martin Luther's appearance at the Diet of Worms (1521). Thereafter he sought to establish evangelicalism in his dominions. He backed the Protestants at the Diets of Speyer (1526 and 1529). In 1530 he signed the Confession of Augsburg, containing the articles of evangelical faith presented to Emperor Charles V. Because of his religious zeal George was known as "the Pious." W. S. REID

GERBILLON, JEAN FRANÇOIS (1654–1707)
Jesuit missionary to China

A native of Verdun (France), Gerbillon completed his novitiate in the Society of Jesus at Nancy (1670). One of the first party of French Jesuits sent to China by Louis XIV, he arrived in Peking in 1687.

The Jesuits provided scholarly service at court and gained influence with the "literati" (scholars). Gerbillon won the favor of Emperor K'ang Hsi, tutoring him in geometry and philosophy and eight times accompanying him into Mongolia.

Gerbillon acted as interpreter and adviser to the embassy that negotiated the first Sino-Russian peace treaty (1689). Consequently, official permission was given to build churches. Gerbillon supervised the construction of the first Catholic church in Peking. He was head of the mission from 1700 to 1706, devoting his last three years to pastoral ministry. P. BEAVER

GERHARD, JOHANN (1582–1637)
German Lutheran theologian who was part of the so-called Trias Johannes, *which included scholars Johann Major and Johann Himmel*

Born at Quedlinburg in Halle, Gerhard studied at Wittenberg, Jena, and Marburg. In 1616 he returned to Jena as professor and worked closely with Major and Himmel. German princes often entrusted him with political and ecclesiastical missions. Gerhard preferred, however, his theological scholarship. He wrote an apologetic of evangelicalism, *Confessio Catholica* (1634–1637), and a treatise on Lutheran theology, *Loci Communes Theologici* (1610–1622). His widely read *Sacred Meditations* (1606) were later translated into English and most European languages. N. HILLYER

GERHARDT, PAUL (1607–1676)
German Lutheran hymn writer

Born at Gräfenhainichen in Saxony, Gerhardt studied at Wittenberg, then taught in Berlin. Not until 1651 did he become a pastor, serving at the Lutheran church at Mittenwalde. Six years later he moved to St. Nicolas Church, Berlin, where he won a great following as a preacher. In 1666 he was banished for refusing to submit to the edicts of the Elector of Brandenburg, Friedrich Wilhelm I. which restricted theological debate between Lutherans and Calvinists in an effort to unite Lutheran and Reformed churches. From 1668 until his death he was archdeacon of Lubben.

Combining deep faith with fine poetry, Gerhardt ranks second only to Luther among German hymn writers. He wrote 133 hymns, unique in that age of baroque for their simple sincerity. Some forty are still sung in Germany. While Luther's hymns are mainly confessional, Gerhardt's are devotional. Among those still popular in English is "Jesus, Thy Boundless Love to Me" (translated by John Wesley). "O Sacred Head, Now Wounded" (translated by J. W. Alexander) was based on a Latin hymn ascribed to Bernard of Clairvaux, whose writings greatly influenced Gerhardt. N. HILLYER

GERMANUS (c. 496–576)

Bishop of Paris, 555–576

Born at Autun (central France), Germanus was an ordained priest by 530. Soon he was also chosen as abbot of Autun's St. Symphorian monastery. Much concerned for the poor, he became known for his open-handed benevolence. In 555, Germanus was appointed bishop of Paris. For the rest of his years, he was active in conciliar work and other broad church matters. He was a leading participant in the Council of Paris III (557), Tours II (566), and Paris IV (573).

Germanus faced many problems involving his era's Frankish kings, but with many pains, he gained extensive influence over Childebert, son of Clovis. Childebert started constructing a church building dedicated to Germanus. This ultimately became the famed St. Germaine-des-Pres in Paris. Now greatly damaged, it has held Germanus's remains through the centuries. There is a contemporary life of the bishop by Venantius Fortunatus. However, nothing of his own writing remains. K. J. BRYER

GERSON, JEAN CHARLIER DE (1363–1429)

Chancellor of the University of Paris; his life spanned the turbulent "Western Schism" and much of the Hundred Years' War between France and England

Gerson left his home near Rethel in Champagne to study theology in Paris and become a priest. Against the war, he zealously advocated the use of peaceful political means. Against the schism, he stalwartly labored to restore church unity. Along with his teacher Cardinal Pierre d'Ailly, Gerson

helped begin the conciliar movement to bring reform through church councils.

Gerson was a prominent member of the Council of Constance (1415–1417), which resolved the "Western Schism" by deposing the two schismatic popes. There he strongly advocated a council's supremacy over popes, although he acquiesced in legitimate authority. Furthermore, he attempted to maintain doctrinal orthodoxy by suppressing the reformer John Huss. Many of his opinions voiced at Constance were unpopular with those in power, so he was not able to return to Paris after the council. Although he retained his title as chancellor, he spent the last decade of his life with his brother at Lyon, ceaselessly writing and preaching.

Gerson, a reputable theologian and orator, delivered countless sermons. Interested in effective teaching and pastoral care, he often preached in the French vernacular (instead of Latin). His extant writings include Latin works on church law, politics, theology, and mysticism. He also wrote poetry, but strongly criticized the moral excesses of the new humanist literary movement emanating from Italy. Gerson was influenced by the philosopher Ockham's "nominalism" (which held that one perceived God only through faith). He never completely abandoned Aristotelian realism, however. Significant as he was for his era, Gerson has been reprehended for condoning the burning of John Huss. A. CABANISS

GERTRUDE THE GREAT (1256–c. 1302)

German mystic and writer who helped start the devotion to the Sacred Heart of Jesus

Gertrude entered a Benedictine convent at Helfta in Thuringia (Germany) at the age of five. She had her first mystical experience when she was twenty-five, and thereafter wrote extensively of her visions.

She is principally remembered for three books: *Spiritual Exercises, Ambassador of Divine Piety,* and *Prayers of Gertrude.* The latter was written by someone in the seventeenth century. Only the second of the five-volume *Ambassador,* which describes her mystical experiences, was written entirely by her.

The other books, which record her actions and her thoughts on the soul's relationship to God, the feasts of the church, and the deaths of friends, were written from her notes. Gertrude has been associated with another mystic, Mechthild of Hackeborn, and has been confused with a contemporaneous abbess, Gertrude of Hackeborn (1232–1292). C. HICKS

GEYMONAT, PAOLO (1827–1907)

Waldensian scholar, evangelist, and apostle of Protestant unity in Italy

Born at Villar Pellici, west of Turin (Italy), Geymonat studied theology at the École de l'Oratoire in Geneva (Switzerland). He was ordained to the Waldensian ministry in 1850. Calvinistic in theology but deeply influenced by the Swiss evangelical revival of the early nineteenth century, Geymonat labored zealously, despite opposition, as a Protestant evangelist in Rome, Florence, Turin, and Genoa.

In 1855 Geymonat was appointed professor of theology at the newly established Waldensian seminary, located first at Torre Pellice and from 1860 at Florence. There he remained until 1902, when he resigned to devote himself to evangelism and the pastoral ministry. He founded a new congregation at Florence, of which he remained pastor until his death. Realizing the urgent need for Protestant solidarity in predominantly Roman Catholic Italy, Geymonat sought strenuously but unsuccessfully to bring about unity among the divided Italian Protestant churches. N. V. HOPE

GIBBON, EDWARD (1737–1794)

English historian

Gibbon was born at Putney, Surrey. While a student at Westminster, he read history voraciously, but in 1749 left because of poor health. After a series of indifferent tutors, he entered Magdalen College, Oxford, in 1752. He was soon expelled for espousing Roman Catholicism. (He later became cynical of Christian beliefs.) Sent to study under a Calvinist minister in Lausanne (Switzer-

land), he received excellent instruction, reading Latin classics, philosophers Locke and Grotius, and French writers Montesquieu and Pascal.

In 1764 he visited Rome, where the ancient ruins inspired him to write a history of antiquity. The seven-volume *Decline and Fall of the Roman Empire* (published, 1776–1788), based on intensive research of original sources, is a monumental study of the late Roman Empire and early church history. Gibbon concluded that the rapid spread of Christianity was primarily due to the strict morality, discipline, and courageous martyrdom of the early church members. Gibbon, however, ridiculed the Christians' belief in the supernatural and derided medieval Christianity as anti-intellectual. N. HILLYER

GIBBONS, JAMES (1834–1921)

Archbishop of Baltimore; leading Roman Catholic "Americanist" of the late nineteenth century

Faced with both internal and external difficulties, Gibbons tried to bring Roman Catholic practice into mainstream American life without forsaking traditional Catholic teaching. As archbishop of the prominent Baltimore archdiocese, and after 1886 as a cardinal, Gibbons was known for his liberal views on the church-state issue. Unlike traditionalists, he thought Roman Catholics could flourish in a society without official state support.

Since Gibbons's family felt the hardship of being immigrants from Ireland, he spent much of his career working to assimilate the millions of Roman Catholic immigrants who entered the United States after the Civil War. Much of his effort was spent rebutting virulent anti-Catholicism and opposition to foreigners. His support of prohibition and cooperation with Protestants earned him the scorn of conservatives. His work *The Faith of Our Fathers* (1877) presented traditional Roman Catholic doctrine for non-Catholic readers. The Catholic University of America in Washington owes its establishment to Gibbons. M. A. NOLL

GIBBONS, ORLANDO (1583–1625)
English composer and organist

Much of Gibbons's career was spent as organist in the chapel of King James I. The last of the great "Elizabethan" school of composers, Gibbons was the first to write anthems with exclusively English texts. His eight-part unaccompanied "Hosanna to the Son of David" is one of the great works in English church music. He also wrote musical settings of the English cathedral service and of the prayerbook responses. Some of the tunes he wrote for George Wither's *Hymnes and Songs of the Church* have been appreciated only in recent years.

Gibbons was also an excellent composer of instrumental and secular vocal music. "The Silver Swan" is one of the most beautiful of all English part-songs. He died suddenly of a stroke in Canterbury, where he had accompanied King Charles I en route to welcome his French bride, Henrietta Maria. J. B. MACMILLAN

GILL, JOHN (1697–1771)
English Baptist theologian

Born to working-class parents in Kettering, Northamptonshire, Gill was educated at the local grammar school. He never attended college or university but learned Greek, Hebrew, and Latin with the help of local Nonconformist ministers. After preaching locally he was called to the pastorate of the Calvinist Baptist church which met at Horsleydown, Southwark, in 1719. Here he remained as pastor until his death. Being near London he was also in demand as a lecturer in various centers.

Many of his books were replies to attacks on high or hyper-Calvinism, which he held. In defense of the doctrine of eternal justification he wrote, *The Doctrine of God's Everlasting Love to His Elect* (1732). Against John Wesley he wrote, *The Doctrine of Predestination Stated and Set in Scripture-Light* (1752). His massive *The Case of God and Truth* (four volumes) was meant to answer Arminian views of divine election. His great *Body of Divinity* (1770), published at the end of his life and often reprinted, was based on the sermons he preached. They were heavily doctrinal in content.

The famous book of Andrew Fuller, *Gospel Worthy of All Acceptation* (1785), which led to a renewal of Baptist churches, was aimed at the denial of that arid Calvinism that Gill and others bequeathed to the Calvinist Baptist Church of England. Yet of Gill, Augustus Toplady wrote, "While true religion and sound learning have a single friend in the British Empire, the works and name of Gill will be precious and revered." P. TOON

GILLESPIE, GEORGE (1613–1649)
Scottish minister

Son of a Kirkcaldy pastor, Gillespie was educated at St. Andrews. He was a strong opponent of the Episcopal system of church government. When it was swept away by the National Covenant of 1638, Gillespie was a chief architect of the newly restored Presbyterianism, ministering at churches in Fife and Edinburgh. He was the youngest commissioner at the Westminster Assembly called to advise Parliament on matters of church government and doctrine (from 1643–1649). By his debating and writing skills Gillespie exercised an influence out of all proportion to his years. His chief book, *Aaron's Rod Blossoming* (1646), was hailed as a masterpiece in its closely knit argument against state influence in church affairs.

Always frail, Gillespie died in Kirkcaldy before his thirty-sixth birthday. "The time that I had in the exercise of the ministry," he said, "is but a moment." "Yes," replied a friend, "but your moment has exceeded the grey heads of others." Gillespie's works encouraged the Covenanters during the times of persecution that followed soon after his death. J. D. DOUGLAS

GILLESPIE, THOMAS (1708–1774)
Scottish minister; founder of the "Relief" Church

Born near Edinburgh and influenced toward the ministry by Thomas Boston, Gillespie was educated at Edinburgh University and at Philip Doddridge's academy in Northampton. Ordained in England in 1741, he became minister of rural Carnock in Fife.

A warm evangelical, Gillespie opposed state interference in church matters, advocating the congregation's right to elect its own minister. He declined to participate in the induction at Inverkeithing of a minister not so elected but "imposed" upon the people. For this he was deposed from the Church of Scotland ministry in 1752. His supporters built him a church in Dunfermline, and in 1761 two other ejected ministers joined him to form an independent presbytery "for relief of Christians oppressed in their Christian privileges." He nonetheless retained an affection for the Church of Scotland and before his death advised his congregation to return to it. J. D. DOUGLAS

GILMOUR, JAMES (1843–1891)
Scottish missionary

Born near Glasgow, Gilmour was educated at the university there and at Congregationalist colleges. After ordination, he left in 1870 for China with the London Missionary Society. (The diary he kept thereafter until his death shows how high anti-missionary feeling was then running in Peking.) By living in a tent among the nomadic Mongolians, he learned their language and lifestyle and thus developed a special ministry among them.

Apart from an eleven-year marriage (his wife died on the field), Gilmour never had a regular missionary colleague. Experiencing loneliness and extreme austerity, he lived for a time on less than five cents a day, traveling great distances in the desert on foot to save the expense of a camel.

Gilmour had two furloughs: after the first his *Among the Mongols* (1883) was published—a work that some have compared to *Robinson Crusoe*. The lack of response to the gospel in predominantly Buddhist areas would have overwhelmed a less dedicated man. His diary for 1886 tells the story: "preached to 24,000 people, treated more than 5,700 patients, distributed 10,000

books and tracts . . . and out of all this there are only two men who have openly confessed Christ." His last six years were spent among the more settled farmers of eastern Mongolia. J. D. DOUGLAS

GILPIN, BERNARD (1517–1583)
English rector and reformer during the turbulent period of the Church of England's establishment

Born in Westmoreland, Gilpin attended Oxford University, where he was attracted by the humanist writings of Dutch reformer Erasmus. After ordination, he became a fellow at Queens College, Oxford, and later at Christ College, founded by Cardinal Wolsey. Through debates with the Protestant professor Peter Martyr, Gilpin began to move toward evangelical theology.

After studying abroad at Louvain, Antwerp, and Paris, Gilpin moved to northern England where he became rector of Houghton-le-Spring. During Mary's (Roman Catholic) reign (1553–1558), Gilpin began to preach reformed doctrine in his own parish and in surrounding counties. His preaching and work with the poor earned him the title "apostle of the North." Gilpin's reformed views were reported to church officials and, in spite of his bishop's protection, he was called to London. Before he could obey the summons Mary died and her more tolerant sister Elizabeth became queen. Although Gilpin found Elizabeth's settlement of religion theologically aberrant, he reluctantly accepted it, at the same time refusing royal offers of benefices. He continued his itinerant ministry and clerical reform work, which won him the support of the Puritan groups. P. TOON

GILSON, ETIENNE (1884–1978)
Roman Catholic philosopher and scholar

Born in Paris, Gilson pursued advanced studies at the Sorbonne and College de France. In 1913, he began his lifelong work of university teaching. As professor of philosophy, he taught at the University of Lille (1913–1918), University of Strassburg

(1919–1920), University of Paris (1921–1932), and College de France (1931–1951). He also lectured at Harvard University (1926–1928). Gilson's specialty was medieval and Scholastic thought. Over the years, he produced detailed studies on Augustine, Bernard, Francis of Assisi, Aquinas, Bonaventure, and John Duns Scotus. For these figures and others, Gilson was one of the twentieth century's major interpreters. He was an important expositor also of Descartes. Beside his individual studies, Gilson wrote superbly on medieval philosophy and life as a whole.

Gilson was one of the founders of the Pontifical Institute of Mediaeval Studies, Toronto, Canada. From its beginnings in 1929, this has enjoyed world renown as a leading medieval research facility. Gilson served as one of its directors from 1929 until his death. After 1951, following retirement from the College de France, Gilson taught regularly at the Institute. Gilson was also a founder of *Archives d'histoire doctrinale et litteraire du moyen age,* a leading journal for intensive and original medieval research. Among many honors, Gilson gave the Gifford Lectures of 1932. These were reproduced as his well-known work *L'Esprit de la philosophie medievale.* Gilson was a major contemporary figure in the Thomist movement. This came partly from his Catholic adherence and twentieth-century Catholicism's dogmatic focus on Aquinas. More importantly, along with d'Arcy, Mercier, Marechal, Maritain, and many others, Gilson participated in Thomism's twentieth-century philosophic revival. Even for the modern world, he saw Thomism as a worthy, fruitful system of philosophy. Gilson's last writings gave expression to his broad knowledge of the fine arts. K. J. BRYER

GIOTTO DI BONDONE (c. 1266–1337)
Italian painter and architect known for his naturalistic approach to religious subject matter

Giotto introduced a method of painting that relied fully on careful observation of nature. This approach led him to a new fidelity to the world of sight. Giotto was more than an imitator of nature; he distilled and revealed fundamental visible order. This new outward vision replaced the medieval inward vision. His figures became solid, weighty bodies within a somewhat illusionistic three-dimensional space. Giotto established painting as a major art for the next seven hundred years. Applauded in his own day, his reputation has never faltered. He continues to be honored as the father of Western pictorial painting.

Primarily, Giotto was a muralist. His fresco cycle in the Arena Chapel at Padua (1305–1306) displays his work at its finest. These frescoes, considered the peak of Giotto's humanistic art, are dramatic moments in the life of Christ and Mary, his mother. He complemented this with the court of heaven over the choir and with the Last Judgment on the entrance wall. In the last years of Giotto's life he was honored by his native city of Florence in being appointed director of its major art activities. Of note was his design of the cathedral bell tower in Florence. A. STEFFLER

GLADDEN, WASHINGTON (1836–1918)
American advocate of the social gospel

An ordained Congregational minister, Gladden served lengthy pastorates in Springfield, Massachusetts, and Columbus, Ohio. He also lectured widely and authored more than thirty-five books. Theologically, Gladden was in the vanguard of liberalism. In such works as *Who Wrote the Bible?* (1891) he adopted the newer evolutionary views of Christian origins and human potential.

A tireless champion of social reform, especially in the economic sphere, Gladden argued against exploitation of industrial workers and for unions' rights and industrial arbitration. He once urged his denomination to refuse a gift from the Standard Oil Company as tainted money. More than most of the evangelicals of his time, Gladden preserved the social activism that had characterized nineteenth-century American Christianity in general. He did not, however, preserve its orthodox theology.

Gladden also wrote hymns, including "O Master, Let Me Walk with Thee." M. A. NOLL

GLADSTONE, WILLIAM EWART
(1809–1898)
British Prime Minister who had strong
Christian convictions

Born into an evangelical Liverpool family, Gladstone attended Eton School and Christ Church, Oxford, before entering Parliament in 1832 as a Conservative. His religious views were decidedly High Church and he was friendly with leaders of the Oxford or Tractarian movement. His first major publication, *The State in Its Relation with the Church* (1838), defended the "establishment" of the Church of England. Two years later he openly showed his commitment to High Church principles in his *Church Principles Considered in Their Results.* Though he believed in a High Church view of apostolic succession, he always opposed Roman Catholicism. He viewed the Tractarian movement as a fulfillment of Wesley's evangelical movement.

Gladstone's career in Parliament, though checkered in the 1840s, reached its heights in 1867, when he became leader of the Liberal party. Later, as prime minister, he saw through the House of Commons the bill to disestablish the Church of England in Ireland (which he confessed involved for him a change of mind). He was also responsible for other legislation of a liberalizing kind, for example, the abolition of compulsory church taxes and the removal of religious tests for entering a university.

Gladstone frequently attended church and took Holy Communion weekly. Generous in his philanthropy and rightly regarded as a Christian statesman, he also had a missionary vision. The Anglican Church overseas benefited in various ways from his help. P. TOON

GLAS, JOHN (1695–1773)
Founder of the Glasites, a splinter group
from the Reformed Church of Scotland

Glas was educated at St. Andrews and Edinburgh, and in 1719 became a minister in Tealing near Dundee. In his parish, he introduced the practice of monthly Communion and stressed the concept of the spiritual nature of Christ's kingdom.

His *Testimony of the King of Martyrs* (1728) brought him before the Scottish ecclesiastical courts. Glas argued three points: (1) a national church had no New Testament basis, (2) civil officials had no right to prosecute people as heretics, and (3) the two Scottish covenants (National, 1638, and Solemn League, 1643,) lacked biblical support. Glas opposed "founding the Church . . . upon any act of Parliament, or covenant, formed by the wisdom of man." Deposed for heresy, Glas ministered to an independent group first in Dundee, then from 1733 in Perth, where the Glasites' first meeting house was set up.

Faith to Glas was an intellectual asset, and he held that Scripture did not authorize missionary tasks. The Glasites followed a strict discipline of dietary laws, caring for the poor, footwashing, giving the kiss of peace, and keeping the "love feast" followed by Communion.

A genial man, Glas remained remarkably serene in the face of trial. Neither he nor his wife regretted leaving the national church for conscience' sake despite subsequent hardships for their family of fifteen. Leadership of the Glasites gradually passed to his son-in-law, Robert Sandeman.
J. D. DOUGLAS

GLEGG, ALEXANDER LINDSAY
(1882–1975)
British lay evangelist

Born in London of Scottish parents, Glegg was converted at a Keswick Convention in 1905, shortly after graduating in electrical engineering. He continued his business career, but spent all his free time in mission work among London's slum dwellers. From that base he traveled all over the British Isles, being used by God to bring thousands into his kingdom. University students and businessmen, laborers and holiday makers all responded to his fresh and lively presentation of the gospel at a convention center he founded at Filey (England). He once even made an appeal for decisions during a sermon in Westminster Abbey.

Glegg was a great encourager of young evangelists. He not only advised them to play golf for their spiritual good, but in a practical way made it possible by his unobtrusive generosity. Probably Britain's best-known evangelist of the twentieth century, he was preaching until just before the end of his life. J. D. DOUGLAS

GODET, FRÉDÉRIC LOUIS (1812–1900)
Swiss Protestant theologian and New Testament scholar

Born at Neuchatel, and educated there and at Bonn and Berlin, Godet served from 1838 to 1844 as tutor to Crown Prince (later King) Frederick Wilhelm III of Prussia. He served as supply preacher in the Val-de-Ruy from 1844 to 1851, and as pastor at Neuchatel from 1851 to 1866. Between 1851 and 1873 he was also professor of exegetical and critical theology in Neuchatel. From 1873 to 1887 he was professor of New Testament exegesis at the newly established Free Evangelical Faculty, which he helped to found.

Godet did much to interpret German theological thought to French-speaking Protestants, and the English translations of his works made him influential in international New Testament scholarship. His conservative viewpoint in New Testament interpretation is clearly expressed in his critical commentaries (John, 1864–1865; Luke, 1871; Romans, 1879–1880; 1 Corinthians, 1886). N. V. HOPE

GOETHE, JOHANN WOLFGANG VON (1749–1832)
Poet, dramatist, scientist, and philosopher; leader of the German intellectual renaissance of the late eighteenth century

Born at Frankfort am Main, Goethe was the son of well-to-do parents with intellectual interest. Goethe received his early schooling at home, with a strong emphasis on languages—Greek, Latin, Hebrew, English, French, and Italian. He also took lessons in music and played the piano and the flute. His first extant poem was written at the age of eight; on his thirteenth birthday he presented his father with a volume of his own poems. He studied law, against his will at the University of Leipzig; five years later, he studied law and medicine at the University of Strassburg. Between his enrollment at the two universities he recuperated at home from a serious illness during the winter of 1768 and all of 1769. While at home he came under the influence of a pietist friend of his mother's, and apparently underwent a deeply personal religious experience which led him into pietism.

At Strassburg he met Johann Gottfried von Herder (1744–1803), the theologian and literary critic who influenced Goethe in becoming a leader of the Sturm und Drang (Storm and Stress) movement, a trend away from restrictions of Classical and French influence on literature toward the intuitive and emotional. The spirit of this movement dominates *The Sorrows of Young Werther* (1774), a sentimental novel, inspired in part by one of his many turbulent love affairs.

In 1775 he accepted an invitation to visit the court of the young Duke of Weimar and, except for an extended journey to Italy a decade later, stayed there the rest of his life, filling various posts in the Weimar government. Here a close friendship with Friedrich von Schiller (1775–1854) developed, and here he conducted significant scientific experiments and published a steady stream of books of the highest order and in a variety of forms. After celebrating in lyrics many of his ardent loves, in 1806 he married Christiane Vulpius, whom he had loved for many years.

In later life Goethe became a generous patron of younger writers, including Byron and Carlisle. In 1790 he published the first version of his life work as *Faust, a Fragment*, but Part I of the completed *Faust* did not appear until 1808, while Part II was finished and published only a few months before Goethe's death. This dramatic poem, which shows Goethe's mental, spiritual, and literary questioning and development from youth to old age, is the eternal saga of man's struggle in his quest for fulfillment and complete joy in his pursuit of the "consummate moment." Disenchanted in turn by knowledge, power, and sensual pleasure, Faust is truly happy when he becomes engaged in a huge project, draining a pestilential swamp, and in a moment of vision sees the community of free people who will flourish on the reclaimed land.

Goethe was buried by the side of his patron, Duke Karl August, and his friend Schiller, in a local mausoleum at Weimar.

E. B. BATSON

GOFORTH, JONATHAN (1859–1936)
Canadian missionary to China

Goforth's conversion at the age of eighteen was simple but complete. For a time he considered becoming a lawyer or a politician, but after reading the *Memoirs of Robert Murray M'Cheyne* he decided to enter full-time Christian service. He was ordained to the Presbyterian ministry in 1886. His call to foreign missions came through an address by George Leslie Mackay, Canadian Presbyterian missionary to Formosa, and the reading of Hudson Taylor's *China's Spiritual Needs and Claims*.

Goforth and his wife, Rosalind, sailed for China in 1887, settling in the province of Honan, where they laid the foundations of the Canadian Presbyterian Mission in central China. Early in his ministry he learned the secret of spiritual power: his favorite text was "Not by might, nor by power, but by my spirit, saith the Lord of hosts" (Zech. 4:6). On a visit to Korea he saw firsthand the results of the mighty 1907 revival there. Carrying members of that revival back to China, he held revival meetings throughout the country. He later recorded those efforts in his book, *By My Spirit*.

When nearly seventy Goforth opened a new field in Manchuria. In one short term he won thousands to Christ and trained some seventy evangelists. Even after becoming suddenly blind, he stayed on for another two or three years. Finally, ill health forced him home at seventy-four years of age.

Upon his return to Canada Goforth was in great demand as a conference and missionary speaker. In eighteen months he spoke at 481 meetings, his last conference being at Ben Lippin in North Carolina. His last Sunday he spoke four times. Three days later he died.

During their service in China the Goforths experienced frequent tribulation. Five of their eleven children died in childhood. Never robust, Goforth suffered from colds, typhoid fever, malaria, jaundice, and pneumonia. On one occasion he had twenty-five carbuncles. During 1900 he and his family narrowly escaped death at the hands of the Boxers. To his dying day he carried the scars inflicted by the Boxers' swords. H. KANE

GOGARTEN, FRIEDRICH (1887–1967)
German Lutheran theologian

Gogarten was born in Dortmund, Germany, and is known mainly as one of a small group of German Protestant theologians allied with Karl Barth. After serving as a pastor in Thuringia, Gogarten was professor of theology at the University of Jena (1927–1933) and later in the University of Göttingen (1935–1953).

Immediately after World War I, Gogarten became one of those creative thinkers (such as Emil Brunner, Eduard Thurneysen, and Rudolf Bultmann) who labored with Barth in publishing the widely read periodical, *Zwischen den Zeiten* (*Between the Times*). But when Barth launched his attack on natural theology, Gogarten and Brunner parted company with the Swiss theologian.

In reaction to Friedrich Schleiermacher's idealistic liberalism (faith is a feeling of absolute dependence), Gogarten adopted the existentialist philosophy of Søren Kierkegaard. As an authority on Martin Luther's theology, he maintained that Luther had intended an existential form of Christianity—not a mere system of truths but a free way of life. He argued that the Reformers had lost Luther's emphasis through interpreting history as created and governed by a power outside human control. Gogarten believed Luther had taught that people create history rather than simply interpret it. The only way to understand history, said Gogarten, is to participate in it. God has actually entrusted the world to human hands. In accepting such responsibility, a person overcomes the subject/object distinction and becomes able to choose the course of his or her own historical existence "under the Word of God which addresses man in Christ." He claimed that the apostle Paul promoted that idea in Galatians.

Gogarten taught that faith is not established by observing the objective events of the past, even though they are recorded in Scripture. Rather, one obtains faith through experiencing one's own existence by participating in history. Gogarten said such ideas were rightly drawn from Luther's doctrine of "faith alone."

Gogarten's writings include *I Believe in the Triune God* (1926), *Political Ethics* (1932), *The Church and the World* (1948), *Demythologizing and History* (1953, 1955), and *Man between God and the World* (1956).

L. A. KALLAND

GOMAR (GOMARUS), FRANCES (1563–1641)
Dutch Calvinist theologian

Born at Bruges, Gomar studied at Strassburg under Johannes Sturm and at Neustadt-on-Hardt under Girolamo Zanchius, and also at Oxford and Cambridge Universities, taking his doctorate at Heidelberg in 1593. Between 1587 and 1593 he was pastor of the Dutch community at Frankfurt am Main, and in 1594 was appointed professor of theology at Leyden University. There he emerged as a strong defender of rigid Calvinistic orthodoxy and engaged in controversy concerning predestination with Jacob Arminius (1560–1609) after the latter joined the Leyden faculty in 1603. On Arminius's death in 1609, Conrad Vorstius, an Arminian, was appointed as his successor—whereupon Gomar left the university. From 1614 to 1618 he taught at the French Huguenot seminary of Saumur, and from 1618 to his death was a professor at Groningen. Gomar was a delegate to the Synod of Dort (1618–1619), and he played a prominent part in that Synod's condemnation of Arminianism in its definitions of election and grace. N. V. HOPE

GOODE, WILLIAM (1801–1868)
Anglican evangelical theologian

Goode was the son of a well-known evangelical preacher by the same name. After study at St. Paul's School, London, and Trinity College, Cambridge, the younger Goode in 1835 became rector of St. Antholin Church, Watling Street, London. In 1849 he moved to Allhallows the Great, Thames Street, and then in 1856 to St. Margaret's, Lothbury, both in London. In 1860 he was appointed by the prime minister, Lord Palmerston, as dean of the Ripon Cathedral.

Goode was the leading evangelical theologian in the Church of England from 1834 until his death. The title of his books reflect the major theological concerns of evangelicals of that period. His *Modern Claims to the Extraordinary Gifts of the Spirit* (1834) attempted to prove as false the claims that Edward Irving (1792–1834) and others were making in support of speaking in tongues. Later, during a long and bitter controversy with the Tractarians, Goode wrote several books and many articles and pamphlets. *The Divine Rule of Faith and Practice* (1842) was a lengthy defense of the view that the early church fathers held the authority of Scripture to be primary. *Tract XC Historically Refuted* (1845) discussed J. H. Newman's famous *Tract 90,* which had seemed to teach Roman Catholic doctrine. *The Doctrine of the Church of England as to the Effects of Baptism in the Case of Infants* (1849) related to the Gorham controversy and attempted to show that the doctrine of baptismal regeneration is not necessarily associated with the rite of infant baptism. *The Nature of Christ's Presence in the Eucharist* (1856) showed that the Tractarian way of stating the doctrine of the "real presence" was not the usual way held by Church of England theologians.

Goode served as editor of the *Christian Observer* from 1847 to 1849 and also published books on biblical prophecy. People of all schools of opinion in the Church of England regarded him as the learned champion of evangelicalism. P. TOON

GOODELL, WILLIAM (1792–1867)

Pioneer missionary of the American Board of Commissioners for Foreign Missions in the Near East; founder of a mission to Armenians

A graduate of Dartmouth College and Andover Seminary, Goodell was sent with his bride, Abigail P. Davis, to Malta in 1822. Then after some years in Beirut, Goodell in 1831 went to Constantinople (modern Istanbul, Turkey). Working toward the spiritual and evangelistic revival of the Armenian Orthodox Church, Goodell undertook Bible translation and distribution, Bible classes, literature work, and personal contacts. At first, the only worship services that could be conducted for foreigners were in English. An evangelical party did develop in the Armenian Orthodox Church, however, which formed an evangelical union in 1839. After suffering persecution for a time, these Protestants were expelled from the area in 1846. Subsequently, the Sultan of Turkey recognized the Evangelical Armenian Church and granted freedom by decrees in 1847, 1850, and 1853. Goodell returned to the United States in 1865 because of infirmities, dying at Philadelphia. P. BEAVER

GOODSPEED, EDGAR JOHNSON (1871–1962)

American scholar in New Testament and early Christian literature

Goodspeed was born in Quincy, Illinois, and educated at Denison University and the University of Chicago. He was a member of the Chicago faculty from 1898 to 1937.

Perhaps Goodspeed's most notable contribution to New Testament studies was his theory on the collection and circulation of the Pauline epistles. He argued that the Letter to the Ephesians was written in the last quarter of the first century by a collector (perhaps the Onesimus of Col. 4:9) of the apostle Paul's correspondence to the Galatians, Philippians, Thessalonians, Corinthians, and Romans. Ephesians was meant to serve as a kind of covering letter for the circulation of Paul's epistles among the churches.

Goodspeed made important translations of the New Testament (*An American Translation*, 1923), the apostolic fathers, and the Apocrypha. His *History of Early Christian Literature* (1942) is considered a classic. P. TOON

GORDON, ADONIRAM JUDSON (1836–1895)

Baptist minister in Boston

Born in Hampton, New Hampshire, Gordon was a leading evangelical in the transitional period between nineteenth-century Protestantism and twentieth-century fundamentalism. In the tradition of nineteenth-century evangelicalism he maintained a very active social witness. His church worked extensively among Boston's poor—white, black, and immigrant—and also campaigned against the misuse of alcohol. As a defender of orthodoxy against modernism, Gordon wrote widely used books on Christ, the Holy Spirit, and the church. He was also a leader in the important prophecy conferences of 1878 and 1886.

With other Bible students in the late nineteenth century, Gordon put new emphasis on the literal interpretation of Scripture. He founded the Boston Missionary Training School (later Gordon College and Divinity School). He also helped compile two hymnals and wrote gospel songs, including "My Jesus I Love Thee." M. A. NOLL

GORDON, CHARLES WILLIAM (1860–1937)

Canadian author and Presbyterian clergyman

Born at Indian Lands, Glengarry County, Canada West (Ontario), the son of a Presbyterian minister, Gordon was educated at the University of Toronto and Knox College. He was ordained in 1890 and in 1894 became minister of St. Stephen's Church, Winnipeg, a position he held until his retirement in 1929. He served as chaplain in the Canadian Expeditionary Force during World War I. In 1921 he was elected moderator of the General Assembly of the Presbyterian Church in Canada. He strongly advocated merger of the Presbyterian, Methodist, and Congregational churches.

Gordon is chiefly remembered as a very popular novelist, writing under the pseudonym of Ralph Connor. He wrote against the background of his early years in Glengarry and his later career in the Canadian West and as a military chaplain. Among his many books was *The Man from Glengarry* (1901), in which Gordon gave a vivid picture of early Canadian Presbyterianism. In *The Sky Pilot* (1899) he described the difficulties of a Protestant minister adjusting his preaching to a western frontier environment: "The preaching was always of the simplest kind, abstract questions being avoided and the concrete in those wonderful Bible tales, dressed in modern and in western garb, set forth." He also wrote *Glengarry School Days* (1902). D. C. MASTERS

GORDON, SAMUEL DICKEY
(1859–1936)
American devotional writer and lecturer

Gordon was born in Philadelphia, Pennsylvania, where he received a public school education. At age twenty-five he became assistant secretary of the Philadelphia YMCA, a role he filled for two years until his appointment as YMCA state secretary for Ohio. During his nine years in that position he developed a speaking style especially suited to devotional themes and characterized by common parables.

Gordon spent the years 1896 to 1900 traveling through Europe and the Orient as a visiting missionary lecturer. The first of his twenty-five books, *Quiet Talks on Power,* was published in 1901. Within the next five years three more titles appeared: *Quiet Talks on Prayer, Quiet Talks on Service*, and *Quiet Talks on Jesus.* An estimated 1.5 million copies from his "Quiet Talks" series have been printed. In 1951 a commemorative collection of Gordon's most popular essays was published. M. FACKLER

GORE, CHARLES (1853–1932)
Anglican bishop and theologian

Born at Wimbledon (England), Gore was educated at Harrow and at Oxford University, where he was elected a fellow of Trinity College in 1875. He became vice-principal of Cuddesdon Theological College in 1880, then served as first principal of Pusey House, Oxford (1884–1893). While there, he founded a religious order, the Community of the Resurrection, of which he remained head until 1901. After six years as a canon (clergyman) of Westminster Cathedral, he was appointed bishop of Worcester (1902).

Largely through Gore's efforts, the new diocese of Birmingham was established. In 1905 he became its first bishop. Transferred to the see of Oxford in 1911, he served there until 1919, when he resigned. Settling in London, he devoted himself to writing and teaching: for example, from 1924 to 1928 he was dean of theology at King's College, London.

Gore was a convinced High Churchman, emphasizing the Church of England's Roman Catholic heritage. His book *The Ministry of the Christian Church* (1880; new edition, 1919, edited by C. H. Turner) became the standard exposition and defense of the principle of the apostolic succession. But he was an Anglo-Catholic of the most liberal kind who accepted the findings of evolutionary science and biblical criticism. This is portrayed, for example, in his essay, "The Holy Spirit and Inspiration," in *Lux Mundi* (1889, a volume of essays that he edited).

Furthermore, Gore had a "permanently troubled conscience" concerning contemporary social and economic problems. A founder of the Christian Social Union (1889), in his book *Christ and Society* (1928) he emphasized the social implications of the gospel and made a strong plea for an unofficial interdenominational organization of Christian forces "to reassert the social meaning of Christianity." In the view of W. R. Inge, a critic of Anglo-Catholicism, Gore was "one of the most powerful spiritual forces of (his) generation." N. V. HOPE

GOSSE, PHILIP HENRY (1810–1888)
Naturalist, schoolmaster, and teacher

Philip Gosse was the son of Thomas Gosse, a painter, and his wife, Hannah Best, the daughter of a Worcestershire yeoman. Philip went to Newfoundland at an early age carrying with him the spirit of Puritanism in which he had been reared, developing further his natural aptitude for zoology and botany, and deepening his understanding of evangelical faith.

At the age of twenty-nine he returned to England to spread his knowledge of the truth in Christianity as well as in science. He became schoolmaster and preacher in Hackney, but once again left England at the insistence of the authorities of the British Museum, as insect collector in the West Indies. Returning to England in 1846, he once more settled in Hackney, met Emily Bowes, a member of the Plymouth Brethren religious group and a successful writer of tracts, and married her in 1848. Their son, Sir Edmund Gosse, the author of *Father and Son*, which records the struggle between the temperaments and consciences of Philip and Edmund, was born in 1849.

Philip Gosse's scientific writings, though earning him fame among the learned, brought little income to the family, but he was intensely happy, immersing himself in scientific pursuits and practicing his evangelical faith.

In 1856 his wife died; in 1858 Philip and his young son moved to Marychurch in Devon where he lived for the next thirty years, continued his scientific work, and exhorted others in evangelical teachings, particularly his son, Edmund, who was entering a literary career.

While studying the stars on a winter night in 1887, Philip Gosse contracted bronchitis; in January it became a serious illness from which he never recovered. E. B. BATSON

GOSSNER, JOHANNES EVANGELISTA (1773–1858)
Founder of the Gossner Mission Society

Born into a devout Catholic home at Hausen near Augsburg (Germany), Gossner studied at Dillingen and Ingolstadt. As a student he came in contact with a Pietist professor, Johann Michael Sailer (1751–1832). In 1796 Gossner was ordained and became an assistant priest at Neuburg. Next he served as cathedral chaplain at Augsburg (1797–1804), where he came into conflict with Catholic authorities because of his evangelical views. Those views no doubt played a part in the evangelical revival his congregation experienced when he was the parish priest of Dirlewang (1804–1811).

After 1811 he accepted an appointment to Munich, where he devoted himself to writing. In 1819, when his friend and spiritual mentor Martin Boos moved to Dusseldorf, Gossner joined him to work for a year as a religion teacher. His next position was pastor of a German Catholic congregation in St. Petersburg (Russia). Doubts regarding the necessity of clerical celibacy, however, led him to resign that post in 1824.

In 1826 Gossner left the Roman Catholic Church and was ordained a Lutheran minister. The only Lutheran parish he served was Bethlehem Church in Berlin (1829–1846). While there he founded several schools, asylums, and a missionary society—the Gossner Mission Society. In 1846 Gossner resigned from the church to devote his entire efforts to the Elizabeth Hospital, which he had also established. W. A. DETZLER

GOTTSCHALK (c. 803–869)
Monk, theologian, and poet whose unorthodox teachings on predestination resulted in his censure and imprisonment

Of noble Saxon origin, Gottschalk was made a child oblate (ward and pupil) of the Benedictine abbey at Fulda (now in Germany). As he grew older he came to resent his condition and sought his freedom. Although his release was resisted by his abbot, Rabanus Maurus, a synod at Mainz (829) granted it. Rabanus then appealed the decision to Frankish emperor Louis. Gottschalk was compelled to return to a monastery at Orbais in Gaul where he was unofficially ordained a priest.

After studying the fourth-century theologian Augustine, Gottschalk adopted an extreme Augustinian teaching of double predestination (that God had sovereignly decreed salvation for some and damnation for others). Allowed some freedom to travel, Gottschalk undertook a visit to Rome (which he called an exile) around 847. His preaching there and in the Balkans was condemned by a synod at Mainz (848), presided over by Rabanus. Gottschalk was consequently remanded to Hincmar, archbishop of Reims, for punishment. He was deprived of the priesthood, severely beaten, denied the sacraments, and imprisoned at Hautvillers. His controversial predestination doctrine, a major subject of debate, divided theologians of the time. The hapless Gottschalk, more or less forgotten in the confutations, died after almost twenty years of misfortune and suffering. Strangely enough, from his pen came some of the most beautiful poems of the Carolingian (French dynasty) renaissance. Gottschalk's poetry was a forerunner to later medieval lyrical expressions. A. CABANISS

GOUNOD, CHARLES FRANÇOIS (1818–1893)
French romantic composer

Gounod was born in Paris, attended the Paris Conservatory, and won the Grand Prix de Rome (1839). During his three years in Rome he was deeply affected by Italian religious choral music, especially that of Palestrina, and began writing church music. For a while he seriously considered becoming a priest, but after completing theological studies he decided to stay with music. A singer urged him to write an opera for her and thus began his successful association with the stage, most celebrated in *Faust,* one of the most popular operas ever written (1859). Altogether Gounod wrote twelve operas; only three, however, received public acclaim.

Gounod's church music included twenty-three masses, six oratorios, and more than eighty motets and canticles. The Sanctus from his *St. Cecilia* mass and the Ave Maria melody written to Bach's C major prelude

are still frequently performed, though many worthwhile pieces have been neglected.

Gounod's well-crafted music has a facile attractiveness. At times, however, it is melodramatic or overly sentimental. Church music in the early twentieth century was given over to many poor imitators of Gounod's style. W. PHEMISTER

GRAFTON, RICHARD (died 1572)
Protestant printer who circulated English Bible translations in and around London

After Grafton converted to the Protestant faith, he collaborated with his colleague Edward Whitchurch in publishing a composite of William Tyndale's and Miles Coverdale's English Bibles (1537). It was printed in Antwerp (now Belgium) and dedicated to English king Henry VIII who soon required every parish to carry a vernacular Bible. Assigned to a fictitious Thomas Matthews (to protect the real editor John Rogers), the translation became known as Matthew's Bible. Grafton then arranged for the printing and distributing of the revised version of Coverdale's New Testament (1538). Grafton's and Whitchurch's next Bible publication began in Paris. French Catholic officials, however, confiscated their work, forcing the printers to flee to England where their Great Bible was made available in 1539.

Grafton also printed Henry VIII's authorized Church of England devotional primer (1545). He was entitled "Printer to the Prince's Grace" in honor of the king's son Prince Edward VI. When Edward became king (1547), Grafton was appointed royal printer and thus had sole rights to print statutes and acts of Parliament. He printed the *First Book of Homilies* (1547) and the first *Book of Common Prayer* (1549). After Edward died (1553), Grafton supported Lady Jane Grey's accession to the throne, publishing her first proclamation as queen. When Henry VIII's Catholic daughter Mary seized power (1553), he lost his post. In 1563 he returned to public life as a Parliament member for the city of Coventry. He also pursued his interest as a chronicler, publishing a rather pedantic history of England. P. Toon

GRAHAM, WILLIAM ("BILLY") FRANKLIN, JR. (born 1918)

International evangelist, writer, and religious leader

Graham was born November 7, 1918, in Charlotte, North Carolina, the first son of William F. and Morrow Graham. His parents owned a dairy farm and were active members of the Associate Presbyterian Church. At the age of sixteen he was converted through the ministry of Mordecai Ham, a well-known southern evangelist.

After a brief period at Bob Jones College (Tennessee), Graham enrolled in Florida Bible Institute in Tampa, Florida (B.Th., 1940). There he not only gained a foundation in the Bible which would greatly influence him the rest of his life, but also received his call to the Christian ministry. During that time he began preaching and was ordained as a Southern Baptist minister in 1940. Later that year he enrolled at Wheaton College (Illinois), where he met his future wife, Ruth McCue Bell, the daughter of L. Nelson and Virginia Bell, Presbyterian medical missionaries to China. They married on August 13, 1943, and have five children.

Upon graduation in 1943 (B.A., Anthropology) he became pastor of a small Baptist church in Western Springs, Illinois. Two years later he resigned to become a full-time evangelist with the newly formed Youth for Christ organization. Almost immediately he began to travel extensively, not only through the United States but to war-scarred Great Britain. In 1947 he reluctantly accepted the presidency of the Northwestern Schools in Minneapolis (which included a Bible college, liberal arts college, and seminary), but continued to travel widely as an evangelist, finally resigning from the presidency in 1951.

Graham skyrocketed to national prominence in 1949 through his meetings in Los Angeles. The meetings in a huge "canvas cathedral" (tent) resulted in the conversion of several well-known personalities and attracted the attention of media giant William Randolph Hearst, whose newspapers gave widespread coverage to the event. Almost overnight Billy Graham became a household name, and in the next few years his citywide evangelistic meetings in stadiums and arenas in some of America's largest cities established a pattern for mass evangelism that would always be associated with his ministry. He has preached in person in more than eighty countries to over 110 million people, more than any other individual in history. Hundreds of millions more have heard him through television, radio, and film.

Graham's primary commitment has always been to proclaim the historic message of the Christian faith to nonbelievers. This desire to reach unbelievers led him to utilize the mass media for the proclamation of the gospel to an unprecedented extent. His worldwide radio program "The Hour of Decision," started in 1950, soon was heard on hundreds of stations. He likewise utilized television extensively almost as soon as it became widespread (choosing to purchase prime time on major stations for several days three or four times a year, rather than attempting a weekly production). As technology has advanced, Graham has used satellites and videotapes to extend single crusade meetings across entire continents. Through its World Wide Pictures unit the Billy Graham Evangelistic Association (founded 1950) has produced and distributed dozens of documentary and dramatic films, becoming the largest producer of religious films in the world. Graham has authored over fifteen books, most of which have hit the best-seller lists and have been widely translated. He also is a frequent guest on major television programs.

While drawing upon the work of such evangelists as Wesley, Whitefield, Finney, Moody, and Sunday, Graham sought to refine and update the methods of mass evangelism. Each citywide crusade is carefully organized, with a trained staff working with local church leaders and volunteers for many months in advance. Early in his work Graham realized the need for more effective follow-up of those making spiritual commitments in his meetings. Working with Dawson Trotman (founder of The Navigators) he developed a system that includes basic Bible studies, personal counseling, and immediate contact with a local church.

Almost from the beginning of his public ministry Graham opted for a cooperative approach to evangelism, i.e., working with all churches and denominations that would cooperate with him. This led to criticism from both fundamentalists and liberals—the former denouncing him for compromising (in their view) with liberal churches and clergymen, the latter rejecting his message and methods as simplistic, out-of-date, and socially irrelevant. Conservative critics also assailed him for integrating his meetings, which he did more than a year before the Supreme Court's landmark decision on civil rights (1954). In the late 1970s and early 1980s others criticized him for accepting invitations to preach in communist-dominated Eastern Europe and the Soviet Union, although many of those same critics later acknowledged that his visits had a significant impact on the later course of religious freedom there.

In spite of these critics, however, Graham's integrity, personal humility, and popular appeal have made him one of the most influential religious leaders of the twentieth century. The annual Gallup poll has ranked him among the ten most admired men in America since 1951. He has sometimes been called the unofficial White House chaplain, due to his friendship with every American president since Harry Truman. He has received numerous honorary degrees, including one from the Debrecen Theological Academy in Hungary (the oldest Protestant seminary in the world), and over fifty major awards, including the Templeton Prize for Progress in Religion (1982) and the Presidential Medal of Freedom (1983), America's highest nonmilitary honor.

Of special significance is Graham's influence on the resurgence of evangelical Christianity in the latter half of the twentieth century. As the most visible proponent of biblical Christianity, Graham has become the symbolic leader of evangelicalism, in spite of his refusal to become associated with special interest groups or causes. His concern for the future of evangelicalism led to the founding of the influential magazine Christianity Today, where he remains chairman of the board. Graham has also used his influence to draw together evangelical leaders and evangelists in a series of international congresses, including the World Congress on Evangelism (Berlin, 1966), the International Congress on World Evangelization (Lausanne, 1974), and the International Conferences for Itinerant Evangelists (Amsterdam, 1983, 1986). He has been chairman of the board of Gordon-Conwell Theological Seminary (Massachusetts) and honorary chairman of the Lausanne Committee for World Evangelization. J. N. AKERS

GRANT, GEORGE MONRO (1835–1902)
Canadian clergyman and educator

Grant was born of Scottish parents at Albion Mines, Nova Scotia, and was educated at Pictou Academy and the University of Glasgow. Ordained to the Church of Scotland ministry in 1860, he was minister of St. Matthew's Church, Halifax, Nova Scotia, from 1863 to 1877. At that time he became principal of Queen's University, Kingston, Ontario, a position he held until his death.

Grant is chiefly remembered as perhaps the greatest single influence in the development of Queen's University. He helped to effect its transition from an orthodox Presbyterian to a nonsectarian institution with a national constituency. He also exercised a liberalizing influence on the Presbyterian Church in Canada, in general priding himself on being a moderate in the controversy over science and religion. Grant was also a strong supporter of the British Empire and a prominent member of the Imperial Federation League. D. C. MASTERS

GRATIAN (twelfth century)
Originator of the science of canon law

Born at Chiusi (Italy), Gratian probably became a Camaldolese monk and lectured at the monastery of saints Felix and Nabor in Bologna, the Roman law study center.

Gratian's famous work, officially entitled *Concordantia Discordantium Canonum* (*Reconciliation of Discordant Regulations*), is better known as the *Decretum*. Gratian compiled about thirty-eight hundred texts on all fields of church discipline into a systematic arrangement of ecclesiastical laws and canons, conciliar and papal decrees, and patristics (writings of the early church leaders). The *Decretum* was published shortly after the second Lateran Council of 1139. Designed to reconcile apparent contradictions, Gratian's orderly and comprehensive work made any further codification efforts unnecessary.

Though not accepted as exclusively authoritative, the *Decretum* became an indispensable legal and catechetical text. Popes Gregory IX, Boniface VIII, and Clement V supplemented Gratian's work, which was then published in 1582 as the *Corpus Juris Canonici* (*The Code of Canon*). N. V. HOPE

GRAY, JAMES MARTIN (1851–1935)
Author and Bible teacher

Gray was associated with Moody Bible Institute of Chicago for over forty years— first as summer lecturer (1892–1903), then as dean (1904–1923), president (1923–1934), and president-emeritus (1934–1935). Before receiving Dwight L. Moody's invitation to teach in Chicago, Gray served as a Reformed Episcopal rector in Brooklyn and Newburgh, New York, and in Boston, Massachusetts. During his administration at Moody, student enrollment, staff, budget, magazine and book outreach, and the physical plant grew markedly.

Gray's "synthetic method" of Bible study involved prayerfully reading each book of the Bible in a single sitting, then reading it repeatedly until mastered, independent of other helps. Moody called Gray "the best Bible teacher I ever met." Gray's verse-by-verse preaching contained a strong evangelistic appeal.

Gray's fifteen books include *How to Master the English Bible* and the *Christian Worker's Commentary*. His best-known songs were "Nor Silver nor Gold" and "Only a Sinner." G. F. ARNOLD

GREBEL, CONRAD (1498–1526)
A founder of the Swiss radical reformers known as Anabaptists

Grebel enjoyed a good education that took him to Basel, Vienna, and Paris and brought him into touch with renaissance influences. Back in Zurich he welcomed the coming of Zwingli as the people's pastor at the Great Minster. With Felix Manz, he joined Zwingli in the study of the Greek New Testament and in plans for reform in the city. In the early stages, however, he found the pace too slow and after trying to hurry up the movement broke with Zwingli over the issue of infant baptism. Probably the deeper issue was whether or not to form a gathered church in the hope that the rest would follow. Initial disputations failed to bridge the gap.

In January 1525 Grebel and others took the decisive step of separation when they held the first baptism, or, as Zwingli would put it, rebaptism. As might be expected the city council saw this as a challenge to its authority and took steps that checked the movement in Zurich but led to its extension elsewhere. Grebel held fast to his convictions. As he had stated in a letter to Thomas Muntzer in September, 1524, he desired a simple administration of the Lord's Supper, rejected singing in public worship, wanted a church based as literally as possible on New Testament statements, renounced any reliance on physical weapons to protect believers on the way of affliction, and demanded baptism only on profession of faith and dedication to a walk "in newness of life and spirit." He disagreed sharply with Muntzer not only on the smaller issue of singing but also on the important one of violence. Yet the revolutionary activities of Muntzer and his like probably explain the great severity of the measures taken to suppress the radical movement in Zurich. Under these measures Grebel himself suffered imprisonment that led to his early death. G. BROMILEY

GREGORY I (THE GREAT) (c. 540–604)

Pope, 590–604—commonly regarded as the
father of the medieval papacy

The fourth and last of the Latin so-called "Doctors of the Church," Gregory was born in Rome of wealthy parents and received a comprehensive education. In legal studies he so distinguished himself that in 573 he was given the imperial appointment of prefect of Rome. His piety, however, led him to renounce the world, and after the death of his father he gave his wealth and energies to good works. He founded seven monasteries in Sicily and one in Rome, and himself entered the latter about 575. Not for long, however, because Pope Benedict I persuaded him to leave the cloisters and ordained him as one of the seven Roman deacons in 577. Two years later, Pope Pelagius II sent him as his delegate to Constantinople. Gregory may have been allowed to retire to his monastery once more in 585, but left again reluctantly when elected pope in 590.

Despite his legal acumen he was not regarded as a scholar, nor was he ever more than a mediocre theologian. He knew none of the biblical languages, had no time for pagan learning, and was not an original thinker. He was preeminently a teacher and a preacher. In theology he followed Augustine of Hippo, whose teaching he is said to have "passed on to the medieval Church in a debased and coarsened form, eked out with conceptions of angels, demons, miracles and purgatory."

Gregory was a believer in the verbal inspiration of Scripture, and thought it a futile exercise to enquire into the authorship of the books of the Bible. He said, "When we are persuaded that the Holy Spirit was its author, in stirring a question about the author, what else do we do than in reading a letter inquire about the pen?" Sin might be forgiven on condition of repentance, which involved contrition, confession, and satisfaction. Satisfaction included penance, and the penance was in proportion to the sin. On this was the vast complex penitential system of the Middle Ages constructed, and—combined with the doctrine of purgatory—it led

to that mechanical theory of penance and indulgences against which Luther protested and which led on to the Reformation in Germany.

Gregory was the first pope who aspired to temporal power. When the emperor abandoned Rome and his Italian possessions, Gregory had to take on secular sovereignty or leave Rome to anarchy and the Lombards. By the time he died in 604, the pope was looked upon as the chief bishop in the West, the natural arbiter and court of appeal in ecclesiastical cases, and the one person who could intervene with authority in cases of serious scandal. One of Gregory's chief claims to fame is that in 596 he sent Augustine on a mission to convert the pagan English (and later to become the first archbishop of Canterbury). Despite being involved in power struggles—notably in resisting the patriarch of Constantinople's assumption of the title "Ecumenical Patriarch"—Gregory in his personal life evinced a marked humility as "the servant of the servants of God."

He was one of the primary organizers and codifiers of the Roman liturgy and its music, together with his predecessors Celestine I (pope, 422–432) and Sixtus III (pope, 432–440). It is believed that Gregory reorganized the Schola cantorum of Rome, a center for singing and for the promulgation of plainsong, which was already active under Celestine I. His contribution to the finalization of musical style in Roman plainsong has taken on less certain status in recent times, owing to discoveries of major liturgical reforms occurring under Frankish rulers during the eighth and early ninth centuries. On the other hand, the musical reforms instituted under Gregory can also be viewed in perspective of his very significant efforts to exterminate the last vestiges of the Arian heresy and to resolve controversy between Rome and Constantinople.

Gregorian Chant is named for him. His role is now seen as that of codifier and collector, though he possibly wrote hymns. The great collection of his undertaking is the *Antiphonarium cento*, with its efforts to unify and distribute musical elements throughout the liturgical year.

Generally Gregory was a prolific author. His *Liber Regulae Pastoralis* (c. 591) deals with the pastoral life of a bishop. His *Dialogues* (c. 593) consisted of biographies of Benedict and other Western saints. Among Gregory's other works were an exposition of the book of Job and *Homilies on the Gospels,* which contained sermons preached on various texts. There is also a collection of Gregory's letters, which gives useful insights into contemporary thinking and events.

D. S. CUSHMAN & J. D. DOUGLAS

GREGORY VII (c. 1021–1085)
Pope, 1073–1085

The son of poor Tuscany parents, Gregory was educated in St. Mary's monastery at Rome. His life of church service began as a Benedictine monk. Deeply affected by the Benedictines' Cluny-inspired reforms, he assumed the name Hildebrand, meaning "brilliant flame." Hildebrand was soon recognized for his exceptional abilities, and by 1046, he was an assistant to Pope Gregory VI, accompanying his exile to Germany. The stay in Germany deeply enhanced the young aide's intense notions about Church renewal. After Gregory VI's death in 1047, Hildebrand returned to Rome. Immediately he became a strong force behind successive reform-minded popes, mainly Leo IX, Victor II, Nicholas II, Alexander II. His influence grew pervasive not only in Rome, but in Christianity at large. For most of these years, his official position was archdeacon or chancellor of the Roman diocese. But frequently he served as papal legate in critical matters. Throughout the period, Hildebrand refused to become a candidate for pope himself. In fact, largely by his efforts, the College of Cardinals gained full control over papal elections.

Hildebrand agreed, however, to assume the papacy on Alexander II's death in 1073. With the cardinals' unanimous support, he now believed his direct leadership was required for the Church's immense renewal needs. Concluding treaties with various Italian princes, Gregory VII's first action was to secure the papacy's political position. To do this, Robert Guiscard, the irascible Norman conqueror of Sicily and southern Italy, had to be removed. For his obstinacy and hostility, Giscard was finally excommunicated in 1075. The new pope also tried to retrieve the separated, declining Eastern Church. But his plans for organizational reunion while repulsing the Muslims gained only meager support. Thus, from 1074 onward, ideas for Western Church reform had Gregory's full attention. In overview, this renewal aimed not just at formal religious changes but Christian spiritual ascendancy in all temporal matters. As outlined in the twenty-seven sentences of his famous *Dictatus papae,* Gregory's plans envisioned all of western Europe's main facets—familial, proprietary, political, dynastic—under Church controls. But essentially, the vehicle of this new design was Church governmental changes. Quickly, at the Lenten Synod of 1074, the pope set forth the principal reform pronouncements. The decrees ordered actions on two primary issues: removal of simony from every clerical election, and enforcement of celibacy rules for all major clergy. To assure implacement of such provisions, Gregory also promulgated two other general decrees. These were reaffirmation of the supreme authority of papal decrees, and, most critically, a final elimination of all non-ecclesiastical investiture of Church office. In the following fast-paced years, Gregory's reform program became one of the Roman Catholic Church's historic turning points. Immediately, of course, there was monumental conflict with European rulers and Church leaders. Thus Gregory is sometimes recalled most for defeats, as inflicted especially by Henry IV, the Holy Roman Emperor. However, to a remarkable extent changes did take hold, and the impact was enduring. Not unexpectedly, responses to Gregory's plans in Germany, France, and England, the three main Western Church regions, were varied. As to the internal issues, simony and celibacy, Germany's clergy was the most and France's the least compliant. In England, Lanfranc, the brilliant archbishop, obtained a grudging but basic submission without wide upheaval. Within France, though, many bishops and other clergy had to be replaced. On the external matters, papal authority and royal or lay investiture, the three chief rulers, England's William I, France's Philip I, and Germany's Henry IV, opposed Gregory vehemently. But given William's sincere support for reform, Gregory readily compromised with the English king. In France, Philip's worldly minded opposition was easily overriden. It was Henry IV, ruler of Germany, and its inextricable church-state interdependence, who induced a climactic struggle. At first, based on his favor with German nobles, Gregory had the upper hand. Thus the year 1077 saw Gregory's deposition of Henry and then, at Canossa, the emperor's famous penitence and submission. But soon Germany's civil war undermined Gregory's position. In one last maneuver, the pope excommunicated Henry again in 1080. But the emperor had renewed power, and he proceeded to put Rome under siege. Though freed by his old nemesis Guiscard, Gregory spent his last two years in exile at Monte Cassino and Salerno. His last words were: "I have loved justice and hated iniquity, therefore I die in exile." Gregory departed one of the great champions of Christian opposition to worldly dominance. K. J. BRYER

GREGORY IX (c. 1148–1241)

Pope, 1227–1241

Born Ugolino de Segni, Gregory was a nephew of Pope Innocent III. He studied at the Universities of Paris and Bologna. In 1198, after years of Church service, his uncle made him a cardinal deacon. In 1206, he was consecrated bishop of Ostia. Subsequently, he served as papal legate in many important matters, and from 1217 to 1219, mediated intercity disputes. Despite the mismanaged Crusade of 1218 to 1221 (Europe's fifth general crusade), much interest in freeing Jerusalem from the Muslims still existed. Promoting this Crusade in northern Italy was Gregory's assignment for several years. In 1220, at Frederick II's coronation,

it was to Gregory the emperor gave his renewed vows for a Crusade.

Gregory faced two main issues: Frederick's desire to unite Italy with the empire, and Gregory's demand that Frederick lead a Holy Land Crusade. Frederick was action-oriented and secular-minded, while Gregory was scholarly and religious-minded. In 1227, after years of delay, Frederick finally started his army toward the Holy Land, but turned back before the halfway mark. His explanation was that his troops suffered a serious epidemic. Deeply disappointed, the pope rejected Frederick's excuses and excommunicated him. Frederick completed his Crusade in 1229; on return he easily defeated the pope's army. Nevertheless, in 1230, both leaders found it useful to conclude the Peace of San Germano. This exchanged Frederick's excommunication and other sanctions for imperial support of Gregory's rule in Sicily and papal lands. Nonetheless, within a few years, it was plain even this pact could not bring peace. By 1239, Frederick's new encroachments in northern Italy had caused another empire-papal breakdown. Once again the pope excommunicated the emperor. To bolster this action, Gregory also convoked a general Church council, scheduled for 1241. However, Frederick found a means for disrupting the pope's strategy. Defeating the Genoese navy, the emperor captured and imprisoned a large contingent of bishops bound for Rome. This required the council to be postponed. And then, momentously, in 1241, while Frederick had Rome under siege, Gregory grew ill and died. Well aware of a growing materialism and worldliness, Gregory sought to renew the Church's spiritual vitality and witness. To this end, one of the pope's crucial actions was support of the new mendicant orders. The Franciscans and Dominicans were now the largest and most prominent of such itinerant groups. Gregory also gave financial and other help to older orders, especially those with Church renewal potential. Moreover, throughout Gregory's tenure, numerous missionaries were commissioned for non-Christian areas. This included such places as Tunis, Morocco, Finland, and other remote parts of Africa and Europe.

As he opposed his era's rising heresies, Gregory's characteristic energy turned into harshness. The Albigensians had multiplied since Innocent III's military suppression. But in 1228, Gregory had Louis IX pursue another armed crusade against the group. Then also Gregory's papacy was the first to deal with heresy through formal Church inquisition. To assure the fairest, most painstaking judgments, the pope assigned Franciscans and Dominicans to this work. Contrastingly, on other matters, Gregory was surprisingly liberal. He was a patron of learning, the university, and the new scholarship of his era. It was also he who revoked the Church's ban against scholarly use of Aristotle's writings. Most crucially, Gregory was also compiler of the canonical decretals, the canon law's all-important second section. This complemented the first section, Gratian's *Decretum*, a summation of Christianity's historic moral doctrine. Mainly comprising Alexander III's and Innocent III's decrees, Gregory's *Decretales* were final statements on many religious and social issues. For medieval and modern times alike, the decretals' basic role, both in Church morality and life, and all Western social development, can hardly be exaggerated.

K. J. BRYER

GREGORY XIII (1502–1585)
Pope, 1572–1585

Born Ugo Buoncompagni in Bologna, he was educated at the city's university and taught canon law there (1531–1539). Such was his expertise in that field that Pius IV sent him to the Council of Trent (1561–1563) and for his services there rewarded him with a cardinal's hat. Shortly after his election to the papacy he provoked bitter hostility by celebrating with a Te Deum the killing of French Huguenots (Protestants), which has gone down in history as the notorious Massacre of St. Bartholomew's Day (1572).

Gregory had a measure of success in promoting the Counter-Reformation. He founded the Gregorian University in Rome as well as a large number of Jesuit colleges,

strove for union with the East, encouraged missions in India and Japan, built magnificent churches in Rome, actively supported the Inquisition, and issued the Gregorian Calendar and a new edition of canon law. The expenses of all his grandiose projects brought financial chaos to the Vatican.

J. D. DOUGLAS

GREGORY XVI (1765–1846)
Pope, 1831–1846

Born Bartolomeo Alberto Cappellari into a noble family at Belluno, he joined the Camaldolese Order in 1783, was ordained in 1787, and in 1805 became abbot of San Gregorio Monastery, Rome. He was forced to leave there when Napoleon threatened the Papal States and did not return until 1814. Made cardinal in 1826, by which time he was vicar-general of his Order, he was a compromise choice as pope. Soon after he assumed the post, revolution broke out in the Papal States; this he put down with Austrian help. Considerable reforms were demanded of him, but he was no friend of Italian nationalism and had a high view of the papal office. An enormous debt piled up. Relations with France became increasingly strained, especially when the Jesuits became unacceptable in France, where they were suppressed in 1845. Meanwhile revolution again beset the Papal States.

Gregory was a supporter of missions and monasticism (during his pontificate the Benedictines and Dominicans were restored in France), and a tireless denouncer of errors in a series of encyclicals. In 1844 he condemned the newly founded Evangelical Alliance and the Bible societies. He was nonetheless a patron of arts and letters, established the Vatican's Etruscan and Egyptian collections, and the Lateran Museum of Christian Antiquities. J. D. DOUGLAS

GREGORY OF NAZIANZUS
(c. 330–389)
Cappadocian monk whose eloquent preaching and scholarly writing earned him the title "the theologian"

Gregory was born at Arianzus near Nazianzus. His father, bishop of Nazianzus, gave young Gregory a serious religious education. Gregory's mother, Nonna, who had guided her husband's conversion, also had a great spiritual impact on her son.

Gregory studied at Caesarea, Caesarea Philippi, Alexandria, and Athens. During that period of time he cultivated a close friendship with Basil, another student from Cappadocia. After teaching rhetoric in Athens for a time, Gregory returned to Nazianzus in about 359. Though he wanted to become a religious hermit, Gregory was persuaded by his father to accept ordination as a church leader. Afterwards he repudiated that action and entered monastic life with Basil.

During the next twenty years Gregory's ascetic life was interrupted intermittently with active church ministry. At the Council of Constantinople (381), his theological disputations won him the bishopric of Constantinople. Gregory refused the appointment.

Theologically, Gregory appears to have been strongly influenced by the early third-century theologian Origen. Gregory defended the Nicene council's view of the Trinity and argued against the Apollinarian view that Christ's humanity was passive. He condemned the emperor Julian, who tried to exclude Christians from higher learning and study of the classics. H. W. HOUSE

GREGORY OF NYSSA (330–c. 395)
Cappadocian rhetorician and theologian; bishop of Nyssa

Gregory, born at Caesarea in Cappadocia, was the younger brother of Basil and Macrina (a sister), whom he called his "teachers." He with Basil and Gregory Nazianzus composed the "three Cappadocians" who powerfully influenced the fourth-century Eastern church.

Gregory received a diverse classical education. Under the direction of his domineering brother, he briefly served as a reader in church, but later chose to teach rhetoric instead. Gregory of Nazianzus urged him to return to Christian ministry. Basil, after asking Gregory to help him in his Caesarea diocese, finally forced the vacant bishopric of

Nyssa upon him (371). Gregory's enthusiastic anti-Arian stance drew opposition, and he was soon ousted from that position by the emperor Valens (about 376). Following Valens's death (378) Gregory was recalled and commissioned to assist churches in Arabia and Palestine. In the Council of Constantinople (381) he defended the Nicene Creed.

Although often eclipsed by Basil's brilliant career, Gregory was a theological prodigy. He elaborated doctrines of resurrection, divine grace, and Christology. He produced treaties on ascetic piety and mystic communion with God. Some scholars believe that his early work *On Virginity* indicated that he was married. H. W. HOUSE

GREGORY OF TOURS (c. 538–594)
Bishop of Tours; historian of medieval Gaul (France)

Born Georgius Florentius, he took the name Gregorius Turonesis ("of Tours"). From his birth in Clermont-Ferrand, he was associated with ecclesiastical life. After his father died, Gregory's mother moved to Cavaillon, where Gregory was educated by his uncle, bishop of Clermont, and his grand uncle Bishop Nicetius. Gregory was ordained deacon in the 560s and bishop in 573. As bishop he was able to end murderous feuds, relieve the people of some burdensome taxation, and influence several Frankish kings.

Gregory produced seven books of *Miracles*, a commentary on *Psalms*, the *Lives of the Fathers*, and a book on Church Offices. His ten-volume *History of the Franks* is the principal sourcebook of sixth-century Gaul. Gregory's propensity for the miraculous often clouded his historical narrative; nevertheless, his writings vividly portrayed the geography, language, and religious sentiments of that era. H. W. HOUSE

GREGORY PALAMAS (c. 1296–1359)
Greek monk and theologian; bishop of Thessalonica

Gregory Palamas left his well-to-do family home in Constantinople at the age of twenty-two to enter the austere monastery of Mount

Athos (Greece). Turkish invasions, however, compelled him to seek refuge in Thessalonica, where he was ordained a priest (in 1326).

Upon his return to Mount Athos (around 1331) he became embroiled in a controversial form of eastern meditation called "hesychasm." Hesychast adherents practiced disciplined yoga meditation positions, breathing exercises, and hypnotic "Jesus prayer" recitation. Borlaam, a monk from southern Italy vigorously opposed hesychasm. Gregory defended it, arguing that God had blessed the material world (hence the body) and thus the total person should be engaged in prayer. Both the council at Constantinople (1341) and a synod at Mount Athos endorsed hesychast contemplation. At one stage Gregory was excommunicated and imprisoned, but in 1347 was vindicated and appointed bishop of Thessalonica. Hesychasm became orthodox in the Eastern church through his adamant defense, theological writings, and canonization (1368). A. CABANISS

GREGORY THAUMATURGUS
(c. 213–c. 270)
Bishop of Neocaesarea in Pontus

Gregory (named Theodore from birth) was a member of a wealthy family. He studied law with his brother Athenodorus in the famous school at Berytus only to become an enthusiastic pupil of the famed theologian Origen from 233 to 238. Gregory's oration on Origen is a first attempt at Christian biography. In turn, details of Gregory's life are related in a similar fashion by Gregory of Nyssa. On return home, Gregory and his brother were consecrated bishops by Phaedimus of Amasea.

Tradition states that Gregory ministered in this diocese in Pontus for thirty years. He began his ministry with seventeen Christians and ended it with as many converts. Gregory assisted with his brother at the first synod of Antioch (264), which condemned Paul of Samosata. There are three or four accounts of Thaumaturgus, which in Greek means "miracle-worker." Gregory of Nyssa's eulogy is a trustworthy account of his life while his own *Panygeric on Origen* preserves some detail. St. Basil in the *De Spirito Sancto* as pre-

served in Eusebius adds material, and Rufinus's account of the miracles in his *Ecclesiastical History* completes the account. These legendary lives, in Greek, Latin, Syriac, and Armenian, preserve details of his life.

The Exposition of Faith given in Nyssa's biography is a brief Trinitarian affirmation. Gregory prepared a Greek exposition of *Ecclesiastes* adapted into classical Greek from the Septuagint. His *Canonical Epistle* answers questions arising from the Gothic invasion of Pontus when Christians pillaged and apostasized. Other writings ascribed to Gregory are doubtful. M. ANDERSON

GRENFELL, GEORGE (1849–1906)
British Baptist missionary and explorer in the Congo

Grenfell was born into an Anglican family, but in 1864 he joined the Heneage Street Baptist Chapel in Birmingham (England). Ten years later he was accepted by the Baptist Missionary Society for work in the Cameroons under the direction of Alfred Saker (1814–1880).

Grenfell explored inland rivers of the Cameroons, then was commissioned to accompany T. J. Combe up the lower Congo. Together they established mission stations at Musuko, Vivi, Isangila, and Manyanga.

In 1884 Grenfell surveyed the Congo up to the equator and at Stanley Pool assembled and launched a river steamer *Peace*. With that vessel, which could be dismantled and carried in sections around cataracts, he undertook six exploratory voyages, which resulted in several more mission stations being set up. In 1886 Grenfell's observations on the areas he had explored were published by the Royal Geographical Society. The following year it honored him with a founder's medal.
D. R. MITCHELL

GRENFELL, SIR WILFRED THOMASON
(1865–1940)
British medical missionary

Born at Parkgate, near Chester (England), Grenfell studied at London Hospital, from which he obtained a medical degree in 1888.

Having committed himself to a life of Christian service at an 1885 meeting addressed by D. L. Moody, in 1888 Grenfell joined the Royal National Mission to Deep Sea Fishermen. He left England in 1892, chosen by the mission to start a pioneer medical service to the fishermen of Labrador and the Coast of Newfoundland.

Responding to "the lure of the Labrador," Grenfell spent more than forty years there, serving in many capacities—doctor, master mariner, geographer, and missionary. He sought to improve the quality of life at all levels among the Labrador natives—Eskimos and Indians, as well as whites. He established churches and schools wherever he found clusters of people to attend them. In addition, he set up five hospitals and seven nursing stations along the Labrador Coast. Further, Grenfell enriched economic life by opening cooperative stores, teaching fox farming, and improving methods of seal fishing. In 1912 he opened the King George V Seamen's Institute at St. Johns, Newfoundland. That same year he organized the International Grenfell Association, which united the groups in the United States, Canada, and Great Britain that supported his work. Knighted by King George V in 1927, Grenfell retired in 1935, dying five years later at Charlotte, Vermont. N. V. HOPE

GRETCHANINOV, ALEXANDER
(1864–1956)
Russian-American composer of church music

Gretchaninov's early compositions followed the Russian Orthodox unaccompanied style with rich, multi-part textures and wide pitch ranges. Later he introduced the organ and other instruments into his choral works, a practice not accepted in Russia but well received in the West. He also was innovative in his use of Russian national melodic patterns.

Gretchaninov studied at the Moscow and St. Petersburg conservatories; at the latter his composition teacher was Rimsky-Korsakov. Not welcome as a church composer in Russia after the revolution, he settled in Paris in 1925 and later in the United States, where he became an American citizen (1946). Besides

church music Gretchaninov wrote three operas, seven cantatas, five symphonies, four string quartets, as well as several orchestral suites, overtures, concertos, and more than three hundred songs. In one of his last church works, the *Missa Oecumenica* (1944), he made use of elements from other religious traditions, including non-Christian. W. PHEMISTER

GRIESBACH, JOHANN JAKOB
(1745–1812)
Noted German New Testament scholar

Griesbach became a private tutor at Tübingen University in 1771. In 1775 he became a professor at Jena, where he taught until his death. He authored numerous critical works on the New Testament.

Griesbach laid the foundations of modern textual criticism. In the long tedious process of making handwritten manuscripts, numerous errors had been incorporated into the biblical text. Griesbach attempted to develop a method to sort out the errors and uncover the original text of the New Testament. He concluded that there are three major groups or "families" of manuscripts—the Alexandrian, Western, and Byzantine—each with its own particular characteristics. He then devised numerous "tests" whereby one could trace back the history of the text of each family and arrive at the earlier, less corrupted, "parent" manuscripts. From 1775 through 1777 he published a text of the New Testament based upon these new principles. R. HESSELGRAVE

GRINDAL, EDMUND (1519–1583)
Archbishop of Canterbury who tried to bring reforming views to the Church of England

Grindal left his family's Cumberland farm to study at Cambridge University, where he became a fellow of Pembroke Hall (in 1538). Common enthusiasm for the Reformation led to a friendship with Nicholas Ridley, bishop of Rochester, through whom he became the precentor (leader of singing) at St. Paul's Cathedral in London. When Ridley and other Protestant leaders were burned by

Catholic Queen Mary, Grindal fled to Europe. After Mary's death, her sister Elizabeth became queen. She appointed Grindal master of Pembroke Hall and bishop of London. A recognized Protestant leader, he helped in the revision of the new English prayer book.

As archbishop of York, he tried to convert Roman Catholics to the Church of England. He was unwilling, however, to root out Puritanism from London after his appointment as Archbishop of Canterbury (in 1575). Grindal supported Puritan meetings or "prophesyings." Elizabeth believed Puritanism was undermining the Church; so when Grindal refused to suppress the group, he was suspended (in 1577). His successor, John Whitgift, proved less tolerant and vigorously implemented the anti-Puritan measure Grindal had opposed. P. TOON

GROOTE, GERARD (1340–1384)
Dutch scholar; founder of the Catholic lay community Brethren of the Common Life

Gerard (Geert) Groote was born in Deventer (the Netherlands). His father, a prosperous cloth merchant, left him a substantial inheritance, making his academic pursuits possible. Groote eagerly delved into Greek, Latin, Hebrew, astrology, medicine, law, philosophy, and theology.

After studying in Paris and Cologne, he received a canonry at Aachen. That appointment, combined with successes in public disputations, paved the way for further advancements. His career was interrupted in 1372, however, by serious illness. When he recovered, he began to pursue a life of living by the Spirit. Seeking to follow the way of Christ, he began preaching his *devotio moderna*, a "modern devotion" based on inner spirituality and charitable service. Soon he established one household for women and another for men devoted to cultivating that practical piety. He briefly stayed in a Carthusian monastery, but soon returned to Deventer. Groote's spiritual renewal, evidenced by his convincing preaching, raised up defenders and opponents to his ministry. When the bishop forbade him to preach publicly, he withdrew to Windesheim near

Deventer and founded an order of Augustinian canons. It was at the Windesheim monastery that the scholar Desiderius Erasmus studied.

Groote kept a diary, which has been entitled *The Following of Christ*. Some scholars believe this is the same work called the *Imitation of Christ*, usually attributed to Thomas à Kempis, who attended the Common Life School at Deventer as a youth. P. VELTMAN

GROSSETESTE, ROBERT (c. 1168–1253)
Bishop of Lincoln, England; prolific writer

Grosseteste was a member of a poor Suffolk family, and the nature of his early education is not known. He did, however, become a teacher at Oxford University, rising to the post of chancellor. From 1229 to 1235 he was a teacher in the new Franciscan House there. Then, on being elected bishop of Lincoln in 1235, he moved there. Lincoln was the largest diocese in England, and Grosseteste attempted to remedy the many abuses he found in its parishes and religious houses, a policy that led him into a prolonged conflict with his cathedral staff. In 1250 he visited Rome and, in further attempts to remove corruption, protested about the appointment of Italians, who spoke no English, to wealthy church offices in England. Nor did he spare royalty in his criticisms. Also, he strongly objected to clergy holding civil offices.

Grosseteste's academic interests were wide ranging, from theology and philosophy to natural science. He translated works by Aristotle of Greece, John of Damascus, and Ignatius of Antioch. He wrote commentaries on philosophical and biblical texts. He was fascinated by light, seeing it as that which God first made. His treatis, *De luce* (*On Light*), develops this theme into a metaphysical system of thought. Further treatises by Grosseteste were on pastoral, devotional, and theological topics. P. TOON

GROTIUS, HUGO (1583–1645)
Humanistic, Arminian writer

Born in Delft (the Netherlands), Hugo

Grotius (Huigh de Groot) was nurtured in an environment conducive to academic life. He wrote Latin poetry at eight, attended the University of Leiden (where his father was curator) at eleven, and received the doctorate from the University of Orleans (France) at fifteen. He was greatly admired by French king Henry IV, who hailed him as "the miracle of Holland."

Grotius, who had studied under Jacobus Arminius (1560–1609) at Leiden, embraced the beliefs of his mentor and supported staunchly grand pensionary Jan van Oldenbarneveldt, champion of the Arminian cause.

In the Netherlands, strife between Remonstrants (reformed Calvinists and followers of Arminius) and Calvinists had intensified with the Union of Utrecht (northern Dutch "declaration of independence" from Catholic Spain) in 1579. The Union guaranteed that each province, supported by militia if necessary, could determine its own religious commitment. Of those northern provinces only Utrecht and Holland chose Arminianism. Embroiled in the political-religious controversy, the States-General beheaded Oldenbarneveldt and sentenced Grotius to life imprisonment. Through clever plotting by his wife Reigersberg, Grotius escaped in 1621 to Paris.

Later Grotius served Queen Christina of Sweden as ambassador. In 1645 he resigned in order to return to his native land. En route, however, he became ill and died at Rostock (now a German port).

Poetry, history, law, and religion all attracted Grotius. His 1625 publication *On the Law of War and Peace* was a comprehensive treatise on international law in which he applied Scripture, theology, classical thought, and political philosophy. The thesis was a systematic polemic against totalitarianism under which Grotius himself suffered.

In 1627 his religious work *De veritate religionis Christianae* brought him tribute for his logic and eloquence, although Christian truth for Grotius was as much natural law as it was God's miraculous intervention.

Because of his zeal for Christian unity, he was labeled a papist by Protestants. Because of his reformed theology on Communion, Catholics branded him a heretic. Neverthe-

less, as religious toleration became normative (especially in the eighteenth century), Grotius's humanistic, Arminian approach was greatly accepted. P. VELTMAN

GROVES, ANTHONY NORRIS
(1795–1853)
Leader among the Plymouth Brethren; missionary to Baghdad

Born in Newton, Hampshire (England), Groves studied dentistry and surgery in London as a young man, then moved to Devon in 1816. Having a strong sense of call to Christian work, he went to Dublin in 1826 to train for the ministry at Trinity College. There he met J. N. Darby, who later became a noted Bible teacher and originator of dispensationalism. With Darby and others he formed a circle of friends who studied and prayed together.

In 1829 Groves determined to use his own money and become a missionary. With his family and a few friends he set off for Baghdad. There he sought to teach Christianity without reference to any denomination or sect. He used his medical skill to help the people. After his wife died of the plague, he visited India to view missions there, returning to England in 1834. He actively recruited non-denominational missionaries for India and, after remarrying, set off for the country again himself. There he continued his evangelistic work and also made use of his dentistry and surgery. In 1852, due to ill health, he had to return home.

Groves's principles for fellowship and evangelism were attractive in their simplicity. With George Müller, he is considered a founding father of the "Open" Brethren. P. TOON

GRUBB, WILFRED BARBROOKE
(1865–1930)
Scottish pioneer missionary to the Gran Chaco

The "Livingstone of South America," Grubb was born at Liberton, Edinburgh. He was accepted by the South American Missionary Society at age nineteen and spent forty years spreading the gospel across the unexplored heart of the continent of South America. His fearlessness and Christian love so won the confidence of the Indians in Paraguay that the government of that country appointed him commissioner for the Chaco.

Grubb's method was to befriend several nomadic families and teach them to build homes, working simultaneously along educational, industrial, medical, and evangelistic lines. In 1911 he wrote about the Lengua Indians of the Paraguayan Chaco in *An Unknown People in an Unknown Land.*

By that time tribal wars had ceased, and strangers could wander safely over the 450 miles of roads that had replaced Indian tracks. Although less than two hundred Lenguas had been baptized, the tone of a whole people had been transformed. Grubb translated hymns, prayers, and much of the New Testament into Lengua. He accomplished his work with never more than four other European missionaries at any one time. N. HILLYER

GUICCIARDINI, PIERO (1806–1866)
Italian Protestant leader

Guicciardini was born in Florence into a well-known family that included in its membership the sixteenth-century historian Francesco. Early in life he made contact with Swiss Protestants who resided in Florence and began to read the Bible; and in 1836, he underwent a conversion experience. Private meetings with like-minded evangelical friends, some of them of the working class, went on for many years. In 1848 revolution broke out in several areas of disunited Italy—the first stage of the Risorgimento, that resurgence of cultural and patriotic fervor that eventually produced an independent and unified Italian nation-state. This movement was accompanied by a small-scale evangelical revival in 1849, in the course of which meetings were held openly. Late that year, however, the revolutionary movement was put down by the Austrian army, and evangelicals became objects of suspicion. In 1851 Guicciardini was arrested and sentenced to six months' imprisonment. On being released, he sought refuge in England, where he came into contact with leaders of the Plymouth Brethren movement, notably Anthony Noris Groves. He also met

another Italian political exile Teodoro Rossetti, whom he converted to the evangelical faith. While in England, Guicciardini helped to prepare a revision of the Italian Bible, which was published in 1853. Next year he was able to return to Italy, followed by Rossetti in 1857. Under the leadership of these two, evangelical congregations of the Brethren Church were started, centering in Florence and Alessandria. By 1870, the year of national unification, some thirty of these had been founded throughout Italy. N. V. HOPE

GUILMANT, ALEXANDRA (1837–1911)
French musician and composer; known as the finest organist of his day

Guilmant served as the organist at La Trinite Church in Paris from 1871 to 1901. In 1894 Guilmant, Charles Bordes, and Vincent D'Indy, also musicians, established the Schola Cantorum (School of Singing) in Paris. At this school, music theory was taught by studying the structure of the Gregorian chants from the Middle Ages. The music of the romantic era from composers such as Bach and Beethoven served as models for modern church music composition. Guilmant, interested in the music of past periods, edited two collections of lesser-known classical organ pieces. Guilmant also wrote original sonatas and symphonies for organ and orchestra. K. LEID

GUINNESS, HENRY GRATTAN (1835–1910)
Evangelist and writer

A native of Dublin and converted at age twenty, Guinness was a man of rare evangelistic passion and missionary vision. He was ordained (as an evangelist) in 1857 and preached in all parts of the British Isles and the United States. Though he himself never became a missionary, he visited many parts of the world and was used of God to promote the cause of home and foreign missions. He helped found several missionary training schools in London, Boston, and Minneapolis, from which hundreds of graduates went to the mission field.

As a direct result of Guinness's influence two well-known missions were founded: North Africa Mission (1881) and the Livingstone Inland Mission (1877), which became part of the Regions Beyond Missionary Union in 1899. His two books, *The Approaching End of the Age* (1886) and *Light for the Last Days* (1888), did much to stir up interest in evangelical circles on both sides of the Atlantic. H. KANE

GUNKEL, HERMANN (1862–1932)
German Protestant theologian

Gunkel is best known for his contributions to the "form criticism" school of biblical theology. Form criticism attempted to trace the origins and history of various literary forms in the Bible. Gunkel was one of the first to apply the method to the Old Testament. Although he wrote commentaries on several biblical books, his best-known book was a study on the psalms (1926–1928).

For Gunkel, the most important part of biblical history was not the events described, but the description itself. He was mainly interested in the setting or source of literary materials (German *Sitz im Leben,* "situation in life"). He thought that Old Testament poetry originated in oral tradition rather than in literary documents, and that the oral tradition had taken a certain form through the process of retelling. By studying the literary forms, one may discover something of the historical process that produced the forms, but not necessarily the history of the events themselves. It is possible to determine why the stories were preserved and what function they served in the communities that preserved them. But no one can tell how or whether they happened.

Gunkel was a professor at a number of leading German universities such as Halle (1889–1893, 1920–1927), Berlin (1894–1907), and Giessen (1907–1920). D. M. LAKE

GUSTAVUS II, ADOLPHUS (1594–1632)
Swedish king whose intervention in the Thirty Years' War helped to save the German Protestant cause

The son of Charles IX and Christina (daughter of German duke Adolphus), Gustavus was brought up as a Lutheran Protestant. Multilingual and well-schooled in politics and diplomacy, he ascended the Swedish throne at age seventeen.

Inherited conflicts with Denmark, Russia, and Poland thrust Gustavus into the position of military commander. He organized well-disciplined, well-equipped artillery and cavalry units and deployed them effectively in battle. As a result he enlarged Sweden's boundaries and secured a prominent share in Baltic commerce. Alarmed by the Austrian emperor's victories against Protestant forces, Gustavus embarked in 1630 for Pomerania (now northern Poland). After several victories, Gustavus was killed in battle. His political mission to end the Thirty Years' War was completed by his daughter, Christian, who as queen contracted the Treaty of Westphalia (1648). N. V. HOPE

GUSTAVUS VASA (1496–1560)
Founder of the Vasa dynasty, which ruled Sweden from 1523 to 1720

In 1520 Gustavus Vasa, a young nobleman, mobilized groups of peasants who won Swedish independence from Denmark. Gustavus was then elected king by a diet at Strangnas (1523).

Because of its opposition to the national independence movement, the Roman Catholic Church incurred unpopularity in Sweden. In addition, the urgent financial needs of the new government made the wealthy Catholic church a tempting target. Gustavus's personal inclination to Lutheranism and the introduction of Protestantism into Sweden in the early 1520s by Olavus Petri resulted in the anti-Catholic decrees of the Diet of Vasteras (1527). As a result, Catholic church property was confiscated, Protestant doctrines were taught in the schools, the king (rather than the pope) had authority to confirm higher clergy. In 1528 the bishop of Vasteras consecrated three Swedish bishops without papal confirmation.

Under Gustavus's leadership, Lutheranism gradually replaced Roman Catholicism as the national religion. Protestantism became so firmly established during his reign that it successfully withstood subsequent rulers' attempts to change the nation's religious allegiance. N. V. HOPE

GUTENBERG, JOHANN (c. 1398-1468)
German pioneer printer

Evidently born into a prosperous Mainz family, he was called Johann Gensfleisch eur Laden, but adopted his mother's name, Gutenberg. Through family connections, he entered the well-known goldsmiths' guild of Mainz. He practiced metalwork there until bitter struggles between guilds forced him to move to Strassburg (France). During that time he experimented with molded type viscous ink for use on metal plates and, in separate reusable letters, developing a printing press with movable metal type. No documents from that time exist, however, to prove Gutenberg's revolutionary inventions.

In 1448, the indebted Gutenberg sought loans from friends in Mainz. Around 1450 he secured the financial backing of Johann Fust, a wealthy banker. A legal battle in 1455 dissolved their partnership, and Fust gained control of Gutenberg's innovative printing equipment. Fust and Peter Schoeffer, who had worked under Gutenberg, published the forty-two-line so-called Mazarin Bible around 1456. Fust and Schoeffer then printed a *Psalter* (1457), whose type is believed to have been originally conceived by Gutenberg. In 1465 Gutenberg received a pension from the archbishop of Mainz, but nothing more is known of his printing. Several Bible editions have been attributed to Gutenberg, but these claims cannot be verified. R. VONDERLACK

GUTHRIE, JAMES (c. 1612-1661)
Scottish minister

Born into an Episcopalian family in Angus, Guthrie came under the influence of Samuel Rutherford at St. Andrews, signed the National Covenant in 1638, and was ordained minister at Lauder in 1642, transferring to Stirling in 1649. He stoutly denied the young King Charles II's authority in spiritual matters. Under the Cromwellian regime, nonetheless, he defended the principle of monarchy, like many

of his Covenanter colleagues. In 1653 his *Causes of God's Wrath against Scotland* upheld both the National Covenant and the Solemn League and Covenant and rejected all suggestion of religious toleration. After the Restoration of the monarchy in 1660, he led a group of twelve strict Covenanters who congratulated Charles, reminded him of his Covenant obligation, and asked him to fill all offices of trust in Scotland, England, and Ireland with Covenanters "of known affection to the cause of God." With other petitioners he was seized. Charged with declining the king's authority in ecclesiastical affairs, he was condemned to the gallows and became the first of a long line of minister martyrs for the Covenant. It was said more recently that the charges against him really involved freedom of the press, to hold public meetings, defend constitutions and conscience, and to have a free church.
J. D. DOUGLAS

GUTHRIE, THOMAS (1803–1873)
Free Church of Scotland minister; advocate for needy children

Born in Brechin, Guthrie studied theology at Edinburgh University (1815–1825) and then medicine in Edinburgh and Paris. In 1830 he became minister at Arbirlot, Forfarshire, and in 1837 became collegiate minister of Old Greyfriars Church, Edinburgh. When evangelicals broke from the Scottish state church (1843), Guthrie joined the new Free Church.

During his subsequent pastorate at Free St. John's, he became deeply interested in the plight of neglected children. Guthrie issued his *Plea for Ragged Schools* (1847) to raise money for a school to feed, clothe, teach, and vocationally train needy children. Guthrie's persistence resulted in two parliamentary acts (1854) that provided more humane treatment for delinquent and vagrant children. In 1862 he was moderator of the Free Church general assembly. N. V. HOPE

GUTHRIE, WILLIAM (1620–1665)
Scottish Covenanter

An Angus landowner's son, Guthrie was

educated at St. Andrews University and influenced toward the ministry by the professor Samuel Rutherford. In 1644 he became minister of Fenwick in Ayrshire and transformed an unspiritual parish, preaching to congregations that overflowed into the churchyard. His was no gloomy religion: he was fisher, fowler, curler, and "given to innocent mirth." When persecution began he appeared on Covenanting battlefields, for he linked his piety with patriotism and good citizenship. His book, *The Christian's Great Interest* (1658), had a wide circulation; John Owen said that it and his New Testament were his constant companions. In 1661 William's cousin, James Guthrie, suffered martyrdom; and Guthrie himself was dismissed from his position by the state-backed episcopacy in 1664. Dogged by ill health all his life, he died at the age of forty-five at Brechin. J. D. DOUGLAS

GUTZLAFF, KARL FRIEDRICH AUGUST (1803–1851)
German missionary to China

Born in Prussia and educated at royal expense at Johannes Janicke's missionary training school in Berlin, Gutzlaff sailed for the East Indies in 1827. A year later he severed his relations with the Netherlands Missionary Society and became a free-lance missionary. His first achievement was the translation of the Bible into Siamese, which he accomplished in just three years. Never able to settle down, he lived in Batavia (now Jakarta, Indonesia), Singapore, Bangkok, Macao, Canton, and Hong Kong. For a time he was Chinese secretary to the British authorities in Macao and Canton. Like J. Hudson Taylor after him, he took a Chinese name and wore Chinese clothes. In the 1830s he made several trips along the China coast distributing Christian literature.

Unable to enter China himself, Gutzlaff organized a band of Chinese preachers and through them planned to evangelize China. This effort attracted much attention and support in Europe, but without proper supervision it ended in failure. Many of the "preachers" turned out to be opium smokers who took advantage of Gutzlaff's credulity and generosity. Among his converts, however, were some earnest and sincere men. He had, moreover, been the means of attracting to China a number of very able German missionaries who later laid the foundations of a successful work. H. KANE

GUYON, MADAME (1648–1717)
French mystic whose Quietist writings had great impact on theological circles of her time

Jeanne Marie Bouvier Guyon was born to aristocratic parents in Montargis (France). Her character was molded by the many convents who educated her and whose religious life she planned to follow until her forced marriage at age fifteen. In her voluminous autobiography Guyon implied that her mother-in-law made her marriage miserable, so that she turned to intense, inward prayer. Widowed in 1676, Guyon had a religious experience four years later, which she interpreted as a special, mystical union with God. As a result of this relationship, she believed she had authority and insight beyond that of official church leaders.

Guyon traveled extensively throughout France, making both disciples and enemies. In 1686 she came to Paris and became influential at court. At that time the church began to suppress unorthodox mystic spiritualists—condemning, for example, Miguel de Molinos, a deviant Spanish priest. In 1687, Guyon's closest disciple and confessor, Father Lacombe, was arrested. And Guyon herself was confined to a convent. She was later released and subsequently precipitated continual conflict among influential bishops, particularly her supporter, François Fénelon, and his ideological rival, Jacques Bossuet, who finally had her censured. Thereafter she lived quietly in Blois until her death. R. D. SHUSTER

H

HALDANE, JAMES ALEXANDER (1768–1851)

Scottish evangelist

Born in Dundee of good family, Haldane lost both parents by the time he was six years old. After studying at Edinburgh University, he joined the navy in 1785 and became captain of an East Indiaman. He resigned his commission in 1794, was converted soon afterwards, and helped to found the Society for Propagating the Gospel at Home (1797) at a time when apathy, unbelief, and moral laxity dominated the Church of Scotland. Three evangelists were soon appointed, Charles Simeon encouraged to return to Scotland for a further tour, and Haldane and a colleague went on the first of a series of preaching tours that covered Scotland from Shetland to the Solway. His written accounts of these itinerancies reflect both the low state of Christianity in the land of John Knox, and the eagerness of the people to hear and respond to the gospel. Opposition came from parish ministers and from the aristocracy, but Haldane's social standing, his reputation as a courageous sea captain, and his earnestness and integrity discomfited his opponents. In 1799 he was ordained as the first congregational minister in Scotland, with more than three hundred at once joining his preaching tabernacle.

Similar congregations were established in other Scottish cities, and they flourished, to the great dismay not only of the national church but of the Secessionists who had formed Presbyterian splinter groups. Like his brother Robert, with whom he always collaborated closely, he later became convinced of the efficacy of believer's baptism, but though this caused serious differences with some old friends, he never saw this as an impediment to cooperation in preaching the Word. It was said that no other since the time of Whitefield had been so used of God in the conversion of sinners. J. D. DOUGLAS

HALDANE, ROBERT (1764–1842)

Scottish evangelist, philanthropist, and writer

Born in London and educated in Scotland, Haldane at first made the sea his career but soon returned to the family estate in Stirlingshire inherited on the early death of his father. After his conversion in 1795, he held that "Christianity is everything or nothing. If it be true, it warrants and commands every sacrifice to promote its influence." He sold his estate in order to start a mission in Bengal—a project never implemented because of the opposition of the East India Company. He devoted himself instead to home missions, in which cause he spent some fifty thousand pounds in eight years. He was prepared to bring twenty-four African children over from Sierra Leone to be educated at his expense (the children did come, but others bore the cost), and established a seminary that at one time had sixty students for whose maintenance and fees he made himself responsible. He founded various tabernacles in Scotland, administered on congregational principles. His evangelistic work took him to Switzerland and France (1816–1819), where his ministry made a significant contribution to the Awakening that so electrified the flagging Protestant cause in those lands. A man of irenic and gracious disposition, he could be unyielding when he felt truth was in jeopardy. Thus he was a foremost critic of the British and Foreign Bible Society when copies of the Scripture with the Apocrypha added were circulated in Europe. As with his brother James, his social standing opened doors of opportunity, yet his preaching was so simple and direct that it reached the hearts of all kinds of people. Haldane's chief written works include *Evidences and Authority of Divine Revelation* (1816) and a commentary on the epistle to the Romans (1834).

J. D. DOUGLAS

HALL, ROBERT (1764–1831)
English Baptist preacher

Born in Leicestershire, Hall became a leading English Baptist preacher. The youngest of fourteen children, he had a thirst for knowledge and was sent to be educated by John Ryland, a Baptist minister in Northampton. Then he studied at the Baptist Academy in Bristol and at King's College, Aberdeen, where he received the M.A. degree in 1785. He became assistant minister at Broadmead Chapel, Bristol, and tutor in the Academy nearby. By this time he had moved away from his earlier Calvinism to an Arminian position that was informed by an interest in the "new" science of Joseph Priestley and others. In 1791 he moved to the Baptist Chapel in Cambridge to succeed Robert Robinson. People were impressed by his oratory and noble sentiments.

A conversion experience, following physical and mental illness, caused him to become more evangelical in his views and in 1807 he took a pastorate in Leicester from where he moved in 1826 to Bristol. Here he succeeded his former teacher, Ryland, as pastor of Broadmead Chapel (Baptist).

His particular gift was his ability to commend Christ to people of good education and of literary tastes. His favorite poet was John Milton, and he even learned Italian in order to be able to read Dante. In later life his enthusiasm for Priestley waned, and he became an admirer of Jeremy Bentham. His *Works* was published in six volumes in 1832.

P. TOON

HALLESBY, OLE KRISTIAN (1879–1961)
Norwegian evangelical leader, writer, and theologian

Born into a farming family whose religion was influenced by the pietism (stressing personal holiness, Bible reading, and experience of God) taught by Hans Nielsen Hauge (1771–1824) of Norway, Hallesby became a student of theology. However, he moved away from his father's position and became more liberal. In 1902 he had a powerful experience of God that caused him to view favorably the interpretation of Christianity called evangelical. Like Hauge, he was for a time an itinerant preacher who saw several significant awakenings. But he was also an academic and so, after doctoral studies in Berlin, he became a professor of dogmatics in the new Free Faculty of Theology in Oslo (the Menighetsfakultetet), which had been founded to counteract the spread of liberalism and to train orthodox pastors for the parishes. In this Faculty he lectured from 1909 to 1952.

Outside Scandinavia he is best known for his participation in the work of Inter-Varsity and the International Fellowship of Evangelical Students, of which he was the first President in 1947. Several of his books, *Prayer* (1948), *Conscience* (1951), and *Why I am a Christian* (1951), were published by Inter-Varsity (United Kingdom) and were very influential among students.

All his life Hallesby was a leader of evangelicals in the Norwegian church as well as being an ardent supporter of foreign missions. He resisted the Nazis and spent the years from 1943 through 1945 in a concentration camp. P. TOON

HAMILTON, JOHN (1512–1571)
Archbishop of St. Andrews, the last Roman Catholic to hold that office

Born in Edinburgh, the son of the first Earl of Arran, Hamilton matriculated from St. Andrews University in 1528 and later studied in Paris (1540–1543). Through family influence he was appointed on his return to Scotland as Keeper of the Privy Seal (1543–1546) and then Lord Treasurer (1543–1554). In 1546 he became Bishop of Dunkeld, and the next year, Archbishop of St. Andrews when Beaton was assassinated. As Archbishop he led the opposition to the Scottish Reformers. From 1548 he summoned a series of synods on clergy morality and the religious education of the laity, and these resulted in the highly regarded *Archbishop Hamilton's Catechism* (1552). A supporter of Mary Queen of Scots, he baptized her son, the future James VI, in 1566. After her flight, he was arrested and hanged as a traitor at Stirling. N. HILLYER

HAMILTON, PATRICK (1503–1528)
First martyr of the Scottish Reformation

Born to an aristocratic family, Hamilton studied at Paris University (1515–1520) and then at St. Andrews, by which time the writings of Luther had fired his enthusiasm. In 1527 he had to flee abroad from Archbishop Beaton's threats. At Wittenberg he met Luther and Melanchthon, and on a visit to Marburg attended the opening of Philip of Nesse's new Evangelical University. He soon returned to Scotland, where his preaching met with a great response. Early in 1528 Beaton lured him to St. Andrews on the pretense of debate. Hamilton was arrested, tried, and by noon was being burnt at the stake before influential friends could save him. His murder, intended to intimidate

others, had the opposite effect. All Scotland began discussing Reformation theology, for as one witness of the execution put it, "The reek [smoke] of Patrick Hamilton has infected as many as it did blow upon." His spirited defense of his faith converted one accuser, Alexander Alesius (1500–1565), who escaped to the continent, later to become the friend of Melanchthon. Hamilton's only work, *Loci Communes*, or "Patrick's Pleas," setting forth the doctrine of justification by faith, is included in Foxe's *Acts and Monuments*. N. HILLYER

HAMMERSCHMIDT, ANDRES (1612–1675)
German organist and composer

Born in Bohemia, Hammerschmidt spent most of his life as organist of various Lutheran churches in Saxony. He was among the first composers in Germany to adapt the new Italian dramatic style to sacred works for the Protestant church. He favored writing for several voices in dialogue with instrumental accompaniment, using episodes drawn from Scripture. His works were received with a good deal of enthusiasm. They represent an important step in the development of the Lutheran church cantatas and passions that later were brought to their highest development by J. S. Bach. Hammerschmidt also wrote important instrumental music. J. B. MACMILLAN

HANDEL, GEORGE FRIDERIC (1685–1759)
German composer; famous for his composition, Messiah

Handel was born in Halle, Saxony. Except for his extraordinary musical gifts and his Lutheran background, Handel's career stands in marked contrast to that of his distinguished contemporary and fellow-countryman, Johann S. Bach. Unlike Bach, Handel did not come from a musical family; his father, a physician, wanted him to study law. Only grudgingly did he permit his son to receive musical instruction. Possessing unqualified genius, at seventeen Handel had mastered harpsichord and organ, violin and oboe, as well as the elements of composition. Handel's career as a composer began about 1703 in Hamburg, where German opera was flourishing at the time. He then moved to Italy where he spent 1707 through 1710 advancing his skills through contact with such noted composers as Arcangelo Corelli, and Alessandro and Giuseppe Scarlatti. Returning to Germany in 1712 he briefly entered the service of the future George I of England, then Elector of Hanover. The next year Handel moved to London, which became his home for the rest of his life. He was buried there in Westminster Abbey.

It was the growing taste of London aristocracy for Italian opera that had drawn Handel there. Throughout his life, he wrote about forty such works. Even after changing taste brought him financial crisis and a resultant physical collapse in 1737, he did not lose interest in the form. But it was with oratorios that he rebuilt his popularity and fortune. The oratorio had begun in Italy as a sort of sacred opera. It was normally performed without costumes, however, and only sometimes with stage scenery. Handel combined his particular gift for the dramatic in music with his mastery of the English choral tradition to create a new type of oratorio that appealed to the cultured English middle class. Although a few of his nearly thirty such works are secular, most employ plots drawn from the Old Testament.

Handel's first English oratorio was *Esther.* Among others are *Jephtha, Samson, Saul, Solomon,* and *Judas Maccabaeus* (from the Apocrypha). Only in *Israel in Egypt* and *Messiah* did he not present soloists as specific characters and use the actual words of Scripture exclusively for his texts.

Messiah (1741) is unique in Handel's output, not because its music is his greatest but because of the way in which the messianic theme from prophecy to fulfillment is given continuity in music of utmost appropriateness. No major work in any category has enjoyed such continuous and widespread popularity over so long a period of time. In addition, it was composed in a remarkably

short time—about three weeks. Handel repeatedly presented it during the rest of his life, making numerous revisions and alterations.

Handel wrote a number of fine anthems, including three for coronation ceremonies, and several festal settings of the *Te Deum.* He also produced numerous cantatas, sonatas, and concertos of great excellence. The English oratorio, however, was his most individual achievement. His works in that genre provided models for such later composers as Joseph Haydn, Ludwig Spohr, and Felix Mendelssohn. J. B. MacMillan

HARDING, STEPHEN (died 1134)
Abbot of Citeaux, France

Harding, born in Sherborne, England, escaped the Norman Conquest by fleeing first to Scotland, then to France. There he came into contact with the relatively new Cistercian Order. Attracted to it, he made his profession at Citeaux in 1098. After a while he was constituted as prior and then in 1109 as the third abbot. By his strong sense of discipline and his effectiveness in administering it, he welded the order into a unity that it had been in danger of losing. Part of such activity was the creation of a uniform text of the Bible. In so doing he employed many scholars including some Jewish savants. He required all daughter-foundations to accept the spiritual, but not financial, jurisdiction of Citeaux. The Benedictine rule was to be observed in its strict interpretation as at Citeaux. And in all abbeys of the order, liturgical texts and practices were to be in conformity with the use at Citeaux. A. Cabaniss

HARNACK, ADOLF (1851–1930)
German church historian and theologian

Born in Dorpat, Estonia, where his father Theodosius was professor of practical theology, Harnack was educated at Dorpat and then at Leipzig. He taught in Leipzig from 1874 to 1879, when he was appointed full professor at Giessen. In 1886 he became professor at Marburg, and in 1889 at Berlin, where he remained until his retirement in 1921.

Harnack was an immensely productive historian of the church of the first five centuries. He displayed his extensive research in over sixteen hundred publications. Significant among them were the *History of Early Christian Literature to Eusebius* (three volumes, 1893–1904), "a monument of exact learning and critical acumen," and *The Mission and Expansion of Christianity in The First Three Centuries* (1902; fourth edition, 1924), "the first detailed survey of the actual growth of Christian communities before the conversion of Constantine." His magnum opus was *Lehrbuch der Dogmengeschichte* (*History of Dogma,* 1886–1889), which traced the history of Christian doctrine down to the Reformation. He expounded there the thesis that as the original fervor of early Christians faded, Greek thought forms and institutions began to influence the church's development.

Harnack was also a theologian of the school of Albrecht Ritschl (1822–1889). He sought to unite Christianity and culture. In order to do so, he deemed it necessary to separate the essential message of Christianity from the theological interpretations by which it had been encrusted. His lectures in Berlin in the winter of 1899–1900, published as *Das Wesen des Christenthums* (*What is Christianity?* 1901), were a major attempt to make such a separation. He believed that Jesus was a man who attained spiritual serenity and strength that he was able to pass on to others. And he believed that Jesus' essential message was not about himself but God the Father. He believed that Jesus' gospel focused on the infinite value of the human soul, the higher righteousness, and the command of love. Though Harnack's interpretation did not win widespread acceptance, it touched off a lively and fruitful international debate on the real meaning of Christianity. N. V. HOPE

HARPER, WILLIAM RAINEY
(1856–1906)
Scholar and educator

Born in Ohio, Harper earned his Ph.D. from Yale at age nineteen. After a brief period as professor of Hebrew at the newly formed Baptist Union Theological Seminary (Chicago), he returned to Yale, but two years later when John D. Rockefeller founded the University of Chicago, Harper was invited to become its president. During his fourteen years as president and professor, Harper led the university to become one of America's greatest academic centers. He was both an able administrator and a prolific scholar. His major written work is a commentary on Amos and Hosea (1905). His linguistic techniques are still widely used. D. M. LAKE

HARRIS, HOWEL (1714–1773)
Welsh preacher

Born in Brecon and of a poor family, Harris determined to enter the ministry of the Anglican Church. After a period as a schoolmaster, he underwent a conversion experience and spent a short time at Oxford University. He soon returned to the life of an itinerant evangelist in Wales, first in the south, then in the north, by 1739. People had to listen to him for he was both handsome and eloquent. The official clergy and their patrons were opposed to his methods, but he did not desire to found a new denomination. However, the result of his labors (as also for Daniel Rowland and George Whitefield) was the formation of Calvinistic Methodist churches. Unfortunately he had quarrels with both Rowland and Whitefield, which did not help the cause of unity in the revival. In 1752 he settled in a house in Trevecca, which became a center for the revival. Later the Countess of Huntingdon gave her support to the new college there. Harris did not write any significant books, but several of his Welsh hymns became well known. P. TOON

HARRIS, JAMES RENDEL (1852–1941)
Biblical scholar, archaeologist, and orientalist

Born at Plymouth, England, Harris was educated at Cambridge University from which he graduated in 1874. In 1880 he changed his religious affiliation from Congregationalism to Quakerism. In 1882 he was called to teach New Testament Greek at Johns Hopkins University, Baltimore, Maryland, and in 1885 became Professor of Biblical Languages and Literature at Haverford College (Pennsylvania). In 1893 he returned to Cambridge University as Lecturer in Paleography. Ten years later he became the first Director of Studies at Woodbrooke, the Quaker settlement for religious and social study at Selly Oak, Birmingham (England). In 1918 he was appointed Curator of Eastern manuscripts at the John Rylands Library, Manchester, in which capacity he traveled extensively in the Near and Middle East. From this position he retired in 1925 because of failing eyesight. The author of many specialist studies in biblical and related texts, Harris is best known for his discovery at the Monastery of St. Catherine on Mount Sinai of the Syriac text of the lost *Apology of Aristides,* which he published in 1891. N. V. HOPE

HARRIS, WILLIAM WADE
(c. 1865–1929)

African Christian prophet; a Grebo of Liberia

Harris attended Methodist schools and was converted at twenty-one. Confirmed in the Episcopal Church, he taught in its schools. While imprisoned due to a Grebo revolt, Harris was called to be a prophet of the Lord. He was imprisoned as a disrupter of the peace. He preached with charismatic power in the Ivory and Gold Coasts in 1913, baptizing, building churches, and gathering up to a hundred thousand followers. The French government expelled him from Ivory Coast when war broke out in 1914. Harris's later preaching was not so successful. He sought an indigenous African Christianity. The "Harrisites" and the Church of the Twelve Apostles claim to be his true followers, but it was the British Methodist Mission that reaped his harvest. Missionaries sent to Ivory Coast in 1924 quickly gathered in twenty-five thousand people and then another large group in the Gold Coast. R. P. BEAVER

HARVARD, JOHN (1607–1638)

Benefactor of Harvard University

Born in Southwark, John Harvard studied at Emmanuel College, Cambridge, and then later joined the Puritan emigration to the New World. In the early 1630s he settled in Massachusetts and became a teaching elder of the Charlestown Congregational church. He died shortly thereafter. His will left half his estate (£780) and his library (three to four hundred books) to the fledgling educational institution, which in 1638, the year of Harvard's death, had hired its first professor and enrolled its first students. This institution, the first American college, had been established by the Massachusetts General Court (legislature) in 1636, a mere six years after the Puritan migration began to the New World. (By contrast, the first college in Virginia, William and Mary, was not founded until 1693.) Out of gratitude for the bequest from John Harvard, the Board of Overseers named the school after him. The institution thus founded pledged itself "to advance Learning" and to provide for a trained ministry. From this humble but godly beginning has emerged Harvard University, America's most prestigious educational institution. M. A. NOLL

HASTINGS, JAMES (1852–1922)

Presbyterian minister; religious editor

Hastings was born in Huntly, Aberdeenshire (Scotland), and educated at Aberdeen University and Aberdeen Free Church College. He was ordained in 1884 as minister of the Free Church and held several pastorates until 1911, when he resigned to devote full time to his duties as a religious editor. He had begun editorial work in 1889, when he founded *The Expository Times,* a monthly journal he edited until his death. He also edited several important scholarly works, including the *Dictionary of the Bible* (five volumes, 1898–1904); *Dictionary of Christ and the Gospels* (two volumes, 1906–1908); an entirely new one-volume *Dictionary of the Bible* (1908); and the *Dictionary of the Apostolic Church* (two volumes, 1915–1918). His most ambitious editorial project was the *En-*

cyclopedia of Religion and Ethics (twelve volumes, 1908–1921; Index, 1926). That massive work has been described as "in some respects the most remarkable achievement of this prince of editors." N. V. HOPE

HASTINGS, THOMAS (1784–1872)
American church musician

Born in Connecticut, Hastings was self-taught. He was an albino, but overcame the handicap of poor sight to become a scholar, editor, and influential educator in the realm of church music. He was active in the Handel and Haydn Society, and with its founder, Lowell Mason, brought out the important collection *Hymns for Social Worship*. He is credited with composing over a thousand hymn tunes, among them that of "Rock of Ages." New York University honored him with a doctorate in music.
J. B. MACMILLAN

HAVERGAL, FRANCES RIDLEY (1836–1879)
English poet whose verse made a significant contribution to Christian hymnody

Havergal's father, William Henry Havergal, was an Anglican rector in Worcestershire. An accomplished musician who wrote about one hundred hymns, he instilled in his daughter a lifelong passion for knowledge. She was educated in boarding schools in England and Germany, where she learned several modern languages plus Greek and Hebrew.

The theology of Frances Havergal's poetry is mildly Calvinistic but not dogmatic. Her poems communicate a simple, childlike faith, yet they are still profound. The most well known of her fifty hymns and two hundred poems are "Take My Life, and Let It Be" (1874), "Like a River Glorious" (1878), "Who Is on the Lord's Side?" (1877), "Thou Art Coming, O My Saviour" (1872), "I Am Trusting Thee, Lord Jesus" (1874), "I Gave My Life for Thee," and "Lord, Speak to Me." Frances Havergal's publications include *Opened Treasures* and *Kept for the Master's Use*. W. PHEMISTER

HAWEIS, THOMAS (1734–1820)
A leading English evangelical preacher

Haweis went to the Grammar School in Truro Cornwall, where one of the first Anglican evangelicals was Curate of St. Mary's. That was Samuel Walker, and he had a decisive influence on Haweis, being responsible both for his conversion and for his call to the ministry. Haweis went to Christ Church, Oxford, but he never took a degree. He was ordained in Oxford and founded a second "Holy Club" (similar to that of the Wesleys). After being assistant to Martin Madan, chaplain of the Lock Hospital, London, he became Rector of Aldwincle in Northamptonshire from 1764 until his death. The parish became a center for the Revival movement. In 1774 he became a chaplain of Lady Huntingdon and a manager of her College at Trevecca. On her death in 1791 he was her trustee and executor.

He took a great interest in foreign missions, especially to the South Seas, was a founding father of the interdenominational London Missionary Society in 1794 and 1795, and wrote over forty books. P. TOON

HAYDN, FRANZ JOSEPH (1732–1809)
Austrian composer; luminary of Western music of the classical era

In early life Haydn was a choirboy at St. Stephen's Cathedral in Vienna. He subsequently studied the theoretical works of Fux and Matthesohn and studied composition under Porpora. After having as patrons Baron K. J. Furnberg and Count F. M. Morzin, Haydn began service in the house of Prince Esterhazy, where he became first *kapellmeister* (chapelmaster) by 1766. Although Haydn had become wealthy, internationally known, and virtually independent by 1790, he remained in the service of the Esterhazys until his retirement in 1801. His contribution as composer of opera, symphonic, and chamber music is of the highest caliber, approaching that of Ludwig van Beethoven and Wolfgang Mozart.

Haydn's music for the church spans nearly his whole career. He wrote fourteen masses, a Stabat Mater, two Te Deums, two major oratorios: *The Creation* (1798), his most popular choral work, and the secular *The Seasons* (1801). He also composed offertories, cantatas, and *The Seven Last Words*—originally seven instrumental sonatas written for the cathedral of Cadiz, later rescored as *String Quartets, Op. 51* and as an oratorio with soloists, chorus, and orchestra.

Among his best-known masses are the "Great Organ Mass" (*Mass in Honor of the Blessed Virgin Mary*, 1766), the *St. Cecilia Mass* (1770), the *Mass in Time of War* (1796), the "Lord Nelson Mass" (*Missa in Angustiis*, 1798), and the *Harmony Mass* (1802).

His techniques are of great historical importance. His uses of fugue, for example, often are symphonic in technique, while operatic influences come into many of his arias. Choral pieces are often written in sonata style, involving the contrasts and developments/recapitulations of instrumental music. His instrumental scorings are very interesting and colorful, particularly in uses of wind instruments. D. S. CUSHMAN

HAYDN, MICHAEL (1737–1806)
Austrian Composer

Johann Michael Haydn followed his older and more famous brother, Franz Josef, as a chorister at St. Stephen's Cathedral in Vienna. After filling several important musical posts, he became organist and music director of the Cathedral in Salzburg, where Mozart had served for a time, and with whom he had friendly relations. He excelled as a teacher and as a composer of masses and other music for the Roman Catholic rite, in which field he is held to have surpassed his brother. He wrote twenty-four masses and two requiems. In the secular field, he composed over thirty symphonies and much instrumental music for various combinations. J. B. MACMILLAN

HAYMO OF FAVERSHAM (died 1244)
English Franciscan

Of English origin, Haymo was already a priest and competent theologian in France when he joined the new Order of Friars Minor (Franciscan) in 1226 or 1228. Almost immediately Haymo became a significant administrator, serving Franciscanism in numerous capacities. By 1240 he was elected minister-general of the Order (the only Englishman ever to hold that position). He made the important and democratic reform of giving the general chapter of the Order authority superior to that of the minister-general. By restricting office to clerical members, however, he virtually halted the active recruitment of lay brothers. Among his other reforms was a carefully studied and large-scale revision of the liturgy, which was ultimately adopted by the entire church. As a result the pre-Tridentine and even Tridentine Roman liturgy basically became Franciscan. Since Vatican II, it has lost much of that particularity. A. CABANISS

HEADLAM, ARTHUR CAYLEY (1862–1947)
Anglican bishop; Bible scholar

Born at Whorlton Hall, Durham County, England, Headlam was educated at Winchester and Oxford University (1881–1885). Ordained Deacon in 1888 and priest in 1889, he taught Theology at Oxford University from 1885 to 1896. In the latter year he became Rector of Welwyn, Hertfordshire. In 1903 he was appointed Professor of Theology and Principal of King's College, London, where he instituted the important administrative reform of separating the theological faculty from the other divisions of the College. In 1913 he resigned as Principal, but retained his theological professorship until 1918 when he was appointed Regius Professor of Divinity at Oxford University. In 1923 he was nominated as Bishop of Gloucester, and remained in this diocese until 1945, when he retired. Headlam's first scholarly interest was in the New Testament; and in 1895, along with William Sanday, he published a learned commentary on Paul's Epistle to the Romans. In churchmanship Headlam belonged to no party, but he was deeply interested in Christian unity. His

Bampton Lectures of 1930, "The Doctrine of the Church and Christian Reunion," dealt with this question. When the Faith and Order Movement started, Headlam became deeply involved. He attended the two Faith and Order Conferences at Lausanne in 1927 and at Edinburgh in 1937, though he unsuccessfully opposed the merger of the Faith and Order Movement with that of Life and Work to form The World Council of Churches. N. V. HOPE

HEBER, REGINALD (1783–1826)
Anglican missionary bishop; hymn writer

Born at Malpas, Cheshire, England, Heber was educated at Oxford University, where he was elected to a Fellowship of All Souls College in 1805. In 1807 he was ordained as a clergyman and became Vicar of Hodnet in Hampshire. In 1815 he delivered the Bampton Lectures at Oxford University on the "Personality and Office of the Holy Comforter." In 1823 he was appointed the second missionary Bishop of Calcutta, a diocese which then included all of British India. Though his episcopate lasted only three years, "perhaps no missionary has ever left on his surroundings so deep an impress of his personality in so short a time" (Stephen C. Neill). Heber is notable also as "the greatest writer of English hymns since Charles Wesley." His fifty-seven hymns include such well-known sacred songs as "Holy, Holy, Holy" and "From Greenland's Icy Mountains" and "The Son of God Goes Forth to War." He also edited a posthumously published (1827) volume entitled *Hymns Written and Adapted to the Weekly Church Services of the Year*; and since this publication did much to popularize the singing of hymns, he has been described as "The Creator of the Modern Church Hymnbook" (W. H. Frere). N. V. HOPE

HECKER, ISAAC (1819–1888)
American "evangelist" to the Roman Catholics

After his years as a Methodist, and after a disappointing experience with the transcen-

dentalists of Brook Far, Hecker was drawn in 1844 to the Roman Catholic Church by his own bent to mystical piety. He served first in the Redemptorist Order until his views on Roman Catholicism in the United States separated him from that body. He then gained Pope Paul IX's permission in 1858 to found the congregation of Missionary Priests of Saint Paul the Apostle (Paulist Fathers). This organization undertook widespread efforts to bring Americans into the Roman Catholic Church. Unlike earlier Roman Catholic missionaries in America, the Paulist Fathers stressed the compatibility of Roman Catholicism with American styles of life. Hecker's books, such as *Aspiration of Nature* (1857), presented Roman Catholicism as a fulfillment of democracy and as the best answer to the spiritual needs of Americans. Hecker edited the influential *Catholic World* from 1865 until his death. A biography of Hecker published posthumously occasioned the "Americanist" controversy and a long debate over the wisdom of Hecker's approach for Roman Catholic missions. M. A. NOLL

HEERMANN, JOHANN (1585–1647)
German hymn writer

Many consider Heermann to be the greatest German hymn writer between Luther and the incomparable Paulus Gerhardt. He was born in Silesia and became distinguished for culture and scholarship. Much of his life as a pastor witnessed the unspeakable horrors of the Thirty Years' War. "Ah, Holy Jesus, How Hast Thou Offended" and "O God, Thou Gracious God" are among the greatest of Lutheran hymns. His work marks a transition from the more objective, didactic style of early Lutheranism to the warm, subjective expression of the Pietists. He published three important collections of hymns. J. B. MACMILLAN

HEGEL, GEORGE WILLIAM FRIEDRICH (1770–1831)
German philosopher

Perhaps the most influential philosopher

of the nineteenth century, Hegel was educated with a view to entering the clergy but reacted against the unimaginative orthodoxy of his professors, and taught philosophy instead at Jena, Heidelberg, and Berlin. He seems to have regarded his philosophy as a defense of Christianity, but his is a Christianity reinterpreted to conform to his philosophy and robbed of its historical and supernatural elements. Hegel thereby contributed to the rise of theological liberalism and the so-called "secular religion."

His early theological writings interpret religion along Kantian lines as a symbolic way of teaching morality. Thus God is pure reason and Jesus is a purely human teacher who acted out of rational duty in opposing the irrational legalism of the Pharisees. His natural religion of reason stands against all the positive religions of any priestly authorities. A little later Hegel changed this to stress not reason but love—the conflict between love and slavery to moral law.

These early ideas, while radically changed later, provide his conception not only of symbol but also of the dialectic: a process in which opposites negate each other yet are united in a synthesis that transcends their conflict. Hegel traced this process through unfolding logical categories into the evolution of nature and of the human spirit and its culture. Unifying this ongoing historical dialectic so that it advances in one direction is the underlying reality of Being, the absolute rational spirit that achieves full self-consciousness and self-expression in the emerging self-consciousness of the human spirit. This underlying absolute is God.

Religion employs imaginative pictorial concepts, sometimes called symbols, in reflecting on man's consciousness of himself as spirit at one with the Absolute. Philosophy dispenses with these symbols by achieving purely rational concepts. Consequently, Hegel took religious beliefs to symbolize his philosophical ideas. This is the case with all religions: primitive nature-religions symbolize the fact that nature is in some way related to Spirit; religions of spiritual individuality, such as Judaism, advance further in recognizing that man is spirit; but the absolute religion is Christianity, whose doctrine of the incarnation means that all finite things embody Absolute Spirit. Hegel, in other words, was an idealist who saw all reality as basically spiritual, and a panentheist who denied that God is numerically or qualitatively distinct from the world.

Other Christian symbols suffer, too. Love means that in the historical dialectic all negation and opposition are finally reconciled by becoming one in the Absolute. Resurrection, the death of death, speaks of Spirit's triumph over negation. Christianity is effectively changed from a religion rooted in historical events into an abstruse metaphysical theory. A. F. HOLMES

HEGESIPPUS (c. 120–190)
Antiheretical Christian author

A converted Jew and probably a native of Palestine, about the year 180 Hegesippus wrote five books of *Recollections,* a work "doctrinal in character and controversial in aim," which survives only in fragments, nearly all of them preserved in Eusebuis's *Ecclesiastical History.* About the middle of the second century Hegesippus set out for Rome, visiting other Christian centers on the way; and there he ascertained for himself that the genuine apostolic doctrinal tradition had been maintained in Rome without interruption down to the time of the then Bishop Anicetus (155–167). From what he learned in the Roman and other Christian churches, he was convinced that "in every succession and in every city the preaching of the Law and the Prophets and the Lord is faithfully followed." This open tradition of Christian orthodoxy, he argued, provided decisive refutation of the Gnostic claim to a secret tradition. N. V. HOPE

HEIDEGGER, MARTIN (1889–1976)
German existentialist

Heidegger studied at Freiberg under the distinguished phenomenologist Edmund Husserl, whom he succeeded there in 1928 as philosophy professor. In 1933, he served briefly as rector of the university under the

Nazis but soon retracted that alignment even though he remained enthusiastic about the superiority of German culture.

In line with existentialism generally, his interest centered in man's "being in the world," marked by temporality, "being unto death," and anxiety. He insists that scientific accounts of man fail to get at this situation. *Being And Time,* his best-known work, offers a detailed phenomenology of human existence, describing the "facticity" of being cast into a life not of our own making, free to pursue all kinds of options yet trapped by our own finiteness. Destiny awaits, however, and conscience calls us to an authentically human existence. In his later writings, Heidegger makes it clear that man is no Promethean, saving himself, but that the Ground of Being is revealed in the depth of his anxiety. This is not a personal God, however, nor a Being distinct from others, but rather a panentheistic kind of Being-Itself within which we find our being.

The theologian Paul Tillich developed this idea further in his account of God as the Ground of Being and of faith as the "courage to be." Rudolph Bultmann's existential hermeneutic also has roots here. Bultmann attempted to break the hold of the scientific mentality in theology by interpreting the gospel as speaking to man's existential predicament in order to elicit faith and authenticity. But Heidegger offers no adequate account of what authentic man is like; he has no appreciation of the image of God in man, nor of the Perfect Man, Jesus, by whom God gave men hope.

His philosophy also contributed to the existential psychoanalysis of Ludwig Binswanger, and even more plainly to the French novelist, playwright, and philosopher Jean-Paul Sartre. A. F. HOLMES

HEIM, KARL (1874–1959)
German Protestant theologian who represented the best in pietistic, conservative theology at a time when Liberal and Neoorthodox theology dominated German scholarship

Heim spent most of his life in the south-ern area of Germany known as Württemberg, and he studied at the leading university of the area, Tübingen. He served both as a schoolmaster and pastor before accepting university posts first at Halle (1907–1914), then at Münster (1914–1920), and finally from 1920 at Tübingen. His own theological position was a moderate and mediating one. Like Karl Barth and other contemporaries, he rejected the liberal view of God that made God identical with human and historical development. Heim was greatly interested in scientific developments and felt that none of these posed any real challenge to the biblical idea of a transcendent, personal God. Atheism and secularism were distortions of the scientific method. The expression of Heim's theology reflects the influence of existentialism (as with Martin Heidegger) and personalistic relationships (as with Martin Buber). Just as Buber distinguished between impersonal "I-It" relationships and "I-Thou" personal relationships, so Heim used these categories, but added the scientific concept of space. In I-It relationships a void exists and God is absent; whereas in I-Thou personal relationships, God fills the space to bring people into real relationships with himself and with one another. Like others of his era, Heim opposed Hitler. His works *God Transcendent (1935) and Christian Faith and Natural Science* (1953) are available to the English reader. D. M. LAKE

HELENA (c. 248–c. 327)
Mother of Constantine the Great

Helena's origins were lowly; her father was an innkeeper in a town near the Bosporus, and some ancient sources indicate that she was merely Constantius's legal concubine. Whatever her status, in 292 she was put away by Constantius so that he could marry the stepdaughter of the Emperor Maximian in order to become a Caesar. Helena was restored to a position of honor when her son Constantine became emperor. She warmly embraced her son's faith, and around the year 326 she went to Palestine and supervised the building of a church over Christ's tomb. When the area was being excavated, she is supposed to have found the "True Cross." Despite her much praised piety, Helena is suspected of having assisted in the condemnation of Constantine's wife Fausta on charges of adultery. C. HICKS

HELMS, EDGAR JAMES (1863–1942)
Founder of Goodwill Industries

Born in New York State, Helms (as a child) traveled in a covered wagon to an Iowa prairie farm. For a while he became a printer's helper for the country newspaper, then later worked his way through Cornell College (Iowa) and Boston University's School of Theology. Thwarted in his plan to go to Bombay, India, as a Methodist missionary, he served as a settlement worker among the foreign emigrants at Morgan Methodist Chapel in Boston. As a part of his ministry efforts to feed the hungry, to clothe the poor, and to give hope to the destitute, he began the Morgan Memorial Co-operative Industries and Stores, later to become the Goodwill Industries (in 1905). His vision was to give needy and handicapped people "not charity, but a chance"—a chance to work and to gain self-respect for themselves. R. VONDERLACK

HELOISE (c. 1098–1164)
Abbess of the Paraclete; niece of Canon Fulbert at Paris; most noted for her love affair with Peter Abelard and later devotion to the religious life

Heloise's love affair began with Peter Abelard in 1118. Abelard suggested to Heloise's uncle, Fulbert, that he might take his meals in their house. Fulbert then entrusted his niece to Abelard's tutelage. Opportunity gave way to indulgence, then to calamity. "When we had opened our books, more works of love appeared than of reading; kisses were more numerous than sentences." The pangs of conscience were aroused by their secret marriage and the son born to them was left in Brittany. Fulbert countered their passion by emasculating Abelard.

Abelard sought refuge in the monastery of St. Denis from where he urged Heloise to also become a monastic. She entered the convent of Argenteuil near Paris until it was closed in 1128. Heloise then moved to the Benedictine Abbey of the Paraclete near Troyes, which Abelard had built. Her passion for Abelard was replaced by intense devotion to God.

Abelard's extensive account of his calamities traces the agonizing question of marriage that the two faced and the disgrace if he would renounce the celibate life. They both were inspired by the Roman writer Cicero whose treatise *On Friendship* described the worth of disinterested love. Their correspondence oscillated between this kind of friendship, an extramarital relationship, marriage, and mental chastity within marriage that would argue against marriage in the end. Heloise's experience in the convent, as described in her correspondence with Abelard, dwelt upon her loss and separation. In the end Abelard discovered a love that bound them on their path to God. Heloise reversed roles and lamented the urge of her heart, which thirteen years of monastic life could not erode. Her career of devotion ended in 1164. Heloise was buried next to Abelard at the Paraclete, and in 1817 both remains were taken to Paris. M. ANDERSON

HENDERSON, ALEXANDER (1583–1646)
Scottish Covenanter

Born in Fife and educated at St. Andrews University, Henderson taught there until becoming the episcopally appointed minister at Leuchars in 1612. Some years later he experienced a spiritual awakening, largely through hearing Robert Bruce preach. Soon Henderson fell foul of the royal policy of making the Church of Scotland more liturgical, but King James VI never quite overstepped the mark, unlike his son Charles I, who from his accession in 1625 determined to make the Scottish Kirk more like the Church of England. Among his leading opponents was Henderson, who had a large part in the National Covenant of 1638, a staunch defense of Reformed faith and church government. A general assembly at Glasgow that year chose Henderson as moderator ("incomparably the ablest man of us all"). Excitement was at fever heat after Presbyterianism had been restored, but steered by Henderson, the assembly was seen to "have been seeking God only and no other thing." He became minister of the High Kirk of Edinburgh two months later. The Scots took up arms against the king, and Henderson was among those sent to negotiate with Charles, who conceded all the Scottish demands. He also appointed Henderson as his chaplain—and was promptly rebuked by him for playing golf on Sunday afternoon. Despite the increasing gulf between king and Covenanter, Charles retained high respect for his chaplain's learning, character, and ability. Henderson was one of the chief drafters of the Solemn League and Covenant (a religious pact between Scotland and England) and one of the Scottish commissioners to the Westminster Assembly of Divines, making significant contributions to its findings. He achieved the rare distinction of being three times moderator of the general assembly and had a key role in Presbyterian resistance against the Stuart theory of the Divine Right of Kings. J. D. DOUGLAS

HENRY II (1133–1189)
King of England, 1154–1189

Son of Empress Matilda and grandson of Henry I, Henry II succeeded to the throne of England after a civil war between his mother and King Stephen (in 1154). By marriage to Eleanor, duchess of Aquitaine and divorced wife of Louis VII of France, Henry was lord of a vast realm extending from the Pyrenees to the Scottish border. In some sense it can be said that he created or rather confirmed the royal exchequer, circuit courts, use of legal writs, and trial by jury. His efforts to reduce the variety of conflicting laws in England to a common law for the realm brought him opposition by the church.

His friend and former courtier was Archbishop Thomas à Becket of Canterbury. The latter, resisting Henry's encroachments on ecclesiastical prerogatives, suffered exile. Six years later he returned to England, but the old difficulties were renewed. Becket excommunicated some of the king's close adherents. Henry, at war in France, was enraged. Several of his knights embarked for England and murdered the archbishop in his cathedral church. Henry was blamed and revolt stirred anew, but he was persuaded to perform a public penance and to relax some of his regulations against the church's legal position. His latter years were troubled: his wife, his sons (especially Richard), and King Philip II of France, all opposed him in one way or another. But the political institutions he had established or strengthened continued and gave stability to the realm. A. CABANISS

HENRY III (1207–1272)
King of England, 1216–1272

Oldest son of King John and Isabella of Angouleme, Henry III succeeded his father in 1216, when he was a very young minor. For a number of years thereafter the realm of England was administered by baronial regents who thus had an opportunity to implement the Magna Carta (1215) and especially to make ineffectual John's acknowledgement of England as a papal fief. In January 1236 Henry was married to Eleanor of Provence, who brought to England many of her relatives eager to secure English properties. Henry III was a weak ruler and was consequently subjected to frequent baronial revolts. For long periods of time the government was dominated by Simon de Montfort, a baronial leader, who is credited with the first Parliament in 1265. The king's weakness contributed to increasing secularity of the government as well as to growing baronial power. Nonetheless, he was responsible for the remodeling of Westminster Abbey into much the form that it has today. A. CABANISS

HENRY IV (1553–1610)
First Bourbon king of France, 1576–1610

Through his father, Antoine de Bourbon,

Henry IV was of the French royal line, and through his mother, Jeanne d'Albret, he was heir to the Kingdom of Navarre. Brought up a Protestant by his staunchly Calvinistic mother, Henry was married in 1572 to Margaret of Valois, sister of French King Charles IX (who died in 1574) and daughter of Catherine de' Medici. After the Massacre of St. Bartholomew's Day in 1572, Henry was held prisoner for over three years; but after his escape in 1576 he became the recognized leader of the Protestant forces in the Wars of Religion, which had been going on between Protestantism and Catholicism intermittently since 1562. Henry won military victories over the Catholic forces, and when his cousin Henry III died in 1589 he became the successor to the French throne. His Protestantism, however, made him unacceptable to the Catholic League and its supporters. In 1593, therefore, Henry embraced Catholicism, and in 1595 Pope Clement VIII removed the ban of excommunication from him. His motives for converting have been variously assessed; but it seems likely that his major reason was the desire to end the long-continued bloodletting and restore something like national unity. After he came to power, he did not forget his Protestant former co-religionists. The Edict of Nantes, which he promulgated in 1598, though it recognized Catholicism as the official religion of the French state, gave Protestants certain important rights—religious rights, such as freedom of conscience and liberty to continue worship in places where they had done so before 1597; civic rights, such as eligibility to hold public offices; and political rights, such as permission to hold public assemblies and maintain 450 places with garrisons as strongholds. This edict, the first in Europe to permit two religions to coexist legally under one political government, was rigidly enforced by Henry until he was assassinated by the Catholic fanatic Ravaillac in 1610. N. V. HOPE

HENRY VIII (1491–1547)
King of England, 1509–1547

Henry VIII, son of Henry VII and Eliza-

beth of York, was born at Greenwich. His two brothers, one of whom, Arthur, was heir to the throne, predeceased their father, with the result that Henry became the crown prince. Sarpi, the contemporary Italian writer, says that Henry was originally trained to enter the Roman Catholic Church, although there is little evidence for this. He was, however given a very thorough humanistic training, becoming adept in poetic and musical composition, as well as in all the warlike arts. A personable young man full of energy and charm, he was very popular when he mounted the English throne in 1509.

Shortly after his accession, Henry married Catherine of Aragon, daughter of Ferdinand and Isabella of Spain and his elder brother Arthur's widow. Although Henry VII had obtained a papal dispensation for the marriage, partially because he did not wish to return the dowry, and partially because Ferdinand wished to maintain a center of influence in England, Henry VIII was always doubtful as to whether his marriage was lawful in the eyes of God.

At the outset of his reign, Henry had little interest in administration, particularly in foreign policy, leaving this to his chancellor, Archbishop Thomas Wolsey of York (c.1475–1530), who sought to maintain an alliance with Spain against France. Ferdinand, however, was completely unreliable and although Henry in person went to the continent in 1512 where he was present at the sieges of Therouanne and Tournay and the Battle of the Spurs at Guinegate, Ferdinand deserted him at the crucial moment and made his peace with France. Henry's only gain was that the Scots, allies of France, who had invaded England in September of 1513 had been virtually wiped out at the Battle of Flodden Field in which their king, James IV, with many of his nobles had been killed. This made the northern borders safe for the moment.

Henry, however, was so angry with Ferdinand that he talked of the possibility of a divorce. Wolsey soon afterwards patched up the quarrel, and once again England and Spain were allied against France, until in

1519 Charles V of Spain deserted Henry and made peace once again with France.

Meanwhile other matters were occupying Henry's attention. Although Catherine bore him a number of children, all of them died at an early age, except Mary (1516–1558). But since the idea of a woman ruling a country was not popular in the sixteenth century, Henry was very worried lest his lack of an heir should mark the end of the Tudor line. He felt that perhaps his lack of a male heir indicated God's displeasure over his marriage to his brother's widow. Furthermore, a certain young lady, Anne Boleyn, had recently come to court and Henry had fallen in love with her. He, therefore, desired a divorce in order that he might marry her, in the hope that she would present him with a son.

In all of this, Henry was still an orthodox Roman Catholic. In 1521 he had written a tract, *The Assertion of the Seven Sacraments,* against Martin Luther, receiving as a reward from Pope Leo X the title of "Defender of the Faith," a title still borne by the British monarchs. Because of his professed religious convictions, he now sought the anullment of his marriage with Catherine, which he might have obtained without much difficulty if it had not been that the pope was really a prisoner in the hands of Charles V of Spain, Catherine's nephew. Although Wolsey did everything he could to forward Henry's cause, nothing came of it. Henry, therefore, deprived Wolsey of his office of chancellor and the latter died in disgrace. Thomas Cranmer, Archbishop of Canterbury, suggested that the matter be submitted to the universities of England and the continent. The former approved the divorce with the result that Henry, after stopping the transmission of revenues to the papacy, had parliament declare him to be the head of the Church of England, had an anullment pronounced by Cranmer and promptly married Anne who was already pregnant and shortly afterwards bore him a daughter, Elizabeth. The marriage, however, did not last long, for Anne was beheaded in 1536 on a charge of adultery.

Henry's wives who followed in Anne's footsteps were Jane Seymour, who gave birth to his one legitimate son, Edward, but who died shortly afterwards; Anne of Cleves, whom he divorced very soon after the marriage; Catherine Howard, who went to the block within a year on a charge of adultery; and Catherine Parr, who had the good fortune and ability to outlive him.

The break with Rome caused Henry many problems. By this time he was becoming increasingly dictatorial and unscrupulous, probably as a result of his declining health, which may have been caused by syphilis. In 1535 he had Wolsey's successor as chancellor, Sir Thomas More, executed because he refused to recognize Henry's claim to be head of the Church of England. In 1540, Thomas Cromwell, More's successor, was executed because he had negotiated the marriage of Henry to Anne of Cleves, whom Henry did not like when he met her.

At the same time, Henry was plagued with financial problems. Inflation was becoming a problem in Europe, the English taxation system was inefficient and Henry had wasted a great amount of money in his foreign policy. The wealth of the church, therefore, became an object of envy and interest with the result that in 1536 the suppression of the monasteries began, with their lands and wealth being taken over by the crown.

In the meantime, the influence of the Reformation had been growing. In 1536 Henry had authorized the publication of Tyndale's translation of the Bible, and Cranmer was pressing for a more Protestant form of liturgy. Henry at this point became more conservative and published his *Six Articles,* which made belief in the specific Roman Catholic doctrines obligatory. Those who had accepted Protestant doctrines either had to submit, flee the country, or face being burned at the stake.

In 1544 Henry determined the succession to his throne: Edward, Mary, and Elizabeth if either of the first two died without issue. He, himself, died January 28, 1547, leaving a country sorely divided. While he had been dictatorial and ruthless, he had by his policies of necessity enhanced the power of par-

liament and laid the groundwork, albeit unwittingly, of the English Reformation.
W. S. REID

HENRY, CARL FERDINAND HOWARD (born 1913)

Theologian and editor

Born in New York City as the son of German immigrants, Henry was converted after having worked for some years as a journalist. Thereafter he graduated from Wheaton College and from Northern Baptist Theological Seminary (Th.D., 1942) where he also taught theology (1940–1947). A Ph.D. from Boston University followed in 1949. Meanwhile, he joined some colleagues in founding Fuller Theological Seminary in Pasadena, where he was to spend the next nine years. In response to an urgent need in the evangelical world, he returned east in 1956 to become the first editor of *Christianity Today*. The periodical was soon highly regarded and respected even by those of other religious traditions. Centered in downtown Washington, D.C., it took full advantage of its location to report and make Christian comment on contemporary events. Henry gathered around himself an able and dedicated staff, and established an office in London in 1960. He was chairman and prime mover in the World Congress on Evangelism in Berlin in 1966. When he left *Christianity Today* in 1968 (he continued as editor-at-large until 1974), he embarked on a wide-ranging ministry as lecturer that extended to many parts of Europe, Asia, and Africa. All this time he was producing a steady stream of publications, among which were *The Uneasy Conscience of Modern Fundamentalism* (1948), *Christian Personal Ethics* (1957), *Frontiers in Modern Theology* (1966), *God, Revelation, and Authority* (six volumes, 1976–1983), and *Toward a Recovery of Christian Belief* (1990). His *Confessions of a Theologian* (1986), with its remarkably candid insights into the world of American evangelicalism, gives also a wealth of detail that confirms his position as one of the twentieth century's leading evangelical spokesmen in the United States. J. D. DOUGLAS

HENRY, MATTHEW (1662–1714)

English non-conformist minister and Bible commentator

Matthew Henry was the son of Philip Henry, a clergyman ejected from the Church of England under the Act of Uniformity of 1662. Henry at first thought of entering a legal career but soon decided on Christian ministry. He prepared for it with two years of study (1680–1682) at the Islington Academy under Thomas Dolittle. Ordained a Presbyterian, he served two parishes, first at Chester from 1687–1712, and then at Hackney from 1712 until his death two years later. He is best remembered for his *Exposition of the Old and New Testament* begun in 1704. This work was completed, and he was well into the New Testament at the time of his sudden and premature death. His Bible commentaries, though long superseded from a critical and academic viewpoint, have always enjoyed much popularity for "their penetrating insight, their exhilarating freshness, and their ingenuity of thought and expression." N. V. HOPE

HENSON, HERBERT HENSLEY (1863–1947)

Church of England bishop

After taking a first-class degree in history at Oxford, Henson became a Fellow of All Souls College (1884). After some hesitancy he was ordained into the ministry in 1887. At this stage he was an Anglo-Catholic, but he gradually moved away from this position during his parish ministry at Barking in Essex. In 1900 he became a Canon of Westminister Abbey and Rector of nearby St. Margaret's. His eloquence and independence of mind attracted large congregations. In 1912 he moved to Durham as Dean of the Cathedral. When he was nominated as Bishop of Hereford there was opposition from Anglo-Catholics because of his now liberal views on biblical interpretation. However, he was consecrated bishop but only remained in that position from 1917 through 1920, when he became the Bishop of Durham. In this northern diocese he continued to be outspoken on matters of

Church and State as he opposed the establishment. However, he gained the confidence of the majority of his clergy and laity and was widely loved.

During his last years he wrote his autobiography, *Retrospect of an Unimportant Life* (1942–1950). His challenging addresses to his clergy were printed as *Ad Clerum* (1937). P. TOON

HEPBURN, JAMES CURTIS (1815–1911)
Pioneer missionary to Japan

Born in Milton, Pennsylvania, Hepburn was later converted at Princeton Seminary. Then, through the Presbyterian Board of Mission, Hepburn arrived in Japan in 1859, the year the nation opened to the West. Earlier he had spent five years in Amoy, China, and then thirteen years in medical practice in New York. At age forty-four, the first Presbyterian missionary to Japan, he plunged into language study and medical practice in an abandoned Buddhist temple near Yokohama. During thirty-four years he opened Japan's first dispensary, held the nation's first classes for medical students, pioneered ophthalmology, and taught the Japanese to make and use soap. He was called the father of medicine in Northeast Asia. His wife, Clara, first taught English to sons of nobility and then pioneered education for women for twenty-five years. One of the greatest foreign scholars of the Japanese language of his time, Hepburn invented the system of writing Japanese in Roman letters, published the first Japanese-English dictionary in 1867, following it with an English-Japanese dictionary and a Japanese grammar. He began Bible translation in 1861 with the Gospel of Matthew. Together with coworkers he translated the entire Bible and published it in 1888, followed by a Dictionary of the Bible in 1891. Along the way he translated the Westminster Shorter Catechism and Confession of Faith. As an educator he helped found and was first president of the Presbyterian Meiji Gakuin (college). Hepburn opened the heart of the nation to the gospel. Small, quiet, kind, and scholarly, he appealed to the Japanese mind, earning

the accolade "the superior man." At his death he was called "the nation's friend." Out of his and his coworkers' evangelistic efforts came the Yokohama band, which contributed several of the first great leaders of the Protestant church in Japan. His character and contributions were foundational to the Christian church in that nation. D. HOKE

HEPBURN, JOHN (1649–1723)
Scottish minister

One of the Church of Scotland's most bewildering figures, Hepburn graduated at Aberdeen and inexplicably turned from episcopacy to presbytery. Ordained by exiled Scots ministers in London (1678), he returned as a field preacher of whom other Covenanters remained suspicious. He was imprisoned at least twice, mysteriously freed, became a fugitive again, yet for over three decades served the parish ministry at Urr without having been legally settled. In 1690 he and his followers, called "Hebronites" and evidently numbering some four thousand, complained that the Kirk had been insufficiently purged of episcopal features. The Hebronites opposed the Act of Union with England (1707) and the Toleration Act (1712) and were ambivalent toward the Jacobite Rising (1715). Though suspended and temporarily deposed, Hepburn continued his ministry and was highly respected in Urr, to which place many walked upwards of twenty miles to hear him. J. D. DOUGLAS

HERBERT, EDWARD (1582–1648)
British historian and philosopher

Lord Herbert of Cherbury was the brother of the poet George Herbert and a follower of John Donne. He is known as the father of English deism.

Dismissing any claim to an infallible church, an authorative priesthood, or a special revelation, Herbert based his thinking on certain eternal and universal truths, "common notions" recognizable by all men, thanks to their God-given faculties. These truths provide the essence of "natural religion" and of "natural law," and by them all religions and all laws should be judged.

In religion, he lists five such "common notions": (1) there is one supreme God, (2) who ought to be worshiped; (3) virtue and piety are the principal parts of worship, so (4) we should repent for our sins; and (5) God administers rewards and punishments in both this world and the next.

Measured by this yardstick, Christianity seemed to Herbert to stand up best, but its "superfluous" supernatural elements should be discarded. Eighteenth-century deism followed the direction he began.

A. F. HOLMES

HERBERT, GEORGE (1593–1633)
English Poet

Herbert was born of a distinguished Welsh family and educated at Westminster and at Trinity College, Cambridge. He was appointed Praelector in Rhetoric in 1618 and became Public Orator to the University in 1620. His career flourished until, in 1624 and 1625, a series of deaths deprived Herbert of influential patrons, including the king. In 1629 he married Joane Dauvers; in 1630 he resolved upon an ecclesiastical life when he accepted the offer as a priest of a village parish at Bemerton. His small book on the duties of his new life, *A Priest to the Temple, or, The Country Prison* (1652), testifies to the earnestness and joy but also to the uneasiness with which he embraced his new role. In chronic bad health, Herbert spent his final three years at Bemerton performing pastoral duties, writing and revising his poems, and playing music.

Almost all of Herbert's poetry is contained in *The Temple* (1633). Shortly before his death he sent the manuscript to Nicholas Ferrar, head of the Anglican community at Little Gidding, with instructions that "if he can think it may turn to the advantage of any dejected poor soul, let it be made public; if not, let him burn it, for I and it are the least of God's mercies."

The Temple is an architectural metaphor, which shows associations with the Old Testament temple, and with Greek and Roman temples, but the latter are now subsumed in the New Testament view of the human heart or the dwelling place of the Spirit of God.

In "The Church Porch," where the classical allusions are most in evidence, the speaker delivers his didactic counsels regarding the behavior befitting the Christian life.

The second section, called "The Church," explores the essence of the relationship between Christ and man. In these poems (except for "The Sacrifice," which is spoken by Christ), the tone of the speaker ranges from the rebellious, colloquial language of "The Collar" to the highly formal praise of "Antiphon (I)" and "Antiphon (II)" to the meditations of "Church-Monuments." The collection begins with poems that treat the basis of the man-God relationship, Christ's sacrifice. Many of the poems of the first half deal with such subjects as sacraments, rituals, feast days, and events of Christ's life. The second part explores the aspirations and distresses attendant upon man's relationship with God. The section concludes with a group of poems on the Last Things, culminating with "Love (III)," which draws together the threads of Eucharistic imagery that run throughout the body of the work.

"The Church Militant," though it may have been written earlier, forms an organic part of the unity of *The Temple*. In contrast to the exploration of the inner dimension of the soul, this poem presents the movement of the Church as a corporate society throughout history.

George Herbert's subject is single, the variety of poems is astounding, and the artistry is as admirable in its totality as in its detail.

E. B. BATSON

HERBST, JOHANNES (1735–1812)
Moravian musician

In the eighteenth century, the finest music in America was to be heard in the Moravian settlements at Bethlehem, Pennsylvania, and Salem, North Carolina. Herbst was perhaps the finest of the composers who exercised his talents to provide such music. Born and trained in Germany, he served as a minister in Lancaster and Lititz, Pennsylvania, and later became bishop in the South. He wrote over a hundred anthems with organ and orchestral accompaniment. Partly because of the German language, and partly because the music was ahead of the cultural level of most other settlers, Moravian church music did not spread its influence in America and has become widely known only in recent times. J. B. MACMILLAN

HERMANN VON REICHENAU (1013–1054)
Medieval church musician

Nicknamed *Contractus* ("the Cripple") because he was lame from childhood, Hermann was one of the most important musical theorists of the Middle Ages. He was educated in the great Swiss monastery of St. Gall, and spent most of his active life as a monk at Reichenau. He played an important role in the later development of Gregorian chant and contributed to the improvement of musical notation. His hymn to the Virgin, "Alma Redemptoris Mater" ("Dear Mother of the Redeemer"), is mentioned in Chaucer's *Canterbury Tales,* and is still sung in the Catholic Church. J. B. MACMILLAN

HERMAS (died c.150)
Christian teacher and moralist

Known very little otherwise, Hermas cites some details about himself in his writing. His extant work is one book, a writing called *The Shepherd* (referring to the work's central shepherd figure). In *The Shepherd,* Hermas states that he was originally a slave, gained his freedom, married and started a business, lost nearly everything material, saw his children lapse, and finally, brought his family together by acts of repentance. Hermas indicates also that he knew Clement of Rome, late first-century bishop of Rome. From internal evidences, it is impossible to tell if this biography is fictional or not. As to external facts, references to Hermas are contradictory. Some authorities, most eminently the Muratorian Canon, a late second-century

document, make Hermas a brother of Pius, bishop of Rome about 150. In the third century, Origen thought Hermas was the individual Paul named in Romans 16:14, an identification upholding Hermas' own statements. Modern scholarly commentators lean much toward the first opinion.

Hermas' book offers a series of visions about Christian life and morality. Specifically, the work contains three principal parts: five visions, twelve mandates, and ten simulitudes. Employing as symbols either a tower under construction, or a woman who becomes youthful, the five visions are extended allegories depicting Christian ethical truths. In the fifth vision, an angel of repentance appears as a shepherd, the book's main symbolic figure. The shepherd introduces the work's remaining segments, the mandates and similitudes. In brief, the twelve mandates are depictions of Christian virtues—humility, chastity, truthfulness, longsuffering, simplicity, respectfulness, good cheer—and exhortations over the purity and repentance such virtues require. Prominent here is the "two ways" pattern of moral instruction (the way of life and the way of death). This mirrors the *Didache* and other respected early Christian ethical writings. Some connect *The Shepherd* with early Christian ethical writings. Others connect *The Shepherd* with early Jewish Christianity and its frequent use of the same instructive device. Finally, the ten similitudes describe principles by which the Christian virtues may be attained, this emphasizing purity and repentance again.

Throughout apostolic and postapostolic times, most church leaders gave Hermas's book high respect. Eusebius of Caesaria believed *The Shepherd* was read widely in the early church; and some important leaders, such as Irenaeus and Clement of Alexandria, even considered it canonical Scripture. For Athanasius, the work was not Scripture but did offer, like the *Didache,* help for Christian learners. In his pre-Montanist days, Tertullian thought highly of the book, but as a Montanist, he opposed its allowances for gravely sinful believers. *The Shepherd* was used more by Western than Eastern Christians after the fourth century. Thus it came through the Middle Ages primarily in various Latin translations from the original Greek. Because of its simplicity and candor, some have compared Hermas's work with Bunyan's *Pilgrim's Progress*. It is at least a valuable index to Christian ethics and the church's moral instruction, in Christianity's earliest decades.

Hermas' work exists in some Greek manuscripts and in many Medieval Latin translations. Printed editions of the book began in the early 1500s. K. J. BRYER

HERZOG, JOHANN JAKOB
(1805–1882)
Swiss-German Reformed theologian

Herzog studied theology at Basle and Berlin and was a student of Schleiermacher. But Herzog was more a historian than an apologist or systematic theologian. He taught historical theology and church history at Lausanne, Halle, and Erlangen. He is best known for his work on the famous German encyclopedia *Realencyklopadie fur protestantische Theologie und Kirche* (1853–1868), which was later reedited and translated to become the *Schaff-Herzog Encyclopedia of Religious Knowledge*. Philip Schaff, the famous German-American historian, did the reediting and translation work. Updating and supplementary volumes have been produced in 1955 (editor, L. A. Loetscher) and in 1991 (editor, J. D. Douglas). D. M. LAKE

HEYLING, PETER (c. 1608–1652)
First German Protestant missionary

Heyling was the son of wealthy, north German Lutheran parents. With six other students from Lubeck, he enrolled at the University of Paris to study law. While there, the group came under the influence of Hugo Grotius, the Dutch lawyer-theologian-statesman. Grotius had left the Netherlands because of his opposition to the "hardening Calvinistic predestinarianism." As a result of discussion with Grotius about Christian faith and life, three of the German students committed themselves to missionary ser-

vice. Heyling was one of these. The trio's aim was "the revitalization of the lapsed churches in the Near East."

After two years in Egypt, living in the desert with the Coptic monks, learning Arabic and Syriac, Heyling set out for Abyssinia (Ethiopia). He traveled with the recently appointed Abuna (Coptic archbishop) to Gondar, the ancient capital. Heyling spent twenty-two years there. He translated portions of the New Testament into the Amharic language. It is said that the emperor gave Heyling his daughter in marriage, indicative of the reception and esteem accorded him.

Heyling experienced opposition from the Jesuits in east Africa. And on a trip back to Egypt, he was martyred by a Muslim Turk. H. EILER

HIGGINBOTTOM, SAM (1874–1958)
First missionary scientific agriculturist and rural reconstruction expert in India

A native of Manchester, England, Higginbottom went to the United States in 1894 to attend Dwight L. Moody's Mt. Hermon School. He graduated from Princeton University in 1903 and was appointed to Ewing Christian College at Allahabad by the Board of Foreign Missions of the Presbyterian Church in the U.S.A. He was so moved by rural poverty that he concentrated on an effort to increase food production. To that end he studied agriculture at Ohio State University, and received the B.S. degree in 1911. He then established the Allahabad Agricultural Institute, which affiliated with Allahabad University in 1932 and awarded its first degrees in 1934. It injected a force for transformation into rural society. Higginbottom saw his ministry as truly evangelistic despite the opposition of some colleagues in his mission. P. BEAVER

HILARY OF ARLES (401–449)
Bishop of Arles

Hilary was bishop of Arles in southern France when the bishop of Rome first actively extended a wide control over other bishops with the aid of the civil authority. Honoratus, the kinsman of Hilary, lead him first into the monastic life at Lerins, an island southwest of Nice. When Honoratus became bishop of Arles, Hilary followed him there and succeeded him as bishop in 428.

Hilary of Arles, like many of the monks at Lerins and Marseilles, was a Semi-Pelagian. These taught that the beginning step in salvation is made by the will of man and that perseverance is also an act of man.

As bishop, Hilary presided over councils at Riez (439), Orange (441), and Vaison (442). The decisions of these councils were directed toward improving discipline and against worldliness in the church. The church in Arles had gained an elevated position in Gaul after the civil authority was transferred from Trier to Arles about 401, but the leading bishops of Gaul had reacted against the elevation of Arles. It was Hilary who asserted this authority with new vigor and then deposed Chelidonius, bishop of Besancon in eastern France (444). Hilary overstepped the accepted practice (canonical procedure) in this case and in others, according to the letters of Leo, the bishop of Rome. After Leo heard the appeals of the parties involved, he restricted Hilary to his see. Hilary submitted to Leo when Valentinian III (died 455), the western emperor, supported the decision of Leo and ordered all bishops in the western provinces to submit to the authority of the Roman bishop. Hilary of Arles, by his confrontation with Leo, contributed to the rise of the papal authority.
J. NEWTON

HILARY OF POITIERS (c. 315–367)
Bishop of Poitiers

Hilary was bishop of Poitiers in west central France. He was the leading orthodox Latin church father during the peak of the Arian power. Hilary was born into a prominent pagan family of Poitiers and was educated in philosophy and rhetoric. Three years after his conversion to Christianity (c. 350), he was elected bishop of his hometown by the people there, even though he was married.

After the Council of Milan (355) agreed to the banishment of the orthodox Athanasius, Hilary organized the bishops of Gaul to resist the Arian emperor and those bishops who supported Arianism. As a result, Emperor Constantius exiled Hilary to Phrygia (Asia Minor) where he wrote his principal work *On the Trinity* (356–359).

This work by Hilary was the best defense of the divinity of Christ against the Arians, who did not consider the Son to be eternal but created by the Father. Hilary held that the Father and the Son have identity of substance yet are two. With his *On the Trinity* and other writings, especially his work *On the Synods*, Hilary did much to bring unity between the followers of Athanasius and other anti-Arians. Unity had not been achieved because many felt that the phrases of the council of Nicea did not make a clear distinction between the Father and the Son. As a mediator, Hilary indicated the areas on each side that needed correction.

Emperor Constantius returned Hilary to Gaul without restoring him to his office. During the rule of Constantius and Valentinian, Hilary continued his opposition to the Arians until his death in 367. Where Hilary failed in his effort to achieve an orthodox church and state, another Latin father, Ambrose, would later succeed.
J. NEWTON

HILDEGARD (1098–1179)
German abbess, mystic, and author

Hildegard was born to noble parents in the diocese of Mainz. According to her later accounts, from the age of three she experienced visions of God, which gradually revealed to her his nature and the nature of the universe. At a very young age her parents sent her to be educated at a Benedictine convent. She entered that order and spent the rest of her life within it.

In 1141, for the first time, she informed her friends and superiors at the convent of her visions. They persuaded her to have the revelations she had experienced written in a book, which was entitled *Scivias*, a classic of medieval mysticism. The highest authorities in the church, including the pope, regarded her as a prophetess. One of her admirers was Bernard of Clairvaux (1090–1153), with whom she carried on a lifelong correspondence dealing, among other topics, with the need for church reform. Because of her leadership abilities, she eventually became abbess of her convent at Disibodenberg and in 1148 founded a new convent at Rupertsberg near Bingen where she remained until her death. Besides her administrative duties she maintained a wide correspondence and authored books on science, medicine, hymnology, and lives of the saints. She joined other leaders of the church in condemning the heresy of the Catharists but unlike others she opposed sentencing them to death. She was never canonized, although the procedure was begun three times in the thirteenth and fourteenth centuries. R. D. SHUSTER

HILL, DAVID (1840–1896)
British Methodist missionary to China

Hill was a native of York. The Wesleyan Missionary Society sent him to its Central China field, where he became its leading representative. Independently wealthy, Hill devoted his income to the work of the church. He was preeminent as an evangelist and church planter. The famous Pastor Hsi was one of his converts. He recruited and trained missionaries, pastors, and lay workers. He founded secondary schools, schools for the blind, orphanages, homes for aged, combated the opium trade, and was a founder of the Christian Literature Society. Hill promoted interchurch cooperation and unity. He had a special vocation to famine relief, ministering as far abroad as the Shansi famine of 1878–1880. He died of typhus at the age of fifty-six, contracting the disease while caring for famine victims in the Wuchang area. Hill was widely revered as a saint. P. BEAVER

HILL, ROWLAND (1744–1833)
English evangelical leader

Hill attended Eton School and St. John's College, Cambridge. While at St. John's he preached the gospel to many of his classmates. He also visited the sick and then later was engaged in itinerant preaching—the latter activity causing six bishops to refuse to ordain him. At last the Bishop of Bath and Wells ordained him deacon. But, because he continued to preach outside the parish to which he was licensed, he found it impossible to persuade a bishop to ordain him priest. So he continued his work as an itinerant preacher of the Evangelical Revival. As he was such a gifted preacher, rich laity built two chapels for him. One was in Wotton, Gloucestershire, and the other was the Surrey Chapel in London, opened in 1783. Attached to the Surrey Chapel were thirteen Sunday schools and a very large congregation, which he delighted with his humorous yet challenging rhetoric.

His interests and concerns were interdenominational, and thus he was known as an "irregular" clergyman (i.e., not keeping to a regular parish). He was the first chairman of the committee of the Religious Tract Society, and he helped to promote the British and Foreign Bible Society and the London Missionary Society. He was concerned with social problems and actively encouraged the use of vaccination for smallpox. P. TOON

HINCMAR (c. 806–882)
Archbishop of Reims, 845–882

Born to a French noble family, Hincmar received his education under Hilduin at the abbey of St. Denis (north of Paris). In 822, both student and teacher joined the court of Louis I (the Pious). Hincmar then remained with Charles II (the Bald) and the Frankish court until 845. That year Sergius II appointed him archbishop of Reims. Opposed by Lothair I, a competitor for the Frankish throne, Hincmar underwent several investigations before his election was final. He was confirmed in the post by Leo IV in 853 and Benedict III in 855.

Hincmar was the Church's dominant leader in Gaul during the 800s. In fact, in a period of many jurisdictional conflicts, Hincmar's ascendant power was a primary issue for the Gaulish church. In 862,

Hincmar deposed Rothad, bishop of Soissons, for repeated attacks on the archbishop and his prerogatives. A short time later, Nicholas I upheld Rothad's appeal, and Hincmar bowed to papal authority in the matter. In 871, for the same reasons, Hincmar forced Hincmar, bishop of Laon, his nephew and namesake, permanently out of office. Finally, however, in 876, Hincmar had to submit to a legate John VIII created for Gaul and Germany. Hincmar's independence presaged various Gallican-papal arguments in later centuries. The most famous episode concerned the archbishop's opposition to Lothair II's divorce from his wife Teutberga. Consonant with Church efforts to enforce its long-standing marriage rules, Hincmar condemned the Synod of Aachen's approval of the divorce. Even more forcibly he rejected Lothair's new marriage to Waldrada and its approval by the bishops of Trier and Cologne. Nicholas I eventually bore the brunt of the controversy. Based on the papacy's adamancy, Lothair finally took Teutberga back a short time before he died.

Besides the Church structural disputes, Hincmar entered into numerous theological and moral controversies. He challenged Gottschalk's position that both saved and damned were predestined by God to their eternal states. Attracting a sizable following, Gottschalk maintained that his views represented ideas taken from Augustine of Hippo. But Hincmar fought Gottschalk vigorously, not only with writings of his own, but arguments solicited from John Scotus Erigena, Rabanus Maurus, and other leading teachers. In essence, Hincmar asserted that divine predestination could not apply to the damned since this made God the author of sin. Finally, at the Synod of Quiercy, 849, Gottschalk was defrocked and imprisoned for his statements. However, Hincmar's position was also rejected. The disagreement went unsettled until the Synod of Tuzey, 860, and its compromise formula. As to practical questions, it is obvious Hincmar acquired and used a vast knowledge of Christian ethical traditions. His writings on marriage and divorce were very important for their support of the Church's strict view of monogamous marriage. But Hincmar involved himself in many marriage cases, as well as the spectrum of moral issues. His decisions and writings greatly influenced formulations of canon law in later centuries.

Reproductions of Hincmar's works may be found in Migne's *Patrologia Latina*. His poems and letters have been printed in the *Monumenta Germaniae historica*.

K. J. BRYER

HINDEMITH, PAUL (1895–1963)
Influential twentieth-century German composer

Hindemith's most well-known composition is the symphony extracted from his opera *Mathis der Maler* (*Mathias the Painter*). This tells the story of Mathias Grunewald painting the altar piece at the church of St. Anthony in Isenheim.

He not only wrote music for the concert hall but also for people to play at home, which he called "useful" music. Thus, he created a steady stream of music of all types for every instrument.

His is clear, logical, well-organized music, the twentieth-century representation of the mainstream of German music since Bach. His influence on many composers today through his theoretical writings is significant.

His overtly religious works are few in number but include the *Marien-leben* (a life of Mary song-cycle on poems by Rilke), the ballet *Nobilissima Visione* on the conversion of St. Francis, thirteen motets, a mass, and the three organ sonatas, which are performed by many church musicians.

W. PHEMISTER

HIPPOLYTUS (c. 160–236)
Roman presbyter and theologian

Though Hippolytus was the most important theologian of the Roman church in the third century, the facts concerning his life were soon forgotten in the West. Probably this was due to his schismatic activities and that he wrote his works in Greek.

Hippolytus was a presbyter while Zephyrinus was bishop of Rome (c. 199–217), whom he attacked as a modalist. Although Hippolytus was recognized as a scholar with many assets, he was passed over for bishop in favor of the deacon Callistus. Hippolytus withdrew from the Roman church with a few followers to become the first anti-pope in history. The major disagreement between him and Callistus concerned the question of absolution for mortal sins. Hippolytus supported a rigorist discipline while Callistus took the opposite view. This attack by Hippolytus continued against Callistus' successors, Urban (222–230) and Pontianus (230–235). Under the persecution of the Emperor Maximin (235–238), however, Hippolytus and Pontianus were exiled together to Sardinia, after which they were united. Both then resigned to allow for a successor, Anteros (235–236), thus ending the schism.

Hippolytus was a champion of the Logos doctrine, which distinguished the persons of the Trinity, as opposed to modalism, which believed the persons of the Trinity to be simply different manifestations of the same person. He was not an original-thinking theologian but rather a dedicated and learned compiler whose writings too often were marked by a bitter, controversial tone. His most important work among several writings was the *Refutation of All Heresies,* which sought to demonstrate that all Christian heresies could be traced to pagan philosophies. H. W. HOUSE

HOBBES, THOMAS (1588–1679)
British political philosopher

The son of a clergyman, educated under Aristotelian tutors at Oxford, Hobbes soon grew dissatisfied with Aristotle's physics and psychology and with theologies built thereon. The work of Kepler and Galileo suggested that nature is ruled by fixed mechanical forces or laws rather than by inherent purposes. His association with Francis Bacon convinced him of the inadequacy of Aristotle's philosophy, and he extended the mechanistic explanation to human psychol-

ogy, treating thought and motives and morals as products of physiological causes. In this way, he aided the development of mechanistic materialism in modern thought.

During the English Civil War (1640–1651) Hobbes lived in France, mostly in Paris, where he tutored the Prince of Wales (later Charles II). In 1651, upon his return to England, Hobbes, concerned about politics and religion, published his *Leviathan.* The book is still read as a classic in political theory. He chose to relate religious belief to politics rather than to philosophy and science, as had previously been the case, because in Stuart England, torn by civil war whose causes were both political and religious, he understandably saw religion as a major cause of discord. Hence he argued that the absolute ruler should decide what form of religious belief and worship the citizens must follow.

To support this conclusion, he pointed out that God's attributes are largely incomprehensible to men, so that our theologies represent pious intentions more than truth. Though we do know that God is the all-powerful cause of this world and its causal forces and that Jesus is the Christ according to the Scriptures, everything else must be decided by the ruler.

Some have thought this a piece of subtle irony to flatter the king, rather than the serious proposal it was taken to be. A. F. HOLMES

HOCKING, WILLIAM ERNEST (1873–1966)
American philosopher of religion

Born in Cleveland and educated at Harvard University, Hocking was a leading philosopher of religion in the twentieth century. His more important works are *The Meaning of God in Human Experience* (1912), *Human Nature and Its Remaking* (1923), *The Dilemma of Religious Knowledge* (1931), *Living Religions and a World Faith* (1940), and *The Coming World Civilization* (1956).

He is best known in mission circles as the Chairman of Commission of Appraisal of the Laymen's Foreign Missions Inquiry, which made an in-depth study of seven American missions working in India, Burma, China, and Japan. This was the most thorough investigation of foreign missions ever undertaken. Its report, edited by Hocking, was published in 1932 as *Re-Thinking Missions*.

The first part of the Report, on "General Principles," written by Hocking himself, was received with a good deal of misgiving by conservatives. He was so appreciative of the value of other religions that he appeared to diminish both the uniqueness of the Christian faith and the urgency of the Christian mission. In his later writings, however, he returned to basic Christian beliefs and his desire to see Christianity as the religion for the world. H. KANE

HODGE, ARCHIBALD ALEXANDER
(1823–1886)
Presbyterian theologian and teacher

Son of Charles Hodge, Archibald Hodge was educated at the College of New Jersey (later Princeton University) and trained for the ministry at Princeton Theological Seminary. Ordained in 1847, he spent the following three years as a missionary to India. Thereafter he served for fourteen years as minister of three Presbyterian parishes in Maryland, Virginia, and Pennsylvania. In 1864 he was appointed Professor of Systematic Theology at Western Seminary; and in 1877 he was called back to Princeton Seminary as Associate to his father, whom he succeeded in the Chair of Theology after his father's death in 1878. This younger Hodge was so deeply influenced by his father that he devoted himself to expounding the father's theology in undiluted form. His published works include *The Life of Charles Hodge* (1880) and *Outlines of Theology* (1860, 1879), a popular textbook of Charles Hodge's thought. N. V. HOPE

HODGE, CHARLES (1797–1878)
American Presbyterian theologian and educator

Born in Philadelphia, Hodge graduated from the College of New Jersey (later Princeton University) in 1815 and from Princeton Theological Seminary in 1819. In 1820 he joined the staff of the Seminary and remained a member of its faculty for the rest of his life, except for two years of study in France and Germany (1826–1828). From 1822 to 1840 he was Professor of Oriental and Biblical Literature, and from 1840 Professor of Theology.

Hodge was involved in several of the controversies that agitated the Presbyterian Church of his day. He wholeheartedly supported the Old School position in the Old School–New School dispute that produced the schism of 1837. He believed that slavery was permitted by the Bible and that only its abuse was condemned; and this set him at odds with the majority opinion in the Northern Presbyterian Church during the Civil War of 1861–1865. N. V. HOPE

HOFMANN, JOHANN CHRISTIAN KONRAD VON (1810–1877)
Lutheran theologian and biblical scholar

Born in Nuremberg, Hofmann studied at Erlangen (1827–1829) and Berlin (1829–1832), where he obtained his doctorate in 1835. After teaching in a gymnasium, he started his university career at Erlangen in 1838, being promoted to a professorship in 1841. In 1842 he became a professor of theology at Rostock, and in 1845 returned to a theological chair at Erlangen, where he remained until his death. Interested in politics, he represented Erlangen and Furth at several sessions of the Bavarian parliament.

One of his major works is *Weissagung und Erfullung im Alten und Neuen Testament* (*Prophecy and Fulfillment in the Old and New Testaments*; two parts, 1841–1844), a study of the theology of biblical prophecy, in which he propounded the idea of prophecy as God's unfolding of his plan of salvation, wherein each step in fulfillment is again turned into a promise, culminating in the Incarnation of Jesus Christ, who prefigures the final glorification of the church of Christian believers. Another of his works, *Der Schriftbeweis* (*Proof from Scripture*; three parts, 1852–1856), is an attempt to prove the authenticity and divine origin of Christianity from its basic documents by showing the biblical revelation to be the necessary transcript and correlate of Christian experience, which is communion of God with man mediated by Jesus Christ. Charged with denying the doctrine of Christ's vicarious atonement, Hofmann replied in yet another massive work, *Schutzschriften* (*Writings in Defense*; five parts, 1856–1859). N. V. HOPE

HOFMANN, MELCHIOR (c. 1496–1544)
German preacher

Born in Swabisch-Hall, Hofmann became a leather dresser. In 1523 he went to Livonia where he became a lay preacher with great effect. He then moved to Womar, but was driven from there by the authorities to Dorpat, where with Luther's and Bugenhagen's support he carried on a feud with the clergy. In 1526 he was in Stockholm preaching, but he was becoming interested in prophecy, claiming that the world would end in 1533. In Holstein (1527–1529) he set forth his views of the Lord's Supper as a spiritual memorial, contrary to Luther. In 1529 he came to Strassburg, but opposition to his prophetic views forced him to join the Anabaptists. After a short time he left to proclaim his views in Emden, East Friesland, and Holland. In 1533 he returned to Strassburg, where he remained until his death, gathering around him a growing number of "Melchiorites." He spent much of his time interpreting the book of Revelation, and also set forth the view that Christ derived his humanity not from Mary, but from a special act of God. W. S. REID

HOLDEN, OLIVER (1765–1844)
Puritan minister; musician

Much of Holden's life was spent in Charlestown, Massachusetts, where he was a musician, carpenter, and Puritan minister. He also served for fourteen years in the State House of Representatives. He was much concerned with the improvement of congregational singing. "Coronation," his best-known tune, is the one most widely used in America for the hymn, "All Hail the Power of Jesus' Name." He was one of the many who wrote songs lamenting the death of Washington. J. B. MACMILLAN

HOLL, KARL (1866–1926)
German Protestant historian of church and theology

After a brief period as a Lutheran pastor, Holl became a lecturer and later a full professor of church history at Tübingen (1901–1906). From 1906 until his death he was a professor of church history in Berlin. He worked with Adolf von Harnack (1851–1930) on a series of the early church fathers. Although he attempted to stay clear of the theological disputes that surfaced at the turn of the century, his studies in Luther's theology, especially his work—*The Cultural Significance of the Reformation*—served to answer the negative charges of Marxist critics and to spur new interest in the Reformation not only as a theological turning point in the life of the church but as a pivotal point in human history. His interest in Eastern Orthodoxy led him to discover the writings of Leo Tolstoy and helped to waken Western Europe to the significance of Russian Christianity. D. M. LAKE

HOLST, GUSTAV (1874–1934)
An English composer influential in the modern revival of interest in English folk song and Elizabethan music

Holst believed strongly in the social value of music and encouraged music making with great enthusiasm in schools, in churches, and in his lifelong association with community organizations such as the YMCA. He wrote much choral music, especially for festive services in Canterbury, Chichester, and other English churches. *The Coming of Christ,* a mystery play to a text by John Masefield, and *The Hymn of Jesus* (1917) from the Apocryphal Acts of St. John are noteworthy. *The Planets* (1918), a symphonic suite of seven movements, is his most well known work. W. PHEMISTER

HOLTZMANN, HEINRICH JULIUS (1832–1910)

German New Testament scholar

Holtzmann became full professor at the University of Heidelberg in 1865 and served as professor at the University of Strassburg from 1874 to 1904. He wrote numerous works on the Synoptic Gospels (1863), New Testament Introduction (1885), and theology of the New Testament (two volumes, 1896–1897). Each reflects the prevailing liberalism of his time. In *The Synoptic Gospels* he questions both the historical accuracy of the Gospel accounts and the deity of Christ. He argues, probably correctly, that Mark was the first of the Synoptic Gospels to be written. Both Matthew and Luke relied upon Mark, and probably also upon a second source of Jesus' sayings that we do not possess. He claimed that these two gospels are unreliable and that only Mark gives a relatively true picture of the progress of Jesus' ministry. According to Holtzmann's view of Mark's Gospel, Jesus—through the force of circumstances—gradually began to see himself as a messiah who must suffer death on a cross.

Holtzmann also wrote studies of Colossians, Ephesians, and the Pastoral Epistles, and commentaries on the Gospels and Acts. In each he develops an unorthodox view that appealed to many later liberal theologians. R. HESSELGRAVE

HONEGGER, ARTHUR (1892–1955)

Modern composer

Though born of Swiss parents, Honegger lived most of his life in France. He trained at the Zurich and Paris conservatories. Fame came to him in the 1920s with two significant works: *Pacific 231* (1924), in which he realistically imitated the power and clangor of an express locomotive, and *Le Roi David* (1921), an impassioned treatment of the story of King David in the grand manner of biblical oratorios.

In his complete works, which cover virtually every type of combination of instruments, voices, and solos, there is a significant amount based on religious themes, including the oratorio *Joan of Arc at the Stake* (1938), the *Third Symphony,* called *"liturgical,"* and the opera on the apocryphal book Judith. W. PHEMISTER

HONORIUS I (died 638)

Pope, 625–638

Apart from his origins in Campania (southern Italy), Honorius's early life cannot be traced. Election to the papacy brought out vigorous leadership capabilities, and he continued many of Gregory I's main objectives. Very concerned over Britain, Honorius sent Birinus and other missionaries to the western Saxons. Gregory's recognition of Honorius as archbishop of Canterbury, and Paulinus as archbishop of York, was important. He also wrote to commend King Edwin of Northumbria on his conversion to Christianity, and his admonishment of Irish bishops about Roman practices seems to have had effect. Elsewhere in western Europe, Honorius provided needed help over the Gothic church's conversion from Arianism to orthodoxy in Spain. He made various efforts to bring northern Italy's Arians under orthodox doctrine and practice. This had little result, but he did end opposition to Rome in the see of Aquileia. Overall, Honorius handled the Church's material and spiritual affairs carefully, and his reputation as a judicious pope seems deserved.

Honorius' papacy generated a controversy whose repercussions have continued to the twentieth century. The conflict revolved about how much Honorius' statements on Monothelitism, a christological doctrine, were or were not heretical. Monothelitism was a doctrine that stated that Christ possessed not two wills but one will only. Subsequent pronouncements by the church declared this a heretical doctrine, one that aligned with monophysitism, a teaching in which Christ has not two natures, divine and human, but one divine-human nature. In various writings, Honorius upheld

Christ's two distinct natures, but he also specified that proper depictions should ascribe Christ only "one will" and not "two wills." Honorius also declared that the dispute was a problem in semantics and not basic doctrine. Nonetheless, not long after his death, the Council of Constantinople (681) pronounced monothelitism heretical and named Honorius along with Sergius among its proponents. This declaration was then ratified by Pope Leo II in 682.

In succeeding centuries, the controversy's main concern has been how error free papal teachings have remained throughout history. The discord between Honorius I and Leo II, along with the Council of Constantinople (681), appears to belie claims that the papacy has never erred on important doctrine. Honorius and monothelitism were a point of conflict at Vatican Council I (twentieth general council, 1868–1870) and its formal definition of papal infallibility.

Reproductions of Honorius I's letters may be found in Migne's *Patrologia Latina*. Jaffe's *Regesta Pontificum Romanorum* lists other important original documents. K. J. BRYER

HOOKER, RICHARD (1554–1600)
Author of a classic on church-state relationships, Laws of Ecclesiastical Polity

Born at Heavitree near Exeter and educated at Exeter Grammar school and Corpus Christi College, Oxford, Hooker was a fellow from 1577–1584. He lectured in Hebrew at Drayton Beauchamp and was appointed master of the Temple in London in 1585. He was rector of Bishopbourne from 1595 until his death.

Hooker was a social and political theorist, as well as an Anglican clergyman and theologian. In Elizabethan England he set out to defend the established relation of church and state against both Roman Catholics and Puritans.

Basic to his thinking is the Anglican tradition of affirming both biblical authority, church tradition, and man's rational powers. The Bible must be accorded absolute authority when it speaks plainly and unambiguously. When it is silent or unclear, then it is interpreted by the traditions of the church. But when both Bible and tradition are silent or unclear, then the Holy Spirit leads men by the light of reason. Consequently, explicit biblical teachings must be regarded as essential, as distinguished from accessory matters, which reason advises. For example, Scripture prescribes no one form of church government or worship, so reason permits churches to develop their own polity and rites.

Hooker understood reason to be God's gift to man whereby he can discern the natural law inherent in creation. Here Hooker follows his Aristotelian teachers and Thomas Aquinas. The Puritans rejected Aristotle and Aquinas because the Puritans believed that fallen man cannot know the natural law adequately, so that civil laws must build directly on the divine law in Scripture. Hooker replied that Scripture is not explicit enough in all matters, but must be supplemented by human laws based on our knowledge of natural law. The fall did not prevent this; rather, it prevented us knowing apart from the biblical revelation what is needed to gain eternal life. Both biblical law and natural law are therefore needed—hence, the need for both church and state. But to avoid division and ruin within either church or state, and since the people of the land make up both, it is reasonable that the one supreme ruler they acknowledge should govern both church and state. This should be the sovereign who holds office by both the wisdom of God and the laws of the land. C. HICKS

HOOKER, THOMAS (1586–1647)
Puritan pastor; often described as the founder of Connecticut

Born in Leicestershire and educated at Cambridge, Hooker was an Anglican clergyman before his Puritan views brought him into conflict with Archbishop William Laud and forced his removal to Holland in 1630. Three years later he crossed the Atlantic and in 1634 became pastor at New Towne (Cambridge), Massachusetts. Partly because of rivalry with Roger Williams, the congregation moved in 1636 to the Connecticut Valley. He took part in the proceedings against Anne Hutchinson in 1637. He held that the people as a whole—and not just church members—should choose their magistrates, and he was a prime mover in organizing in 1643 the "United Colonies of New England" (claimed to be the earliest system of federal government in America). A strong champion of the Congregational polity against Presbyterianism, he wrote a number of books including *The Soul's Preparation for Christ* (1632), *An Exposition of the Principles of Religion* (1640), *A Survey of the Sum of Church Discipline* (1648), and *The Poor Doubting Christian Drawn to Christ* (1684). J. D. DOUGLAS

HOOPER, JOHN (died 1555)
Church of England bishop; Protestant martyr

The date of his birth in Somerset is not known, but Hooper was educated at Oxford, where he then entered a monastic house. When the dissolution of the monasteries came, he moved to London, where he adopted views of the Reformation. After making these known, he was exiled for heresy; he traveled on the Continent, getting to know Protestant leaders like Bullinger and Bucer. Returning to England in 1549 when the young Edward began to rule, he became chaplain first to Protector Somerset and then to Northumberland. In 1550 he was offered the bishopric of Gloucester, but he did not take it up immediately due to various scruples over vestments and the affirmations he had to make publicly. When he became bishop his work was exemplary. He preached regularly, visited parishes, helped the poor, sought to correct social injustice, and attempted to create the habit of Bible-reading. When the sees of Gloucester and Worcester were united, he continued as bishop of both until he was removed by Queen Mary. He was imprisoned in London, tried for heresy, and found guilty. Refusing to recant, he was burned at the stake on February 9, 1555. Some of his writings that exhibit a developed Protestantism were treasured by the Puritans. In 1843 and 1852 the Parker Society published his *Works* in two large volumes. P. TOON

HOPKINS, GERARD MANLEY (1844–1889)
Poet, priest, and teacher

Hopkins was born at Stratford, Essex, of prosperous middle-class parents. He studied at Oxford, where he began his lifelong friendship with Robert Bridges, later Poet Laureate and collector of Hopkins's poems. While at Oxford, he also became a Roman Catholic; in 1867 he took a First-Class honors degree in Classics; for a few months after leaving Oxford taught at John Henry Newman's Oratory School at Edgbaston, and in 1868, he entered the Novitiate of the Society of Jesus.

On becoming a Jesuit, he burned (so he thought) all the poems he had written and resolved not to write poetry unless by the wish of his "Superiors." Hopkins had to write, and in 1875 he composed his first great poem, *The Wreck of the Deutschland,* a lament for the death of four nuns, which incorporated almost all the elements of his "sprung rhythm," his "inscaped" diction, and his Christian view of life.

Between 1877 and 1881 he served as select preacher or parish priest in London, Oxford, Liverpool, and Chesterfield. Many of the poems of these years grew out of his experience as a priest, and most of them, like "The Handsome Heart" and "Felix Randal" show deep concern for the spiritual welfare and destiny of man; others like "God's Grandeur" and "The Windhover" reveal the inexplicable illumination that comes to one who perceives the impact of God in nature.

During his last years he wrote other excellent poems, including *Carrion Comfort,* which reflects Hopkins' faith as the powerful source of comfort. All of his poetry shows his fierce joy in mastering words, which he hammered into compelling patterns. E. B. BATSON

HOPKINS, SAMUEL (1721–1803)
A colonial clergyman whose stern presentation of New England theology and outspoken opposition to slavery made him a leader among Congregationalists

Hopkins was born on a farm in Waterbury, Connecticut, graduated from Yale in 1741, was ordained as a Congregational minister (1743), and took a church of five members in Massachusetts. The small church endured his severe logic and uncompromising homiletical dullness until 1769, when Hopkins was dismissed. He moved to the First Congregational Church of Newport, Rhode Island (1770), and stayed there until his death, though he was forced to flee during the British occupation of 1776.

An intense scholar, Hopkins devoted his mental energies to the elaboration of extreme Calvinistic doctrines. In this endeavor he was influenced by Jonathan Edwards, though Edwards repudiated certain of Hopkins's theses. A sovereign God does all things for his own glory, taught Hopkins. Even sin and evil shine to the glory of God by granting occasion for God's display of justice and mercy. Men should follow their divinely ordained path, willing even to be among the reprobate should this fate accrue to the glory of God. The goal of Christian life was disinterested benevolence. So elaborate and systematic were Hopkins's articulations that his views were known as Hopkinsianism. His *System of Doctrines* (1793) was the product of his study.

That slaveholders were among Hopkins's parishioners did not inhibit the minister's outspokenness against that evil. Hopkins collected money to free some slaves and wrote in favor of nationwide emancipation in 1776. He was one of the first congregational ministers to denounce the practice.
M. FACKLER

HORT, FENTON JOHN ANTHONY (1828–1892)
English New Testament textual critic

Born in Dublin, Ireland, Hort was educated at Rugby, and then Trinity College, Cambridge, becoming a fellow in 1852. He became Huslean Professor of Divinity at Cambridge. He taught most of his life there and became closely associated with two other famous Cambridge scholars, J. B. Lightfoot and B. F. Westcott. There is little doubt that Hort was the greatest genius of the Cambridge school.

Hort is most known for his work in New Testament textual criticism and for purporting the theory that Codex Vaticanus and Codex Sinaiticus (along with a few other early manuscripts) represented a text that most closely replicated the original writing. Hort called this text the Neutral Text. (According to his studies, the Neutral Text described certain manuscripts that had the least amount of textual corruption.) This is the text that Hort, together with his friend B. F. Westcott, relied upon for compiling their edition called *The New Testament in the Original Greek*—a work they took twenty-eight years to complete.

Hort, with his friends B. F. Westcott and J. B. Lightfoot, had planned to collaborate in writing a commentary on all the books of the New Testament, but they did not realize their collective goal. Lightfoot completed commentaries on some Pauline Epistles; Westcott completed his work on Hebrews, John, and the Epistles of John; but Hort did not complete any books before he died because he was very occupied with producing the English Revised Version and was known to be a perfectionist. However, after his death, it was discovered that he had written on James and 1 Peter. A dozen of Hort's works were published posthumously; some of these works include *Judaistic Christianity* (1894), *The Christian Ecclesia* (1897), and his Hulsean Lectures of 1871, which dealt with philosophical theology.

Hort's most influential work was his *Introduction to The New Testament in the Original Greek* (1882), wherein Hort detailed the critical principles that he and Westcott followed in making their edition of the Greek New Testament. Another monograph, *Two Dissertations* (1876), defends the reading "only God" in John 1:18, a reading that appears in the earliest Greek manuscripts.

Hort was more than a brilliant scholar—he was also an involved churchman. He was particularly interested in social issues and supported the work of F. D. Maurice and Charles Kingsley, both leaders in the British social gospel movement. Nevertheless,

Hort's own theological position was conservative. P. W. COMFORT & D. M. LAKE

HOSIUS (OSSIUS) (c. 257–c. 357)
Bishop of Cordova, Spain

Born in Spain and consecrated as Bishop of Cordova (c. 296), Hosius suffered in the persecution that the emperor Diocletian began in 303. He took part in the Council of Elvira (c. 300); and from about 313 to 326 he was ecclesiastical adviser to the emperor Constantine. After Constantine achieved final mastery in the Roman Empire in 323, Hosius was sent to adjudicate the doctrinal dispute at Alexandria between Arius and Athanasius, but failed in this attempt. It was probably on his advice that Constantine summoned the Council of Nicaea in 325 to settle the matter officially. There Hosius presided, and lent his support to the orthodox Christological formula that the Council adopted. After Nicaea, Hosius returned to his diocese in Spain, but surfaced at the Council of Sardica in 343. In 355 he was summoned to Milan by the emperor Constantius to condemn Athanasius and recognize the Arians. This he refused to do; but in 357 at Sirmium, under threats, he was pressured into signing a creed that favored Arianism—an action for which he was later condemned by a Spanish synod.
N. V. HOPE

HOSKYNS, SIR EDWYN CLEMENT (1884–1937)
Anglican clergyman and New Testament scholar

After studies at Jesus College, Cambridge, and the University of Berlin, Hoskyns became a fellow at Corpus Christi College, Cambridge (1919). His personal influence and writings helped to spur the movement known as "biblical theology" both in England and in Germany. He translated Karl Barth's famous commentary on Romans for English readers. At a time when many New Testament scholars were making a sharp distinction between the "real Jesus of history" and the early church creation of the "Christ

of faith," Hoskyns argued that the two could not be separated—not if any credence or reliability was given to the Gospel records. The theme was developed in his book *The Riddle of the New Testament* (with F. N. Davey, 1931). His very thorough examination of the Gospel of John was published in 1940 as a posthumous work entitled *The Fourth Gospel*. His study demonstrated the application of modern linguistic criticism to the gospel writings. D. M. LAKE

HOUGHTON, WILL HENRY (1887–1947)
President of the Moody Bible Institute of Chicago, 1934–1947

Born in Boston and educated in New England, Houghton accepted Christ in 1901 during evangelistic meetings. After four years as an actor, he rededicated his life to Christ in 1909. Houghton attended Eastern Nazarene College in Rhode Island, leaving to assist evangelists including R. A. Torrey and Billy Sunday.

He pastored Baptist churches in Canton (1915–1917), New Bethlehem (1918–1920), and Norristown (1920–1923), Pennsylvania. These ministries were followed by the Baptist Tabernacle in Atlanta, Georgia (1925–1928) and Calvary Baptist Church of New York City (1930–1934).

During his Moody presidency, enrollment increased from 840 to 1428. *Moody Monthly* magazine circulation doubled to seventy thousand. As successor to Dr. James M. Gray, Houghton strengthened the faculty and started the Moody Institute of Science and the America Scientific Affiliation. Houghton was a frequent writer of gospel tracts, articles, editorials, books, poems, songs, and choruses, including "Lead Me to Some Soul Today." G. F. ARNOLD

HOWARD, JOHN (c. 1726–1790)
English philanthropist and prison reformer

Born in London, Howard lost his mother and father early in life; but, being left in a reasonable financial position he traveled on the Continent before settling in Stoke Newington, near London. In 1751 he married his landlady who was twice his age but who had nursed him through a severe illness. She died in 1755 after which he settled at Carding, Bedfordshire, which remained his principal home. He was a Dissenter, a teetotaler, and a vegetarian. In Cardington he built model cottages, provided elementary education, and urged the villages to be industrious. His second wife died soon after childbirth.

His career as a prison reformer began when, as the High Sheriff of Bedfordshire, he inspected prisons and was appalled by the conditions of them in his own and other counties. He gave evidence to a Committee of the House of Commons and agitated for reform. When the House of Commons passed two measures for improvement, he paid for the cost of printing and distributing them. To strengthen his hand he made several lengthy tours of prisons in continental countries as well as in Britain. In 1777 he published his influential *State of Prisons in England* and in 1789 his *Account of the Principal Lazarettos in Europe.* His last journey was to Russia where he died of swamp fever. It is said that he spent thirty thousand pounds of his own money in his reforming activities. Named after him is the Howard League for Penal Reform, founded in 1866. P. TOON

HOWE, JULIA WARD (1819–1910)
Social reformer and author; popularly known for her "Battle Hymn of the Republic"

Julia Ward was born to a wealthy New York couple, Samuel and Julia Rush Cutler Ward. Her mother, a poet, encouraged her writing when she was a child. She later pursued studies in the field of law and literature, receiving the doctorate of law from Tufts and Smith colleges and the doctorate of letters from Brown University.

She married philanthropist and reformer Samuel Gridley Howe in 1843. After extensive travels, they settled in Boston, where they raised a family of six children. Julia Howe was active in the Unitarian Church, occasionally preaching in congregations

throughout New England. An ardent abolitionist, she and her husband edited the Boston *Commonwealth*, an antislavery periodical (1851–1853). She also campaigned for child welfare, prison reform, and equal education. She presided over the New England Woman Suffrage Association and the Woman's International Peace Association.

A prolific writer, she published volumes of poetry, biography, drama, and travel. She was a member of the American Academy of Arts and Letters. T. H. SPENCE

HROMADKA, JOSEF LUKE (1889–1969)
Czech Protestant theologian

Born at Hodslavice, Moravia, Hromadka was educated at the Universities of Vienna, Basel, Heidelberg, Aberdeen, and Prague. From 1912 until 1920 he was pastor of Lutheran congregations in Vsetin, Moravia, and then at Prague. In 1920 he was called to the Chair of Systematic Theology at the John Hus (since 1950 the Comenius) Faculty of Protestant Theology at the University of Prague. In 1939 he left Czechoslovakia and came to the United States, where he taught Theology at Princeton Theological Seminary until 1947. In his latter years he returned to Czechoslovakia and resumed teaching in his former Chair, becoming Dean of the Faculty in 1950. With the Communist takeover of Czechoslovakia in 1947, Hromadka urged Christian and Communist dialogue and East-West understanding. In 1958 he received the Lenin Peace Prize and founded the Christian Peace Conference, which sought to serve as a vehicle of Christian-Marxist dialogue; but in 1968 his vigorous public protest against the Russian invasion of Czechoslovakia led to his forced resignation in 1969 as Chairman of the Christian Peace Conference. He died shortly thereafter.

Long interested in Christian reunion, Hromadka attended the First Assembly of the World Council of Churches in Amsterdam in 1948 and thereafter served a term of office as a member of its Central Committee. N. V. HOPE

HSI, PASTOR (1830–1896)

One of China's greatest preachers

A proud Confucian scholar and one-time opium addict, Hsi was dramatically converted to Christ at the age of forty-nine by reading the Gospel of Matthew in order to enter a literary contest arranged by a Methodist missionary, David Hill. Though definitely of an independent spirit, Hsi managed to work harmoniously with David Hill and later with D. E. Hoste of the China Inland Mission. A man of simple faith and persevering prayer, he became a spiritual giant whose influence extended far beyond the confines of his native province of Shansi. To him God was a living God, and the Bible was a living book. He dared to claim the promises of God and received remarkable answers to prayer. In time he became one of China's greatest preachers, with a rare passion for the glory of God and the souls of men. Remembering his own former bondage to the opium habit, he opened rehabilitation centers where opium addicts could, through the power of Christ, be delivered from drug addiction. He also had a ministry to demon-possessed persons. A man of great self-discipline, he assiduously cultivated his own spiritual life, keeping short accounts with God and ministering always in the power of the Holy Spirit. H. KANE

HUBMAIER, BALTHASAR (c. 1481–1528)

German Anabaptist

Hubmaier was born in Friedberg, and in 1503 he entered the University of Friedberg, where one of his professors was Johann Eck, later one of Luther's principal Roman Catholic opponents. In 1512 he was appointed professor of theology at the University of Ingolstadt and pastor of the town church. In 1516 he became preacher in the cathedral at Regensberg. By 1522, however, he had become a Protestant and the same year pastor of Waldshut in northern Switzerland. Soon after this he accepted the theological position of Ulrich Zwingli of Zurich and opposed the Roman Catholic government of Lower Austria. However, he soon came under the influence of Thomas Munzer, Con-

rad Grebel, and Felix Manz, and moved from Zwinglian to Anabaptist views, demonstrating this by being rebaptized in 1525. The same year the Peasants Revolt took place, in which Waldshut was involved. When the peasants were defeated, Hubmaier fled to Zurich where he abjured Anabaptism, but shortly afterwards in Constance he recanted his recantation. This change brought him into conflict with both Zwinglians and Roman Catholics. As a result he fled to Moravia. In Nikolsburg he gathered a large group of followers from the "Bohemian Brethren" and also established a printing press from which he could issue pamphlets against both the Lutherans and the Zwinglians. The Austrians, however, gained control of Moravia. Then Hubmaier and his wife were arrested and carried to Vienna where they were tried for heresy by a Roman Catholic court. He was burned at the stake, and his wife was drowned in the Danube River. W. S. REID

HUC, EVARISTE REGIS (1813–1860)

French Roman Catholic missionary to China

After ordination to the priesthood in 1839, Huc went as a missionary to China to the valley of Blackwaters. During this period Roman Catholics were being persecuted in China. In 1844, with Joseph Gabet, he began the famous journey through Mongolia and Tibet to gain knowledge of the various peoples. Disguised as lamas to escape attention, they eventually entered Lhasa in January of 1846. They were beginning to establish a mission in Lhasa, but had to make a hasty exit six weeks later. Huc returned to France in 1852 in shattered health, left his religious order in 1853, and devoted himself to writing. Huc wrote the much-read book *Travels in Tartary, Tibet, and China* (two volumes, 1850) and *The Empire in China* (1854), which received recognition from the French Academy. P. TOON

HUGH OF CLUNY (1024–1109)

The sixth abbot of Cluny

Of noble birth, Hugh entered the abbey of

Cluny at the age of fourteen. At the age of twenty he was ordained priest. Only four years later Hugh was made prior of the abbey and one year later, still a very young man, he was elected abbot. For the ensuing sixty years he so ruled the monastery that it reached its peak of influence under him. Hugh even formed the first Cluniac convent of nuns in 1056, extending the influence of Cluny to the female world. Although he remained a devout person of prayer, he was often involved in ecclesiastical activities, such as participating in numerous councils and serving on diplomatic missions for several popes. In the latter capacity he was present at Canossa when the Holy Roman Emperor Henry IV humbled himself before Pope Gregory VII. Hugh was canonized only eleven years after his death. A. CABANISS

HUGH OF ST. VICTOR (1096–1141)
Abbot, mystic, writer

Though one nearly contemporary source calls him Hugh of Lorraine, he probably came from the region of Halberstadt in Saxony, where one of his uncles was a bishop. He entered St. Victor's in 1115, bringing with him the relics of that saint, which he had obtained in Marseilles. His most systematic theological work is the *Sacraments of the Christian Faith*, which deals with the doctrines of Creation, the Trinity, free will, the Fall, the Incarnation, the unity of the Church, and end times. His *Didascalion*, an encyclopedia of science, was designed to introduce students to the study of twenty-one fields of learning, including seven mechanical sciences. He also wrote devotional pieces, commentaries of Scripture and Pseudo-Dionysius, and works on philosophy, grammar, and geography. Hugh was an original thinker who emphasized studying the literal meaning and historical significance of Scripture. C. HICKS

HUGHES, HUGH PRICE (1847–1903)
Methodist minister and social reformer

Born in Carmarthen, Wales, Hughes trained for the ministry (1865–1869) in Lon-

don at Richmond Theological College and London University, from which he graduated with a B.A. in 1869. After ordination to the Methodist ministry he served for eighteen years in Dover, Brighton, Oxford, and London before being appointed in 1887 as First Superintendent of the West London Mission, a position he retained until his death. In 1898 he was elected President of the Methodist Conference. Hughes was one of the founders of the Methodist Forward Movement, an attempt to make Methodism more effective and relevant in the religious life of contemporary England. One important feature of this was the setting up in the great cities vital centers of personal evangelism and social service. In 1885 he founded the *Methodist Times,* which gave the movement publicity. As a social reformer Hughes expressed what was called "the Nonconformist conscience" in opposing such evils as alcoholic intemperance, gambling, militarism, and sexual immorality, and in advocating public health, the well-being of children, and shorter hours and better conditions of work for the laboring class. He was also a leader in that movement for greater solidarity among non-established Protestant churches of England, which resulted in the formation of the National Evangelical Free Church Council (of which he was the first president) in 1896. N. V. HOPE

HUME, DAVID (1711–1776)
Scottish historian and philosopher

Hume's major work was in epistomology, where he argued that men have no a priori knowledge of fact and no empirically based knowledge of facts beyond their present experience. Thus, while people know the experiences they presently have, this provides no foundation for proving anything else. The problem, he pointed out, is that any inference to things beyond present experience depends on a cause-effect relation of which experience itself leaves us ignorant. This skeptical conclusion affects the traditional arguments for the existence of God, the immortality of the soul, and almost every other belief one might hold.

Yet Hume's last word is not of skepticism

but of belief. That is, while we cannot prove even that material things exist outside our present experience, we properly believe that they do. Repeated experiences instill in us the mental expectations and habits we call "belief." And while he criticized the theistic arguments in his *Dialogues Concerning Natural Religion,* he described the psychological grounds of religious belief in *The Natural History of Religion.* His famous essay on miracles appeared in the same context. Defining a miracle as "a violation of natural law," he argued that belief in natural laws is so well established by repeated experiences that only experiences of greater regularity—or else a miracle—could upset that belief and lead one to believe in miracles. But the evidence offered, for miracles, he says, is not that good: it is spotty, inconsistent, from out-of-the-way places, by prejudiced observers. How could it overthrow the better-established belief in uniform natural laws?

Hume was indeed skeptical of man's ability to know, but he allowed the legitimacy of beliefs that have psychological rather than logical grounds. But, it is objected, Hume had too limited a conception of belief. On his criterion, much of history would be quite unbelievable. But his skepticism elicited work on the psychology and justification of belief that continues to the present day.
A. F. HOLMES

HUNT, ARTHUR SURRIDGE (1871–1934)

English papyrologist (one who works with ancient manuscripts)

Born in Rawford, Essex, Hunt studied classics at Queen's College, Oxford, England, and after graduation he joined B. P. Grenfell and D. G. Hogarth in an excavation at the Fayum near Cairo. In 1901 he became a fellow of Lincoln College, Oxford, until 1906, when he replaced an ailing Grenfell as professor of papyrology from 1908 to 1913.

After military service in World War I, he became the sole editor of the papyrus texts issued by the Egypt Exploration Society. Hunt edited volume one of the *Catalog of the Greek Papyri* in the Salem Rylands Library Manchester (1911) and *Tragicorum Graecorum Fragmenti Papyracea* (1912). Together with Grenfell he published much of the literary finds from their excavation at the Fayum (the *Oxyrhynchus Papyri,* seventeen volumes, 1898–1927; and edited the *Amherst Papyri,* volume one, 1902; volume two, 1907).

An excellent scholar with a fine mind and deep devotion to accuracy, Hunt was noted for his quiet sense of humor and reserved nature. He was also known for being generously kind and devoutly religious.
D. CORNELL

HUNT, JOHN (1812–1848)

Pioneer Wesleyan missionary to Fiji

Born in Lincolnshire, England, Hunt was the first missionary to Fiji to have had theological training (Hoxton, 1835). Ordained in 1838, he proved an effective evangelist in Oxford and Australia before he went to Fiji in 1838. He stated his goals for Fiji were (1) the conversion of the Fijian people, (2) the translation of the Fijian Scriptures and training of men to interpret them, and (3) the revival of the doctrine of Scriptural Holiness. He was effective in each of these respects.

The Great Awakening in mainland Fiji began under his ministry at Viwa and spread through his trained preachers. He translated the New Testament into beautiful Bauan idiom (1848) from the Greek. His training program (the Viwa Plan) became the model for all Fiji, and his *Short Sermons* the indigenous teacher's textbook. He wrote a memoir of his colleague, William Cross. His *Letters on Entire Sanctification* (1848) became prescribed reading for Australian Wesleyan ministerial trainees for fifty years. No missionary did more to shape Christianity in Fiji. His notebooks are full of missiological and anthropological insights. Hunt communicated well to the cannibal world. He died at Viwa, Fiji, and was buried with a Fijian ceremonial dirge.
A. R. TIPPETT

HUNT, WILLIAM HOLMAN
(1827–1910)
English painter

Hunt studied art at the Royal Academy Schools in London where he met John Millais and Dante Gabriel Rossetti with whom he founded the Pre-Raphaelite Brotherhood. The primary purpose of the group was to recover and advance the style and spirit of Italian painting before Raphael—to paint nature honestly, as observed. Following his lifelong ambition to paint religious themes realistically, he went to Palestine in 1854 for the first of four trips. His best-known painting, *Christ as The Light of the World,* was made in 1854. These trips provided Hunt with the precise detail needed for the authenticity of works like his paintings *Finding Christ in the Temple* and *The Triumph of the Innocents.* Although the churchmen of England were slow to appreciate his art, he was eventually given the coveted Order of Merit in 1905. The influential art critic John Ruskin was responsible for the defense and promotion of Hunt's work.

In addition to his accomplishments in painting, he was one of the artists chosen to illustrate Alfred, Lord Tennyson's poems (1857) and was author of *Pre-Raphaelitism and the Pre-Raphaelite Brotherhood* (two volumes, 1905). A. STEFFLER

HUSS, JAN (1373–1415)
Bohemian preacher and forerunner of Protestantism; the link between John Wycliffe and Martin Luther

Huss was born in Hussinec (hence his name) into a well-to-do farming family. He received a good elementary education and then attended the University of Prague, where he received his master's degree in 1396. Two years later he began lecturing at the university.

After English king Richard II's marriage to Anne of Bohemia in 1382, Wycliffe's ideas were introduced to Bohemian theological and philosophical circles. Consequently, Huss began to read and study that English reformer's works.

In 1400 Huss was ordained to the priesthood and then made dean of the philosophy faculty (1401). As rector of the university (1402–1403), he wielded considerable influence, but even more important was his preaching activity.

His reputation spread while he was a synodical preacher. He became even better known upon receiving the prestigious position of Bethlehem Chapel's rector. There he upheld the Czech tradition of preaching in the vernacular.

His preaching responsibilities forced him to study the Bible more seriously. He continued reading Wycliffe's works, although he did not abandon the Roman church or Catholic doctrine. In fact, Huss still acted as Archbishop Sbynjek's agent in examining the claims of various churches to be sites of miracles. Those investigations resulted in his first book *Concerning the Glorification of All the Blood of Christ* (1404). Huss attacked forged miracles and urged the faithful not to seek Christ in miraculous signs but in Scripture. Huss simultaneously began translating Wycliffe's works into Bohemian.

The stance Huss took on Wycliffe soon brought reactions from his university colleagues who had condemned Wycliffe's teachings (1403). At the same time, Huss's demands for clerical reforms incited complaints from offended clergy. Huss was also attacked for his criticism of the papacy. As a result, he was forbidden by the archbishop to perform any priestly functions (1408).

Another conflict arose concerning the legitimacy of two papal contenders (Gregory XII and Alexander V). A church council was to be held in Pisa in 1409, and the king of Bohemia requested that until then, the two claimants remain neutral. The papal election directly affected the Czech nation's autonomy in the Holy Roman Empire. In that controversy, Huss, as Bohemia's leader, won strong support from Czech nationalists. His role in the Bohemian separatist movement, however, not only alienated non-Czechs but also many of the clergy.

When Huss was reelected rector of the university (1409), formal charges of heresy were made against him. Pope Alexander V condemned Wycliffism as heresy and forbade most public preaching. That decree was probably directed against Huss, who continued to preach to large audiences in the Bethlehem Chapel. Huss was then excommunicated (1411) but not silenced. When Prague citizens rallied to his support, an interdict was laid on the city, forbidding ecclesiastical services and burial in consecrated ground.

In 1412 a papal envoy sent to Prague announced a crusade against the Vatican's enemy, neighboring king Ladislaus of Naples. Huss boldly protested the crusade and the indulgence (pardon of sin) offered to participants or sold to supporters. As a result, he was forced to leave Prague. During his exile, he completed his work *On the Church* (1413), largely based on Wycliffe's similar book.

From 1414 to 1418, church leaders met at Constance (in present-day Germany) to resolve the recurrent conflict among various papal claimants. Because of his controversial teachings, Huss was summoned to appear. Although promised safe-conduct by Bohemian emperor Sigismund, Huss set out with great misgivings. Soon after arrival, he was jailed. During his seven-month trial, he received little opportunity to respond to the accusations. Throughout the proceedings Huss defended his teachings with Scripture. His connection with Wycliffism, however, harmed his position. Consequently, the testimonies and arguments of powerful Catholic church leaders secured his condemnation for heresy. Sigismund refused to implement his safe-conduct. On July 6, Huss was handed over to the secular authorities with an empty recommendation "for mercy." He was immediately led outside the city where he was defrocked and burned at the stake. He died singing *Kyrie eleēson* (a Greek liturgical prayer, "Lord, have mercy").
W. S. REID

HUTCHINSON, ANNE (1591–1643)

Colonial America's ablest and most controversial female theologian

Anne Marbury was born in Lincolnshire (England), where her father was a clergyman. The Puritan vicar there, John Cotton, influenced her spiritual development. In 1634 she came with her husband, William Hutchinson, and their children to Massachusetts in order to maintain contact with Cotton, who had fled England the year before. In his Boston pastorate, Cotton expounded doctrines of free grace and principles of Puritan government. Anne Hutchinson began a mid-weekly meeting to discuss Cotton's sermons and other spiritual matters.

Hutchinson's friendship with Cotton and meritorious community service as a nurse secured her social status. She was well respected until some ministers began accusing her of theological error. They claimed she taught antinomianism, which infers that Christians do not need the law. The accusations created a fervor and soon sixty to eighty people were flocking to her lectures. She argued that a believer possessing the Holy Spirit was not bound by laws of conduct but was moved by inner spiritual compulsions. Her statements showed a thorough knowledge of the Bible.

Some ministers (including Cotton) supported her views as being legitimate, even if they were a mystical interpretation of Puritan theology. Others, such as Massachusetts governor John Winthrop, feared Hutchinson's opinions would corrupt New England Puritanism. The personal inspiration she attributed to all Christians undermined the theocratic structures of Puritan society.

Finally, Massachusetts leaders demanded a hearing for Hutchinson. During days of discussion she defended herself against the colony's most powerful ministers and magistrates by careful biblical argument and penetrating logic. Although her skillful confutations silenced her opponents, her claim that the Holy Spirit communicated directly to her (apart from Scripture) was not tolerated. As a result of that rash assertion, she and her followers were banished from Massachusetts (1638).

She first moved to Rhode Island, then to Long Island, and finally to inland New York.

There she and most of her family were killed by Indians. M. A. NOLL

HUTTEN, ULRICH VON (1488–1523)
German humanist and reformer

Born in Steckelberg, Hesse, Hutten at the age of eleven was placed in a monastery to train for the "religious" life. But after six years he fled from the monastery, taking with him a strong hatred of that form of religious devotion. For the next few years he spent his time studying at various universities in Germany and Italy, imbibing all the current humanistic ideas and theories.

By 1517 Hutten had become strongly anti-papal, wishing to see the influence of the pope removed from Germany, largely because he felt that Rome was mulcting Germany of large sums of money. Furthermore, in the conflict over Johannes Reuchlin (1455–1522), who had been attacked by Jewish convert Johannes Pfefferkorn for opposing the destruction of Jewish books as being anti-Christian, Hutten took Reuchlin's part and helped to prepare a lampoon on Pfefferkorn and the ideas he supported, in *The Letters of Obscure Men.*

At the same time Hutten had come under the influence of Martin Luther, whom he had heard at the Leipzig debate in 1519. He became increasingly vocal in his antipapalism, hoping to unite the German Imperial Knights and the Imperial Free cities in an alliance to curtail the powers of the princes, whom he seemed to regard as being the mainstay of papal power. He also edited and published Lorenzo Valla's work on the *Donation of Constantine,* which provided Luther with material for attacking the secular claims of the papacy.

As a result of his activities he was ordered arrested, but he fled to the protection of the castle of his friend Franz von Sickingen. When it was quite evident that the latter could not protect him, he was forced to leave and sought refuge in Schlettstadt, Basel, and Mulhausen. All these cities, not yet on the side of the Reformation, refused to receive him. Eventually he arrived in Zurich, where Ulrich Zwingli arranged for him to live on an island in Lake Zurich. There he passed his last days sick and in poverty.

How far Hutten was really a Protestant is uncertain, since it is difficult to untangle his humanism, his nationalism, and his religion, for they all seemed intermingled. But it is certain that he did help to forward the cause of the Reformation in Germany. W. S. REID

HUXLEY, THOMAS HENRY (1825–1895)
English biologist and educator

Born in Ealing, Middlesex, England, Huxley took a medical degree at London University in 1845. His scientific researches won him election to a fellowship of the Royal Society in 1851. In 1854 he was appointed Lecturer in Natural History at the Royal School of Mines, London, a position he held for thirty-one years. After Charles Darwin's *Origin of Species* was published in 1859, Huxley, always interested in promoting the scientific viewpoint, appointed himself "Darwin's bulldog," the "general agent" of the theory of biological evolution. Contending that "we need faith not by justification but by verification," Huxley in 1869 coined the term *agnostic* to describe his religious viewpoint. Though he was no atheist, he could not find adequate scientific proof of the claims of Christianity. Nevertheless, as a member of the London School Board from 1870 to 1872, Huxley contended strenuously for the required reading of the Bible in public schools, and he always had the highest respect and praise for the moral standard that Christianity inculcates. N. V. HOPE

HYDE, JOHN (1865–1912)
Presbyterian missionary to India; known as "Praying Hyde"

Son of a Presbyterian pastor, Hyde was born at Carrolton, Illinois. In 1882 the family moved to a new pastorate in Carthage, Illinois. That same year, at Carthage College, Hyde began his higher education. He was an avid student, and on graduation in 1886, the school invited him to join the faculty. After consideration, Hyde decided on a life of formal Church ministry. Soon he was in Chicago, Illinois, attending the Presbyterian Church's McCormick Seminary. Following his father's footsteps, his aim was toward pastoral work in Illinois. But in 1882, on graduation, Hyde joined a band of Presbyterian missionaries bound for India.

The Presbyterian Church assigned Hyde to the Punjab region of India. For the two decades he was there, Hyde's ministry centered in itinerant outreach to remote villages. Learning several local languages, he became one of rural India's powerful preachers. His spiritually minded, revival-oriented messages were also sought after for Indian missionary conferences. But after several years, Hyde began to concentrate on another ministry. Discouraged by the lack of converts, he turned increasingly to vigilent, persistent prayer. Thus began an intense prayer life that soon formed his greatest work. Remarkably, as Hyde spent sometimes forty or more hours on his knees, significant numbers of conversions began to come. Such prayer eventually occupied large portions of his time. From this point onward, Hyde saw continuing results in lives around him.

In 1904, Hyde helped found the Punjab Prayer Union, an effort to emphasize prayer among missionaries and converts in India. But Hyde's praying seemed to take a heavy toll on his body, and he was frequently ill his last years. Finally forced to leave India, he returned to New York in 1911, where he died a few weeks later. K. J. BRYER

I

IGNATIUS (died c. 107)

Bishop of Antioch in Syria

Ignatius was the Apostolic Father closest in thought to the New Testament writers. He wrote seven letters while en route under armed guard to Rome to suffer martyrdom (probably 107). The letters were to churches in cities through which he passed, Philadelphia and Smyrna, and to churches that sent delegations to visit him during this final journey—namely, Ephesus, Tralles, and Magnesia. He sent a letter ahead to the church in Rome to prevent their intervention with the Roman authorities in delivering him from martyrdom. He also wrote a letter to Polycarp, the bishop of Smyrna.

Similar to the New Testament epistles, these writings reveal a strong commitment to Christ and to the physical facts of his birth, death, and resurrection. Although Ignatius has some statement of the salvation in Christ, he did not have a clear view of grace and forgiveness. In his emphasis on his own martyrdom as "a true sacrifice," he detracts from the finished work of Christ.

The letters of Ignatius are the evidence for the rapid development of the episcopal structure in the early church of Asia Minor and Syria. In the New Testament, the local church was governed by a body of equal officers called elders or bishops, but in these letters there is reference to a single ruling bishop in each city except Rome. Ignatius is the first writer to use the term "catholic" (universal) to describe the church. His use of the term implied a connectional church with a unity in faith toward Christ and with delegations to express concerns between the churches.

He opposed the Ebionite heresy, which demanded the keeping of the Jewish regulations as the way of salvation. According to Ignatius, in order to affirm Christ the believer must reject Jewish practices. The Christian must worship on the Lord's Day, the day of his resurrection, rather than observe the Jewish sabbaths. Yet he did view the church as the continuation of the Old Testament people of God and the prophets as disciples who looked forward to Christ.

Ignatius also attacked Docetism, which held that Christ only appeared to have real birth, death, and resurrection. In reciting the facts of Christ's life, Igantius was the first one outside the New Testament writers to speak of the virgin birth of Jesus. Ignatius also emphasized the fact that the apostles touched the body of their risen Lord. Ignatius said it was the real suffering of Jesus Christ on the cross and his physical resurrection that made it possible for him to face martyrdom. J. NEWTON

IGNATIUS OF LOYOLA (1491–1556)

Spanish ascetic and theologian who founded the Society of Jesus

Ignatius was born into a powerful and wealthy Basque family living in the province of Guipuzcoa (Spain). Little is known of the boyhood of Inigo Lopez de Onaz y de Loyola. In 1506, through the help provided by Juan Velazquez de Cuellar, he was introduced to the court of King Ferdinand. His life of ease and luxury there abruptly ended with the king's death (1516) and the invasion by French armies into Navarre—a territory claimed by Spain. While defending the city of Pamplona, Loyola was seriously wounded in the leg by a cannon ball (1521).

The subsequent painful surgery and recuperation were undertaken at the castle of Loyola. There he was given the *Life of Christ*, a devotional book by a fourteenth-century Carthusian monk Ludolph of Saxony. After reading that and other spiritual writings, Ignatius experienced a mystical vision of Christ and the Virgin Mary. His former desires for chivalric honor were transformed into spiritual desires to serve God. He envisioned companies of men—not knights but soldiers of Christ.

He then visited a monastery at Montserrat and secluded himself in a cave at Manresa. Influenced by other ascetics, he practiced severe mental and physical mortification, including flagellation and fasting. It was here that his *Spiritual Exercises* first formed in his mind, although the book was not published until later.

After a year of intense prayer, confession, and introspection, Ignatius was close to suicide. He decided to leave his hermitage (1523) and continue his spiritual exercises while on pilgrimage to Palestine. He then resumed the education he had abandoned, studying in Barcelona, Alcala, and Salamanca. He finally graduated (1535) with an M.A. from the University of Paris.

While studying, Ignatius had attracted considerable attention. Some faculty criticized his doctrines. A small band of students, however, impressed by his teaching, formed an association with Ignatius. They were dedicated to chastity, poverty, and making a pilgrimage to Jerusalem in order to serve the poor and sick there.

Ignatius then traveled to Rome (1537) to affirm his unqualified allegiance to the pope. He was soon joined by his company and in 1540 the association was constituted the Society of Jesus by Paul III (1534–1549). Recognizing their "prophetic spirit," the pope expressed his hope that they would "reform the Church."

Ignatius then devoted himself to perfecting his *Spiritual Exercises* and compiling the order's *Constitutions*. He served as superior general of the "company" from its inception until he fell ill in 1556. Two attempts to resign were thwarted by his Jesuit brothers.

At Ignatius of Loyola's death, there were approximately one thousand members in the society. Soon Jesuits penetrated every country in Europe as well as Japan, China, the East Indies, the Americas, and Africa. Some European countries expelled them, and Pope Clement XIV suppressed them completely (1773). They were restored, however, by Pope Pius VII (1814). Thereafter, they were highly influential at church councils, in the universities, and in royal courts. The Jesuits' presence in the Roman Catholic Church today continues to be felt through the Gregorian University in Rome as well as through many other educational institutions which they maintain.

Ignatius of Loyola and Martin Luther (1483–1546) were contemporaries whose divergent paths keenly illustrated their different approaches to the church's reform. Both perceived the corruption of the church and both recoiled from the degradation of the Renaissance popes. Ignatius and Luther recognized that the secularism that had permeated the church could not be repelled without far-reaching "reform in head and members." Luther came to pursue his ideal outside the Roman Catholic Church. Ignatius, Luther's junior, pursued his inside the church.

Ignatius saw church reform to be based upon individual reform. His *Spiritual Exercises* was written to foster union with God and unqualified allegiance to the church. The process of purgation, illumination, and union was borrowed from writings of medieval mystics. First, all "inordinate attachments" were to be "purged" and rejected. Second, the will of God would be "illumined" or made plain. Third, if one was obedient to that revealed will, one would experience union with God.

Ignatius saw the need for an intelligent and well-educated clergy, perhaps even before he became aware of the magnitude of the Protestant revolt. His own efforts to secure an education at the best universities of Europe show his esteem for learning. In his choice of followers—Ignatius candidly recruited—he sought men who had distinguished themselves by intellectual achievements. He frankly tried to gather an intellectual elite. Ignatius did not immediately conceive of the mission of his society as educational; his foremost intent was personal and ecclesiastical reform. The men he assembled, however, were immediately in demand by royalty, nobility, and university chancellors. By recognizing and fostering individual talent and giving it freedom to operate, Ignatius made the Jesuits far more influential than their numbers would suggest.

Ignatius was not an original theologian; his only theological work was the *Spiritual Exercises*. That volume's Christocentric, devotional approach to the Christian life did not originate with Ignatius. The originality lay in the disciplined method of prayer that Ignatius developed. He believed that Christians could learn to imitate Christ through prayer in any state of life. The *Exercises* was not written to recruit members for the society. The method of the *Exercises* was basically a close and imaginative study of the person, words, and actions of Jesus as described in the Gospels.

Ignatius's theology of mysticism in particular was affected by his system of meditation. Since he believed truth is communicated through the teaching and functioning of the church, Ignatius declared that mystical experiences should remain within officially sanctioned limits. He stated that what "seems to me white, I will believe black if the hierarchial Church so defines." He proposed a re-vived mysticism set within a rigidly authoritarian view of the church.

Ignatius's unquestioning loyalty to the Roman Catholic Church should be seen in light of his Spanish Catholic heritage. His identification of the Roman Catholic Church with the papacy is not so easily explained. He considered the papacy as the only stable force from which the Roman church could collect its strength. Catholicism's unity was essential to repel the forces of the Reformation. Ignatius of Loyola's allegiance to the Roman church was so unshakable that not even imprisonment under the Inquisition succeeded in muting his devotion to it.

Ignatius did not found his society, however, as an answer to the Protestant Reformation. He put his papal theology in practice with no particular mission in mind. Instead, he placed Jesuit members at the pope's disposal for assignment to those missions that Rome judged most urgent. The pope then sent that small but highly gifted and totally dedicated group of men throughout the world. Papal theology in the following centuries was shaped by the papal theology of Loyola, and many members of his society are counted among its architects.
D. F. WELLS & J. L. McKENZIE

INGE, WILLIAM RALPH (1860–1954)
English theologian and philosopher; dean of St. Paul's Cathedral, London, 1911–1934

Born in Crayke, Yorkshire, the son of a clergyman, Inge was educated at Eton and King's College, Cambridge, winning prizes for his academic ability. He taught briefly at Eton, then in 1888 began teaching classics at Hertford College, Oxford. In 1899 he gave the Bampton Lectures at Oxford on the topic of mysticism, published as *Christian Mysticism*. Inge believed that the nature of religious experience was a major theological problem and that mysticism was the most concentrated form of religious experience. His ideas influenced two famous writers on mysticism: the Catholic Friedrich von Hugel (1852–1925) and the Anglican Evelyn Underhill (1875–1941).

In 1905 Inge married and left Oxford to become vicar of All Saints Church in Ennismore Gardens, London. Two years later he moved to Cambridge as the Lady Margaret Professor of Divinity. There Inge continued his studies, publishing *Personal Idealism and Mysticism* (1907) and *Faith and Its Psychology* (1909). When Inge was appointed dean of St. Paul's Cathedral in 1911, his liberal theology caused concern among many of the cathedral staff. His preaching, however, soon made a great impression. He also became popular as a journalist, writing for the *London Evening Standard* from 1921 to 1946.

Inge considered his Gifford Lectures, delivered in Scotland (1917–1918) and published as *The Philosophy of Plotinus* (two volumes), his major publication. After retirement in 1934 he continued to write mostly at a popular level. Regarded by his critics as more a philosopher than a theologian, Inge saw in a union of Christianity and Platonism the means of providing a satisfactory intellectual system. P. TOON

INGERSOLL, ROBERT GREEN
(1833–1899)
American lawyer and lecturer; called "the great agnostic"

The son of a conservative Protestant minister, Ingersoll was born in Dresden, New York. At the age of twenty-one he was admitted to the bar at Mount Vernon, Illinois. He started to practice law with his brother Ebon Clark Ingersoll in Shawneeville, Illinois, then moved to Peoria in 1857. After fighting in the Civil War, in which he was taken prisoner, Ingersoll served as attorney general of Illinois (1867–1869). In 1879 he moved to Washington, D.C., to engage in the practice of federal law; in 1885 he settled in New York City, where he continued to be a successful trial lawyer.

Ingersoll rebelled against what he considered an unduly harsh Calvinistic upbringing. When Charles Darwin's *Origin of Species* (1859) caused an acute religious controversy over the question of biblical infallibility, Ingersoll became an ardent exponent of the doctrine of evolution. He began attacking orthodox Christian beliefs and defending agnosticism in public lectures. One of his lectures was on what he called "Some Mistakes of Moses." Known for his oratorical gifts, exemplary private life, and noble character, he was an effective champion of agnosticism. N. V. HOPE

INNOCENT I (died 417)
Pope, 402–417

Except that he probably grew up in Rome, nothing certain is known about Innocent before he became bishop of Rome. His papacy opposed heterodoxy forcefully, especially the Novatian schism and the Photian heresy. Innocent also supported Honorius I, the (western) emperor, in his decrees against the Donatists in 404, and against Manicheans, Montanists, and Priscillianists in 407. It was during Innocent's tenure that Alaric and the Goths sacked Rome. Engulfed by the empire's waning political control, Innocent sought to enlarge the Church's power, particularly the Roman bishopric's rule. His claims for the Roman see's supremacy were firmer than those of any predecessor, extending to the entire Church.

Twenty-six of Innocent's letters are still extant. Occupied with doctrinal and jurisdictional concerns, the letters document Innocent's assertion of papal rule in both eastern and western portions of the Church. As to western issues, there were exchanges with Augustine and other African bishops on action against Pelagius and his views. Innocent upheld Pelagius's condemnation, but he also insisted on the papacy's right to review all such cases. Letters to Aurelius, bishop of Carthage, expressed Innocent's solace toward Jerome after attacks on his Bethlehem monastery, his denunciation of the culprits, certain violent Pelagians, and his reproof of John, bishop of Jerusalem, for deliberate neglect of the matter. An obvious purpose here was to reduce John's ill-will toward Jerome over the latter's repudiation of Origenism. Demonstrating Innocent's wide-reaching vision, other letters went to Victricius, bishop of Rouen; Exuperis, bishop of Toulouse; and to Spain, England, and other distant sites.

Concerning eastern church issues, Innocent's correspondence with Thessalonican bishops successfully preserved the Roman see's authority throughout Illyricum (northern Greece). Theophilus, bishop of Alexandria, also received highly important correspondence from Innocent. This affirmed the innocence of John Chrysostom, deposed bishop of Constantinople, and reproached Theophilus for his persecution and imprisonment of the great preacher. Though backed by Honorius, Innocent could not free Chrysostom because Theophilus had the favor of Arcadius, the (eastern) emperor. The Roman bishop and Chrysostom did exchange several communications before the latter's death in 407. In general, Innocent's eastern letters also blanketed a wide area. A letter from Innocent to Decentius, bishop of Eugubium (central Italy) in 416, is significant for its description of the mass, confirmation, unction, and penance in the early fifth century. Copies of Innocent I's letters may be found in Migne's *Patrologia Latina.* K. J. BRYER

INNOCENT III (1160–1216)
Pope, 1198–1216

Son of an Italian noble, Innocent's family name was Lotario de Conti de Segni. He began advanced studies at Paris, and he also pursued work at the University of Bologna. Completing his education, he joined the papal court, and by 1189, he was a cardinal deacon. During this time Innocent produced two great works: *De contemptu mundi, sive de miseria conditionis humanae* and *De sacro altaris mysterio.* Both writings reflect the inner intensity and spiritual depth he showed in later years.

Innocent was a unanimous choice for the papacy on Celestine III's death. The new electee, still in his thirties, accepted the office only reluctantly, but eventually became the most eminent of medieval popes. During his tenure the papacy reached the apex of its western European political dominance. In Innocent's decrees, particularly Lateran IV's

many canons, medieval religous ideals had their fullest, most representative expression. Such ideals had two aims: Christian spiritual primacy over all worldly interest, and Christian unity through the Church and its life. During his reign, western Europe saw long-building religious, intellectual, political, economic, legal, and social forces come to fruition.

Innocent initially faced political problems on three fronts: consolidation of full papal authority in Rome and the papal states; establishment of secure, deferent rule in the Holy Roman Empire; correction of misrule and improprieties in France and England.

The first front was the simplest to manage. Drawing on his popular local support, Innocent quickly obtained obedience from Rome's prefect. This accomplished, there was little struggle in gaining authority over the papal lands. Innocent believed that without direct political controls, Europe's secular power would overwhelm Christianity and its witness.

The second front's problems, however, necessitated long-term concentration and finesse. Since Henry VI's death in 1197, ruling power in the empire had been unsettled. Innocent worked both for his choice for emperor and papal rights to review imperial elections. To this end, he first expelled imperial troops from Italy. Then in 1202, Innocent issued his famous letter *Venerabilem.* This asserted a papal right to accept or refuse any newly elected emperor. In 1211, the young Hohenstaufen heir, Frederick II, consented to the pope's policies, including the critical one, guarantee of papal rights in Sicily. Hence, with Innocent's support, Frederick gained the German throne in 1212.

The third front occasioned Innocent's most colorful political activities. In 1198 the pope forced a truce on Richard I of England and Philip II of France by threats of an interdict. Then soon, by an actual year-long interdict, Innocent also gained Philip II's compliance on another crucial matter. Previously, in 1196, aided by certain French bishops, Philip had divorced his legitimate queen, Ingeborg, and married Agnes. But in 1200, faced with Innocent's potent action,

Philip reversed his violations of Church marriage rules. After numerous delays, Ingeborg even regained her place as Philip's wife and queen.

However dramatic his political successes, Innocent's most enduring actions concerned Church doctrine and practice. The high point of his papacy was Lateran Council IV (1215). Issued as papal decrees, this council's canons epitomized and consolidated medieval Christianity at its peak.

Consistently, from the mid-twelfth to the mid-thirteenth century, western Europe brought nearly every issue to the Church courts. And Innocent, like his great predecessor Alexander III, was seen as this system's final arbiter. Hence, from the financial and material to the abstract and spiritual, Innocent's hundreds of letters engage the West's basic problems broadly. Quite a few of these letters, along with Lateran IV canons, passed into the Church's canon law. Innocent also saw the expansion of Christianity as a major objective. Like many predecessors, one of his main thoughts was military war with Islam. In 1202, Innocent approved another Holy Land Crusade (Europe's fourth general Crusade) under various French nobles. But on the way, against the pope's wishes, Venetian financers persuaded the crusaders to fight rebels at Constantinople, the eastern empire's capital. This led eventually to a Latin takeover of both Constantinople and the Eastern Church. Rejecting the crusade's many wrongs, Innocent ruefully accepted its results, hoping they might reunite a long divided Christianity. Undaunted, Innocent started arrangements for yet another crusade at Lateran Council IV.

Innocent was the first pope to grant Franciscans and Dominicans, and other mendicant orders, formal approval. But Innocent was also responsible for crushing the Albigensians with military force. In general, Innocent sought to use his great power in the service of God. K. J. BRYER

IRELAND, JOHN (1838–1918)
Roman Catholic leader who sought

accommodation between the Roman Catholic Church and the American way of life

As the archbishop of St. Paul, Minnesota, Ireland campaigned for full Roman Catholic participation in American education and politics. Himself an immigrant (born in Burnchurch, Ireland), the archbishop maintained a lifelong commitment to aiding the immigrants and laborers whose experiences in the new world matched his own family's. Ireland aligned himself with other "Americanizing" leaders, like Cardinal James Gibbons of Baltimore, against German, Polish, and conservative Irish Catholics who wanted to see a European-style Roman Catholicism established in the United States. With the other "Americanists" Ireland argued for strong Roman Catholic education in both public schools and a separate parochial system. He supported the Catholic University of America (opened in 1889 in Washington, D.C.) but also showed an active concern for public higher education.

Ireland urged American Catholics to be active in politics. Unlike many of his fellow religionists, he leaned toward the Republican party, in large measure so that the Democrats would not take the immigrant Roman Catholic vote for granted. His enthusiasm for America led him to work with the railroads in bringing immigrants to the upper Midwest.

Ireland summed up his feelings on the place of Roman Catholics in the United States with these words in 1894: "There is no conflict between the Catholic Church and America . . . the principles of the Church are in thorough harmony with the interests of the Republic." M. A. NOLL

IRENAEUS (fl. c. 175–195)
Bishop of Lyons in southern France; one of the most important Christian writers of the second century

Irenaeus grew up in Asia Minor under the preaching of the apostolic father Polycarp and moved to southern France, becoming "elder" (presbyter) in Lyons. When the aging bishop was martyred, Irenaeus succeeded him as bishop in the West.

In his primary work, *Against Heresies,* Irenaeus gave his theology as statements of the Christian faith to refute the heresies of Valentinus (the Gnostic) and Marcion. For Irenaeus the authority of "the faith" is established through the direct line of elders in the church back to the apostles. This authentic message of the church confirms the Christian Bible. He was the first to state four Gospels as canon. To these he also added a list of apostolic writings, quoting all as "Scripture" along with the Old Testament. In his argument for the direct line of elders, he was the first to list the succession of Roman bishops as an example of this line, and thus he opened the way for later church officials to elevate the bishop of Rome.

Irenaeus opposed the Gnostic attitude toward creation by affirming both creation and redemption as the acts of God. From the beginning, the "One Creator God" worked through his "two hands," the Son and the Spirit, without intermediary angels. He considered the Atonement as a "recapitulation" made by Christ—that is, his going over the ground again in obedience where Adam and man failed. To this biblical thought he added the theme "the Virgin Mary is the obedient Eve." As others in the second century, Irenaeus taught an earthly millennial kingdom at the second coming of Christ.

Irenaeus was more Pauline than the apostolic fathers. He was also more biblical and less philosophical than the Greek church fathers who came later. Although a contemporary with the apologists and their work, Irenaeus was the first to write as a theologian for the church. J. NEWTON

IRVING, EDWARD (1792–1834)
Scottish Presbyterian Pentecostalist

Born in Annan (Scotland), Irving was educated at the University of Edinburgh. He then worked as a schoolmaster, learning foreign languages while waiting for ordination. In 1819 he became Thomas Chalmers's assistant at St. John's Church, Glasgow. Finding his powerful oratorical gifts somewhat overshadowed by Chalmers, in 1822 Irving accepted a call to London, becoming minister of the Scottish church in Hatton Garden and chaplain of the Caledonian Asylum. His preaching attracted large numbers of fashionable London society. His friends included writer Thomas Carlyle (1795–1881).

Irving gave himself enthusiastically to the study of prophecy, then common in evangelical circles. He translated from Spanish a book by a Jesuit priest entitled *The Coming of the Messiah in Glory and Majesty* (1827). From 1826 onward, he took part in a series of prophetic conferences held at the home of banker Henry Drummond at Albury in Surrey. Irving wrote for *The Morning Watch,* a journal on unfulfilled prophecy.

Meanwhile Irving's church had moved into a large building in Regent Square. His sermons continued to fill the church even when his views on basic doctrines began to change. His doctrine of baptism appeared to include baptismal regeneration. His doctrine of Christ attributed to Jesus a fallen human nature. Irving's Christology was the basis for his trial for heresy by the Church of Scotland and his removal from its ministry (1833).

In the late 1820s prophetic study had led Irving to teach that churches could expect a spiritual renewal with the manifestation of the gifts of the Spirit. He was thus somewhat prepared for the claims of divine healing and speaking in tongues occurring first in Scotland and then in his own congregation in 1831. Irving supported those who claimed to exercise such gifts. That unpopular position, plus the heresy charges, cost him his post at Regent Square.

Other believers in the validity of the gifts of the Spirit soon organized what was known as the Catholic Apostolic Church, in which Irving was ordained as a minister. His last two or three years of life were sad; he had lost his previous fame and was a member of a strange new sect. P. TOON

ISAAC, HEINRICH (c. 1450–1517)
Composer of church music

A versatile genius in an age when musical giants abounded, Isaac was born near the present-day Dutch-Belgian border. About

1484 he entered the service of Lorenzo di Medici in Florence (Italy), where Isaac was known as Arrigo Tedesco ("Harry the German"). When Savonarola came to power in 1494, Isaac moved to the imperial court in Vienna. Later he returned to Italy and died there.

Isaac was a truly international composer, writing music to Latin, German, and Italian texts with equal facility. His output was tremendous. His *Chroalis Constantius,* consisting of over a thousand works for the diocese of Constance, included music appropriate to every occasion of the Christian year. That work was completed after Isaac's death by his pupil, Ludwig Senfl, who was admired by Martin Luther. The melody of Isaac's beautiful song, "Innsbruck," became a Lutheran hymn tune. J. B. MACMILLAN

ISIDORE OF SEVILLE (560–636)
Spanish archbishop and scholar

Isidore was educated by his older brother Leander, who was then archbishop of Seville. Isidore succeeded Leander in that office in 600. An able administrator, Isidore presided at a number of important church councils, founded schools in each diocese under his supervision for training young clergymen, and forbade the forcible baptism of Jews in Spain. His major importance lay in his scholarship and in his successful attempt to prepare summaries of ancient knowledge for the benefit of the Visigothic peoples. By contemporaries he was looked on as the most learned man of his age.

Isidore's literary output was amazing in view of the troubled times in which he lived and his preoccupation with administrative affairs. He wrote Bible commentaries, spiritual exercises, theology, and history. His most extensive and famous work was his *Etymologiae (Etymologies)*, a treatment of the liberal arts, medicine, law, the divisions of times, the Bible, theology, natural science, agriculture, warfare, games, architecture, and other matters. That work became an encyclopedic authority for a thousand years of European history; much of what medieval people knew of learning came from Isidore's

compilation. The title derives from Isidore's assumption that knowledge of a subject begins with a precise consideration of the word that describes it. Some of Isidore's encyclopedia is naive, but much of it is substantial. A. CABANISS

IVES, CHARLES (1874–1954)
American composer

Born in Danbury, Connecticut, Ives was influenced by his bandmaster father's love for experiment in sound, but he also studied music in traditional European contexts under Horatio Parker at Yale. Ives decided to enter the insurance business as a profession, which brought him financial security and the leisure to create music. Ives anticipated certain musical developments; in fact, many techniques considered avante-garde in the 1920s were already present in his music more than a decade earlier. Yet almost none of his major works received public performance until after 1938.

Much of Ives's significance in religious music comes from his ability to blend diverse musical elements. In a complicated way he joined in serious music the kinds of popular song and hymnody that are also joined in another way in what is known as "gospel music." Ives took seriously the cultural perspectives associated with the gospel-music synthesis, believing that religious and national or regional expressions are bound together. Thus, the popular patriotic song; the gospel hymn of the era of Sankey, Stebbins, and Bliss; the sentimental parlor piece of the late nineteenth century; and the emerging repertories of ragtime and jazz all find intricate interrelation in Ives's music. European classic and romantic elements are also present, usually transformed or parodied by the context of the other elements.

Among Ives's sacred works are pieces for chorus ("Psalm 67" and "Three Harvest Home Chorales") and a cantata (*The Celestial Country*). A work belonging more in the category of cultural/religious fusion is his Symphony No. 2; it alludes continually to popular songs and to gospel hymns such as "Bringing in the Sheaves," "Beulah Land,"

and "When I Survey the Wondrous Cross." Another work of that kind is the Sonata No. 4 for Violin and Piano ("*Children's Day at the Camp Meeting*"), which includes the tunes "Work for the Night Is Coming," "Jesus Loves Me," and "Shall We Gather at the River?" D. S. CUSHMAN

IVO OF CHARTRES (1040–1116)

French bishop who played an important part in the "investiture controversy" (appointment of bishops by secular rulers)

Ivo served as priest at Nesle in Picardy (France), then became provost of the community of Augustinian canons regular (monks who lived by Augustine's rule) at St. Quentin in Beauvais. From 1090 until his death he was bishop of Chartres. As bishop he took an active part in various French ecclesiastical councils. Because of his reputation for being well-informed, his advice was often sought, even by the French king. Ivo's literary output included letters, sermons, and collections of canons (ecclesiastical rules), the last being perhaps his most significant contribution to church life.

In a period of tension in which Pope Gregory VII tried to get rid of lay investiture, Ivo upheld the liberties of bishops and the freedom of monastic orders from secular control. But he was dubious about the growing centralization of power in the pope's hands. It was probably Ivo's proposal that resulted in the compromise Concordat of Worms (1122). That document restored elections of bishops and abbots to clerical control but allowed the emperor to invest them with certain insignia of feudal allegiance to himself and with control of church lands. Without being a final solution to the investiture controversy, the concordat allayed tensions for a time. A. CABANISS

J

JACKSON, FREDERICK JOHN FOAKES (1855–1941)

English church historian and educator

Born in Ipswich in Suffolk, Jackson entered Trinity College, Cambridge, in 1876 to study theology. He won several prizes and graduated with highest honors. In 1886, after ordination, he became a fellow of Jesus College, a position he retained for fifty-five years. Jackson wrote *History of the Christian Church* (1891) and many other books. Best known was a five-volume work (with Kirsopp Lake) entitled *The Beginnings of Christianity: Part 1: The Acts of the Apostles* (1919–1933). Jackson was known as a brilliant teacher. After delivering the Lowell Lectures in Boston in 1916 he accepted an invitation to become the Briggs Professor at Union Seminary, New York, where he remained until 1934. P. TOON

JACKSON, SHELDON (1834–1909)

Presbyterian missionary to Alaska

After graduating from Princeton Theological Seminary (1858), Jackson began a remarkable missionary career in the western United States and Alaska. After ten years in Indian territory and in Minnesota, Jackson accepted the post of superintendent of missions for most of the western frontier. An intrepid traveler, Jackson roamed the frontier from 1870 to 1882, preaching wherever he could gather a group of listeners. Often he was the first preacher in a settlement or mining camp. He founded a large number of churches, began schools, and sought to recruit others for frontier missions.

In 1877 Jackson visited Alaska. He supervised Alaskan missions for the Presbyterian Church from 1884 to 1907. In a government-appointed role as General Agent of Education for Alaska, he established numerous schools for Eskimos. His activities for the social betterment of Alaskans also included setting up a postal system for remote areas, campaigning for limited territorial government, and completing surveys on Alaska's agricultural potential. Concerned about the possibility of famine among the Eskimos due to unrestrained whale and seal hunting, he began a successful program of introducing reindeer from Siberia and Lapland (1892). Jackson was elected moderator of the Presbyterian Church in 1897. J. N. AKERS

JAESCHKE, HEINRICH AUGUST (1817–1883)

Moravian linguist and translator specializing in Tibetan

Jaeschke was born in the Bohemian Protestant refugee community of Herrnhut, Saxony (present-day Germany), established in 1722 by Count Nikolaus Ludwig von Zinzendorf. Considered the greatest linguist in the missionary-minded Moravian church, Jaeschke as a young man mastered Latin, Greek, Polish, and Swedish. Later he learned Arabic, Sanskrit, and Persian. After teaching at Herrnhut, in 1857 he went as a missionary to Tibet. Settling at Kyelang he studied Tibetan and produced a *Short Practical Grammar to the Tibetan Language* (1865). In 1866 Jaeschke presented to the Berlin Academy a paper describing the phonetic laws of Tibetan. In 1868 poor health forced him to return to Herrnhut, where in 1871 he completed work on Tibetan-English and English-Tibetan lexicons. Together with F. A. Redslob and A. W. Heyde, Jaeschke produced a Tibetan New Testament, which appeared in 1885. W. A. DETZLER

JAFFRAY, ROBERT A. (1873–1945)
Noted Alliance missionary who pioneered in South China, Indo-China, and the Netherland East Indies

Born in 1873 in an influential Canadian family, Jaffray declined the prestige and wealth promised him and worked his way through A. B. Simpson's Missionary Training Institute in New York. Upon graduation he and other new recruits, including Robert H. Glover, joined a small Christian and Missionary Alliance contingent who had just opened a work in Wuchow, China. For over forty years Wuchow became both home and headquarters for Jaffray and his ever-expanding ministries. He served as chairman of the Wuchow Bible School, editor of *The Bible Magazine,* founder and director of the South China Alliance Press, and author of numerous articles and booklets written in flawless Cantonese. In 1916 Jaffray added to his duties the direction of the new French Indo-China field and in 1927 was responsible for the missionary outreach to the East Indies with strong support from Chinese nationals through the Chinese Foreign Missionary Union, which Jaffray helped found.

All this from a man who suffered from diabetes and heart disease!

Increasingly burdened for the expanding East Indies work that spread from Sumatra to New Guinea and from Borneo south to the island of Lombok, Robert and Minnie Jaffray left their much-loved land of China and their only child, Margaret, who had since returned to the land of her birth as an Alliance missionary. They moved to the Celebes (Indonesia) in 1931. The terrors of World War II brought havoc to missions in the South Seas and eventual imprisonment and death to scores of dedicated missionaries, among them Jaffray. He died in 1945, weakened from starvation rations and ill treatment in a Japanese concentration camp. J. R. BLUE

JAMES II OF ENGLAND AND VII OF SCOTLAND (1633–1701)
Ruler of England and Scotland, 1685–1688

The second surviving son of Charles I and Henrietta Maria, James was made duke of York in 1643. In the English civil war James was captured by Lord Fairfax but escaped to Holland. After fighting in both the French and Spanish (Roman Catholic) armies, he returned to England in 1660 when his brother Charles was crowned king in London. James was made lord high admiral and won some notable victories against the Dutch fleet.

About 1670 James was received into the Roman Catholic Church. News of his Catholicism, made public in 1672, caused a constitutional crisis. The House of Commons favored passing a bill to exclude him from succession to the throne. Nonetheless, because Charles II was childless, James succeeded him in 1685. As king, James introduced Roman Catholics into both his court and the universities. In 1687 and 1688 he issued "declarations of indulgence" to both Protestant nonconformists and Roman Catholics, acts which cost him much support in the state church. He also required the clergy of the Church of England to read from the pulpit his "Declaration of Liberty of Conscience." Archbishop Sancroft and six other bishops who refused to do so were put in the Tower of London and sent to trial.

By that time rumors of the arrival of William of Orange (son of Anne and grandson of Charles I) on English soil to preserve England's Protestant tradition were becoming strong. James attempted to reverse his policies, but it was too late; William invaded, and James fled to France. Later, when trying to recapture Ireland, James was defeated at the Battle of the Boyne (1690). His exclusion from the throne gave rise to the British Jacobite movement. P. TOON

JAMES VI OF SCOTLAND AND I OF ENGLAND (1566–1625)
Ruler of Scotland (1567–1625) and of England (1603–1625)

The only child of Mary, Queen of Scots, and her husband Henry Stuart (Lord Darnley), James was born in Edinburgh and proclaimed king at the age of one year when his mother abdicated. He was kept in safety at Stirling Castle; there his tutor, George Buchanan, gave him a good education, especially in languages. Assuming active rule in 1578, James sought to strengthen the monarchy's power in Scotland. He entered an alliance with England in 1586 and married Anne of Denmark three years later.

When Elizabeth I died in 1603, James succeeded her on the English throne because of his mother's descent from Henry VII. As James traveled to London to be crowned, he was handed the "Millenary Petition" (with a thousand signatures), an appeal by Puritans for concessions to be made to their consciences. To discuss their grievances he called a conference at Hampton Court in 1604. A positive result of that meeting was the decision to prepare a new translation of the Bible, published in 1611 and known as the King James Version. The Puritans, however, gained only minimal concessions. Clearly James considered that kings and bishops stood together. He pressed for the establishment of episcopacy (church rule by bishops) in Scotland and saw it introduced in 1610.

Though he intended to be lenient to Roman Catholics, James failed to make leniency an official government policy. Hence a group of Catholics plotted to kill him when he visited Parliament in the unsuccessful "gunpowder plot" of 1605. In 1618 James offended both the Scottish Calvinists and the English Puritans over the issue of the *Book of Sports,* which approved lawful sport on the Sabbath. It was during his reign that English and Scottish Protestants developed the settlement of Ulster in northern Ireland.

Among James's writings, which included treatises on the divine right of kings and on witchcraft, were several works on biblical themes (for example, on the Lord's Prayer and Revelation 20). James was succeeded by his son, Charles I. P. TOON

JAMES, BROTHER OF JESUS
Leading elder in the church at Jerusalem; author of epistle bearing his name

The only two references to James in the Gospels mention him with his brothers Joses, Simon, and Judas (Matt. 13:55; Mark 6:3). This James may have been, after Jesus, the oldest of the brothers.

The question has been raised about whether these were indeed full brothers of Jesus by Mary, for such a situation has created difficulty for some of those who cannot square it with their views on the perpetual virginity of Mary, but there seems no good reason to challenge the fact from Scripture. As with the other brothers, James apparently did not accept Jesus' authority during his earthly life (John 7:5).

There is no specific mention of James's conversion; it may have dated from Jesus' appearance to him and the others after the Resurrection (1 Cor. 15:7). He became head of the church at Jerusalem (Gal. 2:9; Acts 12:17; 21:18). Although Jesus had always taught the relative subordination of family ties (Matt. 12:48-50; Mark 3:33-35; Luke 8:21), it is hard to believe that James's authority was not somehow enhanced because of his relationship to the Master.

James was regarded as an apostle (Gal. 1:19), although he was not one of the

Twelve. Some suggest he was a replacement for the martyred son of Zebedee; others infer his apostleship by widening the scope of that term to embrace both the Twelve and "all the apostles" (see the two separate categories cited in 1 Cor. 15:5, 7).

Tradition stated that James was appointed the first bishop of Jerusalem by the Lord himself and the apostles. What is certain is that he presided over the first Council of Jerusalem, called to consider the terms of admission of Gentiles into the Christian church, and he may have formulated the decree that met with the approval of all his colleagues and was sent to the churches of Antioch, Syria, and Cilicia (Acts 15:19). James evidently regarded his own special ministry as being to the Jews, and his was a mediating role in the controversy that arose in the young church around the place of the law for those who had become Christians, from both Gentile and Jewish origins.

That he continued to have strong Jewish Christian sympathies is apparent from the request made to Paul when the latter visited Jerusalem for the last time (Acts 21:18-25). This was also the last mention in Acts of James's career. His name occurs again in the New Testament as the traditional author of the Epistle of James, where he describes himself as "a servant of God and of the Lord Jesus Christ" (James 1:1).

According to Hegesippus (c. 180), James's faithful adherence to the Jewish law and his austere life-style led to the designation "the Just." It seems clear that he suffered martyrdom. Josephus places it in the year 61 when there was a Jewish uprising after the death of Festus the procurator and before his successor had been appointed.

Jerome (c. 345–c. 419) speaks of an apocryphal Gospel of the Hebrews (fragments of which appear in various patristic writings), which contained a passage recounting the appearance of the risen Christ to James. In contrast to 1 Corinthians 15:7, the Gospel of the Hebrews claims that this was the first appearance of the Lord after the Resurrection. The same writing is alleged to have noted James's vow to eat no bread from the time of the Last Supper until he had seen the risen Lord. This raises questions, especially the assumption that James was in fact present at the Last Supper. J. D. DOUGLAS

JAMES, SON OF ALPHAEUS
One of the twelve apostles

James, son of Alphaeus, is always listed as one of the twelve apostles (Matt. 10:3; Mark 3:18; Luke 6:15; Acts 1:13), but nothing is known for certain about him. As Levi (also known as Matthew) is also described as "the son of Alphaeus" (Mark 2:14), he and James may have been brothers. Many scholars have identified him with the one called "James, the less" or "James, the smaller." The description "the less" seems to have been given to distinguish him from the son of Zebedee, and may signify that he was either smaller or younger than his namesake (the Greek word can cover both interpretations). J. D. DOUGLAS

JAMES, SON OF ZEBEDEE (died c. 44)
One of the twelve apostles; the first of them to be martyred

James was a Galilean fisherman whose circumstances we can suppose to have been comfortable (Mark 1:19-20) and who was called to be one of the twelve apostles at the same time as his brother John (Matt. 4:21; Mark 1:19-20). It is reasonable to assume that he was older than John, both because he is nearly always mentioned first, and because John is sometimes identified as "the brother of James" (Mark 3:17; 5:37; Matt. 10:2; 17:1).

James, John, and Simon Peter, who were part of a fishing partnership that included Andrew, Simon's brother (Luke 5:10), were a trio who attained in some sense a place of primacy among the disciples. They are found at the center of things—for example, when Jairus's daughter was raised (Mark 5:37; Luke 8:51), at the Transfiguration (Matt. 17:1; Mark 9:2; Luke 9:28), on the Mount of Olives (Mark 13:3), and in the Garden of Gethsemane (Matt. 26:37; Mark 14:33). It was James and John, moreover, who had earlier accompanied Jesus to the home of Simon and Andrew (Mark 1:29).

James and John were given by Jesus the nickname "Boanerges" or "sons of thunder" (Mark 3:17) when they were rebuked by the Lord for impetuous speech and for having totally misconceived the purpose of his coming. This may have been the consequence of the suggestion made by them that they should pray for the destruction of the Samaritan village, the inhabitants of which had repulsed the Lord's messengers (Luke 9:54; cf. Mark 9:38; Luke 9:49).

The presumptuous and ill-considered thinking of the two brothers was obvious also when, after asking with his brother a place of honor in the kingdom, James was corecipient of the prophecy that they would drink the cup their Master was to drink (Mark 10:35-40; cf. Matt. 20:20-23). The two sons of Zebedee are also assumed to have been present with the other disciples when the risen Christ appeared by the Sea of Tiberias (John 21:1), though curiously James's name is nowhere mentioned in the fourth Gospel.

We know nothing about James's career subsequently until about the year 44 when Jesus' prophecy was fulfilled: James was slain "with the sword" by Herod Agrippa I, and thus became the first of the Twelve whose martyrdom was referred to in the New Testament (Acts 12:1-2).

The wife of Zebedee was Salome (Matthew 27:56), who may have been a sister of the Lord's mother (John 19:25). If this were so, it would mean that James and John were first cousins of Jesus and that they may have considered themselves to have been in a privileged position. J. D. DOUGLAS

JAMES, WILLIAM (1842–1910)
American philosopher and psychologist

Born in New York City, James was educated primarily at home through spirited family discussions. His father, Henry James, Sr., an eccentric Swedenborgian theologian, also enrolled William and his brother Henry (later a famous novelist) in various private schools across Europe. James's early inter-

ests were natural science and painting. In 1861 he entered Lawrence Scientific School at Harvard University, studying first chemistry and later medicine. After a period of ill health, James began teaching at Harvard in 1873. He remained closely associated with that school until his resignation in 1907.

In *Principles of Psychology* (1890), his major work in that field, James argued that there are mental states that are known through introspective observation. Consciousness is a stream rather than a set of states or isolated sensations, as many had claimed. Instead of thinking of mind or consciousness as a substance, James thought of it as an activity.

In 1901 and 1902 James delivered the Gifford lectures, published as *The Varieties of Religious Experience*. In that work he gave a descriptive survey of many kinds of religious experience with a view to explaining them according to scientific laws and principles, as other kinds of experiences are explained. James did not claim that such study of the sources of religious phenomena could determine their worth.

Pragmatism: A New Name for Some Old Ways of Thinking appeared in 1907. Although C. S. Peirce had already outlined the pragmatist position in 1878, as James himself noted, it remained for James to present it in a form that would catch the public eye and seem to present a truly American philosophy. According to James, human ideas are "true" if they "work," or are useful in solving problems. However, what "works" varies from context to context and according to the question one is asking; hence, it is not surprising that the pragmatic theory of truth has produced a variety of interpretations. A. VOS

JANÁČEK, LEOŠ (1854–1928)
Intensely nationalistic Czech composer who was influenced by Antonín Dvořák and later by Bedřich Smetana

Born in Hukvaldy in what was then northern Moravia, Janáček received his training at Brno, Prague, Leipzig, and Vienna. Though he rarely quoted folk songs directly, he absorbed their style into his music in a natural manner. His melodies captured the rhythms and inflections of Moravian and Slovakian languages. Of his ten operas, *Jenufa* (1904) is best known, but the others are also performed frequently.

Janáček's training was in church music schools and the Leipzig (Germany) Conservatory. In 1881 he founded an organ school in Brno (Czechoslovakia), where he taught until 1919, gaining a reputation as a choral director and composer. His religious masterpiece is the "Glagolitic Mass" (1926), a setting of the Ordinary of the Mass in the Old Church Slavonic language of the ninth century (once written in the Glagolitic alphabet). A musically assertive, theatrical composition, his mass suggests an individual's approach to God as his equal—in contrast to a more typically worshipful style usually associated with the text. Janáček also wrote many other masses, motets, and canticles. W. PHEMISTER

JANES, LEROY LANSING (1837–1909)
Educational missionary to Japan

Born in Ohio and educated at West Point Military Academy, as a retired Army captain Janes was confronted with an unusual opportunity at Kumamoto, Japan, in 1871 immediately following the Imperial Restoration. In the revolutionary period that overthrew the Shogunate and opened Japan to Western influence, the local clan had not fared well. So the Daimyo (feudal lord) decided to start the Kumamoto School to train promising young Samurai in Western learning. He asked the famous Dutch-American missionary Guido Verbeck (1830–1898) to recommend a teacher with a military background. Janes was nominated and accepted. When he arrived to take up his duties in 1872, the resident Japanese faculty resigned in a body, leaving him a free hand.

Janes organized the school on West Point lines: all students lived together in a dormitory and were under a regimen marked by discipline, moral strictness, and hard work. At first Janes attempted no religious proselytizing, but in 1875 he told some of

his abler students that since Christianity formed the basis of Western civilization, he would conduct a home Bible class for anyone interested. Ten students enrolled, and before a year was over, the number had risen to around fifty. In January 1876, thirty-five of these students signed a Covenant of Belief, expressing their adherence to Christianity and their desire to propagate it in Japan. They were strongly opposed by their families, and the school was closed in October 1876. Janes recommended the students to prepare for Christian work at the Doshisha School in Kyoto, run by J. E. Neesima (1843–1890); and many did so. Janes left Japan, but returned in 1893 to become a teacher in a government school at Kyoto. Though by then he opposed the teaching of the Christian missionaries, his Kumamoto Band—which included men like Hiromichi Kozaki, Ebina Danjo, and Shimomura Kotaro—were influential Christian teachers in Japan. N. V. HOPE

JANSEN, CORNELIUS OTTO (1585–1638)
Dutch theologian; inspired a reform movement in the Roman Catholic Church

Jansen was born in Leerdam (Netherlands). After studying theology at the University of Louvain (Belgium), he became head of the Dutch college there in 1617. Two years later he became a doctor of the university and in 1630 was appointed professor of theology. His primary contribution was interpreting the Pentateuch, the first five books of the Old Testament. In 1637 he was consecrated bishop of Ypres (Belgium).

Jansen wrote his main work, *Augustinus* in 1627 but it was not published until 1640. In 1643 Pope Urban VIII consigned it to the Index of prohibited books because it attacked the ethics of the Jesuits.

Following Jansen's death the "Jansenist movement" arose under the leadership of Jansen's friend, Jean Du Vergier. The Jansenists stressed the primacy of God's grace in human redemption. W. A. DETZLER

JASPERS, KARL (1883–1969)
German philosopher; one of the founders of the existentialist movement

Jaspers received the M.D. degree from the University of Heidelberg. In 1913 he became a lecturer there in psychology, and in 1921, in philosophy. The National Socialists relieved him of his duties in 1937, but he was reinstated in 1945. His major systematic work is the three-volume *Philosophie* (1932). *The Way to Wisdom* (1951), *Truth and Symbol* (1959), and *The Great Philosophers* (1962) are three of his other books that have been translated into English.

According to Jaspers, the basic questions of philosophy grow from life. Yet the form that they take at a given moment is in accord with the historical situation. In the twentieth century, science plays a large role, but science does not embrace the totality of being. It gives no aim to life and has no answer to essential human problems. Philosophy, by contrast, is the thinking by which a person becomes aware of "being" itself. Unlike science, which can be merely contemplative, philosophy necessarily includes practice. Philosophy is the clarification of *Existenz* (existence or being). *Existenz* is what is real and valuable, the authentic in human beings.

The focus on human "being" leads to the question of God or "Transcendence," as Jaspers put it. Humanity cannot be comprehended on the basis of itself. As one confronts one's "being," transcendence is disclosed as the "other" through which one exists. Philosophizing aims to gain certainty about Transcendence, even though Transcendence is not fathomable and its "being" is doubtful. Hence, people need both philosophy and religion. Those who limit themselves to one or the other become dogmatic and fanatical. Philosophy cannot rely on revelation but must rely instead on the "self-disclosures of the Encompassing" that are present in human beings as human beings. Jaspers proposed a philosophic faith in which individuals are open to Transcendence. In such a philosophic faith Jaspers saw an openness which he contrasted with the "absolutism" of traditional Christianity.
A. VOS

JEFFERSON, THOMAS (1743–1826)
Third president of the United States, 1801–1809

Jefferson wrote these words as his epitaph: "Here was buried Thomas Jefferson, Author of the Declaration of American Independence, of the Statute of the State of Virginia for Religious Freedom, and Father of the University of Virginia." He also served his country as ambassador to France, secretary of state, vice-president, and president, and his native Virginia as legislator and governor.

Jefferson was a man with wide interests and talents; he was a plantation farmer, lawyer and legal scholar, architect, inventor, violinist, student of the classics, author of works on natural science, and one of the United States' greatest political theorists. Overarching all these things, Jefferson had an interest in the spiritual aspects of life.

Though a professing member of the Episcopal Church, Jefferson rejected many orthodox Christian beliefs. His edition of the Gospels, *The Life and Morals of Jesus of Nazareth,* deleted every mention of the supernatural in Christ's life. Jefferson's view of God was based not so much on Scripture as on the English Enlightenment and the Enlightenment's moral philosophy. He conceived of God as the universe's supreme architect and builder (whose character bore an uncanny resemblance to the ideals of the Virginia aristocracy).

Jefferson believed, in the words of the Declaration of Independence, that "all men are created equal" and have certain "unalienable rights." Although suffering pangs of conscience about it, Jefferson retained black slaves throughout his life. Black people, however equal in the abstract, were thought to be deficient in natural capacities. History to Jefferson was a record of an inhumanity that education alone could overcome. Jefferson's ideal was the yeoman farmer—in his self-sufficiency and his intimate relationship with nature.

Above all else Jefferson feared tyranny in matters of the intellect, politics, and religion. His life was devoted to the service of freedom as he understood it. His confidence in humanity's ability to discover the secrets of life and make use of them in government, science, and education was unbounded.

M. A. NOLL

JEROME (c. 345–c. 419)
Latin Bible translator; biblical scholar

Born into wealth near Aquileia (Adriatic Sea's northernmost point), Jerome spent his youth acquiring broad education in Rome. No descriptions of his conversion remain, but at about age twenty he underwent baptism. Soon thereafter, Jerome embarked on a twenty-year period of travel, a pilgrimage traversing the empire. This pilgrimage began at Trier, in Gaul, where Jerome studied theology several years, and gained his lifelong attraction to monasticism. Returning then to Aquileia, he remained three years with Bishop Valerianus and an elite group promoting ascetic teachings and life. But in 375, very discontented, Jerome moved to Antioch, in Syria, where in a conscience-stricken dream he faced vivid accusations of following, not Christ, but Cicero. As he pictured it later, he felt his Christian commitment underwent basic transformation through this incident.

Shortly after the dream, Jerome removed to the desert around Chalcis (east of Antioch). Here he began intense study of Scripture—mixed with learning Hebrew and Greek—and tried to find himself as a Christian. On return two years later to Antioch, Jerome was ordained priest by Bishop Paulinus and became engrossed with lectures by Apollinaris of Laodicea. Moving to Constantinople, he spent two years as a disciple of Gregory of Nazianzus, the great teacher whose circle included Basil of Caesaria, Gregory of Nyssa, and other eminent Church figures. It was now that the writings of Origen heavily impressed themselves on his consciousness. Jerome's wandering concluded in the years 382 to 385, his pilgrimage's happiest and most fruitful segment. Once again in Rome, and serving as Pope Damasus's personal secretary, Jerome pursued his chief interests: thoroughgoing study of Scripture and active promotion of monastic asceticism. Yet this time ended abruptly due to Damascus's death and persecutory attacks stirred up by Jerome's acerbic personality. In much disarray, Jerome departed Rome to seek a place for the remote, unfettered monastic life he found so important. He settled finally in 386 in Bethlehem. Here he spent his last thirty-five years engaged deeply in the biblical scholarship and Bible translation his gifted mind so acquisitively pursued.

Jerome's many works may be grouped under six headings: translations of the Bible, commentaries on Scripture, translations of others' works, historical treatises, theological essays, letters and miscellaneous works. In outline, the important writings fall under two divisions of the early period, and four divisions of the Bethlehem years. Up to 382, first, the principal works are the translations of Origen's Bible commentaries and Eusebius of Caesara's world history. Then, Jerome's extensive Latin New Testament revisions are the highlight of 382 through 385, his time with Damasus. In the initial years at Bethlehem, 386 to 390, the emphasis was on New Testament commentaries, with efforts on Ephesians and Galatians prominent here. Jerome reached his time of maximum production between 390 and 398. Among this period's labors, most significant are final revisions of the Latin New Testament; initiation of the Hebrew to Latin New Testament work; *Vita Malchi monachi captivi,* and other saints' lives narratives; *De viris illustribus,* a catalog of Christian authors; *Liber Hebraicarum quaestionum in Genesim,* a work illuminating Palestinian geography; and *Adversus Jovinianum,* an attack on opposition to Christian asceticism, this revealing Jerome at his worst. Then, amid the still incessant efforts of 398 through 405, Jerome completed his great project, the full Latin translation of the Hebrew Old Testament. This period also included various commentaries on Old Testament books; numerous personal letters, most conspicuously exchanges with Augustine and other church leaders; and *Contra Joannem Hierosolymitanum* and *Apologeticum adversus Rufinum,* works in which Jerome turned against not only

Origenism but former close Origenist friends. In the last years, 405 to 420, Jerome slowed down but continued prolific output nearly to the end. The main writings here were *Contra Vigilantium,* his major defense of Christian monasticism; commentaries on previously missed Old and New Testament books; *Dialogi contra Pelagianos,* the best antiheretical effort; and devotional sermons on countless subjects.

It is the translation labors and exegetical works that are the most valuable of Jerome's profuse efforts. Indisputably, over the centuries, the most influential of all versions of Scripture has been its Latin rendering. Since it is Jerome's Latin version that the Roman Church used almost exclusively throughout its history until modern times, Jerome's translation work was clearly one of Christianity's watershed events. One cannot overstate the axial importance of the Latin Scriptures for Church doctrine and rule, and for Western law and custom at large. Jerome's care in translating from the Bible's original languages is vital here also. His methods have been an example of proper translation approaches for all succeeding eras. In their literal emphasis and comprehensiveness, Jerome's Bible commentaries also have enduring value. Though sometimes mixed with Origen-like allegorical devices, Jerome's attempts at critical exegesis—his respect of history, geography, custom, and other facts—again have been a prototype for subsequent biblical scholarship. Jerome's writings show a high regard for the Apocrypha; but, generally, his understanding coincided with the eventual orthodox position on scriptural canon. In all instances, his view is that Scripture is divinely inspired and fully authoritative for Christian faith and practice.

Some of Jerome's writings are well known because of provocative views on moral and social issues. Obviously not a profound abstract thinker, Jerome nonetheless resisted heterodoxies such as Origenism, Apollinarianism, and Pelagianism, and upheld unwavering theological orthodoxy throughout his life. But in contrast, immersed in ascetic proclivities, Jerome's ethical teachings succumbed to some serious misdirection. Ascetic monasticism offered Jerome a potent vehicle for scholarly pursuits and the purity of life he desired. Yet simultaneously, his feverish advocacy here plainly led his moral doctrine into basic error, especially a legalistic extremism, this including insistence on abstinence from normal eating, employment, and marriage (even marital sexuality). An evidence perhaps of his misjudgment, Jerome's stringent monasticism, despite very heavy promotions, largely attracted only female followers. It was the wealthy Roman widow Paula who became Jerome's best friend and who followed him to Bethlehem; and it was the women around Paula who were his chief disciples the last thirty-five years. And the Palestinian monastic facilities established and accomplished many good works.

As far as is determinable, none of Jerome's works have been lost over the centuries. There are a few medieval copies of the Bible translation. Otherwise various sixteenth-century collections are now the earliest extant copies of Jerome's writings. Through the years, Jerome has been a favorite subject for religious artists, especially Italian Renaissance painters. K. J. BRYER

JEROME OF PRAGUE (c. 1370–1416)
Bohemian reformer

After acquiring a basic education in Prague (present-day Czechoslovakia), Jerome pursued his studies at Paris and then at Oxford. At Oxford he became imbued with the teachings of an early reformer, John Wycliffe (c. 1329–1384), whose views encouraged a degree of opposition to the papacy and stressed apostolic poverty. Both emphases fit well with a resurgent Czech nationalism that resisted German imperial domination.

On his return to Prague Jerome began to expound his new ideas. They were similar to, but evidently independent of, those of John Huss, another slightly younger Czech reformer, with whom Jerome had a friendly relationship. Because of his teaching and other activities, Jerome had to leave Prague. He went from one city to another, meanwhile gaining a considerable reputation. The king of Poland was impressed enough to invite him to establish a university at Kraków. It was not long, however, before the Polish bishops took offense—so Jerome resumed his wanderings.

When Huss was arrested and put on trial at the Council of Constance (1414–1418), Jerome courageously went to that city to see him. Before the council Jerome offered a spirited but unsuccessful defense of his countryman. That act sealed his own doom. In 1415 he was arrested and held for trial. During the prolonged questioning he was impelled to renounce his opinions. Later his courage revived and he retracted those statements, an action that resulted in his condemnation as a lapsed heretic. Almost a year after Huss's death, Jerome of Prague, too, was burned at the stake. A. CABANISS

JESUS CHRIST (c. 6 B.C.–c. A.D. 30)
Messiah, Savior, and Founder of the Christian Church

In approaching a biography of Jesus Christ it must be borne in mind that each of the Gospels has its own distinctive purpose. Matthew, for instance, presents Jesus as the messianic King, whereas the emphasis in Mark is more on Jesus as the servant of all. Luke tends to present Jesus in a softer light, showing particularly his amazing compassion to the less fortunate, whereas John plunges the reader into a deeper and more spiritual understanding of Jesus. These different aims caused the four evangelists to select and arrange the events of Jesus' life differently, resulting in a fourfold portrait of the same man. It was undoubtedly for this reason that the Christian church preserved four Gospels instead of one.

The following sections present the main events in what may be regarded as the chief stages of the life of Jesus. These stages show a definite progression from Christ's incarnation to his cross. The amount of space devoted to each stage in each of the Gospels is dictated by theological rather than biographical interest. The whole presentation of Christ's life centers on the Cross and the subsequent triumphant Resurrection and is more an account of God's message to man than a plain historic account of the life of Jesus.

THE INCARNATION
The major event of this initial stage was the Incarnation. Only Matthew and Luke give accounts of Jesus' birth. John goes back and reflects on what preceded the birth.

It may seem strange that John began his Gospel with a reference to the Word (John 1:1), but it is in this way that he delivers to the reader an exalted view of Jesus. John saw Jesus as existing even before the creation of the world (John 1:2). In fact he saw him as having a part in the act of creation (John 1:3). Therefore when Jesus was born it was both an act of humiliation and of illumination. The light shone, but the world preferred to remain in darkness (John 1:4-5). Therefore anyone coming to John's records of the life of Jesus would know at once, before even being introduced to the man named Jesus, that here was the record of no ordinary man. The account of his life and teaching that followed could not be properly understood except against this background of his preexistence.

THE BIRTH OF JESUS
John simply wrote that the Word became flesh and dwelt among us. Matthew and Luke fill in some of the details of how this happened. There is little in common between the two accounts. Each approaches the subject from a different point of view, but the supernatural character is clear in both. The coming of Jesus is announced beforehand, through dreams to Joseph in Matthew's account (Matt. 1:20-21) and through an angel to Mary in Luke's account (Luke 1:26-33). Matthew leaves his readers in no doubt that the one to be born had a mission to accomplish—to save people from their sins (Matt. 1:21). Luke sets his story of Jesus' coming in an atmosphere of great rejoicing. This is seen in the inclusion of some exquisite songs, which have formed part of the church's worship ever since (Luke 1:47-

55, 68-79). The homage of the wise men in Matthew 2:1-12 is significant because it sets the scene for a universalistic emphasis that links the beginning of the Gospel to its ending (cf. Matt. 28:19-20). A similar emphasis is introduced in the angel's announcement to the shepherds in Luke 2:14 and in Simeon's song (Luke 2:32), where he predicts that Jesus would be a light for Gentiles as well as glory for Israel. The flight into Egypt for safety (Matt. 2:13-15) shows the contribution of a Gentile nation in providing protection for a Jewish child.

One feature of the birth stories in Matthew and Luke is that they are both linked to genealogies. It is difficult to harmonize these genealogies since they appear to be drawn from different sources, but the purpose in both cases is to show that Jesus was descended from Abraham and David. The latter fact gave rise to Jesus' title Son of David.

Luke was the only Gospel writer who attempted to link the coming of Jesus with events in secular history. Although problems arise over the dating of the census of Quirinius (Luke 2:1-2), the firm setting of the contemporary scene is highly significant because the Christian faith is a historic faith centered in a historic person.

LIFE IN NAZARETH

The years of Jesus Christ's human development are given only a few lines in the Gospels. Details are given of only one incident belonging to the period of childhood, the discussion of the twelve-year-old Jesus with the Jewish teachers in the temple (Luke 2:41-50). This event is a pointer to one of the most characteristic features of Jesus' later ministry: his display of irrefutable wisdom in dialogue with his Jewish contemporaries. It also reveals that at an early age Jesus was acutely aware of a divine mission. Nevertheless, Luke notes that in Jesus' formative years he was obedient to his parents (Luke 2:51). It is assumed that during thirty years at Nazareth Jesus learned the carpenter's trade from Joseph and became the village carpenter after Joseph's death. However, there is no account of this period in the Gospels. This fact has led to many fantastic imaginings about Jesus' childhood. Many of these fables are recorded in the apocryphal Gospels, but Luke's account could not be more unembellished. Its remarkable reserve is a strong indication of its historical reliability.

PREPARATORY EVENTS

All four Gospels refer to a brief preparatory period which immediately preceded the commencement of Christ's public ministry. This period focused on three important events.

THE PREACHING OF
JOHN THE BAPTIST

John the Baptist appeared in the wilderness and caused an immediate stir in Judea, particularly as a result of his call to repentance and to baptism (Matt. 3:1-4). John was like one of the Old Testament prophets, but he disclaimed any importance in his own office except as a herald of a greater person to come. His stern appearance and uncompromising moral challenge effectively prepared the way for the public appearance of Jesus (Luke 3:4-6). It is important to note that John the Baptist's announcement of the imminent coming of the kingdom (Matt. 3:2) was the same theme with which Jesus began his own ministry (Matt. 4:17). This shows that John the Baptist's work was an integral part of the preparation for the public ministry of Jesus. The same may be said of the rite of baptism, although John recognized that Jesus would add a new dimension in that he would baptize with the Holy Spirit and with fire (Matt. 3:11). As the forerunner of Jesus Christ, John proclaimed that the one to follow would not only be greater than he, but would come with high standards of judgment (Matt. 3:12). The stage was therefore set in stern terms for the initial public act of Jesus—his willingness to be baptized (Matt. 3:13-16; Luke 3:21).

THE BAPTISM OF JESUS

John's baptism was a baptism of repentance. Since Jesus submitted to this, are we to suppose that Jesus himself needed to repent? If this were the case, it would involve the assumption that Jesus had sinned. This is contrary to other evidence in the New Testament. But if Jesus did not need to repent, what was the point of his requesting baptism at the hands of John? Jesus had come on a mission to others and it is possible that he deliberately submitted to John's baptism in order to show that he was prepared to take the place of others. This explanation is in line with Paul's later understanding of the work of Jesus Christ (2 Cor. 5:21). Matthew is the one evangelist who records John's hesitation to baptize Jesus (Matt. 3:14-15).

The most important part of the baptism of Jesus was the heavenly voice, which declared pleasure in the beloved Son (Matt. 3:17). This announcement by God was the real starting point of the public ministry of Jesus. It revealed that the ministry was no accident or sudden inspiration on the part of Jesus. He went into his work with the full approval of the Father. A further important feature is the part played by the Holy Spirit in this scene. The dove-like description is full of symbolic meaning (Matt. 3:16). It was not just an inner experience that Jesus had. The activity of the Spirit in the ministry of Jesus, although not much emphasized in the Gospels, is nevertheless sufficiently evident to be indispensable to a true understanding of Jesus Christ.

THE TEMPTATION OF JESUS

Jesus' baptism showed the nature of his mission. The temptation showed the nature of the environment in which he was to minister (Matt. 4:1; Luke 4:1-2). Confrontation with adverse spiritual forces characterized Jesus' whole ministry. Only Matthew and Luke record details of the temptations to which Jesus was subjected by the devil. All these temptations present short-cuts which, if pursued, would have deflected Jesus from his vocation. The record leaves us in no doubt that Jesus gained the victory. Both Gospels show that he accomplished this by appealing to Scripture. Jesus is also seen in this event as a genuine man who, like all other men, was subject to temptation. The writer of the letter to the Hebrews notes that this fact qualified Jesus to act as high priest

and to intercede on behalf of his people (Heb. 2:18; 4:15).

THE EARLY MINISTRY OF JESUS IN JUDEA AND SAMARIA

Only John's gospel tells of the work of Jesus in Judea following his baptism. It first describes his calling of two disciples, John and Andrew (John 1:35-39). This event is set against the background of John the Baptist's announcement of Jesus as the Lamb of God who was to take away the sin of the world (John 1:29). These first two disciples were soon joined by three others, Peter, Philip, and Nathaniel (John 1:41-51). These five formed the nucleus of the band of Jesus' followers who came to be known as the Twelve. Jesus' initial calling of these five was followed by a more definite call (Matt. 4:18-22) to leave their occupations and become "fishers of men" (Matt. 4:19). One feature of John's account is the early recognition by the disciples of Jesus as Messiah (John 1:41) and as Son of God (John 1:49).

Soon after Jesus began his ministry in Jerusalem, John relates an incident at Cana in Galilee in which water was turned into wine (John 2:1-11). This event is important in John's account because it is the first of the signs that he records (John 2:11). He saw Jesus' miracles as signs of the truth of the gospel rather than as mere wonders.

John sets two incidents at Jerusalem in this initial period. The first is the cleansing of the temple (John 2:13-16). Matthew, Mark, and Luke all place this event just before Jesus' trial, but John places it at this early stage. The moral intention of Jesus' work is seen in his driving out the money changers who were profiting from worshipers more than was appropriate. This was apparently acceptable to Judaism, but was unacceptable to Jesus. The other evangelists imply that this authoritative act was the event that sparked the final hostility of his opponents. John tells the story for a theological reason. To him the cleansing of the temple was a parable telling of what Jesus had come to do.

The other incident in Jerusalem is the meeting between Jesus and Nicodemus

(John 3). Nicodemus was closely associated with Judaism, yet he was also searching for truth. He was unable to understand, however, the spiritual truth about being born again through the Spirit.

John's story then moves from Judea to Samaria and the story of the Samaritan woman at the well (John 4:1-42). Jesus used her physical thirst to point to her deeper spiritual thirst. She realized that Jesus had something to offer her that she had not previously known. As a result of this woman's experience and testimony, many of the Samaritan people came to believe in Jesus as the Savior of the world (John 4:42). In this case John intends that his readers would appreciate the fuller significance of the words of Jesus by viewing them in the light of the Resurrection.

THE PERIOD OF THE GALILEAN MINISTRY

Almost all the information on this period is found in the Synoptic Gospels (Matthew, Mark, and Luke.) It may be conveniently divided into three sections. The first briefly outlines the events leading up to the choosing of the Twelve, the second deals with Jesus' withdrawal from northern Galilee, and the third with his departure for Jerusalem. While the Synoptic Gospels concentrate exclusively on the events in Galilee, John's account indicates there were some visits by Jesus to Jerusalem during this period. Also, John records another incident at Cana, where the son of a Capernaum official was healed. This is noted as the second sign Jesus performed (John 4:54). It is chiefly important because of the extraordinary faith of the father who was prepared to take Jesus at his word.

THE CALLING OF THE DISCIPLES

In the Synoptic Gospels there is an account of the initial call to four of the disciples to leave their fishing boats and to accompany Jesus (Matt. 4:18-22; Mark 1:16-20; Luke 5:1-11). They had already met Jesus and must have had some idea what was involved in following him. Jesus did not at this time appoint them to be apostles, but this call was an indispensable step toward the establishment of the Twelve as a group. Setting apart a particular number of disciples formed an important part of the ministry of Jesus. The miraculous catch of fish, which preceded the call of the disciples in Luke's account, served to highlight the superiority of the spiritual task of catching people rather than fish.

Another significant call came to Levi, otherwise known as Matthew (Matt. 9:9; Mark 2:13-14; Luke 5:27). As a tax collector he was no doubt of a different type from most of the other disciples. He would certainly have been despised by his Jewish contemporaries because of his profession. But his inclusion in the special circle of Jesus' disciples shows the broad basis on which these men were chosen. One of the others, Simon the Zealot, may have belonged to a group of revolutionaries who were religious as well as political. Even a man like Judas Iscariot was numbered among the Twelve. His allegiance to the cause of Jesus was so questionable that he betrayed Jesus to his enemies for a small sum of money. In training the Twelve, Jesus accepted them as they were and molded them into men who later came to learn how to be totally dependent on God and the power of his Spirit.

THE SERMON ON THE MOUNT

The Gospel of Matthew presents a substantial sample of Jesus' teaching commonly called the Sermon on the Mount (Matt. 5:1–7:29). Some of the same material occurs in Luke in a different context, so some scholars regard the arrangement of the Sermon on the Mount as Matthew's work. It is possible, however, that Jesus often repeated his teachings on different occasions and with different combinations. Matthew's record of the Sermon on the Mount presents an impressive body of teaching, mainly of an ethical character. In it Jesus upholds the Mosaic law and at the same time goes beyond it. The beginning of this sermon has been called the Beatitudes (Matt. 5:3-12). It commends moral and spiritual values. The teaching recorded in this section was radical, but not in a political sense. The Sermon on the Mount may be taken as a fair sample of the kind of discourses which must have abounded in the ministry of Jesus.

JESUS AS HEALER

Throughout the Gospels there are cases of healing miracles. There are more of these miracles than any other type. In a section in Matthew devoted to a sequence of healings (Matt. 8:1–9:34), a leper, a centurion's servant, Peter's mother-in-law, a demoniac, a paralytic, a woman with hemorrhage, blind men, and a dumb man all were healed. In addition, Jairus's daughter was raised from the dead. This concentration of healings focuses on Jesus as a miracle worker, but throughout the Gospels there is no suggestion that Jesus healed by magical means. His power of healing was in some cases dependent on an individual's faith (Matt. 8:10; 9:22). In at least one incident the healing was accompanied by an announcement of the forgiveness of the sins of the one healed (Matt. 9:2; Mark 2:5). This shows that Jesus considered spiritual problems to be of greater consequence than the physical needs.

In view of the widespread belief in the powerful influence of evil spirits over human lives, it is of great significance that Jesus is seen exercising his power of exorcism over demons. Jesus' ministry was set in an atmosphere of spiritual conflict, so the confrontations between the forces of darkness and the Light of the world were to be expected. Those who explain away these cases of demon possession in psychiatric terms miss this key feature of Jesus' ministry. Each time he exorcised a demon he was demonstrating victory, which reached its most dramatic expression in his victory over death at his resurrection.

In addition to the healing miracles in this early section, one nature miracle is recorded, that of the stilling of the storm (Matt. 8:23-27; Mark 4:35-41; Luke 8:22-25). This miracle focused both on the lack of faith in the disciples and the mysterious power of the presence of Jesus.

THE REACTION TO JESUS
BY HIS CONTEMPORARIES

In the early stages of his ministry Jesus was very popular with the ordinary people. There are several notices to this effect (Matt. 4:23-25; Mark 3:7-8). This popularity showed no appreciation of the spiritual purpose of Jesus' mission (Luke 13:17). Nevertheless it stands in stark contrast to the nit-picking opposition of the religious leaders who even plotted to kill Jesus in the early period of his ministry (Mark 3:6).

Jesus and the religious leaders often clashed over the observance of the Sabbath (Matt. 12:1-14; Luke 13:10-17; John 5:9-18). Jesus adopted a more liberal view than the rigid and often illogical interpretation of some of his religious contemporaries. For instance, he was criticized for healing a woman on the Sabbath when the Jewish law allowed the rescuing of trapped animals on the Sabbath (Luke 13:15; Matt. 12:11). To the Pharisaic mind Jesus was regarded as a lawbreaker. The Pharisees feared that it would undermine their authority if his teaching were permitted to permeate popular opinion.

PREPARING THE TWELVE

The Synoptic Gospels supply a list of the names of the twelve apostles (Matt. 10:2-4; Mark 3:16-19; Luke 6;14-16). Both Matthew and Mark name them in the context of their exercising authority over evil spirits, thereby showing that these men were being called to enter the same spiritual conflict as Jesus.

The Synoptic Gospels also give details of the instructions Jesus gave to these disciples before sending them to minister in Israel (Matt. 10:5-41; Luke 9:1-6; Mark 6:7-13). Matthew included material in his discourse that appears in a different context in Mark and Luke, but the discourse still shows the concern of Jesus to prepare his disciples for their future work. They were to proclaim the kingdom as he had done, but they were not to suppose that all would respond to it. They were warned about coming hostility and even persecution. It is important to note that Jesus warned his disciples against encumbering themselves with material possessions. Although the instructions given related immediately to a ministry tour, he was laying the foundation for the future work of the church.

THE RELATION OF JESUS TO JOHN THE BAPTIST

For a while there were parallel preaching and parallel baptisms by John the Baptist and his followers and Jesus and his disciples (John 4:1-2). When John the Baptist was imprisoned by Herod because of his uncompromising condemnation of Herod's marriage to Herodias, his brother's wife (Matt. 14:3-4), it is not surprising that he began to have doubts about Jesus (Matt. 11:1-19; Luke 7:18-35). He may have been expecting Jesus, if he really was the Messiah, to come to his rescue. When John sent his disciples to Jesus to express his doubts, Jesus took the opportunity to tell the crowds of the greatness of John the Baptist. He said there was none born of women who was greater than John. Nevertheless, that was in the old order, and Jesus made clear that his kingdom demanded new methods.

VARIOUS CONTROVERSIES

Jesus did not hesitate to confront his contemporaries on issues that involved moral or religious questions. John's Gospel records a controversy concerning the keeping of the Sabbath that arose when a lame man was healed on that day (John 5:1-18). Once again ritual observance of the Sabbath was regarded as of greater importance than a compassionate concern for the physical welfare of the lame man. This was typical of the Jewish approach and led at once to a persecuting attitude toward Jesus, particularly because he claimed to be doing the work of God.

A similar conflict arose after Jesus' disciples had plucked grain in the fields on the Sabbath day (Matt. 12:1-8). The Pharisees assumed that this act constituted work and saw it as a sufficient reason to plot how to destroy Jesus. After this event he healed a paralytic on the same Sabbath day (Matt. 12:9-14). The Jewish leaders clearly regarded him as a direct threat to their position among the people.

The rising opposition did not deter Jesus from further healings (Matt. 12:15-32), which Matthew depicts as the fulfillment of Scripture. But when Jesus healed a blind and dumb demoniac, the Pharisees charged him with casting out demons by Beelzebub, the prince of the demons. Jesus reminded them that to blaspheme the Holy Spirit was an unforgivable sin. This incident not only brings out the perversity of the religious leaders, but also shows that the ministry of Jesus was under the direct control of the Spirit. Other notable miracles were the healing of the centurion's servant as recorded by Luke (7:1-10) and the raising from the dead of the widow's son at Nain (Luke 7:11-17). The former of these is notable because of the remarkable faith of a Gentile.

Another example of Pharisaic criticism was when Jesus attended a meal in Simon the Pharisee's house (Luke 7:36-50). His host had not provided for the usual courtesies towards guests and yet was critical of Jesus for allowing an immoral woman to wash his feet with tears, dry them with her hair, and anoint them with ointment. There is no doubt that most of Simon's Pharisaic colleagues would have shared his reaction, but Jesus did not prevent the woman because he knew that the motive impelling her to do it was love. He told Simon a parable to press home his point.

John records two visits by Jesus to Jerusalem. These are difficult to date, but they probably occurred during the early period of the ministry. He attended the Feast of Tabernacles (John 7:2) and the Feast of Dedication (John 10:22). At these times Jesus taught in the temple area and entered into dialogue with the religious leaders. The chief priests became alarmed at his presence and sent officers to arrest him (John 7:32). They were unable to do this; instead, they themselves were captivated by his teachings. More discussions with the Jews followed. They charged Jesus with being demon possessed (John 8:48). Both in this case and in the event of the healing of the blind man (John 9), the hostility of the Jews to Jesus surfaces. When Jesus spoke of himself as the Shepherd, his teaching again raised the anger of his Jewish hearers who took up stones to kill him (John 10:31).

TEACHING IN PARABLES

Matthew's Gospel gives a sample of a continuous discourse by Jesus (Matt 5:1–7:29). But Jesus more often spoke in parables. Matthew has collected some of these which concern the theme of the kingdom into a group (Matt. 13). Luke tends to preserve parables of a different kind that are not specially linked to the kingdom. Mark has the least number of parables among the Synoptic Gospels, but his writing shows little interest in Jesus' teaching. John does not relate any parables, although he does preserve two allegories of Jesus—the Sheepfold and the Vine—which could be regarded as extended parables. The parable was a form of teaching particularly characteristic of Jesus. In addition Jesus interspersed even his discourses with metaphors akin to the parabolic form. The parable was valuable because it could stimulate thought and challenge the hearer. This is because the form of the parable is easy to retain in the mind. Jesus did not speak in parables in order to obscure his meaning. This would be contrary to all that he aimed to do through his work and teaching.

SIGNIFICANT EVENTS IN GALILEE

In Nazareth there was a striking instance of the unwillingness to respond to the ministry of Jesus. The people of his hometown proved so hostile that he could perform very few miracles there (Matt. 13:53-58; Mark 6:1-6). This incident is important because it shows there were limitations to what Jesus could do. Faith was especially necessary for people to receive his healing miracles.

The one miracle performed by Jesus that all four evangelists describe is the feeding of the five thousand (Matt. 14:13-21; Mark 6:30-44; Luke 9:10-17; John 6:1-15). This occasion shows the great popularity of Jesus at this stage of his ministry. It also reveals that he was not unmindful of the physical needs of people. After this miracle some wanted to make Jesus king. This casts considerable light on their real motives. They were more concerned with material and political expediency than with spiritual truth. This is why Jesus immediately withdrew

from them and proceeded to instruct his disciples about the spiritual bread that comes from heaven (John 6:25-40).

At this point in John's Gospel Jesus is often seen in dialogue with his opponents. This style of teaching is different from the Synoptic parables but familiar in Jewish-style debate. Many of the people found the spiritual themes in the teaching of Jesus too difficult to accept and consequently ceased to be his disciples (John 6:51-52, 60, 66). This incident demonstrates the uniqueness of the challenge of Jesus and his teaching. Another miracle closely linked with this is when Jesus walked on the water, demonstrating his power in the natural world. Many have sought to rationalize the event by supposing that Jesus was really walking on the shore, and that the disciples did not realize this in the haze. But this miracle is no more extraordinary than the massive multiplication of loaves and fishes, and neither is inconceivable if the miracle worker was all that he claimed to be.

LEAVING NORTHERN GALILEE

Jesus spent a brief time in the region of Tyre and Sidon, where he performed further healings and made clear that his main mission was to the house of Israel (Matt. 15:21-28). He then moved on to Caesarea Philippi; this was the turning point of his ministry (Matt. 16:13-20; Mark 8:27-37; Luke 9:18-27). It was there that Jesus asked his disciples: "Who do people say the Son of Man is?" This caused Peter to confess: "You are the Christ, the Son of the living God." This impressive confession led Jesus to promise that he would build his church on "this rock." There has been much discussion about the meaning of this saying. It is open to some doubt whether Jesus intended to build his church on Peter, on his confession, or on Peter making the confession. Historically Peter was the instrument God used for the entrance into the church of both Jews and Gentiles (Acts 2 and Acts 10). There is no doubt about Jesus' intention to found a church since the word occurs again in Matthew 18:17. Despite the glorious revelation of Jesus on this occasion, he took it as an opportunity to begin to inform his disciples of his death and resurrection (Matt. 16:21-23).

This revelation of Jesus was considerably reinforced by the event known as the Transfiguration, when Jesus was transformed in the presence of three of his disciples (Matt. 17:1-8). It was natural for them to want to keep this glorious vision of Jesus for themselves, but the vision vanished as rapidly as it came. Its purpose was evidently to show the three leading disciples something of the nature of Jesus, which was obscured by his normal human form. A further feature of the vision was the appearance with Jesus of Moses and Elijah, representatives of the Law and the Prophets.

After the Transfiguration Jesus made two predictions concerning his approaching death. These announcements were a total perplexity to the disciples. In Matthew 16, when Jesus mentioned his death, Peter attempts to rebuke Jesus and is rebuked by Jesus in kind. When Jesus mentions his death again in chapter 17, Matthew notes that the disciples were greatly distressed (Matt. 17:23), while Mark and Luke mention the disciples' lack of understanding (Mark 9:32; Luke 9:45). Jesus was approaching the cross with no support from those closest to him. It is not surprising that when the hour arrived they all forsook him.

After the Transfiguration revealed that Jesus was greater than Moses and Elijah and in fact was the beloved Son of God, he was asked to pay the temple tax (Matt. 17:24-27). This incident illustrates the attitude of Jesus toward the authorities and practical responsibilities. He paid the tax, although he did not acknowledge any obligation to do so. The method of payment was extraordinary, for it involved the miracle of the coin in the fish. But the greater importance of the incident is the light it throws on Jesus' independence from the Jewish law.

Luke devotes more than half his Gospel to the period that begins with Jesus leaving Galilee and ends with his death and resurrection in Jerusalem. In this section of his Gospel, Luke introduces a great deal of material that does not occur elsewhere. We can do no more than summarize some of the more striking items that throw light on the life of Jesus.

In addition to the mission of the Twelve, Luke records the mission of the Seventy (or Seventy-two—see Luke 10:17-20). Special parables are recorded by Luke in this section—the Good Samaritan (Luke 10:29-37), the lost sheep (Luke 15:3-7), the lost coin (Luke 15:8-10), and the prodigal son (Luke 15:11-32). As Jesus moved toward Jerusalem he was concerned with developing the spiritual life of his disciples. He was mindful of the fact that he would not be long with them and wished to prepare them for the future. He taught them about prayer (Luke 11:1-13), the Father's care for them (Luke 12:13-34), and preparation for the coming of the Son of Man (Luke 12:35-56).

ON THE WAY TO JERUSALEM

On the approach to Jerusalem Jesus visited both Jericho and Bethany. At Jericho he healed Bartimaeus (Luke 18:35-43) and had a fruitful encounter with Zacchaeus, who reformed his ways as a tax collector (Luke 19:1-10). Bethany was the home of Mary, Martha, and their brother Lazarus, whom Jesus had raised from the dead (John 11). Jesus spent his remaining days in Jerusalem but returned each night to stay at Simon the Leper's house in Bethany in the presence of those who loved him (Matt. 26:6). It was there that a woman anointed his body with costly ointment. This was a controversial and prophetic act preparing Jesus for his burial and enhancing the gospel with loving consecration (Matt. 26:6-13).

THE FINAL DAYS IN JERUSALEM

All four Gospels relate the entry of Jesus into Jerusalem (Matt. 21:1-11; Mark 11:1-10; Luke 19:29-38; John 12:12-15). At this time multitudes greeted Jesus with praises acclaiming him as their king. This welcome stands in stark contrast with the crowd's later cry for his crucifixion. In fact, it was the second crowd that was doing God's bidding since Jesus had not come to Jerusalem to reign but to die.

The Synoptic Gospels place the cleansing

of the temple as the first main event following Jesus' entry into the city (Matt. 21:12-13;
Mark 11:15-17; Luke 19:45-46). The clouds
of opposition had been thickening, but the
audacity of Jesus in clearing out the money
changers from the temple area was too much
for the authorities (Mark 11:18; Luke
19:47). The die was cast and the crucifixion
loomed closer.

It was during this period that further controversies developed between Jesus and the
Pharisees and Sadducees (Matt. 21:23–
22:46). In several cases trick questions were
posed in order to trap Jesus, but with consummate skill he turned their questions
against them. His opposers eventually
reached the point where they dared not ask
him any more questions (Matt. 22:46).

Nearing his final hour, Jesus took the opportunity to instruct his disciples about future events, especially the end of the world.
He reiterated the certainty of his return and
mentioned various signs that would precede
that coming (Matt. 24,25; Mark 13; Luke
21). The purpose of this teaching was to
provide a challenge to the disciples to be
watchful (Matt. 25:13) and diligent (Matt.
25:14-30). This section prepares the way for
the events of the arrest, the trial, the scourging, and the cross-carrying and crucifixion
that followed soon after. But first we must
note the importance of the Last Supper.

When Jesus sat at the table with his disciples on the night before he died (Matt.
26:26-30; Mark 14:22-25; Luke 22:19-20;
1 Cor. 11:23-26), he wished to give them a
simple means by which the significance of
his death could be grasped. The use of the
bread and wine for this purpose was a happy
choice because they were basic elements in
everyday life. Through this symbolic significance Jesus gave an interpretation of his
approaching death—his body broken and
his blood poured out for others. It was necessary for Jesus to provide this reminder that
his sacrificial death would seal a completely
new covenant. It was to be an authentic
memorial to prevent the church from losing
sight of the centrality of the Cross.

John's Gospel does not relate the institution of the Last Supper. Nevertheless, it does
record a significant act in which Jesus
washed the feet of the disciples as an example of humility (John 13:1-20). He impressed on the disciples the principle of
service to others. John follows this display of
humility with a series of teaching Jesus gave
on the eve of the Passion (John 14-17). The
most important feature of this teaching was
the promise of the coming of the Holy Spirit
to the disciples after Jesus had gone. With
his mind occupied with thoughts of approaching death, Jesus showed himself more
concerned about his disciples than about
himself. This is evident in the prayer of Jesus
in John 17. All the evangelists refer in advance to the betrayal by Judas (Matt. 26:21-
25; Mark 14:18-21; Luke 22:21-23; John
13:21-30), which prepares the readers for
the final stages of the way of Jesus to the
cross.

THE BETRAYAL AND ARREST
There is a sense in which the whole gospel
story has been working up to a climax of
rejection. The various outbursts of popular
support were soon over and the determined
opposition emerged as seemingly in control.
In John's Gospel the sense of approaching
climax is expressed in terms of "his hour"
(John 13:1). When this at length comes, the
betrayal and arrest are seen as part of a larger
plan. From the upper room where the Last
Supper was eaten, Jesus went straight to the
Garden of Gethsemane (Matt. 26:36-46;
Mark 14:32-42; Luke 22:40-46), where he
prayed to his Father with deep intensity and
agony. In this we see part of what it cost
Jesus to identify himself with man's need. He
prayed for the cup of suffering to pass from
him, but at the same time submitted to the
Father's will. The three disciples he took
with him all fell asleep, while one of his
other disciples, having betrayed his master,
appeared at the gates at the head of the
group who had come to arrest him. At the
moment of confrontation with Judas, Jesus
exhibits an amazing dignity when he addressed the betrayer as "friend" (Matt.
26:50). He offered no resistance when he
was arrested and chided the crowd of people
for their swords and clubs (Matt. 26:55).

THE TRIAL

Jesus was first taken to the house of Annas, one of the high priests, for a preliminary examination (John 18:13). During his trial, scorn was poured upon him by his enemies, and one of his disciples, Peter, denied him three times (Matt. 26:69-75, Mark 14:66-72; Luke 22:55-62; John 18:15-27), as Jesus predicted he would (Matt. 26:34; Mark 14:30; John 13:38). Before the Sanhedrin the official trial was presided over by Caiaphas, who was nonplussed when Jesus at first refused to speak. At length Jesus predicted that the Son of Man would come on the clouds of heaven; this was enough to make the high priest charge him with blasphemy (Mark 14:62-64). Although he was spat upon and his face was struck, Jesus remained calm and his dignity never deserted him. He showed how much greater he was than those who were treating him with contempt.

The further examinations before Pilate (Matt. 27:1-2; Mark 15:1; Luke 23:1; John 18:28) and Herod (Luke 23:7-12) were no better examples of impartial justice. Again Jesus did not answer when asked about the charges either before Pilate (Matt. 27:14) or Herod (Luke 23:9). He remained majestically silent, except to make a comment to Pilate about the true nature of his kingship (John 18:33-38). The pathetic governor declared Jesus innocent, offered the crowds the release of either Jesus or Barabbas, and then publicly disclaimed responsibility by washing his hands. Pilate then cruelly scourged Jesus and handed him over to be crucified. This judge has ever since been judged by the prisoner.

THE CRUCIFIXION

Many indications have been given throughout the Gospels that Jesus was the incarnated God, yet a genuine man. For this reason the details of the crucifixion are challenging. The soldiers' ribald mockery (Matt. 27:27-30), mixing a royal robe with a frightful crown of thorns (Mark 15:17), compelling a passerby to carry the cross (Luke 23:26), the cruel procedure of nailing Jesus to the cross, the callous casting of lots for his

garment (John 19;23-24), and the scornful challenge to him to use his power to escape (Matt. 27:40-44) all showed man's inhumanity in vivid light. But against this is Jesus' concern about the repentant criminal who was crucified with him (Luke 23:39-43), his concern for his mother (John 19:25-27), his prayer for forgiveness for those responsible for the crucifixion (Luke 23:34), and his final triumphant cry (Mark 15:37), all of which show a nobility of mind that contrasted strongly with the meanness of those about him. A few observers showed a better appreciation, like the centurion who was convinced of Jesus' innocence (Mark 15:39) and the women who followed him and stood at a distance (Matt. 27:55-56). There was one dark moment, as far as Jesus was concerned—his forsaken cry which quickly passed (Mark 15:34). There was an accompanying darkness and an earthquake—as if nature itself was acknowledging the significance of the event. Even the temple veil was torn in two as if it had no longer any right to bar the way into the Holy of Holies (Matt. 27:45, 51).

THE BURIAL, RESURRECTION, AND ASCENSION

Jesus' body was placed in a tomb that belonged to Joseph of Arimathea, who was assisted by Nicodemus in laying the body to rest (Matt 27:57-60; John 19:39). But the tomb played only an incidental part in the Resurrection. The evangelists concentrate on the appearances of Jesus not only on the day of Resurrection, but subsequently. The disciples were convinced that Jesus was alive. Some, like Thomas, had doubts to overcome (John 20:24-29). Others, like John, were more ready to believe when they saw the empty tomb (John 20:2-10). It is not without significance that the first to see the risen Lord was a woman, Mary Magdalene (Matt. 27:61; 28:1, 5-9), whose presence at the cross put to shame those disciples who had run away (Matt 26:56; John 19:25).

We may note that in his glorified, risen state Jesus was in a human form, although he was not at once recognized (John 20:15-16). There was a definite continuity with the

Jesus the disciples had known. The appearances were occasions of both joy and instruction (cf. Luke 24:44 and Acts 1:3). The Resurrection, in fact, had transformed the Cross from a tragedy into a triumph. Forty days after his resurrection, Jesus ascended into heaven to join his Father in glory (Luke 24:51; John 20:17; Acts 1:9-11).

D. GUTHRIE

JEWEL, JOHN (1522–1571)
Bishop of Salisbury; defender of the Protestant Church of England

Born in Devon, Jewel was educated at Merton College, Oxford, where he was introduced to recent English translations of the New Testament. Later he moved to Corpus Christi College. There he worked so hard that he damaged his health. His Protestant opinions were strengthened through the influence of Peter Martyr, the new professor of divinity. When Mary Tudor, a Roman Catholic, became queen in 1553, Jewel was deprived of his position at Corpus Christi.

Jewel was prepared at first to compromise with Roman Catholicism, but later decided to join other Protestants in exile. He arrived in Frankfurt (present-day Germany) in 1555. The British exiles there were divided into an advanced reforming party (future Puritans) and a moderate party, with whom Jewel worked. After visiting other centers of reform and learning, he returned to England when Elizabeth became queen. The letters he wrote to Peter Martyr reveal the problems that faced the queen as she worked for a way to settle religious conflicts. In 1559 Jewel made his famous challenge as he preached at St. Paul's Cross, London: "If any learned man of our adversaries be able to bring any one sufficient sentence out of any old doctor or father, or out of any old general council, or out of the holy scripture, or any one example out of the primitive church for the space of six hundred years after Christ [that is, in proof of specifically Roman doctrine and practices] I will go over to him."

In 1560 Jewel was appointed bishop of Salisbury. Apart from his work as a preacher

and visitor of the diocese, he decided that he would take up the pen to defend the Protestant faith. The result was his celebrated *Apology for the Church of England* (1562), which, in the light of the Council of Trent (1545–1563), set forth the Church of England's claims to be the true church of Christ. The book was written in Latin since it was intended for scholars, but archbishop of Canterbury, Matthew Parker, required that it be translated into English. Since then it has often been reprinted.

The leading Roman Catholic opponent of Jewel's teaching was Thomas Harding (1516–1572), a contemporary at Oxford. In their battle of words the main points of the controversy between Protestants and Roman Catholics over the next several centuries were put forth.

Jewel also promoted the education of poor, bright boys. One of them was Richard Hooker, whose book *Ecclesiastical Polity* extended and developed his benefactor's teaching. P. TOON

JIMÉNEZ DE CISNEROS, FRANCISCO (1436–1517)
Spanish church leader; known for his spirituality, scholarship, austerity, and sound administration

Baptized in Torrelaguna as Gonzalo, Jiménez took the name Francisco in religion. Except that he was of humble origin, little is known of his life before 1492. He studied at Alcala, Salamanca, and Rome, eventually earning his doctor's degree in both civil and canon law. After entering the strict order of Observantine Franciscans, he became a confessor of Isabella, queen of Castile. In 1495 he was elected archbishop of Toledo.

Jiménez was responsible for preserving the Mozarabic (or Visigothic) liturgy. He also founded the University of Alcala de Henares and the major college of San Ildefonso. Like many other Spanish churchmen of his time, Jiménez was concerned about the renewal of spiritual life on the Iberian Peninsula. The renewal he and his fellow religionists spawned, which spread into other Roman Catholic lands before the Council of Trent (1545–1563), became the foundation of the Counter-Reformation.

Jiménez considered a reliable text of Scripture a necessary basis of reform. Therefore he sponsored preparation of the Complutensian Polyglot. That six-volume work, published in 1520, included the Bible in the original languages together with the Vulgate, a Latin version. Erasmus's edition of the Greek New Testament had appeared several years earlier. Based on inferior manuscripts and hurriedly published, it was not as carefully researched as the Complutensian. Its popularity, however, was greater because of both its handiness as a manual and its cheaper price.

Spirituality and scholarship were not the cardinal's sole interests. In political activities he performed just as capably. Twice he served briefly as regent of the realm. He was a vigorous promoter of the Spanish Inquisition as it affected Spain's Moorish population. That fact hurt his reputation in later centuries. Yet his fervor for the Inquisition reflected the severity he practiced in his personal life. He disliked ostentation among the clergy and lived in Franciscan austerity, requiring his clerical associates to live the canonical life under a rule. A. CABANISS

JOACHIM OF FIORE (c. 1130–1202)
Christian mystic, philosopher of history

Born at Celico in the Kingdom of the Two Sicilies, as a young man Joachim is said to have made a pilgrimage to the Holy Land in the course of which he received a divine revelation that determined his future life's work. On his return to Italy, he joined the Cistercian order of monks, was ordained to the priesthood in 1168, and in 1177 was elected abbot of Corazzo. In 1191 he left Corazzo, and the next year settled at Fiore (Flora), where he founded a new Order of St. John, which received papal approval in 1196.

Joachim wrote three major works: *Concordance to the New and Old Testaments* (1189), *Exposition of the Apocalypse* (1196), and *Psaltery of Ten Strings* (1200). In 1254

his works were published in Paris by the Franciscan Gerard of Borgo San Donnino under the title *The Eternal Gospel.*

Joachim's central conception is that human history unfolds in three great overlapping dispensations, identified respectively with the Father, Son, and Holy Spirit. The first stage reaches from Adam to Christ, and in it men live a carnal life, marrying and giving in marriage. The second extends from King Uzziah to the year 1260, and in it men live a mixed life, between the flesh and spirit. The third stage extends from St. Benedict to the end of the world, and in it men live a spiritual life: it is the age of monks.

Some of Joachim's ideas were considered heretical in official church circles, and were condemned at the Lateran Council of 1215 and the Synod of Arles in 1263. But he markedly influenced such groups of later medieval church reformers as the Spiritual Franciscans. N. V. HOPE

JOAN OF ARC (1412–1431)
Peasant who became a national heroine and France's patron saint

Born Jeanne la Pucelle, Joan's early life in Domremy, troubled by the Hundred Years' War, was that of a typical French peasant girl, except for her unusual piety. At about the age of thirteen, Joan thought she began hearing the voices of the archangel Michael and the saints Catherine and Margaret. They told her she must go to aid France's king in the struggle against England. She kept that commission to herself until early 1429, when after passing various tests, she secured the king's consent to lead his troops against Orleans. At that time she predicted she had only slightly more than a year to live. The assault at Orleans was successful, although Joan was wounded. She then stood with Charles VII as he was crowned and anointed at Rheims.

The war, however, dragged on. Joan was captured on May 23, 1430, by the English's Burgundian allies. They sold her to the English, who tried her for sorcery. She was held in prison until her trial, which lasted from February to May, 1431. Questioned at length, she met the examiners with uncannily shrewd, perceptive, and unfaltering replies, despite threats of torture. Finally, when told that death by fire faced her, she renounced the voices—but soon retracted her denial. Condemned as a lapsed heretic, she was burned at the stake. Her last words were "Jesus, Jesus."

In her death Joan of Arc became an even greater inspiration to the French, who at last drove the English out of their country in 1453. In 1456 her trial was reopened and her reputation cleared of the earlier charges. Later in the century, French poet François Villon named her in his "Ballade of Ladies of Former Times." Since then, she has been the subject of many literary and artistic works, including those of two twentieth-century dramatists: *Saint Joan* by George Bernard Shaw (1923) and *The Lark* by Jean Anouilh (1955). She was canonized in 1920.

A. CABANISS

JOHN (1167–1216)
King of England, 1199–1216

Youngest child of Henry II and Eleanor of Aquitaine, John was his father's favorite. "Lackland" was his early nickname because Henry endowed him with castles, not landed estates. In 1185, Henry sent John to rule Ireland, but his abusive, irresponsible conduct forced his recall. Encouraged by his mother, John also plotted with Richard, his elder brother, against their father. Thus John's unruly, treacherous nature came out very early. In 1189, when on Henry's death he became king, Richard invested John with lands, but ordered him to stay in France. Richard then made Arthur of Brittany, son of Geoffrey, Henry's oldest son, his official heir. Angered, John returned to England when Richard departed on the Third Crusade and attempted with little success to take over the throne. In 1194, when finally ransomed from Henry VI, Richard banished John and deprived him of his lands. But two years later, John gained a reconciliation, and in 1197, the elder made the younger brother his heir. On Richard's death in 1199, John assumed the office he greatly coveted.

Three momentous struggles marked John's sixteen-year reign in England. The great conflicts were John's protracted clashes with the French monarch, with the papacy, and with the English nobility. Each of the struggles had a spectacular climax: respectively, disbandment of Angevin holdings in France, imposition of papal lordship over England, and ratification of English noble rights. Unmistakably, the chief elements each time were some baneful action by John, and a reaction duly exacting John's capitulation. All three clashes permanently affected England's subsequent history.

Thoroughly routed in France, John began to concentrate on England with repressive energy. This most immediately affected his relations with the Church. John's one restraining influence, Hubert Walter, the great archbishop of Canterbury, died in 1205. Then, despite the insistence of Innocent III, John refused to install Stephen Langton, a strong, independent-minded leader, as the new archbishop. At the same time, he devised new taxes and other extractions of revenue from the Church. The king and the papacy thus engaged in an acrimonious standoff for the next three years. Finally, in 1208, Innocent placed England under an interdict, and in 1209 he excommunicated John, who then yielded to all of Innocent's terms. These included not only installation of Langton and retreat from Church taxes, but John's consent to papal lordship over England. Thereafter, until the Reformation, papal influence remained very potent in England.

In his last years, whatever his submission to the Church, John's misrule otherwise only grew worse. Distrusting the king for his unscrupulous, unpredictable conduct, a group of rebellious nobles incited England to incipient civil war in 1215. With no other recourse, John placated the rebels by signing the Great Charter, or Magna Carta, a document granting English nobles certain basic rights. But typically, not long after the ceremony at Runnymede, John abandoned the new agreement, and very quickly, civil war commenced in England. John died during this conflict and left England in much chaos and distress. Historians have debated if, besides the negative acts, any benefits for England came from positive deeds by John. It is possible to point to endowments he made to churches and monasteries, and to improvements he obtained in England's financial structure. Nonetheless, overall, John's violence, ruthlessness, profligacy, and ineptness dominated his life and acts as king.

Pertinent sections of the *Cambridge Medieval History* list the original sources describing John and his reign. The appropriate bibliography in the *Oxford History of England* indicates other relevant materials.
K. J. BRYER

JOHN XXII (1249–1334)
Pope, 1316–1334

Born Jacques Duèse, John lived originally in Cahors (southwest France). His studies at the University of Paris and elsewhere concentrated upon law. After ordination, John gained successive appointments as bishop of Frejus (1300), bishop of Avignon (1310), and cardinal bishop of Porto (1312). A compromise candidate on election as pope, John became the principal early figure in the papacy's Avignon residency. This removal from Rome, the so-called Babylonian Captivity (1309–1377), resulted from the papal states' dangerous instability in the era. Despite strenuous efforts, John could not break the Ghibelline hold on Rome and the papal territories. He thus settled at Avignon, where his predecessors had fled. As events turned out, John found Avignon very conducive to the enlargement and centralization he desired for the papal court. Hence he made his time one of wide-scale administrative advance. This carried over into improvements at large in the Church's diocesan boundaries and other jurisdictional spheres.

John held to a highly theocratic understanding of papal sovereignty. In his view, European monarchs all owed their ultimate fidelity to the pope, God's supreme earthly ruler for Church affairs and secular matters. John's main opponent here was Louis of Bavaria, who claimed the Holy Roman Emperor's role and authority over the papacy's temporal acts. In 1324, for such assertions, John summarily excommunicated Louis. In response, Louis allied formally with the Roman Ghibellines and, in 1328, had himself crowned as emperor. He also declared John deposed and Nicholas V the bishop of Rome. Along the way, Louis gained support from Franciscan Spirituals who left their order over ideas on poverty. Most importantly, he also obtained the backing of Marsilius of Padua. His writing, *Defensor Pacis,* was the Middle Ages' greatest defense of general imperial sovereignty. Nonetheless, John excommunicated these supporters and others, and the Church at large soon gave its assent to his papacy. Eventually, Louis was forced out of Italy, and in 1330 Nicholas V submitted his abjuration. In retrospect, John's energies put papal finances and supervisory functions on their soundest basis in years. His additions to the canon law also were important. Migne's *Patrologia Latina* has reproductions of John I's letter. The famous prayer, "Anima Christi," has sometimes been attributed to him. K. J. BRYER

JOHN XXIII (1881–1963)
Pope, 1958–1963; convener of the Second Vatican Council

Born Angelo Guiseppe Roncalli into a humble family near Bergamo, northern Italy, John was ordained in 1904 and later earned a doctorate in theology in Rome. Nine years as secretary to the bishop of Bergamo were followed by a number of other posts from 1914 before he began his involvement in the Vatican diplomatic corps (1925–1953). During those years he served in Bulgaria, Turkey, Greece, and France. While he was in France (beginning in 1944), he encountered thorny issues such as alleged cooperation by French bishops with Nazis, repatriation of German prisoners of war, and the development of the worker-priest movement.

In 1953 Roncalli was made cardinal and patriarch of Venice before his life took an unexpected turn in his election as pope in 1958. Expected to be merely a caretaker in the office, he in turn surprised the church by announcing three intentions: to call a synod of the church in the diocese of Rome, to summon an ecumenical council to promote Christian unity and regenerate spiritual life among Catholics (*aggiornamento*), and to reform canon law. Vatican traditionalists were predictably appalled, but this self-styled "pope who keeps pressing on the accelerator" was undaunted. He and his council sent a prolonged blast of fresh air through church and curia. He kept a close eye on the conciliar proceedings through closed-circuit television, but his personal interventions were few. At the opening of the council he had exhorted the bishops to address the twentieth-century world and its needs; in an informal gesture he invited journalists to the Sistine Chapel one day, and with good-humored and winsome words reminded them of their duty to report the council accurately to that world.

How far Vatican II affected the church's doctrine is still hard to pinpoint precisely. What is not in doubt was John's success in changing his church's attitudes toward non-Catholics. Those who previously had been wandering in uncertain status outside the gate were welcomed as "separated brethren" and invited to send observers to the council. John improved relations with the European communist bloc so that many of its bishops were allowed to go to Rome. The Church of England's spiritual head was received in audience—the first archbishop of Canterbury to visit Rome since the Reformation—and so too, in an even more revolutionary gesture, was the moderator of the (Presbyterian) Church of Scotland's general assembly. John seized the opportunity also to renew and confirm his earlier close relations with the Eastern Orthodox Church.

A further sign of his worldview was his increase in the number of cardinals to an all-time high of eighty-seven, representing a record number of countries. Theologically, however, John kept generally to well-worn paths, particularly with regard to birth control, clerical marriage, and the veneration of the Virgin Mary. Perhaps the most significant of his eight encyclicals were *Mater et magistra* (1961), dealing with social ques-

tions and colonialism; and *Pacem in terris* (1963), an appeal for world peace and cooperation. The pope's *Journal of a Soul* appeared in English in 1965. J. D. DOUGLAS

JOHN, GRIFFITH (1831–1912)
Welshman sent to interior China by the London Missionary Society

Born at Swansea, educated at Brecon College, and ordained to the ministry of the Congregational Church (1855), John was an explorer for the London Missionary Society (LMS) after China's ports were opened to foreign commerce (1842). He passed through the Yangtse gorges and penetrated Szechuan province even before Hudson Taylor, the first missionary to inland China. He eventually settled in the city of Hankow.

John was as fluent, eloquent, and persuasive a public preacher in Chinese as in Welsh and English. Mighty with his pen, he also contributed greatly to the united Protestant literary ministry. He chaired the Central China Tract Society. He produced in Mandarin (the national spoken language) the New Testament, Psalms, and Proverbs, as well as the New Testament in Wenli (the literary language).

Protestant lay people and missionaries throughout China held him in high honor, and he was equally esteemed in Great Britain. The University of Edinburgh bestowed the D.D. degree on him (1889). The Congregational Union of England and Wales elected him chairman (1888). The large Griffith John College (a high school for boys) in Hankow kept his memory fresh until the communist regime closed the institution about 1950. P. BEAVER

JOHN, THE APOSTLE
The apostle known as the "the disciple whom Jesus loved"; author of the fourth Gospel, three epistles, and probably Revelation

The apostle John has a high reputation among Christian people, and his influence has been felt throughout the centuries. Despite this, he is a surprisingly shadowy figure. When he appears in the pages of the

New Testament it is almost always in company with Peter or James, and if there is speaking to be done, it is usually his companion who does it; thus there is not a great deal on which to base a biography.

John's father's name was Zebedee, and John had a brother called James (Matt. 4:21). Among the women at the cross, Matthew names Mary Magdalene, Mary the mother of James and Joseph, and "the mother of Zebedee's children" (Matt. 27:56). Mark names the two Marys and adds Salome (Mark 15:40). This indicates that Salome may be the name of John's mother. If Matthew and Mark are naming the same women as does John, then Salome was Jesus' "mother's sister" (John 19:25). This would make John a cousin of Jesus. We cannot be certain of this, for there were many women there (Matt. 27:55) and there is no way of being sure that Matthew, Mark, and John all name the same three. Many accept the identification, but we can scarcely say more.

John was among those whom Jesus called by the Sea of Galilee (Matt. 4:21-22; Mark 1:19-20). This makes him one of the first disciples. It is also possible that he was the unnamed companion of Andrew when that apostle first followed Jesus (John 1:35-37). John was important in the little group around Jesus since he was one of three who were especially close to the Master. These disciples were selected to be with Jesus on many great occasions. John, along with his brother James and Peter, was present at the transfiguration (Matt. 17:1-2; Mark 9:2; Luke 9:28-29). Jesus also took just these three into the house of Jairus when he brought that man's daughter back to life (Mark 5:37; Luke 8:51). Before Jesus' arrest, it was this trio that he took to pray with him in the Garden of Gethsemane (Matt. 26:37; Mark 14:33). Though the three were admonished for sleeping instead of watching in prayer, we must not overlook the fact that in that time of great difficulty, when Jesus faced the prospect of death on a cross, it was to these three that he looked for support.

There are other occasions when John is mentioned in the Gospels. Luke tells us of John's surprise when the miraculous catch of fish took place (Luke 5:9-10). This is especially noteworthy since John was a fisherman. Toward the close of Jesus' ministry, we find John coming to Jesus with Peter, James, and Andrew, to ask when the end would come and what would be the sign when all things come to their climax (Mark 13:3-4). And on the last evening, Jesus sent Peter and John to prepare the Passover meal (Luke 22:8).

Passages like these show that John was highly esteemed among the apostles and that he stood specially close to Jesus. But there are indications that at first John was far from appreciating what Jesus stood for. When Mark gives his list of the Twelve, he tells us that Jesus gave to James and John the name *Boanerges,* which means *sons of thunder* (Mark 3:17). Some in the early church understood this name as a compliment, thinking it meant that James's and John's witness to Jesus would be as strong as thunder. But most see it as pointing to their tempestuousness of character. We see this, for example, when John encounters a man who was casting out demons in Jesus' name. John instructs him not to, "for he isn't one of our group" (Mark 9:38, TLB; Luke 9:49).

Mark also tells us of an occasion when the sons of Zebedee asked Jesus for the two chief places when he came in glory, one to be on his right and the other on his left (Mark 10:35-40). Matthew adds the point that the words were spoken by the men's mother, but he leaves us no doubt that James and John were in on it (Matt. 20:20-22). Jesus proceeded to ask them whether they could drink the cup he would drink and be baptized with the baptism he would receive. (Clearly, these are metaphors for the suffering Jesus would in due course undergo.) James and John affirmed that they could, and Jesus assured them that they would indeed do this. However, he gave them no assurance about their places in the Father's kingdom. (But it is plain that James and John would suffer for Christ.) At that time, they also failed to understand the loving spirit that moved their Master and was required of them as well.

Another incident that shows the same

tempestuous spirit is one involving Samaritan villagers who refused to receive the little band as they travelled. When James and John heard of it, they asked Jesus whether he wanted them to call down fire from heaven to consume the villagers (Luke 9:54). They were clearly at variance with Jesus, and indeed he rebuked them; but we should not miss the zeal they displayed for their Lord, nor their conviction that if they did call down fire it would come. They were sure that God would not fail to answer the prayer of those who asked for vengeance on the opponents of Jesus. There is zeal here and faith, if also a spirit of lovelessness.

The synoptic Gospels then show us John as a zealous and loyal follower of Jesus. He is not depicted as gentle and considerate. At this time, he knew little of the love that should characterize a follower of Jesus, but he did have faith and a passionate conviction that God would prosper Jesus and those who served him.

John is not mentioned by name in the fourth Gospel, but there are passages which speak about "the disciple whom Jesus loved" (John 13:23; 19:26; 20:2; 21:7, 20). We are not told who this was, but the evidence seems to indicate that it was the apostle John. For example, there is an account of a fishing trip in chapter 21, with a listing of those who went fishing. It includes Peter, who must be ruled out as "the disciple whom Jesus loved" because he is often mentioned along with the beloved disciple. Thomas and Nathaniel were there, but there seems to be no reason for seeing either as a likely candidate. Two unnamed men and the sons of Zebedee make up the remainder of the party. James is excluded by his early death (Acts 12:2). This leaves us with John or one of the unnamed men. John is favored by the fact that the beloved disciple is linked with Peter on a number of occasions (John 13:23-24; 20:2; 21:7). We know from the other Gospels that Peter and John (together with James) were especially close (see also Acts 3; 8:14; Gal. 2:9). Of course, one of the unnamed disciples may have been the beloved disciple, but we have no reasons to assume this. Further, such a supposition

faces the problem of the omission of the name of John the apostle throughout the entire fourth Gospel. If John wrote this book, we can understand his not mentioning himself. But if it was written by someone else, why would that person omit all mention of a man as prominent in the apostolic band as the other Gospels show John to have been? In addition, if John is the author, it would explain why John the Baptist is called simply "John."

It is argued that "the disciple whom Jesus loved" is not the kind of title a man would naturally use of himself, but it must be said also that it is not the kind of title a man would naturally use of someone else, either. And it may be that John uses it in a modest fashion—partly because he did not want to draw attention to himself by using his name, and partly because he wanted to emphasize the truth that it was the fact that Jesus loved him that made him what he was.

If this identification may be accepted, we learn more about the apostle. We should not, of course, read the words "the disciple whom Jesus loved" as though they meant that Jesus did not love the other disciples. He loved them all. But, as applied to John, they mean that he was indeed beloved, probably also that he recognized that he owed all he had and all he was to that love. That he was specially close to Jesus is indicated by the fact that he leaned on Jesus' breast at the Last Supper (John 13:23). It also tells us something of his relationship to the Master that he was at the cross when Christ was crucified and that it was to him that Jesus gave the charge to look after his mother (John 19:26-27). One would have expected that Jesus would have selected one of his family for this responsibility. But his brothers did not believe in him, whereas both John and Mary did. This event certainly shows that a close relationship existed between Jesus and the disciple he loved.

On the first Easter morning, John raced with Peter to the tomb when Mary Magdalene told them it was empty. He won the race, but stood outside the tomb until Peter came. Peter, the leader of men, went right in, and John followed. We read that he "saw and believed" (John 20:8). Then in chapter 21 we read of the beloved disciple fishing with the others. Significantly, it was he who recognized that it was Jesus who stood on the shore and told them where to cast the net (John 21:7).

There is not much to add to this picture when we turn to Acts. At the beginning, John's name occurs in a list of the Twelve (Acts 1:13); and later, when we are told of James's death, it is noted that he was John's brother (Acts 12:2). In every other reference to John, he is in the company of Peter. These two were the instruments God used in bringing healing to a lame man (Acts 3). At that time, they were going to the temple at the hour of prayer. This says something about their habits of devotion. Prayer at the ninth hour apparently refers to the Jewish service of prayer that was held at the same time as the evening offering (i.e., at about three o'clock in the afternoon). Evidently Peter and John were continuing the devotional habits of pious Jews with an interest in the temple and all its doings. On another occasion, these two were arrested and jailed on account of their preaching about Jesus' resurrection (Acts 4:1-3). They were brought before the council, where Peter spoke for them. The council saw that these two men were "uneducated, common men" (Acts 4:13). This means that they had never had the normal rabbinic education. By the standards of the council, they were uneducated. The council forbade them to speak about Jesus, but the apostles' reply displays John's typical boldness: "Whether it is right in the sight of God to listen to you rather than to God, you must judge; for we cannot but speak of what we have seen and heard" (Acts 4:19-20, RSV).

John was associated with Peter again when the gospel was first preached in Samaria. Philip was the evangelist to the Samaritans, but the apostles in Jerusalem decided to send Peter and John to Samaria when they heard how the people had accepted the gospel message. "As soon as they arrived, they began praying for these new Christians to receive the Holy Spirit" (Acts 8:15, TLB), a revealing illustration of apos-

tolic priorities. In due course, they laid their hands on the new believers and they received the Holy Spirit (8:17). John is not specifically mentioned, but he no doubt was included in "the apostles" who were arrested and jailed because of the jealousy of prominent Jews (Acts 5:17-18). But that imprisonment did not last long, for an angel released them at night, so that they resumed their preaching in the early morning (5:21). John is mentioned by name in Galatians 2:9, where he is joined with Peter and James and the three are called "the pillars of the church."

This appears to be the extent of the New Testament's record of the apostle John. Clearly he was an important figure in the little band of the early Christians. On almost every occasion when he comes before us in the record, he is in the company of someone else and normally the speaking is done by his companion, not by John. But we may justly conclude that he stood very close to Jesus. Perhaps he had entered into the mind of Jesus more than any of the others. The best evidence of this is the Gospel of John. Clearly the man who wrote this had great spiritual insight. John may have been more the thinker than a man of action and leader of men.

We have seen that there is good reason to think that the fourth Gospel was written by the apostle John. The Epistles of John probably came from him also (though, as they stand, they are anonymous). All the Johannine writings probably emanate from the province of Asia. The heretics alluded to in 1 John resemble the Cerinthians (followers of the heretic Cerinthus), who were in Asia Minor at the end of the first century, and tradition connects the author of 1 John with Ephesus. It is certain that the same person wrote all three letters, and reasonably certain that this author also wrote the Gospel of John; the Gospel and the letters certainly represent the same mind at work in different situations.

An author named John wrote the book of Revelation (Rev. 1:1), though it is not clear whether this is the apostle or another John. Tradition has identified the John of Revelation (see Rev. 1:1, 9; 22:8) with John the apostle, the author of the Gospel of John and the three letters of John. This view was held by Justin Martyr as early as 140. The main objection to this view is that the original Greek is unlike that of the other Johannine writings, showing scant respect for the rules of the language. Some have suggested that a different John wrote Revelation, others that John's disciples wrote the Gospel and letters and John himself wrote Revelation. But it is still plausible that the apostle John (or one of his close disciples) wrote the Gospel and the letters.

Assuming John the apostle wrote Revelation, he was exiled to Patmos (Rev. 1:9). But the date of this is uncertain. Some probably unreliable evidence from the late fifth century suggests that John was martyred at about the same time as his brother James (c. 44; see also Acts 12:2). Jesus' prophecy in Mark 10:39 need not imply that both met with a simultaneous and violent end. Much stronger is the tradition reflected by Polycrates, bishop of Ephesus (fl. c. 190), that John died a natural death in Ephesus, and by Irenaeus (fl. c. 175–195) that John lingered on in Ephesus until the time of the emperor Trajan (ruled c. 97–117).
L. MORRIS

JOHN OF AVILA (1502–1569)
Roman Catholic saint

Born near Toledo in the Spanish kingdom of Castile, John studied law at Salamanca (1514–1515), then turned to the ascetic life and the study of theology at Alcala. He was ordained to the priesthood in 1525. After his parents' death he gave the family fortune away to the poor.

In 1527 John planned to go to Mexico as a missionary. He was sent instead in 1529 to Andalusia in southern Spain. There he worked for nine years, becoming a popular preacher. He called for moral reform in the Roman Catholic Church, while criticizing the vices of the wealthy. Many people sought his spiritual counsel. His work especially influenced the Spanish clergy, as he helped establish schools to improve both their

knowledge and their morals. His opponents within the church brought him before the Spanish Inquisition in 1533, but he was cleared of charges.

For the last twenty years of his life, because of poor health, John withdrew to a monastery, where he continued to teach and write. His writings, in the tradition of Spanish mystical theology, pointed the way to Christian perfection. His collected works fill nine volumes.

At the time of his death in 1569 his influence was widely felt in Spain. He had encouraged the Jesuits, and he had been friend and adviser to such influential mystics as Theresa of Avila and John of God. He became known in the Roman Catholic Church as the "Apostle of Andalusia." John of Avila was beatified in 1894 and canonized in 1970. W. R. GODFREY

JOHN OF DAMASCUS (c. 675–749)
Greek Orthodox theologian; poet

John was born in Damascus to a wealthy Christian family. His father represented the Christians in the caliph's court. John succeeded his father at court, but then in about 716 joined the monastery of St. Sabas near Jerusalem.

John opposed the iconoclastic movement in the Eastern church. In three treatises written between 726 and 730 he defended the use of icons as a stimulus to Christian devotion. He maintained that those who opposed icons had an unduly pessimistic view of matter.

John expressed his religious devotion beautifully in poetry and hymns. Much of his work was incorporated into the liturgy of the Greek Orthodox Church. Two of his hymns are widely used among Protestants at Easter: "Come, Ye Faithful, Raise the Strain" and "The Day of Resurrection! Earth, Tell It Out Abroad." He also wrote commentaries on the Pauline Epistles and the life of the saints.

John's greatest work was *The Fountain of Knowledge*. The first part, largely philosophical, examined Aristotle's dialectics and applied them to theology in a way that later became the practice of many theologians of the Middle Ages. The second part dealt with heresies. John followed closely the work of Epiphanius (c. 315–403), who described and refuted early heresies. John continued that work by attacking fifth- and sixth-century heresies.

The third part of *The Fountain of Knowledge* was titled "An Accurate Exposition of the Orthodox Faith." It discussed key elements of Christian theology: the Trinity, the Creation, the Incarnation, and the sacraments. John taught a negative theology; that is, he believed human beings can only say what God is not. He offered various proofs for God's existence. On the doctrine of the Trinity his thought was similar to that of the Cappadocian Fathers. He exalted Mary, teaching both her immaculate conception and her bodily assumption into heaven. He supported all his opinions with extensive citation from the church fathers. The third part circulated independently and, through a later Latin translation, influenced Peter Lombard (c. 1100–1160) and Thomas Aquinas (c. 1225–1274).

John of Damascus is known as the last great doctor of the Greek church. His thought was not original, but it was clear and comprehensive. He systematized the theology of Eastern Christianity. The basic structures of his thought remain authoritative for Eastern Orthodoxy. W. R. GODFREY

JOHN OF GOD (1495–1550)
Founder of the Brothers Hospitallers

Born in Portugal, John Ciudad spent most of his life in Spain. As a youth he was a shepherd for a count in Castile. In 1522 he enlisted to fight against both France and the Turks. While a soldier he lived an immoral life.

When he was about forty, John returned to Spain and again became a shepherd. He began to feel remorse over his sinful past, so he sought ways to become a martyr. After his confessor assured him that that approach was wrong, John opened a small shop selling books and religious pictures. On hearing a sermon by John of Avila, he ran about the city praying for mercy until many thought him insane.

John next rented a house in which he cared for the poor and the abandoned who were sick. Because John was an able administrator who ran his hospital in a business-like way, he was consulted by people who wanted to set up hospitals in other parts of the country. He does not seem to have had any thought of founding a religious community. But, after his work drew others into caring for the sick, the bishop of Tuy gave him the name John of God and prescribed a habit and rule for John and his companions. After his death an order was formed that was given John's name. A. VOS

JOHN OF LEYDEN (1509–1536)
Anabaptist leader in Münster (also known as Jan Beukelssen or John Bockelsohn)

John, a tailor of Leyden, was one of many Anabaptists, followers of Melchior Hofmann, who flocked to Münster after a public disputation in which both the Lutheran and Roman Catholic speakers were thought to have been defeated. In 1533 the Anabaptists took control of the city, expelled the bishop, and set up what they believed was a Christian society.

John, who thought Münster would be the site of the New Jerusalem, was made king. He surrounded himself with a large guard and brilliant court. He and his fellow leaders practiced polygamy, claiming they did so on divine command. John himself is said to have taken sixteen wives. Any resistance to John's regime was put down by force. Opinion varies on just how far John went in insisting on community of property, polygamy, and suppression of opposition.

The Anabaptist rule was short-lived, for the bishop, aided by Lutheran and Catholic forces retook the city after an eighteen-month seige. John and the other leaders were tortured and killed. Their bodies were encased in iron cages, then hoisted to the cathedral belfry, where they remained for years as a warning to citizens. The brief, chaotic rule of John and his companions helped shape the popular view that Anabaptists overthrow government, society, morals, and religion. A. Vos

JOHN OF MONTE CORVINO
(died c. 1330)

Italian Franciscan; first Western missionary to reach China

The Mongol Empire opened the doors to missionaries from the Roman Catholic Church just when the Dominicans and Franciscans, the church's two chief missionary orders, were beginning to expand. In 1289 John, already an experienced missionary familiar with the Persian and Armenian languages, was entrusted by Pope Nicholas IV with various letters, including one to the Mongol great khan at Khanbalik (later Peking).

In 1291 John set out through Persia, passed a year in India, and then traveled up the China coast to the Mongol capital. The Mongol ruler received him courteously, but the Nestorian clergy, who were powerful at the court, strongly opposed him. In spite of opposition, John had by 1305 built a church, made about six thousand converts, and translated the New Testament and Psalter into the native language. In letters John reported his successes to the pope, which caused great excitement in the West. Pope Clement V named him an archbishop in 1307. When he died, John was mourned by Christians and non-Christians alike.

Because of the difficulty of the journey, attempts to send reinforcements to the Franciscan mission in China were not successful. The last medieval missionaries to reach China arrived in 1342 and returned in 1353. A. Vos

JOHN OF SALISBURY (1115–1180)

Medieval scholar and churchman

English-born, John attended the lectures of the brilliant French theologian Abelard and other scholars who flourished in Paris. He was also a friend of Bernard of Clairvaux, one of Abelard's enemies. Later John studied in the school of Chartres and afterward taught at Paris. During the interval (1153–

1574) he was attached to the court of Canterbury, where he performed diplomatic service.

John's major work was in the realm of scholarship. His *Metalogicon*—a presentation of grammar, rhetoric, and dialectic—showed the first knowledge since antiquity of the entire range of Aristotle's logical treatises. The *Policraticus*, probably John's most influential publication, was a discussion of medieval political theory. Still considered a landmark in the history of political thought, it was dedicated to King Henry II's chancellor, Thomas à Becket.

John was with Archbishop Becket at the time of Becket's murder in 1170. Later he produced a biography of the martyr and also one of Anselm, archbishop of Canterbury. John of Salisbury wrote the best Latin prose of his time. In 1176 he was elected bishop of Chartres. Despite his association with Paris and Chartres, John was always designated by his birthplace. A. CABANISS

JOHN OF THE CROSS (1542–1591)

Spanish Roman Catholic reformer, mystic, and poet

John's father married beneath his status, and consequently his family repudiated him. Shortly after John's birth the father died in poverty. The child was therefore reared in an institution established for the education of young children. At seventeen John worked for awhile, then entered the Jesuit college at Medina in 1563. There he received excellent training in the new humanistic learning. At twenty-one, however, he made his profession as a Carmelite monk. Sent in 1564 by his superiors to the order's college at Salamanca, he studied the liberal arts and theology. For awhile he taught at that school. In 1567 he was ordained a priest.

At some point John came under the influence of the vibrant Carmelite nun, Teresa of Avila (1515–1582). After being her confessor for five years, he became an ardent proponent of reform within his own order. Because many of the leaders resented his efforts, he was held in close confinement in Toledo for a year (1577–1578) in a vain attempt to force him to give up his activities. In those cramped quarters John turned to writing poetry. Finally he escaped from prison and resumed his reforms.

A period of humiliation and misunderstanding followed, so he retired to a monastery as a solitary. In 1591, an inflamed leg impaired his health; despite treatment, his condition grew worse. He was therefore placed in the grudging care of a monastery at Ubeda, where he died shortly thereafter.

John's major works, poems and commentaries on them, are quasi-mystical. Best known is *The Dark Night* (of the Soul) or *The Ascent of Mount Carmel*. Others of perhaps equal importance are *The Spiritual Canticle and The Living Flame of Love*. Written in Spanish, not Latin, they are landmarks in the history of Spanish spirituality as well as masterpieces of world literature. In thorough conformity with Roman Catholic orthodoxy, John's works taught that union with God (or perfection) can be attained by practice of the theological virtues of faith, hope, and charity.

Although John died in obscurity, his treatises had a profound influence on later Catholicism and even on Protestantism. He and Teresa of Avila, in their own way, represented the Counter-Reformation as truly as did Ignatius Loyola, founder of the Jesuit order (Society of Jesus). In his painting *Christ of St. John of the Cross* (1951), the surrealist artist Salvador Dali depicted one of John's mystic visions of the crucifixion. A. CABANISS

JOHN OF WESEL (1400–1481)
German Catholic scholar

John's surname, seldom used, was Richrat or Ruchrat. Little is known of his early life. In 1440 he was engaged in studying theology at Erfurt, but did not receive the doctor of theology degree until 1456. His great learning and prestige were attested by his contemporary Wimpheling and by his appointment as vice-rector of Erfurt. John's lectures on Peter Lombard's *Sentences* were published as *Lectiones* (*Readings*) and *Quaestiones* (*Inquiries*).

John concerned himself with the abuse of the doctrine of indulgences. He also refused to attribute infallibility to the institutional church (his view, however, has little to do with the tenth-century dogma of papal infallibility). His outspoken utterances inevitably provoked a summons to appear before a local inquisition at Mainz in 1479. Either from sincere conviction or lack of courage, he chose to recant his positions. He was then banished to the obscurity of an Augustinian community at Mainz where he died.

Since Martin Luther claimed to have learned much from John of Wesel, John may be looked on as a precursor of the Reformation. John of Wesel is not to be confused with his Dutch contemporary, John Wessel Gansfort. A. CABANISS

JOHN PAUL I (1912–1978)
Pope for thirty-three days in 1978

Born Albino Lucia in Candle d'Agordo, in the Dolomite Alps of northern Italy, John Paul studied at the Gregorian Seminary in his native diocese of Belluno and at Rome's Pontifical University, and was ordained to the priesthood in 1935. After working in parishes of his home diocese, in 1937 he became vice-rector and professor of dogmatic theology at the Belluno Seminary. In 1958 he was named Bishop of Vittorio Veneto in northern Italy by Pope John XXIII, and in 1969 was appointed Archbishop and Patriarch of Venice by Pope Paul VI, who in 1973 made him a cardinal. In August 1978 he was elected Pope, combining in his official title the names of his two immediate predecessors; but thirty-three days later he died, after the briefest pontificate in three and one-half centuries. He authored two books: *Catechetical Crumbs,* based on his pastoral and teaching experience, and *Illustrissimi,* a series of essays written as letters to famous thinkers of the past and present. N. V. HOPE

JOHN PAUL II (born 1920)
Pope, 1978–present

Born Karol Wotyla, John Paul began life

in Kraków, Poland. His first advanced eduJ-cation was at Kraków's Jagiellonian University. Poetry and drama were his great initial interests. Reduced to manual labor in World War II, John Paul participated in the clandestine Rhapsodic Theatre. Most importantly, he also studied with an underground Catholic seminary. A life of formal church service increasingly attracted him, and in 1946, he became a priest. Immersing himself in higher study, John Paul earned doctorates at Angelicum University (now Pontifical University of St. Thomas), Rome, and Kraków University, Kraków. In 1954, he joined the Catholic University of Lublin, Poland, as professor of philosophy.

John Paul's administrative gifts did not leave him an academic for long. By 1958, he had become a bishop, and in 1964, the Vatican made him archbishop of Kraków. A prominent participant in Vatican Council II, John Paul became known for his balanced progressivism. He was a major contributor to the Vatican II's *Pastoral Constitution on the Church in the Modern World*. In 1967, Pope Paul VI gave him a cardinal's hat. Then in 1978, John Paul I died only a month after succeeding Paul VI. Elected quickly under upset circumstances, John Paul II took a name symbolizing continuance of his predecessors' reforms. He became the first non-Italian pope since the 1500s, and the very first from Poland.

From the outset, John Paul II's papacy has maintained certain emphases for the Roman Catholic Church. In general, these have combined selected modern ideas with an adamant and traditional conservatism. Outside the Church, John Paul's large concern for the masses, especially the poor and oppressed, has been plain. Further, as a former battler of Polish communism, no question exists about his distaste for communism. He has opposed radical liberalism and Marxism alike. His censures have excoriated both socialist and dictatorial and capitalist and democratic regimes.

Within the Church, John Paul has based his papacy on Vatican II's reforms. These have upheld historic Christianity as regards God's creation, man's sin, redemption in Christ, Christian life and worship, and other basics. But they also decreed deep liturgical and disciplinary changes. Subsequently, on one side, John Paul has acted against conservatives resisting the Council's changes. Further, he has curtailed the Jesuit order and other clergy who have sought political power. But on another side, he has aggressively opposed extreme modernists. This has resulted in the public stifling of leading radical theologians and ethicists. But John Paul's conservatism is most obvious as regards intermediate social structures. Above all, concerning priestly orders and marriage, Roman Catholicism's two main vocations, the pope has refused to relax the Church's chief traditions. In the one area, he has maintained unwavering strictness on both a priest's celibate discipline and prohibition of women's ordination. In the other, he has upheld the Church's centuries-old antipathy to contraception, abortion, homosexuality, and divorce. Certainly the integrity of marriage and family life has been one his deepest, most discussed concerns. More than any pope in history, John Paul has attempted face-to-face pastoral work throughout the world. Even after 1981, and a near-fatal attempt on his life, his far-reaching pastoral travels were not curtailed. The immediacy of John Paul's influence has been unparalleled.

John Paul's writings include various important prepapal works. In English translation, the most significant are two books, *Love and Responsibility* and *Sources of Renewal—The Implementation of the Second Vatican Council*; his plays, *The Jeweller's Shop* and *Brother of Our Lord*; and his poetry, *Collected Poems*. The especially important papal letters are "The Redeemer of Man," "On the Mercy of God," "On the Family," "On Social Concern," "On the Dignity and Vocation of Women," and "On the Laity." John Paul's second journey to the United States occurred in 1987. The speeches from this visit, published in *Unity in the Work of Service*, are exceptionally fine statements on a Christian's confrontation with modernity.
K. J. BRYER

JOHNSON, RICHARD (1753–1827)
First gospel preacher in Australia

In 1787, through William Wilberforce's influence, Johnson, an ardent evangelical, was appointed chaplain to the 730 convicts being transported in the first fleet of ships sent out to Botany Bay, New South Wales. As Botany Bay proved too poor in land and water for a settlement, the company sailed north to Port Jackson (Sydney Harbor). There Johnson conducted the first Christian worship service on Australian soil on February 3, 1788, preaching on the text, "What shall I render unto the Lord for all his benefits toward me?" (Ps. 116:12).

At his own expense Johnson built the first Australian church. It was burned down in 1798 by convicts enraged by the governor's decree for compulsory church attendance—an attempt to improve the community's morals. Johnson also established the first schools in the colony in 1793. He returned to England in 1800. N. HILLYER

JOHNSON, SAMUEL (1709–1784)
English essayist, poet, moralist, and lexicographer

Johnson, son of a Litchfield, Staffordshire, bookseller, attended Pembroke College, Oxford, in 1728 though he had to leave the next year for financial reasons. He taught school for two years after marrying Elizabeth Porter, a woman twenty years his senior. Johnson then moved to London to try to make his living as a writer. His earliest works included "London" (1739) and "The Vanity of Human Wishes" (1749), two satirically penetrating poems. He also published two short-lived periodicals, *The Rambler* (1750–1752) and *The Idler* (1758–1760).

Johnson's first major work was his *Dictionary of the English Language* (1755), the first adequate dictionary in English. His edition of Shakespeare, with the preface and notes (1765), continues to be one of the major critical interpretations of the great dramatist's art. In 1759 he published his only novel, *Rasselas*, a moral fable with an Afri-

can setting. His *Lives of the Poets* (1779–1781) were distinguished essays written to accompany new editions of their works. Despite his large output, Johnson lived close to poverty until the Earl of Bute granted him a pension of three hundred pounds in 1762.

In 1763 Johnson met James Boswell, a young Scot. That meeting proved to be one of the most fortunate encounters in English literature. *Boswell's Life of Johnson* (1791) is generally acclaimed one of the world's greatest biographies. The *Life* records in detail the words of Johnson, a brilliant conversationalist, and offers memorable portraits of many of the leading figures of the time.

In 1764, at the suggestion of Sir Joshua Reynolds, the painter, Johnson founded "The Club," which included Edmund Burke, Oliver Goldsmith, Edward Gibbon, David Garrick, and Fanny Burney. For the last twenty years of his life Johnson so dominated the literary tastes of London that the era is sometimes known as "The Age of Johnson."

Johnson, a faithful Anglican, was one of England's most pious writers. He acknowledged human sinfulness and the need for redemption through Christ. He readily confessed his failures, often speaking of his sloth. After his death his *Prayers and Meditations* (1785) were issued, revealing a continual self-searching and a touching humility of spirit. In his final illness he refused sedatives so that his soul might come unclouded into God's presence.
P. M. BECHTEL

JONES, BOB (1883–1968)
American evangelist; founder of Bob Jones University

Born in Dale County, Alabama, Jones as a boy practiced sermon delivery as he walked behind the mules plowing his father's farm. Having conducted revival meetings at the age of thirteen, he eventually became an internationally known evangelist.

Recognized as a "rugged fundamentalist," Jones opposed alcoholic beverages, card games, dancing, jazz, Hollywood movies, and casual close association of the sexes. He believed racial segregation to be a principle taught in the Bible. He strenuously worked against Alfred E. Smith in the 1928 United States presidential campaign, delivering more than a hundred speeches for Smith's Republican opponent, Herbert Hoover.

In 1927 Jones established his own institute of higher learning in Lynn Haven, Florida. Its intent, he said was to resist the "atheistic drift in educational institutions." In 1933, Bob Jones College moved to Cleveland, Tennessee, and in 1947 was relocated as a university in Greenville, South Carolina.

Bob Jones University has maintained its adherence to its founder's doctrinal and behavioral standards. Yet in carrying out Jones's belief that the message of atonement through Jesus Christ should be conveyed with a respectable image, the university has developed a large fine art collection and an impressive drama department. It also conducts an outstanding concert series. Though some of the school's alumni maintain its strict religious and cultural viewpoints in their mature years, other of Jones's "preacher boys" and female graduates have gone on to pursue careers in the Christian community that Jones would have regarded as "beyond the pale." P. VELTMAN

JONES, DAVID (1796–1841)

Congregational missionary to Hova; Bible translator

Born in Cardiganshire (Wales), Jones studied at a dissenting academy before going with Thomas Bevan to Madagascar in 1818. The London Missionary Society supported the two men. A tribal chief—Radama, king of the Hova—welcomed them to the island. Sadly, both their wives and two babies soon died; so also did Bevan.

In 1821 Jones married again. David Griffiths joined him as a colleague. Together they reduced the Hova language to writing. Jones educated the king's sons. Spelling books, catechisms, and the Gospel of Luke were soon available in Hova. The Malagasy people began to respond to the Christian message.

When Radama died (1828), Queen Ranavalona I, one of his four wives, ordered a severe persecution of the Christians. In 1830 the missionaries were expelled, leaving behind a complete text of the Hova Bible. Jones later returned but was placed under house arrest. He left once more and died in Mauritius. After his death the Hova Bible was printed and many natives accepted the gospel. P. TOON

JONES, ELI STANLEY (1884–1973)

Writer, world traveler, and missionary statesman

Jones was converted to Christianity at age seventeen, studied law, and worked in a Baltimore courthouse law library. His first attempt at preaching was a failure. He quit and walked away from the pulpit. While a student at Asbury College (Wilmore, Kentucky), he was "flooded by the Spirit" for four days. Out of that experience grew his call to missionary service. Jones left for India as a Methodist missionary in 1907. On arrival at Lucknow he was made pastor of Lal Bagh Church. He married Mabel Lossing, a teacher he met there.

After Jones had spent eight years in India, a ruptured appendix complicated by tetanus forced his first furlough. That development gave him a chance to think about the direction of his career as an evangelist to Indian intellectuals. Jones's strategy was to develop Christian *ashrams,* centers for meditation and community worship. The adaptation was so popular that the movement spread to the United States, where in 1940 an ashram was established in Saugatuck, Michigan.

Jones moved comfortably in prestigious circles. He was acquainted with Mahatma Gandhi, Jawaharlal Nehru, and Rabindranath Tagore. Just prior to Pearl Harbor he became involved in negotiations between Japanese envoys and President Franklin D. Roosevelt. He believed that war with Japan might have been averted had his plan been followed.

Jones was twice nominated for the Nobel Peace Prize, received seven honorary doctorates, and wrote twenty-nine books. His first and best-known title was *The Christ of the Indian Road*. His crusades took him around the world. He refused consecration as a Methodist bishop (1928), preferring the work of evangelism.

Jones held tenaciously to the uniqueness of Christ and the gospel, though his advocacy of church union offended many evangelicals, as did his view of Scripture. So intense was his focus on Christ that he considered the Old Testament "pre-Christian and sub-Christian." M. FACKLER

leader in the ecumenical movement. Second, in 1917 he helped found the American Friends Service Committee to relieve human suffering caused by natural and manmade catastrophes. Jones hoped the committee would serve as a Christian testimony of pacifism and love. He himself served twice as chairperson. Jones was especially active in attempts to feed starving European children after World War I and to aid Jewish refugees in the late 1930s.

R. D. SHUSTER

JONES, RUFUS MATTHEW (1863–1948)

Society of Friends' scholar, educator, and humanitarian

Jones was born in the rural community of South China, Maine. He was deeply impressed, as he grew up there, with the unity and simple Christianity of that community's Society of Friends. After graduating from the Quaker Haverford College in Pennsylvania in 1886 with an M.A. in American history, Jones spent six years studying and teaching in America and Europe.

Recorded as a minister in the Society of Friends in 1890, he returned to Haverford in 1893 to accept the joint appointment of instructor of philosophy and editor of the *Friends Review* (later *The American Friend*). He remained connected with the college until his death fifty-five years later. Through his students, his writings, and his life he became internationally recognized as a spokesman for Quakerism.

Jones's achievements as a scholar included his historical studies of the Society of Friends, studies that placed it within the larger context of Christian mysticism. Also among his fifty-four books and hundreds of articles were many works on mystical experience, a lifelong interest.

Jones had two major accomplishments besides his decades of teaching and counseling at Haverford. First, he helped bring together factions in his denomination by emphasizing the need for fellowship and by preparing a statement of beliefs that stressed unity. He was a theological liberal and a

JONES, SAMUEL PORTER (1847–1906)

Revivalist and temperance reformer

Born in Chambers County, Alabama, Jones moved with his family to Cartersville, Georgia in 1856. There in 1868 he married and began to practice law. Indulgence in alcohol ended his legal career, and he became a drifter until in 1872 he promised his dying father to become a teetotaler—a promise which he kept. Receiving a license to preach from the North Georgia Conference of the Methodist Episcopal Church South, he served several parishes until in 1880 he was made manager of the North Georgia Orphan Home in Decatur—a position in which he proved to be a successful money raiser. In 1884 he started evangelistic work in Memphis, Tennessee, and the next year he was engaged for similar work by Dr. T. de Witt Talmage of Brooklyn, New York. Until 1900 he was a national revivalist, conducting successful evangelistic missions in such large cities as Chicago, Cincinnati, and Baltimore, for three to six weeks at a time. After the turn of the century he concentrated his evangelistic efforts in the southern states, becoming known as "the Moody of the south." His emphasis was always practical: he attacked the typical vices of city life—especially alcohol, and gave full support to the Prohibition movement.

N. V. HOPE

JONES, THOMAS (1756–1820)

Calvinistic Methodist preacher and author

Born at Penucha, near Caerwys,

Flintshire, Wales, Jones attended school at nearby Holywell until he was fifteen. He was expected to attend the university and become a clergyman of the Church of England; but instead he joined the Methodists in 1772 and began to preach under their auspices in 1783. He supervised Methodist societies in Mold (1795–1804), Ruthin (1804–1806), and Denbigh (1806–1820); and in 1811 when his denomination finally broke with the Church of England, he was one of the first Calvinistic Methodists to be ordained for service in North Wales. In Ruthin he set up a printing establishment and began to translate into Welsh William Gurnall's *Christian in Full Armor,* a four-volume work he eventually completed in 1819. In 1801, along with his friend Thomas Charles of Bala, he drew up the *Rules and Designs of Welsh Methodists.* When the controversy over Arminianism broke out in 1808, Jones published a defense of moderate Calvinism entitled *The Theological Mirror.* That same year he issued a Welsh translation of the Larger Catechism of the Church of England. In Denbigh he wrote *History of the Martyrs,* completed in 1813; and the next year he published a small volume of hymns, some of which remained in vogue for many years.
N. V. HOPE

JOSEPHUS, FLAVIUS (37–c. 100)
Jewish military officer and historian

Josephus was born into an aristocratic priestly family in Jerusalem. Through his mother he was related to the Hasmonean dynasty. In his youth he was noted for his memory and ease in learning. As a teenager he attached himself to a member of an ascetic sect. Then he became a Pharisee.

In the year 64 Josephus was a member of an official party sent to Rome to secure the release of some priests. The empire's capital made an indelible impression on him. After his return to Jerusalem the Jewish war erupted (66). The Sanhedrin (the Jewish governing body) appointed Josephus commander of Galilee. He organized the province well but incurred the opposition of John of Giscala, Galilee's former leader.

Conflict between the two men's forces continued until the arrival of the Roman general Vespasian in the spring of 67.

Josephus and the Galileans entrenched themselves at Jotapata. After a siege of six weeks the Roman army captured and destroyed the city, but Josephus and forty soldiers escaped to a cave. Josephus, whose life was assured by the Romans through a friend's intervention, persuaded his fellow soldiers to kill each other rather than be captured. When only he and one other remained alive, he surrendered to the Romans.

When Josephus appeared before Vespasian and prophesied that Vespasian would become emperor, his life was spared. Nonetheless, Josephus was held prisoner. Vespasian was proclaimed emperor in the year 69 and Josephus was set free. He then adopted Vespasian's family name, "Flavius." In 70, when Vespasian's son Titus marched on Jerusalem, Josephus accompanied him. Several times Josephus tried unsuccessfully to persuade the Jews to surrender.

After Titus's destruction of Jerusalem, Josephus went to Rome where Vespasian favored him with Roman citizenship and a pension. Free to write, Josephus produced a number of books of considerable historical value. In *The Jewish War* (77–78) Josephus described Roman-Jewish conflict from the time of Antiochus Ephiphanes to slightly beyond the fall of Jerusalem. Perhaps Josephus' greatest work was *The Antiquities of the Jews* (c. 94), a twenty-volume work designed to glorify the Jews and eliminate Gentile hostility, traced Jewish history from the creation to the outbreak of war with Rome in 66. His autobiography, *Life,* was primarily a vindication of his activities as governor of Galilee. Josephus wrote *Against Apion* to counteract claims of anti-Semites, using logical arguments as well as derision.

As a historian, Josephus sometimes distorted facts in favor of his patrons. However, he was witness to many of the events about which he wrote. His works illumine the period in which the church came into existence—especially concerning the religion, politics, geography, and prominent persons of the early Christian era. Of particular interest to Christians are his references to John the Baptist, Jesus, and James the Just (Jesus' brother). C. W. HENSLEY

JOVINIAN (died c. 405)
Monk who attacked monastic celibacy

Although the book written by Jovinian is lost, its general content can be established from the writing against it of Jerome (c. 342–420), an early biblical scholar. Jovinian taught that marriage is equal to virginity in God's eyes. He also held that fasting is of no greater merit than eating with thanksgiving. In fact he said there is no scale of rewards in heaven. He taught, as did Helvidius, a fourth-century theologian, that Mary was not a perpetual virgin, but that she had other children by Joseph after Jesus' birth. He was able to show from Jerome's cynical letters that the church could not elevate virginity without at the same time degrading marriage.

Jovinian caused a stir in Rome. After his sermons, individuals who had formerly chosen virginity decided to marry. Augustine of Hippo (345–430) later tried to answer Jovinian with two books, the first on marriage and the second on virginity. Synods in Rome under Siricus (392), and in Milan under Ambrose (393), condemned Jovinian and his followers. J. NEWTON

JOWETT, BENJAMIN (1817–1893)
Master of Balliol College; liberal theologian

Born and educated in London, Jowett had a splendid academic career in classics at Balliol College, Oxford. In 1842 he became a tutor there and also entered holy orders. Beginning life as an evangelical, he was influenced by the Tractarians at Oxford before he came under the influence of German biblical scholars and the philosopher, George W. F. Hegel (1770–1831).

In 1855 Jowett published a critical edition of part of the apostle Paul's Epistles. Several essays in that volume revealed that he did not hold to Christian doctrine in the same way as most of his colleagues. Some viewed him as a heretic and therefore opposed his promotion to the professorship of Greek.

His opponents felt justified when Jowett published "On the Interpretation of Scripture" in *Essays and Reviews* (1860). The essay caused panic in the church because of its radical views. In 1870 he was elected master of Balliol and from then on much of his energy was directed into promoting college affairs and building programs.

Jowett also maintained his wider interests. The new University College at Bristol, for example, owed much to him for its creation. His translations of Plato's *Works* began to appear. Many people in government and the civil service sought his advice. But the strain of work took its toll, and after two serious illnesses he died. Jowett's fame rests on his critical judgments, which anticipated the views of New Testament scholars decades later. P. TOON

JOWETT, JOHN HENRY (1863–1923)
English Congregationalist preacher

Born at Halifax, Yorkshire, Jowett studied for the ministry at Airedale College, Bradford. From there he went to Edinburgh University where, apart from academic influence, he was spiritually moved by the preaching of Henry Drummond, a friend of D. L. Moody. Jowett's first pastorate was at Newcastle-on-Tyne, where he developed his powers of oratory.

From then on, Jowett lived to preach, concentrating all his energies on preaching and preparation for it. On the death of R. W. Dale in 1895 he was called to be minister of the famous Carr's Lane Chapel in Birmingham. By then a national figure, he chaired the congregational Union in 1906 and was made president of the National Council of Evangelical Free Churches in 1910–1911.

Following a holiday in the United States, when he preached at the Northfield Conference (founded by Moody) he was called to the pastorate of the Fifth Avenue Presbyterian Church in New York. The arrival in that city of the leading British preacher caused great interest. He remained there until near the end of World War I.

From Westminster Chapel, London, he received a call to succeed G. Campbell Morgan. The British prime minister urged him to

accept; President Woodrow Wilson urged him to stay in New York. Love for home prevailed, and he became minister of Westminster Chapel. His ministry there was short because of ill health, but he regarded it as a proper climax to his life as a preacher.
P. TOON

JUD, LEO (1482–1542)
Leader of the Reformed church in Zurich (Switzerland) after Ulrich Zwingli

Born in Germany near Alsace, Jud entered the University of Basel at the age of seventeen. There he came under the influence of Thomas Wyttenbach, who was lecturing on the apostle Paul's Epistle to the Romans. As a result of this experience, Jud gave his support to Zwingli when the latter began his reforming work in Zurich.

In 1510 Jud began to preach in St. Pilt, Alsace. In 1518 he succeeded Zwingli at Einsiedeln when the reformer moved to Zurich. Five years later Jud became pastor of St. Peter's in Zurich. At that time he also married a nun who had left the life of the convent.

As one of Zurich's pastors Jud collaborated with Zwingli in his discussions with both the Anabaptists and Lutherans, translating a number of Zwingli's works into German from Latin. After the Battle of Kappel (1532), in which Zwingli was killed, Jud became leader of the Reformed church in Zurich. However, because many blamed him for being one of the instigators of the war against the Forest Cantons, he lost his place of leadership to Henry Bullinger, whom (nonetheless) he supported loyally.

Opposed to compulsion in matters of religion, Jud worked hard for the union of the Reformed and Lutheran movements. He helped prepare the First Helvetic Confession, translated the Old Testament into Latin, prepared the Swiss-German version of the Prophets for the Zurich Bible, and wrote a number of German tracts and catechism.
W. S. REID

JUDSON, ADONIRAM (1788–1850)
Pioneer American missionary to Burma

Judson was born in a Congregationalist manse at Malden, Massachusetts, and graduated from Brown University. He studied for the ministry at Andover Seminary, where he became a member of a foreign mission interest group. As one of its leaders he played a key role in the establishment of the American Board of Commissioners for Foreign Missions in 1810. Appointed to India, he and his wife Ann sailed there in 1812.

Expecting to meet the English Baptists at Calcutta and Serampore, the two studied the subject of baptism on shipboard. They, along with Luther Rice, embraced the Baptist view, which severed their Congregationalist ties. Rice returned to the United States to call Baptists into a missionary organization (begun in 1814) while the Judsons went on to Rangoon (Burma).

Judson had the wisdom to discern that he had little chance of communicating the gospel unless he mastered the language and understood Theravada Buddhism, thereby obtaining a means of interacting with the people. Although he was head of the mission that soon made great headway among the Karens, Kachins, and other tribal peoples, he himself was not drawn to those tribes. Instead he spent his whole life in a difficult witness to the politically and culturally dominant Burmans. He learned their language thoroughly, produced a dictionary, translated the Bible, and composed much literature. Judson engaged in public preaching and learned to sit in an open-air pavilion conversing leisurely with inquirers, especially Buddhist monks.

Judson was not inclined to establish schools. Rather, he trained evangelists and pastors informally. Unlike most Protestant missionaries of the time, he was not interested in propagating European-American civilization and using it as a weapon against Buddhism. He had no illusions about the difficulty of presenting a theistic religion to atheistic Theravada Buddhists, but he dared to hope that the countless pagodas would one day be matched by church spires.

Because the early years of Judson's ministry occurred at a time when the British were trying to establish control over the native

Burmese kingdom, he was caught up in warfare. The Burmans did not distinguish between a Briton and an American, and by moving from Rangoon to the capital, Ava, Judson became the object of suspicion. He was imprisoned under dreadful conditions and barely escaped death. Ann remained with him and attended to him daily. Ann died in 1826 and became the foremost missionary heroine of the American people. Later Judson married Sarah Boardman, widow of another Baptist pioneer. After her death he married Emily Chubbuck, a novelist, while on his only furlough in America. Later, he died during a sea voyage.
P. BEAVER

JULIAN THE APOSTATE (332–363)
Roman emperor who was committed to a revival of paganism

Born in Constantinople, Julian was the nephew of Emperor Constantine (reigned 311–337) and the cousin of Emperor Constantius (reigned 337–361). He was carefully reared by Constantius, who sought to convince him of the truth of Christianity.

Julian seemed to conform to the faith, but in reality he was more deeply influenced by Neoplatonism. The designation "the Apostate" referred to his eventual abandonment of Christian faith. When he became emperor in 361, as Flavius Claudius Julianus, he hoped to strengthen the Roman Empire by restoring the traditional religion. He repaired and reopened temples to the old classical gods in order to encourage people to return to the ancient forms of worship. He had the pagan religion taught in the empire's schools and wrote treatises defending it. He reserved the best government posts for non-Christians.

Julian sought to reverse the inroads Christianity had made within the empire. Although he did not openly persecute Christians, he tried to make life difficult for them. He ended all the legal and financial privileges that previous emperors had given to Christians, and he took opportunity to reward apostasy. His most famous work, *Against the Galileans*, was an attack on Christianity.

Julian ordered all exiled bishops to return to their dioceses, seeking in that way to create dissension in the church and to weaken Christianity internally. One bishop who returned under Julian's order was Athanasius of Alexandria. Athanasius, however, became so effective in converting pagans to Christianity that Julian soon exiled him again.

Julian died while leading an unsuccessful war against Persia. He sought the guidance of the pagan gods in the war, hoping to win a victory that would vindicate his religious views. W. R. GODFREY

JULIAN OF NORWICH
(c. 1342–c. 1413)
English writer on mystical experience

Almost nothing is known about Julian, but reliable tradition associates her with St. Julian's church, Norwich, near which she lived a solitary life of prayer and meditation. Her fame rests on her book *The Sixteen Revelations of Divine Love*, which she wrote in 1393. She claimed to have received fifteen revelations on one day in 1373 and another on the following day. In prolonged states of ecstasy, she saw visions of the sufferings of Christ and of the Trinity. She meditated on these visions for twenty years, concentrating on the love of God, which supplies the answer to all life's problems—and especially to the evil in the world. Her book contains both the original visions and her meditations on them.

Scholars hold that Julian of Norwich was influenced by a famous book on mystical experience, *The Cloud of Unknowing*, as well as by Neoplatonic philosophy. She summed up her doctrine of God in these words: "And I saw full surely that ere God made us He loved us; which love was never slacked nor ever shall be. And in this love He hath done all His works, and in this love He hath made all things profitable to us, and in this love our life is everlasting." P. TOON

JÜLICHER, ADOLF (1867–1938)
German biblical scholar

Born at Falkenberg, Jülicher was a pastor at Rummelsburg near Berlin before becoming a professor. He remained professor of theology at Marburg University from 1889 to 1923. His fame rests primarily on two influential books. The first, *Die Gleichnisreden Jesu* (*The Parables of Jesus*), was published in two volumes in 1888 and 1889. The book argued that parables convey one basic point and are not allegories. The second, *Die Einleitung in das Neue Testament* (1894), appeared in English as *Introduction to the New Testament* in 1904. That volume, widely used as a textbook, gave a careful statement of the critical theories of New Testament scholarship. Jülicher also wrote *Paulus und Jesus* (1907). In scholarly circles he was known for his work on the old Latin versions of the New Testament and for his interest in the early Latin Fathers. P. TOON

JULIUS II (1443–1513)
Pope, 1503–1513

Named Giulaino della Rovere, Julius began life as son of a poor but noble Italian family. He was educated and ordained among Franciscans in Perugia, Italy. In 1471, an uncle of his became Pope Sixtus IV. Soon Julius was made a cardinal, and thereafter, his life centered in varied roles at the papal court. In the years from 1480 to 1482, he served as papal legate to France's Louis XI, but after Sixtus IV died, he returned to Rome and became a confidant of Innocent VIII. When in 1492 his chief curial enemy, Rodrigo Borgia, was elected Pope Alexander VI, Julius fled to the court of France's Charles VIII.

Alexander VI's death in 1503 prompted Julius to return to Rome. And following Pius IV's short reign, he himself gained the papal office, largely by pledges favoring the cardinals' views on war, church reform, and an ecumenical council. But on election, Julius immediately retracted his promises and became immersed in efforts to enlarge the papacy's political power. His political aims now largely swallowed up western Europe's growing call for church reform. Austere, choleric in personality and bearing, proba-

bly no pope was better suited to Julius's aims, and by worldly standards his well-planned actions were highly successful. He was first able to regain former papal territories, and then to bring other parts of Italy, such as Venice, under papal domination. And notwithstanding France's help in defeating Venice, Julius also soon drove French forces out of Italy. Simultaneously, he also restructured the papacy's alliances by founding the Holy League. This was a coalition with Spain, Venice, and later England, primarily against France and the Holy Roman Empire. In 1511, France's Louis XII and the emperor, Maximillian, tried to depose Julius in an antipapal council at Pisa and Milan. But persuading Maximilian back to his side, the pope turned the tables through his own gathering, Lateran Council V, called ostensibly over the Church's deep reform needs. Lateran V did thwart France's efforts against Julius, but concerning the demand for church reformation, it took almost no effective action.

But however temporally minded his rule, Julius was a multi-faceted individual whose interests and activity ranged broadly. He was not disinclined toward genuine church reform, and he initiated many clerical reorganizations, including reconstruction of the papal curia and strict rules against simony. His papacy also instituted numerous improvements in monastic orders and was much involved with missionary work in the West Indies, India, and Africa. Despite his preoccupation with politics, Julius probably is most remembered as one of the papacy's greatest patrons of fine art. It was he who recognized and employed the genius of Raphael and Michelangelo, and also Bramante, and other superlative artists of the Italian Renaissance. Julius's patronage underwrote Raphael's Vatican frescoes and Michelangelo's paintings on the Sistine Chapel. He also laid the cornerstone for the modern rebuilding of St. Peter's Cathedral in Rome.

Lists of original sources concerned with Julius II may be found in Pastor's *History of the Popes*, volume six. Brosch's *Papst Julius II* provides other information about source materials. K. J. BRYER

JULIUS AFRICANUS, SEXTUS
(born c. 160, died after 240)
First Christian scholar to write on subjects other than religion

Julius was born in Jerusalem and was well educated. In his younger years he traveled extensively, visiting various biblical sites. For a time he lived in Emmaus and eventually went as an ambassador from that city to Rome. He so impressed Emperor Alexander Severus with his learning that the emperor appointed him to build the library at the Pantheon.

Julius's most famous work was a five-volume world history, *Chronographia*. The complete manuscript has been lost, but fragments are preserved in the writings of Eusebius, an early church historian. Julius argued that the world was created fifty-five hundred years before Christ and would come to an end five hundred years after Christ's birth. His presentation was so powerful that the Neoplatonic philosopher Porphyry wrote to refute it.

Other writings reveal Julius's scholarship, antiquarian interests, and critical abilities. He prepared an impressive collection of miscellaneous writings ranging from military science to magic. He entered into debate with Origen, an early Christian theologian, on whether the story of Susanna was a genuine part of the Old Testament book of Daniel. Julius's linguistic insights caused him to argue correctly that the story had been written in Greek and could not have been part of Daniel's original work. W. R. GODFREY

JUNG, CARL GUSTAV (1875–1961)
Swiss psychiatrist; founder of analytical psychology

Born in Basel, the son of a clergyman, Jung studied medicine at the University of Basel and psychology in Paris. Jung was interested in natural science but also in religion, philosophy, and the human search for value and meaning. He decided to specialize in psychiatry. From 1907 to 1913 Jung was Sigmund Freud's friend and collaborator. Then Jung broke with Freud to found his own school of psychology.

The orientation of Jung's psychology differed fundamentally from Freud's psychoanalysis. Freud attributed supreme value to sexual release, but Jung found supreme value in the unifying experience of religion. Thus Freud tended to treat religious and emotional experience as an expression of a basic sexual drive whereas Jung interpreted sexuality itself as symbolic. Sex has religious significance, especially since it is a nonrational union of opposites.

Jung is best known for his theory of psychological types. He distinguished between an extroverted type of personality (which is sociable, outgoing, and optimistic) and an introverted type (which is withdrawn from external reality, less sociable, and more absorbed in its own inner life). In addition, he distinguished four functions of personality: sensation, thinking, feeling, and intuition. No person is ever a pure example of one of these types, but often one function is dominant.

Jung introduced the term *complex*. A complex is a collection of associations linked by the same feeling-tone. The personal "unconscious" consists of complexes that have been repressed because they are too painful to acknowledge, and of perceptions of reality that have never made their way into consciousness. Although each individual's unconscious is in part explainable by that person's own life history, some features common to every individual are derived from a "collective unconscious." The collective unconscious contains certain archetypes, or inherited tendencies of psychic functioning.

Although Jung accepted Freud's opinion that many neuroses arise out of repressed sexuality and Alfred Adler's view that other neuroses stem from an unrecognized will to exercise power, Jung felt that behind those causes were more fundamental causes of a religious dimension. He taught that human beings need religious beliefs and experiences; in religious form people are able to encounter and accept the contents of the collective unconscious. Thus Jung argued for the usefulness of religious beliefs, although he recognized that scientifically most religious beliefs cannot be shown to be either true or false. A. Vos

JURIEU, PIERRE (1637–1713)
Leading Huguenot theologian

Jurieu, the grandson of Pierre du Moulin (1568–1658), was born at Mer in the dioceses of Blois. He studied philosophy at the Huguenot academy in Saumur. Theological studies took him to Sedan, where a Protestant academy existed. Later he heard theological teachers in the Netherlands and England, where Reformed theology flourished in the seventeenth century.

After ordination Jurieu returned to Mer. He served as pastor of the Reformed congregation there between 1660 and 1674. From 1674 to 1681 he was professor of Hebrew at Sedan. In 1681 he was appointed professor and pastor in Rotterdam, where he remained until his death.

When the Edict of Nantes (which had granted religious and political freedom to French Protestants) was suspended in 1685, Jurieu threw all his strength into the defense of his persecuted Huguenot brethren. He enlisted the aid of William of Orange for this cause. On behalf of the Huguenots, Jurieu wrote several books, among which were *Reflections on the Cruel Persecutions Suffered by the Reformed Church in France* (1685) and *Pastoral Letters to the Faithful in France* (1686–1689).

Jurieu vigorously attacked Roman Catholic theologians such as Antoine Arnauld, Jacques Bossuet, and Louis Maimbourg. Meanwhile, he actively sought unity with Lutherans on the basis of the Fundamental Articles. Jurieu also opposed the Arminians and Socinians, as well as the moderate Protestant theologians such as Pierre Bayle and Jacques Basnage. He likewise rejected the extreme view on predestination of Claude Pajon at Saumur. W. A. DETZLER

JUSTIN MARTYR (c. 100–165)
Early Christian writer and martyr

Of Greek parents, Justin was born in Palestine near the modern city of Nablus in Samaria. He went to Ephesus and studied the philosophies of the time, especially Platonism. Although deeply impressed by the death of Christian martyrs, he was actually converted (as he himself related) by a humble old Christian. For awhile he taught Christian philosophy at Ephesus, but left in 135 and went to Rome, where he taught and wrote until he was martyred under Marcus Aurelius.

Only two or three of his treatises are still extant: his first *Apology* (the second may not be authentic) and his *Dialogue with Trypho*. The *Apology* was addressed to Emperor Antoninus Pius (adoptive father of Marcus Aurelius); the *Dialogue* was earlier. The *Dialogue* was a discussion with a Jewish rabbi (possibly the historical Rabbi Tarphon) about the superiority of Christianity over Judaism. The *Apologies* were defenses of Christianity presented to Roman authority. Justin was one of the first apologists striving to offer Christianity to the world of his day in the current Hellenistic modes of thought. He believed, as did Philo the Jew, that the pagan philosophers had studied and learned from the Old Testament. To him Christianity was Platonism and Stoicism corrected and completed by the Bible and by the Logos that enlightens everyone. He opposed the early Christian heresies of Gnostic origin, in particular Docetism, by standing for the historicity of Jesus. He also opposed Marcionism, which tried to separate Christianity from its Old Testament precedents. To Justin the culminating act of God was the Incarnation—when God became man. He remained within the early Palestinian tradition by his stress on the church as the true Israel and by his doctrine of the Millennium.

It is in Justin's writings that one first encounters, outside of Scripture, the teaching that Mary by her obedience reversed the effects of Eve's disobedience. And it is from his first *Apology* that the church has its first description, apart from Scripture, of early Christian worship. He also gave evidence of the emerging canon of the New Testament. A. CABANISS

JUSTINIAN I (482–565)

Byzantine emperor (ruled 527–565); known especially for revising the Roman law codes

Born in Tauresium in eastern Illyricum, Justinian was reared in the Orthodox Christian tradition and received an excellent education in Constantinople. He acquitted himself well as an administrator under Emperor Justin I, his uncle. Justin adopted Justinian and, on Justin's death, Justinian became the emperor.

Justinian was a highly energetic emperor. He hoped to restore political and religious unity in the East and West. He conquered the Vandals, destroyed the Ostrogoths, federated the Arab Kingdom, subdued the upper Nile, stabilized the Byzantine position on the Black Sea, reorganized Armenia, and conquered various peoples in the Balkans.

Justinian's religious activities were equally energetic. He pursued a strong policy of repression against nonbelievers, Jews, and heretics. His legislation against the pagans resulted in the closing of the University of Athens. He forbade the Jews to read the Old Testament in Hebrew. When his attempts to convert heretics failed, he persecuted them vigorously.

As emperor, Justinian was convinced that he held special authority over the church. He freely selected and deposed patriarchs and bishops. He created legislation for the clergy and even dictated to the pope. Believing that full power over the empire was his by divine right, he intended to exercise it for the empire's well-being and to spread the faith.

In 542 and 543 Justinian condemned the teaching of the church father Origen (c. 185–254), whose teaching was popular with Palestinian monks. The emperor's edict placed Origen himself under anathema, an action taken with the support of the bishops and Pope Vigilius.

Justinian also stepped into a major controversy that had festered since the Council of Chalcedon in 451. In the western part of the empire, church leaders generally accepted the doctrinal statement of the council that both a divine and a human nature coexist in Christ. In the East many, including Justinian's wife, Theodora, supported the Monophysites, who emphasized Christ's divine nature. Justinian tried to placate the Monophysites by condemning what came to be called the Three Chapters (sections from the writings of Theodore of Mopsuestia, Theodoret of Cyrrhus, and Ibas of Edessa). The emperor accused their writings of Nestorianism, a heresy (condemned in 431) that tended to split Christ into two distinct persons. The Council of Constantinople (553) upheld the Chalcedonian position but condemned the so-called Three Chapters. The whole incident proved fruitless, angering the Monophysites in the East and the pope in the West. The resulting schism between Rome and Constantinople lasted until 610.

Justinian actively commissioned the construction of churches. In Constantinople alone he supervised the building of twenty-five basilicas, including the famous cathedral Hagia Sophia (Holy Wisdom).

R. E. WEBBER

K

KAEHLER, CARL MARTIN AUGUST (1835–1912)

German Protestant Theologian

Born at Neuhausen near Königsberg in Prussia, Kaehler became an influential theologian. He studied law at Königsberg (1853–1854) and theology at Heidelberg (1854–1855), Halle (1855–1858), and Tübingen (1858–1859). After several junior appointments at Bonn and Halle, he became professor of systematic theology and New Testament exegesis at Halle in 1879. Here he stayed for the rest of his working life. His major work on theology, *Die Wissenschaft der Christlichen Lehre* (*The Knowledge of Christian Doctrine*, published in three volumes, 1883–1887, but never translated into English), developed justification by faith. He is best known in America for his *Der Sogenannte Historische Jesus und der Geschichtliche Biblische Christus* (1896), which appeared in part in 1964 as *The So-called Historical Jesus and the Historical Biblical Christ*. The translation of this book some seventy years after its original appearance reflects the continuing interest in the so-called problem of the relation of the historical Jesus and the Christ in whom we believe for salvation. Another book by Kaehler, on the history of German theology,

edited by his son, was published posthumously (1962). P. Toon

KAGAWA, TOYOHIKO (1888–1960)

Japanese evangelist and social reformer

Born in Kobe as an illegitimate child of a geisha, Kagawa's boyhood was lonely and bitter. During his high-school days in Shikoku, American missionaries led him to Christ. Though his conversion resulted in his being disinherited by his family, he decided nonetheless to go into the ministry. He studied at Meiji Gakuin College and later at Kobe Seminary, where he became seriously concerned about the needs of the underprivileged. In 1909, after recovering from tuberculosis, he moved into the slums in Kobe to work among the poor.

From 1914 to 1916 Kagawa studied at Princeton University and Seminary. On returning to Japan he devoted himself to improving social conditions. He founded the first labor union (1919), the first peasant union (1921), relief work at the time of the Kanto earthquake (1923), the Mission to Lepers (1925), the Consumers' Union (1927), and the Credit Co-operative (1928). From 1926 on he concerned himself more with the spiritual side of life by starting the Kingdom of God movement. In the following year he initiated a series of mass evangelistic campaigns called the Million Souls movement. After World War II he risked his health to continue his evangelistic work. He also became a leader of Japan's democratization and pacifist movement.

Kagawa was the author and translator of 169 books on religion, sociology, and science. His basic philosophy was stated in *The Cosmic Teleology* (1957), in which he interpreted the whole of human history as God-directed cosmic evolution overcoming cosmic evils. S. UDA

KANT, IMMANUEL (1724–1804)
German philosopher

A native of Königsberg, East Prussia, where he was educated, taught (from 1770), and lived his entire life, Kant was probably the most influential philosopher of modern times. He reacted against the mystical pietism in which he was reared, regarding it as an uncriticized superstition that could not be a substitute for morality. At the same time he grew dissatisfied with the Protestant scholasticism that constructed rationalistic proofs of God's existence and made theology into a deductive system. He contended that it violated the limits of reason and that its God was of little interest to faith. In place of pietism and rationalism, he argued that morality is not the basis and the meaning of religion and that true morality consists basically of an unbending sense of duty to moral law. By this and other emphases he contributed to the rise of theological liberalism in the nineteenth century.

To understand Kant's position and influence, it is necessary to start with his epistemology (theory of knowledge). Confronted by tendencies in mechanistic science that denied the freedom of the will and reduced religious faith to an intellectual acceptance of deism, Kant undertook in his *Critique of Pure Reason* (1781) to examine the nature and limitations of human knowledge. Whereas previous theories of knowledge had been either "dogmatic" in their knowledge claims or else "skeptical" about gaining any knowledge at all, Kant introduced a "critical" philosophy that scrutinized the logical bases of all human knowledge, that is, bases within the human mind.

Kant claimed that space and time are forms we impose on sense experience and that concepts like substance and causation are subjective categories we bring to all our judgments. Thus the scientific world of space-time substances and causal relations is only the way things appear to us, subjectively structured (the "phenomenal"), not necessarily the way things are in themselves (the "noumenal") apart from the observer. Science and the similar kinds of knowledge, Enlightenment philosophy claimed, tell us only about appearances and not about reality. Kant tried to show that we only create paradoxes and antinomies when we try to argue as Enlightenment philosophy did about either nature, man, or God. This is why the classic proofs for God's existence fail to be logically conclusive.

While Kant saved God and human values from the encroachments of science, he had to find another way of establishing the credibility of religion, human freedom, and morality. The role of reason, he said, is twofold: first, regulative, in that it assures us that the idea of God, for instance, is not self-contradictory; and second, postulational (theoretical or directional), in that it proposes what ideals are needed to fulfill our intellectual and moral expectations. Thus while we cannot logically demonstrate the existence of God or the immortality and freedom of the soul, we can know that these are not self-contradictory beliefs and that they are the most reasonable postulates, both for completing a philosophical worldview and in making sense out of moral duty.

In his *Critique of Practical Reason* (1788) Kant developed a moral argument for God, immortality, and freedom. The sense of moral duty, which is the universal and necessary principle in all moral judgments, presupposes the freedom to act out of duty rather than desire for happiness. And since duty and happiness are then not always conjoined in this life, it is necessary to postulate another life in which happiness does reward virtue, and a divine lawgiver and judge to guarantee that outcome. But God, immortality, and freedom are the presuppositions we uncover, not conclusions that we demonstrate. A. F. HOLMES

KARG-ELERT, SIGFRIED (1877–1933)
One of the greatest composers of organ music after J. S. Bach

Of his copious output, Karg-Elert (a German) is best remembered for his chorale improvisations, most of which were published in 1909. These organ compositions based on church hymns remain popular with congregations in Germany and in English-speaking countries. His music is characterized by inventiveness, energy, and color; brilliant harmony, and striking counterpoint; it is sometimes, however, distractingly flashy in its technique and bizarre in its registration (use of organ stops). A student and the professor (1919) at Leipzig Conservatory in Germany, Karg-Elert also composed notable works for violin, piano, and harmonium. A. L. HAYES

KEBLE, JOHN (1792–1866)
Church of England minister; coleader of the Oxford Movement; poet

Keble's early career centered in Oxford University. After compiling a brilliant undergraduate record, he became a tutor of Oriel College. Keble gained fame first as the author of what became a nineteenth-century devotional classic, *The Christian Year* (1827). His hymn verses, such as "Sun of My Soul, Thou Savior Dear," based on a Scripture passage from each day in the Church of England lectionary, won approval from evangelicals and other Christians.

During the 1820s Keble attracted the close friendship of three younger men, John Henry Newman, Richard Hurrell Froude, and Edward Bouverie Pusey, who shared his alarm over decreasing respect for the Church. In a sermon, "National Apostasy," before the university on July 14, 1833, Keble attacked doctrinal indifference and disrespect for the office of bishop. That formally began the Oxford Movement. Keble, how-

ever, lacked John Henry Newman's organizing drive. Keble largely served behind the scenes in advising and encouraging Newman and others.

In 1836 opposition to the Oxford Movement kept Keble from a coveted royal professorship, so Keble spent the rest of his life in rural ministries, chiefly in the parish of Hursley. There his personal devotional life, faithful visitation, catechizing of parishioners, and attentiveness to the Church services provided a model of the Oxford Movement's principles.

Throughout his life, Keble expressed dislike for the independent tendencies and principles of evangelicals. His main conflicts, though, were with the growing liberal, or Broad Church, party. Keble College at Oxford was founded as a memorial to him. D. MUNSON

KEIL, JOHAN KARL FRIEDRICH (1807–1888)
Lutheran biblical scholar

Born at Lauterbach in Saxony (Germany), Keil studied at the Universities of Dorpat and Berlin. In 1833 he was appointed to the theological faculty at Dorpat, laboring there for twenty-five years as teacher of Old Testament and New Testament exegesis and oriental languages and helping to train young men for the Lutheran ministry. In 1859 he settled in Leipzig, where he devoted himself to writing and to the practical programs of the Lutheran church, especially its missionary work. In 1887 he moved to Rodlitz in Saxony, where he died.

His theological viewpoint was one of Lutheran orthodoxy, after the pattern of his conservative master Ernst Wilhelm Hangstenberg (1802–1869). Keil was a voluminous author, his major work being *Biblical Commentary on the Old Testament,* which he jointly coauthored with Franz Delitzsch between 1861 and 1875. To this work Keil contributed commentaries on all the books of the Old Testament from Genesis to Esther inclusive, and on Jeremiah, Ezekiel, Daniel, and the Minor Prophets. He also published commentaries on the apocryphal books of Maccabees (1875), the four Gospels (1877–1881), Peter and Jude (1883), and Hebrews (1885). Keil was also interested in biblical archaeology, on which he wrote a *Handbook* (1858–1859, second edition 1875). N. V. HOPE

KEITH-FALCONER, ION GRANT NEVILLE (1856–1887)
Arabic scholar and missionary

Born in Edinburgh, son of an evangelical Scottish earl, Keith-Falconer distinguished himself at Cambridge, where he taught Hebrew and was later appointed to a nominal chair of Arabic (it called for only one lecture annually). He also worked among the poor, was a nationally acclaimed cycling champion, and wrote the entry on shorthand for *Encyclopedia Britannica*.

His attention directed to Africa by David Livingstone, Keith-Falconer visited Aden and saw its strategic position as a point of communication with the interior of the continent. In 1886, at his own expense but recognized by the Free Church of Scotland, he and his wife established at Sheikh Othman a mission and hospital. Only a few weeks later he had an attack of Aden fever. After successive recurrences, aggravated by primitive living conditions, Keith-Falconer died in May 1887. J. D. DOUGLAS

KELLY, THOMAS (1769–1855)
Hymn writer and preacher

Kelly was born to a socially and politically important family, his father being a judge of the Irish Court of Common Pleas. Educated at some of the best schools in Ireland, he began to study law in London in accordance with his father's wishes. His own nature, however, was more inclined to the ministry. After reading some of the works of evangelist William Romaine (1714–1795), he was converted and felt a call to preach. He was ordained a priest in the Anglican Church in 1792.

Returning to Ireland Kelly drew large crowds with his gospel messages. But the clergy of Dublin, including the archbishop,

became hostile. Kelly eventually left the Anglican Church and, using his own and his wife's great wealth, built churches to preach in.

Kelly's greatest influence probably came through his 765 hymns, which were popular in the British Isles and America. They have continued to be sung long after his death. Among the best known are "Look, Ye Saints! The Sight Is Glorious"; "The Head That Once Was Crowned with Thorns"; "Ground of My Hope, the Cross Appears"; "Come See the Place Where Jesus Lay"; and "We Sing the Praise of Him Who Died." Kelly's musical works were distinguished by an orthodox, joyful theology and the use of unusual meters. R. D. SHUSTER

KELLY, WILLIAM (1821–1906)
Plymouth Brethren leader

Kelly was born in Ulster and educated at Trinity College, Dublin. Although at one time he was attracted by the Anglican Tractarian movement, he decided in 1841 to join the new Brethren movement instead. Later he became friends with John Nelson Darby (1800–1882) and edited his writings (thirty-four volumes, 1867–1883). From 1844 to 1871 he lived in Guernsey, and from 1871 to 1906 in Blackheath, Kent.

As an editor and writer Kelly exercised a wide influence. He edited *The Prospect* (1848–1850) and *The Bible Treasury* (1857–1906). Some of his books were on prophetic subjects, including a commentary on the Greek text of Revelation. He also published studies of Matthew, John, and the books of Moses. Just before his death he gave his library of fifteen thousand volumes to the town of Middlesborough.

In theology Kelly had views similar to J. N. Darby's. He helped popularize the dispensationalist doctrine of the premillennial advent of Christ. Kelly was also an opponent of higher critical views of the Bible, readily engaging in controversy to resist them. P. TOON

KEMPIS, THOMAS À
See THOMAS À KEMPIS

KEN, THOMAS (1637–1711)
Bishop of Bath and Wells (England); hymn writer

Born in Hertfordshire, Ken lost his parents early in life. He attended Winchester School and Hart Hall, Oxford. Ordained into the ministry of the Church of England, he held a series of appointments, including a position at Winchester School and Cathedral. For the boys there he wrote many devotional pieces, among them the hymns "Awake, My Soul, and with the Sun" and "Glory to Thee, My God, This Night."

In 1679 Ken was appointed chaplain to Charles II's sister, Mary, wife of William II, the prince of Orange. He resided at The Hague and performed his difficult task honorably. In 1683, by then the king's chaplain, he refused the use of his house in Winchester to the royal mistress, Eleanor (Nell) Gwynne. The king respected Ken's principles and personally appointed him to the bishopric of Bath and Wells in 1684. Later Ken gave the king the last rites.

In the troubles surrounding the short reign of James II and the arrival in England of William and Mary, Ken stood by his principles and lost his bishopric. He became a Non-juror but was not active for that cause. He lived a simple life as a celibate and died peacefully, affirming his commitment to the Catholic and Reformed Church of England. P. TOON

KENTIGERN (c. 518–603)
Apostle of the Strathclyde Britons

Illegitimate grandson of a semipagan British prince, Kentigern (otherwise Mungo) with his mother was baptized by a Christian pastor at Culross in Fife where Kentigern trained at the monastic school. He became a missionary to his own people, living in what is now Glasgow. Chosen as bishop, he suffered persecution from local heathen and finally moved to Wales. There he founded a monastery with nearly a thousand monks engaged in agriculture, education, and religious pursuits. The more experienced monks accompanied Kentigern on missionary travels. He traveled extensively, founding churches and ordaining clergy.

When in 573 the Christian party triumphed among North Britons, the king recalled Kentigern, who settled in Glasgow. Of that city he is the patron saint and in that city is the great church that bears his name and houses his tomb. J. D. DOUGLAS

KENYON, SIR FREDERICK GEORGE (1863–1952)
Greek manuscript scholar; chief librarian of the British Museum

Born in London, Kenyon studied at Winchester and New College, Oxford, where he joined the staff of the British Museum in 1889. Eventually he became director and chief librarian (1909–1930). His scholarly interests ranged from editing the poems of Bacchylides to writing several books on Robert and Elizabeth Barrett Browning. But his main work was on Greek papyri and, in particular, New Testament manuscripts. In that field he wrote *Our Bible and the Ancient Manuscripts* (1895; revised 1939), *A Handbook to the Textual Criticism of the New Testament* (1901), *Recent Developments in the Textual Criticism of the Greek Bible* (1933), *The Bible and Archeology* (1940), and *The Bible and Modern Scholarship* (1948). He used his expertise in the knowledge of ancient manuscripts to demonstrate the faithfulness of the text and historicity of the New Testament. N. HILLYER

KENYON, KATHLEEN (1906–1978)
Leading Palestinian archaeologist

Kenyon's contributions to the field of Palestinian studies include improved archaeological techniques, excavations at biblical sites, and several publications. She began her archaeological career with excavations at Zimbabwe, Rhodesia, in 1929. Subsequently she learned the craft of excavation under the tutelage of Sir Mortimer Wheeler at the Roman site of Verulamium in Britain.

Since she has made contributions to that technique herself, the technique presently used in Palestine is commonly called the Wheeler-Kenyon method.

Miss Kenyon held the post of secretary of the Institute of Archaeology at the University of London (1935–1948), when she became lecturer in Palestinian archaeology at the Institute. From 1951 to 1962 she was director of the British School of Archaeology in Jerusalem, and in 1962 she became principal of St. Hugh's College, Oxford. Miss Kenyon's major excavations were conducted at Jericho (1952–1958) and Jebusite Jerusalem (1961–1967). She also worked at Samaria, in Tripolitania, and at various sites in England.

Her publications concerning Palestinian archaeology include *Beginning in Archaeology* (1952), *Digging up Jericho* (1957), *Archaeology in the Holy Land* (1960), *Amorites and Canaanites* (1966), *Jerusalem: Excavating 3,000 Years of History* (1967), and *Royal Cities of the Old Testament* (1971).
H. F. VOS

KEPLER, JOHANNES (1571–1630)
German mathematician and astronomer

Trained in Lutheran theology at Tübingen (Germany), Kepler received his degree in 1591. At the university he learned the new Copernican astronomy. In 1594 he went to teach mathematics in Graz (Austria), after which he worked in Prague with the Danish astronomer Tycho Brahe. On Brahe's death, Kepler succeeded him as imperial mathematician.

Kepler was the formulator of several laws of planetary motion: (1) planets move in ellipses with the center of the sun as one focus; (2) the radius vector moves equal areas in equal times; and (3) the square of the revolution of a planet is in proportion to the cube of its mean distance from the sun.

Kepler stood within the Christian tradition but held to nonorthodox views derived from the Neoplatonists. For him, the universe was an expression of God's being rather than being God's creation. Kepler proposed an ingenious explanation for the star

that led the magi to Bethlehem. His calculations placed the event in 6 B.C., when several planets were in unusual conjunction.
A. CABANISS

KIDD, BERESFORD JAMES (1864–1948)
English Anglo-Catholic clergyman; best known as a church historian

Educated at Keble College, Oxford, Kidd remained in that city until his retirement. After ordination he held both pastoral and academic posts, as tutor in theology at Pembroke College (1902–1911) and vicar of St. Paul's Church (1904–1920). In 1920 he became head of Keble College. He remained in that position for nineteen years.

Among his publications were *A History of the Church to* A.D. *461* (three volumes, 1933), *The Roman Primacy to* A.D. *461* (1936), and various collections of documents for students of church history—for example, *Of the Continental Reformation* (1911) and the general *History of the Church* (two volumes, 1923). His theological books included an exposition of the *Thirty-Nine Articles* (two volumes, 1909) and *The Later Medieval Doctrine of Eucharistic Sacrifice* (1898, reprinted 1958). P. TOON

KIERKEGAARD, SØREN AABYE (1813–1855)
Danish Christian philosopher and author

Within the fourteen large volumes that make up Kierkegaard's collected published writings (Danish edition) can be found works that fall under the categories of literature, philosophy, and theology, plus a large volume of writings that are sermonic or devotional in form, but which the author called "discourses," since he was not ordained to preach. His authorship culminated in an open attack on the state church in Denmark, waged in newspapers and pamphlets.

Kierkegaard was reared in the wealthy home of Michael Pedersen Kierkegaard, who was a devout but strict father. There he absorbed Lutheran orthodoxy, laced with a strong pietistic influence. Kierkegaard was an extremely reflective person, who from an early age struggled with feelings of guilt and depression. The causes for this seemed to stem in large measure from his relationship with his father, who also struggled with guilt and what was then termed "melancholy." This was aggravated by a series of deaths in the family: five of Søren's brothers and sisters died within a relatively short time.

As a young man Kierkegaard became engaged to Regina Olsen and then broke the engagement, partly because he felt he was unfit for marriage. He continued to love the girl, however, and interpreted his sacrifice as religious in character. This experience marked the beginning of his "authorship," much of which concerned the necessity of "dying to self"—acquiring a willingness to sacrifice any earthly good if necessary—in order to achieve a genuine "God-relationship." One other external event also shaped his work: a conflict with the *Corsair,* a Danish satirical magazine, in which Kierkegaard became convinced that "the crowd is untruth." The person who wishes to stand firm for the truth must be prepared to be "the individual" who does not fear the laughter nor seek the praise of the public.

Kierkegaard's authorship is an attempt to help the individual acquire the inward personal concern or "subjectivity" he believed was essential to becoming a true Christian. He saw Christianity as the final and most adequate answer to the question, How should I exist? Basically, he believed there were three major ways of answering this question. These three answers made up what Kierkegaard termed three "spheres of existence" or "stages on life's way."

The first stage he termed the aesthetic stage; this is the life view in which a person is urged to enjoy life by developing his natural drives and abilities. The aesthete lives "for the moment." This life is symbolized by the casual love affair, and it culminates in despair.

The second stage is the ethical life—a life of duty and commitment, which is symbolized by marriage. A truly earnest attempt to live such a life culminates in the discovering

of a person's own moral shortcomings and therefore the recognition of guilt.

The final and highest stage is the religious, which involves a recognition that man is unable to become a whole person on his own and must seek the help of God. Kierkegaard saw Christianity as differing from all other religions, however, in that Christianity alone says that man is not even able to establish a relationship with God on his own. Since man is sinful, it was necessary for God to take the initiative by becoming a man himself.

Kierkegaard stressed that Christianity sees the Incarnation as an actual historical event; thus a Christian acquires salvation not through trying to live a moral life (as many liberal theologians who were Kierkegaard's contemporaries said) but through faith in the Jesus of history. Kierkegaard believed that God's loving self-sacrifice in Christ could not be understood by finite, sinful human beings. He thus opposed any attempts to philosophically understand the Incarnation or scientifically "prove" the truth of Christianity. For Kierkegaard, one becomes a Christian only through faith, which is produced by the consciousness of sin through the work of God. The Incarnation was and remains a "paradox" to human reason, which is only competent to ascertain its own incompetency with respect to the content of Christianity. For the proud man who will not acknowledge his sinful limits, the Incarnation will necessarily be an "offense."

A significant feature of Kierkegaard's authorship is his attempt to utilize "indirect communication." He believed that moral and religious truth could only be acquired by an individual through personal appropriation, unlike mathematical and scientific truth, which can be directly and "objectively" given by one person to another. To help stimulate his readers to concern themselves personally with the "three states on life's way," Kierkegaard wrote a series of books attributed to pseudonymous authors who actually embody the life views they represent. Thus, Kierkegaard's readers not only read about the aesthetic, ethical, and religious ways of life—they encounter these views and are forced to reflect about their own life.

When reading Kierkegaard it is important not to attribute all the opinions of these pseudonymous "characters" to Kierkegaard himself. Kierkegaard's own deepest beliefs are contained in the series of "discourses"— both in those he termed "edifying" and more especially in those he termed "Christian." The beginning reader of Kierkegaard is well advised to start with these latter sorts of works, such as *Purity of Heart Is to Will One Thing* or *Works of Love,* before reading such pseudonymous works as *Either-Or* and *Fear and Trembling.*

Kierkegaard culminated his life with an attack on the Danish state church, which he saw as an embodiment of "Christendom." In Christendom, Christianity is abolished by being made into a triviality. Nobody can become a Christian because it is assumed that everybody is a Christian. Being a Christian has been reduced to being a "nice person" who conforms to the established human order. Kierkegaard saw his task as that of "reintroducing Christianity into Christendom" by helping his contemporaries see that being a Christian requires a radical, courageous decision to follow Christ. This is a decision that must be continually renewed and that may bring the individual into conflict with "the established order," which is permeated by worldly values. C. S. EVANS

KILHAM, ALEXANDER (1762–1798)
Founder of the "Methodist New Connexion"

Born at Epworth, Lincolnshire (England) of Methodist parents, Kilham joined the local Methodist society and became a preacher when he was twenty-five. At first he traveled as assistant to Robert C. Brackenbury, a rich man who had preached with John Wesley. In 1758 he became an official itinerant preacher, working in the Grimsby circuit.

After Wesley's death in 1791, Kilham became a leader of those Methodists who wanted their societies to become Protestant Dissenters, severing all relationships with the parish churches of the national church.

But he and his friends were a minority whose views the Methodist leaders opposed. The controversy led to Kilham's expulsion from the "Methodist Connexion" in 1796. With his sympathizers he began on August 9, 1797, the "Methodist New Connexion." The first society (using a Baptist chapel) met at Leeds. About five thousand people joined within the first year. Societies were eventually established in most towns in northern England. P. TOON

KIMBANGU, SIMON (1889–1951)
Zairian prophet and martyr-figure; founder of the Kimbanguist Church

Kimbangu, born in the Lower Congo, attended the English Baptist mission school at Ngombe Lutete. At twenty-six he was baptized and named Simon. He became a village teacher and catechist working under the Baptist mission.

In 1918 Kimbangu felt a strong sense of God's call to witness to his African brothers and sisters. He tried to escape the call, finally returning home. In April 1921, he felt an urge to pray for a sick woman nearby. She was healed. Kimbangu's reputation as a healer spread, causing great excitement in the region. Healings and "wonders" drew large, excited crowds.

Kimbangu attributed the healings to God's power, not his own, and called a group of "helpers" to join him in dealing with the crowds. Fearing nationalistic overtones and anticolonial feelings in the gatherings, the Belgians accused Kimbangu of inciting sedition. He escaped arrest, hiding with his followers for several months. In September 1921, he gave himself up. He was tried, flogged, and sentenced to death. Due to the intervention of Protestant missionaries and the Belgian king, his sentence was commuted to life imprisonment. He died a prisoner in Elizabethville. J. R. CRAWFORD

KING, MARTIN LUTHER, JR. (1929–1968)
America's most visible civil rights leader from 1955 until his assassination in April 1968

The son of a prominent black Baptist pastor in Atlanta, King studied at Morehouse College, Crozer Theological Seminary, and Boston University (Ph.D.) before becoming the pastor of the Drexler Avenue Baptist Church in Montgomery, Alabama. He vaulted into national prominence when he led the successful Montgomery bus boycott (1955–1956), which sought to end racial segregation on the city's public transportation. In 1957 King helped organize the Southern Christian Leadership Conference (SCLC), which rapidly became one of the foremost civil rights groups in the country. Most of its leaders were, like King, black Baptist ministers.

King was beyond question the most important Christian voice in the drive for civil rights since World War II. His prestige was at its height in the early and mid-1960s. He keynoted the massive march on Washington in August 1963 with his moving "I have a dream" speech, and he helped organize the well-publicized Selma-to-Montgomery march in the spring of 1965. The first of those events provided major support for the Civil Rights Act of 1964, the second for the Voter Registration Act of 1965. King was awarded the Nobel Peace Prize in 1964.

Toward the end of his life King's influence was somewhat in decline. His excursions into the North (Chicago, 1966, for example) cost him the support of those who saw civil rights as a strictly Southern problem. His criticism of the Vietnam War angered other Americans. He was caught in the ideological crossfire caused by the rioting in American cities. Some whites held King responsible for those outbursts because of his promotion of black civil rights. Some blacks felt King betrayed their cause by continuing to repudiate the use of violence to attain racial justice.

During the 1950s and 1960s King was a living example on American television screens of black preaching at its best. His speeches and writings drew heavily on the vocabulary provided by the rich reservoirs of black Christian history. His ideology was constructed on an evangelical realism about the nature of human evil and a scriptural

defense of nonviolence ("love your enemies"). In classic black fashion he made little distinction between spiritual and social problems involved in the civil rights struggle.

It was often hard to tell where the Christian substratum of his thought left off and the superstructure of his social theory began. Other influences on his thinking were the pacifism of Gandhi, the civil disobedience of Thoreau, the philosophical idealism he had studied at Boston University, and the American public faith in democratic equality.

King's books included *Stride Toward Freedom* (1958) and *Where Do We Go from Here: Chaos or Community?* (1967). M. A. NOLL

KINGSLEY, CHARLES (1819–1875)
English clergyman and novelist

Born in Devonshire, Kingsley studied at King's College, London, and at Cambridge. While serving as rector at Eversley in Hampshire, he published tracts urging Christian socialism. The tracts, concerned with improving the lot of the poor and working class, were written under the name "Pastor Lot." He developed his ideas most fully in two novels, *Yeast* (1848) and *Alton Locke* (1850), which vividly describe the poverty of the era. Kingsley did much to create a social consciousness in England, though he lacked the organizing ability to initiate a reform movement.

Kingsley also wrote other novels. *Hypatia* (1853) is a remarkably accurate historical novel picturing fifth-century Alexandria. Kingsley's most popular novel was *Westward Ho* (1855), an exciting adventure story of Elizabethan England. Some think the book is flawed by its anti–Roman Catholic tone. Also widely read was *Water Babies* (1863), a children's story about a chimney sweep's adventures.

Kingsley was one of the few Christians to commend *The Origin of Species* when it appeared in 1859. In the same year he was appointed chaplain to Queen Victoria. In 1860 he became professor of modern history at Cambridge, though he was not a scholar and not widely read in history. In 1863 Kingsley engaged in controversy with John Henry Newman, though he proved not to be the Catholic prelate's intellectual equal. Newman undertook to vindicate himself in *Apologia Pro Vita Sua,* one of the classic spiritual autobiographies. By his early fifties Kingsley had exhausted his energies through his many involvements.

P. M. BECHTEL

KITTEL, GERHARD (1888–1948)

German Protestant theological scholar

Kittel was born in Breslau. He taught successively at Kiel, Leipzig, Greifswald, Tübingen, and Vienna for thirty years (1913–1943). Because he contributed to anti-Semitic publications in the 1930s, the Allies imprisoned him after World War II. On his release he was received by the Benedictine abbey of Beuron.

Kittel's great service was his work on the massive *Theologisches Worterbuch zum Neuen Testament* (*Theological Dictionary of the New Testament*—English translation by G. Bromiley in 1964–1974, nine volumes). He was both editor and contributor. The dictionary includes every major New Testament word and gives all of its appearances in secular and religious, classical and common dialect, Septuagint and New Testament literature. It stresses the New Testament's Jewish background, insisting that a Jewish interpretation should always prevail over a Hellenistic one. A. CABANISS

KNOX, JOHN (1514–1572)

Scottish reformer

Born in or near Haddington, East Lothian, Scotland, Knox was the son of a middle-class farmer. The Knoxes apparently held their lands from the earl of Bothwell whom Knox later acknowledged as his feudal superior. After school at Haddington, Knox probably attended St. Andrews University, studying under John Mair, one of the leading Scottish scholars of the day and also a strong advocate of the conciliar ideal for the government of the church. On graduation,

Knox took orders as a priest in the Catholic Church (1536), and apparently because of legal studies became a papal notary (1540). At the same time, while serving as a tutor to some landholders' sons, he came into contact with a number of Protestant families.

How or when Knox himself became a Protestant is not known, for he never reveals anything about his conversion, but it is known that it was by 1545. At that time a certain George Wishart, a Scot who had spent some time in Switzerland and England, returned to his native land where he began preaching the gospel. In January 1545, after preaching in other places, he came to East Lothian where Knox acted as his bodyguard, carrying a two-handed sword. Despite Wishart's acceptance by the local gentry, however, he was arrested by the earl of Bothwell and taken to St. Andrew's, where after a trial before Cardinal Beaton he was burned at the stake as a heretic in March 1546.

In May 1546, partially as a reprisal for the execution of Wishart but more because of a conflict with some of the local lairds, Cardinal Beaton was murdered in his castle of St. Andrews, which the assassins then continued to hold against the forces of the government. It was to St. Andrews Castle that Knox felt he had to go, since he was under some harassment by the ecclesiastical authorities because of his former support of Wishart. Entering the castle in April 1547 with his young charges, the sons of his employers, he not only continued to teach them but was soon called to become the minister of the garrison and also began to preach in one of the local churches, since the government's siege operations were not very rigorous. In this capacity he spoke out strongly against the Roman Catholic Church and also against the sinful lives of the castle's garrison.

Although the conspirators hoped that the English would come to their rescue, they were disappointed in this, for instead of an English fleet, a French fleet appeared in June 1547 and forced them to surrender. Knox and the garrison were then carried to France where the gentlemen were imprisoned in Rouen and Mont St. Michel and the common individuals, such as Knox, were put in the naval galleys as slaves. But even while in this position Knox never lost hope, nor did he cease to occupy the position of a leader, as he kept in touch with the various lairds in their prisons, presumably with the help of some of the French Protestants.

In March 1549 Knox and Alexander Clerk were released from the galley *Notre Dame,* probably through the influence of England, now ruled by the Protestant Edward VI. Knox was placed in Berwick-on-Tweed as minister of the Protestant congregation, some of whom were Scottish Protestant refugees. In 1551 he was moved to Newcastle-on-Tyne where he became the first Protestant pastor. It was while in this position that he became acquainted with Elizabeth Bowes, wife of the captain of Norham Castle and mother of Marjorie, the woman who would become Knox's first wife. His answers to Mrs. Bowes's letters concerning her spiritual problems provide us with an intimate picture of the man himself and his spiritual struggles.

His conflicts, however, were not just within, but were also with various opponents who did not accept the Reformed or Calvinistic position he now adopted. In 1550 he had to defend his attacks upon the Roman doctrine of the Mass before Tunstall, bishop of Durham. His vigor in attacking such doctrines led in turn to his being removed by the earl of Northumberland, head of the English government to the south of England. Although offered a bishopric in Rochester and a parish in London, he refused both, but continued to act as a preacher against the Anabaptists. At the same time he came into disfavor with Archbishop Cranmer for his criticism of the liturgy of the Lord's Supper in the second Edwardian *Book of Common Prayer* and its requirement of kneeling to receive the elements.

In 1553 Edward VI died and was succeeded by his sister Mary, a staunch Roman Catholic. This brought the Reformation in England to a sudden halt, and within a short time Knox was back in France—this time as a refugee. While waiting in Dieppe to see

what would happen in England he wrote a number of open letters to the Protestants, urging them to stand firm. He then took a short tour through Switzerland and settled in Geneva to study under Calvin's direction.

Knox's stay in Geneva was not long, for he soon received a call from the English refugee congregation in Frankfurt am Main to be their pastor. Reluctantly he consented under pressure from Calvin but soon found himself in trouble owing to the insistence of the English refugees in Strasburg that his congregation should use the English prayer book. When he refused, the English had him expelled from Frankfurt. He returned to Geneva to be followed by some two hundred members of his former congregation who set up what has been called the first Puritan congregation with a confession and form of service somewhat different from the Anglican one. Knox was elected to be the pastor of this body.

In the meantime, however, he had departed to Scotland where he preached for some months until the Roman Catholic bishops prepared to have him arrested and his Genevan congregation called for his return. He therefore left for Geneva, taking with him his wife and his mother-in-law. He was not left in peace, however; the following year (1558) he received another summons to go back to Scotland. But when he arrived in Dieppe ready to board ship, he received another letter telling him not to come since Mary of Guise, the queen regent, seemed more favorable to the Protestant cause. Thoroughly annoyed at this change Knox wrote the nobles such a strongly worded letter that they felt obliged to organize themselves for the furtherance and protection of the Reformation in Scotland. They were known as the Lords of the Congregation of Jesus Christ. Knox followed this letter by a series of pamphlets calling upon the queen regent, the nobles, and the common people to reform the Scottish church. Finally he produced his most notorious pamphlet against female monarchy: *The First Blast of the Trumpet against the Monstrous Regiment of Women.* This made him many female enemies, including Elizabeth of England, who shortly afterwards succeeded her half sister Mary on the throne.

With the accession of Elizabeth, most of Knox's congregation left for home, and he could only follow suit. Since Elizabeth would not let him into England, he sailed directly to Scotland (1559) where he assumed a position of leadership in the movement for reform, becoming minister of St. Giles Church, Edinburgh, which had been taken over by the Protestant forces.

One of the major problems the Protestants faced at this time was the presence of French troops sent over to support the queen regent in her attempts to overcome the Lords of the Congregation. Finally, though, the English were prevailed upon to lend their assistance to the Protestants, and by the Treaty of Edinburgh the French withdrew. Almost immediately afterwards, the Scottish parliament met and abolished papal authority in Scotland, banned the Mass, and adopted a Reformed Confession of Faith largely designed by Knox.

This move, however, did not settle the question of religion in Scotland, for Protestants formed a small minority. Furthermore, many of the nobles had supported the Reformation more to obtain possession of church lands than to glorify God. The new church as established, therefore, soon found itself in serious difficulties financially. Queen Mary, who returned from France in 1561, was no help, for—hoping to restore Romanism in Scotland—she persuaded many of the nobles, even Protestants, to support her against the claims of the new church to the old church's lands. The result was a constant battle in which Knox took a leading part.

The period from 1561 to 1567 was one of constant conflict within the country, to a large extent due to Mary's willfulness and political ineptitude, with the final outcome her deposition, imprisonment, and eventual exile in England. She was succeeded by her son James VI, but a party led by William Maitland of Lethington and Sir William Kirkcaldy of the Grange kept up a guerrilla war, seeking to have her restored to the throne. Knox withstood them strongly, but

was eventually forced to retire to St. Andrews where he remained until 1572, returning to Edinburgh only shortly before his death.

Even before his death Knox was a figure of controversy, and he has continued to be such down to the present. He has been attacked personally, his *History of the Reformation in Scotland* has been criticized as mere propaganda, and his place in the Scottish Reformation has been belittled by many. But the fact that he incites such animosity as well as loyalty and that there have been so many works written about him in the last century and a half would seem to indicate that he was a man of influence who had a powerful impact on the development of the Scottish church. W. S. REID

KNOX, RONALD ARBUTHNOTT (1888–1957)
Roman Catholic priest and Bible translator

Son of the anglican bishop of Manchester (E. D. Knox), Ronald Knox was educated at Eton College and then Balliol College, Oxford. He won many prizes for his academic ability. He rejected his father's evangelicalism and adopted high-church views. After ordination he was a fellow and chaplain of Trinity College, Oxford. He vigorously opposed modernism and defended the Church of England as a true branch of the church of Christ (against Roman Catholic teaching).

During the First World War, however, Knox felt the need to join the Roman Catholic Church. Ordained a priest in 1917, he taught at St. Edmund's College, Ware, before becoming the chaplain to Roman Catholic students at Oxford University in 1926. He remained at Oxford until 1939.

Knox then set out to complete a longtime ambition, the translation of the Bible into modern English, a task the bishops encouraged him to do. Though delayed by duties he performed during World War II, he saw the whole Bible printed in 1949. Based on the Latin Vulgate, it was intended to be written in timeless English. Most people regarded it as a great achievement.

Another of Knox's books was *Enthusiasm*

(1950), which dealt with the phenomenon of individualistic religious experience. Knox gave his reasons for joining the Roman Catholic Church in *A Spiritual Aeneid* (1918). He also wrote many popular religious books and detective stories. P. TOON

KODÁLY, ZOLTÁN (1882–1967)
Hungarian composer and educator

Kodály, together with Béla Bartók, was one of the pioneer collectors of folk music. Hungarian folk songs, in particular, greatly influenced his style of composition. From that source he developed an effective and widely used method of teaching sight-singing. He wrote both vocal and instrumental music but was only incidentally a composer of sacred works. Nonetheless, one of his masterpieces was his *Psalmus Hungaricus* (1923) for soloist, chorus, and orchestra, based on Psalm 55. Kodály also wrote a setting of the Te Deum (1936), a mass, and a cantata entitled *Jesus and the Traders*. J. B. MACMILLAN

KRAEMER, HENDRICK (1888–1965)
Dutch linguist and missionary statesman

Born in Amsterdam, Kraemer earned doctorates from Leyden University in oriental languages and religions. In 1922 the Netherlands Bible Society sent him to Java on behalf of the Dutch Reformed Church to translate the Bible into the Indonesian language. He remained in Java until 1937, when he was appointed professor of history of religions at Leyden.

Kraemer proved to be anything but an ivory tower academician. During World War II he led opposition to the Nazis' plan to dispatch non-Aryan professors to concentration camps. Eventually he himself was interned (1942–1943).

Kraemer, a pioneer in thinking about Christianity's place in industry, business, and the professions, founded the Church in the World Institute at Driebergen. For the Third World Missionary Conference at Tambaran, India (1938), he produced a study guide that became famous as the book *The Christian Message in a Non-Christian World*. Stressing the uniqueness of the biblical message and the discontinuity between Christianity and other religions, it shocked liberal opinion of the day. He returned to the theme in *Religion and the Christian Faith* (1957). Another influential book, *A Theology of the Laity* (1958), stressed the importance of the vocation of ordinary Christians.

From 1946 to 1955, when he retired, Kraemer was first director of the Ecumenical Institute of the World Council of Churches at Bossey, near Geneva, Switzerland. N. HILLYER

KRAPF, JOHANN LUDWIG (1810–1881)
German pioneer missionary to East Africa

Born near Tübingen, Krapf studied at Basle Mission House. He served briefly as a Lutheran parish minister, then joined the Anglican Church Missionary Society, which sent him to Ethiopia in 1838. In 1840 he surveyed the Gallas, 8 million people untouched by the gospel.

After frustrating expulsions from his base in Ethiopia, Krapf established a mission site at Mombasa in 1844 from which he hoped to minister to the Gallas. At Mombasa his wife and newborn child died of fever. Krapf threw himself into language study and the exploration of East Africa. Johann Rebmann joined him in 1846. The two began work among the inland Wanika tribe.

Krapf returned to Germany in 1853 because of failing health. He produced vocabularies of six African languages and a Swahili New Testament, grammar, dictionary, and prayer book. He wrote *Travels, Researches, and Missionary Labors in East Africa* (1860). M. FACKLER

KRUMMACHER, FRIEDRICH WILHELM (1796–1868)
German Reformed pastor

Born at Moers near Dusseldorf, Krummacher studied theology at the Universities of Halle and Jena. In 1819 he became pastor of a Reformed church at Frankfurt. In 1823 he moved to a church at

Ruhrort, in the Ruhr Valley. Two years later he went to Gemarke in Wuppertal.

Krummacher's main pastoral success occurred in Elberfeld (Wuppertal), where he served a Reformed congregation from 1834 until 1847. Then he was called to Trinity Church in Berlin, where Schleiermacher had served as pastor from 1809 until his death in 1834. In 1853 Krummacher became chaplain to the royal court at Potsdam.

Krummacher took an active lead in the early years of the Evangelical Alliance. He was known as a powerful preacher and staunch opponent of rationalism. His most famous writing was *Elijah the Tishbite* (1826). W. A. DETZLER

KUENEN, ABRAHAM (1828–1891)
Dutch theologian

Born in Haarlem (the Netherlands), Kuenen studied at Leyden University, where he attracted his teachers' attention because of his aptitude for theological studies. From 1855 onward he served on the faculty at Leyden, variously in Old Testament, New Testament, and ethics. He developed a reputation as a liberal theologian. With K. H. Graf he introduced the "literary-historical school," elaborated on by Julius Wellhausen. He supported the thesis that the priestly code represents the latest contribution to the Pentateuch. An expert in the analysis of the structure of Hebrew poetry, he contributed to translations of the Bible for children and youth.

Although he was a spokesperson against the Dutch Reformed Church's Calvinistic doctrine, Kuenen frequently opposed the extreme positions of the liberal school. In 1882 he gave the Hibbert lectures, aimed toward "heterodox" anti-Trinitarians to encourage "the unfettered exercise of the rights of private judgment in matters of religion." He was an editor for the *Theologische Tijdscrift*. A major work was his *Historisch-Kritisch Onderzoek* (three volumes, 1861–1865). Kuenen's writings have appeared in Dutch, German, French, and English.
P. VELTMAN

KUHNAU, JOHANN (1660–1722)
Classical scholar; organist and composer

Kuhnau, composer Johann Sebastian Bach's immediate predecessor at St. Thomas Church and School in Leipzig, contributed to the development of the Lutheran church cantata, which Bach brought to its final stage of perfection. Kuhnau is credited with being the first to write pieces entitled *sonata* for keyboard instruments. He wrote a series of such works with descriptive biblical titles like "David and Goliath" and "Hezekiah's Illness and Recovery." J. B. MACMILLAN

KUYPER, ABRAHAM (1837–1920)
Theologian and statesman of the Netherlands

Widely recognized as historian, theologian, philosopher, writer, and professor-educator, Kuyper was born in Maassluis, the son of a State Church (Reformed) pastor, later to accompany his family to the university town of Leyden, where his father accepted a charge. In 1862 Kuyper was awarded the doctor of theology from Leyden University.

Having fully embraced orthodox Calvinism, Kuyper held pastorates in Utrecht, Amsterdam, and elsewhere. Prompted by his interest in the legitimacy of private schools, he became affiliated with the Anti-Revolutionary Party (opposition to godless revolution and support for the Word of God and its implications for life), ultimately becoming its head. He edited a weekly, *De Heraut* (*The Herald*), "for a free church and a free church school in a free land," as well as a daily party organ, *De Standaard* (*The Standard*).

Beginning in 1874, Kuyper served repeatedly as a member of one or the other of the two houses of the Netherlands' legislature. He continued to champion the recognition of private education (common and higher) by government. On October 20, 1880, through the work of Kuyper and cofounders, the Amsterdam Free University was opened, dedicated to a Calvinistic orientation, a tribute to Kuyper's persistence in striving for the right of private higher education in the Netherlands.

In 1886 he led the break from the State

Church, establishing the Reformed Churches in the Netherlands. Kampen became the seminary of the denomination. Kuyper's close association with Herman Bavinck, professor of systematic theology at the seminary, came during this period. In 1901 Kuyper became prime minister of his homeland, a position he held for four years.

Kuyper's copious writings include some 16,800 *Standard* editorials, nineteen major convention addresses, sermons, *Encyclopedia of Sacred Theology* (1898), *Calvinism* (1899), and *The Work of the Holy Spirit* (1900). P. VELTMAN

L

LACHMANN, KARL KONRAD FRIEDRICH WILHELM (1793–1851)

German philologist; considered the founder of modern textual criticism

Lachmann, who studied at Leipzig and Göttingen, became a professor at Friedrich Wilhelm University in Berlin in 1825. He developed guidelines by which more accurate texts of ancient literary works could be derived from existing manuscripts. He is best known for his textual studies of various Latin writers (such as Catullus and Lucretius) and of Homer's *Iliad*.

Lachmann's work in the New Testament was also significant, and in some ways more lasting. He applied to the New Testament the guidelines for textual criticism he had developed for other ancient literature. Lachmann published a new Greek text, which became the basis for the work of later textual critics like Tischendorf, Tregelles, Westcott and Hort. He published a smaller edition of his Greek Testament in 1831 and a more comprehensive Testament in two volumes between 1842–1850. Lachmann was the first scholar to propose (in 1835) that Mark was the earliest synoptic Gospel. J. N. AKERS

LACTANTIUS (c. 240–c. 320)

Christian apologist and historian; most frequently reported of the Latin Fathers of the Church

Very little is known about Lactantius's life. Born probably in North Africa, and said to have been a pupil of Arnobius, he was in mid-life appointed by the emperor Diocletian as a teacher of rhetoric in Nicomedia, the imperial capital. After Diocletian began to persecute Christians, Lactantius returned to the West about 305.

His *Divinae institutiones* (seven volumes, c. 304–313), his principal work, is hailed as the first systematic Latin account of the Christian attitude toward life. It combats polytheism as the basis of all errors, identifies the demons as the source of error, and exposes the frailty of philosophy. The latter part of the work discusses fundamental ethical ideas, the proper way of worshiping God, and immortality. Although he was later called the "Christian Cicero" by Pico della Mirandola, Lactantius's theology was considered somewhat superficial, perhaps because he became a Christian only in mature years. Other works of his that have survived include *De Ira Dei*, which upholds God's punitive justice, and *De Mortibus persecutorium*, a product of his last years, which is a valuable historical source, though criticized for having dwelt overmuch on the terrible fates of persecuting emperors. About 317

Lactantius evidently came out of retirement to tutor Crispus, son of the emperor Constantine. J. D. DOUGLAS

LAGRANGE, MARIE JOSEPH (1855–1938)
Roman Catholic biblical scholar

A priest of the Dominican order, Lagrange began the journal *Revue Biblique* (*International Biblical Review*) in 1892 to promote "critical" study of the Bible in the Roman Catholic Church. Two years earlier he had opened the École Pratique d'Études Bibliques (Practical College of Biblical Studies). In 1902 he was made a member of the Biblical Commission, founded by the pope, to guide the development of Roman Catholic study of Scripture. His commentaries on Mark (1911), Luke (1920), Matthew (1923), and John (1925) were widely used up to World War II. That work on the New Testament presented a change of direction from Lagrange's earlier interest in the Old Testament. F. M. Braun wrote a biography of Lagrange, which was published in English in 1963. P. TOON

LAKE, KIRSOPP (1872–1946)
Biblical scholar

Born at Southampton (England), Lake attended St. Paul's School, London, and Lincoln College, Oxford. After ordination into the Church of England he was curate of St. Mary the Virgin, Oxford, from 1897 to 1904. There he began his career as an academic writer, publishing *The Text of the New Testament* (1900).

For the next ten years Lake was professor of early Christian literature at the University of Leyden (Holland), where he wrote more books, including *The Historical Evidence for the Resurrection of Jesus Christ* (1907). In 1914 he crossed the Atlantic to become a professor at Harvard. He remained at that school until his retirement in 1938.

Perhaps Lake's greatest contribution to learning was the series of volumes he wrote with F. J. Foakes-Jackson entitled *The Beginnings of Christianity: Part 1; The Acts of the Apostles* (1920–1923). In the study of Christianity's origins and in New Testament textual criticism, Lake was a pioneer. P. TOON

LANFRANC (c. 1005–c. 1089)
Archbishop of Canterbury; church reformer

Born in Pavia (Italy), Lanfranc after practicing law set up a school at Avranches (Normandy) in 1039. Two years later he became a Benedictine at Bec. By 1045 he was prior. His brilliant teaching drew students from afar, including Ivo of Chartres, the future pope Alexander II, and Anselm, later to succeed Lanfranc at Bec and then at Canterbury.

Lanfranc at first condemned William of Normandy's marriage to a cousin, but in 1059 he traveled to Rome to secure a papal dispensation. William made Lanfranc abbot of Caen in 1063. After the conquest of England, William chose him to replace the deposed Stigand as archbishop of Canterbury (1070).

Lanfranc, warmly supported by the king, reorganized the English Church. He established the primacy of the archbishopric of Canterbury over York, called regular diocesan synods, appointed archdeacons, and prohibited simony. But replacing Saxons with Normans as abbots and bishops and discouraging clergy from marrying were unpopular measures. Lanfranc wisely moved several sees from smaller places to growing towns. He reformed monasteries and composed the standard constitutions for Benedictine houses in England. Lanfranc shared with Wulfstan the credit for suppressing the Bristol slave trade with Ireland.

As a theologian, Lanfranc is best known for his development of the doctrine of transubstantiation and his stand at the Council of Rome and Verceli (1050) against Berengar's views on the subject. He is also known for his subsequent treatise *Concerning the Body and Blood of Our Lord.* N. HILLYER

LANG, (WILLIAM) COSMO GORDON (1864–1945)
Church of England prelate

Born in Fyvie, Aberdeenshire, Scotland,

the son of a well-known Presbyterian minister, Lang was educated at the Universities of Glasgow and Oxford and studied for the English bar. Converting to Anglicanism and deciding to take holy orders, he was confirmed in 1889 and ordained deacon in 1890 and priest in 1891. From 1890 to 1893 he served as a curate in Leeds; from 1894 to 1896 he was vicar of St. Mary's, Oxford; and between 1896 and 1901 he was vicar of Portsea in Hampshire. In 1901 he was appointed suffragan bishop of Stepney in the diocese of London; in 1908 he was made archbishop of York; and in 1928 he succeeded Randall T. Davidson as archbishop of Canterbury, resigning in 1942. Lang played a significant role in the events that led to the abdication of King Edward VIII (the Duke of Windsor) in December, 1936. N. V. HOPE

LANGE, JOHANN PETER (1802–1884)
Evangelical theologian

Born in Prussia, Lange studied at Bonn University. After his ordination he pastored Reformed churches until 1841. He gained the theological world's attention through two publications. First, he wrote articles in *Evangelische Kirchenzeitung*. Appearing between 1830 and 1840, those articles revealed his commitment to orthodoxy. Second, he wrote a powerful criticism of the view of Jesus presented by D. F. Strauss in *Leben Jesu* (1835). Lange's book, published at Duisburg in 1836, was an attempt to show that the portrayal of Jesus in the Gospels is a reliable record and not, as Strauss held, "mythical."

In 1841 Lange became professor of theology at Zurich, a position originally offered to Strauss. His first major work at Zurich was *Leben Jesu nach den Evangelien* (five volumes, 1844–1847), translated into English in 1864 as *The Life of the Lord Jesus Christ*. In 1854 he succeeded I. A. Dorner as professor of dogmatics at Bonn.

Lange was a prolific author whose writings included hymns. His name is primarily known in America through the translation edited by Philip Schaff of his *Theologisch-homiletisches Bibelwerk* (twenty-five volumes, 1864–1874). That work, intended to help preachers prepare sermons, comments on the whole Bible. Lange's evangelicalism was of the school known as "Vermittlungstheologie," which attempted to combine the emphases of the Protestant Reformation with the proved achievements of modern science. P. TOON

LANGTON, STEPHEN (died 1228)
Greatest of the medieval archbishops of Canterbury

Educated at Paris University, Langton excelled as a student, then became a teacher and a prolific writer. Gifted at bringing the Bible's moral teaching before his readers, he commented on the entire Bible as well as on various theological books. He was probably responsible for the division of the Bible into chapters.

In 1206 Pope Innocent III, whom Langton had known in Paris, made him a cardinal. A year later the pope consecrated him as the archbishop of Canterbury. King John of England, however, did not agree with Innocent's decision, so Langton could not go to his cathedral until 1213. Langton's name appears on the Magna Carta as a counselor to the king, but he had previously supported the English barons in their desire for more freedom. In 1222 Langton guided the English church into accepting new rules at the Council of Oseney. P. TOON

LA SALLE, JEAN BAPTISTE DE (1651–1719)
Educational reformer; founder of the Brothers of the Christian Schools

Born in Reims, La Salle was educated at the local College des Bons Enfants, graduating in 1669. After studying in Paris at the Sorbonne and the Seminary of St. Sulpice, he was ordained priest in 1678. Becoming interested in the educational needs of the neglected poor, in 1679 he started a charity school in Reims and thereafter organized others in the surrounding area. Realizing the need for an adequate supply of trained and dedicated teachers for his schools, in 1684, along with twelve schoolmasters, he founded a lay order, the Brothers of the Christian Schools. In 1688 he moved his headquarters to Paris; in 1694 lifelong vows were introduced for members of the order; in 1705 Rouen became the headquarters of the movement; and in 1718 La Salle drew up for his order a definitive Rule, which was approved by Pope Benedict XIII in 1725. Before La Salle's death the Brothers had founded twenty-two communities in France and one in Rome; and though he had to contend with opposition from jealous members of other educational organizations, his movement took hold and expanded, until by 1950 it had 15,000 members and over 1,350 schools. La Salle's teachers used vernacular French instead of the traditional Latin in their classrooms, and the Christian faith was the inspiration of the whole program. Its purpose was described by La Salle as being that the children might "learn to live uprightly, be initiated into the mysteries of their religion, inspired by Christian maxims, and thus receive the education they require." La Salle wrote several books, among them *The Duties of a Christian* (three volumes, 1703), a simple exposition of Christian doctrine; and *The Conduct of Schools* (1720), a manual of practical pedagogy. He was canonized in 1900. N. V. HOPE

LASKI (A LASCO), JAN (1499–1560)
Polish reformer

Jan Laski the Younger (also called Johannes a Lasco) was helped by his uncle Jan Laski (the Elder), archbishop of Gniezno and primate of Poland, with his education and with obtaining ecclesiastical preferments. In 1521 he was ordained to the Roman Catholic priesthood and became dean of Gniezno. With his brother Jerome he traveled abroad for study and to represent his uncle on diplomatic missions. During this period he made the acquaintance of humanists such as Erasmus and reformers such as Zwingli and Oecolampadius. Returning to Poland in 1526 he was made bishop of Vezprem in Hungary, canon of Kraków, and royal secretary. In 1531 he resigned all his

benefices and went to Frankfurt am Main in Germany, but his reasons for doing so remain unclear. Some say that it was because he had become a Protestant, others that he did not wish to give up a woman whom he had secretly married.

At any rate, by 1543 he was in Emden where he accepted the Augsburg Confession and became the superintendent of the Lutheran churches of the Countess of Anna of Oldenburg. Here he established a church organization similar to that developed by Calvin in Geneva, with the clergy meeting each week between Easter and Michaelmas, in what was called the "coetus" or assembly. In 1548 he was forced out of this position by the Augsburg Interim of Charles V, and by 1550 he was in London as the superintendent of the churches of the strangers, which met in the Church of the Austin Friars and had German, Dutch, Belgian, and French congregations. Despite the opposition of Bishop Ridley, Laski was given a free hand in organizing his congregations and in formulating their liturgies, in all of which he clearly followed the Genevan model. Two of his friends in London were Bishop John Hooper, later martyred, and John Knox, the Scottish reformer.

When Mary Tudor, a staunch Roman Catholic, succeeded her brother, Edward VI, on the throne, Laski and his congregations were forced to leave for the Continent where they attempted to settle in Emden; but because of Laski's acceptance of Reformed theology the Lutheran authorities forbade this. As a result, the congregations were broken up and scattered. Laski himself, after some wandering in western Europe, returned to Poland in 1556 during a brief period of Protestant triumph, where he attended the Synod of Bzesc and ended his days as the superintendent of the Reformed churches of south Poland. W. S. REID

LASSO, ORLANDO DI (c. 1532–1594)
Roman Catholic composer

Known also as Orlandus Lassus, Lasso was born in Mons, probably in 1532. As a choir boy, he was kidnapped three times because of his beautiful voice, the third time being taken to Italy, where he served at different courts. In 1554 he came north to Antwerp, where some of his first compositions were published. Lasso was also active in France, but settled at the Bavarian court in Munich about 1557, where he remained for the rest of his life. He composed music with equal expertise for French, Italian, German, and Latin texts, and was the most versatile and international composer of his age.

Since he was Catholic, all of his church music is with Latin texts, although he composed some sacred pieces in the other languages mentioned, a few being based on Calvinistic psalms and Lutheran chorales. It is not surprising that he had a great influence on a number of Lutheran composers. Lasso wrote over fifty settings of the Mass, but it is among his great number of motets that his artistry is most evident. He set his texts with the utmost sensitivity to the meaning of the words. Ten years after his death, his sons published 516 motets under the title *Magnum Opus Musicum* (*Great Work of Music*). His total output considerably exceeds twelve hundred compositions. His settings of the seven *Penitential Psalms* (published in 1580) were particularly famous. His magnificent motet for double chorus drawn from Ecclesiastes 3 is especially notable, while *Tristis est* (Christ's words in Gethsemane) achieves the utmost poignancy. J. B. MACMILLAN

LATIMER, HUGH (c. 1485–1555)
Protestant Reformer and martyr

Son of a yeoman-farmer, Latimer was educated at Cambridge University, where he became a fellow of Clare Hall. He was ordained in 1510. Gifted as a speaker, he was licensed by the university to preach anywhere in the kingdom. At that stage of his life he wished to reform only obvious abuses; he was not a full-fledged Protestant. But soon, through the influence of the Protestant martyr Thomas Bilney (died 1531), he adopted Protestant views.

After Henry VIII severed links with Rome,

Latimer became one of his senior advisers. In 1535 he was made bishop of Worcester. Five years later he had to resign that bishopric because he was not able to sign the Six Articles (1539), which were designed to prevent the progress of Protestant doctrines. So until 1546 he lived quietly. He emerged into prominence at Edward VI's accession. His gifts as a preacher were then much appreciated. One of his famous series of sermons was "On the Plough," delivered at St. Paul's Cross, London, in 1547.

When Mary I, a Roman Catholic, became queen in 1553, Latimer was placed in the Tower of London. In 1554 he was taken with Thomas Cranmer and Nicholas Ridley to dispute with Roman Catholic theologians on the doctrine of the Mass. Because the three men refused to accept the medieval Roman doctrine, they were excommunicated and condemned to death. They were burned at the stake on October 16, 1555. The Martyrs Memorial in Oxford commemorates their martyrdom. P. TOON

LATOURETTE, KENNETH SCOTT
(1884–1968)
Church historian

Born in Oregon City, Oregon, Latourette was educated at Linfield College and Yale University. He received a Ph.D. from Yale in 1909. He served as a faculty member of Yale-in-China until illness forced him to return to the United States in 1912. After convalescing he taught at Reed College, Oregon (1914–1916), and Denison College, Granville, Ohio (1916–1921). In 1921 he went to Yale as professor of missions, becoming Sterling Professor in 1949. He retired from full-time teaching in 1953.

Latourette held several important offices. He was president of the American Society of Church History, president of the American Historical Association, president of Japan International Christian University, and president of the American Baptist Convention.

Latourette's major work was to teach and write church history, particularly the story of Christian missions. He published over three hundred articles and more than thirty books, which may be put into three categories: (1) works dealing with the Far East, especially China (in which he had an abiding interest after his sojourn there)—for example, *History of Christian Missions in China* (1929) and *A History of the Far East* (1946); (2) volumes describing the growth and spread of Christianity as a missionary movement—for example, *History of the Expansion of Christianity* (seven volumes, 1937–1945); (3) books dealing with "the entire spread of Christianity in all its phases and in its setting in the human scene"—for example, *A History of Christianity* (1953) and *Christianity in a Revolutionary Age* (five volumes, 1958–1962).

Latourette believed that Christianity has exerted a deep influence on the world through the ever-widening impact of Jesus on individuals. His interpretation has not won universal acceptance, but no one doubts that his work on the Christian missionary movement, particularly during what he called "the great century" (1815–1914), will be of lasting significance. Among his many honorary degrees was an Oxford University D.D. awarded him in 1947.
N. V. HOPE

LAUBACH, FRANK CHARLES
(1884–1970)
American missionary; apostle of literacy

Born in Benton, Pennsylvania, Laubach was educated at Princeton University (A.B. 1909), Union Theological Seminary, New York City (1911–1914), and Columbia University (M.A. and Ph.D., 1915). In 1915 he was sent by the American Board of Commissioners for Foreign Missions to Mindanao in the Philippines, and there he became interested in the Muslim Moros. He was transferred to Manila to teach in Union Theological Seminary, but in 1929 he returned to Mindanao and set up a program for teaching illiterates to read by phonetic symbols and pictures. He took as a slogan "Each one teach one," which meant that each illiterate, after learning to read, was expected to teach another. This work proved so successful that it was adopted elsewhere

in the Philippines and eventually was officially sponsored by the government. Laubach's literacy program grew so extensively that finally he had produced more than 300 primers in 235 languages covering 100 countries; and out of his efforts grew the Committee on World Literacy and Christian Literature of the Foreign Missions Conference of North America. All Laubach's efforts were undergirded and sustained by fervent prayer, which he regarded as "the mightiest force in the world." N. V. HOPE

LAUD, WILLIAM (1573–1645)
Controversial archbishop of Canterbury

Born at Reading, Berkshire, Laud studied at St. John's College, Oxford, where he became a fellow and was ordained. Reacting against the dominant Calvinism and Puritanism of his day, he adopted a high doctrine of the visible church and its means of grace. He stood fearlessly by his opinions.

After various church appointments Laud became president of St. John's in 1611. Since he desired to be involved in reform of the worship and maintenance of churches, he looked, too, for an ecclesiastical appointment. In 1616 he became dean of Gloucester Cathedral, in which role he initiated various reforms—to the annoyance of the clergy, whom he did not consult. He resigned the presidency of St. John's in 1621 when he was consecrated bishop of St. David's. (The Welsh church was then part of the English church.)

With the death of James I in 1625 and the accession of Charles I, Laud's dominance in English religion began. He used the royal power to advance his view of the English church as a halfway house between the church of Rome and the church of Geneva. In 1626 he became bishop of Bath and Wells, and two years later, bishop of London. As chancellor of Oxford University beginning in 1629 he was responsible for introducing much-needed reform of the statutes and discipline. In 1633 he became archbishop of Canterbury.

Laud opposed both Roman Catholics and Puritans, especially the latter, who looked on him as a disguised papist and an Arminian. When he attempted in 1637 to force a new prayer book on the Calvinistic Scottish Church, he met powerful opposition. Three years later English clergy opposed him when he tried to pass in convocation a church law requiring clergy to teach the divine right of kings and to promise never to change the current episcopal system of government.

As the Puritan revolution began, Laud was impeached by Parliament and put in the Tower of London in 1641. He was tried in 1644, found guilty of treason, and executed on January 10, 1645. Due to the inflamed passions of the time, he did not get a fair trial. He died as a symbol of the repudiation of Charles I's policies by Parliament and the people.

Seen through Puritan eyes Laud's career was a disaster. But it is possible to give credit for his insistence that churches be kept clean and tidy and that worship in them be dignified. He also worked to improve the Church's economic position. In doctrinal matters, Laud was more broad-minded than many of his critics realized. P. TOON

LAVIGERIE, CHARLES MARTIAL ALLEMAND, CARDINAL (1825–1892)
Roman Catholic missionary to Africa; founder of the White Fathers

Lavigerie was born in Bayonne. He became bishop of Nancy in 1863, archbishop of Algiers in 1866, and cardinal in 1882. In 1884 he was given the title of archbishop of Carthage and primate of Africa, with authority extending over Algeria, Tunisia, and the Sahara. Lavigerie had the vision of evangelizing the whole of Africa by spreading Christianity among both Muslims and pagans. For this purpose he founded the Society of Missionaries of our Lady of Africa (1868), and a corresponding order for women, the Congregation of Missionary Sisters (1869). The secular priests and lay brothers who made up the Society were soon known as the White Fathers on account of their clothes, an adaptation of Arab dress. They have lived in communities and have been bound by oath to lifelong service in the Society's work in Africa. The White Fathers do not take the usual vows of religious communities, except that of obedience to their superiors.

Beginning in Algeria and Tunisia, the first missionaries—after setbacks in the Sahara—spread their work rapidly through Uganda, Tanganyika (now Tanzania), Nyasaland (now Malawi), and parts of the Congo (now Zaire). Lavigerie taught his White Fathers to take four years in preparing African converts for baptism, and then to continue their training, some in trades and agriculture, and others for the priesthood. His life work had considerable influence in the abolition of slavery, secured great improvements in local agricultural methods, and contributed much to the scientific exploration of Africa. N. HILLYER

LAW, WILLIAM (1686–1761)
English devotional writer and mystic

Law was born at King's Cliffe, Northamptonshire, to a family of substantial means. He attended Emmanuel College, Cambridge, where he became a fellow. In 1712, a year after his ordination, he was awarded the M.A. degree following intensive study in the classics and philosophy. It was probably at this time that he began to read the early English mystics and became acquainted with classical devotional writers such as St. Francis de Sales and Thomas à Kempis.

When George I, the Hanoverian king, came to the throne, Law refused to take the oath of allegiance. In consequence he forfeited his fellowship at the university and lost permanently the right to preach in the Church of England. His action gave evidence of a sturdy commitment to conscience.

Little is known of Law's actions after that disappointment, but it is believed he went to London. In 1723 Law became attached to the Gibbon family in Putney, where he served as tutor to Edward Gibbon, father of the famous historian, and as chaplain to the household. With the elder Gibbon's death and the breakup of the household in 1737,

Law returned to his native King's Cliffe, where he remained for the rest of his life.

Law's first significant writing was *Three Letters to the Bishop of Bangor* (1717), an effective apologetic for orthodox Christianity. In *Practical Treatise Upon Christian Perfection* (1726) he laid down rules for achieving a life of piety. Law's reputation rests principally on *A Serious Call to a Devout and Holy Life* (1728). Law lived in the Enlightenment, when many secularists wanted to abandon the prayers of the church. He urged retaining the prayers and bringing people back to a rule of devotion. The first half of *A Serious Call* sets a standard for honoring God in outward affairs. The second half is a guide to prayer and the ordering of the interior life. Though Law's writings lack an emphasis on Christ's redemptive ministry, their insight into the devotional life influenced many evangelicals, such as George Whitefield and John Wesley. In his later years Law, together with Sarah Hutchinson and Hester Gibbon, founded a school and almshouses—evidence of Law's concept of piety. P. M. BECHTEL

LAWES, WILLIAM GEORGE (1839–1907)
London Missionary Society missionary to the Pacific Islands; Bible translator

Born at Aldermaston, Berkshire, England, Lawes started in business at Reading in 1853. In 1858 he began to think of missionary work. Being accepted by the London Missionary Society (LMS), he was trained at Bedford and in 1860 was ordained to the Congregational ministry. That year he was appointed as the first resident LMS missionary on the island of Niue (Savage Island), where he labored until 1872. There he translated the New Testament into the Niue language, completing it in 1870. He also trained native evangelists and promoted the industrial program of the mission. In 1872 he returned to England on furlough, and was appointed to the New Guinea mission, for which he sailed in 1874. Settling at Port Moresby, he reduced the Motu language to writing, pre-

pared a grammar, and completed the translation of the New Testament into this language by 1891. He also founded a training institution for New Guinea natives; and when this was moved to Vatorata in 1894, Lawes moved with it. That year Glasgow University conferred a Doctor of Divinity degree on him. In 1906 he retired to Sydney, New South Wales, Australia, where he died the next year. N. V. HOPE

LAWRENCE, BROTHER
See BROTHER LAWRENCE

LAWS, ROBERT (1851–1934)
Scottish pioneer missionary

Born in Aberdeen and apprenticed to his cabinet-maker father, Laws attended evening school and university classes. Later came study in arts, theology, and medicine; his aim was to follow in David Livingstone's footsteps. Ordained in 1875 in the United Presbyterian Church, he joined a Free Church expedition charged to found a mission in Central Africa to be named Livingstonia. After an eventful journey, a mission was established near remote Lake Nyasa. Laws, in charge from 1877, planned a series of mission stations at strategic lakeside and interior sites. He opened his first school in 1876; when he left Africa in 1927 there were over seven hundred primary schools plus facilities for further education in theology, medicine, agriculture, and technical subjects—and a Christian community of sixty thousand with thirteen ordained African pastors.

Robert Laws of Livingstonia was a clearsighted pioneer. His goal: a Bible-reading, self-governing, self-supporting, self-extending church, with schools staffed by African Christian teachers, as the basic evangelizing agency. He visited Canada, the United States, Germany, and Nigeria; was United Free Church of Scotland moderator in 1908; and served on the legislative council of Nyasaland (now Malawi). J. D. DOUGLAS

LAYARD, AUSTEN H. (1817–1894)
Pioneer excavator in Mesopotamia

Layard excavated at Nimrud (biblical Calah) and later Nineveh (1845–1857), where he discovered part of Ashurbanipal's great library. On his return to England he published *Nineveh and Its Remains,* one of the first archaeological best-sellers. The book did much to arouse public interest in Assyrian discoveries and encourage further excavation.

In 1849 and 1850 Layard went on a second expedition. He made soundings at Babylon, Borsippa, and Nippur. The antiquities he sent to England form the greater part of the Assyrian collection in the British Museum. Later Layard turned to politics and diplomacy, becoming a member of Parliament (1852), envoy extraordinary at Madrid (1869–1877), and ambassador at Constantinople (1877–1880). H. Vos

LAYNEZ, JAMES (1512–1565)
Founding member and second general of the Jesuits

Born in Almazan (Spain), Laynez studied philosophy and theology at Alcala between 1528 and 1533. He then moved to the University of Paris, where he met Ignatius of Loyola. In 1534 Laynez and five others took vows with Ignatius in the Church of Montmartre, Paris, to form the Society of Jesus. The group soon moved to Italy, where Laynez was appointed professor of scholastic theology at Rome. On Ignatius's death in 1556 he became vicar-general of the Jesuits and then general (1558). He had early demonstrated his formidable ability in crushing incipient Protestant movements in northern Italy.

Laynez gained an immense reputation in the Roman Catholic Church as a theologian and teacher. He played a decisive part in three sessions of the Council of Trent (1546, 1551, 1562–1563), particularly on the subjects of justification, the sacraments, penance, purgatory, and papal absolutism. N. HILLYER

LEE, ANN (1736–1784)
Founder of the "Shakers," a communalistic and celibate organization arising near

Manchester, England, about 1758 and later spreading to America

Lee was convinced by Quaker preachers that Christ's return was imminent. Placed in the jail of her native town, Manchester, for her own vigorous preaching, she received a vision ordaining herself as the "Second Pillar of the Church of God." Her followers held that Jesus had revealed the male principle of Christ, "Mother Ann" the female. With seven disciples, Lee came to America in 1774, where her teaching proved attractive to many caught up in the American revivals over the next seventy years. The first permanent settlement of the United Society of Believers in Christ's Second Coming (the Shakers' official name) was established in 1787 in New Lebanon, New York. By the Civil War the group numbered six thousand in nineteen communities. Lee, who had lost four infant children, left her husband in 1766 and then forbade sexual intercourse for her followers. She encouraged instead the frugality, communalism, millennialism, pacifism, vegetarianism, spiritualism, and industriousness that marked her followers and their communities. The group's name came from its ecstatic worship practices, which included shaking as well as singing, dancing, laughing, barking, and marching. M. A. NOLL

LEFÈVRE D'ÉTAPLES, JACQUES (FABER STAPULENSIS, JACOBUS) (1455–1536)
Humanist scholar who prepared the way for the Reformation in France

Lefèvre was born at Étaples in Picardy, took his master's and doctor's degrees at Paris, and was ordained to the priesthood. After a period in Italy, where he felt the influence of Pico della Mirandola, he returned to Paris as a teacher in 1492. He attracted many students, including William Farel, the future reformer of Geneva and Neuchatel.

Lefèvre's writings on Scripture created suspicion among the traditionalists. Two essays criticizing the Roman Church and showing some Lutheran sympathies brought down on him the censure of the

Sorbonne in 1521. He therefore moved for a time to Meaux under the protection of the bishop, another former pupil called Briconnet. Here he helped initiate some practical reforms, being appointed vicar general in 1523. He was also the center of a little group (the "Meaux circle") that included Farel, Roussel, and Margaret, the sister of King Francis I.

Further accusations caused him to leave Meaux for Strassburg and later Basel. But he was soon back in Paris, where he met Calvin around 1534. He spent his final years in Navarre, where Margaret was queen.

Lefèvre's most important work was done in biblical studies between 1509, when his edition of the Psalms appeared, and 1530, when his complete translation of the Bible into French was published in Antwerp. A commentary on the Pauline Epistles came out in 1512 and commentaries on the four Gospels in 1522. The French translation of the New Testament first came out in 1523 and that of the Old Testament in 1528.

Lefèvre never broke with the Roman Catholic Church, and the extent of his theological agreement with the Reformation has been debated. Nevertheless, his scholarly work on the Bible provided a basis for the reformers. His thinking and activity had an evangelical element that was expressed in his famous preface to the commentaries on the Gospels (written in 1522): "The Word of God suffices . . . This rule alone is the guide to eternal life . . . . Understanding [of it] must be sought through the gift and grace of God . . . granted not according to the merits of anyone, but according to the pure generosity of Him who gives. . . . Beseech the Lord of the Word, who is the Lord Christ, that His Word, does not fall without fruit, but that throughout the world it bears fruit unto life everlasting." G. BROMILEY

LEGGE, JAMES (1815–1897)
Congregational missionary and scholar

Born in Scotland, Legge was educated at Aberdeen University before becoming a missionary to Asia. He was minister of the Union Church, Hong Kong, from 1843 to 1873. He was also head of the Anglo-Chinese College in the colony. He developed that institution both as a theological college and a boys' school.

As a scholar, Legge became famous for his translation into English of the Chinese classics. Appearing in five volumes, the work included the Confucian classics and the texts of Taoism. On his return to Britain, Legge had an academic career at Oxford University, being a fellow of Corpus Christi College and the first professor of Chinese. P. TOON

LEIBNIZ, GOTTFRIED WILHELM (1646–1716)
German Protestant statesman, mathematician, and philosopher

Leibniz was born at Leipzig, received a broad education at Leipzig and Jena in classics, philosophy, theology, mathematics, and law, and spent the most active years of his life as a diplomat. Concerned about wars between the "Christian states" of Europe, he devised a variety of plans during the years 1686 to 1691 for the avoidance of conflict through closer federation. Since religious differences were somewhat involved, he worked for a reunion of Protestant and Roman Catholic churches on the basis of the many common elements in their creeds. This scheme failed, as did his further ecumenical plan for church union between Reformed and Lutheran groups. To this end Leibniz helped establish the Collegium Irenicum at Berlin (1703).

He found greater success in mathematical and philosophical investigations. He invented a calculating machine and discovered calculus—disputing at length with Isaac Newton over which one of them discovered it first. But his most lasting contribution is undoubtedly in philosophy.

He repudiated the Cartesian and mechanistic philosophies, which tried to explain all natural processes in terms of cause-effect mechanisms; he insisted instead that nature has inbuilt purposes. This is perhaps the pivotal doctrine of his entire philosophy. Nature consists not of inert matter moved by purposeless forces, but of units of energy. He called them "monads" and conceived of them in conscious beings as souls. In Leibniz's view God creates by generating energy and life; God himself is the supreme monad who created the entire world of monads to fulfill his ends. Everything therefore has its place in the universe and finds sufficient reason for its existence in God.

This led Leibniz to argue for the existence of God, using both the cosmological and the teleological proofs. In his famous *Theodicy* (1710) he accounted for evil as a purposeful part of the overall scheme of things. This is the best of all possible worlds—best not in terms of our purposes, but of God's. The French skeptic Voltaire, who ridiculed this idea, failed to observe that Leibniz's claim applies not to the present cross section of history, riddled as it is with conflict and suffering, but to the overall history and triumph of the kingdom of God on earth. Leibniz's philosophy was dedicated to that, and so to furthering God's purposes in the creation. A. F. HOLMES

LEO I (died 461)
Pope, 440–461

Aside from locating him originally in Tuscany, records on Leo offer nothing for reconstructing his early life. Young adulthood brought him wide recognition, though, for service in the Church at Rome: first as a prominent deacon under Celestine I, then as imperial diplomat (for Valentinian III) under Sixtus III. Leo's exceptional abilities made him a natural choice for pope in 440. Under his leadership, the church experienced deep changes during one of Western history's most turbulent eras.

Leo's papacy faced two immense problems: the emergence of heresies greatly threatening basic church integrity; and the rapid political disintegration of the Roman (Western) Empire. To combat these difficulties, Leo offered three main tactics: actions to provide essential church doctrine with well-drawn, orthodox formulation; efforts to unify church government under a sovereign papacy; and attempts at general peace by negotiation with the empire's enemies. Leo's establishment of orthodox teaching followed several lines. On the negative side, as he opposed the period's major heresies, Manicheanism, Pelagianism, Priscillianism, Leo unhesitantly utilized imperial criminal prosecution and banishment. More positively, Leo's finest achievement was probably the formation and acceptance he gained for orthodox Christological dogma. In particular, though Arianism was in retreat, the 400s battled with Eutychianism, another misrepresentation about Christ from the empire's eastern regions. Rather than rely on suppression, Leo brought Eutychus to Rome for lengthy discussions and, after painstaking adjudication, issued a carefully written letter, the now famous *Tome of Leo*. Setting forth a remarkably clear exposition of Christ's two natures in one person, Leo's *Tome* became the basis in 451 for the Council of Chalcedon's enduring formulation of Christological doctrine.

Regarding consolidation of papal power, Leo had numerous vigorous approaches. At one point, during Valentinian III's rule, Leo even acquired formal imperial sanction for a papacy with ultimate church authority. But predominantly, Leo relied on frequent letters and sermons, always models of skillful polemic, to give ideas of papal power cogent, persuasive expression. With no reservation, Leo pressed the papacy's claims to general supremacy in church doctrine and rule on all institutional Christianity of the period. By the time of his death, this campaign exhibited extensive success in western areas, including the major sees of Italy, Africa, Gaul, and Spain; and there were partial submissions from many eastern bishops as well. Toward ameliorating Rome's political troubles, Leo's activities included some dramatic confrontations with leaders of the empire's military foes. His journey to Lombardy in 451 won general agreement from Attila the Hun to remain north of the Danube River; and in 452 Leo persuaded Genseric, chief of the Vandals, to refrain from killing residents and destroying buildings in Rome. Through his doctrinal and church governmental actions and his interventions for the empire, Leo very significantly bolstered church unity and stability, this affecting not only the fifth century's upheavals, but all subsequent Christian history. These attainments place him among the greatest papal figures in respect to institutional church development and life. Leo also could enter effectively into local church needs. With a transparent style, Leo's sermons reveal much genuine, thoughtful engagement with the spiritual welfare of individual believers.

Among Leo I's surviving works, the 96 sermons and 142 letters are most important. But some thirty letters received by Leo also are still extant. Early sources of information about the great pope exist mainly in these letters. K. J. BRYER

LEO III (died 816)
Pope, 795–816

Born in Rome of humble origins, Leo is little known to history until his election to the papacy. Right from the start he incurred the hostility of his predecessor Pius IX's aristocratic entourage, who had been deprived of their power. When in 799 his opponents attempted his physical mutilation (which would have disqualified him from office), Leo fled to the court of Charlemagne, whose guardianship he had prudently acknowledged earlier. The Frankish ruler saw to it that Leo was reestablished in Rome, but further unrest and serious charges alleged against the pope brought Charlemagne south to investigate the situation personally in 800. Leo purged himself on oath and on Christmas Day enterprisingly and dramatically crowned Charlemagne as Roman emperor—an act whose legality and significance has provoked much scholarly controversy. While the coronation enhanced Leo's prestige in Rome, it caused Charlemagne to consider the pope as his subject, as were all the other bishops. The event also put a strain on relations with the eastern part of the empire by appearing to cast doubts on the status of the latter. Until the death of Charlemagne in 814, pronouncements even on theological issues were made by the voice of Leo, but the scriptwriter was

clearly the emperor. Leo's final two years were again bedeviled by conspirators and dissidents. J. D. DOUGLAS

LEO XIII (1810–1903)
Pope, 1878–1903

Born into a noble family in Carpineto near Rome, Joachim Vincent Pecci was educated by Jesuits before entering the prestigious Roman College in 1825. A brilliant student, he took his doctor's degree from Rome's Gregorian University in 1832 and was made a domestic prelate by Gregory XVI. Having become expert in canon and civil law, he was ordained in 1837 and served in the Vatican diplomatic service until appointment as bishop of Perugia (1846–1878). He was made cardinal in 1853. He succeeded Pius IX eight years after the papacy's temporal power was lost, his task made harder because of his predecessor's ultraconservative policies. He ended the feud with the German government, reestablished the Roman Catholic hierarchy in Presbyterian Scotland, and in 1893 sent the first apostolic delegate to America. His wide-ranging interests were reflected in his encyclicals, which included significant pronouncements on Socialism (1878) and Scripture (1893). He promoted learning (opening the Vatican archives to historical research), had a deep social concern, and campaigned against the African slave trade. He sought the reunion of all Christendom, but in 1896 denied the validity of Anglican clerical orders. A likeable man who wrote Latin poetry in leisure hours, he spent his entire pontificate within the Vatican. J. D. DOUGLAS

LEONARDO DA VINCI (1452–1519)
Italian artist, inventor, and scholar

Leonardo da Vinci first studied art under the sculptor/painter Verrochio in Florence. In 1482 he left Florence for Milan, where he served the duke of Milan until 1499. During that period he produced some of his best-known works, including the *Last Supper* for the Dominican brothers of S. Maria della Grazie. Leonardo's innovative genius in that painting lay in the moment Leonardo chose to depict. He did not paint the institution of the Eucharist but Jesus' announcement of the betrayal. Leonardo's desire to show the humanity of Jesus Christ and his disciples gave the painting a feeling that is this-worldly rather than other-worldly. Such realism was to become one of the key features of High Renaissance art. When the French invaded Milan in 1499, Leonardo began to lead a wanderer's life, devoting himself mainly to scientific and scholarly work. His artistic output included *St. Anne* and *Mona Lisa*. In 1517 he settled in France under the patronage of the king. Two years later, at the age of sixty-five, he died.

Although Leonardo was one of the great geniuses of the Renaissance, not until the twentieth century were many of his notations (related to such diverse fields as geology, physics, anatomy, and philosophy) understood and appreciated. Leonardo was centuries ahead of his time in his ideas about the airplane, the water turbine, and machines of war. A. STEFFLER

LESSING, GOTTHOLD EPHRAIM
(1729–1781)
German writer who became a transitional figure between the Enlightenment and Romanticism and was a significant influence in the development of liberal theology and religious humanism

The son of a German Lutheran pastor, Lessing studied theology at Leipzig but spent most of his life as a playwright, poet, essayist, and literary critic. Not until the final decade of his life did his attention return to theology; yet this was enough to produce a considerable influence.

As a student, he had absorbed the rationalism of the German Enlightenment, complete with the religious views of the English deists. Yet by his final decade he had assimilated Spinoza's pantheism, substituting a wholly immanentistic basis for ethical values in place of the transcendent Creator. For him, the essence of religion was the practice of love and universal brotherhood, without either a transcendent God or a traditional

theology. He endorsed "natural religion" without divine revelation.

Some examples will serve to illustrate this. Lessing's publication of some writings by the deist Reimarus stirred up a controversy with a Hamburg pastor, which in turn initiated the nineteenth-century "quest for the historical Jesus" as distinct from the Christ of theology. Basically, Lessing's point was that a logical gulf exists between the truth of the historical narrative (which biblical inerrantists eagerly defended) and the truth of divine revelation. The historical accuracy of a document does not prove that it was specially revealed, nor does it imply the truth of the theological significance ascribed to the events recorded. Thus it may be true that Jesus died under Pontius Pilate, but that he died "for our sins" does not logically follow. This gap in the traditional argument, sometimes called "Lessing's ditch," is alluded to by Kierkegaard in his more orthodox criticism of Enlightenment theology: it poses the still current problem of the relation between history and faith.

Again, Lessing engaged in a critical study of the synoptic Gospels. But, being forbidden by the civil authorities to engage in further theological controversy, he put his dramatic powers to theological use in a play, *Nathan the Wise*. Its outcome is a plea for theological indifferentism that regards doctrine and historical questions as inconsequential. A "Christian" ethic of love, sincerity, and tolerance stands independently of traditional dogma.

Finally, Lessing's pantheistic tendencies led him to the view that everything exists within the divine mind, for God is the harmonizing ground of all being that determines whatever shall be. If this denies individual freedom, that is good; for whatever must be is good, if it is divine work. Thus arises the optimistic characteristic of a nineteenth-century theology that allows no special acts of revelation or redemption. In some regards, it is like Hegel's panentheism. In other regards, it anticipates the humanistic religion of Auguste Comte.
A. F. HOLMES

LEWIS, C.S. (CLIVE STAPLES)
(1898–1963)
Christian writer and scholar

C. S. Lewis spent most of his life as tutor and lecturer at Oxford and Cambridge Universities and as writer of many scholarly and Christian books. His best-known scholarly work is *English Literature in the Sixteenth Century* (1954). His first scholarly work, *The Allegory of Love* (1936), was called by at least one critic a classic in its field.

Lewis is best known as the author of more than twenty-five Christian works. He had been a "happy atheist" at fourteen and over a long period was slowly persuaded that the Christian religion is the only logical way by which to understand man and his universe. Becoming a Christian at about thirty, he shortly afterwards wrote an autobiographical novel called *The Pilgrim's Regress* (1933). Later he told of his birth and upbringing in *Surprised by Joy* (1955).

Millions of copies of his books were sold during his lifetime and an increasing number have followed since his death. One person, asked which of Lewis's books he thought best, said, "The one I am now reading." For a long time his *Screwtape Letters* (1942), being letters from a major devil to a lesser one in charge of a young man's soul, was Lewis's most popular work. Another much-read work is *Mere Christianity* (1952), a simple but profound delineation of the rationale of the Christian position. He also wrote *Miracles* (1947), *The Problem of Pain* (1940), *Reflections on the Psalms* (1958), and many others. His *Abolition of Man* (1943) was admitted by the Britannica Encyclopedia to the Great Books of the World.

Lewis's fiction is also much read, especially the Chronicles of Narnia (1950–1956), seven books for children that were illustrated by Pauline Baynes—a set of stories guaranteed to delight children from five years onward. They tell of adventures that ensue upon passing through a magical wardrobe and other similar entrances into entrancing lands watched over by a magnificent lion called Aslan, actually the symbol of Christ. While these books have been instrumental in the conversion of many people, they are not sermons but exciting stories.

The Space Trilogy, consisting of *Out of the Silent Planet* (1938), *Perelandra* (1943), and *That Hideous Strength* (1945), take the reader, in the first two volumes, to Mars and then Venus, while the third is mainly anti-utopian with events occurring in England. *Perelandra* recounts the adventures of a good and a bad man who in an Edenic world try to persuade an "Eve" to their respective viewpoints. But in this story Eve does not fall. *The Great Divorce* (1946) involves a dream visit of a busload of people going from hell to heaven and there being warmly invited in but refusing the glory they can see over the mountains ahead. Their trouble is that they cannot give up, even after the punishments of hell itself, their claim to self over God.

The great interest in Lewis has resulted in many books, many doctoral dissertations, and many societies devoted to his writings. Other works include *Till We Have Faces* (1956) and *Christian Reflections* (1967).

C. KILBY

LIDDELL, ERIC HENRY (1902–1945)
Scottish athlete and missionary

Born in China of missionary parents, Liddell went to school in England and later graduated in science from Edinburgh University. He excelled in sports, representing Scotland on the international rugby field. At the 1924 Paris Olympics, having disqualified himself from the one hundred meters because Christian conviction would not permit him to run a preliminary heat on Sunday, he won the gold medal and achieved a world record in the four hundred meters. Before that race a note slipped into his hand reminded him of 1 Samuel 2:30: "Them that honour me I will honour."

Liddell became a prominent member of student teams pledged to actively evangelize central Scotland. His participation undoubtedly brought thousands within sound of the gospel for the first time. In 1925, to the dismay of the athletic world, he returned to China under the London Missionary Society

to teach at the Anglo-Chinese Christian College, Tientsin. Both there and in a Japanese internment camp from 1942, the humility and the serene testimony of "Scotland's greatest athlete," not least in the trying days before his death from a brain tumor, greatly encouraged his colleagues and gave him a unique outreach to all who heard him.
J. D. DOUGLAS

LIDDON, HENRY PARR (1829–1890)
Leading Tractarian; canon of St. Paul's Cathedral

Educated at King's College School, London, and Christ Church, Oxford, Liddon was ordained and served his curacy under the Tractarian vicar of Wantage, W. J. Butler. Later he was appointed to a canonry at St. Paul's Cathedral, London (1870), and to a professorship at Oxford (1870). He held both appointments at the same time.

Liddon used his influence to defend traditional doctrine and the use of the Athanasian Creed in worship. His widely read book *The Divinity of Our Lord and Savior, Jesus Christ* (1867) is a gem of orthodoxy. It was much appreciated by evangelicals who could not accept his high-church practices and views.

Out of his admiration for E. B. Pusey, one of the founders of the Tractarian movement, Liddon gave up his professorship to devote himself to writing a massive biography of Pusey (four volumes, 1893–1897). Because he could not adapt himself to the new learning and higher criticism, Liddon represented the older, conservative Tractarianism, while Bishop Gore represented the new Tractarianism. P. TOON

LIETZMANN, HANS (1875–1942)
Church historian

Born in Berlin, educated in classical philology and theology, Lietzmann taught at several universities before 1924. In that year he was appointed as successor to Adolf Harnack at the University of Berlin. In time he became a scholar in church history, archaeology, canon law, history of the creeds,

and papyrology. In his autobiography he stated that his purpose was to combine theology and classical philology.

Significant treatises flowed from Lietzmann's pen, the most monumental being his four-volume *History of the Early Church* (1932–1944). His *Peter and Paul in Rome* (1915, 1927) removed that subject from polemics and gave it a firm, impartial, historical foundation. Perhaps his most enduring work was his *Mass and Lord's Supper* (1926), only recently translated into English. It has been questioned in its details but probably not in its overall impact. It made liturgics an important study for Protestants of non-Anglican traditions. A. CABANISS

LIGHTFOOT, JOHN (1601–1675)
British expert on rabbinical studies

Born at Stoke on Trent, Lightfoot was educated at Christ's College, Cambridge. After several curacies he became rector of Ashley, Staffordshire, where he built a special study in his garden in which to study Hebrew. After supporting Parliament in the civil war, he was appointed by that body both to the rectory of Much Munden, Hertfordshire (1644) and to the Mastership of Catherine Hall, Cambridge (1650). He retained both those preferments at the Restoration in 1660 because royalists valued his learning.

From 1643 to 1647 Lightfoot made valuable contributions to the Westminster Assembly in London. He was known as an Erastian because, though he held presbyterian views of church organization, he believed the state had the right to intervene in church affairs.

Lightfoot's fame rests on his learning. It was said of him that "by constant reading of the rabbis he became almost a rabbi himself." The truth of that statement is seen in his greatest work *Horae Hebraicae et Talmudicae* (six volumes, 1658–1678). Lightfoot bequeathed his oriental books to Harvard, where they perished in a fire in 1769. P. TOON

LIGHTFOOT, JOSEPH BARBER
(1828–1889)
Bishop of Durham; biblical scholar

Born in Liverpool, Lightfoot was educated at King Edward's School, Birmingham, and Trinity College, Cambridge, where he became a fellow in 1852. He was ordained an Anglican priest in 1858 and taught classics in his college. In 1861 he became Hulsean professor of divinity. Lecturing mainly on the Epistles of Paul, he attracted large audiences. In 1870 he persuaded his friend B. F. Westcott to make himself available for the vacant regius professorship of divinity, to which Westcott was then elected. The two friends worked side by side, doing much to make critical study of the New Testament attractive.

Having refused the bishopric of Lichfield, Lightfoot accepted that of Durham in 1870. He gave himself wholeheartedly to his large diocese with its mines and ports. He organized a biennial diocesan conference, increased the number of full-time lay workers, started a church building fund, and traveled many miles to visit the parishes. Exhausted, he died in December 1889 and was buried in the chapel of Auckland Castle, the traditional home of the bishops of Durham.

Lightfoot's scholarly output was immense. He was a leading member of the team of New Testament translators for the Revised Version. He filled his commentaries on Galatians (1865), Philippians (1868), and Colossians with Philemon (1875) with erudition. Likewise, his editions of the apostolic fathers (1869, 1885), especially the two volumes on Ignatius, were very important in their day. In his *Leaders of the Northern Church* (1890) he used his historical gifts to communicate at a more popular level. Lightfoot will be remembered, along with Westcott and Hort (his two companions), for providing the best in English biblical scholarship. P. TOON

LIGHTFOOT, ROBERT HENRY
(1883–1953)
Anglican New Testament scholar

Born at Wellingborough, Northampton-shire, England, Lightfoot was educated at Eton and at Worcester College, Oxford University, where he won first-class honors in theology in 1907. Ordained a deacon in 1909 and to the Anglican priesthood in 1910, he served as curate at Haslemere (1909–1912) before becoming successively bursar (1912–1913), vice-principal (1913–1916), and principal (1916–1919) of Wells Theological College. For thirty years he taught at Oxford, as chaplain of Lincoln College (1919–1921) and fellow of New College (1924–1950). In 1934 he was appointed Ireland Professor of the Exegesis of Holy Scripture, and he occupied this chair until his retirement in 1949.

Lightfoot's distinctive contribution to New Testament studies was his adoption of the "form critical" method of the German Ernest Lohmeyer (1890–1946). In his 1934 Bampton Lectures, published the next year under the title *History and Interpretation in the Gospels,* Lightfoot maintained that in the New Testament Gospels there is no such thing as pure history—history and theology are always intermingled, even in Mark, and the history cannot be properly understood unless the theology is taken seriously. In his later book *Locality and Doctrine in the Gospels* (1938), Lightfoot contended that places and place-names in the New Testament have theological as well as topographical significance. Lightfoot also wrote a commentary on Mark (1950) and on John (published posthumously in 1956), and from 1941 until his death he edited the *Journal of Theological Studies.* N. V. HOPE

LIGUORI, ALPHONSIUS (1696–1787)
Roman Catholic moral theologian; founder of the Redemptorists

Born at Marianella, near Naples (Italy), Liguori practiced law for eight years. He left that profession to join an association of mission preachers. Ordained a priest in 1726, he became an effective evangelist among country people around Naples.

In 1729 Liguori entered a Naples missionary college. There he came to know Tomaso Falcoia (1663–1743), whose founding of an order for religious women prompted Liguori to similar work. In 1731 Liguori reorganized the nuns in Scala, in the diocese where Falcoia was now bishop. The following year he founded the Congregation of the Most Holy Redeemer (Redemptorists) for men. The Redemptorists devoted themselves to pastoral work among poor peasants in rural areas.

In a worldly and unbelieving generation, Liguori commended the gospel by gentle, simple, direct preaching, in contrast to the lurid oratory of the day. He opposed the prevailing rigoristic attitude over the confessional. He wrote an immense amount of devotional literature, running to seventy volumes. His influential *Moral Theology* (two volumes, 1753 and 1755), reprinted seven times before his death, steered a midway course between rigorism and laxity.

Liguori declined the archbishopric of Palermo in 1747. In 1762 he reluctantly agreed to be made bishop of Saint Agatha of the Goths near Naples. He resigned in 1775 and returned to his order. Liguori was canonized in 1839. N. HILLYER

LINCOLN, ABRAHAM (1809–1865)
Sixteenth president of the United States, 1861–1865

Lincoln's extraordinary leadership preserved the American Union through even the Civil War. Possessor of extraordinary humor, piety, conviction, and common sense, he created some of America's most enduring literature, powerful in simplicity and fitness.

Lincoln never formally joined any church, nor is there any explicit record of a conversion experience, but his confidence and trust in the Sovereign God and the Scriptures are a dominant theme in the historical records of Lincoln's life and work. He was a constant reader of the Bible, quoting frequently from it in his speeches, letters, and conversation.

Born February 12, 1809, in a rough log cabin on a Kentucky farm, Lincoln moved to Indiana in 1816. He had a total of less than one year's formal education, a fact he regret-

ted all his life. As a young boy, he learned "to cipher"—to read and write. Books were scarce on the frontier, but Lincoln read and reread what was available—*Robinson Crusoe, Pilgrim's Progress*, and Weems's *Life of Washington*. On the Sundays of Lincoln's boyhood, he no doubt read and reread the Bible.

Another source of biblical knowledge and religious influence was the preaching of the Hardshell Baptist Church the Lincoln family attended in Indiana. The wilderness preachers whom Lincoln heard in the church had little education but thorough biblical knowledge with a strong Calvinistic emphasis. Young Lincoln, an excellent mimic of these preachers, would mount a tree stump and delight his hearers with his "preaching."

At age twenty-one, Lincoln moved to the frontier village of New Salem, Illinois, where he was a store clerk, postmaster, store owner, and land surveyor. In 1834 he was elected to the state legislature, receiving his license to practice law two years later. Six months out of the year, Lincoln traveled the judicial circuit around Illinois, loving the days in court and the evenings of storytelling. In 1842 he married Mary Todd, an educated socialite of Springfield, Illinois. Of the four children born to Abe and Mary, only one grew to adulthood.

Lincoln, the young man, on occasion used his tough, legal mind to analyze and critique religion. In running for the Illinois legislature in 1834, he was charged by his opponent as being anti-Christian. Lincoln responded in a circulated handbill saying in part: "That I am not a member of any Christian church is true; but I have never denied the truth of Scripture." When Lincoln learned that his father was dying, he wrote in a letter to his stepbrother: "I sincerely hope father may recover his health; but at all events tell him to remember to call upon and confide in our great and good and merciful Maker, who will not turn away from him in any extremity. He notes the fall of a sparrow and numbers the hair of our head, and He will not forget the dying man who puts his trust in Him."

In 1858 Lincoln lost the Senate race to

Stephen Douglas, but the famous Lincoln-Douglas debates catapulted him to national prominence. When the newly formed Republican Party met in Chicago in 1860, Lincoln became their presidential candidate.

A month after Lincoln was inaugurated President, Fort Sumter was fired upon, signaling the start of the Civil War. The tragedy of the war was capsulized by Lincoln in his great Gettysburg Address in November 1863. He had declared the slaves free in his Emancipation Proclamation of September 1862. It was Lincoln's burning desire to free the slaves, a passion that had been ignited and inflamed from the truth of the dignity of man that he found in the Scriptures.

Lincoln suffered the hardest blow of his life when his son, Willie, died in 1864. Dr. Phineas D. Gurley, minister of the Presbyterian Church in Washington where Lincoln attended as often as he could, spent long hours with Lincoln at this crisis. A change came to Lincoln, an even deeper confidence in the Bible and prayer. "Take all this book upon reason that you can, and the balance on faith," Lincoln said of the Bible to his friend Joshua Speed in 1864, "and you will live and die a better man."

Elected to a second presidential term in 1864, the war was clearly near its end. Nowhere can one find a more Christian analysis of the Civil War than in Lincoln's Second Inaugural Address: "Both (North and South) read the same Bible, and pray to the same God; and each invokes His aid against the other. It may seem strange that any men should dare to ask a just God's assistance in wringing their bread from the sweat of other men's faces; but let us judge not that we be not judged. The prayers of both could not be answered; that of neither has been answered fully. The Almighty has His own purposes." Even more to the point was his reply when a minister from the North told the president he hoped "the Lord is on our side." Responded Lincoln: "I am not at all concerned about that. . . . But it is my constant anxiety and prayer that I and this nation should be on the Lord's side."

After a year in his second term as President, the war ended. On April 9, 1865, Lee surrendered to Grant. On the night of April 14, while attending a play at Ford's Theater in Washington, Lincoln was shot by assassin John Wilkes Booth. Lincoln died the next morning. He is buried in Springfield, Illinois, and remains a beloved symbol of union and democracy and trust in God.

D. P. AMSLER

LIPPI, FRA FILIPPO (c. 1406–1469)

Main contributor to the humanization of religious art that was to become a key feature of Renaissance art

Lippi entered the community of the Carmelite friars when he was fourteen, but in about 1431 he was permitted to leave the monastery to paint. He developed a linear style that emphasized the contours of his figures and gave him a device for suggesting movement in his forms.

One of Lippi's most inventive works from his later years, *Madonna and Child with Angels,* shows his skill at humanizing a religious theme. All the figures suggest the painter used individual models for them. They reflect the real rather than the ideal common in earlier religious art. For background Lippi used a particular scene of the Arno River valley rather than an imaginary, stylized landscape.

Lippi's most important pupil was Sandro Bottecelli. Lippi had a son, Filippino Lippi, who was also an influential painter.

A. STEFFLER

LISZT, FRANZ (1811–1886)

Hungarian pianist

Although born in Hungary and famed for his Hungarian Rhapsodies, Liszt was a thoroughly international figure. From his youth he rightfully won fame as the greatest pianist of his day. In later life he gave himself to composition and teaching, in which fields he was enormously influential. In addition to a very great number of works for piano that evince both extreme Romantic characteristics and the utmost in technical difficulty, he also wrote much for orchestra and a considerable number of songs. Not so well known are his over sixty religious works, including settings of a number of Psalms, several elaborate masses, and three oratorios. Little that he wrote is suitable for church performance today. The tune we know as "Fairest Lord Jesus" is used by Liszt in the "Crusader's March" in his oratorio *The Legend of St. Elizabeth.* It is probably a German chorale, or a folksong, but its origin is obscure. Liszt made great numbers of arrangements of works by many composers for the piano that were welcome in an era before the advent of the recording industry. J. B. MacMILLAN

LIVINGSTONE, DAVID (1813–1873)
Scottish missionary and explorer

Born at Blantyre of "poor and pious parents," Livingstone was only ten when he began working fourteen-hour days in the cotton mill. Snatched sentences from a book on his spinning jenny, followed by two hours of night school, augmented his scanty education. Converted at twelve, he had a profound spiritual awakening at twenty and resolved to be a medical missionary in China.

Livingstone studied Greek, theology, and medicine at Glasgow, returning to the mill during vacations to help pay expenses. Qualified in medicine, he was sent by the London Missionary Society in 1840 to South Africa, since China had been closed by the Opium War. Livingstone's heart had been fired by missionary Robert Moffat's words about having seen "the smoke of a thousand villages" where no missionary had ever been.

At Cape Town, before heading for his station at Kuruman, Livingstone preached against white exploitation of blacks. Later he criticized the deployment of missionaries in the south while innumerable villages in the north remained untouched. Another conviction alarming to his colleagues was that greater use be made of the Africans in missionary work.

Livingstone and his wife, Mary, Moffat's daughter, stayed in three homes in three years, ever moving further up-country. He was evangelist, doctor, teacher, builder, gardener, shoemaker, carpenter. But all the time his eyes were on the "unknown north" beyond the fearsome Kalahari Desert.

In 1852 Livingstone sent his wife and children home before he embarked on a four-year, six-thousand-mile journey that took him to Angola's Atlantic coast, then east to the Indian Ocean at Mozambique. During long weary journeys, debilitating illnesses, danger from wild animals and hostile tribes, he never relaxed his self-imposed discipline, but made observations, studied languages, kept his famous *Diaries,* and prepared scientific reports that brought him fame. He retained his humility, writing in 1853: "I will place no value on anything I have . . . except in relation to the Kingdom of Christ."

In 1857, during his first furlough, Livingstone gave at Cambridge University a challenging address that led to the founding of the Universities' Mission to Central Africa. That year he also led a government-appointed expedition to explore the Zambesi region. His outrage at slave-trading displeased diplomatic circles; the expedition was recalled but not before it had discovered Victoria Falls.

When Livingstone's wife died in 1861, he threw himself fiercely into his work. He disappeared from sight; and when found by Henry Morton Stanley of the *New York Herald* in 1871, Livingstone refused to go home. Stanley's kindness probably saved Livingstone's life for another eighteen months until at Ilala (now in Zambia) he was discovered dead, kneeling by his bedside.

Such was their love for him that native assistants bore his body fifteen hundred miles to the coast. One of them was among the huge crowd at the funeral in Westminster Abbey. Some words on Livingstone's tombstone there summarize his achievements: "For thirty years his life was spent in an unwearied effort to evangelize the native races, to explore the undiscovered secrets, to abolish the desolating slave trade of Central Africa." J. D. DOUGLAS

LLOYD-JONES, DAVID MARTYN (1899–1981)
Welsh preacher and writer

Born in Newcastle Emlyn, Lloyd-Jones was brought up in Calvinistic Methodism and trained in medicine at London, where his brilliance was soon acknowledged. Suddenly he changed direction and entered the ministry, convinced that many of his patients needed not ordinary medicine but the gospel of Jesus Christ.

His change of direction was confirmed during his first pastorate at Port Talbot in industrial Wales (1927–1938). Chosen in 1938 by G. Campbell Morgan as his colleague at London's Westminster Chapel, the Welshman saw the congregation through difficult wartime years (Morgan retired in 1943). Under his thirty-two-year ministry the chapel was established as the foremost evangelical pulpit in England, chiefly because of his conviction that preaching is "the highest and greatest and the most glorious calling." He held strong views on controversial subjects, but these were always the outcome of keen analytic reasoning. He believed in evangelical unity so long as theological principles were not jeopardized. He was suspicious of syncretism and in 1966 challenged evangelicals to leave mainline churches (perhaps especially the Church of England) whose witness he felt to be hopelessly compromised. Because of his strong pastoral faith and counseling, marriages were saved, fellow physicians kept the track, and students were guided through theological thickets and personal problems. His many published works include *Truth Unchanged, Unchanging* (1951), *From Fear to Faith* (1953), *Conversions: Psychological and Spiritual* (1959), and *Studies in the Sermon on the Mount* (two volumes, 1959–1960).
J. D. DOUGLAS

LOCKE, JOHN (1632–1704)
Most influential British philosopher of the Enlightenment

Locke was a devout Christian, an Anglican with Puritan leanings. His education, completed at Oxford, included biblical languages as well as science, medicine, and philosophy. His writings ranged from ethics, politics, and education to epistemology and theology.

Locke is best known for his *Essay Concerning Human Understanding* (1690), which presents a systematic exposition of the empiricism that has shaped British philosophy ever since. The essay applies to both our common awareness of the world and the main concepts of Newtonian science—the thesis that all knowledge is derived from the simple ideas that make up our sensory and reflective experience. Even the idea of God arises from these simple ideas, combined with the recognition of God's infinity. Our moral beliefs are learned from experiencing the pleasures and pains God has established as a moral guide.

Locke's political ideas helped shape Western democratic ideals. His *Two Treatises on Civil Government* (1689) argue for God-given rights to life, liberty, and property, as laws of nature. Government exists by the consent of the governed to protect those rights, so that significant moral limitations are placed on political power (he rejected the divine right of kings), as well as on war and other government activities. The right to property stems ultimately from the fact that God gave the resources of his creation to all people to share. The individual's right is limited, then, to what he can appropriate by his work and what is needful in sustaining a human quality of life. He must leave sufficient resources for the needs of others. The self-centeredness of an unbridled capitalism has no place in Locke's thinking, for human beings are to be responsible stewards in God's creation.

Locke also wrote *An Essay on Religious Toleration* (1667), a progressive document at the time, in which he advocated freedom of religious belief and practice—provided only that that freedom does not endanger the community. Locke's most extended religious work was *The Reasonableness of Christianity* (1695), which argues that while the Christian revelation adds to what we can discover by reason alone, it does not contradict reason.

Locke tried to diminish the theological schisms in the church by returning attention

to the inspired Scriptures. There he found that being a Christian involves two essentials: one must accept Jesus as God's Messiah and so be justified by faith, and one must live in accordance with Christ's teaching.
A. F. HOLMES

LOHMEYER, ERNST (1890–1946)
New Testament scholar and exegete

Born at Dorsten, Westphalia, Germany, Lohmeyer in 1918 was appointed privatdozent in New Testament studies at Heidelberg. In 1920 he became associate professor at Breslau and was promoted to a full professorship the next year. In 1935 he was transferred for political reasons to Greifswald, where in 1945 he became rector of the university. In February 1946, during the night before the official reopening of the university after World War II, he was arrested and disappeared. R. Gregor Smith says that "nothing is known of his fate, but it is assumed that his life ended somewhere in Russia in September 1946."

In his New Testament research, Lohmeyer was an exponent of *Redactionsgeschichte* (redaction criticism), which seeks to determine the influences and intentions that motivated the various editors of the biblical material. He wrote extensively on the New Testament—for example, the commentary on Revelation (1916) in Lietzmann's *Handbook to the New Testament* and the commentaries on Matthew and Mark in Meyer's Critical Exegetical series. He also wrote *The Foundations of Pauline Theology* (1929) and a scholarly study of *The Lord's Prayer* (1946; English translation, 1965). Lohmeyer also contributed to the study of early church history in his two books *Christian Worship and Caesar Worship* (1919) and *Social Questions in Primitive Christianity* (1921). N. V. HOPE

LOISY, ALFRED FIRMIN (1857–1940)
New Testament scholar; leading French Catholic modernist

Born at Ambrieres in French Lorraine, Loisy entered the seminary at Châlons-sur-Marne in 1874. In 1878 he was sent from Châlons to complete his training at the newly constituted theological faculty of the Catholic Institute of Paris, and the next year he was ordained priest. After serving as pastor of two village churches, in 1881 he resumed his studies at the Catholic Institute, where he was deeply influenced by the church historian Louis Duchesne. From 1882 to 1885 he attended the lectures of Ernest Renan at the College de France. In 1890 Loisy was appointed professor of holy Scripture at the Catholic Institute and earned his doctorate for a thesis on the history of the canon of the Old Testament; but his unorthodox views on the Bible led to his dismissal in 1893. From 1894 to 1899 he was chaplain to the Dominican teaching nuns at Neuilly; and in 1900 he became a lecturer at the École des Hautes Études, a department of the state university, from which he resigned in 1904 and retired to the country.

In 1902 he published his book *L'Évangile et l'Église* (*The Gospel and the Church*) in which, though he sought to justify the place and authority of the Catholic Church as the organized expression of the Christian faith, he insinuated the need for an essential reform in the Church's exegesis of the Gospels, in its official theology, and in its methods of government. This book—along with some other writings of Loisy—was put on the Index of prohibited books late in 1903. Loisy refused to submit to this judgment of the papacy. In 1906 he was deprived of his authority to say mass, and in 1908 he was excommunicated. From 1909 to 1926 he was professor of the history of religions at the College de France.

Loisy was a New Testament scholar of considerable distinction. He published commentaries on various New Testament books but most notably on the four Gospels: *Le Quatrieme Évangile* (*The Fourth Gospel*, 1903); *Les Évangiles Synoptiques* (*The Synoptic Gospels*; two volumes, 1907–1908).
N. V. HOPE

LOUIS IX (1214–1270)
King of France, 1226–1270; saint

Son of King Louis VIII and Blanche of

Castile, Louis IX acceded to the throne upon his father's death in November 1226. Only twelve at the time, he ruled under the regency of his strong-willed mother, who continued to exercise a powerful influence on him until her death in 1252. In 1234 he was married to Marguerite of Provence, by whom he had ten children.

Louis's life, written by his companion, Jean, Sire de Joinville, is one of the most famous biographies of the Middle Ages. It gives an intimate picture of the sovereign— of his impelling sense of duty, his warm piety, and his meticulous administration of justice. The latter became so well known in his own day that some cases arising in other lands were appealed to Louis for adjudication. So trusted was the king that he inaugurated the practice of issuing decrees on his own initiative without consulting his curia. He thus established the right of a French monarch to rule absolutely—and this at the time when his English royal counterpart and kinsman, Henry III, was being forced to accede to the growing powers of Parliament.

Louis's piety gained him canonization only twenty-seven years after his death. It also expressed itself in zeal for crusade. He led two of them. The first (1248–1254) began with an attack on Egypt, in which Louis was captured. When finally paroled, Louis spent much time in the Holy Land trying vainly to secure European support. On his return to France he continued to agitate and at length sailed to North Africa in 1270. But he had hardly landed when he fell ill and died. His piety also led him to construct the Sainte Chapelle in Paris (1245–1248), a gem of Gothic architecture built to house the crown of thorns, which he supposedly had obtained from Constantinople.

Because of Louis IX's popularity, a crusading order was created bearing his name. To it belonged so many of the explorers of the Americas that his memory is maintained all over the New World in place-names such as Louisiana, St. Louis, Louisville, and San Luis Rey. A. CABANISS

LOUIS XIV (1638–1715)
King of France, 1660–1715

Louis XIV was known as the Sun King. His reign began in 1660, when France was recognized as the strongest nation in Europe. In 1682 he moved to the palace of Versailles, which was finally completed in 1710. Under Louis the administration of the French government was concentrated in the king's hands. The monarch's potential enemies were held in check; the Estates-General (parliament) was not even convened. Louis himself claimed, "I am the state."

The Sun King had almost uninterrupted conflict with the pope over the subject of papal authority. In 1682 the conflict came to a head when the subject was referred to an assembly of the French clergy. Bossuet, bishop of Meaux, drafted the Declaration of Gallican Liberties. Papal authority, it said, was limited to matters of doctrine. Even there the pope was subject to a general council. The movement arising out of that declaration was called Gallicanism. Pursuant to that policy Louis initiated a persecution of the Jansenists, who had their headquarters at Port-Royal. In 1710 Port-Royal was desecrated. The remaining Jansenists fled to Belgium and the Netherlands.

Louis XIV's most dramatic stroke of religious repression was the suspension in 1685 of the Edict of Nantes, which had guaranteed the Huguenots (French Protestants) toleration since 1598. That action unleashed a ruinous emigration of Huguenot craftsmen from France. Many went to Germany, England, or America. A minority remained in France to endure persecution at the hands of the Sun King's absolutism.

Louis XIV built not only a strong internal administration but also an extremely powerful war machine. He attempted to extend the boundaries of France by four major wars. After 1685, however, his fortunes turned. Personal tragedy and political disaster accompanied the last days of the Grand Monarch. W. A. DETZLER

LOVEJOY, ELIJAH PARISH (1802–1837)
Presbyterian editor; martyred abolitionist

Lovejoy was born in Albion, Maine, the son of a Congregational pastor. After graduating from Baptist-sponsored Waterville College (Maine), Lovejoy went to St. Louis, Missouri, where he established a private high school. He found teaching dull, however, so in 1830 he joined the *St. Louis Times.* The move sharpened his interest in moral reform movements.

In 1832 Lovejoy was converted under the ministry of Presbyterian revivalist David Nelson. The same year he enrolled at Princeton Theological Seminary. In 1833 he was licensed by the Second Presbytery of Philadelphia. Later that year he returned to St. Louis as editor of a new Presbyterian-sponsored paper, *St. Louis Observer.* Although the paper spoke out against a number of social evils, Lovejoy at first refused to adopt an abolitionist stance, holding instead to a program of gradual emancipation.

By 1835, however, Lovejoy's position had changed, largely through the influence of his spiritual mentor, David Nelson. Before long Lovejoy was espousing firm abolitionist views. Missouri, on the other hand, was growing increasingly proslavery. Lovejoy therefore found extreme hostility toward his new position.

The threat of violence led Lovejoy to move his newspaper a few miles across the Mississippi River to Alton, Illinois, a free state. The new location proved just as dangerous. Mobs several times destroyed Lovejoy's press. On November 7, 1837, a mob again attacked. In the ensuing riot Lovejoy was killed. News of his death electrified abolitionist forces, bringing new strength to the antislavery movement.
J. N. AKERS

LUCAR, CYRIL (1572–1638)
Patriarch of Constantinople

Lucar is best known in Christian history as the Eastern patriarch who became influenced by Calvinism and attempted to reform the Orthodox Church along Calvinistic lines.

He was born in Crete and studied at Venice and Padua, where he came into contact with Roman theology. He did not appreciate Roman thought and became particularly antagonistic toward the Roman Church after the union of Brest-Litovsk (1596), which brought the Ruthenian bishops and several million orthodox Christians under the jurisdiction of the pope.

He became particularly interested in Reformed thought and the Church of England. This interest was expressed in the gift of Codex Alexandrinus, an early fifth-century manuscript of the Greek Bible, which Lucar sent to England's King James I through the British ambassador. He became friends with the Calvinist theologian, Antoine Leger, and with his support and encouragement, sponsored a translation of the Bible into the vernacular. In 1629 a confession of faith (*confessio fidei*) that reinterprets the traditional Eastern Orthodox faith in Calvinistic terms was published. Lucar affixed his name to this document.

Lucar was appointed patriarch of Constantinople in 1620. His administration, which was as unacceptable to the Catholics as it was acceptable to the Protestants, was one of constant turmoil. In 1623 he was removed from his throne. He was removed twice in 1633 and again in 1634.

Although he was the most important eastern theologian since the fall of Constantinople in 1453, his sympathies with Calvinism led to his condemnation. His teachings were condemned by synods held in Constantinople in 1638 and again in 1642. His teachings were condemned again at the synod of Jassy in 1642, which ratified a confession strongly influenced by Roman theology. He was again condemned at a synod in Jerusalem in 1672.

In spite of his controversial reign, Lucar is regarded as a most brilliant and politically astute national leader. R. E. WEBBER

LUDLOW, JOHN MALCOLM FORBES (1821–1911)
Founder of the Christian Socialist movement in England

Born in India and familiar with social problems and reform there, Ludlow was a sympathetic observer of the revolutions of

1830 and 1848 in France. Moved by the plight of slaves during visits to the West Indies, Ludlow devoted his life from mid-century on to the cause of the poor in England. Friend and coworker of Charles Kingsley, Thomas Hughes, and Frederick Denison Maurice, he helped enlist many others in that cause.

Ludlow became a leader and tireless worker in humane programs and institutions while practicing law from 1843 to 1874. He helped establish enterprises that included the papers *Politics for the People* (1848) and *The Christian Socialist* (1850), a night school for the poor, the Working Men's College (1854), and London's first "Co-operative Congress" (1869). Ludlow lectured in those schools, contributed to numerous periodicals, and authored books, among which were *Popular Epics of the Middle Ages* (1865), *President Lincoln* (1866), *Progress of the Working Class* (1867), and *Woman's Work in the Church* (1865).

Secretary of the Royal Commission on Friendly Societies from 1870 to 1874, Ludlow held the post of Chief Registrar of Friendly Societies from 1875 until 1891. His active interest in humane causes continued until his death at age ninety. A small and gentle man, Ludlow's energetic efforts on behalf of the poor were undergirded by his deep Christian commitment.

N. MAGNUSON

LUKE (first century)
Companion of the apostle Paul; author of the third Gospel and Acts

Accepting the author of Luke-Acts as Luke the companion of Paul, much can be gleaned about him from this two-volume work. The preface to the Gospel indicates that Luke was not an eyewitness or immediate disciple of the Lord. Luke states that he had carried out extensive research and had written an orderly account about Jesus.

An examination of his work over against the other Gospels indicates the emphases that were of special concern to Luke. The extraordinary feature of Luke's work is the presence of Acts, which conveys the distinc-

tive and comprehensive perspective of Luke. The essence of this perspective is to show the actual fulfilling of the prophecies of Isaiah in the proclamation of the gospel to the ends of the earth. This inclusion of the Gentiles is often referred to as Luke's universalism or concern for all humanity (Luke 2:14; 24:47). The Gospel of Luke displays a keen interest in individuals, social outcasts, women, children, and social relationships, especially situations involving poverty or wealth. This Gospel has a special stress on prayer and the Holy Spirit, which results in a striking note of joyfulness and praise. These features tell us something about Luke as a person and his understanding of Christianity.

If Luke is accepted as the companion of Paul, then the "we" passages of Acts disclose that Luke was in Philippi (possibly his hometown), and that there he joined Paul (Acts 16:10-17). Then he later rejoined Paul when the latter returned to Philippi (Acts 20:5-15). Luke then journeyed with Paul on his way to Jerusalem and stayed with Philip at Caesarea (Acts 21:1-18). Then, after Paul's two-year imprisonment in Caesarea, Luke sailed with him to Rome (Acts 27:1–28:16).

Further references to Luke in the Epistles of Paul (Col. 4:14; Philem. 24; 2 Tim. 4:11) give some valuable information about Luke. Colossians 4:11 and 14 seem to indicate that Luke was a Gentile and a physician. The latter is supported, but not proved, by the interest shown by Luke in medical matters, as in Luke 4:38; 5:12; and 8:43. It is also interesting that early tradition adds that Luke was a physician of Antioch who wrote his Gospel in Achaia and died at the age of eighty-four. H. K. FARRELL

LULL, RAYMOND (c. 1232–1316)
Spanish mystic, missionary, and scholar

Married quite young, Lull led a chivalric life as a seneschal at the Aragonese court. During the decade of 1262 to 1272, however, he experienced a series of visions, which caused him to devote himself to missionary activity, mainly among Muslims. Tradition records that on a third preaching tour to Tunis he suffered martyrdom by stoning.

Lull was a mystic, deeply influenced by the Franciscan movement and by Muslim Sufism. Restlessly active, nonetheless, he traveled far and wide (Italy, France, England, and Germany), seeking support for his efforts. Having learned Arabic from the large Muslim element around him, he wrote in that language as well as in Latin and his native Catalan. His writings were not only theological and philosophical (in the Augustinian tradition); they also included poetry in the troubadour fashion and allegorical novels. A manual of chivalry by Lull was printed in an English version by William Caxton.

Strongly attracted by the mendicant orders, both Dominican and Franciscan, Lull may have become a Franciscan tertiary. But he probably remained all his life, like Dante, one of those unusual medieval phenomena, a literate layperson. He taught Arabic metaphysics briefly at the University of Paris. He also established a school of oriental languages under the patronage of King James II of Majorca. One of his books purports to present a conversation held by a Christian, a Jew, and a Muslim in search of common ground for the three religions of Iberia.

Despite his activity and productivity, Lull did not impress his own day. Although one of the brightest flowers of the Spanish Middle Ages, Lull had to wait until recent times to begin receiving serious study.

A. CABANISS

LUTHER, MARTIN (1483–1546)
Father of the German Reformation

THE EARLY YEARS

Born at Eisleben in Thüringe, Saxony, Luther attended school at Mansfeld, at Magdeburg under the Brethren of the Common Life, and at Eisleben. He then went to university at Erfurt (1501), where he came under Nominalist influence and learned Greek, graduating B.A. in 1502 and M.A. in 1505. He had intended to study law, but due to a narrow escape from death by lightning,

he changed his mind and in spite of his father's objections became an Augustinian monk in 1506.

In the Erfurt monastery he did further theological study, was made a priest in 1507, and with his transfer to Wittenberg in 1508 read for the B.D. (1509) and began to teach moral theology, the *Sentences* of Peter Lombard, and the holy Scriptures. A visit to Rome on Augustinian business (1510–1511) opened his eyes to the corruption prevalent among the higher clergy. Returning to Wittenberg he took the degree of D.Th. in 1512 and was appointed to the chair of biblical studies, which he occupied for the rest of his life. He also became subprior of the Wittenberg house.

Outwardly Luther was building up a successful monastic and academic career but inwardly he was troubled by a conviction of sin that his diligence in monastery life could not relieve. John Staupitz, his vicar-general, proved to be a good counselor at this period. And Luther also read widely in Augustine, Tauler, and the German mystics collected in the volume called *German Theology*. He also received help from the work of contemporary French theologian Lefèvre d'Étaples on the Psalms. His biblical reading, especially in preparation for his classes on the Psalms (1513–1515), Romans (1515–1516), and Galatians (1517) proved to be the decisive factor. It was probably during this period, perhaps in 1514, that he had the famous Tower experience when he came to realize that God's righteousness in Romans 1 is not the justice that we have to fear but the positive righteousness that God gives believers in Christ—it is a righteousness they receive by personally trusting in Christ.

THE YEARS OF PROTEST

Luther might easily have held and taught his new understanding of justification without interference or vital reforming impact. His colleagues at Wittenberg both on the theological faculty and in the monastery supported him, and church life went on undisturbed. In 1517, however, Luther was aroused when just across the border from Saxony John Tetzel preached an indulgence in which crude theology was accompanied by the crassest materialism. In protest Luther rapidly drew up ninety-five theses for debate, which he posted on the door of the Castle church on October 31, 1517. When translated and widely circulated, these theses brought an explosion of anti-church feeling that wrecked the indulgence. Given practical application in this way, Luther's theology could no longer go unnoticed, and he came at once under ecclesiastical pressures ranging from attempts at intimidation to promised favors for compliance.

Luther refused to be silenced. He won over many Augustinians at the Heidelberg disputation in 1518. He argued, not incorrectly, that he was defying no dogmatic definition of the church. Pressed by Eck at the Leipzig disputation in 1519, he claimed the supremacy of the authority of Scripture over all ecclesiastical authority. Continuing his own preaching and teaching, he defended the theses in his *Explanations* (1518) and showed how the righteousness of sinners lies in the alien righteousness of Christ in his *Two Kinds of Righteousness* (1518). When Charles V, the newly elected emperor, stepped up the pressure, Luther responded in 1520 with three powerful works that have come to be called his primary treatises. In the *Address to the German Nobility* he appealed to the princes to throw off papal oppression. In the *Babylonian Captivity* he attacked the current sacramental system. In *The Freedom of a Christian Man* he expounded the complementary theses that the Christian is both a free lord subject to none and also a servant subject to all. The writings of this period also include his *Treatise on Good Works*, which shows how faith finds expression in works, and his *Sermon on the Mass,* which teaches the priesthood of all believers.

By the middle of 1520 papal patience was at an end, and a bull was drawn up ordering Luther's recantation and the burning of his works. Protected by the elector Frederick, Luther denounced the bull, and the theology faculty solemnly burned a copy at a ceremony on December 10, 1520. Early in 1521 a stronger bull of excommunication

was prepared that, if carried out, would have deprived Luther of civil rights and protection. Before its execution Charles V agreed to give Luther the chance to recant at the diet to be held at Worms. Here Luther made his resounding confession before the emperor, princes, and other rulers: "My conscience is captive to the Word of God . . . Here I stand, I can do no other."

THE YEARS OF RECONSTRUCTION
The situation after Worms seemed hardly favorable for positive reform. A majority at the diet decided to apply the papal bull. In order to shield Luther against violence, Frederick arranged his "kidnapping" on the way home and hid him in the safe castle of the Wartburg under the guise of George the Knight. Luther, however, grasped the opportunity to begin the work of translating the New Testament directly from the Greek into superbly simple and idiomatic German, which served as a model for William Tyndale's English rendering. He finished this work in the fall of 1522 and followed it up with an Old Testament translation from the Hebrew. This, of course, took much longer and was not finished until 1534. The completed Luther Bible proved to be no less tremendous a force in the German-speaking world than the King James Version was later to be in the English sphere, and it must be regarded as one of Luther's most valuable contributions to the German church.

Able to return from the Wartburg in 1522, Luther turned his attention to the sphere of worship. The main step here, as in relation to Scripture, was to make the services understandable by putting them in the native tongue. Luther, indeed, had no wish to cause friction by unnecessary changes in liturgical structure. The spiritual and theological reformation formed the heart of the matter for him. He thus produced conservative orders for baptism and the mass in 1523. The order of 1526, which included collects, canticles, and a litany, brought some reduction in the baptismal service. Even more significantly, however, it introduced new paraphrases and hymns for congregational use. Luther's own skill as a hymn writer and his musical interest and ability gave special importance to his work in this field, and even in translation some of his hymns—especially "A Mighty Fortress"—have been a constant source of spiritual strength and inspiration.

During his time in the Wartburg Luther had given much thought to the question of celibacy. Even earlier he had come to think that the only lifelong vow a Christian ought to take is that of baptism, i.e., of general discipleship. While in the Wartburg he wrote *On Monastic Vows*. His reforming work when he came back to Wittenberg included the dissolution of monasteries and the ending of clerical celibacy. The resources of the monasteries were made available for the relief of the poor, and marriages between former celibates became the order of the day so that, as Erasmus noted, the tragedy of the break with Rome looked like it finished as a comedy—with everyone getting married and living happily ever after. Luther himself married the former nun Katherine of Bora, and they had a happy life with six children. Luther continued to live in what had been the Augustinian convent, and some of the students he had in for meals took down his conversation, now published in the volumes of *Table Talk*.

Spreading reform to the parishes formed an essential part of reconstruction. Luther saw clearly the need for education, and he thus issued an appeal for Christian schools in 1524, worked with Melanchthon on a plan for popular education in the instructions for the Saxon visitation of 1528, and preached to parents on the duty of sending children to school in 1530. Spiritual as well as secular instruction was needed to remedy the ignorance prevalent in the later Middle Ages. To help pastors provide this, Luther composed a Large Catechism in 1528 and then a more popular Small Catechism in 1529. In the latter he gave a simple exposition of the Creed, the Lord's Prayer, the Ten Commandments, and the two sacraments. He also offered forms for confession, morning and evening prayers, and grace at meals. To supply more able pastors and teachers for the parishes he supported Melanchthon in

university reforms, especially in the theological faculties.

The work of reconstruction could hardly be completed without a doctrinal statement. Luther had not begun the reformation with a prepared and developed theological position. He saw his way clearly in the matter of justification by grace and faith. When his applying of this teaching to indulgences brought it under attack, he quickly saw that Scripture must be the supreme authority in the church. He then began to work out the ramifications of these basic tenets in other areas but not in a systematic way. His colleague and friend Melanchthon issued a first doctrinal presentation in his work *Theological Common Places* (1521). Later Luther himself had a hand in the framing of the articles discussed at Marburg (1529), which were then incorporated into the *Confession of Augsburg* (1530)—although in relation to the latter he played more of the role of a consultant, and Melanchthon acted as principal writer. In 1536 Luther accepted the agreement with the South Germans expressed in the Wittenberg Concord, and in 1537 he offered a restatement of his essential theology in the *Articles of Schmalcald*, which reaffirm the early creeds, condemn medieval abuses, and give positive teaching on sin, law and gospel, the sacraments, justification, and the church.

Finally Luther contributed to positive reform through his constant preaching and writing. Collections of his sermons are available in the comprehensive editions of his works. His writings include many polemical pieces, but there were many constructive works too. Worthy of special mention are his justifiably renowned *Lectures on Galatians* of 1535, which are among the finest of his works and have had an influence extending well beyond the reformation period.

THE YEARS OF CONTROVERSY

From the publication of his *95 Theses* Luther was engaged in unending debate with the Roman Church. In addition, he soon found himself in disagreement with other reforming groups. Since he was plain, outspoken, and pugnacious, and came into collision with equally militant opponents, these controversies often took on a bitter edge that brought personal alienation and greatly hampered the general movement of reform.

A first problem arose in 1521 when Luther was in Wartburg. A little group from Zwickau, the Zwickau Prophets, came to Wittenberg and caused great confusion in the church. Visiting the city to deal with the issue Luther preached against the group and later summed up his criticisms in the work *Against the Heavenly Prophets*. Radicalism took a violent turn with Thomas Munzer, who savagely denounced Luther and was himself denounced in return. When the peasants began to revolt in 1524, Luther sympathized with their demands, attempted mediation, and issued a call for peace. The uprisings increased in 1525 and under the influence of men like Munzer often took on a fanatical character. This led Luther to leave his mediatorial role and to call for the ruthless suppression of the rebels in the interests of divinely willed law and order. Although he still made a plea for economic justice, his attitude alienated many of the peasants and brought a rift.

At the very same period Luther became entangled in an unfortunate if unavoidable controversy with the humanist scholar and reformer Erasmus. The two had much in common, sharing concerns for scholarship, for opening up the Scriptures, and for doctrinal and practical reform. Nevertheless, they differed sharply in character and also in theological approach. Under pressure to declare himself either for Luther or against him, Erasmus turned to the important issue of the freedom of the will and published a *Diatribe on Free Will* (1524). To this Luther made a sharp and almost scornful reply in his *Bondage of the Will* (1525). This work is a powerful statement of the Augustinian position that in matters of right conduct and salvation the will has no power to act apart from the divine initiative. Erasmus came out with a counter-reply, but Luther ignored this. Erasmus then aligned himself with the opponents of the Reformation, although still urging reform and maintaining friendly relations with various reformers.

The disruptive eucharistic controversy that split the Lutherans from the South Germans and the Swiss also began at this time. In answer to the Swiss, Luther defended his literal reading of the words "This is my body" in various works, especially *The Sacrament of the Body and Blood of Christ* in 1526 and *That These Words of Christ "This is my Body" Still Stand* in 1527. Unfortunately Luther adopted in this debate a coarse and vituperative style that did little to win over his opponents or commend his teaching. Philip of Hesse tried to achieve agreement at Marburg in 1529, but in the discussions Luther showed from the first a rigidity that doomed the effort to failure. Later Luther accepted the uneasy concord with Bucer and the South Germans at Wittenberg (1536). No progress was made with the Swiss, however, although it has been thought that if Luther had lived, Calvin might have broken the deadlock. Luther's concern was that in the saying "This is my body" the word "is" should be given its true force, but he opened the door to controversy by admitting a special mode of Christ's presence in the relation to bread and wine. The controversy became christological when, in reply to the truth that Christ in the body is now in heaven, Luther claimed that the body enjoys omnipresence through the communicating of the attributes of Christ's deity to his humanity. As a result christological as well as eucharistic differences continued between the Reformed and the Lutherans long after the death of Luther himself.

Luther ran into other difficulties, too. He hoped at first that the renewing of the gospel would open the way for the conversion of the Jews. When this hope was not realized, he made intemperate attacks on the Jews, thus putting a dark blot on his record. Philip of Hesse, the great champion of the Reformation, became a serious embarrassment when he secured the unwilling assent of Luther to his bigamous marriage in 1540. The development of armed religious alliances in the empire also worried Luther, for while he accepted the divine authorization of princes and valued their help in practical reformation, he struggled hard for the principle that the gospel does not need to be advanced or defended by military power. He was mercifully spared the conflict that came so soon after his death.

THE CLOSING YEARS
Pressured by ill health and harassed constantly by political and theological problems, Luther tended to display in his last years the less pleasant aspects of his virtues. His courage increasingly appeared as pugnacity, his bluntness as crudity, and his steadfastness as obstinacy. Instead of mellowing with the years, his opposition to the papists, the radicals, and other reformers became even more bitter. Nevertheless, he continued to work for military peace in the empire—and it is a tribute to his underlying desire for peace and reconciliation that the aim of his final journey was to bring together the quarreling rulers of Anhaldt. As chance would have it, his itinerary brought him to the town of his birth, and it was in Eisleben that he died on February 18, 1546.

Luther stands out as a very human figure. As he said at Worms, he made no claim to special sanctity. He recognized himself when he stated that believers are at the same time both righteous and sinners. His faults were as easy to see as his virtues. He was not characterized by any hypocrisy or pretense. He saw and told things as they were, whether in relation to the gospel or in relation to himself.

This very human figure had extraordinary gifts. Perhaps the most striking thing of all about him was his versatility. Without being an outstanding linguist, he had a mastery of the biblical languages. This mastery went hand-in-hand with a rare theological insight. Luther could see to the heart of theological questions and express himself with astonishing originality and force. If he never put his theology together in a dogmatic, he contributed more to real theology than the vast majority of dogmaticians.

Yet Luther was no academician or theological theorist. His daily job was that of a professor, but he put his learning to work on many practical fronts. Theological and pastoral concern launched him into the attack on indulgences that toppled the medieval system. His linguistic skills produced one of the greatest Bible translations of all time. His combination of biblical knowledge with graphic simplicity of utterance and a vital reality of faith made him no less eminent and effective as a preacher. That he should have such lavish liturgical gifts, as well, seems almost incredible. Behind it all, of course, lay the passionate sincerity of one who had been brought to his thought and mission not by abstract speculation but by the realities of sin, grace, forgiveness, and faith. His written works fill many bulky volumes, but the words are all vibrant and challenging, for they came not merely from the study or podium but from life and action.

Luther did a work that probably no one else in his highly gifted age could have done. He did it because he had the required combination of learning, insight, character, and faith. When under God the hour struck in 1517, the man for the hour was there. The Reformation that had been arrested so long could no longer be delayed.
G. BROMILEY

LYTE, HENRY FRANCIS (1793–1847)
Hymn writer and poet

Born in Scotland and educated at Trinity College, Dublin, Lyte entered the ministry of the Church of Ireland. After a curacy in Ireland, he moved to England, where he married and held several more curacies, the last being at Lower Brixham, Devon. Plagued by ill health, he made frequent foreign visits in search of sunshine and cures. He died at Nice in France and was buried in the British cemetery there.

Some of his hymns are well known: "Abide with Me, Fast Falls the Eventide," "Pleasant are Thy Courts Above," "Praise, My Soul, the King of Heaven," and "Jesus, I My Cross Have Taken." He published some of his hymns in *Poems Chiefly Religious* (1833) and his metrical psalms in *Spirit of the Psalter* (1834). He also published several volumes of secular verse. After his death his daughter published his *Remains* (1850), in which are poems, letters, sermons, plus a brief biography. Because of his constant sickness and his experience of God's peace, Lyte's hymns were written out of deep spiritual experience. P. TOON

M

MABILLON, JEAN (1632–1707)
Church historian

Born in Champagne, France, and of peasant stock, Mabillon became a noted historian. He entered the Abbey of St. Remi at Reims, becoming a full member of the Maurist Congregation in 1654. His zeal for the ascetic religious life affected his health; thus, from 1658 to 1663 he was at the Abbey of Corbie regaining health. It was here that he developed his gifts as a historian. From 1664 until his death he was at the Abbey of St. Germain des Prés, where there was a society of learned scholars. In this group Mabillon showed his own brilliance. He produced twenty folio works of which a large proportion was devoted to the history of the Benedictine order of monks, of which the Maurists were a part. He also produced an edition of the works of Bernard, the medieval theologian. In a lively volume, *Treatise on Study in Monasteries* (1691), he defended the right of monks to pursue scholarly studies. It may be said that he put the study of paleography on a scientific basis. P. TOON

MACALISTER, R. A. S. (1870–1950)
Irish archaeologist

A professor of Celtic archaeology at the Univeristy of Dublin, Macalister became interested in Palestinian archaeology. He directed the Palestine Exploration Fund for many years and conducted extensive excavations at Gezer (1902–1909) and a dig on the hill Ophel in Jerusalem (1923–1924). The Gezer dig was the largest excavation undertaken in Palestine to that time, employing up to two hundred workers on a year-round basis. Macalister also worked at Marisa, Azekah, Mareshah, and Tell el-Judeideh. Among his several publications are *Excavations at Gezer, Studies in Irish Epigraphy,* and *A Century of Excavation in Palestine.* H. F. VOS

MACAULAY, ZACHARY (1768–1838)
Evangelical philanthropist and abolitionist

Born in Argyllshire, Scotland, the son of a clergyman, Macaulay went at the age of sixteen to Jamaica to act as bookkeeper on an estate that used slave labor. Eventually he became manager of that estate. Unhappy about slavery, he returned to Great Britain, where, after meeting members of the Clapham Group, he became involved in the scheme to repatriate some black slaves in Sierra Leone. He went out to the colony as the representative of the Sierra Leone Company and became governor in 1793. Ill health forced him to return to Britain in

1795, but he insisted on returning via the West Indies so that he could experience personally the crossing of the Atlantic on a slave ship from Africa to the West Indies. After a rest he returned to the colony for another four years and attempted in a variety of ways to give the repatriated slaves good homes and surroundings. Returning to London he acted as the secretary of the company until the government took over the colony in 1808.

He was an able writer and edited *The Christian Observer*, a monthly journal financed by the Clapham Sect, from 1802 to 1816. Also he ran his own merchant business with his nephew and used his knowledge of the slave trade to fight for its abolition. A founding member of the Anti-Slavery Society (1823), he never spared himself in the fight for the liberation of slaves. Also he was an active member of the big evangelical societies—the British and Foreign Bible Society and the Church Missionary Society. Further, he was greatly interested in education and was, with others, responsible for the foundation of the University of London. P. TOON

McCHEYNE, R.M. (1813–1843)
Scottish minister

Born in Edinburgh, McCheyne studied arts and divinity at the university there and in 1836 became minister of St. Peter's Church, Dundee. His life and ministry were short and punctuated by severe illnesses, yet McCheyne's impact on Scotland was like that of Samuel Rutherford. There was the same self-discipline, fervent prayer, Bible study, assiduous preparation for the pulpit, sense of urgency that time was short, and the same deep concern for souls. He once said he blessed God every morning that he lived in witnessing times. Ordered to take an extended rest from parish work, he went to the Holy Land and contributed to the later development of a Scottish mission to Jews. He wrote letters, tracts, poems, used his artistic and musical gifts effectively, and accepted invitations to preach all over Scotland. When the encroachment of civil authority

on spiritual matters came before parliament he wrote: "Once more King Jesus stands at an earthly tribunal, and they know Him not!" The outcome was the 1843 Disruption when the national church lost most of its evangelicals. McCheyne would have joined them but—not quite thirty—he had died a few months earlier.

In his remarkable memoir, Dr. Andrew Bonar said of McCheyne: "He cared for no question unless his Master cared for it; and his main anxiety was to know the mind of Christ." McCheyne is widely known through Bonar's biography, *Memoir and Remains of Robert Murray McCheyne* (1862). J. D. DOUGLAS

MACDONALD, GEORGE (1824–1905)
Scottish writer and poet

Almost as popular as Charles Dickens in the latter part of the nineteenth century, George Macdonald belonged at his best among the great writers of English. Unhappily, he could not always maintain the fine quality often noteworthy in his writing. He produced more than fifty books, including twenty-five novels, a great many stories for children, poetry, essays, and sermons. In all that he wrote there is a distinctive Christian flavor and meaning. Indeed, his works sometimes suffer from too much exhortation.

Macdonald knew many of the other great writers of his time, such as Emerson, Longfellow, and Whittier in the United States and Thackeray, Ruskin, Tennyson, Dickens, and Carlyle in England. He was the close friend of Lewis Carroll. Lady Byron, after the death of her husband, provided her longtime friend Macdonald with funds to help him sustain his family and protect his own precarious health.

Macdonald's novels are not much read today, but his so-called fairy stories have remained popular since they were written. *At the Back of the North Wind* (1871) is the story of Diamond the cab horse and of a little boy, also named Diamond, who slept in the straw in an attic and was visited by the North Wind in the form of a lovely lady who took him for visits high in the air and at last taught him of a still more lovely Being. Perhaps his best book is *The Princess and the Goblin* (1872), where a small boy and girl have adventures with evil goblins in underground mines and overcome the goblins. In *The Princess and Curdie* (1883) the same two undergo further adventures and grow up and get married. *The Lost Princess* (1875) is a memorable account of Rosamund, a spoiled princess, and Agnes, a spoiled shepherd's daughter, who are taught better ways by the Wise Woman.

Some of the adult books frequently reprinted are two mythopoetic novels: *Phantastes* (1858), the story which played a large part in starting C. S. Lewis on his journey to God, and *Lilith* (1895), the story of a man indifferent to anything religious who is converted by the efforts of a redeemed Adam and Eve. Other works are *Diary of an Old Soul* (1880), *The Hope of the Gospel* (1892), *Unspoken Sermons* (1867, 1886, 1889), and *The Miracles of Our Lord* (1870).

Macdonald had revolted against a rigid Calvinistic teaching given to him in his youth—that only the "elect" could be saved. He turned radical and accepted the opposite view of universal salvation. Nonetheless, he remained a warmhearted and persuasive preacher of the gospel throughout his life. C. KILBY

McGIFFERT, ARTHUR CUSHMAN (1861–1933)
Leading church historian of American liberalism at the beginning of the twentieth century

After graduating from Union Seminary in New York (1885), McGiffert did doctoral work under the famed Adolph Von Harnack in Germany. For five years he taught church history at Lane Seminary in Cincinnati before succeeding Philip Schaff, founder of the American Society of Church History, as professor of church history at Union in 1893. He later served as Union's president from 1917 to 1926. McGiffert was an ordained Presbyterian whose ideas brought him into conflict with the majority of that denomina-

tion. The three most important principles of his teaching were concern for the life of Christ, commitment to "scientific" history, and belief in social ethics. For him, Jesus possessed "a vivid realization of God as his father and the father of his brethren." The apostle Paul, on the other hand, propounded ideas "totally at variance with Christ's." It was Paul who founded historic Christianity, a movement distorted (until the enlightened nineteenth century) by its overemphasis on the divinity of Christ and on the institutional church. McGiffert's historical work was strongly influenced by his training in Germany, particularly by the idea that "scientific" history, which excluded the supernatural, was somehow more "objective" than that which allowed for the possibility of God's action. He believed so thoroughly in the virtue of doing good that virtually every kind of humanitarian service became a form of Christianity. With these views it is not surprising that he fell afoul of the evangelical and conservative majority in the Presbyterian church. Under heavy fire, McGiffert left the denomination voluntarily in 1900 and became a Congregationalist. His books, such as *A History of Christianity in the Apostolic Age* (1897) and *A History of Christian Thought* (two volumes, 1931–1933), remain lucid examples of church history from a liberal perspective. M. NOLL

McGREADY, JAMES (c. 1758–1817)
Frontier revivalist; credited with originating the outdoor camp meeting

McGready was born in western Pennsylvania of Scottish parents. Educated at John McMillan's log college in Canonsburg, Pennsylvania, he was ordained in 1788 to the Presbyterian ministry. He preached in Orange County, North Carolina, but his revivalistic zeal began to show significant results when he moved to Logan County, Kentucky. There he made a solemn covenant with his congregations to pray and fast on the third Saturday of every month, and every week at dusk on Saturday and dawn on Sunday. A year later a revival began that spread to six states and became the momentum for the Second Great Awakening (1800–1805).

The Cumberland revival has given McGready his place in American church history. Camp meetings were organized by McGready and two Methodists at Cane Ridge, Kentucky, in 1800. The meetings drew thousands of people. It was the first of its kind; many more followed. New converts flocked into churches, one of which was the newly formed Cumberland Presbyterian Church. M. FACKLER

MACHEN, J. GRESHAM (1881–1937)
American Presbyterian apologist, theologian, and educator

Born in Baltimore, Maryland, Machen was the son of a prosperous lawyer. His mother came from a prominent family in Georgia, and both parents, who were strong Christians, exerted a deep influence on Machen through most of his life. Machen graduated from Johns Hopkins University and Princeton Theological Seminary. He was greatly influenced by the strong Calvinism of Princeton, especially as held by Benjamin Warfield and Francis Patton. Following his graduation from Princeton in 1905, he studied in Germany at Marburg and Göttingen. At Marburg he was greatly impressed by Professor Wilhelm Herrmann, whose attractive presentation of liberal theology captivated him for a time. However, Machen gradually came to the conviction there was a vast gulf between religious liberalism and orthodox Christianity. The experience affected him profoundly and made him determined to stand firm against religious liberalism.

After his studies in Germany, Machen returned to Princeton in 1906 as an instructor in New Testament. As a bachelor he was free to devote his full time to his work and gradually became well known in Presbyterian circles as an excellent scholar, teacher, and preacher. Following ordination in 1914, Machen was elevated to full faculty status at Princeton.

During this time many American denominations were becoming increasingly divided over the fundamentalist-modernist controversy. The Presbyterian Church in the U.S.A. was no exception, and Princeton, as that denomination's leading seminary, found itself reluctantly drawn into the struggle. In 1914 Dr. J. Ross Stevenson became the seminary's new president. It soon became clear that Stevenson, while not, strictly speaking, a theological liberal, favored a policy of tolerance and inclusivism toward those who held modernist views. In this attitude Stevenson was clearly reflecting the opinion of many in the Presbyterian Church.

Machen found such ideas repugnant, believing that they would eventually lead to the rejection of the basic reformed beliefs for which Presbyterians—and Princeton—were noted. Before long, after a stint with the YMCA in France during World War I, Machen found himself thrust into the leadership of the conservative Presbyterian ranks. A proposal to allow united efforts with non-Reformed bodies was passed by the Presbyterian General Assembly in 1920. Machen vigorously fought against its approval by the Presbyterians, and was unquestionably a major influence in its defeat. His books *The Origin of Paul's Religion* (1921) and *Christianity and Liberalism* (1923) further established his reputation as a scholarly and articulate conservative apologist, as did his later (and possibly most significant) work, *The Virgin Birth of Christ* (1930).

Machen's role in the Presbyterian Church became increasingly prominent, especially after the publication of the Auburn Affirmation (1924), which showed the depth of liberal sentiment among Presbyterian ministers. Confirmation of Machen's election to the chair of apologetics at Princeton was tabled by the 1925 General Assembly, which also appointed a committee to investigate the growing tensions in the seminary faculty and governing bodies. The committee recommended that the seminary be reorganized, a move that would bring much greater liberal influence to the seminary. By 1929 the proposed reorganization had been passed by the General Assembly in spite of the objections of Machen and other conservative Presbyterians. The move was widely seen as heralding the end of Princeton's strict Reformed theological stance.

Almost immediately Machen and other conservatives began plans for a new seminary that would carry on Princeton's tradition of close adherence to the Westminster Standards. The new institution (known as Westminster Seminary) opened its doors in the fall of 1929, with Machen as president and professor of New Testament.

The controversy over liberalism continued. The publication of *Rethinking Missions* (1932), a liberal attack on many traditional missionary concepts, led to new tensions. The refusal of the Presbyterian Board of Foreign Missions to renounce unequivocally the book's position led to heightened conservative worries over the direction of denominational missions. Again Machen became the principal defender of the conservative course. When it became clear the denomination's mission program was moving toward doctrinal latitude, Machen led in the formation of an independent mission board. The move caused widespread dispute and led to Machen's suspension from the ministry by his presbytery (1935). This action gave impetus to the formation in 1936 of a new denomination, the Presbyterian Church of America (later renamed the Orthodox Presbyterian Church) with Machen as the first moderator. To his disappointment, many Presbyterian conservatives who had supported him elected not to join the new denomination. J. N. AKERS

MACK, ALEXANDER (1679–1735)
Leader of the German Church of the Brethren

Born in Schriesheim, Germany, Mack became a miller by trade. Mack was attracted by the radical pietist movement that developed in Germany in the seventeenth and eighteenth centuries. He was associated in preaching missions with E. C. Hochmann von Hochenau, the German mystic. Suffering persecution, Mack took refuge in the village of Schwarzenau in the county of Wittgenstein. Here, in 1708, he and seven others formed a religious group, the begin-

ning of what was to become the Church of the Brethren. The group stressed believers' baptism and the separated church. They practiced primitive rites with a biblical precedent including foot washing, the holy kiss after Communion, and the love feast. The most distinctive practice (not derived from biblical precedent) was triple immersion. Increasing persecution of the Brethren groups at Schwarzenau and Marienborn led them to move to West Friesland and Crefeld. In 1719 Peter Becker, another Brethren leader, led a group to Germantown, Pennsylvania. Here he was joined by Mack and his group in 1729. The Brethren were the basis of a church which, by the time of the American Revolution, was located in eastern Pennsylvania, New Jersey, and Maryland. In 1871 the group adopted the name of the German Baptist Brethren, but they are now known as the Church of the Brethren. Mack continued as the Brethren leader in America until his death. D.C. MASTERS

MACKAY, GEORGE LESLIE (1844–1901)
Canadian Presbyterian missionary to Taiwan

Mackay was born at Zorra, Ontario. He was educated at Knox College, Toronto, Princeton Theological Seminary and Edinburgh University and was appointed by the Canada Presbyterian Church as its first missionary to China in 1871.

For the next thirty years he labored indefatigably in the northern half of the island of Taiwan. Mackay quickly mastered the Chinese language and classics and by 1875 had developed a Christian community with nine chapels and three schools. He adopted Chinese clothes and customs and in 1878 married one of his converts. Returning for a visit to Canada in 1880, he had great success in raising money for his mission and also received some medical training. In thirty years he established some sixty churches with three thousand members. His work was interrupted by a wave of anti-foreign feeling that developed as a result of the French invasion of Taiwan in 1884. In 1893 Mackay again returned for a visit to Canada and subsequently published a book, *From Far*

Formosa: The Island, Its People and Missions (1896). Mackay's mission churches suffered more persecution after the Japanese annexation of Taiwan in 1895 but in the long run profited from the more liberal attitude of the Japanese to foreigners. D. C. MASTERS

McKENDREE, WILLIAM (1757–1835)
The first American-born bishop of the Methodist Church

Born in Virginia, McKendree was attracted to the Methodist movement in his late teens but only later (at about the age of thirty) did he experience conversion. Shortly afterward he was appointed by Bishop Francis Asbury to work on a trial basis among Methodists in Virginia, and before long he was ordained an elder in charge of a circuit. He held numerous circuits, not only in Virginia, but in several frontier areas as well. In 1801 he was appointed presiding elder of the Western Conference, which covered a vast area from Ohio to Georgia. He played a major role in the rapid expansion of Methodism along the frontier during this time. In 1808 McKendree was elected bishop, replacing Bishop Whatcoat (who had died in 1806). He acted as Bishop Asbury's assistant until Asbury's death in 1816. Although plagued by ill health, McKendree continued to travel extensively (especially to visit quarterly and annual conference meetings) until his death. J. N. AKERS

MACKINTOSH, HUGH ROSS (1870–1936)
Scottish theologian

Born in Paisley of Highland stock, Mackintosh had an extraordinarily brilliant record as a student at Edinburgh and at various German universities. In 1897 he was ordained in the Free Church of Scotland and ministered successively in Tayport and Aberdeen. In 1904 his academic gifts were recognized when he was appointed to the chair of systematic theology in New College, Edinburgh. (Both Mackintosh and the college were by this time part of the new United Free Church.) A tireless worker, he won

international fame as a theologian and, unusual for a minister of the Kirk, earned an Oxford D.D. In strict evangelical circles he came under some criticism for his preoccupation with German Protestant theology, but he was also widely acknowledged to be a transparently devout man. Says one of his former students, "Step by step he led us into the great deeps where we knew the abasement of our sin, and thought of the love of God that could reach even deeper than our sin." The redoubtable Alexander Whyte of Free St. George's also had no doubts about Mackintosh's orthodoxy and often called on the professor to fill that famous pulpit in his absence, realizing (as he put it) that here was "a very rich possession to our own church and to all the churches." In 1929 New College came into the national church after the great union, and three years later Mackintosh was called to be moderator of the general assembly. Among his best-remembered and still-used works are *The Christian Experience of Forgiveness* (1927) and *Types of Modern Theology* (1937). J. D. DOUGLAS

MACLAREN, ALEXANDER (1826–1910)
British Baptist pastor

Born in Glasgow, son of a businessman who was also a Baptist lay pastor, Maclaren took classes at the local university before going south to train for the ministry at Stepney (later Regents Park) College, London. A diligent student, he was awarded London University's B.A. degree in 1845. In the following year he became pastor at Portland Chapel, Southampton, and during his twelve years there made it a well-known center of Christian witness. In 1858 he began his forty-five-year ministry at Union Chapel, Manchester. This small building had to be replaced by another that could accommodate the crowds who wanted to hear "the prince of expository preachers." He was tireless in preparation; he maintained the habit of daily reading in the original language one chapter from each Testament. He was an evangelical sympathetic to other views. He attacked the

Church of Rome while conceding it contained "true and devout souls" and maintained good relations with Roman and Anglican bishops. He warmly advocated union between Baptists and Congregationalists. Maclaren sponsored preaching stations, with a particular concern that the poor hear the gospel. Honored with doctorates from several British universities, twice president of the Baptist Union, and the first president of the Baptist World Alliance (1905), Maclaren remained a humble man. Next to Spurgeon's, his sermons were highly regarded in Victorian England; both message and method still offer valuable lessons more than eighty years after his death.
J. D. DOUGLAS

MacLEOD, GEORGE FIELDEN (LORD MacLEOD OF FUINARY) (1895–1991)
Church of Scotland minister; founder of the Iona community

Son of a baronet and parliamentarian, MacLeod was educated at Oxford and Edinburgh universities, and won two medals for valor in World War I (he later became an ardent pacifist). After ordination he ministered at fashionable St. Cuthbert's, Edinburgh (1926–1930), and in industrial Glasgow (1930–1938). Convinced that his message was not getting through to local shipyard and factory workers in those depression years, he embarked on a striking experiment to bring ministry and laity together. Resigning his charge, he settled with eight young craftsmen and ministers on the historic island of Iona, and set about rebuilding its abbey (associated with sixth-century Columba). He formed the Iona Community, which stressed four things: the church is committed to mission; parishioners must be trained to take responsible political action; the church must recover the ministry of healing; and worship must be related to daily life. MacLeod has lectured throughout the world, was made a royal chaplain in 1956 and moderator of the Kirk's general assembly in 1957, and was given a life peerage in 1967. Under him Iona again became a place of pilgrimage, and his name

was given to the island's youth and reconciliation center, which opened in 1988. He is the author of two books: *We Shall Rebuild* (1944) and *Only One Way Left* (1956). In 1989 MacLeod was given the Templeton Prize, the major award in religion, for adapting "the monastic ideal and spirit to modern life and religious activity." J. D. DOUGLAS

McPHERSON, AIMEE SEMPLE (1890–1944)
One of America's most flamboyant revivalists in the 1920s and 1930s

Born in Ingersoll, Ontario (Canada), McPherson married the man who had been influential in her conversion, Robert Semple, a Pentecostal preacher, with whom she went to China as a missionary in 1908. When Robert died, Aimee returned to the United States with their son, Robert. She then married Harold McPherson, from whom she was subsequently divorced. A third marriage and another divorce came later. With her mother as companion, Aimee Semple McPherson began after World War I a very successful series of revival tours across the United States. "Sister Aimee," as she was known to her followers, was a physically attractive woman who knew how to exploit her good looks and vibrant personality to capture the attention of the media. She pioneered in radio evangelism (1922) and may have participated in a staged kidnapping of herself in 1926, a case that remains clothed in mystery. Her teaching was probably not as important as her personality in her great success, but it did include standard fundamentalist and Pentecostal emphases: sanctification, baptism of the Holy Spirit with the gift of tongues, Christ as Savior and healer (hence faith healing), and the imminent return of Christ. In 1922 she settled in Los Angeles, where she preached to thousands each week at her $1.5 million Los Angeles Temple. The International Church of the Foursquare Gospel arose as a result of her ministry in 1927. It continued under the direction of her son after she died. Part of the sensation surrounding McPherson's career arose from allegations linking her romantically to other men. Even her death in 1944 was not free from sensation— some ascribing it to a heart attack, others to an overdose of sleeping pills. M. A. NOLL

MacVICAR, DONALD HARVEY (1831–1902)
Canadian Presbyterian clergyman and educator

MacVicar was born in Argyleshire, Scotland, and came to Canada with his parents as a child. He was educated at the University of Toronto and Knox College, Toronto, and in 1859 entered the Presbyterian ministry.

In 1868 MacVicar helped to found Presbyterian College in Montreal. His appointment as principal in 1868 represented a triumph for those who wanted the appointment of a Canadian-trained Scot rather than one trained in Scotland. From the time of his appointment until his death in 1902, the fortunes of Presbyterian College depended largely upon his energy and devotion. In the early period of the college's history almost the whole burden of teaching fell on him.

MacVicar was a fine preacher. His sermon at a precommunion service in the Glengarry district in Ontario has been vividly recorded by the Canadian writer Ralph Connor in his novel, *The Man from Glengarry*. MacVicar wrote widely, publishing articles in the *Presbyterian College Journal* and in magazines in Ontario and New York.

MacVicar's theology was the solid, Calvinist theology of the Reformed faith. His lectures showed the influence of American Calvinists such as Jonathan Edwards and Charles Hodge. He was anxious that his students should preach the gospel of salvation and urged them, "You are sent to preach the Gospel, to proclaim the great doctrines of grace in the proportions and relations to each other in which you find them stated in the Word of God." He was a firm believer in the Presbyterian form of church organization which, he said, afforded "proper rights and powers to clergy and laity alike."

MacVicar was Moderator of the General Assembly of the Presbyterian Church in Canada in 1881. He was a powerful factor in shaping the church as a Calvinist and evangelizing body. D. C. MASTERS

MAIER, WALTER ARTHUR (1893–1950)
Lutheran radio broadcaster

Maier was the Boston-born son of German immigrants. He was educated at Concordia Collegiate Institute (Bronxville), Boston University, Concordia Theological Seminary (St. Louis), and Harvard University (Ph.D., 1929). He was an outstanding student with a predilection for baseball, business, and practical jokes. While at Harvard on a graduate scholarship in Semitic studies he was ordained to the Lutheran ministry in 1917. During World War I he served briefly as Protestant chaplain at Camp Gordon, Georgia, and after the armistice returned to Harvard and Lutheran welfare work aiding POWs and their families. Then followed two years' service as executive secretary of the Walther League in Milwaukee and Chicago. In the fall of 1922 he was appointed professor of Old Testament interpretation and history at Concordia. He settled in St. Louis, married in 1924, and was on the verge of a distinguished academic career when he was introduced to radio broadcasting by a friend. Within a short time Maier was preaching from an attic radio station at the seminary and caught the vision of a nationwide radio ministry of "Bringing Christ to the Nation." In 1930 he persuaded the Lutheran Laymen's League to sponsor the "Lutheran Hour" on radio network, a venture which would eventually reach more than 20 million listeners a week and elicit half a million letters annually. By the time of his death, his religious program was broadcast by more than 1,230 stations in fifty-five countries in almost forty languages. E. A. HOLLATZ

MAIMONIDES (MOSES BEN MAIMON) (1135–1204)
Medieval Jewish philosopher and theologian

Maimonides was born at Cordova in Islamic Spain, but because of persecution his family wandered in Spain for twelve years before trying to settle at Fez in Morocco. Persecution also raged there and they escaped to Palestine. Conditions in the Holy Land were not good, and so they settled in Egypt, south of Cairo. Maimonides was thoroughly educated in Rabbinical teaching by his father. He also had access to the wealth of Arabic learning. At this time the Arabs, unlike Western Europe, had access to the major works of the Greek philosophers, most notably Aristotle. Maimonides became a physician. Later he was appointed chief of all the Jewish communities in Egypt.

Outside of Judaism, Maimonides' major influence has been through his *Guide of the Perplexed*. This work was originally published in Arabic in 1190 and translated into Hebrew in 1204. A Latin translation was made before 1240, and through it such Christian thinkers as Albertus Magnus (1193–1280), Thomas Aquinas (1224–1274), and Duns Scotus (1266–1308) came to know Maimonides' thought. Indeed, except for the doctrine of the soul, the philosophies of Maimonides and Thomas Aquinas are in harmony on all major points.

Maimonides was persuaded that faith has nothing to fear from applying reason to Scripture. Still the confrontation of science and Scripture can lead to perplexity, and so he wrote his *Guide* to aid learned believers. The purpose of the *Guide* is to illuminate Scripture, the Torah. It gives an exegesis of biblical terms and similes. This is necessary because many terms used to describe God have an outer and an inner meaning. When men understand the Bible according to its literal meaning, grave errors and tormenting perplexities arise. Other parts of the *Guide* are devoted to the themes of "Creation" and "The Chariot." In twenty-six propositions Maimonides presents the main theses from which philosophers have proved God's existence. He rejected only one thesis—that which asserted the eternity of the world.

Concerning God, Maimonides believed that he is one and that he has nothing in common with creatures; and so human language is radically inadequate to express him. Terms used to describe God in Scripture are only metaphors. Concerning the human soul, Maimonides held that the possession of intellectual qualities assures a man of immortality. The eternal life promised by faith is attained through knowledge which unites one to a higher Intellect. This position did not seem to lend support to the resurrection of the body. This is one of the reasons why Maimonides' work was attacked by Hasdai Crescas (c. 1340–1412) and other Jewish leaders after his death.

In holding that philosophy alone is not capable of attaining certain truths that we know through revelation, and in his conviction that theologians should not employ pseudorational arguments whose only merit is that they agree with the teaching of faith, Maimonides was an inspiration to Thomas Aquinas and other Christian thinkers. A. VOS

MAJOR, JOHN (1469–1550)
Scottish historian; scholastic divine

Born in East Lothian, Major studied and taught at Paris, took his D.D. there, and won wide fame as a lecturer at the Sorbonne. In 1518 he returned to Scotland as principal of Glasgow University, transferred to St. Andrews in 1522 to teach philosophy and logic and, except for a further six-year stint in Paris, remained there for the rest of his life. Major, who wrote entirely in Latin, published many works, notably the renowned commentary on Peter Lombard's *Sentences* (1509–1517) and the *History of Greater Britain* (1521). Though he wrote against tyranny and advocated reformation of the church, he approved of persecution and defended doctrines such as transubstantiation. His students at St. Andrews included Patrick Hamilton (the first martyr for the Reformation, 1528) and George Buchanan. Major died ten years before the Reformation triumphed in his native land. J. D. DOUGLAS

MAKARIOS III (1913–1977)
Orthodox archbishop; first president of the Republic of Cyprus

Born Mihail Christodoulou Mouskos near Paphos, Makarios was ordained priest in 1946, was recalled from studies in the United States on election as bishop of Kition in 1948, and became archbishop and primate of the autocephalous Church of Cyprus in 1950. A vigorous opponent of British rule, he was suspected of collaborating with guerrilla forces and was exiled to the Seychelles. He later resided in Athens, but returned after a 1959 agreement gave Cyprus independence and made Makarios also head of state. An astute and complex figure, he had to cope with a restive Turkish Muslim minority, extremists who sought union with Greece, fellow bishops who criticized his dual role, and a small but active Communist presence, which Makarios exploited for his own ends. A short-lived coup removed him briefly from leadership in 1974, but he was reinstated in 1975. When he died the two chief posts in the republic were separated. J. D. DOUGLAS

MAKEMIE, FRANCIS (1658–1708)
Founder of American Presbyterianism

Makemie was born in Ireland, educated in Glasgow (Scotland), and commissioned in Northern Ireland to serve as a missionary in America (1682). Makemie evangelized throughout the English-speaking New World—in New England, New York, Maryland, Virginia, and North Carolina, as well as in Barbados. He established the first Presbyterian congregation in America at Snow Hill, Maryland, in 1684. Cotton and Increase Mather of New England spoke highly of his work, and Congregationalists in general wished him well.

In 1706 he succeeded in bringing together Presbyterians of different backgrounds (English, Welsh, Scottish, Scots-Irish, and from New England) as the Presbytery of Philadelphia. Its purpose was "to meet yearly and oftener, if necessary, to consult the most proper measure for advancing religion and propagating Christianity in our various stations." In spite of differences in emphasis and custom, these Presbyterians could agree to take their stand on the Westminster Confession's presentation of biblical truth. In 1707 Makemie was arrested by New York's governor, Lord Cornbury, for preaching without a license in a private home on Long Island. Makemie

defended himself by appealing to the English Toleration Act of 1689, which granted religious freedom to Quakers whose views were much further from the establishment's than those of the Presbyterians. He was acquitted, although he did have to pay the high costs of his trial. This event solidified the image of Presbyterians as defenders of freedom in the public mind and won new respect for the denomination in America. M. A. NOLL

MALAN, CESAR HENRI ABRAHAM (1787–1864)
Swiss Reformed pastor

Born in Geneva, Malan studied Protestant theology there and was ordained to the ministry of the Reformed Church. In early years he was strongly influenced by the rationalistic thinkers Voltaire and Rousseau. In 1817 the Scot Robert Haldane came to Geneva, where he conducted a series of Bible studies on the Epistle to the Romans. Through these Bible studies Malan was converted to personal faith in Christ. Church authorities immediately attacked him for evangelical preaching, and he was forbidden to mention such subjects as original sin and election. Having disregarded the ban on preaching, Malan was ultimately shut out of his pulpit. Although he never formally left the established church, Malan did gather a group of ten believers. Soon they were celebrating the Lord's Supper. Later they met in the Capelle du Temoignage. Among the members of Malan's circle were Henry Pyt, François Gaussen, Jean G. Gonthier, and M. Jean Guerin. These men carried forward the "Reveil" revival movement in French-speaking Switzerland. Malan later wrote several hymns that continue in use. He also made several missionary journeys to Switzerland, Germany, France, the Netherlands, and Scotland. W. A. DETZLER

MALEBRANCHE, NICHOLAS (1638–1715)
French philosopher

Malebranche was son of the secretary to Louis XIII of France. After study at the Sorbonne, he joined the Paris House of the Oratory of St. Philip Neri. After some research in both history and biblical studies he read a book by René Descartes, the great philosopher. This captivated his interest, and henceforth he gave himself to the study of philosophy (or philosophical theology).

Though it may be said that he is a disciple of both Augustine of Hippo and of Descartes, he was a truly original thinker. Of his works the two most important are *De la Recherche de la verite* (two volumes, 1674) and *Traite de la nature et de la grace* (1680). The first was written at the beginning of his philosophic career; it sets out the views that are developed in his later writings. His views on the grace of God were challenged by leading Roman Catholic theologians, including J. B. Bossuet. P. TOON

MANALO, FELIX (1886–1963)

Founder of the "Iglesia ni cristo," an indigenous religion in the Philippines

Born near Manila to Catholic parents, Manalo left Catholicism in 1902 after witnessing the defeat of a Catholic priest by a Protestant missionary in a public debate. Thereafter he aligned himself successively with the Methodists, the Disciple's Mission, and the Seventh-day Adventists. Following quarrels with missionaries, Felix lapsed into agnosticism in 1912. During this period he exposed himself to Unitarian theology. Then giving religion another chance, he went into seclusion for fasting and meditation, after which he launched out on his own, preaching a new doctrine. In 1914 he formally founded "Iglesia ni cristo," functioning as "Executive Minister" until his death. His son, Erano, succeeded him.

Manalo denied the divinity of Christ. To him Christ was the man appointed by God to be the Savior of all who joined his church. Outside this church there is no salvation. Christ founded his church, "Iglesia ni cristo," in A.D. 33, but following the apostle Paul's death the church gradually disappeared because of apostasy. This apostasy took its ultimate form in Roman Catholicism. Not until 1914, when God commissioned his last messenger, Felix Manalo himself, did the church of Christ reappear in the Philippines. This was said to fulfill the prophecy of Revelation 7:2.

Every member of this religion is indoctrinated to defend its theology and all members are regimented into small committees for militant evangelism. Life-style is policed and tithing is mandatory. Magnificent church buildings, executive mansion, and palatial headquarters have been built from monies exacted from members. A nationalistic spirit is fostered by the use of the Philippines' national language and by teaching that there are many specific references to the Philippines in Bible prophecy. In the latest Philippine census, about 500,000 were listed as members. Following Filipino immigrants abroad, this religion has spread to Germany, Britain, and the United States. P. E. DORMAN

MANNING, BERNARD LORD (1892–1941)

Church historian

Born in Lincolnshire, the son of a Congregationalist minister, Manning became a distinguished church historian. He was educated at Cambridge University in Jesus College, where he later became a fellow and, for a period, college bursar. From 1933 to his death he was also a university lecturer in medieval history.

Although he never sacrificed his Congregationalist convictions, Manning had wide sympathies and appreciated many different Christian traditions. This is shown in his writings, which apart from obvious scholarship reveal his humor and wit. These are *The People's Faith in the Time of Wyclif* (1919), *The Making of Modern English Religion* (1929), *Essays in Orthodox Dissent* (1939), and *The Hymns of Wesley and Watts* (1942). In the Cambridge Medieval History he wrote two chapters in the seventh volume on "Wyclif" and "Edward III" and "Richard II." He also published two volumes of sermons. As a teacher of young men in Cambridge he treated his students as equals, while maintaining good discipline. P. TOON

MANNING, HENRY EDWARD
(1808–1892)
Roman Catholic cardinal

Born at Totteridge Hertfordshire, the son of a merchant, Manning attended Harrow School and Balliol College, Oxford. He was a fine athlete. In 1832 he was ordained and became a fellow of Merton College, Oxford. His background was in the evangelicalism of the Clapham Sect, but he became friendly with the Tractarians and adopted a high-church position. He wrote Number 78 of the *Tracts for the Times* and printed various other literature that supported the Tractarian viewpoint. In 1841 he became arch-deacon of Chichester where some of his sermons upset the evangelical clergy. After the secession of John Henry Newman to Rome in 1845 he was regarded as a leader of the Tractarian party along with E. B. Pusey and John Keble.

In 1850 he was appalled at the interference (as he saw it) of the state in the affairs of the Church of England with regard to the doctrine of baptism—in the controversy surrounding G. C. Gorham and the bishop of Exeter. This led him to believe that the only true church must be the Roman Catholic Church. Since his wife had died he was able to be ordained as a Roman Catholic priest after he had studied for two years in Rome. Thereafter he quickly rose in the hierarchy of the Roman Catholic Church. In 1865 he became archbishop of Westminster and in 1875 was made a cardinal. At the Vatican Council (1869–1870) he established himself as a firm supporter of the doctrine of the infallibility of the pope and advocated this for the rest of his life. Though he did not live to see its completion, he was responsible for the building of Westminister Cathedral, half a mile from the older Westminster Abbey (Anglican). Despite his rigid conservative frame of mind he had a keen social conscience and promoted all kinds of useful work for the poor. P. TOON

MANSON, THOMAS WALTER
(1893–1958)
English New Testament scholar

Born in Northumberland, Manson became an outstanding Bible scholar. He studied at Glasgow University and Westminster College, Cambridge. In 1925 he entered the ministry of the Presbyterian Church of England and became a pastor in Northumberland. Here he wrote his *The Teaching of Jesus* (1931), which led on to his academic career. First he was Yates professor of New Testament Greek at Mansfield College, Oxford, and then the Rylands professor of biblical criticism and exegesis at Manchester University. In both positions he followed C. H. Dodd. His books on the Gospels included *The Servant Messiah* (1953) and *Ethics and the Gospel* (1960). He also wrote two influential books on the ministry: *Ministry and Priesthood* (1958) and *The Church's Ministry* (1948). He was a Doctor of Divinity of the Universities of Cambridge, Dublin, Durham, and Glasgow. He had the reputation of combining scholarship with a concern for the welfare of the church. P. TOON

MANTON, THOMAS (1620–1677)
English minister

Son of a Somerset clergyman, Manton graduated in arts from Oxford. In 1640, at the age of twenty, he was reportedly ordained deacon by the bishop of Exeter (the official minimum age was twenty-three). He was one of the scribes at the Westminister Assembly (1642–1649) and soon achieved prominence among London's Presbyterians. He preached many times before Parliament (1647–1658) and generally supported Oliver Cromwell's regime while disapproving of the execution of Charles I. From 1656 he was rector of St. Paul's, Covent Garden, where crowds flocked to hear him. With others he drew up the "Fundamentals of Religion" (1658). Manton, honored with an Oxford D.D. in 1660, was nicknamed by a critic the "prelate of the Protectorate." The Restoration church settlement was too liturgical for him; he resigned his living and preached in private houses until arrested in 1670 for declining to take an oath against attempting any change in church and state. His six-month imprisonment was spent, however, in comfortable circumstances, and he preached occasionally thereafter. With Baxter and others he tried unsuccessfully to come to "an accommodation" with the bishops. A Puritan concerned with religion, not politics, Manton was said to have used his influence "for the public tranquillity." A very large number of ministers attended his funeral, walking in pairs, a conformist and a nonconformist together. His many works include six volumes of sermons published after his death and highly prized commentaries on James (1651) and Jude (1658). J. D. DOUGLAS

MANZ, FELIX (c. 1498–1527)
Swiss Protestant and martyr

Manz was the son of a canon of the Zurich cathedral. After studying in Austria and being well trained in Latin, Greek, and Hebrew, he returned to Zurich, where in 1519 he joined Ulrich Zwingli, who was at that time leading a movement for the reform of the church in that city. Manz, however, came to reject Zwingli's view that the ultimate authority in any reform movement must be the civil authorities, and he did not accept the other reformers' distinction between the "visible" and the "invisible" church—i.e., those who professed faith and those who truly did believe. He believed that the church must be made up of only those who have true faith in Jesus Christ as Savior. Therefore, he denied the right of infants to baptism. As a result he turned from Zwingli to give his support to Conrad Grebel, with whom he organized the Swiss Brethren, using the tracts of the German radical Carlstadt. In 1525 he took part in the first dispute with Zwingli on baptism and then participated in the first service of "believer's baptism," which was held in his house. As a result of this, Manz was imprisoned for a time. In 1526 there were further disputations with Zwingli, which led to Manz's and Georg Blaurock's arrest. Then, on January 5, 1527, Manz was drowned in the River Liemat, the first Protestant martyred by Protestants. W. S. REID

MARBECK, PILGRIM (c. 1495–c. 1557)
Austrian Anabaptist

Marbeck was born in Rattenberg in the Tyrol, Austria, where he became an engineer. He was, however, expelled from the town because he had become an Anabaptist. In 1528 he went to Strassburg, where he was the engineer of the water works, but he was soon in trouble there for disputing with the religious leaders of the city—Bucer, Capito, and Zell—on the subject of baptism. Within three years he was expelled, eventually settling with some of his followers in Augsburg, where he died. He wrote a number of polemical theological works against another Anabaptist, Kaspar Schwenkenfeld, which had considerable influence. His followers were absorbed by the Swiss Brethren shortly after his death. W. S. REID

MARCEL, GABRIEL (1889–1973)
French Catholic existential philosopher

Marcel traveled a tortuous road to the faith and the philosophy he eventually embraced. His mother, a Jewess, died when he was four. Raised by his agnostic father and a liberal Protestant aunt, his early education stressed only intellectual achievement. During World War I, he worked with the Red Cross, locating missing soldiers, and this opened up new dimensions of human existence, including the quest for meaning in life. He gravitated away from rationalism and toward the idealism of philosophers like F. H. Bradley and Josiah Royce, who stressed man's immediate awareness of the Divine Presence. In 1929 he converted to Roman Catholicism, and then gradually he developed a Christian existentialism.

Like other existentialists, Marcel held that philosophy begins with the fact of my existence rather than with some theoretical abstraction or indubitable truth. Abstract thinking can deal objectively and analytically with logical and scientific problems, but existential thinking concerns itself more with the concrete experience of individuals and explores concepts that illuminate their existence. He therefore refused to construct a logical system, contenting himself with more tentative descriptions of our being incarnated in the world. Man is a traveler (*homo viator*), alienated from himself, from those he loves, and from God. He seeks dialogue and communication that can overcome his solitude and give life meaning. Meantime the soul's existence is inseparable from its body, its world, and its alienated condition.

But Marcel is not the nihilist without hope, and he is critical of Sartre's pessimistic and atheistic existentialism. Like Martin Buber, he sees a hope-filled difference between how we relate to things and how we can relate to persons: the latter is filled with possibilities of faith and love and therefore hope. The hope for men, then, is that we too might become one in our interpersonal communion, and this in relation to God.
A. F. HOLMES

MARCELLA (c. 325–c. 410)
A Roman lady of the noble family of Marcelli

After seven months of marriage Marcella's husband died, leaving her childless. She then decided not to marry again but to give her life to celibacy. She thereupon turned her home on the Aventine hill into a center for like-minded women, unmarried and widowed, of origin similar to hers. During the interval of 382 to 385, they received instruction from Jerome, an ardent advocate of celibate life. Marcella herself was a serious student of Scripture who plied Jerome with many exegetical questions. His letters indicate her queries and his replies. It is from his letters that information about her has been preserved. During Alaric's sack of Rome in 410, she was beaten by the marauders and died from the maltreatment. A. CABANISS

MARCION (second century)
Prominent heretic of the second century

Marcion was a native of Sinope in Pontus, where his father was said to have been bishop and to have excommunicated his son from the church for immorality. In subsequent years he was reportedly a wealthy shipowner. Around 140 he arrived in Rome,

where he became a disciple of the heretic Cerdo. In the next few years he worked out a theological system of his own and soon outshone his teacher. From Rome he organized the propagation of his views. He was successful in gaining a large following throughout the empire. This group became a major threat to the Christian faith and provoked a wide response among Christian scholars who refuted the wrong notions of Marcionism.

At the heart of Marcion's theology is a dualistic notion of God. The God of the Old Testament and the God of the New are not the same. The God of the Old Testament is the cause of the world and of evil. He is legal-minded, violent, vindictive. The religion of this God is oriented around laws and demands. The God of Jesus Christ, however, is the opposite. He is the forgiving and saving God. He is "unknown" except that he is revealed in Jesus. And in Jesus he is revealed as pure love and mercy. The religion of this God is oriented around love. It is the purpose of Jesus and his love to overthrow the God of the Old Testament and the religion of law.

According to Marcion, Paul was the only one who really understood the difference between the two religions. He was the one who had received his revelation not from man, but directly from God. His understanding was clearly set forth in the antithesis between law and grace. Consequently Marcion developed a canon of scripture that consisted of ten of the Epistles of Paul (he either rejected the pastoral epistles or did not know of their existence) and an altered form of Luke (because he was the friend and companion of Paul). Marcion also rejected the humanity of Jesus. Jesus was a mere appearance (the docetic heresy). He appeared as a full grown man in the fifteenth year of Tiberius.

In reaction to Marcion, the orthodox Christians set forth the true canon of Scripture. (Irenaeus, for example, is the first one to cite Matthew, Mark, Luke, and John as comprising the four Gospels of the received tradition.) They also produced "rules of faith," which are brief summaries of orthodox doctrine; and they appealed to apostolic tradition and apostolic succession as the only reliable source through which the truth has been preserved and handed down in the church. By the end of the second century Marcionism had lost its strength as a movement. R. E. WEBBER

MARCUS AURELIUS (121–180)
Roman emperor

Born in Rome, the adoptive son of Emperor Antoninus Pius, Marcus Aurelius married a daughter of Antoninus Pius. Of Spanish ancestry with noble Roman affiliation, he received excellent training in rhetoric and literature, in philosophy and law. He succeeded Antoninus on March 7, 161, and for eight years ruled conjointly with his brother Lucius Aurelius Verus. Turbulent revolts in various parts of the empire required his presence with the military forces. In a frontier camp he began his treatise *To Himself* (usually called his *Mediations*), a classic statement of Stoic philosophy. He looked upon Christianity as a "theatrical obstinacy" and Christians as a threat to the well-being of the state. Consequently, although Marcus Aurelius did not institute persecutions, he allowed them. Many martyrs, therefore, died under this emperor, among them the Christian philosopher Justin as well as many at Lyons and Vienne. A. CABANISS

MARGARET OF NAVARRE (1492–1549)
Champion of the reformed movement in France

As sister of King Francis I of France, Margaret married Charles, Duke of Aleuzon in 1509. After the death of her first husband she married Henry d'Albret, King of Navarre. Thereafter she came under the influence of the French reformers. She patronized the men and women of the Meaux Group, among whom were the Bible translator Jacques Lefèvre d'Étaples, the Swiss reformer William Farel, and the Hebraist Vatable. Later Margaret sheltered the reformers at her estates in Angouleme and also in Navarre. At the urging of her friends, she

sought to reform the churches within her realm; she also exerted influence on Francis I in favor of the French reformers. She maintained a lively correspondence with the reformers, and ultimately Margaret herself became a convinced Calvinist. She wrote several books of poetry and prose.

At the command of Henry II, Margaret was forced to offer her daughter in marriage to Antoine de Bourbon. Out of this marriage came Henry of Navarre, later Henry IV of France. W. A. DETZLER

MARGARET OF SCOTLAND (c. 1045–1093)
Wife of the Scottish King Malcolm III Canmore

Brought up at the Hungarian court where her English father was in exile, Margaret came to Scotland after the Normans had conquered England at Hastings in 1066. About four years later, despite her ascetic tendencies, she married Malcolm, and showed herself to be one of those few redoubtable women in the Middle Ages who improved the lot of their sex through innate goodness.

Margaret not only championed the cause of orphans, lepers, and prisoners, but thought nothing of stooping to wash the feet of beggars. Such was her influence in the kingdom that she succeeded in settling an age-old tension by ridding Scotland of Celtic church practices and bringing the country into the mainstream of Roman Catholicism. Shortly after Malcolm had been killed, Margaret died in Edinburgh. She was canonized by Innocent IV in 1250. J. D. DOUGLAS

MARIE OF FRANCE (c. 1140–1220)
French poet

Obtainable only from her works, present knowledge about Marie is meager. Her poetry does provide her name and indicates she lived and wrote in twelfth-century France. One may also infer she was well educated and her family was aristocratic. And from her writings' dedicatory lines, it is clear she participated in the English and

French court life of Henry II of England and his wife, Eleanor of Aquitaine. As far as known, Marie produced just three works, *Lais, Ysopet,* and *L'Espurgatoire seint Patriz.* All three consist of longer or shorter narrative poems set in octosyllabic couplet verse.

Marie's poetry is significant both for its unique literary position and its moral and social insights. Marie is the first important female French poet. Her writings also are among the earliest of any works to use the French vernacular. After the fashion of her period, Marie constructed her *Lais* as courtly love songs; but unlike many troubadours' works, her stories reveal much sensitivity both to strict moral standards and real problems in love and marriage. While inexplicit, a Christian understanding of love can be imagined of the author's mind and background. An intriguing selection of reconstructed ancient fables forms the content of *Ysopet.* It discloses Marie's perceptiveness over moral issues in her time, and her interest in speaking to such issues. *L'Espurgatoire seint Patriz* offers an allegorical tale about an Irish knight, St. Patrick, and his observation of the contrasting end results of evil life and good life. Very evident in the last work is the author's acceptance of certain basic Christian doctrines. This includes teaching on atonement and redemption as well as God's final judgment. K. J. BRYER

MARITAIN, JACQUES (1882–1973)
French Christian philosopher

As a student in Paris, Maritain grew disillusioned with the Liberal Protestantism in which he was reared and with the "scientism" it had taught him (i.e., since only science yields knowledge of reality, man's hope lies in better science). His thinking took more constructive direction under the influence of his teacher, Henry Bergson (1859–1941), and of biological vitalism— the view that life is a creative force not altogether subject to examination or prediction. Meanwhile he made an intensive study of Thomas Aquinas, and in 1906 he and his wife (a Russian Jew) converted to Roman Catholicism.

Maritain wrote over fifty philosophical books and numerous periodical articles, which together with his teaching have significantly influenced Western culture and Christian thought. Basic to all his work is the insistence on various ways of knowing reality. We are not limited to the methods of science, for philosophy, art, and religious experience have their ways, too. This led him to speak of prephilosophical approaches to God in personal religious life. It guided his work in ethics, where he insisted that we attend not only to the behavioral and social sciences but also to what theology and the Christian revelation say about the human condition. Man's propensity to evil is best understood in terms of concupiscence and original sin. Man's moral struggle is aided by the availability of divine grace. Likewise in the political sphere, Maritain believed that human rights are God-given and that they are based in the value of individuals as persons. A. F. HOLMES

MARK (JOHN MARK)
Cousin of Barnabas; companion to both Paul and Peter; author of the second Gospel

A member of a Jewish family in Jerusalem who were early believers in Jesus Christ, John Mark bore both a Jewish and a Roman name. The Roman name "Mark" was perhaps a badge of Roman citizenship, as in Paul's case, or was adopted when he left Jerusalem to serve the Gentile church in Antioch (Acts 12:25). When an angel of the Lord freed Peter from prison, the apostle went directly to "the house of Mary, the mother of John whose other name was Mark" (Acts 12:12, NRSV). This house, described as having an outer gate, being of adequate size to accommodate a gathering of many believers, and served by a slave named Rhoda (Acts 12:12-13), was obviously the dwelling of a wealthy family. By the time of this event (c. A.D. 44) Mark may have already been converted through the personal influence of Peter (1 Pet. 5:13). The fact that he was chosen to accompany Barnabas and Saul (Paul) to Antioch indicates that Mark was held in high esteem by the church in Jerusalem (Acts 12:25).

John Mark accompanied Barnabas and Saul to "assist them" (Acts 13:5, NRSV) on their expedition into Asia with the gospel. He soon left the apostles, however, and returned to Jerusalem (Acts 13:13). Scripture does not reveal the cause of this desertion. Perhaps the rigors and hardships of the journey overwhelmed the young man. Another possible explanation was that at Paphos, shortly into the journey, Paul stepped to the front as leader and spokesman (Acts 13:13). Thereafter Acts (with the natural exception of Acts 15:12, 25) speaks of Paul and Barnabas rather than Barnabas and Paul. Perhaps it offended Mark to see his kinsman Barnabas, who had preceded Paul in the faith (Acts 4:36-37) and had ushered him into the apostles' fellowship (Acts 9:27), take second place in the work of the gospel.

But there may have been a deeper and more significant cause for Mark's withdrawal. Like Paul, Mark was "a Hebrew born of Hebrews" (Phil. 3:5, NRSV). Because of this Mark may have objected to Paul's offer of salvation to the Gentiles based only on faith without the prerequisite of keeping the Jewish law. It is noteworthy that the Bible uses only the Hebrew name "John" when recording Mark's presence on the Gospel journey (13:5) and his departure at Perga in Pamphylia (Acts 13:13). Also important is the fact that John Mark returned, not to the Gentile church in Antioch, the site of his former service, but to the Jewish church in Jerusalem (Acts 13:13). Luke's history records that later "the disagreement [between Paul and Barnabas over Mark] became so sharp that they parted company" (Acts 15:39, NRSV). Nothing stirred Paul's feelings more than the question of justification by faith, and Barnabas had already demonstrated his weakness on this point (Gal. 2:13). Therefore it may have been the cause of their separation: Barnabas and Mark to Cyprus, and Paul and Silas into Asia to strengthen the new churches (Acts 15:39-41).

About eleven years pass before Mark again appears in the biblical record. In Co-

lossians 4:10 and Philemon 24, he is in Rome with "Paul the aged," who is there as "a prisoner of Jesus Christ" (Philem. 19). The fracture has been healed, such that Paul says that Mark and others are "the only ones of the circumcision [the Jews] among my co-workers for the kingdom of God" (Col. 4:11, NRSV). Paul, in his last epistle, pays Mark his final tribute. He tells Timothy, "Do your best to come to me soon. . . . Only Luke is with me. Get Mark and bring him with you, for *he is useful in my ministry*" (2 Tim. 4:9, 11, NRSV, italics added). Although all had deserted Paul in his trial before Caesar Nero (2 Tim. 4:16), Mark, who in his youth had also deserted the apostle, traveled from Ephesus to Rome, endeavoring to come to the beloved Paul with Timothy.

In 1 Peter 5:13 the apostle Peter sends Mark's greeting along with that of the church in Babylon (signifying Rome), indicating Mark's close relationship with the apostle to the circumcision (Gal. 2:9). The most important and reliable extrascriptural tradition concerning Mark is that he was the close attendant of Peter. The early church Fathers said this association produced the Gospel of Mark, inasmuch as Mark took account of Peter's teachings about Jesus and then used them to shape his Gospel—perhaps written in Rome between A.D. 55 and 65. D. PARTNER

MAROT, CLÉMENT (1497–1544)
Outstanding poet at the court of Francis I of France

Born in Cahors, Marot began writing poetry at about age twenty and became court poet to Margaret, queen of Navarre, whose Protestantism influenced him. His style exerted a great influence on the future of French poetry. It was likely the influence of one of his patronesses, Margaret of Navarre, that attracted him to Protestant ideas at this staunchly Catholic court. He applied his superior talent to rendering a number of Psalms into elegant French verse. His renderings of Psalm 23, 42, and 130 are worthy of mention. These and others were sung with enthusiasm by members of the court to already existent melodies, probably with lute accompaniment. His aim was to substitute edifying words in place of the frivolous and often suggestive ones then current. Of course, the words of Scripture were paraphrased to fit into varied and sophisticated stanza patterns, but never at the expense of the meaning. Similar versions of the Psalms were appearing elsewhere at this time, in English and Flemish for instance, but all were inferior to those of Marot.

It is not clear how Marot's verses came to Calvin's attention in Strassburg, but when the poet was forced to flee to Geneva from the Inquisition, he met Calvin there in 1547 and was persuaded to continue his activity. The French courtier found Geneva intolerably restrictive and soon left for Ferrara, but not before he had completed forty-nine of the Psalms and *The Song of Simeon* (Luke 2:29-32). The task of versifying the whole *Psalter* was completed by Calvin's colleague Theodore Beza in 1562. J. B. MACMILLAN

MARQUETTE, JACQUES (1637–1675)

Jesuit missionary and explorer in North America

Marquette was born in Laon, France, and entered the Jesuit novitiate in France in 1654. He arrived in Canada in 1666 and served in missions to the Algonquin Indians at Sault St. Marie and to refugee Ottawa and Huron Indians at the western end of Lake Superior. In the summer of 1671 he founded a mission at St. Ignace on the straits of Michilimackinac. In 1673 Marquette and Louis Joliet set out from St. Ignace, proceeded southwest to the Wisconsin River, and then to the Mississippi at a point near the present boundary of Arkansas and Louisiana. They returned to Lake Michigan by way of the Chicago River. In 1674 and 1675 Marquette ministered to the Indians in the Illinois country. He died near the present site of Ludington, Michigan. Marquette is justly honored for his part in the discovery of the Mississippi, but the question of his place in history has been the subject of controversy. D. C. MASTERS

MARSDEN, SAMUEL (1764–1838)

English prison chaplain; missionary to New Zealand and Australia

Born at Farsley, Yorkshire, Marsden was educated at Cambridge. William Wilberforce persuaded Pitt to establish a chaplaincy for the New South Wales convict settlement. When the post opened in 1793, he persuaded Marsden to accept it. Marsden's lifework had two facets: (1) as chaplain and colonial developer; and (2) in pioneering missionary activity in the South Seas.

In the former capacity he established a model homestead at Parramatta, a pilot project in farm development and soil husbandry. Previously experienced in wool-spinning and weaving, he introduced sheep, trained ex-convicts in self-support, and transformed them into respectable citizens. He helped develop colonial trade and education. Despite his association with the penal system as chaplain (for which he had his critics), he was primarily a pastor, accepting the system as a "given" and working within it as a rehabilitator. He believed evangelism and civilizing should go together, though before he died he confessed doubts about this theory of mission.

His evangelical and missionary spirit was stimulated by Maori visitors at Parramatta. Failing to interest the Church Missionary Society (CMS) in a New Zealand mission, he bought a vessel himself and visited that country, preaching the gospel there for the first time. Between 1814 and 1837 he made seven missionary voyages, fought the trade in firearms, and won a reputation among the Maoris as friend and peacemaker. Meanwhile the CMS had taken over the missionary program. He also served as the London Missionary Society agent, performing a notable service in 1810 by persuading the discouraged Tahiti missionaries to return to their deserted posts and pleading their cause with their London Board.

Many Marsden documents have been preserved in New Zealand and Australia, and his *Life and Letters* has been published. A. R. TIPPETT

MARSHALL, PETER (1902–1949)
Presbyterian pastor

Born in Coatbridge, Scotland, Marshall emigrated to the United States in 1927. Feeling a call to the Christian ministry, he attended Columbia Theological Seminary in Decatur, Georgia, from 1928 to 1931. After pastoring churches in Covington and Atlanta, Georgia, he succeeded Dr. Joseph R. Sizoo as minister of the New York Avenue Presbyterian Church of Washington, D.C. (1937). From 1947 he also served as chaplain to the United States Senate. He died of a heart attack in 1949. He had enjoyed great popularity as a preacher, and some of his sermons were posthumously published under the title, *Mr. Jones, Meet the Master* (1949). His story became widely known through his widow's biography, *A Man Called Peter* (1951), a filmed version of which was widely circulated. The chair of homiletics at Columbia Theological Seminary was endowed in Marshall's memory in 1955. N. V. HOPE

MARSHMAN, JOSHUA (1768–1837)
Formed the famous Serampore Trio with colleagues William Carey and William Ward

Marshman was a weaver until 1794 and then taught school at Bristol while attaining a classical education. The Baptist Missionary Society (BMS) in 1799 sent him to India to join William Carey. Unable to locate at Calcutta he settled at Danish Serampore. BMS support was insufficient, so Marshman and his wife opened two schools for European children and one for Indian children. The income they generated, along with Carey's Fort William College salary, made the mission independent, and the BMS severed relations with them until 1837. Marshman was an expert linguist, especially in Bengali, Sanskrit, and Chinese. He, with Carey, made a great impact on Bengali literature. He produced a Bengali-English dictionary, a Sanskrit grammar (with Carey), a Chinese grammar, and even a translation of the Confucian Classics into English. He was active in Bible translation. Brown University in Providence, Rhode Island, gave him the D.D. degree. P. BEAVER

MARSILIUS (MARSIGLIO) OF PADUA (c. 1275–1342)
Medieval political philosopher who strongly opposed papal claims to temporal power

Little is known about Marsilius's early life, but he seems to have studied at Padua and completed his education in medicine and philosophy at Paris. He was made rector of the University of Paris in 1313 and was teaching there when he published his one major work, *The Defender of the Peace* (1324). When his authorship became known, he was forced to leave Paris, and he took refuge at the Court of Louis IV of Bavaria, who was then involved in a dispute with Pope John XXII.

From 1327 to 1329 Marsilius accompanied Louis as he occupied Rome. In accord with Marsilius's political theories, assemblies of the Roman people were held, and these proclaimed Louis emperor, denounced the pope as a heretic, and installed a new pope in his place. Marsilius was appointed spiritual vicar of the city in 1328. When the people turned against Louis a few months later, he was forced to leave Rome, and Marsilius accompanied him back to Germany and spent the rest of his life at the imperial court.

Marsilius's work, *The Defender of the Peace,* was divided into three discourses. The first presented a philosophy of the state, based on reason alone. The second, which was the major portion of the work, was a long indictment of papal claims to temporal power. The third summed up the results of the first two discourses and drew some conclusions.

Marsilius distinguished two modes of life: the temporal life, which princes regulate according to the teachings of philosophy, and eternal life, to which the priests lead man with the help of revelation. The needs of the temporal life are cared for by craftsmen and civil servants. The priests have a role to play in the city, but philosophers have not been able to demonstrate what that role is. Nations agree that it is important to have priests to honor God and to worship him. Most religious sects promise that the good life will be rewarded and the wicked punished in another life. These beliefs are not proved but are useful, for they encourage citizens to live peacefully and to respect the rules of private morality. The only authority competent to enact law for the state is the whole body of citizens or the weightier part of it. Laws are made to promote civil justice and the common well-being, and the best judge of the usefulness of a law is the whole body of citizens.

The second discourse was a long condemnation of the papacy, based on Scripture and other Christian authorities. Marsilius rebuked the papacy for its desire for temporal power, which he saw as being the major source of strife in cities and states. Christ said, "My kingdom is not of this world." He gave the apostles only a power to administer sacraments, no temporal power of any kind. Marsilius wanted the church stripped of all its power, privileges, and property. He also attacked the claim that the pope is the successor of the apostle Peter. According to Marsilius, all the apostles shared equally in the same priestly power.

Marsilius did not present a complete political philosophy but was concerned with one evil, the influence of the papacy in temporal affairs with its dire consequence for society. As the title of his work indicates, he was not a defender of the faith but a defender of the peace. In Marsilius and in William of Ockham, who had also taken refuge with Louis, one can find most of the arguments against the papacy that were later taken up by the Reformers. Marsilius's views had a significant influence upon the political thought of the Reformation. A. VOS

MARTIN V (1368–1431)

Pope, 1417–1431

Born Oddo Colonna at Genazzano near Rome, Martin was educated at the University of Perugia. With his election at the Council of Constance (1414–1418) there ended the Great Schism in the Western

Church that had lasted for four decades. During that time the Western Church had seen nations line up behind various competing popes. One antipapal line associated with Avignon stumbled on until 1429 in the Spanish province of Aragon.

The French would have liked Martin to remain on their soil, but he determined to reestablish the papacy in Rome. There was some delay about this, for the city was in the hand of the Neapolitan army, and other parts of the Papal States were also in turmoil. Papal control was eventually reasserted, extending gradually to the whole of the Western Church.

Martin corresponded with several monarchs and sought actively to mediate in the Hundred Years' War between England and France. He joined with the emperor Sigismund in crushing the followers of Jan Hus, who had never forgotten the treachery that led to their leader's execution at Constance in 1415. Martin successfully opposed limitation of the papal rule, and six weeks after his election he banned appeals from the pope to any other court. This went contrary to his earlier commitment to the principles of conciliarism (which claimed authority over the pope). He made attempts to end the other "Great Schism" (between Eastern and Western churches). He died suddenly, shortly after calling the Council of Basel in 1431—a decision made only with the utmost reluctance in response to irresistible pressure put upon him. J. D. DOUGLAS

MARTIN OF TOURS (c. 335–397)

Bishop of Tours and patron saint of France

Martin was born in Sabaria, Pannonia (modern Hungary), of pagan parents, but early in life he became a catechumen in the church. At fifteen he became a soldier and served for three years until, through a vision of Christ, he was converted and then baptized. After a period of activity against the Arians, he embraced the monastic life. In 360 he joined with Hilary of Poitiers to establish the monastery of Ligugé, the first in Gaul.

In 372 Martin became the bishop of

Tours. At first he resided at his cathedral. Later, however, along with eighty disciples he returned to the monastic way of life at Marmoutier, near Tours. He supported the spread of monasticism in Gaul and encouraged the evangelization of the countryside. Many rural parishes were established as a result of these evangelistic efforts. Another result was the formation of a rudimentary parochial system.

Martin was occasionally consulted by the emperor Maximus. He secured a promise from the emperor that Priscillian, a Gnostic heretic, would not be executed. When Maximus broke the promise, Martin broke communion with the Spanish bishops until he received a promise that measures against the Priscillianists would be dropped.

He died while on a pastoral visit at Candes. Three days later a huge crowd of mourners attended his funeral at Tours. A chapel was erected in his memory by his successor. R. E. WEBBER

MARTYN, HENRY (1781–1812)
Anglican pioneer missionary

Born in Truro, Cornwall, Martyn was educated at Truro Grammar School and St. John's College, Cambridge, where he became a fellow and was ordained. Through the influence of Charles Simeon, vicar of Holy Trinity Church, whom he assisted, and the reading of the life of David Brainerd, he resolved by God's grace to become a missionary. He intended to offer his services to the new Church Missionary Society but the need to maintain his sister made him take a chaplaincy with the East India Company in Bengal. He arrived in Calcutta in April 1806 and primarily served the European congregations. But he learned the local language in order to be able to preach to the people and to assist them with educational facilities. He also began the work of translating the New Testament into Hindustani. After he moved to Cawnpore in 1809 he finished this task and also worked at a Persian translation. On doctor's advice he took a sea journey but used the opportunity to visit Persia in order to perfect his translation. Through the assis-

tance of the British ambassador to the Persian court at Shiraz, this translation was printed.

Martyn was seriously ill in Persia, but on recovering he resolved to travel overland to Turkey and from there take a boat to England, where he hoped to marry his first-love, Lydia Grenfell. On the way he fell ill at Tokat and died. He was buried in the Armenian cemetery with the honors usually reserved for an archbishop. His *Journals and Letters* appeared in 1837, edited by Samuel Wilberforce, and they made a profound impression on many young men, just as reports of his life and work in the press had previously done. His translation of the New Testament into Hindustani appeared in 1814, as well as his translation of the Anglican *Book of Common Prayer*. P. TOON

MARVELL, ANDREW (1621–1678)
English poet

Best known in his own time for his political interests, Marvell won recognition as a gifted metaphysical poet in the twentieth century. He was born at Winestead, Yorkshire, where his father was a Calvinist clergyman. At thirteen he entered Cambridge and took his B.A. at Trinity in 1639. At eighteen he was briefly converted to Roman Catholicism. From 1642 to 1646 he traveled on the continent and thus missed the civil war, although he allied himself with the anti-Royalist side.

Cromwell's courage and leadership ability won Marvell to the Commonwealth cause. For a time he was tutor to William Dutton, Cromwell's prospective son-in-law. Several of his poems honor the Puritan leader: "An Horatian Ode on Cromwell's Return from Ireland" (1650), "The First Anniversary of the Government under His Highness the Lord Protector" (1655), and "A Poem upon the Death of His Late Highness the Lord Protector" (1658). In 1657 he became Latin Secretary as a colleague of Milton. He was elected to Parliament in 1659 and continued in that body for the rest of his life.

After his death, friends of Marvell published a group of his works under the title

Miscellaneous Poems of Andrew Marvell, Esq. (1681). Marvell fused the graces of the Elizabethans with the ingenuity of both Donne and the metaphysicals to create skillfully graceful verse often touched with wit. His most commonly anthologized poem is "To His Coy Mistress." P. M. BECHTEL

MARY, QUEEN OF SCOTS (1542–1587)
Queen of Scots, 1542–1567

Daughter of James V and Mary of Guise, Mary became Queen of Scots upon the death of her father when she was only six days old. At the time of her accession to the throne Scotland was in a state of turbulence owing to English intrigues and a growing Protestant movement. Although the Earl of Hamilton, the regent, at first agreed to Mary's marriage to Edward, Henry VIII's heir, he was forced to renounce the treaty. This led to conflict with England and the dispatch of Mary to France in 1548 for education and marriage to Francis, the Dauphin. She became queen of France as Francis II's consort in 1559, but he died in 1560, resulting in her return to Scotland in August of that year.

In the thirteen intervening years between her departure and return much had happened in Scotland, the most important being the triumph of the cause of Protestantism. This had resulted in the abolition of the Mass, the renouncing of papal ecclesiastical supremacy, and the establishment of a church with a Reformed or Calvinistic confession. The country was divided on the issue, and Mary hoped to be able to restore Roman Catholicism by the exercise of both royal power and her own personal charm. One of the principal obstacles in her path was the reformer John Knox, who had the support of many of the lairds and burgesses of the towns, as well as some of the nobles. Mary might have succeeded in her plan, but she alienated most of the more moderate element who might have supported her. At the same time, by claiming that she was the true heir to the English throne, she alienated Elizabeth and frightened the Protestant element in England.

Her downfall began when she married

Henry Darnley, who had a strong claim to the English throne. Then when Darnley was murdered, she married the suspected murderer, the earl of Bothwell. The result was her deposition and eventual flight into England. There she was kept as a prisoner by Elizabeth until she was executed at Fotheringay because of her suspected involvement in a number of Roman Catholic plots against the English queen. W. S. REID

MARY TUDOR (1516–1558)
Mary I, Queen of England; often called "Bloody Mary" because of the persecution of Protestants in her reign

Daughter of Henry VIII and Catherine of Aragon, Mary was born in Greenwich and received the very best liberal arts education so that she knew Latin and several foreign languages well. She was brought up as a Roman Catholic. When Henry sought a divorce from Catherine (1527), Mary's life was made miserable. Later, when Henry married Anne Boleyn (1533), Mary's circumstances became worse. She had to give up the dignity of a princess and was required to acknowledge that she was illegitimate. She refused to do the latter and suffered privation, which did not help her delicate health. After Anne's death her position improved when she accepted in 1536 that her father was the "Supreme Head of the Church of England under Christ." Before his death Henry restored her to the royal succession. Thus after the brief reign (1547–1553) of her half brother, Edward VI, during which she endured further privation, she became Queen in 1553, having much support from the common people.

She was crowned by Stephen Gardiner, bishop of Winchester and her trusted guide. At first she showed leniency to the leading Protestants who had enjoyed ascendancy during Edward's reign. Yet she caused the Church of England to return to the use of Latin and to the Roman services. Protestant doctrine and worship were forbidden. Meanwhile she married Philip II of Spain, but this proved an unhappy and unpopular match. Since there were no children, he returned to Spain, leaving behind a sad queen.

With Mary's agreement, Gardiner set in motion the legal processes to try heretics. Leading Protestants—Thomas Cranmer, Hugh Latimer, Nicholas Ridley, and John Hooper—were tried for heresy and burned at the stake. This helped to diminish Mary's popularity. So also did the loss of the port of Calais to France during the war against France in which England was engaged with Spain. Her health deteriorated, and she died at St. James's Palace. She is a sad figure whose sincerity was never in question but who was caught between two powerful movements and suffered in the confrontation. She was succeeded by Elizabeth I, her half sister. P. TOON

MASON, LOWELL (1792–1872)

American composer

Mason was entirely self-taught in music. In his youth he directed a church choir in his native Medford, Massachusetts, and one in Savannah, Georgia, where he was a bank clerk. After 1827 he devoted himself entirely to teaching and lecturing about music. Through the balance of his long life, he edited an enormous number of musical instruction books, and collections of hymn tunes and anthems. He visited Europe to observe musical practices in the churches there as well as methods of musical pedagogy. New York University honored him with one of the first musical doctorates given in America. He founded the Handel and Haydn Society of Boston and also the Boston Academy of Music.

Mason exercised an enormous influence on church music in nineteenth-century America. He also composed and adapted a great number of hymn tunes, including those for "Joy to the World" (often attributed to Handel) and "When I Survey the Wondrous Cross." The tunes for "From Greenland's Icy Mountains" and "My Faith Looks Up to Thee" are known worldwide. Unfortunately, Mason looked down on the rich heritage of early American folk tunes.

They have only recently begun to find their way into our hymn books once again.
J. B. MACMILLAN

MATHER, COTTON (1663–1728)

A leading Congregational minister; scientist; the most celebrated New England writer of his day; one of the founders of Yale University

Born in Boston, Mather graduated from Harvard (1678) and in 1685 became a colleague of his father, Increase Mather, as pastor of Boston's Second Church. Intellectually gifted and very learned, Mather was also quick-tempered and his life was marked by numerous controversies. His *Memorable Providences Relating to Witchcrafts* (1689), along with two other works on the same subject, may have contributed to the hysteria that led to the Salem witch trials of 1692. Although he expressed concern about the kind of evidence the judges were accepting in the trials and urged fasting and prayer instead of death for the convicted, he made no public protest. When Mather was denied the privilege of succeeding his father as president of Harvard, he became one of the founders of Yale College, which he hoped would carry on the orthodox Congregationalist tradition.

Like his father, Mather was keenly interested in scientific phenomena. His scientific papers won him a coveted election to the Royal Society of London (1713). When smallpox broke out in Boston in 1721, the practice of inoculation, which Mather so vigorously advocated, may be said to mark the beginning of preventive medicine in the Western world. Mather was incredibly productive as a writer, turning out over 450 books on a variety of subjects. In his greatest work, *Magnalia Christi Americana* (1702), he described in rich detail the Puritan experience in early New England. And in *The Christian Philosopher* (1721) he sought to reconcile the Puritan faith with the recent scientific discoveries of Sir Isaac Newton. Historians have often emphasized the less attractive features of Mather's personality at the expense of his more humane qualities. He gave generously of his time and money

to the poor, established a school for educating slaves, supported the building of churches in poor communities, and came to the aid of needy ministers.
R. L. TROUTMAN

MATHER, INCREASE (1639–1723)
An important Congregational minister; a leading clergyman in colonial Massachusetts

Born in Dorchester, Massachusetts, in 1639, Mather was a graduate of Harvard College (1565) and Trinity College, Dublin, Ireland (1658). After holding several pastorates in England, he returned to America and in 1664 became minister of Boston's Second Church, a position he held for fifty-nine years. Although he devoted himself principally to his church, Mather accomplished a great deal in other areas as well. In 1683 he established himself as a leader in the science of astronomy with the publication of his *Discourse Concerning Comets*. As president of Harvard College from 1685 to 1701, Mather sought to make it more than simply a training school for ministers, but at the same time he carefully guarded its Congregational distinctions. When Charles II in 1684 revoked the Massachusetts Bay charter by which the colony elected its own governor, it was Increase Mather who was sent to London in 1688 on behalf of the Congregational churches to petition the king.

When he returned in 1692 the Salem witch trials were just beginning. Mather's role in the proceedings is somewhat controversial. Although he never questioned the existence of witches and at first approved the trials, Mather publicly protested the acceptance of "spectral evidence," such as visions by those who claimed to be bewitched. He was the first important minister to call for an end to the trials. After 1693 Mather's influence waned. In 1701 less orthodox elements forced his resignation as president of Harvard College. He spent his last years in pastoring Second Church, continuing his voluminous writing, and giving his support to Yale College, which he hoped would replace Harvard as a stronghold of orthodoxy.

When Mather died, he was universally mourned as "the patriarch . . . among us."
R. L. TROUTMAN

MATHESON, GEORGE (1842–1906)
Scottish minister and writer

Born in Glasgow and virtually blind by the time he completed his arts degree there in 1862, Matheson surmounted almost impossible obstacles to become a minister. He served the parishes of Innellan (Argyll) from 1868 to 1886, and St. Bernard's, Edinburgh, from 1886 to 1899, attracting overflowing congregations from all walks of life who were stirred not only by his preaching but by his remarkable prayers with which he used to open the service. The blind preacher had a rare gift of language that had both artistic and spiritual appeal. Fellow ministers confessed to having been almost afraid to read Matheson's sermons because their freshness, originality, and arresting power of expression tempted them to plagiarism. Matheson's prose works include *Studies of the Portrait of Christ* (two volumes; 1899, 1900), hailed by Alexander Whyte as a work of genius, and a widely popular series on representative Bible characters. His verse has a winsome, haunting quality as evidenced in his *Sacred Songs* (1890). The latter collection contains a hymn that has gone all over the world: "O Love That Wilt Not Let Me Go." Written out of what Matheson called "the most severe mental suffering," it was finished in five minutes, "dictated to me by some inward voice." J. D. DOUGLAS

MATHEWS, SHAILER (1863–1941)
American educator and advocate of the social gospel

Born in Portland, Maine, and educated at Colby College (1884) and Newton (Massachusetts) Theological Institute (1887), Mathews served on the Colby faculty from 1887 until 1894. Then he joined the faculty of the University of Chicago Divinity School, teaching New Testament until 1906 and thereafter historical and comparative theology until his retirement in 1933. For twenty-five years (1908–1933) he also served as dean of the faculty. Along with Washington Gladden and Walter Rauschenbusch, Mathews was an early exponent of the social gospel. In this area he published *The Social Teaching of Jesus* (1897)—a pioneer work in stating the biblical basis of the social gospel movement. An active churchman, Mathews was president of the Federal Council of Churches from 1912 to 1916 and of the Northern Baptist Convention in 1915. N. V. HOPE

MATTHEW

Son of Alphaeus; a tax collector by occupation; chosen by Jesus to be one of the twelve apostles; credited with the authorship of the Gospel of Matthew

Matthew is listed in each of the four rosters of the Twelve (Matt. 10:3; Mark 3:18; Luke 6:15; Acts 1:13). Aside from these lists Matthew is only mentioned in the record of his calling by Christ (Matt. 9:9; Mark 2:13-14; Luke 5:27). Before his apostolic call, the Gospels refer to Matthew as Levi (Mark 2:14; Luke 5:27; compare Matt. 9:9). The identity of Levi as Matthew is beyond all doubt. It is improbable that Matthew was the brother of James the Less whose father was also named Alphaeus (Matt. 10:3) since this fact would have been mentioned in the record of Scripture as it is in the cases of Peter and Andrew and the sons of Zebedee.

Matthew served King Herod Antipas in Capernaum of Galilee collecting tariffs on goods passing on the road from Damascus to the Mediterranean Sea. To function in this capacity Matthew would have been an educated man, acquainted with the Greek language as well as the native Aramaic, thus qualifying him to write the Gospel of Matthew. As a tax collector Matthew may have been a man of wealth, but this occupation also caused him to be despised by the Jews and considered among the lowest of people. The Pharisees consistently spoke of tax collectors in the same breath with sinners (Matt. 11:19; Mark 2:16; Luke 7:34; 15:1).

Matthew was called while he was working at his toll booth. Jesus passed by on the road

and said to him, "Follow me" (Mark 2:14). Matthew left everything and did so (Luke 5:28). Immediately he gave Jesus a great banquet at his house and a large crowd of his fellow tax collectors and others were there to enjoy it. It was at this feast that the Pharisees and their scribes made the well-known complaint: "Why do you eat and drink with tax collectors and sinners?" (Luke 5:29-32, RSV).

It is not certain when Matthew was called, but it is probable that the first six disciples were present on that day since the Pharisees complained to Christ's disciples during Matthew's feast. Unlike the first men Jesus called, Matthew was not originally a follower of John the Baptist. P. W. COMFORT & D. PARTNER

MATTHEW PARIS (c. 1199–1259)

English medieval historian

Matthew became a monk in the Benedictine monastery of St. Albans at eighteen years of age. Here he became an expert at writing manuscripts (a scribe) and at illustrating them (an illuminator). From 1236 he was the official historian of the monastery and was chiefly responsible for the history known as *Gesta Monasterii Sancti Albani* (see modern edition edited by H. T. Riley in 1867). All his writings were in Latin and carefully adorned. His fame primarily rests upon his *Chronica Majora*. This was a history of the world from the Creation to his own day. In fact his own research, conducted in several countries of Europe, gave him the primary material to write about the years 1235 to 1258. For the rest he relied heavily on Roger of Wendover's *Flores Historiarum*. His chronicles contained many criticisms of the Church, the papacy, and Henry II of England. They were, therefore, enthusiastically read by later reformers such as John Wycliffe. P. TOON

MAURIAC, FRANÇOIS (1885–1970)

Roman Catholic novelist; recipient of the Nobel prize in 1952

Mauriac was born in Bordeaux and educated at Institute Saint Marie and College Grand Lebrun. In 1933 he became a member of the French Academy. Lyric poetry captured Mauriac's imagination, and his first two published books were poetry. His first novel, *Young Man in Chains,* appeared in 1913. With the publication of *A Kiss for Lepers* in 1922, he became an established novelist. There followed a steady stream of novels: *Viper's Tangle* (1947), *A Woman of the Pharisees* (1946), *The Lamb* (1955), and others. Among his other writings is *Life of Jesus* (1937), as well as books of essays, criticism, and biography. Mauriac was also a well-known political columnist and drama critic.

When Mauriac was asked about his work as a novelist, he said: "If there is a reason for the existence of the novelist on earth it is this: to show the element which holds out against God in the highest and noblest characters—the innermost evils and dissimulations; and also to light up the secret sources of sanctity in creatures which seem to us to have failed."

Mauriac understood the psychology of human nature. His concerns were religious, and in his works he expressed the problems of sin and salvation. His characters seek fulfillment in human loves but fail to find real fulfillment until they encounter the love of God. D. ROETHLESBERGER

MAURICE, FREDERICK DENISON
(1805–1872)
Anglican theologian

Son of a Unitarian minister who lived in East Anglia, England, Maurice was supposed to go into the Nonconformist ministry. He rebelled against his father's views and went to study at Trinity College, Cambridge, intending to become a lawyer. During his residency (1823–1826) his intellectual qualities and gifts as a writer were recognized. Yet, because of conscientious scruples he did not remain to take up a fellowship. After a period living at home and writing for magazines he went to Exeter College, Oxford, and having become an Anglican, was ordained in 1834 to a curacy in Warwickshire. Here he

wrote several pieces including his autobiographical novel, *Eustace Conway* (1834). In January of 1836 he became chaplain of Guy's Hospital, London, where he lectured to students on moral philosophy and wrote the book by which he is often known: *The Kingdom of Christ* (1938). Most thought it was brilliant but confusing, for the author did not easily fit into any of the parties or schools of churchmanship familiar in the Church of England. Certainly it helped to make him well known.

In 1840 he became professor of English literature in the new King's College, London; six years later he became the professor of theology. He possessed an independent mind and worked things out for himself; however, when he denied the doctrine of eternal punishment in his *Theological Essays* (1853), he was accused of heresy and he had to resign his professorship. Meanwhile he had become intensely interested in the idea of Christian Socialism and in 1854 started a Working Men's College in London to put his theories into practice. After several years as a parish priest he returned to the academic scene in 1866, when he became the Knightsbridge professor of moral philosophy at Cambridge University, publishing his *Social Morality* in 1869. He also wrote several popular books that enjoyed large circulations in his lifetime. In recent years he has proved very attractive to historians, and there have been many studies made of his life, thought, and influence. He combined a warm spirituality with a depth of intellect, and if his views were not always orthodox, they were usually worthy of study. P. TOON

MAXIMILLA (died c. 179)
Second-century Montanist prophetess

According to Jerome, Maximilla was a rich and well-born woman who, with the encouragement of the self-styled prophet Montanus, left her husband to join the charismatic movement that Montanus headed in Asia Minor. Preaching the imminent return of Christ, the end of the world, and the establishment of the new Jerusalem in Phrygia (Asia Minor), she was deeply convinced of her divinely ordered role, saying, "The Lord sent me as a devotee, revealer, and interpreter of this promise and covenant. I was compelled, willing or unwilling, to learn the knowledge of God." When the orthodox Catholic Church rejected her and her message, she complained: "I am driven from the sheep like a wolf; I am not a wolf. I am Word and Spirit and Power." Two bishops of Asia Minor tried to exorcise her, but in vain. When she died, she was unreconciled to the church. She had prophesied that her death would be followed by fierce persecution of Christians; but in fact, there was a period of thirteen years of freedom from government interference. N. V. HOPE

MAXIMUS THE CONFESSOR
(c. 580–662)
Byzantine theologian

Maximus's theological system brought together the principles of classical philosophy and the teachings of the early church fathers. He built his theology around Christ as the cosmic center of the universe. History prior to the Incarnation was a preparation for God's becoming man. History after the Incarnation is the story of how man is made divine through the presence of the Word in his life. Man's nature tends toward God. The supernatural union with God that takes place through baptism and is nurtured in the life of the church gives man the capacity to avoid sin and practice virtue. This is all couched, however, in man's love for God and his rejection of the world. Accepting the absolute supremacy of God, denying one's personal will, and actualizing the love of neighbor is the basis of an ecstatic experience with God.

In his emphasis on spirituality Maximus cultivated three steps toward God: self-control through mortification; contemplation of nature leading to God; contemplation-union with God. He always insisted that contemplation had to be assisted by charity—thus maintaining two approaches to spiritual perfection: the practical and the contemplative.

He wrote more than ninety works and participated in a number of theological controversies, including the Monothelite issue. His most important work is the *Mystagogia,* a commentary on the meaning of the liturgy. R. E. WEBBER

MAYHEW, JONATHAN (1720–1766)
Noted American clergyman and patriot

Mayhew was the son of a missionary to the American Indians. After graduation from Harvard he became pastor of West Church in Boston, where he stayed until his death in 1766. Mayhew adopted rationalistic views in theology that varied from the prevailing Calvinism of most New England Congregationalists, and in many respects he accepted Unitarian ideas. An avowed patriot, Mayhew urged united action among the colonies against British domination. He also opposed the Society for the Propagation of the Gospel in Foreign Parts, believing that the British-based missionary society was attempting to bring about the downfall of congregationalism and replace it with prelacy. J. A. AKERS

MAYOR, JOSEPH BICKERSTETH
(1828–1916)
Classical and New Testament scholar

Educated at Rugby School (1841–1847) and St. John's College, Cambridge University, Mayor graduated B.A. in 1851 and M.A. in 1854. He was a fellow and lecturer at St. John's College from 1852 to 1863 and from 1860 to 1863 acted also as a tutor in the college. He was ordained a deacon in the Church of England in 1859 and a priest in 1860 by the bishop of Ely. Between 1864 and 1868 he was headmaster of Kensington Preparatory School in London, and from 1870 to 1879 he was professor of classics at Kings College, London University. From 1887 to 1893 he edited the *Classical Review.* His publications in the classical area include *A Guide to the Choice of Classical Books* (third edition in 1885, with a supplement in 1869) and an edition of Cicero's *De Natura Deorum* in three volumes (1880–1885). In the area of philosophy he edited Professor Grote's posthumous works—*An Examination of Utilitarian Philosophy* (1870) and *A Treatise on the Moral Ideals* (1876). His major works in the new Testament field are *The Epistle of St. James: Greek Text with Introductory Notes and Comments* (1892; 3rd edition 1910), which he described as "a work which for some years has been my main preoccupation"; and *The Epistle of St. Jude and the Second Epistle of St. Peter,* which he called "a sort of appendix" to his edition of *The Epistle of St. James.* N. V. HOPE

MEDINA, BARTHOLOMEO DE (1527–1578)

Dominican theologian; usually held to be the father of probabilism

Medina entered the Dominican Order at Salamanca, taught at Alcala and later at Salamanca. His principal works are his commentaries on Thomas Aquinas's *Summa Theologiae.* Medina espoused the philosophy known as "probabilism." Probabilism is a moral system that arose from facing this question: suppose Christian freedom suggests one course of action but legal considerations suggest another—what ought a Christian to do in case of such a conflict of duties? In the Roman Catholic Church the presence of many contradictory moral authorities made legal considerations almost endless. Probabiliorists said that the two courses of action should be examined, and the one that seems more probably correct should be followed. Probabilists, by contrast, hold that one may follow the opinion for liberty, provided it is truly probable, even though the opinion for law is more definitely probable. Medina wrote, "It seems to me that if there is a probable opinion, it is lawful to follow it, even though the opposite is more probable." Others went far beyond Medina with regard to what constitutes a probable opinion, and this opened the way to excesses that were opposed by the Jansenists, most notably by Pascal. Probabilist teaching was condemned in 1665. A. VOS

MELANCHTHON, PHILIP (1497–1560)

Scholar and theologian; associated with Martin Luther in the German reformation

Born in Bretten, Baden, the son of George Scharzerd, Philip was given the Greek name "Melanchthon" (meaning "black earth") by his great-uncle John Reuchlin, the famous Hebraist, when he showed signs of academic ability. He graduated at the age of fourteen (1511) and received an M.A. from Tübingen the following year. On Reuchlin's recommendation he came to Wittenberg University as professor of Greek in 1518, took his B.D. in 1519, and published his *Rhetoric* and *Dialectics* the same year. He married Katherine Krapp in 1520, and the pair had four children.

THE THEOLOGIAN

Melanchthon quickly identified himself with his older colleague Luther in the struggle that began in 1517. He attended the Leipzig disputation in 1519 and in his own B.D. disputation championed the supreme authority of Scripture against that of popes and councils. In his lectures on Romans he expounded the doctrine of justification by faith through the nonimputation of our sin and the imputed righteousness of Christ. By 1521 he had given the Reformation its first dogmatics, the *Loci communes theologici* (*Theological Common Places*), which he was to reissue in various editions during the next decades. This work dealt especially with the themes of law and gospel, the bondage of the will, and justification by faith. At a more directly practical level Melanchthon helped to spread the Reformation with the injunctions he drew up for the Saxon visitation of 1528. On a broader front he formulated, with Luther's help, the basic Lutheran statement, the *Augsburg Confession,* for presentation to the imperial diet in 1530. To explain the confession to its papal opponents he also wrote a longer *Apology* in 1531. As a third contribution to confessional Lutheranism he added to Luther's Schmalcald Articles of 1537 a discussion on *The Power and the Primacy of the Papacy.* For use in Saxony itself he later compiled the *Saxon Confession* (1551).

THE EDUCATOR

Melanchthon is remembered for the leadership he gave the German Reformation in educational reform. In his inaugural address as a professor in 1518, he contended strongly for the reform of learning along classical lines. His own work led him to emphasize the need for Greek in theological training, and he combined humanist and reforming insights in his plans for university reconstruction. At this level he had a hand in the reorganization of existing universities, such as Heidelberg and Tübingen, and also in the forming of new ones at Marburg and Königsberg. Along with Luther he had a concern for the schools as well, initiating curricular reforms and in his Visitation Articles (1528) drawing up pioneering plans for free public education.

THE ECUMENIST

Of a mild and peaceful disposition, displayed in his horrified reaction to the Peasants' War (1525), Melanchthon worked hard for reconciliation both with the papists and also with other reformers. With Luther he took part as a principal in the unsuccessful Marburg Colloquy (1529) with the Swiss (Zwingli and Oecolampadius) on the eucharistic question. He helped to achieve agreement with Bucer and the South Germans on the same issue in the Wittenberg Concord of 1536. Along the same lines he contributed to the Thirteen Articles that the Lutherans and the Anglicans agreed on unofficially in 1538. With Bucer he also participated in the discussions with Romanists at Hagenau and Worms that led to the famous Colloquy of Regensburg of 1541. (There Cardinal Contarini made a serious bid for agreement, but the differences finally proved to be insoluble.) A decade later Melanchthon did not prove to be so enthusiastic about Cranmer's plan for a pan-reformation conference in London, but by this time he was under serious attack from within for alleged weakening of Lutheran teaching.

THE CONTROVERSIALIST

In spite of his own desire for harmony, Melanchthon could not avoid controversy.

Already in 1522, when Luther was in the Wartburg, he had difficulties with Carlstadt over the Zwickau Prophets. In 1540 he brought out an edition of the Augsburg Confession with alterations that offended many Lutherans and brought him under considerable criticism after Luther's death in 1546. The defeat of the Lutheran forces in 1547 and the imposing of the interim agreements of Augsburg and Leipzig (1548) caused further problems when Melanchthon recommended the acceptance of many papal practices on the ground they were indifferent or nonessential matters (*adiaphora*). Matthias Flacius accused him of betraying the Reformation. His mediating views on predestination and the eucharistic concessions he was thought to have made to the Swiss increased the opposition, and his followers at Wittenberg and Leipzig were scornfully referred to as Philippists and even as Crypto-Calvinists. Although Melanchthon's essential Lutheranism was later vindicated, and he was honorably buried beside Luther when he died in 1560. The attacks caused him a good deal of mental stress in his closing years.

THE MAN

Melanchthon was more the scholar and the reflective theologian than the man of action. In this regard he proved to be complementary to Luther, and their close friendship probably owed much to this fact. His worth came out when it was a matter defending Reformation teaching and carrying through educational reconstruction. His weakness was quickly revealed when decisive leadership was demanded. In 1522, fortunately, Luther was at hand to restore the situation, but after Luther's death, although he was the natural successor, Melanchthon lacked the moral force to deal adequately with the practical and theological problems that arose. His sincerity and piety, of course, were beyond question. Indeed, it was his overscrupulous conscience about trifles that once caused Luther to give him the startling advice to "sin boldly"—which was naturally misunderstood when taken out of context. Less vital and dramatic than Luther, yet no less able and dedicated in his own way, Melanchthon must be regarded as a pivotal figure in the early days of the Reformation. He not only left his mark on Lutheranism but also had a more extended educational and theological influence. G. BROMILEY

MELITIUS OF ANTIOCH (died 381)
Bishop of Antioch, 360–381

Melitius was born in Melitene, Armenia Minor, to a wealthy and noble family. He became a member of the Antiochene School of exegetical literalism. Consecrated bishop of Sabaste in 357, Melitius was called to Antioch in 360 by Arians and Nicenes who disagreed over whether the Son was merely *like* the Father or of the same essence as the Father. Both parties were hoping for the support of Melitius, but his inaugural address on Proverbs 8:22 suggested Nicene sympathies, and the Arians had him immediately exiled. Melitius represented a mediating position between extreme Arianism and rigid orthodoxy, and consequently he was unable to gain the support of either party. In 362 he was called from exile by Julius but before he could return, the Eustathians, an orthodox party, consecrated Paulinus as bishop of Antioch. This provoked a schism, known as the Melitian Schism (not to be confused with the schism by the same name in Egypt half a century earlier). Paulinus served as bishop over his schismatic church with the support of Rome and, to some extent, Alexandria. Melitius also retained his bishopric with the support of the moderate Nicenes. The churches were eventually reunited in 418. Melitius was banished twice under Valens and was finally reinstated in 378. He presided over the Council of Constantinople of 381, during which he died. C. WHITACRE

MELITIUS OF LYCOPOLIS (died c. 325)
Bishop of Lycopolis; responsible for the Melitian schism in Egypt around 305

Melitius disagreed with Peter, bishop of Alexandria, over how to deal with lapsed Christians during the Diocletian persecu-

tion. Peter merely required backsliders to do penance in order to be reinstated in the church, while Melitius considered these terms lax. Melitius declared himself bishop of Alexandria and began ordaining clergy in Peter's jurisdiction. Peter (who was ruling his church from exile) and a synod of bishops excommunicated Melitius. Peter was killed in another wave of persecution and Melitius, who had also been exiled, returned to Egypt to head his schismatic church. The Council of Nicea (325) tried to heal the schism by acknowledging Melitius's ordinations as valid but requiring his clergy to yield to Alexander, the successor to Peter. Melitius was permitted to retain the title of bishop but was given no see. After Melitius's death, Athanasius became bishop of Alexandria (in 328). Athanasius did not recognize the clergy put in position by Melitius, so the Melitians sided with Arius against Athanasius, and the sect continued under the leadership of John Arkaph of Memphis.
C. WHITACRE

MELITO (second century)
Bishop of Sardis; the first known Christian pilgrim

Little is known of Melito's life. Eusebius supplies a list of the works of Melito (most of which have not survived), who was evidently bishop of Sardis during the reign of Emperor Marcus Aurelius (161–180), a Stoic. According to Eusebius, Melito shortly after 169 (by which time Christianity was regarded as a direct crime against the state) had addressed to the emperor an apologetical work which begged him to examine the charges made against believers. It suggested that Christianity be made the official religion, for church and empire were complementary divine works intended for the benefit of mankind. We do not know that this made any impression on Marcus Aurelius who, for all his general mildness, turned out to be an implacable persecutor of Christians.

Melito was apparently involved also in the problem of the dating of Easter, and he pioneered the pilgrim path to places significant in Christian origins and provided the first list of Old Testament canonical writings (he separated the Apocrypha from the canonical books). It has been noted that an extant fragment of his treatise *On Baptism* shows how he adapted Homeric exegetical method into Christian thought. A twentieth-century discovery of Melito's *Homily on the Passion* discussed the link between the old law and the new, a vital mid-second-century problem because of the attacks on the old law made by Gnostics. This work confirms Melito's status as a prominent theologian and Christian spokesman in the post-apostolic era. An unmarried bishop, according to Eusebius, Melito seems to have been interested in Montanism (his book titles suggest this). Polycrates in 195 speaks of Melito as one who "in his whole life was full of the Holy Ghost." J. D. DOUGLAS

MELVILLE, ANDREW (1545–1622)

Scottish reformer; often described as "the Father of Presbyterianism"

Born in Angus and educated in Scotland, France, and Switzerland, Melville became a professor of humanity in Geneva in 1569. He returned to Scotland in 1574, filling the vacuum left by Knox's death two years earlier. Soon Melville was principal of Glasgow University, where he overhauled and enlarged the curriculum until he transferred to St. Andrews in 1580 as principal of St. Mary's College. Melville became the champion of the Reformed Kirk against the efforts first of Regent Morton and then the young King James VI to impose a form of episcopacy on the country. He rejected all threats, bribes, and blandishments, even the offer of the archbishopric of St. Andrews, and fearlessly stood against the royal claim to supremacy over the church. He led the general assembly in ratifying the 1578 Second Book of Discipline, a work often referred to as the Magna Carta of Presbyterianism.

King James saw episcopacy as more amenable to his brand of kingcraft than presbytery and resolved to be no ministers' king. Melville in 1596, calling James "God's sillie vassal," reminded him in a memorable speech that there was in Scotland another kingdom of which James was but a member, and of which Christ Jesus was King. As with Knox in rebuking Mary Queen of Scots, there was with Melville no tempering of the tongue where eternal verities were at stake. It was James, however, who triumphed, for shortly after another defiant speech in 1606, Melville was consigned to the Tower of London for four years, at first in solitary confinement—without even pen and paper. He was released in 1611 to become professor of biblical theology in the University of Sedan, France, and never again set foot in his native land.

Melville was a superb scholar with an encyclopedic mind that absorbed learning of many kinds: theological, philosophical, legal, linguistic, and scientific. Through his activities and counsel, the three oldest Scottish universities (St. Andrews, Glasgow, and Aberdeen) acquired a reputation for sound learning among the even more ancient institutions on the continent. As a Presbyterian leader he could be as impetuous and abrasive as his predecessor John Knox had been. Concerned as he was with crucial matters of church-state relations, Melville never lost sight of his chief object: to make Christianity a matter of popular concern. Church, school, and state alike were for the people—and the people were the Lord's. One might question whether the attempt to transplant Genevan thinking into the political circumstances of Scotland was prudent or practicable. That the threat to spiritual liberty was a very real one, however, was seen when the House of Stuart still further developed the theory of the Divine Right of Kings, and what Melville had feared and fought came to pass. It was Presbyterianism of the type Melville had forged that ultimately won the victory some eighty years after his banishment and which still forms the basis of the national Church of Scotland today. J. D. DOUGLAS

MENDELSSOHN, FELIX (1809–1847)

German composer

The composer's complete name was Jakob

Ludwig Felix Mendelssohn-Bartholdy. His grandfather was a famous literary figure, and his parents were wealthy and cultured. Although they were Jewish, they converted to Lutheranism. Mendelssohn was confirmed in the Lutheran church, an act which seems to have moved him deeply. He was born in Hamburg, but the family moved to Berlin, where their home became a center of musical and other cultural activity. Mendelssohn was greatly gifted both as a pianist and composer. As a boy he wrote twelve symphonies and several concertos for the concerts given in the parental household. He also played the viola and was an expert painter in watercolors.

He studied composition with Zelter, the musical mentor of the great poet Goethe, who was greatly impressed by the gifted boy. Zelter introduced young Mendelssohn to the music of J. S. Bach, which was then known only to a small circle of admirers. Mendelssohn, at twenty, conducted Bach's *St. Matthew Passion* for the first time since the death of its composer, an event that began the revival of Bach's music.

Mendelssohn composed important works in all genres except opera. His first oratorio, *St. Paul* (1835), is much influenced by Bach in its use of Lutheran church melodies, while his *Elijah* (1846) is probably the greatest dramatic oratorio of the nineteenth century. It was first performed in England, where Mendelssohn's music had great success. *The Hymn of Praise* is a symphony with several choral movements using texts from the Bible and from Lutheran hymnody. It was written to commemorate the four hundredth anniversary of the invention of printing. He also wrote *The Reformation Symphony* for the third centennial of the Augsburg Confession. His choral settings of Psalm 42 and Psalm 43 are notable. Inspired by Bach, he also composed important works for the organ, several of which draw on Lutheran hymn tunes.

Although marred at times by the overfacile use of clichés, Mendelssohn's music has stood the test of time. His contribution as performer, composer, and conductor, and the excellence of his choral music assure

him of a continuing place among the great musicians of the nineteenth century.
J. B. MacMillan

MENNO SIMONS (1496–1561)
Spiritual leader of sixteenth-century Anabaptists; person from whom modern Mennonites take their name

Menno was born in Witmarsum, Friesland. Ordination as a Catholic priest came in 1524. For twelve years he served the Roman church, but in 1536, after a study of the New Testament to resolve doubts about transubstantiation, Menno converted to the Anabaptist movement. He was baptized by Obbe Philips, founder of Holland's first Anabaptist congregation. The following year he began preaching in a church in Groningen.

Convinced that Anabaptism was the New Testament pattern, Menno became a moderating influence among the radical reformers. He worked to purge Anabaptism of the millennial fantasies that had led to its ruin in Munster, but his ministry was primarily one of moral and devotional enthusiasm.

Menno adopted a literalistic and sometimes legalistic interpretation of Scripture and was suspicious of attempts to systematize theology. He refused to use the term "Trinity" because it did not appear in Scripture, though he accepted the Apocrypha as past canon. Menno opposed the Chalcedonian (451) interpretation of Christ's two natures. He believed Christ was "entirely the true Son of the true and living God" born "through" Mary but not "by" Mary. The church he defined as the "assembly of the pious." Church purity was to be preserved by the "ban" and by "shunning," both gestures of brotherly love when rightly applied. Infant baptism was considered "idolatrous, useless, and vain," since original sin was not damnatory in children. The ordinances—adult baptism and the Lord's Supper—were outward symbols only; they mediated no grace. Foot washing was practiced, not as an ordinance, but as a sign of Christian humility. Menno was millennarian and a pacifist. So clear was the separation of God's kingdom from the world that civil magistrates were not granted membership in Menno's churches. Oath taking was unlawful for Christians. The church was to be a tightly knit circle (marriage to outsiders not permitted) of "brethren" (their identifying term until after Menno's death). The church was to be withdrawn from the secular world.

For twenty-five years Menno traveled the Netherlands and Germany, planting churches and preaching. He finally settled in Wustenfeld, where he died in 1561. He wrote twenty-four books and booklets; the best known is *Foundations of Christian Doctrine* (1539). The Mennonites, an offshoot of the Anabaptists, continue to follow Menno's teachings. M. FACKLER

MERTON, THOMAS (1915–1968)
American poet and mystic

Though Merton was born in France, his father was an English landscape painter and his mother was an American Quaker. He went to England where he studied at Cambridge and then came to the United States, where he graduated from Columbia University with an M.A. In 1938 he converted to Roman Catholicism and shortly thereafter entered the Trappist monastery of Gethsemani in Kentucky. Merton had led a full and worldy life prior to his conversion and entrance to the strict monastery. The profound spiritual experiences he encountered in prompting him to join the monastery are described in his autobiography, *The Seven Storey Mountain* (1941). A sequel autobiography, *The Sign of Jonas* (1952), provides a vivid description of life in a Trappist monastery.

Merton is best known for his personal mysticism as expressed in his poems: *Thirty Poems* (1944), a volume that was written in "the first flush of his conversion"; *Figs for an Apocalypse* (1947) and *Tears of the Blind Lions* (1949), two volumes that express his Catholic spirituality in vigorous verse. P. W. COMFORT

MERULO, CLAUDIO (1533–1604)
Composer

Merulo was an outstanding composer and printer of music. Between 1564 and 1584 he was first organist of St. Mark's Cathedral in Venice, where two organs were used. This was a position of great prestige, and was held successively by musicians of renown throughout the sixteenth century. He was one of the first to develop a distinctive style of organ music. A collection of his organ toccatas was published in 1598. Such music was intended, of course, to adorn the services of the church. J. B. MACMILLAN

METHODIUS
See CYRIL AND METHODIUS

METZGER, BRUCE MANNING (born 1914)
New Testament scholar and textual critic; Bible translator

Born in Middleton, Pennsylvania, Metzger was educated at Lebanon Valley College (A.B., 1935) and Princeton Theological Seminary (Th.B., 1938; Th.M., 1939). He was ordained to the ministry of the Presbyterian Church U.S.A. in 1939. Thereafter he studied at Princeton University, receiving an M.A. (1940) and Ph.D. in Greek and Latin Classics (1942). He taught New Testament at Princeton Theological Seminary from 1938 to 1984, serving as the George L. Collord Professor of New Testament language and literature from 1964 to 1984.

Metzger is best known for his work in New Testament textual criticism. He is regarded as one of the foremost American textual critics, having published many significant articles and books in this field, as well as serving on the committee that produced the United Bible Societies' *Greek New Testament,* a standard edition in the late twentieth century. Among his books on textual criticism are *The Text of the New Testament: Its Transmission, Corruption, and Restoration* (1964, 1968, 1991); *A Textual Commentary on the Greek New Testament: A Companion Volume to the United Bible Societies' Greek New Testament* (third edition, 1971); and *Manuscripts of the Greek Bible: An Introduction to Palaeography* (1981).

Metzger has also gained recognition for his work in Bible translation. He has served on the committees of both the Revised Standard Version and the New Revised Standard Version. For the NRSV, published in 1990, he was the chairperson during the fourteen years it took to complete the revision. He is the author or editor of more than thirty books, including *The Text, Canon, and Principle Versions of the Bible* (1956); *The Early Versions of the New Testament: Their Origin, Transmission, and Limitations* (1977); and *The Canon of the New Testament: Its Origin, Development, and Significance* (1987). Since 1978 he has been a corresponding fellow of the British Academy, an honor accorded to few American scholars. P. W. COMFORT

MEYER, EDUARD (1855–1930)
German historian

Born in Hamburg, Meyer was, after studying at Bonn and Leipzig, appointed professor of ancient history at Breslau (1885), Halle (1889), and finally Berlin, where he taught from 1902 to 1923. He made a major and pioneering contribution to the critical study of ancient history by recognizing the historical value of folklore, numismatics, and monuments. He established Egyptian chronology and wrote a book on that subject (1904) and another on Caesar and Pompeii (1918). But he specialized in the history of early Judaism and of primitive Christianity. In *Ursprung und Anfange des Christentums* (*The Origins and Beginnings of Christianity,* three volumes; 1921–1923) he contradicted accepted German theological opinion by powerfully arguing for the historical value and early date of Luke-Acts. Luke himself, claimed Meyer, was assured of a conspicuous place among the most important historical writers of any age and ranked in class with the church historian Eusebius. Though appreciating the person of Jesus, Meyer dismissed Christianity and all other faiths. In his opinion any religion was merely the product of the mythical thinking of the masses. His lifework was enshrined in a massive history of the ancient world,

Geschichte des Altertums (eight volumes, 1884–1902). N. HILLYER

MEYER, FREDERICK BROTHERTON (1847–1929)
British preacher, author, and spokesman for public righteousness

Meyer's ministry was worldwide, but his base was London. He was born and educated there, held pastorates at some of London's largest free churches, and conducted his moral crusades from that city.

An ardent Baptist and premillennialist, Meyer applied Christian principles to social ills such as drunkenness, prostitution, unmarried mothers, and unwanted children. One of his best crusades occurred in 1911 when he successfully stopped a prize fight that was to be held at Earl's Court between Jack Johnson of the United States and a British contender. Meyer endured scorn for his efforts: a London newspaper called him "Meddling, Maudlin Meyer."

Meyer was involved in the Blue Ribbon movement (prohibition); the Purity, Rescue, and Temperance work of the Central South London Free Church Council (which closed brothels and counseled prostitutes); and the Homeless Children's Aid and Adoption Society. He served as president of the National and World Sunday School Unions, president of the National Union of Christian Endeavor, and founder of South London Missionary Training College. He was also the author of more than seventy books. He preached around the world. Melbourne Hall (Leicester), a center of social and evangelistic activity, was built in 1881 under his leadership. M. FACKLER

MEYER, HEINRICH AUGUST WILHELM (1800–1873)
German Protestant clergyman and New Testament scholar

Born in Gotha, Meyer studied theology at the University of Jena. Thereafter he taught in a private school at Grone and then pastored churches in various German cities—such as Grone, Hoya, Neustadt, and

Hanover from 1822 to 1848. In addition to pastoring, he devoted his time to writing commentaries on the New Testament based on the principle of historico-grammatical exegesis. His commentary series, *Kritisch-exegetischer Komentar über das Neuen Testamentum,* begun in 1829, set a standard for modern critical exegesis of the New Testament; it is a series that continues to be consulted by scholars. Meyer wrote the first two volumes of the series on the Greek text and German translation, and then commentaries on the four Gospels, Acts, and eight Pauline Epistles. Meyer also worked on the revision of Luther's translation of the Bible.
P. W. COMFORT

MICHAELIS, JOHANN DAVID
(1717–1791)
German biblical scholar and Bible translator

Born at Halle, Michaelis became professor of philosophy (1746–1750) and oriental languages (1750–1791) at Göttingen. In his annotated translation of the Old Testament (thirteen volumes, 1769–1791) and New Testament (two volumes, 1790–1792), he provided the cultured public with an introduction to the new critical views of Scripture. This was continued in his *Introductions* to the Old Testament and New Testament. The latter was translated into English and published in four volumes (1793–1801). His achievements in the world of scholarship lay in his attempts to free the study of Hebrew from its traditional Jewish, rabbinical assumptions. He compared it with other ancient Middle Eastern languages and to this end published grammars of Chaldean and Syriac. In his *Mosaisches Recht* (six volumes, 1770–1775) he argued that the laws of the Pentateuch reflected the statesmanship of Moses rather than the direct action of God. In translation this book was entitled *Commentaries on the Laws of Moses* (four volumes, 1814), and it helped to label Michaelis as a rationalist theologian. He also published works in geography and archaeology and revealed his independent thinking about doctrine in books on dogmatic and moral theology. P. TOON

MICHELANGELO BUONARROTI
(MICHELAGNIOLO DI LODOVICO
BUONARROTI-SIMONI) (1475–1654)
An Italian artist whose genius found expression in painting, sculpture, and architecture

Michelangelo was born in the Tuscan village of Caprese. At age thirteen he was sent to Florence to study painting with the Ghirlandaio brothers. Within the year his work caught the eye of Lorenzo de' Medici, who invited the boy to join the Medici household. There he came under the influence of the most brilliant intellectuals in all of Europe. In 1496 after spending some time in Venice and Bologna, he went to Rome where he carved his first Pieta, now in St. Peter's. In 1501 he returned to Florence, where he was commissioned to do several civic works including the eighteen-foot-tall David, now in Florence. In 1505 he was called back to Rome by Pope Julius II to do work for this powerful patron. From 1508 to 1512 Michelangelo painted the story of creation on the ceiling of the Sistine Chapel. At the same time he continued work on the enormous, and preferred, project of sculpture for the Pope's tomb. Of this only *Moses* and the series of *Bound Slaves* were completed. From 1518 to 1534 Michelangelo worked in Rome and Florence on commissions both in sculpture and architecture. For Pope Leo X he worked on the Medici Chapel in Florence. From 1534 until his death he concentrated on major projects in Rome including the *Last Judgment,* again in the Sistine Chapel, and the frescoes of the Pauline Chapel. In 1546 he was made chief architect for the rebuilding of St. Peter's. At this time he also became involved in a number of other architectural projects. Two sculptures that were never completed, both on the theme of Christ's death, were begun in the last two years of his life.

Michelangelo was the most technically gifted artist as well as one of the greatest intellectuals of his time. As an artist he was obsessed with God's infinite and mysterious nature and God's crowning work of creation—man. His was a God- and man-centered art. By Michelangelo's own testimony,

God was his greatest influence. Great art, he believed, depended upon the artist having first within himself a perfect God-given idea. Then the physical beauty of the art that was made was not an end in itself. It was to be a reflection of a spiritual beauty and was meant to lift the thoughts of the viewer above material things. A. STEFFLER

MIGNE, JACQUES PAUL (1800–1875)
French editor and printer of theological books

Born at St. Flour in France, Migne was ordained in 1824 as a Roman Catholic priest and worked in the diocese of Orleans. After a disagreement with his bishop he went to live in Paris in 1833. He started a paper called *L'Univers,* which he ran until 1836. Then he moved to nearby Petit Montrouge, where he set up a printing works called "Imprimerie catholique." At the same establishment organs and church fittings were made. The output of books was tremendous. Perhaps the most important of the works printed was that of the Greek and Latin Fathers— *Patrolotiae cursus completus* (Latin, 217 volumes; Greek, 162 volumes). A majority of the time the Roman hierarchy disapproved of his work, but the books he printed soon found homes in Roman Catholic centers of learning. In February 1868 his establishment, then employing some three hundred men, was destroyed by fire. It was never restored to its early size and was eventually sold. P. TOON

MILL, JOHN STUART (1806–1873)
Utilitarian philosopher and social scientist

Born in London, Mill was educated privately (1809–1820) by his father, the Scottish-born philosopher and historian James Mill (1773–1826). In 1823 Mill became a clerk at India House, the London headquarters of the East India Company, where in 1856 he became chief examiner of India correspondence. When Parliament ended the rule of this company in India in 1858, Mill was retired on pension. Between 1865 and 1868 he represented Westminster in the House of Commons. Thereafter he

lived most of each year at St. Veran, near Avignon, in France, where he died.

Mill was a voluminous writer on almost every branch of social science, to which he hoped to give something of the exactness and predictability of the physical sciences. Among his most important publications are *The System of Logic* (1843), *Principles of Political Economy* (1848), *On Liberty* (1859), *On Representative Government* (1861), and *On the Subjection of Women* (1867). His interests were primarily practical. He aspired to be a reformer of the world in accordance with the utilitarian principle of promoting "the greatest happiness of the greatest number," and he interpreted his social objective thus: "How to unite the greatest individual liberty of action with a common ownership of the raw material of the globe, and an equal partnership of all in the benefits of combined labor."

Mill was a man of high moral character; he has been described as "the saint of rationalism." Since his father had abandoned all belief in revealed religion, Mill was brought up without any formal religious interest. But in his later years he grew more sympathetic to religion and to Christianity in particular, declaring in an essay on theism that the balance of evidence favors the idea of creation by intelligence, that science does not rule out belief in immortality, and that Jesus Christ might possibly be what he claimed— namely "a man charged with a special, express, and unique commission from God to lead mankind to truth and virtue."
N. V. HOPE

MILLER, WILLIAM (1782–1849)
Founder of the Adventist movement; ardent nineteenth-century spokesman for premillennialism

Miller was born in Pittsfield, Massachusetts, took up farming, and served as a captain in the War of 1812. His conversion from Deism in 1816 launched him on a fourteen-year study of Bible prophecy. He concluded that the 2300 year-days of Daniel 8:14 had started in 457 B.C. and that the Lord would return within twelve months of March 1843.

Miller was licensed to preach by a Baptist church in 1833 and published his views in 1836 under the title *Evidence from Scripture and History of the Second Coming of Christ, about the Year 1843*. When Christ did not return by March 1844, Miller recalculated the event for October 22, 1844. When that date also passed, many followers dropped away. Others who were scattered among traditional denominations began to band together. Miller became first president of the new Advent Church in 1845. M. FACKLER

MILLIGAN, GEORGE (1860–1934)
Scottish New Testament scholar

Born in Fife, Milligan studied arts and divinity at Scottish and German universities, and thereafter ministered in Edinburgh (1883–1894) and Caputh (1894–1910). In his quiet Perthshire parish he developed an interest in Greek papyri. He lectured on the subject at Oxford, Cambridge, and in the United States and used his expertise to produce a highly praised commentary on Paul's Epistles to the Thessalonians. In 1910 he became professor of divinity and biblical criticism at Glasgow. Milligan is best remembered for his remarkable *Vocabulary of the Greek New Testament* (1914–1929), a project which, after the first year, he carried out single-handedly. Moderator of the Church of Scotland general assembly in 1923, and active in the more general field of religious education, he was a friendly man who brought objectivity and lucidity to all his sermons, lectures, and writings.
J. D. DOUGLAS

MILLS, SAMUEL J. (1783–1818)
One of the founders of the modern missionary movement in the United States

With several other students at Williams College, Williamstown, Massachusetts, Mills formed the Society of the Brethren in 1808. The purpose of the society was to take the gospel to the ends of the earth. These young men met frequently for discussion and prayer. One day they were caught in a sudden downpour and took shelter in the lee of a haystack. When the storm was over they stood to their feet and said, "We can do it if we will." Mills went on to Andover where he was joined by Adoniram Judson from Brown, Samuel Newell from Harvard, and Samuel Nott, Jr., from Union College. In June 1810 these four young men offered themselves for missionary service to the General Assembly of the Congregational Church. As a direct result there came into being the American Board of Commissioners for Foreign Missions, which in 1812 dispatched the first American missionaries to India. Ill health prevented Mills himself from going overseas. But from 1812 to 1814 he was sent by the Congregational Home Missions Societies of Massachusetts and Connecticut on extensive tours of the western United States to assess the need for missionaries there. Soon thereafter pastors began to be sent to frontier areas.

Mills was equally concerned for the evangelization of Africa and the plight of the slaves in the U.S.A. To this end he helped to found the American Colonization Society in 1817. The purpose of the society was to evangelize and liberate the slaves and then repatriate them to Africa. Mills never lived to see his dream come true. Returning from a visit to Africa he died at sea on June 15, 1818. After Mills's death his concern for spreading the gospel on the frontier bore fruit in the establishment of the American Home Missionary Society (1826).
M. A. NOLL

MILMAN, HENRY HART (1791–1868)
Poet and church historian

Milman was born in London, the youngest son of Sir Francis Milman, physician to King George III. During a brilliant career at Oxford University, he won the Newdigate Prize with an English poem on the *Apollo Belvidere* (1812). He wrote several hymns, including "Ride on, Ride on, in Majesty." Ordained in 1816, Milman became rector of St. Margaret's, Westminster (1835). As dean of St. Paul's Cathedral (1849–1868), he popularized public worship and in 1858 began evening services under the dome. He was professor of poetry at Oxford (1821–1831), a pioneer in the study and translation of Sanskrit poetry, but an undistinguished Bampton Lecturer (1827). In 1830 his *History of the Jews* aroused great criticism for his liberal and unorthodox views, while two of his books on early Christianity (1840, 1854) won Macaulay's praise. He wrote a life of Gibbon and in 1838 edited his *Decline and Fall of the Roman Empire*. His delightful history, *Annals of St. Paul's,* was published posthumously. N. HILLYER

MILNE, WILLIAM (1785–1822)
Missionary to the Far East

Born at Kennethmont, Aberdeenshire, Scotland, Milne was converted at the age of sixteen and joined an independent church in nearby Huntly. Accepted as a candidate for the mission field by the London Missionary Society (LMS), he was trained at the society's college at Gosport and ordained to the ministry in 1812. Selected by LMS directors to join Robert Morrison as a missionary to China, he arrived in Macao in July 1813; but being ordered to leave by the Portuguese governor, he proceeded to Canton, where Morrison joined him. The next two years he spent in distributing Christian literature in Canton and the East Indies—particularly Java—before setting up headquarters at Malacca in 1815 for what became known as the Ultra Ganges Mission. There he mastered the Chinese language, opened a school for Chinese children, and set up a printing press from which he issued a monthly magazine, *The Indo-Chinese Gleaner.* He also translated parts of the Old Testament into Chinese and in 1818 became principal of the Anglo-Chinese College that was founded at Malacca "to impart the knowledge of the English language and the principles of the Christian religion to Chinese youth, and the instruction of missionaries and others in the Chinese language." That same year Milne received the D.D. degree from Glasgow University. He died in Malacca four years later. N. V. HOPE

MILNER, ISAAC (1750–1820)
Mathematician, chemist, and evangelical leader

Born at Leeds and educated at Queens College, Cambridge, Milner became a fellow and was ordained. He remained in Cambridge all his life. In 1776 he was elected a fellow of the Royal Society and in 1778 he became head (president) of his college. He aimed to make it an important educational center and a promoter of evangelical principles. Critics came to refer to it as "a nursery of evangelical neophytes."

On several occasions he was vice-chancellor of the university, and in 1798 he was elected Lucasian Professor of mathematics. Ecclesiastical promotion came his way also, for in 1791 he became dean of Carlisle Cathedral, which he visited as often as possible to preach and to preside over the chapter. He edited and completed his brother, Joseph's, book, *History of the Church of Christ* (1800) and also wrote a biography of Joseph (1801), for whom he had a deep affection. He also enjoyed a close friendship with William Wilberforce. P. TOON

MILNER, JOSEPH (1744–1797)
Evangelical Anglican leader

Born at Leeds (England) and educated at Catherine Hall, Cambridge University, Milner was ordained to serve both as a schoolmaster and a curate. In 1768 he became headmaster of Hull Grammar School. From 1770 when he adopted evangelical principles, he became an enthusiastic preacher in both Holy Trinity Church, Hull, and in nearby North Ferriby. He offended the respectable middle classes but attracted the poor and laboring classes in great numbers. By his influence the town became a center of the new Anglican evangelicalism. As a writer he is best known for *The History of the Church of Christ* (three volumes, 1794–1809). He wrote this because he believed that most histories of the church played into the hands of unbelievers, for they concentrated on controversies. Therefore he painted the brighter side of the history. His work was completed by his brother, Isaac, then revised by John Scott. Also, after his death four volumes (1800–1830) of his sermons were printed by his friends. Like his brother, he was a lifelong friend of William Wilberforce, whom he had taught at Hull Grammar School. P. TOON

MILTON, JOHN (1608–1674)
Eminent English poet

Milton's father, who was a scrivener and an accomplished musician, afforded Milton an extraordinary education including seven years at Christ's College, Cambridge; six years of "postgraduate" private study; and fifteen months of travel, primarily in Italy.

Milton enjoyed languages. He loved Latin and wrote Latin poems. He loved Italian (and Dante and Petrarch) and wrote sonnets in Italian. He read Homer, Plato, and the New Testament in the original language, Greek; and his knowledge of Hebrew and Aramaic enabled him to read the Old Testament and the Jewish commentators like a scholar. In addition to French and Spanish he probably read Anglo-Saxon. He agreed to teach Roger Williams Greek in return for lessons in one of the languages of the American Indians. Hardly a single area of study and culture escaped Milton's attention; the keystone of all his learning was the Bible.

With the outbreak of the English civil war in 1642, Milton allied himself with the Parliamentary party. When Cromwell came into power, Milton was sought out by Parliament to serve as Latin secretary to the council of state and as chief apologist for the government.

In 1643, Milton married Mary Powell, the daughter of a prominent Royalist. A few months after the wedding, Mary returned to the home of her parents. She remained separated from Milton for three years but returned and, within a year, bore her first child, a daughter. She gave birth to three other children and died giving birth to the last one. The third child, a son named John, died one month after his mother had died. Four years later, at the age of forty-seven, after he had become almost totally blind, Milton married Katherine Woodcock, who

within a year bore a daughter. Within a few months the mother and daughter died.

Cromwell's death in 1658 resulted in the loss of Milton's secretaryship. In 1660 shortly before Charles II returned from France to restore monarchy, Milton published *A Free and Easy Way to Establish a Free Commonwealth.* Immediately following the Restoration, Milton faced great danger. He was forced to go into hiding until influential friends interceded on his behalf. From the early to mid 1660s until his death in 1674, Milton lived a quiet life, arranged in part by his third wife, Elizabeth Minsul.

Milton's writings may be roughly divided into three periods. He produced his first group of poems and prose before the outbreak of the civil war in 1642. By the age of twenty-four, he had written three excellent poems: "On the Meaning of Christ's Nativity," "L'Allegro," and "Il Penseroso." During the next six years he wrote poems that would guarantee his immortality in literature—among them "Commus" and "Lycidas."

The second period of Milton's productivity coincides roughly with the outbreak of the civil war. He wrote scholarly and polemical essays on religious, social, educational, and domestic responsibility. His first essays were against the powers of the bishop in an ecclesiastical hierarchy not authorized by Scripture. He also published *Of Education,* a plea for qualitative Christian education; and *Areopagetica,* an argument against a law requiring that any piece of writing be approved by censors before publication. The first of his essays on divorce appeared in 1644, and *Eikonoklastes,* a defense of the action of the Commonwealth, appeared in 1649. Between 1655 and 1661, working from a remarkable memory and with the help of people who read to him and took dictation from him, Milton completed *De Doctrina Christiana,* an exposition of Christian doctrine derived from his interpretation of the Bible.

The period from 1660 to the end of his life was devoted to his greatest works. The epic *Paradise Lost* (1667), showing his story of man's creation and fall; *Paradise Regained*

(1671), depicting the temptation of Jesus, who unlike Adam, would not fall; and *Samson Agonistes* (1671), showing Samson's tribulation and triumph in the form of Greek tragedy, assured Milton's reputation as a great poet. E. B. BATSON

MINDSZENTY, JOZSEF (1892–1975)
Roman Catholic archbishop of Esztergom; primate of Hungary

Born Jozsef Pehm in Mindszent, western Hungary, and educated at the seminary in Szombathely, Mindszenty became assistant pastor in two small villages after his ordination to the Roman Catholic priesthood in 1915. In 1917 he was called to teach religion at the State Gymnasium in Zalaegerszeg, where two years later he became the parish priest. In 1944 he was appointed bishop of Veszprem and the next year was promoted to be archbishop of Esztergom and primate of the Catholic Church in Hungary. In 1946 he was made a cardinal.

As an early opponent of totalitarianism, Mindszenty was twice arrested in 1919, first by the revolutionary government of Count Michael Karolyi and then by the Communist regime of Bela Kun. He was imprisoned again in 1944 by the Hungarian Nazis, who were then in power. During the period of Communist takeover in Hungary, Mindszenty's refusal to permit Catholic parochial schools to be secularized brought about his arrest, and in 1949 he was convicted of treason. Sentenced to life imprisonment, in the course of the Hungarian uprising of 1956 he was released; but when the Communist party regained control, he sought refuge in the American embassy in Budapest. In 1971 he left Hungary and settled in Vienna. In 1974, when he criticized the papal dealings with the Hungarian government, his see was declared vacant. He died in Vienna the next year. N. V. HOPE

MOFFAT, ROBERT (1795–1883)
Pioneer Scottish missionary in South Africa

Born at Ormiston, East Lothian, Moffat was the son of a customhouse keeper. Apprenticed as a gardener at High Leigh, Cheshire (1813), he came under the Christian influence of Wesleyan Methodists. At a missionary meeting at Warrington led by William Roby, he decided to go overseas in full-time Christian work. Because of his poor education, the London Missionary Society accepted him only reluctantly (1815). In 1816 he left for South Africa, and two years later in Cape Town he married Mary Smith, his employer's daughter. She shared his labors for the next fifty years. After eight years in Great Namaqualand, he made his base in Kuruman, Bechuanaland (1825), until he left Africa for the last time over forty years later.

By 1830 Moffat had produced the Gospel of Luke in Bechuana. He went on to translate the complete New Testament (1840) and Old Testament (1857), many hymns, *Pilgrim's Progress*, and a number of educational textbooks for Bechuana Africans. But his considerable literary output did not prevent Moffat from taking the gospel further afield. On his first arrival in South Africa, little was known of the country north of Cape Colony beyond the Orange River. By the time he left (1870), the continent had been opened up beyond the Zambesi. Thanks to his labors and those of his son-in-law David Livingstone, Christian churches led by trained African ministers were established.

A tall man with shaggy hair and beard, clear-cut features, and piercing eyes, Moffat had an impressive appearance. A consecrated man of faith, the father of South African missionary work proved to be a staunch friend to the Africans, a persevering teacher, a determined explorer, and a skillful organizer. Moffat had an enthusiastic welcome when on furlough in England (1838–1843). During this period he published *Missionary Labors and Scenes in South Africa* (1842) and inspired David Livingstone to go out to areas then untouched by the gospel—first to South and then to Central Africa. Moffat's eldest daughter, Mary, married Livingstone in 1844. In failing health, Moffat finally left Africa in 1870. Edinburgh University awarded him an honorary doctorate in 1872. N. HILLYER

MOFFATT, JAMES (1870–1944)
Scottish Bible translator

Born in Glasgow, Moffatt was educated at the University and the Free Church College in that city. After ordination in 1896, he spent fifteen years in parish work for the Free Church of Scotland. He then lectured at Mansfield College, Oxford, for four years, and Glasgow for twelve, before being appointed Washburn professor of church history at Union Theological Seminary, New York, in 1927. He retired in 1939. Among his many books on biblical criticism, *An Introduction to the Literature of the New Testament* (1911), which is a wide-ranging survey of modern critical scholarship, reveals his own very liberal standpoint. But his most widely known work was the popular "Moffatt Bible," a single-handed and somewhat colloquial translation of the entire Scriptures (New Testament, 1913; Old Testament, 1924). This was a remarkable achievement for one man, even though he attracted much criticism from other scholars for trying to overcome literary difficulties by freely rearranging verses and even chapters. He also depended far too heavily on critical theories for his rendering of the Old Testament in particular. Subsequent findings in the fields of archaeology and philology have shown his theories to be untenable. Moffatt also edited a series of commentaries covering all the books of the New Testament (seventeen volumes, 1928–1949), which were all based on his translation. He himself contributed the volumes on 1 Corinthians and the general Epistles. In addition to theological and biblical works, Moffatt wrote several books on English literature. N. HILLYER

MOFFETT, SAMUEL AUSTIN (1864–1939)
Pioneer Presbyterian missionary to Korea

Born in Madison, Indiana, Moffett was educated at Hanover College (A.B., 1884; M.S., 1885; D.D., 1901) and McCormick Seminary (1888). He sailed to Korea in 1889 under the Presbyterian Church U.S.A. Board of Foreign Missions. Korea had only recently (1884) been opened to Protestant missions when he landed in 1890. Public preaching was forbidden. Foreigners were restricted to the treaty ports. When Moffett was assigned all North Korea as his field and moved into the interior in 1892, a hostile mob stoned him in the streets of Pyongyang. But he lived to see that same city become the center of the country's phenomenal church growth, and later he ordained the leader of the mob (that had stoned him) as one of the first ministers of the Korean church.

His missionary strategy stressed personal evangelism, instruction in Bible for all Christians, and self-government and self-support for the church. In 1901 he founded the first theological school in Korea, the Presbyterian Theological Seminary. In 1907 he was elected the first moderator of the Independent Presbyterian Church of Korea. Moffett's work laid the foundation for the rapid growth and organization of the Presbyterian Church of Korea, one of the largest in the Third World.

Moffett advocated a working partnership between evangelism and education. He is credited with founding over two hundred Christian schools ranging from one-room primary schools to Korea's first modern college, Soongsil (now Soongjun University), of which he was cofounder in 1906. He helped to organize the Korea Red Cross, and he was president of the Presbyterian Seminary (1902–1924) and of Soongsil College (1918–1828). He represented Korea at the International Missionary Conference in Edinburgh (1910) and then in Jerusalem (1928). For advances in education he was awarded the gold medal of the Japanese empire in 1925 and 1935, but in 1936 he was expelled from Korea for refusing to permit Christian schools to participate in Shinto shrine worship. However, he was posthumously decorated by the Republic of Korea in 1963 for his identification with the cause of Korean independence. S. H. MOFFETT

MOHR, JOSEPH (1792–1848)
An Austrian priest best known for his poem "Silent Night, Holy Night"

Born in Salzburg, Mohr became a Roman

Catholic priest in 1815 and served several parishes around Salzburg. On December 24, 1818, Mohr asked Franz Grüber, village schoolmaster and organist, to set his poem to suitable music for two solo voices, chorus, and guitar accompaniment. The guitar accompaniment was needed because the church organ had broken down. In a few hours the organist composed the simple melody. That same Christmas evening it was sung. In a short time the tender carol had attained such popularity that it was translated into many modern languages. Joseph Mohr also helped restore to general use, especially in German-speaking areas, those melodies and texts sung in the church prior to the Reformation. These less sentimental hymns were published, along with Mohr's own hymn tunes, in his various hymn and prayer book collections. A. STEFFLER

MOLINA, LUIS DE (1535–1600)

Spanish Jesuit theologian who tried to resolve the apparent contradiction between the doctrines of grace and free will by holding that God has a "middle knowledge" (scientia media)

In his writings Molina wanted to affirm that God has foreknowledge of human affairs, without lapsing into determinism. In his *On the Agreement of God's Grace and Free Will*, published in 1588, he argued that there is a cooperation of man's will with divine grace. This view contrasts with the Thomist view that God predetermines man's will to act freely. Molina saw in the Thomist view a disguised determinism.

The key element in Molina's solution of the problem is his account of God's "middle knowledge." This knowledge receives its name from the fact that it falls between two kinds of knowledge that Thomas Aquinas (1224–1274) described. Aquinas held that God's knowledge may be one of "vision," which is a knowledge of that which *has* existed, *does* exist, and *will* exist. This is knowledge of what follows from the absolute divine decree. Aquinas also held that God has a knowledge of the purely possible, which is a knowledge of "simple under-

standing," of things and events that have not existed, do not exist, and will not exist. This knowledge supposes no divine decrees. Molina's "middle knowledge," which falls between these two kinds of knowledge, is the knowledge that God has of conditional future events. God knows what an individual will do in certain circumstances if grace is offered, and so he decrees the circumstances and the grace necessary to effect the cooperative action of the individual. In the conditional order then, God's grace is efficacious entirely from man's free futurable consent.

Thomists opposed Molina's position, for they saw in Molina's "middle knowledge" a denial of God's universal causality. Debate on this view continued for over three centuries. In the Roman Catholic Church this remains one of the accepted solutions of the problem of grace and free will. Molina's position was adopted by Francisco Suarez (1548–1617), whose thought came to dominate Roman Catholic and many Protestant universities during the seventeenth and eighteenth centuries. Consequently, Molina's views have been far more influential in Protestant discussions of grace and free will than is usually recognized. A. VOS

MOLINOS, MIGUEL DE (1640–1697)

Spanish theologian whose life and writings greatly influenced seventeenth-century mysticism

Born of noble parents in Muniesa, Spain, Molinos studied at Valencia, where he was ordained and received a doctorate in theology. In 1663 he settled in Rome where he became a well-known priest and confessor. In 1675 he published *A Spiritual Guide,* which was immediately popular and translated into several languages. According to Molinos, contemplation distinguishes the perfect from the imperfect Christian. The imperfect Christian lives an active life and uses the prayer of meditation. The contemplation of the perfect Christian consists in a total abandonment of the self to the will and operation of God in the soul. The soul has to rid itself of all efforts to act virtuously, to form thoughts and desires, or even to repel temptations. Hence, his view is sometimes called Quietist.

The Jesuits attacked Molinos's work, claiming it to be Jansenist in character, because it undercuts the role of the church. At first Molinos defended himself successfully, and the books of his opponents were placed on the Index in 1681. However, in 1685 he was suddenly arrested and investigated by the Holy Office. In 1687 Molinos retracted a number of errors attributed to him and pleaded guilty to charges of moral misconduct. The *Guide* was susceptible to dangerous and even heretical interpretations; but this hardly seems reason enough for the sudden and drastic action taken against so respected a person. Non-Catholics have tended to think that political considerations caused Molinos's downfall, but Roman Catholic sources tend to attribute it to the charges of moral misconduct. Molinos's conviction caused a great stir. He was sentenced to a life of penitential imprisonment and died after living nine years of pious and exemplary behavior. A. VOS

MONICA (c. 331–387)
Mother of Augustine of Hippo

Born in Numidia, Monica was a Christian of Christian parents. She married the pagan Patricius (whom she ultimately saw converted). By him she had two sons and one daughter; Augustine was her favorite. Her serenity, simplicity, and deep devotion were probably the most important early influences in the life of her son; but these were not enough to prevent him from falling into debauchery. He has left vivid vignettes of her in his writings, especially his *Confessions*. Like her son, Monica was an admirer of Bishop Ambrose of Milan, who tried to purge her religious devotion of superstition.

Monica accompanied Augustine when he left North Africa for study and teaching— first in Rome, then in Milan. She disapproved of his liaison with the woman who became the mother of his son, Adeodatus, and tried unsuccessfully to secure for him a suitable wife. When Augustine finally became a Christian at the age of thirty-three and decided upon the celibate life and priesthood, she felt that her work was accomplished. She died shortly thereafter, just as they were about to set sail to return to North Africa. A. CABANISS

MONOD, ADOLPHE (1802–1856)
Noted French Protestant preacher of the nineteenth century

Monod was the leader of the "Réveil," the Protestant awakening which swept French-speaking Europe in the first half of the last century. Although his brother, Frédéric, was converted to evangelical beliefs early in the nineteenth century, Adolphe steadfastly resisted this teaching. Adolphe pursued theological studies from 1820 to 1824, then took up pastoral charge of a French congregation at Naples from 1825 to 1827.

Through contacts with the Scottish lay theologian Thomas Erskine (1788–1870), Monod was won to orthodoxy. For a short period he became schismatic (during his pastoral ministry in Lyon), but Monod soon returned to the Reformed fold. In 1836 he was appointed to the chair of theology at Montauban, where he served with distinction until 1847. At that time he was installed as pastor of the great Oratoire Church in Paris, where he preached until his death. The powerful sermons of Monod were published in French and also in many other languages. W. A. DETZLER

MONOD, FRÉDÉRIC (1794–1863)
French Protestant pastor and editor

Frédéric Monod was the elder brother of Adolphe, the famous preacher of the French Protestant revival. Frédéric had in many ways a larger sphere of influence than his brother. Frédéric was converted under the ministry of the Scot Robert Haldane at Geneva in 1817. (Haldane conducted regular Bible studies for theological students in the Swiss city.) After completion of his theological studies, Frédéric served as assistant to his father, pastor Jean Monod of Paris. In 1832 he became pastor of the Oratoire

Church, preceding his famous brother in that role. For forty-three years Frédéric edited the *Archives du christianisme au dix-neuvieme siècle,* a periodical designed to promote evangelicalism among the French Protestants. As editor, Monod fought the subservience of the church to the state, and he urged the acceptance of a conservative creed by his coreligionists. In 1849 he helped to organize the dissident Reformed congregations into an association of free churches. This union exists to this day as a monument to Monod's incessant activity on behalf of revived French Protestantism. W. A. DETZLER

MONTALEMBERT, CHARLES-FORBES-RENÉ, COMTE DE (1810–1870)

Roman Catholic historian

Born in London of a French father and Scottish mother, Montalembert became a historian and an enthusiastic liberal Roman Catholic. He sat in the French Chamber of Deputies from 1848 to 1857, where he was noted for his advocacy of Roman Catholic principles. He became a member of the French Academy in 1851. His best-known historical works are *Les Moines d'Occident* (two volumes, 1860), which deals with the origin of monasticism, and the *Vie de Sainte Elizabeth de Hongrie* (1836). The latter book restored hagiography in France and brought back to Roman Catholics a taste for the supernatural. Also Montalembert was a writer who did more than any other to foster in Europe the taste for Gothic art. His letter to Victor Hugo, entitled "Vandalisme en France" (March, 1833), made a strong impression everywhere and thus helped to save many Gothic buildings from destruction. P. TOON

MONTANUS (second century)

Promoter of a widespread early schism in Christianity occurring about the middle of the second century

Montanus was a convert to Christianity from the rather peculiar paganism of his area, Phrygia. He and two prophetesses, Prisca (Priscilla) and Maximilla, began what

is known as Montanism or the Phrygian heresy. Their emphasis was on the Paraclete's continuing gift of prophecy, severe asceticism, a gradual restriction of the term *church* to a charismatic group of "spiritual" persons, and vibrant millenialism. At first Rome tended to look upon the movement with favor, but ultimately disapproved it.

Montanus introduced the practice of ecstatic utterances into their gatherings. His followers were often seized with mass hysteria evoked by millenarian hopes that the Asia Minor city of Pepuza would be the apocalyptic new Jerusalem and the site of Christ's second coming. The prophetesses Prisca and Maximilla were looked upon as instruments of the Holy Spirit extending the process of revelation beyond the data of Scripture. The failure of the ecclesiastic officials to embrace and approve the movement caused it to become anti-institutional, schismatic, and heretical.

Perhaps the most famous convert to Montanism was the eminent North African theologian Tertullian, whose later writings came from his Montanist period. The movement disintegrated not long after Tertullian's death. In fact, his conversion to it culminated in a deviation within the movement, many of the Montanists following him into a sect named for Tertullian. Vestiges of it, however, lingered into the fifth and sixth centuries. A. CABANISS

MONTEVERDI, CLAUDIO (1567–1643)

Noted Italian composer of the early Baroque era

Born in Cremona, Italy, Monteverdi served at the court of Mantua for twenty-one years, functioning as a singer and violinist, then as music director. It was for this court that Monteverdi created opera's earliest masterpiece, *Orfeo (Orpheus),* in 1607. As was the case with other composers, he received little pay or respect for his creative output. He was widely recognized in Mantua, yet he had to beg the treasurer for his pay.

Things turned around for him in 1613 when he was appointed music director at St.

Mark's in Venice. This was the most important church position in Italy. He stayed at St. Mark's for thirty years, until his death in 1643. He composed the required sacred music as well as secular music for the aristocracy. He wrote operas for Venice's San Cassiario, the first public opera house in Europe. At the age of seventy-five, Monteverdi wrote his last opera, *L'incoronation di Pappea* (*The Coronation of Pappea*, 1642).

Monteverdi was the first composer of operatic masterpieces. Only three of the twelve operas he wrote are preserved, but they truly blend music and drama. He wanted to create music of emotional intensity. He believed that earlier music had not expressed any emotional intensity, so he composed in a fashion that his music would include passion and excitement. To achieve this he used dissonance with great freedom. To express anger and warlike feelings he included pizzicato and tremelo in the texts. His vocal lines responded marvelously to the inflections of Italian while maintaining melodic flow.

In *Orfeo*, he adapted the Florentine recitative style to the use of closed forms such as the aria and dance song. He was equally adept at using the Renaissance polyphonic and the Baroque monophonic idioms. His madrigals are among the finest in the Italian school, but here he showed his association with the modern school of Baroque through his close attention to word and mood expression.

Besides his previously mentioned operas, *El Piterno Di Ulisse* should be mentioned along with his eight books of madrigals. He also wrote dramatic scenes, and his religious music was used greatly by the church.
G. A. COMFORT

MONTGOMERY, JAMES (1771–1854)
Scottish hymn writer

Relatively few great hymn writers have been laymen. Such, however, was Montgomery, a newspaper publisher and editor and a determined advocate of social reform. Indeed, he was twice imprisoned for his outspoken articles.

Montgomery was born in Scotland, the son of Moravian missionaries to the West Indies, both of whom died while he was still a boy. His early years were difficult ones, but eventually he found his place on the staff of a journal in Sheffield, England. In time he became the owner of the publication, which he renamed *The Iris*. Through it he championed many causes, such as the struggle to abolish child labor in the factories. Not surprisingly, his Moravian background gave him an ardent concern for foreign missionary endeavors.

He was closely associated with the efforts of evangelical Anglicans to win acceptance for hymn-singing in their churches, a practice still opposed by many of the bishops. Together with his friend and minister, Thomas Cotterill, who was also a hymn writer, he won the approval of the archbishop of York for the use of a hymnal they had compiled. Montgomery had a keen sense of literary style, as well as a fine lyrical gift. He was one of the finest hymn writers of his generation and one of the first to write critical articles on the subject of hymnody.

Of his own fine hymns, the best-known is probably "Angels from the Realms of Glory." "Go to Dark Gethsemane" is a masterpiece in its poignant brevity. "O Spirit of the Living God," among the greatest of missionary hymns, contains a couplet that epitomizes his sense of urgent mission: "Give tongues of fire and hearts of love, To preach the reconciling Word." J. B. MACMILLAN

MOODY, D. L. (DWIGHT LYMAN) (1837–1899)
American evangelist

From 1875 until 1899 Dwight L. Moody was unquestionably the chief spokesman for the revivalist wing of the flourishing American evangelicals of his day. In addition to regular evangelistic tours through American and British cities, Moody through personal contacts helped shape a network of Christian activities that he or his close associates controlled. His central leadership role was very similar to that played by Charles

Finney before the Civil War or that of Billy Graham in the era after 1950.

Moody himself was a Horatio Alger figure—the boy born in modest circumstances who through initiative and imagination rose to fame and success. In this sense he was a man of his era. Moody left his boyhood home of Northfield, Massachusetts, at age seventeen to seek a career in Boston. There he was converted and joined a Congregational church. He soon left Boston, however, moving in 1856 to Chicago, where in a few years he developed a very successful business as a shoe salesman. In the meantime he was touched by the enthusiasm of the city revivals that spread through America in 1858, and he turned more and more toward Christian work. He was especially concerned with the spiritual needs of persons in the growing American cities. Accordingly, in 1860 he abandoned his shoe business to work full time with YMCA evangelism to young men in the cities and to found a Sunday school for poor children. These activities were partially interrupted by the Civil War, during which Moody spent some time doing Christian work among soldiers. Soon after the war he became president of the Chicago YMCA and also built the Sunday school into the independent Illinois Street Church. Throughout his career it was characteristic of Moody to carry on his work independent of denominational structures, even though he was sympathetic to many denominations and cooperated with them in his revival campaigns. This move by Moody toward independent nondenominational work had important influences on later American fundamentalism and evangelicalism.

By the early 1870s Moody was a well-known local Chicago evangelical leader, but he was unknown nationally. His rise to fame resulted from a modestly conceived evangelistic tour of Great Britain in which Moody was accompanied by his singing associate, Ira Sankey. In Scotland the evangelists suddenly met with immense success, which was followed by similar triumphs in other British cities, especially London. When Moody and Sankey returned home after this tour, which had lasted from 1873 to 1875, they

were virtually national heroes. Moody needed only to choose the cities in which to hold his campaigns, since religious leaders of every metropolis were eager to supply him with whatever cooperation or accommodations he wanted if Moody would supply his services. Some even built giant auditoriums especially for his meetings. Moody's success continued throughout America much as it had in Britain, reaching not so much the poor and immigrant elements of the cities who had never heard the gospel as those in the middle classes whose encounters with Christianity and God needed to be renewed or intensified.

Moody's style on the platform was not sensational or spectacular, but more like that of a nineteenth-century businessman who won the hearts of his audiences by homely illustrations that effectively appealed to their sentiments. His message was essentially simple. It has been characterized by the "Three R's: Ruin by sin, Redemption by Christ, and Regeneration by the Holy Ghost." Moody focused his ministry on saving souls. His most famous remark was, "I look upon this world as a wrecked vessel. God has given me a lifeboat and said to me, 'Moody, save all you can.'" To do this he thought that one should concentrate on verbal proclamation. This was a departure from his earlier city work in which he had combined speaking the Word with acts to relieve poverty. This change in emphasis, which was part of an important shift taking place in American revivalist evangelicalism, was not due to a lessening of interest on Moody's part in the welfare of the poor. Rather, he was convinced that the best way to help the poor was to lead them to seek first the kingdom of God, after which other things would be added to them.

This shift toward emphasizing rescuing souls out of the world was accompanied by the growth in America after the Civil War of the premillennial movement, of which Moody became an important part. Although Moody did not espouse any precise dispensational schemes, he did regularly preach on the hope of Christ's coming to rescue God's people out of the world and then with them to set up a kingdom on earth. Many of Moody's close friends and associates—notably Reuben A. Torrey, James M. Gray, A. J. Gordon, C. I. Scofield, and A. T. Pierson—were deeply involved in promoting a more exact and doctrinally militant form of dispensational premillennialism. Moody, however, refused to become involved in any theological debates that might detract from his evangelistic work. He therefore remained moderate on millennial questions. And unlike many of his younger followers who eventually became militant fundamentalists, he was most reluctant to condemn professed Christian leaders because of their liberal leanings.

Other than through his personal work, Moody's principal means for perpetuating his influence was through establishing educational institutions. In 1879 he founded a school for girls at his home base, which was in Northfield, Massachusetts, and in 1881 followed it with the Mount Hermon School for boys. In 1886 he adopted Emma Dryer's recently founded Bible training school, the Chicago Bible Institute (later Moody Bible Institute) to quickly train "gapmen" or laymen in those things necessary for them to become effective Christian workers. Perhaps more important at the time were Moody's summer Bible conferences held at Northfield beginning in 1880. At these conferences Christian leaders from all parts of the English-speaking world assembled to learn particularly about evangelism and the necessity of Spirit-filled lives of holiness. The outstanding outgrowth of these Northfield conferences was the formation of the immensely influential Student Volunteer Movement in 1886. This movement inspired missionary efforts by thousands of young persons during the succeeding decades, carrying with them the motto of the Student Volunteers, which also summarized the goal of the lifework of D. L. Moody, "the evangelization of the world in this generation."

G. M. MARSDEN

MORE, HANNAH (1745–1833)

English religious writer

More was born at Stapleton near Bristol, the fourth daughter of the village schoolmaster, who taught her to read before she was four. At eight she was startling her father by her abilities in Latin, mathematics, and verse making. Later she acquired knowledge of French, Italian, and Spanish. She taught at the school run by her sisters in Bristol and before she was eighteen had written a pastoral drama, *A Search after Happiness* (1762), for use in young ladies' schools. In 1773 she made the first of a number of annual visits to London. There she was introduced to the literary society of David Garrick, Sir Joshua Reynolds, Samuel Johnson, Edward Gibbon, and Edmund Burke.

The deaths of Garrick (1779) and Johnson (1784) made her think seriously about spiritual matters. She gradually found less pleasure in society and literary life and turned to the evangelicals of the Clapham Sect. She determined to use her talents for God and henceforth wielded, as her friend John Newton said, "a consecrated pen." In 1785 she moved to Cowslip Green near Bristol. There she published, at first anonymously, *Thoughts on the Importance of the Manners of the Great to General Society* (1788). Seven large editions were sold out in five months. Then she turned from the "great" to the humble. In 1792 a clever and simply written volume, *Village Politics by Will Chip,* aimed at counteracting revolutionary literature among the English poor, had such a huge success that she embarked upon a series of *Cheap Repository Tracts,* plainly setting forth religious truth and civil duty. The venture was financed by Henry Thornton and William Wilberforce. Two million copies were sold the first year and inspired the work of the Religious Tract Society. She distributed Bibles and began Sunday schools in the Vale of Cheddar, and that neglected district was morally transformed. During 1808 and 1809 her witty satire on the foibles of irreligious society, *Coelebs in Search of a Wife,* sold out thirty editions in twenty-five years. She wrote incessantly and was the first evangelical to dare to enlist novels and drama in the service of religion and morality. N. HILLYER

MORE, HENRY (1614–1687)
English philosopher

Born at Grantham, More became an Anglican theologian. He entered Christ's College, Cambridge, in 1631 and remained there for the rest of his life. He turned down offers of bishoprics and headships of colleges, preferring the life of solitude, contemplation, and study. During the English civil war he supported the king and remained a firm royalist all his life. Though he shrank from theological controversy, he did have definite views. He belonged to the small group of Cambridge men known as the Cambridge Platonists who believed in the reconciliation of reason and revelation, making use of Platonic philosophy. His works include *Antidote Against Atheism* (1653), *Manual of Ethics* (1666), *Divine Dialogues* (1668), and *Manual of Metaphysics* (1671). Of the group he was probably the most interesting but yet the most unreadable. From 1672 to 1675 he spent most of his time translating his English works into Latin for the use of a European audience. His philosophical theology represents a rejection of the Calvinism of his parents and an attempt to defend Christianity against atheism and Roman Catholicism. P. Toon

MORE, SIR THOMAS (1478–1535)
Lord Chancellor of England

Grandson of a London sheriff and son of a lawyer, More received a good education in his youth and was made a member of the household of Archbishop Morton. He later studied at Oxford, where he was well trained in Latin, Greek, and French. He then proceeded to study law, becoming a member of Furnival's Inn. Between 1499 and 1503 he went through a deep religious experience, which affected his whole life thereafter. He was very ascetic, wearing sackcloth next to his skin at all times. In 1504 he was elected to Parliament and was used by the king on a number of foreign diplomatic missions. He was later given various royal offices, eventually succeeding Cardinal Thomas Wolsey as chancelor in 1529. He was knighted in 1521.

A brilliant man with a sense of humor, he was also a humanist with a sound classical training, which brought him the friendship of men such as Desiderius Erasmus, John Colet, and Hans Holbein. Erasmus lived in his home for a number of years while he wrote some of his works.

More was convinced of the need for social reform, but reform from within society. He expressed his views in his *Utopia* (1516), in which he set forth the view that all things should be held in common and that there should be freedom of religion. In practice, however, he did not follow his own theories. He was very much opposed to Lutheranism, aiding Henry VIII in writing a book in defense of the seven sacraments against Martin Luther. He also wrote pamphlets against Luther, William Tyndale, and John Frith. As a judge he showed himself severe in dealing with heretics who were brought before him.

More had his time of testing when Henry had his marriage to Catherine of Aragon annulled by Archbishop Thomas Cranmer and then was declared by Parliament to be head of the Church of England. In 1532 More retired from office rather than acknowledge Henry's divorce. But when he refused to acknowledge Henry as head of the church he was sent to the Tower of London. On July 1, 1535, he was indicted for treason, but claimed that history supported the claims of the papacy. Although More was sentenced to be hanged, Henry commuted the sentence to beheading. He was canonized by Pope Pius XI in 1935. W. S. Reid

MORGAN, GEORGE CAMPBELL (1863–1945)
British preacher, prolific writer, Bible teacher

Morgan was born in Gloucestershire, the son of a Baptist preacher who, inspired by Plymouth Brethren doctrine, resigned his pulpit to start a faith mission in a rented hall. Morgan preached his first sermon at age thirteen, a symmetrical four-part sermon on salvation. He became a school teacher to make a living, although his youthful ambition was to join the Salvation Army. In 1888, he was a candidate for the Wesleyan ministry, but was turned down after failing his trial sermon—an ironic prelude to a brilliant pulpit career.

A struggle of faith occurred after he read Darwin, Huxley, and other progressive thinkers. After three ambivalent years, Morgan locked all his books, save one, in a cupboard. "The Bible found me," he wrote. Later he was ordained by the Congregationalists.

Although he had no formal training for the ministry, his skill at oratory and biblical insight eventually led to a position at Westminster Chapel in London, where he served from 1904 to 1917 and from 1933 to 1943. Morgan inaugurated the Friday Night Bible School in 1904 when Westminster was in a period of decline.

Morgan crossed the Atlantic fifty-four times, ministering in the United States at the Northfield (Massachusetts) conference, teaching for a short time at the Bible Institute of Los Angeles, and at Gordon College of Theology in Boston. His only pastorate in the United States was at Tabernacle Presbyterian Church in Philadelphia from 1929 to 1932. His wife Annie (called Nancy) was a source of lifelong inspiration and a great help in the preparation of his books.

Chicago Theological Seminary granted Morgan the doctor of divinity degree in 1902. His writings include more than sixty books. Among them are *Discipleship* (1898), *God's Methods with Man* (1898), *The Crisis of the Christ* (1903), *The Great Physician* (1937), and *The Christ of Today* (1943).
M. FACKLER

MORISON, JAMES (1816–1893)
Scottish minister; founder of the Evangelical Union

Born into a Seceder manse in West Lothian, Morison was educated at Edinburgh University and in 1839 was ordained and inducted into a United Secession charge in Kilmarnock. From the beginning Morison proved himself a compelling preacher. People flocked to hear him both on Sundays and on weekdays when he expounded Scripture. His preaching tours were accompanied by spiritual revival. In one village, it is re-

ported, there were "seven hundred people sitting or standing quite contentedly for nearly two hours listening to the Gospel." Soon, however, he ran into trouble in his own denomination. Publication of a booklet resulted in his suspension from the ministry for preaching the universal nature of Christ's atonement.

Joined by his father and two other ministers, he founded in 1843 the Evangelical Union, a body conspicuous for its evangelical spirit and its zeal in the cause of temperance. Morison quickly founded a theological college with himself as principal, which post he later held in conjunction with the pastorate of Dundas Street Church, Glasgow. This, too, became a preaching center with a strong biblical basis. He frequently told his theological students that it was unimportant to the people what the preachers thought on any subject, but it was of unutterable moment that they should know what Jesus thought.

Morison, who published a famous and durable exposition of Romans 9, as well as commentaries on Matthew (1870) and Mark (1873), was widely acclaimed as a theologian and received honorary doctorates from Glasgow and Michigan. In America he found a great affinity with the Cumberland Presbyterians, by whom he was warmly welcomed. The Evangelical Union united with Scottish Congregationalism three years after Morison's death. J. D. DOUGLAS

MORRISON, ROBERT (1782–1834)
Pioneer of Protestant missions in China

Born in Northumberland of Scottish parentage, Morrison received a Christian upbringing and was himself converted while apprenticed in the shoemaking trade at Newcastle. He improved his scanty education and went south to study at Hoxton College, a Non-conformist institution. With a good grounding in theology, astronomy, and medicine, and having learned the rudiments of Chinese, Morrison was ordained and sent to China by the London Misionary Society in 1807. He got as far as Canton and was allowed to remain there only because his proficiency in Chinese made him useful as an interpreter with the East India Company—a post he held until his death. In the most unsuitable circumstances for missionary work, with obstacles placed in his way by Chinese and British alike, he began his great task of translating the Bible into Chinese. Aided by his colleague William Milne, he completed the work by 1821. His Chinese dictionary (1815–1823) remained a standard work for many years. In 1818 he was largely responsible for founding the Anglo-Chinese College at Malacca for "the cultivation of English and Chinese literature in order to encourage the spread of the Gospel of Jesus Christ." Milne set up a printing press there so that Christian literature could go where missionaries could not.

Morrison returned to Britain in 1824 a famous man. His goal was to promote an understanding of China and its evangelization. He soon returned to China, however, and continued the work until his death, laying the foundations of many future missionary endeavors. During his twenty-seven years in China only a handful of Chinese were baptized—yet all of them kept the faith. J. D. DOUGLAS

MORSE, JEDIDIAH (1761–1826)
American clergyman and geographer

Born in Connecticut, Morse graduated in 1783 from Yale (where he had first publicly professed his Christian faith). Thereafter he taught school and studied theology. It was during this time that he became interested in geography, due largely to the lack of adequate textbooks in the field. In a series of publications (beginning in 1784), Morse established a reputation as the father of American geography. His works remained as standard textbooks until after his death in 1826.

Morse was equally significant, however, for his leadership in New England Congregationalism. After brief pastorates in several areas of New England (and one period among Congregationalists in Georgia), Morse became pastor of the church in Charlestown, Massachusetts, where he re-

mained from 1789 until his retirement in 1820.

Morse viewed with alarm the secular drift of American society, and particularly the growing denial of orthodoxy within the churches of New England. As a member of the Board of Overseers of Harvard University, Morse led those demanding that orthodox Christians be appointed to the divinity school faculty. Morse's efforts were in vain; the election in 1805 of Henry Ware, a Unitarian, as Hollis Professor of divinity was only the first in a series of liberal appointments to the Harvard faculty, and it marked a major turning point in New England religion. Undaunted, Morse rallied orthodox forces to form Andover Theological Seminary, which soon became one of the leading centers of ministerial training in America. Morse also established an influential religious periodical, *The Panoplist,* and wrote numerous books and pamphlets to defend orthodoxy.

His work was especially important in giving encouragement to the Second Great Awakening. He also gave strong support in the New England area to Indian and foreign missions. Morse's eldest son, Samuel, was the inventor of the telegraph. J. N. AKERS

MORTON, JOHN (1839–1912)
Canadian Presbyterian missionary to the East Indians of Trinidad

Morton, the son of Scottish immigrants in Pictou county, Nova Scotia, was trained at the Presbyterian Free Church College in Halifax. He was ordained to a Presbyterian charge in Bridgewater, Nova Scotia, in 1861. Later, he was to become the leader of the first successful mission to the East Indians of Trinidad.

While on a voyage to the West Indies for reasons of ill health, Morton visited Trinidad in 1864. Here he was attracted by the East Indian workers who had been brought in by sugar planters in the 1850s. He urged the Presbyterians in Trinidad to help the East Indians and received a promise of partial support from one of the sugar planters. When he went back to Nova Scotia, Morton tried to obtain support for work among the East Indians. He finally secured permission to revive a defunct American mission at Iere on condition that he look after the small congregation of blacks in the area. Returning to Trinidad in 1868, he used the Iere mission as a point of departure for work among the East Indians. By 1881 he had moved to Tunapuna and had established four stations to serve every part of the island. He also supervised missionary ventures to the East Indians in other West Indian Islands, including St. Lucia, Grenada, and Jamaica.

Morton and his colleagues on the other islands developed an effective pattern of missions, combining education and evangelism. He also sought to train leaders by establishing a teachers' training college and a theological college in San Fernando.

Morton was a theological conservative, but he did not worry unduly about higher criticism or the social gospel. He was preoccupied with the need to bring the East Indians to Christ. He was also a secular conservative, a strong advocate of the British empire and of plantation agriculture. He died at Tunapuna, leaving a mission which in 1914 possessed sixty-six day schools, two colleges, two ordained East Indians, and fifty catechists. D. C. MASTERS

MOTHER TERESA (born 1910)
Roman Catholic missionary to India

Named Agnes Gonxha Bojaxhiu, Teresa was born an Albanian in Skopje, Yugoslavia. Her father was a prominent businessman and her mother a helper of the poor. As early as age twelve, Teresa saw herself as a devout Catholic with missionary interest in India. In 1928, on graduating from high school, she joined the Sisters of Loretto, an Irish order of missionary nuns. After a year's study of English in Ireland, she arrived in Calcutta, India, in 1929. Two years later, vows of poverty, chastity, and obedience concluded her novitiate. She took her name from Teresa de Lisieux, who emphasized joy in menial tasks. In 1937, she became Mother Teresa through further vows. From 1931 to

1948, Teresa taught geography and history at St. Mary's School, her order's high school in Calcutta. But by 1946, she believed God had given her another special call: to live among and assist Calcutta's most desperate poor.

Mother Teresa secured permission to begin her new ministry in 1948. After a year's training as a nurse, she founded a school in one of Calcutta's slums. Before long, she had attracted numbers of dedicated workers. In 1950, the Vatican approved organization of her work as the Missionaries of Charity. A fourth vow became basic to this group: wholehearted free service to the poor. As her efforts proceeded, Teresa was appalled at some of the slums' hideous conditions. Consequently, she resolved to concentrate on the worst of the diseased and destitute. With her various helpers, she approached Calcutta's most afflicted lepers, trash-disposed infants, starving families, and dismembered beggars—the deformed and helpless of all ages and backgrounds. Thus, among other facilities, Teresa's Calcutta work eventually included a home for the dying, an orphanage, a leper colony, an employment workshop, various medical centers, and countless shelters. But soon Calcutta could not contain Teresa's vision. In 1965, she was permitted to extend her ministries to other parts of the world. By 1986 the Missionaries of Charity had founded centers in Venezuela, Ceylon, Tanzania, Rome, Cuba, and other locations. These all implemented Teresa's call to the "poorest of the poor."

In the last twenty years, Mother Teresa and her work have had wide recognition. She received the Jawaharlal Nehru Award for International Understanding in 1969, and in 1971 the Vatican gave her its Pope John XXIII Peace Prize. In 1979, she accepted the Nobel Peace Prize. Overruling critics, the Nobel Committee stated that she made efforts for peace by her "confirmation of the inviolability of human dignity." In the name of "the hungry, the naked, the homeless," Teresa accepted all prizes, using any monetary awards toward purchasing more facilities. Above all, in describing her motives, she spoke of Christ's love and his commands to respect each human life. In recent years, Mother Teresa has sometimes acted as Pope John Paul II's emissary for peace. Momentously, in 1985, on its fortieth anniversary, she addressed the general assembly of the United Nations. She again reminded the world of God's love for all human life.

There are many printings of Mother Teresa's writings. In the English translation, the best-known are *A Gift for God; Life in the Spirit: Reflections, Meditations, Prayers; My Life for the Poor;* and *Jesus, the Word to be Spoken: Prayers and Meditations.* Despite feminists' complaints, Teresa has emphasized domestic roles for women and a wife's subjection to her husband. She has staunchly opposed all forms of abortion. Once asked if civilization had declined, she replied: Can it descend lower than "to allow a mother to kill her own child?" About her ministries, she claims to have done no great things, only small tasks in the power of Jesus' love. K. J. BRYER

MOTT, JOHN RALEIGH (1865–1955)
Outstanding ecumenical leader and missionary statesman of the twentieth century

Born at Postville, Iowa, Mott studied at Upper Iowa and Cornell universities. Experience as president of the Cornell collegiate YMCA launched him into the student movement. During the famous Mount Hermon Conference of 1886, Mott was one of the hundred who signed the first Student Volunteer pledge to missionary service. While secretary of the Intercollegiate YMCA (1888), he organized the Student Volunteer Movement (SVM) and for the next twenty-seven years was its chairman. He presided over the first ten great Quadrennials. He was instrumental in introducing it into the United Kingdom and other countries and was the foremost apologist for its watchword, "The evangelization of the world in this generation." As general secretary of the Intercollegiate YMCA of the United States and Canada, he kept it and the SVM closely integrated. Mott founded the World Student Christian Federation in 1895 and was its general secretary and then chairman until 1929. In 1915

he became general secretary of the entire American YMCA organization. He developed its foreign service and was the chief architect of the World's Committee of the YMCAs, resigning the chairmanship in 1948. As much of Mott's time and energy during his travels was equally divided between student evangelism and administering these organizations; he was very effective in both.

Much of the success of the World Missionary Conference at Edinburgh in 1910 was due to Mott's planning, organization, and presiding as chairman. Then as chairman of its Continuation Committee he traveled around the world in 1912 and 1913, holding regional conferences and establishing national missionary conferences. World War I delayed organization of a world mission organization; and Mott mediated between mission leaders on both sides of the battle lines, created the YMCA service to the Armed Services and prisoners of war, and was appointed by President Wilson as a member of the Root Mission to Russia. The International Missionary Council was founded at Lake Mohonk in 1921, and Mott was chairman through the Madras Conference of 1938. He was business chairman of the Oxford Conference on Church, Community, and State in 1937, vice-chairman of the Provisional Committee of the World Council of Churches, and honorary president of the World Council of Churches from 1948. His range of service to the Foreign Missions Conference, the Federal Council of Churches, other organizations in America, and his raising 300 million dollars in support of them all were significant accomplishments. He undergirded all his work with prayer. Throughout his long and fruitful life, Mott remained a Methodist layman. P. BEAVER

MOULE, HENDLEY CARR GLYN (1841–1920)
Church of England bishop

Born in Dorset, the son of a clergyman, Moule studied at Trinity College, Cambridge University, where he became a fellow in 1865. After ordination he assisted his father as well as pursuing his academic career. In

1881, when Ridley Hall was opened in Cambridge, he became the first principal of this evangelical theological college. In 1899 he was appointed the Norrisian professor of divinity, but this appointment only lasted for two years because in 1901 he succeeded B. F. Westcott, the bishop of Durham.

As a bishop his strength lay in his personal and spiritual appeal. Also he was fearless in proclaiming what he believed was the truth. Before moving to Durham, and certainly afterwards, he was regarded as a leader of evangelicals in the Church of England. Also he was one of the most popular of the speakers at the Keswick Convention. His books included the following titles: *Thoughts on Christian Sanctity* (1885), *Outlines of Christian Doctrine* (1889), *Veni Creator* (1890), *Studies in Philippians, Colossians, and Ephesians* (1897–1900), and *Christus Consolator* (1915). P. TOON

MOULTON, JAMES HOPE (1863–1917)
British New Testament scholar

Moulton's father, William Fiddian Moulton, was a noted Greek scholar, and young Moulton grew up in an atmosphere of serious biblical scholarship. After graduation from Cambridge, Moulton was ordained in 1886 to the Methodist ministry and became a lecturer at Leys School, where his father was headmaster. He later held various academic appointments, the most important of which was Greenwood professor of Hellenistic Greek and Indo-European philology at the University of Manchester.

Moulton is best known for his significant work in applying to New Testament linguistics insights from the study of newly discovered Greek papyri. These papyri manuscripts showed clearly that the language of the New Testament was the common (or "Koine") Greek of the first century. These papyri clarified the grammar and meaning of numerous biblical passages. In some ways his most significant work (in collaboration with George Milligan) was *Vocabulary of the Greek New Testament, illustrated from the Papyri and other non-literary Sources* (1914–1915). He also produced the first volume of a major

New Testament Greek grammar (1906); the work was later completed by other scholars. Other important works include *The Science of Language and the Study of the New Testament* and *Religions and Religion.* Moulton also had a keen interest in ancient Iranian studies.

Moulton was awarded a number of honorary degrees by leading British and German universities. He died of exposure after the ship on which he was returning from a tour of India was torpedoed and sunk.
J. N. AKERS

MOULTON, WILLIAM FIDDIAN (1835–1898)
British Bible scholar and teacher

Born of strong Methodist parents, Moulton attended various Methodist schools and graduated from London University. He was ordained in 1858 and became a tutor in classics at Wesley College, Surrey. The position allowed him to devote much time to scholarly research, and in 1870 he published his first work, a translation from German of Winer's *Grammar of New Testament Greek.* The same year he was appointed the youngest member of the committee responsible for the Revised Version of the New Testament. He was generally acknowledged to be one of the finest Greek scholars of his generation. In addition to the translation of Winer's grammar, Moulton's writings include *A History of the English Bible* (1878) and a Commentary on Hebrews in the Ellicott series (1879). He also collaborated with William Milligan on a commentary on the Gospel of John (1880) and with A. S. Geden on *A Concordance of the Greek New Testament* (1897).

A respected Methodist leader, Moulton was elected president of the Wesleyan Conference in 1890. He also was appointed the first headmaster of The Leys School, Cambridge (1874), a position he held until his death. He received honorary degrees from Cambridge and Edinburgh Universities for his contributions to the study of Greek grammar. J. N. AKERS

MOWLL, HOWARD WEST KILVINTON
(1890–1958)
Australian archbishop

Born in Dover, England, into a godly home where service of God and community intertwined, Mowll was educated at King's School Canterbury, and King's and Ridley Colleges, Cambridge. From 1913 to 1922 he taught at Wycliffe College, Toronto, and traveled extensively for the gospel throughout Canada. He was later assistant bishop and bishop of West China, playing an important part in developing indigenous leaders in unsettled times. In 1934 he went to Sydney, Australia, as archbishop. His solid leadership, evangelical convictions, and missionary vision were recognized in his election as primate of Australia in 1947. With rare gifts of leadership based on deep personal faith in God and simple trust in the Scriptures, he gave the Anglican Church in Sydney (and beyond) wise guidance in war and postwar expansion. Deep interest in missions characterized his episcopate, as did enormous capacity for work and mastery of detail. By 1958, his spiritual stature had left a deep imprint on the Sydney diocese and enhanced its strong evangelical tradition.

I. BREWARD

MOZART, WOLFGANG AMADEUS (JOANNES CHRYSOSTOMUS WOLFGANGUS THEOPHILUS)
(1756–1791)
Austrian composer

Wolfgang Amadeus Mozart was born in Salzburg, Austria. He was the son of a court musician, Leopold Mozart. Wolfgang had the single-mindedness of a genius. From the age of four until he was thirty-five, he rarely rested from composition and performance. By the age of six he could play the harpsichord and violin, improvise fugues, write minuets, and read music perfectly at first sight. At eight, he wrote a symphony; at eleven, an oratorio; and at twelve, an opera. By his early teens Mozart had created many works that would have brought credit to a composer well beyond his age.

A strong influence in his youth was the youngest son of J. S. Bach, Johann Christian Bach. Johann introduced Mozart to the spirit of Italian music. Bach, who worshiped the Italian ideals of "beauty and form," devoted a lot of time to Mozart and inspired him. Leopold, Mozart's father, saw to it that Mozart was steeped in every form of Italian music. Prior to this he studied with his father along with his older sister, Maria Anna.

At fifteen, Mozart returned to Salzburg, which was ruled by a new prince, archbishop Hieronymus Colleredo. The archbishop was a tyrant who did not appreciate Mozart's genius; he refused to grant him more than a subordinate seat in the court orchestra. With his father's help, Mozart tried to find a suitable position over the next decade, but to no avail. Although he was usually suffering from lack of money and poor health, this distress rarely showed through in his music. It was as though he transcended his physical life when he composed. Perhaps this is why listeners sense such a carefree spirit in much of his music.

The irony of Mozart's life was that he won more acclaim as a boy wonder than as an adult musician. His early life of performing for the kings throughout Europe actually spoiled him so that when he became an adult musician he couldn't tolerate being treated as a court servant and became totally insubordinate to the prince archbishop he worked for in Salzburg.

In 1781, when he was twenty-five, Mozart left Salzburg to be a free-lance musician. He went to Vienna and experienced success the first few years there. His opera *The Abduction from the Seraglio* (1782) was acclaimed. He married Constanze Weber, who was as poor and as impractical as he was. Contributing to the brightness of these years was Mozart's friendship with Haydn, who told his father, "Your son is the greatest composer that I know, either personally or by reputation; he has taste and beyond that, the most consummate knowledge of the art of composition." In gratitude for all that he learned from Haydn, he dedicated six string quartets to him. The variety and richness of the music is beyond description.

Mozart may well be called the father of the modern concerto. He was the first to play a piano concerto in public, and his improvisations were much admired. The piano was his favorite instrument, and he used it for some of his most personal expressions. His sensitivity in composition gives one delight.

In 1786 he wrote his opera *The Marriage of Figaro*. Vienna and Prague loved it dearly. Then the Prague opera company performed *Don Giovanni*, his opera written after *Figaro*. The Viennese could not appreciate the dark qualities and dissonance because they were accustomed to light and more frivolous opera.

The events of Mozart's last year would have been good material for a grim opera plot. Though his health was failing in 1791, he was very happy to receive a commission for a German comic opera *The Magic Flute*. While he was working on this opera a stranger dressed entirely in gray brought an anonymous letter commissioning a requiem, a mass for the dead. Mozart did not know that the request was from an unscrupulous nobleman who wanted to claim this requiem as his own composition. Since Mozart's health was failing rapidly, he thought the requiem was for himself and rushed to finish it on his deathbed. He had the happiness at this time of knowing that *The Magic Flute* was a wonderful success, but he died before he could enjoy the financial rewards. His student Sussmayr finished the requiem for Mozart.

Mozart died in misery and was buried in a pauper's tomb. He died an unsung hero at the time; but the beauty, perfection, and profundity of his music outlived him and has delighted the world through the years. Some of Mozart's more noteworthy sacred works are a madrigal, "God is Our Refuge"; a Rauzzini motet, *Exsultate, jubilate*; Mozart's first mass (K. 139/47a); a coronation mass (K. 13); two complete settings of the Vesper Psalms; *Requiem*; "Alleluia"; "Psalm 117"; and "Ave Verum Corpus." G. A. COMFORT

MUHAMMAD, ELIJAH (ELIJAH POOLE) (1897-1975)
Leader of the Black Muslims

Elijah Poole was born to two former slaves, Wali and Marie Poole, outside of Sanderville, Georgia. His father was a sharecropper and a Baptist preacher. Because Elijah had to work as a field hand, he attended school only to the age of nine. A witness to social injustice, Poole came to hate the white man. At sixteen he left home and began wandering the United States, working on railroad gangs and doing other odd jobs. In 1923 he settled in Detroit, Michigan, with his wife, and became an assembly worker in the Chevrolet automobile plant. It was in Detroit in 1930 that he encountered "Allah" through W. D. Ford.

When Ford mysteriously disappeared in 1934, Poole changed his name to Elijah Muhammad and announced that the "Master" had designated him his "messenger" or "apostle," the custodian of revelation. He was made head of the Nation of Islam. During the 1950s and 1960s Muhammad saw his religion grow in numbers, but his movement met a crucial blow with Malcolm X's defection and death in 1965. This split the movement into two opposing groups.

Muhammad headed the Black Muslim movement, a Chicago-based black militant organization with tens of thousands of adherents, for more than forty years. He preached separation and declared that whites are morally and intellectually inferior to blacks. He advocated social dignity and economic self-improvement. He also headed a multi-million-dollar network of business enterprises, schools, and other institutions. R. VONDERLACK

MÜHLENBERG, HENRY MELCHOIR (1711–1787)
Lutheran leader during the American colonial period

Mühlenberg was born in Eimbeck (Hanover), Germany, and studied theology at Göttingen, where he was influenced by German pietism, especially as represented by A. H. Francke. Following his ordination to the Lutheran ministry in 1739, he became a pastor. At the urging of German pietist leaders, however, Mühlenberg resigned in 1741 to go to America as pastor of three Lutheran congregations in Pennsylvania.

The early decades of the eighteenth century had seen a large influx of German immigrants to America. Although most were of Lutheran background, Mühlenberg found the Lutheran Church in America was struggling for survival. Under his leadership the three churches he initially pastored prospered in spite of initial difficulties. Mühlenberg's administrative and pastoral abilities became well known, and he soon found himself traveling widely to minister to scattered congregations and individuals—often in the face of harsh frontier conditions.

Mühlenberg was instrumental in persuading other Lutheran pastors to migrate to America from Germany, thus meeting the need for an educated ministry. However, he was determined to make the American Lutheran Church less dependent on its European heritage. Accordingly, he organized the first synod of American Lutherans (1748). He also wrote a constitution for the Lutheran Church in Philadelphia that was especially suited to the American situation and soon became a model for many other Lutheran congregations. Mühlenberg also edited a hymnal for the American churches. By the time of his death in 1787, Lutherans in America had become a vigorous and influential denomination. J. N. AKERS

MÜLLER, GEORGE (1805–1898)
Leader in the Plymouth Brethren movement; founder of Christian orphanages

Müller was born in Kroppenstadt, Prussia, and later became a British citizen. Although intended by his father for the Lutheran ministry, his early years were profligate until in 1825 he was converted at a prayer meeting in a private house. In 1829 he went to London to train with the Society for Promoting Christianity among the Jews, but ill-health caused him to retire to Teignmouth in Devon. There he joined the Plymouth Brethren, resigned from the Jews' Society, and became a preacher at Ebenezer Chapel, which grew from 18 members to 227 in under three years. Believing that his

material needs could be supplied through believing prayer alone, he abolished pew rents, refused a salary, and relied entirely on gifts from Christians for his work and personal support. At Teignmouth he met Henry Craik, who had once taught the children of the Brethren leader A. N. Groves. Müller married Groves's sister Mary and in 1832 began a joint ministry with Craik in Bristol. In 1834 Müller founded the Scriptural Knowledge Institution for Home and Abroad to promote education of biblical principles, to circulate Scriptures, and to support missionary work.

In Germany he had lodged for two months at the orphanage established in Halle by A. H. Francke, a project run in entire dependence upon God for its support. In 1835 a copy of Francke's life prompted Müller to begin a similar work for orphan children in Bristol. He devoted the rest of his long life to demonstrating by faith and prayer alone that the "Father to the fatherless" (Psalm 68:5) still provided for his children. Beginning with a few orphans, Müller was eventually housing, educating, and training two thousand boys and girls in five great houses on Ashley Down, near Bristol. At the age of seventy, Müller set out with his second wife on a worldwide mission, which lasted for seventeen years. His witness to the prayer-hearing God of the Bible, through sermons, tracts, and books, including his *Narrative of the Lord's Dealings with George Müller,* prompted the establishment of orphanages based on similar faith principles in many lands. N. HILLYER

MÜNZER, THOMAS (c. 1490–1525)
Radical leader in the Reformation

Born at Stolberg, Münzer studied at Leipzig and Frankfurt an der Oder, learning Greek and Hebrew and reading widely in Scripture, the Fathers, and the mystic Tauler. He was at Leipzig for the 1519 disputation and with Luther's help was appointed preacher at Zwickau in 1520. Associating with the Zwickau Prophets he became violently anticlerical. He opposed infant baptism, quarreled with the Zwickau reformer

Egrinus, and was dismissed in 1522. After a stay in Prague, where he issued a Manifesto asking for a new beginning of the church in Bohemia, he took various posts, coming as parish priest to Allstedt in 1523. Here he promoted liturgical reform, organized covenant bands to establish Christian truth, and with H. Pfeiffer caused disturbances that brought his expulsion in 1524. While at Allstedt he defended his view of the Spirit against Luther and wrote his tracts on *Faith and Baptism* and *The Exposure of False Faith.* Then, in a famous sermon on Daniel 2, he demanded the dukes of Saxony to use force in establishing the true gospel. When summoned to a hearing with the dukes, he left Allstedt. From there he went to Muhlausen, Nuremberg, Basel, and back to Muhlhausen, where he preached participation in the Peasants' War (1524). Caught up in this, he met with decisive defeat at Frankenhausen; he was captured and executed.

Münzer had much influence in spite of his early death. Some Lutheran services incorporated his liturgies, and he left his mark on nonviolent Anabaptists with his rejection of infant baptism, his stress on suffering discipleship, and his call for judgment. Not very convincingly, some Marxists have tried to portray him as a proletarian revolutionary. G. BROMILEY

MURILLO, BARTOLOMÉ ESTEBAN (1617–1682)

A Spanish painter known especially for his painting of the Immaculate Conception

Murillo supported himself by making small religious paintings, which he exported to South America. For most of his life he resided in Seville, Spain, where he was the most sought-after religious painter of his day. His numerous commissions included work for churches, convents, and monasteries. His influence as an artist extended to students through the Seville Academy of Painting, which he founded in 1660. His realistic religious paintings, characterized by softness, sweetness, and warmth helped him achieve enormous popularity in European countries outside Spain. His popularity continued well

into the nineteenth century. In addition to his famous religious subjects, he also painted genre paintings and excellent portraits.

Among his major works are *Birth of the Virgin* (Louvre, Paris), *Flight into Egypt* (Institute of Art, Detroit), *Return of the Prodigal Son* (National Gallery, Washington, D.C.), and *Madonna and Child* (Walker Art Gallery, Liverpool). A. STEFFLER

MURRAY, ANDREW (1828–1917)

South-African Dutch Reformed leader; author of many devotional writings

Born in Cape Town, South Africa, Murray became a noted missionary leader. His father was a Scottish Presbyterian serving the Dutch Reformed Church of South Africa, and his mother had connections with both French Huguenots and German Lutherans. This background to some extent explains his ecumenical spirit. He was educated at Aberdeen University, Scotland, and at Utrecht University in the Netherlands. After ordination in 1848 he served pastorates at Bloemfontein, Worcester, Cape Town, and Wellington. He helped to found what are now the University College of the Orange Free State and the Stellenbosch Seminary. He served as Moderator of the Cape Synod of the Dutch Reformed Church and was president of both the YMCA (1865) and the South Africa General Mission (1888–1917), now the Africa Evangelical Fellowship.

He was one of the chief promoters of the call to missions in South Africa. This led to the Dutch Reformed Church missions to blacks in the Transvaal and Malawi. Apart from his evangelistic tours in South Africa, he spoke at the Keswick and Northfield Conventions in 1895, making a great impression upon his British and American audiences. For his contribution to world missions he was given an honorary doctorate by the universities of Aberdeen (1898) and Cape of Good Hope (1907).

Murray is best known today for his devotional writings, which place great emphasis on the need for a rich, personal devotional life. Many of his 240 publications explain how he saw this devotion and its outworking in the life of the Christian. Several of his books have become devotional classics; among these are *Abide in Christ, Absolute Surrender, With Christ in the School of Prayer, The Spirit of Christ,* and *Waiting on God.* P. TOON

MURRAY, JOHN (1898–1974)
Reformed theologian

Murray was born in Creich, Sutherlandshire (Scotland), and brought up in a strict Free Presbyterian home. He learned the Westminster Shorter Catechism at an early age. From 1919 to 1923 he attended the University of Glasgow where he obtained his M.A. After further studies at Princeton Seminary and Edinburgh, he returned to Princeton as assistant to Professor Casper Wistar Hodge in theology. With the formation of Westminster Theological Seminary, Philadelphia, he was persuaded to move there in 1930 and remained as a member of the theological department until his retirement in 1966. During his time at Westminster he became well known as both a lecturer and writer. His theological articles appeared in many journals, and he was the author of books, such as *Redemption, Accomplished and Applied* (1955) and a commentary on Romans (two volumes, 1959 and 1965). His collected writings were published in four volumes, beginning in 1976. He took an active part in the work of the Orthodox Presbyterian Church, serving as moderator of its general assembly in 1961. He was one of the original trustees of the Banner of Truth Trust. He was also known and appreciated widely as an able Reformed preacher. Having trained a large number of theological students and written extensively, Murray was one of the most influential Reformed theologians of the mid-twentieth century. W. S. REID

MUSCULUS (MAUSLEIN), WOLFGANG (1497–1563)
German Reformer

A lesser figure of the Reformation, Musculus came from Drieuze, Lothringen. He studied at Schlettstadt, where he met Martin Bucer, the future reformer of Strassburg, who was to play an important role in Musculus's life. In 1512 he joined the Benedictine order at Lixheim and while there was won over to Lutheran teaching through copies of Luther's writings that may have been sent to him by Bucer. In 1527 he left the monastery to join Bucer as his secretary in Strassburg, where he also served in the Cathedral Church. Through Bucer's influence he secured a preaching position in Augsburg in 1531, where, in a tangled situation, he upheld Bucer's position on the Eucharist and church discipline. While at Augsburg he participated in the important discussions at Wittenberg (1536) and Regensburg (1541). He also provided a catechism for the reformation at Donauworth. Forced out by the Augsburg Interim in 1548 he found a friend in Heinrich Bullinger of Zurich, who helped him to a theological professorship at Bern (1549). Here he supported the Bern position on church discipline against Calvin's program in Geneva. Although he himself agreed with Bullinger on eucharistic teaching, Bern would not endorse the consensus of Zurich accepted by the other reformed Swiss churches. Musculus was no polemicist but strongly supported toleration on non-essentials. He wrote several commentaries, a history of the early Reformation in Hungary, and above all *Common Places* (1560), which enjoyed a wide circulation and was soon translated into English. G. BROMILEY

MYCONIUS, FRIEDRICH (1490–1546)
German reformer

Myconius was born at Lichtenfels in Upper Franconia. He went to school at Annaberg, where he met Tetzel, the preacher of indulgences. In 1510 he joined the Franciscan order and served first at Leipzig and then at Weimar, becoming a priest and preacher in 1516. A student of the Bible and of Augustine, Lombard, and Bonaventura, he was won over by Luther's teaching and after meeting considerable resistance escaped from the monastery in 1526. After a stay at Zwickau he settled at Gotha and in association with Duke John reformed the church and reorganized the schools. He also undertook preaching missions (e.g., to Gologne) and visitations (in Thüringenia). He corresponded with Luther and Melanchthon and participated in the discussions at Marburg (1529), Wittenberg (1536), Schmalcald (1537), and Hagenau (1540). He also served as a theologian on the Lutheran embassy to England in 1538 and helped to bring reformation to Ducal Saxony, especially at Annaberg and Leipig. Bronchial troubles curtailed his activity after 1539. Two of his writings made a considerable impression; his tract *On Instructing the Simple, and especially the Sick, in Christianity* and his *History of the Reformation, 1517–1542,* which tells the story from the standpoint of a contemporary participant. G. W. BROMILEY

MYCONIUS, OSWALD (1488–1552)
Swiss reformer

Myconius (Geisshusler) was born at Lucerne. After studying at Basel, where he became a friend of Zwingli and was given the name Myconius by Erasmus, he taught classics at the canons' school in Zurich (1516–1520). Here he played a big part in securing the momentous appointment of Zwingli as people's priest in 1519. Moving to Lucerne in 1520, he had to leave in 1522; and after a short stay at Einsiedeln, he returned to Zurich in 1523 to lecture on the New Testament in German. Although not ordained, he was appointed to a church in Basel in 1531 and in 1532 succeeded Oecolampadius as chief pastor of the city and New Testament professor at the university. His early days in Basel were made difficult by Carlstadt, who had to seek refuge in Switzerland. Constructively, he took the lead in drawing up the Basel Confession of 1534, which attempted reconciliation on the issue of the Eucharist by stressing the positive side of Zwingli's teaching. On the debated question of church and state, especially in relation to discipline, he promoted Oecolampadius' policy of a measure of separation. His works include the first biography of Zwingli and a commentary on Mark's Gospel (1538).
G. W. BROMILEY

N

NEAL, DANIEL (1678–1743)
Historian of the Puritans

Neal was born in London and educated at the Merchant Taylors' School. He could have gone to St. John's College, Oxford, but declined due to the conformity required by the established Church of England and studied instead at Utrecht and at Leyden. He returned to England, where he became an assistant at the Congregational church on Aldersgate Street in London. He soon became the pastor and the congregation flourished under his lifelong leadership and ministry at that post.

Neal's scholarly gifts were first manifested in the publication of *A History of New England* (two volumes, 1720), for which he was given an M.A. degree from Harvard College. But his major contribution was a massive four-volume *History of the Puritans*. The first volume appeared in 1732 and the fourth in 1738. The whole work covers the period from the Reformation to the Act of Toleration in 1689.

This work immediately drew criticism from Anglicans. The first came from Isaac Maddox (later bishop of St. Asaph), to which Neal replied; and the second, and more formidable, came from Zachary Grey, who claimed that Neal had misrepresented issues and had failed to cite sources. In spite of the criticisms, the *History of the Puritans* was received with enthusiasm by the dissenting tradition and was translated into Dutch in 1752. Zachary Grey's copy of Neal's work, with notes and criticism, is in St. John's College, Cambridge. In 1797 Joshua Toulmin published an elaborate edition of Neal's history in five volumes, which included a life of the author and a response to Grey's criticism. This history not only nurtured Congregationalists but also gave the general dissenting tradition a renewed sense of its identity and dignity in the eighteenth and nineteenth centuries.

Neal is also known for his history and defense of inoculation for smallpox, which was opposed at the time by a majority of both physicians and clergy.   C. F. ALLISON

NEALE, JOHN MASON (1818–1866)
Anglican hymnologist, liturgist, and historian

Born in London, educated at Trinity College, Cambridge, Neale was ordained deacon in 1841 and priest in 1842. As an undergraduate at Cambridge, he was one of the founders of the Cambridge Camden Society. Neale's strong High Church views and support of Puseyism embroiled him in lifelong controversy and militated against any ecclesiastical appointments. After a brief pastorate in Crawley, Sussex, in 1842, his poor health prompted residence in Madeira. He returned to England in 1845. The following year he became warden of Sackville College, a charitable institution in East Grinstead. That position he held until his death two decades later. In it he had the opportunity to exercise his interests in human welfare and in writing. His extensive charitable efforts included prominently the founding of the nursing Sisterhood of St. Margaret, which eventually came to include an orphanage, a school for girls, and a home for fallen women.

An accomplished linguist, said to have known as many as twenty languages, he was a prolific writer, authoring some seventy publications and numerous hymns. His works include essays, commentaries, books for children, and a compilation of hymns. Neal's fame as a hymnologist rests not only in his numerous original compositions but also in his translations of ancient and medieval hymns, an area in which he has hardly had an equal. His translations include works of Bernard of Cluny, Theodolf, and Prudentius. His poetical works won him the Seatonian prize on eleven occasions. His frail health, in combination with his heavy labors and years of controversy, contributed to his early death. His works include *Hymns of the Eastern Church* (1862), *Essays on Liturgiology and Church History* (1863), and *The History of the Holy Eastern Church* (five volumes, 1847–1873). N. MAGNUSON

NEANDER, JOHANN AUGUST WILHELM (1789–1850)

Church historian; known as the father of modern church history

Neander belonged to a Jewish family and originally bore the name of David Mendel. He changed his name to Neander when he became a Christian in 1806. A German Lutheran, he studied with F. D. Schleiermacher (1768–1834) in Berlin, but soon switched his interest from speculative theology to church history. After a year of teaching in Heidelberg (1812), he returned to Berlin as professor of ecclesiastical history (1813).

Here he attracted many students not only by the quality of his scholarship but also by the spirit of piety he brought to his work and the interest he showed in the personal aspects of history. From the first he wrote extensively on historical themes, beginning with biographical studies of significant figures like Julian the Apostate (1812), Bernard of Clairvaux (1813), John Chrysostom (1822), and Tertullian (1824). Turning to a whole movement, he offered a history of Gnosticism in 1818. When F. C. Baur and D. F. Strauss introduced a rationalistic interpretation of the New Testament and early Christian history, he strongly opposed them. He wrote a life of Christ (1837) in answer to the theory puported by Strauss in *Life of Jesus* (1835–1836) that the Gospel record is simply a myth in historical dress. With the maturing of his scholarship, Neander began to put together his more detailed monographs in broader historical works. His history of the apostolic age came out in two volumes under the title *History of the Planting and Training of the Christian Church by the Apostles* (1832–1833). Even before the publication of this work he had launched his most ambitious project, *A General History of the Christian Religion and Church,* which came out in six volumes beginning in 1826 and ending only after his death in 1852. Both these larger works were translated into English, the latter appearing in five volumes (1882) and the former in two volumes (1887–1888).

Neander had considerable influence not only in his own church and country but also further afield through the combination of scholarly excellence and personal interest that he achieved in his teaching and writing. This influence lived on in the American and English-speaking world through the historical work and writing of Philip Schaff (1819–1893), who studied and taught with Neander in Berlin prior to his appointment to Mercersburg in 1844. A basic conviction of Neander was that church history is not just an academic pursuit but part of the mission and ministry of the church. As he himself put it in the Preface to Part III of his *General History*: "The truth alone, which is its own witness, should here, as it instructs, also edify. . . . This is the objectivity which I aim at." G. BROMILEY

NEE, WATCHMAN (1903–1972)

Leader of indigenous local church movement in China

Watchman Nee (whose real name was Nee Tao Shu) was born in Swatow but soon moved with his parents to Foochow, where he spent the early part of his life. Converted when he was eighteen, he gave up the opportunity of attending university and devoted himself to Bible study and gospel preaching. He was greatly influenced by Margaret Barber, an English missionary who introduced him to the writings of Jessie Penn-Lewis, D. M. Panton, and J. N. Darby. He produced a magazine, *The Christian*, which soon had a wide influence. When he was only twenty-five he wrote and published *The Spiritual Man*, a three-volume work explaining the full process of spiritual maturity. For a time he was linked with an exclusive group of Brethren in England. This fellowship was later broken because he could not accept their exclusive principles. Later he started work in Shanghai and had close fellowship with Charles Judd of the China Inland Mission.

In 1930, while teaching Christians in Chefoo, he met Witness Lee, who later was to become a leader in the work. During this third decade, the work spread rapidly and "Church Assemblies" (known to others as the "Little Flock") were established in many parts of China. Two of his fellow workers, Simon Meek and Faithful Luke, started the work in Manila and Singapore. The "Church Assemblies," which often started as small house churches, were completely independent of foreign missionary organizations and were used to bring many into the kingdom of God. He was, however, often criticized for his insistence that there could be only one true local church in each city. As a result of this emphasis, together with the zeal and warmth of fellowship and the attraction of a movement that was free from all foreign connections, quite a number of people were drawn away from other churches.

After Pearl Harbor, while living under the Japanese, he organized a pharmaceutical company for the sake of raising money for the work of the ministry. This business venture caused him much suffering because his fellow workers misunderstod his intentions; this resulted in Nee's withdrawal from active ministry for several years. Later it provided an excuse for his arrest by the Communists.

Following the end of the war with Japan, Watchman Nee was restored to leadership, and the work in Shanghai prospered with large numbers of assemblies springing up in many parts of the country. From them have come many of the house churches, which have continued a faithful witness in a communist society. Watchman Nee was arrested in 1952 while on a trip to Manchuria in connection with the disposal of the pharmaceutical business. Four years later, he was brought to Shanghai for a public trial and found guilty of a large number of charges brought against him—all of which were false. After serving his fifteen-year sentence, he was kept in prison and remained faithful to his Lord until his death.

Watchman Nee will be remembered not only for his leadership of an indigenous church movement in China, but also for the books that continue to enrich Christians throughout the world. Some of the more noteworthy works are *The Normal Christian Life; Changed into His Likeness; Love Not the World; What Shall This Man Do; A Living Sacrifice; Spiritual Man*; and *Sit, Walk, Stand*. His biography, *Against the Tide,* was written by Angus Kinnear. D. ADENEY

NERI, SAINT PHILIP (1515–1595)

Founder of the Congregation of the Oratory

Born in Florence, Italy, and educated by the Dominican friars, Neri went to Rome in 1533, where he acted as a tutor while studying philosophy and theology. In 1538 he decided to dedicate his life to the service of the poor and the sick, and in 1548 he helped to found the Confraternity of the Most Holy Trinity. Its purpose was to assist convalescents discharged from hospitals and the pilgrims who thronged the city of Rome. In 1551 he was ordained to the Roman Catholic priesthood and went to live in a clergy house at San Girolamo, where in 1556 he began the Oratory for the conduct of religious meetings of a special kind. These meetings were held in the evening, and consisted of prayers, Scripture readings, and addresses designed to appeal to the unchurched. In these meeting hymns and music played a prominent part, and Palestrina (c. 1525–1594) did much of the composing for them. In 1575 the Oratory was given official approval by Pope Gregory XIII as a community of priests bound to obedience but making no formal vows. The movement spread to Italy, Spain, and France, though each house was independent of the others. The movement contributed greatly to the success of the Catholic Counter-Reformation. Neri died in Rome and was later canonized in 1622. N. V. HOPE

NESTLE, EBERHARD (1851–1913)
German New Testament scholar

Nestle was born in Stuttgart. After being educated at several schools and seminaries, he received the Ph.D. degree from Tübingen in 1874. He held several teaching posts, including positions at Ulm, Tübingen, and the Evangelical Theological Seminary at Maulbronn (Württemberg).

Nestle was a skilled linguist and textual critic. His early interest was in the Greek text of the Old Testament (the Septuagint), and he was the editor of major editions of Tischendorf's text of the Septuagint. He also contributed numerous writings on the Syriac language, including an important grammar.

Nestle's main contribution, however, was in the field of New Testament language and textual criticism. While he wrote various works in this field, his most lasting work was his edition of the text of the Greek New Testament (first edition, 1898). Nestle used the best editions of the Greek New Testament produced in the nineteenth century to compile a text that represented the majority

consensus. The work of making new editions was carried on by his son for several years and then came under the editorship of Kurt Aland. The latest edition (the 26th) of Nestle-Aland's *Novum Testamentum Graece* appeared in 1979 (with a corrected edition in 1986). The twenty-sixth edition of the Nestle-Aland text is regarded by many as representing the latest and best in textual scholarship. J. N. AKERS

NESTORIUS (late fourth century–c. 451)
Patriarch of Constantinople whose Christological views led to a still-existent split in Christendom

Born in Germanicia (modern Maras, Turkey), Nestorius studied in Antioch under the famous Theodore of Mopsuestia, became a monk, and earned a reputation as a preacher. Little more is known of Nestorius until in 428 he was brought in by Emperor Theodosius II to head the see of Constantinople after bitter wranglings among local candidates for the post. Nestorius promptly launched an attack on heretics of various hues and sought the emperor's support by promising him heaven and the patriarchal backing against the Persians.

More particularly, Nestorius imported an Antiochene presbyter called Anastasius, who from the pulpit vehemently denounced the widespread use of the term *Theotokos* (God-bearer) to describe the Virgin Mary. When this brought howls of protest, Nestorius reiterated the presbyter's contention that "Mary was but a woman, and it is impossible that God should be born of a woman." Convinced that the reality of Christ's human nature had been challenged, Nestorius pointed out that Mary was also *anthropotokos* (man-bearer), but his preferred word was *Christotokos* (Christ-bearer).

The whole controversy was a natural development from the Council of Constantinople (381), which had condemned Bishop Apollinarius's assertion that Jesus' humanity was imperfect. The storm that blew up around Nestorius in 428 originated partly also in the traditional rivalry between the patriarchates of Antioch and Alexandria. The former school of thought tended to a literal interpretation of Scripture; the latter's exegesis gave full rein to the allegorical. Nestorius was true to his training under fellow Antiochene, Theodore of Mopsuestia, (whom many regard as the real founder of Nestorianism) in stressing the Lord's humanity.

Nestorius found formidable adversaries in the patriarch of Alexandria (Cyril) and the bishop of Rome (Celestine I), both of whom convened synods that declared Nestorius to be a heretic. After heated exchanges, the emperor (who favored Nestorius) in 431 summoned the church's third ecumenical council, held at Ephesus. Before the tardy arrival of the accused's Syrian supporters and of the papal representatives from Rome, Cyril opened the proceedings. Nestorius was subsequently declared to be deposed and excommunicated, and *Theotokos* was pronounced to be a fitting title for the Virgin Mary.

The Syrian latecomers held a rival meeting that did not discuss the point at issue but which excommunicated Cyril. It was the latter's gathering (which Nestorius had pointedly boycotted) that was finally held by the Romans to be valid. The emperor Theodosius, whose vacillations during the dispute did him little credit, banished Nestorius first to his monastery in Antioch and later to Upper Egypt, where he died. Rejected by the Roman Empire, Nestorianism not only persisted but expanded in the East, evincing a remarkable missionary activity that extended as far as China. Modern representatives of Nestorianism are to be found in the Persian or Assyrian Church, located in Iraq, Syria, and Iran.

J. D. DOUGLAS

NEVIN, JOHN WILLIAMSON
(1803–1886)
German Reformed theologian

Nevin was born in Strasburg, Pennsylvania, and educated at Union College, Schenectady (1817–1821) and Princeton Theological Seminary (1823–1826). From 1830 to 1840 he was professor of biblical literature at the (Presbyterian) Western Theological Seminary at Allegheny, Pennsylvania, where his interest in church history was aroused through his discovery of the works of Neander (1789–1850), the "father of modern church history."

In 1840 he accepted a call to the German Reformed Seminary at Mercersburg, Pennsylvania, where in 1843 he attacked the then prevailing revivalistic methods in his book *The Anxious Bench*. In 1844 Nevin was joined by Philip Schaff, and these two colleagues developed what came to be known as the Mercersburg theology. This emphasized the organic—as contrasted with the individualistic—doctrine of the Christian church, the centrality of the person of Jesus Christ and his incarnation in Christian thought and experience, and the real spiritual presence of Christ in the sacrament of the Lord's Supper, "which forms the very heart of the whole Christian worship." Nevin's High Church views were expounded in his major work, *The Mystical Presence: A Vindication of the Reformed or Calvinistic Doctrine of the Holy Eucharist,* published in 1846. He also expounded his views in the *Mercersburg Review,* which he edited from 1849 to 1853, and which has been described as "one of the great theological journals of pre–Civil War America." In 1853 ill health compelled Nevin to retire from his academic chair; but in 1861 he was appointed professor of philosophy, history, and esthetics at Franklin and Marshall College in Lancaster, Pennsylvania, which he headed as president from 1866 to 1876. N. V. HOPE

NEVIUS, JOHN LIVINGSTON
(1829–1893)
American Presbyterian missionary to China

Nevius served in China at Ningpo and Hangchow (1854–1893) and in Shantung Province (1861–1893), founding Chefoo Station. He created the modern fruit orchard industry of the area by distributing seeds and cuttings. His books are *China and the Chinese; Demon Possession;* and *The Planting and Development of Missionary Churches* (which first appeared in 1886 as articles in the *Chinese Recorder*). The last book explained the famous "Nevius Plan," rejected by his colleagues in Shantung but adopted by the Presbyterian missionaries in the new field of Korea in 1890. It is credited with the rapid growth of churches there. Nevius is best known for the plan that bears his name. It included four points: (1) each Christian should "abide in the calling wherein he was called," support himself by his own work, and be a witness for Christ by life and word; (2) church methods and machinery should be developed only in so far as the church was able to bear responsibility for the same; (3) the church itself should select and support those best qualified for full-time service; (4) church buildings were to be constructed by the Christians at their expense and were to conform to indigenous architecture. Nevius was a firm believer in the three-self principle: self-government, self-support, and self-propagation, as the best way to establish strong national churches. He also stressed Bible study, preaching, and church discipline.

P. BEAVER

NEWMAN, JOHN HENRY (1801–1890)

English clergyman and tractarian

Newman's life was divided into a Church of England period (wherein he was the chief instigator and leader of the High Church or Anglo-Catholic Oxford Movement) and a Roman Catholic period after his conversion in 1845 (wherein he attained national stature as a cardinal of the Roman Church).

From youth, Newman showed determination to make his mark in the world. At fifteen, just before entering Oxford University, he experienced a profound awakening to God through the influence of a Calvinist teacher and William Law's *Serious Call to a Devout and Holy Life*. Later, his sermons consistently reflected deep moral earnestness.

He drew strength from believing that God had a work for him to do and was providentially directing his life. He regularly sorted through his letters and papers, seeking some clue to God's direction. While on a ship that was in a becalming fog, he wrote his hymn, "Lead Kindly Light, Amidst the Encircling Gloom," itching to take up the work that was to become the Oxford movement.

After ordination in 1824, and soon after becoming an Oxford tutor, Newman toyed with liberalism or rationalism. He became convinced, though, that liberalism was the enemy of respect for God, defining it as the rejection of authority, subjecting to human judgment God's Word. In theological matters he became one of the strongest anti-liberals of the nineteenth century.

Newman also had rejected his early evangelical associations, arguing that the Protestant principle of private interpretation of the Bible led to sanctioning rebellion, and that belief in the forgiveness of sin by faith in Christ only produced moral and religious indifference. The only hope he saw for defense of the faith and the Bible was in the catholic religion of the church fathers. The Roman Church could not offer that, for it had added corruptions during the Middle Ages. He believed that a Catholic Church of England, which the Reformation had recognized and Thirty-nine Articles of faith accepted, was the logical defense.

During the early 1830s a reforming spirit swept Britain and threatened the organization and constitution of the Church. Newman was then vicar of St. Mary's, the university church, and a fellow of one of the most prestigious colleges, Oriel. In the summer of 1833, while others debated what to do, Newman began to pour forth his Anglo-Catholic interpretation of the Reformation and the Church with great energy. He wrote four- to eight-page treatises, which he then had published anonymously under the title *Tracts for the Times*. He preached and lectured at St. Mary's, later publishing these productions. Whenever possible he aroused the University against proposed liberal actions or appointments affecting the Church, and in time he took over the editorship of the journal, *British Critic*. He reached the height of his influence by 1838, becoming a greatly admired model to many undergraduates.

At that time he was beginning to defend

his theory also against criticism by Roman Catholics. As he studied their arguments and the church fathers, doubts began to rise. The fatal blow came in 1841 when his Tract 90, arguing a catholic interpretation of the Thirty-nine Articles, brought rebuke from the bishop of Oxford and others. Slowly and painfully he began to resign his Anglican offices. He retired to a monastic life outside Oxford. His submission to the Roman Church four years later represented his new belief that she was the only true church.

Although a hero or trophy to English Roman Catholics, Newman became almost forgotten by the public until in 1864 he found his truthfulness attacked by Charles Kingsley. Again demonstrating his skill in debate, he wrote his life's defense, *Apologia pro Vita Sua*. He offered insight into the struggle he had passed through as an Anglican and won great sympathy. He also began to reissue his Anglican sermons, eventually producing thirty-six volumes. His elevation in 1879 to the College of Cardinals proved quite popular. He saw himself as still fighting "the doctrine that there is no positive truth in religion, but that one creed is as good as another."

Evangelicals today may find themselves sharing a surprising number of doctrinal concerns with Newman. His differences grew out of his considering the institutional church a divine and therefore an infallible institution. That belief lead him to adopt Roman Catholicism. D. MUNSON

NEWTON, BENJAMIN WILLS (1807–1899)
Plymouth Brethren leader; Bible interpreter

Born in Plymouth, England, at the age of seventeen Newton entered Exeter College, Oxford, where the next year he was elected to a fellowship, and then graduated in 1828 with first-class honors in Classics. Converted to a saving Christian faith in 1827, he continued at Oxford until 1832, when he returned to Plymouth. There he first became a private tutor and later conducted a school. In Plymouth he became a leader of the Assembly of Brethren, a congregation of about

one thousand members, among whom he labored as pastor and preacher until 1847. In 1835 under Newton's influence, Samuel P. Tregelles was converted, and his subsequent research in the Greek text of the New Testament was generously supported by Newton both morally and financially. In 1847 Newton broke with John Nelson Darby, whom he had persuaded to join him in his Plymouth ministry. Thereafter he left Plymouth and the Brethren and for years held meetings in a hall built for him in Bayswater, London; and in 1896 he moved to Tunbridge Wells, where he died. A voluminous author of books and pamphlets expounding the biblical message from an orthodox evangelical standpoint, Newton devoted special attention to biblical prophecy, which he interpreted in a premillennial sense—that is, foretelling the fast-approaching end of the age and the divine cataclysmic intervention prior to the bringing-in of God's manifest kingdom. N. V. HOPE

NEWTON, SIR ISAAC (1642–1727)
English mathematician and physicist

Born at Woolsthorpe, in Lincolnshire, Newton was educated at Grantham School and Trinity College, Cambridge, of which he was elected a fellow in 1667. In 1669 he became Lucasian Professor of mathematics at Cambridge University. In 1694 he moved to London, was appointed master of the mint in 1699, and knighted by Queen Anne in 1705. He had been a member of the Royal Society since 1672 and was its president from 1703 until his death.

Newton was a scientific genius of the highest order. Among his many achievements were the formulation of the law of gravitation, the discovery of the differential calculus, and the first correct analysis of white light. His *Principia Mathematica*, published in 1687, constitutes a landmark in the history of physical science.

Newton was deeply interested in religion. A conforming member of the Church of England, he criticized Roman Catholicism both for its doctrine and its record of persecution. Concerning his theology, although he reverenced Jesus Christ as the Savior of the world, he did not believe in his essential deity. As a student of the Bible, he was particularly fascinated by its prophetical books, especially Daniel and Revelation, and suggested a method of interpreting them meaningfully. N. V. HOPE

NEWTON, JOHN (1725–1807)
Anglican clergyman and hymn writer

Born in London, for a few years of his very early life Newton attended school at Stratford in Essex. But from the age of eleven until seventeen he served on a merchant ship of which his father was commander, plying the Mediterranean. At the age of nineteen he was impressed into the British naval service aboard the man-of-war *Harwich*. Through his father's influence he was made a midshipman, but when he tried to escape he was flogged and degraded. Not long thereafter he entered the service of a slave dealer who was sailing the ocean between Africa and ports in which he could sell the slaves. In 1747, at the age of twenty-two, Newton himself became master of a slave ship. During his voyages he applied himself to learning mathematics, the classics, and later the Bible.

During a storm at sea in 1748 he experienced conversion from what he himself later called a life of debauchery. He abandoned shipping in 1755 and until 1760 held the post of surveyor of the tides at Liverpool. There he met George Whitefield and somewhat later John Wesley and came under their influence. So deep was his experience that he began to study Greek and Hebrew privately in preparation for the ministry, hesitating for a while between the free churches and the Anglican priesthood. Although not at first acceptable to the authorities of the state church, he ultimately received presentation as curate of the church at Olney, where at the age of thirty-nine he was ordained (1764).

In that same year he published an autobiographical account of his sea-going and religious experiences, *The Authentic Narrative*. In 1767 the poet William Cowper set-

tled at Olney and became a parishioner and friend of Newton. The latter had developed some poetic talent, and in 1779 he and Cowper collaborated in preparing and publishing a collection called *Olney Hymns*. Earlier Newton had published his *Olney Sermons*. Troubles arose that caused him to remove in 1780 to a London parish where his "extempore" preaching attracted a large following. An extensive religious correspondence gave rise to a collection of his letters called *Cardiphonia* (1781). In 1792 he was awarded the D.D. degree by the College of New Jersey (now Princeton). Toward the end of his life he became blind, but he still continued his incessant preaching.

Like many of his contemporary clerics, Newton was essentially Calvinistic in his theology. But in his fervor and zeal he found his closest associates among the Wesleyans. He also took great interest in some social concerns, especially the abolition of the slave trade. After he left Olney for his London parish, he is reputed to have exercised some influence on William Wilberforce in that regard.

But it is for his hymns that Newton has his permanent recognition. There are four in particular that are still in general use. Two are in the popular common meter: "How Sweet the Name of Jesus Sounds in a Believer's Ear" and "Amazing Grace, How Sweet the Sound." By itself the latter would be almost sufficient for Newton's continuing fame. A third, "Safely through Another Week God Hath Brought Us on Our Way," is probably the most widely known hymn in English in honor of the Sabbath. But a fourth, "Glorious Things of Thee Are Spoken, Zion, City of Our God," is remarkable for three reasons. As a praise of the church, it shows that Newton, for all his evangelical fervor (which was primarily individualistic), did not neglect the total company of God's people, the holy catholic church. It is also in part a version of Psalm 87, showing that Newton was in the stalwart tradition of metrical psalmody. Lastly, the particular rhythm of the hymn is noteworthy. It is the popular Goliardic rhythm used in both secular and religious poetry of the Middle Ages.

Thomas Aquinas employed it in his "Pange, lingua, gloriosi corporis mysterium." Thus Newton was a representative of the incipient Romantic movement, which followed the rationalism of the eighteenth century.

A. CABANISS

NICHOLAS I (died 867)
Pope, 858–867

Son of a distinguished Roman family, Nicholas began his life of church service with a superior education and high connections. He entered the papal court in 844, and during the fourteen following years, he filled various important roles. Well prepared for his election, Nicholas became one of the papacy's most powerful occupants and one of its strongest spokesmen for Rome's primacy in the church. His decisions and actions influenced Christianity and western European society for the remainder of the Middle Ages.

Nicholas's tenure as pope was especially historic for two fundamental church controversies, one Eastern and one Western in origin. Both conflicts centered around the supremacy of papal authority over the church's hierarchy. For the Eastern church, the great issue was control of the bishop's office at Constantinople, Christianity's second most important center. In 857, the Byzantine emperor Michael III replaced Ignatius, the duly elected bishop, with his own man, Photius, as head of the Constantinopolitan church. Nicholas immediately opposed this decision with actions culminating with excommunication of Photius at the synod of Rome (863). About the same time, Nicholas also claimed papal authority over the newly converted Bulgars. Incensed by such drastic actions, Photius secured the emperor's support and excommunicated Nicholas in 867. Photius also accused the Western church of heresy in its acceptance of the Filoque doctrine, a dogma portraying the Holy Spirit as proceeding from both the Father and the Son. The episode was a large step toward Eastern Orthodoxy's full break with Roman Catholicism in the 1000s.

Concerning the Western church, the prominent issue was control of the bishop's office at Soissons (northwest Gaul). In 861, Rothad, bishop of Soissons, appealed to Nicholas after being deposed by Hincmar, Gaul's leading church figure. The pope decided in favor of Rothad and ordered Hincmar to accept Roman jurisdiction in the matter. The pope also prevailed against John, bishop of Ravenna (northern Italy), who appealed his deposition by Nicholas to Louis II, the Frankish emperor. John lost his case, but eventually Nicholas restored him to Ravenna on agreement that he would reform certain longstanding abuses. The acceptance Nicholas gained for papal power was a critical element in the Western church's development through the Middle Ages, as well as centuries thereafter. Nicholas also attended to issues affecting western Europe as a whole. His most significant action here was an active enforcement of the church's strict marriage rules.

Nicholas I's letters have been printed in Migne's *Patrologia Latina*. Roy's *Nicholas I* lists other important original materials.

K. J. BRYER

NICHOLAS OF CUSA (1401–1464)
German cardinal and philosopher

Nicholas was born in Cues (in the diocese of Treves), from which town he took his appellative "Cusanus." At the age of twenty-two he received the doctorate in canon law from the University of Padua. The exact date of his ordination to the priesthood is unknown, but it occurred between 1436 and 1440. Skilled in mathematics, theology, philosophy, and above all in church politics, he went to the council of Basel in 1432. There he defended the council's authority above that of the pope. He recognized, for instance, the defectiveness of the so-called Donation of Constantine and the pseudo-Isidorian decretals, either in anticipation of or about the same time as his contemporary, Lorenzo Valla. But the claim that he was the first to make that recognition is not accurate. He had as a matter of fact been preceded by the Holy Roman Emperor Otto III and by the English archbishop Grosseteste, if not by many nontheoretical medieval challengers of papal authority.

At Basel, Nicholas became disillusioned by the bickering. He changed sides and joined the pope when the latter removed a portion of the council to Ferrara (ultimately to Florence). There he took an interest in healing the four-hundred-year-old schism with the Greek Church. Consequently, he was made a member of the papal group that secured the Greek emperor's willingness to deal with the council in 1438.

After the council, Nicholas was appointed papal legate in Germany during the interval of 1450 to 1452 to correct abuses in the church. In 1452 he was elected bishop of Brixen (he had already been rewarded with the red hat of a cardinal). At Brixen he strove to reform it and make it a model diocese, and did so with much success. But within a few years he clashed with civil authorities over feudal claims and had to leave his see. In that struggle he was stalwartly defended by Pope Pius II, but to no avail.

Despite a very active life in practical affairs of the church, he found time to write. Many of his sermons have survived. Some were treatises concerned with epistemology; others were dialogues in the Platonic manner and dealt with many philosophical problems. His most renowned study, *De docta ignorantia* (*On Learned Ignorance*, 1440), proposed that all man's vast knowledge about God was in reality a form of ignorance. His *De coniecturis* (*On Guesses*, 1442) concluded that positive statements about truth, however good, were mere guesses. It is obvious, therefore, that Nicholas of Cusa was far from the tradition of Thomas Aquinas's scholasticism. Indeed Nicholas was not a Christian Aristotelian, but a Christian Neoplatonist. He has even been called a mystic. But the truth of the matter is that he adhered to no single particular school of thought. The concept of a totality (*summa*) of theological data, which had flourished in the high Middle Ages, held no appeal for him. On the contrary, he believed, in quasi-mathematical terms, that all contradictions would be resolved at infinity. He thus broke with most ancient and medieval concepts

and appeared on the historical scene as a representative of the high Renaissance, much like his superior, Pius II. Despite obvious antitheses in the world, he sought to discern such a harmony as would encompass everything. A. CABANISS

NICHOLAS OF HEREFORD (died 1420)
Bible translator

Probably born at Hereford, Nicholas studied at Queen's College, Oxford, where he became a supporter of John Wycliffe. He participated with Wycliffe in the production of the *Early Version* of the Wycliffe Bible (1382) and is usually credited with translating much of the Old Testament from the Latin Vulgate into English. The translators' original copy is still in the Bodleian Library, Oxford.

For preaching Wycliffe's views, Nicholas was condemned and excommunicated by the pope. When he traveled to Rome to appeal the sentence, he was put in prison. Escaping in 1385, he returned to England and resumed preaching Lollard doctrines.

A few years later he was imprisoned at Nottingham, tortured, and kept behind bars until he recanted—which left his followers depressed and bewildered. Released from prison (1391), Nicholas was taken under royal protection and made chancellor and later treasurer of Hereford Cathedral. In 1417 he resigned these offices and became a Carthusian monk.

That he had anything to do with the *Later Version* of the Wycliffe Bible (as sometimes claimed) is doubtful, for it was produced between 1395 and 1397, after he had returned to the Roman Catholic fold. The *Later Version* seems to have been largely the work of John Purvey. H. F. VOS

NICHOLAS OF LYRA (c. 1270–c. 1349)
Franciscan scholar

Born in Lire, France (hence his name), Nicholas joined the Franciscans in 1300. He received a doctorate from the University of Paris (c. 1308) and taught in the theological faculty there. He was an unusual student of Hebrew, perhaps the best of his time, going beyond the Vulgate to the original. Nicholas also knew and studied rabbinical and other commentators on Scripture, especially Rashi. His belief was that the literal sense of the Bible was primary, and that only on a firm literal foundation should one establish other meanings of the text. In many respects he was like the church father and translator Jerome. Some authorities have deemed him the best Hebrew scholar after Jerome. It is certain that Martin Luther relied quite heavily on him for rabbinical lore. One writer even quipped, "If Lyra had not played on his lyre," the Lutheran reformation might not have been what it was. A. CABANISS

NICHOLSON, WILLIAM PATTESON
(1876–1959)
Northern Ireland evangelist

After a dramatic conversion to Christ in 1898 while living as a rough seaman, Nicholson studied at the Bible Training Institute in Glasgow in order to become a preacher. Before going to the United States he worked as an evangelist with the Lanarkshire Christian Union in Scotland. In the United States he was an official evangelist of the Presbyterian Church of the U.S.A. and a teacher at Moody Bible Institute (a sister institution to that in Glasgow). Soon he returned to Ulster, where his evangelistic missions attracted great crowds in the 1920s. His greatest success was in the dockland area of Belfast, where many professed conversion. There was also an improvement in the morality of those living in the area. Because of this his name is legendary among Northern Irish Protestants; he is especially known as the preacher who drove people into the kingdom of God by preaching about hellfire. He also preached in South Africa and Australia. P. TOON

NICOLAI (KASATKIN), IVAN
(c. 1835–1912)
Founder of the Japanese mission of the Orthodox church in Japan

After graduating from the St. Petersburg Ecclesiastical Academy, Nicolai became a monk and was ordained a monk-priest. In 1860 he was sent to Japan as chaplain to the Russian diplomatic consulate in Nagasaki. His first years were spent in the study of the language. To this day he is considered to be one of the greatest experts in the Japanese language. His mastery of the language was used particularly in the translation of the Eastern liturgical books.

In the 1860s solitary proselytes began to join the church. Nicholas was the only monk-priest in Japan. Gradually the work became larger than he alone could handle. Support began to increase from Russia. Money was sent, and students began to prepare to travel to Japan. More important, however, was the fact that Nicholas sent Japanese converts to Russia to study theology.

Small orthodox communities began to appear throughout Japan. By 1880 Orthodox Christianity had spread to the extent that Nicholas was raised to Archimandrite (bishop). Within the next few years Nicholas erected a cathedral in Tokyo and built a few houses around it in which he located an Ecclesiastical Seminary, a girls' school, the Missionary Administration, a printing office, and a domicile for himself and his assistants.

The Orthodox Church of Japan is national and independent in character. The staff of clergy and missionaries are largely Japanese. All the publications are in Japanese as well as is school education. R. E. WEBBER

NICOLL, SIR WILLIAM ROBERTSON
(1851–1923)
Religious journalist

Born into the Free Church of Scotland manse at Auchindoir, Aberdeenshire, Nicoll's reading habits began early among his minister father's seventeen thousand volumes. William graduated from Aberdeen (1870), and after theological training in his church's divinity hall, he served parishes at Dufftown (1874–1877) and Kelso (1877–1885) and established his reputation as a preacher. Ill health forced his resignation from the ministry. He went to London and began his editorship of *The Expositor* (1885) and the *British Weekly* (1886), posts which he held for the rest of his life. His aim in the latter publication was to handle everything in a Christian spirit. In 1896 he visited America with his friend Sir J. M. Barrie, and he maintained a fruitful correspondence with many American writers, politicians, and preachers. He engaged increasingly in political controversies, was a friend of Lloyd George with whose social legislation he identified himself, and helped overcome Nonconformist pacifist views in World War II. Like a good Free Kirkman, Nicoll was a formidable foe of Erastianism. He made the *British Weekly* widely influential, published several religious and secular books, edited *The Expositor's Greek Testament*, was knighted (1909), and was made a companion of honor (a prestigious order) two years before his death. J. D. DOUGLAS

NIDA, EUGENE ALBERT (born 1914)
American linguist and Bible translator

Born in Oklahoma City, Oklahoma, Nida studied at the University of Southern California at Los Angeles (M.A., 1939) and the University of Michigan (Ph.D., 1943). Thereafter he received D.D. degrees from Eastern Baptist Seminary (1956) and California Baptist Seminary (1959), as well as a Th.D. from the University of Münster (1967). He was ordained to the ministry in the American Baptist Church in 1943.

Nida's lifelong ministry has been his involvement with Bible translation work all around the world. He served as a field investigator for the Wycliffe Bible Translators from 1936 to 1937 and continued to teach translators until 1952. He served as secretary for translations in the American Bible Society from 1943 to 1984, and as translations research coordinator for the United Bible Societies from 1972 to 1984. At present he is a consultant for the American Bible Society and the United Bible Societies. He and his wife Althea, have traveled to over eighty countries and worked with Bible translators in over two hundred languages.

Nida is best known for developing theories and methodologies for linguistics and Bible translation. These are clearly expressed in his books *Toward a Science of Translating* (1964), *Theory and Practice of Translation* (1969), and *From One Language to Another* (1986, with Jan de Waard). Nida purports a translation theory known as *dynamic equivalence* (later named as *functional equivalence*). According to Nida, dynamic equivalence is "the reproduction in a receptor language [for example, English] of the closest natural equivalent of the source language [Hebrew or Greek] message, first in terms of meaning, and second in terms of style." Nida thinks the receptors should be able to understand and appreciate the message in essentially the same way as the original receptors understood and appreciated the original message. Of course, this response can never be identical, for the cultural and historical settings are too different, but there should be a high degree of equivalence of response.

Nida's theory of dynamic equivalence has been extensively used in the making of many modern, idiomatic translations of the Bible all around the world and has been even more widely accepted in the secular world. The Contemporary English Version (1991), prepared by a team of translators under the direction of Barclay Newman and in cooperation with Eugene Nida, is a good example of this kind of translation in English.

Among Nida's many other accomplishments, he was responsible for bringing together the international committee that produced the United Bible Societies' third edition of the *Greek New Testament* (1975), followed by the Nestle-Aland 26th edition of *Novum Testamentum Graece* (1979). Nida was also responsible for setting up and guiding the work of the Hebrew Old Testament project, which is concerned with five thousand textual problems in the Old Testament. In collaboration with Newman and others, Nida has produced a series of helpful handbooks for Bible translators. And, finally, he has written several books dealing with missions; among these are *Customs and Cultures* (1954), *Message and Missions* (1960), and *Religion Across Cultures* (1968). P. W. COMFORT

NIEBUHR, HELMUT RICHARD
(1894–1962)
American Neoorthodox theologian

Helmut (with his brother, Reinhold) was among the leaders of a new "Christian Realism" in America that arose out of modernism in the late 1920s. His work shared his brother's criticisms of theological liberalism and its debt to European neoorthodoxy. It offered, in its own right, serious consideration of vital theological themes and path-breaking analyses of the church in society.

Niebuhr was ordained in the Evangelical and Reformed Church after attending the denomination's schools, Elmhurst College and Eden Theological Seminary. He served three years as a pastor in St. Louis (1916–1918), then taught theology at Eden Seminary, pursued doctoral studies at Yale University, served as president of Elmhurst, and again as theological professor at Eden. In 1931 he accepted a position at Yale Divinity School where he remained until his death.

Niebuhr's published work drew on diverse influences. From the older liberalism he took a commitment to the essentially experiential nature of religion. From the same source he took the view that mankind, immersed in history, can never transcend that history to see truth unbiased and whole. From European neoorthodoxy he took a sharply critical view of liberal optimism concerning man and his potential. This new realism about the human prospect was the most notable contribution of the Niebuhrs to American neoorthodoxy. From the classical orthodoxy of Augustine, the reformers, and Jonathan Edwards he took a high conception of God's sovereignty and a firm belief in the utter dependency of all existence upon God.

Niebuhr created a stimulating flow of influential books. One group of them dealt broadly with the church in society. *The Social Sources of Denominationalism* (1929) showed how securely church structures were bound up with the cultural customs and patterns of Western life. *The Kingdom of God in America* (1937) provided a brilliant portrait of the way in which the idea of God's kingdom had shifted content throughout American history—from God's sovereignty in the time of Jonathan Edwards, to the kingdom of Christ during the 1800s, and finally to the coming kingdom for twentieth-century liberals. The book has sharp criticisms to make of each period but looks most fondly on the earliest period when some Americans truly believed in the ultimacy of God. The book also contains the best critical description of theological liberalism ever written: "A God without wrath brought men without sin into a kingdom without judgment through the ministrations of a Christ without a cross."

Christ and Culture (1951) provides a classic schematization for the different ways in which believers over the centuries have interacted with their surrounding worlds. Its five categories—Christ against culture, the Christ of culture, Christ above culture, Christ and culture in paradox, and Christ the transformer of culture—have become standard ways to describe Christian approaches to political, economic, and social affairs.

Niebuhr's more directly theological works have not been as widely read but have exerted a special influence on American religious thought. *The Meaning of Revelation* (1941) argues that when God reveals himself to people, all other events and questions become relative. The work has been criticized for making revelation overly subjective, but here and elsewhere Niebuhr pointed to the Christian community as a body providing standards (though they are relative also) for describing and communicating God's revelation. *Radical Monotheism and Western Culture* (1960) was Niebuhr's last full statement of his convictions. In it he looked to God as the source of all being, as Being itself, and decried all that would detract from his all-sufficiency.

Evangelicals sometimes find Niebuhr's reliance on Scripture insufficient and his picture of Christ's work incomplete. But with all Christians they, too, profit from the depth of learning and profundity of insight that is Niebuhr's gift to the church. M. A. NOLL

NIEBUHR, REINHOLD (1892–1971)

Best-known spokesman for American neoorthodoxy

Niebuhr's neoorthodoxy was quite different from that on the European continent; it was more concerned with ethics than theology proper, it focused more on the doctrine of man than on the doctrine of God, and it showed more concern for life in society than for life in the church. It shared nonetheless the conviction of European neoorthodoxy that liberalism had placed too much faith in man and too little reliance in God.

Niebuhr was the son of a pastor in the German Evangelical church. (Niebuhr moved with this small denomination into the Evangelical and Reformed Church and eventually the United Church of Christ.) He attended his denomination's college and seminary (Elmhurst and Eden) before doing two years of graduate work at Yale. In 1915 he accepted the pastorate of Bethel Evangelical Church in Detroit, where he served for thirteen years. Niebuhr came of age theologically in this urban church as his liberalism encountered the harsh realities of industrial America. He was particularly upset with what industrial life did to the laborers. He wondered what hope there was for American civilization when "naive gentlemen with a genius for mechanics suddenly become the arbiters over the lives and fortunes of hundreds of thousands." While still in Detroit, Niebuhr began to advocate radical solutions to the human crisis as he saw it—socialism and pacifism for life in society, a new "Christian Realism" for theology.

When Niebuhr moved to New York's Union Theological Seminary in 1928, he carried with him the commitments formed in Detroit. The coming of World War II led him to abandon his socialism and pacifism, but he remained a dedicated social activist—serving on scores of committees in the 1930s and 1940s, helping to form Americans for Democratic Action and New York's Liberal Party, editing the journal *Christianity and Crisis,* and writing prolifically for newspapers and magazines.

His theological ethics were developed more systematically in a long list of major books. The two most important are *Moral Man and Immoral Society* (1932) and *The Nature and Destiny of Man* (1941, 1943). The first severely criticized the liberal optimism concerning man. It pointed out that social groups are selfish almost by their very definition. It gave a sharp rebuke to the notion that human beings were perfectible as individuals and inherently good in groups. The second provided a more systematic discussion of what Niebuhr called mankind's "most vexing problem. How shall he think of himself?" In this work and elsewhere Niebuhr proposed to answer his own question: man as sinner and saint, man as subject to history and social forces but also as shaper of history and society, man as creature of the Creator but potential lord of the creation, man as egotistical but capable of living for others. In explaining these tensions or paradoxes, Niebuhr drew on the Bible. What he called the biblical "myth" of creation helped show man's potential (made in the image of God) for both true good and radical evil. Niebuhr believed that Scripture supported his contention that man sins inevitably but not by moral necessity. In the person of Christ, Niebuhr found a unique example of an individual who used power only for good and not—as all other people—for evil. The cross of Christ was a particularly important theme for Niebuhr since it revealed the great paradox of powerlessness turned into power.

Niebuhr showed little interest in the doctrines of Christ or grace except where they aided his study of man. In so doing he can be criticized for being more interested in the paradoxes of human life than in the salvation offered through Christ. A similar criticism relates to Niebuhr's use of Scripture. The Bible seemed to mean more to him because it was relevant to the modern condition than because it was God's Word to us. In spite of such criticisms, Niebuhr's work retains its importance. Even if it does not present an entirely evangelical solution to life's dilemmas, it does share an evangelical analysis of man as sinner in need of divine help. M. A. NOLL

NIEMOLLER, MARTIN (1892–1984)
Lutheran pastor and political activist

Born in Lippstadt, Germany, Niemoller was a German submarine commander during World War I. He completed theological studies after the war, and in 1924 he was ordained as an Evangelical Church (Lutheran) pastor. From 1931 to 1937, Niemoller served a congregation in Dahlem, Germany (near Berlin). Here he attracted notice both for his church work and his outspokenness as a German nationalist and patriot. As the 1930s progressed, however, he developed increasing conflicts with Germany's radical political upheavals. At first Niemoller was a Hitler supporter, but he soon saw the destructive, anti-Christian character of Nazism's objectives. By the mid-1930s, he had helped found and become a leader of Germany's confessing church movement. Only a small contingent, this represented German churchmen who openly opposed Hitler and his designs.

Niemoller's World War I service prevented his arrest for several years. Finally Hitler's government seized him, and he spent most of World War II in a concentration camp. Several times government agents offered Niemoller release if he would compromise his express opposition to Nazism. With typical bluntness, he refused all such offers and remained in prison. Niemoller returned to church work after his release in 1945. Very quickly, in many dramatic statements, he began to excoriate his countrymen, especially fellow ministers, for their failure to reject Nazism. Among other results, in 1945, this brought about the Stuttgart Declaration of Guilt. In the postwar years, Niemoller occupied various general offices in Germany's Evangelical Church, and from 1961 to 1968 he served as one of the World Council of Churches' presidents. Regarding politics, it was now evident his war experiences had given Niemoller a radical pacifist outlook. This view hardened and became more extreme in succeeding years. He eventually advocated complete neutrality between Communist East and Democratic West Germany. Perceived as a compromiser with communism, he lost much of his influence both inside and outside Germany. His last years

were spent in obscurity. Over the years, Niemoller produced numerous written works, his autobiography, *Vom U-Boot zur Kanzel,* being the most important. His work for the Evangelical Church of Germany continued until his death. K. J. BRYER

NIETZSCHE, FRIEDRICH (1844–1900)
German philosopher

Nietzsche has been called the most influential German philosopher since Kant and Hegel. Certainly he is one of the most original, and his influence is still felt in literature, philosophy, and theology.

He was born in Rocher, Prussia, the son of a Lutheran minister, and both his parents were themselves children of Lutheran ministers. He was educated at the University of Basel, where he taught classical philology. He rejected all religions, regarded supernaturalism as anti-intellectual, and was revolted by what he saw as its otherworldliness. He criticized Christianity, yet admired Jesus. The disciples, he maintained, so misunderstood Jesus that their Christianity was the opposite of what Jesus intended: it pitted believer against unbeliever, faith against reason, and meekness against strength.

To understand Nietzsche one must see the central thesis of his philosophy. It is a voluntaristic interpretation of life, to the effect that all of history and human existence is an evolutionary struggle, in which the conflict and balance of weak and strong wills holds the destiny of mankind. This is symbolized by the contrast in ancient Greece between the Apollonian emphasis on rational restraint, harmony and order on the one hand, and Dionysian revelry without restraint on the other. Greek tragedy combined the two by affirming the ordered nature of life and destiny in the face of suffering and conflict. But Christianity has upset that balance with its Apollonian stress on order and its ethic of meekness and love. The result is a crisis of Western civilization grown weak and effete, in which even God for all practical purposes is dead, and there is none to save us. Strength and vitality of will must be affirmed anew. Nietzsche therefore pictured an old man, Zarathustra, journeying through the towns and villages of Europe announcing the death of God and proclaiming that man must now become the meaning of the earth—a superman whose forceful strength of purpose will revitalize culture, turn the course of history, and save the day.

Nietzsche was not swayed by traditional arguments to the contrary. He believed that our reasons at root are rationalizations, expressions of what we want—of weak or strong wills. What we call truth is simply what we will. The criteria we adopt for testing truth simply enhance our feelings of power. He was a pragmatist: whatever we can make work in achieving our purposes—that is truth.

Nor was he impressed by a Christian ethic, diluted in the nineteenth century with evolutionary optimism and unrealistic attitudes about the rule of reason and love. He advocated a "transvaluation of values" from the herd morality of democratic equality and asceticism's self-denial, to a strong-willed self-assertiveness with racist overtones. The Christianity that he rejected is otherworldly and weak-willed; it says no to the vitality of nature and to life. The ethic he embraced is this-worldly: it says yes to strength and vitality and no to all that is meek and mild. Christians, he argued, have weakened Jesus into one without the power to save anything at all.

Nietzsche retired from the University of Basel in 1879 and went insane in 1889. He wrote *The Antichrist* (1895), an attack on Christian dogma. Nietzsche's influence is seen in some forms of existentialism, and more specifically in the "death of God" theology of the 1960s. A. F. HOLMES

NINIAN (c.360–c.432)
Described as the first authentic figure in the story of Christianity in North Britain

We have few details of Ninian's life and work. As a young man he set out on a pilgrimage to Rome where, according to Bede, he was "accurately instructed . . . in the Faith and mysteries of the Truth." The pope, who evidently took a personal interest in the

young Briton, consecrated him as a bishop and sent him back to his native land to convert his own countrymen. On the return journey his education continued when he spent some time with his fellow bishop Martin of Tours, pioneer of the monastic life in Gaul. Martin is said to have encouraged some masons to accompany Ninian to help in the building of a stone church, which Ninian called Candida Casa, meaning the White House, at what is now Whithorn, Scotland. Thus, on the shores of the Solway Firth, the Church of Scotland was born among the Southern Picts.

This became his base as the first bishop of Galloway. To the monastery he founded there came students from Ireland and Wales; from it many took monastic ideals to other parts. Ninian and his preachers went out with the gospel through Strathclyde and north at least to the Grampians, as well as to Ireland and northern England.

Ninian thus laid the missionary foundation that was continued a century after his death by Columba and Kentigern (Mungo). St. Ninian's Cave near Whithorn, where the saint is reported to have retired regularly for prayer, can still be seen, with its rocky walls displaying the symbol of the cross said to have been carved by his followers. J. D. DOUGLAS

NOMMENSEN, LUDWIG INGWER (1834–1918)
Apostle to the Bataks of Sumatra

Nommensen was born on the island of Nordstrand, Schleswig (then Danish). Illness led to a vow of missionary service. After completing studies in the seminary of the Rhenish Missionary Society at Barmen, he was sent to Sumatra in 1862. Despite the opposition of colleagues and Dutch officials, Nommensen began pioneering among the Bataks in the interior. He was befriended and protected by the powerful chief Radja Pontas Lumbantobing, but in the midst of death threats, Nommensen's greatest assets were his personal courage, simple faith, ability to make friends, and his medical skill. He constructed a church order based on the Batak *adat* or traditional social and cultural order. Convinced that a great people could be converted only by its own agents, he instituted the "preacher-teacher system." The radjas and elders were given leadership in the church. The people supported their own ministries and were ardent evangelists. German missionaries were kept at a minimum. By Nommensen's death in 1918, the Church had 180,000 baptized members, as many adherents, 510 schools, 32,700 pupils, 788 teacher-preachers, 2,200 elders, and 34 ordained pastors. Nommensen was Ephorus of the Church until his death. P. BEAVER

NORBERT OF XANTEN (c. 1080–1134)
Founder of the Premonstratensian order

Norbert was born in Xanten, Germany, of noble parentage. He was thirty-five when, after a very worldly life at the imperial court, he barely escaped being struck by a bolt of lightning. Like Luther much later, he interpreted his experience as a call—in his case to a life as a wandering preacher of penance. He undertook his work seriously, and some time afterwards he was made a priest. Opposed by many clerics but favored by the popes, he established a monastery in 1120 near Laon at a place appropriately called *Premontre* (meaning "foreshown"). From thence the order he founded took its name, Premonstratensian. Confirmed by pope Honorius II in 1126, the order spread rapidly, especially in England. It exercised considerable influence on Dominicanism and the Society of Jesus. Although intended to be primarily contemplative, the order encouraged active and vigorous preaching. In the latter part of his life, Norbert was elected bishop of Magdeburg, where he died. He was canonized in 1582.
A. CABANISS

NOYES, JOHN HUMPHREY (1811–1886)
The best known Christian communitarian in nineteenth-century America

A graduate of Dartmouth, Noyes was con-

verted during a revival in 1831. He then attended Andover Theological Seminary and Yale Divinity School, where his opinions brought him into disfavor. He advocated sinless perfection through union with Christ and in 1839 proclaimed that Jesus had returned to earth in A.D. 70. He also thought that socialism was the means for perfected Christians to bring the kingdom of heaven to earth. With these views he organized a group of "Bible Communists" who in 1840 settled near Putney, Vermont. In 1846 Noyes's communalism advanced a step when he declared that holding all things in common should extend to wives. This view of "complex marriage" caused a sensation and led to legal charges. In 1848 Noyes led his group to Oneida in western New York state where the community was reestablished. Here they prospered, having over two hundred residents by 1851 and being successful in farming and in light industry. The community expressed Noyes's belief in evangelical perfectionism, Christian communalism, and rational American efficiency. These principles also shaped Noyes's *History of American Socialism* (1870). The group's "free love" was carefully, even eugenically, controlled. Gradually, however, secularization invaded the community; less and less concern came to be paid to sinless perfection and evangelical zeal. And the scandal of Oneida's marriage customs kept pressure on from the outside. Noyes finally fled to Canada to escape lawsuits and warrants in 1879.
M. A. NOLL

NUTTALL, ENOS (1842–1916)
First archbishop of the West Indies

Born at Clitheroe, Lancashire, England, Nuttal went out to Jamaica as a missionary in 1862. Ordained in the Anglican Church in 1866, he helped to reorganize the Church of England in Jamaica on its disestablishment (1870), drafting its canons and setting up and running its financial system. In 1879 he received the Lambeth B.D. from Archbishop Tait and was chosen by the diocesan synod the next year as bishop of Jamaica. He was made primate of the West Indies in 1893 and styled archbishop from 1897. His coolness in the Jamaican earthquake of 1907 and his prompt relief measures won high praise. For fifty-four years he showed his constant concern for Jamaican daily welfare in education, nursing, housing, and agriculture, in close consultation with the government of the United Kingdom. He founded the first Jamaican diocesan theological college in 1893. N. HILLYER

O

OATES, TITUS (1649–1703)
A leader in the so-called "Popish Plot" of 1678

Born in Oakham, England, Oates was said to have been "distinguished for the effrontery of his demeanor no less than by the superior villainy of his private life." Although expelled from school, the navy, and the church, publicly flogged and imprisoned, he managed to lie or bribe his way out of scandals concerning sex, religion, and politics. As an Anglican clergyman, a Jesuit scholar, or Baptist preacher, he was an impostor and perjurer remembered for his foul mouth and blasphemy that accompanied his dramatic behavior. Playing on the fears and prejudice of the populace in regard to Roman Catholicism, he instigated in 1678 the notorious "Popish Plot" to overthrow the Protestant rule of Charles II. It was the cause of the execution of innocent men as well as increased bitterness between Catholics and Protestants. A reversed decision of his jail sentence for this crime and a fortunate marriage allowed him to continue his disreputable life until his death. A biography and engraving of a portrait of Oates is found in *The Lives of Twelve Bad Men* by Seccombe; representations of him in the pillory surrounded by the heads of his victims became the subject of fashionable portraits at the time of the plot. C. F. ALLISON

OCCOM, SAMSON (1723–1792)
Best-known American Indian preacher of the eighteenth century

Converted during the Great Awakening at New London, Connecticut, in 1740, Occom began studies with Eleazar Wheelock in Lebanon, Connecticut, about two years later in order to equip himself for Indian missionary work. Wheelock's school later was to move to Hanover, New Hampshire, and reincorporate as Dartmouth College.

Occom, a Mohican, ministered to the Montauk Indians of Long Island (1749–1764) and was ordained in 1759 by the Suffolk Presbytery on Long Island. He was in England from 1765 to 1768 to raise money for Wheelock's Indian training school at Lebanon. Occom caught the popular fancy in England, where he preached over three hundred sermons and raised more than ten thousand pounds. Returning to North America, he engaged in an extended period of missionary work among the Oneida Indians of New York, founding Brotherstown, an Indian village, in 1784. H. F. VOS

OCHINO, BERNARDINO (1487–1564)
Italian Catholic–turned–Protestant Reformer

A native of Siena, Ochino joined the Franciscan Order around 1504 and then became vicar-general of the stricter, newly founded order of the Capuchins (1538–1542). He became a renowned penitential preacher, and after being commissioned to read and dispute Protestant teachings, he was converted to the belief that the clergy cannot be mediators for another man's sins. Ochino kept his new beliefs confidential, but in a sermon he gave at Venice in 1542, he criticized the Inquisition. When he was summoned to Rome, he escaped over the Alps to Geneva, Switzerland, where Calvin received him warmly. In a final break with Rome, he married a refugee from Lucca. He resided in Geneva from 1542 to 1545, using these years for preaching and for writing several works, including his *Apologhi*. In 1545 he became pastor of the Italian church at Augsburg.

During the war between Charles V and the Schmalkaldic League, Augsburg fell, and Ochino was forced to flee to England where he was influential in the Reformation under Edward VI. Thomas Cranmer acted as his protector and secured a royal pension for him. During this time (1547–1553) he preached to the Italians in London and wrote *The Usurped Primacy of the Bishop of Rome* and the *Labyrinth*, dedicated to Elizabeth I, in which he attacked Calvin's doctrine of predestination, greatly angering the Calvinists. Upon the ascension of the Catholic Queen Mary to the throne of England, Ochino was forced to return to the European mainland.

He became minister to the Italian congregation in Zurich but seemed to have a talent for offending and alienating the magistrates and ministers of the city. In 1563 he published *Thirty Dialogues*, which was thought to mishandle the doctrine of the Trinity and monogamy. As a result, he was banished along with his four children (his wife had died). His next residence was Cracow, Poland, where he preached for a time, but the Catholics urged the king to expel all foreign dissidents and he moved, again, to Slavkov,

Moravia. Soon after, he died, reportedly from the plague. L. LEONARD

ODILO (962–1049)
Fifth abbot of Cluny

Born of a noble family of Mercoeur in the Auvergne, Odilo was professed as a Benedictine monk at Cluny in 990. He became assistant to the abbot only two years later, then became an abbot himself in 994. Odilo often served as a diplomat in negotiating the tense relations between the French kings and Holy Roman Emperors. He actively pursued his efforts at peace by striving to further the Truce of God. Under him the number of Cluniac communities was almost doubled. Known far and wide for his largess to those in want, he also had occasion to prepare sermons, compose hymns, and write letters intended to strengthen the religious life. A work of major significance was an account of Majolus, his very great predecessor as abbot of Cluny. Odilo did not inaugurate the solemnity of All Souls' Day (November 2), but he encouraged it and made it an annual observance for those houses under his control. According to his biographer, Odilo declared just before he died, "I approach this journey with the holy cross, which is my life." Referred to by his contemporaries as "the archangel of monks," Odilo was canonized in 1063, not very long after his death. A. CABANISS

ODO (879–942)
Second abbot of Cluny

Born in Maine, France, Odo was trained at the school of St. Martin at Tours and was made a canon of that church. In 909 he became a Benedictine monk. At the new foundation of Cluny (910), he attracted by his profound humility the attention of Berno, its first abbot. The latter soon had Odo ordained to the priesthood. In 926, he succeeded as abbot upon Berno's retirement (Berno died a year later). Under Odo the abbey began its great work, the so-called Cluniac reform, which was destined to evoke and be absorbed by the Hildebrandine reformation of the eleventh century. Its program was an effort to liberate the church from secular control, and it used the following measures: advocating clerical celibacy, imposing restraints upon lay investiture, abolishing simony (bribery) in the disposition of ecclesiastical functions and offices, and securing supremacy of the papacy in church affairs. A by-product of this program was that he gained papal approval. Odo's zeal brought to Cluny almost two hundred important donations of property, making it a mighty force in its day.

Odo wrote poems, sermons, and lectures, all of which illustrate his patristic and humane culture. They, together with his other activities, increased the prestige of Cluny. A. CABANISS

OECOLAMPADIUS (JOHANNES HEUSSGEN) (1482–1531)
One of the leaders of the Reformation in Switzerland

A brilliant philologist in Latin, Greek, and Hebrew, Oecolampadius studied at Heilbronn, Bologna, and Heidelberg. Well-versed in the thought of Thomas Aquinas and the medieval mystics, he acted as the tutor of a noble's sons and also obtained the prebend of Weinsberg, which he held until 1512. For the next three years, he studied at various universities and in 1515 settled in Basel for a short time. There he met Erasmus, whom he helped with the translation of the New Testament. In his travels he also made contact with Melanchthon and Reuchlin. Although he was being influenced by Luther's thought, in 1520 he gave up his pastorate in Augsburg to enter a monastery, only to withdraw in 1522. For a short time he acted as the chaplain of Franz von Sickingen but soon received a call to go to Basel, where the Reformation was already becoming strong. In 1523 he was named a professor of holy Scripture but had difficulties with the Roman Catholic university authorities. By this time he was moving over to the views of Zwingli on the subject of the Lord's Supper. He then became a pastor in the city, using his influence to have the

people demand a complete Reformation. This resulted in a series of riots aimed at ridding churches of pictures and images. In 1523 the city council ordered the free preaching of the gospel and allowed a number of theological disputations to take place. During the Peasants' Revolt in Germany (1524), there was fear that they might attack Basel, but this did not happen.

Though Roman Catholic opposition to Protestantism was strong, Oecolampadius succeeded in having services conducted in German and in 1529 established a new Reformed church order. In the same year he took part in the Marburg Colloquy, in which he supported Zwingli against Luther, although also advocating moderation on both sides. In Basel he sought to introduce church discipline, without state interference, but was considered too rigorous by many. He was one of the most important of the early Swiss reformers. W. S. REID

OLDHAM, JOSEPH HOULDSWORTH (1874–1969)
Lay theologian, missionary, statesman, and ecumenical pioneer

Born in India, Oldham was educated at Edinburgh Academy and Trinity College, Oxford University. In 1896 he became secretary of the Student Christian Movement. In 1908 he was appointed secretary of the committee preparing for the World Missionary Conference in Edinburgh in 1910. He also served as secretary of the continuation committee (1910–1912) established by the Edinburgh conference. When the International Missionary Council was founded in 1921, Oldham was appointed joint secretary along with A. L. Warnshuis.

From 1912 to 1927 Oldham edited the *International Review of Missions*. In 1934 he accepted the chair of the research committee of the Life and Work movement, helping plan the Oxford Conference on "Church, Community, and State" (1937) and editing its official report. Oldham was secretary of the Council on the Christian Faith and the Common Life (1939–1942) and of the Christian Frontier Council (1942–1945).

Between 1939 and 1945 he edited the *Christian News Letter,* which sought to encourage Christian lay witness in secular life.

Deeply interested throughout much of his life in relations between the races, Oldham wrote *Christianity and the Race Problem* in 1924. In his later years he worked to improve the lot of African nationals. All his activities were undergirded by a rich devotional life, the basis of his widely circulated book, *A Devotional Diary* (1929).
N. V. HOPE

OLEVIANUS, KASPAR (1536–1587)
Reformed theologian

Olevianus was born at Trier (Treves) and educated at Paris, Orleans, and Bourges. His education brought him to a reformation faith, and through the accidental death of a friend he received a clear call to the preaching ministry. This call led him to seek theological training, and to this end he visited Geneva, Zurich, and Lausanne, where he came to know such leading reformers as Farel, Calvin, Bullinger, and Peter Martyr. In 1559 he went back as a teacher to his native Trier, but there his reformed preaching led to opposition, a short imprisonment, and expulsion. At this juncture Frederic III, elector of the Palatinate, who had opted for Reformed as distinct from Lutheran teaching, invited him to a pastorate at Heidelberg, where he helped to reform the church along Presbyterian lines. It was while in Heidelberg that he teamed up with Ursinus, professor of theology, to produce the renowned Heidelberg Catechism (1563), which has come down to posterity as perhaps the most balanced, elegant, and beautiful of all the confessional and catechetical statements of the Reformation period.

During the rest of Frederick's reign Olevianus seems to have been his chief adviser in church affairs, as well as court preacher and theological teacher. A reaction to Lutheranism came with Frederick's death and the accession of his son Louis VI. No longer at home in the Palatinate, Olevianus moved to Nassau, where he found an opportunity for further reforming work. Theolog-

ically Olevianus is best remembered for his work in covenant theology, his chief writing being *On the Substance of the Covenant of God with Man and the Means of Its Communication to Us.* G. BROMILEY

OLIVÉTAN, PIERRE ROBERT (c. 1506–c. 1540)
French Protestant reformer and Bible translator

His name "Olivétan" was given to him because as a student he burned the midnight (olive) oil. Born in Noyon, France, he was a cousin of John Calvin. He studied law at Paris and at Orleans, in the latter place being won over to Protestantism, to which also he is said to have brought Calvin. In 1528 he found it wise to retire to Strassburg, where Bucer and Capito persuaded him to work on the Greek and Hebrew Scriptures, with a view to making a translation into French. In 1531 he was in Geneva and for a short time taught school in Neuchatel. The following year at the Synod of Chamforans, he made contact with the Waldenses, who asked him to translate the Bible into French. He did, having his cousin, John Calvin, write the preface. (This was Calvin's first acknowledgment that he had become a Protestant.) In 1536 or 1537 he taught for a time in Geneva at the new gymnasium, but sometime after 1538 he left to visit Renée, duchess of Ferrara, who was giving protection to Protestant refugees. He then traveled for a time in Italy, but no more is heard of him after that. Some believe that he died in Ferrara, but there does not seem to be any certain information as to what happened to him.

His most important contribution to the Reformation was his translation of the Bible into French, for it became the text employed by the French reformers in their preaching and teaching. The translation was published in Neuchatel in 1535. He also translated the Psalms into French (published in 1537) and the same year also brought out *Instruction des Enfants.* Although not in the front rank of Reformers, his contribution was of great importance. W. S. REID

OMAN, JOHN WOOD (1860–1939)
Presbyterian theologian

Born in Orkney, Oman studied at Edinburgh, Erlangen, Heidelberg, and Neuchatel, then became a minister at Alnwick, Northumberland, in 1889. Eighteen years later he went as professor of systematic theology and apologetics to Westminster College, Cambridge (1907–1935), and was also principal of the college from 1925 to 1935. He was greatly influenced in his philosophical and theological thought by the emphasis of Schleiermacher on subjective feeling as forming the basis of religion. He translated Schleiermacher's *Reden uber die Religion* (*Speeches on Religion to Its Cultural Despisers,* 1799) in 1893. Oman set out his own, strongly personalistic doctrine of man and of God's dealings with him in his best-known book *The Natural and the Supernatural* (1931). He argued that man could be directly aware of the supernatural and that he achieved his true end through an awareness of and reverence for sacred values (as against relying on motives of expediency or personal profit). There were risks in freedom, but man must walk in accordance with the insights of his own sincerity. God respected the personality of man since it was his own gift to him, a thought Oman had earlier brought out in *Grace and Personality* (1917). He also wrote *Vision and Authority* (1902, revised 1928) and *The Church and the Divine Order* (1911). Moderator of the Presbyterian Church of England general assembly in 1931, he received honorary doctorates from Oxford and Edinburgh and was elected a fellow of the British Academy in 1938.

N. HILLYER

ORIGEN (ORIGENES ADAMANTIUS) (c. 185–c. 254)
Alexandrian theologian

Born of a Christian family (most likely in Alexandria), the oldest of seven children, Origen was initially trained in both secular and religious literature by his father Leonides (who was exceedingly proud of his son's learning). Very early Origen developed a passion for martyrdom, but he was restrained by his mother when he attempted to join his father in martyrdom. The burden of caring for the family fell upon Origen at the age of seventeen, so he began to teach. His classes proved so popular that he had to divide them, leaving beginners to an assistant, reserving the more advanced for himself.

Origen lived in extreme austerity. Eusebius related that in his rashness he castrated himself, but that account may not be accurate. He was bold in his admiration for martyrs, and many of his students suffered in the persecutions. Despite his lack of care for his own life, he was spared because many pagan philosophers and Christian heretics came to him for instruction. (The Neoplatonist Porphyry was an early acquaintance.) Origen was apparently free to travel, for he visited Rome, Palestine, and Arabia briefly, where he gained approval from many foreign bishops.

His range of learning was vast. In addition to his father's instruction, Origen also studied under Ammonius Saccas and Clement of Alexandria. For the sake of biblical exegesis, he learned Hebrew. His knowledge of the philosophies of the day, especially Platonism, was profound. While still living in Alexandria, he began to write and compile books. One of the earliest and most significant was *De principiis,* one of the first efforts toward a systematic theology. Another work was his *Hexapla,* an enormous edition of the Bible arranged in six columns. It contained the Hebrew text, a Greek transliteration of the Hebrew, the Septuagint, and the Greek versions by Symmachus, Aquila, and Theodotion. The *Hexapla* was a great aid in the study of the Scriptures.

So famous did he become that Mamaea, mother of Emperor Alexander Severus, summoned him to Antioch to instruct her. On his way to Greece, he was ordained as a priest by the bishop of Caesarea. That action was uncanonical and was protested by his own bishop of Alexandria. As a result, he never returned to Egypt but settled down in Caesarea, where he taught for the remainder of his life.

Constantly called upon all his life to

preach (even when he was a layman), he finally, after he had passed the age of sixty, allowed his homilies to be recorded by shorthand experts. Toward the end of his life (250), he was seized by civil authorities and tortured in an effort to make him apostatize. The persecution, although very severe, failed in its purpose. But it may have contributed to his death a few years later. Thus he died, not a martyr, but a confessor.

Origen wrote an incredible number of books. Many have been lost. What has been preserved has come down only in part in Greek, the rest in Latin translation. His leading Western interpreter was Tyrannius Rufinus, a friend of Jerome. All of Origen's work was, at least in theory, based on the literal text of Scripture, which he believed to be historical. Origen's exegesis of the text was often allegorical and typological—a style following that adopted by Alexandrian commentators on the Homeric epics. To Origen, Christ was the center—all Scripture must be interpreted in his light. That meant, for Origen, speculation on the spiritual significance of the literal. Basically he was not terribly systematic. The very size of his literary output gave rise to paradoxes and dilemmas in his expression, even to contradictions. As a consequence, he was admired and hated in his own lifetime and afterwards. But many who disagreed with him were deeply influenced by him.

His De principiis and Hexapla have already been mentioned. He also wrote commentaries on Genesis, the Psalms, Song of Songs, Lamentations, the prophets, Matthew, John, and the Pauline corpus. (He is the one who made the well-known remark, "But who wrote the letter to the Hebrews, only God really knows.") His homilies treated Genesis, Exodus, Leviticus, Numbers, Joshua, Judges, Ruth, 1 Samuel, Song of Songs, Isaiah, Jeremiah, Ezekiel, and Luke. The total body of his work has not been preserved.

The details of Origen's life were recorded by his student Gregory Thaumaturgus in a panegyric, by Eusebius in his history, and by Jerome in several references. The first two were favorable. So was Jerome at first, but he later came to disapprove of Origen's exege-sis. Yet, Jerome called him the second teacher of the church after Paul. Some of Origen's teachings were condemned by the Fifth Ecumenical Council. The West was more favorable to his writings, albeit usually not by name. But in quite modern times, his fame and his thought have been more or less rehabilitated, owing to the effort to distinguish his doctrines from those attributed to him by his later followers. A. CABANISS

OROSIUS, PAULUS (c. 390–after 418)
Spanish historian

Orosius first appeared in the historical record in 414, when he was already a priest. In that year he fled the Vandal invasion of his native Spain and visited Bishop Augustine at Hippo. Concerned at the moment with the challenge of Pelagianism, Augustine dispatched Orosius to Palestine to confront the heresiarch, Pelagius. But Orosius was not able to make a favorable impression on the hierarchy there, the Council of Diospolis (415) deciding in favor of Pelagius. Back in Hippo (416) Augustine requested that he prepare a study that could provide a historical foundation for the latter's City of God. The work was completed in two years. After that Orosius disappeared from the historical scene as mysteriously as he had appeared on it only four years earlier.

His work, Seven Books of Histories Against the Pagans, is considered the first universal chronicle by a Christian scholar. It purported to show the calamitous state of the world before Christianity and the improvement of the world after its introduction and proliferation. A. CABANISS

ORR, JAMES (1844–1913)
Scottish theologian

Born in Glasgow and educated at the university there, Orr went on to the United Presbyterian Church's college in Edinburgh. After ordination he ministered in the Scottish border town of Hawick (1874–1891). He was then appointed professor of church history in his old college, transferring in 1900 to the Glasgow college. There he taught apologetics and systematic theology—with classes augmented by the union between his church and the Free Church (a development in which he played a prominent part). Orr was critical of established religion. "A State Church," he declared, "speaks in bonds; its guns are spiked." Yet, he himself came under fire from conservatives in the continuing Free Church for teaching a modified Calvinism and for holding a defective doctrine of the inspiration of Scripture. The allegations were open to question; from another Presbyterian church came a different assessment. "Some make Christianity a doubtful thing," said the *Original Secession Church* magazine. "Dr. Orr made it to many a stable, imperishable, reliable thing."

Orr became one of the best-known theologians in the English-speaking world. He had four lecture tours in North America. One of his books, *The Virgin Birth of Christ* (1907), came out of lectures given in New York to the Bible Teachers' Training School. His many publications include *The Christian View of God and the World* (1893), *The Progress of Dogma* (1901), *The Resurrection of Jesus* (1908), and *The Faith of a Modern Christian* (1910). To many scholars he is known as the general editor of *The International Standard Bible Encyclopedia*, a comprehensive and conservative work durable enough to have undergone a complete revision nearly seventy years after Orr's death. J. D. DOUGLAS

OSIANDER, ANDREAS (1498–1552)
German reformer

Born in Gunzenhausen, Osiander was a clever and able man, but he was also irascible and was constantly involved in personal and theological battles. Having studied at the University of Ingoldstadt, he was ordained to the priesthood in 1520 and taught Hebrew in the Augustinian cloister in Nuremberg. In 1522 he published a new improved edition of the Latin Bible. By this time he had become a Protestant and was made preacher in the St. Lorenz Kirche, from which pulpit he made violent attacks upon the Roman Catholic Church's doctrines. In constant conflict with his colleagues in Nuremberg, he also opposed Luther at the meeting of the Protestant princes at Schmalkald (1526). However, at the Colloquy of Marburg (1529) he supported Luther against Zwingli, and at the Diet of Augsburg (1530) he advocated the Lutheran position. At the conference in Worms (1540) he met Calvin, who did not approve of his bad manners.

Osiander had gained a reputation as a mathematician and was invited by Copernicus to check his mathematics in his forthcoming book on astronomy in which he set forth a theory of a solar-centered universe. Osiander agreed, but secretly added a preface in which he stated that Copernicus's views were purely hypothetical and presented for discussion. Copernicus never knew of this, for he died just as the book came off the press.

Meanwhile, Osiander had become strongly anti-Zwinglian, which caused him some trouble. He was finally forced to leave Nuremberg by the Augsburg Interim (1548). He then went to Königsberg in Prussia, where he held a pastorate, but was soon in trouble as he attacked Melanchthon over the doctrine of forensic justification. While he accepted the doctrine of justification by faith alone, he held that the believer also partook of the divine nature mystically. This view was opposed by Lutherans outside Prussia and by Reformed theologians such as John Calvin. While carrying on this controversy, he also prepared the Brandenburg-Nuremberg Church Orders, containing sermons on Luther's catechism later used by Archbishop Cranmer in his own catechism (1548). The controversy over justification, however, continued and Osiander died in the midst of it. His views were rejected in Article III of the Formula of Concord (1577). W. S. REID

OTTO I (912–973)
Holy Roman Emperor, 962–973

Son of Henry I of the Saxon dynasty, Otto was elected king of Germany on his father's death in 936. His first years provoked much conflict with rebellious nobles, including Henry, a younger brother. But eventually relatives of Otto took over most of Germany's estates. Such supremacy established, Otto began to extend his rule and influence to surrounding regions. Success attended such conquests, and in 962 Pope John XII crowned Otto the new Roman emperor. As distinguished from the original Roman Empire, and Charlemagne's dominions, Otto's kingdom came to be called the Holy Roman Empire.

It was first and foremost military conquest that created Otto's empire. To the east, nobles devoted to Otto campaigned for years beyond the Elbe River. The founding of the Magdeburg monastery (937) and the Brandenburg bishopric (948) climaxed the general subjugation of this territory. By 950, after some initial losses, Otto brought the prince of Bohemia under submission. And momentously, in 955, Germany's forces won victories over both the Slavs and the Magyars. Further, while active in the east, Otto also extended his power to the far north. This was made concrete through establishment of several new bishoprics in Denmark. As for the west, Otto repulsed France's attempts to claim Lorraine, while simultaneously securing ascendancy in Burgundy. The latter resulted mainly from Otto's marriage to Adelaide, a Burgundian princess, whom in 951 he freed from Berengar's Italian imprisonment. (Otto's first wife, Eadgyth, died in 946.) Now increasingly driven by his empire's prospects, Otto again pressed into Italian territory in 960. Once again Berengar, who was harassing Pope John XII, was encountered and defeated. Thus in 962, the pope crowned Otto as emperor and also agreed to a treaty specifying their respective powers.

Like the Carolingian Empire before it, the Holy Roman Empire arose also from the creation of an integral Church-state unity. This began with Otto's reconstruction of Germany as a so-called Reich, or closely conjoined Church-state entity. And as he expanded his rule, Otto settled his conquests around new monasteries and bishop-

rics, these forming the main centers of government and society. In Otto's eyes, the treaty had exchanged papal entitlement to certain lands for an imperial right to ratify papal elections. Hence, in 963, when John XII consorted with Berengar, Otto secured the pope's deposition. And the next two popes, Leo VIII and John XIII, gained election through the emperor's influence. Most of Otto's time between 963 and 972 was spent acquiring further hegemony in Italy. In 972, the emperor's son and heir, the future Otto II, married Theophano, a Byzantine princess. This cemented agreeable relations with the Eastern empire for years to come. In 973, on his final return to Germany, Otto held a grand assembly and died shortly thereafter. Besides its political and religious consolidation, Otto's time saw some cultural resurgence, the Ottonian Renaissance, develop. Variously expanding or contracting in size and power, the Holy Roman Empire continued as a major western European political entity through the Middle Ages. It was important also in the Reformation era, and its final decline did not come until the early nineteenth century.

Many original sources depicting Otto I's life and rule are reproduced in the *Monumenta Germaniae Historica*. Gunter's *Kaiser Otto der Grosse* lists other relevant materials. K. J. BRYER

OTTO, RUDOLPH (1869–1937)
German theologian

Born in Hanover, he was educated at Erlangen and Göttingen. He then taught theology at Göttingen (1904–1914), at Breslau (1914–1917), and at Marburg (1917–1937). Otto is best known for his discussion of religious feeling and religious knowledge. These topics were treated in a series of works that culminated in *The Idea of the Holy* (1917).

In his earliest work Otto discussed the relation of religion to naturalism. Naturalism, which represents the philosophical position associated with modern science, attempts to explain everything in terms of mechanical laws and so eliminates the mystery essential to religion. Religion makes claims that are truths, not just metaphors, but these truths cannot be derived from the naturalist's view of nature. Religious claims differ in kind from those of science and common sense. They have their own ground in the heart and conscience. Consequently, science does not conflict with religious claims nor can it judge their value.

In *The Idea of the Holy*, Otto described religious feelings. He distinguished two aspects: a feeling of religious dread and of religious fascination. A close parallel to religious dread is the terror one may experience from a ghost story. The feeling of fascination creates both a desire to approach the object and a feeling that one has no value compared to the religious object. Thus in religious experience there is a mystery that evokes both fascination and awe.

Religious feelings were called "numinous feelings" by Otto, because their object is the *numen*, that is, the divine. Through these feelings one receives both a concept and the object to which the concept applies. When the concept of the numinous is united with goodness, completeness, necessity, and substantiality, one has the "complex category of the 'holy' itself." Love and similar concepts apply both in ordinary situations and to the numen, but their form differs in the two cases. In ordinary situations they are limited in scope, but with the numen they apply absolutely, without any limit. A. Vos

OWEN, JAMES (1654–1706)
Influential Nonconformist minister

James, the second son of John Owen, received his early education under a Quaker, James Picton, at Carmarthen and later studied philosophy at Brynllywarch. He was converted at age thirteen after listening to a Nonconformist minister preach on Malachi 4:1.

Owen lived in a time of religious turmoil caused by conflict between the established Church of England and Nonconformists (or dissenters), who objected to official teachings and practices. He became convinced of the truth of the Nonconformist position at an early age. His first years of preaching, as an assistant to Stephen Hughes at Swansea, brought him into frequent conflict with the ecclesiastical courts, and he was forced to move for safety's sake to North Wales. In 1676 he was given charge of a small dissenting congregation at Oswestry and also became a personal chaplain to Mrs. Baker in the nearby town of Swiney. Thirteen years later he started a dissenting academy in Oswestry for the purpose of training students from the ministry. In 1700 he moved to Shrewsbury, where he continued the work of the academy and served as a cominister, with Francis Tallents, of the High Street Chapel.

Owen was widely respected as a church leader, scholar, and tutor. He debated with William Lloyd (1681) on ordination and published a work, *A Plea for Scripture Ordination* (1694), arguing for the right to ordain presbyters without diocesan bishops. He published other works in English and Welsh. The best known are *Moderation, a Virtue* (1703) and *Moderation, Still a Virtue* (1704). R. HESSELGRAVE

OWEN, JOHN (1616–1683)
Leading theologian of the Congregational churches

Born at Stadhampton, Oxfordshire, Owen was educated at Queen's College, Oxford, where he studied classics and theology and was ordained. Because of the "high-church" innovations introduced by Archbishop William Laud, he left the university to be a chaplain to the family of a noble lord. His first parish was at Fordham in Essex, to which he went while the nation was involved in civil war. Here he became convinced that the Congregational way was the scriptural form of church government. In his next charge, the parish of Coggeshall in Essex, he acted both as the pastor of a gathered church and as the minister of the parish. This was possible because the parliament, at war with the king, had removed bishops. In practice, this meant that the parishes could go their own way in worship and organization. Oliver Cromwell liked Owen and took him as his chaplain on his expeditions both to Ireland and Scotland (1649–1651).

Owen's fame was at its height from 1651 to 1660 when he played a prominent part in the religious, political, and academic life of the nation. Appointed dean of Christ Church, Oxford, in 1651, he became also vice-chancellor of the university in 1652, a post he held for five years with great distinction and with a marked impartiality not often found in Puritan divines. This led him also to disagreement, even with Cromwell, over the latter's assumption of the protectorship. Owen retained his deanery until 1659. Shortly after the Restoration of the monarchy in 1660, he moved to London, where he was active in preaching and writing until his death. He declined invitations to the ministry in Boston (1663) and the presidency of Harvard (1670) and chided New England Congregationalists

for intolerance. He turned aside also from high preferment when his influence was acknowledged by governmental attempts to persuade him to relinquish Nonconformity in favor of the established church.

His numerous works include *The Display of Arminianism* (1642); *Eshcol, or Rules of Direction for the Walking of the Saints in Fellowship* (1648), an exposition of Congregational principles; *Salus Electorum, Sanguis Jesu* (1648), another anti-Arminian polemic; *Diatriba de Divina Justitia* (1658), an attack on Socinianism; *Of the Divine Original Authority . . . of the Scriptures* (1659); *Theologoumena Pantodapa* (1661), a history from creation to Reformation; *Animadversions to Fiat Lux* (1662), replying to a Roman Catholic treatise; *Doctrine of Justification by Faith* (1677); and *Exercitationes on the Epistle to the Hebrews* (1668–1684).

J. D. DOUGLAS

P

PACHOMIUS (290–346)

Founder of cenobitic monasticism; one of the greatest of the monastic fathers

Born in Esneh, Egypt, Pachomius was converted from paganism as a young man while serving in the army, because of the love seen in the lives of some Christians with whom he had contact. About 316 he became a solitary at Schenesit under the guidance of the hermit Palaemon. A few years later he founded the first monastery of the full communal life at Tabennisi. Considered a man of true vision, he sought to counteract the possible dangers that are often inherent in monastic living by centering the group on communal love and sharing.

From a small group of adherents there was a steady increase of followers. Along with this growth came a development in Pachomius's view of mortification. He stressed the necessity of complete obedience to superiors, under whom all the work was organized, and also complete community ownership of goods. By the time of his death thousands of monks were involved in his monasteries. Throughout his life his headquarters were at Pebou, at which location there was a meeting of the superiors each Easter and August. The organizational structure resulted in spiritual and economic communion and allowed freedom for greater rigor on the part of the individual monk.

There are six extant biographies of Pachomius by his contemporaries, as well as several of his own instructions to his monks, and instructions and letters to his two successors, Horsiesi (died 368) and Theodore (died 380). To his credit are eleven monasteries—nine for men and two for women—established in the Thebaid. H. W. HOUSE

PADWICK, CONSTANCE EVELYN (1886–1968)

Missionary to the Muslim world; interpreter of Islam to Western Christianity

Born in Sussex, England, Padwick began her missionary career in 1916 in Egypt. There she worked with the Nile Mission Press before joining the Church Missionary Society in 1923. For three decades her work was based in Egypt and Palestine. She worked with Canon Temple Gairdner in Cairo and produced his biography in 1929. She served as secretary for the Central Literature Committee for Moslems, a position that gave her worldwide influence. Forced out of Palestine in 1937, Padwick relocated in the Sudan, where she prepared a text on basic Arabic for the Nuba people.

Padwick's most enduring contribution

was published in 1961, a definitive study on Muslim personal religion entitled *Muslim Devotions*. The book was a compilation of material gathered from twenty years of friendships and travel from Morocco to Singapore. Padwick also wrote a biography of Henry Martyn, pioneer missionary to India and Persia. M. FACKLER

PAISLEY, IAN RICHARD KYLE (born 1926)
British parliamentarian; founder of the Free Presbyterian Church of Ulster

Born in Northern Ireland and ordained at a Baptist service, Paisley began his own denomination in 1951. By 1985 his Free Presbyterian Church (a misleading description unlinked to historic Presbyterianism) had nearly eleven thousand members, with Paisley himself as pastor of its largest congregation, in Belfast—a position he still holds. Strongly pro-British and violently opposed to the unification of Ireland, the Roman Catholic Church, and the World Council of Churches, he has been for more than twenty years a member of the House of Commons (M.P.); and he is one of three Northern Ireland members of the European Parliament, in which he dramatically protested against the pope as guest speaker in 1988. A rousing orator who inspires both fanatical devotion and deep distrust, he is regarded by many as the spokesman for Northern Ireland's Protestants. As a parliamentarian, however, he is credited with having made no distinction in religious affiliation when dealing with constituency matters—an observation that would be superfluous to make anywhere else than in Northern Ireland.
J. D. DOUGLAS

PALESTRINA, GIOVANNI PIERLUIGI SANTI DA (1525–1594)
Italian composer

Born in the city of Palestrina, he became the organist and choirmaster at the cathedral of Palestrina (1544–1551). In 1551 the former bishop of Palestrina became Pope Julius II, who soon sent for the composer to be master of the Capella Juliana, the choir responsible for services at St. Peter's. He composed a mass in the pope's honor, and in 1555 the pope repaid him by making him a member of the pontifical choir.

He served under Pope Marcellus (pope for about four weeks, later in 1555) and then was dismissed by Pope Paul IV, apparently because he was married. He was appointed music director at St. John Lateran (succeeding Orlando di Lasso). He resigned in 1560 and from 1561 was choirmaster at Santa Maria Maggiore.

From 1567 he spent summers in the service of Cardinal Ippolito d'Este at Tivoli and was music master at a new Roman seminary. From 1571 he was again director of the Julian choir at St. Peter's. On the death of his wife in 1580, he decided to become a priest and received the tonsure, but three months later he married a wealthy widow. He took charge of her business and earned enough money to publish his music, and he continued to compose.

He was the most celebrated musician in Rome. In 1578 the title of master of music was bestowed on him at the Vatican Basilica. While he never had the title of head of the papal choir, successive popes evidently considered him to be the official composer for the choir.

The reforms of church music instituted by the Council of Trent forbade the singing of masses whose music was so elaborately polyphonic as to obscure the words and which contained words foreign to the liturgy of the Mass. Palestrina's church works, beginning with the famous *Missa Papae Marcelli* (*Pope Marcellus Mass*, 1560), were in conformity with those decrees. He also produced a "reformed" version of the plainsong of the Mass, published in the "Mediciean" Gradual of 1614, which has been replaced in this century by the Solesmes versions of the medieval chant.

Palestrina composed over ninety musical settings of the Latin Mass, about 250 motets, and other liturgical music (lamentations, magnificats, litanies, and psalms), and a number of sacred madrigals (in Italian) and secular madrigals. A study of Palestrina's musical style by J. J. Fux, called *Gradus ad*

Parnassum (*Steps to Parnassus*, 1725), formed the basis for modern study of sixteenth-century polyphonic music (especially devotional music). D. HAYES

PALEY, WILLIAM (1743–1805)
English theologian

After graduating from Christ's College, Cambridge, Paley was elected fellow and tutor (1766–1776). His first book, *Principles of Moral and Political Philosophy* (1785), was based on his Cambridge ethics lectures and expounded a form of utilitarianism that anticipated Jeremy Bentham. The work quickly became a popular standard textbook, with a reputation that exceeded its true value. It expounded the dictum "Whatever is expedient is right," in terms of a strict theological orthodoxy. *Horae Paulinae* (1790) was his ablest and only really original work. In it he demonstrated the historicity of the New Testament by pointing out undesigned coincidences between Acts and the Pauline letters. Paley's famous book *A View of the Evidences of Christianity* (1794) was written to defend the faith against such critics as David Hume and Edward Gibbon. Paley argued that miracles, supported by the evidence of faithful witnesses, attest the truth of the divine revelation in Jesus Christ. Paley was archdeacon of Carlisle from 1782 until his death. N. HILLYER

PALLADIUS, PEDER (1503–1560)
Danish reformer; Bible translator

Palladius studied at Wittenberg (1531–1537), where he was influenced profoundly by the German reformers Philip Melanchthon (1497–1560) and Johann Bugenhagen (1485–1558). Upon the recommendation of Bugenhagen, Palladius was chosen to be the first Protestant bishop of Zealand, Denmark's largest diocese. In 1538 he was appointed also to the chair of theology at the University of Copenhagen. Palladius helped shape the Danish Lutheran Church through the exercise of his exceptional gifts as a theologian, administrator, and eloquent preacher. He also penned several founda-

tional books. His *Book of Visitations* applied evangelical teaching to Protestant parish ministries. In 1556 his *Service Book* provided a liturgy for Lutheran worship in Danish. Palladius also collaborated with others to translate a Danish Bible by 1550. W. A. DETZLER

PAMMACHIUS (c. 340–c. 410)
A Roman senator of noble origin; friend of Jerome

Several of Jerome's letters discussing theological topics were addressed to Pammachius. A letter Augustine wrote him is extant. He married Paulina, daughter of Jerome's friend Paula. After she died near the end of the century, Pammachius devoted himself to a life of religion and charity. His wealth paid for the erection of a hospice at Ostia and may have led to the founding of the church of Saints John and Paul on the Coelian. He died just before the sack of Rome by Alaric. A. CABANISS

PAMPHILUS (c. 250–310)
Christian martyr

Pamphilus was born in Berytus (modern Beirut) and died in Caesarea in Palestine. He was arrested in 307, held in prison for two years, and decapitated during the persecution of Maximinus Daia. He is best known for his understanding of the theology of Origen and for the support he gave to Origen's views.

He had studied under Pierius, a theologian who became known as Origen the Younger because of his ardent support for Origen. This enthusiasm was passed down to Pamphilus, who reopened the school of Caesarea founded by Origen. Pamphilus reorganized the library at the school of Caesarea and employed a band of copyists to keep the tradition of the school alive.

The only known writing of Pamphilus is his *Apology for Origen*, which was written during his two years in prison. He defends Origen in those areas where accusations had been made against his orthodoxy. R. E. WEBBER

PAPIAS (60–130)

Early church leader of Hierapolis; chronicler of early Christianity

The information we have about Papias and his work was given by Eusebius of Caesarea and Irenaeus of Lyons. Irenaeus stated that Papias had heard the apostle John preach and also knew Polycarp. Eusebius mentioned his *Explanation of the Sayings of the Lord*. In the preface to this work Papias maintains that his primary purpose is to bring forth a truthful record of a collection of the words and deeds of the Apostles that were told to him by a presbyter. Irenaeus understood him to be alluding to the apostle John, but Eusebius contended that he referred to two Johns, one who was the apostle and the other who was the companion of Aristion.

Papias claimed that Mark, the Evangelist, who had never heard Christ, was the interpreter of Peter, and that he carefully gave an account of everything he remembered from the preaching of Peter. The statement that Matthew wrote down sayings of Jesus in Hebrew was affirmed by Papias. Irenaeus understood this as a reference to Hebraisms in Matthew's Gospel, whereas Origen took this to mean that Matthew originally wrote his Gospel in Hebrew.

The statements of Papias have raised many questions on the formation of the Gospels, a possible Aramaic version of Matthew, the possibility and identity of two Johns, and other problems in the history of the early church. According to tradition, Papias died a martyr. H. W. HOUSE

PARKER, JOSEPH (1830–1902)

English Congregational preacher; writer

Born into a Christian stonemason's family in Northumberland, Parker showed an early aptitude for preaching. Without theological training he went to London in 1852 and was assistant to John Campbell of Whitefield Tabernacle. In 1853 he was called to minister in Banbury, where a larger chapel had to be built to accommodate all who wished to hear him. Similar success attended an eleven-year ministry in Manchester, before he assumed the pastorate of the rundown Poultry Chapel in London in 1869. He so rejuvenated the charge that the outcome was a new three-thousand-seat building opened in 1874 as the City Temple. An evangelical with an impressive pulpit presence and a dramatic delivery, he conducted for over thirty years a Thursday noon service that attracted people of all classes. He was twice chairman of the Congregational Union of England and Wales. His numerous published works included *Hidden Springs* (1864), *Paraclete* (1874), *The Priesthood of Christ* (1876), *The People's Bible* (twenty-five volumes, 1884), the autobiographical *Preacher's Life* (1899), and *Studies in Texts* (six volumes, 1901). J. D. DOUGLAS

PARKER, MATTHEW (1504–1575)

Archbishop of Canterbury

Born in Norwich, Parker was educated at Corpus Christi College, Cambridge. His academic performance was good, and he became a fellow of the college. Ordained in 1527, he was also attracted by the new theology of reformation. After being appointed chaplain to Anne Boleyn, he became master of his college in 1544 and was known as a moderate reformer. During the reign of the Protestant Edward VI (1547–1553), Parker was made dean of Lincoln Cathedral. In this same period, he cultivated a friendship with Martin Bucer, the Strassburg reformer, who was in Cambridge. When Queen Mary came to the throne in 1553, he soon lost all his academic and ecclesiastical positions and had to live in obscurity. However, with the death of Mary and the crowning of Elizabeth (1558), he rose to prominence. Elizabeth appointed him as archbishop of Canterbury (1559). He was duly consecrated to this position by the laying on of the hands of four men who had been bishops in the reign of Edward VI. His main task was to preserve and implement the settlement of religion agreed by Elizabeth and her parliament. This meant he played a major part in the publication of the Bishops' Bible (1568) and the Thirty-nine Articles of Religion (1563, 1571). It also meant that he was not popular with the Puritans, who wanted further reformation of the Church. He disliked controversy and was probably happiest when editing the works of medieval chroniclers such as Matthew of Westminster. His own researches were embodied in a book about the antiquity of the British church and the archbishopric of Canterbury, *De Antiquitate Britannicae Ecclesiae* (1572). P. TOON

PARKER, PETER (1804–1888)
First medical missionary to China

Born near Farmington, Massachusetts, Parker took his A.B. at Yale College in 1831 and then returned for further study and received his B.D. and M.D. in 1834. The American Board of Commissioners for Foreign Missions sent him to Canton before China was officially opened in 1842, and he resided in the foreign factory district. His Ophthalmic Hospital was an immediate success. He was a founder of the China Medical Missionary Society in 1837 and head of its hospital. He was an excellent linguist. He was interpreter for the American diplomatic mission that negotiated a treaty after the Opium War. Henceforth he was engaged in the United States foreign service, devoting his income to his hospital. The American Board objected to his diplomatic work and terminated his service in August of 1847. Parker continued to support his ministry through his part-time diplomatic work, often being the acting commissioner (or head of mission). He was commissioner from 1855 to 1857. Parker will be remembered as the most influential person in introducing Western scientific medicine into China. P. BEAVER

PASCAL, BLAISE (1623–1662)
French mathematician and scientist; Christian apologist

Pascal was born at Clermont-Ferrond, where his father, Etienne, a lawyer, presided over the Court of Aids. When Pascal was three, his mother died, leaving him and two sisters in the care of their father. In 1631 the family moved to Paris, where the elder Pas-

cal could provide better cultural and educational opportunities for his children. Blaise Pascal was extraordinarily precocious, especially in mathematics. By the time he was twelve, he had worked out the equivalent of many of Euclid's geometrical theorems. Subsequently, he made original contributions to geometry and calculus.

The elder Pascal, much interested in the science and arts of his day, had a wide circle of like-minded friends, intellectuals like himself. Blaise Pascal was often present when these eminent men gathered for conversation. In this way Pascal met René Descartes, the noted philosopher, who has been called the father of modern rationalism and whose ideas Pascal was soon to regard as enemies of the Christian faith. At nineteen Pascal invented the first workable calculating machine to help his father complete his burdensome daily reports as a tax collector. The machine was based on a system of rotating discs—the foundation of arithmetical machines until modern times. In physics, "Pascal's law" stated the principle that makes possible all modern hydraulic operations. Some people credit Pascal with having created the first wristwatch and having set up the first bus route in Paris.

In 1646 the entire Pascal family was converted to Jansenism, a reform movement in Roman Catholicism. But Blaise Pascal's devotion to the Christian faith really began with a mystical vision in November 1654. He described the details of his experience on a piece of parchment, which he sewed into the lining of his coat and which was found there at his death. In 1657 Pascal published his *Provincial Letters,* a masterpiece of irony and satire written to support the Jansenists' demand for a reemphasis on Augustine's doctrine of grace within the Catholic church.

Around 1658 Pascal undertook to prepare an *Apology for the Christian Religion.* The work was never completed, for Pascal died at the age of thirty-nine. He left only a series of remarkable notes, first published in 1670, eight years after his death, as *Pensées (Thoughts).* The work is a classic of literature and apologetics. It puts the case for vital Christianity against the rationalism of Descartes and the skepticism of the French writer Montaigne.

Pascal noted that man's need for God is made evident by his misery apart from God, his constant need for diversion, and his resort to the world of the imagination. God can be known through an act of faith, itself given by God. Pascal held that the supporting evidence for the truth of Christianity is overwhelming: fulfilled prophecies, miracles, the witness of history, the self-authentication of Scripture. In spite of the strong external evidences, God is known by the heart. "The heart has its reasons which the reason does not know," wrote Pascal.
P. M. BECHTEL

PASCHAL II (died 1118)
Pope, 1099–1118

Born Ramerius, at Bieda di Galeata (Ravenna), Paschal entered a monastery as a boy and around 1080 was made a cardinal by Gregory VII. In 1099 he succeeded Urban II, who had inaugurated the First Crusade. His most important problem as pope was that of the conflict with civil rulers over the secular investiture of church prelates who held feudal lands. In 1107 the matter was settled in England when Henry II agreed that he would not invest the bishops with the insignia of their spiritual office if they did homage to him for their lands. The same year the pope and Philip I of France also reached an agreement. Philip had been excommunicated in 1100 for an illegal marriage, but absolved in 1104. He agreed to accept a simple oath of fealty from the prelates.

The principal conflict was with the emperors Henry IV and V. Paschal supported Henry V in his rebellion against his father, but found that Henry V was no more inclined to submit to papal dictates than his predecessor. At Sutri, Henry took Paschal prisoner, forcing him to come to an agreement, by which the pope surrendered all crown lands in return for the abolition of investiture. This, however, caused opposition within the German church, resulting in a riot at Henry's coronation (April 13, 1111). Paschal revoked all concessions in 1116, and the controversy was not settled until 1122 in the Council of Worms held by Pope Calixtus II. W. S. REID

PATON, JOHN GIBSON (1824–1907)
Pioneer Presbyterian missionary to the New Hebrides, a group of islands in the southwest Pacific (now Vanuata)

Born at Kirkmahoe, Dumfriesshire (Scotland), Paton was educated in theology and medicine at the University of Glasgow while serving as a city missioner (1847–1856). Ordained in 1858, he sailed for Tanna in the New Hebrides. During his first term of missionary service, he suffered many privations. In 1859 he lost his wife and infant son. Constantly under threat, Paton himself escaped, taking with him only his Bible and some translations. He then traveled widely in Australia and Scotland seeking support for mission work in the New Hebrides. In Scotland the Reformed Presbyterian Church elected him moderator in 1864. After remarriage, he returned in 1866 to the New Hebrides, where he worked successfully for fifteen years on the island of Aniwa.

Paton was a forceful, descriptive speaker and writer. He was an aggressive crusader against the social evils of the white man in the Pacific: the traffic in liquor, in western arms and ammunition, and particularly in laborers, which displaced many islanders and cost many lives. Thus incurring the wrath of his enemies, he became a controversial figure.

Paton is said to have raised the equivalent of more than four hundred thousand dollars for South Pacific missions. His autobiography, edited by his brother, suited the popular Christian market and became a best-seller; the missionary promotional literature of his day probably idealized Paton somewhat. Cambridge University awarded him an honorary D.D., and a fund in Paton's honor was established for New Hebrides missions.
A. R. TIPPETT

PATON, WILLIAM (1886–1943)
British ecumenist and writer

Born in England of Scottish parents, Paton studied at Whitgift School and Pembroke College, Oxford University. He was active in the Student Christian Movement (SCM) and the Student Volunteer Movement, and he attended the World Student Christian Fellowship conference at Istanbul. His first book, *Jesus Christ and the World's Religions*, appeared in 1916. He was ordained in 1917 by the Presbyterian Church of England and went to India for a year of YMCA work with the Army. Paton returned to England to be the SCM's secretary for missions and began his lifelong association with J. H. Oldham. The YMCA called him back to India in 1921 as secretary for student work. He participated in the formation of the International Missionary Council (IMC) at Lake Mohonk in 1921 and then accepted a call to be a secretary of the National Christian Council of India. Paton was next called to Edinburgh House, London, in 1927 as a secretary of the International Missionary Council. He plunged at once into preparation for the Jerusalem Conference of the IMC in 1928. In the IMC, he had responsibility for Indian and Muslim affairs especially. He was editor of the *International Review of Missions*. Paton also worked closely with the Committee on the Christian Approach to the Jews and with the Lindsay Commission on Christian Higher Education in India.

Paton and Oldham were deeply involved in the planning and execution of the two 1937 ecumenical conferences: The Oxford Life and Work Conference on "Church, Community, and State" and the Faith and Order Conference at Edinburgh. Paton wrote for the former the book *Christianity in the Eastern Conflicts*. It was decided at those two conferences to merge into the World Council of Churches, and a provisional committee was organized. Paton was made a secretary, with the IMC paying his salary, on a part-time basis. He was largely responsible for the preparation for the Madras Conference of 1938. In 1939 the University of Edinburgh bestowed the D.D. degree on him in recognition of his missionary statesman-

ship. World War II brought Paton especially heavy responsibilities for prisoners of war and refugees and for religious broadcasting. He was involved in the organization of the British Council of Churches and in the Religion and Life Weeks. Other responsibilities were peace efforts and orphaned missions. It is said that overwork contributed to his death, which occurred after what should have been a routine operation. P. BEAVER

PATRICK (c. 390–c. 461)
Chief apostle of Ireland

Born at Ailclyde, now Dumbarton, Patrick was the son of a deacon named Calpurnius. At age sixteen he was captured in a raid by Irish pirates and sold to Milchu, an Antrim chieftain. After six years as a slave he escaped to Gaul, where he became a monk, first under Martin of Tours and later at Lerins. After returning to his family in Britain, he was called in a vision to preach to the heathen Irish. He was made a bishop and landed at Wicklow with a missionary party about 431. But the hostile reception he received drove him up the east coast to Strangford Lough. There he set his base until he had converted all the Ulstermen to Christianity. Among his converts was his old master Milchu. Patrick took advantage of the spirit of clanship by first winning chiefs for Christ and then using their influence to reach their people. Subsequently, he made missionary journeys throughout Ireland. After Patrick had converted Ireland, it became a center of Christian influence throughout Europe. He died at Saulpatrick about 461, though the exact date is much debated. His burial place at Armagh soon attracted pilgrims to the spot.

Patrick's only authentic literary remains are the *Confessions*, written to answer foes who attacked him over a moral lapse when he was fifteen, and a letter addressed to the Christian subjects of the tyrant Coroticus, a British chieftain, in which Patrick protested against the ill-treatment of some Irish Christians he had carried off as slaves. Later versions of these writings were elaborated by others to bring the works more in line with the popular life of the apostle, according to which, legendary foreign travels delayed his arrival in Ireland until he was sixty. Irish Christians felt that the culture and learning of Augustine of Canterbury and other Roman missionaries made the Irish saint appear too simple and crude. So, national pride ascribed to Patrick a learning he never claimed and a Roman mission of which he knew nothing, protracted his stay in Gaul, and extended his travels to Italy. Of the many legends about Patrick the best known is the story of his expelling snakes from Ireland. His being called a saint also comes from popular tradition; he was never formally canonized at Rome. N. HILLYER

PATTESON, JOHN COLERIDGE
(1827–1871)
First bishop of Melanesia

Born in London, educated at Oxford, Patteson joined Selwyn in the New Zealand mission in 1853. In 1861 Selwyn consecrated him the first bishop of Melanesia—an ideal choice because Patteson had a tremendous gift for languages and navigational skill.

Patteson founded a training institution at Norfolk Island, where he transported island youths for education in the Christian way of life. Many returned to their homes to become evangelists. They used Mota, not English, as the "lingua franca." Patteson's linguistic skill is still manifest in the indigenous liturgy and catechism, for which he sought patiently the best Melanesian terms.

His missionary policy, spoken of as the "Melanesian ethos," preserved many cultural features, like art forms and skills; required a large team of catechists; demanded linguistic proficiency from the missionaries; and produced some good missionary anthropologists, like Codrington and Fox.

The bishop's tragic death resulted directly from the notorious labor trade. It was a retaliatory murder against white traders who took natives to labor in Austrailia. The symbols of that event have been woven into the ecclesiastical art of the island church. In Sydney, Patteson's eulogy was delivered by

Lorimer Fison (who, more than anyone, fought the labor trade) and was published in the *Sydney Morning Herald*. A. R. TIPPETT

PAUL III (1468–1549)
Pope, 1534–1549

Born Alessandro Farnese, Paul was son of an important Italian family. He received a broad humanist education in Rome and Florence. At a young age, he entered the papal court and rose rapidly. In 1493 he was appointed a cardinal deacon, probably due to family influences. However, an eventual election as the College of Cardinals' dean showed his exceptional talents, especially in diplomatic matters. Before 1519, when he finally attained priestly ordination, Paul led a sexually profligate life. He had at least four illegitimate children. His large number of important benefices also allowed him a very lavish material existence. Paul was known also for his unrestrained nepotism. Illustrated in the two adolescent nephews he made cardinals, this penchant continued even while he was pope.

Paul's tenure as pope raggedly combined an indulgence of Renaissance wealth and excess with efforts to bring reformation to the Church. Amid his glaring weaknesses, Paul was a figure of high intelligence and vision, and his papacy provided the Church with vast material and structural improvements. He was a very eminent papal patron of scholarship and the arts. His support brought many of the best theologians to Rome's universities and numbers of valuable manuscripts to the Vatican Library. He commissioned innumerable art projects, such as works by Michelangelo and Titian, some of them among history's greatest pieces. Under Paul, much progress also took place in the rebuilding of St. Peter's Cathedral. His spending included great sums for the renovation of Rome's buildings and roads. Moreover, both in Rome and the Church at large, Paul brought about many far-reaching organizational changes. He initiated improvements, for example, in the papal curia and College of Cardinals, this mainly by elevating outstanding figures such as Reginald Pole, Gasparo Contarini, Giampietro Canaffa (later Paul IV), and Giovanni Morone. In 1540, it was also Paul's letter, *Regimini militantis ecclesiae,* that gave Ignatius Loyola's Society of Jesus its formal beginning. Other reform orders, such as the Ursilines, came into existence by his approval.

Responding to his era's broad-scale upheavals, Paul also sought to lead the movement for basic doctrinal reform. Inadequately conceived and developed, many of these actions were destined to fail from the first. This certainly was true of Paul's cultivation of Charles V. The emperor's conflicts with Francis I and desires for war with Islam completely distracted his dealings with Church dissidents. Similarly inept was Paul's attack on Henry VIII, already precariously balanced between Catholics and Protestants. But there were other actions that seemed promising for authentic reformation. This appeared true of *Concilium de emendenda ecclesia,* the broad-ranging report of Paul's main commission on reform. Although criticized by Protestants, the report set in motion various Catholic-Protestant colloquies, including in 1541 the last and most famous, the Conference of Ratisbon (Germany), called by Charles V. Tragically, while its leaders—Catholics Eck, Pflug, Gropper; Protestants Melanchthon, Bucer, Pistorius—gained basic agreement on most issues (including believers' justification), the Ratisbon Conference's results were totally destroyed by Martin Luther's hostility and opposition. Thus was ruined what proved to be Catholics' and Protestants' last hope for unity. Results, however, did accompany what is deservedly Paul's most acclaimed action: his call for an ecumenical church council. This call bore fruit in 1545 at the opening sessions of the Council of Trent. As it went on, the Council of Trent had enormous problems, and Paul died before its end in 1563.

Original sources of information on Paul III are listed in Pastor's *History of the Popes* (volumes eleven and twelve). Friedensburg's *Karl V* and *Papat Paul III* provide other important materials. K. J. BRYER

PAUL VI (1897–1978)
Pope, 1963–1978

Born Giovanni Battista Montini near Brescia, where his wealthy father was editor of a Catholic daily newspaper, Paul received his early education from the Jesuits. At seventeen he went on to the diocesan seminary, but during his training there he lived at home because of his fitful health. Ordained in 1920, he went on for further study at the Gregorian University and the University of Rome. Four years later he entered the Vatican's diplomatic wing; his career flourished especially from 1937 when the future Pope Pius XII promoted him and subsequently (as pope) made him de facto secretary of state.

In 1954 Montini was appointed archbishop of Milan, where he espoused the cause of the workers. Made cardinal in 1958, he was elected to succeed John XXIII as pope in 1963. He continued the latter's Vatican II work by convening sessions two, three, and four. Although Paul VI was conservative in doctrinal matters, his pontificate saw some remarkable changes in Vatican administration and attitudes. The much-criticized Index of prohibited books was at last abolished, as was the rule against meat eating on Fridays. Even more revolutionary, Latin was replaced by other languages in church worship. Paul, on the other hand, rejected the idea of women priests and in two notable encyclicals upheld priestly celibacy (*Sacerdotalis caelibates,* 1967) and the ban on birth control (*Humanae vitae,* 1968). A new permanent Synod of Bishops was set up to advise the pope on a wide variety of topics, including canon law and human rights. The normal retirement age for bishops was decreed to be seventy-five. Paul VI was the first pope since 1809 to travel outside Italy and the first to travel by plane; his destinations took in not only Europe, but also Asia, the Americas, Africa, and Australia. He also improved relations with the Eastern Orthodox Church and in his pastoral capacity visited prisoners and the sick in Rome itself. J. D. DOUGLAS

PAUL, THE APOSTLE (SAUL OF TARSUS) (c. 10–67)

Prominent leader of the first-century church; apostle to the Gentiles; author of thirteen New Testament Epistles

FAMILY AND CULTURAL BACKGROUND

Paul was born a Jew in a family of Pharisees (Acts 23:6) of the tribe of Benjamin (Phil. 3:5) in Tarsus of Cilicia (Acts 9:11; 21:39; 22:3), a center of commerce and learning that embraced the Hellenistic spirit and Roman politics. It was a city of which he could be proud (Acts 21:39). His parents named him Saul after the first king of Israel, who was also a Benjaminite (1 Sam. 11:15; Acts 13:21), but Acts 13:9 notes that he "was also called Paul" (NIV).He uses the Roman name Paul throughout his letters.

From religious parents Paul received knowledge of the Law and Prophets and the Hebrew and Aramaic languages (Acts 21:40; 22:2-3; 23:6; Gal. 1:14; Phil. 3:56). Tarsus, however, was not a Jewish city. Rather it had a Greek character where the Greek language was spoken and Greek literature was cultivated. This accounts for Paul's familiarity with Greek (Acts 21:37), the language of the streets and shops of Tarsus.

Jews were brought to Tarsus, the capital of the Roman province of Cilicia, in 171 B.C. to promote business in the region. At that time Paul's ancestors were probably given Roman citizenship. Paul inherited from his father both Tarsisian and Roman citizenship, which would prove to be of great value to Paul in his later life as he traveled with the gospel through the Roman Empire (Acts 16:37; 22:25-29; 23:27). Paul may have had several brothers and sisters, but Acts 23:16 mentions only one sister whose son performed a lifesaving act for his uncle. Like all Jewish sons Paul called his father "Abba," an Aramaic word Paul later wove into the fabric of the Christian faith as an affectionate and intimate title for God the Father (Rom 8:15; Gal. 4:6).

Paul was a tentmaker (Acts 18:3). He may have learned this trade from his father, or he may have selected it as a means of self-support as was the custom of those in rab-

binical training. Tarsus was well known for the goat's hair cloth called *cilicium*. It was the weaving of this cloth and the fashioning of it into tents, sails, awnings, and cloaks that gave Paul his economic independence during his apostolic ministry (Acts 18:3; 20:34; 28:30; 2 Cor 11:9; 1 Thess. 2:9; 2 Thess. 3:8).

EDUCATION

Although born in Tarsus, Paul testified to the Jews in Jerusalem that he had been "brought up in this city at the feet of Gamaliel" (Acts 22:3). It is not clear when Paul was first brought to Jerusalem, but it is likely that sometime between the ages of thirteen and twenty he began his formal rabbinical studies. His teacher, Gamaliel, was the grandson of Hillel, who began the Pharisaic school whose teachings run through the Talmudical writings to this day. This is the same Gamaliel whose wisdom persuaded the Sanhedrin to spare the lives of Peter and the apostles (Acts 5:33-40). No doubt it was while studying under Gamaliel in Hillel's school that Paul began to advance in Judaism beyond many Jews of his own age and became extremely zealous for the traditions of his fathers (Gal. 1:14). Perhaps then also Paul began to experience the struggles with the law he would later describe in Romans chapter 7.

While Paul was studying the Jewish law in Jerusalem, Jesus was working as a carpenter in Nazareth. Then Jesus gathered the disciples who would one day be Paul's fellow workers in the gospel, fulfilled his ministry, and accomplished redemption on the cross of Calvary (A.D. 30). Christ's resurrection gave birth to the church, which was baptized in the Holy Spirit at the feast of Pentecost in Jerusalem.

THE PERSECUTOR

Shortly after these world-changing events, the members of certain synagogues in Jerusalem, including the Cilician synagogue, that of Paul's native land (Acts 6:9), could not withstand the wisdom and spirit (Acts 6:10) of a member of the church in Jerusalem named Stephen (Acts 6:5, 8). They accused him of blasphemy before the Sanhedrin (Acts 6:11-15) and after his eloquent defense (Acts 7:1-53) dragged him out of the city, where he was stoned to death, thereby becoming the first Christian martyr. The record does not fully reveal the role Paul played in these proceedings, but we know that he was present and prominent because the witnesses against Stephen, who were required to throw the first stones in the execution, "laid their clothes at the feet of a young man called Saul" (Acts 7:58, NIV).

At Stephen's trial, Paul heard Stephen's historical method of defense, and he later used it himself at Antioch of Pisidia (Acts 13:16-41). He witnessed the man with the face of an angel (Acts 6:15), full of the Holy Spirit, looking above and proclaiming "the heavens opened, and the Son of man standing on the right hand of God" (Acts 7:56). Later Paul would write to the Colossians to "seek those things which are above, where Christ sitteth at the right hand of God" (Col. 3:1). Stephen's death initiated the events that would culminate in Paul's conversion and commission as the apostle to the Gentiles. But at the time, "Saul was consenting unto his death" (Acts 8:1).

Paul became a leader of the oppressors of the church. He breathed threats and murder against the disciples of the Lord (Acts 9:1) and "persecuted the church of God, and wasted it" (Gal. 1:13), "binding and delivering into prisons both men and women" (Acts 22:4), "and being exceedingly mad against them, I persecuted them even unto strange cities" (Acts 26:10-11).

CONVERSION AND CALLING

One of these foreign cities was Damascus. Paul had obtained letters from the high priest in Jerusalem to the synagogues in Damascus authorizing him to arrest the believers there and bring them to Jerusalem for trial (Acts 9:1-2). Paul traveled to Damascus for this purpose. Then on the outskirts of the city came the event that was to transform this law-keeping persecutor of Jesus Christ and blasphemous destroyer of the infant church into the chief propagator of the gospel of grace and master builder of the church of God (1 Tim. 1:13; 1 Cor. 3:10). This was

the occasion of Paul's conversion (c. 31–33). It was of such revolutionary and lasting importance that three detailed accounts of it are given in the New Testament (Acts 9:1-19; 22:1-21; 26:1-23), and many references are given to it in Paul's own writing (1 Cor. 9:1; 15:8; Gal. 1:15-16; Eph. 3:3; Phil. 3:12).

At that time a light from heaven, brighter than the midday sun shone around Paul and his traveling companions, and they fell to the ground (Acts 26:13-14). Only Paul, however, heard the voice of Jesus instruct him in his commission as a minister and witness to the Gentiles (Acts 26:14-18). Temporarily blinded, Paul was led into Damascus (Acts 9:8). There, the disciple Ananias and the Christian community forgave Paul, baptized him, and helped him through the bewildering event of his conversion (Acts 9:10-22). After a short time with the church there, Paul was threatened with death by the Jews to whom he preached Jesus (Acts 9:20-22) but was protected by the believers and ingeniously delivered from his persecutors (Acts 9:23-25).

PREPARATION

Then began a period of preparation, which lasted about thirteen years. During this time, Paul first was in the desert of Arabia for three years. Here was his opportunity to pray and reflect on Stephen's defense to the Sanhedrin, the momentous significance of his conversion, the vision he received of Jesus Christ, and the meaning of all this in the light of Jewish theology. Following this Paul returned to Damascus and then visited Peter in Jerusalem for fifteen days (Gal. 1:17-18).

At first the disciples in Jerusalem were afraid of him, not believing that he was also a disciple of Jesus (Acts 9:26), but he was championed by Barnabas and thus accepted by the believers in Jerusalem (Acts 9:27-28). While there, Paul may have heard the oral gospel, a summary of the words and deeds of Jesus, handed down to all converts. This would have included the institution of the Lord's Supper (1 Cor. 11:23-25), specific words of the Lord (Acts 20:35; 1 Cor. 7:10; 9:14), the appearances of the resurrected

Christ (1 Cor. 15:3-8), and the spirit and character of Jesus (2 Cor. 10:1; Phil. 2:5-8). Paul also preached in Jerusalem, perhaps in the same synagogues in which he had heard Stephen; but when his life was again threatened by the Jews, the believers sent him away to Tarsus (Acts 9:29-30; Gal. 1:21).

The end of Paul's preparation came when Barnabas went to Tarsus to look for him and bring him to Antioch. By this time Paul had lived for ten years in Cilicia. Since his conversion, before being sent to Tarsus, he had proclaimed Jesus (Acts 9:20), speaking boldly in the name of the Lord (Acts 9:27). There is no reason to think he did otherwise while living among the Gentiles in Cilicia. In fact, his work may have been so effective that he began to attract attention in Antioch. During these years, Paul probably underwent many of the sufferings mentioned in 2 Corinthians 11:24-26. Several scholars think that the ecstatic experience mentioned in 2 Corinthians 12:1-9, with its accompanying thorn in the flesh, also took place before he came to Antioch.

SENT OUT FROM ANTIOCH

The church in Antioch had its origins in the persecution fomented by Paul after the death of Stephen (Acts 11:19). Until they arrived in Antioch, the scattered believers had only spoken the word to Jews (Acts 11:19). It was here that the Gentiles first heard the Good News (Acts 11:20), and many became believers (Acts 11:21). It is fitting that Paul, the apostle to the Gentiles (Rom. 11:13; Acts 22:21), who was as yet unknown by sight to the churches of Judea (Gal. 1:22), should appear in Antioch to formally begin the ministry to which he was called (Acts 26:17-18).

Barnabas and Paul stayed with the church in Antioch for a year. Their work there was so blessed that a new name, "Christian," was coined to distinguish the believers in Antioch from Gentiles and Jews (Acts 11:26). Hearing of a famine in Judea, the disciples in Antioch determined to send relief to the believers in Judea and did so by Barnabas and Paul (Acts 11:30). Such a gift displayed to the Jewish churches the potency of the

gospel among the Gentiles. Their mission complete, Barnabas and Paul returned to Antioch with John Mark (Acts 12:25), Barnabas's cousin (Col. 4:10).

Beginning from the day of Pentecost the work in the gospel had been casual and incidental. Contacts were made in the homes, the marketplace, the streets, synagogues, highways, etc. (Acts 3:1; 5:12, 42; 8:26-29; 10:22). But in Antioch, the Holy Spirit initiated a determined effort to evangelize a section of the Roman Empire (Acts 13:1-3). By the Holy Spirit's instructions, the church separated Barnabas and Paul for this work. With the prayers and encouragement of this church and with John Mark as their assistant, Barnabas and Paul, sent out by the Holy Spirit, sailed for Cyprus (Acts 13:4).

TRAVEL WITH BARNABAS

Arriving in Salamis, they preached in the synagogues as they traveled the length of the island to Paphos (Acts 13:5-6). There the Roman proconsul, Sergius Paulus, wanted to hear the word of God (Acts 13:7). A magician named Elymas Bar-Jesus tried to prevent the proconsul from believing but was stricken with temporary blindness by Paul's command (Acts 13:8-11). This was the first manifestation in Paul of the signs of an apostle (2 Cor. 12:12). From then on the name Paul, not Saul, is used in Luke's record of the Acts of the Apostles (Acts 13:9), and Paul replaced Barnabas as the leader of the party. So "Paul and his company" set sail from Paphos and arrived in Perga of Pamphylia (Acts 13:13). John Mark deserted them at Perga and returned to his home in Jerusalem (Acts 13:13). This caused discord (Acts 15:38), but Paul and Mark were later reconciled (Col. 4:10; 2 Tim. 4:11).

Paul's travels with the gospel now continued on the Asia Minor mainland specifically in the southern portion of the Roman province of Galatia, the areas of Pamphylia, Pisidia, and Lycaonia. The coastal area where the party landed is a hot malarial region. It is thought that Paul contracted malaria there and so traveled inland through the mountains to the four-thousand-foot-high tablelands. Such a journey would have been full of dangerous rivers and bandits (2 Cor. 11:26), but Paul was well cared for by the Galatian highlanders when he arrived (Gal. 4:13-15) and was rewarded with a warm reception to his message (Acts 13:48-49).

Paul and Barnabas were asked to speak at the synagogue of Antioch in Pisidia (Acts 13:15), and Paul delivered a discourse full of the characteristics of the gospel he would later record in his letters to the churches (Acts 13:16-41). He was invited to speak the next week (Acts 13:42) and "almost the whole city gathered together to hear the word of God" (Acts 13:44, RSV). This stirred up jealousy in the Jews who opposed Paul's words (Acts 13:45), causing the apostles' dramatic turn to the Gentiles (Acts 13:46-47). Many Gentiles in Antioch believed and spread the word throughout the region, but Paul and Barnabas were forced out and went to Iconium in Lycaonia (Acts 13:48-51).

The success in Antioch was duplicated in Iconium as was the Jews' opposition (Acts 14:1), and the apostles fled from the threat of a stoning to Lystra and Derbe in Lycaonia (Acts 14:5-6). In Lystra the signs of an apostle were again seen when Paul healed a man who had been crippled since birth (Acts 14:8-10). The idolatrous citizens of the town, however, primed by the popular belief that Jupiter, accompanied by Mercury, had once visited their region, worshiped Paul and Barnabas as these deities (Acts 14:11-13). Even the convincing words of Paul, whom they mistook for Mercury, hardly restrained the crowds from offering a sacrifice (Acts 14:14-18).

It was in Lystra that Paul was first given a taste of the same medicine he had once administered to Christians. The Jews stoned him, dragged him out of the city, and left him for dead (Acts 14:19). Timothy (Acts 16:1-3) may have been among the new disciples surrounding Paul as he lay outside the gate (Acts 14:20). Timothy was Paul's son in the faith (1 Tim. 1:2; 1 Cor. 4:17), eyewitness to his suffering (2 Tim. 3:10-11), faithful companion, and fellow worker (Acts 19:22; 20:4; Rom. 16:21; 1 Thess. 3:2). The next day Barnabas and Paul went on to Derbe (Acts 14:20).

After making many disciples in Derbe the apostles retraced their steps through Lystra, Iconium, and Antioch of Pisidia, strengthening and encouraging the new believers and appointing elders in each church (Acts 14:21-23). Arriving again in Perga, they sailed back to Antioch, where they reported to the church the wonderful news that God had opened a door of faith for the Gentiles (Acts 14:25-27).

THE COUNCIL OF JERUSALEM
The Jews, who had dogged the steps of Paul and Barnabas throughout Galatia, followed on their heels to bewitch the Gentiles there, convincing them to desert the grace of Christ and submit to the Jewish law (Gal. 1:6; 3:1). Shortly after the apostles' return to Antioch, Judaizers came from Judea to Antioch, teaching salvation by the law (Acts 15:1). This began the war against the gospel of grace, which Paul preached.

The church in Antioch sent Paul, Barnabas, and others to Jerusalem to settle the controversy of the law versus grace with the apostles and elders there (A.D. 49, Acts 15:2). Along the way to Jerusalem they spread the news of the conversion of the Gentiles. This brought great joy to the believers (Acts 15:3). Such joy was not shared by some in Jerusalem, who in the first meeting of the council said that the Gentiles should be ordered "to keep the law of Moses" (Acts 15:5).

After this meeting, Paul and Barnabas met privately with Peter, John, and James (Gal. 2:1-10) and explained the gospel they had been preaching to the Gentiles. These three leaders of the church in Jerusalem saw the grace that had been given to Paul to bring the gospel to the Gentiles and extended to him the "right hand of fellowship." This private meeting seems to have decided the question of compliance to the Jewish law because in the next general meeting Peter said, "We believe that we shall be saved through the grace of the Lord Jesus" (Acts 15:11, RSV), and James reached the decision that "we should not trouble those of the Gentiles who turn to God" (Acts 15:19, RSV). This was a great victory for Paul and

Barnabas, and the news was received with rejoicing by the church in Antioch (Acts 15:30-35).

Later Peter visited Antioch and freely associated with the Gentile believers as he had timidly done in Cornelius's house (Acts 10:28). This continued until "certain men came from James." Their presence brought fear to Peter, clouding the light of the gospel of grace, and causing him to separate himself from the Gentiles. Peter's action influenced others, including Barnabas, to do the same (Gal. 2:12-13, RSV). Paul rose to the challenge of this serious crisis, confronted Peter publicly, and charged him with Judaizing and hypocrisy (Gal. 2:14). Paul won the battle and rescued Peter and Barnabas with eloquent words on justification by faith (Gal. 2:15-21), but the Judaizers had resumed their war. From this time on they did not rest; rather they tormented and persecuted Paul all over the world, but the apostle did not submit to them for a moment. He was engaged in the fight of his life "that the truth of the gospel might remain with you" (Gal.2:5, NIV).

FURTHER TRAVEL

Paul desired to visit the new believers and see how they were doing and proposed to Barnabas that they return to the cities where they proclaimed the word of the Lord (Acts 15:36). Barnabas wanted to take John Mark with them, but Paul would not take him since he had deserted them during their earlier journey (Acts 13:13). This sharp disagreement ended Barnabas's association with Paul (Acts 15:37-39). Silas, a leader among the brothers in Jerusalem (Acts 15:22), accompanied Paul as he set out by land through Syria and Cilicia strengthening the churches (Acts 15:40-41).

Beginning from Derbe in Galatia, Paul and Silas revisited the churches Paul had established with Barnabas. While in Lystra they were joined by Timothy (Acts 16:1-3). The apostles delivered to these young churches the letter drafted by the elders and apostles in Jerusalem concerning the observance of the law (Acts 15:23-29), thus

strengthening and increasing them (Acts 16:4-5).

It is likely that Ephesus, a major city in the Roman province of Asia, was the party's main objective for the advancement of the gospel, but they were "forbidden by the Holy Spirit to speak the word in Asia" (Acts 16:6, RSV). Then they attempted to turn north and enter the region of Bythinia, "but the Spirit of Jesus did not allow them" (Acts 16:7, RSV). In this way they were forced by God to continue straight westward to Troas on the Aegean Sea where Luke joined them ("we" in Acts 16:10), and Paul had a vision in which he was called out of Asia into Macedonia (Acts 16:8-9). Paul and his party immediately crossed by boat into Europe (Acts 16:11) where they carried the gospel to Philippi, Thessalonica, Beroea, Athens, and Corinth.

Philippi was a Roman colony and military outpost where there were few Jews, so Paul went to a place by the river where the local Jews prayed. He spoke to some women there, notably Lydia, who believed and with her household was baptized (Acts 16:12-15), beginning the first church in Europe. Paul cast a spirit of divination out of a girl in Philippi, and as a result he and Silas were jailed (Acts 16:16-24). The events of their night in jail made the jailer a believer in God (Acts 16:25-34), and he and his family were added to the church in Philippi, which met in Lydia's home (Acts 16:40). When Paul disclosed his Roman citizenship he was released and was asked to leave the city (Acts 16:35-39).

At Thessalonica the Jews, aroused to jealousy by the success of Paul's gospel message, raised a mob to search for the apostles. They complained to the city authorities that the people "who have turned the world upside down have come here also" and accused the apostles of "saying that there is another king [besides Caesar], Jesus" (Acts 17:5-7, RSV).

Paul and Silas quickly left Thessalonica by night and arrived in Beroea, a city thereafter distinguished by its citizens who eagerly and thoughtfully received the gospel (Acts 17:10-12). The Thessalonian Jews did not rest, but trailed Paul to Beroea to incite the crowds. The believers then sent Paul away to Athens, while Silas and Timothy stayed behind (Acts 17:13-15).

The Athenians called Paul a babbler but let him air his views before the Areopagus. Paul's speech there was alive with his broad knowledge. He alluded to Graeco-Roman philosophy (Acts 17:27), poetry (Acts 17:28), sculpture (Acts 17:25, 29), architecture (Acts 17:24), and religion while proclaiming the existence of an "unknown god" (Acts 17:23), but he was rudely cut short by scoffing and indifference when he mentioned the Resurrection (Acts 17:32). Paul's words delighted the minds of many but influenced the wills of few, so when he arrived in Corinth he determined not to proclaim the mystery of God in lofty words of wisdom so that the believers' faith would not rest on human wisdom but on the power of God (1 Cor 2:1-5).

In Corinth Paul met Aquila and Priscilla (Acts 18:2-3), Roman Jews with whom he lived and worked as a tentmaker and who would become prominent among the churches (Acts 18:26; Rom. 16:3; 1 Cor. 16:19; 2 Tim. 4:19). He stayed in Corinth eighteen months from A.D. 50 to 51 raising up a church (Acts 18:11) on the strength of a vision from God (Acts 18:9-10) and in spite of the attacks of the Jews (Acts 18:12-17). Paul wrote the first and second letters to the Thessalonians from Corinth to establish the believers in a holy, industrious life (1 Thess. 3:13; 5:23; 2 Thess. 3:7-12) in hope of the second coming of Jesus Christ (1 Thess. 4:15-18; 2 Thess. 2:1ff).

Accompanied by Priscilla and Aquila, Paul sailed from Corinth for Syria. He left his fellow workers in Ephesus, sailed to Caesarea, briefly visited Jerusalem, and returned to Antioch (Acts 18:18-22). Paul stayed "some time" in Antioch but did not remain absent from the field of his labors for long. Alone he departed from Antioch, went from place to place in Galatia and Phrygia strengthening all the disciples, and eventually arrived in Ephesus (Acts 18:23; 19:1).

LABOR IN THE GOSPEL

Apollos ministered in Ephesus prior to Paul's arrival and had recently gone over to

Corinth (Acts 18:24-28). There Apollos innocently became the cause of such discord (1 Cor. 3:3-9) that he left and refused to return even at Paul's request (1 Cor. 16:12). Paul's earlier visit to Ephesus (Acts 18:19-20), Apollos's ministry, and the presence of Priscilla and Aquila had prepared Ephesus for the apostle's preaching of the gospel of Christ.

Paul began his work in Ephesus by setting straight some ill-informed disciples of John the Baptist (Acts 19:1-7). He then spent three months preaching at the local synagogue until members of the congregation "spoke evil of the Way." Paul then took the disciples and continued his arguments on the neutral ground of Tyrannus's school (Acts 19.8-9, NRSV) where Jews and Greeks were free to come. He continued there for two years and "all the residents of Asia, both Jews and Greeks, heard the word of the Lord" (Acts 19.10, NRSV).

The work in Ephesus was a great success (Acts 19:10, 20, 26). Paul enjoyed an open door for effective work (1 Cor. 16:9), bolstered by extraordinary miracles (Acts 19:11-17), a public burning of valuable books of sorcery (Acts 19:18-19), and the assistance of friendly officials from the province of Asia (Acts 19:31). There were also many adversaries (1 Cor. 15:32; 16:9), especially among the artisans associated with the temple of Diana. Paul's ministry had hurt their trade to the extent that they were incited to riot (Acts 19:23-41). Paul had intended to stay in Ephesus until Pentecost (1 Cor. 16:8), but this tumult seems to have hastened his departure (Acts 20:1).

During his stay in Ephesus the household of Chloe sent word to Paul from Corinth that there were divisions in the church there (1 Cor. 1:10-13). This report generated a flurry of letters and travels. Paul wrote a letter, which is now lost, to this church (1 Cor. 5:9). The church in Corinth wrote a letter (1 Cor. 7:1) and sent messengers to Paul (1 Cor. 16:17), and Paul sent Timothy to them (1 Cor. 4:17; 16:10). Paul then wrote 1 Corinthians (A.D. 53) and sent it by Titus, who was to meet him in Troas to report the results (2 Cor. 2:12-13).

After his hasty exit from Ephesus Paul found an open door for the gospel in Troas, but he so longed to hear from Corinth that he pushed on into Macedonia (2 Cor. 2:12-13). There he was finally comforted by Titus (2 Cor. 7:5-7) and rejoiced at the news of the Corinthians' repentance, earnestness, longing, and zeal (2 Cor. 7:8-16). From Macedonia Paul wrote 2 Corinthians (A.D. 54), toured northwest to proclaim the good news of Christ in Illyricum (Rom 15:19), and then turned south for Achaia and his third visit to Corinth (Acts 19:21; 20:1-3; 2 Cor. 13:1).

The time and place from which Paul wrote his letter to the Galatians is a topic of controversy. Some date it before the council at Jerusalem, about A.D. 45. Others say he wrote it from Corinth at this stage in his history. The latter opinion is the choice of this narrative.

A three-month winter stay in Corinth (A.D. 55–56) produced the letter to the Romans, which firmly set the benchmark of the gospel for all the ages. Paul had many personal friends in Rome (Rom. 16) and had long intended to visit there (Rom. 1:10, 13, 15). His plans were to deliver a collection from the Gentile churches to Jerusalem (Acts 20:35; Rom. 15:25-26; 1 Cor. 16:1) and then "see Rome" (Acts 19:21) on his way to Spain (Rom. 15:23-24).

THE ARREST IN JERUSALEM

Paul's trip from Corinth to Jerusalem was marked by abundant warnings of the danger awaiting him in Jerusalem. The Judaizers' acrimony toward Paul was common talk everywhere, but all alarms went unheeded (Acts 20:22-24, 38; 21:4, 10-15). However, the request for prayer in Romans 15:30-32 shows that Paul knew he might soon need a divine rescue from the unbelievers in Judea.

The travelers, carrying the collection for Jerusalem, journeyed swiftly in order to reach Jerusalem by Pentecost (Acts 20:16). They proceeded by land from Achaia, through Macedonia, to Philippi in time for the Passover (spring A.D. 56, Acts 20:6). Crossing by sea to Troas they visited the believers there (Acts 20:7-12) and then sailed through the archipelago of the eastern

Aegean Sea to Miletus (Acts 20:13-16). From Miletus Paul sent for the elders of Ephesus to whom he delivered an impassioned speech containing his own dire warnings for them (Acts 20:17-38).

Parting from them Paul and his companions set sail to Cos, to Rhodes, and then to Patara where they changed ships for Phoenicia (Acts 21:1-2). A straight course to Tyre brought them within sight of Cyprus with its memories of Barnabas and Sergius Paulus (Acts 21:3). "Through the Spirit" the disciples in Tyre "told Paul not to go on to Jerusalem" (Acts 21.4, NRSV), but he pressed on to Caesarea where he and his company stayed with Philip, who had formerly served with the martyred Stephen (Acts 21:8; 6:5). In Caesarea Paul would not be persuaded by an especially dramatic prophecy of his coming arrest (Acts 21:10-14).

In Jerusalem the apostolic band stayed with Mnason, an early disciple, and were warmly welcomed by the brothers there (Acts 21:15-17). James and the elders of the church praised God when they heard of the things he had done through Paul among the Gentiles (Acts 21:18-20) and when they received the collection from the churches (Acts 24:17). They told Paul of his bad reputation among the thousands of Jewish believers in Jerusalem and urged him to set right the Judaizers' misrepresentation that he encouraged Jewish Christians to forsake the Mosaic customs (Acts 21:21-24). Acts 21:25 shows the Jerusalem elders understood that the Gentiles were under no obligation to Moses; their concern was for Paul to demonstrate that Jewish believers were free to continue their traditional observances. Paul's action would not contradict the gospel's truth that Jews and Gentiles both are justified before God only by faith in Jesus Christ.

Paul had kept the Jewish feasts (Acts 20:6), as had Jesus and the early disciples in Jerusalem. He had also cut his hair in a vow at Cenchreae (Acts 18:18), so it was a small matter for him, a Jew, to ceremonially purify himself after becoming a Christian, especially if it would undermine the arguments of the Judaizers. To have refused the elders' request would have lent credence to the

Judaizers' charge. The success of this plan is seen in that it was the Jews from Asia, visiting Jerusalem for the Pentecost feast of A.D. 57, who stirred up trouble for Paul (Acts 21:27-29)—not the Judaizers from Jerusalem.

The whole city was aroused by Paul's persistent persecutors. A violent crowd dragged him out of the temple just as Stephen had once been hauled to his martyrdom. They tried to kill him, but he was rescued by Roman soldiers as the mob cried, "Away with him!"—just as they had done to Jesus (Acts 21.30-36, NRSV). At this juncture the educational and cultural diversity of Paul's life came to his rescue. As he was carried for safety to the Roman barracks, he spoke in Greek to the tribune who had mistaken him for an Egyptian assassin (Acts 21:37-38). Given permission to speak to the crowd, he did so in the Aramaic language then common in Israel (Acts 21:39-40). The hushed crowd eagerly heard Paul's defense until he uttered the word *Gentiles*. At this the crowd resumed its threatening and violence, and Paul was brought into the barracks (Acts 22:1-24). There the Romans prepared to flog him until Paul revealed that he was not only a Jew from Tarsus, but also a freeborn Roman citizen. The tribune was afraid for his own freedom since he had bound a Roman citizen and, wishing to know the charges against Paul, brought him to the Sanhedrin (Acts 22:25-30).

This meeting of the Jewish judiciary was shortly reduced to dissension and violence. Paul resorted to tactics justifiable in such a war and hopelessly divided the Sanhedrin on the subject of the Resurrection (Acts 23:1-9). Paul again was rescued, this time from the contending factions of the Jewish leadership, and taken to the barracks where "the Lord stood near him" and encouraged him, promising that he would go to Rome (A.D. 56, Acts 23.10-11, NRSV).

In the meantime forty Jews entered into a murderous plot against Paul. They vowed not to eat or drink until they had killed the apostle (Acts 23:12-15). They almost succeeded, but with the help of "the son of Paul's sister" (Acts 23.16, NRSV) the conspiracy was exposed. For safety, Paul was taken from Jerusalem to Caesarea under guard of 470 soldiers and handed over to the custody of Felix the governor (Acts 23:16-35). Inconclusive hearings before Felix (Acts 24), his successor Festus (Acts 25:1-12), and King Agrippa (Acts 25:23–26:32) occupied Paul in his two years of imprisonment in Ceasarea. Festus, wanting to please the Jews, suggested that Paul be returned to Jerusalem for trial, but Paul knew the murderous intent of his accusers and again utilized his Roman citizenship by making a dramatic appeal to Caesar (Acts 25:9-12).

VOYAGE AND STAY IN ROME

To plead his case at Caesar's court Paul and his companions, Aristarchus and Luke, were taken on a perilous voyage (A.D. 58, Acts 27:1–28:16). Their passage by ship from Caesarea to Rome is one of the most remarkable on record. Luke's detailed account is a treasure of information on ancient ships, navigation, and seamanship. It is also a beautiful portrait of a heroic and dignified apostle Paul, the gospel's ambassador in chains (Eph. 6:20), who with the guidance and assurance of his God (Acts 27:23-26), led the 276 souls on board to safety (Acts 27:37).

Luke traces the voyage stage by stage through every crisis, with a change of ship at Myra, delay at Fair Havens on Crete, and the shipwreck on Malta. Finally, in the spring of A.D. 59, they arrived at Puteoli, Italy, and made their way to Rome, welcomed by the believers along the Appian Way (Acts 28:13-16).

Luke provided a peaceful denouement to the Acts, notwithstanding the fact that the apostle was an imperial prisoner of Caesar Nero. Paul lived by himself in his own house chained to a Roman guard (Acts 28:16, 30). There he received the local Jewish leaders—to calm any misgivings they may have had about him and, at the same time, to convince them about Jesus. His efforts had mixed success (Acts 28:17-28). During Paul's two or more years in Rome, the Judaizers seem to have withdrawn, only to be replaced by the peril of eastern Gnosticism. This is seen in Paul's letters to the Philippians, Colossians, and Ephesians, and to Philemon, all written at this time. It is unlikely that Paul's accusers appeared in Rome to bring formal charges before Caesar, so Paul was released in A.D. 61.

FINAL YEARS AND MARTYRDOM

It is here assumed that the Pastoral Letters (1 Timothy, 2 Timothy, and Titus) are truly Paul's work. Only through them can the probable course of events in Paul's final years be traced. Romans 15.28 shows that Paul intended to deliver the collection to Jerusalem and then to "set out by way of you [Rome] to Spain" (NRSV). The arrest and imprisonment in Jerusalem not only destroyed these plans but also extracted five precious years from the prime of a most productive life. Although Clement of Rome implied that Paul did fulfill his desire to go to Spain (*Clement to the Corinthians* 5), it is certain that the "daily pressure" of Paul's "anxiety for all the churches" (2 Cor. 11.28, NRSV) did not abate.

If Paul went to Spain, he may have been there when Rome was burned on July 19, A.D. 64. Tradition says that Paul traveled as far as Britain, but there is no evidence to confirm this. Returning east, he left Titus in Crete (Titus 1:5) and traveled through Miletus, south of Ephesus, where he left Trophimus sick (2 Tim. 4:20). Traveling toward Macedonia, Paul visited Timothy in Ephesus (1 Tim. 1:3). On the way Paul left his cloak and books with Carpus in Troas (2 Tim. 4:13). This indicates that he intended to return there for his possessions. From Macedonia Paul wrote his loving yet apprehensive first letter to Timothy (A.D. 62–64). He had decided to spend the winter in Nicopolis (Titus 3:12), northwest of Corinth on the Adriatic Sea, but was still in Macedonia when he wrote his letter to Titus. This letter is similar to 1 Timothy, yet with a somewhat harsher tone. In it is a final glimpse of the eloquent and zealous Apollos (Titus 3:13), who is still in association with Paul ten or more years after his first appearance in Ephesus (Acts 18:24).

From here Paul's path is obscure. He may have wintered in Nicopolis, but he did not return to Troas for his winter cloak (2 Tim. 4:13). At some point he was arrested by the Romans because he spent a winter in Rome's Mamertine Prison suffering from the cold in that rock cell before he wrote his second letter to Timothy (A.D. 66–67). He may have been anticipating the coming winter when he requested that Timothy bring his cloak (2 Tim. 4:13, 21). It is possible that the charges against Paul were related to the burning of Rome; this is unknown. It was, however, now "illegal" to be a Christian since the "new religion" was no longer protected by Roman law as being part of Judaism (which was a legalized, recognized religion by Roman law).

It was dangerous to be associated with Paul at this time. Many deserted him (2 Tim. 4:16), including "all . . . in Asia" (2 Tim. 1:15) and Demas who loved the world (2 Tim. 4:10). Only Luke, the physician and author of Luke and Acts, was with him when he wrote his second letter to Timothy (2 Tim. 4:11). Faithful believers still in hiding in Rome were also in contact with the apostle (2 Tim. 1:16; 4:19, 21). He told Timothy to come to him in Rome and bring Mark also (2 Tim. 4:11). Apparently Timothy did come and was imprisoned (Heb. 13:23). Paul's request for the books and parchments (2 Tim. 4:13) discloses that he was reading and studying the Scripture to the end.

The apostle Paul had two hearings before Caesar Nero. At his first defense only the Lord stood by him (2 Tim. 4:16). There he not only pleaded his own cause but also that of the gospel, still longing that all the Gentiles would hear its message (2 Tim. 4:17). Perhaps no decision was made, and thus he was "rescued from the lion's mouth" (2 Tim. 4.17, NRSV). Though he knew he would soon die, he was not afraid, but was assured that the Lord would give him a crown of righteousness on the last day (2 Tim. 4:8). Finally, the apostle himself recorded his seminal encouragement to all believers: "The Lord be with your spirit. Grace be with you" (2 Tim. 4.22, NRSV). After this the Scripture is silent regarding Paul.

Nothing is known of Paul's second hearing but that it resulted in the sentence of capital punishment. History does not record Paul's end. Nero died in the summer of A.D. 68, so Paul was executed before that date. As a Roman citizen he must have been spared the lingering torture that had recently been suffered by his fellow martyrs. Tradition says that the apostle to the Gentiles, the man who had revealed "the plan of the mystery hidden for ages in God" (Eph. 3.9, NRSV), was decapitated by the sword of an imperial headsman on the Ostian Road just outside of Rome, and buried nearby. This fulfilled Paul's desire "to depart and be with Christ, for that is far better" (Phil. 1.23, NRSV).

It has been rightly suggested that Paul wrote his own epitaph in 2 Timothy 4.6-8 (NRSV): "As for me, I am already being poured out as a libation, and the time of my departure has come. I have fought the good fight, I have finished the race, I have kept the faith. From now on there is reserved for me the crown of righteousness, which the Lord, the righteous judge, will give me on that day, and not only to me but also to all who have longed for his appearing."
D. PARTNER

PAUL OF SAMOSATA (third century)
Bishop of Antioch charged with heresy

Paul was named Samosata since he was born at Samosata on the Euphrates. Having acquired considerable wealth and position under the king of Palmyra, he went on to succeed Demetrianus as bishop of Antioch, while retaining his secular position. Because of severe criticism of his conduct and doctrine, a synod was held in Antioch in 264, presided by Firmilian of Caesarea and Helenus, to consider charges against Paul. He was accused of improprieties as well as the doctrinal error of forbidding hymns of worship to Christ since Paul viewed him only as a man. After three synods he was finally deposed in 268. His heresy is known only from the records of his debate with Malchion and preserved in the works of Hilary of Poitiers. His error seems to have been that he taught that Jesus was only a man and a manifestation of God, not himself deity. He distinguished the "heavenly Word" (who is God) from the man Jesus.
H. W. HOUSE

PAUL OF THE CROSS (PAOLO FRANCESCO DANEI) (1694–1775)
Founder of the "Congregation of the Discalced Clerks of the Most Holy Cross and Passion of our Lord Jesus Christ" (also known as the Passionists)

Born in Ovada, Italy, Paul became a hermit and had visions of the Virgin Mary. Shortly afterwards he drew up a rule and was permitted by Pope Benedict XIII to receive novices, and in 1727 he was ordained. He worked as a missionary in Monte Argantaro, and in 1746 Benedict XIV authorized the formation of a monastic order of which he became general (1747). In 1771 he founded the Passionist Nuns in Tarquinia. By the time of his death the order had twelve monasteries throughout Italy. He was regarded as a very powerful preacher, especially on the passion of Christ, and also as a miracle worker. W. S. REID

PAULA (347–404)
Founder of nunneries

Born in Rome of a noble Roman family that had long been Christian, Paula was married in 362 to Toxotius. She bore him four daughters and one son. But upon Toxotius's death (378), she turned her residence into a center of celibate asceticism for Roman women, unmarried and widowed. Jerome became their spiritual director. In 385 Paula and her daughter Eustochium withdrew to Palestine. In Bethlehem she subsidized construction of a monastery, a nunnery, and a hospice for pilgrims. Jerome, who wrote her eulogy, said that she knew the Scripture by memory. A. CABANISS

PAULINUS (c. 353–431)
Bishop of Nola, Italy

Born to a noble Bordeaux family, Paulinus began adulthood with a broad education and enormous wealth. Public service was his interest for several years, but about 390 he became a Christian. After baptism by Delphinus, bishop of Bordeaux, Paulinus was greatly influenced by Martin of Tours and Ambrose of Milan. Soon he decided on a life of church service. Together Paulinus and his wife, Therasia, distributed their vast assets to the church and the poor. In 394, Paulinus underwent priestly ordination at Barcelona.

Paulinus and his wife settled at Nola (central Italy) in 396. Remarkably like-minded, the two began an austere life centered in ministries to the needy. They founded various monasteries and facilities for the poor and sick of their vicinity. In 409, Paulinus was appointed bishop of Nola. An indefatigable letter writer, the bishop corresponded with churchmen far and wide. He exchanged letters with many of his era's prominent Christians. Among well-known figures, he could claim friendships with Martin, Ambrose, Augustine of Hippo, and Pope Anastasius II. Many of these letters are extant. Paulinus also had other writing gifts. For the early church period he was one of Christianity's most talented Latin poets. His works are notable for their buoyant hopefulness and love. Throughout his letters and poems, Paulinus makes many references to church customs and conditions. There are some historic disclosures about saints, cults, church buildings, and other specifics of that time. K. J. BRYER

PEAKE, ARTHUR SAMUEL (1865–1929)
Methodist biblical scholar

Peake was born in Staffordshire, England, the son of a Primitive Methodist preacher. He studied at St. John's College, Oxford, and became a lecturer at the Congregationalist Mansfield College nearby. In 1890 he achieved a rare distinction for a Nonconformist: he obtained a theological fellowship at Merton College. But two years later he responded to a call from his own denomination to become senior tutor at the new Primitive Methodist (later Hartley Victoria) College in Manchester. Here he remained for the rest of his life, giving the college an international reputation. In 1904 he added to his duties the Rylands Chair of biblical criticism and exegesis at Manchester University.

He combined a warm, attractive piety with critical scholarship—a mixture that confounded many ordinary Methodists. He is best remembered for his editorship of a *Commentary on the Bible* (1919) in one volume, usually known as *Peake's Commentary*. Other books he wrote include *The Bible, Its Origin, Its Significance and Its Abiding Worth* (1913), *The Problem of Suffering in the Old Testament* (1904), and *A Critical Introduction to the New Testament* (1919). Though he worked to unite the various Methodist churches in England, he died before their union in 1932. P. TOON

PELAGIUS (c. 354–after 418)
Monk who founded a school of thought that rejected the doctrines of original sin and predestination and that believed in man's free will and inherent capacity for good

Born probably in Britain (Jerome says Ireland), Pelagius went to Rome about 380 and for three decades thereafter seems to have been regarded as orthodox. He wrote an acceptable treatise on *Faith in the Trinity* and a commentary on the Pauline Epistles, condemned the Manichaean heresy, and gained a reputation as a spiritual director, though he held no official position.

Distressed by the apathy he found among Christians in Rome (he himself was said to have sold all his possessions), Pelagius contended that they were encouraged in this by Augustine's view of divine grace, which asserted man's inability to earn salvation. Pelagius particularly disliked the prayer of Augustine in his *Confessions*, "Give what Thou commandest—and command what Thou wilt." The controversy expanded when the Goths invaded Rome (410) and forced Pelagius and his ex-lawyer colleague Celestius to migrate to North Africa. This was the territory of Augustine, who lost no time in confronting what he denounced as a dangerous heresy.

It is not clear how much Celestius contributed to the latter, but Augustine took issue with it chiefly on three points: the denial of original sin; the view that justifying grace is not given freely, but according to merit; and the assertion that after baptism sinless perfection is possible. About 412

Pelagius went on to Palestine, where at the synod of Jerusalem in 415 he contrived to avoid censure on charge of heresy. Meanwhile the more aggressive Celestius had been condemned by the church at Carthage for expressing opinions of which Pelagius might not have approved (for example, the outright rejection of infant baptism).

A two-pronged attack by Augustine and Jerome (a powerful combination) led to Pelagius's condemnation by two African councils in 416, a decision upheld by Pope Innocent I, who in 417 excommunicated Pelagius and Celestius. Though Innocent's successor, Zosimus, at first overturned this verdict and action, he was shaken by such a storm from the African bishops that he not only changed his mind, but wrote a letter requiring Western bishops to endorse the condemnation (418). After this nothing more is heard of Pelagius. One source has him dead by 420, another report says he lived for at least another twenty years. A modified form of his views, known as semi-Pelagianism, lingered on for many years, with echoes of it still detectable in some modern holiness groups. J. D. DOUGLAS

PELOUBET, FRANCIS NATHAN (1831–1920)
Writer, principally of Sunday school material; Congregational minister

Peloubet was born in New York City, the grandson of a French royalist officer who was exiled during the French Revolution. He graduated from Williams College in 1855. He intended to be a missionary, studied Tamil, and was appointed to India. But instead, he was ordained (1857) and took pastorates in Massachusetts. Peloubet could not find publishers for his first two books. But two other works were published and met with immediate success: his question books based on the International Sunday School Lessons (1874) and his commentary for teachers (1875). His *Select Notes* were published annually for forty-five years (1875–1920). Peloubet also wrote commentaries and edited several Bible reference works. M. FACKLER

PENN, WILLIAM (1644–1718)
The founder of Pennsylvania; one of the most engaging religious figures of his age

Penn was born in London, reared there and in Ireland, and given all the privileges befitting his station as the eldest son of Admiral Sir William Penn, who had captured Jamaica from the Dutch in 1655. By 1661, however, a very worldly William Penn had begun to fall under the sway of a radical new religious force in England, the Society of Friends, or Quakers. By 1666 he had become a Quaker. A prolific writer throughout his life, Penn ran afoul of the law in 1668 for a tract attacking the doctrines of the Church of England. While in prison in 1669 he wrote the devotional classic *No Cross, No Crown*, an exposition concerning Christian suffering that has been printed in over thirty editions to the present. After his release from prison he grew steadily disillusioned about the prospects for Quakers in England.

Penn took his first step toward finding a refuge for Friends by backing a Quaker expedition to New Jersey in 1677 and 1678. In 1681 he acquired a huge tract of land from King Charles II to settle a large debt owed to his father. Pennsylvania ("Penn's Woods") thereafter became the most secure home for religious toleration in the world. In 1682 the city of Philadelphia was laid out and, of certainly equal importance, Pennsylvania's "Frame of Government" was published. This constitution set out the terms of Penn's "Holy Experiment" in the new world. It allowed unprecedented freedom of religion to any who believed in one God; it was also a politically liberal document for its time. Although Penn realized very little profit from his colony, Pennsylvania flourished from the start. One of the reasons for this was Penn's vigorous promotion of the colony on the European continent; another was Pennsylvania's spreading reputation for toleration. The source of many of the early immigrants was memorialized in the name chosen for a town founded in 1683, Germantown, as a grant from Penn to a group of German Mennonites and Dutch Quakers. One of the most appealing features of the Penn administration was its fair and just treatment of the Indians.

Penn himself experienced serious personal difficulties during the rest of his life. He was able to remain in his colony for only two brief periods (1682–1684, 1699–1701). He lost control of Pennsylvania from 1692 to 1694 because of his friendship with the deposed English king, James II. And his financial reverses landed him in debtors' prison briefly. Through it all he continued to write, publishing more than a hundred tracts, pamphlets, and books on a wide variety of subjects. Modern historians have written correctly in calling Penn a "compassionate humanitarian, mystic, theologian, and profound political theorist"—or more simply "the Renaissance Quaker." M. A. NOLL

PEPIN III (c. 714–768)

Frankish mayor of the palace, 741–751; king of the Franks, 751–768

Pepin was a son of Charles Martel, who had stemmed the tide of Muslim advance at Tours in 732. At first, in typical fashion of the time, Pepin exercised joint authority with his brother Carloman. In 747, however, Carloman retired to a monastery, and Pepin became sole ruler. In 751, with papal consent, he set aside the last of the Merovingian dynasty, Childeric III, and secured his own elevation to kingship, the first of the Carolingian line. Elected by his magnates, he was anointed by Archbishop Boniface in 752 and again by Pope Stephen II in 754, in a revival of the biblical practice recorded of the Davidic monarchy. Pepin worked closely with the reforms of Boniface. He took seriously his title as "patrician of the Romans" and defended the papacy against Lombard assaults. In 756 Pepin established the States of the Church by his grant of Lombard lands to the pope. His wife, Bertrada (Bartha), bore him the illustrious Charles in 742, the ruler later called Charlemagne. The son had the fame, but the father laid the foundation for his son. A. CABANISS

PERKINS, JUSTIN (1805–1869)

Pioneer missionary to Persia (Iran)

Born in West Springfield, Massachusetts,

Perkins studied at Amherst College and Andover Theological Seminary. He was ordained in 1833. Perkins and his wife, members of the American Board of Commissioners for Foreign Missions (ABCFM), left for Persia the same year and arrived in Urmia in 1835. There they began a work among Nestorian Christians that included schools (the first opened in 1836 with seven boys), Bible translation (Henry Martyn had translated the New Testament into Persian in 1812), medical work, publication of Christian literature (the first press arrived in 1840), and church growth (three thousand converts when the ABCFM turned its work over to Northern Presbyterians in 1870). Perkins's books, notably *Eight Years' Residence in Persia* (1843) and *Missionary Life in Persia* (1861), brought the Persian field to the attention of the Christian public. Failing health forced his return to Massachusetts, where he died the same year. M. FACKLER

PERKINS, WILLIAM (1558–1602)

English Puritan scholar

Born in Marston Jabbet, Warwickshire, Perkins was educated at Christ's College, Cambridge, and was a fellow until his marriage in 1595. His early writings showed pastoral concern and deep psychological insight into the work of God's grace in the human heart. Though one of the leaders of the Puritan movement, he placed his emphasis on the renewal of family and church. He was not a public advocate for Presbyterian polity. Instead he wrote widely read spiritual guides for the laity that popularized Reformed theology and Ramist logic. (His writings were extensively translated throughout Europe.) He was concerned that theology be lived and experienced. This did much to establish the school of English practical divinity, which influenced continental Pietism in the seventeenth century.

As a reputed lecturer and preacher at Great St. Andrew's Church, Cambridge, from 1595 until his death, Perkins exercised a unique influence on students and townsmen alike. His plain and intensely serious preaching profoundly affected the ethos of the Church of England ministry. His theological writings, such as *De Praedestinatione* (*Concerning Predestination*, 1597), were widely used by scholars and ministers. Commentaries on Scripture; writings on patristics, preaching, ministry, ethics and the spiritual life; as well as vigorous polemics against Roman Catholicism, witchcraft, and astrology gave him an international reputation that was unique among Elizabethan churchmen of his day. He continued to be read and quoted throughout the seventeenth century in England and New England, as well as throughout Europe. Disciples like William Ames ensured the continuing vitality of the theological and pastoral tradition Perkins established—with its careful attention to conscience and the rule of the Word of God over every aspect of life.

I. BREWARD

PERPETUA (c. 180–203)

Christian martyr

A native of Carthage and young believer in Christ, Perpetua, along with her slave Felicitas and several others, was martyred in the arena at Carthage. First subjected to severe flogging, then exposed to wild beasts, they were ultimately beheaded. Only catechumens at the time of their arrest, they were baptized while in confinement. Perpetua wrote an account of her visions. To that were added some chapters by her catechist—and an introduction and conclusion by a witness of the martyrdom. Thus the *Passion of St. Perpetua* is one of the most reliable martyrologies. Afterwards the women's names were entered in the canon of the Mass and commemorated until modern canons were composed. A. CABANISS

PETER, THE APOSTLE

One of the twelve disciples; rose to prominence both among the disciples during Jesus' ministry and among the apostles afterwards

There are actually four forms of Peter's name in the New Testament: the Hebrew translated into Greek, "Simeon" to "Simon," and the Aramaic translated into Greek, "Cephas" to "Petros" (meaning "rock"). His given name was Simeon bar-Jonah (Matt. 16:17; cf. John 1:42), "Simon the son of John," which was common Semitic nomenclature. It is most likely that "Simon" was not merely the Greek equivalent of "Simeon" but that, having his home in bilingual Galilee, "Simon" was the alternate form he used in dealings with Gentiles. In fact, it was quite common for a cosmopolitan Jew to employ three forms of his name depending on the occasion: Aramaic, Latin, and Greek. The double name "Simon Peter" (or "Simon called Peter") demonstrates that the second name was a later addition, similar to "Jesus, the Christ." The number of times that the Aramaic equivalent "Cephas" is used (once in John, four times each in Galatians and 1 Corinthians), as well as its translation into the Greek (not common with proper names), indicates the importance of the secondary name. Both Aramaic and Greek forms mean "the rock," an obvious indication of Peter's stature in the early church (see below on Matt. 16:18). It is obvious that he was called "Simon" throughout Jesus' ministry but came to be known as "Peter" more and more in the apostolic age.

PETER'S BACKGROUND

Peter was raised in bilingual Galilee. John 1:44 says that the home of Andrew (his brother) and Peter was Bethsaida, the whereabouts of which is difficult to place archaeologically. The only site about which we know is east of the Jordan in the district called Gaulanitis. Yet John 12:21 places Bethsaida in Galilee; however, it is possible that John is reflecting the popular use of the term "Galilee" rather than the legally correct one. Peter and Andrew had a fishing business centered in Capernaum (Mark 1:21, 29) and perhaps were partners with James and John (Luke 5:10). It is also likely that they intermittently continued in their business while disciples, as indicated in the fishing scene in John 21:1-8.

One difficulty with this is the series of statements saying, "We have left all and followed You" (Matt. 19:27; Mark 10:28; Luke

549

18:28, NKJV). The majority of interpreters have given this an absolute sense of "sold" or "left" their business. However, Luke 18:28 occurs in the context of leaving their homes but obviously is not meant in an absolute sense. It seems most likely that the disciples did leave the practice of their fishing businesses to follow Christ, but kept the tools of their trade and returned to their trades when necessary.

They certainly did not abandon their families, as evidenced by Peter, who returned to his home at the end of each tour. The New Testament tells us that Peter was married. In Mark 1:29-31 Jesus heals his mother-in-law, who perhaps was living with Peter. In fact, it is possible that his home became Jesus' headquarters in Galilee. (Matthew 8:14 may indicate that Jesus dwelt there.) First Corinthians 9:5 says that Peter, along with the other married apostles, often took his wife with him on his missionary journeys. Later tradition speaks of his children (Clement of Alexandria's *Stromateis* 2.6.52) and says that Peter was present at the martyrdom of his wife (Eusebius's *Ecclesiastical History* 3.30.2).

PETER'S CONVERSION AND CALL
Peter's brother, Andrew, was a disciple of John the Baptist, according to John 1:35-40. This follows the witness of John in 1:29-34 and is the second stage of John's discipleship drama in chapter one—i.e., after bearing witness he now sends his own followers to Jesus. Andrew and the unnamed disciple (perhaps Philip as in John 1:43 or the "beloved disciple," whom many identify with John himself) then "follow" Jesus (a term used often in John for discipleship). The next day Andrew follows the Baptist's example and looks up his brother Simon, saying, "We have found the Messiah" (John 1:41, NKJV). Peter's conversion is presupposed in John 1:42, where Simon is brought to Jesus by Andrew and there given a new name.

There are three separate episodes in the Gospels in which Simon is called, and these overlap with three episodes in which he is given the name "Cephas" ("Peter," which means "rock") by Jesus. John locates the event in Judea where John the Baptist was

baptizing. The synoptic Gospels have two different scenes. The first call takes place at the Sea of Galilee (Mark 1:16-20; Matt. 4:18-22). Jesus is walking along the shore and sees Peter and Andrew along with James and John casting their nets into the sea. At this time he calls them to become "fishers of men." Luke then expands this into a fishing scene (Luke 5:1-11), in which the disciples have fished all night and caught nothing but at the command of Jesus lower their nets and catch an amount of fish so great that the boat starts to sink. The episode concludes exactly like the Markan abbreviated form: Jesus says that from now on they will "catch men," and as a result they leave everything and follow him.

The second synoptic episode involving Peter's call (and his new name) is the official choice of the Twelve upon the mountain (Mark 3:13-19 and parallels); in the list of the names we have "Simon he surnamed Peter." The final occurrence dealing with Peter's new name is found in Matthew 16:17-19, in connection with Peter's confession at Caesarea Philippi.

It is somewhat difficult to harmonize these episodes properly. Were there three different episodes in which Simon was called (John 1:42; Mark 1:20; 3:16) and three separate incidents in which he was given the name Cephas/Peter (John 1:42; Mark 3:16; Matt. 16:18)? It is attractive to a broad spectrum of academia to assume that one single event, which happened at some indeterminate time toward the beginning of Jesus' ministry, was later expanded into these diverse traditions. However, a closer examination of the Gospel data does not necessitate such a conclusion. John 1:35-42 is not an institutional scene that connotes an official call. Rather, it describes the first encounter with Jesus and realization regarding his significance. The "renaming" is in the future tense and looks to a later event. Moreover, John deliberately omits most of the crisis events in Jesus' life (the baptism, the choice of the Twelve, the Transfiguration, the words of institution at the Last Supper, Gethsemane) and replaces them with highly theological scenes that teach the spiritual significance of the events. This is what he has done here.

The same is true of the first synoptic call, i.e., the fishing scene. Again, there is no hint of official ordination to office here but rather a proleptic or prophetic hint of future ministry. This is especially true of the highly theological scene in Luke, which promises abundant results. Again in all three accounts the future tense is employed: "I will make you fishers of men" (Matthew and Mark), "You will catch men" (Luke, NKJV). The call in Mark 1:20 and Matthew 4:21 and their reaction (leaving all behind and following Jesus) is the opening gambit that is finalized in the actual institutional scene in Mark 3:13-19 and parallels. The wording does not indicate that these two episodes are doublets, for the actual appointment of the disciples occurs in the second passage. We must differentiate between the original call to one segment (who became the so-called "inner circle" of the Twelve) and the final choice of all the disciples.

PETER'S PLACE AMONG THE TWELVE

The prominence of Simon Peter in the Gospels and Acts cannot be disputed. While some have attempted to attribute this to his leadership role in the later church, there is no basis for that in the text of the New Testament. From the very beginning Simon attained preeminence above the others. In the lists of the Twelve just mentioned, Simon's name always appears first, and in Matthew 10:2 it introduces his name as "the first." Moreover, the Twelve are often designated "Peter and those with him" (Mark 1:36; Luke 9:32; 8:45, NKJV).

Throughout the accounts Peter acted and spoke on behalf of the other disciples. At the Transfiguration it is Peter who wanted to erect tents (Mark 9:5), and he alone had sufficient faith to attempt walking on the water (Matt. 14:28-31). It is Peter who asks the Lord to explain his teaching on forgiveness (Matt. 18:21) and parables (Matt. 15:15; Luke 12:41) and who speaks the disciples' minds in Matthew 19:27, "Behold, we have left everything and followed you; what's in it for us?" (paraphrased). The col-

lectors of the temple tax come to Peter as leader of the group (Matt. 17:24). As a member of the inner circle (with James and John, possibly Andrew in Mark 13:3) he was often alone with Jesus (at the raising of Jairus's daughter, Mark 5:37 and parallels; at the Transfiguration, Mark 9:2 and parallels; at Gethsemane, Mark 14:33 and Matt. 26:37). Jesus asks Peter and John to prepare the Passover meal in Luke 22:8, and in Mark 14:37 (and Matt. 26:40) he directs his rebuke to Peter as representing the others ("Could ye not watch with me one hour?"). Finally, the message of the angel at the tomb as recorded in Mark 16:7 said, "Go your way, tell his disciples and Peter." Certainly Peter held a very special place among the Twelve.

This was especially evident in the Caesarea Philippi episode (Mark 8:27-33 and parallels). It was Peter whose confession became the high point of the Gospel accounts, "Thou art the Christ" (Luke adds "of God"; Matthew, "the Son of the living God"). After Jesus then spoke of the suffering of the Son of Man, Peter rebuked him, and in Mark's description Jesus then turned, gazed at all the disciples, and said to Peter, "Get thee behind me, Satan: for thou savourest not the things that be of God, but the things that be of men." This was obviously directed at them all through Peter.

The portrait of Peter that comes through all four accounts pictures him as impulsive, often rash; he is the first to act and speak his mind and was typified by his enthusiasm for everything in which he had a part. At the sight of Jesus walking on the water, Peter asked that the Lord command him to do the same and then immediately leaped out of the boat and began doing just that. At the Transfiguration, while the others were awed into silence by the appearance of Moses and Elijah, Peter the man of action said, "If thou wilt, let us make three tabernacles here" (Matt. 17:4). Mark and Luke both add here that Peter did not know what he was saying. Peter's unguarded and unthinking tendency to protest Jesus' statements is seen not only at Caesarea Philippi but also at the footwashing scene in John 13:4-11 when he said first, "You shall never ever wash my feet";

and then after Jesus' strong retort, "If I do not wash you, you have no part with Me," he reversed himself completely, stating, "Lord, not my feet only, but also my hands and head" (13:8-9, NKJV). Finally, in the account of the race to the tomb (John 20:2-10), the beloved disciple, reaching the tomb first, paused while Peter immediately and impulsively entered it. Peter was certainly one who "rushed in where angels fear to tread." However, this very trait aligns him with all of us and may be one of the major reasons why he becomes the representative disciple throughout the Gospels.

PETER THE ROCK

The key to the significance of Simon Peter is obviously the controversial addendum to the Caesarea Philippi episode, found only in Matthew 16:17-19, Jesus' testimonial to Peter. There are several crucial aspects of this saying. The most important for this study is verse 18, "And I say also unto thee, That thou art Peter, and upon this rock I will build my church." There have been many interpretations of this down through history: (1) It refers to Peter as the "rock" or first bishop of the church. This was the Roman Catholic interpretation from the third century on and was employed as a prooftext for apostolic succession, but it is not hinted at anywhere in the context or even in the epistles: it was not a first-century concept. (2) The majority of Protestants since the Reformation have taken this to be a reference to Peter's statement of faith rather than to Peter himself; but this neglects the wordplay, which is even more pronounced in Aramaic, which has only one form for "Cephas" (rock). (3) An alternative has been to take "this rock" as a reference to Jesus himself, but that is fanciful and is hardly in the context. In conclusion, "this rock" is almost certainly a reference to Peter, but it must be understood in two ways. First, Peter was to become the foundation upon which Christ would build his church, a position clearly attested to in Acts. This does not mean that Peter had an authority above the other apostles. Paul's rebuke of Peter in Galatians 2:11-14 dem-

onstrates that he was not above them, and at the Jerusalem council in Acts 15 it is James who has the position of leadership. Second, Peter is seen here not merely as an individual but as the representative of the disciples. This view is coming to increasing prominence today. It recognized the Jewish concept of "corporate identity" in which the leader was identified with the corporate body (e.g., the king or high priest representing the nation before God). This concept is also in keeping with Matthew 18:18-20, which passes on the same authority to the church as is here given to Peter. In this view Peter as the rock becomes the first of the building blocks upon which Christ, the chief cornerstone (to continue the metaphor), will build his church (see Eph. 2:19-20).

Two other aspects are worthy of note here. First, verse 18 says, "the gates of hell shall not prevail against it." The "gates of hell" is a common Jewish euphemism for death's inevitable and irrevocable power. Jesus is saying that Satan will not be triumphant over the church, and his sphere of operations, death, will be defeated (cf. 1 Cor. 15:26, 54-55). The church would undergo persecution and martyrdom, but the church would be triumphant.

Second, verse 19 promises, "I will give unto thee [singular] the keys of the kingdom," another statement used of apostolic succession by the medieval church. Again, this must be understood in light of corporate identity; Peter, as the preeminent figure in the early church, here embodies the community in his leadership. The "keys of the kingdom" are in direct contrast to the "gates of hell" (cf. Rev. 1:18, "the keys of hell and death" and Rev. 3:7, the "key of David"), and this follows the imagery of the building seen in the rock upon which Christ will build his church. Here Peter is given the keys that will unlock the power of the kingdom in building God's community, the church. The future tense ("will give") undoubtedly points to the postresurrection period, when that power was unleashed and the church erected.

PETER THE APOSTLE

Two events led to the new Peter who fills the pages of Acts: his reinstatement described in John 21:15-17 and the resurrection appearance of the Lord, which is never described but alluded to in Luke 24:34 and 1 Corinthians 15:5. His denial was certainly proof that he was not yet able to assume his predicted position as the rock of the church. Both Luke and Paul seem to state that the risen Lord appeared to Simon Peter before the others, which would be fitting in light of his preeminence in the early church. During the Palestinian era, the fifteen-year period prior to the Gentile mission, Peter was the leading figure. The others mentioned in Acts 1–12 are all secondary to Peter, the dominant director of church policy. These include John, who is with Peter in the temple (3:1), the prison (4:13), and Samaria (8:14); Stephen, who was one of the Seven and whose revolutionary preaching led to his martyrdom (chapters 6–7); Philip, another of the Seven who proclaimed the gospel in Samaria and to the Ethiopian Eunuch (chapter 8); Barnabas, who set an example of communal sharing (4:36-37) and was an official delegate to Antioch (11:20-30); Paul, a miraculous convert and witness (9:1-30; 11:25-30; 12:25); and James, who became the first apostolic martyr (12:2). It is Peter who proposes the choice of the twelfth disciple (1:15-17), who proclaims the gospel at Pentecost (2:14-40), who utters the healing word (3:6), and who defends the gospel before the Sanhedrin (4:8-12, 19-20; 5:29-32). The episode regarding Ananias and Sapphira is particularly poignant, for here Peter functions as the avenging messenger of God; nowhere is his authority more evident. We would also note his authority in the scene at Samaria concerning the attempt of Simon the Sorcerer to buy the charismatic power (8:18-24). Again, it is Peter whose influence commands the situation. In these two incidents we certainly see the "binding and loosing" jurisdiction (cf. Matt. 16:19) exhibited in Peter.

Yet Peter and the church still came under the strictures of their Jewish heritage. The evidence points to a Jewish proselyte self-consciousness on the part of the early church. They viewed themselves as the righteous remnant, living in the age of Messianic fulfillment, but still interpreted themselves in a Jewish sense and conducted their evangelism in the proselyte form of Jewish particularism (i.e., Gentiles could only be converted through Judaism). Two events altered this. First, the Hellenistic Jewish branch of the church rebelled against the Hebrew Christians, which resulted in the appointment of the seven deacons and a change in the orthodox policy of the Palestinian church. Second, this then led to a new preaching ministry, first by Stephen, whose insights ended in his martyrdom and the dispersal of the Hellenistic branch in chapter 8; then by Philip and others, who extended the gospel even further, to the Samaritans and God-fearers. As a further result, Peter and John came to Samaria (8:14), the next significant step toward the Gentile mission. Thus ended the centrality of Jerusalem in the unfolding story.

The two miracles of Peter, at Lydda (the paralytic) and Joppa (raising the dead woman) in Acts 9:32-42, are probably intended to parallel similar miracles of Jesus in Luke's first work (Luke 5:18-26; 8:49-56). This is part of a major theme in Acts whereby Jesus' life and ministry are paralleled and continued in the work of the Spirit through the church. Again Peter is seen in a representative role.

The new relationships are extended in two further scenes. First, Peter stays with "Simon, a tanner," in Joppa, an unclean trade; no pious Jew would knowingly have social contact with such a one. Even more important, God teaches Peter through a dream (10:10-16) that the old dichotomy between clean and unclean has been broken. This then leads Peter to the home of an uncircumcised Gentile, the most serious social taboo for the Jew, and subsequent events force Peter to admit Gentiles into the church without the necessity of Jewish proselyte requirements. The serious consequences of this are seen in the debate that ensued in Jerusalem (Acts 11:2-3) and later at the council (Acts

15:1-21). The centrality of this event is demonstrated in the extent to which Luke reproduces Peter's speech, which seems to be a repetition of chapter 10 but is meant to highlight this crucial episode. Often forgotten in the significance of this for the early church is the fact that for Luke the Gentile mission begins with Peter, not Paul. He is the one upon whom the salvific act of God descends; and as the leader of the church, he was the first important witness to it.

The persecution of Herod Agrippa (Acts 12:1-4) was likely due to the furor caused by this free intercourse with Gentiles; and it ended the period of Peter's leadership in Jerusalem. The Jewish people were greatly offended by the new Christian push; and according to Luke in Acts, the idyllic period of popularity, in which the common people supported the church, effectively ceased at this time. Peter's miraculous release and the dramatic scene at Mary's house typified the special place of Peter, but the momentum shifts. Peter is forced to flee Jerusalem, and in the interim James arises to leadership (Acts 12:17); at the Jerusalem council it is the latter who has the chair and presents the council's decision (Acts 15:6-29).

The exact relationship between Peter and the other disciples, especially with the so-called pillars—James and John—and the apostle Paul, cannot be ascertained. The evidence is too vague. Many have thought that indeed there were no truly universal leaders, for the early church was too diverse. However, that is unlikely, and Luke's portrayal in Acts parallels Paul's statement in Galatians 2:8 that Peter was the apostle par excellence to the "circumcised" and Paul to the "Gentiles." They were the universal leaders, while James became the local leader of the Jerusalem eldership. However, neither Peter nor Paul had dominical status similar to that of later popes (i.e., neither was the absolute spokesman of the church and above criticism). So-called emissaries from James could have such an influence on Peter that he would hypocritically change his behavior before Gentiles (Gal. 2:12), and Paul could rebuke Peter publicly for doing so (Gal. 2:11-14). Paul never claimed

authority over the other disciples and even sought their approval and "the right hands of fellowship" for his ministry to the Gentiles (Gal. 2:1-10).

PETER'S FUTURE MINISTRY

We have very little hard evidence for Peter's other movements. It seems as though Peter gradually turned from leadership to missionary work. However, this is an oversimplification. It is most likely that, following the similar pattern of Paul, he combined the two. The presence of a "Cephas party" at Corinth (1 Cor. 1:12; 3:22) may indicate that Peter had spent some time there. This is made even more likely when Paul uses Peter as the main example for taking one's wife on missionary expeditions (1 Cor. 9:5). The "Cephas party" probably consisted of those who were converted under his ministry; it is probable that they were Jewish Christians and opposed the "Paul party" on Jewish-Gentile debates reflected elsewhere in 1 Corinthians.

The First Epistle of Peter was sent to churches in northern Asia Minor—the provinces of Pontus, Galatia, Cappadocia, Asia, and Bithynia. The problem here is that there is no hint that Peter had been there and no personal notations in the epistle to demonstrate his acquaintance with these churches. However, it does show that he was very interested in them. In fact, some believe that the reason why Paul was not allowed into this district according to Acts 16:7-8 was that Peter was already ministering there. In short, the question of Peter's involvement in Asia Minor must remain an open one.

There is no final New Testament evidence that Peter went to Rome. First Peter 5:13 says that the epistle was sent from "Babylon," and it is doubtful that this was the literal Babylon, because there is no tradition that Peter ever went there, and Babylon was sparsely populated back then. It is probably a cryptic symbol for Rome, the "Babylon of the West." It is most likely that the "Babylon" of Revelation 14:8 and 16:19 is also a symbol of Rome. This would fit the strong tradition in the early church that indeed Peter did minister there.

There are four early external witnesses concerning Peter's death. John 21:18 mentions only the martyrdom of Peter but does not give any hint as to the place. First Clement was written at the end of the first century and reports the martyrdom of Peter and Paul among others. While 1 Clement 5:4 testifies only to the fact and not the place of Peter's martyrdom, a study of two aspects favors Rome—the reference to a "great multitude" of martyrdoms, which best fits the Neronian persecution, and the phrase "glorious example among us," which shows that the people of Clement's own church (Rome) were involved. Ignatius's letter to the Romans (4:3) also testifies generally to the martyrdom of Peter and Paul, and again the context favors Rome as the place. He says, "I did not command you as did Peter and Paul," which shows that they had ministries in Rome. The Ascension of Isaiah 4:2-3, a Jewish Christian work of the same period, speaks of Beliar (probably Nero) who martyrs "one of the Twelve," almost certainly Peter. Therefore the earliest evidence does not explicitly point to Rome as the place of Peter's death, but that is the most likely hypothesis.

Definite statements to that effect appear toward the end of the second century. Dionysius, bishop of Corinth, in a letter dated c. 170 (preserved in Eusebius's *Ecclesiastical History* 2.25.8) says that Peter and Paul taught together in Italy. At the end of that century Irenaeus says (in *Against Heresies* 2.1-3) that Peter and Paul preached in Rome, and Tertullian in the same general period adds that Peter was martyred "like . . . the Lord" (*Scorpiace* 15). Clement of Alexandria and Origen both allude to Peter's presence in Rome, and the latter adds the belief that he was "crucified head-downwards" (Eusebius's *Ecclesiastical History* 2.15.2; 3.1.2). The tradition that Peter was crucified may be supported in John 21:18: "when thou shalt be old, thou shalt stretch forth thy hands, and another shall . . . carry thee wither thou wouldest not."

The fact that Paul's Epistle to the Romans (c. 55–57) does not mention Peter tells us that he could not have gone there earlier than that. If 1 Peter was written during the Neronian persecution, as those who hold to Petrine authorship believe, he must have gone there sometime in the late 50s or early 60s. Of course, the extent of his ministry in Rome also cannot be known. Some indeed have posited that he had little or no extensive stay in Rome. The facts, as they can be recovered, point to certain tentative conclusions. Peter did have some type of ministry in Rome, though the extent of it cannot be known. However, it is doubtful, in light of the early testimony to his preaching ministry there, that he was merely passing through Rome when caught in Nero's pogrom. Therefore he most likely spent the last years of his ministry in Rome and there suffered martyrdom under Nero, perhaps by crucifixion.

Simon Peter, along with Paul, was the leading figure in the early church. His impact has been tragically dimmed by the acrimonious debates of Roman Catholic–Protestant circles, but the biblical evidence is clear. He was the leading disciple of Jesus and indeed the "rock" who provided the foundation for the church. As the representative disciple, his enthusiasm and even his weaknesses have made him the supreme example of the developing disciple, one who, through the power of the risen Lord, rose above his faults to become a towering figure on the church scene. G. R. OSBORNE

PETER CANTOR (died 1197)
Theologian and teacher

A member of a French knightly family, Peter was educated at the cathedral schools of Reims and Paris. In the early 1170s he gained a teaching appointment at the Paris school, and he soon became one of his era's masters of church doctrine. He was also elected to various lower church offices, including the post of cantor, the title of which was appended to his name. (A cantor led the congregation in singing and prayer.) Based on his respected capabilities and reputation, the papacy frequently also chose Peter as judge for important cases. He was one of the judges in the matter of Ingeborg and Philip II of France, perhaps the high Middle Ages' most famous divorce dispute.

Peter's many writings include commentaries or glosses on most Old and New Testament books. His importance, however, rests mainly on his systematic theological and moral treatises. Among works on theology, a unique work is *De tropis theologicis,* an introduction to the Bible resolving its apparent contradictions by varied reasoned approaches. He also produced *Summa quae dicitur Abel,* a dictionary of basic theological terms. But it is Peter's works on Christian social ethics, especially *Summa de sacramentis et animae consiliis* and *Verbum abbreviatum,* that deserve high esteem. These were not only originally significant for their superb moral exposition, but have great continuing value for their information on social manners and customs of that time. Great church figures of the early 1200s, such as Stephen Langton, archbishop of Canterbury, and Pope Innocent III, were influenced by Peter's wide-ranging moral instruction. Only the *Verbum abbreviatum* of Peter's many works has been printed, but his other writings are extant in manuscript form.
K. J. BRYER

PETER DE BRUYS (died c. 1130)
Heretical preacher

Very little is known of Peter de Bruys's life; most of the information concerning him comes from the writings of his opponents, especially Peter the Venerable, abbot of Cluny, and the early scholastic theologian, Peter Abelard. Peter was an itinerant preacher in southern France whose utterances moved from scornful criticism of clerical worldliness and unworthiness to fanatical attacks on all clergy and the sacraments. Peter repudiated the baptism of infants and crasser versions of the Real Presence, as well as hymnody and art forms. He is even reputed to have rejected all the books of the Bible except the Gospels. It was a time of great ferment—religious, cultural, and political—in part evoked by the enthusiasm accompanying the Crusading movement. For a long time, therefore, his preaching was tolerated. He gained a number of followers called Petrobrusians. But after approxi-

mately twenty years of preaching he was finally arrested, tried, and executed for heresy. His movement ultimately disintegrated, or quite probably it was absorbed by more dynamic heretical movements. A. CABANISS

PETER LOMBARD (c. 1095–c. 1164)
Italian theologian and bishop

Peter Lombard was an important figure in the history of scholasticism—the theology and philosophy taught in the medieval schools from the eleventh to the fourteenth centuries. Peter was born at Novara, which was then in Lombardy. He studied at Bologna and afterwards in France, where he went around 1134. He taught in the cathedral school at Notre Dame in Paris and during the same period produced a large body of writing. He also achieved a position of honor in the Roman Church. By 1156 he was an archdeacon of Paris, and in 1159 he became bishop of Paris.

Peter's most famous work, and the one on which his reputation largely depends, was *Libri quatuor sententiarum (Four Books of Sentences),* which was written between 1147 and 1150 and which attained final form about 1158. This volume was a sort of textbook of the beliefs and practices of the Roman Catholic Church. Peter's method was to state the doctrine of the Church on each issue and then to confirm it by reference to the Bible, the writing of the early Christian fathers, and later Christian writers. The work included many quotations from Augustine of Hippo.

Book I of Peter's *Sentences* was concerned with the nature of God. He described the relation between God's sovereignty and the events of history, stressing God's role as the cause of good in the elect. Book II dealt with the Creation, emphasizing the sinful nature of man and his dependence upon divine grace. Book III described man's redemption through the death of Christ. Book IV was concerned with the sacraments and with eschatology (the doctrine of the "last things"). Peter seems to have been the first to declare that there are seven sacraments. The number was finally accepted by the

Council of Florence in 1439. Peter asserted that a sacrament was not only a symbol of divine grace but also a means of actually conveying divine grace. In addition to the *Sentences,* Peter also wrote commentaries on the Psalms, Job, and the Pauline Epistles, which still exist in various manuscripts.

Peter was not an original thinker in the sense that Augustine and Thomas Aquinas were. He compiled other people's writings and was strongly influenced by Augustine and by Peter Abelard, a great scholastic philosopher who had raised a number of important doctrinal questions in his book *Yes and No.* But by contriving to show the doctrinal position of the Roman Catholic Church Peter exercised a considerable influence right down to the seventeenth century. In spite of his attempt at objectivity he was accused of heresy by various contemporaries, particularly by his great enemy, Walter St. Victor. However, at the Fourth Lateran Council (1215) Peter was declared to be orthodox. Peter's heavy reliance on Augustine and his consequent views on election made him acceptable to Protestant Reformed historians and less acceptable to Roman Catholic theologians. D. C. MASTERS

PETER MARTYR (c. 1205–1252)
Dominican reformer

Born in Verona, Italy, a child of heretical parents, he later abjured their heresy and became a stalwart orthodox Christian. When he was about the age of sixteen he was professed as a member of the relatively new Order of Preachers (commonly called Dominicans), an order specifically devoted to homiletic and intellectual activity against heresies. Peter became a staunch and vigorous representative of Dominicanism in that respect. As a result he was twice appointed papal inquisitor, once in 1232 and later in 1251. (It should be remembered that the word *inquisitor* simply means "investigator.") Peter's duty was, therefore, to seek out heretics and preach to them in an effort to convert them to the truth. At the time of his activity the prominent heretics were the dualistic Cathari (in France called Albigen-

sians), who had actively infested northern Italy and southern France. Peter's sermons were so persuasive that many persons were converted to orthodoxy. As a result angered Albigensian leaders hated him, finally assassinating him. He thus became the first martyr of the Dominican order and as such was canonized after his death. In the next century he was the subject of a painting by his fellow friar Fra Angelico. A. CABANISS

PETER MARTYR VERMIGLI
(1500–1562)
Italian Protestant reformer

Peter was born in Florence and named by his father (a follower of Savonarola) after the Dominican Peter Martyr, who had been killed by the Cathari in 1252. Vermigli joined the Augustinian order in 1516 and became prior at Naples in 1532. Through contacts with Juan de Valdés, study of the Bible, and the influence of writings by Bucer and Zwingli, he became sympathetic to reformation teaching and as a result was transferred to Lucca, where he preached effectively and enlisted the aid of two other significant people, Tremellius and Zanchius. Forced to leave Italy with his fellow reformer Bernardino Ochino in 1542, he moved through Zurich and Basel to Strassburg, where he was appointed to a chair in theology and also married the former nun Catherine Dammartin. The imposing of the Augsburg Interim (1548) led him, with Martin Bucer and Ochino, to seek refuge in England, where Archbishop Thomas Cranmer first secured for him a government pension and then the position of professor of divinity at Oxford (1548). During his stay in England Peter did much to promote the English Reformation, not only by his general teaching and preaching, but also by his suggestions for the 1552 Prayer Book, and above all by his sponsoring of Reformed eucharistic doctrine. He also made some solid friendships with future Elizabethan leaders such as John Parkhurst and John Jewel, with whom he enjoyed many theological discussions over a cup of perry made with pears from Parkhurst's vicarage garden.

The death of Edward IV and the accession of (Bloody) Mary (1553) brought his career in England to an abrupt end. After a brief imprisonment he was allowed to return to Strassburg and resumed his professorship there. Owing to debates over the Eucharist he moved on to Zurich, where he succeeded Pelikan as professor of Hebrew in 1556. In Zurich he was able to repay hospitality to the English refugees, including Jewel, with whom he exchanged interesting and informative letters after the latter's return to England under Elizabeth (1558). Apart from his many writings he made two important contributions during the Zurich years. First, he opposed the weakened doctrine of election advocated by the brilliant linguist Theodore Bibliander. Second, he made suggestions to Heinrich Bullinger in the preparation of what later became the Second Helvetic Confession (1566). He enjoyed a happy relation with Bullinger, as he had with Cranmer in England. Although he preached and taught on many subjects, perhaps he did his most significant work in formulating a doctrine of Christ's eucharistic presence that was in keeping with the doctrine of Christ's incarnation. Not unlike the view of John Calvin, this helped to strengthen the recently established harmony between Geneva and Zurich. Resembling also the view of Nicholas Ridley, Cranmer, and the younger Anglicans, it confirmed and clarified the understanding of the Church of England as this finally came to expression in the final draft of the Thirty-nine Articles prepared under the chairmanship of Jewel (1571). G. BROMILEY

PETER THE HERMIT (c.1050–1115)
Catholic hermit who supported the First Crusade

Peter was famous as an eloquent supporter and proclaimer of the First Crusade against the Turks (1095–1096). He was a hermit when Pope Urban II announced the Crusade at the Council of Clermont in 1095. He responded by enthusiastically commending it, and he gained a tremendous following among the peasants of southern France and the Rhine Valley. Part of his appeal was his promise of blessings from God to a poor and often starving people. In 1096 a great but undisciplined crowd of perhaps twenty thousand men marched with him towards Palestine. But they were overcome, and many were massacred by the Turks at Civitot while Peter was visiting Constantinople. The survivors joined the main army under Godfrey of Bouillon, and thus Peter and his followers entered Jerusalem with the victorious army. After he returned to Europe he became prior of the Augustinian monastery of Neufmoutier. He also became the subject of many legends, and a bronze statue of him was erected in Amiens (France) in 1854. P. TOON

PETRARCH (1304–1374)
Italian scholar and poet

Born in Arezzo, Petrarch followed his father's wishes and studied law at Bologna, but abandoned this pursuit to take minor orders in the church. In Avignon, where his family had moved, he was at home among the refined society of the papal court. In 1327, at the Church of St. Claire, he saw for the first time Laura, who was to become the subject of his idealized love. Since she was already married, his love was romantically celebrated from afar and memorialized in his sonnets, for which he is best known. In 1337 he paid his first visit to Rome, to him the center of antiquity and Christianity.

Petrarch received an invitation to be honored as poet laureate by both Paris and Rome in 1340. Choosing Rome, he received the crown in the Eternal City. In 1350 he met Boccaccio, another of the great Italian humanists. The two are often linked together as ushering in the new spirit of the Italian Renaissance. Though he did not know Greek, Petrarch studied the old Latin manuscripts and edited a number of them. He was not a speculative thinker like many churchmen and scholars of his time. He stood somewhat between the Aristotelian thought of his age and the new humanist devotion to the study of texts. His favorite Christian author was Augustine. After a life

filled with achievement and honor, he died at his country home near Padua.
P. M. BECHTEL

PETRI, OLAVUS (1493–1552)
Swedish reformer

Born at Oerebro, Petri studied at Uppsala, Leipzig, and Wittenberg (at the latter he was a contemporary of Luther and Melanchthon). He returned in 1520 to become a deacon in Strengnas Cathedral. In 1527, at the prompting of Gustavus Vasa (king from 1523 to 1560), the Reformation was introduced, the church was freed from Rome (which had opposed the national movement of independence from Denmark), and its possessions placed at the king's disposal. Petri's wisdom and prudence guided the spiritual work of the Reformation. Petri, who in 1524 had been transferred to be preacher and secretary for Stockholm, translated Luther's prayer book (1526), the first Reformation publication in Sweden. He also gave the people a Swedish translation of the New Testament and with his brother Laurentius (who became the first Protestant archbishop of Sweden) later provided a translation of the whole Bible. He collaborated in other publications to help the people and consolidate the reestablished church. Thereafter Petri ran into trouble with the king, who tried to alter the form of church government. Popular opposition forced a royal reversal of policy, but Petri, whose life was in danger at one point from court allegations, never regained his former influence. J. D. DOUGLAS

PETRIE, SIR WILLIAM MATTHEWS FLINDERS (1853–1942)
British archaeologist

Petrie is considered to have instituted modern scientific archaeology in Egypt and was called the "greatest genius among biblical archaeologists" by W. F. Albright. He founded the British School of Archaeology in Egypt and directed its excavations in Egypt and Palestine (1880–1937); researched in Sinai and found the famous early

alphabetic inscriptions at Serabit el-Khadem (now dated c. 1500 B.C.); developed the system of sequence dating for early Egypt from excavations at Naqada; developed the system of pottery chronology for Palestine from work at Tell el-Hesy; excavated at over thirty-nine sites all over Egypt during a period of fifty years, including Amarna, Naqada, and Naucratis; and excavated at several sites in Palestine, including Tell Jemmeh, Tell el-Ajjul, and Tell el-Far'ah (southern). Knighted in 1923, he wrote over one hundred books, including *Pyramids and Temples of Giza, The Making of Egypt, Wisdom of the Egyptians,* and *Seventy Years in Archaeology* (1931). H. F. VOS

PHILIP II (1527–1598)
King of Spain

Born in Valladolid, Philip was the son of Emperor Charles V and Isabella of Portugal and great-grandson of Ferdinand and Isabella, the Catholic sovereigns. Philip was married four times, first, to Maria of Portugal in 1543. She died only two years later. In 1554 he married Queen Mary I of England, at which time he bore the shadowy crowns of Jerusalem and Sicily. Mary died in 1558. In the following year Philip married Elizabeth of Valois, who died in 1568. He married Anne of Austria in 1570 by whom he had a surviving son and successor, Philip III. In the meanwhile his father had abdicated in 1556, leaving, out of his vast possessions, the Low Countries, Castile, Navarre, Aragon, Sardinia, and Spanish holdings in the New World to his son Philip II. The remainder passed to his brother, Emperor Ferdinand I.

Philip II was regent of Spain from 1543, while his father pursued his activities in the empire. His government was strong, and Philip took a personal interest in it, serving it as nearly as possible without too much interference from advisers. Part of his diligence was directed toward the church. He was appreciative of native efforts to reform the church from within, but intolerant of influences derived from the Reformation movement. It is at that point that the peculiar arm of the state called the Spanish Inquisition gained its notoriety. Through it Philip was successful in nipping Spanish Protestantism in the bud. In 1570 he suppressed the Moriscos in Grenada. To him any significant deviation from Spanish Catholicism was a factor that threatened the stability and unity of the Spanish state. He was, however, favorable to the Counter-Reformation as it expressed itself through the Council of Trent. But he opposed (as his father had) any effort on the part of the papacy to encroach upon the liberties of the Spanish church.

As a true Hapsburg Philip was always sensitive to the growth of French power. That led him to interfere in the religious wars that wracked France. The enduring memorial that he left was El Excorial, built in the shape of an inverted griddle. He failed in his attempt to subdue England with his great Armada. A. CABANISS

PHILIP IV (1268–1314)
King of France, 1285–1314

Born to France's Philip III and Isabella of Aragon, Philip became king at his father's death. Joan of Navarre was his wife. More than any prior ruler, Philip sought to make royal government supreme in France. Overall, this meant subduing dissident political elements and centralizing and expanding royal administration. At many costs, Philip's reign went far in achieving these aims. The king's major innovation was the legists, a new order of nobles supporting and imposing royal authority in France. But above all, an obsession with revenue characterized Philip's government. Some of this had benefits. The assemblies gathered to approve taxes led to France's national estates-general. French finances came under much greater efficiency and accountability. But Philip's rule became despotic as well. Within France at large, the king imposed many new and heavier taxes. For special groups, such as the Jews, unjust exactions or confiscations took place.

Philip's aims also elicited an intense struggle with Pope Boniface VIII. In the late 1290s, England's Edward I and France were near war over Gascony. To halt hostilities,

Boniface acted to curtail the combatants' finances, mainly clerical taxation revenues. The pope demanded full authority over such taxes. By 1299, Boniface had pursuaded the two kings to sign a marriage treaty. All the same, Philip became highly belligerent over Boniface's claims, and he shut down French funds to Rome. In response, the pope broadened his assertions of sovereignty and prepared to excommunicate Philip. This broke relations completely, and the king declared Boniface an outright enemy. In 1303, forces aligned with Philip took the pope prisoner. Though quickly released, the harried pontiff died a short time later. Thereafter, papal authority in France was never the same. Beginning in 1305, Philip gained a conciliatory pontiff in Clement V. Needing exile, Clement had Philip's encouragement to move to Avignon in 1309, and here the papacy's "Babylonian Captivity" continued for the next seventy years. Though Clement generally indulged him, Philip brought contrived charges against the Templars and confiscated their wealth. This was French royal tyranny and avarice at its worst. In sum, during Philip IV's time, France's political consolidation and ecclesiastical independence both reached major turning points. K. J. BRYER

PHILIP OF HESSE (1504–1567)
Prince of Hesse; supporter of the Reformation

Born at Marburg, Philip succeeded as Landgrave of Hesse when he was only five years old. He ended regency squabbles by taking power in 1519, met Luther at Worms in 1521, and after theological discussion with Melanchthon came out for the Reformation with his marriage to Christina of Saxony in 1524. As part of the reconstruction of religious and educational life in Hesse, he founded the university of Marburg in 1527. At Speyer in 1529 he signed the famous Protest (or Protestation), and he also signed the Augsburg Confession in 1530. Interested both in the uniting of reforming forces and also in self-protection against the papal princes, he tried to bring about a theological agreement between Luther and

Zwingli at the Colloquy of Marburg in 1529. Most issues gave little trouble, but the discussions broke down over the question of the eucharistic presence. In view of the threatening political situation in 1530, Philip took the lead with John of Saxony in forming the League of Schmalcald, which included such cities as Strassburg and Ulm, and demanded of its members a commitment to reformation according to the Word of God and the Augsburg Confession. The Wittenberg Agreement of 1536 temporarily strengthened the league, although the Swiss remained aloof and attempts to make alliance with England failed. Philip seriously weakened his own position and damaged the Reformation cause when for dynastic reasons he committed bigamy with Margaret von der Saale in 1540. Luther and Melanchthon foolishly, if reluctantly, assented to this step and made matters worse with an attempted cover-up. For a time Philip found it best to make peace with the emperor Charles V, but he rejoined the league in 1546. With the defeat of the following year he became Charles's prisoner for five years (1547–1552) and had to agree to the imposing on Hesse of the Augsburg Interim (1548) and its pre-reformed practices.

Released with the Peace of Passau (1552), he devoted his final years to the pursuit of theological and political unity among the Reformers and the backing of reforming groups such as the French Huguenots. Just before his death he crowned his work in Hesse by consolidating the Reformation into a territorial church. G. BROMILEY

PHILIPS, DIRK (DIETRICH) (1502–1568)

Mennonite theologian

The son of a Dutch priest, Dirk Philips was well-trained in Latin, Greek, and Hebrew. At an early age he entered the Franciscan order, but by 1533 he had joined the Anabaptists. At the request of the Anabaptists of Groningen, his brother, Obbe, ordained him an elder. With Obbe and Menno Simons, Dirk took a strong stand against the rebels who seized Münster, help-

ing to gather the dispersed Münsterites after the fall of the city. He also wrote extensively, becoming the leading Dutch and North German Mennonite theologian. W. S. REID

PHILIPS, OBBE (c. 1500–1568)

Netherlands Anabaptist leader

Obbe Philips was the son of a Dutch priest and elder brother of Dirk Philips. Obbe witnessed the execution of the first Anabaptist martyr in the Netherlands, Sicke Freercks, in 1531. Greatly influenced by Melchior Hofman, Philips was baptized in 1533, after which he began preaching and baptizing throughout the Netherlands. He baptized and ordained two men who became leading Anabaptists: David Joris in 1534 and Menno Simons around 1536. He agreed with Simons in opposing the violence of the Münsterites and helped to organize the dispersed radicals after the fall of the city. They came to be known as "Obbenites." When he relinquished the leadership of the group, Simons took over. After his death in 1568 his *Confession* was published, describing his religious pilgrimage. W. S. REID

PHILLIPS, JOHN BERTRAM (1906–1982)

English pastor known for his paraphrase,
The New Testament in Modern English

Phillips was born in London, the son of a civil servant. In 1930 he became a priest for St. Katherine's Church in London. When Phillips was pastoring London youth, he discovered that they couldn't understand the authorized King James Version. This prompted him to produce a paraphrase of the New Testament for youth. C. S. Lewis saw the first book Phillips completed (Colossians) and encouraged him to do more. He did so and in 1947 published *Letters to Young Churches*. Many people who read this fresh paraphrase of the Pauline Epistles encouraged Phillips to do the entire New Testament. Responding to their encouragement, he completed the Gospels in 1952, the book of Acts in 1955, and the book of Revelation in 1957. The entire New Testament was published in 1958, called *The New Testament in Modern English*. Due to its popularity this version (revised in 1973) has been reprinted many times. Some of his other popular writings include *Your God Is Too Small* (1952), *A Man Called Jesus* (1959), and *Ring of Truth: A Translator's Testimony* (1977). P. W. COMFORT

PHILO, JUDAEUS (c. 25 B.C.–c. A.D. 40)
Hellenistic Jewish philosopher whose thought presents the first major confrontation of biblical faith with Greek thought

Son of a prominent Alexandrian family, Philo was educated both in the Jewish faith and in Greek philosophy and culture. Of the events of his life we know little, except that in A.D. 40 he headed a delegation from the Jewish community in Alexandria to the emperor Caligula in Rome.

The Jewish community in Alexandria was thoroughly hellenized. Even the Scriptures were read in the Greek translation called the Septuagint. In spite of the fact that these Jews were living and participating in Greek culture, they remained orthodox. Philo was no exception. On the one hand, he carefully observed the Mosaic law and held that it is the infallibly revealed will of God both for God's chosen people, the Jews, and for the Gentiles. On the other hand, Philo was very Greek. He probably knew Hebrew only imperfectly and received a liberal education under Greek tutors. His Bible was the Old Testament, especially the Pentateuch, which he held to be most authoritative, but he read it in Greek translation. Because he held that the Septuagint was divinely inspired, Philo had no need to refer to the original Hebrew text.

To understand Philo's work, one must recognize that the need to come to terms with Greek culture stemmed not merely from practical necessity but also from the fact that Judaism is a missionary religion. Jews could not simply turn their backs on the Greek world, for the prophets had called Israel to be a light to the Gentiles. From his studies Philo was also convinced that there is much that is true in Greek philosophy. Conse-

quently, he was anxious to find some way of correlating and harmonizing biblically revealed truth with the teachings of the philosophers. As a Jewish believer considering the claims of Greek philosophy, Philo was confronted with problems very similar to those posed for a Christian by scientific theories of evolution in our day.

The method that Philo used to harmonize Scripture with the teachings of the philosophers was allegorical interpretation. This method of interpretation had been practiced by many before Philo, and many others followed his example. Through the use of this method Genesis could be read as a contemporary myth about the human condition and man's search for salvation, rather than as an ancient and somewhat crude legend. The proper reading of the text gives not ancient history and geography, but philosophical and moral truth. According to Philo, Moses, both because he was divinely instructed and because he had attained the summit of philosophy, did not resort to mythical fictions, as poets and sophists do; he was able to make ideas visible. By using allegorical interpretation, Philo found in the historical narrative and ceremonial law an inward, spiritual meaning that incorporates the truth he found in Greek thought.

In dealing with the conception of God, Philo approached Greek views critically and rejected what was opposed to Scripture. However, in dealing with the structure and composition of the world, Scripture is quite vague, and so Philo felt free to adopt whatever seemed most reasonable in the writings of the philosophers. He believed that God is the source of both the Mosaic law and the truths of Greek philosophy. The human mind is made in the image of the divine *Logos*, and so it has some capacity to receive and discover truths about realities beyond the sensible.

Among the philosophers, Philo found Plato's view closest to the truth. God existed from eternity without a world, and after he made the world he continued to exist above and beyond it. God is the active cause, and this world is passive, incapable of life and motion by itself, but a most perfect masterpiece when set in motion, shaped, and quickened by God. Moreover, God does not neglect his creation but cares for it and preserves it. This care is called providence. While the Greeks had spoken of a universal providence that preserves natural processes, providence, for Philo, acquired a new meaning. It is God's care for individual beings, so that it includes the power to suspend the laws of nature.

God is One, but the source of all multiplicity. He is immutable, self-sufficient, and hence does not need the world. Creation has its source in his goodness. Although Moses said that the world was created in six days, God must be thought of as doing all things simultaneously. The account of six days serves to show that there is order in things. The visible world was created out of non-being, from nothing. All the available matter was used in creation, so the world is unique. The world was created by God's will, and it may be imperishable. Philo thought that Plato followed Moses in thinking that the world was created by God.

Concerning the doctrine of the *Logos*, Philo is both dependent upon and yet critical of the Greek philosophers. Plato had affirmed that there are eternal ideas to which the Craftsman or Maker looked when forming the world. Philo could not accept this position because God alone is eternal. He harmonized the two views by affirming that from eternity the ideas existed as thoughts of God, but they became a fully formed intelligible world only when God willed to create the visible world. The universe of the ideas, which has no location other than the divine reason, is the pattern according to which the sensible world was made.

To Philo, the *Logos* is much more than just the instrument by which the visible world was made. It is also described as "the idea of ideas," the first-begotten Son of the uncreated Father and "second God," the archetype of human reason, and "the man of God." The *Logos* is the vital power that holds together the entire hierarchy of created beings. As God's viceroy he mediates revelation to the created order. He stands on the frontier between Creator and creature.

He is the high priest who intercedes with God on behalf of mortals. He appeared in the burning bush and dwelt in Moses. Some think that the *Logos* is God, but he is really God's image. While one can be quite certain that the *Logos* was not a person for Philo, the exact status of this power in relation to God is by no means clear. Various aspects of this teaching have been taken up by Christian writers, most notably John, who taught that the *Logos* (the Word) is the instrument by means of which God created the world (see John 1:1-4). About the origins of this view much less is known. It appears that the notion of the *Logos* was current in Hellenistic Judaism. Its function in Philo's thought seems to indicate that it was philosophical considerations, rather than biblical ones, that were most significant in his teaching.

Philo had other views about the creation. He believed that while the heavenly bodies are living creatures endowed with mind and not susceptible to evil, man is of a mixed nature, liable to failure. He can be both wise and foolish, just and unjust. God made all good things by himself, but man, because he is liable to both good and evil, must have been made by lesser deities. This is why we are told by Moses that God said, "Let us make man." In the case of man, then, being created involved a fall. Here also there are two steps in creation. First there is man created after the divine image, and this is an idea or type, an object of thought only, incorporeal, neither male nor female and by nature incorruptible (Gen.1:26). Later it says that "God formed man of the dust of the ground, and breathed into his nostrils the breath of life" (Gen. 2:7). This man became an object of sense-perception, consisting of body and soul, man or woman, by nature mortal. Woman became for man the beginning of blameworthy life. When man and woman saw each other, desire was aroused, and this desire produced bodily pleasure. This pleasure is the beginning of wrongs and violation of law. The Garden of Eden is also meant to be taken symbolically rather than literally. There never have been trees of life or of understanding, nor is it likely that any will ever appear on earth. The tree of life signifies reverence toward God; the tree of knowledge of good and evil signifies moral prudence.

One sees in Philo, then, a tendency to dualism in which spirit is good and matter evil, a tendency derived from Platonism and read into the Old Testament. This led Philo to agree with the Stoics that the only good is the good of the soul. God gives the world to use, not to possess. To rise to the eternal world of mind, a man must suppress all responses to the sensible world. In general, Philo tended toward a world-denying asceticism.

The only temple worthy of God is a pure soul. True religion consists in inner devotion, rather than externals. In this life the soul is a pilgrim, like Abraham or like the Israelites wandering in the desert. Through spiritual self-discipline the soul comes to realize that the body is a major obstacle to perfection. The goal is the vision of God, "drawing near to God who has drawn the mind to himself." God is knowable by the mind, but he is unknowable in himself. We can know only that he is, not what he is. For Philo the soul in its search for perfection ultimately comes to discover that it must cease to rely on itself and must acknowledge that virtue is a gift of God. The man who has discovered his own limitations comes to know God and his own dependence upon God.

Although Josephus borrowed some from Philo, his greatest influence was on Christian writers. Hellenistic Judaism became less significant as the Judaism of the rabbis became the norm during the next two centuries. By contrast second- and third-century Christians had much in common with Philo. Parts of his work were translated into Latin and Armenian. Clement and Origin, among the Greek fathers, and Ambrose, among the Latin fathers, were especially indebted to him. A. Vos

PHOTIUS (c. 820–891)
Patriarch of Constantinople

Born into a prominent and wealthy family in Constantinople, Photius became the most

versatile scholar of his age and of the ninth-century Byzantine Renaissance. He was not originally a theologian, but a courtier and diplomat. In 858, while he was professor of philosophy in the Imperial Academy, he was chosen to be patriarch of Constantinople—and as a layman was hurried through the five ecclesiastical orders in six days before he could be consecrated. His predecessor, Ignatius, had resigned while in exile, but his followers did not consider the resignation valid and met to excommunicate Photius. He, in turn, convened a synod in 859 that declared Ignatius deposed, an action confirmed by the papal legates present at the Council of Constantinople in 861. Pope Nicholas I, however, disowned the decision of his representatives when they returned to Rome and, holding that his dominion extended also over the Eastern Church, had Photius formally deposed and Ignatius reinstated—a decision pointedly ignored in the East.

This claim to supremacy over the whole of Christendom on the part of the pope further widened the breach between the two wings, with the situation further aggravated by doctrinal differences. These included minor matters such as fasts, celibacy, and anointing with oil, but the real problem here was the Western dogma of the Double Procession of the Holy Spirit (i.e., the Holy Spirit proceeds from the Father and the Son). Photius not only repudiated this, but in an encyclical letter to his three Eastern patriarchal colleagues he portrayed the difference in worship and practice between East and West as a difference between orthodoxy and heretical Christianity.

Language was a further barrier between pope and patriarch; few theologians in East or West spoke the other's language. Photius, with all his gifts, could not read Latin, which his emperor, Michael III, dismissed as a "barbarian tongue." There was conflict also on the mission field, when both sides vied for the souls of the Slavs. Photius had sent a bishop to Russia in 864, but the real battlefield was in Bulgaria where the Roman missionaries had the support of Boris the khan (king) for a time before he reverted to

Eastern Orthodoxy. But Photius had other problems in 867. After the Council of Constantinople had that year solemnly excommunicated Nicholas, the emperor Michael III was murdered. His successor, Basil, deposed Photius and reinstated Ignatius as patriarch. On Ignatius's death in 877, however, Basil brought back Photius. The new pope, John VIII, neither pressed the question of Double Procession (known technically as "Filioque" from the Latin phrase "and the Son"), nor did he try to enforce papal claims in the East. Photius's stout defense of his church's position may have persuaded John how much his predecessor's intransigence had endangered the unity of Christendom. Yet the damage had been done and the ground laid for the final split between the Eastern and Western churches in 1054.

There is much about the life and times of Photius that remains obscure; we do know that on the accession of Leo VI as emperor in 886 Photius was either again deposed or resigned under pressure. He retired to a monastery in Armenia and died there. Despite a sporadic, almost impetuous, arrogance, Photius seems to have been enlightened and charitable—for his relations with Ignatius remained cordial, and Photius was responsible for his canonization. Photius has been called "the most distinguished thinker, the most outstanding politician, and the most skillful diplomat ever to hold office as patriarch of Constantinople." J. D. DOUGLAS

PICO DELLA MIRANDOLA, GIOVANNI (1463–1494)

Renaissance humanist and philosopher

Born in Mirandola, Italy, a younger son in a family of feudal lords, Pico della Mirandola was destined for a career in the church. He studied at Bologna, Ferrara, and Padua. In 1486 he composed nine hundred theses and offered to defend them in public disputation in Rome the following year. Theologians objected to some of these theses. Seven were condemned as unorthodox and six more declared to be dubious. Pico published a defense in 1488, and then the pope con-

demned all nine hundred theses. Pico fled to France, was arrested, but freed through the influence of Italian princes, and was allowed to return to Italy and to settle in Florence. There he was in contact with the Platonic Academy of Ficino and Savonarola.

Unlike many of the humanists who despised scholastic philosophers simply because of their lack of elegance and classical training, Pico recognized the soundness of the scholastics' thought. Consequently, he was willing to learn whatever he could from them. More generally, Pico was convinced that all known philosophical and theological schools contain valid insights that are compatible. Each thinker participates in the truth to some extent, and Pico wished to gather that truth from Jewish, Greek, and Arabic sources. This historical and philosophical attitude is known as syncretism. Two examples will illustrate Pico's attitude: Christian writers had long tried to show that the Old Testament is an anticipation of Christian truth, and Pico tried to show that the Jewish cabalistic tradition, in addition to the Hebrew Scriptures, is in basic agreement with Christian teaching. Again, Pico tended to assume that Plato and Aristotle are in basic agreement, even though their words and apparent meaning do not coincide.

Pico is most famous, however, for his doctrine of man. In the *Oration* (1486), which is the most widely known early Renaissance writing, he assigns man a privileged place in the universe. Ficino had described the human soul as the bond of the universe, the link between the intelligible and sensible worlds. Pico goes beyond this, placing the emphasis not so much on man's universality, but on his freedom. Man is completely apart from the universal hierarchy, able to occupy any degree of life from the highest to the lowest, as he chooses. This emphasis accounts for Pico's attack on astrology, which is found in his longest work, *Disputations against Astrology*.

Pico's attempts to harmonize various intellectual traditions and to point to a truth beyond the limits of schools were influential on Renaissance thinkers. A. VOS

PIERSON, ARTHUR TAPPAN
(1837–1911)

American preacher, writer, and missionary enthusiast

Born in New York City, Pierson studied at Hamilton College (1857) and Union Seminary (1860). Pastorates in Binghamton and Waterford, New York, followed his ordination. He also ministered at Fort Street Church, Detroit (1869–1882), and Bethany Church, Philadelphia (1883–1889). A two-year missionary tour of England brought him into contact with C. H. Spurgeon, and Pierson preached at Metropolitan Tabernacle for two years after Spurgeon's death. A Presbyterian by training, Pierson became a Baptist in 1896. He lectured on missions at Rutgers College and New College (Edinburgh) around 1891–1892. He wrote a biography of George Müller, and helped found the Student Volunteer Movement. His interest in prophecy and adherence to dispensationalism are reflected in his work as consulting editor on the Scofield Reference Bible. Pierson was editor of *Missionary Review of the World* for several years.
M. FACKLER

PIKE, JAMES ALBERT (1913–1969)
Episcopal bishop

Born in Oklahoma City, Pike was educated at the University of Southern California (1936) and Yale University Law School (J.S.D., 1938). He served as an attorney with the Securities and Exchange Commission from 1938 to 1941 and in Naval Intelligence from 1942 to 1945. Renouncing the Roman Catholicism in which he was brought up, he entered the Episcopal ministry, being ordained deacon in 1944 and priest in 1946. From 1947 to 1949 he was rector of Christ Church, Poughkeepsie, New York, and between 1949 and 1952 he was chaplain and chairman of the religion department at Columbia University. In 1951 he was appointed dean of the Cathedral of St. John the Divine in New York City, and in 1958 he was elected bishop of California. In 1966 he resigned from his diocese to become theologian in residence at the Center for the Study of Democratic Institutions at Santa Barbara, California.

During his public career Pike was a controversial figure, partly because he was not firm about such classical Christian doctrines as the Trinity, partly because of his supposed social radicalism, and partly because he became a spiritualist. In 1966 when his son committed suicide, Pike began to explore spiritualism in an attempt to contact his deceased son. He was censured by the House of Bishops of the Protestant Episcopal Church. In 1969 he announced his intention to leave the institutional church and establish the Foundation for Religious Transition at Santa Barbara. In September of that year he died in the Judean desert in Israeli-occupied Jordan. N. V. HOPE

PILKINGTON, GEORGE LAWRENCE
(1865–1897)

British missionary to Uganda; Bible translator

Born in Dublin to an Irish Protestant landlord family, Pilkington was educated at Uppingham Public School and Pembroke College, Cambridge. In 1885 the young student of classics underwent a profound conversion experience and turned from a promising career in teaching to enter Christian service. Although lacking theological training, he volunteered for service in Africa and went to Uganda as a lay worker under the Church Missionary Society. A competent linguist, he mastered the Luganda language and prepared a basic grammar and the first Bible translation. A man of simple but deep piety, he emphasized the baptism of the Holy Spirit in his personal ministry. He vigorously promoted the idea of the self-supporting and self-propagating indigenous church and identified with the Africans among whom he worked. He felt European missionaries should go to those areas where strong national churches existed, provide leadership for the national Christians, and reinforce their endeavors. He was killed during an anti-British militia uprising in Uganda.
R. V. PIERARD

PIUS II (1405–1464)
Pope, 1458–1464

Named Enea Silvio Piccolomini, Pius was born to a wealthy Italian family. He excelled in his studies at the University of Siena. And under Filelfo of Florence he gained a love for the classics and poetry. For years, Pius had an extraordinary career. He was at once a brilliant humanist writer and an unordained assistant to high church leaders. From 1431 to 1435, Pius attended the Council of Basle as Cardinal Capranica's secretary. Designed to continue the Council of Constance (1414–1417), the Basle gathering was much taken by conciliarist ideas. (Conciliarists held that a general council was higher than the pope in authority.) Eventually the papacy saw Basle's work as antipapal and repealed its decrees. But Pius became deeply impressed with conciliarist views. His famous work, *Libellus dialogorum de generalis concilii,* advocated the position.

Holy Roman Emperor Frederick III made Pius imperial poet laureate in 1441. Pius's humanist works in this period were much celebrated. Among many items, the best perhaps are *De duobus amantibus Eurialo et Lucresi,* and *Chrysis.* Despite his high-church connections, Pius was still immersed in a sensuous life. In 1445, however, Pius underwent a basic change of heart. He announced he was commmitting himself to a life of church service. To show his sincerity, he gave up most of his worldly pursuits, and then he renounced his conciliarist views. The latter was needed to reconcile with the papacy. Within a short time, Pius was granted priestly ordination, and in 1447 he was consecrated as bishop of Trieste, Italy. He gained a cardinal's hat in 1456. Further, it was in this period that Pius completed his largest body of writings. These cover an array of topics. Among scholarly items, the most important were his histories. There were also some influential satirical pieces, including *Miseriae Curilium,* and also numerous orations and poetical works.

With much humanist support, Pius was a popular choice for pope in 1458. However, his dedication to conservative Christianity and papal traditions at least outwardly was very strong. Thus in 1460, in his letter *Execrabilis,* Pius once again repudiated his conciliarist ideas. For the time being, this undid opposition to Louis XI's repeal of the *Pragmatic Sanction.* Supreme papal authority thus returned to France for a time. But largely, like other church leaders, Pius's main concern now was the Islamic conquest of Constantinople. Since their victory in 1453, Muslims had increasingly dominated the center of Eastern Christianity. Hence, much of Pius's energy went into fighting the Turks and their continuing expansion. Above all the pope hoped for a full-scale Crusade led by western European rulers. But as typical, the monarchs' disputes, both among themselves and with the papacy, ruined all effective action. Finally, as a last resort, Pius gathered some troops and put himself at their head. But while meeting with his forces, he took seriously ill. His death followed quickly.

In retrospect, while belittled by some for his radical turnabouts, Pius's last years seemingly saw a deeply committed believer and pope. Without question, he was the most literarily gifted of all supreme pontiffs. Coming at so crucial a point, his anti-conciliarism also certainly affected church history significantly. Pius II's *Pii II Commentarii rerum memorabilium* is the only autobiography left by a pope. His *Cosmographiae in Asiae et Europae* also is an important study of geography and ethnography. Complete editions of Pius's works were published in the 1500s. There are modern editions and some translations of his autobiography and letters. K. J. BRYER

PIUS VII (1740–1823)
Pope, 1800–1823

Born Barnaba Chiaramonti in Cesena, he joined the Benedictines at sixteen, lectured in Parma and Rome, was bishop of Tivoli (1782) and then of Imola (1785), and was a cardinal. It was a time of trouble with France and Germany; and because of French occupation of Rome, the conclave that elected Pius was held in Venice. He made a famous concordat with Napoleon in 1801, but relations between them soon soured. In 1809

Pius was carried away captive, and Napoleon declared the Papal States annexed to France. Not until that emperor's fortunes began to wane was the pope freed and allowed to return to Rome (1814). Near the end of his life Pius strove with Spain and Portugal, partly because of his recognition of the new Latin-American republics. But this was also an era of artistic achievement and educational reform, and under the patronage of various monarchs Rome took on a new splendor. Pius revived the Jesuit Order in 1814, condemned Freemasonry, and was an enthusiastic supporter of missions. J. D. DOUGLAS

PIUS IX (1792–1878)
Pope, 1846–1878

Born Giovanni Maria Mastai-Ferretti in the Papal States, he studied in Rome and after ordination served in Chile (1823–1825). He became archbishop of Spoleto (1827), then bishop of Imola (1832), and was made cardinal in 1840. Though widely thought to be a liberal pope, he ran into trouble with dissident elements (backed by Austria) in administering the Papal States, which were badly in need of reform. In 1848 the movement toward Italian nationalism forced his flight from Rome until 1850, when he was restored by the French army. In the Papal States there was corruption, illiteracy, bad administration, and neglected trade and industry. The hearts of many Italians were set on unification. In 1854 Pius declared the dogma of the Immaculate Conception largely on his own initiative. Under his rule Vatican Council I declared the infallibility of the pope in 1870. Meanwhile the Italian army had occupied Rome, and a plebiscite showed an overwhelming majority for the incorporation of Rome into the Italian kingdom.

Pius pretended to be the prisoner in the Vatican, and in a sense he was. His pontificate was the longest in history. He would at first have nothing to do with the unified kingdom. He was awarded an annual sum to compensate for the loss of his temporal domains, allowed to have exclusive authority within the Vatican and its immediate envi-

rons, and to conduct his own diplomatic relations with other powers.

His pontificate saw the restoration of the hierarchy in England (1850) and the Netherlands (1853). In the rest of Italy, church and state were separated. The vexed Roman question had thus been resolved at last, though the papacy did not acknowledge this formally until 1929. Pius latterly was concerned that liberalism in the church had to be destroyed and that all ecclesiastical authority should be concentrated in the pope's hands (thus paving the way for papal infallibility). Pius produced also the Syllabus of Errors (1864) and condemned Bismarck's Kulturkampf. J. D. DOUGLAS

PIUS X (1835–1914)
Pope, 1903–1914

Born Giuseppe Melchiorre Sarto near Venice, he was ordained in 1858. After extensive parish experience he became bishop of Mantua in 1884 and cardinal and patriarch of Venice in 1893. He was elected to the papacy after Emperor Francis Joseph I of Austria opposed the first choice of the cardinals (the last time such a veto operated). Pius decided that his chief task was the defense of the church in a time of secularism among most European nations, creeping modernism in the church itself, and hostility from Protestant countries because of papal encyclicals directed against them. In secularist France, differences between church and state on the appointment of bishops and on the legal status of church property led to the severance of diplomatic relations and to separation of church and state in 1905. Differences arose also with the governments of Spain and Italy.

Doctrinally it was an age of struggle, and Pius took robust action against lay movements not directly controlled by the hierarchy, especially those with social or political tendencies. He aimed at the revival of Christian life and devotion, and in 1907 he urged frequent reception of Holy Communion, even to the extent of allowing young children to communicate if they understood its doctrine. He reformed the Breviary, revived the use of Gregorian church music in liturgical worship, and founded the Pontifical Biblical Institute in Rome (1909). He had earlier (1904) begun the simplification of canon law. He died much grieved by the outbreak of World War I in 1914, was beatified in 1951, and canonized in 1954. J. D. DOUGLAS

PIUS XI (1857–1939)
Pope, 1922–1939

Born Ambrogio Damiano Achille Ratti in Milan province, he studied at Milan and Rome, was ordained in 1879, and earned doctorates in theology, canon law, and philosophy. Expert also in paleography, he served the church in various scholarly capacities (taking his leisure in mountaineering), then was in Vatican diplomatic service in Poland (1919), and was briefly archbishop of Milan before election to the papacy.

In the Lateran Treaty of 1929 he came to an agreement with Mussolini's Fascist government about their respective areas of authority. Roman Catholicism was declared to be the official religion of Italy. Pius, whose motto was The Peace of Christ in the Kingdom of Christ, tried, usually without success, to improve relations with and between secular states. France continued to pose a problem, though Pius improved relations with that secularist nation in 1928. And the pope had reason to condemn the dictatorships of Italy (1931) and Germany (1937). Atheistic communism was also rejected in a 1937 encyclical. A great supporter and organizer of foreign missions, he encouraged the formation of indigenous churches with their own bishops and clergy, and consecrated the first six Chinese bishops in 1926 and a Japanese one in 1927. He promoted Catholic Action as "the participation of the laity in the apostolate of the Church's hierarchy," expanded on Roman ecumenism, encouraged the growth of Uniate churches and the understanding of Eastern Orthodoxy, and sought greater integration of all churches within the Roman obedience (a 1928 encyclical showed his dislike of Protestantism). He reaffirmed Thomism as the normal expression of Catholic doctrine and, in biblical research, would make no compromise with modernism. J. D. DOUGLAS

PIUS XII (1876–1958)
Pope, 1939–1958

Born Eugenio Pacelli near Rome, he studied at the Gregorian University, obtaining two doctorates. He was ordained in 1899, entered Vatican service in 1901 and rose rapidly in its ranks, specializing in law. In 1917 at a delicate period in World War I, he went as an archbishop to Munich to negotiate a concordat with Bavaria. He was in Berlin (1925–1929) on similar business before being recalled to Rome. He was made cardinal, became Pius XI's secretary of state in 1930, and traveled widely, notably to the Americas. He was elected pope, in the shortest conclave since 1623, just before World War II began, sought vainly the preservation of peace, and tried to keep communications open with warring nations.

His twelve years in Germany and his knowledge of and affection for that nation was no unmixed blessing. The 1933 Concordat with Hitler had largely been his work, though just previous to World War II he had criticized Nazi policies. He was deeply disappointed by Italy's entry into the war. He protested against the violation of human rights, but was criticized later for not speaking out more clearly when millions of Jews were rounded up and executed by the Nazis. He condemned atheistic communism, upheld the privileged position of his church in Italy and Spain, but resisted freedom for non-Catholic churches and individuals. A 1943 encyclical freed Catholic biblical studies from some of the inhibitions that had surrounded it for decades. Pius strove to maintain the independence of the church behind the Iron Curtain and in 1950 defined the dogma of the Assumption of the Virgin Mary. J. D. DOUGLAS

PLATO (428–347 B.C.)
Greek philosopher

Plato was born into a prominent and rich family in Athens. He lived the luxurious life natural to such a position. However, his friendship with Socrates made him feel that his vocation or calling was to be a thinker rather than an active political leader like his relatives and friends.

After Socrates' death, Plato entered into a spiritual discipleship of this great man and friend, now departed from him. Plato traveled widely, visiting many parts of the Mediterranean world. He also founded a school, the Academy, in Athens, for young men who wished to learn how to think. The Academy was the "university" of the ancient world. Plato served as the Academy's director, and took a real part in the teaching and in the supervision of his students.

Plato spoke of God as the self-moving source of "good motions," which he believed was scientific proof of the existence of God. Plato brought the idea of God into philosophy for the first time, and he believed that God was a living soul, and that he was good. Plato's God is a personal God; he is not a form, but a soul, and he is the "self-moved" mover. Human souls, though inferior, exist as truly as the divine soul; therefore Plato thought it possible to reconcile the existence of evil with the absolute goodness of God. Plato was a great thinker who, for the first time in Western thought, believed in the supremacy of the soul and the spiritual life. These ideas accorded very well with the teachings of the Bible. Plato wrote in the *Theaetetus*, "We are to become like God so far as it is possible to become like him—to be as holy, just, and wise. He of us who is most righteous is the most like him. To know this is true wisdom and virtue. If a man loves goodness, truth, and beauty, he then knows the highest happiness. Virtue is its own reward!" Plato refers to the Good as being positively divine. If our knowledge could be to see real objects, not shadows, we would be in touch with the true world of goodness, truth, and beauty. We could see the Lord of Light in this world and the source of reason and truth in this intellectual world. We could also see the existence of a spiritual world, to which we really belong, and come to realize our true nature as man.

God, the Creator, fashioned the world using the material of goodness, truth, and beauty, which he wanted to share with others. When he was framing the universe, he put intelligence in soul and soul in body, so as to create a most beautiful work. In the work *Laws*, Plato refers to man "as the measure of all things, meaning that he who would be dear to God must be like him, and such as he is." Plato's religion was his most profound personal conviction. In his work *Republic*, he said something that Christian writers used to think was almost a prediction of Jesus. He wrote that the "truly righteous man" may very well not be accepted and will be killed in the world as it is now.

Christianity, in so far as it has been given a philosophical shape, owes a great deal to Plato. He believed God to be "the supremely good soul that takes forethought for the universe and guides along its path." He passionately asserted that there are many gods of varying powers, but there is a God who is supremely good, and nothing can be better than he. G. RISER

PLINY THE YOUNGER (c. 61–c. 113)
Roman writer and administrator

Born into a wealthy family at Novum Comum (modern Como in northern Italy), Pliny (Gaius Plinius Caecilius Secundus) early joined the legal profession and soon gained a reputation as a crusading prosecutor of corrupt provincial officials. After holding also key posts in financial departments he attained the rank of consul by A.D. 100. About ten years later the emperor Trajan sent him to govern the province of Bithynia and to look into irregularities in its administration. There he ran into the problem of how to deal with the local Christians, and this became the subject of correspondence with Trajan. A number of Christians were executed at Pliny's command, but closer investigation seems to have convinced him that, while they were "unboundably superstitious," the Christians generally were of good character and guiltless of the charges made against them of gross immorality. It is likely that he followed the imperial advice to disregard anonymous and unsubstantiated accusations against the believers and to take action only against the most blatantly defiant. An accomplished and sophisticated writer, Pliny had earlier written nine books of letters to friends. Apart from their literary merit, the letters give fascinating insights into contemporary Roman society. J. D. DOUGLAS

PLOTINUS (205–270)
Egyptian philosopher

At age twenty-eight Plotinus began to study philosophy. He went to Alexandria to study, but only after several disappointing experiences did he find a satisfying teacher, Ammonius Saccas, with whom he studied for eleven years. In 242 Plotinus accompanied the emperor Gordian on an expedition to the east in order to study Persian and Indian philosophy. When Gordian was killed, Plotinus had to flee. He escaped to Antioch and went on to Rome. He established a school in 244–245 and taught there for the rest of his life. A group of devoted disciples gathered about Plotinus, and he was often approached for help and advice, thus serving as a spiritual adviser.

Most of what we know of Plotinus's life comes down to us from the biography of his devoted student Porphyry. Also the only version of Plotinus's writings that are extant have come to us in Porphyry's edition. Porphyry attempted to arrange Plotinus's writings in a systematic form. He divided them into six books of nine chapters each. From this comes their name, *The Enneads*, which means nines. All of these works were written during the last fifteen years of Plotinus's life.

Plotinus attempts to give a complete account of reality and a guide to spiritual life. The account of reality shows how everything is derived from the highest of the three Primary Principles, The One. There is an outgoing or movement of descent that brings into being the various levels of reality. This outward movement is complemented by a return or ascent in which the individual soul passes upward through all the stages of being to a final union with The One.

The highest cause or first principle in Plotinus's philosophy is The One or Good. Plotinus sometimes calls it Father, but rarely God. Because it is the source of everything that is, it is itself above being. The One is complete unity, but all plurality comes from it.

After The One comes the Divine Mind, or Intelligence, as it is sometimes called. Divine Mind emanates from The One, and in general in Plotinus's thought each lower stage of reality emanates from the one above it. The One is not affected in any way by this process. There is no activity on the part of The One; it does not will or plan. Emanation is a kind of necessary, but also spontaneous, giving-out or flowing forth. This factor makes the Plotinian universe quite different from the Christian view where God freely creates the world.

In several ways, the Divine Mind is similar to Plato's world of ideas. This realm is the level of true being. However, whereas for Plato the ideas were self-sufficient entities outside of the mind that contemplates them, for Plotinus they exist only in the Divine Mind. The Divine Mind is a single, living reality, infinite in power and beyond all measuring and limitation. Unlike Plato, Plotinus believed that there are forms of individuals, and yet the total number of forms is finite.

The third principle is Soul. Soul provides the link between the higher, spiritual and the lower, material worlds. Soul emanates from Mind, just as Mind emanated from The One. The Divine Mind is the source of the soul's reality and all that is good and beautiful in it. Soul returns to Mind. There is a distinction between the higher or Universal Soul, which is not confined in or bound to body, and the lower Soul or Nature, which is found in body. Because of the presence of Soul, the material universe is an organic whole. The matter to which the lower Soul is joined is a principle of evil in the material world; it resists the ordering and informing activity of Soul.

Man finds himself in the midst of the disorder and suffering that are inevitable in the only kind of harmony there can be in the material world. He has, however, no right to complain, for suffering is a necessary consequence of embodiment. The wise man gets beyond the turmoil and conflict of bodily life; he abides above in the spiritual world. In knowledge he attains the level of Divine Mind and in mystical experience, overcoming all duality, he is united with The One. But it is only to the philosopher that this path is open. For the ordinary man, who is not aware of the divine in himself and who consequently cannot give an account of divine things, Plotinus offers little hope. The weak, the foolish, and the wicked suffer what they deserve, and they have no right to expect gods or good men to come to their aid. A century later the young Augustine was attracted briefly by the view that makes the wise man self-sufficient and promises him the possibility of growing godlike through his own powers, but he ultimately rejected it completely, affirming instead the biblical view that salvation for all is through God's grace.

Plotinus is usually considered to be the founder of Neoplatonism, the movement through which he had a profound influence on both pagan and Christian thought. Along with Plato and Aristotle, he was one of the great masters of Greek philosophy. A. Vos

POLE, REGINALD (1500–1558)
Cardinal and archbishop of Canterbury

Pole was born at Stourbridge and educated at Oxford, Padua, and Paris. Henry VIII gave him several church preferments while only a layman and still a teenager. At Padua in 1521 Pole met the Italian Renaissance firsthand and made friends with many who were eager for church reform, including Thomas More and Erasmus. On his return to England in 1530 Henry tried to secure his support over the divorce by offering him the sees of York and Winchester. But Pole, unwilling to take sides, declined and was allowed to return to Padua in 1532. At Henry's request he compiled a report on the royal divorce and on papal supremacy. But Pole's treatise, *Pro Ecclesiasticae Unitatis Defensione* (1536), severely censured the king's conduct. Henry promptly canceled Pole's pension and preferments, but Pope Paul III made Pole a cardinal

and then nominated him as papal legate to England. When Henry denounced him as a rebel, Pole went to the Continent and conferred with English malcontents in the Low Countries. Henry retaliated by executing members of Pole's family, including his mother, Countess of Salisbury (1541).

A president at the Council of Trent (1545), Pole was nearly elected pope in 1549. On Mary's accession Pole returned to London as legate (1554) and reconciled the Church of England to Rome. He succeeded Cranmer as archbishop of Canterbury (two days after the latter's execution) in 1556; but, worn out by anxieties over the war between Pope Paul IV and Philip II and by the pope's personal animosity against him, Pole died on November 17, 1558, twelve hours after Mary died. N. HILLYER

POLLARD, SAMUEL (1864–1915)
Missionary to China

Pollard was the son of a minister of the Bible Christian Church (now known as the United Methodist Church). He spent five years in civil service in London and then in 1887 was sent by his church to Chaot'ung, Yunnan, China. Evangelism and philanthropy among the Chinese were his ministry until 1905. There were no baptisms during the first five years, but after the Boxer uprising a response came. Pollard made a first approach to the aboriginal Nosu and Miao in 1903 and from 1905 worked exclusively with the Miao. The Chinese and Nosu landlords opposed the mission, but Pollard became proficient in the language and persisted. A mass movement developed, and after ten years there were ten thousand Christians, including forty-eight hundred adult communicants, plus five thousand under instruction for baptism. Pollard's life and mission were cut short by typhoid.
P. BEAVER

POLYCARP (c. 70–156)
Bishop of Smyrna and martyr

Born of a Christian family, Polycarp claimed to have been a disciple of John, presumably the apostle. Ignatius of Antioch, on his way to Roman martyrdom (c. 116), wrote letters both to Polycarp and to the church of Smyrna. In the days of Pope Anicetus, Polycarp visited Rome as representative of the Asia Minor churches that observed 14 Nisan as Easter. Although he and the pope could not come to an agreement on that question, they maintained fellowship with each other. While there Polycarp met some of the Valentinian heretics and encountered Marcion, whom he characterized as "firstborn of Satan."

The account of Polycarp's death (a letter from the church of Smyrna to the church of Philomelium) is the earliest extant Christian martyrology. The civil authorities importuned the bishop to apostatize because of his age, but he replied dramatically, "I have served Christ eighty-six years and He has done me no wrong. How can I blaspheme my King? I am a Christian." Miraculously the flames did not harm him, so he was dispatched with a dagger, then burned. His followers gathered up his bones as holy relics "more precious than precious stones and finer than gold," and put them in a suitable place where they could celebrate the anniversary of his martyrdom. According to the record, the Jews were as avid for his death as the pagans were.

Only one of Polycarp's letters has been preserved. Addressed to the Philippians in response to one from them, it has to do with the assembling of Ignatius's letters into a single volume. It alludes to more than one letter by the apostle Paul to the Philippians. It is also an attestation of certain New Testament books as canonical. A. CABANISS

POOLE, MATTHEW (1624–1679)
Presbyterian biblical scholar

Born at York, Poole studied at Emmanuel College, Cambridge. He adopted presbyterian views of church polity, believing them to be ordained by God. In 1649 he became rector of St. Michael-le-Querne in London and was involved in the presbyterian organization that temporarily was effective in the London area by order of the "Puritan" Par-

liament. He was very concerned about the education of young men for the ordained ministry and put forward plans in 1658 to raise funds for this project. With the restoration of monarchy in 1660 this project had to be abandoned, and he had to give up his rectory. Without pastoral charge he devoted himself to the great work of his life, a *Synopsis* (in Latin) of the critical writings of biblical commentators. This was published between 1669 and 1676 in five folio volumes. Also he produced a more popular *Annotations upon the Holy Bible* in two volumes. When his name was linked with the "Popish Plot" in 1678 he feared murder; so he went to live in Holland, where he remained until his death. P. TOON

PRIDEAUX, HUMPHREY (1648–1724)
Dean of Norwich Cathedral; scholar of ancient civilizations in the Middle East

Prideaux was born in Cornwall and educated at Westminster and Christ Church, Oxford, where he graduated in 1672 and went on to take several advanced degrees. He entered the Anglican ministry and had several churches in the Oxford area while engaging in research under the direction of John Fell, dean of Christ Church and bishop of Oxford. Prideaux belonged to the "Low Church" (or Protestant) wing of the Church of England, and he left Oxford for Norwich in 1686 when a Roman Catholic was named as dean of his college. In Norwich he became canon, archdeacon (1688), and dean (1702). He welcomed the revolution of 1688 that ousted the Roman Catholic King James II. He was unsuccessful in attempts to revise the Book of Common Prayer so as to give representation to the views of the Puritan dissenters.

Of Prideaux's writings, two were influential. The first work, *Life of Mahomet* (1697), purported to be a study of the founder of Islam, but was actually a polemical tract against the deists, who believed that God was not involved in the natural order. The second work, *The Old and New Testaments Connected in the History of the Jews* (two volumes, 1716–1718), was a history of the

Jewish people in the intertestamental period. Prideaux wrote numerous tracts that dealt with ecclesiastical issues. P. TOON

PRIESTLEY, JOSEPH (1733–1804)
English Unitarian clergyman; scientist

Born in Yorkshire, Priestley attended Daventry Nonconformist Academy from 1751 to 1755, when the ancient universities were closed to Nonconformists. His first pastorate was in Suffolk, and he followed this with another short one in Nantwich Cheshire. In this period he followed the rational mood of the time and began to question basic orthodox doctrines. In particular he came to reject the traditional view of Christ presented in the Nicene Creed; he also rejected the divine inspiration of the Scriptures. In 1761 he became a tutor at the Warrington Academy and moved six years later to the pastorate of Mill Hill Unitarian Chapel in Leeds. From here he propagated his radical views in a magazine, *The Theological Repository*. Alongside his theological interests he had maintained an absorbing interest in chemistry. From 1722 to 1780 he devoted himself to this scientific pursuit supported financially by Lord Shelbourne. In this period he "discovered" oxygen and wrote his monumental *Experiments and Observations on Different Kinds of Air* (1774–1786).

From 1780 to 1791 he resumed his pastoral ministry in Birmingham at the chapel of the New Meeting Society. Here he published several widely read books in which orthodoxy was attacked, such as *History of the Corruptions of Christianity* (1782) and *History of Early Opinions concerning Jesus Christ* (1786). Bishop Horsley, a learned Anglican, wrote against the latter work. Priestley's political views were also radical inasmuch as he publicly supported the French Revolution. His religious and political views provoked great hostility, forcing him to leave Birmingham and flee to London in 1791. From here he went three years later to Northumberland, Pennsylvania, where he died. P. TOON

PRITCHARD, JAMES BENNETT
(born 1909)
American archaeologist

Born in Louisville, Kentucky, Pritchard was educated at Asbury College, Drew Seminary, and the University of Pennsylvania (Ph.D., 1942). He taught Old Testament at Crozer Seminary from 1942 to 1954, and at the Church Divinity School of the Pacific from 1954 to 1962; and beginning in 1962 he served as professor of religious thought at the University of Pennsylvania. He was involved in archaeological excavations under the auspices of the American School of Oriental Research intermittently since 1950. Thus, he directed expeditions to Jericho (1950); El-Jib, Jordan (1956–1962); Tel es Sa-Diveh, Jordan (1964–1972); and Sarafand, Lebanon (1967–1972). He published several books in the field of archaeology—notably *Archaeology and the New Testament* (1956) and *The Ancient Near East* (1958). N. V. HOPE

PRUDENTIUS CLEMENS, AURELIUS
(348–c. 410)
Christian Latin poet and hymn writer

Prudentius was born in Spain, trained in the legal profession, and rose high in the civil service as a provincial governor in Spain. He ended his successful career at the age of fifty-seven to devote his life to Christ. At this time he published his writings, which were to have a great influence on subsequent Christian poetry and hymnology.

His poetic style was modeled after classical Latin forms and was clearly an attempt to take the best of Roman culture and consecrate it to the church. His poetry was lengthy and rich in doctrine. Three works dealt directly with apologetical and theological themes: the *Apotheosis* (on the divinity of Christ), the *Hamartigenia* (on the origin of sin against the heretical Marcion), and the *Contra Symmachum* (against a brief reappearance of paganism in Rome). His charming *Cathemerinon* was a collection of hymns and prayers for use at various times in daily life. The *Psychomachia* was a very influential allegory of spiritual warfare within the soul. This work marks the beginning of a new literary form in Christian letters, the allegorical epic. *Peri Stephanon* (*On Crowns*) is a collection of poems praising Roman and Spanish martyrs. In a very different style is his *Dittochaeon*, a series of pithy portraits of biblical themes and events that may have been intended as inscriptions for mosaics or paintings.

Prudentius's hymns are used by Christians even to this day. The most popular is as follows:

Of the Father's love begotten
Ere the worlds began to be,
He is Alpha and Omega,
He the source, the ending he,
Of the things that are,
that have been,
And that future years shall see,
Evermore and evermore!

P. TOON

PRYNNE, WILLIAM (1600–1669)

Puritan pamphleteer

Born in Somerset and educated at Oxford University, Prynne entered law school at Lincoln's Inn, London, in 1621. Here he was strongly influenced by Puritan and Calvinistic ideas, and he wrote a series of pamphlets against what he called Arminianism, the theological views of the leaders of the English State and Church. In 1632 he also wrote against stage plays. His attacks were understood by those in authority to be directed against the monarch, and so in 1634 he was sentenced by the Court of Star Chamber to life imprisonment, a fine of five thousand pounds, the loss of his university degree, and the pillory where both his ears were cut off. But all this could not silence him. In 1640 he was released from prison, and in the following years during the Long Parliament he played a major role in preparing the case against Archbishop Laud (an Arminian). Later he found that his principles also made him oppose Oliver Cromwell, and in 1650 he was again imprisoned, this time by Puritans. In 1659 he returned to active politics and had a part in the restora-

tion of Charles II to the throne. He became a member of the Cavalier Parliament. In all he wrote over two hundred books or pamphlets. P. TOON

PUSEY, EDWARD BOUVERIE (1800–1882)

Leader in the Anglo-Catholic Oxford movement within the Church of England

Pusey was Regius Professor of Hebrew and canon of Christ Church at Oxford. He shared with other brilliant young Oxford conservatives concern about the rising tide of biblical and theological liberalism and the reform spirit rampant in Britain during the late 1820s and 1830s. He contributed to reviving a "dead" High Church orthodoxy by stimulating knowledge of the early church fathers and of non-Puritan Anglicans of the seventeenth century. Their teaching had been obscured, in his estimation, by Deism, Broad Church theological indifference, and the evangelicals' concentration upon God's work alone in justification and the experience of that.

Pusey began to warn against the dangers of the new German theology, which he had studied firsthand. He began in late 1833 to contribute to the *Tracts for the Times* edited by John Henry Newman and to make the *Tracts* significant expressions of Anglo-Catholic teaching. He established a residence for theological students and a society for professors, tutors, and graduates in order to spread his principles. In 1836, he commenced editing translations of early Christian writers under the title *The Library of the Fathers*, which became a lifetime project, the last of the forty-eight volumes being published after his death. He was the first person of prominence to identify himself publicly with the movement, causing "Puseyism" to become the sometimes popular designation for it.

Because of an 1843 sermon, "The Holy Eucharist," he was suspended two years from preaching at Oxford for the Romish views expressed, an event that contributed to the conversion of Newman and others to Roman Catholicism. Pusey, however, remained steadfastly within the Church of England. He had learned to bear much sorrow in his private life through strict discipline and such practices as the wearing of a hair shirt. Nor did he share Newman's view that officials were to be obeyed absolutely. Pusey's strength helped retain others.

He was instrumental in 1845 in establishing an order of sisters in London. This was evidence of his personal charity and of new vitality among Anglo-Catholics in reaching the poor, as well as of the Church's ability to accept Anglo-Catholic concepts. In 1846, he resumed his university preaching, taking up theologically where he had left off. Later, a new wave of liberalism in the church provided Pusey his final thrusts of public activity against the influence of Benjamin Jowett and biblical higher criticism. D. MUNSON

PYM, JOHN (c. 1583–1643)

Leader of the parliamentary opposition to Charles I in the period before the English Civil War

Pym was born in Somerset and educated at Oxford and the law school of the Middle Temple, London. Though he was in Parliament from 1614, he became prominent in 1621 when he was identified with the faction that wanted to impose penal laws against Roman Catholics. He maintained opposition to Roman Catholicism for the rest of his career. It was in 1640, as a mature parliamentarian, that he became a leader of the opposition to Charles I. During the hectic events of the next two years as the nation moved toward civil war, he was one of the most vocal opponents of the policy of the king and his advisers. When war did break out in 1642 he was one of the members of the parliamentary committee who promoted the war. Despite his reluctance to accept Scottish Presbyterianism he was prominent in negotiating the alliance with Scotland against the king in 1643—which was his last political achievement. P. TOON

Q

QUARRIER, WILLIAM (1829–1903)

Founder of the Orphan Homes of Scotland

Born in the Clydeside Valley of Scotland, Quarrier lost his father three years later, went to work at the age of six, knew grinding poverty in the Glasgow slums, and became a shoemaker. He was converted at seventeen, excelled and prospered in his trade, won others to Christ (including his own mother), and in 1864 began work for destitute and orphan children in Glasgow. Having taken as his motto Have Faith in God, he testified to God's faithfulness near the end of his life in saying, "He gave me the utmost of my asking, and I felt that I would need to give Him the utmost of the power I pledged."

Quarrier, who became one of the first multiple storeowners in Glasgow, opened his Orphan Homes of Scotland at Bridge of Weir in 1878. Thousands of children were trained in its church and school. A prevalent scourge was countered by the addition of Scotland's first tuberculosis sanatorium; later it became a colony for epileptics. In Glasgow a huge night shelter and evangelistic center was built. Quarrier established a base also in Canada, and many Scottish orphans were happily settled in families there.

The homes have never appealed for money. The work was the Lord's—Quarrier regarded himself only as the agent. The work still continues as an enterprise of faith.

J. D. DOUGLAS

QUESNEL, PASQUIER (1634–1719)

French Roman Catholic Jansenist theologian

After studying at the University of the Sorbonne, Paris, Quesnel joined the Oratory in 1657. He showed gifts as a spiritual director and was placed in charge of the moral and spiritual development of young men. His teaching to them, based on close study of the Bible, is found in his well-known work *The New Testament in French, with Moral Comments on Each Verse* (1672). By 1675 he had adopted Jansenist views, believing that people become Christians through the irresistible grace of God and must live lives of strict moral discipline. In his edition of the *Works of St. Leo,* these views appeared in the notes. Jansensim was not acceptable to the papacy. So in 1681 he had to leave Paris for Orleans, and three years later he moved to Brussels, living with Antoine Arnaul, another distinguished Jansenist. During 1703 through 1704, he spent time in prison but escaped to Holland. He bravely defended his views but was further condemned by the pope in 1708 and then again in the papal bull *Unigenitus* (1713), which condemned 101 of his statements taken from his book of the New Testament. He held to his beliefs, however, and died in Amsterdam in 1719. P. TOON

QUIMBY, PHINEAS PARKHURST
(1802–1866)
Leader of the mental healing movement in America; spiritual father of several mentalist cults

Quimby founded no organization, but the disciples who adopted his teachings (most notably, Mary Baker Eddy) organized several: Divine Science, Unity, Practical Christianity, Livable Christianity, Home of Truth, and Christian Science.

Quimby was born in Lebanon, New Hampshire. He gave up clock making to become a mesmerist in 1838, after hearing Charles Poyen, who practiced mental healing in Portland, Maine. Disease was mental, taught Quimby; God, or Wisdom, was everything real (as opposed to illusory matter).

The term *New Thought* was used by the 1890s to describe Quimby's teaching and the diverse groups it produced. The movement became formalized when the International New Thought Alliance was organized in 1914. M. FACKLER

R

RAHNER, KARL (1904–1984)
German Jesuit priest and scholar

Born in Freiburg, Germany, Rahner became a Jesuit in 1922 and, in 1932, underwent priestly ordination. His final advanced degree work was accomplished at Freiburg University and Innsbruck University. In 1936, he joined the Innsbruck faculty. Serving as instructor in theology, Rahner became a prominent academic figure at both Innsbruck University and München University between 1936 and 1964. His great work in these years was his many books and articles, an enormous output on every conceivable religious topic. He was also editor of various important collected works. Among the most notable were the *Lexikon fur Theologie und Kirche* and *Sacramentum Mundi*. Trenchant as well as prolific, Rahner was equally at home both with formal, abstract teaching and popular discussion of theological themes.

Rahner's writings are a highly significant exposition of twentieth-century Roman Catholic theology. Based in vast philosophical erudition, Rahner's work has, in fact, had broad influence on contemporary Roman Catholic doctrinal thought. The substance and methods of his work have been publicly admired by various popes. Appointed as one of its theological experts, Rahner also had an impact on Vatican Council II and its doctrinal statements. In many ways, Rahner's place in Roman Catholicism is comparable to Karl Barth's in Protestantism. In general, Rahner's thought upholds a traditional Christian supernaturalism, sometimes adjusted deeply for modern philosophy. For Rahner, as for Barth, this has meant a combining of traditional and orthodox doctrine with existentialism and its insights. Through his superb expressive skills, Rahner made his abstract teachings highly appealing to a wide academic audience. But at the same time, his writings and lectures for the public have compelling pastoral insights and evangelistic promptings. Rahner's works have given recent Roman Catholic theology one of its ablest expositions.
K. J. BRYER

RAIKES, ROBERT (1735–1811)
One of the founders of Sunday schools

Raikes was born in Gloucester, England, and was educated at the cathedral school there. His father was a newspaper publisher, and on his death in 1757 Raikes followed in his footsteps. Raikes had a keen social conscience and used his newspaper to support his philanthropic concerns. In 1768 he led a campaign for the reform of the Gloucester prisons. In 1780, in response to the neglected condition of many of the city's children, he set up a Sunday school in his own parish after consulting with the curate of a neighboring parish, the Reverend Thomas Stock (1749–1803), who himself had begun one. The school was in session weekdays and Sundays, teaching Bible, reading, and other basic subjects. The project was a controversial one, for many opposed free popular education, fearing civil unrest and revolution. In 1783, Raikes used his newspaper to promote the Sunday school movement; this attracted wide attention. By 1786 it was said that some two hundred thousand children were receiving this basic education throughout England. William Fox, who had for some time been interested in such an educational system, approved of Raikes's plan and in 1785 set up a London society to help establish these schools. The movement spread into Wales, Scotland, Ireland, and the Americas. John Wesley promoted them, and the Queen's interest in them also gave impetus to the movement. Raikes himself developed a reputation that his benevolence and philanthropy were matched only by his vanity. But generally, his contemporaries forgave him this sin, recognizing the great good he helped bring about. Teachers were at first paid, but after 1810 the schools were usually staffed by volunteers. P. TOON

RAINY, ROBERT (1826–1906)
Scottish theologian; ecclesiastical statesman

Born in Glasgow, where he graduated with a liberal arts degree, Rainy was among the first of Thomas Chalmers's students at New College, Edinburgh, after the 1843 Disruption. He ministered in the Free Church at Huntly (1851–1854) and in Edinburgh (1854–1862) before his appointment at thirty-six as church history professor at New College, a post which he held (with that of principal from 1874) until his death. Rainy needed all his great physical stamina and spiritual serenity during those momentous Free Church years. He routed Dean A. P. Stanley of Westminster by showing that his lectures on the Church of Scotland (1872)

were riddled with superficialities and errors. With heavy heart, and only for the sake of the unity of the church, he supported the deposition for heresy of Professor Robertson Smith in 1881. Rainy was one of the architects of the 1900 union between the Free Church and the United Presbyterian Church and was the automatic choice as moderator of the first assembly. Prime Minister Gladstone called him "the greatest of living Scotsmen." He was sometimes misunderstood in standing firm for unpopular causes, but his integrity and dedication were never questioned. Amid all the turbulence that surrounded him, one biographer commented, "He held the keys of inward peace." J. D. DOUGLAS

RAMSAY, SIR WILLIAM MITCHELL (1851–1939)
Classical and New Testament scholar; archaeologist

Born at Glasgow, Scotland, Ramsay was educated at Aberdeen and Oxford. As professor of humanity (Latin) at Aberdeen (1886–1911), he was able to spend many of the long vacations in Asia Minor, continuing his research as an archaeologist, a practice he had begun in 1880. He soon made himself the foremost authority of his day on the geography and early history of the area. His *Historical Geography of Asia Minor* (1890) and *The Church in the Roman Empire before A.D. 170* (1893) remain of basic importance for their subjects. In 1883 he had discovered the funerary inscription of Abercius, bishop of Hierapolis in the late second century.

Ramsay increasingly concentrated on early Christian history and remains. His work led him to abandon his previous acceptance of the Tübingen school's skepticism of the historical reliability of the Lucan writings, for he found that Luke was minutely accurate in his use of titles. Every person, said Ramsay, was found just where he ought to be: *proconsuls* in senatorial provinces, *asiarchs* in Ephesus, *politarchs* in Thessalonica, magicians and soothsayers everywhere. The title *politarch* (Acts 17:6) is particularly striking; it was unknown in other Greek literature until the discovery of inscriptions, including five of them in Thessalonica. Besides demonstrating Luke's reliability as a historian, Ramsay filled in much of Paul's historical background in *The Cities of St. Paul* (1907), while *A Historical Commentary on St. Paul's Epistle to the Galatians* (1899) powerfully argued that the letter was addressed to south, not north, Galatia.

N. HILLYER

RAMUS, PETER (1515–1572)
French humanist, logician, and educational reformer

Born Pierre de la Ramée, Ramus was the son of an impoverished noble family of Liege, in northern France. He studied at Paris and received the master of arts degree there. In 1543 he published two Latin works, "The Structure of Dialectic" and "Remarks on Aristotle." The latter was highly critical of both Aristotle and the university curriculum. The university faculty secured a decree forbidding Ramus to teach philosophy, but two years later the ban was lifted. In 1551 Henry II appointed him professor of eloquence and philosophy in the school later known as the College de France. He was converted to Calvinism about 1561. During the religious wars he left Paris, moved to Germany, and then to Switzerland. In 1570 he returned to Paris and was murdered in the St. Bartholomew's Day Massacre (1572).

Ramus wrote about sixty works and collaborated on a number of others. They include classical editions and commentaries; lectures on physics, metaphysics, and mathematics; textbooks and a posthumously published theological work. By far the most influential were his writings on logic and rhetoric. The extent of his influence can be seen in the fact that his *Dialectica* (1555), also called *Logica*, appeared in nearly 250 editions or adaptations.

In his logic, Ramus proposed an "art of discourse" to replace the complex quantified logic of the Middle Ages. Previous logicians had distinguished scientific logic (which argues from certainties or necessity) from dialectic (which argues from probabilities). Ramus reduced all argumentation to the art of discourse. This was supposed to be a natural logic that formulated the laws governing man's spontaneous thinking and reasoning. Natural logic has two parts: discovery and judgment. The first stage in thought consists in the discovery of arguments, or categories. These categories, or *loci* as they were called, included original categories such as cause and effect but also derived categories such as genus, species, division, and definition. The second stage, judgment, consists in applying these categories, or arranging the arguments. Here there are three stages: the syllogism, the system that is the formation of a systematic chain of conclusions, and finally the bringing of all sciences and knowledge in relation to God. The model of dichotomized division, where every subject is subdivided into two parts and these subdivided in turn, was extremely prominent in his work.

Although there is little that is original in Ramus's work, it was extremely popular and influential. It represents a humanist reaction to scholastic logic, a reform in the interest of cultured expression and the development of the personality. It did little to develop the method of logic or empirical science. Still, Descartes studied a post-Ramist logic text with a section on method—a debate roused by Ramus's work. The modern encyclopedia owes much of its organization to the Ramist tradition. Ramus's views were especially popular in Calvinist "middle," or secondary, schools, though this was probably for cultural and psychological rather than religious reasons. A. Vos

RANDALL, BENJAMIN (1749–1808)
New England evangelist; founder of the northern branch of the Freewill Baptists

Randall was born in New Castle, New Hampshire, and went to sea with his sailor father. He was converted in 1770 under Whitefield's ministry. Ordained ten years later, he abandoned the doctrine of sovereign election and adopted Baptistic views on the sacrament. He wrote the covenant that

became the basis for the Freewill Baptist Church and preached for twenty-five years throughout northeastern United States. The Free Baptist Church numbered about six thousand at the time of his death.
M. FACKLER

RANKE, LEOPOLD VON (1795–1886)
German historian

Born in Wiehe, Thüringen, in the kingdom of Saxony and educated at Leipzig, Ranke taught classics at a gymnasium in Frankfurt for seven years before becoming professor of history in 1825 at Berlin University, a position he retained until 1871. He published fifty-four volumes in the historical field, of which the most important are *History of the Popes* (two volumes, eight editions, 1834–1885), "in which he treated the papacy as a great historical phenomenon without regard to the controversies of the day and without romantic enthusiasm"; *German History in the Reformation Era* (five volumes, 1839–1847); *French History* (five volumes, 1852–1861); *English History* (seven volumes, 1859–1868). Through these and his other publications, as G. P. Gooch has said, "It is Ranke's glory to have rendered the history of modern Europe more fully intelligible, to have established its unity and portrayed the leading characters in the drama." A pioneer in the field of "scientific history," Ranke's greatness as a historian lies chiefly in the objectivity of his presentation, his insistence on a thorough study of contemporary sources, and his critical evaluation of such sources in the light of their origin. In 1841 he was appointed historiographer to the Prussian State, and in 1865 he was ennobled by the King of Prussia. N. V. HOPE

RAPP, J. G. (1757–1847)
Founder of the Harmony Society, a communal society

Rapp and a few followers, fleeing persecution, left Württemberg, Germany, to settle in Pennsylvania in 1803. The Harmony Society was organized in 1805, moved to (New Harmony) Indiana in 1814, and then moved

again to Economy (now Ambridge), Pennsylvania, in 1824. Rapp was a pietist who believed in an imminent regeneration of the world, at which time the "harmony" of male and female elements in man would be restored. His group prospered, save in numbers (they were celibates). Rapp dominated the group until the end of his life.
M. FACKLER

RAUSCHENBUSCH, WALTER (1861–1918)
Known as the "father of the social gospel"

Rauschenbusch was born in Rochester, New York, where his father was a professor in the "German Department" of Rochester's Baptist Theological Seminary. Rauschenbusch lived in Rochester most of his life, attending college and seminary there and teaching for his last twenty-one years in the seminary. His one lengthy excursion from Rochester, however, gave him experiences that changed his life.

Rauschenbusch became the pastor of the Second German Baptist Church in New York City in 1886. The church was largely made up of immigrants who lived on New York's lower East Side, an area aptly called "Hell's Kitchen." What Rauschenbusch saw there of the immigrants' sordid living conditions, of labor exploitation by industrial giants, and of governmental indifference to the suffering of the poor led to a personal revolution. Rauschenbusch looked back in 1913 on what had happened: "I began to work in New York and there, among the working people, . . . I began to understand the connection between religious and social questions." Rauschenbusch asked himself if his Christian heritage had anything to offer the suffering thousands in the immediate vicinity of his church. His question forced him to rethink his religious categories and to begin a fresh study of the Bible. It also encouraged him to explore the views of dynamic social critics, like Henry George, who ran for mayor of New York as a socialist in the year Rauschenbusch began his pastorate, or like Jacob Riis, with whom Rauschenbusch later campaigned for children's playgrounds and better housing.

Rauschenbusch left New York City in 1897 to return to Rochester, but these experiences formed the context out of which his first book, *Christianity and the Social Crisis* (1907), was written. This volume became an immediate sensation and catapulted Rauschenbusch into national prominence as a spokesman for a socially committed Christianity. The book noted the great interest Old Testament prophets had shown in social matters and how socially powerful the life of the early church had been. It also called for a faith joining Christian beliefs and social ethics. The book manifested Rauschenbusch's continuing evangelical sentiments ("In personal religion the first requirement is to repent and believe the gospel"); but it also made provocative new statements ("Social religions, too, demand repentance and faith: repentance for our social sins; faith in the possibility of a new social order").

In subsequent books, Rauschenbusch fleshed out his picture of a "social gospel." His *Prayers for the Social Awakening* (1910) has been described as a modern devotional classic. The prayers also reflect the combined reliance on Christian faith and human potential that was characteristic of the early social gospel.

His *Christianizing the Social Order* (1912) contained his most sustained criticism of American capitalism. It was, according to Rauschenbusch, blinded to human needs by its competitiveness and its drive for profit. Its major firms tyrannized the weak and defenseless; it fostered values through advertising and the mass market, which debased the spiritual qualities of life. In the place of capitalism, Rauschenbusch called for a social order characterized by justice, collective ownership of most property, democracy in the organization of industry, and a much more equal distribution of goods. Rauschenbusch frequently called himself a Christian socialist, but he also took pains to disavow Marxist or doctrinaire formulas for overhauling American economic life.

Rauschenbusch's last major work appeared shortly before his death, *A Theology for the Social Gospel* (1917). This influential volume set out systematically what a Christian theology would look like if it took seriously the needs of modern society. It was somewhat less optimistic than earlier books about the possibilities for human improvement. Yet Rauschenbusch had always been the one leader of the social gospel who had never underestimated the reality of evil or its permanent roots in the human heart. The volume also warned of how dangerous mere social movements could be if they lost the backing of Christian theology.

In *A Theology for the Social Gospel*, Rauschenbusch laid great stress on the theme of the kingdom of God. During his pastorate in New York, he had helped found an informal "Brotherhood of the Kingdom" in which the ideas of the social gospel were developed in discussion with other likeminded men. Rauschenbusch admitted that his conception of the kingdom represented an effort to Christianize Darwinistic evolution. But he also maintained that progress for the kingdom of God against the kingdom of evil could never take place without the presence of Christ and the work of the Holy Spirit.

Rauschenbusch was an "evangelical liberal" who combined many elements of orthodoxy with many convictions of the modern age. His reputation as the leader of the *social* gospel, however, has blinded both liberals and evangelicals to how much orthodoxy remained in his social *gospel*. Specific evaluation of Rauschenbusch aside, he was undoubtedly the most influential American Christian thinker in the first third of the twentieth century. M. A. NOLL

RAWLINSON, ALFRED EDWARD JOHN (1884–1960)
Anglican bishop; New Testament theologian

Born at Newton le Willows, Lancashire, England, Rawlinson was educated at Corpus Christi College, Oxford University, graduating in 1907 with high honors. Ordained in the Church of England as deacon in 1909 and priest in 1910, he was a tutor at Keble College (1909–1913) and student and tutor at Christ Church College (1914–1929). In the latter year he was made canon residentiary of Durham and archdeacon of Auckland; and in 1936 he was appointed bishop of Derby, where he remained until his retirement in 1959. Between 1930 and 1936 he was chaplain to the king. Rawlinson published a commentary on Mark's Gospel in the Westminster Commentaries series. He delivered Bampton Lectures in 1926 on the subject "The New Testament Doctrine of the Christ." He authored books on theology such as *Dogma, Fact, and Experience* (1915) and *Authority and Freedom* (1924). He also contributed to publication of several theological symposia—for example, *Foundations* (1912), *Essays Catholic and Critical* (1926), and *Essays on the Trinity and Incarnation* (1928). N. V. HOPE

RAWLINSON, SIR HENRY CRESWICKE (1810–1895)
Orientalist

Born at Challington, Oxfordshire, England, in 1827 Rawlinson was nominated to a military cadetship in the East India Company. His next twenty years were spent as a political agent of the company and as a military and consular officer of the British Crown, in which capacities he saw service in India, Afghanistan, and Iran. He early developed a taste for Oriental studies; and in 1833 when he, along with other British officers, went to Iran to reorganize the Shah's army, he became keenly interested in Persian antiquities. In particular he was so fascinated by the cuneiform inscriptions at Behistun, Iran, that he determined to decipher the Old Persian portions of them. In this self-appointed task he succeeded, publishing his findings in his book *Persian Cuneiform Inscriptions at Behistun* (1846–1851). By 1857 Rawlinson and other students succeeded in deciphering the Mesopotamian cuneiform. These important discoveries led to a greatly increased understanding of ancient Babylonia and Assyria and much of biblical history as well. Rawlinson was made a knight in 1856 and a baronet in 1891 "in recognition

of his distinguished services to the state, stretching over a long period of years." N. V. HOPE

REBMAN, JOHANNES (1819–1876)
Pioneer missionary of the Church Missionary Society to East Africa

A German Lutheran from Württemberg, Rebman graduated from the Basel Mission Seminary and the Anglican Theological College in Islington. With J. L. Krapf, Rebman established Rabai Station, one thousand feet above Mombasa, in 1846, and there Rebman died in 1876 without ever having returned to Europe. He was blind during the last years. The two missionaries made six important trips of exploration, and Rebman discovered Mount Kilimanjaro in May 1848. He said of these travels: "Our grand aim was but the spreading of the kingdom of God," and "I took possession of the pagan land for the militant Church of Christ." He at first vigorously attacked pagan beliefs and customs until God taught him to preach only the love of Christ. P. BEAVER

REES, THOMAS BONNER (1911–1970)
English evangelist

Rees was born in Blackburn, the son of a clothing wholesaler. He was not a good student, and he left grammar school to work in London. He was converted at the age of fifteen and soon thereafter became involved in various evangelistic activities. He became a lay worker at St. Nicholas's Anglican Church, Sevenoaks. In 1931 he resigned his position there when some Anglican churchmen criticized his involvement in Nonconformist missions. He went throughout Great Britain on an itinerant mission, and he carried out large evangelistic rallies, particularly in Northern Ireland. For several years he worked on the staff of Scripture Union. In the late 1930s he took a pastorate at the Banwell Baptist Church for several years, but during World War II he returned again to evangelism. He founded three evangelistic conference centers, the most famous of these being Hildenborough in 1945. He conducted over fifty mass evangelistic rallies in the Royal Albert Hall, London, and his missions took him all over Great Britain and forty-eight times to North America. He was a participant at the Keswick and Port Stewart conventions, and he was instrumental in launching Billy Graham's first crusade in England. His son, Justyn, continued his father's work at Hildenborough, and his wife, Jean, wrote a biography of him, *His Name Was Tom* (1971). P. TOON

REIMARUS, HERMANN SAMUEL
(1694–1768)
German Deist; biblical critic

Born at Hamburg, Reimarus studied at Jena under J. A. Fabricius, whose son-in-law he became. Subsequently, Reimarus taught philosophy at Wittenberg. He came under the influence of English Deists, and this was a primary source of destructive biblical criticism. After serving from 1723 to 1727 as rector of the *Hochschule* at Wismar, he became in 1727 professor of Hebrew and Oriental languages at the Johanneum Gymnasium in Hamburg. Reimarus remained in this post until his death. From 1744 he worked on a comprehensive study of biblical criticism. Although the work remained largely unpublished, portions were released (1774–1778) by G. E. Lessing under the title of *Wolfenbuettel Fragments*. These declared the biblical writers to be frauds and deceivers, and the publication unleashed a sensation throughout Germany. One fragment, "The Object of Jesus and His Disciples," presented a humanistic view of Jesus and fueled the speculations that appeared in Albert Schweitzer's *Quest of the Historical Jesus* (1901). W. A. DETZLER

REMBRANDT HARMENSZ VAN RIJN
(1606–1669)
Dutch painter

Rembrandt was born in Leyden, the son of a prosperous miller. From age seven until age fourteen he attended a humanist school in his home city. For a short time he went to the University of Leyden, where he came into contact with the great literature that was to influence his later art. In 1620 he began a three-year study of art in the studio of an unimportant Leyden artist. In the latter part of 1631 he moved to Amsterdam, where he began to have success as a portrait painter after a brief six-month apprenticeship to the celebrated artist Lastman. Two years later he married the wealthy Saskia van Uylenburch, who died in 1641. Later (in 1649), Hendrickje Stoffels became Rembrandt's common-law wife. This brought her hardship and persecution at the hands of the local rigidly Calvinist society. She remained with Rembrandt through the artist's increasing financial difficulties brought about by mismanagement of his money and particularly by his great appetite for possessing antiques and other objects of art. By 1657 Rembrandt was bankrupt and had lost his house and art collection. Contrary to popular belief that he then lived a life of poverty and neglect, he continued to receive good commissions. In 1658, after bankruptcy, he worked for an art firm set up by his only son, Titus, and Hendrickje. In 1663 Hendrickje died, and in 1668 Rembrandt lost Titus, one year before his own death.

Of great lasting influence on Rembrandt's art were the memories of his mother reading the Bible to him. He also drew freely from older art, literature, history, and contemporary life. The development of his highly personal style was founded upon continuous work, which in over forty years yielded about 650 paintings, 280 etchings, and 1400 drawings.

Rembrandt's religious art was never intended for use in a church. His works might be called private devotional paintings. They were small in size and intended for contemplation in the home. His development as an individual and painter is seen in a single painting, *John the Baptist Teaching* (Stratliche Museum, Berlin), that he started in 1636 and worked over for the next fourteen years. For the most part Rembrandt saw the Bible in terms of men and women with distinct personalities that were not unlike the average person he knew in Amsterdam. His Christ, like the one in the painting *Christ at*

Emmaus (Louvre, c. 1648), attempts at fathoming the Jesus of the Gospels—the historic Jesus. A. STEFFLER

RENAN, JOSEPH ERNST (1823–1892)

French historian; orientalist

Renan was given a scholarship in 1838 by F. A. Dupanloup to join the seminary of St.-Nicholas-du-Chardonnet at Paris. Through the study of German theology, historical criticism, and Semitic languages he came to doubt the truth of Christianity. These doubts led him in 1845 to leave the seminary of St. Sulpice. His most notable writing was *La Vie de Jésus* (*Life of Jesus*), which appeared in 1863. Using the results of biblical criticism, he portrayed Jesus as a gifted itinerant preacher, but he was not the Son of God. Immediately Renan set about to enlarge the book, and the result was his *Histoire de Origines du Christiansme* (*History of the Origins of Christianity*; seven volumes, 1863–1881). This major work embraced the early expansion of Christianity under the apostle Paul throughout the ancient world. Subsequently, Renan penned a parallel work bearing the title *Histoire du Peuple d'Israel* (*History of the People of Israel*; five volumes, 1887–1893). Throughout his career, Renan made frequent forays to the Near East, where he participated in archaeological digs. He was called to the chair of Hebrew at the Collège de France in 1862, but he was summarily removed after the publication of his *Life of Jesus*. In 1870 he was reinstated to the post, and under the secularist Third Republic the skeptic Renan was elevated to be director of the college in 1879. W. A. DETZLER

REUCHLIN, JOHANNES (1455–1522)

German Hebraist

Reuchlin was born in Pforzhem, near Stuttgart. He studied under Brethren of the Common Life in Schlettstadt and attended the University of Paris, where he concentrated on Greek. After his graduation in 1470 he obtained his M.A. at the University of Basel in 1474, following which he studied law at Poitiers and Orleans, receiving his licentiate in 1481. He then spent some time traveling in Italy. On his return to Germany he taught both jurisprudence and arts at the University of Tübingen. He also acted as a legal adviser to the Duke of Württemberg and from 1502 to 1512 was a judge in the Swabian League.

Reuchlin's primary interest, however, was in the study of Hebrew at which he worked from 1486 to 1506. He thus became the leading Hebraist among the humanists in the early sixteenth century. As a result of his studies he published both a Hebrew dictionary and a Hebrew grammar: *Rudimenta Hebraica* (1506). He also studied the Hebrew commentaries on the Old Testament and the Jewish Cabala. He sought to combine the ideas found in these works with his Greek Pythagorean philosophy. As a result he published two works: *On the Wonderworking Word* (1494) and *On the Cabalistic Art* (1517).

Reuchlin's interest in the so-called cabalistic science caused him trouble. Johann Pfefferkorn, a converted Jew, writing in *A Mirror for the Jews* (1511), declared that all Jewish books should be confiscated and burned. Reuchlin opposed this on the ground that only those that were blasphemous should be destroyed, but that works such as the Talmud, the Cabala, the Old Testament manuscripts, and prayer and hymn books should be preserved. For this statement, Jakob Hoogstraten cited him to appear before his Court of Inquisition, but Reuchlin successfully appealed to Rome. He then wrote a work justifying himself: *Augenspiegel* (*A Mirror for the Eyes*). He received support from many of the humanists who published a collection of defensive letters entitled *Letters of Famous Men* (1514). But more important was the work edited by Cortus Rubeanus and Ulrich von Hutten: *Letters of Obscure Men* (1515), a scathing attack on the obscurantism of the church's leaders. Reuchlin was appointed professor of Hebrew and Greek at the University of Ingelstadt, (1519–1520) and then at Tübingen. Reuchlin died before he could assume the latter office. His works were condemned by Pope Leo X in 1520. W. S. REID

REUSS, EDWARD (1804–1891)

Protestant biblical scholar who influenced later critical theories about the composition of the Old Testament

Reuss was born in Strassburg, France. From 1834 he taught at the Protestant seminary in that city and from 1838 was a member of the state theological faculty. He became dean of the theological faculty in the newly organized University of Strassburg in 1872.

Reuss was one of the first biblical scholars to suggest that the earliest parts of the Old Testament were collected and written in stages. His views paved the way for scholars such as K. H. Graf, Abraham Kuenen, and Julius Wellhausen. Reuss believed that one section of the Pentateuch, the *Grundschrift*, (*Priestly Document*, or *P*) was composed at a late date, perhaps as late as the Exile in the sixth century B.C. The *P* material was thought to be the developed ritual and ceremony sections (much of Numbers, all of Leviticus, Exodus 25–40, also Genesis 1:1–2:3). Reuss also attacked the view of F. C. Baur that the dominant note in the apostolic church was the conflict between Jewish and Gentile interpretations of Christianity.

During his long and productive scholarly career, Reuss helped edit a standard edition of John Calvin's works (sixteen volumes, 1863–1900), founded the journal *Theologische Gesellschaft*, and produced a sixteen-volume French translation and commentary on the Bible (1874–1881). Of his many writings, *Das Alte Testament* (published posthumously in six volumes, 1892–1894) was his most developed study of the Old Testament. P. TOON

RHENIUS, KARL (1790–1838)

German missionary to India

Rhenius was one of the first German missionaries to India under the Church Missionary Society of London, which at the time could not recruit enough Anglican priests.

Sent to Palamcottah, he built on the work done by the chaplain of the British East India Company, James Hough, from 1816 to 1820 and the earlier pioneering of the famous Danish-Halle missionary, C. F. Schwartz. Rhenius led a mass movement of the Shanan caste, and by 1835 there were 11,186 members in 261 villages. His method was based on the village school, of which the teacher was also the local catechist. Rhenius produced a Tamil grammar and revised the Bible. He established a seminary for catechists, out of which high schools and training colleges eventually developed. He came into conflict with the Church Missionary Society over the ordination powers of bishops, withdrew from the Society, but remained at Palamcottah. P. BEAVER

RICCI, MATTEO (1552–1610)

First Roman Catholic missionary to China

Born of a noble family at Macareta, Italy, Ricci entered the Society of Jesus in 1571 and was sent to Macao, the Portuguese trading settlement on the Kwangtung coast, in 1582. He was directed to learn Chinese. Eventually he gained admittance to Chaoching and spent six years there in experimentation. His map of the world, books, paintings, and mechanical instruments gained the interest of the literati. Ricci dressed like a Buddhist monk and built a chapel like a Buddhist temple; but finding this an obstacle rather than an advantage, he then dressed as a Confucian scholar and lived like the literati. Ricci was a remarkable linguist. He came to a profound understanding and appreciation of Chinese civilization and became expert in philosophy. He studied the Classics at Shaochow. After abortive trips to Peking in 1595 and 1598 he settled in Nanking. There he made influential friends and converts. The church began to grow through his approach to individuals.

Ricci was able to gain residence in Peking in 1601 and remained there until death. His policy was radical adaptation. Opposing Buddhism and Taoism, he allied with classical Confucianism, making it a bridge to the gospel. He recognized the cult of Confucius as civil only and permitted ancestor rites to be purged of certain features. His most influential writing was *The True Knowledge of God* (1603). Ricci regarded his apostolate to intellectuals as preparatory; he planted the church, and his successors built on his foundation. P. BEAVER

RICHARD I (1157–1199)

Known as the "Lion Heart"; king of England, 1189–1199

Born at Oxford, Richard was king of England for ten years but was not in England more than six months—the country being ruled by various regents. His major interest was the Crusade; he was one of the three royal leaders of the Third. Before he inherited the throne, he was in almost constant revolt against his father, King Henry II, but he was especially beloved by his mother, the famous Eleanor of Aquitaine. From her, Richard inherited a love for the troubadour civilization of southern France.

At the end of the Third Crusade, Richard was held for ransom by the duke of Austria. The "king's ransom" raised by his mother became a quasipermanent tax in England, and the phrase passed into common usage. He had earlier imposed the "Saladin tithe" to raise money for the Crusade, the first direct taxation in England, and one that endured for a long time after the death of both Richard and Saladin. Despite his serious incapacity for government, Richard has gone down in legend as a heroic-romantic figure, probably because of reaction to his capable—but disliked—brother and successor, King John. Richard was married to Berengaria of Navarre, a queen of England who never set foot on the island. A. CABANISS

RICHARD, TIMOTHY (1845–1919)

Missionary to China

Richard, a Welshman under the Baptist Missionary Society of London (BMS), is generally regarded as one of the greatest missionaries ever sent to China. After his arrival in 1870, he ranged widely over the country and then in 1877 was drawn to Shansi prov-

ince by the great famine. He remained there eight years, hoping to induce the officials and intellectuals to eliminate famines through using Western science. Richard was a great sinologist and highly appreciative of Chinese culture. He hoped to reach the literati, intellectuals, and officials by presenting the gospel and Christian faith through terms, concepts, and methods that would appeal to them. However, he believed that the country needed both the gospel and Western learning to solve its problems; so he called the missions to contribute to the reconstruction of China.

Richard proposed to establish Christian colleges in the capital of each province, but failed to get the BMS to found such a college in either Shansi or Shantung. Leaving the BMS, he joined the Society for the Diffusion of Christian and General Knowledge, founded in 1887 (called the Christian Literature Society after 1906). He became general secretary in 1891. The Society was very influential with the reformers, and even the young emperor read its literature. Richard was successful in having a large part of the Boxer Indemnity Fund in Shansi applied to the founding of a state university where Western learning would be taught, and he was given complete control of it for ten years. P. BEAVER

RICHARD ROLLE OF HAMPOLE (c. 1300–1349)

English scholar and hermit

Born in Thorton Dale, Yorkshire, Rolle studied at Oxford, then began the life of a hermit at the age of nineteen. His last years were spent in Hampole, where he was the spiritual guide to a convent of Cisterian nuns.

Rolle is known primarily because of his writings rather than his deeds. He wrote in Latin as well as English, which indicates a superior degree of learning. He wrote lyrical poetry as well as prose and has latterly gained some notoriety as a literary figure. Some of his poems, although quite uneven in quality, are delicate, delightful, alliterative variations on themes from the biblical Song of Songs. In his own day, as revealed in his writings, he was a bitter, sharp, and complaining person against those whom he deemed as his enemies. At the same time he is also revealed as a quasimystic who preferred his solitude and contemplation to the active life. He was probably also an ecstatic who saw visions. Such theology as he had was quite simple and almost undefined in its lack of clarity. Rolle's writings belong to a preromantic tradition. His major works are *Incendium Amoris*, which presents his mystical theology, and *Melum Contemplativorum*. He also translated portions of the Scripture into Latin and English and wrote several commentaries. A. CABANISS

RICHELIEU, ARMAND-JEAN DU PLESSIS, DUC DE (1585–1642)
French cardinal and politician

Born in Paris of a noble family, Richelieu trained for the army at the Collège de Navarre in Paris. Because of the poverty of his family, he was put forward in 1606 for the bishopric of Lucon. In 1614 he was chosen to represent the clergy of Poitou in the States General (parliament). Two years later he was elevated to the post of secretary of state by Louis XIII. When his patron Concini died in 1617, Richelieu was exiled to Avignon. There he wrote a defense of Catholicism against the Huguenots. Recalled to Paris in 1619, he soon was raised to court favor as principal advisor to Marie de' Medici, mother of the king. In 1622 Gregory XV created him cardinal. Two years later he became president of the council of ministers. After 1629 he became chief minister and virtual ruler of France. He supported Gallicanism and thus fought ruthlessly the international dominance of the Spanish and Hapsburgs. To this end he entered the Thirty Years' War on the Protestant side. To wipe away political and military resistance to the throne, the cardinal attacked both the Huguenots and the French nobility. The Huguenots finally were defeated at La Rochelle (1628).

Richelieu was a patron of the arts and founder in 1635 of the Royal Academy. At his behest the Palais Royale and Sorbonne Chapel were built. W. A. DETZLER

RICHTER, JULIUS (1862–1940)
German professor of missiology

Pastor Richter led many missionary organizations in Germany, and he became interested in missiology, the scientific study of missions. In 1911 he succeeded Gustav Warneck as editor of the *Allgemeine Missionszeitschrift*. Warneck had given to missiology a degree of academic respectability by his service as professor of missions at Halle. In 1920 Richter was appointed to a similar academic chair at Berlin, a post he held until his death. Subsequently Richter became a well-known leader in the emerging ecumenical movement. Although more than thirty books and many essays were written by him, his most ambitious writing was the five-volume *History of Protestant Missionary Activities*. It appeared from 1906 through 1932 under the title *Allgemeine Evangelische Missionsgeschichte*. Parts of this work have been translated into English. W. A. DETZLER

RIDLEY, NICHOLAS (1500–1555)
Protestant reformer and martyr

Ridley was born in Northumberland, and in 1518 he went to Pembroke College, Cambridge. In 1524 he was elected a fellow of the college, and went on to continue his studies at the Sorbonne in Paris and at Louvain. He returned to his college in Cambridge in 1530. In 1537 he became a chaplain to Thomas Cranmer, the archbishop of Canterbury, and the following year became vicar of Herne, Kent. He was said to have had a deep influence upon Cranmer's thinking. Throughout the 1530s there was little indication that Ridley was abandoning traditional Catholic teaching: he accepted the doctrine of transubstantiation, auricular confession, and clerical celibacy. But his views changed dramatically the next decade. In 1540 he became master of Pembroke and chaplain to King Henry VIII; in 1541 he was made canon of Canterbury, and in 1543 canon of

Westminster. During these years he gradually made up his mind against the doctrine of transubstantiation. In 1547, the year Edward VI came to the throne, he was made bishop of Rochester. In 1550, when Edmund Bonner refused to reject the doctrine of transubstantiation, Ridley succeeded him as bishop of London. Ridley was instrumental in the production of the first edition of the Book of Common Prayer in 1549 and its revision in 1552, where his theology of the Eucharist was given special place in the order of service for Holy Communion. As the bishop of London, Ridley succeeded in having stone altars replaced by wooden tables for the observance of Holy Communion. He also instituted important pastoral work in the city, aiding the poor and founding hospitals and schools.

Just before the death of King Edward in 1553, Ridley ill-advisedly supported the claim of Lady Jane Grey to the throne and publicly denounced Mary and Elizabeth, the daughters of Henry VIII, as illegitimate. When Mary was made Queen shortly thereafter, she had Ridley imprisoned in the Tower of London and reinstated Bonner. He was joined there by Cranmer and Hugh Latimer. In the spring of 1554 the three were taken to Oxford, where their opinions were examined. There Ridley and his companions were given opportunities to renounce their Protestant views. Only Cranmer recanted (but in 1556 he again affirmed his Protestant beliefs and was burned); Ridley and Latimer held firm and were condemned to be burned at the stake on October 16, 1555. The execution was held near Balliol College in Oxford, where a martyrs' memorial was erected in 1841. Ridley was fastened to the stake by an iron chain, and a bag of gunpowder was hung around his neck. As the fire was lit, Latimer shouted encouragement: "Be of good comfort, Master Ridley, and play the man. We shall this day light such a candle by God's grace in England as, I trust, shall never be put out!" Latimer was said to have died quickly, but death for Ridley came more slowly with great pain. The scene was memorably described in Foxe's *Book of Martyrs*.
P. TOON

RIENZI, COLA DI (1312–1354)
Italian leader

Rienzi (or Rienzo) was an Italian patriot who figured prominently in the history of Rome in the mid-fourteenth century. He first came to prominence in 1343, when he was sent to Avignon to persuade Pope Clement VI to return to Rome and end the "Babylonian Captivity" of the papacy. Though unsuccessful, he did win the pope's favor.

Rienzi next gained prominence in 1347, when a popular revolution swept him into power as tribune in the city of Rome. By supporting the popular cause against the ruling families, Rienzi lost the support of the latter. By seeking to convene a meeting of all the Italian states to establish a common Italian policy, he lost support of the pope, whose temporal powers would be destroyed in a united Italy. And, by his arbitrary policies and ostentation, he lost the support of the populace.

Expelled in 1348, Rienzi experienced the decline of his fortunes until he was sentenced to death by a church court in Avignon in 1352. But before the sentence was carried out, Pope Clement died and his successor Innocent VI (desiring to strike a blow at the Roman aristocracy) sent Rienzi back to Rome with some mercenary soldiers and the title of senator. He entered Rome in 1354 and easily regained his position of leadership but was murdered in a riot later in the year. He was the hero of Bulwer-Lytton's novel *Rienzi* (1835), on which Richard Wagner based his opera *Rienzi* (1840).
H. F. VOS

RILEY, WILLIAM BELL (1861–1947)
Conservative Baptist minister and educator

Born in Green County, Indiana, Riley was educated at Hanover College (1885) and Southern Baptist Seminary (1888). After several brief pastorates in Baptist churches in Kentucky, Indiana, and Illinois, Riley became minister of Calvary Baptist Church in Chicago in 1893. In 1897 he accepted a call to the First Baptist Church of Minneapolis, where he remained until 1942. In the course of his ministry the membership of this church increased from 585 to 3,550. Riley founded three educational institutions: (1) Northwestern Bible and Missionary Training School (1902)—to provide pastoral leadership for neglected small-town churches; (2) Northwestern Evangelical Seminary (1938)—to meet the needs of urban congregations seeking ministers; (3) Northwestern College (1944)—to provide a liberal arts education under conservative auspices. A leading opponent of theological liberalism, Riley expounded his fundamentalist viewpoint in more than sixty books and many articles and in such religious magazines as the *Baptist Beacon* and the *Christian Fundamentalist*. He was one of the organizers of the World Christian Fundamentals Association in 1919; and while he was president of the Minnesota Baptist Convention (1944–1945), that body severed its connection with the Northern Baptist Convention. N. V. HOPE

RITSCHL, ALBRECHT BENJAMIN (1822–1889)
German liberal systematic theologian

At the peak of his career Ritschl was a professor at the Universities of Tübingen and Göttingen. His writings include *The Christian Doctrine of Justification and Reconciliation* (1870–1874) and a *History of Pietism* (1880–1886), both in three volumes.

Ritschl stood opposed to the Tübingen school's (1) skepticism about Christian origins; (2) mysticism, with its indifference to historical Christianity; (3) pietism, with its stress on private religious experience; and (4) idealist philosophy, with its vast and unprovable speculations about the outworking of the divine spirit in the universe. Ritschl was deeply influenced by the philosophy of Immanuel Kant (1724–1804), who maintained that the human mind was not equipped to grapple with anything beyond the immediate experience of the senses and the dictates of reason. Like Kant, he gave a strong ethical interpretation to Christianity. For though the mind could not penetrate mysteries beyond the experience of everyday life, it could appreciate moral issues.

Ritschl drew a distinction between judgments of fact and judgments of value. The former could be proven objectively; the latter involved subjective interpretation. Thus the divinity of Christ is not to be understood as a statement of fact but as the expression of Jesus' revelational value. It does not tell us about something that can be proved; it tells us what Christ means to the church.

Ritschl's theology centered on his understanding of justification and the kingdom of God. Justification is God's acceptance of sinners into fellowship with himself. Although he spoke about salvation and eternal life, he did not understand the terms in any orthodox sense. God already loves the sinner. Justification is the removal of the sense of guilt that causes men to feel alienated from God. For Ritschl, the kingdom meant God's rule among men. It was Jesus' mission to bring this about by changing men's moral attitudes and causing them to accept God's rule in their lives. Christ died as a martyr to this vocation, preferring death rather than deviation of his loyalty.

Ritschlian theology found its last great exponent in the church historian Adolf Harnack (1851–1930). Its influence waned in the twentieth century because of its neglect of the eschatological dimension of the kingdom of God and its failure to treat revelation seriously. C. BROWN

ROBBIA, LUCA DELLA (c. 1399–1482)
Italian sculptor

Robbia spent his lifetime making religious art for the churches in the city of Florence. He is best known for the images that he modeled out of clay and then color-glazed according to a process he perfected and applied for the first time to monumental sculpture. The *Resurrection* and *Ascension*, above the portals of the cathedral in Florence, are among his finest accomplishments in this glazed terra-cotta technique.

Robbia's work was in such demand that he was compelled to open a workshop to aid in the production of his sculpture. Pieces made in this factory became known as Della Robbia ware. His most ambitious work was the bronze doors of the sacristy (a room in a church where sacred vessels and vestments are kept) of the cathedral in Florence. It took Robbia thirty years to finish this labor of religious devotion. A. STEFFLER

ROBERTS, EVAN JOHN (1878–1951)
Welsh revivalist and evangelist; leader of the famous 1904–1908 revival in Wales

Roberts was born in Glamorgan, the ninth of fourteen children of a Welsh miner. His formal education was interrupted when, at the age of twelve, he began work in the mines to help his father, who had suffered a foot injury. In 1902, at the age of twenty-four, he was apprenticed to an uncle as a blacksmith. Two years later he felt a call to enter the ministry, was accepted as a candidate by the Calvinist Methodist Church, and began studies at the Ministers' Training College at Newcastle Emlyn. In the months prior to taking up studies at this school, he wrote of his experiences of God appearing to him each night. But while at school, he spoke of how his heart was hardened and how these appearances stopped. His sense of the presence of God returned to him in a powerful way during that first year of study.

In 1904 he returned from a spiritual retreat convinced that he had been anointed by the Holy Spirit to preach Jesus to the Welsh and urge them from their spiritual lethargy. He returned to his home in Loughor and began to hold nightly meetings. People began to respond with a remarkable spontaneity, for Roberts emphasized in his preaching the gifts of the Holy Spirit that must be freely expressed. In an amazingly short period of time, the revival had spread throughout Wales. Roberts and his friends began an itinerant ministry, from November 1904 to January 1906 traveling through Glamorgan, Liverpool, Anglesey, and Caernarvonshire. Roberts quickly was identified as the center of the revival, and he soon achieved worldwide notice. Calculations put the number of conversions at one hundred thousand. Naturally, the Welsh revival and Roberts provoked many skeptical responses, and it was often charged that he

was playing off an unseemly emotionalism. Roberts's public life was short-lived; as the revival fires cooled, he went to live in Leicester. He returned to Wales in 1925 and died at Cardiff. P. TOON

ROBERTS, RICHARD (1874–1945)
Canadian United Church minister

Roberts was born in North Wales and was educated at the University of Wales and at the theological college in Bala, North Wales. He was ordained to the Presbyterian ministry and served in a number of churches in England. In 1917 he came to the United States as pastor of the Church of the Pilgrims in Brooklyn, New York. In 1922 he became pastor of the American Presbyterian Church in Montreal.

Roberts became a leading Canadian liberal theologian, impatient with discussions on fine points of doctrine and mainly concerned with the humanitarian aspects of Christianity. He wrote a number of books on religious topics, including *The Ascending Life* (1924), *The New Man and the Divine Society* (1926), and *The Contemporary Christ* (1938). In an article published in 1929, he repudiated the traditional concept of God as a being who combined justice and mercy in his relations with men. Roberts stressed God's mercy but objected to the orthodox emphasis on divine justice, which he regarded as smacking of "retaliation."

Roberts was a leading advocate of the union of the Presbyterian, Methodist, and Congregational churches, which was accomplished in 1925. In the movement that culminated in union, he tried to minimize discussions about doctrine. He regarded the statement of faith of the United Church as unduly conservative, yet he accepted it because it left "considerable elbow room for interpretation."

Roberts was an eloquent preacher with a rich, Welsh voice. He was the minister of Sherbourne Street United Church in Toronto from 1928 to 1938 and was moderator of the United Church of Canada from 1934 to 1936. D. C. MASTERS

ROBERTSON, FREDERICK WILLIAM (1816–1853)
English preacher

Born in London, son of an artillery officer, Robertson was educated at Edinburgh and Oxford, declined a commission in the army, and was ordained in the Church of England in 1840. After curacies in Winchester and Cheltenham, punctuated by physical and mental breakdowns, he ministered briefly at St. Ebbe's, Oxford, before becoming the incumbent of Trinity Chapel, Brighton. His zeal was attributable to an evangelical upbringing, but he gradually moved away as the base of his preaching broadened. He professed no party label, but the (liberal) Broad Church party, with some justification, claimed him as their own. Robertson once compared the evangelical view of the Atonement to Juggernaut and said its principles were derived from the heathen shambles. His sermons, which always stressed the humanity of Jesus, were strikingly delivered and were relevant to the times. He established a rare rapport with working people and founded a working men's institute; no one, it was said, had the same influence on those totally unreached by the clergy. Not surprisingly in society-conscious Brighton, Robertson was resented for his social concern and political remarks in his preaching.

He could be morbid, uncertain of temper, and hypersensitive, causing him to see things out of proportion; yet he realized his faults and constantly strove against them. With the constant tension accentuated by his own temperament and by the lack of a saving sense of humor, his health further deteriorated, and he died on the sixth anniversary of his settlement at Brighton. More than two thousand people followed to the cemetery the coffin of a man who has come down in history as simply Robertson of Brighton. The accolade would have been bewildering had it not been for the extraordinary vitality of his preaching, which can be sensed in the five series of *Sermons Preached at Brighton* published from 1855 and often reprinted. J. D. DOUGLAS

ROBINSON, HENRY WHEELER (1872–1945)
English Old Testament scholar

Born at Northampton, Robinson was educated at Edinburgh, Oxford, and Göttingen. After pastorates at Pitlochry, Perthshire, and Coventry (1900–1906), he became a skilled tutor at Rawdon Baptist College (1906–1920). As principal of Regent Park College from 1920 until his retirement in 1942, he employed his administrative gifts in the transfer of the college to Oxford in 1927. By this move he was able to give prospective Baptist ministers the benefit of a university environment. He was appointed reader in biblical criticism at Oxford (1934–1941) and chairman of the theology faculty (1937–1939). With the help of his studies in Germany, he made himself thoroughly familiar with German scholarship in his specialist field of the Old Testament, but he retained his evangelical convictions and emphasis and was influential far beyond his own denomination. He edited a series called Library of Constructive Theology, and his many books include *The Christian Doctrine of Man* (1911), *The Religious Ideas of the Old Testament* (1913, revised 1956), and *Redemption and Revelation* (1942). After a serious illness in 1913, which led to deeper thought on the Holy Spirit and the problem of suffering, he wrote *The Christian Experience of the Holy Spirit* (1928) and *Suffering, Human and Divine* (1940). N. HILLYER

ROBINSON, JOHN (c. 1576–1625)
Beloved pastor of the Pilgrims before their departure to America in 1620

Robinson was born not far from Scrooby, in eastern England. He attended Cambridge University in the 1590s and later held a benefice at Norfolk from 1600 to 1604. Because of his Puritan views he was suspended from his position, so he joined the small band of Separatists meeting at Scrooby. The congregation quickly elected him as their "teacher," a position second only to the pastor. Robinson accompanied the Pilgrims in 1608 when they fled to Amsterdam, Holland. When the group removed to Leyden in

1609, he was ordained as their pastor. In the years that followed, Robinson not only ministered faithfully to his congregation, he also found time to do a considerable amount of writing, in which he upheld the doctrines of Calvin, defended the Separatist position, and advocated the congregational form of church government.

By 1617 he was also actively involved in the effort to establish a refuge for the Pilgrims in the New World. Although Robinson wanted very much to accompany the members of his flock who decided to emigrate, his hopes were never realized. Nevertheless, he continued to exert a deep influence on the Pilgrims through his published sermons, tracts, and his pastoral letters to the settlers. R. L. TROUTMAN

ROBINSON, JOHN ARTHUR THOMAS (1919–1983)
Anglican theologian and bishop

Born into a clerical family in Canterbury, Robinson graduated from Cambridge, where external examiner John Baillie hailed Robinson's Ph.D. thesis as "the best ever to have come my way." Ordained in 1945, he ministered in the west of England (1945–1951) and was fellow and dean of Clare College, Cambridge (1951–1958). In 1959 he became suffragan bishop of Woolwich and was soon recognized as the leading radical of the Church of England. In a court case he spoke in defense of D. H. Lawrence's *Lady Chatterley's Lover,* but he caused even more of a stir when his *Honest to God* (1963), which sold over a million copies, was held to deny some aspects of basic Christian doctrine—notably the traditional view of the Atonement. The archbishop of Canterbury (A. M. Ramsey) was critical of that work, which may explain why Robinson was given no further preferment. He returned to Cambridge in 1969 as fellow, dean of chapel, and lecturer in theology at Trinity College. He participated in the translation of the New English Bible and published other works regarded as more orthodox. Among them are *The Human Face of God* (1973), *Truth Is*

Two-Eyed (1979), *The Priority of John* (1985), and *Where Three Ways Meet* (1987). J. D. DOUGLAS

RODEHEAVER, HOMER ALVAN (1880–1955)
Publisher of gospel music; musical innovator

Rodeheaver was born in Cinco Hollow, Ohio, and grew up in Jellico, Tennessee. He learned to play the cornet as a youth and enrolled at Ohio Wesleyan University as a music student in 1896. His studies were interrupted by financial need and the Spanish American War. In 1904 he left college without a degree to work with evangelist William E. Biederwolf.

"Rody" was a buoyant, affable personality, and the music he selected for crusade meetings reflected his own disposition. His selections emphasized the optimistic aspects of the gospel. The mood he sought was triumphant, confident, nondoctrinaire, and occasionally syncopated. "Brighten the Corner" became his trademark.

In 1909, Rodeheaver met Billy Sunday. For the next twenty years, the two formed one of America's most popular evangelistic teams. Rodeheaver served as master of ceremonies, trombonist, and choir director in Billy Sunday's campaigns. He helped to maintain the team's public image by mollifying Sunday's abrasiveness.

The Rodeheaver Publishers of sacred music was organized in 1910 and began distributing phonographs, as well as printed music, in 1916. Rodeheaver founded a ranch for deprived boys in Florida and for many years conducted a sacred music conference at Winona Lake, Indiana. M. FACKLER

ROGERS, JOHN (c. 1500–1555)
Editor of Matthew's Bible, the second complete Bible in English; first Protestant to be executed in the reign of Queen Mary

Rogers was born near Birmingham and educated at Pembroke Hall in Cambridge. In 1532 he became rector of Holy Trinity, London, a position he resigned two years later to become chaplain to British merchants in Antwerp, Belgium. Here he met William Tyndale, who was busy translating the Old Testament into English, and came to be influenced by Reformed beliefs. After Tyndale was burned at the stake, Rogers threw off the mantle of clerical celibacy by taking a wife. When Tyndale was arrested, he had given to Rogers his incomplete translation of the Old Testament. Rogers took this, completed the Old Testament from the 1535 translation of Miles Coverdale (the earliest English Bible), added Tyndale's earlier translation of the New Testament, and in 1537 published the whole Bible in Antwerp under the name of Thomas Matthew. Rogers himself contributed the marginal notes, which constituted the first English commentary on the Bible. In the first printing fifteen hundred copies were made, three of which are preserved in the British Museum.

Rogers next spent some time in Germany, ministering to a Protestant congregation in Wittenberg. He returned to London in the summer of 1548. In 1550 he was given charge of two parishes in London and a year later was appointed prebendary and divinity lecturer at St. Paul's Cathedral in the city. On August 6, 1553, a sermon he preached on behalf of Protestantism at Paul's Cross got him into trouble with the newly established government of Queen Mary. He was put under house arrest that year and early in 1554 imprisoned at Newgate. He went to trial in January, 1555, on charges of heresy. His views against the Roman doctrine of transubstantiation and against the papacy led to a death sentence. He was excommunicated and taken to Smithfield to be burned at the stake, in full view of his wife and children. Just before the flame was kindled, Rogers was offered a pardon if he would recant his views, an offer he rejected.
P. TOON

ROMAINE, WILLIAM (1714–1795)
English leader in evangelical revival

Of Huguenot stock, Romaine was born in the county of Durham. He proceeded from there to Christ Church, Oxford, where he

was an able student. After ordination he served parishes in Devon and Surrey before beginning his great work in London in 1748. He was appointed lecturer first at St. George's, Billingsgate, and then at St.-Dunstan-in-the-West. He preached a message similar to that of the great George Whitefield, a warm evangelical message with a Calvinistic flavor. He was friendly with all the leaders in the revival and, like them, made preaching tours around the country. In 1766 he was appointed rector of St. Anne's, Blackfriars, and remained there until his death. He set an example of how the power of the revival could be contained within the parish structures of the Church of England, thereby helping to form what is now the evangelical party in that Church. He wrote several books, but his most famous is his trilogy, *The Life, Walk and Triumph of Faith*, published in three parts between 1771 and 1794 and often reprinted. P. TOON

ROSCELLINUS (c. 1050–c. 1125)
Founder of Nominalism

Roscellinus was a French scholastic philosopher who purported a philosophy known as Nominalism. This position held that general conceptions are merely products of human reason, mere intellectual abstractions (*nomina*) derived from the common attributes of things. Applied to Christian doctrine, this approach concluded, for instance, that the Trinity was merely a subjective conception with no real existence. Furthermore, this view stressed the separate reality of the three Persons in such a way as to approach tritheism.

Roscellinus was born at Compiegne, studied at Soissons and Reims, was attached to the cathedral at Chartres, and became canon at Compiegne. To deal with his teachings on the Trinity, the archbishop of Reims called a council at Soissons in 1092. Though Roscellinus repudiated the charge of tritheism, the council condemned him. In danger of being stoned to death by the orthodox populace there, he recanted his position and later fled to England. There he got into trouble by attacking the teachings of Anselm of Canterbury.

Thereafter he went to Rome, was reconciled to the Church, and returned to France, where he taught at Tours and later at Loches in Brittany. At the latter, Abelard was his pupil. While at Loches, he once again taught his original position on the Trinity and was attacked by Abelard for his views.

It is difficult to know exactly what Roscellinus taught because his views are known almost exclusively through the accounts of others, mostly his enemies, who would be expected to distort them to some degree. Of his writings, nothing remains except a letter to Abelard on the doctrine of the Trinity. H. F. VOS

ROSSETTI, CHRISTINA (1830–1894)
English poet

Christina Rossetti, born in London, was the daughter of a Dante scholar and the sister of Dante Gabriel Rossetti, also a poet and a pre-Raphaelite enthusiast. Christina began to write poetry at an early age and as a young woman assisted her mother in the management of a school. She was interested in Italian culture and, like her brother, composed some poems in Italian. Her first volume of poems, *Goblin Market, and Other Poems* (1862), was much praised for its style and originality. The volume revealed spiritual insights that were a reflection of the author's religious nature.

The ritual and beauty of the High Church (Anglican) party suited Rossetti's nature perfectly. She was often busy with church work and the preparation of devotional manuals. She published *Commonplace,* a collection of stories, in 1870, followed by *Sing Song,* a collection of nursery rhymes (1872) and *Sleeping Likenesses,* tales for children (1874). Her religious works were widely circulated and did more to win acclaim for her than any other of her writing, although most of this work was of only modest literary quality.

Christina Rossetti spent many of the late years of her life as an invalid. She died of cancer at her London residence in 1894.

Following her death, her unpublished poems were collected and issued by her brother William as *New Poems* (1896). P. M. BECHTEL

ROTHMAN, BRENT (c. 1495–1535)
German Anabaptist leader

In 1532 Rothman introduced Lutheranism to his native city of Münster, despite strong opposition by the city officials. In 1533 he adopted Anabaptist views, and, when large numbers of Melchiorites led by Jan Matthijs came to the city, he threw in his lot with them, accepting the radical millenarianism of Melchior Hoffman. In 1534 the Melchiorites seized the city and attempted to set up a kingdom in preparation for the imminent return of Christ. Protestants and Roman Catholics, meanwhile, joined forces to besiege the city, and in a skirmish Matthijs was killed, his place being taken by Jan of Leyden. Rothman apparently agreed wholeheartedly with the practice of communism and polygamy. According to some reports, he had nine wives. He also served as the state preacher, giving his full support to this regime. In 1535 the besieging force assaulted the city and massacred most of the garrison and its supporters. In this holocaust, Rothman was killed. He left behind a number of books he had written over the years that showed his changing views of the Christian faith, including his most famous work, *Restitution* (1534), which set forth and defended the religious position of the Münsterites. W. S. REID

ROUAULT, GEORGES (1871–1958)
French painter and engraver

At fourteen Rouault was apprenticed as a stained-glass-window painter, restoring medieval windows. During these five years he became interested in religious art. Throughout his life his luminous color and use of black linear elements similar to the leading of stained glass windows demonstrate the influence of the stained glass medium upon his style of painting.

His inclination toward religious art was

further developed through his training at the École des Beaux-Arts in Paris, where he studied with Gustave Moreau, whose highly imaginative style stimulated Rouault's mystical direction. Other important influences came to Rouault through contacts with the work of the philosopher Jacques Maritain and the converted Roman Catholic writer J. K. Huysmans.

Rouault frequently exhibited in Paris, first at the Salon des Artistes Francais (1895–1901) and then at the Salon d'Automne (1903–1918), where in 1905 his work was associated with that of the Fauves (Wild Beasts). Rouault's production included paintings, watercolors, gouaches, tapestries, enamels, plus prints in all media, generally for book illustrations.

His themes included many religious subjects. Most outstanding of these were his paintings of the suffering and sorrowing Christ. Later his subjects changed to those dealing with pathetic outcasts of society—prostitutes, clowns, and lawyers—whom he treated as tragic metaphors of good and evil. Rouault combined modern idioms with traditional Christian subjects. His work stands among the greatest religious art of the twentieth century. A. STEFFLER

ROUSSEAU, JEAN-JACQUES
(1712–1778)
French-Swiss philosopher and author

Rousseau was born into a French refugee family at Geneva. Although brought up as a Calvinist, he became a Catholic through the influence of his benefactress and mistress, Madame de Warens, whose own faith was hardly orthodox. His final position was a unique blend of rationalism and Deism.

Rousseau was a man of many talents. He devised a new system of musical notation, which he presented to the Academy of Sciences in Paris. He composed a ballet and an opera, which was performed before the court of Louis XV. His writings, which touched on education, religion, and political theory, sometimes took the form of novels.

Rousseau's private life combined pathos with paradox. His theories on education

helped to revolutionize modern teaching, yet he deposited his five illegitimate children in an orphanage. He craved for appreciation, yet repeatedly rewarded his friends with gross ingratitude, not least his fellow philosophers and the several women in his life.

Rousseau found fame with his prize-winning *Discourse on the Sciences and Arts* (1750), in which he argued that civilization and progress corrupt morals. It was a theme he developed at length in later works. *Julie, or The New Heloise* (1760) attacked the conventions of society that divorced love from marriage; it also contained a defense of natural religion. *Emile, or On Education* (1762) was a treatise on education in the form of a novel. The young Emile is brought up in a kind of moral quarantine, apart from the corrupting influences of society. He had a private tutor whose role was to direct his pupil's inquiring mind. This program of learning anticipated modern theories of project studies, unstructured curricula, and the assumption that the child is best helped when he is given freedom to explore and learn. Among the harmful influences to be kept at bay are church bells and toy weapons, lest the child be tempted to think of religion and fighting.

Emile contains a lengthy excursus entitled "The Creed of a Savoyard Priest," in which an aged Catholic priest quietly renounces the teaching of the church in favor of a deistic religion based on feeling. God is the Being of beings. He is to be held in awe, but it is not safe for man with his limited mind to say anything about him.

In the same year that saw the publication of *Emile*, Rousseau set out his political theory in *The Social Contract*. He rejected the idea that government has anything to do with the will of God. States exist for the benefit of the people and may be changed at will. Government presupposes the idea of a social contract by which the citizens of any state voluntarily limit their freedom for the common benefit. Laws exist for promoting this public good. Where they do not, they may be democratically changed.

Rousseau's last main works were his

Confessions (1765) and *The Reveries of a Solitary Stroller* (1778), which combined biography with personal apologia. Despite the religious tinge of much of his writing, Rousseau helped to pioneer the modern secular outlook. His political theories were among the influences that contributed to the American and French revolutions. C. BROWN

ROWLEY, HAROLD HENRY
(1890–1969)
Old Testament scholar

Rowley was born in Leicester, England, and educated at Bristol and Mansfield College, Oxford. He was minister of a united Baptist-Congregationalist church in Wells, Somerset, from 1917 to 1922. He spent the next eight years under the Baptist Missionary Society in China, where he was professor of Old Testament at Christian College, Shantung. In 1930 he returned to Great Britain and took up duties as a lecturer in Semitic languages at the University College of South Wales (Cardiff). In 1935 he became professor of Semitic languages at the University College of North Wales (Bangor). In 1945 he went to the University of Manchester as professor of Semitic languages, and from 1949 until his retirement in 1959 he was professor of Hebrew language and literature in the university.

Rowley was a prolific writer and has left many books on Old Testament subjects. His best work is generally acknowledged to be on the book of Daniel. He was the Old Testament editor of two important reference works, *Peake's Commentary on the Bible* and James Hastings's *Dictionary of the Bible*. Old Testament scholars owe him a great debt for the work he did to reestablish Old Testament studies in Europe after World War II. As the foreign secretary of the Society for Old Testament Study, Rowley was able to gather together Old Testament studies during the war, particularly in Germany, and bring them to the attention of other scholars. P. TOON

RUBENS, PETER PAUL (1577–1640)
Flemish painter

Rubens, Flemish painter of the Counter-Reformation, combined the best elements of the more idealized monumental Italian schools of art with an individual vigor and descriptive tradition of his native land. He was one of the most popular, sought-after artists of the Baroque period.

At the age of twenty-three Rubens went to Italy, where he served the duke of Mantua in Venice. A diplomatic mission to Spain on behalf of the duke brought him favor from both the duke and the Spanish court. It was at this time in Spain that he did a number of portaits and palace decorations. From there he traveled to England in the service of the Spanish king and incidentally assumed the job of decorating the ceiling of the banquet hall in Whitehall Palace. Later he returned to Antwerp where he became the city's foremost painter. Because of the demands upon him, he organized an art studio that operated on the assembly-line method of painting. He would make the preliminary sketches, and then his assistants would develop the painting, after which Rubens would add the finishing touches.

Rubens's sympathy with the Jesuit movement afforded him the opportunity to do a number of paintings for them, particularly for their church in Antwerp. Among his most famous works are the *Raising of the Cross* (1610) and *Descent from the Cross* (1610–1611), both in Antwerp Cathedral. A. STEFFLER

RUFINUS TYRANNIUS (345–410)
Latin ecclesiastical translator

Born at Concordia, Italy, and baptized at Aquileia about 371, Rufinus became the friend and then the adversary of Jerome. After eight years in Alexandria, Rufinus lived in Palestine (371–397), being ordained in Jerusalem about 390. He studied under Didymus the Blind and Gregory of Nazianzus and founded a monastery on the Mount of Olives. His many translations of Greek theological works into Latin helped to promote Western asceticism and theology. The translations include *The Monastic Rule of Basil*, ten works of Gregory of Nazianzus, some of Origen's commentaries, the *Clementine Recognitions*, and Eusebius's *History of the Church*. His own commentary on the Apostles' Creed gives the earliest continuous fourth-century Latin text we have. His translation of Origen's *De Principiis* is the only complete text surviving. But his rather free rendering was also intended to put Origen's teaching in a more orthodox light, and this led to a lifelong quarrel with Jerome. N. HILLYER

RUNCIE, ROBERT ALEXANDER KENNEDY (born 1921)
Archbishop of Canterbury, 1980–1991

Son of a Scots engineer, Runcie won the Military Cross as a combatant officer in World War II. He graduated at Oxford, trained for the priesthood at Cambridge, and was ordained in 1950. After several pastoral and teaching ministries, he was consecrated as bishop of St. Albans in 1970 before succeeding Donald Coggan at Canterbury. Criticized for taking too much or too little part in contemporary controversies and for theological liberalism, he was greatly concerned with humanitarian causes worldwide and reportedly angered the British establishment when after the Falklands War his St. Paul's Cathedral address hit no triumphalist notes. His interest in ecumenicity was seen in his longtime relations with Eastern Orthodoxy and in the visit to Canterbury in 1982 of Pope John Paul—the first pontiff since the Reformation to see the spiritual home of Anglicanism. Runcie wrote *Windows onto God* and *Seasons of the Spirit,* both published in 1983. J. D. DOUGLAS

RUPERT OF DEUTZ (c. 1075–c. 1130)
German medieval theologian

Rupert of Deutz, monk at Liege—then, after 1119, abbot of the Cluniac monastery at Deutz—is remembered primarily as a Bible scholar, but he was also a theologian, an effective critic of developing scholasticism, and a church reformer.

Visions in adolescence convinced him that he was specially endowed to interpret Scriptures. He apparently wrote commentaries on most of the biblical books, interpreting allegorically, with keen interest in the prefiguration of the New Testament within the Old and with keen interest in Christian liturgics in both. For him, the central biblical doctrine is Christ's incarnation, to which all else must relate.

Commenting on the belief that God has two wills (passive and approving), Rupert criticized the new scholasticism: "Any notion that can be conceived apart from sacred Scripture or constructed from argumentation is irrational and is thus in no way pertinent to the praise of God. . . ." For him, the goal of study was redemptive knowledge of God; the method was meditation. He considered the dialectic approach, with its goal of objective knowledge, to be spiritually useless. P. M. BASSETT

RUSKIN, JOHN (1819–1900)
Writer, artist, social critic

Ruskin was the son of a prosperous wine merchant. During his early years he developed an enthusiasm for the classics and great art from his father and for Bible reading from his mother. In many of Ruskin's works the moral force of the Bible is clear. At fourteen he began a series of European tours with his family, during which he developed a devotion to the beauties of nature. In 1836 he went to Christ Church, Oxford, where his achievements as a student were modest, though he did win a prize for poetry.

Resources provided by his father enabled Ruskin to begin a collection of the paintings of J. M. W. Turner. From 1843 to 1845 he published *Modern Painters* (two volumes), a study of the masters of landscape painting, in which Turner was always the most admired of these artists. In 1845 he set out for another trip to Italy, enjoying the beauty and making sketches of much of the medieval architecture and sculpture he saw. His marriage to Effie Chalmers Gray in 1848 was a failure, for she was a demanding social climber, incapable of appreciating or complimenting her husband's talents.

The Seven Lamps of Architecture (1848), a study of Gothic architecture, was a very successful, well-written book with an elevated moral tone. Applying similar principles of moral judgment to architecture, Ruskin published *The Stones of Venice* (1851–1853), noting that the rise and fall of the city was dictated by spiritual principles. Over the years he continued to work on *Modern Painters,* completing the fifth volume in 1860. At his father's death Ruskin was left a substantial fortune, some of which he used to encourage social and economic reform. This interest can be seen in *Flors Clavingera* (1871), a series of letters to working men. For ten years (1869–1879) he held a lectureship at Oxford. During the last years of his life he was frequently ill, but he was able to prepare, though not complete, a delightful autobiography, *Praeteria* (1871–1874). Ruskin exercised a significant moral influence in his time and is a valuable mirror of the Victorian era. P. BECHTEL

RUSSELL, CHARLES TAZE (1852–1916)
Founder of the Jehovah's Witnesses

Russell spent most of his early years in Pittsburgh and Allegheny, Pennsylvania. At the age of twenty-five he became the manager of several men's furnishing stores. Reacting to his early training in the Congregational Church, he rejected the doctrine of eternal judgment and reliability of the Bible. By 1872 Russell had gathered around himself a small group of believers to study the Bible "relative to the coming of Christ and his kingdom." In 1879 he began the publication of his *Zion's Watchtower* and *Herald of Christ's Presence,* whose circulation grew from six thousand to 244 million by 1975; the following year he published his first book, *Food for Thinking Christians.* By 1884 he had won enough followers to form Zion's Watchtower Tract Society in Pittsburgh, Pennsylvania, to spread his new gospel. "Pastor" Russell is said to have traveled a million miles in the course of his ministry to train new workers and establish new churches. His organiza-

tion, the Jehovah's Witnesses, has also been called Millennial Darwinists, International Bible Students, members of the Watchtower Bible and Tract Society, Russellites, and Rutherfordites. R. VONDERLACK

RUTHERFORD, JOSEPH FRANKLIN (1869–1942)
Successor to Charles Russell as the leader of the Jehovah's Witnesses

Rutherford was a descendant of a Baptist family in Morgan County, Missouri; and although he never studied law, he was given a license to practice law in 1892. He gained the special title "Judge" when in his early years he served as a special judge of the Eighth Judicial Circuit Court of Boonville, Missouri. He became the legal counsel of the Jehovah's Witnesses Society and Charles Taze Russell's attorney in his divorce proceedings and his "miracle wheat" scandal.

Judge Rutherford assumed power over the Society in 1917 after Russell's death. He injected new life into the Society, substituting his writings for Russell's, popularizing the slogan "Millions now living will never die," introducing the name "Jehovah's Witnesses," and equipping the Witnesses with phonographs so that they could utilize transcriptions of his talks in their house-to-house calls. He replaced Pastor Russell as the authoritative teacher and leader. He wrote over one hundred books and pamphlets. As of 1941, his works had been translated into eighty languages.

An outspoken personality, he was accused of violating the "Espionage Act" in 1918 on the basis that his views were considered disloyal to his country. He served a term of imprisonment in 1918 and 1919 at Atlanta, Georgia. He was frequently accused of fraudulent practices, even by his own followers. He acquitted himself nobly in the eyes of the Society by attacking the doctrines of "organized religion," which he called "rackets," with unparalleled vigor in his radio talks, phonograph recordings, and numerous books. R. VONDERLACK

RUTHERFORD, SAMUEL (1600–1661)
Scottish minister and covenanter

Born a farmer's son near the border town of Jedburgh, Rutherford graduated at Edinburgh in arts and divinity and in 1627 became minister of Anwoth on the Solway Firth. It was said of him that he was always visiting the sick, always praying, always preaching, always writing and studying. His serene faith never faltered, even when he lost his wife and two children. Alarmed at the spread of Arminianism in Scotland, Rutherford wrote strongly against it. For this the ruling Episcopalian party deprived him of his charge, forbade him to preach, and exiled him to Aberdeen ("the first in the kingdom put to utter silence"). During those eighteen months, nonetheless, he wrote more than half of those seraphic *Letters* hailed by Richard Baxter and C. H. Spurgeon as the nearest thing to inspiration—after the Bible—in evangelical literature.

With the triumph of Presbyterianism and the signing of the National Covenant in 1638, Rutherford became professor of divinity at St. Andrews. In 1643 he was one of the Scottish commissioners sent to the Westminster Assembly, to which he made a substantial contribution. In 1644 his *Lex Rex* appeared, a long and devastating reply to the Divine Right of Kings theory. Rutherford held, with his fellow covenanters, that the people have the true majesty; that the law, and no autocrat on the throne, is king; and that limitless sovereignty is the property of God alone. Much of this doctrine became the constitutional inheritance of modern democracies, but understandably the Stuart dynasty took a marked dislike to it. With the restoration of the monarchy in 1660, Rutherford narrowly escaped the hands of the public hangman. Summoned to appear before the council, the dying scholar sent a message to say he had had a prior summons before "a Superior Judge and Judicatory." J. D. DOUGLAS

RUYSBROECK, JAN VAN (1293–1381)
Flemish mystic

Born near Brussels, at an early date Ruysbroeck was taken to be reared by his uncle, a canon of St. Gudule's church in Brussels. At the age of twenty-four he was made a priest. His life thereafter was mainly involved with writing and exercising his pastoral duties. The times were those of great religious ferment, aroused perhaps by the so-called "Babylonian Captivity" of the papacy, which disturbed many devout papalists. It was also the period of the disastrous Hundred Years' War. Ruysbroeck's area was particularly affected by conflicting loyalties both in church and in state. Many intellectuals gave themselves to a non-mediatorial kind of religion, usually called mysticism, in which there was great devotion to the ideal of "deification." Ruysbroeck was attracted by this movement, but sought to keep it in orthodox channels.

His writings were in both the vernacular and Latin, but only the latter have survived. In them Ruysbroeck taught mystical union with Christ—that Christ should be experienced in active life, in the interior life, and in the supernatural life of contemplation. At the same time, Christians must adhere to the priesthood and sacramental system. His best-known work is *Die Chierheit der Gheestelijke Brulocht* (*The Spiritual Espousals*, translated in 1952). In 1349 Ruysbroeck organized a community of canons at Groenendael, where he spent the remainder of his years. He has been given the title of "ecstatic doctor," suggesting both his mystical and orthodox character. A. CABANISS

RYERSON, ADOLPHUS EGERTON (1803–1882)
Canadian Methodist leader and educationalist

Ryerson was born in Norfolk County, Upper Canada, of United Empire Loyalist parents. Having experienced a religious conversion, he entered the ministry of the Methodist Episcopal Church in 1825. Ryerson soon became the great apologist of Canadian Methodism against the claims of John Strachan (Anglican bishop of Toronto, 1839) to special privileges for the Church of England. Ryerson became editor of the *Christian Guardian* in 1829 and used the paper in the 1830s to attack the claims of the

Church of England for exclusive control of the Clergy Reserves (crown lands set aside for the support of a Protestant clergy).

Ryerson was a voluntaryist, claiming that the churches should be financed by their own supporters. He maintained that the proceeds of the Reserves should be devoted to education. His voluntaryist opinions were unacceptable to the British Wesleyans who had joined with the Methodist Episcopal Church in Upper Canada in 1833. In politics Ryerson was a moderate conservative, although he worked with William Lyon Mackenzie and the Reformers prior to 1833.

Ryerson was an active leader in the field of education. He helped to establish the Methodist school, Upper Canada Academy, at Cobourg in 1836; and when it became Victoria College in 1841, he was its first principal. Ryerson's most important achievement was in the field of primary and secondary education. He was appointed chief superintendent of education for Canada West (later Ontario) in 1844, a position he occupied until 1876. Ryerson was the great architect of the public school system in Ontario. On the vexed question of the place of religion in the schools, he contended, in his famous *Report* of 1846, that students should be instructed in Christian ethics but not in "sectarian dogma." He stressed the role of the state in using education in the development of socially and politically desirable attitudes. D. C. MASTERS

RYLE, JOHN CHARLES (1816–1900)
Leader of evangelicals in the Church of England

Born in Cheshire into a nominally Chris-tian home, Ryle was sent to Eton College and then to Christ Church, Oxford. He proved to be a good athlete and an able scholar. Toward the end of his period at Oxford he experienced an evangelical conversion. He worked in his father's bank from 1838 to 1841 and intended to enter Parliament. After the failure of the bank, he decided to become a clergyman and began with a poorly paid curacy in the diocese of Winchester.

He began his significant work in 1844 when he moved to East Anglia. Here he was at Helmingham (1844–1861) and Stradbroke (1861–1880). With the arrival of the railway system he was able to travel and develop his gifts as a public speaker. In the quiet of the countryside he was able to write many powerful tracts and booklets on basic evangelical topics. Also he wrote his influential *Expository Thoughts on the Gospels*. By 1875 he was a leader of the evangelical party in the Church of England. So it is not surprising that, in 1880, he was first offered the deanery of a cathedral and then the bishopric of the new diocese of Liverpool. He chose to go to Liverpool, where he had to organize the work of the churches in this great port and industrial area. Estimates vary as to his effectiveness. He had various problems—whether to build a new cathedral, how to treat the Anglo-Catholic priests, and how to relate to the poverty of the city. What is clear is that he set before his clergy and laity the ideal of preaching Christ and doing good to all men. He died in East Anglia but was buried in Liverpool. Among his descendants are Sir Martin Ryle, the astronomer royal, and Gilbert Ryle, the philosopher. P. TOON

S

SABATIER, LOUIS AUGUSTE (1839–1901)

French Protestant theologian

Born at Vallon, Ardeche, of a Huguenot family, Sabatier was educated at Montpelier and Montauben. He accepted the methods of historical criticism and development in his study of the New Testament, and as a result gradually moved from an orthodox position to become a prominent leader of French liberal Protestantism. He was influential among both Protestants and Roman Catholics in spreading the theological views of F. D. E. Schleiermacher and A. Ritschl in France, and, by interpreting Christian dogma in terms of the symbolism of religious feelings, he helped to promote the modernist movement in that country. In 1867 he was appointed professor of Reformed dogmatics at Strassburg University and, ten years later, became dean of the Protestant theological faculty when it was moved to Paris. From 1886 he also lectured in the religious studies department of the Sorbonne. Among his best-known books are *The Apostle Paul* (1870; English translation, 1891), *Outlines of a Philosophy of Religion* (1897), and *The Religions of Authority and the Religion of the Spirit* (published posthumously in 1903). N. HILLYER

SABATIER, PAUL (1858–1928)

Franciscan scholar

Born at Strassburg in 1858, Sabatier studied letters at Besancon and Lille, and medicine at Montpelier. Later he enrolled in the faculty of theology at Paris, where he was taught by the skeptical professor Joseph Ernst Renan. From 1885 until 1889 Sabatier served as pastor of St. Nicholas Church at Strassburg, but his unorthodox, Protestant views led to his expulsion from Germany in 1889. Thereafter he served as pastor at St.-Cierge-la-Serre in France until 1894, when he resigned and devoted himself completely to the study of St. Francis of Assisi. His studies centered mainly in Assisi but also included visits to Italy. From 1919 until his death, Sabatier was professor of theology at Strassburg. In 1883 Sabatier published his *Life of St. Francis of Assisi* (English translation, 1894). Arguing that St. Francis had hoped to purify the Catholic Church, Sabatier was soon accused of liberalism. Consequently, his biography was consigned in 1894 to the Index of prohibited books. Nevertheless, the biography went through forty editions during the lifetime of the author. In 1902 Sabatier formed at Assisi the International Society of Franciscan studies, and a British society was established in 1908 at London. W. A. DETZLER

SABATIER, PIERRE (1683–1742)
French Bible scholar

Born at Poitiers, Pierre Sabatier achieved fame as a Bible scholar. While studying at the monastery of St.-Germain-des-Pres, he was thoroughly indoctrinated with the Maurist ideal of reform. The congregation of St. Maurus sought reformation of the Benedictine order and eventually established about two hundred Maurist houses. More than seven hundred erudite works issued from these centers of religious scholarship. Sabatier's primary mentor was Thierry Ruinart (1657–1709), a major proponent of Maurism. Accused of Jansenist theological tendencies, Sabatier was exiled in 1727 to Reims, where he continued his academic pursuits. After his death, his remarkable collection of pre-Vulgate manuscripts in Old Latin was published in three folio volumes under the title *Bibliorum Sacrorum Latinae Versiones Antiquae* (1743). W. A. DETZLER

SADOLETO, JACOPO (1477–1547)
Cardinal, humanist, and biblical scholar

Sadoleto was born in Modena, the son of a lawyer. Interested in humanistic studies, he became a poet and moved in 1498 to Rome, where he enjoyed the patronage of Oliviero Cardinal Caraffa, through whom he became the secretary of Pope Leo X in 1514, along with Pietro Bembo. In 1517 he was made bishop of Carpentras in France, but remained in Rome as a member of the papal curia until after the sack of the city in 1527 by Spanish troops. He then moved to his diocese, where he spent much of his time writing.

Sadoleto was an irenic person who sought to bring the Protestants back to Rome and, at the same time, to reform the church. To this end he was one of those who helped to lay the foundation for the organization of the oratory of Divine Love, formally established in 1562. He also wrote a number of works aimed at attracting the Protestants. The first was a commentary on Romans (1535), which was disapproved of both by Rome and the University of Paris. Three years later he published the *De Laudibus*

Philosophiae but insisted that the Gospels alone contained the knowledge of salvation. His most famous work would seem to have been the letter he wrote to the city of Geneva in 1539, urging the Genevans to return to Rome. As the ministers in Geneva could not answer the arguments, they sent the letter to Calvin in Strassburg; and he answered it in six days. Made a cardinal in 1536, he was also a member of the papal commission on reform from 1536 to 1538, but the commission's report was ignored. Although he sought diligently for reform and reconciliation, he was able to accomplish little by the time of his death in 1547. W. S. REID

SAINT-CYRAN, ABBÉ DE (1581–1643)
Jansenist scholar

Born Jean Duvergier de Hauranne, Saint-Cyran was, along with his friend Cornelius Jansen, one of the principal leaders of the Jansenist movement, which sought to reform the Roman Catholic Church from the inside. He received his education in Jesuit schools, and in 1620 he was made commendatory abbot of Saint-Cyran and settled in Paris. Being especially influenced by the writings of St. Augustine, he began to work out an outline for the reform of the Church—the chief emphasis was upon the necessity and irresistibility of grace. Also advocated was a stricter approach to matters of morality and discipline. He was an opponent of the Protestant Reformation as well, charging that the Reformers had taken Augustine's theology while abandoning his high view of the Church. In 1623 he became connected with the Arnauld family and with the convent at Port-Royal, which were to be important elements in the Jansenist movement. In 1633 he became the influential spiritual director for the convent. He was imprisoned by Cardinal Richelieu for the last five years of his life. P. TOON

SALMON, GEORGE (1819–1904)
Theologian and mathematician

A strong-minded Protestant, Salmon was educated at Trinity College in Dublin, Ireland. He was made a fellow of Trinity in 1841, became Regius professor of divinity in 1866, and was made provost in 1888. In 1845 he was ordained as a priest in the Church of Ireland (Anglican). He was an important figure in the restructuring of that church when it lost its established status through an act of Parliament in 1869. Salmon engaged in controversy on at least two fronts during his career—against Roman Catholicism and against the historical-critical methods of biblical scholarship. His *Infallibility of the Church* (1888) defended the Protestant view of the Church; his other book, *An Historical Introduction to the Study of the Books of the New Testament* (1885), refuted various critical theories about the New Testament documents. The latter book was widely read in its day. Among his other published writings are his sermons delivered at Trinity College chapel and his mathematical studies. P. TOON

SANCHEZ, THOMAS (1550–1610)
Jesuit teacher and moralist

Born in Cordova, Sanchez became a Jesuit in 1567. His life of church service began in the College of Granada, and here he remained until his death. After many years of diligent effort, Sanchez became the college's main teacher of canon law and moral theology. He was known all his life for his conscientious piety.

Sanchez's great work was his treatise on marriage, *Disputationes de sancto matrimonii sacramento*. In its final form, this was one of Christianity's most elaborate works on marital life's nature and function. It had a wide influence among Catholics (and some Protestants) in the seventeenth century. Even in modern times, its detailed insights have been regarded as a classic discussion. In general, the work upholds Christian marital doctrine in its traditional conservative conception. It is thus based on affirmations of the principle of monogamy (i.e., marriage always a union until death) and the principle of patriarchy (i.e., marriage always led by male headship). The *Disputationes'* last edition appeared in Venice in 1754.

On issues other than marriage, Blaise Pascal attacked Sanchez's views as morally lax. However, this was part of the Jansenists' intense battle with the Jesuits in the 1600s. Some of Sanchez's writings might be verbose and lack clarity. On essentials, his moral theology made no significant departures from mainstream Christian thought. K. J. BRYER

SANDAY, WILLIAM (1843–1920)
English Bible scholar

Born at Holme Pierrepont, Nottingham, Sanday was educated at Repton and Oxford. After a fellowship at Trinity College, Oxford (1866–1869), he spent some years as a clergyman in country parishes before being made principal of Hatfield Hall, Durham (1876). He returned to Oxford in 1882 on his appointment as Dean Ireland's professor of exegesis of Holy Scripture. He became Lady Margaret's professor of divinity and canon of Christ Church (1895–1919) and was elected a fellow of the British Academy in 1903. With A. C. Headlam he wrote a famous commentary on Romans in the International Critical Commentary series (1895) but later devoted his studies to the Gospels. A projected *Life of Christ* was never written, but a number of preparatory works were published. Among these were *The Authorship and Historical Character of the Fourth Gospel* (1872), rebutting in title and content some extreme critical views on the continent; *Outlines of the Life of Christ* (1905) and *Oxford Studies in the Synoptic Problem* (1911), the fruit of his Oxford seminar, which included eminent biblical scholars such as J. C. Hawkins, W. C. Allen, J. V. Bartlett, and B. H. Streeter. Sanday's patient scholarship was influential in encouraging the wide acceptance of modern critical methods in Britain. N. HILLYER

SANGSTER, WILLIAM EDWYN ROBERT (1900–1960)
English Methodist preacher and writer

Born in London, Sangster trained for the ministry at Richmond College and was ordained in 1926. He ministered in Bognor Regis, Colwyn Bay, Liverpool, Scarborough, and Leeds before taking over at Westminster Central Hall. There for sixteen years his preaching drew great crowds. His doctoral dissertation, published as *The Path to Perfection* (1943), made him a Ph.D. of London University. His other works included *He Is Able* (1936), *Methodism Can Be Born Again* (1938), *The Craft of Sermon Construction* (1949), *Power in Preaching* (1958), and *Give God a Chance* (1959). J. D. Douglas

SANKEY, IRA DAVID (1840–1908)
Evangelistic singer; composer of gospel hymns; hymnbook compiler

Sankey was born in Brooklyn, New York. He became famous as a music director during a series of revival meetings held in England from 1873 to 1875, in which he accompanied the evangelist Dwight L. Moody. He made "singing the gospel" popular. He would sing as he accompanied himself on a portable organ. Sankey's tunes were very rousing and greatly complimented Moody's preaching.

He performed the songs of William Bradbury, Philip Philip, and Philip Bliss, and he employed the musical effects of rubato and parlando. He also directed the congregations in singing. He became as effective a revivalist with song as Moody was in his sermons. He elevated music to an equal role with preaching, in evangelism. As a result, gospel music became one of the first forms of American music to be accepted in England. However, it should be noted that Sankey did not originate the gospel song during his first campaign to England, as is often stated. The English people had been using Bradbury's and Root's tunes and Sunday school songs before Sankey's time.

Sankey compiled a twenty-four-page pamphlet, *Sacred Songs and Solos* (London, 1873), to meet the request of Christian congregations. This pamphlet was expanded to a volume containing about twelve hundred pieces, which sold more than 80 million copies and is still in print. When he returned to America, Sankey merged his works with Bliss's *Gospel Songs* (1874) to produce *Gospel Hymns* and *Gospel Hymns and Sacred Songs* (Cincinnati, 1875). This was followed by five more volumes; the whole was published as *Gospel Hymns* (volumes 1–6 complete). This series contains many of Sankey's own songs for hymns such as "The Ninety and Nine" (1874), "I'm Praying for You" (1875), "Hiding in Thee" (1877), "A Shelter in the Time of Storm" (1885), and "Faith Is the Victory" (1891). The latter became the "bible" of gospel melody and helped to popularize the term "gospel song." From 1895 to his death in 1908 Sankey was president of Biglow and Main, the publishing firm responsible for issuing many of his works. G. A. Comfort

SAPHIR, ADOLPH (1831–1891)
Presbyterian minister and writer

Son of a Jewish merchant in Pesth, Hungary, Adolph and his father were both converted there in 1843 through the Scottish Mission to the Jews. The rest of the family followed, and all were baptized together—the splendid firstfruits of the mission's work. After schooling in the gymnasium in Berlin, Saphir went on to the universities of Glasgow and Aberdeen and trained for the Free Church of Scotland ministry in Edinburgh (1848–1854). He was appointed a missionary to the Jews, a ministry never lost sight of later when he pastored Presbyterian churches on Tyneside and in London. Highly respected as a theologian (Edinburgh gave him a D.D. in 1878), he used his intimate knowledge of Judaism to contribute to scholarship and to counteract, in pamphlets and lectures, the rationalistic theologians of Germany. His many books include *Christ and the Scriptures* (1867), *Expository Lectures on the Epistle to the Hebrews* (two volumes, 1874–1876), and *The Divine Unity of Scripture* (1892). J. D. Douglas

LUIS DE SARRIA (1504–1588)
Dominican preacher and writer

Son of a poor Spanish family, Luis obtained advanced education through benefactors, mainly Dominicans, who recognized his abilities. He distinguished himself both in theological studies and in his era's newly revived humanist (classical) scholarship. Ordained as a priest, Luis joined the Dominicans and served his order at Cordova from 1534 to 1545. Here the contemplative life attracted him deeply, and he became a disciple of John of Avila. Calling himself Luis of Granada, he also became known for his powerful, intensely spiritual preaching. In 1555 he transferred to the Dominicans of Portugal. Devoting his remaining years mostly to the Portuguese, Luis served both the nobility and lower classes as a counselor and confessor.

Luis refused varied offers to head bishoprics in Spain and Portugal. The pope's offer of a cardinal's hat was also declined. With singleness of purpose, Luis centered his life in preaching, writing, and inward worship of Christ. He emphasized strict inner discipline as the basis for illumination and power, confidence and wisdom, in the Christian life. His views drew on insights from both Thomas Kempis and John of Avila, as well as Savonarola and Erasmus. With an exceptionally beautiful Spanish style, Luis's writings were remarkable both for doctrinal purity and popular appeal. His devotional works are his most enduring legacy. The greatest of these works, *Book on Prayer and Meditation* and *Guide to Sinners*, have undergone many translations and exist in various modern editions. Luis also produced biographical and historical works, as well as writings on theology and ethics.

K. J. BRYER

SAVONAROLA, GIROLAMO
(1452–1498)
Italian reformer

Savonarola was a forceful preacher against the worldliness and corruption of church and society in northern Italy. A native of Ferrara, he was at first destined for the medical profession; but his revulsion against the evils of society led him to enter the Dominican order in 1474. Transferred to the convent of San Marco in Florence in

1482, he rose to the position of prior there and was invited to preach in the cathedral.

His studies in the Old Testament prophets and the book of Revelation helped to make him a powerful preacher against the evils and corruption of society, with a prophetic tinge to his utterances. He believed that God had given him the mission of calling people to repentance before the impending day of judgment. The populace was greatly moved—in fact struck with terror—by his utterances, especially after some of his predictions came true: the death of Pope Innocent VIII, the coming of a foreign power with a large army as a scourge of God (fulfilled by the invasion of Charles VIII of France in 1494), and the collapse of the Medici power in Florence. Savonarola preached against the worldliness of the clergy and the corruption of secular life and was especially opposed to the ruling class.

Thus he became the spiritual leader of the democratic party, which came to power with the invasion of Charles VIII and the flight of Piero de' Medici, ruler of Florence, in 1494. Savonarola gained additional prestige because he twice persuaded Charles not to sack the city; the French king finally left without doing any significant damage.

Thereafter Savonarola exercised virtual dictatorship in Florence; and he tried to reform both the state and church there, changing the city into an ascetic type of community. He brought about tax reform and court reform and instituted programs to aid the poor. The new constitution of 1495 was similar to that of the Republic of Venice. With the passage of time, opposition to Savonarola heightened, and his power began to slip. Some of his political views became unpopular, and the masses began to waver in their support. Adherents of the deposed Medici took the offensive against him, as did Pope Alexander VI, whose evil character and misrule Savonarola openly condemned. He suffered attacks from the rival Franciscans, and his "bonfire of vanities" in 1496 and 1497 offended many of the moderates of the city. Moreover, he found that he could no longer depend on Charles VIII of France, and Venice opposed him for his pro-French stance. Alexander excommunicated him in 1497, and in April 1498 he was arrested, tried for sedition and heresy, and cruelly tortured. Finally, on May 23 he was hanged and his body burned.

While Savonarola demanded reform in the church, he never took the more advanced position of Wycliffe and Huss. He had no quarrel with the teaching or the organization of the church, but seems to have believed in justification by faith. He was characterized by religious zeal and personal piety. H. F. VOS

SAYCE, ARCHIBALD HENRY
(1845–1933)
English Oriental scholar; defender of the Mosaic authorship of the Pentateuch

Sayce was born near Bristol, the son of an Anglican priest. He studied at Queen's College, Oxford, from 1865 to 1869; he was then elected a fellow of the college and a classics lecturer. The next year he was ordained. Unmarried, he did a great deal of traveling the next years of his life throughout Europe, Asia, North Africa, and the United States; in this period he became an expert in Near Eastern languages. From 1874 to 1884 he worked on a team that produced the Revised Version of the Old Testament. From then on, he devoted himself to the history of religion, especially in Babylon, Egypt, and Israel. In 1891 he was named the first professor of Assyriology at Oxford, a post he held until 1915. The remaining years of his life were spent in England and Egypt writing many scholarly articles. He suffered from ill health throughout much of his life.

In 1894 he published The "Higher Criticism" and the Verdict of the Monuments, which was a significant contribution to Old Testament scholarship. He was especially critical of a theory put forward by the German biblical scholar Julius Wellhausen (1844–1918), that Moses could not have written the first five books of the Bible, in part because of the belief that before the fifth century B.C. there was no writing. Sayce challenged this supposition on archeological grounds. P. TOON

SAYERS, DOROTHY LEIGH
(1893–1957)
Anglican writer

Born in Oxford, Sayers graduated at the university there, specializing in medieval literature. Although she became highly successful as a writer of detective stories, she decided to relinquish that career and turn to weightier topics. While hiding in an air-raid shelter during World War II, she read Dante's *Divine Comedy* and, stunned with its greatness, promptly began to learn Italian to savor it in the original. Later, she translated this monumental work into English. She had not totally completed the translation at the time of her death, so her friend Barbara Reynolds completed the task.

People who love her detective works and her translation of Dante do not always know that Dorothy L. Sayers was also a Christian writer. Her best-known Christian work is *The Man Born to be King* (1941), twelve dramatic episodes in the life of Christ. Though it ran into strong objections at first, the main one being the use of Christ actually speaking, the drama became so popular that it was broadcast over the BBC, Christmas after Christmas. Her long play *The Emperor Constantine* (1951) is an effort to show this Roman emperor's complicated relationships with Christianity and especially his involvements with the Council of Nicea. Other Christian dramas she wrote are *The Zeal of Thy House* (1937) and *Four Sacred Plays*.

She also produced many profitable Christian essays, including "The Other Six Deadly Sins," "What Do We Believe," "Strong Meat," and "The Greatest Drama Ever Staged." She was concerned about the relationship of Christianity and the arts and wrote "Towards a Christian Aesthetic," "Creative Mind," and "The Image of God." Undoubtedly one of her finest works is *The Mind of the Maker* (1941), based on the proposition that ". . . every work of creation is threefold, an earthly trinity to match the heavenly"; the creative *idea* being the

Father, the creative *energy* being the Word, and the creative *power* being the indwelling Spirit. C. KILBY

SCHAEFFER, FRANCIS AUGUST (1912–1984)

Evangelical missionary, philosopher, author, and lecturer

Schaeffer was born in Philadelphia, Pennsylvania, into a Lutheran family, but became an agnostic during his teen years. While a student engineer at Drexel Institute in Philadelphia he became a believer. In 1935 he completed his college work *magna cum laude* at Hampden Sidney College, Virginia, a Southern Presbyterian school, receiving his bachelor of arts degree. During this year he married Edith Seville. Schaeffer further attended Westminster Theological Seminary in Philadelphia, studying under Cornelius van Til, a Reformed apologist from the Netherlands; and he finished his training at Faith Theological Seminary, Wilmington, Delaware, receiving his bachelor of divinity degree in 1938. He became the first ordained minister of the Bible Presbyterian Church and went on to pastor other churches in Pennsylvania and St. Louis, Missouri. In 1971 he was awarded a doctor of laws degree by Gordon College, Wenham, Massachusetts.

In 1948 the Schaeffer family was moved to Switzerland by the Independent Board for Presbyterian Foreign Missions. Francis and Edith became vitally concerned for the youth from all nations they observed there, and in 1955 they founded an international study and ministry community in the Swiss Alps at Huemoz, which they called L'Abri (shelter). Students from all cultures and beliefs were welcome to stay with the Schaeffers and discuss secular culture and ideas. Through study and prayer many of the thousands of internationals who visited at L'Abri became Christians. The story of the founding and development of the L'Abri community is told by Edith Schaeffer in the book, *L'Abri* (1969). Eventually there was L'Abri work in Milan, London, Amsterdam, and Rochester, Minnesota.

The ministry gained worldwide recognition through the distribution of Schaeffer's books: *The God Who Is There* (1968); *Escape from Reason* (1968); *Pollution and the Death of Man* (1970); *The Church at the End of the Twentieth Century* (1970); *True Spirituality* (1971); *He Is There and He Is Not Silent* (1972); *How Should We Then Live; The Rise and Decline of Western Thought and Culture* (1976) to name a few.

Schaeffer attributed much of today's social ills to the teaching of the philosopher Hegel, who promoted the thought that truth is relative and not absolute. Schaeffer's writings, twenty-four books in all, describe the disastrous political and moral consequences of adopting Hegel's view, and contend that the only remedy for our world is a return to biblical absolutes.

In 1979 Schaeffer toured the United States with Dr. C. Everett Koop (later surgeon general of the United States). They lectured and showed a film entitled "Whatever Happened to the Human Race?" This film, produced by his son, Franky Schaeffer, contended that secular humanism had replaced God's laws as the basis of contemporary ethics.

After battling cancer for several years, Dr. Schaeffer died in Rochester, Minnesota, where he and his wife had settled. Two collections about Schaeffer, compiled by Lane T. Dennis, were published by Crossway books in 1986 (*Francis A. Schaeffer: Portraits of the Man and His Work; The Letters of Francis Schaeffer: Spiritual Reality in the Personal Christian Life*). L. LEONARD

SCHAFF, PHILIP (1819–1893)

Swiss-American church historian and ecumenical pioneer

Born in Chur, Switzerland, Schaff was educated in the Universities of Tübingen, Halle, and Berlin, where in 1842 he was appointed privatdozent. Called to Mercersburg, Pennsylvania, to teach church history and biblical literature, he was ordained as a minister of the Reformed Church in April 1844 and in July of that year arrived in the United States. For nineteen years he taught at Mercersburg Academy, where, along with

J. W. Nevin, he helped to develop the Mercersburg Theology, with its emphasis on the church and the sacraments. In 1863 he moved to New York City, where he became secretary of the New York Sabbath Committee, an organization opposed to the secularization of Sunday. In 1870 he joined the faculty of Union Theological Seminary in New York City, where he served until his death. His ecumenical interests were shown in his strong support of the Evangelical Alliance, of which he was the American secretary, and of the Alliance of Reformed Churches.

Schaff was a prolific author. His best-known work is his *History of the Christian Church* (seven volumes, 1882–1892). He also edited the Schaff-Herzog *Encyclopedia of Religious Knowledge* (three volumes, 1882–1884), and the set of patristic translations known as *The Nicene and Post-Nicene Fathers* (1886–1900); and he compiled a valuable collection of confessional documents in his *Creeds of Christendom* (three volumes, 1877). Schaff was also active in the preparation of the Revised Version of the Bible, which was published in 1881 (New Testament) and 1885 (Old Testament). N. V. HOPE

SCHEIN, JOHANN HERMANN (1586–1630)

German composer

Born in Saxony, the son of a Lutheran pastor, Schein lost his father at a young age and was taken to be a chorister at the court chapel in Dresden. In 1615 he was appointed cantor to St. Thomas' School at Leipzig, a post he held until his death.

Schein is primarily known for his *Cantional* first published in 1627. A second, enlarged edition appeared posthumously in 1645. This work, which consists of chorale tunes harmonized for church use, shows that Schein was a poet, melodist, and harmonist. Out of the two hundred or so melodies in this book, eighty are Schein's own. Many have held their own in modern German hymnbooks.

With Michael Praetorius and Heinrich Schütz (and probably through their influence), Schein was one of the pioneers, in Germany, of the new movement in music proceeding from Italy at the beginning of the seventeenth century.

He composed sixteen secular strophic songs and a work containing thirty sacred motets, some set to Latin texts, others to German. Another major work was dedicated to Duke Johann Ernst of Weimar and contains twenty instrumental suites. *Opella Nova* contains thirty sacred compositions on German texts, based on choral tunes. *Musica Boscareccia* contains fifty secular compositions, three based on a poem written by Schein himself. *Fontana d'Israel* and *Dilette postorali* contain motets and madrigals. Then he composed thirty-two more sacred pieces, also giving specific directions for their performance. Besides these major works, he composed many pieces for weddings and funerals. G. A. COMFORT

SCHERESCHEWSKY, SAMUEL ISAAC JOSEPH (1831–1906)

Bishop of the Episcopal Church in Shanghai; Bible translator

Schereschewsky was born into an orthodox Jewish family in Russian Lithuania, studied in rabbinical schools and the University of Breslau. He was converted to Christianity through Bible study. While a student at General Theological Seminary in New York he resolved to become a missionary and translate the Bible into Chinese. He translated the Anglican Book of Common Prayer. He and others published the New Testament in Mandarin in 1872, and his Mandarin Old Testament was published in 1874. He was consecrated bishop while in the United States in 1878. Schereschewsky founded St. John's College (later University), first of the Protestant colleges and long the leading one. The bishop was paralyzed in 1881 and only partially recovered. He resigned the episcopate and spent his remaining years in Bible translation, although he could not use a pen and could type only with one finger. He produced a Wenli, or

Literary, Chinese Bible. He died in Tokyo in 1906 while having some of his work printed.
R. P. BEAVER

SCHLATTER, ADOLF VON (1852–1938)
Theologian, historian, and New Testament scholar

Born at St. Gall, Switzerland, Schlatter studied at the universities of Basel and Tübingen (1872–1875). After serving two Swiss pastorates, in 1880 he began to teach at Bern, first as privatdozent and then as associate professor. In 1886 he became professor of New Testament exegesis at Greifswald; in 1893 he went to Berlin as professor of systematic theology; and in 1898 he accepted a chair of New Testament at Tübingen, where he remained until his retirement in 1922. In such theological works as *Die Theologie des Neuen Testaments* (1909) and *Das Christliche Dogma* (1911), Schlatter insisted that the only valid foundation for systematic theology lay in sound biblical exegesis, and he stressed the central importance of the historical Jesus for a true understanding of the Christian faith. In New Testament studies he wrote *Die Sprach und Heimat des vierten Evangelisten* (1902), in which he showed, from his deep knowledge of the Semitic background of the New Testament, that many phrases in the Gospel of John that were commonly held to be Hellenistic could be paralleled from Rabbinic writings. Schlatter also produced such historical works as *A History of Israel from Alexander to Hadrian* (1901) and *A History of the Early Church* (1926). From 1897, along with A. H. Cremer, he edited the *Beitrage zur Forderung Christliche Theologie*. N. V. HOPE

SCHLEIERMACHER, FRIEDRICH ERNST DANIEL (1768–1834)
Influential German liberal theologian

Schleiermacher, born into a clerical family, had a pietistic background. He studied at Halle, where he was irritated by the pious and narrow outlook of his Moravian teachers. As a university student, he was fascinated by the debates instigated by the teaching of Immanuel Kant (1724–1804).

After a brief period as a tutor and as an assistant minister to his uncle, Schleiermacher came to Berlin as chaplain to the Charity Hospital in 1796. Here he was drawn into the brilliant circle of Romantic novelists and poets who formed the *avant garde* intellectuals of the day. It was in this period that Schleiermacher published his famous *On Religion: Speeches to Its Cultured Despisers*.

In 1804 Schleiermacher became an assistant professor in the University of Halle, where he wrote on biblical criticism and began his edition of Plato. His translation was to remain for many years the standard in the German language. The years at Halle were overshadowed by the Napoleonic Wars and the collapse of the German armies before the French invaders. In 1809 Schleiermacher returned to Berlin, where he helped to found the new university. The university was a symbol of national revival, and Schleiermacher became the leading preacher of Prussian renewal.

At Berlin, Schleiermacher was a professor of theology and also minister of the Trinity Church. The church itself was an early venture in ecumenical relations. It was shared by the Reformed and Lutheran churches, which the king of Prussia was anxious to bring together as an instrument of unification and renewal. Schleiermacher represented the Reformed Church. His greatest work, *The Christian Faith* (1821), was the first attempt to write an ecumenical systematic theology for the two churches. His collected writings fill some thirty volumes, dividing almost equally into sermons, theology, and philosophical writings. He was a prominent member of the Academy of Sciences. It was his ideal to bring together the academic world, the church, the state, and family life.

Schleiermacher's theology steered a middle course between traditional Protestant theology, based on the Bible as the Word of God, and the philosophical theology of the Age of Enlightenment. He could no longer regard Scripture as the inspired Word of God; but neither could he embrace a purely philosophical approach. Like Kant, he believed that one could not speculate about reality beyond man's immediate experience. Schleiermacher based his approach on religious experience, the essence of which he saw as the feeling or sense of absolute dependence. This led to a restatement of the whole range of Christian doctrine. God is that being upon whom man feels utterly dependent. Sin is man's attempt to be independent, when he should be dependent. Redemption is the restoration of man's true dependence.

Schleiermacher wished to revise the teaching of the creeds about Christ. He saw him as a man in whom the feeling of dependence was developed to perfection. Hence, one could speak of an existence of God in him and of Christ as the mediator of this experience of God. But he was not fully God and fully man in the same sense of the creeds. Schleiermacher pioneered the way for the later liberal views of Jesus as a divinely inspired man. In the twentieth century, Karl Barth and Emil Brunner voiced the criticism of many when they pointed out that Schleiermacher's theology, being man-centered, neglected the revelation of God in his Word. C. BROWN

SCHLIEMANN, HEINRICH (1822–1890)
Known as the founder of prehistoric Greek archaeology

Born at Neu Buckow in Mecklenberg-Schwerin, north Germany, Schliemann at age fourteen was apprenticed to a grocer. Pursuing a business career, he became a bookkeeper for an Amsterdam trading firm, which in 1846 sent him to St. Petersburg, the Russian capital. There Schliemann established his own business, and at the time of the Crimean War (1854–1855) he made a fortune, mainly as a military contractor. At the age of thirty-six he retired from business to devote himself to the study and practice of prehistoric archaeology. After some training in Paris and extensive world travel, in 1856 he took his large fortune to Greece, visiting Homeric shrines there and in Asia Minor. He began his excavations in 1870 and carried them on, with some interrup-

tions, until his death. Schliemann identified the site of ancient Troy in Asia Minor, and that of Mycenae in northeast Peloponnesus, Greece; he published his findings in such books as *Mycenae* (1877), *Ilios* (1880), and *Troja* (1884). Projects of archaeological work at Ithaca and at Knossos were cut short by Schliemann's death in Naples.
N. V. HOPE

SCHMUCKER, SAMUEL SIMON (1799–1873)
Leader of the "American" or "New School" Lutheranism

Schmucker, although a graduate of the Presbyterian seminary at Princeton, worked throughout his life for causes he felt would benefit both Lutherans and other evangelicals in the United States. He helped strengthen the General Synod of Lutheran churches formed in 1820. He was a founder, professor of theology, and president of Gettysburg Lutheran Seminary. He pledged himself to fight rationalism and religious indifference with the weapons of the Augsburg Confession and Luther's Small Catechism.

At the same time, his concerns moved beyond Lutheranism. He supported revivalism. He favored the development of interdenominational agencies, such as the Sunday school movement, to spread the gospel and improve national morality. He spoke out on American national issues by expressing fears, for example, concerning immigrants and Roman Catholics. He also was a founder of the American branch of the interdenominational Evangelical Alliance (1846). And, what was most upsetting to traditional Lutherans, he favored certain modifications in the Augsburg Confession—he did not believe in a Real Presence of Christ's body in the Lord's Supper; he rejected private confession; and he desired a much stronger emphasis on keeping the Sabbath. Schmucker's opponents failed to note his general commitment to Lutheranism as they called into question his "modern American Puritanism."

Schmucker's form of Lutheranism became

known as "American" or "New School" Lutheranism, as opposed to "European" or "Old" Lutheranism, inasmuch as he attempted to join characteristics of American Protestantism to traditional Lutheran distinctives. His point of view prevailed among American Lutherans until about the time of the Civil War. Then, however, growing numbers of German and Scandinavian immigrants, and a revival of interest in the roots of the Reformation, combined to lessen its influence. His own works—such as *Elements of Popular Theology* (1834) and *A Fraternal Appeal to the American Churches* (1838)—illustrated the blend of his traditionally Lutheran and modern American convictions. The anonymous *Definite Synodical Platform* of 1855, which proposed a revision of the Augsburg Confession along lines favored by Schmucker, precipitated a clash of interests, which eventually led to the triumph of "European" Lutheranism over Schmucker's "American" variation. M. A. NOLL

SCHUBERT, FRANZ (1797–1828)
Viennese composer

Born in Vienna, the son of a schoolmaster, Schubert was a younger contemporary of Beethoven. He is perhaps best known for his over six hundred songs (*Lieder*) for voice and piano, which blend music and poetry into a highly expressive form. He also wrote operas, symphonies, piano sonatas, string quartets, piano trios, and other chamber music, works for male chorus, female chorus, and mixed chorus, for a total of at least one thousand works.

His sacred works include six settings of the Mass for solo voices, chorus, and orchestra, as well as much other church music such as hymns (e.g., "Stabat Mater"), antiphons (e.g., "Salve Regina"), offertories, and other texts. Of the masses, four are early works: the F-major Mass (1814, revised 1815), the G-major (1815), the B-flat major (also 1815), and the C-major (1816, revised in 1825 and 1828). The two remaining masses are considered important works: the A-flat major Mass (1819–1822, with a re-

vised version later, both still extant) and the E-flat major Mass (1828). D. HAYES

SCHÜRER, EMIL (1844–1910)
German New Testament scholar

After studying at Erlangen, Berlin, Heidelberg, and Leipzig, Schürer lectured at Leipzig (1896–1878), Giessen (1878–1890), Kiel (1890–1895), and Göttingen (1895–1910). In 1876 he founded the journal *Theologische Literaturzeitung* and edited it for twenty-six years. He devoted his life to the study of Judaism around the beginning of the Christian era. Over the years he gradually expanded his handbook of New Testament history (1874) into a famous, massive, and standard five-volume treatise entitled *A History of the Jewish People in the Time of Christ* (1886–1890; English translation, 1890–1891). This monumental work covers the period from the Maccabees to the Trojan wars (175 B.C.–A.D. 135) from the political, social, religious, and literary viewpoints. A completely revised edition under the editorship of M. Black, G. Vermes, and F. Millar appeared in 1973, incorporating new insights from the Dead Sea Scrolls and other discoveries this century. N. HILLYER

SCHÜTZ, HEINRICH (1585–1672)
German composer

Schütz had a good early musical training and a very good general education. He then continued his studies in law at the University of Marburg. At this time he was also manifesting a talent for music and decided to go to Venice to study with Giovanni Gabrieli.

After two years Gabrieli died, and Schütz went to Leipzig to continue the study of law. However, he returned to music as a vocation, establishing himself as director of the electoral chapel in 1617 at a salary of four hundred florins.

He then married Magdalene Wildeck, who died a short while later, in 1625. To distract himself from deep sorrow and to familiarize himself with the new Italian music, especially the works of Claudio Monteverdi, he returned to Italy. Then in 1641 he returned to Dresden, and after a few years he continued his musical service until the end of his life. In his later years his hearing was poor, and he spent most of his time reading the Holy Scripture and spiritual books. He loved the Psalms, and one of his last creative tasks was a setting of Psalm 119: "Thy statutes have been my songs in the house of my pilgrimage."

Schütz holds a place of unique importance in the relationship between the German and Italian music of the seventeenth century. He was well-fitted to endow German music with the brilliance of the Italian style. His first compositions were done while studying with Giovanni Gabrieli in his early years. From these modest madrigals Schütz passed directly to the grand manner of the new "concerted style" in his next important publication *Psalmen Davids sammt etlichen Mottetten and Concerten mit und Mehr Stimmen* (1619). Almost every one of these Psalms of 1619 exploits a different kind of sonority, imaginatively suited to its exposition.

The year 1627 marked an event of great historical importance, the production of the first German opera, Schütz's *Dafne*. The ensuing period until 1636 was an unproductive one, owing to the upheavals caused by the Thirty Years' War. However, at the end of this time *Musicalische Exequien,* described as a "concert in the form of a German funeral Mass" was composed. In 1664, when Schütz was nearly eighty, he experienced a remarkable resurgence of creative activity. In this and the following year, he composed a Christmas oratorio and at least three settings of the story of the Passion, all outstanding works. He continued to produce substantial works until the end of his life—the remarkable *Deutsches Magnificat* of 1671 bearing witness.

Though Schütz was recognized as the heir of Gabrieli's rich heritage, Schütz never forsook his original German ancestry. One of the most impressive features of his style is the precision in his musical thoughts. His ideas have had an enduring significance born out of his deep reflections and realizations of God and Christ. Thus, his gift to the church has been profound, and his contribution to the transitional musical era in which he lived was greatly significant. As a predecessor to Bach, Heinrich Schütz was indeed a gift and a master. G. A. COMFORT

SCHWARTZ, CHRISTIAN FRIEDRICH (1726–1798)
German missionary to India

Born a baker's son at Sonnenburg, Prussia, Schwartz studied theology at Halle University, mastered the Tamil language (to which were later added several others), was ordained in Copenhagen, and in 1750 was sent by the Danish Missionary Society to Tranquebar, India. He extended his outreach to Ceylon in 1760 and in 1762 went to Trichinopoly, where he was appointed chaplain to the British community, including the army. Coming under the London-based Society for the Promotion of Christian Knowledge in 1767, he went five years later to Tanjore, where he served and wielded enormous political influence for good. He never forgot that he was first and foremost a missionary—and one concerned to strengthen the indigenous church in India. He founded many congregations, encouraged the education of native pastors and laity, was a peacemaker in turbulent times, and contributed much to making Europeans trusted and respected. Schwartz never returned home. An extraordinary tribute was paid after his death when two marble monuments were set up: one from a Hindu prince, the other by the directors of the East India Company—an institution not always sympathetic to missionaries. J. D. DOUGLAS

SCHWEITZER, ALBERT (1875–1965)
Theologian, medical missionary, organist, and musical historian

Born in Alsace, Schweitzer was the son of a Protestant minister. He was trained in Greek and Latin at a gymnasium and then went on to attend the University of Strassburg from 1893 to 1898, where he studied theology. From 1905 to 1913 he studied medicine at the University of Strassburg. Beginning in 1903 he went as a medical missionary to establish a hospital in Lambarene. Throughout his life, he had three main passions: theology, medicine, and music.

As a theologian, Schweitzer was intensely interested in recovering the historical Jesus. In his study of Jesus, as presented in *The Quest of the Historical Jesus* (1906), he believed he had discovered the real Jesus by reconstructing his historicity through a study of the Gospels. Schweitzer claimed that this Jesus was not at all like the one imagined by Protestants; rather, he pictured Jesus as one who accepted as true the Jewish messianic expectations and whose thought, word, and action were based on his expectation that the end of the world was near and that the kingdom of God would be revealed. This implied that Jesus' life was driven by a mistaken expectation. Other significiant theological works written by Schweitzer are *Mystery of the Kingdom of God* (1901), *Psychiatric Study of Jesus* (1913), and *Christianity and the Religions of the World* (1923).

After receiving his M.D. from the University of Strassburg in 1913, Schweitzer set out as a medical missionary to the Congo, wherein he established a hospital at Lambarene. Basically, for the rest of his life Schweitzer labored at this hospital, healing the Congolese of their many diseases. His experiences are captured in his books, such as *On the Edge of the Primeval Forest* (1921) and *The Jungle Hospital* (1948).

As a musician, Schweitzer was organist of the Strassburg Bach concerts from 1896 and of the Paris Bach society concerts from 1906. While a medical missionary in Africa, he made visits to Europe to give lectures and organ recitals—often to raise funds for his hospital in Lambarene. He is known especially as an interpreter of the music of J. S. Bach, whom he saw as a kind of poet-musician, conceiving musical ideas as various kinds of emotion suggested by his texts. This is expressed in his book *J. S. Bach le Musicien-Poète* (1905). He also published *J. S. Bach* (1908) and Bach's *Complete Organ Works* (1954). Schweitzer's discussion of

Bach's music, in relation to his cantata texts and the words of chorales, has brought a deeper understanding of Bach's sacred music.

Schweitzer, a man of many talents and great energy, is best known for his philosophy of "reverence for life." Indeed, this philosophy is expressed in a posthumous work of the same title, *Reverence for Life* (1966). Schweitzer is also known for his quest for world peace, for which he received the Nobel Peace Prize for 1952. His autobiography is *Out of My Life and Thought* (1933, updated in 1949 and 1990).

P. W. COMFORT & D. HAYES

SCHWENKFELD, KASPAR VON OSSIG (1489–1561)
German theologian; leader of the Schwenkfelders

Born in 1489 near Luben, Schwenkfeld was the eldest son of an aristocratic family. He studied at Cologne, Frankfurt an der Oder, and possibly Erfurt, and seems to have been won to the Reformation by reading Martin Luther's tracts. He visited Wittenberg while Luther was in Wartburg and began to correspond with Luther. In 1524, however, he was disillusioned by the results of Luther's work and moved closer to the radicals, especially Andreas Carlstadt. Claiming a special revelation, he intervened in the debate about Christ's eucharistic presence in 1525 and for a while gained some support from Zwingli. His increasing association with the Anabaptists forced him to leave Silesia in 1529 and Strassburg in 1534.

Schwenkfeld spent the rest of his life as a wanderer, mostly in Swabia. During this time he continued to publish his distinctive views on the Lord's Supper, the relationship of the Word and Spirit, and especially the Incarnation. It was his doctrine of the deification of Christ's humanity, stated in the *Great Confession* of 1540, which brought about his denunciation not only by the Swiss but also by the Lutherans. After 1540 his followers, originally called Confessors of the Glory of Christ, later Schwenkfelders, formed their own congregations, mainly in

Silesia and Swabia, then in Prussia. Coming under persecution in 1720, they moved to Holland, England, and Pennsylvania, where a small group still remains. Schwenkfeld himself continued his active preaching and writing ministry until 1561, when he died at Ulm. His works were collected and published in thirteen volumes during the years 1907 to 1937. G. BROMILEY

SCOFIELD, CYRUS INGERSON
(1843–1921)
Lawyer and frontier politician; best known for his reference Bible

Born in Lenawee County, Michigan, Scofield grew up near Lebanon, Tennessee. He read assiduously, always making careful notes and tracing the identity of unknown terms or names. He enlisted in the Confederate army and won the Cross of Honor for valor at Antietam. Following the Civil War, he took work as a clerk in a land abstract office, became an expert in the field, and attached himself to a St. Louis, Missouri, law firm that specialized in land titles. He was admitted to the Kansas bar, elected to the state legislature, and in 1873 appointed United States Attorney for Kansas by President Ulysses S. Grant.

In 1879, during a business trip in St. Louis, the young attorney was converted by a YMCA evangelist. His attention turned to theology, especially prophecy. Scofield's enthusiasm for the system of doctrine and history known as dispensationalism began during his friendship with James H. Brookes, a Presbyterian clergyman. Scofield was ordained as a Congregational minister in 1882, accepted a pastorate at First Congregational Church in Dallas (now Scofield Memorial Church), and three years later issued his first dispensational book, *Rightly Dividing the Word of Truth* (1907).

During his Dallas pastorate, Scofield founded the Central American Mission (1890). From 1895 to 1902, at D. L. Moody's request, he temporarily took over the East Northfield, Massachusetts, Congregational Church. During this same period, he was also president of the East Northfield and Mount Hermon schools.

Scofield returned to Dallas in 1902, a year after he first proposed the idea of an annotated Bible. Financial backing was found, and the giant task was done in the course of his second Dallas pastorate and a Bible conference ministry in the United States and England. Publication of the *Scofield Reference Bible* in 1909 drew mixed reactions. He had projected into the text the seven-era dispensational scheme first proposed by John N. Darby in 1830. Critics suggested that his peculiar approach to Christ's return (two returns, two resurrections, etc.) supplanted the Crucifixion as the central point of history. Despite the controversy, the *Scofield Bible* continued to be the best-selling study Bible for many years. M. FACKLER

SCRIVENER, FREDERICK HENRY AMBROSE (1813–1891)
English New Testament textual critic

Born at Southwark, Scrivener was educated at Falmouth School and Trinity College, Cambridge. He later became the headmaster of Falmouth (1846–1856) and prebendary of Exeter (1874–1891). Scrivener spent his entire career working on New Testament manuscripts. He published the texts of twenty manuscripts (including Codex Augiensis and the miniscule 81), produced a list of all extant manuscripts, and created a system for classifying manuscripts. As an enthusiastic supporter of the Textus Receptus, he opposed the text produced by Westcott and Hort but did not gain a following among biblical scholars. He is well known for his book, *A Plain Introduction to the Criticism of the New Testament* (1894). P. W. COMFORT

SCUDDER, IDA SOPHIA (1870–1959)
Founder of Vellore Medical College and hospital in Madras State, India

Ida Scudder was born in Ranipet, Arcot (India), the daughter of a medical missionary of the Reformed Church in America and granddaughter of the very first American medical missionary anywhere. She studied at Northfield Seminary, Massachusetts, and went back to India for a short term because her mother was ill. An unusually traumatic experience in 1893 turned Scudder to her medical vocation. Three men came to her in one night asking her to assist their wives in childbirth, since her missionary father, as a man, was not allowed to approach those women. All three women died that night. Scudder then studied at the Women's Medical College in Philadelphia and graduated from Cornell University Medical College. She went back to India in 1900 and opened a women's hospital at Vellore. A branch and roadside clinics were added. Indian women doctors were urgently needed, and after five years of pleading Dr. Scudder was allowed to open a medical college in 1918. Six boards united to support it, and many others later joined. A Vellore College Board was set up in New York to raise continuing support. The institution was raised to university status in 1942. It was opened to men also in 1947. P. BEAVER

SEABURY, SAMUEL (1729–1796)
First bishop of the Protestant Episcopal Church in the United States

Seabury was born in Connecticut to a former Congregationalist minister who had left that communion to become a missionary for the Church of England. Seabury graduated from Yale, studied medicine in Edinburgh, and was ordained to the Anglican priesthood in England in 1753. He returned to America to serve first as a missionary in New Brunswick, then as a parish minister on Long Island, and finally as a pastor in Connecticut. With the coming of the American Revolution, Seabury found himself swimming against the tide. Religiously, he was "High Church," one who emphasized Catholic characteristics of Anglicanism, such as its teaching on the apostolic succession through bishops. Politically, he was loyal to the king. His political views led him to an exchange of pamphlets with Alexander Hamilton, future secretary of the treasury of the United States. They also led to his im-

prisonment in 1775. When released from jail Seabury served as a chaplain with British forces. In spite of this service to the king, he eventually became a solid friend of the American republic.

Seabury's greatest work was his effort to rebuild an Episcopal Church in the new United States. With the connection to the Church of England destroyed by the war and with great confusion concerning the leadership of American Episcopalians, firm measures were necessary. In Connecticut a convention of Episcopalian ministers met in 1783 and elected Seabury a prospective bishop. Consecration, however, proved a difficult matter. Seabury waited in England an entire year for consecration. When circumstances made that impossible, he traveled to Scotland, where he was consecrated in November 1784 by bishops of the Episcopalian Church there.

Much work remained in America. Many of Seabury's fellow Americans distrusted him—some because of his actions during the war, others because of his High Church views. Jurisdictional difficulties also arose when two other Americans, William White of Philadelphia and Samuel Provoost of New York, finally received ordination as bishops from the Church of England itself. Finally in 1789, mistrust was set aside, and Seabury, who was recognized as presiding bishop, joined with White, Provoost, other clergymen, and lay delegates in establishing the Protestant Episcopal Church in the United States.

Something of Seabury's energy and of his Christian spirit can be glimpsed in this journal entry made only three months before his death. It describes a visit to several churches in which "I traveled 134 miles, preached 10 times, administered the Communion 5 times, and confirmed 198 persons. . . . And now, All glory to God for his innumerable benefits." M. A. NOLL

SEBASTIAN (died c. 303)
Fourth-century Christian Roman martyr

Bishop Ambrose states that Sebastian was a native of Milan who died for his faith during the persecution unleashed by the emperor Diocletian against Christianity in the Roman Empire (303). According to the *Passio S. Sebastiani,* a romance compiled around the mid-400s, Sebastian was an army officer condemned for his Christian faith to be shot to death with arrows by his fellow soldiers, after which he was buried by the matron Lucina in a cemetery in a catacomb on the Appian Way in Rome. A later legend maintained that Sebastian survived his shooting, was restored to health by the widow Irene, and presented himself before the emperor, who ordered him to be clubbed to death. This legend, however, lacks authenticity and is no longer believed. N. V. HOPE

SEELEY, JOHN ROBERT (1834–1895)
English historian and theologian

Born in London, Seeley entered Cambridge University in 1852 and graduated in 1857. After teaching school for some years, in 1863 he was appointed professor of Latin at University College, London, and in 1869 he succeeded Charles Kingsley as professor of modern history at Cambridge University. His chief historical works are *The Life and Times of Stein, or Germany and Prussia in the Napoleonic Age* (1878); *The Expansion of England* (1883), which emphasized the colonial aspect of British history between 1688 and 1815; and *The Growth of British Policy* (two volumes, 1895). Seeley's major theological work is *Ecce Homo* (*Behold the Man*), published anonymously in 1865. It was an attempt—one of the very earliest—to interpret the religious and moral teaching of Jesus in a simple and positive form. Though it aroused considerable controversy because it seemed to ignore Jesus' deity, it won recognition as a fresh and perceptive treatment of its subject, and it achieved a large circulation. In 1894 Seeley was knighted by Queen Victoria. N. V. HOPE

SELWYN, GEORGE AUGUSTUS (1809–1878)
First Anglican bishop of New Zealand

Born in London and educated at St. John's,

Cambridge, Selwyn was ordained in 1833 and appointed bishop of New Zealand in 1841. Missionaries from the Church Missionary Society (CMS) had entered New Zealand in 1814 and witnessed widespread conversions among the Maori people. It was Selwyn's responsibility to engineer their passage from the mission to the church. He established good rapport with the Maoris and learned their language, expecting the same from his clergy. He experienced problems with the CMS board over the transfer of authority, with other missionaries over the theology of the ministry, and with the colonists over land alienation. The latter was aggravated by the Maori Wars, the bishop being spiritual shepherd for both sides.

Selwyn founded St. John's College, Auckland, was appointed an archdeacon (1844), and developed the structures for a colonial church. His first synod (1846) explored the kind of structure required in a mission field situation so different from England. In 1847 he introduced the laity into his synod and proposed a constitution in 1857 (confirmed in 1865) that gave autonomy to the colonial church.

An error of latitude in his letters patent gave him jurisdiction over Melanesia. He voyaged through the islands and then established the Melanesian Mission, consecrating J. C. Patteson as its first bishop (1861). His directives were to retain as much of the culture as could be spiritually Christianized and to raise native leaders. He had already ordained Maoris since 1853. He brought suitable young islanders to New Zealand for training and return to their homelands. This became a permanent policy. A. R. TIPPETT

SEMLER, JOHANN SALOMO (1725–1791)
German theologian and church historian

Born in Thüringen, Semler in his early years was strongly influenced by his father's Pietism. Later, while attending the University of Halle (1743–1750), he was attracted to the rationalism of J. S. Baumgarten. After teaching at Coberg and Altdorf, he returned to Halle as professor of theology (1753–

1791) and soon became one of the most popular theologians in Germany.

Semler was a prolific writer. Most of his 171 publications are on ecclesiastical history and history of the canon. In his *Treatise on the Free Investigation of the Canon* (1771–1775) he maintained that theology and ethics were historically conditioned and subject to constant change and development as writers respond to various circumstances. Consequently, there is much in the Bible that is not inspired. The value of any one portion must be left to the judgment of each individual as guided by the Holy Spirit. Although his views pointed in the direction of naturalism, Semler steadfastly opposed the conclusions of naturalism. He highly valued the marks of piety—such as prayer, singing of hymns, and Christian morality—that were promoted by the church. Thus, while one's private beliefs must be free from coercion, public dogma must be preserved from its influences and strictly regulated by the state. R. HESSELGRAVE

SENFL, LUDWIG (c. 1490–1543)
German composer

Born in Zurich, Senfl was a student of Heinrich Isaac, and in 1517 he was successor to him as court kapellmeister at Vienna. In 1520 he was in Augsburg. In 1523 he became kapellmeister at München (a Roman Catholic court). He corresponded with Luther and composed polyphonic choral settings of Luther's chorales. In 1530 and 1531 he completed an unfinished sequence in Isaac's *Choralis Constantinus* (settings of parts of the proper of the Mass for the whole liturgical year) and supervised the copying of the whole work. He was a prolific and versatile composer. He wrote settings of German secular songs and Latin hymns, motets, and settings of the Magnificat. D. HAYES

SERRA, JUNÍPERO (1713–1784)
Franciscan missionary to the Indians of Mexico and the California coast

Though born into a poor family on the Mediterranean island of Majorca in 1713, Serra had an extensive education. His doctorate in theology could have opened the doors to privilege; instead, after a period of university professorship, he sailed to America (1749) and established and administered missions. The California cities of San Diego, San Gabriel, San Luis Obispo, San Francisco, San Juan Capistrano, and Santa Clara, among others, grew up around missions that Serra founded.

While Serra originally entered California with a Spanish army of conquest (1769), he was quick to defend the Indians from bad treatment. To this purpose, he presented his *Representación* (1773), a treatise on the conduct of missions, to the Spanish viceroy in Mexico City. In 1778, Serra was granted the right to confirm, a right usually reserved to bishops.

Calculations made just before his death showed that he had baptized six thousand and confirmed five thousand in his almost continuous walking through the mission territories. He was buried at San Carlos Mission, California. P. M. BASSETT

SERVETUS, MICHAEL (1511–1553)
Anti-Trinitarian theologian and physician

Servetus was born in the Aragon region (Spain) of a pious Roman Catholic family. Although he studied law at the University of Tolouse, he was more interested in biblical languages, theology, and philosophy. For a time he served as secretary to Charles V's confessor, but then left to travel in northern Europe, where he visited Lyons, Geneva, Basel, and Strassburg. In the latter city he met Protestant Reformer Martin Bucer and also had dealings with some of the Anabaptist leaders.

As a result of these contacts and his studies in Neoplatonic and Cabalistic philosophy, he came to the conclusion that in order to win Jews and Muslims to Christ, the doctrine of the Trinity had to be revised, and to this end he published *De Trinitatis Erroribus* (1531), which was immediately attacked by both Roman Catholics and Reformers such as Zwingli, Oecolampadius, and Bucer. In

1538 he spent some time studying medicine in Paris and also lectured on astrology. After that he also studied Hebrew and theology at Louvain. As his heretical opinions on the Trinity, however, had brought him to the notice of the Roman Catholic authorities, he turned to the practice of medicine in Avignon and Vienne. About this time he apparently worked out the pulmonary circulation of the blood, an account of which he published.

His real interest, however, was in theology, and for this reason he opened a correspondence with Calvin in Geneva (1545–1546). Between 1547 and 1553 he worked on his major book, *Restitutio Christianismi*, which was primarily an attack on Calvin's *Institutes*, based on what might be called a kind of Christocentric pantheism. The work was published anonymously, but it was soon discovered that he was the author. He was then arrested and condemned by the Inquisition in Vienne, but escaped, and despite previous warnings from Calvin, came to Geneva where he apparently made contact with some of those opposed to Calvin. But he was recognized, arrested, and condemned to be burned at the stake. W. S. REID

SETON, ELIZABETH ANN BAYLEY (1774–1821)
Known as mother of the American parochial school system

Born in New York City, reared an Episcopalian, Elizabeth married William Seton in 1794 and moved with him to Italy. She became the mother of five children and after her husband's death in 1803 turned to an Italian family for help. Under their influence and after a spiritual struggle, she converted to Roman Catholicism.

Shortly after her conversion Seton opened a boarding school in Baltimore, Maryland, and quickly earned the approval of John Carroll, the city's first Roman Catholic archbishop. Carroll appointed her as "mother" of the group of young women who had joined her at the school. Modeling themselves after the French Daughters of Charity

of Saint Vincent de Paul, they took vows of poverty, chastity, and obedience; adopted a habit; and thus founded the American Sisters of Chastity, the first native American sisterhood. Seton later expanded her school and moved it to near Emmitsburg in northern Maryland.

On September 14, 1975, by declaration of Pope Paul VI, she became the first American-born person to be declared a saint. E. G. ROHR

SHAFTESBURY, ANTHONY ASHLEY COOPER (1801–1885)
Christian statesman; England's seventh Earl of Shaftesbury

Now known as Lord Shaftesbury instead of Lord Ashley, he attended Harrow School and Christ Church, Oxford, where he gained academic distinction. When his father inherited the earldom, Ashley inherited his baronetcy (the lowest British hereditary title), becoming Lord Ashley in 1811. In 1830 he married Lady Emily Cowper, daughter of the Earl and Lady Cowper. After the earl's death, his widow married Lord Palmerston, who became prime minister of Britain in 1855. As his son-in-law, Ashley (by then Lord Shaftesbury) was able to recommend evangelical clergymen to the prime minister for senior appointments in the Church of England.

As a social reformer, Shaftesbury campaigned on such matters as the treatment of lunatics; the terms of employment of workers in factories, mills, and collieries (mines); and the use of boys as chimney sweepers. He continued to press for social action as a member of the House of Commons between 1830 and 1850. Later, as a member of the House of Lords, he especially called attention to the need to improve the dwelling houses of industrial workers. As a landowner he built a model village in Dorset. He was the best type of Victorian philanthropist who wanted to improve the conditions of the poor. To look in him for modern ideas of social reform (that is, for changing the social structures) is to look in vain. Whereas other reformers like Wilberforce, Fry, and Howard tended to concentrate on a single issue, Shaftesbury managed to focus attention on many.

As a committed member of the Church of England, he allied himself with the evangelical party within it. The list of Anglican evangelical societies of which he was president is virtually a complete list of all such societies. He was also a friend of Nonconformists and gladly cooperated with them in the British and Foreign Bible Society, the YMCA, and other ventures. Among clergymen his closest friend was Edward Bickersteth and among laity it was Alexander Haldane, editor of the *Record* newspaper.

Shaftesbury's theological commitment was to moderate Calvinism and nondispensational premillennialism. He believed in the restoration of Jews to Palestine and to that end supported the establishment of the Protestant bishopric in Jerusalem in 1841 (a joint venture of Prussian Lutherans and the Church of England). As a strong Protestant he opposed both the Tractarian movement in the English church and the "papal aggression" of 1851 (the establishment of Roman Catholic dioceses in England and Wales). To the joy of historians his diaries have been preserved and are kept in the Palmerston House (Broadlands Archives) in England.

P. TOON

SHARP, GRANVILLE (1735–1813)
English abolitionist, philanthropist, and Bible scholar

Sharp was born in Durham, the grandson of the archbishop of York. He had little formal education, but he did teach himself such subjects as Greek. Eventually he entered the civil service in London. In 1765 he befriended a destitute Negro slave who had been abandoned by his owner, and this marked the beginning of his passionate campaign to eradicate slavery in England. He attempted to press charges against the owner but lost in court. He then spent his next years studying the law of personal liberty in England, wrote on the issue, and in 1772 saw the courts affirm the principle he worked so tirelessly to secure: the moment a slave sets foot on English soil he is free. In 1787 he founded the Society for the Abolition of Slavery and helped to found a colony for freed slaves in Sierra Leone.

Sharp was an advocate for the interests and concerns of the American colonies and a fierce opponent of press gangs, a method of forced conscription into military service. Toward the end of the American war for independence, he played an important role in providing bishops for the Episcopal (Anglican) congregations in the colonies. The consecration of the Episcopal bishops of New York and Pennsylvania in 1787 was largely arranged by him. Such efforts won him honorary degrees from Harvard and elsewhere. In 1804 he helped to found the British and Foreign Bible Society, and in 1813 the Protestant Union (which opposed Catholic emancipation, a stand uncharacteristic of Sharp).

In 1798 he wrote on the use of the definite article in the Greek New Testament and formulated a principle that came to be known as "Granville Sharp's canon": when two nouns are connected by *kai* (and), the former with the definite article, the latter without, both refer to the same person. For instance, in Titus 2:13 the reading would be "our great God and Savior, Jesus Christ" (see NRSV). His theory was hotly debated in the unitarian controversies, but it is now a well-established principle in Greek grammar.

P. TOON

SHEDD, WILLIAM GREENOUGH THAYER (1820–1894)
American systematic theologian

Shedd was educated at the University of Vermont and Andover Theological Seminary and then began a wide-ranging career. He was briefly a Congregational minister in Vermont, then a professor of English at the university of that state, a professor of preaching at Auburn Seminary, professor of church history at Andover, briefly an associate minister of Brick Presbyterian Church in New York, and finally a professor of Bible and theology at New York's Union Seminary. His best-known writing is his *Dogmatic*

Theology, published in three volumes from 1888 to 1894. As with the *Systematic Theology* of Hodge (1872–1873), Shedd's weighty work advocated the "high Calvinism" of the Westminster Confession. Shedd's work lacks a little of the comprehension which has made Hodge's theology so influential; but more than Hodge, Shedd took account of modern intellectual trends. Against ancient and more recent detractions from orthodoxy he posed the riches of the Christian tradition: Athanasius on the Trinity, Augustine on the nature of sin, Anselm on the existence of God, and the Reformers on salvation. His interests extended well beyond theology, however, to include literature, church history, homiletics, and Bible commentary. He published works in each of these areas. His concern for modern learning bore fruit in the application of the idea of the organic development of history (*Lectures on the Philosophy of History,* 1856) and in his editing of the complete works of Samuel Taylor Coleridge (published in 1894).
M. A. NOLL

SHEEN, FULTON JOHN (1895–1979)
Roman Catholic archbishop and broadcaster

Son of an El Paso, Illinois, family, Sheen began higher education at St. Viator's College, Illinois, and St. Paul's Seminary, Minnesota. By 1924, he also had obtained degrees from Catholic University of America, Louvain University, University of Paris, and the Collegio Angelico, Rome. In 1926, after teaching a year in England, Sheen returned to the Catholic University of America. Here he taught philosophy from 1926 to 1950. As his career developed, Sheen showed remarkable ability as a preacher and explicator of Catholic belief. From 1930 to 1950, he appeared on the "Catholic Hour" radio broadcasts. His talks were a regular feature in the program's later years.

Sheen's expressive gifts made his entrance into Catholic Church television broadcasting inevitable. Thus from 1951 to 1957, he was the featured speaker on the "Life Is Worth Living" program, an ABC broadcast attracting eventually some 30 million weekly viewers. The program received an Emmy award in 1952. Later, from 1966 to 1969, Sheen conducted the "Bishop Sheen Program," an even more popular ABC broadcast. Both programs were notable for their appealing introduction to Catholic ideas and practice. During these same years, Sheen wrote two widely syndicated newspaper columns. These were "Bishop Sheen Writes," designed for the secular press and "God Loves You," produced for Catholic publications. As to conventional church duties, Sheen in 1951 was named director of the Society for the Propagation of the Faith, the Catholic Church's main American missions agency. He remained at this post until 1966, seeing it become the largest Catholic missions fund-raising agency in the world. Simultaneously Sheen also was editor of *World Mission* and *Mission,* American Catholicism's principal missions periodicals. From 1951 to 1966, Sheen held the position of auxilliary bishop of New York. In 1966, he was consecrated as bishop of Rochester, New York, and also titular archbishop of Newport, Wales. However, he resigned his church offices in 1969 and spent the rest of life writing and occasionally speaking. Sheen was the author of many academic and popular books. His depictions of Catholic doctrine and life often appeared on national best-seller lists. K. J. BRYER

SHELDON, CHARLES MONROE (1857–1946)
American Congregational clergyman; religious publicist

Born in Wellsville, New York, and educated at Phillips Academy, Andover (1879), Brown University (1883), and Andover Theological Seminary (1886), Sheldon's first pastorate was at the Congregational church of Waterbury, Vermont, where he served from 1886 to 1889. In the latter year he became minister of the newly founded Central Community Church of Topeka, Kansas, with which he retained an official connection until 1919. From 1920 to 1925 he was editor-in-chief of the *Christian Herald,* continuing thereafter as contributing editor.

Sheldon wrote more than fifty books, most of them inspirational works that expressed a liberal Protestant viewpoint on current social and religious issues. His best-known work is *In His Steps* (1896), of which more than six million copies have been sold. Within a simple narrative framework, this book describes the experiences of several church members who had made a pledge to guide their lives by the principle, "What would Jesus do?" in any given situation. Sheldon was an active participant in the Prohibition movement, in support of which in 1914 to 1915 he was a member of the "Flying Squad" that spoke in its behalf in 247 American churches in the course of 243 days. N. V. HOPE

SHEMBE, ISAIAH (c. 1870–1935)
Zulu prophet; founder of the Nazarites (ama-Nazaretha), a South African sect

Shembe was raised in Natal and baptized in 1906 in the African Native Baptist Church. He broke with that church in 1911 to found his own. Shembe had no schooling, but his magnetic personality and preaching drew followers. He applied all Old Testament references to Nazarites to his people, who came to regard him as semidivine. Shembe wrote several hymns, some after he was raised from the dead, followers believe. He practiced healing, exorcism, and claimed to have had three revelations from Jehovah that turned him from a life of immorality into a type of Zulu messiah. His hymns, for example, "Praise Father and Holy Spirit," suggesting that Shembe himself was the "Promised One" from God. He gained incredible influence over Zulu chiefs and passed leadership on to his son, Johannes Galilee Shembe. M. FACKLER

SHEPPARD, HUGH RICHARD LAWRIE (1880–1937)
English clergyman

Born at Windsor, Sheppard graduated from Cambridge, trained for the ministry at Oxford, and served in London's East End (1907–1911). At the other end of the social scale, he was curate of St. George's, Hanover Square (1911–1914), before embarking on his memorable ministry at St. Martin-in-the-Fields in central London (1914–1926). There he not only attracted the aristocracy, but opened the premises and his own heart to the poorest, lowliest, and lost ("You can't preach Christ to empty bellies"). He brought a breath of fresh air into the stuffiest institutions, he pioneered the broadcasting of church services, and he wrote articles for Sunday newspapers, which nonchurchgoers read and appreciated. His parish magazine went all over the world. Later in life he became a strong pacifist and founded the Peace Pledge Union in 1936. His best-selling book, *The Impatience of a Parson* (1937), reflected the convictions and prejudices of one who "would like to smash Canterbury and then try to rebuild it again." Persistent ill-health forced his resignation first from St. Martin's, then from the deanery of Canterbury (1929–1931). He was dogged also by domestic disappointment and even considered leaving the church, but he remained greatly beloved. He died alone, but a hundred thousand people filed past his coffin. J. D. DOUGLAS

SHIELDS, THOMAS TODHUNTER (1873–1955)
Canadian Baptist preacher; defender of conservative Protestant beliefs

Self-educated, Shields held several pastorates in small Baptist churches in Canada before accepting a call in 1910 to Jarvis Street Church in Toronto. Under Shields's leadership Jarvis Street Church became one of the largest Protestant churches in Canada. Shields spoke out strongly against the acceptance of liberal teachers into the faculty of McMaster University in Hamilton, Ontario, a school under the direction of the Ontario and Quebec Convention (Baptist). In 1927 the Ontario and Quebec Convention dismissed the Jarvis Street Church, largely because of Shields's conservative views. In 1923 Shields joined with concerned Baptist leaders in the United States to form the Baptist Bible Union (BBU). Shields served as president of the BBU for seven years. In 1932 the BBU was dissolved, and many of its members (but not Shields) organized the General Association of Regular Baptist Churches (GARBC). During the 1920s and 1930s Shields published a magazine, the *Gospel Witness,* in which he monitored what he considered to be the growing threat of liberalism to the Baptist church. After the mid-1930s Shields centered his ministry in Canada and directed the construction of a new building for Jarvis Street Church. K. LEID

SICKINGEN, FRANZ VON (1481–1523)
German knight; supporter of the early Reformation

Sickingen was man of the sword throughout his life, fighting—he claimed—for the lowly and oppressed, but never turning aside from the opportunity to plunder either. He fought for the German emperor Maximilian I and for Francis I of France. He was also a supporter of the new emperor Charles V at his election in 1519. But his greatest claim to fame was his support of Martin Luther.

Sickingen was won to the side of the reform through another colorful figure of the age, Ulrich von Hutten, to whom Sickingen had given refuge in his castle Ebernburg. Hutten, a wandering humanistic scholar and soldier, won over the illiterate Sickingen by reading to him from Luther's works and the works of humanistic reformers. Thereafter Sickingen opened his castles as places of refuge for harried reformers. He and his troops succeeded in relieving the Hebrew scholar Johannes Reuchlin from penalties imposed by the church. And some, who would later play important roles in the Reformation, found protection with him, including Martin Bucer, the reformer of Strassburg, and John Oecolampadius, reformer of Basel.

In the crucial year of 1520 Sickingen made a direct offer of refuge and military support to Luther. Luther took this offer, and similar ones, into serious consideration. Ultimately, however, he decided to put his trust in the power of God's Word alone. Luther's attitude toward Sickingen—and toward others who sought to accomplish spiritual goals through force of arms—was revealed in the dedication of a sermon on confession to Sickingen in 1521. Luther sent this booklet to Sickingen "to show my good will and gratitude for the many encouragements and offers you have given to me." He went on to add, however, that he "had an advantage" over Sickingen: "I walk unencumbered"—i.e., Luther did not wear the armor of a knight, and that made his journey through life a simpler one.

It was good for Luther that he did not take advantage of Sickingen's offer. When Sickingen attacked the archbishop of Trier in 1522, the archbishop and others whom Sickingen had preyed upon united to strike back. The next year Sickingen was killed in battle at his castle Landstuhl when the vastly superior forces of his opponents routed his own. M. A. NOLL

SIGISMUND (1368–1437)
Holy Roman Emperor, 1433–1437

Born in Nuremburg and reared at the Hungarian court, Sigismund became king in 1387 by virtue of his marriage to the daughter of his predecessor. In 1410 he was elected king of the Romans, in succession to his brother. That was tantamount to becoming Holy Roman Emperor, but he did not gain the crown until 1433. In the meanwhile, although bitterly opposed, he became king of Bohemia in 1419 and king of the Lombards in 1419. The succession of titles indicates that he spent most of his life in ceaseless fighting, especially for the imperial crown. In 1396 he and his Western troops were defeated by the Turkish Sultan Bajazet I at Nicopolis on the Black Sea. That campaign was one of the last expressions of the Crusading movement. His kingdom of Bohemia was deeply affected by the thought of John Wycliffe, as expressed and interpreted by John Huss. The so-called Hussite heresy allied itself with Czech nationalism and became so strong that it was one of the reasons for the Council of Constance

(1414–1418). The immediate provocation, however, was the papal schism with three claimants to the title—Roman, Avignonese, and Pisan. Sigismund was persuaded to convoke the council.

Sigismund's latter days were troubled with the Hussite wars and struggle against the encroaching Osmanli Turks. In an effort to perpetuate the conciliar movement he also convoked the Council of Basel in 1431, but he died long before that council wasted away. When he died he was succeeded by his son-in-law Albert II, by no means the first Hapsburg but one of those who made the title permanent in that family. A. CABANISS

SIMEON, CHARLES (1759–1836)
Evangelical leader in the Church of England

After an initial education at Eton College, Simeon entered King's College, Cambridge. Here the compulsory attendance at Holy Communion was the means used by God to bring about his spiritual awakening. He became a fellow of the college and was ordained. At the tender age of twenty-three he was appointed vicar of Holy Trinity Church, Cambridge, where he remained until his death. In the view of Lord Macaulay, Simeon's influence here on the Church of England was greater than that of any archbishop. Overcoming the opposition of some parishioners, he made the church the center of a teaching and preaching ministry. It could be claimed to have been the center of Anglican evangelicalism. Undergraduates who were converted and enthusiastic about the gospel took the liberating message to all parts of the British Empire. His curate, Henry Martyn, became a missionary in India and by his example encouraged others to offer themselves as missionaries.

Simeon also played a major role in the establishment of important evangelical societies—the British and Foreign Bible Society, the Religious Tract Society, the Church Missionary Society, and the London Jews Society. He organized what is now called the Simeon Trust. This trust bought the right to act as patron of parishes so that it could appoint evangelical clergy to them. It still

exists. Though he did support William Wilberforce in the efforts to abolish slavery, he put the converting of souls first. His ministry took place between the French wars and revolution and the passing of the British Reform Bill, and in all that time he never preached on politics. If Wilberforce is the most famous evangelical layman in the Church of England, then Simeon is the most famous evangelical clergyman. P. TOON

SIMPSON, A. B. (ALBERT BENJAMIN) (1844–1919)
Founder of what became the Christian and Missionary Alliance

Simpson was born on Prince Edward Island, Canada, to parents of Scottish descent. His father was involved in the export-import trade, as well as in the shipbuilding industry. Prompted by business depression, the family later moved to a farm in Ontario. Albert and the eight other children were raised in a home of strong biblical commitment and disciplined Christian living.

In 1861, young Simpson began study for the ministry at Knox College, Toronto. The recipient of scholarships and prizes, he graduated in 1865 and accepted his first charge at Knox Church, Hamilton. Additional churches served were in Louisville, Kentucky, and New York City. Widely hailed as an outstanding pulpiteer, Simpson totally rejected such praise. He favored pastoral visitation and evangelism as emphases in his ministry. Ultimately he devoted much of his energy to addressing conventions and concentrated his interest on missions. In 1887 Simpson became the prime mover in the establishment of the Evangelical Missionary Alliance, later to become the Christian and Missionary Alliance.

Simpson authored some seventy books, edited his denomination's publication (*Alliance Weekly*), wrote numerous poems, and composed a large number of songs. Emphases in his writing and preaching include the sanctified life and confidence in divine healing. Some of his more noteworthy books are *The Gospel of Healing, Holy Spirit, Christ in the Tabernacle,* and *The Life of Prayer.*
P. VELTMAN

SIMPSON, SIR JAMES YOUNG (1811–1870)

Scottish doctor who discovered the anesthetic effect of chloroform

Born a baker's son in West Lothian, Simpson graduated in medicine at Edinburgh and became professor of midwifery there at the early age of twenty-eight. Having heard in 1847 how ether had been used in surgery in Massachusetts, he experimented with it, then with chloroform, in the relief of pain in childbirth. The effects were far-reaching, though clergy and medical conservatives complained that anesthesia was unnatural, that pain was part of God's purpose—according to Genesis 3:16. Simpson produced statistics to show how anesthesia not only did away with pain, but saved lives. Had not Genesis 2:21 also given divine approval in recording the first operation, "And the Lord God caused a deep sleep to fall upon Adam"?

Opposition diminished in 1853 when Queen Victoria was delighted by the effect of chloroform in her eighth confinement. Simpson became a baronet, internationally acclaimed, yet always his skill and money were at the disposal of the needy. At fifty years of age he sought a deeper meaning in life and in 1862 told a gathering of medical missionary students, "I am the oldest sinner and the youngest believer in this room," going on to testify to his conversion. For some years he presided over the Carrubers Close Mission meetings in Edinburgh that brought over two thousand listeners. When he died his family declined an invitation to have him buried in Westminster Abbey. Instead, his mile-long funeral procession in Edinburgh brought traffic and business to a halt. J. D. DOUGLAS

SLEIDANUS, JOHANNES (1506–1556)

Chronicler of the Reformation

Born in Schleidan, near Aachen, Sleidanus studied ancient languages at Liege and Cologne, and later, law and jurisprudence at Paris and Orleans. He probably became a Protestant around 1541 while a student at Liege. He then entered the service of Cardinal Jean DuBellay, acting as an envoy for Francis I in his negotiations with the German princes for an alliance against the emperor Charles V. While in the cardinal's service he also was in close contact with the cardinal's brother, Guillaume DuBellay, who was writing a history of France, and from him he learned some of the historical techniques that he afterwards employed. He formed the habit of copying all documents that came to his notice, even transcribing some of those in the royal library in Paris, and in some cases he furnished copies to men such as John Calvin.

In 1542 he left DuBellay's service and settled in Strassburg, where he began the preparation of a history of the Reformation. He had already edited the works of Jean Froissard and Philip de Comines and was regarded as an authority in this field. Through the influence of Martin Bucer he was, therefore, appointed historian of the Schmalkaldic League, which gave him access to the archives of various principalities. By 1545 the first volume of the *De Statu Religionis et Republicae Carolo V Caesare Commentari* was completed. His historical work was interrupted, however, by his being sent on missions to England and France, although he used the opportunity so provided to obtain more documentation. He also represented the city of Strassburg at the diets of Frankfort and Worms. As a result of the Schmalkaldic War, he did not receive his salary from the league, but Archbishop Cranmer persuaded Edward VI of England to confer on him a pension. In 1551 he represented a number of German cities at the Council of Trent. In 1555 the second volume of his commentary appeared, an impartial, well-documented work. It was eventually translated into a number of languages, as was his *Key to History*, in which he sought to use the four kingdoms of Daniel as an explanation of world history. Although appointed a professor at the University of Strassburg in 1554, he died in poverty two years later. W. S. REID

SLESSOR, MARY (1848–1915)

Scottish missionary to West Africa

Born in Aberdeen and reared in a poor home in Dundee, Slessor worked long hours in a factory and acquired only a meagre education. She became a Sunday school teacher and mission helper and in 1876 was sent by the United Presbyterian Church to Calabar. That part of West Africa, uncontrolled by any colonial power, was divided among warring tribes ruled by witchcraft and barbarous customs that included the killing of twins at birth. Though her life was in constant danger, Slessor finally won the confidence of the tribal chiefs and their peoples by her fearlessness and dedication, her medical and linguistic skills, and her great sense of humor.

Like David Livingstone, she contributed greatly to the opening up of Africa for commerce and Christianity in her encouragement of healthy trade and her opposition to slavery. She improved the lot of women in the community. Seeing the need for training Africans in industrial work, she was the moving spirit behind the opening in 1895 of the famous Hope Waddell Institute. When British rule was extended over the territory, Slessor was appointed a magistrate and acted as a consular agent. She undertook the work and reluctantly declined remuneration. There was much to do, but she learned serenity through Jesus' example: "Every day's duties were done as every day brought them, but the rest was left with God." From 1903 she worked at Itu, and was still opening up new territory to the north and west when she died at sixty-six, worn out by her service to Africa. J. D. DOUGLAS

SMITH, ELI (1801–1857)
American missionary to the Middle East; Bible translator

Born in Northford, Connecticut, Smith later attended Yale (1821) and Andover Seminary (1826). Then he was ordained to the Congregational ministry and went to Malta under the American Board of Commissioners for Foreign Missions. In 1827 Smith was transferred to Beirut. At the request of the American Board of Commissioners for Foreign Missions, he undertook an extended journey in 1830 through Persia, Georgia, and other areas of the Middle East.

The result was the establishment of a mission to Nestorian Christians who would be, it was felt, more open to evangelism than Muslims. He also traveled with the noted explorer Edward Robinson into the Sinai Desert in 1838, which was largely unknown in the West.

Smith's major work was the translation of the Bible into Arabic. A skilled linguist, he began his project in 1846, and by the time of his death in 1857 he had completed the New Testament and large sections of the Old Testament. J. N. AKERS

SMITH, GEORGE ADAM (1856–1942)
Scottish Old Testament scholar

Born at Calcutta, Smith's father was editor of the *Calcutta Review*. After study at Edinburgh, Tübingen, and Leipzig, he became minister of Queen's Cross Free Church, Aberdeen (1882), then professor of Old Testament at the United Free Church College, Glasgow (1892), and principal of the University of Aberdeen (1909–1935). Among his many books were volumes in the Expositor's Bible series of commentaries on *Isaiah* (two volumes, 1888–1890) and *The Twelve Prophets* (two volumes, 1896–1897); *Life of Henry Drummond* (1898); *Jerusalem* (two volumes, 1907); *The Early Poetry of Israel* (Schweich Lectures, 1912); *Deuteronomy* (Cambridge Bible, 1918); and *Jeremiah* (1923). One work in particular that has stood the test of time was first published in 1894 and has been frequently reprinted. This is his *Historical Geography of the Holy Land in relation to the History of Israel and the Early Church,* the fruit of frequent and extensive travels in Egypt, Syria, and Palestine.

His Yale lectures on *Modern Criticism* (1899) and *The Preaching of the Old Testament to the Age* (1901), together with the work of his contemporaries William Robertson Smith and A. S. Peake, were influential in carrying the canons of higher criticism from classroom to pulpit and pew. They also aroused misgivings in some conservative quarters in Scotland. There were moves made to charge him with heresy, but these were quashed by a vote of confidence in the

General Assembly of his church in 1902. He was knighted in 1916 and elected a fellow of the British Academy. N. HILLYER

SMITH, HANNA WHITALL (1832–1911)

Spokesperson for inner piety and author of the spiritual classic, The Christian's Secret of a Happy Life *(1875)*

Hanna was raised in a strict Quaker home and was given to morbid introspection that found little relief until her marriage to Robert Piersall Smith in 1851. They were both converted under Plymouth Brethren influence in 1858 and in 1867 had a new experience of faith that propelled them on a speaking tour of the United States and Europe. Their "Higher Christian Life" meetings in England were exceedingly popular, partly because of D. L. Moody's success there. They remained in England due to Robert's declining health and observed the founding of the Keswick Convention in 1874, an outgrowth of their conferences. Trouble followed, however. Robert began to entertain notions of spiritual wifery, was criticized, and eventually claimed to be a Buddhist. Hanna developed ideas on the final restitution of all things, diverted herself into social causes and writing. She produced *The Unselfishness of God and How I Discovered It* in 1903. A year later she was stricken with arthritis. Although confined to a wheelchair and in much pain, she maintained an optimistic spiritual outlook until her death. M. FACKLER

SMITH, HENRY PRESERVED (1847–1927)

Old Testament scholar

Born in Troy, Ohio, Smith graduated from Amherst College in 1869, from Lane Theological Seminary in Cincinnati in 1872, and did postgraduate work at the Universities of Berlin and Leipzig. Appointed in 1874 to a teaching position in Lane Seminary, where he became professor of Hebrew and Old Testament in 1877, he changed from a conservative to a liberal position on questions of Old Testament critical scholarship. In 1882

he published an article in the *Presbyterian Review,* in which he questioned the Mosaic authorship of the Pentateuch and the verbal infallibility of the Bible. When Charles A. Briggs of Union Theological Seminary was accused of heresy in 1891, Smith defended him. For this he was convicted of heresy by the Cincinnati Presbytery in 1892, a verdict that was upheld by the General Assembly in 1894. Suspended from the Presbyterian ministry, he resigned from his chair in 1893 and in 1899 became a Congregationalist. After leaving Cincinnati he taught at Amherst College (1898–1907), Meadville Theological School, Pennsylvania (1907–1913), and Union Theological Seminary (1913–1925), where he served both as professor of Hebrew and as librarian. His books include *The Religion of Israel* (1914), *Essays in Biblical Interpretation* (1921), and his autobiography, *Heretic's Defense* (1926). N. V. HOPE

SMITH, JOSEPH (1805–1844)

Founder of the Mormon church, formulator of its creeds; called a prophet by its followers, and finally a martyr for its cause

Joseph Smith, Jr., was born in Sharon, Vermont, the fourth of ten children. His family moved to Palmyra, New York, when he was ten years old and soon thereafter became embroiled in the sectarian movements vying for converts in that region. Smith was troubled; and, as he reports, he was instructed by two angelic visitors in 1819 not to join any of the sects. The two apparitions he later identified as God the Father and Jesus Christ. More visions followed. In September of 1823, the angel Moroni led Smith to golden tablets, which he allegedly translated and published as the *Book of Mormon* in 1830. It contained a bizarre history of the North American peoples.

On April 6, 1830, the Church of Jesus Christ of Latter-Day Saints was formally organized with six members. Peter, James, and John had previously conferred upon Smith and Oliver Cowdery the Melchizedek priesthood. Missionaries were quickly sent out.

Smith established a base in Kirtland, Ohio, then in Independence, Missouri, which he believed would be the site of the millennial Zion.

A dynamic leader, Smith was nonetheless unable to control the periphery of the movement. Bank failures, disputes with local officials, and finally his "revelation" concerning polygamy all brought persecution upon the tightly-knit band. Smith was arrested in Missouri and threatened with death. He was permitted to bribe his jailers and thus escaped to Illinois. There he settled his followers at Commerce, on the Mississippi River, and changed the town's name to Nauvoo. Smith became mayor, commander of the Nauvoo Legion (a state militia unit), and in February of 1844 announced his intention to run for the United States presidency. When a group of locals and Mormon defectors published a broadside critical of him, Smith ordered the presses destroyed.

For that action, he was taken into custody by state authorities, along with his brother Hyrum and John Taylor. The three men were lodged in a Carthage, Illinois, jail where, on June 27, 1844, a mob killed the Smiths. Taylor survived to become third president of the Latter-Day Saint's church.

Smith's personal life was as irregular as his ecclesiastical affairs. For example, he publicly acknowledged only one wife, Emma Hale (married in 1827), by whom he had nine children; but his actual wives may have numbered as high as fifty.

Mormons regard Smith as God's prophet for the restoration of the Christian church. His writings include the *Book of Mormon, Doctrine and Covenants,* and *The Pearl of Great Price.* M. FACKLER

SMITH, SYDNEY (1771–1845)
English clergyman and essayist

Born in Essex, Smith was educated at Winchester and New College, Oxford. He was ordained in the Church of England in 1794 and went to Edinburgh, where he served as a tutor and where in 1802 he was the cofounder of the famous journal the *Edinburgh Review.* In 1804 he went to London, where he secured posts as preacher in Foundling Hospital and lecturer in moral philosophy at the Royal Institution. It was here that his wit caught the eyes of Whig politicians, who, when in power, were to help him advance in his ecclesiastical career. From 1809 to 1828 he lived as a country gentleman, village parson, and doctor in Yorkshire. In 1828 he became prebendary at Bristol, and in 1831 he was made canon of St. Paul's Cathedral, London. He wrote some sixty-five articles for the *Edinburgh Review,* but his most influential writing was the *Peter Letters of Plymley* (1807), written in defense of Roman Catholic emancipation. Theologically he was a rationalist and usually identified with the latitudinarian outlook. He disliked evangelicals, Methodists, and the Anglo-Catholic Tractarians. He distrusted anything that gave the appearance of being mystical in religion or literature. He was a great admirer of William Paley (1743–1805), a proponent of natural theology, which looked for evidences in nature for the existence of God. His biography was written by Hesketh Pearson, entitled *The Smith of Smiths* (1934, reprinted in 1972 and 1988). P. TOON

SMITH, SIR WILLIAM ALEXANDER (1854–1914)
Founder of the Boys' Brigade

Born near Thurso in northern Scotland, Smith became a businessman in Glasgow and an active member of the Free Church of Scotland. The sight of bored teenagers too old for Sunday school led Smith to originate a movement that would permit religious instruction to continue, but which would also include games, discipline and physical training. So emerged the Boys' Brigade's famous basis: "The advancement of Christ's kingdom among boys and the promotion of habits of reverence, discipline, self-respect, and all that tends towards a true Christian manliness." He enlisted the support of many eminent people, including George Adam Smith and Henry Drummond. In Queen Victoria's Jubilee Year (1897) one of the BB's captains was lord mayor of London. Smith would never make boys sing hymns with words unreal to them, nor would he permit officers to use the annual camp for proselytizing purposes—camp was for health and enjoyment. The BB spread throughout the world, and Smith is honored for his tremendous contribution in the development of voluntary organizations. His own movement was consistently church-centered; his insistence on this was reaffirmed in recent times when its executive declared that the BB's purpose was that of "helping boys to achieve a true Christian faith."

J. D. DOUGLAS

SMITH, WILLIAM ROBERTSON (1846–1894)

Scottish Semitics scholar

Born the son of a Free Church minister in Aberdeenshire, he was educated at Aberdeen, Edinburgh, Bonn, and Göttingen. In 1870 he was ordained on appointment as professor of Oriental languages and Old Testament exegesis at the Free Church College in Aberdeen. In 1875 he became a member of the company working on the Revised Version (Old Testament) of the Bible. That same year, a storm was raised when the *Encyclopaedia Britannica* carried articles by Smith that allegedly undermined belief in the inspiration of Scripture. The chief source of offense was Smith's exposition and partial acceptance of the composite nature of the Pentateuch (a theory associated with the German radical scholar Wellhausen). In 1877 Smith was suspended from teaching. The 1880 assembly dropped the charges against him, but a second wave of criticism led to his removal from his chair in 1881. The case of Smith, who has been called a martyr for the cause of biblical scholarship, nearly split the Free Church in two.

He became joint editor, then editor-in-chief, of the *Encyclopaedia Britannica* (1881–1888), was appointed chair of Arabic at Cambridge (1883–1894), and was chief librarian there (1886–1889). Smith traveled widely in pursuance of his studies, especially in the Near East. His books include *The Old Testament in the Jewish Church* (1881), *The Prophets of Israel* (1882), and *Lectures on the Religion of the Semites* (1889).

J. D. DOUGLAS

SMYTH, JOHN (c. 1560–1612)

Founder of the English General Baptists

John Smyth (pronounced "Smith") was educated at Cambridge University and ordained a minister of the Church of England. While attached to the Anglican cathedral at Lincoln, he was drawn to Puritan and separatistic views. For these he was dismissed from the Church of England in 1602. His belief that churches should be made up only of confessed Christians led him to gather a separatistic congregation in Gainsborough. He also assisted in forming a separated congregation at Scrooby in the home of William Brewster. Members of both congregations would eventually wind up in the New World among the Pilgrims.

For the moment, however, the path led to Amsterdam. With most of his Gainsborough congregation, Smyth ran foul of the English authorities and moved in 1607 or 1608 to the freer climate of Holland. There Smyth encountered the Mennonites, who had practiced adult baptism based on a personal confession of faith for two generations. Under this influence Smyth broke with the Gainsborough Separates. In 1609 he baptized himself by pouring (hence he was called a se-baptist, or "self-baptizer"). He then baptized several others upon their confessions of faith. Among these was Thomas Helwys, who later returned to England and established the first permanent Baptist church in that country. Before that, the Baptists in Holland organized an Arminian ("General") Baptist church. The continuing influence of the Mennonites on Smyth's thought led to a break with Helwys and the other English Baptists. In fact, Smyth probably would have joined the Mennonites if death had not intervened in 1612. In his published works, Smyth set out the case of the Separates against the Church of England; he tried to explain the nature of the differences separating the Separates from each other; and he argued for freedom of religious thought and practice. M. A. NOLL

SOCRATES (469 or 470–399 B.C.)
Greek philosopher

Socrates' life is so important in standard Western histories that Greek philosophy is separated into pre-Socratic and post-Socratic periods. Probably he is most commonly known for strolling about Athens, questioning and talking with the young men of the city, trying to help them learn the "truth." He raised questions about what is accepted as truth and urged people to know themselves and live virtuous, moral lives.

Socrates taught by the oral method; as far as we know, he never put anything into writing. He is known through the works of others who "interpreted" him, especially his understanding friend and student Plato. Another who interpreted him was Xenophon. Both of these men knew Socrates personally. They had much in common, but they did not interpret Socrates the same in all cases. For instance, Plato believed that Socrates felt that it is not right to respond to evil with evil; Xenophon affirmed the established position of the times: that a good person will aid his friends and do injury to his enemies.

Socrates searched for the self-believed objective patterns, or "forms," that were available to define human excellence; he felt that these could be discovered by philosophic inquiry. He used the inductive method—that of reasoning from particular facts to a general idea, or a universal definition, which applied to all examples. This was carried on by means of dialectic conversation and became known as the "Socratic method." This method results in exposing people's ignorance. And when Socrates maintained his own ignorance, he reminded others that they were ignorant. It goes without saying that this method alienates and offends people.

Later in Socrates' life, the Athenian power structure wanted unquestioning patriotism, because they had just been defeated in war. Religion was a civic function, a reflection of the local ways and customs. To act piously was to follow the custom, or law, of the city; this was established by tradition. The city was the state, and the state decided which gods to venerate. The city regulated the religious practices—the rites, the temples, the sacrifices, and the festivals. The city officials tried to scare the "questioning" Socrates away by bringing him to trial on three charges: not recognizing gods espoused by the city, introducing new divinities, and corrupting the youth.

Socrates told the judges that God gave him the mission of awakening the consciences of his fellow Athenians. He was trying to educate the young, not corrupt them. He was trying to awaken people to the fact that God, not man, is the measure of all things.

By his method of asking questions to guide the thinking of others, he tried to start them searching for answers for themselves, but he also wanted them to be confident of finding answers. He did not hand down wisdom, rather he worked to make others find it. He felt that a person, by forthright thinking and with God's help, could arrive at the truth.

Socrates believed in the traditional gods; he made sacrifices to them and took part in the festivals. He observed his religion appropriately and found it the ground upon which everything else is based. He believed that what should be done in actual situations cannot always be decided by reason. He felt that the gods came to aid us and there is a limit beyond which one must obey the gods without understanding necessarily why one must obey.

He practiced the art of conversation with everyone—to arouse, to compel a person to examine his innermost soul, to know himself. Education is communication, to come to oneself and have the truth open up, for truth is what joins men together. Each individual is important for his own sake; independence comes from having self-mastery. True freedom comes with knowledge: these are the ultimate bases upon which man can meet the godhead.

Socrates believed in a divine power in a higher sense than his accusers did and was ready to accept the decision of the gods concerning the outcome of his trial. He had several chances to escape from prison, but refused to leave. Socrates was found guilty by the jury and sentenced to death. The sentence was carried out when he drank a cup of hemlock poison.

To the church fathers, Socrates was a great person, a precursor of every Christian martyr; each was accused of blasphemy against the traditional religions of the times and each died for those beliefs. G. RISER

SOCRATES SCHOLASTICUS
(c. 380–c. 450)
Church historian

Born at Constantinople, Socrates was trained in pagan grammar and rhetoric; then he studied law and became an advocate (*scholasticus*) in the imperial city. The work for which he is noted, however, lay in the field of historical writing. He undertook to supplement Eusebius's work by treating the period 305 to 439. Each of his seven books is organized around the reign of an emperor. Much of the later part depends upon his own knowledge and oral tradition. The first-known layman to write church history, he dealt with the secular world as well as the religious. The book is particularly valuable for its extensive quotation of sources. Stylistically his work is not as good as Sozomen's, but critically it is better.

He admired Origen despite criticisms surrounding that name, and he stressed the importance of Greek learning for the church. Socrates has been suspected of Novatianism, and he did insist that it and orthodoxy were brothers. In dogmatic matters he preferred to adore the ineffable mysteries of the faith in silence. A. CABANISS

SODERBLOM, NATHAN (1866–1931)
Swedish archbishop and ecumenist

Born a pastor's son at Trono, Soderblom studied first at Uppsala, then at Paris, where after Lutheran ordination he was chaplain to the Swedish community (1894–1901). Having earned a reputation as a comparative

religionist he was professor at Uppsala and Leipzig before his surprise election in 1914 as archbishop of Uppsala and primate of Sweden. A lifelong advocate of church unity (his outreach extended to Rome and the Orthodox churches), he was chief organizer of the historic Conference on Life and Work at Stockholm in 1925. He was awarded the Nobel peace prize in 1930. Though he had moved appreciably from his Pietistic roots, he continually reminded the budding ecumenical movement that worship and prayer should be at its heart. He once astounded an American audience by breaking off an address and launching into all five verses of "There Were Ninety and Nine." A piece of advice urged upon his own clergy was, "Work yourselves to death—but slowly, please." Apart from his erudite Orientalist works, he published three significant volumes, available in English as *Christian Fellowship* (1923), *The Living God* (1933), and *The Nature of Revelation* (1933). J. D. DOUGLAS

SPALATIN, GEORGE (1484–1545)
German reformer

An important if less publicized figure in the Lutheran Reformation, Spalatin was born at Spalt near Nuremberg. His real name was George Burkhard, but he adopted the Latinized surname Spalatin. At university in Erfurt and Wittenberg he came under the influence of the prevailing humanism. In 1505 he became a monk in Erfurt, in 1507 he began pastoral work at Hohenkirchen, and in 1508 he was consecrated priest.

Perhaps the most important turn in his life came in 1509, when he entered the service of the elector of Saxony as tutor to the future ruler John Frederick. This did not end his monastic career, for in 1511 he became a member of the monastery chapter in Altenburg. Nevertheless, his future lay with the electoral house. He tutored the princes of Brunswick from 1511 to 1516. In 1512 he also became librarian of the elector's castle library. Finally, at a crucial moment, he became in 1516 the closest aide to the elector Frederick the Wise—serving him as his private secretary, historiographer, father confessor, and court chaplain, with special responsibilities for church and university affairs.

It was in this capacity that Spalatin was able to forge the vital link between Frederick and Martin Luther. Spalatin and Luther had been friends since 1513. When Luther launched the Reformation in 1517, Spalatin supported him and gained Frederick's support as well. For years he served as the go-between who made possible the working relation between ruler and reformer that secured the Reformation in its first and fragile period. His extensive correspondence with Luther shows how important his role was.

On Frederick's death in 1525, Spalatin became pastor at Altenburg and brought reform to the city. He continued to advise Frederick's successors in church affairs. He took part in the Saxon visitations, played a notable part in educational and pastoral reform, and worked with Melanchthon and Luther on the Augsburg Confession of 1530. His works include translations of the Latin writings of Luther, Melanchthon, and Erasmus and his own *Annals of Saxony*.

G. BROMILEY

SPEER, ROBERT ELLIOTT (1867–1947)

Leader in the modern American missionary movement

Speer was an early participant and then a pioneer administrator in the Student Volunteer Movement, the organization that arose in the 1880s from meetings held at D. L. Moody's Mt. Hermon summer conferences. He then served from 1891 to 1937 as secretary of the Board of Foreign Missions for the Presbyterian Church of the U.S.A. (forerunner of the present United Presbyterian Church). Speer's lifelong commitment to the Presbyterian church was rewarded in 1927 when he was named the second lay moderator of his denomination's General Assembly.

But Speer was also an active promoter of cooperative missionary work and a leader in ecumenical ventures at home. In pursuit of missionary harmony, he was chairman of the

Committee on Cooperation in Latin America. For ecumenicism at home he served a term as president of the Federal Council of Churches and, during World War I, as the chairman of the General Wartime Committee of Churches.

Speer's commitment to Christianity's missionary mandate was the major theme of his nearly seventy published books and his many articles. This was the burden of the two articles that he contributed to *The Fundamentals* (1910–1915). In an age during which Westerners were learning more and more about non-Christian religions, many modernists questioned the need for Christian missions. To such ones, Speer replied that Christian missions are indispensable because Christ is indispensable. *Christianity and the Nations* (1910) admitted that missionaries had often made mistakes in spreading the gospel. But it also argued that, in spite of such errors, the gospel still needed to be spread. One of his last books, *The Finality of Jesus Christ* (1933), put the case eloquently—Christian missions will be necessary so long as Christ is the only Savior of mankind.

Speer's forthright defense of the uniqueness of Christ cost him the support of liberals in his own denomination. On the other side, however, his relatively loose oversight of Presbyterian missionaries earned him the wrath of conservatives. As early as 1921 Speer was being criticized for letting funds go to missionaries holding to a more liberal theology. This criticism intensified as the Presbyterian General Assembly relaxed its inspection of the theological positions of its missionaries. Such criticism reflected part of the fundamentalist-modernist struggle that embroiled the northern Presbyterians in the 1920s and early 1930s. Speer, for his part, tried to stay clear of the battle. In 1921 he expressed his strong feelings on theological wrangling in words that summed up the concerns of his life: "I wish we could get up such a glow and fervor and onrush of evangelical and evangelistic conviction and action that we would be swept clear past issues like the present one so that men who want to dispute over these things could stay behind and do so while the rest of us could march ahead." M. A. NOLL

SPENER, PHILIPP JAKOB (1635–1705)

German Lutheran Pietist leader and reformer

Spener was born in the Alsatian village of Rappoltstein when the Thirty Years' War was at its height. The spiritual climate could accurately be described as dry, formal—a religion of the disciplined mind. Ministers were trained in the propositions of orthodox Lutheranism and the art of philosophical debate, necessary tools for defending the tenents of their rote theology. Their close cousins in the Reformation, the Calvinists, and the Roman Catholic Church both were considered enemies of the true faith. Debates were numerous; the Christian Church was divided. Lutheranism in Spener's day had degenerated to a religion of the mind and had little relevance for the common man.

Spener was raised in a highly protective and deeply religious atmosphere. As a youth he was an avid reader, and his favorite book next to the Bible was *True Christianity,* by Johann Arndt. This book did much to shape Spener's thought, asserting the limited value of orthodox doctrine and the importance of pious living and active love. Spener became a student of theology at Strassburg, studying under the strict Lutheran J. K. Dannhauer (1651–1659). He then spent a number of years as a wandering student (1659–1662), studying in Basle, Geneva, Stuttgart, and Tübingen. In Geneva he came into contact with Reformed theology and Jean de Labadie, who preached the doctrines of repentance and regeneration. All these experiences were formative to Spener's life and thought.

In 1663 Spener became a free preacher at Strassburg, at which time he received his doctor of theology degree (1664). During this time he also served as pastor and senior of the ministerium in Frankfurt am Main (1666–1685). It was there that he emerged as the leader of the Pietist movement in Germany. He was appointed court chaplain at Dresden in 1686, but a poor relationship

with the ruling Saxon family made his stay there short-lived. In 1691 he accepted the invitation to the pastorate of Saint Nicholas Church in Berlin.

While at Frankfurt, Spener did much to reform the standard religious instruction of his day. He advocated a contextual approach to biblical preaching, restored the confirmation service, set aside days of fasting and prayer, and argued for the necessity of conversion and holy living. He is probably best known for setting up what he called *collegia pietatis*—small groups of pastors and laymen that met together for Bible study and prayer. He saw these as small churches within the church and believed them to be a necessity for strengthening pastors and laity alike. Spener modeled his small groups upon similar bodies among the Reformed churches, and with time, these became an important feature in much of German Lutheranism.

Spener's best-known writing, "Pia Desideria" ("Pious Desires"), was originally written to preface an edition of Johann Arndt's book, *True Christianity.* In this tract, Spener set forth the important truths of Pietism—the importance of Bible study, the priesthood of believers, faith expressed not in knowledge but in acts of love toward others, and the avoidance of theological argumentation. He believed the spiritual life to be more important than "correct" doctrine and felt that preaching should call its hearers to more pious living rather than deeper philosophical thinking. Spener's approach brought a radical critique on the ministerial training of his day, while also calling the laity to a pious and active faith.

As the Pietist movement gained momentum, Spener became an increasingly controversial figure. In 1690, August Herman Francke, probably Spener's best-known follower, was forced from his teaching post at the University of Leipzig for his views. Francke would move on to the University of Halle, which became fertile ground for the Pietist movement, a place where scholarship was balanced with devotion. In assessment, little of Spener's teaching was original, but it was timely and forcefully argued. His emphasis upon the new birth and holy living effectively undermined the position of scholastic Lutheran orthodoxy, doing much to revitalize the German Lutheran Church of his day. He called the church to a life of piety, to a faith that not only used the mind, but touched the heart and inspired the hands as well. M. R. NORTON

SPINOZA, BENEDICT DE (1632–1677)
Dutch Jewish philosopher

Spinoza was a Jew of Portuguese descent, his parents being refugees from an inquisition-like persecution. Born in Amsterdam, originally named "Baruch," though later Latinized, he attended Jewish schools and was apparently being prepared for life as a Jewish merchant. But he early questioned whether the Bible in fact teaches that God is an immaterial and transcendent being, that angels exist, or that the soul is immortal—these items all having in common the concept of immaterial or spiritual being. He also questioned the Mosaic authorship of the Pentateuch.

For most of his life he supported himself by the new trade of grinding and polishing lenses for spectacles, telescopes, and microscopes—a significant thing in itself, since the science of optics had only recently been furthered by the French scientist and philosopher René Descartes (1596–1650).

Spinoza became acquainted with Descartes's philosophy—both its method and its content. Its method he adopted, starting in geometrical fashion, working from axioms and deducing from there a whole system of thought. Even the literary structure of Spinoza's major work, *Ethics*, follows this pattern. He also adopted Descartes's physics, with its mechanistic explanation of nature in terms of cause-effect processes. But he rejected Descartes's dualistic metaphysics, with its immaterial and transcendent God and its immaterial and immortal soul, in addition to matter. Rather he viewed both thought and physical extension (i.e., mind and matter) as attributes of one underlying substance, and he viewed that one substance as God or Nature. The result was a kind of pantheism, in which all events are determined by their place in the whole, so that freedom of will is denied to both God and man. Although he was denounced by Jews and Christians alike, Spinoza's pantheism exerted profound influence on liberal theologians of the nineteenth century, who wanted to see everything as somehow in God and God in everything.

In 1670, Spinoza published his Tractatus Theologico-Politicus, undertaking historical criticism of the Old Testament. He concluded that the Old Testament was inspired only in its morality and not in its account of nature, miracles, and God. A. F. HOLMES

SPITTA, FRIEDRICH ADOLF WILHELM (1852–1924)
New Testament scholar; liturgiologist

Born at Wittingen, near Brunswick, Germany, Spitta studied at Göttingen and Erlangen from 1871 to 1875. He taught high school at Hanover (1876–1877), became inspector of Tholuck Seminary in Halle (1877–1879), and then served two pastorates, one at Bonn (1879–1881) and the other at nearby Ober Kassel (1881–1887). In 1880 he was appointed privatdozent at Bonn and in 1887 professor of New Testament exegesis and practical theology at Strassburg, where he also served as university preacher. In 1919 he moved to his final teaching appointment at Göttingen. Spitta published works in New Testament studies and in the history of the Apostolic Church—for example, *Das Johannes-Evangelium als Quelle der Geschichte Jesu* (The Fourth Gospel as a Historical Source, 1910) and *Zur Geschichte und Litteratur des Urchristentums* (The History and Literature of Apostolic Christianity; three volumes, 1891–1901), respectively. He was also deeply interested in church music and in liturgics. In 1901 he published *Der Gottesdienst des Urchristentum* (The Worship Service in Apostolic Christianity); and from 1896 he was joint editor with Julius Smend—and after 1914 sole editor—of the *Monatsschrift für Gottesdienst und Kirchliche Kunst* (Monthly Magazine of Worship and Christian Art). N. V. HOPE

SPURGEON, CHARLES HADDON
(1834–1892)
Baptist preacher

Spurgeon was the son of a Congregational minister, but among his ancestors were Huguenots and Quakers. Born at Kelvedon, Essex, he spent much of his youth with his grandfather, himself a Congregational minister in Essex. He was sent to school in Colchester from 1845 to 1849, and it was in the same town, in a Primitive Methodist Chapel, that he was converted in 1850. Rejecting the tradition of his father, he decided to be baptized as an adult believer. After his baptism, he joined a Baptist church in Cambridge, where he was helping at a school; then he started his own private school.

By this time he had discovered his gifts as a preacher, and he was much in demand. After a brief pastorate near Cambridge at Waterbeach (1852–1854), he was called to the pastorate of the Baptist church in New Park Street, Southwark, London. The congregation was small when he arrived, but within a few weeks he was attracting large crowds, even though he was only twenty years of age. The chapel proved too small, and it was decided to extend it. While this was proceeding he preached at the Exeter Hall, but again the crowds could not be accommodated. When he returned to the extended chapel in New Park Street, this quickly proved too small; so a great tabernacle was planned. While this was being built, he preached to great crowds at the Surrey Gardens Music Hall.

The Metropolitan tabernacle cost thirty-one thousand pounds and could hold six thousand people. Spurgeon preached here from 1861 until just before his death. His preaching was powerful and even humorous. In theology he was a Calvinist. He was a careful expositor of the Scriptures and a dedicated evangelist. The excellency of his sermons is proved by the fact that in their printed form they are still popular and eminently readable today, a century later.

The Tabernacle was more than a preaching place; it was also an educational and social center. Spurgeon founded a pastor's college in 1856 and an orphanage in 1867—both still exist. He also founded a colportage association; and from the church, various societies operated to help in the local slums.

Spurgeon was a prolific writer. From 1855 a sermon by him was printed each week. These have been collected in many volumes. In 1865 he started a monthly magazine, *The Sword and the Trowel*. His comments on the Psalms are in *The Treasury of David* (1870–1885). The advice he gave to preachers is found in his *Lectures to My Students* (1875, 1877) and *Commenting and Commentaries* (1876). His autobiography, edited by his wife and two friends and taken from his letters, diaries, etc., was published in four volumes between 1897 and 1900. Many of his writings still remain in print.

In such a position he could not escape from controversy. Sometimes he was drawn into it, and at other times he initiated it. He attacked both extremes of Protestant theology—hyper-Calvinism and Arminianism. In 1864 he deeply offended the evangelical Anglicans by accusing them of dishonesty. By using the Prayer Book Service of Holy Baptism and at the same time denying the doctrine of instantaneous baptismal regeneration, the Anglicans were being dishonest, said Spurgeon. Then there was the famous "Downgrade Controversy" of 1887 to 1889. He accused some of his fellow Baptists of teaching radical and "modernist" theology. This caused great troubles in the Baptist Union and caused his withdrawal from the Union. Despite these controversies, Spurgeon will always be known as the great preacher and orator. P. TOON

SPURGEON, THOMAS (1856–1917)
Baptist pastor and successor of Charles H. Spurgeon

Thomas and his twin brother, Charles, were born in London, the sons of Charles and Susannah Spurgeon. Even as children both brothers were allowed to share in their famous father's ministry. In 1877 Thomas went on a voyage to Australia, where he did some preaching but also pursued his trade as a wood engraver. He returned to share in some preaching at his father's London church, the Metropolitan Tabernacle, and also studied at Pastor's (Spurgeon's) College. In 1879 he returned to Australia; in 1881 he assumed a temporary pastorate in Dunedin, New Zealand; the following year he took a Baptist pastorate in Auckland. It was there that he built the Baptist Tabernacle. From 1889 to 1893 he served as an evangelist for the New Zealand Baptist Union. He then returned to London to succeed his father as pastor of the Metropolitan Tabernacle, a position which he held until retiring for health reasons in 1908. He also continued other ministries started by his father. P. TOON

STAINER, SIR JOHN (1840–1901)
English composer

Like many English composers, Stainer was trained as a choirboy and grew up in the tradition of English cathedral music. He served as university organist at Oxford, where he received bachelor and doctor degrees in music. As organist of St. Paul's Cathedral in London, he restored the choral program there to excellence and exerted a wide influence toward the improvement of church music throughout England. He was also a professor at the Royal College of Music, where he continued to teach after poor eyesight ended his career at St. Paul's.

His simple oratorio, *The Crucifixion,* gave to English-speaking churches a new, appropriate type of music. Although not artistically great music, it met the comprehension of the average churchgoer and gained an extraordinary popularity that has not yet entirely passed away. Many of his anthems long enjoyed wide acceptance. Stainer was a scholar as well as a composer. He wrote a book on the music of the Bible and published an important anthology of early fifteenth-century music. He also produced an excellent manual on organ playing, as well as several theoretical works. He was a man of sincerity and integrity, and he exercised a lasting influence for good in the realm of church music. J. B. MACMILLAN

STALKER, JAMES (1848–1927)
Scottish scholar and pastor

Born at Crieff, Perthshire, and educated at the Universities of Edinburgh, Berlin, and Halle, Stalker ministered in Kirkcaldy and Glasgow before appointment as professor of church history in the United Free Church College, Aberdeen (1902–1926). Much in demand as a lecturer at home and abroad, he was known as a theologian who rested his faith "on the threefold foundation of scripture, tradition, and personal experience, with emphasis on the third." His publications included works on the life of Jesus (1879), Paul (1884), and John Knox (1904); other titles were *The Preacher and His Models* (1891), *The Seven Deadly Sins* (1901), *The Seven Cardinal Virtues* (1902), *The Atonement* (1908), and *The Ethic of Jesus according to the Synoptic Gospels* (1909).
J. D. DOUGLAS

STANFORD, SIR CHARLES VILLIERS (1852–1924)
Irish composer

Born in Ireland, Stanford studied at Cambridge University and was for a time organist of Trinity College Chapel there. He also studied in Europe and taught at the Royal College of Music. He became professor of music at Cambridge and was the author of books on music history and theory. As a teacher, he had a wide and prolonged influence, for among his pupils were such men as Ralph Vaughan Williams and Tertius Noble, who did great service to better the cause of church music in the United States.

Stanford was a prolific composer in all the major categories; but it is his choral music, especially that for the church, that has lasted. He was the first to bring to Anglican services the technical refinement and coherence of the German classics. The "Te Deum" and "Magnificat" from his *Cathedral Service in B-flat* are among his best-known compositions and exemplify the aspects of his style noted above. He wrote several complete services in the Anglican liturgical manner and many anthems, among which are an attractive setting of "The Lord Is My Shepherd" and "How Beauteous Are Their Feet"—making use of Isaac Watts's fine scriptural paraphrase.

Along with Sir Edward Elgar and Sir Hubert Parry, Stanford was one of the generation of composers who brought about what is often referred to as the "Renaissance" in British music at the end of the nineteenth century, also helping to create a recognizable English style in composition.
J. B. MacMillan

STANISLAUS (c. 1030–1079)
Polish bishop and martyr

Born in Szczepanow, Stanislaus was educated at Gnesen and at Paris, and at about the age of forty-two he was designated bishop of Kraków. He is said to have joined Polish nobles in an attempt to overthrow King Boleslaw II (called the Cruel). In any case he did excommunicate the king for his evil life. Consequently, he was deemed a traitor and was murdered by the king during Mass. The pope laid Poland under an interdict; the king fled to Hungary and may have become a monk. Like Thomas à Becket, Stanislaus was immediately acknowledged as a true martyr, but unlike the English prelate his canonization waited almost one hundred seventy-five years. His cult was immensely popular—not only in Poland, but also in the related areas of Lithuania, Byelorussia, and the Ukraine. His body now rests in his cathedral church renamed for him. A little before and a little after his canonization in 1253, two biographies of him were written, giving the essential information about his life. A. Cabaniss

STAUPITZ, JOHANNES VON (1460–1524)
Roman Catholic theologian

Staupitz was born in Motterwitz, Saxony, and received his early education in Leipzig and Cologne, completing his studies at Tübingen, where he obtained his Th.D. in 1500. Having joined the Order of Hermits of St. Augustine, he became prior of the house in Munich, then he moved to Wittenberg to take up an appointment as professor of Bible in the new university. As vicar general of his order in Saxony, he exercised a strong influence on Martin Luther, whom he brought to the University of Wittenberg in 1508. While his theology was strongly Augustinian, he was not prepared to follow Luther's break with the Church of Rome. In 1521 he left the Augustinians to join the Benedictine Order in Salzburg, where he remained to the end of his life. He developed a covenant theology in which the doctrine of election held a central position. He was also quite mystical in his view of the Christian's personal devotional life. W. S. Reid

STEINER, RUDOLPH (1861–1925)
Founder of anthroposophy

Steiner was born in Hungary of Roman Catholic parents. He became convinced that most people are blinded by material things to spiritual realities, and, influenced by the German poet Goethe, he developed an idealistic philosophy of freedom. An early interest in theosophy and the occult did not last, because he had no room for any kind of God in his thinking. Rather he stressed the ongoing evolution of the human spirit through intuitive knowledge to the point where mind transcends matter and so is finally liberated. He taught a perception of spiritual processes going on in man's higher self, a perception that is independent of the senses; and he established a cultural center in Switzerland that was to contribute to this liberation of the spirit of man.
A. F. Holmes

STERN, HENRY AARON (1820–1885)
German missionary to Jews

Born to Jewish parents at Unterreichenbach, Hesse-Cassel, Stern was educated at Frankfurt. After commercial training, he came to London in 1839 and the next year was converted to Christianity. Ordained a deacon in 1844 by Bishop Alexander of Jerusalem, he traveled widely in Iraq, Persia, and Kurdistan as a missionary of the London Jews' Society and made a number of converts. In 1853 he became one of the few Europeans to penetrate the interior of South Arabia. He went to Ethiopia in 1859 and obtained permission from King Theodore for J. M. Flad's work among black Falasha Jews on the condition that converts were baptized into the Ethiopian Church. Later, however (1863–1868), Stern and his fellow Europeans were imprisoned and tortured by the unpredictable king, who felt offended by the British government. Stern returned to London and, despite ill-health, spent his remaining years in Spitalfields and Whitechapel winning many converts among Jews. He wrote *Dawning of Light in the East* (1854) and *The Captive Missionary* (1864). The archbishop of Canterbury awarded him a D.D. in 1881. N. HILLYER

STEWART, JAMES (1831–1905)
Presbyterian missionary statesman.

Born in Edinburgh, Scotland, Stewart took his liberal arts courses at the Universities of Edinburgh and St. Andrews (1850–1855), trained in theology at New College (1855–1859), and studied medicine at Edinburgh and Glasgow universities, graduating from the latter as a doctor in 1866. In 1865 he was ordained as a missionary of the Free Church of Scotland and in 1867 arrived in Lovedale, Southeast Africa, a missionary settlement seven hundred miles northeast of Capetown, which had been begun in 1841 by the Glasgow Missionary Society. When Lovedale's first principal, W. Govan, retired in 1870, Stewart succeeded him; and under his leadership for the next thirty-five years the mission developed into a comprehensive religious, medical, and educational establishment, whose teaching program embraced "the rudiments of education for all, industrial training for the many, and a higher education for the talented few." In 1873 Stewart founded the Blythswood Missionary Institute in Transkei, which was opened in 1877. In 1875 he founded another mission in Myasaland, Central Africa, named *Livingstonia* in honor of the recently deceased David Livingstone. In 1891 he established the Kibwezi (now Kikuyu) mis-

sion in East Africa. In 1899 he presided as moderator of the Free Church General Assembly. Stewart wrote several books, the most important of which were *Lovedale Past and Present* (1884), a powerful defense of African education; and *Dawn in the Dark Continent* (1903), a missionary classic. He has rightly been described by James Wells as "one of the greatest of modern missionary pioneers." N. V. HOPE

STODDARD, SOLOMON (1643–1729)
Leader of American Protestantism

Stoddard was one of the most influential leaders of American Protestantism from the time of John Cotton (died 1652) to that of Jonathan Edwards (born 1703). From his pulpit in Northampton, Massachusetts, where he served from 1672 to 1729, Stoddard's ideas exerted a powerful influence, not only in the Connecticut River Valley, but in Boston and the coast as well.

"Pope" Stoddard, as his opponents called him, was best known for his innovations in church discipline. By Stoddard's time the New England Congregational churches had adopted the Half Way Covenant. This allowed baptized members who had not made a personal profession of faith to bring their infants to be baptized; but it kept all except those who could personally confess their faith from participating in the Lord's Supper. Stoddard proposed that all people who lived outwardly decent lives should be allowed to take Communion. At the same time he also urged the churches of Massachusetts to develop a "connectional" or "Presbyterian" plan of oversight to keep local churches and ministers in the straight and narrow of orthodoxy. These varying sides of Stoddard's thought have led some historians to praise him for his democratic principles (in opening up the Lord's Supper) and others to condemn him for being anti-democratic (in proposing tighter outside controls for local churches).

In fact, Stoddard was most interested in revivals and the conversion of the lost. He regarded the Lord's Supper given at "open" Communion as "a converting ordinance."

He claimed that participation in Communion was an excellent way for people to "learn the necessity and sufficiency of the death of Christ in order to [find] pardon." Likewise, Stoddard intended tighter control over the churches to preserve the purity of the gospel.

For his labors, Stoddard experienced five "harvests" of souls in Northampton. In general, however, those who followed his teachings on church discipline were not as eager to see the lost converted. Stoddard's concern for revival was shared by his grandson, Jonathan Edwards, who became his colleague minister in 1724 and his successor when he died. Edwards did eventually repudiate his grandfather's ideas on church membership, for which he lost his pulpit in Northampton. But his efforts in the 1730s and 1740s to promote the revival that came to be known as the Great Awakening proved that the spirit of Stoddard lived on. M. A. NOLL

STONE, BARTON WARREN
(1772–1844)
American evangelist; founder of the
Christian Church denomination

Born in Maryland, Stone studied at a Presbyterian Academy in North Carolina and was ordained as the minister of several Presbyterian churches in frontier Kentucky in 1798. He was a participant in the frontier revivals of the period, including the famous Cane Ridge Meeting (1801).

Increasing doubts about Calvinistic doctrines, especially the doctrines of unconditional election and limited atonement, led Stone to renounce his Presbyterian heritage, and in 1803 he and several others formed the Springfield Presbytery. This became the foundation of the Christian Church denomination. A dedicated evangelist, he traveled widely in the Western frontier, establishing churches in Kentucky, Tennessee, and Ohio. He published several books defending his theological views, including *Letters on the Atonement* and *Address to the Christian Churches,* as well as edited church newspapers that spread his views.

Stone came in contact with Alexander Campbell, whose doctrines and interest in Christian unity were similar to his own. He was instrumental in bringing about a union between many of the Christian Churches and Campbell's Disciples of Christ (or "Campbellites") in 1832. J. N. AKERS

STONEHOUSE, NED BERNARD
(1902–1962)
New Testament scholar

Born in Grand Rapids, Michigan, Stonehouse was educated at Calvin College (1924), Princeton Theological Seminary (1927), and the Free University of Amsterdam (Th.D., 1929). He was ordained to the ministry of the Presbyterian Church in the U.S.A. in 1932. In 1929 he became an instructor in New Testament at Westminster Theological Seminary; from 1930 to 1937 he was assistant professor, and then full professor from 1937 until his death. He was also dean of the faculty from 1955 to 1962. In 1936 he helped to organize the Presbyterian Church of America, later named the Orthodox Presbyterian Church; and he edited the *Presbyterian Guardian* (1936–1937, 1945–1948, 1956–1958).

His published works include New Testament studies, especially *The Apocalypse and the Ancient Church* (1929), *The Witness of Luke to Christ* (1951), and *The Origins of the Synoptic Gospels* (1963).

Stonehouse was deeply influenced by J. Gresham Machen, whose biography he published in 1954, and he edited two volumes of Machen's work after the latter's death—namely, *God Transcendent* (1949) and *What Is Christianity?* (1951). He was a founding editor of the seven-volume *New International Commentary on the New Testament,* for which he labored from 1951 until his death. N. V. HOPE

STOTT, JOHN ROBERT WALMSLEY
(born 1921)
English preacher and scholar

Born in London, Stott had a brilliant career at Cambridge, was ordained in the Church of England, and was curate (1945–

1950) and rector (1950–1975) of All Souls' Church, Langham Place, in London's West End district. In addition to a busy and influential ministry, he became a leader in the movement to restore evangelical Christianity and expository preaching to the mainstream of the church's life and thinking. He also had a wide appeal, at home and abroad, in conducting university missions; and he supported the work of bodies such as the Scripture Union and the Evangelical Alliance. His deepening social concern was reflected in the Lausanne Covenant (1974), in which he was the prime mover. Even after his 1975 resignation as rector, he kept his ties with All Souls' Church and made it his base when he founded the Institute for Contemporary Christianity, of which he was director (1982–1986) and then president. His sermons and lectures are models of precision and lucidity. He has been actively involved in sending Christian literature to Third World churches, and he has been a royal chaplain since 1959. His numerous publications include *Basic Christianity* (1958), *Fundamentalism and Evangelism* (1959), *The Epistles of John* (1964), *Our Guilty Silence* (1967), *Christ the Controversialist* (1970), *God's New Society* (1979), *I Believe in Preaching* (1982), *Issues Facing Christians Today* (1984), and *The Cross of Christ* (1986). J. D. DOUGLAS

STOWE, HARRIET BEECHER (1811–1896)
Abolitionist and writer

Stowe was born in Litchfield, Connecticut, the daughter of Lyman and Roxana (Foote) Beecher and sister of Henry Ward Beecher. In 1832 the family moved to Cincinnati, Ohio, where her father became president of Lane Theological Seminary. About this time she began to write magazine sketches. In 1836 she married Calvin Ellis Stowe, a professor at Lane. In 1850 the Stowes moved to Bowdoin College in Brunswick, Maine; and in 1852 to Andover, Massachusetts, where her husband joined the faculty of Andover Seminary. She then became more and more concerned with the

elimination of slavery. Besides her *Uncle Tom's Cabin* (1851–1853), which gave great impetus to the anti-slavery movement, Mrs. Stowe wrote numerous volumes, including several novels. T. H. SPENCE

STRACHAN, JOHN (1778–1867)
Anglican bishop of Toronto

Born in Aberdeen, Strachan's father was a Scottish Episcopalian and his mother a Presbyterian. He was educated at the Universities of Aberdeen and St. Andrews. He went to Canada in 1799 and served as tutor to the children of Richard Cartwright and a few other prominent Kingston citizens. He was ordained to the Anglican diaconate in 1803 and made a priest in 1804. He served as the rector of Cornwall, Upper Canada, from 1803 to 1812. He also conducted a school at Cornwall in which he taught the sons of many prominent men in Upper Canadian society.

He became rector of York (later known as Toronto) in 1812 and archdeacon of York in 1827. When York was captured by American forces in 1813, during the War of 1812, Strachan negotiated the terms of surrender. During the years between 1812 and 1839 Strachan pursued an active political role at York where he was associated with the powerful group of Tories, commonly known as the Family Compact. He was a strong advocate of the position of the Anglican Church in Canada, particularly in regard to control of the Clergy Reserves.

After his removal to York, Strachan continued to play an active part in education. He conducted the Home District School in York, until 1823, and from 1823 to 1833 he was president of the Upper Canada Board of Education. Strachan was a strong believer in Anglican control of the schools. He also attempted to make education available for all classes in Upper Canada. While he failed to secure Anglican dominance, Strachan helped to establish the place of religion in the schools of the area that later became Ontario. Strachan was also active in the field of higher education. He secured a charter for King's College, York, in 1827 as a dominantly

Anglican institution. After King's was secularized in 1849, Strachan established Trinity College in 1851 as an Anglican institution.

Strachan was consecrated bishop of Toronto in 1839. He was a vigorous and forthright bishop who maintained strong control over his clergy in a period when the Anglican Church was threatened with serious internal divisions. He stressed the importance of developing a local Canadian clergy.
D. C. MASTERS

STRACHAN, ROBERT KENNETH (1910–1965)
Director of Latin American Mission

Born in Buenos Aires, Argentina, Strachan was the son of Harry and Susan Strachan, founders in 1921 of the Latin America Mission. Raised in Costa Rica, he graduated from Wheaton College (1935) and from Dallas (1936) and Princeton Theological Seminaries (Th.M., 1943). He was awarded a doctorate in laws by Wheaton (1957) in recognition of his missionary statesmanship. He returned to Costa Rica in 1936 with the Latin America Mission (LAM) as professor in the Latin America Biblical Seminary. In 1945 he became codirector of the LAM upon the death of his father and in 1950 became general director following his mother's death.

Always a progressive thinker and writer, he was in the vanguard of missionary advance in strategy, as well as in principles and theory. Long before it was popular, he pioneered such concepts as "latinamericanization," whereby Latin leaders became full and equal members of the LAM with their North American colleagues, many assuming positions of top leadership in the mission. His greatest contribution was the development of Evangelism-in-Depth, a concept of total mobilization of the church for evangelization of an entire nation. His theorem— "The success of any movement is in direct proportion to its ability to mobilize its entire membership in constant propagation of its belief"—has become a standard axiom of missions.

His ability to develop leadership potential

in others enabled him to build a strong team ready to carry on his vision when Hodgkin's disease caused his untimely death in 1965. The impact of his life on individuals and on the mission of the church around the world is incalculable. D. M. HOWARD

STRANG, JAMES JESSE (1813–1856)
Mormon leader

Strang was a lawyer, taught school, edited a weekly paper, and was a country postmaster before he went to Burlington, Wisconsin, in 1843 with his wife's family. By means of his wife's brother-in-law, a Mormon, he visited Joseph Smith at Nauvoo, Illinois, and was converted to Mormonism. He was ordained an elder by Smith in February 1844. After Smith's assassination, Strong exhibited a letter, supposedly written by Smith, proclaiming himself to be Smith's successor. He claimed to be the new "seer, revelatory, and prophet" of the Mormon Church. With twenty-five hundred followers he moved to Vorce, Wisconsin, to be crowned King James I, after translating *The Book of the Law of the Lord* from the golden plates from the ark of the covenant. In 1849 his followers moved to Beaver Island in Lake Michigan. Under a new revelation, polygamy was sanctioned, and Strang was married to four wives. His followers grew to five thousand in Michigan and Wisconsin; but he made many enemies. He was assassinated on July 9, 1856.
R. VONDERLACK

STRAUSS, DAVID FRIEDRICH (1808–1874)
German theologian

Born at Ludwigsburg, near Stuttgart, Strauss studied theology under F. C. Baur at Tübingen. Already in these early years he found it impossible to believe in a personal God and inclined toward pantheism and the philosophy of Hegel. After a few frustrating months as a curate, he returned to the academic world, obtaining his doctorate and becoming in 1832 a tutor in the seminary at Tübingen.

In 1835 Strauss published his *Das Leben*

Jesu (*Life of Jesus;* English translation by George Eliot, 1846). Strauss was immediately catapulted into international fame and bitter controversy because he purported that Jesus' life as presented in the Gospels was a myth. Because his views were widely regarded as heretical, he was forced to resign his position in the seminary. He never again was able to hold an academic post. After some polemical writing in which he defended himself against his opponents, Strauss produced a systematic exposition of theology, *The Doctrine of the Christian Faith* (two volumes 1840–1841), and then for twenty years turned entirely away from theology to politics and then to the writing of biographies. His return to theology was marked by writing a new, popular *Life of Jesus* (1864) "for the German people," no less radical than his earlier *Life.* His last book, *The Old Faith and the New* (1872), provides a final statement of the radical revisions of theology demanded by "the modern worldview" and reflects the influence of Charles Darwin. Reaction to this book was almost unanimously negative, and Strauss came to the last of his days again in the midst of the controversy, severed relationships, rejection, and bitterness that had been so true of most of his life.

The *Life of Jesus* makes 1835 a turning point in the history of biblical scholarship because of the powerful way in which it called attention to the unchallengeable importance of historical criticism, the necessary extent of its application, and its radical character. Strauss said almost nothing that was totally new, but he wrote with a comprehensiveness, a forcefulness, and a frankness that provided enormous impact. What dominates and invalidates his entire approach, however, is a bias against the supernatural. With the presuppositions that the personal God of the Bible does not exist and that supernatural events cannot occur in history, it was inevitable that Strauss should produce a portrait of Jesus that was outrageous and unsatisfactory. Down to the present, however, New Testament scholarship has been forced to grapple with the questions and problems raised by Strauss. He is the early forerunner of form and redaction criticism, and many contemporary radical critical scholars (e.g., Bultmann and his followers) are rightly regarded as his descendants.
D. A. HAGNER

STRAVINSKY, IGOR (1882–1971)
Russian composer

Born in Oranienbaum, near St. Petersburg, Stravinsky was one of the greatest masters of modern music. His contribution to the evolution of music in the areas of rhythm, melody, and harmony are significant. Igor was the son of a famous opera singer, the bass at the Russian Imperial Opera, Feodor Stravinsky; so he was brought up in a musical environment. He studied piano and music theory as a youth, then he met a son of Rimsky-Korsakov, another famous Russian composer, who introduced Stravinsky to Rimsky-Korsakov. He then studied composition with Rimsky-Korsakov for three years.

Stravinsky found sudden fame after the performance of the ballet *The Firebird.* This was the first modern ballet, created with brilliant music and steeped in the colors of Russian fairy tales. His second ballet, *Petrouchka*, was also performed in Paris with great success. His third ballet, *Le Sacre du Printemps,* still stands as one of the most daring creations of the modern musical mind. Many of the first listeners considered the music "barbaric."

In 1917 the Russian Revolution shook the world. Stravinsky had been living in Switzerland, so his concern for family and friends, while being cut off from his financial resources, put him into a nervous affliction. Some of his friends helped him financially through this crisis, and when he was better he wrote various piano works and began appearing as a concert pianist and conductor.

In 1930 Stravinsky composed his *Symphony of Psalms* dedicated to the glory of God. Grout says that it is one of the great works of the twentieth century, a masterpiece of invention, musical architecture, and religious devotion. Robert Craft, in his book

Conversations with Igor Stravinsky, tells of the incident when Stravinsky was asked if one must be a believer to compose in the forms related to the church. Characteristically, Stravinsky answered with directness: "Certainly, and not merely a believer in 'symbolic figures,' but in the Person of the Lord, the Person of the Devil, and the miracles of the church."

Stravinsky had a genuine humility before God. It is not surprising to learn that he began his day with prayer. He recognized that the principal virtue of music is a means of communication with God. Stravinsky started the "Back to Bach" movement and said that the heart of every musician's study should be the cantatas of J. S. Bach.

Threni was his first work to be conceived exclusively in the twelve-tone technique. It is a work of enormous dignity and restraint. It was written in 1958, and the words were taken from the Lamentations of the prophet Jeremiah. Ill health caused Stravinsky to slow down in his last years. He died in New York City, but he was buried next to his Russian friend and colleague Sergey Diaghilev on the island of San Michele near Venice. G. A. COMFORT

STREETER, BURNETT HILLMAN (1874–1937)
English New Testament scholar and theologian

Streeter received a first-class degree in classics from Queen's College, Oxford, and remained with that college in various capacities for most of his life (except from 1899 to 1905, when he was dean of Pembroke College, Oxford). He always had a deep concern for people, an attitude which won for him devoted students and colleagues; and this concern led him to be ordained in 1899 in the Church of England, despite some doubts he had about Christian orthodoxy. In 1912 he contributed an essay on the historical Jesus to the controversial book *Foundations,* which helped to establish his reputation as a liberal theologian. The year previous, he published an essay in *Studies in the Synoptic*

Problem, which set him out as a leading New Testament scholar.

In 1924 his most famous and important book was published, *The Four Gospels: A Study of Origins,* a work that has had lasting influence. He argued that one of the important early Greek texts of the Gospels emerged from Caesarea in Palestine. Streeter also argued for the existence of an original source behind the Gospel of Luke, which he called Proto-Luke. This he thought to be a first draft of Luke that lacked the infancy narratives (chapters 1 and 2) and the material which Luke is thought to have borrowed from the Gospel of Mark. He also wrote on science and theology (*Reality: A New Correlation of Science and Religion,* 1926) as well as comparative religion (*The Buddha and the Christ,* 1932).

Streeter was always a supporter of Christian student groups. He and his wife were killed in an airplane crash in Switzerland while working with one such movement, the Oxford Group of Frank Buchman, subsequently known as Moral Re-Armament. P. TOON

STRONG, AUGUSTUS HOPKINS (1836–1921)
America's leading Baptist theologian at the turn of the twentieth century

After serving Baptist churches in Haverhill, Massachusetts, and Cleveland, Strong was elected president of Rochester Theological Seminary in 1872. He was an active promoter of Baptist missions throughout his life, and from 1907 to 1910 he served as the first president of the Northern Baptist Convention (now the American Baptist Churches in the U.S.A.).

In his forty years at Rochester Seminary, Strong taught a theology that combined traditional Reformed emphases, distinctive Baptist convictions on the ordinances and the organization of churches, and a relative openness to modern ideas. He published his multivolume *Systematic Theology* in 1886. This influential work was revised several times by Strong himself and continues in print to this day. Although Strong was con-

sistently orthodox, he did use the results of modern critical scholarship more than, for example, his near Presbyterian contemporary Charles Hodge. Also, unlike Hodge, Strong was comfortable with the idea that God may have created the world through the processes of evolution. In the 1907 edition of his theology, Strong summarized his views on modern thought: "Neither evolution nor the higher criticism has any terrors to one who regards them as part of Christ's creating and education process." Yet late in his life Strong spoke out strongly against those who used modern thought to compromise belief in Christ's divinity or his saving work. In the 1907 revision, Strong proposed the counter to modernism that he maintained until he died: Christ as "the one and only Revealer of God, in nature, in humanity, in history, in science, in Scripture." For Baptists, and many more Americans, Strong's *Systematics* and other carefully crafted books have proved themselves enduring guides to the riches of the faith.
M. A. NOLL

STUBBS, WILLIAM (1825–1901)
Anglican bishop of Oxford; historian

Stubbs, considered to be the greatest British historian of his time, was born in Knaresborough, Yorkshire, educated at the Ripon Grammar School, and in 1844 began studies at Christ Church, Oxford. In 1848 he was elected a fellow of Trinity College, Oxford. From 1850 to 1866 he was rector of Navestock. In 1866 he was elected to the Regius Professorship of Modern History at Oxford, a chair he held until 1884. During the last five years of that period he was a canon of St. Paul's Cathedral, London. In 1884 he was chosen bishop of Chester. He was identified with the High Church party in Anglicanism and was an admirer of Edward Pusey. His important writings include nineteen editions of the medieval *Chronicles and Memorials* (1864–1889); the three-volume *Constitutional History of England to 1485* (1873–1878) and its companion, *Select Charters* (1870), which are considered classics; and the three-volume *Councils and Ec-*

clesiastical Documents relating to Great Britain and Ireland (1869–1873, with A. W. Haddan). P. TOON

STUDD, CHARLES THOMAS (1862–1931)
English missionary to China, India, and Africa

Son of a wealthy plantation owner who had been converted under D. L. Moody, Studd was educated at Eton and Trinity College, Cambridge, where he won fame as an all-England cricketer. Influenced by his father, he volunteered for missionary service; and as one of the "Cambridge Seven," he helped to lay the foundation of the Student Volunteer Movement, with its special interest in recruiting college students as foreign missionaries. In 1885 Studd sailed for China under the auspices of the China Inland Mission. Giving away the fortune he had inherited, he sought to live in native Chinese fashion. In 1900 he went to India, where he served as minister of the Union Church of Ootacamund in southern India. Ill health compelled him to give up this work in 1906; but in 1910, contrary to medical advice, he sailed for central Africa, where he labored until his death. In 1912 he founded the Heart of Africa Mission, which later became the Worldwide Evangelization Crusade, taking as its watchword "the evangelization of every part of the unevangelized world in the shortest possible time."
N. V. HOPE

STURM, JAKOB (1489–1553)
German Reformer and statesman

Born at Strassburg, Sturm studied at Heidelberg and Freiburg with the Protestant Wolfgang Fabricius Capito (1478–1541) and the Catholic polemicist Johann Eck (1486–1543). At Freiburg, Sturm came under the influence of Jakob Wimpfeling (1450–1528), the humanist scholar. In 1503 Sturm joined the Freiburg faculty, and later he became a city counselor. Returning to his native Strassburg in 1517, he served until 1523 as secretary to the dean of the cathedral. The next year he became a magistrate and served from 1526 as chief magistrate at Strassburg. From 1528 he was commissioner of education. In all, he represented Strassburg ninety-one times at the imperial councils. As a scholar and statesman, Sturm took part in several major Reformation convocations. In 1529 he was one of the original "Protestants" at the Diet of Speyer. During the same year he participated in the Marburg Colloquy. In 1530 he presented the Tetrapolitan Confession to the Diet of Augsburg. This was done in the name of the cities of Strassburg, Mammingen, Lindau, and Constance. One year later Sturm led Strassburg into the Schmalkaldic League (1531), thus giving concrete expression to Sturm's long-standing desire for unity among the Protestant princes of Europe. W. A. DETZLER

STURM, JOHANNES (1507–1589)
Protestant Reformer and educationalist

Born at Schleiden, in the German region of Eifel, Sturm was educated by the Brethren of the Common Life at Liege. Later he studied at Louvain University. Soon thereafter he took up with the French humanists, best known for the Meaux circle, which gathered under the patronage of Margaret of Navarre. From 1530 to 1536 Sturm lectured in classics at the University of Paris. In a pattern similar to that of Calvin, Sturm was driven from Paris in 1536 and aligned himself with Protestants in Strassburg. Bucer had attracted him to that center. His humanism led him to seek a reconciliation between Protestant and Catholic humanists, a dream condemned to perpetual frustration. In 1538 Sturm organized at Strassburg a humanistic gymnasium (high school). An academy of further education was set up in 1564. In fact, both Calvin and Thomas Platter of Basel sought his advice in shaping Reformed educational practices. Sturm's influence even extended to the German Reformation and surprisingly also to the Jesuits, who emulated some of his activities. After a sharp disagreement with the Lutheran leaders Johannes Marbach (1521–1581) and Johan-

nes Pappus (1549–1610), Sturm was expelled from Strassburg as a Roman Catholic sympathizer. Although he later was permitted to return, his old age was clouded by extreme poverty; this resulted when he loaned his personal wealth to the distressed Huguenots. W. A. DETZLER

SUÁREZ, FRANCISCO DE (1548–1617)
Spanish Jesuit philosopher and scholar

Born in Granada, Suárez studied law in Salamanca. In 1564, he joined the Jesuits. He then studied theology and taught philosophy at Segovia and Rome. He taught theology in Acala and Salamanca (1585–1597), then at Coimbra until his death.

Suárez spent his entire professional life studying, lecturing, and writing. He developed his own philosophical method and agenda based on a refusal to distinguish between essence and existence. Like Aquinas and Aristotle (his models), he attempted to synthesize into one system all of the available data of experience. Following Aquinas, he sought to weld all valid thought, pagan or Christian, into a Christian whole. His most significant work in this respect was *Metaphysical Disputations* (late 1590s), a work so basic that it was even used in Protestant universities until the Enlightenment. He wrote many other important works, including *Concerning Law* (1612) and *On the Defence of the Faith* (1613).

Suárez's most enduring ideas related to civil government and to moral responsibility. Opposing the divine right of kings, he advocated a social contract, based on each individual's natural right to life, liberty, and property. Countering both Protestant Augustinianism and Catholic Molinism, he argued that one may do righteous deeds out of the resources of his own will, because God in his foreknowledge sees one's desire and grants grace to fulfill it.

Suárez's industry and freshness of thought earned him the sobriquet *Doctor eximius et pius* ("distinguished and pious Teacher"). P. M. BASSETT

SUGER (c. 1081–1151)
French abbot, statesman, and patron of art and architecture

Born in Saint-Denis, Suger's humble parents presented him as an oblate at the abbey of Saint-Denis when he was ten years old. The abbey became his life. Fortunately for him, it was a royal foundation. During his early years in school there, he was befriended by a fellow pupil, the future King Louis VI of France. For the rest of his life he was an intimate of the royal family. In 1122 he was elected abbot. Some years later, in 1135, he began the process of rebuilding the church with royal help. That church is reputed to be the first representative of Gothic architecture in Europe (the claim is, of course, debatable). In any case, that structure probably contributed to the immense popularity of the Gothic style. Suger was also able to enrich Saint-Denis with vast amounts of art treasure in which he gloried (to the dismay of Bernard of Clairvaux). During the absence of Louis VII on the Second Crusade, Suger served as regent of the French state. His ability expressed itself not so much in the religious life as in his patronage of art, in statesmanship, and in administration. In the debate over Peter Abelard, he often served in a mediatorial capacity between the severity of Bernard and the generosity of Peter the Venerable of Cluny.
A. CABANNIS

SUNDAR SINGH, SADHU (1889–c. 1929)
Indian Christian mystic

Born into a wealthy Sikh family, Sundar Singh was raised in the Sikh tradition and in Hinduism. His mother strongly desired him to be a "Sadhu" or holy man. In 1904, at the age of fifteen, he claimed to have a vision of Christ and converted to Christianity. He was baptized in 1905 and experienced extreme persecution from his relatives. He attempted to bring Christianity to India in the form of a Sadhu. He adopted the proper apparel and went about preaching. His initial excursions took him to the Punjab, Kashmir, Baluchistan, and Afghanistan. He later ventured into Tibet, the Himalayas, and also south to Madras. In the early 1920s he ventured into East Asia, North America, Australia, Britain, and Europe. The goal of Singh's life was to live as Christ did. He claims to have received many visions and experienced many miracles. He preached to vast audiences and wrote prolifically. He widely influenced great numbers of people by his life. Nothing is known about his death except that after April of 1929, while on an evangelistic journey into Tibet, he was never heard from again. One of Sundar Singh's works available in English is *With and without Christ:* (Being Incidents Taken from the Lives of Christians and of Non-Christians Which Illustrate the Difference in Lives Lived with Christ and without Christ). T. FIRAK

SUNDAY, WILLIAM ("BILLY") ASHLEY (1862–1935)
American evangelist

Billy Sunday was born in Iowa, the youngest son of a Union soldier who died without ever seeing the child. The boy, after having moved several times with his mother and siblings and having spent a period in an orphanage, set out on his own at the age of fourteen. He managed to earn a high-school education and, because of his skill as a runner and ball player on amateur teams, was signed in 1883 to play for the Chicago Whitestockings.

In Chicago two major events in his life occurred. He was led, through the preaching at the Pacific Garden Mission, to commit his life to Christ, and, in 1888, he married Helen Amelia Thompson. After years of gradually increasing lay evangelism work, Sunday quit baseball to work full-time for the YMCA at a great financial sacrifice. From 1893 to 1895 he assisted evangelist J. Wilbur Chapman (1859–1918) and learned thoroughly the details of revival meeting work. When Chapman suddenly left mass evangelism in 1895, Sunday began holding his own meetings, although he was not licensed to preach by the Presbyterian Church until 1898 and was not ordained until 1903.

During the decade following 1895, Sunday

developed a knack for publicity and a slangy direct style of preaching that attracted large crowds. The climax of his meetings came after the sermon, when large numbers of the audience would accept Sunday's invitation to walk "the sawdust trail" to the front of the tabernacle, to indicate their decision to live a Christian life. As he was invited to larger cities, Sunday and his wife put together a varied and expert staff to take care of tabernacle construction, prayer meetings, special services, counseling, and publicity. The best known of these staff members was Homer Rodeheaver, Sunday's choir leader, soloist, and master of ceremonies.

Criticisms of Sunday accumulated as his fame grew. Some reporters accused him—perhaps because of the enthusiastic support he received from men like John D. Rockefeller, Jr., and John Wanamaker—of being a tool of the rich for channeling the discontent of the poor. Some clergy felt he ignored the social aspects of the gospel, while others did not like his frequent blasting of ministerial failings, and what they felt was sensationalism and a lack of convert follow-up. Another common source of criticism was the large "love offerings" taken for Sunday toward the end of the meetings. Sunday and his supporters defended his methods by pointing to the results they generated and by defining nurture of the convert as the job of the church, not the evangelist. The "love offering" was upheld as the traditional remuneration of an evangelist. During World War I, Sunday often donated the entire offering to relief organizations.

Sunday reached the peak of his fame from 1914 to 1919 when he preached in the nation's richest and most populous cities. For example, from May to June of 1917, Sunday preached over 120 sermons to overflowing crowds in New York City. During the same period the eighteenth amendment was passed, prohibiting the sale and manufacture of alcoholic beverages. Sunday's long fight against "Mr. Booze" climaxed during this time.

After the war Sunday's drawing power among the general public declined. Until his death he never lacked invitations to hold meetings, but they were no longer for union meetings in the larger cities. His decreasing appeal was probably due to a change in the country rather than a change in him, since he continued to preach the same message of salvation, although with less vigour and spontaneity, as financial troubles and the death of two of his four children saddened his life. Unlike other major evangelists such as Finney, Moody, and Graham, he preached only in North America and left no institutions to carry on his work. His legacy was in the lives of those (estimated at one million) who walked "the sawdust trail" shortly afterward at his invitation. R. D. SHUSTER

SUNG, JOHN (1901–1944)
Chinese evangelist

Sung was born in the village of Hong Chek in the Fukien province of southeast China, the sixth of ten children of a Methodist minister. In 1907 the family moved to the city of Hinghwa where John's father was appointed the assistant principal of the Methodist Bible School. A great evangelical revival occurred in Hinghwa, and among those touched by it was nine-year old John Sung. Following this, Sung's life became characterized by love for the Bible, prayer, and preaching. By the age of thirteen he traveled the circuit covered by local preachers and often helped his father who was now the senior city pastor. Sung applied himself to his studies and finished high school at the top of his class. He became the chief editor of *Revival*, his father's magazine, and carried out evangelical work among children.

In 1919 China was embroiled in political tumult. Sung felt that he could not study well in such an atmosphere and decided to go to America. His father was indignant since the family was not well-to-do. John prayed and subsequently received a letter from an American missionary in Peking who offered free tuition, room, and board at Ohio Wesleyan University. During this period he had a dream that found him rescuing people out of a stream onto a platform shaped like a cross and then rejoicing with a joyful throng in the heavens. He interpreted this as the story of his life—and, indeed, he would become a great evangelist. He graduated in 1923 *cum laude,* was elected to Phi Beta Kappa, and received the gold medal and a cash prize for physics and chemistry. Being the first Chinese to achieve such scholastic heights, news of him spread across the country and abroad. Sung was now offered positions and scholarships from various institutions, Harvard among them. He accepted a scholarship for an M.S. degree at Ohio State University. He finished his degree in nine months, then went on to obtain a Ph.D. in chemistry in just twenty-one months.

Following this, Sung went to Union Theological Seminary in New York City, where he planned to finish three years of study in one year. With his usual intensity he pursued his studies but found that his faith in Christ was declining as rationalism, Buddhism, and Taoism took its place. By his own account his heart was filled with great unhappiness. A turn of events began when he attended an evangelistic campaign at a Baptist church and listened to a fifteen-year old girl read the Scriptures and preach on the cross of Christ. Sung's heart was moved, and he felt God's presence. This drove him to read Christian biographies and attend meetings to discover the power he had seen in that young girl. One night the struggles in his heart reached a pinnacle as he read Luke 23 and realized his sins were forgiven. Such a peace filled his heart that he couldn't contain it; he began to shout for joy, running through the dormitory. This began a new life for the enthusiastic Sung, who spoke to all about his experience.

The president of the seminary thought that he had lost his mind due to his extreme scholastic efforts and had him committed to a psychopathic ward. Sung spent six months in the hospital and utilized his time to rest and study the Bible. He was finally released due to intervention by the Chinese consul and Dr. Rollin Walker, a professor of Bible at Ohio Wesleyan, who was Sung's friend. He was released on the terms that he should return to China.

Upon returning to China in the fall of 1927, Sung, to the initial disappointment of his parents, forsook careers in academia and industry to become a gospel preacher. He took a part-time position at a Methodist Christian high school teaching chemistry and the Bible but was mainly occupied with preaching. Sung viewed bowing to Sun Yat-Sen's portrait as idolatry and soon fell into disrepute with the Nationalist party. This turn of events led to the resignation of his teaching position. Despite a growing anti-Christian mood in the country, Sung and those working with him effected great revival among rural Christians and churches. The grounding of new Christians in the Bible was a major concern for Sung. He held Bible trainings and then sent the trainees out to share what they had learned in numerous village churches.

Eventually Sung's preaching began to turn from Bible exposition to the conviction of sin and the remedy of the cross. At this point he began to experience heart trouble, but he carried on with the same fervor. He joined up with the Bethel bands on their tours, who brought revival in numerous places.After three years with the Bethel band, Sung became an independent evangelist. His reputation was growing, and invitations to preach poured in from many regions. His unconventional preaching methods and scathing reproaches of lukewarm leaders had a great effect wherever he went. Christians in Tientsin had invited him there, but no church would let him use their buildings. A new meeting hall was built after eight thousand dollars were donated by Christians who felt the need for a place where the gospel could be preached freely. In and around Amoy (Xiamen) great revival occurred, resulting in the formation of numerous preaching bands that Sung sent out. In 1935 he got a united invitation from three denominations in the Philippines. Overflow crowds packed in to see the dramatic, illustrative, and piercing preaching of Sung. His preaching would usually last over two hours, punctuated by singing and always denouncing sin.

In the following years, Sung preached in Malaysia, northern Sumatra, Taiwan, Canton,

Hong Kong, Kowloon, Singapore, and Sibu. Many of those who heard Sung's preaching were truly changed; their new birth empowered them to leave sinful habits behind, reconcile with family members, and spread the gospel to others.

Sung had neglected his health for years, and by 1940 his pain was so intense that he was forced to receive medical attention. He was found to have both cancer and tuberculosis. He underwent three operations over the span of about two and a half years. As his health returned he met with Christian leaders to help them to continue the work of the Lord, always stressing prayer as the first mode of action along with grounding in the Scripture. He wrote a book entitled *Allegories,* in which he taught the main thoughts from the books of the Bible. The main emphasis of the book was to illustrate the proper Christian worker and how to build the church.

John Sung was an unconventional and extremely powerful preacher of the gospel, bringing Christians and non-Christians alike to repentance. He, like Watchman Nee, a contemporary of his, felt that many of the foreign missions were ineffectual. Sung was extremely outspoken and public about this, as well as about the political situation; therefore, he was a highly controversial figure. Christians today in China and Taiwan owe much to Sung's ministry; he was one of God's greatest gifts to the Far East in the twentieth century. T. FIRAK

SWAIN, CLARA A. (1834–1910)

Pioneer medical missionary to India

Born at Elmira, New York, for several years Swain taught school in western New York, near her birthplace and childhood home. In 1865 she began medical training in her hometown and, thereafter, continued it at the Women's Medical College of Pennsylvania, from which she graduated in 1869. On graduation she accepted a call from Mrs. D. W. Thomas, who with her husband conducted a Methodist girls' orphanage in Bareilly, a city of over one hundred thousand inhabitants in northwest India. The position

was for a "lady physician" to teach medicine. Swain went out under the auspices of the Boston-based New England branch of the Woman's Foreign Missionary Society of the Methodist Episcopal Church. She sailed with Isabella Thoburn as the first qualified woman medical practitioner in India. During the first year she was successful in training seventeen young women, who finally passed the required civil service examination and were duly licensed to practice medicine "in all ordinary diseases." In 1871 the Nawab of Rampore, though not a Christian, donated forty acres of land, upon which Swain built a six-room dispensary (1873) and then (1874) the first modern women's hospital in India. In May of 1876 she left Bareilly for Castile, New York, to recuperate from poor health, but resumed her medical missionary labors in 1880. In 1885, while treating the Rhani Saheba of Khetri, wife of the Rajah of Rajputana, she accepted a royal invitation to remain as court physician in order to open a women's dispensary—a position she held for the next ten years. In 1896 she retired from her labors in India to Castile, New York, where she lived for the rest of her life—except for a farewell visit she paid to India between 1906 and 1908. In 1909 she published *A Glimpse of India.* N. V. HOPE

SWEDENBORG, EMANUEL (1688–1772)

Swedish scientist, philosopher, and theologian

A native of Stockholm, Swedenborg demonstrated a scholar's interest in a variety of subjects: mathematics, engineering, physics, general science, music, astronomy, natural history. He studied Isaac Newton intensely. Many inventions resulted from his research, among which was a design of a submarine and a flying machine. Some of his conclusions reached by inductive argument alone are close to the theories of modern nuclear physics. Swedenborg published widely in scientific fields, began a respected periodical, and produced the first treatise on algebra in the Swedish language. He was regarded as one of the leading thinkers of his day.

In spite of his many scientific achievements, Swedenborg is known chiefly for his work in theology. In 1743 he asserted that he gained spiritual insight in direct response to a divine vision and call. From that time, he felt as consciously attuned in the spiritual world as he was in the natural world, noting that he was in communication with angels and spirits. He claimed to have conversed on various theological points with Martin Luther, the apostle Paul, and other deceased authorities. His otherworld experiences have caused some to regard him as a "medium."

Swedenborg's previous purpose had been to explore nature, chemistry, and the sciences of mining and anatomy. After 1743, he held that God had selected him for revealing the spiritual meaning of sacred Scriptures. Swedenborg saw a logical progression from the natural to the spiritual, and for this reason, he believed, he was introduced first to the natural sciences as preparation for the spiritual. According to Swedenborg, man is born natural, by education becomes moral, and afterwards by regeneration from the Lord, he becomes spiritual. He argued that the many volumes of theological works he penned on such subjects as the last judgment and heaven and hell constituted a revelation from God for a new age of truth and reason in religion that provided the meaning of the second advent.

Swedenborg's theology maintained the absolute unity of God in essence and person, rejecting what he regarded as the traditional doctrine of the Trinity as three persons in one God. Instead, he held that the Trinity is one person uniting the Father (Creator Divine), the Son (embodiment of that Divine), and the Holy Spirit (outflowing activity of the Divine Human). He was averse to the doctrine of salvation by faith alone. Rather, he thought that God imparts righteousness to whomever he chooses, even to those who have not repented.

Swedenborg did not found a new church. Around 1784 some of his disciples, however, founded The New Jerusalem Church, which remains small in size, with branches throughout the world. E. G. ROHR

SWEELINCK, JAN PIETERSZOON (1562–1621)
Dutch organist and composer

Born either at Deventer or Amsterdam, Sweelinck studied music with Andrea Zarlino in Venice. His father, Pieter, the organist of the Old Church in Amsterdam, died in 1573; and, sometime between 1577 and 1580, the son succeeded to this position and retained it until his death. Sweelinck wrote much sacred and secular vocal music. For example, he set all the Psalms to music, and they were published in four volumes between 1604 and 1623. But his chief importance lies in the fact that he was the first major Protestant composer of music for the organ. He wrote the first organ music that provided an independent part for the pedals; and in constructing fugues, he set a style that developed continuously until it reached its climax in Johann Sebastian Bach (1685–1750). Sweelinck was also a teacher of uncommon brilliance; virtually all the eminent North German organists of the following generation were his pupils. N. V. HOPE

SWEET, WILLIAM WARREN (1881–1958)
American church historian

Born at Baldwin, Kansas, Sweet was educated at Ohio Wesleyan University, Drew Theological Seminary, Crozer Theological Seminary, and the University of Pennsylvania (Ph.D., 1912). He served two Methodist churches in the Philadelphia area (1909–1911) before teaching history at Ohio Wesleyan University (1911–1913) and at DePauw University (1913–1927). He was professor of history of American Christianity, University of Chicago (1927–1946). After official retirement, he taught church history at Garrett Biblical Institute (1946–1948) and from 1948 was professor of history and chairman of faculty at Perkins School of Theology. His writings include *The Story of Religion in America* (1930), *Methodism in American History* (1933), *Religion on the American Frontier* (four volumes, 1931–1946), *Religion in Colonial America* (1942), *Revivalism in America* (1944), *The American*

Churches (1947), and *Religion in the Development of American Culture, 1740–1865* (1952). J. D. Douglas

SWETE, HENRY BARCLAY (1835–1917)
New Testament and patristics scholar

Swete was born in Bristol, England, the only son of an Anglican clergyman. He received his education at Bishop's College, Bristol; King's College, London; and Gonville and Caius College, Cambridge, from which he graduated in 1858. He was ordained and for the next several years served as an assistant to his father at Blagdon, Somerset. In 1865 he returned to his college in Cambridge, where he served as dean, tutor, and theological lecturer. In 1877 he took a parish job at Ashdon, Essex. From 1882 to 1890 he was professor of pastoral theology at King's College, London.

In 1890 he succeeded B. F. Westcott in the prestigious Regius Professorship of Divinity at Cambridge University. His appointment was a controversial one because many did not think he was of the stature of his predecessor. But he served the professorship brilliantly over the twenty-five years he held the post. He managed successfully to combine theological scholarship of the highest quality with a deep, pastoral concern for students preparing for the ministry. He became the most popular lecturer in the divinity faculty at Cambridge.

Swete published several important essays on the Holy Spirit (1909), and he prepared critical editions of the Septuagint (Greek) version of the Old Testament and the commentaries of Theodore of Mopsuestia on the Minor Epistles of St. Paul (1912). He edited Greek texts of Mark and Revelation, as well as the apocryphal Gospel of Peter (1893). He was the editor of the influential *Essays on the Early History of the Church and the Ministry* (published in 1918). He helped to found the *Journal of Theological Studies* (1899) and established series of publications in liturgical studies and texts of early Christian writers. He began the massive project that led to the publication, over a half-century later, of the *Patristic Greek Lexicon* (1961–1969).
P. Toon

SWIFT, JONATHAN (1667–1745)
English satirist

Swift was born in Ireland of English parents. Since his father died before Jonathan was born, Swift was dependent on relatives for his education at Trinity College, Dublin. In the aftermath of the Revolution of 1688, he went to England for safety, finding a place in the household of Sir William Temple. There he remained until 1699, reading in Temple's library and growing to intellectual maturity. His genius first found expression in *A Tale of a Tub* (1704), a satire against "corruptions in religion and learning." Later he produced a religious satire called *Argument to Prove the Inconvenience of Abolishing Christianity* (1708).

Swift became vicar of a small Anglican church at Larancornear, Dublin, in 1700. In the years that followed he had numerous contacts with High Churchmen and hoped for an appointment in England. Instead, he was made dean of St. Patrick's, Dublin, in 1713. Throughout his life he was an ardent and devoted defender of the Anglican Church. For him it was equal with the monarchy itself. Swift saw as enemies all who would undermine the established Church—Deists, Nonconformists, Roman Catholics, freethinkers, and liberal politicians. He was active in politics as both a Whig and a Tory, and his strong convictions found their way into his writing, where it is clear he believed that power derives from the people. *A Modest Proposal* (1729) suggested satirically that Irish children be sold by their parents and eaten to keep the population down. He was really protesting the ignorance and poverty in which children were reared. *The Journal to Stella* (1710–1713) was a series of letters to Esther Johnson, whom Swift had tutored in the Temple household. They are a vivid picture of London life and politics. *Gulliver's Travels* (1725) is Swift's masterpiece, one of the greatest satires ever written. It brings under severe judgment the political, economic, and social institutions of Swift's day—and the human race in general. P. M. Bechtel

SYMMACHUS (died 514)

Pope, 498–514

Symmachus is best known for the controversy that resulted from his election to the chair of Peter. At the time, two parties in Rome were seeking power. Symmachus was elected by the majority party that opposed a conciliatory policy toward Constantinople. A minority group elected the archpriest Laurentius. Both parties appealed to King Theodoric, who decided in favor of Symmachus. The next year Pope Symmachus held a synod in Rome that stipulated a majority vote should prevail in the election of a pope.

The supporters of Laurentius, however, refused to give up. Before Theodoric, they accused Symmachus of immorality, fixing his own election, and ordering the celebration of Easter on a date other than that observed in Alexandria. Symmachus was summoned to appear before the king. He agreed to meet with a synod in Rome but on his way was attacked by members of the opposing parties. The synod declared that the pope could not be tried, since no earthly power could sit in judgment over a pope. King Theodoric, displeased with their action, decreed Laurentius to be the pope.

For the next four years Rome was the scene of many brawls and fights between the opposing parties. The central issue was whether the bishop of Rome could be judged by civil law or God alone. The "Symmachan Forgeries" appeared when Ennodius of Milan argued that only God could judge the bishops of Rome. These documents contain arguments based on what appear to be spurious historical precedents. Nonetheless, peace was eventually restored, and the Laurentians supported Pope Symmachus. R. E. WEBBER

T

TACITUS, CORNELIUS (c. 55–120)
Roman historian

Little is known of Tacitus personally, but his surviving writings present an invaluable picture of Roman life during the first century A.D. These works are *Dialogus de Oratoribus* (c. 77); *The Life of Agricola*, his father-in-law (c. 98); *Germania* (c. 98); *Histories* (c. 116); *Annals* (c. 116). In this last-named work, Tacitus refered to the persecution of the Christians in Rome in A.D. 64, when the emperor Nero made them the scapegoats for the fire that he had ordered set. Though Tacitus believed the Christians to be innocent of the arson of which they were accused, he refered to their faith as "a detestable superstition," named Christ as the founder of this sect, and stated that he was crucified "in the reign of Emperor Tiberius by the Procurator Pontius Pilate." He further said that Nero accused the Roman Christians not only of arson but of "hatred of the human race," and that Nero had some of them thrown to dogs, others crucified, still others burned in the imperial garden. Thus Tacitus provides independent secular confirmation for some basic events recorded in the New Testament, including Jesus' crucifixion.

N. V. HOPE

TAIT, ARCHIBALD CAMPBELL (1811–1882)
Archbishop of Canterbury

Born in Edinburgh into a family that originally came from England, Tait was brought up as a Presbyterian. His mother died when he was only three. After attending school in Edinburgh he went to Glasgow University (1827–1830). While there he determined to enter the ministry of the Church of England. He won a scholarship to Balliol College, Oxford, and distinguished himself academically. He also made many important friendships with men who were to become leaders in church and state. He became a fellow of his college and was ordained into the ministry.

Among his personal friends were the leaders of the Oxford Tractarian (Anglo-Catholic) movement. While he sympathized with their call for a greater devotion and discipline by clergy, he could not accept their narrow definition of the Church as only Episcopalian. He had too many Scottish Presbyterian friends!

In 1842 he succeeded Dr. Thomas Arnold as Headmaster of the famous Rugby School. He continued the policy of Arnold, developing new methods of education. After a serious illness he resigned in 1850 to take the less demanding post of dean of Carlisle

Cathedral. Here in 1856 he and his wife suffered the loss of five of their seven children from scarlet fever. Soon after this tragedy he was offered the bishopric of London, which he accepted.

As bishop he encouraged evangelistic efforts and caused Westminster Abbey and St. Paul's Cathedral to hold popular preaching services on Sunday evenings. He faced with justice and tact the many problems raised by the introduction of ritualism into parishes. In the cholera epidemic of August 1866 he risked his own life to minister to the dying. To help the poorer parishes of London he formed the Bishop of London's Fund to which more than a hundred thousand pounds were subscribed in the first year (1863).

In February 1869 he was consecrated archbishop of Canterbury. Winds of change were blowing in the state and church and these made his task difficult. Parliament was passing legislation to disestablish the Church in Ireland, and in the Church of England the problems caused by ritualism were many and complex. It is generally recognised that Tait was a great statesman at a time when the archbishop of Canterbury was an important political figure. He was often involved in debates in the House of Lords and in speaking publicly on contemporary issues. In his period of office the archbishopric of Canterbury began effectively to be the senior bishopric of the growing Anglican communion of churches.
P. TOON

TALLIS, THOMAS (c. 1505–1585)
English composer

Little is known of this composer's early career. Tallis was the organist of Waltham Abbey, a position that he lost when King Henry VIII dissolved the monasteries in 1540. He then became a member of the Royal Chapel. Together with William Byrd, he was granted by Queen Elizabeth I the first patent to print music in England. In all probability much of his music has been lost, but the significant portion that remains reveals him to be a most polished craftsman.

He wrote not only music with Latin text, but anthems with English words for the new Anglican liturgy. Among his Latin works are an exceedingly beautiful set of *Lamentations for Holy Week* and choir settings using some of the great Latin plainsong hymns. A beautiful little anthem is "If Ye Love Me, Keep My Commandments." A set of choral responses for the Anglican liturgy is still widely used. He also wrote tunes for Archbishop Parker's *Psalter,* from which a couple of tunes have found wide acceptance. Tallis also wrote music for organ and for virginals (an early form of harpsichord). A great twentieth-century piece for string orchestra is Vaughan Williams's *Fantasia on a Theme by Tallis,* and so the contribution of this great Elizabethan is kept alive today. J. B. MacMILLAN

TATIAN (died c. 180)
Apologist and heretic

Originally from Assyria (upper Mesopotamia), Tatian acquired extensive Greek learning. He became a Christian in Rome following a long period of travel. For several years, Tatian was an adherent of Justin and his teaching. But after Justin's death, he retreated into the Encratite sect and lived mostly thereafter in the empire's far eastern provinces. The Encratite doctrines were heavily Gnostic in character. The sect believed that matter is evil and maintained varied ascetic practices, including prohibition of marriage.

Tatian was the author of numerous early works defending Christianity. According to Eusebius of Caesaria, some of these writings were entitled *On Animals, On Demons, On Perfection,* and *Book of Problems.* But just two of Tatian's works are still extant: *Address to the Greeks,* a defense of Christian ideas and life, and *Diatessaron,* a harmony of the four Gospel accounts of Christ's life. The first was a generally orthodox presentation of Christian apologetics. Its main theme was the superiority of Christianity over Greek learning and culture. Not an attractive work, it assumes a harsh, denunciatory posture and fails to depict the person of Christ, the Incarnation, and atonement for sins. The second writing was used widely by the Syrian Church until the fifth century. Its value lies with its easy use for educational and liturgical purposes. But in the early 400s, Rabbula, bishop of Edessa, pronounced Tatian a heretic and ordered employment of other translations of the Gospels. A little later, Theodoret, another Syrian bishop, did the same. K. J. BRYER

TAVERNER, JOHN (1495–1545)
English composer

Taverner was master of the choristers at Cardinal College (later Christ Church) in Oxford (1526–1530). He was accused of heresy (the College was a hotbed of Lutheranism) and imprisoned for a time in 1528, and he later worked as an agent of Thomas Cromwell in the suppression of monasteries. He composed eight masses, three Magnificats, motets, and other church music, all highly regarded since the sixteenth century. D. HAYES

TAYLOR, EDWARD (1642–1729)
First American poet

Born in Leicestershire, England, Taylor was the son of a successful farmer. He was educated by a Nonconformist schoolmaster and was given a good foundation in Latin, Greek, and Hebrew. At this time, he very likely studied the works of George Herbert. If the regime of Cromwell had endured, Taylor, a Puritan, could have remained in England, studied theology, and then become a teacher. However, the Restoration and Act of Uniformity (1662) meant that he could not enter Cambridge or Oxford without subscribing to the act. He and his fellow Nonconformists were not allowed to preach or congregate. As a result, in 1668 he embarked on a ship headed for the Bay Colony (Massachusetts). After arriving in Massachusetts, Taylor attended Harvard College and graduated in 1671. He intended to stay at Harvard as a resident scholar, but then answered a call to become a minister for the church in Westfield, a small town one hundred miles west of Bos-

ton. He remained there until his death fifty-eight years later.

During all the years Taylor was a minister he wrote poetry. One of his volumes, *Preparatory Meditations*, is a collection of over two hundred spiritual meditations written in preparation for the Lord's Supper. Another collection, entitled *God's Determinations*, is a series of short poems written as a dramatic allegory wherein Taylor affirms God's predestination of the elect. Another large work, called *The Metrical History of Christianity*, describes the history of the Christian church in decasyllabic couplets. Taylor was a metaphysical poet who wrote in the tradition of George Herbert—but was not as polished and refined as Herbert or the other great metaphysical poets such as Donne and Crashaw. Nonetheless, he contributed to our American heritage of Christian poetry and is credited with being the first American poet. This recognition did not come until the twentieth century, when his poetry was discovered in the Yale University library. P. W. COMFORT

TAYLOR, JAMES HUDSON (1832–1905)
Founder of the China Inland Mission

Born into a Methodist Christian family in Barnsley, Yorkshire, Taylor was much influenced as to spiritual things by both his parents and his grandparents who had received John Wesley as a guest in their home. His father, a pharmacist, had a deep concern for the spiritual condition of China. At a very young age, around five years old, Taylor indicated that he would like to be a missionary to China one day. He was basically home schooled out of necessity, as he was a frail and often infirm child. He had a strong spiritual relationship with his mother and sister, who both prayed much for him when he was in spiritual turmoil. In June 1849, at the age of seventeen, while reading a tract on the finished work of Christ in his father's study, he felt that he had finally understood what Christ had done for him. At this point he offered his life to Christ and his service. In 1849 Taylor felt the Lord's call to China. He responded to this call and began to prepare every facet of his life toward the goal of leaving for China. At this point he felt his life was on a higher plane.

Two books helped shape the future for Taylor. One was a copy of the Gospel of Luke in Mandarin; the other, a book that told of the value of medical missions to China. By comparing the Mandarin version to the English version of Luke, Taylor was able to begin learning Mandarin Chinese. His career preparation turned from pharmacy to medicine. He also contacted different societies that involved themselves in missionary work in China to express his interest in the missions. Taylor gave of his income to such endeavors. His medical training began in Hull and continued in London. It was during this time that Taylor, convinced in himself that he could by no means be prepared for work in China without depending on God for everything, put himself under a strict daily life training. He studied theology, Latin, and Greek, as well as medicine before attending to his duties. He often put himself into situations that demanded that God would meet his financial needs. While at Hull, Taylor lived mainly on oatmeal and rice, giving a good part of his income to Christian work.

One time as he was out ministering to the poor, a man asked him to come and pray for his wife, who was near death. Upon entering the house he saw a house full of starving children and their sick mother with a tiny infant moaning next to her. He was moved by the scene and told them that the Father in heaven loved them so they should not be downcast. Hesitant at first, Taylor was emboldened by God to give them the only coin he had. The money was used to save the woman's life. Later that day a person brought Taylor a package with money. This experience led Taylor to depend solely on God for his needs.

In association with the Chinese Evangelization Society Taylor set sail for China in 1853. Unexpected conditions met Taylor as he got off the ship. Those whom he expected to meet had either died or left the country, and Shanghai had been taken over by rebels. Introductions were made with other Chris-

tians, and Taylor began to learn more Chinese as well as evangelize. His desire was to go deep inland, where few missionaries ever ventured. Such an undertaking was dangerous, since there was much political strife at that time and Westerners were not always looked upon with favor. Evangelistic excursions often consisted of Taylor and another missionary, who took turns speaking the gospel and handing out tracts or portions of the Bible to the natives. Taylor adopted native dress, which did much to win the respect of the Chinese.

By 1856 Taylor had begun work in Ningpo, an influential coastal city. It was here that, because of his conviction that a Christian should "owe no man anything," he severed his connection with the Chinese Evangelization Society. The society, from which he drew a salary, had been running on borrowed money, and Taylor felt that because of this he could no longer associate with it. He felt that if a work had a lack of funds, God must no longer support it. This was a bold move, since he had no friends who could assure him of supplies. He married Maria J. Dyer in January 1858, and in the fall of 1859 he took charge of the London Mission Hospital in Ningpo. After nine months Taylor resigned because of failing health and left more funds with the hospital than he had started with. Even better, many of the patients rapidly recovered and came to know Christ.

By 1860 the work was growing, but the laborers were few. Taylor, in his late twenties, had to return to England so that his health could be restored. This was extremely difficult for one had who directed his whole life toward serving the Lord in China, especially now when the work had begun to blossom. Doctors in England assured him that it would be years, if it were at all possible, before he could revisit China. Every day he prayed for workers to go to China, viewing a large map of it on his wall. He worked with F. F. Gough on a revision of the New Testament in colloquial Ningpo Chinese for the British and Foreign Bible Society. Slowly, new workers set out for China, and Taylor felt the need for an agency that was especially suited for the gospel work in the interior of China. To meet this need, the China Inland Mission was founded. The revision work on the Ningpo New Testament had given Taylor a fresh insight on how the Mission should proceed. There was to be dependence upon God for all financial needs. No personal solicitations or collections were to be made at public meetings where Taylor might be speaking.

In 1865 Taylor asked the Lord for twenty-four fellow workers, two for each of the evangelized inland provinces and two for Mongolia. United prayer beseeching the Lord to meet the needs of the mission was offered daily. In 1866 Taylor, his wife, Maria, and a party of new missionaries sailed for China. From bases there in Ningpo and Hangchow, the work spread southward to the province of Chekiang; ten years later it was spreading north to Kiangsu, west to Anhwei, and southwest to Kiangsi. It was during this period, in 1870, that Maria died of cholera. This occurred shortly after the death of her fifth son, an infant, also from cholera. Taylor remarried in 1872 to Miss J. E. Faulding, who was a leader of the women's work in Hangchow.

Between 1876 and 1878 a great many more workers entered the field. This pioneering work spread throughout the whole interior of China. Christians from all over the world, agreeing to overlook denominational differences, joined the ranks of the China Inland Mission. By the end of the century, half of the evangelical missionaries in China were from the China Inland Mission. Taylor withdrew from active work in 1901 and died in Changsha in 1905.

James Hudson Taylor proved to be one of the most profound pioneering spiritual influences in China. Going to regions where none had ventured with the gospel of Christ before, in native garb and in full dependence upon God for all his needs, Taylor carried on a work that would culminate in the China Inland Mission. He believed that by deepening the spiritual life of Christians, new converts and otherwise, the mission field would never lack workers. Taylor's love for the Bible was profound. When out in the field

with other workers he would wait until everyone was asleep in their shared hut and then light a match to read his Bible so as not to disturb the others. The field work was exhausting, but he always made time for the Bible. Through numerous trials, persecutions, and hardships Taylor and those with him toiled by faith to bring Christ to a politically unstable nation where foreigners were not always welcome. Through the years China has gone through many changes, but whatever Christian vitality exists there today must be due in great part to his pioneering work. Taylor, having no formal connections with other missions, became greatly respected for his deep spirituality and living faith in God for all aspects of mission work.

His writings include *China: Its Spiritual Need and Claims* (1865), *A Retrospect* (1884, also issued under the titles: *To China with Love* and *Hudson Taylor*) and *Union and Communion* (1894). The latter is devotional in nature, concerned with the Song of Solomon, revealing Taylor's spiritual roots in Christ. For a thorough description of his life and work, see the two-volume work of Dr. and Mrs. Howard Taylor, *Hudson Taylor in Early Years* (1911) and *Hudson Taylor and the China Inland Mission* (1918). T. FIRAK

TAYLOR, JEREMY (1613–1667)
Anglican bishop and writer

Born in Cambridge, England, where he entered the university in 1626, Taylor had as a fellow student John Milton, with whom he was to differ radically in politics and theology. He was ordained in 1633 and made a fellow of All Souls, Oxford, in 1638. As chaplain to King Charles I, Taylor left his rural church to serve with the royalist forces at the outbreak of the English Civil War in 1642. When the king's forces were defeated at Cardigan Castle in Wales, he was briefly taken prisoner. After his release he remained in Wales and found a new patron in the earl of Carbery, who made him his chaplain and invited him to live in his castle, Golden Grove. Here Taylor wrote *The Liberty of Prophesying* (1647) and one of his most famous works, *Holy Living* (1650). Holy living requires, Taylor wrote, that a man prepare for his heavenly destiny by limiting his attractions to this world. These resolutions must be made before one loses his strength, for Taylor rejected deathbed repentance. In 1651 Taylor published *Holy Dying*, in which he declared that heaven is reserved for those who live and die in a holy manner, having been sober and godly in their earthly lives. The beauty of Taylor's writing style led to his being called the "Shakespeare of English divines." In 1660 he was consecrated bishop of Down and Connor (Ireland) and became vice-chancellor of Dublin University. In Ireland the Presbyterian clergymen refused to acknowledge his authority over them; perhaps they had not forgotten his broadside against them entitled *The Sacred Order and Offices of Episcopacy.* For Roman Catholics he had even less tolerance, as seen in his somewhat violent *Dissuasive from Popery.* His last years filled with conflict, he died in Ireland, where he is buried in the cemetery of a church he himself built. P. M. BECHTEL

TAYLOR, KENNETH NATHANIEL
(born 1917)
Translator of The Living Bible; *publisher; writer*

Born in Portland, Oregon, son of George Nathaniel Taylor, a minister in the United Presbyterian denomination, young Kenneth made an early profession of faith under his parents' guidance. Taylor attended Wheaton College (Illinois) from 1934 to 1938, graduating with a B.S. degree in zoology. Early in his college years he had aspired to a prestigious career in medicine, but shortly before his junior year his motivations were dramatically changed as he read *Borden of Yale '09.* Profoundly challenged by Borden's dedication to God, Taylor made a complete and permanent surrender of his own life.

After graduating from college, Taylor served on the staff of Inter-Varsity Christian Fellowship in Canada, then attended Dallas Theological Seminary (1940–1943). He completed his seminary training at Northern Baptist Theological Seminary in Chicago, at the same time working as editor of *HIS* magazine. Upon receiving the Th.M. degree from Northern Baptist in 1944, he was ordained to the Christian ministry at Central Bible Church in Portland.

He continued as editor of *HIS* magazine until 1946, when he joined the staff of Good News Publishers in Chicago. In 1947 he became director of Moody Literature Mission, a division of Moody Bible Institute in Chicago, and remained there until 1963. During thirteen of those years he was also director of Moody Press.

As the father of ten children, Taylor was keenly aware of his responsibility to communicate the Christian faith to his own and other children. This led to his writing several books for children, the best known of which is *The Bible in Pictures for Little Eyes* (1956), with more than a million copies in print and fifty-four foreign translations.

This same concern for his children's knowledge of the Bible was the impetus for Taylor's early efforts in the 1950s to rephrase Bible passages to make them more understandable. The first result was the publication of *Living Letters* in 1962; this volume contained his modern-language translation of all the Epistles of the New Testament. Unable to find a publisher for *Living Letters,* Kenneth and his wife, Margaret, formed a new publishing company, which they named Tyndale House Publishers in honor of William Tyndale, sixteenth-century translator of the Bible into English.

The warm reception of *Living Letters,* owing in part to Billy Graham's endorsement of it and his offering it as a premium gift on his television programs, led Taylor to prepare and publish similar versions of all the other parts of the Bible: *Living Prophecies* (1965), *Living Gospels and the Book of Acts* (1966), *Living Psalms and Proverbs* (1967), *Living Lessons of Life and Love* (1968), *Living Books of Moses* (1969), and *Living History of Israel* (1970). These seven component volumes were combined to form *The Living Bible,* published in 1971. Its large distribution made publishing history, and by 1991 some 38 million copies were in print.

Although best known for his work with

The Living Bible, Taylor has always been characterized by concern for missions and for the literature needs of the world. Acknowledging God as the Author of the Bible, Taylor has not received author royalties on *The Living Bible,* instead chanelling those funds through Tyndale House Foundation and Living Bibles International. These organizations were founded to support the production of modern-language Bibles in foreign countries and language groups around the world.

Taylor has always demonstrated personal gifts as a creative entrepreneur. Some of his outstanding innovations are the following: the Christian Booksellers Association (1950), which provides Christian publishers and bookstore owners a Christian counterpart of the American Booksellers Association; Evangelical Literature Overseas (1953), bringing the literature efforts of mission boards into a cooperative and more productive program; and Short Terms Abroad (1965), one of the first groups to research and catalogue the needs of mission stations around the world for short-term missionaries.

Several colleges have honored Kenneth Taylor, author of twenty-four books, with Ph.D.s in literature (Wheaton College of Illinois, 1965; Trinity Evangelical Divinity School, 1972) and in humane letters (Huntington College, 1974; Taylor University, 1989). He is also the recipient of more than twenty-five other honors, recognitions, and awards, many of them related to his contributions to biblical literature worldwide. His autobiography is *My Life: A Guided Tour* (1991). V. J. MUIR

TAYLOR, NATHANIEL WILLIAM (1786–1858)
American theologian and educator

Born in New Milford, Connecticut, Taylor graduated from Yale University in 1807. After studying theology under President Timothy Dwight of Yale, in 1812 he was ordained to the Congregational ministry and called as pastor of the First Church of New Haven, where he had a distinguished ministry for ten years. When the Divinity School

was established at Yale University in 1822, Taylor was appointed its first professor of theology, a position he occupied for the rest of his life. His chief intellectual endeavor was to construct a theological system that would remain true to traditional New England Calvinism, with its predestinarian viewpoint, and yet make room for the experiences of the Second Great Awakening, with its emphasis on human freewill decision. His views aroused such controversy that some of the more orthodox Calvinists departed from Yale and set up a rival seminary at Hartford in 1834. N. V. HOPE

TEMPLE, FREDERICK (1821–1902)
Archbishop of Canterbury, 1896–1902

The thirteenth of fifteen children, Temple was the son of a British colonial administrator. After his father's death in Sierra Leone the family settled in Devon. Here he did extremely well at school and went to Balliol College, Oxford, in 1839, where he studied classics and mathematics. He also gained a wide circle of influential friends and was ordained. He developed a broad-minded approach to questions of churchmanship and a progressive attitude to the social questions of the day. He then became a government inspector of education and gained a reputation as an expert on educational matters. He believed that the laboring classes could be taught to help themselves and improve their lot by proper education. He also believed that alcohol was a serious problem and supported temperance schemes. He wrote on "National Education" for the *Oxford Essays* (1856) and on "The Education of the World" for *Essays and Reviews* (1860).

In 1857 he became headmaster of Rugby School, where he introduced a series of reforms and increased its size. Here he remained until 1869, when he left to become bishop of Exeter. His appointment was challenged by both Anglo-Catholics and evangelicals because of his participation in *Essays and Reviews.* Eventually he took up the post and proved to be both a faithful pastor and a popular bishop. He was influential in having the bishopric of Truro carved out of that of Exeter in 1876.

In 1885 he became the bishop of London, involving himself in the major social questions of the day. He was responsible for the move to build what is now called Church House, Westminster, as a memorial of the Jubilee of Queen Victoria. He made a great impression in London and it was not surprising that he became archbishop of Canterbury in 1897. As such he presided over the fourth Lambeth Conference. He purchased a large house next to Canterbury Cathedral to function as the palace of the archbishop. In 1898 he addressed the General Assembly of the Church of Scotland on the subject of temperance.

Known as a man who got straight to the point, he was respected for the strength of his arguments and his character. His publications were mostly sermons and addresses, but they did include the printing of his Bampton Lectures on *The Relation between Religion and Science* (1884). One of his sons, William, also became archbishop of Canterbury. P. TOON

TEMPLE, WILLIAM (1881–1944)
Archbishop of Canterbury, 1942–1944

Son of Frederick Temple, also archbishop of Canterbury, William attended Rugby School before entering Balliol College, Oxford. Here he gained high academic honors, showed great ability as a speaker, was president of the Students' Union, and took a practical interest in the poor of London's East End. The primary intellectual influence upon him was that of Edward Caird, Master of Balliol. In 1904 he became a fellow of Queen's College and, with a light teaching load, was able to visit Europe and hear the leading theologians and philosophers. He committed himself to the Workers' Educational Association, which aimed to offer the "culture" usually reserved for the middle classes to the working classes. When he applied to the bishop of Oxford for ordination in 1906, he was refused because of his liberal views on the Virgin Birth and the bodily resurrection of Jesus Christ. However, the archbishop of Canterbury, Randall Davidson, ordained him in Canterbury Cathedral in 1908.

He became headmaster of Repton School in 1910 and while there wrote his first major book, *Mens Creatix* (1917), a philosophical argument for Christian theism. During World War I he came into prominence, especially through his leadership of the Life and Liberty Movement (which worked for greater freedom for the church). After a period as canon of Westminster Abbey, where his preaching attracted large congregations, he became bishop of Manchester in 1920. There he distinguished himself in his concern for the welfare of people of all kinds. He also took a leading part in the young ecumenical movement, attending the conferences at Lausanne (1927) and Jerusalem (1928).

From 1929 to 1942 he was archbishop of York and from 1942 to 1944 the archbishop of Canterbury. In these places of leadership he devoted himself to three aims. First, he attempted to present a reasoned exposition of the Christian faith, which is expounded in *Christian Faith and Life* (1931), *Reading in St. John's Gospel* (1939–1940), and *Nature, Man, and God* (Gifford Lectures, 1934). He emphasized the Incarnation and a Christ-centered metaphysical philosophy. Second, he worked for the union of the churches. He was president of the Edinburgh Ecumenical Conference of 1937 and in 1942 presided over the inauguration of the British Council of Churches. Third, he was passionately concerned about national and social righteousness. He was a committed Christian socialist. His popular *Christianity and the Social Order* (1942) quickly sold 139,000 copies in the war years. P. TOON

TENNENT, GILBERT (1703–1764)
Presbyterian minister and revivalist

Born in the county of Armagh, Ireland, Gilbert Tennent immigrated to Pennsylvania in 1718 with his father, William Tennent. He received the majority of his theological education under his father and was awarded an honorary M.A. degree from Yale College in

1725. After a period of doubting his suitability for the ministry and a year of pursuing a course of medicine, he submitted himself to the Presbytery of Philadelphia and was licensed in May 1725. In December of that year he accepted a call to Newcastle, Delaware, but left abruptly after a very short time and assisted his father in the Log College. In 1726 he accepted a call to New Brunswick, New Jersey, and was ordained by the Philadelphia Presbytery in the same year. Soon after settling in New Brunswick he met Theodorus Frelinghuysen, revivalist and minister of a neighboring Dutch Reformed church. Frelinghuysen's evangelistic fervor and personal piety left a lasting impression on the young Tennent and helped to shape his powerful preaching style and revivalist agenda. He routinely attacked the formal religion of his day as harboring dead forms of piety and emphasized the necessity of a personal experience of conversion evidenced by moral reformation.

Tennent met George Whitefield in November 1739, and a year later, at the invitation of several New England ministers, was persuaded by Whitefield to accompany him on a preaching tour of New England. He spent almost three months in Boston and preached in nearly twenty other towns of Massachusetts and Connecticut with great success. In the middle colonies he became the leader of the Great Awakening and the center of controversy. As the leader of the newly formed New Brunswick Presbytery (1738), he was responsible for the first split in the Presbyterian Church. Conflict arose over the synod's opposition to New Brunswick's support of ordaining graduates from the Log College, itinerant preaching, lay exhorters, and the revivalism of the Great Awakening. Tensions reached their zenith when, on March 8, 1740, in Nottingham, Pennsylvania, Tennent preached a sermon entitled "The Dangers of an Unconverted Ministry," in which he characterized the majority of ministers as hypocrites and unreliable guides, and then urged the people to abandon their ministry for the itinerants. The Synod of Philadelphia published a formal protest and Tennent and the New Brunswick Presbytery withdrew in 1741, causing the division between the Old Side and the New Side.

In 1743 Tennent moved to Philadelphia to pastor a newly formed New Side church, where he remained until his death on July 23, 1764. While in Philadelpia, he experienced a change of heart. Regretting his former censoriousness, he worked during the remaining years of his life for the union of the two Presbyteries, publishing toward this end *Irenicum Ecclesiasticum, or a Humble, Impartial Essay upon the Peace of Jerusalem* (1749). In 1753 he became one of the trustees of the College of New Jersey (now Princeton University) and, along with Samuel Davies, was sent to Britain (1753–1755) to raise money for the college.

C. MITCHELL

TENNENT, WILLIAM (c. 1673–1746)
Presbyterian minister and theological educator

Born probably in Scotland, Tennent was educated at the University of Edinburgh, from which he graduated with the M.A. degree in 1695. For reasons now unknown, he took orders in the Episcopal Church of Ireland, as deacon in 1704 and as priest in 1706. He is said to have acted as chaplain to a nobleman in northern Ireland, but never served an Episcopal parish. In 1718 with his wife, four sons, and a daughter, he emigrated to Philadelphia, where his wife's cousin James Logan was a prominent Pennsylvania official. In September 1718 he applied for admission as a Presbyterian minister to the Synod of Philadelphia, then in session; and after stating that he had renounced Episcopalianism because of its form of government and Arminian trends in its theology, he was accepted without reordination. Thereafter he served in East Chester, New York (1718–1720), and Bedford, New York (1720–1726); and then he accepted a call to Nashaminy, northeast of Philadelphia, where he labored until his death. There, in 1735 and 1736, he established his Log College, where he trained about a score of capable and dedicated ministers, including his three younger sons, William, John, and Charles, and Samuel Finley, who became president of the College of New Jersey (now Princeton University). Tennent was a teacher of unusual ability, who succeeded in imparting to his students a deep concern for a vital religious faith. The graduates of his Log College became effective exponents of that evangelical revival known as the Great Awakening, which did much to revitalize American Protestantism in the 1730s and 1740s. At the same time, they contributed to the Old Side–New Side schism that divided the Presbyterian Church between 1741 and 1758. N. V. HOPE

TENNYSON, LORD ALFRED
(1809–1892)
English poet

The most popular English poet of the latter half of the nineteenth century, Tennyson was born in Somersby, Lincolnshire, the son of a country rector. He and his brother began to write verse and published a volume titled *Poems by Two Brothers* in 1827, the year Alfred left for Cambridge. He remained there until 1831, when financial need obligated him to return home, where he devoted himself to the craft of poetry. At Cambridge he developed a close friendship with Arthur Henry Hallam, who later became engaged to Tennyson's sister. Hallam's sudden death in Vienna at age twenty-two led to the publication of a long sequence of elegies by the poet in tribute to his friend. Finally completed and published in 1850, *In Memoriam,* is generally considered to be Tennyson's finest work. Some parts of the poem have been made into hymns. Also in 1850 Tennyson was appointed Poet Laureate as successor to William Wordsworth.

His earlier poems—"Mariana," "The Palace of Art," "The Lotus Eaters," "The Lady of Shalott," "Ulysses," and "Locksley Hall"—won for Tennyson wide acclaim. His poetry is always touched with the spirit of romanticism that early reminded critics of Keats. With the publication of *In Memoriam* Tennyson was secure, his income substantial, enabling him to buy a house in the

country and to marry Emily Sellwood. *Idylls of the King,* a twelve-part narrative poem based on the Arthurian legends, occupied much of the latter part of Tennyson's life. A good portion of Tennyson's work is idealistic and morally high-minded. His religious convictions were expressed in terms of hope for an afterlife, but these hopes were rarely supported by strong doctrinal commitment. "Crossing the Bar," his best known single poem, was written when the poet was eighty years old. Tennyson's "Strong Son of God, Immortal Love" (1850) found its way into Christian hymnody when it was set to music by Leo Sowerby in 1941. He was buried in Westminster Abbey next to Robert Browning. P. M. BECHTEL

TERESA, MOTHER
See MOTHER TERESA

TERESA OF AVILA (1515–1582)
Spanish mystic; founder of a reformed Carmelite order, the Discalced (barefooted) Carmelites

Calling herself Teresa of Jesus, she became a nun at sixteen; but even the relaxed or mitigated rule of the community in which she lived was too restrictive for her, and she suffered both emotionally and physically. Yet, little by little she sought new depths of contemplation and at age forty experienced a trance in which for the first time she had a vision of Christ. Increasing spiritual sensitivity led also to increasing dissatisfaction with the mitigated rule, and the combination of spiritual accomplishment and dissatisfaction led Teresa to dispute with local authorities and those of her order. Thus she resolved to found a reformed order. This was accomplished, against protests, in 1562. From the new convent of St. Joseph in Avila, Teresa, a semi-invalid, traveled incessantly throughout Spain, founding and administering seventeen convents, all obedient to the original, strict, Carmelite rule. This rule emphasized strict enclosure, discipline, and mental prayer. She was herself a model of rigorous discipline, wearing a hair shirt and often scourging herself.

A very practical-minded person, with genuine genius for administration, her literary legacy, nonetheless, is her books on the mystical way: *Autobiography* (1562), *Way of Perfection*, *Book of Foundations*, and *Interior Castle*. These brought her the title Doctor (i.e., teacher) of the Church. Her saintliness and miracles reported to have been done by her led to her canonization in 1622, only a generation after her death. P. M. BASSETT

TERESA OF LISIEUX (1873–1897)
Carmelite nun; devotional writer

Teresa was born at Alençon, Normandy. In 1886 she underwent a religious conversion and thereafter dedicated herself to monastic life. Entering the Carmelite convent at Lisieux at fifteen, she was appointed assistant novice mistress in 1893. One year before her death (1897) from tuberculosis, she volunteered to join the Carmelite missionaries in China. Her devotional book, *The Little Way*, was widely acclaimed, as was her autobiography, *The Story of a Soul*. Miracles of healing and prophecy soon were attributed to her name, and an account of these was appended in 1907 to the autobiography. Teresa was beatified in 1923 and canonized in 1925. One year later a basilica was erected in her honor at Lisieux. In 1929 she became patroness of foreign missions, and in 1947 she was named patroness of France, together with Joan of Arc. Churches and shrines dedicated to her memory often bear the title "Little Flower," reflecting the subtitle of her autobiography.
W. A. DETZLER

TERTULLIAN (c. 160–225)
African Latin theologian and moralist

Besides what is known about Tertullian through his lifelong residency in Carthage, personal facts about him can be traced only in outline. He enjoyed a superior education, including literary, rhetorical, and legal training, and instruction in Greek and Latin. Very probably he practiced law at some point. Sometime in his late thirties, Tertullian was converted to belief in Christ. He was married to a Christian wife, and after her death he remained a widower. In succeeding years, he served the church at Carthage as a gifted teacher. Out of his intense Christian commitment, Tertullian's experiences with the Carthage church prompted much dissatisfaction over perceived laxities. Consequently, about 206, he joined the Montanists, a separatist yet largely unheretical Christian sect. Eventually he led a segment of this group called the Tertullianists. Except for separatist ideas on Church life, Tertullian remained doctrinally orthodox until his death. The Tertullianists rejoined the church at Carthage several decades later.

Soon after conversion, Tertullian began the large output of Christian writings occupying his last twenty-five years. Sizable portions of this production, thirty-one Latin works, are yet extant; and these may be divided by three types of content: apologetic, dogmatic, and moral. While the moral essays exhibit a rigorist outlook, Tertullian's essentially mainstream posture changed little in the apologetic and dogmatic treatises. Within the apologetic works, most important are *Ad Nationes* and *Apologeticum*, both very early efforts. The first is a refutation of pagan slanders, such as accusations of infanticide and incest, against Christian practices; and the second offers a polished general appeal—from reason, literature, many other sources—for fair appraisal of Christian belief and life. Still other potent defenses of Christianity appear in *De testimonio animae* and *Adversus Judaeos*. Justly, some of Christianity's most time-honored sayings derive from Tertullian's apologetics: "See how they [Christians] love one another," and "The blood of the martyrs is the seed of the Church." These also are the works in which such common expressions as "If God will," "God bless," and "God grant" made their first appearance in writing.

Most of Tertullian's dogmatic works are acutely polemical in nature. In survey, the prominent writings here are *De prae-*

scriptione haereticorum, Adversus Paxean, De carne Christi, and *De resurrectione carnis.* These constitute a crucial body of works in which many of Christianity's central doctrines have their most influential initial formation. Amid numerous basic discussions, most critical are probably Tertullian's treatment of the Trinity as being three persons in one substance; the divine and human natures of Christ; the subjection of man to original sin; and Christ's virgin birth and bodily resurrection. The high significance here lies with the direct, fundamental effect Tertullian's ideas had on later expositions by Athanasius and Augustine and other church fathers, and on the Councils of Nicea (325) and Chalcedon (451) and their lasting formularies. One might note Tertullian's use of the Latin *trinitas* as the first application of the term *trinity* to Deity. In the writings against Marcion, researchers also possess a major source of knowledge about this period's heretical teachings. Although accepting Apocryphal books sometimes as revelatory, Tertullian's dogmatic writings gave authoritative status mainly just to the Old and New Testament books eventually seen as canonical.

For many people, the moral writings give Tertullian's life and teachings memorable distinction. Even before the Montanist period, this category's primary works, *De baptismo, De oratione, De paenitentia, De spectaculis, De cultu feminarum,* and *De patientia,* showed an austere approach to Christian morality. But such essays were tempered by Tertullian's wit and periodic humor (as in the remarks on patience, and his temerity to treat a virtue so personally unapparent). From the above items, the first three, all catechetical writings, were the earliest formal doctrinal works on baptism, the Lord's prayer, and penance, respectively. Containing some of Tertullian's most piquant social ideas, these also are the essays with his conservative views on Christian women and their conduct. With the departure into Montanism, Tertullian's moral discussions took on some extremist elements. This is true not so much of the earlier *De virginibus velandis, De corona,* and *De*

idololatria as it is of the later *De fuga, De ieiunio, De pudicitia,* and *De pallio.* But further, very prominent here also are basic treatments of marriage and celibacy: the pre-Montanist *Ad uxorum,* and the Montanist *De exhortatione Castitatis* and *De monogamia.* Parallel to other topics treated by Tertullian, these essays are the earliest attempts at providing systematic teaching on Christian wedlock. In this capacity, such works provide a critical disclosure of Christianity's original ideas on the principle of monogamy (i.e. marriage always a union until death), and the principle of patriarchy (i.e. marriage always led by male headship), and the strict regard early believers gave these axial marital precepts.

Tertullian's works were influenced, on the one hand, by Stoicism and Roman legalism, and on the other, a highly impetuous, obdurate personality. Yet, overall, even the Montanist writings were respectful reflections of the scriptural teachings Tertullian honored as divine revelation. Literarily, his special attainment was a pungent, aphoristic style, and a confrontational force unequalled by any other early Christian authority. Theologically, Tertullian's teachings place him among the great early Christian fathers, positioning him as founder of Latin Christian doctrine and proponent of much in orthodox Western Church dogmas as a whole. Concerning church life, Tertullian presaged Protestantism, with results similarly negative and positive, in asserting that a local body remains truly Christian even separate from the church at large. Above all an archetype of uncompromising commitment to Christ's practical demands, Tertullian left much valuable doctrinal instruction and many stirring challenges concerning Christian morality and its warfare with pagan ideology and corruption.

Except for the indicated thirty-one works, everything by Tertullian, including his Greek writings, has been lost. While Jerome and Augustine and a few others give him brief mention, Tertullian's own works are the only extensive early source of information about him. K. J. BRYER

TETZEL, JOHANN (c. 1465–1519)
Dominican prior who was criticized by
Luther for selling indulgences

Johann Tetzel is chiefly famous for his selling of indulgences, which provoked Martin Luther to write his ninety-five theses, which marked the beginning of the Reformation. Born in Leipzig, he graduated from the university in 1487 and two years later entered the Dominican convent, of which he later became prior. He early made a name for himself as a preacher of indulgences, his first major work of this type being the selling of indulgences for Cardinal-legate Raymond Peraud. In 1517 Pope Leo X made him inquisitor and commissioner of indulgences for all Germany. The same year he began preaching the indulgence to obtain funds for Albrecht of Hohenzollern, who had borrowed money from the Augsburg bankers, the Fuggers, to pay his firstfruits for his provision to the Archbishopric of Mainz, and for the financing of Leo X's extension of St. Peter's Basilica in Rome. His shameless commercialization of the indulgence provoked Luther's attack, to which Tetzel replied with 106 theses. The papal legate, von Miltitz, rebuked him for avarice, dishonesty, and sexual immorality. He was so unpopular as a result of the reform movement that he found it necessary to hide in the Dominican convent at Leipzig for fear of popular violence. It was in this convent, during Luther's debate in the city with Johann Eck on the subject of indulgences, that he died. W. S. REID

THEOBALD (died 1161)
Archbishop of Canterbury, 1138–1161

A Norman by birth, Theobald became a Benedictine monk early in life. In 1137 he was appointed abbot of Bec, the famous French monastery. A year later, though, the English church chose him as archbishop of Canterbury. While together at Lateran Council II, Pope Innocent II invested Theobald with his office. This confirmation left Henry, bishop of Winchester, disappointed. Consequently, when Henry became England's papal legate, Theobald faced numerous jurisdictional disputes. But these ended with Henry's death in 1143, and in 1150 Pope Eugenius III transferred the legate post to the archbishopric. In 1139 Theobald was the church representative who crowned Stephen, the last of England's Norman kings. Throughout Stephen's troubled reign, the archbishop was a quiet supporter, even when exiled. In the end, Theobald favored the Plantagenets' assumption of the English throne. It was he who crowned Henry II in 1154.

Theobald drew many of his era's outstanding aspiring churchmen to his residence. Numerous vital influences came to English Christianity through these individuals. Among famous figures, the most prominent was Thomas Becket, Theobald's successor. Further, it was Theobald who invited Vacarius, the Italian expert in Roman law, to England. On this basis, the archbishop had a hand in the Roman law's impact on English common law. But the archbishop was much more important to England and the canon law. Increasingly throughout western Europe, the canon law was a potent, facile instrument through Gratian's *Concordia* and attendant commentaries. And it was by Theobald's Council of London (1151), and other means, that the canon law began its pervasive affect on English morals and life. Eventually, on marriage and numerous social issues, English common law took much from the canon law. Besides his history-making church role, Theobald thus had a critical part in English juristic and social developments. During his last years, Theobald tried to keep church arguments with Henry II as irenic as possible. One of his suggestions was that a churchman assume the chancellor's post. This Henry accepted, albeit with tragic results for Thomas Becket. After 1148, John of Salisbury, the eminent scholar, served as Theobald's secretary. This enhanced English Christianity's involvement in humanist learning and literature. Editions of *John of Salisbury's Works,* as well as Migne's *Patrologia Latina,* contain many of the archbishop's letters.

K. J. BRYER

THEODORE (602–690)

Archbishop of Canterbury, 668–690

Born in Tarsus (south Asia Minor), Theodore was an eastern church scholar who migrated to Rome. He became admired for both his knowledge and his administrative gifts. In 667, these gifts led Pope Vitalian to make Theodore archbishop of Canterbury. Simultaneously, the pope also commissioned Hadrian, a Latin scholar, and Benedict Biscop, an English churchman, to assist Theodore in England. This was to ensure that Western and Roman—not Eastern—church practices arose from the archbishop's leadership. In 668, as Theodore assumed his post, Hadrian was appointed his archepiscopal assistant. Biscop went on to found many of northern England's leading monasteries. The three worked well together until their deaths. Despite his advanced age, Theodore became one of his office's most energetic, influential occupants.

Theodore's efforts had immediate, profound effects on English Christianity. First, based in Theodore's directives, Hadrian's headship at the Canterbury archepiscopal school was foundational for English church scholarship. Other academic groundwork also resulted from Biscop's monastic endowments. This soon produced such great figures as Aldheim at Canterbury, Bede at Jarrow, and many scholarly descendants. Further, rooted in his diocesan changes, the archbishop also unified English church administration for the first time. This was achieved both by asserting supremacy claims and by filling and reassigning various prominent posts. In 669, for example, Theodore established Wilfrid as bishop of York. Under Wilfrid's headship, the diocese of York gained a preeminence second only to Canterbury's. Theodore did try to divide York into four parts about ten years later. By that time, however, York was secure as England's chief northern church center. Unquestionably, all subsequent English church unity and subdivision owes much to Theodore's fundamental work. Moreover, English political unity lagged for centuries. Consequently, the archbishop's acts were basic to England's general unification as well.

In 673, after much preparation, Theodore convoked the Synod of Hertford. This was England's first general church council. Primarily, Hertford's decrees confirmed Theodore's organizational decisions, outlining limits for the church's varied elements. But most importantly, the Synod also now officially affirmed Roman Christian traditions as English church requirements. In its decree establishing Rome's Easter practices, Hertford plainly denied further English use of Celtic church customs. Among other matters, the Synod also supported the Western church's strict marriage and divorce traditions. Significantly, this overruled Theodore's support for liberal Eastern church rules. All the Synod's decrees were basic to England's subsequent church life, as well as English society at large. Then further, it was Theodore's *Penitential* that instigated wide use of confessional and moral instruction books in England. For the next six hundred years, this instrument had deep influences on English law and social custom.

In general, Theodore's work was integral to the permanence that Roman Christianity gained in the English church. Not one of Theodore's scholarly works has been preserved. His *Penitential*, however, exists in many early and modern editions.

K. J. BRYER

THEODORE OF MOPSUESTIA (c. 350–427)

Bishop of Mopsuestia in Cilicia, 392–427

Raised in Antioch by wealthy parents, Theodore studied under eminent rhetorician and philosopher Libanius. Under the influence of his fellow student John Chrysostom, he entered the monastic school of Diodore (of Tarsus) around 369. When he left the monastery nearly ten years later to pursue marriage and a career in law, it was John who encouraged him to return to the monastery. Theodore returned as a pupil but later served as a teacher until his election as archbishop of Mopsuestia. He is best known as the founder of Antiochene Christology, which asserted the two independent natures of Christ. Because the eternal God could not be born, suffer, or die, Theodore concluded that Jesus was born simply a man. He *became* the Son of God through the indwelling of the divine Logos, somewhat like the indwelling of the Spirit in the prophets and apostles. However, the man Jesus and the divine Logos were uniquely related by a moral union initiated by divine grace and perfected by the human obedience of Jesus. His emphasis on both the human and divine natures of Christ made him an effective opponent of Arianism and Apollinarianism and won him honor as an orthodox teacher throughout his lifetime. Shortly after his death, however, his most famous student, Nestorius, was anathematized at the Council of Ephesus in 431. In the controversy that followed the council, Theodore was posthumously condemned at the Council of Constantinople in 553.

Theodore wrote extensive biblical commentaries defending the literal and typological interpretation of Scripture, characteristic of the Antiochene tradition. While most of his writings are not extant, fragments of such works as *Commentary on the Minor Prophets* and *Disputation with Macedonians* still exist. C. WHITACRE

THEODORET (c. 393–c. 458)
Bishop, theologian, and Bible commentator

Born into a wealthy family in Antioch, Theodoret received an excellent classical education. When his parents died he decided to enter monastic life. About the age of thirty-three he was made bishop of Cyrrhus (Syria), becoming thereby a prominent figure in church activities.

Theodoret was a prolific writer. His commentaries, exegeting most of the books of Scripture, stand somewhere between the literal and allegorical interpretations. He wrote polemics against Jews, Persians, and Greek paganism. Occasionally he adopted the Platonic style of dialogue, as in a debate between proponents of orthodoxy and of the Monophysite heresy. Theodoret also compiled a continuation of Eusebius's history from the year 323 to 428, a discussion of

heresies down to Eutyches, and a book about the Syrian monks.

A leading heresy of the time, which Theodoret vigorously opposed, was Apollinarianism. In comparison to it he gave the impression of being favorable to Nestorianism. Emperor Theodosius II thereupon sent him back to his monastery. Theodoret appealed to the pope; and the next emperor, Marcian, restored him to his see. Present at the Council of Chalcedon in 451, he joined in anathematizing Nestorius. He refused, however, to accept the interchange of divine and human characteristics. There is still some question about his precise doctrine of Christ. His life after the council of Chalcedon has not been recorded.
A. CABANISS

THEODOSIUS I (347–395)
Roman emperor, 379–395

Named after his father, Theodosius was born to a distinguished Spanish family. The elder Theodosius was an important Roman general and landowner. In 378, on his uncle Valens's death, Gratian became emperor of Rome. A year later, Gratian asked Theodosius, well-known through his father, to serve as coemperor for Rome's eastern provinces. Even before Gratian died in 383, Theodosius was the entire empire's dominant ruler. He was the last emperor to give simultaneous rule to Rome's Eastern and Western segments.

Amid years plainly revealing Rome's disintegration, Theodosius achieved a notable stability for the empire. Nonetheless, throughout his reign, difficulties with both insurrectionists and invaders were severe. Probably the empire's chief overt problem came from the breach of Rome's defenses in the western Goths' momentous victory at Adrianople in 378. For several years Theodosius campaigned strenuously against the Goths, and in 382 he settled for a treaty, one mainly favorable to the Goths and their occupation of Rome's northern sections. Yet various other invaders and usurpers Theodosius repulsed in effective fashion, bringing the empire comparatively good order for the times.

But it was not military operations or political changes, but religious practices and the use of religion for Rome's improvement, that primarily occupied Theodosius's years as emperor. Early in life Theodosius had become a seriously committed Christian, and now he strove not only to conform his own actions to Christian tenets, but he also tried to establish Christian ideas and standards in the populace at large. First, toward these ends, Theodosius eliminated his office's pagan title, pontifex maximus, and then promulgated laws against pagan religious accoutrements in government and other public affairs. Then, going further, he also constructed laws that essentially and practically made Christianity the empire's official religion. The critical enactments here were the provisions specifying orthodox doctrine as the church's only legally acceptable creed, this outlawing all other positions, especially Arianism, the nearly dominant heterodoxy of the Eastern empire, a teaching Theodosius saw as dangerous.

Theodosius did not stop simply at the creation of laws on orthodox religion. He also gave direct attention to their enforcement and embedment in the church and empire at large. Thus detailed edicts were drawn up against the Manicheans and other heretical and separatist groups. And, particularly in and around Constantinople, Theodosius oversaw the deposition of as many Arian bishops as possible. The emperor also battled Arianism with numerous positive means. Primarily, this entailed many summonings of church gatherings, including the Council of Constantinople (381), a meeting designed to bring orthodox and Arian leaders face to face. Basically, Theodosius sought peaceful agreement between orthodox and Arian Christians if feasible. Some degree of settlement was reached, but in the end, the emperor's elevation of orthodoxy clearly did not defeat Arianism. Theodosius was unmistakably a genuine believer who sought the broad furtherance of true Christianity. And however egregious his political establishment of religion, his efforts, in many ways, did stimulate Christianity and its benefits within the empire as a whole.

Original information on Theodosius I may be obtained from lengthy sections in works by Socrates, Sozomen, Libanius, Zosimus, and other fifth-century church historians. Mommsen has produced an edition of the *Codex Theodosianus*. K. J. BRYER

THIERRY OF CHARTRES
(c. 1100–c. 1156)
French philosopher and theologian

Thierry's Latinized name was Theodericus Brito, the last probably indicating Britain or Brittany as his place of origin. He and his work were known by his bishop, John of Salisbury (an Englishman), and by Peter Abelard. After teaching for a while in Paris (c. 1139), and at Chartres, he was made chancellor of the diocese of Chartres in 1141. There he entered into the stream of grammatical and humanistic learning that made Chartres famous. His erudition gave him notoriety as the leading philosopher of Europe. His stress on the inadequacy of human language to express the meaning of theology, and the speculative quality of his thought, leaned toward a quasi-mysticism.

At about the age of fifty, Thierry retired from public affairs and entered the quiet of monastic seclusion. He wrote commentaries on the great pagan humanist Cicero, on the great Christian humanist Boethius, and on the Heptateuch, especially Genesis, thereby displaying a vast range of learning. Despite his significance for his time, materials for a biography are remarkably sparse. He had a brother, Bernard, who preceded him as a teacher at Chartres, and a pupil Bernard Silvestris of Tours, both of whom should be distinguished from the abbot of Clairvaux of the same name and approximately the same time. The humane learning of Chartres with its stress on grammar did not last long before the emerging and growing Parisian stress on Aristotle. The latter ultimately dominated the earlier Platonism that had been so characteristic until the High Middle Ages.
A. CABANISS

THOBURN, JAMES MILLS (1836–1922)
Methodist missionary bishop

Born at St. Clairsville, Ohio, Thoburn was educated at Allegheny College, Pennsylvania, where he graduated in 1857. After preaching in several churches in Ohio from 1857 to 1859 and being ordained to the Methodist ministry in 1858, Thoburn went out to India as a missionary in 1859. There he served in various stations, and in 1888 was appointed Bishop of India and Malaysia—the first resident Methodist bishop in Asia. He founded Methodism in Burma in 1879, in Malaysia in 1885, and in the Philippines in 1899. His missionary program embraced wide-ranging medical and social work, and education for both girls and boys; and under his leadership an organizational structure was developed for Methodism in India, which in principle covered the whole country. He authored various books, including the autobiographical volume *My Missionary Apprenticeship* (1886); *The Life of Isabella Thoburn*—his sister and fellow missionary to India (1903); and *The Christian Conquest of India* (1906). John R. Mott called him "possibly the greatest ecclesiastic of the nineteenth century." N. V. HOPE

THOMAS, NORMAN MATTOON (1884–1968)
Presbyterian minister; socialist leader

Born in Marion, Ohio, Thomas was educated at Princeton University and Union Theological Seminary, New York. In 1911 he was ordained to the Presbyterian ministry and became pastor of the East Harlem Church and chairman of the American Parish, a New York City Settlement House. In 1918 he resigned from both these positions and was appointed secretary of the recently formed pacifist organization, the Fellowship of Reconciliation (FOR). He founded the FOR's magazine *The World Tomorrow* and edited it for the next three years. In 1921 he became associate editor of the liberal weekly *The Nation,* and in 1922 executive coordinator of the League for Industrial Democracy, a position which he held for ten years. In 1931 he demitted the ministry. A member of the Socialist party since 1918, Thomas became one of its leading spokesmen and a candidate for public office on its behalf. He ran for governor of New York in 1924, for mayor of New York City in 1925 and 1929, and for the presidency of the United States six successive times between 1928 and 1948, but never won any election.

Following World War II, as chairman of the Post-War World Council, Thomas devoted much of his energy to the problem of international peace; and in the 1960s he urged the cessation of the Vietnam war. He was a popular radio speaker and the author of numerous articles and books. Among the latter were *The Conscientious Objector in America* (1923), *A Socialist's Faith* (1951), and *Socialism Re-examined* (1963). N. V. HOPE

THOMAS, OWEN (1812–1891)
Welsh preacher and theologian

Born in Holyhead, the son of a stonemason, Thomas took up his father's occupation before becoming a schoolmaster. He felt a call to the ordained ministry and studied first at Bala College, Wales, and then at Edinburgh University. At the age of thirty-two he was ordained into the ministry of the Calvinistic Methodist Church (now the Presbyterian Church in Wales). He spent the major part of his ministry serving two Welsh congregations in Liverpool (1865–1871, and 1871 to his death). In 1868 and 1888 he was moderator of the assembly of his church. In his day he was one of the most eloquent of Welsh preachers.

He combined his pastoral and preaching duties with historical and theological writing. He was given the D.D. degree by Princeton University in recognition of his academic labors. These included a translation into Welsh of three important books: Kitto's New Testament commentary, and two major biographies of great Welsh preachers, John Jones (1796–1857) and Henry Rees (1798–1869). And he wrote most of the articles in the ten-volume Welsh encyclopedia, *Gwyddoniadur* (1857–1877). P. TOON

THOMAS À KEMPIS
(1379 or 1380–1471)
The best-known representative of the Brethren of the Common Life (Devotio moderna); usually thought to be the author of the Imitation of Christ

Thomas Hemerken was born in Kempen, a town in the Rhine valley not far from Cologne. From this town Thomas got his name. He was the younger of two sons in a peasant family. In 1392 Thomas entered the famous cathedral school at Deventer, a town in the Yssel valley in what is now the Netherlands.

Through his older brother, John, who had earlier gone to Windesheim, near Deventer, Thomas came into contact with Florentius Radewijns, a highly respected member of the Brethren of the Common Life and a famous preacher. Thomas was not wealthy and was unable to pay for his board and lodging, so Radewijns invited him to stay at his house. Radewijns provided him with books and paid his tuition at the school of St. Lebwin's. (Radewijns's support of Thomas was typical among members of the Brethren of the Common Life, who aided and educated many poor youngsters.) Later Thomas seems to have lived with the Brethren in the Brethren house at Deventer. He wrote about this time: "All I earned, I gave to the community. Here I learned to read and write the Holy Scriptures and books on moral subjects, but it was chiefly through the sweet conversation of the Brethren that I was inspired yet more strongly to despise the world. I took pleasure in their godly conduct."

About 1399 Thomas à Kempis went to Mount St. Agnes, a newly founded monastery of the Canons Regular of St. Augustine. He was ordained a priest about 1413 and spent the remainder of his life there, except for a brief period when the community moved. He was sub-prior in 1425 and again in 1448. Other monks were greatly impressed with his great religious fervor. By the time he died, his name had made the monastery of Mount St. Agnes well known.

Thomas copied many manuscripts, which was one of the main activities of the Brethren. He wrote devotional works, sermons, and chronicles. His *Soliloquy of the Soul* contains practical counsels on how to be faithful to the movements of grace. Other works treat poverty, humility, and chastity, as well as give counsel to the person in charge of the goods of the monastery. There are sermons to novices and a number of lives of saints. However, the principal work for which Thomas is known is the *Imitation of Christ,* a classic devotional.

Thomas's life and work are the best-known examples of the religious renewal brought about by the Brethren of the Common Life. Thomas and his fellow brethren did much to raise the level of religious life in the Low Countries, both through their work with the common people and through reform of existing religious institutions, such as monasteries and convents. Although the Brethren did not join the Protestant Reformation, their work among the common people undoubtedly contributed much to the vast success of the Reformation in the Low Countries. A. VOS

THOMPSON, FRANCIS (1859–1907)
English poet

Thompson was born at Preston, Lancashire, where his father was a doctor. Following his parents' conversion to Roman Catholicism, Thompson was educated in that faith with some thought of his being prepared for the priesthood. Rejecting that prospect, Thompson began the study of medicine at Owen's College, Manchester. However, he was more interested in literature than medicine and failed his examinations. In London, ill and impoverished, he took to the use of opium, which habit reduced him to selling matches and papers. Thompson was rescued by Wilfred Meynell, a magazine editor who recognized his poetic talents. Two of his poems published in *Merry England* by Meynell won the commendation of Browning. His first volume, *Poems* (1893), was also favorably received. *Sister Songs,* dedicated to the Meynells' children, appeared in 1895 and *New Poems* in 1897. Thompson's output was not impressive, but a few of his poems are notable. *The Hound of Heaven,* his best poem and best known, is generally regarded as one of the finest odes in English literature, in spite of its rather ornate language. In the poem the fugitive sinner seeks to escape the relentless pursuit of God, but the divine love is greater than the sin of man—the hunted is finally brought to bay. Thompson was much attracted to Richard Crashaw, the seventeenth-century Roman Catholic devotional poet, with whom he is frequently compared. He died of tuberculosis in London.

P. M. BECHTEL

THOMSON, WILLIAM (LORD KELVIN) (1824–1907)

Irish scientist and inventor

Born at Belfast and educated at Glasgow, Cambridge, and Paris, Thomson made his mark in mathematics and physical science. As Professor of Natural History at Glasgow (1846–1899), he concentrated on developing the hypothesis of Sadi Carnot in 1824 and James Prescott Joule in 1847 that work and heat were convertible. In papers to the Royal Society of Edinburgh in 1851 and 1854 he formulated the two great laws of thermodynamics—of equivalence and transformation—and later enunciated the doctrine of available energy. Throughout his long life he sought practical applications of scientific work. He made great improvements in signalling apparatus, invented a sounding machine for determining depths at sea (1872), and made a new form of mariner's compass (1873–1878). It was mainly due to his refined researches into the transmission of electric currents in submarine cables that the Atlantic cable was successful (1866). He was the first to define the Absolute or Kelvin Scale of temperature. In 1892 he was raised to the peerage and awarded the Order of Merit, and in 1902 made a Privy Councillor. In a day when it was widely assumed that religion and science were of necessity hostile to one another, he held to a strong personal religious faith. He was buried in Westminster Abbey.

N. HILLYER

THOREAU, HENRY DAVID (1817–1862)

American philosopher and writer

Thoreau was born in Concord, Massachusetts, the son of a pencil maker. As a boy he roamed the woods of the area and developed a lifelong love of nature. At sixteen, he entered Harvard, where he familiarized himself with the classics and English literature. After graduation he returned to Concord, where he worked with his father for a year in pencil making. From 1838 to 1841 he ran a private school and developed a friendship with the famous townsman Ralph Waldo Emerson. For two years (1841–1843) Thoreau lived with the Emerson family, earning his keep as a handyman. During his residence with Emerson, Thoreau absorbed the Transcendentalist teachings of Emerson and became a member of the Transcendentalist Club. Transcendentalism taught that man has the capacity of knowing the truth intuitively and of attaining knowledge transcending the reach of the senses. It is more of a philosophical concept than a religion, though some of Thoreau's contemporaries seemed to use it as a substitute for religion.

In March 1845 Thoreau borrowed an axe and on a small plot of ground purchased from Emerson built a cabin at Walden Pond, about a mile from Concord. There he lived alone for two years and two months, his purpose being, he wrote, "not to live cheaply nor to live dearly, but to transact some private business." In this experiment Thoreau wished to free himself from the burdens that, he believed, kept most people from devoting themselves to life's highest values. At Walden he watched the seasons come and go, cultivated his garden, observed the wild life, occasionally entertained a guest in his one-room cabin. Above all, he kept notes of his experiences that grew into *Walden* (1854), one of the most distinguished American books for its beauty of style and depth of thought. Thoreau's most famous single essay is "Civil Disobedience," which came out of his imprisonment for one night in 1845 for failure to pay his poll tax. *A Week on the Concord and Merrimack Rivers* (1849) describes a trip that Thoreau made with his brother in 1839. Though *Walden* has had great popularity in the twentieth century, neither it nor any of Thoreau's other works sold well in his lifetime.

Thoreau had a high sense of social justice, self-reliance, and moral obligation, but his theological sympathies were Unitarian rather than Christian. P. M. BECHTEL

THORNTON, HENRY (1760–1815)
Christian philanthropist and economist

Thornton's father, John, was a leading layman of the Evangelical party of the Church of England and a great financial supporter of evangelical schemes. Henry was a partner for a brief period in his father's business before becoming a partner in a London bank. In 1782 he was elected to Parliament as member for Southwark and kept the seat all his working life. Though not a good debater, he was a recognized authority on financial matters. His *Enquiry into the Nature and Effects of the Paper Credit of Great Britain* (1802) was highly valued by those involved or interested in economics.

He was a member of the influential evangelical club known as the Clapham Sect. At his home in Battersea Rise on Clapham Common the group met and planned its major work for the liberation of slaves and the formation of the colony of Sierre Leone. Thornton was heavily committed financially in these expressions of Christian social concern. He was also treasurer of the Church Missionary Society and of the British and Foreign Bible Society. Until his marriage in 1796 he gave away six-sevenths of his income; after his marriage he reduced this to one-third. In his will he deliberately left his children only nominal amounts of money. After his death Sir R. Inglis published some of Thornton's religious writings—such as *Family Prayers* and *Lectures on the Ten Commandments*. P. TOON

TILAK, NARAYAN VAMAN (1862–1919)
Marathi hymn writer and poet

Tilak was born a Chitpawan Brahman, the highest caste of the Hindus of western India, in the Ratnagiri area of Maharashtra. At the age of eighteen he married an eleven-year-old girl. As a young man he questioned Hindu orthodoxy, and became interested in Christianity after a chance encounter with an unknown European whom he met during a train journey in 1893. This European gave Tilak a New Testament, and as he read the Sermon on the Mount the Word had a profound effect on his spirit. He became a believer and was baptized in 1895 at Byculla, Bombay. Tilak began a ministry of teaching, lecturing, and writing and is most remembered, perhaps, for his hymns. Many of the hymns in the Marathi hymnbook are his. This hymnbook gave the Christians in India the opportunity to praise God in their own medium, although Tilak also translated many Western hymns into Marathi. He began a work on the life of Christ in verse, the *Christayan*, which was never completed. Although he never received formal theological training, he was ordained in the American Marathi (Presbyterian) Mission. L. LEONARD

TILLICH, PAUL (1886–1965)
German-American Protestant philosophical theologian

Paul Tillich was born in East Prussia. Following research at Breslau and Halle and an army chaplaincy in World War I, Tillich embarked on a teaching career that took him to the Universities of Berlin, Marburg, Dresden, Leipzig, and Frankfurt. It was a period marked by an interest in philosophy, particularly that of the early nineteenth-century idealist Friedrich Schelling (1775–1854). But this was combined with contemporary existentialism and religious socialism. The advent of Hitler terminated his academic career in Germany.

Thanks to Reinhold Niebuhr (1893–1971), Tillich obtained a post at Union Theological Seminary, New York, in 1933. In 1940 he became an American citizen and subsequently held professorships at Harvard and Chicago. Tillich published a large number of shorter writings, including sermons, which attracted the attention of the intellectual public. His chief work was his three-volume *Systematic Theology* (1951–1963), which sets out the philosophical position that underlies his shorter works. After his death Tillich's widow, Hannah, published a revealing and controversial biography entitled *From Time to Time.*

To those familiar with traditional theology, Tillich's *Systematic Theology* is like a museum of Picassos. While some of the subjects have an oddly familiar look, the perspectives are often startling and strange. His whole approach has a highly abstract quality. The Bible is rarely quoted, and only occasional reference is made to the classical theologians. Instead, there is a great deal of talk about existence and being. The reason for this is Tillich's desire to investigate the structure of reality which, for him, is represented symbolically in the Bible.

Basic to Tillich's approach is his rejection of what he calls supranaturalism—belief in God over and above the world. Instead, Tillich believed in being. Tillich's God was a purely immanent God. He is the ground of our being or Being itself. At this point Tillich's position is scarcely distinguishable from pantheism. He maintained, however, that there was a break between what he called essence (or pure being) and existence (our life and that of all other creatures as it actually is). For Tillich, the biblical story of the Fall was a symbol of this alienation between ourselves and the ground of our being. The alienation is overcome by Jesus as the Christ or (to use Tillich's language) the Bearer of the New Being. For Christ lived so close to the ground of his being that in him there was no existential estrangement. This closeness to the ground of his being is for Tillich what in other theologies is the divinity of Christ. For him, Christ is the key symbolic figure who mediates the overcoming of estrangement between ourselves and the ground of our being.

All this is combined with a radical skepticism about the historical value of the Gospel accounts. For Tillich, what matters is not historical truth but the symbolic value of the biblical stories. This explains the tension between the vivid realism of Tillich's preaching and the profound historical skepticism of his other writings. A story may make great impact as a symbol giving insight into the structure of reality (as in a fictional novel, play, or film), and at the same time be without historical foundation.

Tillich's position is best described as an existential ontology, since it combines the existentialist's interest in the tensions of human existence with a theory of being. Although it was presented in a modern idiom, it was essentially a restatement of the early nineteenth-century idealism of men like Schelling, on whose writings Tillich conducted his postgraduate research. It has strong affinities with Buddhism, with which Tillich expressed considerable sympathy towards the end of his life. He rejected the need for Christian missions in Japan on the grounds that many Japanese already had a greater insight into the reality of being through their own religion than the missionaries who came to convert them.

Other important works include *The Protestant Era* (1948), *The Shaking of Foundations* (1948), *The New Being* (1955), *The Eternal Now* (1963), and *Morality and Beyond* (1963). C. BROWN

TINDAL, MATTHEW (1655–1733)
English proponent of Deism

Born in Devon, Tindal entered Lincoln College, Oxford, in 1673, transferred to Exeter College, and was then elected to a fellowship in law at All Souls' College. He was a high churchman as a young man but became a Roman Catholic for a short time during the reign of James II. He returned to the Church of England in 1688. The books for which he is best known were not on law but on theology. He held that God, having created the world, left it to run by the laws he placed within it. His God was transcendent but not immanent. The idea of the laws of nature featured strongly in the books. His most important publication was *Christianity as Old as the Creation, or the Gospel a Republication of the Religion of Nature* (1730). In this he denied that Christ brought anything new to mankind; he merely taught what was always evident to discerning people. Many literary opponents thought differently, and over a hundred titles appeared against his position. P. TOON

TINTORETTO (JACOPO ROBUSTI)
(1518–1594)
Italian painter

Born in Venice, the son of a dyer, Tintoretto was a largely self-taught painter (*Tintoretto* is Italian for "little dyer"). Nonetheless, his work shows the influence of Michelangelo and Titian. By 1539 he was an independent master. In 1548 the Confraternity of St. Mark sponsored a competition for the best painting of Mark delivering a slave. Tintoretto's *The Miracle of St. Mark* won this competition and brought him public fame. Between 1562 and 1566 he painted various scenes from the life of St. Mark for this group. About 1556 he began his work for the Venetian aristocracy, when he received a commission to paint canvases for the Ducal Palace. From then until the 1580s his work for the Senate covered such classical themes as *Ariadne, Venus and Bacchus,* and such historical incidents as *Frederick Barbarossa Receiving Envoys from the Pope and the Doge* and *The Battle of Zara*. His long association with the Confraternity of St. Roch began in 1564, and this provided him with a retainer of one hundred ducats per year in return for his delivering three pictures annually. Under this contract Tintoretto did some of his finest work—for example, *The Crucifixion* (1565), described by John Ruskin as "beyond all analysis and above all praise." Of almost incredible versatility, in the spirit of the Counter-Reformation Tintoretto depicted "the mighty epic of the Christian cosmology, theology and eschatology, from the Creation to the Last Judgment," with unusual imagination, power, and technical skill. He deeply influenced such later artists as El Greco and Rubens. N. V. HOPE

TISCHENDORF, LOBEGOTT FRIEDRICH KONSTANTIN VON (1815–1874)
German New Testament textual critic

Born in Lengenfeld, Tischendorf studied at Leipzig (1834–1838) under J. G. B. Winer,

a noted Greek grammarian whose grammar of New Testament Greek (1822) had become a standard for many generations. For many years thereafter Tischendorf also taught in the theology department at Leipzig. Influenced by Winer, Tischendorf developed an intense desire to utilize the most ancient manuscripts and thereby recover the purest and earliest form of the Greek New Testament. To that end Tischendorf devoted a lifetime of labor to discovering manuscripts and producing accurate editions of the Greek New Testament. In a letter to his fiancée he wrote, "I am confronted with a sacred task, the struggle to regain the original form of the New Testament." In fulfillment of his desire, he discovered Codex Sinaiticus, deciphered the palimpsest Codex Ephraemi Rescriptus, collated countless manuscripts, and produced several editions of the Greek New Testament (the eighth edition is the best).

Of all Tischendorf's accomplishments, the best known is his discovery of Codex Sinaiticus at St. Catherine's Monastery (located near Mount Sinai). The manuscript, dated around A.D. 360 to 375, is one of the two oldest vellum (treated animal hide) manuscripts of the Greek New Testament. The first time Tischendorf visited the monastery (1844), he retrieved several leaves of an ancient Septuagint from a wastebasket. Many other leaves, he was told, had already been used to stoke fires! On another visit (1859) he was shown a copy of the Greek Scriptures (containing books of the Old Testament and all of the New Testament) by the steward of the monastery. Recognizing it as the oldest extant copy of the Greek Scriptures, Tischendorf attempted to purchase the manuscript but was refused. After making a transcription of the text, Tischendorf did some political maneuvering wherein the czar of Russia was given the manuscript in exchange for favors conferred upon the authorities of the monastery. Tischendorf greatly used the textual evidence of Codex Sinaiticus in preparing his critical editions of the Greek New Testament. P. W. COMFORT

TOLKIEN, J. R. R. (JOHN RONALD REUEL) (1892–1973)

Authority on Anglo-Saxon and Middle English literature; author of mythopoetic tales

Born in Bloemfontein, South Africa, J. R. R. Tolkien graduated from Oxford and later became professor at Merton College. He was, however, far better known among millions for *The Hobbit* (1937) and a lengthy story called *The Lord of the Rings* (1954–1955). The latter is perhaps the best example of mythopoetic creation in this century. It is the story of a gentle and peace-loving Hobbit who prefers, above everything else, to lead a quiet and uneventful life but who is called upon, and quietly accepts the commission, to save the whole of Middle-earth. He can do this only by destroying a powerful ring that is sought by Sauron (an evil spirit) and his henchmen, the Black Riders. He does this, finally, with the aid of another Hobbit, but almost at the cost of their lives. *The Lord of the Rings* is an exciting story, and some readers find nothing more in it than that. Yet it is difficult to avoid the intuition of deeper meaning, and in the latter part of his life Tolkien stated this meaning to be vitally Christian. C. KILBY

TOLSTOY, LEO (1828–1910)

Russian novelist

Tolstoy, born of a noble Russian family, attempted throughout much of his life to alleviate the suffering that surrounded him. In 1845 he entered the university but became restless with academic life and was unable or unwilling to concentrate on his work. He left two years later and returned to the family estate with serious intentions of helping the peasants who were working the lands. Under the influence of Jean-Jacques Rousseau's writings, he tried to empathize with the problems of the serfs, but at that time they were only suspicious of his interests.

While in the army at Sebastapol during the Crimean War, he wrote *Tales from Sebastapol* (1853–1855), which won him instant literary fame. Between 1857 and 1861, after the war, he made three trips to the continent; he visited Germany, Italy, Paris, Lucerne, and London. On his return he settled at Yasnaya Polyana, ran a school for peasants' children for two years, and ultimately became the father of thirteen children. He set to work writing again soon after his marriage, and began *War and Peace* (1863–1869) and *Anna Karenina* (1873–1877), his two greatest literary achievements. *War and Peace* has to do not exclusively with the conflict between one half of Europe and the other, but rather it also embodies the struggling movements of human souls from war to peace. It is further the story of love—love between men and women, love of country, but particularly Christian love. *Anna Karenina* is a probing story of multifaceted Russian society, including "rules" for happiness in family life as well as the complex meaning of life and death.

In 1873 two of Tolstoy's children died, and he became more troubled and restless than usual. He began to study the Bible and subsequently yearned to serve God. In 1880 he devoted himself to a life of physical labor. He rose at dawn and worked in the fields, helping the poor with their crops. He volunteered for census taking, a job that allowed him to see misery among the poor. This condition so sickened him that had his family and government permitted, he would have given up all he owned. *What Are We to Do?* (1886) is a graphic record of his discoveries while taking the census. In 1888 he decided that he could no longer remain a landed proprietor; he gave everything he owned over to his wife and family and wrote tales exposing the evils to which peasants were subjected. During this same period Tolstoy wrote *My Confession* (1879–1882), a statement of his relentless spiritual pilgrimage. Other writings include *My Religion* (1883), *The Death of Ivan Ilyich* (1886), *The Kreutzer Sonata* (1891), and *What Is Art?* (1897).

In 1895 Tolstoy rushed to the defense of a sect of pacifists, the Dukhobors, who were persecuted for not serving in the army, and won sympathy for them all over the world. Because of this sect, he wrote *Resurrection*

(1899), which depicted the essence of his mature views on most fundamental questions of life. The work contained an attack on the Orthodox Church, and the Synod excommunicated Tolstoy. Included in his response was: "I believe that the will of God is most intelligibly expressed in the teachings of the man Jesus." E. B. BATSON

TOMLINSON, AMBROSE JESSUP
(1865–1943)
Missionary to Appalachia; early leader of the Church of God

Born into a Quaker household near Westfield, Indiana, Tomlinson became a dedicated Christian in 1892. Moving to North Carolina, he became a door-to-door salesman for the American Bible Society. During this time he came under the influence of Richard G. Spurling, who was influential in starting the Pentecostal Church of God movement in Tennessee. Tomlinson joined the group in 1896 and rapidly rose to leadership status. From 1903 to 1923 he was designated "moderator" and "general overseer." Shortly after he became moderator the group decided their organization should be called the Church of God to indicate biblical patterns of worship, and in 1908 headquarters were established at Cleveland, Tennessee. In addition to faith in the baptism of the Holy Spirit, the church stressed bodily healing.

By 1922 the Church of God had 666 churches with over twenty-one thousand members. In 1921 a constitution was adopted that divided Tomlinson's authority between more elders and committees. A schism developed, and thereafter the churches under Tomlinson's headship designated themselves the Original Church of God. Tomlinson worked very hard to build up congregations, especially in the southeastern states and as far away as the Caribbean Islands, with mission stations around the world. After his death two of his sons, Homer A. and M. A. Tomlinson, continued to lead new branches of the organization, known as Tomlinson groups. L. LEONARD

TORQUEMADA, TOMÁS DE
(1420–1498)
Grand Inquisitor of Spain

Possessing a paradoxical personality, Torquemada gained fame as Grand Inquisitor of Spain in the reign of Ferdinand and Isabella. Born of a distinguished family, Torquemada became a Dominican, and whatever offers of high ecclesiastical office were made to him he refused, choosing the simple life of a friar to the end of his days. Yet he insisted that pomp and grandeur attend inquisitorial activities. Though of Jewish ancestry, he was always suspicious of the faith of Jewish converts and forged the policy expelling all non-converted Jews from Spain. Declaring orthodoxy dearer than life, he retained a bodyguard.

In 1478, Pope Sixtus IV placed the Inquisition in the hands of Ferdinand and Isabella, at their urging. Their intention was to purify Christianity of allegedly widespread Judaizing. For five years, their Inquisition had fitful success. It lacked central administration. To remedy this, Isabella nominated Assistant Inquisitor Torquemada, her confessor, as Grand Inquisitor for Castile in 1483. This was approved by Pope Innocent VIII. By year's end, Torquemada was also Grand Inquisitor for Ferdinand's Aragon.

Quickly, he established tribunals in Valladolid, Seville, Jaen, Avila, Cordoba, and Villareal, then in Saragossa; and, in 1484, he presented guidelines for inquisitors. The Pope, fearful of Torquemada's zeal, insisted that he establish an appelate court. This was the *Suprema*, with Torquemada as president. Now he was papal representative, intimate of royalty, nominator of inquisitors and their superior, and funnel for any appeals of decision to Rome—the most powerful figure in Spain, except for the sovereigns, to whom he was completely loyal.

The sovereigns, in turn, fully supported Torquemada as an instrument of national unity and orthodoxy. Severe complaints from both nobility and some churchmen objecting to various Inquisition tactics were scarcely recognized. So he had powerful critics but even more powerful friends.

In 1492, aided by a fabricated tale of a

Jewish ritual infanticide, Torquemada prodded a reluctant throne to order the expulsion of all non-converted Jews. One hundred sixty thousand Jews, many of them among the intellectual and commercial elite of Spain, were forced to convert or leave.

Figures concerning the number burned at the stake during Torquemada's presidency vary from two thousand to more than ten thousand. And estimates of his character vary as widely as these figures. Generally, even the most indulgent assessments condemn Torquemada's cruelty while lauding his zeal and integrity. P. M. BASSETT

TORRANCE, THOMAS FORSYTH
(born 1913)
Scottish theologian

Born of missionary parents in Szechwan, China, Torrance was educated at the Universities of Edinburgh, Basel (Th.D., 1946), and Oxford, and taught briefly at Auburn Theological Seminary. He was ordained in the Church of Scotland and ministered at Alyth (1940–1947) and Aberdeen (1947–1950) before returning to academic life as professor of church history (1950–1952) and Christian dogmatics (1952–1979) at New College, Edinburgh. He was a cofounder of *Scottish Journal of Theology*, an editor of Karl Barth's works, and moderator of the Church of Scotland general assembly in 1976. Specially interested in the relation between science and theology, he was awarded in 1978 the Templeton Prize, given to "those who through original and pioneering ways advanced the knowledge and love of God." His numerous books include *Calvin's Doctrine of Man* (1948), *Royal Priesthood* (1955), *Theological Science* (1969), *Space, Time and Resurrection* (1976), *Divine and Contingent Order* (1981), *Reality and Scientific Theology* (1985), and *The Trinitarian Faith* (1988). J. D. DOUGLAS

TORREY, CHARLES CUTLER
(1863–1956)
Semitic scholar; biblical textual critic

Born in East Hardwick, Vermont, Torrey

was educated at Bowdoin College (A.B., 1884), Andover Seminary (B.D. 1889), and Strassburg University (Ph.D., 1892). From 1892 to 1900 he was instructor in Semitic languages at Andover Seminary. Between 1900 and 1932 he was professor of Semitic languages at Yale University, and on his retirement he was made professor emeritus. He founded the American School of Oriental Research in Jerusalem, serving as its first president. As an Old Testament scholar he offered a fresh critical appraisal and reconstruction of Ezra and Nehemiah in *The Composition and Historical Value of Ezra-Nehemiah* (1896). In *The Second Isaiah: A New Interpretation* (1920) he argued that Isaiah 34–35 and 40–66 should be dated 400 B.C. In several volumes—*Translations Made from the Original Aramaic Gospels* (1912); *The Four Gospels: A New Translation* (1933); and *Our Translated Gospels* (1936)—Torrey argued that the four Gospels of the New Testament are Greek translations from Aramaic originals—a viewpoint that, however, has not found widespread scholarly acceptance. Torrey's Islamic studies bore fruit in *The Mohammedan Conquest of Egypt and North Africa* (1901) and *The Jewish Foundation of Islam* (1932). N. V. HOPE

TORREY, REUBEN ARCHER
(1856–1928)
Independent Congregationalist educator; evangelist

Son of a Hoboken, New Jersey, family, Torrey graduated from Yale University and Yale Divinity School. He was ordained in 1883 as a Congregationalist minister. Moving to Minneapolis, he served as a pastor and missions supervisor (1883–1889). In 1889 D. L. Moody asked Torrey to become the first superintendent of the Moody Bible Institute (then Institute of the Chicago Evangelistic Society). He remained in this post until 1908, laying the strong foundations the Institute displayed in its later development. From 1894 to 1906 Torrey served also as pastor of Chicago's Moody Memorial Church (then Chicago Avenue Church). Further, in the years 1902 to 1906, Torrey pursued his great interest in mass evangelism with Charles M. Alexander. This involved a remarkable series of overseas tours, including meetings in Australia, New Zealand, India, China, Japan, Germany, Great Britain, Canada, and elsewhere.

Torrey consented in 1912 to head the newly formed Bible Institute of Los Angeles (Biola). Again his leadership was foundational for an institution destined for enlargement and wide-ranging service. Torrey stayed at Biola until 1924. In addition, for most of these years he was pastor of the Church of the Open Door in downtown Los Angeles. Until 1911, he also continued his evangelistic campaigns in the United States and Canada. Despite his various demanding duties, Torrey produced a large number of written works. These were notable for their acute opposition to Protestant liberalism and advocacy of highly conservative doctrine and practice. Torrey was one of the compilers of *The Fundamentals,* for which he wrote many famous articles expounding conservative Protestantism (published from 1910 to 1915). In his later years, Torrey was active in summer Bible conference activities. He also returned to Moody Bible Institute as a lecturer from 1924 to 1928. Torrey carried out several crucial roles and wide-reaching ministries that had few parallels among American leaders of conservative Protestantism in the early twentieth century. K. J. BRYER

TOZER, A. W. (AIDEN WILSON) (1897–1963)
Christian writer

Born in Newburg, Pennsylvania, Tozer was converted to Christ at the age of eighteen. Without any formal education beyond grade school, in 1919 he began a lifelong ministry of pastoring in several Christian and Missionary Alliance churches in the United States and Canada.

Throughout his Christian life, Tozer was intensely devotional and mystical. He deeply appreciated mystics such as Fénelon, Bernard of Cluny, Bernard of Clairvaux, and Julian of Norwich. He enjoyed devotional poetry, the hymns of the mystics, and the writings of Emerson and Shakespeare. His

pulpit ministry, enriched by his spirituality and breadth of reading, was greatly appreciated and in much demand.

Tozer made his greatest impact as a writer. Many of his writings were developed from his sermons, which he arduously shaped into written form. Most of his best-known books went through this process: *The Pursuit of God* (1948), *The Divine Conquest* (1950), and *The Knowledge of the Holy* (1961). In his writings he encourages his readers to know God personally and experientially. This was his constant aspiration and proclamation. P. W. COMFORT

TRAHERNE, THOMAS (1637–1674)
English clergyman, philosopher, writer, and metaphysical poet

Thomas Traherne was the son of a Herefordshire shoemaker, descendant of an ancient Welsh family that had once been prominent. He graduated from Brasenose College, Oxford, in 1656. He then took holy orders in 1660 and retired to a country parish near Hereford.

Traherne was scarcely known even to scholars until the discovery of his poems in a manuscript in a bookstall in 1896. The poems were initially attributed to Henry Vaughan, but were identified as Traherne's by the publisher Bertram Dobell. Acclaim followed the publication of his *Poetical Works* in 1903, *The Centuries of Meditations* in 1908, and, in 1910 *Poems of Felicity.* He also wrote *Roman Forgeries* (1673), a theological polemic against the Roman Church, and *A Serious and Pathetical Contemplation of the Mercies of God* (1699). The latter showed real affinities with the works for which he is remembered, the poems and the *Centuries.*

Prominent themes are the sanctity of childhood, the validity of intuition, and the immanence of God in nature. *Centuries* focuses on the soul's journey to Glory or to a knowledge and love of all things in time and eternity.

His perception of a divinely directed cosmos surrounding individuals and active within them was a common one in the early seventeenth century. But in his preoccupation with infinity (both inner and outer) and

in his aspirations toward the Absolute he anticipated Blake and the Romantics.
E. B. BATSON

TREGELLES, SAMUEL PRIDEAUX (1813–1875)
English New Testament textual critic

Born the son of an English iron worker, Tregelles was recognized for his brilliance when he was still a teenager. However, he was unable to pursue a university career because he had been brought up among the Society of Friends. Tregelles taught himself Aramaic, Hebrew, Greek, and Welsh, then spent the rest of his life examining and collating nearly all the extant New Testament manuscripts then known. He is especially known for his work on Codex Zacynthius and Codex Vaticanus, which had been in the Vatican's library since at least 1481 but had not been made available to scholars until the middle of the nineteenth century.

Tregelles concentrated all of his efforts on publishing one Greek text, which came out in six parts, from 1857 to 1872. His goal was "to exhibit the text of the New Testament in the very words in which it has been transmitted on the evidence of ancient authority." Working according to similar principles as Lachmann (without knowing it), he compiled a text based on the evidence of the earliest manuscripts. His philosophy and methodology are described in his work, *An Account of the Printed Text of the New Testament* (1854). Along with Tischendorf, Tregelles is known as the best New Testament textual critic of the nineteenth century.

Tregelles is also known for his translation of Gesenius's *Hebrew Lexicon* into English and his books on prophecy: *The Man of Sin* (1840), *The Prophetic Visions of Daniel* (1845), and *The Hope of Christ's Second Coming* (1865). P. W. COMFORT

TRENCH, RICHARD CHENEVIX (1807–1886)
Archbishop of Dublin; biblical scholar

Born in Dublin, the son of a barrister-at-law, Trench was educated at Harrow School and Trinity College, Cambridge. He left Cambridge in 1829 and after a period of depression and despondency, which he relieved by writing poetry, was ordained in 1832. After brief curacies, he became professor of divinity in King's College, London (1846–1858), dean of Westminster (1856–1863), and finally archbishop of Dublin (1863–1884). In the latter position he opposed Prime Minister W. E. Gladstone's proposals for the disestablishment of the Church in Ireland. His efforts failed.

Apart from the publication of poetry, he wrote two well-known books on the Gospels: *Notes on the Parables of Our Lord* (1841) and *Notes on the Miracles of Our Lord* (1846). More technical were his *Study of Words* (1851) and *Synonyms of the New Testament* (1854). This interest in philology also took practical form in his activity in helping with the publication of the now famous *Oxford English Dictionary*. P. TOON

TROELTSCH, ERNST PETER WILHELM (1865–1923)
German theologian and religious philosopher

Born near Augsburg, from 1883 to 1888 Troeltsch studied theology at Erlangen, Göttingen, and Berlin. Ordained a Lutheran clergyman, he served as a curate in Munich from 1888 to 1891. In 1891 he was appointed to a lectureship at Göttingen; in 1892 he became associate professor at Bonn; and from 1894 to 1914 he occupied the chair of systematic theology at Heidelberg, and while there sat as an elected member of the Baden Upper House. In 1915 he succeeded Otto Pfleiderer as professor of philosophy at Berlin, where he remained until his death. From 1919 to 1921 he was a member of the Prussian Landtag and Undersecretary of State in the Ministry of Public Worship and Education.

Troeltsch was the systematic theologian of the "history of religions" (*religionsgeschichtliche*) school, a group of German scholars who flourished between 1890 and 1920 and employed extensive data from the comparative study of religion in their interpretation of Christianity. Since

Troeltsch's religious viewpoint was one that denied the existence of facts of a unique or absolute character in history, he came to doubt the finality and perpetual validity of Christianity among the religions of the world. Nevertheless, he asserted that "the Christian religion, tied as it is to a European and ancient heritage of civilization, is the highest form and power of spiritual life, in spite of all the defects, contradictions and impurities of our civilization"; and in his chief work, *The Social Teachings of the Christian Churches and Groups* (1912), he produced a classic treatise on Christian social thought—that is, Christian teaching concerning the most important nonreligious sociological structures that the church has encountered in its history. N. V. HOPE

TROTTER, ISABELLA LILIAS (1853–1928)
Founder of the Algiers Mission Band (AMB) in 1888; missionary to Muslim North Africa

Trotter was privileged by birth. Her father, a London businessman, gave her a private education. She developed a friendship with John Ruskin, who strongly urged that she pursue a career in art. But Trotter's conversion under Robert and Hanna Whitall Smith convinced her that a missionary career in North Africa must take priority. She began work in Algeria in 1888. Dangerous journeys into Muslim regions won converts among Arabs, the French, Jews, and Black Africans. The AMB was organized the same year, an evangelical, interdenominational agency that was more a national organization than a mission, though it received funds from the U.S.A. and Great Britain. The AMB grew from three to thirty workers, mostly single women, and merged in 1964 with the North Africa Mission. Trotter translated the New Testament into the common tongue of Algeria, produced tracts in Arabic and French, and through her society sought to establish self-governing and self-supporting North African churches. M. FACKLER

TRUMBULL, DAVID (1817–1899)
Missionary to Chile

Trumbull was born in Elizabethtown, New Jersey, and educated at Yale University and Princeton Seminary. He was influenced by Charles Hodge at Princeton and became a lifelong proponent of Reformed theology. Trumbull left for Chile in 1845, settling in Valparaiso. Non-Catholic worship was prohibited by that country's constitution, but Trumbull established the Union Church in 1847. Church members met privately for twenty years before they could erect a building for public worship.

Trumbull was an energetic churchman. He helped organize the Bible Society of Valparaiso in 1861 and served as its president. His Gospel Union (1856) brought together several Protestant denominations for cooperative effort. He conducted a school for girls over the objection of Catholic authorities. He discipled the first Spanish-speaking Protestant minister in Latin America.

A social activist, Trumbull campaigned for temperance, mixed marriages, and state-controlled cemeteries and birth records. When his reforms were adopted by the government, he became a citizen of Chile in 1886. M. FACKLER

TUCKER, ALFRED ROBERT (1849–1914)
Missionary statesman in East Africa who campaigned for equality between missionary and national citizens

Tucker was born in Woolwich, England, the son of artists. He had established a promising career in art, including an exhibit in the Royal Academy, when he decided to give up art for Anglican ordination in 1878. After seven years in parishes, he was sent out by the Church Missionary Society, having been appointed bishop of Eastern Equatorial Africa, a post he held from 1890 to 1898. He was bishop of Uganda from 1898 to 1911, though ill health compelled his return to England in 1908. His progressive views on church government were issued in a constitution that he drew up for a Native Anglican Church (adopted 1909) and in his ordination of African priests (1896). He viewed the indigenous church as one within which missionaries should serve. His contemporaries favored a clearer missionary-native church demarcation. When he resigned from the Church Missionary Society in 1912, he became canon of Durham cathedral. The greatest gains in Uganda were made by Bishop Tucker between 1890 and 1911. Of rugged physique, unflinching courage, sound judgment, and superior organizational ability, Tucker made an ideal bishop. When he arrived, his flock had numbered two hundred; before he died church membership had climbed to sixty-five thousand. Perhaps his greatest legacy is the Bishop Tucker Theological College, one of the most prestigious institutions of its kind in Africa. M. FACKLER

TURNER, CUTHBERT HAMILTON (1860–1930)
New Testament and patristic scholar; textual critic

Born in London, the son of a solicitor, Turner attended Winchester School before going to New College, Oxford. Here he gained distinction in his classical and theological studies. After a lectureship at St. John's College, he became a fellow of Madgalen. Also he acted as assistant to the regius professor of Church history, William Bright. Eventually, after serving the faculty of theology in various ways, he was appointed Dean Ireland Professor of Exegesis in 1920. From 1899 to 1902 he was the first editor of the *Journal of Theological Studies.*

His main work as a scholar was to edit the successive fasciculi (parts of a book) of his monumental collection of early documents relating to the law of the church: *Ecclesiae Occidentalis Monumenta Juris Antiquissima.* The only published interpretation he gave of this evidence was in his essay, "The Organisation of the Church," in the *Cambridge Mediaeval History* (volume one, 1911). In biblical studies his article on "Chronology of the New Testament" was printed in *Hastings Dictionary of the Bible.* It was deemed to be a masterpiece. So thorough was the way he did his textual work that when he revised Bishop Gore's book on

Church and Ministry in 1919, the finished product seemed to be a new book altogether. In churchmanship he was an Anglo-Catholic and took over the editing from H. B. Swete of the influential *Essays on the Early History of the Church and Ministry* (1918). As a textual critic he was of similar ability to the great F. J. A. Hort. P. TOON

TURRETIN, FRANCIS (1623–1687)
Noted Reformed pastor and theologian

Turretin received his education at Geneva, Leyden, Utrecht, Paris, Saumer, Montauban, and Nîmes. He became pastor of an Italian congregation in Geneva in 1648 and professor of theology in 1653—a position he held until his death.

Turretin is best known as an able and vigorous defender of orthodox Calvinism as set forth in the Canons of Dort (1619). He lived in a time of critical change when many of Dort's doctrines were being challenged by new intellectual movements. He was one of the authors of the Helvetic Consensus, a response, in part, to the "liberal" teachings of the school of Saumer, which questioned the doctrines of original sin, predestination, and inspiration of Scripture. The Calvinistic view of predestination was prominent in Turretin's own theological system. But while he held to the views of limited atonement and double predestination, he attempted to balance these with an emphasis upon God's loving and covenantal purpose.

Turretin's most significant work is his *Theological Institutes* (1688), which, along with his four-volume *Works* (1701), was reprinted in 1847. His work was very influential in the development of American theology in the nineteenth century, particularly American Presbyterianism. R. HESSELGRAVE

TYNDALE, WILLIAM (c. 1494–1536)
English reformer and Bible translator

Tyndale was born in the western part of England. In 1515 he graduated from Oxford, where he had studied the Scriptures in Greek and in Hebrew. By the time he was thirty, Tyndale had committed his life to translating the Bible from the original languages into English. His heart's desire is exemplified in a statement he made to a clergyman when refuting the view that only the clergy were qualified to read and correctly interpret the Scriptures. Tyndale said, "If God spare my life, ere many years, I will cause a boy that driveth the plough to know more of the Scripture than thou dost."

In 1523 Tyndale went to London seeking a place to work on his translation. When the bishop of London would not give him hospitality, he was provided a place by Humphrey Munmouth, a cloth merchant. Then, in 1524, Tyndale left England for Germany because the English church, which was still under the papal authority of Rome, strongly opposed putting the Bible into the hands of the laity. Tyndale first settled in Hamburg, Germany. Quite possibly, he met Luther in Wittenberg soon thereafter. Even if he didn't meet Luther, he was well acquainted with Luther's writings and Luther's German translation of the New Testament (published in 1522). Both Luther and Tyndale used the same Greek text (one compiled by Erasmus in 1516) in making their translations.

Tyndale completed his translation of the New Testament in 1525. Fifteen thousand copies, in six editions, were smuggled into England between the years 1525 and 1530. Church authorities did their best to confiscate copies of Tyndale's translation and burn them, but they couldn't stop the flow of Bibles from Germany into England. Tyndale himself could not return to England because he was considered an outlaw at the same time his translation had been banned. However, he continued to work abroad—correcting, revising, and reissuing his translation until his final revision appeared in 1535. After finishing the New Testament, Tyndale had begun work on a translation of the Hebrew Old Testament, but he did not live long enough to complete his task. He had, however, translated the Pentateuch (the first five books of the Old Testament), Jonah, and some historical books.

In May 1535, Tyndale was arrested and carried off to a castle near Brussels, where he was imprisoned. While he was in prison, an associate of his named Miles Coverdale

(1488–1569) brought to completion an entire Bible in English—based largely on Tyndale's translation of the New Testament and other Old Testament books. After being in prison for over a year, Tyndale was tried and condemned to death. He was strangled and burnt at the stake on October 6, 1536. His final words were so very poignant: "Lord, open the King of England's eyes."

P. M. BECHTEL & P. W. COMFORT

TYRRELL, GEORGE (1861–1909)
English Roman Catholic modernist theologian

Born in Dublin into an evangelical Anglican family, Tyrrell was educated at Trinity College, Dublin. He moved first toward an Anglo-Catholic and then into a Roman Catholic position. He joined the Church of Rome, trained as a Jesuit, and was ordained in 1891. After a period as a lecturer in moral theology, he went to the Jesuit Church in Farm Street, London. Here he was much in demand as a counsellor and confessor. He published two books of meditations and a series of lectures *On External Religion* (1899). His friendship with Baron Frederick von Hügel made it possible for him to meet Roman Catholics from France who shared his growing dissatisfaction with traditional, scholastic, systematic theology.

After the publication of an article on "Hell" for a magazine in 1899 his superiors decided to move him to Richmond, Yorkshire. Here, while his growing away from much traditionalism continued, he did develop his commitment to the devotional, spiritual life. His last book to gain the official stamp of approval was on prayer, *Lex Orandi* (1903). Eventually, after his request to leave the order had been refused, his superiors expelled him and also barred him from receiving the sacrament of the Lord's Supper. However, he continued to write and his views became very liberal. In a book published just after his death, *Christianity at the Cross-Roads,* he expressed doubts about the final authority of the Christian faith. He was not given a Roman Catholic burial; instead, he was buried in the Church of England parish of Storrington. P. TOON

U

UDALL, JOHN (c. 1560–1592)
Elizabethan Puritan

Educated at Christ's and Trinity Colleges, Cambridge, Udall graduated in 1581. In this period he adopted Puritan views and was friendly with John Perry, the Puritan extremist. After ordination he put his new ideas into practice in the parish of Kingston-on-Thames beginning in 1583. Here he preached to large audiences and published some of his sermons. He publicly criticized the organization of the church and the behavior of bishops. Such views were not favored by Queen Elizabeth or her advisers, so Udall was severely reprimanded.

In cooperation with a Puritan printer, Robert Waldegrave (who moved into Udall's parish), Udall wrote and published several anonymous tracts against the church's organization and discipline, such as *The State of the Church* and *A Demonstration of the truth of that Discipline which Christ hath prescribed.* In 1588 he was removed from his parish for his critical views and moved to Newcastle-on-Tyne, where he preached for a year. Then he was summoned to London to answer charges. He was actually condemned to death for his sedition, but the sentence was never carried out. After a period in prison his influential friends gained his release, but it was too late—for shortly thereafter, being weakened by his ordeal, he died. After his death two of his works were published: his Hebrew grammar, *A Key of the Holy Tongue* (1593), and his *Commentary on Jeremiah* (1595). P. TOON

UEMURA, MASAHISA (1858–1925)
Prominent Japanese church leader; foremost representative of evangelical Christianity in the 1890s and early 1900s

Born into a *Samurai* family during a period of declining Samurai influence, Uemura attended schools conducted by J. Ballagh and S. Brown, members of the first generation of American Protestant missionaries. Their influence opened a new world to him, liberating him from the bondage of feudalism. Baptized in 1873 at the age of sixteen, he was led immediately to dedicate his life to the gospel of Christ. He entered Tokyo United Seminary in 1877 and began a preaching mission that became the first instance of Protestant evangelism conducted under Japanese leadership. Later he became the pastor of Fujimicho Church in Tokyo, the historic center of the Presbyterian-Reformed tradition in Japan for many years. Concerned with the independence of the Japanese churches, he played an important role in the formation of Nihon Kirisuto

Kyokai (The Church of Christ in Japan) in 1891, using the Apostles' Creed as a doctrinal basis, a Presbyterian form of government, and the principle of indigeneity. He also helped found Tokyo Shingakusha (Tokyo Seminary) in 1904, the first seminary independently administered and financed by Japanese churches.

Though widely known for his vigorous defense of classical orthodoxy, Uemura virtually denied the doctrines of substitutionary atonement and verbal inspiration of the Bible. As a gifted writer and publisher, he translated hymns, helped with Bible translation, wrote the first systematic theology in 1884, and published two periodicals in 1890: *Fukuin Shinpo* (*The Gospel Weekly*) for Christian people and *Japan Review,* considered one of the most influential journals of its time because it introduced Christian concepts to the educated public. He helped to elevate the status of women, becoming the first minister to support the ordination of women elders. His seven-volume collected works continue to exercise a significant influence on the contemporary Japanese clergy. S. UDA

ULFILAS (c. 311–383)
Bible translator and missionary bishop
to the Goths

Born in Cappadocia (east Asia Minor), Ulfilas may have been captured by Gothic raiders as a youth. Yet his residence by early adulthood was Constantinople, the Roman Empire's eastern capital. Here undoubtedly he received his education and began his life of service to the church. In 341 Eusebius of Nicomedia, bishop of Constantinople, consecrated Ulfilas as bishop. Soon afterward the young bishop proceeded to Dacia (north of the Danube River), and for his remaining years he served as the church's principal missionary to the western Goths in this region. The many converts indicate that Ulfilas's efforts to spread the gospel had extensive results. After several years, persecution forced Ulfilas out of Dacia, and his work thereafter originated from a residence in

Moesia (south of the Danube), an area within the empire's borders.

Ulfilas's removal to Moesia also saw the beginnings of the project for which he is best remembered. This was his translation of the Old and New Testaments into the Goths' vernacular language. Toward this end, Ulfilas first had to reduce Gothic speech to writing, a task involving the invention of an alphabet based on Greek. Surviving remnants of this translation, as copied in the early Middle Ages, represent the earliest extant examples of Gothic literature. Ulfilas appears to have translated the whole New Testament and also the Old Testament except for the Books of Kings (1 and 2 Samuel, 1 and 2 Kings). It is supposed that the missing Old Testament sections were omitted purposely because of Ulfilas's fear that they would only encourage the aggressive Goths.

In his education and early experience, Ulfilas probably was orthodox in his doctrinal views. Nevertheless, he was already a firm Arian at his consecration, and he retained at least some of this heterodoxy until his death. In this regard Ulfilas was a product of Constantinople, a stronghold of the Arian beliefs that dominated much of the empire in the fourth century. Ulfilas was present at a synod held in Constantinople in 360, and he seems to have assumed a mild form of Arianism that emerged at this point. Yet even under pressure from Theodosius, the staunchly orthodox emperor, and official consultations in 379, Ulfilas remained Arian to the end. He occupied a central position in the initial evangelization of the Goths and related peoples. In this role he deserves an honored place among the great missionaries of Christian history. Yet simultaneously Ulfilas's heterodoxy had far-reaching consequences, not only for Christian missionary effort, but also for general early Germanic and western European history. The Arianism Ulfilas established with the Goths' conversion remained integral to western Gothic Christianity for centuries. And as a critical, fixed element in the western Goths' national life, Arianism spread and took hold among some eastern Goths and other Germanic groups. The larger significance here appears in the fact that Arian beliefs became one of the main sources of division between Goths and the Roman Empire. Arian Goths also had many disruptive conflicts with other western European peoples prior to the triumph of orthodox doctrine in the early Middle Ages.

Among Ulfilas's known writings, the only modern survivals are the Bible translation and possibly a creedal statement. The sermons and interpretive writings are no longer extant. Portions of a beautiful copy of the Gothic Bible have been preserved at the University of Uppsala, Sweden. Early sources of information about Ulfilas exist mainly in works by fifth-century church historians, primarily Philostorgius, Socrates, and Sozomen. K. J. BRYER

UNAMUNO, MIGUEL DE (1864–1937)
Spanish existentialist writer and philosopher

Don Miguel de Unamuno y Jugo was born in Bilbao in the Basque country of Northern Spain. He studied classics and philosophy in the University of Madrid, moving to Salamanca in 1891 as professor of Greek, and later serving as rector of the university. In 1924 he was deported to the Canary Islands for his repeated attacks on the totalitarian government. He succeeded in escaping to France, where he remained in exile until 1930. The following year he was reinstated as rector of the University of Salamanca. He served briefly as an independent republican in the Spanish constituent assembly. In the Spanish Civil War he favored the nationalists at first, but later felt that neither side served the best interests of Spain and humanity. During the last year of his life he was placed under house arrest.

Unamuno is remembered as a novelist. His first novel, *Peace in War* (1897), is regarded as the first existentialist novel. Later works treated the failure of science to deal with human problems and the tension between faith and reason. His last novel, *Saint Emanuel the Good, Martyr* (1933), describes the agony of a priest who lost his faith. Unamuno's earlier masterpiece, *The Tragic Sense of Life in Men and Peoples* (1913), ex-

plores man's craving for solace amidst hopelessness. Its title draws attention to man's helplessness in so many situations in life. So many evils are beyond redemption. But if man recognizes his impossible plight, he may at least experience a sense of brotherhood with his fellow man who finds himself in the same condition.

For Unamuno, philosophy was no abstract academic exercise. Philosophy in its deepest sense was reflection on human existence. Man philosophizes in order to live. He does so in order to resign himself to life, to seek some finality in it, or to distract himself. Man has a perennial hunger for immortality and craving for the divine. This consuming desire is in constant tension with man's reason, which pulls him towards skepticism. But out of this hunger and tension come hope, faith, charity, and man's sense of beauty and goodness. This is the message of Unamuno's writings. C. BROWN

UNDERHILL, EVELYN (1875–1941)
English mystic and writer

Evelyn Underhill was born in London, the only child of Sir Arthur Underhill, a distinguished lawyer and enthusiastic yachtsman. Educated at King's College for Women in London, she early showed interest in writing fiction, though her first book was a work of humorous verse. As a girl she began annual trips to the continent with her parents and was charmed by Paris, Chartres, Florence, and Rome. Though she had been raised an Anglican, she was strongly drawn toward Catholicism when in 1907 she visited a friend at the Franciscan convent of St. Mary in Southampton. In the same year she began *Mysticism: A Study in the Nature and Development of Man's Spiritual Consciousness.* Published in 1911, this classic work is a superb evaluation of spirituality from the early Christian era to the beginning of the twentieth century. In 1907 she was married to Hubert Stuart Moore, and in 1911 began her friendship with Baron Friedrich von Hügel, with whom she corresponded extensively and who exercised a strong influence upon her spiritual life, especially between 1921 and the time of his death in 1925. Though she was impressed with Roman Catholicism, she remained an Anglican, giving herself to social services, speaking at church retreats, and writing. She combined the good ethical life with a deep sense of devotion to God. Other writings on the devotional life are *The Mystical Way, Practical Mysticism* (1915) and *The Essential of Mysticism* (1920). Her much-praised work *Worship* (1937) is a study in liturgical practices in various church traditions. P. BECHTEL

UNDERWOOD, HORACE GRANT
(1859–1916)

Missionary to Korea; sometimes called "the father of Korean Presbyterianism"

Born in London, England, Underwood was educated at New York University (A.B., 1881) and New Brunswick Seminary (B.D., 1884). Ordained to the ministry by the Reformed Church in America in 1884, he served its Pompton, New Jersey, church before going out in 1885 under the Presbyterian Board of Foreign Missions as its first ordained missionary to Korea. He founded the first Presbyterian church in Korea, of which he became the pastor. In 1891 he persuaded the Presbyterian church to adopt the Nevius plan for church growth: self-support, self-government, and self-propagation.

From 1887 to 1889 Underwood taught chemistry and physics at Royal Korea Medical College. He was chairman of the Board of Bible Translators (1887–1911). He became treasurer of the Korean Presbyterian Mission (1885–1889) and chairman of the same organization (1889–1890). He was first chairman of the General Council of Evangelical Missions in Korea in 1905, and first moderator of the Presbyterian Church of Korea in 1912. From 1907 he served as professor of theology at the Presbyterian Theological Seminary of Korea in Pyong-Yang. Between 1901 and 1905 he helped to form Union Medical College, which, with Severance Hospital Nurses Training School, was later merged with Chosen Christian University— now known as Yonsei University in Seoul. Besides compiling a Korean grammar and

dictionary, Underwood wrote *The Call to Korea* (1908) and *Religions of Eastern Asia* (1910). N. V. HOPE

URBAN I (died 230)
Pope, 222–230

Little is said of Urban's reign in the *Liber Pontificalis* (*Pope's Lives,* an authority for the early period). Although there was a continuation of Hippolytus's schism and of the Adoptionist and Montanist heresies, the church was at relative peace. He was deemed a martyr and is so listed in the Roman Martyrology, but that is probably a mistake in the evidence. Buried in the cemetery of St. Calixtus, he was commemorated by an epitaph in Greek, testifying to the persistence of the Greek language in the early Roman church. He was the only Pope Urban who used his baptismal name as his papal name. A. CABANISS

URBAN II (1042–1099)
Pope, 1088–1099

Born as Odo of Lagery, in Châtillon sur Marne, near Rheims, he first became a diocesan cleric and archdeacon of Rheims and then a Benedictine monk at Cluny in 1070. There he entered into the spirit of the Cluniac reform and developed as a theologian. Soon made prior, he was appointed by Gregory VII as cardinal bishop of Ostia in 1078. Employed as a papal diplomat he proved capable and flexible yet true to Gregorian ideas. When he was elected pope, he was refused admission to Rome by the Holy Roman Emperor Henry IV, who supported an antipope, Clement III. Various troubles, however, soon beset the emperor. Support for the antipope fell away, and Urban was able to gain access to Rome. As pope he often asked advice of Bruno, founder of the Carthusian order.

Despite serious difficulties with the French king, Urban visited France in 1095. There at Clermont he proclaimed the first Crusade. It was an effort to unite the Christian world against the Turks of Palestine, as well as to unite it under the papal aegis. His forceful sermon (which has been preserved) was immediately effective, with its ringing battle-cry of "God wills it"—strangely reminiscent of the similar Muslim battle-cry, "It is the will of God." The Crusaders left for the Holy Land in mid-1096 and pushed on to the Holy Sepulcher. In July of 1099 the victorious armies captured Jerusalem and set about establishing a feudal state in Palestine. A few weeks later Pope Urban II died without having received news of the successful outcome of his project. He was beatified in 1881. A. CABANISS

URBAN III (died 1187)
Pope, 1185–1187

Born Uberto Crivelli in Milan, he became the archbishop of Milan. On the very day his predecessor (Lucius III) died, he was elected pope. The papacy, in alliance with the city-states of northern Italy, was engaged in conflict with Holy Roman Emperor Frederick Barbarossa concerning his effort to dominate the Italian peninsula. The latter sought, by the marriage of his son, Henry, to the heiress of Sicily, to hem in the papal state from both north and south. Urban prepared to excommunicate Frederick, but the fearful citizens of Verona, where the pope had taken refuge, begged that the decree not be issued from their city. Urban thereupon removed to Ferrara, where he died, never having occupied the Vatican. A. CABANISS

URBAN IV (c. 1200–1264)
Pope, 1261–1264

Born Jacques Pantaleon in Troyes, France, he was the son of a French cobbler. Made bishop of Verdun in 1255, he was two years later translated to the patriarchal see of Jerusalem, by that time largely an honorary function. Only eight cardinals constituted the conclave at which Urban was chosen as pope. Immediately afterwards, therefore, he created fourteen new cardinals, most of them French. Crowned at Viterbo, he made his residence chiefly at Orvieto and later at Perugia. He was never permitted to occupy Rome. In general he favored his own coun-

trymen and thus paved the way for later papal residence at Avignon. In the year he died he elevated the popular festival of Corpus Christi to the rank of a universal observance. He was virtually an older contemporary of Thomas Aquinas, who composed the beautiful hymns for that occasion, "Tantum ergo sacramentum" and "O salutaris hostia," also employed at the service called Benediction. A. CABANISS

URBAN V (1310–1370)
Pope, 1363–1370

Born Guillaume de Grimoard of a noble family at Grisac, France, he was educated at Montpellier and Toulouse and then became a monk. For a while he taught canon law at Montpellier, Paris, and Avignon. And he was instrumental in founding the medical school at Montpellier. Not a cardinal when he was elected pope, he chose the name Urban because he mistakenly thought that all his predecessors so named had been saints. He strove desperately to return the papacy from Avignon to Rome; and in 1369 he actually went to the city. But Rome proved too turbulent, so in the autumn of 1370 he and his cardinals reluctantly went back to Avignon. That action was vigorously opposed by the protests of many important people, among them Bridget, a Swedish princess, and the poet laureate Petrarch. The princess indeed prophesied that Urban would die if he left Rome—and he did, in December of the same year. A good and saintly man, he was not sufficiently strong for the pressures of his day. He was beatified in 1870, five hundred years after his death. A. CABANISS

URBAN VI (c. 1318–1389)
Pope, 1378–1389

Born Bartolomeo Prignano, he lived in Naples. His predecessor, Gregory XI, had returned to Rome from Avignon in 1377, but the disorder of the city drove him to decide to go back to Avignon. He died before he could do so. Thus the cardinals were forced by threats of the mob to elect a non-Frenchman. They chose the archbishop of

Bari as Urban VI. Upon his arrival in Rome he was harsh and rude to his electors, giving substance of a kind to rumors about his sanity. Secretly they conspired to leave Rome. At Anagni they declared Urban's election null and void, as having been made under duress. Then they sailed to Avignon, after having elected Cardinal Robert of Geneva as Clement VII. It was the first time the same group of cardinals had elected a pope, then declared his election void and had another pope elected. But Urban promptly retaliated by creating a college of Italian cardinals, and the rift was complete.

Both popes excommunicated each other's adherents. The Great Western Schism began and Europe was torn assunder by conflicting loyalties, chiefly along nationalistic lines. France and its satellites opted for the Avignonese pope, while England and its satellites opted for the Roman pope. Urban continued through the remainder of his reign to act crudely and disastrously and without any intention of negotiating with Avignon. Even the saintly Catherine of Siena implored him unsuccessfully to curb the sudden impulses of his nature. A. CABANISS

URBAN VII (1521–1590)
Pope for two weeks in 1590

Born Giambattista Castagna in Rome, he was the son of Roman and Genoese nobility. He was early noted both for his charities and for his diplomacy. He was a prudent leader in the council of Trent, but his reign as pope was cut short, for he died twelve days after his election. A. CABANISS

URBAN VIII (1568–1644)
Pope, 1623–1644

Born Maffeo Barberini, he was the member of a wealthy Florentine family. Urban's reign was signalized by open and notorious nepotism. The Romans are said to have whispered in reply a pungent aphorism, "Quod non fecerunt barbari, fecerunt Barberini" ("What the barbarians did not do, the Barberini did"). Although the prestige of the papacy declined notably, Urban was an able diplomat. He overtly approved the action of Cardinal Richelieu in supporting the Protestants during the Thirty Years' War, correctly deeming it a political, rather than a religious, war.

Although Galileo was tried by the Inquisition during his reign, Urban never officially made a pronouncement against the scientist. He actually gave him a pension for the rest of his life and sent him his blessing at his death. Urban solemnly condemned the book *Augustinus* by Bishop Cornelius Jansenius of Ypres, but its strong Augustinian teaching continued into the eighteenth century. He sponsored the sculptor Bernini, whose Baroque columns still support the canopy over the high altar of St. Peter's basilica. In his own right Urban was a respectable composer of hymns and poems. But his long reign was essentially that of head of a greedy family and prince of a petty Italian state rather than of a real leader of the Christian church. His excesses apparently cured the later papacy of obvious nepotism. A. CABANISS

URSINUS, ZACHARIAS (1534–1583)
German reformer and theologian

A reforming theologian, Ursinus was born at Breslau in 1534 and studied at Wittenberg from 1550 to 1557. He then moved to Geneva for further study and from there took a teaching post in his native city of Breslau. His doctrine of the Lord's Supper led to his dismissal from Breslau in 1559. But in 1561, thanks to his mentor Peter Martyr Vermigli, he received an invitation from Elector Frederick III to come to Heidelberg as director of the theological academy. It was at Heidelberg that with Caspar Olevianus he made his most notable contribution to church life by drafting the Heidelberg Catechism (1563). He also undertook the defense of the Catechism against Lutheran objections. From 1562 he added the professorship of dogmatics to his administrative duties and also prepared a new liturgy. Zanchius relieved him of the burden of teaching in 1568, but Ursinus became involved in a difficult struggle to bring in a new discipline on the Genevan model (1570). The death of the elector in 1577 opened the way for Lutheran influences; Ursinus, with Zanchius, moved to Neustadt in 1578 and spent his last years there. In addition to his work on the Catechism, he also wrote an important treatise on the Lutheran Book of Concord and did much to promote Peter Martyr's *Loci*.

G. BROMILEY

USSHER, JAMES (1581–1656)
Archbishop of Armagh; Calvinist theologian

Ussher was educated in Dublin at the new university founded by Elizabeth I called Trinity College. He became a fellow in 1600, was ordained in 1601, and became chancellor of St. Patrick's Cathedral in 1606 and regius professor of divinity in Trinity College in 1607. Early in his life he sought to understand and to argue against the theology of the Roman Catholic Church. His career as a writer began in 1613 with the publication of a book on the history of the Church in the West (the Latin Church): *Gravissimae Quaestionis de Christianarum Ecclesiarum*. He compiled the 104 (Calvinist) articles of faith known as the Irish Articles, which were accepted by the Convocation of the Church in Ireland in 1615. After an interview with King Charles I in London, he was made bishop of Meath in 1621 and Archbishop of Armagh in 1625. He kept himself busy with diocesan and academic affairs, making periodic visits to England to consult books and people. On one of these visits in 1640 he found himself caught in the struggle between king and Parliament. His Calvinistic theological sympathies tended to be with the Presbyterian divines who supported Parliament, but his general culture and outlook led him to support the crown. He refused to be a member of the Westminster Assembly of divines and preferred to advise the king when and where asked. After the war he never returned to Ireland but acted as preacher to the Society of Lincoln's Inn, London, a post he held from 1647 to 1656. He had been removed by Parliament from his Irish offices.

He was a man of prodigious learning and was respected by Puritan, Royalist, and Roman Catholic. He is famous for a chronology of the Bible that he worked out, and which for many years was printed in editions of the King James Version. Oliver Cromwell thought so highly of him as to give him a State funeral and bury him in Westminster Abbey. Much of his writing was in Latin and (whether in English or Latin) was written for scholars dealing with such matters as the Protestant character of the Irish Church, the genuine seven letters of Ignatius of Antioch, predestination, biblical exposition, and church order. His scheme for a modified form of episcopacy was widely studied in the seventeenth century. P. TOON

V

VALDÉS, ALFONSO DE (c. 1500–1532)
Spanish diplomat and writer

With his brother, Juan, Alfonso Valdés appropriated the ideas of Erasmus. With Juan's collaboration, he wrote *Diálogo de Lactancio y un arcediano* (*The Dialogue of Lactancio and the Archdeacon*) and *Diálogo de Mercurio y Carón* (*The Dialogue of Mercury and Charon*). Both works advocate evangelical poverty, the superiority of inner to merely external religion, and the cause of Emperor Charles V against the papacy. The papal nuncio to Spain, stung by Valdés's pen, urged the Inquisition to examine Valdés's works. The verdict exonerated Valdés of doctrinal error.

Valdés's criticisms of the Church, for whom he was secretary and sometime emissary, criticized its political pretensions and the moral laxity of the clergy, not Catholic doctrine or sacramental theology. Nonetheless, he placed sufficient emphasis upon the inner working of the Holy Spirit, at the expense of the rites and ordinances of the institutional Church, that he was repeatedly accused of Illuminism. His early death left many of his ideas undeveloped.
P. M. BASSETT

VALDÉS, JUAN DE (c. 1500–1541)
Spanish humanist and lay theologian

Deeply influenced by Erasmus, Valdés anonymously wrote an exposition of the Lord's Prayer, the *Diálogo de doctrina cristiana* (*Dialogue on Christian Doctrine,* 1529) that so vexed the clergy that it was consigned to the Inquisition. It was condemned, but Valdés himself was allowed to expatriate to Italy.

After several years as a papal secretary, Valdés lived in Naples, where he was secretary to the viceroy and inspector of fortifications. More importantly, he there gathered about him a devoted group of aristocrats and friends concerned with the reform of Roman Catholicism and personal piety. The group included Bernardino Ochino and Peter Martyr Vermigli, both of whom later became Protestants.

In Naples, too, he wrote his most significant works; some in Spanish, some in Italian. Most were published after his death, though they circulated widely before then. The *Alphabeto cristiano* (*Christian Alphabet,* 1536) advocated evangelical poverty and a simple life-style as the path to Christian perfection. *Le cento e dieci considerazione* (*110 Considerations*), his principal doctrinal work, is intensely Christocentric and emphasizes the Christian's appropriation of the Atonement in his inner religious experience and his application of it to his pattern of living.

Like his brother, Alfonso, Juan was sharply critical of both Catholics and Protestants, though he was at least nominally Catholic. Such doctrinal criticisms as he made were not theological but aimed at ethical indifference. Such was his critique of infant baptism. It was not theologically or biblically wrong, but it bred false security and ethical carelessness.

According to Valdés, who later came close to a Protestant understanding of justification, the true Christian must heed the personal inspiration and illumination of the Holy Spirit working within him. Such persons constitute the authentic church, the mystical Body of Christ. Both Catholicism and Protestantism inhibit that kind of spiritual sensitivity: Catholicism by its ecclesiasticism, Protestantism by its bibliolatry. This line of thought, with its emphasis on the internal life and the illumination of the Spirit, brought Valdés under considerable suspicion, but he was not condemned during his lifetime.

Among Valdés's other works were the first non-rabbinic translation of the Psalms into Spanish, translations of most of the New Testament books, and commentaries on Matthew, Romans, and 1 Corinthians. These, and his *Diálogo de la lengua* (*Dialogue of Language*), establish him among the very greatest masters of Spanish and in the front rank of her sixteenth-century thinkers. P. M. BASSETT

VALLA, LORENZO (1407–1457)

Italian humanist; best known for his exposure of the Donation of Constantin (1440)

Born in Rome, Valla learned Latin and Greek there and perhaps in Florence. From 1431 to 1433 he taught rhetoric at the University of Pavia, a lively humanist center. In 1435 he entered the service of King Alfonso of Aragon, remaining until 1448. He spent his last years in Rome in the service of Pope Nicholas V.

It is probably in connection with Alfonso's quarrels with the pope that Valla wrote his work exposing the *Donation of Constantine*. This document was supposed to indicate that the emperor Constantine of the Western Empire had given central Italy to papal control when he moved his capital to the East. The document had been used by the papacy to exert power in secular affairs. By means of very effective historical criticism, Valla showed that the Donation was an eighth-century forgery. Others had made this claim, but it remained for Valla to make a definitive case. That Valla was accepted into papal service after exposure of this forgery is not as surprising as it may seem, for he accompanied his argument with a plea for the spiritual purity of the Holy See.

Valla was a brilliant philologist and made substantial contributions to textual and historical criticism. Like many other humanists, he was interested in a return to the spirit of the Gospel. Preferring the Church Fathers, both Greek and Latin, to the obscurity of the scholastics, he attacked scholastic logic, theology, and law. In Valla's opinion Aristotelian logic was sophistry, based on empty subtleties and wordplays. The purpose of thought is to know things, but many terms in Aristotelian logic are artificial constructions that fail to express reality and give no insight into the concrete characteristics of things. He held that philosophy and dialectic should not depart from the customary manner of speaking, from natural sense and common usage.

Valla has had a reputation for hedonism, based on his early work "On Pleasure" (1431), which is probably not deserved. In this work two speakers present the Stoic and the Epicurean ethics and then a third speaker replies to both. The third speaker, clearly representing Valla's views, argues that the true Christian should disregard the goals of this life and concentrate on the joys that await him in heaven. He accepted, however, the Epicurean view that it is good to strive after pleasure and happiness, but he insisted that the complete happiness of man is not to be found in this life. H. F. VOS

VANDERKEMP, JOHANNES THEODORUS (1747–1811)

Pioneer Dutch medical missionary to South Africa

Born in Rotterdam, Vanderkemp was the son of a Lutheran professor of theology. After serving fifteen years in the army, Vanderkemp completed his medical studies at Edinburgh University, graduating in 1782. He practiced medicine in Middleburg (1782–1791) and at Dordrecht (1791–1793) and served as a Dutch Army doctor from 1793 to 1795. In 1791 he was converted from Deism to a vital Christian faith; and in 1796 he was accepted for foreign service by the recently founded London Missionary Society, receiving ordination in London in 1797 as a minister of the Church of Scotland. Appointed to lead a mission to South Africa, along with three companions, he arrived in Cape Town in 1799. There were two major African peoples with whom Vanderkemp had to deal—the "Kaffirs" (Xhosa) and the Hottentots. Though he was deeply interested in the Kaffirs and carried out a sixteen-month mission among them between 1799 and 1801, his main efforts were directed to the Hottentots. He labored among them first in the Graaff-Reinet area, then at Bota's Place, near Algoa Bay, and finally in 1803 settled at Bethelsdorp, about four hundred miles east of Cape Town, where he set up an industrial missionary center. He soon found himself in trouble with the governmental authorities—Dutch and British—partly because he identified so closely with the natives as to marry an African wife, but mainly because he defended the rights of the Kaffirs and Hottentots against the injustice and oppression by the white colonists.

Among his publications was a catechism entitled *The Principles of the Word of God for the Hottentot Mission*, published in 1804. N. V. HOPE

VAN ESS, LEANDER (1772–1847)
German Roman Catholic theologian

Born at Warburg in Westphalia, Van Ess was christened Johann Heinrich. Upon entering the Benedictine Cloister at Marienmünster in 1790 he changed his name to Leander. In 1793 he was ordained a subdeacon and two years later deacon. He took orders as a priest in 1796. Because of the Napoleonic invasion, the cloister was closed in 1802, and Van Ess became a parish priest at Schwalenburg. Meanwhile, he collaborated with his cousin, Karl, to produce a Catholic translation of the New Testament (1807). As a consequence of his scholarly reputation, Van Ess was appointed to the chair of Catholic theology at Marburg in 1812, where he remained until 1822. In 1821 his fortunes declined when his translation was placed on the Index of prohibited books. This occurred despite several episcopal imprimaturs. Van Ess was generously supported in the production and distribution of his translation by the British and Foreign Bible Society. However, when he insisted on including the Apocrypha in his 1822 Old Testament translation, the British society withdrew its support. After several personal and ecclesiastical disasters, Van Ess died in relative obscurity. W. A. DETZLER

VAUGHAN, HENRY (c. 1621–1695)
Welsh poet

Born in Breconshire, Vaughn retained an explicit relation to the Welsh tradition by adopting the title the Silurist, in honor of the Celtic tribe, the Silures, that had once inhabited Southeast Wales. He attended Jesus College, Oxford, but left without taking a degree in order to study law at the Inns of Court, London. With the commencement of the civil war he returned to Wales, and it is reasonably certain that he served with the royalist forces.

Vaughan underwent a conversion experience in the late 1640s and wrote the major part of his poetry in the early 1650s, although he wrote little after 1655. Later he turned to the study and practice of medicine.

Major influences on his writing were George Herbert (to whom he pays tribute in the preface to his *Sacred Poems,* 1650; second part, 1655), the Scriptures, his Welsh heritage, and the Augustinian tradition of meditation. His poetry depicts a keen awareness of the Fall and of his belief in the Incarnation. He looked to Christ as mediator, but the Incarnation also meant the immanence of the Divine in nature as is evident in the poem "The Incarnation, and Passion." He rejoices in the way creatures always follow an order and fulfill God's plan for them in contrast to man's vacillation and disobedience.

The emblem introducing his *Sacred Poems* calls attention to two dominant images in Vaughan's poetry: the stony heart and the fire of God acting upon it. His verse lacks the polish of Herbert's poetry, but some poems contain sections that equal anything in English devotional poetry. E. B. BATSON

VAUGHAN WILLIAMS, RALPH (1872–1958)
English composer

It is seldom that a major composer of international renown has concerned himself with hymn tunes. Vaughan Williams was such a one. His father, a clergyman in the west of England, died when the composer was a small boy, and he was raised in his mother's home, a wealthy and aristocratic household. He turned to music at any early age, but was relatively slow in his development and never a skillful performer. It was in composition that he excelled. He attended Trinity College, Oxford, and the Royal College of Music, London. He also studied with Max Bruch in Berlin (1897–1898) and with Ravel in Paris (1909).

Vaughan Williams became greatly interested in folk song and Elizabethan music. After a brief period as a church organist, he gave himself to research, lecturing, and composition. For many years he conducted the Leith Hill music festival, which was open to participants from the community and for which he wrote many works. His activity as a composer increased with age. He finished his Ninth Symphony, a work of seemingly youthful vigor, shortly before his death at eighty-six.

In 1906 Vaughan Williams was musical editor of *The English Hymnal* (revised 1933). This work proved a landmark in hymnal editing. High Anglican in viewpoint, it contained plainsong at one extreme and gospel songs at the other. Many English folk songs were successfully adapted to sacred words, and a good sampling of the then little-known Welsh hymn tunes were introduced to English congregations. Tunes like *Aberystwyth, Ebenezer,* and *Hyfrydol* are now known the world over. *Sine Nomine (Without a Name)* is his own superb tune to the hymn "For All the Saints." The tune to "All Creatures of our God and King" was recast by him from German origin. He was also coeditor of the famous *Oxford Carol Book* and the ecumenical and eclectic *Songs of Praise.* His early oratorio, *Sancta Civitas,* was written in a harmonic idiom daring for its time. Several cantatas on episodes from *Pilgrim's Progress* eventually led to the opera (1951), which he termed "A Morality." A ballet on *Job,* inspired by Blake's illustrations, *Five Mystical Songs* with texts by George Herbert, a Christmas cantata, *Hodie (This Day),* and a variety of other sacred works and anthems give Vaughan Williams a unique place in twentieth-century sacred music. J. B. MACMILLAN

VENN, HENRY (1796–1873)
British missionary leader

Henry Venn was the grandson of Henry Venn (1724–1797) and son of John Venn, who was rector of Clapham, and a well-known Anglican evangelical. Henry studied at Queens' College, Cambridge, where he became a fellow in 1819. After ordination he became curate of a church in London for four years. Then, after a short time in Cambridge, he went to Drypool, Hull, where his friend William Wilberforce lived. He remained in this parish until 1834 and then returned to London to work in St. John's, Holloway. After twelve years he became the secretary of the Church Missionary Society, an evangelical Anglican society his father had helped to found. He held this post for thirty-two years.

He is remembered as a missionary strategist; he had the vision of the creation of indigenous churches that were self-supporting, self-governing, and self-extending. Some missionaries did not like his advanced views, and they proved to be difficult to implement in Victorian times. However, when he became secretary, the society had 107 European and 9 native clergy; when he retired it had 230 and 148 respectively.

As a leader of the evangelicals in the Church of England he was placed on two royal commissions of enquiry: clerical subscription and ritualism. He was known as a man of broad sympathies and distinct evangelical principles. He wrote a life of his grandfather entitled *The Life and Letters of Henry Venn* (1834). P. TOON

VENN, JOHN (1758–1813)
Anglican evangelical leader

Son of Henry Venn, one of the early evangelicals in the Church of England, John Venn was born at Clapham where his father was curate. He studied at Sidney Sussex College, Cambridge, graduating with a B.A. in 1781. From 1783 to 1792 he was a rector in Norfolk and from 1792 until his death, rector of Clapham. He was thus at the center of the religious life of the Clapham Sect, the evangelical group that worked for the abolition of the slave trade and the application of biblical principles to social life. He was a founding member of the Church Missionary Society and acted as its organizer for several years. He helped to found the magazine *Christian Observer*, which represented the cultured type of evangelicalism practiced at Clapham. He had two sons, one of whom, Henry, was the secretary of the Church Missionary Society for thirty-two years. The other, also a clergyman, was vicar of St. Peter's Hereford for many years. Not so famous as his father or his son (both named Henry), John was nevertheless an important member of the Clapham Sect even if less well known than Wilberforce and Thornton. P. TOON

VERBECK, GUIDO (1830–1898)
Dutch missionary and educator

Born in Zeist, the Netherlands, and Moravian by heritage, Verbeck was nurtured in a cultural, refined environment. Verbeck was destined to become a major maker of modern Japan.

Following his graduation from the Moravian School in Zeist, he enrolled in the Polytechnic Institute of Utrecht. For some time he was involved in metal work, then accepted an invitation to invest his talent in the developing steamboat industry in America. Upon completion of his study at the Presbyterian Theological Seminary in Auburn, New York, he accepted a call for an "Americanized Dutchman" for missionary service in Japan by what is now the Reformed Church in America. By the close of 1859 the Japanese work had been established.

Verbeck served as missionary and Bible teacher, translator, diplomat, governmental advisor, and educator, as he sought to open Japan peacefully to the benefits of Christianity and the Western way of life. He conducted a school for Japanese-English interpreters. In 1869 he became head of what was to become the Japanese Imperial University. In recognition of his services to the Japanese, he was issued membership in the Order of the Rising Sun in 1877.

Verbeck lost his Netherlands citizenship because of his long departure from his homeland, was refused United States citizenship because of his short time there, and was not assigned Japanese citizenship. He died a man without a country. P. VELTMAN

VIGILIUS (c. 500–555)
Pope, 537–555

Son of a Roman noble, Vigilius was ordained and sent to represent Pope Agapetus I in Constantinople. There he became friendly with the empress Theodora, a firm Monophysite, wife of Justinian I, who was concerned to placate the powerful Monophysite party in order to maintain unity in church and state. (He made considerable concessions to them in what became known as the Three Chapter Controversy.)

When the Goths finally abandoned Rome, Theodora saw the advantages of a pope who could be manipulated. Under the pretext of his supposed treacherous alliance with the

Goths, she had Pope Silverius deposed and banished (he died the following year) and Vigilius installed in his place. For his part, Vigilius undertook to help restore a Monophysite as patriarch of Constantinople and to be generally tolerant toward the party. After he became pope, however, Vigilius tried to extricate himself from Eastern influence and to uphold theological orthodoxy. There followed an incredible series of events wherein pressure was put upon him, including forcible removal to Constantinople, and no fewer than four major changes of mind on the part of this most vacillating of all popes. He refused to take part in the 553 Council of Constantinople, but eventually he gave in once more and (in 555) was given leave to return to Rome but died on the way. His behavior is often used as an argument against papal infallibility in questions of doctrine. J. D. DOUGLAS

VINCENT DE PAUL (1581–c. 1660)
Founder of the Lazarists and the Sisters of Charity

Born at Ranquine in southwest France of peasant stock, Vincent de Paul studied humanities at Dax (1595–1597). Later he pursued theological studies at Toulouse (1604). He had been ordained as a priest in 1600. When pirates captured him, he was condemned to two years (1605–1607) as a slave in Tunisia. In 1607 he escaped to Avignon. Two years later he went to Paris, where he came under the influence of Pierre de Bérulle. This awakened in Vincent a concern for the poor. As parish priest at Clichy (1612–1626), he ministered selflessly to the paupers. At the same time he served as chaplain to the family of Philippe-Emmanuel do Gondi (1613–1625), ultimately assuming responsibility for the household. In 1617 he founded the Confraternity of Charity. He became superior of the visitation convents at Paris (1622) and soon was appointed principal of the Collège des Bons-Enfants (1624). In 1625 he was named superior of the Congregation of Missions, known as the Lazarists (or Vincentians). At his prompting the first enclosed order of women dedicated

to serving the sick and poor was established in 1633 under the name Daughters of Charity. He served the wider interests of the Roman Church by conducting retreats for clergy and ordinands and by founding seminaries. During the Wars of Religion he undertook relief work and was recognized for this by Louis XIII. In 1643 the Queen Regent appointed him to the Council of Conscience, which functioned during the reign of Louis XIV. Canonized in 1737, he was named in 1885 as patron of all works of charity. W. A. DETZLER

VINES, RICHARD (c. 1600–1656)
English Puritan; Presbyterian divine

Born at Blaston, Leicestershire, Vines was educated at Magdalene College, Cambridge, where he graduated with a B.A. in 1622 and an M.A. in 1627. He ran a school at Hinckley, Leicestershire, from 1624 to 1642 and during this period oversaw two parishes, where curates appear to have done the work for him. He achieved fame in London by a sermon entitled "Caleb's integrity in following the Lord fully," delivered to Parliament on a day of fasting. His support of the parliamentary cause against the king brought quick promotion. He became rector of St. Clement Danes, London, in 1643 and Master of Pembroke College, Cambridge, in 1644, holding both positions until 1649. He also became a prominent member of the Westminster Assembly of divines and served on the drafting committee for the Confession of Faith. He believed the Puritan cause was going too far with the execution of Charles I in 1649 and this opposition cost him his favor with Parliament. Losing his Cambridge and London positions, he became the minister of St. Lawrence Jewry. For the last years of his life he participated minimally in ecclesiastical affairs because he had been disillusioned by the Puritan movement. He had wanted a reform of the National Church on Presbyterian lines, but the supporters of Cromwell had gone too far and fast for his liking. Among his posthumous publications was *A Treatise on the Institution of the Lord's Supper* (1657). P. TOON

VINET, ALEXANDRE RUDOLPHE
(1797–1847)

Swiss Reformed theologian

Vinet was born into a French Huguenot family at Ouchy, near Lausanne, and there he also died. Vinet studied theology at Lausanne. Although he was ordained into the Reformed ministry in 1819, Vinet took up a post teaching French language and literature at Basel. During this time he stoutly defended the rationalistic theology of Germany as it was taught by W. L. deWette. A serious illness in 1823 and 1824 led to a spiritual crisis, which was to Vinet almost an evangelical conversion. In 1837 he was called to the chair of practical theology at the Academy in Lausanne. Here he gained a reputation that led to his being nicknamed "the Schleiermacher of French Protestantism." In fact, his theology was very much a mixture of the mysticism and rationalism that characterized Schleiermacher. In 1843 an English translation of Vinet's work on the separation of church and state was published. Two years later he participated in the establishment of the Free Church of Vaud. His support was due mainly to his convictions concerning religious freedom, not to a strong sympathy with the Swiss revival. In 1848 Vinet published his studies of Blaise Pascal.
W. A. DETZLER

VIROLLEAUD, CHARLES (1879–1968)

French orientalist and historian

Born in Barbezieux, Virolleaud studied at the École des Langues Orientales, specializing in Arabic and Persian. His academic career was spent mainly at the University of Paris. Founder and editor in 1966 of *Babylonica*, he was particularly interested in astrology, in which field he published between 1906 and 1912 his monumental work *L'Astrologie Chaldéene*. For nine years (1920–1929) he served as director of the Archaeological Service of France, in which capacity he supervised all archaeological activity conducted under official French auspices in Syria and Lebanon. In 1929 some archaeologists headed by Charles F. A. Schaeffer began to find ancient tablets in cuneiform script at Ugarit (Ras Shamra) near Latakia on the Mediterranean coast of north Syria. These discoveries were given to Virolleaud, who thereafter gave himself to their decipherment and publication, culminating in his *Textes Mythologiques et Liturgiques de Ras Shamra—Ugaritica 5* shortly before his death in 1968. His work did much to uncover the civilization of ancient Phoenicia. N. V. HOPE

VISSER 'T HOOFT, WILLEM ADOLF
(1900–1985)

First general secretary of the World Council of Churches

Born in Haarlem, the Netherlands, Visser't Hooft graduated in theology from Leyden University and served first with the YMCA, then with the World Student Christian Federation. In 1938 he became General Secretary of the Provisional Committee of the World Council of Churches, which remained "in process of formation" until 1948. In the latter year, at the Amsterdam Assembly at which the World Council of Churches was officially constituted, Visser 't Hooft was made General Secretary, a position he retained until his retirement in 1966. Long before his retirement this multilingual Dutchman was hailed as the foremost ecumenical statesman of his generation. It has been well said that "during his administration the World Council moved from tentative and provisional beginnings to become the acknowledged chief instrument and channel of the ecumenical movement." Apart from his many publications on the ecumenical movement, his works include *The Background of the Social Gospel in America* (1928), *Anglo-Catholicism and Orthodoxy* (1933), *None Other Gods* (1937), *The Kingship of Christ* (1947), *No Other Name* (1963), *Memoirs* (1973), and *The Fatherhood of God in an Age of Emancipation* (1982). J. D. DOUGLAS & N. V. HOPE

VITUS (died 303)

One of fourteen auxiliary saints or Holy Helpers venerated in the Roman Catholic Church for their prayers on behalf of human need

Vitus is invoked against sudden death, hydrophobia, and convulsions known as St. Vitus' Dance. The saint is represented as immersed in a burning cauldron, a graphic symbol of his martyrdom under Diocletian. He was born to pagan parents in southern Italy and raised by a Christian nurse, Crescentia, and her husband, Modestus, who were also martyred. His cult spread among Germans and Slavs in the Middle Ages, when relics of the saint were moved from Saint Denis in Paris to Saxony and to Prague. M. FACKLER

VOLTAIRE, FRANÇOIS-MARIE AROUET (1694–1778)

French philosopher of the Enlightenment; opponent of Christianity

Born François-Marie Arouet, Voltaire became the best known and perhaps also the most widely disdained French philosopher. Certainly, he was a most eloquent and influential spokesman for the Enlightenment. Although his primary and secondary education was at the hands of the Jesuits, he developed an intense hatred for their superstition and fanaticism. While studying at Paris, he became familiar with the writings and philosophy of Descartes, Montaigne Montague, and Pierre Bayle.

Exiled to England (1726–1729), he became acquainted with the Deists, especially with the thinking of the philosopher John Locke and the mathematician Sir Isaac Newton. After returning to France, Voltaire published his *Lettres Philosophiques* (1734). The revolutionary character of these led to his expulsion from Paris, and he took refuge in the estate of the Marquise du Châtelet at Cirey in provincial Lorraine. Together with the marquise he pursued his interests in the works of Newton and the philosophy of Leibniz. He also enjoyed the cultural life of the region, attending with the marquise theatrical performances and lavish receptions. Voltaire remained in rather luxurious exile for almost a decade (1734–1743).

After the death of the marquise, Voltaire left France (1750) to reside at the court of Frederick II in Prussia. The king had a deep interest in French literature generally and in the work of Voltaire in particular. For some years Voltaire had corresponded with the Prussian monarch. During his stay at the court, honors and distinctions were showered by Frederick II upon Voltaire. When estrangement separated Voltaire from the king, the philosopher returned to France.

In search of political tolerance, Voltaire bought property near Geneva in 1755. Later he purchased the two estates of Tournay and Ferney (1758) along the Swiss frontier. Here he implemented his social theories by experimenting with the village population of two thousand. After 1759 Voltaire actually lived at Ferney. He instituted practical reforms and established a successful silk industry to support the community. He sought to establish tolerance as the primary trait of society. Soon Ferney became a shrine of enlightenment, and pilgrims came from every quarter to see Voltaire. In 1778 he returned to an enthusiastic welcome at Paris, but his enjoyment was short-lived. Death overtook him there on May 30, 1778.

His writings are loosely representative of three categories: literature, history, and philosophy. In the field of literature he is known for such lyrical poems as *The Worldly Man, Poem on Natural Law,* and *Poem on the Disaster of Lisbon.* His philosophical tales included *Micromegas* (1752), *Zadig* (1747), and *Candide* (1759). He introduced scientific methods to the study of history, concentrating mainly on contemporary or recent history and questioning the traditional emphasis on the working of divine providence in human affairs. He encouraged the ideal of impartial reporting, but his own work was often biased by his distaste for organized religion and for any evidence of the supernatural. In 1765 he published his *Philosophy of History.* Voltaire's main field of endeavor was, however, philosophy. Two representative works are his *Lettres Philosophiques* (1734) and his social theory, *Oedipe* (1718).

He also wrote many articles on religious and cultural ethics for the *Dictionnaire Philosophique* (1764). He constantly attacked superstition in churchmen and waged two campaigns in favor of people who were victims of cruel treatment by ecclesiastical authorities. During his lifetime he penned more than twenty thousand letters to twelve hundred important people. Because of his critical approach to the Roman Catholic Church, thirty-nine of Voltaire's works were placed on the Index of prohibited books. His writings were at the root of much of the anticlerical expression that continues to be part of the French culture. W. A. DETZLER

VON HÜGEL, FRIEDRICH (1852–1925)
Roman Catholic lay theologian, philosopher, and spiritual adviser

Friedrich von Hügel was born in Florence, the elder son of Baron Carl von Hügel, whose title he inherited. His mother was a Scottish Presbyterian who became a convert to Roman Catholicism. His father was an Austrian diplomat, and the boy grew up in an atmosphere of familiarity with the leading figures of the Catholic Church. Friedrich never went to school but was taught by a succession of private tutors. An attack of typhus in 1870 left him deaf and his health permanently impaired. Shortly afterwards he came to a firm faith. He married in 1873, and from 1876 until his death he made his home in London.

Baron von Hügel was a private scholar of independent means. His studies embraced science, philosophy, biblical criticism, and religious history. His early interest in geology taught him the value of cumulative evidence and made him aware of successive stages in development. By 1890 he had begun to study Wellhausen's critical approach to the Old Testament.

Von Hügel was a personal friend of several leaders of the Modernist movement in the Roman Catholic Church at the turn of the century. They included the French scholar Alfred Loisy (1857–1940) and the English Jesuit George Tyrrell (1861–1909). Both Loisy and Tyrrell were excommunicated, but von Hügel, perhaps because he was a layman holding no official position, escaped formal censure. At the same time von Hügel was less openly critical of the Church and less skeptical about the historicity of its early origins.

Von Hügel was critical of developments within the Roman Catholic Church since the Reformation. He believed that undue emphasis was being placed on papal infallibility, the authority of the hierarchy, and the juridical aspect of the church. This was coupled with a neglect of its sacramental and spiritual life. His own position combined a critical approach to the Bible with a mystical faith and a deep commitment to the Church. His friendships and influence extended far beyond the confines of Roman Catholicism, and he was valued as a spiritual adviser by many among the ranks of cultured society. His published works include *Essays and Addresses* (1921), *Selected Letters* (1928), and *The Reality of God* (1931). C. BROWN

W

WALDENSTROM, PAUL PETER (1838–1917)

Swedish theologian; organizer of the Swedish Mission Covenant

Born at Lulea, Waldenstrom studied at Uppsala, where he graduated with a Ph.D. in 1863. In the following year he was ordained in the (Lutheran) Church of Sweden, but found its theological outlook depressing to a man more interested in revivals and who put the Bible above creedal statements. Though he was at heart an evangelical, as a biblical theologian he acknowledged a debt to Albrecht Ritschl (1822–1889), the German Protestant theologian who rejected the idea of Christ's propitiatory sacrifice and God's penal wrath. Waldenstrom insisted that man had to be reconciled to God, not God to man—that man needed to take up God's offer of salvation. This was not regarded as consistent with mainline Lutheranism. In 1878, still within the umbrella of the national church, he organized the Swedish Mission Covenant, which held to congregational principles. Four years later Waldenstrom resigned from the national church's ministry and served the Evangelical National Association, a movement founded in 1856 for the reform of religion in Sweden. He became its leader and its publications editor. He visited America several times after 1889. He formed what was subsequently known as the Evangelical Covenant Church among the many covenant members who had gone there.

Waldenstrom was not only an accomplished scholar who early in his career had taught theology and biblical languages, he was also a member of the state diet (*Riksdag*) for more than two decades from 1884. His devotional writings were warmly acclaimed and widely used. J. D. DOUGLAS

WALDO, PETER (c. 1150–1218)

Mendicant preacher; founder of the Waldenses

His early life obscure, Peter Waldo (or Valdes) dispersed his wealth and began a mendicant life about 1173. He was soon a prominent itinerant preacher in Lyons and elsewhere in France. Amid a simple gospel presentation, Waldo's message strongly criticized prevailing Church abuses. This focused on the regular clergy's worldliness and heresies of the Cathar sect. Until his death, Waldo's ministry attracted ever-increasing numbers. Such adherents, often called the Poor Men of Lyons, or the Poor of Spirit, became a loosely identifiable Christian body. As the movement spread in the 1200s and 1300s, it was known as the Waldenses. Quite uniquely, Waldo preached from a vernacular French translation of the Scriptures. This eschewal of the authorized Latin Bible distinguished the Waldenses, especially compared to Francis of Assisi's similar movement.

Waldo and his followers sought legitimization at Lateran Council III (eleventh general council) in 1179. In a respectful response, Alexander III approved the Waldenses' poverty vows but prohibited any preaching except by clerical invitation. Waldo and other Waldenses, however, felt compelled to continue public proclamation of their views. Thus shortly after Alexander's statement, Bellesmains, archbishop of Lyons, condemned the movement. Waldo made a fully orthodox declaration of faith to Cardinal Henry Albano in 1180. But at the Council of Verona (1184) Lucius III excommunicated the Waldenses as a group, banding them with Cathars and other heretics. From this point, the Church and the Waldenses became radically separated, and the movement joined with other Nonconformist groups and doctrines in many places. Frequently Waldensian teachings approximated later Protestant ideas: rejection of purgatory and some sacraments, refusal to venerate saints or pray for the dead. Waldenses also were usually Donatist separatists, opponents of any recognition of unworthy priests. Some Waldenses joined with the extremist Humiliati and Arnoldists of Italy. Except for separatist concepts, most, however, seem to have remained generally orthodox.

Despite their doctrinal orthodoxy, Waldo and his adherents were persecuted heavily after Lucius's condemnation. In some places, this included not only excommunication but imprisonment and capital punishment. Such measures forced many Waldenses to conform to the Church. A few retained poverty vows in their renewed Church obedience. In the later 1200s and 1300s, therefore, explicit Waldensianism flourished primarily in France's and Italy's remote mountain areas. The name Waldenses became synonymous with heretic, but some adherents escaped persecution and kept their identity into the 1400s. Many

at that time united with Hussites and other pre-Reformation groups. Clearly, the Waldenses were important forerunners of the Protestant Reformation. A few distinct Waldenses continued into the Reformation era, and these organized a formal church in France and Italy. This small group has remained intact until now.

One may find original materials on Waldo and his movement in the *Archivum Fratrum Praedicatorum*. Other sources are printed in the *Enchiridion Fontium Valdensium*. K. J. BRYER

WALKER, THOMAS (1859–1912)
Anglican missionary to South India

Born at Matlock Bath, Derbyshire, Walker attended St. John's College at Cambridge and was ordained to the ministry in 1882. In 1885 he was commissioned by the Church Missionary Society to go to Tirunelveli, where he became known as Walker of Tinnevelly. The Syrian Orthodox Church invited him to conduct preaching tours in Kerala. He became a well-known evangelist and Bible teacher in the Tamil region, preaching at Keswick-type conventions and exerting a great influence on Amy Carmichael, the first Keswick missionary. Walker was closely linked with Carmichael's work at Dohnavur. L. LEONARD

WARFIELD, BENJAMIN BRECKENRIDGE (1851–1921)
American Presbyterian theologian and educator

Born in Lexington, Kentucky, Warfield graduated from the College of New Jersey (Princeton University) in 1871 and from Princeton Theological Seminary in 1876. He spent a year in postgraduate study at Leipzig University (1876–1877) and then became assistant minister of the First Presbyterian Church of Baltimore, Maryland (1877–1878). In 1878 he was appointed instructor in New Testament Language and Literature at Western Theological Seminary, Allegheny, Pennsylvania, being promoted to a full professorship in 1879. In 1887 he succeeded

A. Hodge as professor of didactic and polemical theology at Princeton Seminary, a position he retained until his death. He was chief editor of the quarterly *Presbyterian and Reformed Review* from 1890 to 1902, and a frequent contributor to its successor, the *Princeton Theological Review.* Theologically, Warfield held to the doctrines of biblical inerrancy (which he defended against such opponents as C. A. Briggs and Henry P. Smith), original sin, predestination, and limited atonement; and since he found these doctrines clearly set forth in the Westminster Confession of Faith, he honored it as "the final crystallization of the very essence of evangelical religion." During his lifetime he published twenty volumes of sermons, lectures, doctrinal treatises, reviews, and critical essays on contemporary theological issues, and under the terms of his will, ten volumes of his most important articles were posthumously collected and published—for example, *Revelation and Inspiration* (1927), *Calvin and Calvinism* (1931), *Perfectionism* (1931–1932), and *The Inspiration and Authority of the Bible* (1948). N. V. HOPE

WARNECK, GUSTAV (1834–1910)
Missionary statesman; founder of the science of missiology

Born in Naumburg, and educated at nearby Halle University, Warneck served as an official of the Barmen (Rhine) mission from 1871 to 1875 before becoming pastor in the latter year at Rothen Schirmbach, where he remained until 1896. In that year he retired from his pastorate in order to occupy the first German university chair of missions at Halle, which he occupied for the next twelve years. In the *Allgemeine Missionszeitschrift* (*General Missionary Journal*), which he founded in 1874 and edited for the next thirty-seven years, and more particularly in his monumental five-volume *Evangelische Missionslehre: Ein Missionstheoretiker Versuch* (1897–1903), he founded the science of missiology. Stephen Neill says that "all later writers have borrowed much, directly or indirectly, from Warneck." In his *Sketch of a History of Protestant Missions*

(1882; tenth edition, 1913), Warneck traced the story of the Protestant missionary movement as it had developed since the Reformation. He also contributed to missionary strategy the idea of holding regular conferences among missionaries and missionary organizations in order to coordinate their activities and thus make them more effective. In 1879 he founded the Saxon Provincial Missionary Conference, of which he became president; and in 1888 at the London Centenary Conference on Foreign Missions, he presented a plan for worldwide cooperation among Protestants in foreign missions, which was practically a blueprint for the International Missionary Council when it was founded in 1921. N. V. HOPE

WATTS, ISAAC (1674–1748)
English hymn writer

Isaac Watts was the first Englishman to succeed in overcoming the prejudices that opposed the introduction of hymns into English public worship. Today it is difficult to realize that such a prejudice ever existed. The objection to singing usually was not an objection to the singing of the Psalms, but an objection to the singing of hymns that had been composed in modern time.

In 1707 Watts published a book of hymns, some of which were of such enduring worth that scarcely any hymnal in modern times omits them: "When I Survey the Wondrous Cross," "Joy to the World," "O God Our Help in Ages Past," "Jesus Shall Reign Where'er the Sun," "Lord of the Worlds Above," and "Give Me the Wings of Faith to Rise." They were by no means the first English hymns, but they were the first considerable collection. It is not surprising that Independent Congregations sang no other songs for seventy years or so, or that Watts's hymns have retained their popularity after generations of hymn writers.

As a result of Watts's writings, the need of the human heart to express its religious feelings found vent in a new and more expressive direction. The lyric impulse that again and again had manifested itself in sacred hymns, despite the shackles of the Calvinistic devotion to the Psalms, found its expression first in these freer and more spontaneous versions by Watts. These new versions of the Psalms had a freedom and spiritual fervency unknown before. This gives place to a more spontaneous and emotional expression of the general thought of the Psalms. The tunes to which these new hymns were to be sung were emotional, spontaneous, and popular. This "new wine" burst the old bottles of rigid psalmody and created a new church music of its own.

When Isaac Watts's hymns began to find their way into favor, many conservative religious people disdainfully called them "Watts's whims." While Martin Luther's hymns were being sung widely in Germany, Watts's hymns were still fighting their way into some churches, sometimes as much as thirty to forty years later.

Watts wrote over five hundred hymns; however, not all were the best quality. He said that Charles Wesley's hymn "Wrestling Jacob" was worth all that he (Watts) had ever written. Despite his modesty, his output was very significant to English hymnody.

In 1719, Watts introduced Psalm paraphrases written with greater freedom than those that had been in use. He managed to express faithfully the sentiment of the Psalms and enriched them for Christian people by references to New Testament thought.

Isaac Watts's *Hymns and Psalms of David Imitates* was also well known in the United States colonies in the eighteenth century. He kept in touch with the colonies, carrying on regular correspondence with different religious leaders such as Cotton Mather. Benjamin Franklin published Watts's *Psalms* in 1729. By 1740 it was clear that it strongly caught the interest of the American colonists. One of the earliest American books for children was *Divine and Moral Songs*, published by Isaac Watts in 1720. G. A. COMFORT

WEATHERHEAD, LESLIE DIXON
(1893–1976)
British preacher and religious author

Born in London of Scottish parentage and brought up in Leicester, Weatherhead was educated for the Methodist ministry at Richmond College, London, from 1913 to 1915. From 1917 to 1919 he served as an officer in the Indian army, and after World War I ended he became a chaplain, taking charge of the English Methodist Church in Madras, India, in 1919. In 1922 he returned to England and served as minister of the Methodist Church of Oxford Road, Manchester, until 1925. In 1925 he became minister of the Brunswick Methodist Church, Leeds, where he remained for eleven years. In 1936 he became minister of the London City Temple, a Congregational church. (This church was destroyed by enemy action in 1941, but was rebuilt in 1958.) Weatherhead resigned in 1960. He was president of the Methodist Conference in 1955 and 1956.

Weatherhead authored more than thirty books, most of them with wide circulation. They embraced three categories: (1) sermons, such as *When The Lamp Flickers* (1948), *That Immortal Sea* (1953), and *Key Next Door* (1960); (2) popular theology, such as *Why Do Men Suffer?* (1936) and *The Christian Agnostic* (1965); (3) treatises on the relation of psychology to the Christian faith, such as *Psychology in the Service of the Soul* (1930), *Psychology and Life* (1934), and *Psychology, Religion, and Healing* (1951).

The story of Weatherhead's life has been written by his son, A. Kingsley Weatherhead, and was published in 1975 under the title *Leslie Weatherhead, A Personal Portrait*. N. V. HOPE

WEIL, SIMONE (1909–1943)
French writer, philosopher, and mystic

Simone Weil was born in Paris, the daughter of prosperous, free-thinking Jewish parents. Throughout her early schooling and her years at the university she demonstrated exceptional intellectual gifts. During the same time she developed a compassionate concern for the socially underprivileged and the working class. Between 1931 and 1938 she taught philosophy at several French universities. During the Spanish Civil War she served briefly with an anarchist unit, evidencing her leftist political tendencies.

During the late 1930s Weil began to experience mystical visions and engaged in talks and correspondence with Father J. M. Perrin, who brought her close to the threshold of faith and conversion. In 1942, during World War II, she came to America with her parents and in 1943 went to England to work with the French Resistance. There she died of tuberculosis and malnutrition, having refused to eat more than her countrymen were getting in occupied France.

Most of her books appeared after her death. While it contains passages of moving and probing simplicity, much of her writing taxes the understanding. *Waiting for God* (1950), her spiritual autobiography, is her best-known work. Admired also is *Gravity and Grace* (1952), which declares that all things in the world tend downward through gravity, but only grace can raise that which has fallen. Some observers have seen in the intensity and thought patterns of Weil's writing a similarity with Pascal. Other works, notebooks, and letters were published during the 1950s. Simone Weil's writing and her activitist involvements had a great influence after her death on intellectuals in the West. P. M. BECHTEL

WEISS, JOHANNES (1863–1914)
Theologian; New Testament scholar

Born at Kiel, son of the distinguished theological professor Bernard Weiss (1827–1918), Johannes was educated at the Universities of Marburg, Berlin, Göttingen, and Breslau. In 1888 he began his career as a New Testament teacher as privatdozent at Göttingen, where he remained until 1895. From 1895 to 1908 he taught at Marburg, and from 1908 until his death, at Heidelberg. In 1892, in his book *Die Predigt Jesu vom Reiche Gottes* (*Jesus' Preaching Concerning the Kingdom of God*), he propounded the view that the central purpose of Jesus' mission was to proclaim the future transcendent kingdom of God, in which he (Jesus) would be manifested as Messiah, and which would come only through a great and cataclysmic act of God himself. This apocalyptic view of the kingdom, which was subsequently taken up and developed in thoroughgoing

fashion by Albert Schweitzer, dealt a serious blow to the prevalent liberal and this-worldly conception of the kingdom of God as an inward spiritual experience or an ethical society, and provoked widespread debate. Furthermore, Weiss was a pioneer exponent of the principles of form criticism—i.e., the scientific study of the history of literary forms—which was subsequently elaborated upon by Weiss' successor at Heidelberg, Martin Dibelius, and his pupil Rudolf Bultmann. Weiss' principles were laid forth in an article he wrote in 1912 for the publication *Religion in Geschichte und Gegenwart* (*Religion in History and the Present*) on "Literatur Geschichte des Neuen Testament" ("Literary History of the New Testament"). In 1914 Weiss also began a comprehensive work on the history of primitive Christianity (*Das Urchristentum*), which was left unfinished at his untimely death but was subsequently completed and edited by R. Knopf in 1917. N. V. HOPE

WELLHAUSEN, JULIUS (1844–1918)
German theologian and biblical critic

Born in Hameln, Westphalia, Wellhausen studied at Göttingen and then taught there for two years. Then he was appointed professor of theology at Greifswald University in 1880, but shortly thereafter he resigned because he did not believe in the inspiration of Scripture. Thereafter he became a professor of Oriental languages at Halle (1882), Marburg (1885), and Göttingen (1892). Wellhausen acheived fame by purporting the view that the Pentateuch was written by different authors at different times—as late as the postexilic period. Many archaelogical discoveries in the past century have discredited this view. Most of his writings focused on Old Testament criticism and Jewish history; his most acclaimed book is *History of Israel* (1878, translated into English in 1883). P. W. COMFORT

WELZ (WELTZ), JUSTINIAN VON (1621–1668)
Promoter of Protestant missions

Justinian von Welz was the third of seven children born to the Lutheran couple of noble lineage, Gotthard and Rosine von Welz, living in Roman Catholic Austria. Little is known about Justinian's early years. At the age of twenty, Justinian went to Leyden, probably as a university student. Following a dramatic conversion he was a transformed person, ready to become an overseas missionary. Welz was prepared to give up his baronial title and be a missionary but proceeded cautiously. Upon extensive correspondence with leading theologians to test his ideas, he took steps to form a "Jesus-Loving Society."

In 1664 Welz issued a clarion call to the church to assume its missionary responsibilities. In three pamphlets he set forth the missionary obligation of the church, called for the organization of a missionary association to get the job done, and advocated the opening of a training school for missionary candidates. But the times were not propitious. The churches, though orthodox in doctrine, were lacking in spiritual life and missionary vision. Before the Protestant churches could launch an ongoing missionary endeavor they had to be renewed.

Even though Welz failed to mobilize the Protestant Church for mission, he remained faithful to the cause. Leaving Germany for Holland, he gained support from pastor Friedrich Breckling in Zwolle. Welz became the first and only missionary ever to be sent out by the Jesus-Loving Society. In 1666 he departed as missionary for Suriname, where he died two years later. H. KASDORF

WESLEY, CHARLES (1707–1788)
Celebrated hymn writer; cofounder of Methodism

Charles Wesley was the younger brother of the famous John Wesley. He was as committed to Christian work as John was, but of a gentler spirit. Historically, he was absolutely indispensable to the Methodist movement. His contribution was no less than his illustrious brother's.

Charles Wesley was converted in May 1738, three days before John. Both men went to Oxford and were instrumental in keeping the Holy Club alive. Charles Wesley's ministry began at Bristol in 1739, and like his brother he suffered a good deal of persecution in the early days. He lived into his eighties, long enough to see an acceptance of his preaching and principles.

It is by his hymns that Charles Wesley is known worldwide. The number of hymns he wrote is approximately eight thousand. It could be said that he wrote three hymns a week for fifty-seven years.

The first hymnal of the Evangelical revival was edited by Wesley. It was called *Collection of Psalms and Hymns* (1738). A year later a joint effort by Charles and John was published called *Hymns and Sacred Poems*. Charles's last hymn book was called *A Pocket Hymn Book* (1786).

Charles's purposes in writing hymns were to provide Christian teaching and material for public praise and to objectify his rich personal faith. He equaled the Calvinist hymn writer Isaac Watts in his use of the Scriptures and excelled him in his faculty for juxtaposing scriptural references and allusions. For example, "Love Divine" quotes from 2 Corinthians 3, Psalm 106, and Malachi 3, among other sources. Not only was Scripture his guide; classical and contemporary literature provide some of his sources. "Love Divine" finishes with a quotation from Joseph Addison and was written with a tune by Purcell in mind. Wesley was filled with the best of literature in the English, Latin, and Greek languages. He associated this literature with Scripture and used it to illuminate Scripture, producing the amazing lyrics by which his people were taught.

As Charles Wesley composed his hymns, Germany was ready for his music as it was ready for Handel's music. The individualism of Wesley's religious approach and that of Handel's music flow from a common cultural source. The music that came naturally to the composer (who furnished the tunes for the early evangelical hymn books) was the music of the opera house and the concert room—solo and chorus, melody and bass, aria and continuo.

Wesley wrote a seasonal hymn for each of the great Christian seasons. Many of these have survived into contemporary use, such as "Lo, He Comes" for Advent, "Hark the Herald Angels Sing" for Christmas, "Christ the Lord is Risen Today" for Easter, and "Hail the Day That Sees Him Rise" for Ascension.

Hymn books from the time of Isaac Watts onward were written also for reading as well as for congregational singing. This is why most Christians carried with them a "pocket hymnal"; they were used daily for devotions—either read or sung.

Wesley raised two musical sons who both contributed greatly to the music of the church. They were Charles II and Samuel. Both of the sons followed in the footsteps of their father, and Samuel was the most prolific in composition, fashioning much of his work after the great J. S. Bach. When Charles Wesley died, he left the Methodist church a wealth of hymns and songs that have endured through these ages as timeless treasures. G. A. COMFORT

WESLEY, JOHN (1703–1791)
English evangelist; theologian; cofounder of Methodism

Born in Epworth, Lincolnshire, England, John Wesley was the fifteenth child and second surviving son of Susanna and Samuel Wesley. Samuel was a former Nonconformist and rector at Epworth who, with Susanna, raised his children in an atmosphere of piety and Puritan discipline. John's dramatic rescue at age five from a fire that destroyed his father's rectory gave occasion for him in later life to refer to himself as "a brand plucked from the burning [fire]."

Wesley was educated at the Charterhouse School, London, and Christ Church, Oxford. He was elected fellow of Lincoln College, Oxford in 1726, and received his M.A. in 1727. Wesley's short tenure as assistant to his father as curate at Wroote (1727–1729) was his only experience in a parish. A letter from the rector of Lincoln brought Wesley back to his duties at Oxford, where he joined his brother Charles, George Whitefield, and others in a venture that was to be the cradle of the Methodist movement.

These earnest young men caused a sensation at Oxford by frequently meeting together for Bible study, communion, and prayer. They were derisively referred to as the Holy Club, Sacramentarians, Bible moths (feeding on the Bible as moths on cloth), Bible bigots, and Methodists. John was called the "curator" or "father" of the Holy Club.

Charles had started the group while John was away serving at Wroote. He said the word *Methodist* "was bestowed on himself and his friends because of their strict conformity to the method of study prescribed by the university." John did not care for the nickname but wore it as a badge of honor and in an early sermon spoke of his associates as "the people in derision called Methodists." Later, in his *English Dictionary,* he defined a Methodist as "one that lives according to the *method* laid down in the Bible."

On January 1, 1733, in the midst of the controversy surrounding the "Oxford Methodists," John preached his second university sermon, "The Circumcision of the Heart." This sermon helped establish him as a theologian because it won approval from both the vice-chancellor and the rector of Lincoln. In it Wesley set forth the two doctrines that were basic to his position at that time: Christian perfection and the witness of the Spirit (that we are the children of God—Rom. 8:16).

Although the Methodist fracas cost him the loss of earnings, of friends, and of reputation, John Wesley placed higher value on "a clean heart, a single eye, a soul full of God! A fair exchange, if by loss of reputation we can purchase the lowest degree of purity of heart!" In 1735 John and his brothers were summoned to the deathbed of their father. There Samuel Wesley said to John, "The inward witness, son, the inward witness—this is the proof, the strongest proof of Christianity."

That same year the Holy Club began to dissolve when John, Charles, and two others of its members sailed for the American colony of Georgia. John was to be missionary to the native Americans and pastor of the Savannah parish, but his naïve pursuit of a romance with Sophia Hopkey, niece of the chief magistrate of Savannah, contributed to the failure of this endeavor. Sophia, rejected by John, married another man and Wesley excluded her from Holy Communion. Wesley had faithfully served his flock but had exhibited a stiff high churchmanship that antagonized the parish. The Hopkey affair produced enough misunderstanding and persecution to cause John to flee Georgia and return to England.

John Wesley failed decisively in Georgia, but the experience proved to be important to his future career. The preface to this American disaster came during a violent storm on the voyage from England. Wesley was cowering in fear of death yet witnessed the unexplainable peace experienced by a group of Moravian Brethren who were his fellow travelers. An interview with the Moravians' leader upon landing in Georgia set in motion John's search for the living reality of the doctrines he preached.

Wesley left Georgia on December 2, 1737. On January 24, 1738, he wrote in his *Journal*: "I went to America to convert the Indians; but O! who shall convert me? Who, what is he that shall deliver me from this evil heart of unbelief? I have a fair summer religion. I can talk well; nay, and believe myself while no danger is near; but let death look me in the face, and my spirit is troubled. Nor can I say, 'To die is gain.' . . . I show my faith by my works by staking my all upon it . . . . O who will deliver me from this fear of death?"

Back in London John met Peter Bohler, a Moravian who instructed him in the assurance of salvation by faith. This and his reading of Luther's commentary on Galatians, which emphasized justification by faith alone, prepared him for the day he attended a Moravian meeting near his old school, Charterhouse. What followed is described in the famous entry for May 24, 1738, in John Wesley's *Journal*:

In the evening I went very unwillingly to a society in Aldersgate Street, where one was reading Luther's preface to the Epistle to the Romans. About a quarter before nine, while he was describing the change which God

works in the heart through faith in Christ, I felt my heart strangely warmed. I felt I did trust in Christ, Christ alone for salvation; and an assurance was given to me that he had taken away my sins, even mine, and saved me from the law of sin and death.

Charles Wesley had preceded John in forming the Holy Club and in true faith in Jesus Christ. But now at last they were together prepared to lead the great Methodist revival that revolutionized English society. On June 11, 1738, eighteen days after Aldersgate and one week before his thirty-fifth birthday, John preached at Oxford University his famous sermon "By Grace Ye Are Saved through Faith" and struck the chord that was to be the theme of his life thereafter.

Wesley immediately left for Germany, where he visited the Moravian Brethren leader Count Zinzendorf. He returned to England in September 1738, joining Charles in preaching the truth of the gospel wherever he was permitted. Such places were becoming harder to find, since the Anglican congregations soon closed their doors to the Wesleys because of their enthusiasm, but they were invited to the religious societies that existed at that time within the Church of England. In May 1738 they had founded their own "little society" on Fetter Lane, London. By autumn the Fetter Lane society numbered fifty-six men and eight women.

Encouraged by an account of the Great Awakening in New England by Jonathan Edwards and by George Whitefield's successes at outdoor preaching, Wesley swept away his ecclesiastical and High Church views and began preaching in fields at Bristol (1739). The Methodist revival in England had begun. "I look upon the world as my parish," he wrote, "Thus far, I mean, that in whatever part I am in, I judge it meet, right, and my bounden duty to declare unto all that are willing to hear the glad tidings of salvation."

Wesley was a member of the Church of England until his death. He would not schedule Methodist meetings to conflict with Anglican services. However, during the following fifty years John Wesley rode

250,000 miles on the roads of England, Scotland, and Ireland to preach 42,000 sermons. Besides this he published 233 books. His tireless and incessant activity changed the face of British society and the nature of its religion forever.

In 1739 Wesley bought and renovated an abandoned cannon foundry near London. Seating fifteen hundred, the foundry served as the Methodists' headquarters for thirty-eight years until, in 1777, City Road Chapel was built.

John followed his younger brother Charles in evangelical conversion and George Whitefield in outdoor preaching, but his unique practical genius, seen in his ability to organize, preserved his work as the Methodist societies. In 1742 he organized "class meetings," with admission only to those holding "society tickets," to exclude undesirables. He published *Rules* for the Methodist societies in 1743 to avoid the scandal of unworthy members. In 1744 the societies imitated the primitive church in holding love feasts and broke new ground by gathering in the first annual conference. This gathering of preachers at Wesley's invitation developed into a sort of parliament deciding doctrinal and administrative questions. The conference perpetuated Wesley's authority among the British Methodists after his death.

The Methodist Revival caused great tumult in England. Rioting mobs often threatened the lives of Wesley and his followers. Methodism eventually emerged as an evangelical order within the Church of England, though it was never appreciated or approved by the Church hierarchy. Church doors continued to be closed to Wesley's teaching. This produced a poignant and triumphant scene at Epworth in May 1742. Refused the pulpit in the parish where he was born and where his father devoted nearly forty years to the service of God, John stood on his father's tombstone in the churchyard and preached for eight evenings to the greatest crowds Epworth had ever seen. He returned to London and described the scene to his ailing mother. Susanna Wesley died in July 1742, happy to have witnessed the revival of religion her husband had long desired.

Wesley broke the mold of the settled Anglican curate and became a widely traveled itinerant preacher. Most ordained clergymen of the day had no taste for this approach to the service of God. So Wesley was forced to enlist a band of dedicated laymen who also became itinerant preachers and administrators of the Methodist societies. These Methodist "circuit riders" became an important element in American life after the American Revolution.

His rejection of the doctrine of election caused a temporary split with George Whitefield in 1741 and the division of the Welsh Calvinistic Methodists in 1743. Wesley organized societies in Ireland on forty-two trips beginning in 1747 and in Scotland on twenty-two trips beginning in 1751. In 1770 he sent Francis Asbury to America to strengthen and enlarge the societies there and in 1772 ordained Thomas Coke as general superintendent of the Methodists in America. Coke then ordained Asbury. This development horrified Charles, who said that his brother had "assumed the *episcopal character.*" John later ordained several others "to administer the sacraments of baptism and the Lord's Supper according to the usage of the Church of England . . ." yet continued to hold that Methodism was simply a society of Christians who would remain loyal to their own church or denomination.

Wesley had another serious problem—a difficult marriage. His wife, Mary, had a troubled spirit. She lied about her husband, destroyed his papers, and resented the regimen he followed in his work. In 1771 she left without warning. Attempts at reconciliation were made, but when his wife was buried on October 12, 1781, John had not even heard of her death.

Wesley enjoyed good health for most of his long life. His *Journal* records the sources of his bodily strength: (1) the power of God, fitting Wesley for his calling; (2) traveling four or five thousand miles a year; (3) the ability to sleep at command, day or night; (4) having risen at four in the morning for over sixty years; (5) having preached at five in the morning for over fifty years; (6) "Lastly, evenness of temper. I feel and grieve, but by the grace of God I fret at nothing. But still, 'the help that is done upon earth He doeth it Himself.' And this He doeth in answer to many prayers."

His "desire to furnish poor people with cheaper, shorter and plainer books" caused Wesley to become a prolific author of educational treatises, translations from Greek, Latin, and Hebrew, histories of Rome and England, an ecclesiastical history, and biblical commentaries. He edited *Imitation of Christ* and works by Bunyan, Baxter, Edwards, Rutherford, and Law; he compiled an English dictionary, published twenty-three collections of hymns, and recorded his activities, travels, and spiritual life in his *Journal* (1735–1790). His medical handbook *Primitive Physick* went through twenty-three editions in his lifetime and nine after his death. Concerning his publications he wrote, "Some of these have such a sale as I never thought of; and by this means I became unawares rich." He gave all of the riches away.

Beginning in the days of the Holy Club until his death Wesley was concerned "to reform the nation." He pioneered or participated in most of the good causes of his day: legal and prison reform, the abolition of slavery, civil rights, and popular education. In fact, his last act was to dictate a letter to William Wilberforce, who was fighting in Parliament to abolish the slave trade. He encouraged the young man's "glorious enterprise in opposing that execrable villainy which is the scandal of religion, of England and of human nature . . . . O be not weary in well doing! Go on, in the name of God in the power of his might, till even American slavery (the vilest that ever saw the sun) shall vanish away before it."

At age eighty-six Wesley preached a hundred sermons in sixty towns in nine weeks. On October 7, 1790, he preached his last outdoor sermon under an ash tree in the churchyard of Rye in Kent. On February 23, 1791, he preached from Isaiah 55:6, "Seek ye the Lord while he may be found; call ye upon him while he is near," in Kingston House in the country village of Leatherhead. This was the last time the world heard John

Wesley raise his voice to proclaim the glad tidings of Jesus Christ.

At ten o'clock on Wednesday morning, March 2, 1791, John Wesley spoke his final word, "Farewell," and the beloved servant of God entered the joy of his Lord. Thousands filed by his open coffin in City Road Chapel. At the funeral John Whitehead preached, "Know ye not that there is a prince and a great man fallen this day in Israel?" (2 Sam. 3:38). Memorial services were held throughout England, Scotland, and Ireland. Newspapers and magazines published scores of sermons and articles. One, the *Gentleman's Magazine*, a secular publication that had often criticized Wesley, was most eloquent:

> *Where much good is done we should not mark every little excess. The great point in which his name and mission will be honored is this: he directed his labors towards those who had no instructor; to the highways and hedges; to the miners in Cornwall and the colliers in Kingswood. . . . By the humane and active endeavors of him and his brother Charles, a sense of decency, morals, and religion was introduced into the lowest classes of mankind; the ignorant were instructed; the wretched relieved; and the abandoned reclaimed. . . .*
>
> *Though his taste was classic, and his manners elegant, he sacrificed that society in which he was particularly calculated to shine; gave up those preferments which his abilities must have obtained, and devoted a long life in practicing and enforcing the plainest duties. Instead of being "an ornament to literature," he was a blessing to his fellow creatures; instead of "the genius of the age," he was the servant of God!*

D. PARTNER

WESLEY, SAMUEL SEBASTIAN (1810–1876)
Christian hymn writer

The Wesley family produced men of remarkable talent through five generations. This Wesley was a grandson of Charles, the great hymn writer. His father, Samuel, and uncle were both accomplished organists and composers, the former being one of the first in England to appreciate the genius of Johann Sebastian Bach, thus giving his son Samuel the same middle name. In his maturer years, he was organist successively of several cathedrals of the Church of England. Like his namesake he found the ecclesiastical authorities penurious and unappreciative. In 1849, he published a sharp attack on their indifference toward the maintenance of adequate choirs and instruments. Unfortunately he did not live to see the improvements brought about by his crusading or the efforts of such men as Ouseley and Stainer. Wesley's output of musical compositions was not great, but his Cathedral Service in E and such anthems as "The Wilderness" are superior to anything by his contemporaries. He wrote a good many hymn tunes, of which the best known is *Aurelia,* written for "Jerusalem, the Golden" but now universally sung to "The Church's One Foundation."

J. B. MacMILLAN

WESSEL, GANSFORT (c. 1419–1489)
Dutch scholar

Born in Groningen, the Netherlands, Wessel added the name Johann to his baptized name, supposedly to distinguish himself from John (Richrath) of Wesel, his virtual contemporary. A student of the schools of the Brethren of the Common Life, he taught at Zwolle from 1432 to 1449. Under the profound influence of the *Devotio moderna,* he went in 1449 to Cologne. There he studied Greek, philosophy, and the relatively new discipline of Hebrew. He was particularly interested in the writings of Augustine, Bernard of Clairvaux, and Rupert of Deutz. All of that indicates that he belonged to the new humanism, but it was the particularly Christian phase of it that characterized northern European countries. It also carried with it a strain of Platonic realism and elements of mysticism.

About 1458 he migrated to Paris, where he became involved in the nominalist controversy that was raging at that time. After a lengthy interval Wessel returned about 1475 to the Netherlands. Many later students, notably Luther, looked upon him as an authentic precursor of the Reformation. It is possible that there was some (almost inevitable) confusion of him with his slightly older contemporary. Wessel did in fact question the church's infallibility, whether of pope or of councils, the doctrines of indulgences, of priestly absolution, and of purgatory, as well as the efficacy of sacraments apart from faith. Yet he was protected by his ecclesiastical superior, the bishop of Utrecht.

A. CABANISS

WEST, JOHN (c. 1775–1845)
Anglican missionary to western Canada

Born at Farnham, Surrey, England, John West was educated at St. Edmund's Hall, Oxford. He was ordained to the Anglican ministry in 1804 and spent fifteen years in curacies in England. Having been appointed to the parish of Chettle in Dorsetshire, England, West temporarily absented himself in order to undertake missionary work in the Red River district in western Canada.

In 1820 he reached the Red River settlement, in what was later the Winnipeg area, where he served as chaplain to personnel of the Hudson's Bay Company, a fur-trading organization. In 1822 he was accepted as a missionary by the Church Missionary Society of Britain. West made several missionary journeys in the area north and west of Red River, conducting services and performing marriages and baptisms. In 1821 and 1822 he visited York Factory on Hudson Bay, where he established an Auxiliary Bible Society on contributions from Hudson's Bay Company personnel.

West was a pioneer in the early history of Manitoba. He helped to raise the moral tone of the Red River settlement and laid the groundwork for the education of both whites and Indians. Three of the Indian pupils of the school he established became missionaries. He suffered from the hostility of Scots in the Hudson's Bay Company who resented the fact that they had not been given a Presbyterian minister. In 1823 West returned to his parish at Chettle in England, where he spent the rest of his life.

D. C. MASTERS

WESTCOTT, BROOKE FOSS
(1825–1901)
Bishop of Durham (England); New Testament scholar

Raised in Birmingham, Westcott later attended Trinity College, Cambridge, where he became a fellow in 1849. From his college days on he remained a close friend of J. B. Lightfoot and Fenton Hort, with whom he labored in producing some of the best Christian scholarship of the nineteenth century.

Beginning in 1853 Westcott and Hort worked together for twenty-eight years to produce a volume entitled *The New Testament in the Original Greek* (1881). Along with this publication, they made known their theory (which was chiefly Hort's) that Codex Vaticanus and Codex Sinaiticus (along with a few other early manuscripts) represented a text that most closely replicated the original writing. They called this text the Neutral Text. (According to their studies, the Neutral Text described certain manuscripts that had the least amount of textual corruption.) This is the text that Westcott and Hort relied upon for compiling their edition of the Greek New Testament.

In 1870 Westcott was appointed regius professor of Divinity at Cambridge, and in 1890 he succeeded Lightfoot as bishop of Durham. He built upon the good foundation laid by Lightfoot, who had done much to reorganize the diocese. Westcott had a deep concern for the social and industrial problems of his diocese and on several occasions helped the coal miners.

Westcott, with Hort and Lightfoot, had planned to collaborate in writing a commentary on all the books of the New Testament, but the three did not realize their collective goal. (Lightfoot completed commentaries on some Pauline Epistles, and Hort made little progress.) Westcott, however, completed his portion—on Hebrews, John, and the Epistles of John. These became classic commentaries—still consulted and quoted by modern scholars. Among other noted works, Westcott wrote *History of the New Testament Canon* and *A History of the English Bible*. He also served on the committee that produced the English Revised Version.
P. W. COMFORT

WESTON, FRANK (1871–1924)
Anglican bishop of Zanzibar

Born into an evangelical home in London, Weston became a strong Anglo-Catholic during a brilliant career at Oxford. After ordination in 1894, he served parishes in slum areas, then joined the largely celibate Universities' Mission to Central Africa in 1898. Ten years were spent chiefly in the educational field, notably in the training of ordinands, before his consecration as bishop. Indefatigable and of strong views that he never hesitated to express (he once pronounced excommunication on a fellow English bishop who had promoted a very liberal clergyman), Weston was said to have understood the mind of Africans as few have done. In *Serfs of Great Britain* (1920), he protested against the system of forced labor in East Africa. While in principle supporting church reunion, he is remembered most for fierce opposition to a particular scheme that would have brought together Christian missionary work in Kenya, thus stirring a controversy that spread throughout the English-speaking world. His antimodernism was reflected in his best-known work, *The One Christ* (1907), which espoused a modified kenotic (i.e., "emptying out") theory of Christ's incarnation. J. D. DOUGLAS

WHEELOCK, ELEAZER (1711–1779)
Congregational pastor; founder of Dartmouth College

Born in Windham, Connecticut, Wheelock graduated from Yale University in 1733. After graduation he pastored a Congregationalist church in Lebanon, Connecticut, where he achieved success as a revivalist preacher during the Great Awakening of the 1730s. Several years later, in an attempt to increase his income, he began to take pupils, including Indians, into his home. His interest turned more and more to education and the conversion of Indians. In advancing these causes, Wheelock founded a school in 1754 to prepare Indians as missionaries to their own tribes. And in 1769 he secured a charter from the colony of New Hampshire for the establishment of a school known as Dartmouth College. The institution was named after the earl of Dartmouth, who had contributed ten thousand pounds to the effort. Wheelock proved to be an able and dedicated administrator, supervising the construction of the campus at Hanover, New Hampshire, directing farming operations, preaching, teaching, recruiting students, and continually raising funds. R. L. TROUTMAN

WHITBY, DANIEL (1638–1726)
Anglican scholar; controversialist

Born in the English county of Northampton, Whitby graduated from Oxford and was elected fellow of Trinity College there in 1664. He published that year *Romish Doctrines Not from the Beginning*—one of his many broadsides against Roman Catholicism. From 1668 he ministered in the diocese of Salisbury and in 1682 produced *The Protestant Reconciler.* This attempt to gain concessions from Nonconformists so that they would be attracted to the Church of England drew considerable criticism. Whitby's bishop forced him to sign a retraction, and the work was publicly burnt at Oxford, condemned for "want of prudence and deference to authority" and for containing "false and schismatical principles." He also wrote in characteristically robust fashion against Calvinism. His somewhat dogmatic views on eschatological matters were remarkably influential, but heterodox notes crept into his theology. He latterly inclined toward Arianism, and his *Last Thoughts* (1727, posthumous) show that he had become a convinced Unitarian. Of all his works, his *Paraphrase and Commentary on the New Testament* (two volumes, 1703) was the most lasting; it maintained a wide circulation for two centuries.
J. D. DOUGLAS

WHITE, ELLEN GOULD (1827–1915)
Early leader in the Seventh Day Adventist Church

White was born at Gorham, Maine, the daughter of Robert and Eunice Harmon. When she was still a child, her family moved to Portland, Maine. When Ellen was ten she was struck by a stone, putting her in a coma for three weeks. When she recovered, her devout mother believed she was spared for some divine purpose. For the next six years, the young girl fought a battle to return to a normal state of health.

During a moving evangelistic campaign of William Miller in 1840, Ellen embraced the Adventist faith and looked for the personal return of Christ in October 1844. Being disappointed by this false expectation, and in a state of depression, in December of that year she held a prayer meeting with four women. Subsequently, she had a vision of being transported to heaven and realized that Christ's second advent could not take place unless the great commission was fulfilled.

On August 30, 1846, she married the Reverend James White, born in Palmyra, Maine. He was ordained a minister to the Adventist faith in 1843. In 1864 he became ill and his wife nursed him back to health. This experience turned their thoughts to health reform, and in response to a vision that came to Ellen, the Western Health Reform Institute was founded in 1866 at Battle Creek, Michigan.

After her husband's death in 1881, Ellen traveled about visiting churches and attending conferences and camp meetings. She labored in Europe from 1885 to 1888, and in 1891 she went to Australia, remaining there nine years. In 1901 she directed her interests to the southern states and founded Southern Publishing Association at Nashville, Tennessee, in 1903. She had a definite part in moving the national denominational headquarters to Washington, D.C., in 1907. Ellen White was a constant contributor to denominational newspapers and authored several volumes such as *Life Sketches.*
R. VONDERLACK

WHITE, JOHN (1866–1933)

British Wesleyan missionary to the Mashona of Rhodesia

Besides his ministry in Mashonaland, White introduced Methodist missions beyond the Zambesi River and into the Copperbelt of Katonga, Congo. From beginning to end White championed the rights of the native peoples against the government, the Chartered Company, the white settlers, and even officers of the Church. Perhaps his greatest achievement was the founding of Waddilove Institution, a coeducational enterprise with a school, crafts shops, a farm, and a hospital. He established other schools, trained catechists, and translated the Scriptures. After 1901 he was chairman of the Missionary District and later superintendent. White was stationed at Bulawayo in urban ministry after 1904, but illness sent him back to Waddilove in 1921. The great famine of 1922 challenged his talents. He went to England for an operation for cancer, and died August 7, 1933. P. BEAVER

WHITEFIELD, GEORGE (1714–1770)

Revivalist and well-known evangelist of the eighteenth century

Whitefield was born in Gloucester, England, where he received his early education. Later he entered Pembroke College, Oxford, where in exchange for tuition he served several more highly placed students. At Oxford he was befriended by John and Charles Wesley and became part of the Holy Club, a group of young men devoted to the regular practice of Christian duties. While at Oxford he experienced an evangelical conversion and became convinced of the absolute necessity of spiritual regeneration for salvation. After receiving ordination as a deacon in the Church of England in 1736, he began preaching on the necessity of the "New Birth."

When opposition to his preaching resulted in churches closing their doors to him, he began preaching wherever and whenever the opportunity presented itself, such as in meeting houses of religious societies, public halls, barns, and (far more scandalous at the time) open fields. As an itinerant preacher he was tireless. In his nearly thirty-four years of ministry he spoke more than fifteen thousand times to literally millions of people. In addition to Wales, Ireland, and his own England, he made fourteen visits to Scotland and seven trips across the Atlantic to the American colonies (1738, 1739–1741, 1744–1748, 1751–1752, 1754–1755, 1763–1765, 1769–1770), where he died in Newburyport, Massachusetts, in 1770. Whitefield's friendship with the Wesleys became strained as differences in theology became apparent. Whitefield, a decided Calvinist, freely preached on the bound will, God's electing grace, and the definite Atonement, themes that were at odds with John Wesley's Arminianism. In 1741 they officially broke from each other but maintained a mutual respect for the rest of their lives. Whitefield was neither a theologian nor the organizer that John Wesley was, but for sheer oratory he was unsurpassed, and as a preacher he did not allow doctrinal issues to determine where he would minister. He freely crossed ecclesiastical boundaries, and though Anglican, he cooperated readily with all denominations and was equally at home in America and in England.

Routinely claimed as the founder of American revivalism, Whitefield was the leading figure in the eighteenth-century American revival known as the Great Awakening. In his first visit to the American colonies in 1738 he helped to found an orphanage in Georgia. During his second visit, beginning in 1739, his preaching set the colonies ablaze with revival. The height of his success came in 1740 during a six-week tour of New England. In just forty-five days he preached over one hundred and seventy-five sermons to tens of thousands of people, leaving the region in a spiritual uproar, marking one of the most remarkable periods of American Christianity. His aggressive method of preaching wherever and whenever the opportunity presented itself was new to America and especially to Puritan New England. While ministers would occasionally exchange pulpits by mutual consent, the whirlwind itinerant ministry of Whitefield set an example that was later imitated by evangelical ministers of all denominations. Unlike the preaching of his day, which was heavily doctrinal and full of multiple points and subpoints and delivered in a "plain style," he preached with simplicity and directness and with much life and passion. His free use of natural gestures, illustrations, and a more extemporaneous style permanently altered American evangelical preaching. He was also a preacher of extraordinary power and possessed a supreme ability to hold audiences, attracting people from every rank and station in life. Benjamin Franklin estimated that he could be heard clearly by up to thirty thousand people at one time.

He was one of the first to enlist the aid of laymen, thereby helping to break down the rigid clergy-laity distinction in ministry. While not despising educated and ordained clergy, he was led to emphasize piety and gifts over official sanction. What was needed were men truly converted, called, gifted, and living a godly life. In addition, he believed that personal study was an indispensable part of the Christian life; thus he was directly involved in helping to found three American educational institutions: the College of New Jersey (now Princeton University), the College of Philadelphia (now the University of Pennsylvania), and Dartmouth; and at the time of his death he was intending to begin one in Georgia.

By his successive trips to the American colonies and extensive preaching tours throughout Britain, Whitefield helped to knit into a unified movement an evangelical network of revivalism that transcended denominational barriers. He inspired such figures as Jonathan Edwards and Gilbert Tennent in America and fanned into flame the revival fires that swept through Scotland and Wales in the early 1740s. His network of correspondence was staggering; he often received his letters by the trunkload. While he enjoyed unprecedented success, he also experienced great censureship and abuse. In the first years of his ministry he committed several indiscretions that were forcefully brought to his attention. When confronted with his own mistakes he characteristically owned up to them and gave public apology for them. His willingness to confess and redress such errors early in his ministry enabled him to avoid committing others for the greater part of his life. By the time of his death he had won the admiration and commanded the attention, if not the assent, of the entire English-speaking world, leaving a legacy that has helped shape American Christianity. C. MITCHELL

WHITMAN, MARCUS (1802–1847)
American physician, missionary, and pioneer

Born at Rushville, New York, Whitman in 1832 was awarded the M.D. degree by the College of Physicians and Surgeons of the Western District of New York. After practicing medicine in Canada and at Wheeler, New York, in 1834 he offered his services to the American Board of Commissioners for Foreign Missions as "physician, teacher, or agriculturist." In 1835, along with Samuel Parker, he was sent to explore the region of the Oregon, but did not go beyond Green River. In March 1836 with his wife and three other fellow missionaries, he left the East to engage in Christian work among the Cayuse Indians of the upper Columbia River. In September the party reached Fort Walla Walla at the junction of the Columbia and Walla Walla rivers. Thereafter three mission stations were founded: at Waiilatpu in the Walla Walla valley, at Lapwai near the present Lewiston, Idaho, and at Spokane, Washington, in 1838. In 1842, because of dissension among the missionary fraternity, the American Board decided to close down one of the stations. In 1842 and 1843 Whitman journeyed three thousand miles back east to persuade the board to rescind this decision. He succeeded in doing so and returned with a group of immigrants to the Oregon territory. In 1847 an epidemic of measles caused such fatalities that Whitman and the other missionaries were suspected of using black magic against the Indians. Whitman, his wife, and twelve others were murdered by Indians at their Waiilatpu station. It may be claimed that Whitman, more than anyone else, aroused popular interest in Oregon and thus greatly helped to promote its settlement. N. V. HOPE

WHITTIER, JOHN GREENLEAF
(1807–1892)
American poet

Whittier was born to poor parents of Quaker and Puritan ancestry on a farm near Haverhill, Massachusetts, north of Boston. His schooling beyond the elementary grades consisted of two terms in a local academy, financed by Whittier's schoolteaching and shoemaking. He quite early showed skill as a poet and secured a position as editor of a weekly published in Boston. His first published volume, including poetry and prose, drew largely from his local New England experience and appeared under the title *Legends of New England* (1831). Like his parents, Whittier was a Quaker and a pacifist, but in matters of social reform he was an energetic activist. He was intensely involved in antislavery agitation, and his writing is said to have helped elect Lincoln. The height of his fame came in the 1880s, when he was regarded as one of the "schoolroom poets," was studied in classrooms everywhere, and was readily understood by student readers. His poetry was admired for its piety, compassion, and commendation of goodness, but it lacks evidence of depth and wide learning. Whittier's most admired poem is "Snow-Bound" (1866). Well known also are "Maud Muller," "Barbara Frietchie," "Telling the Bees," "Ichabod," and "Skipper Ireson's Ride." Among Whittier's fine hymns are "Dear Lord and Father of Mankind" and "We May Not Climb the Heavenly Steeps." P. M. BECHTEL

WHITTINGHAM, WILLIAM
(c. 1524–1579)
Puritan scholar; Anglican dean; Bible translator

Born at Chester, Whittingham was educated at Oxford; and after further studies in France, Germany, and Switzerland he returned to England a convinced Protestant. The temper of the time was not congenial, however, for this was the reign of Mary Tudor (1553–1558), who was set on suppressing Protestantism. After four months Whittingham left for Frankfurt, which became a gathering place for exiles, including the Scot John Knox. Divisions rose among the group. Knox was expelled in 1555 for insisting on a more thorough Reformation (such as he was to effect in Scotland five years later). Whittingham followed Knox to Geneva and, though he evidently had not been ordained, succeeded him as minister in the city of Calvin. Whittingham published there an English version of the New Testament and was to a large extent responsible also for the so-called Geneva Bible (1560) and for metrical versions of the Ten Commandments and many psalms. In 1563, after the Protestant Elizabeth succeeded the Catholic Mary on the English throne, Whittingham was made dean of Durham—a surprising choice, for Elizabeth normally disliked Puritans. Whittingham fell foul of his bishop, Edwin Sandys, fellow biblical scholar and moderate Puritan, who questioned the validity of Whittingham's clerical orders. The matter had not been resolved when the dean suddenly died. J. D. DOUGLAS

WHYTE, ALEXANDER (1836–1921)
Scottish minister

Born in the small Angus town of Kirriemuir, Whyte was educated at Aberdeen University and the Free Church College in Edinburgh. After four years as assistant minister at Free St. John's, Glasgow (1866–1870), he became colleague and successor to the famous R. S. Candlish at Free St. George's, Edinburgh. His appearance in the pulpit was as arresting and impressive as the preaching itself, which attracted people of every class and kind. A deep appreciation of God's grace to save sinners gave him rare passion and power. "Let your imagination sweep up through the whole visible heavens, up to the heaven of heavens," he would urge. A dramatic quality captivated his congregations with its depth of spiritual fervor. "To know Dr. Whyte," said J. M. Barrie, himself a native of Kirriemuir, "was to know what the Covenanters were like in their most splendid hours." In the month after Dr. Candlish died (1873), Whyte welcomed to Edinburgh two unknown American evangelists, Dwight L. Moody and Ira D. Sankey, and warmly supported both their meetings and the follow-up work. Such was the atten-

dance at his own Tuesday prayer meeting that it had to move from the hall into the church itself. His addresses to men on personal morality were unusually forthright, and some were "shaken to the foundations of their being." Whyte also had a breadth of culture (he lectured on Dante and corresponded with Newman) not often found in evangelicals of his day. In 1909 he became principal of New College, a post he held until three years before his death. He was moderator of his church's general assembly in 1898, and he wrote much, but it is as a preacher that he will always be remembered.
J. D. DOUGLAS

WILBERFORCE, SAMUEL (1805–1873)
Anglican bishop

Born in London, the third son of William Wilberforce, the emancipator of slaves, Wilberforce was educated at Oriel College, Oxford University, where he obtained the B.A. degree in 1826. Ordained deacon in 1828 and priest in 1829, from 1830 to 1840 he was rector of Brightstone on the Isle of Wight. In 1840 he was appointed chaplain to Albert, Queen Victoria's prince consort, and that year he left Brightstone to become the rector of Alverstoke in Hampshire. In March 1845 he was nominated to the deanery of Westminster, and in October of that year he became bishop of Oxford. In 1869 he was translated to the see of Winchester, where four years later he was killed by a fall from his horse.

Wilberforce has been called "the remodeler of the episcopate," since he projected the image of the pastoral, as contrasted with the political or prelatical, bishop. Believing that the bishop should be "the mainspring of all spiritual and religious agency in the diocese," he compelled the rural deans to assemble their clergy in regular chapters and report to him personally on their activities. He established diocesan societies for the building of churches, for augmentation of clerical salaries, for the provision of additional clergy, and for the relief of the poor. The total amount thus expended in the diocese of Oxford under Wilberforce's episcopate was upwards of two million pounds. In

his service to the national Church of England, he encouraged the formation of some of the earliest Anglican religious communities, notably sisterhoods at Wantage (1849–1850) and Clewer (1852) and the Society of St. John the Evangelist at Cowley (1865). In 1854 he founded Cuddesdon Theological College as an Anglo-Catholic training school for future clergymen. One of his last achievements was to sponsor the revision of the King James New Testament. In 1870 a joint committee of both Houses of Convocation was appointed for this purpose. Until his death Wilberforce presided over the activities of this committee, which eventually produced a revised translation in 1881.
N. V. HOPE

WILBERFORCE, WILLIAM (1759–1833)
English philanthropist; antislavery crusader

Born in Hull, Wilberforce studied in desultory fashion at Cambridge, then in 1780 entered Parliament and became a strong supporter of William Pitt, who persuaded Wilberforce to devote himself to the abolition of the slave trade. In this cause he opposed many in the empire who had powerful vested interests, and he opposed those who regarded slavery as "a natural and scriptural institution." The reformers finally triumphed in 1807 when the slave trade was done away with, though abolition of slavery itself had to wait until 1833.

Wilberforce, who had been converted at twenty-five, was the most famous figure associated with the Clapham Sect, which sought to do for the upper classes what Wesley had done for the lower. They used their wealth and influence in Christian outreach. He supported missions, fought to improve the condition of the poor and prisoners, and in 1804 helped to form the British and Foreign Bible Society. He also supported Catholic emancipation. Wilberforce, who was once described as "the authorized interpreter of the national conscience," published in 1797 his *Practical View of the Prevailing Religious System*, which ran through many editions.
J. D. DOUGLAS

WILFRID (634–709)
Northumbrian bishop and evangelist

Son of a noble Saxon family, Wilfrid received his main education at the Lindsfarne abbey. He also studied at Canterbury, where he became strongly devoted to Roman Christian ideas and traditions. To the end, Wilfrid's great desire was the establishment of Roman—as opposed to Celtic—Church practices in England. In 653, he traveled to Rome, and then, going on to Lyons, he remained three more years on the Continent. Returning in 658 to Northumbria, Wilfrid assumed the abbacy of the monastery at Ripon (near York). His ordination as priest came in 664 through Agilberht, a Gaulish bishop serving northern England. Momentously, that same year the Synod of Whitby, largely through Wilfrid's advocacy, made Roman traditions the official practices of the Northumbrian church. Celtic Christian leaders immediately departed the area, leaving many bishoprics entirely leaderless. In the ensuing reorganization, Wilfrid was selected for the prominent see of York, the principal vacated jurisdiction.

Wilfrid's trials over the York post were a continuing thorn for the rest of his days. Yet overall, amid the difficulties, his long life was one of highly committed, effective Christian service. Wilfrid's first business was his consecration as bishop, this necessitating a journey to a convocation at Campiegne, France. On return after many delays, however, he found York taken over by Chad, another Northumbrian leader. Wilfrid retired temporarily to his old post at Ripon, and he soon entered into various ministries in Mercia (south of Northumbria). But then in 669, Theodore, archbishop of Canterbury, on his visit to Northumbria, ordered Wilfrid brought back and installed at York. Wilfrid came immediately, and under his leadership the York bishopric, always central to Northumbrian Christianity, soon expanded greatly in size and dominance. Wide implementation was given the great bishop's emphases on Benedictine monastic rule and Roman practice in general. Yet as time went on, Theodore found York's expansion objectionable, and in 678 he directed that the York jurisdiction become four separate bishoprics. Fearing mostly the new Roman ways' demise, Wilfrid vehemently opposed this action. His response was the innovative decision to travel to Rome and appeal to the pope. And by 679, Wilfrid was on his way back with Pope Agatho's order to restore York's undivided state. But unexpectedly, on his arrival at York, Wilfrid faced Egfrith, the Northumbrian king, who not only rejected the papal order but had the great bishop imprisoned. Though quickly released, Wilfrid decided his fight over York should be suspended.

For the next seven years, Wilfrid threw himself into evangelistic work among the Saxons of Sussex (southernmost England). In 686, a new Northumbrian king, Aldfrith, reinstated Wilfrid at York. This lasted only until 691, when disputes with Aldfrith forced Wilfrid to leave. Responding to a request by Ethelred, king of Mercia, Wilfrid then again journeyed south, and for the next eleven years he administered the bishopric of Lichfield. These were years of uplift for the Mercian church. In 703, Brihtwald, Theodore's successor at Canterbury, decided Wilfrid should resign his position at York and resume the abbacy at Ripon. Still in dissent about York, Wilfrid quickly departed once more for a personal appeal to Rome. Once again the papacy upheld his claims to the bishop's office at York. After consideration, however, on return to England, Wilfrid reconciled with Brihtwald and agreed to exchange York for the bishopric of Hexham (near York) as well as the Ripon abbacy. His last years were relatively quiet.

It is unjust to picture Wilfrid's life as a quest for mere ecclesiastical power. Wilfrid primarily sought the advantages he thought Benedictine monasticism and Roman authority could bring English Christianity. And in the end, a chief reason for these traditions' ascendancy in England came from Wilfrid's efforts. Perhaps more importantly, Wilfrid, despite his exiles and travel, had many fruitful years as an evangelist and administrator in southern England. Wilfrid's influences also contributed much to

Willibrord's and others' interest in bringing the Gospel to the Continent.

Not one of Wilfrid's writings has been preserved. However, there are contemporary accounts of his life by Eddi in his *Vidi Wilfridi*, and by Bede in his *Historia ecclesiastica*. K. J. BRYER

WILLIAM I (WILLIAM THE CONQUEROR) (c. 1028–1087)
King of England 1066–1087

Born illegitimately to Robert, Duke of Normandy, and Herleva, William was nonetheless designated Normandy's heir in 1035. His youth was immersed in the problems of consolidating his rule over Normandy's vast area. While a young adult, William was respected for his piety, strict conduct, and leadership. In 1047, he could claim to have bested all of Normandy's rebellious nobles and also to have conquered Maine, an adjacent province. Besides the king, William was France's most powerful noble.

In 1053, William married Mathilda, daughter of Baldwin V, earl of Flanders. He was fastidious in obtaining the papal dispensation required for overcoming the prohibition against close relatives marrying. In deference to the church, William revealed not just his piety and strict views on wedlock but also his interest in the English throne, to which the marriage would offer greater claims. Actually, William, closely related by blood to Edward, England's king, had already considered this prospect on other grounds. But on Edward's death, the situation was inflamed when another relative, Harold, took the English crown despite a pledge of loyalty to William. Thus, in October 1066, William gathered his forces, crossed the channel, and defeated Harold's army in a climactic battle at Hastings, England. He was officially crowned king of England on December 25, 1066. Due to his legitimate if distant claims and his well-known capabilities, William received immediate support from the papacy and the English hierarchy, and even from many English nobles. Some rebellious landholders presented obstacles to the conquest. But by 1070, after many characteristically brutal campaigns, William had succeeded in uniting the kingdom of England under his reign.

William proved to be even better as an administrator than as a warrior in his rule of England. His policies and laws were an insightful mixture of established Saxon practice and innovative Norman ideas. In both political and ecclesiastical spheres, the foundations created by William became an enduring basis for England's further development and advance. Amid very many memorable achievements, William's Domesday survey of 1086 is probably the most widely remembered. Truly an extraordinary project, the Domesday records detail the material resources and social divisions for all of late-eleventh-century England. William's last year was occupied with suppressing revolt in his native Normandy. According to attendants at his death in Rouen, his last few days showed much constancy of devotion to Christ.

Throughout his reconstruction of English life, William enjoyed the English hierarchy's unreserved consideration and support. In general, the church viewed William's rule as a vehicle for the powerful reform movements sweeping over England and all western Europe. In retrospect, it seems unequivocal that William's church policies—his effort to bring England the best in Norman Christianity—had lasting benefits. He thus deserves recognition as one of England's most important religious reformers. In practical terms, William's most provident action was his installation of Lanfranc, former abbot of Bec (near Paris), as archbishop of Canterbury. Lanfranc was a supremely capable, far-seeing leader who brought to English Christianity much wisdom over church-state relations and zeal for clerical and lay revival. William was generally submissive to the papacy regarding church affairs (except on investiture of bishops by secular monarchs). And even Gregory VII, the great zealot for investiture reform, kept quiet about England because of William's beneficence toward church progress and renewal. K. J. BRYER

WILLIAM I (THE SILENT) (1533–1584)

Governor (Stadtholder) of Holland; Prince of Orange; Dutch patriot; "father of his country"

Born at Dillenburg in Germany, in 1544 William inherited from his cousin René large estates in the Low Countries (Netherlands and nearby regions) and Germany. Educated as a Roman Catholic for service at the court of the emperor Charles V, when Charles abdicated in 1555 William was appointed by Charles's son and heir Philip II as a member of the Council of State and was later made Governor (Stadtholder) of Holland, Zealand, and Utrecht. Along with his colleagues Egmond and Hoorn, however, William opposed Philip's policy of persecuting Dutch Protestants by means of the Inquisition.

In 1567, when Philip sent the Duke of Alva to the Netherlands to carry out this persecution with thoroughness, William retired to his Dillenburg estate, thus escaping the fate of Egmond and Hoorn, who were executed for high treason in 1568. That year William mobilized an army to free the Netherlands from Spain, but this attempt failed. Then he sought help from the French Protestants (Huguenots), but the Massacre of St. Bartholomew's Day in 1572 made this impossible. William now pinned his hopes for Dutch independence on the Calvinists of Holland and Zealand. He landed at Enkhuizen in 1572 and embraced Calvinism the next year. Though he suffered some defeats in the campaigns that followed, by 1576 Spanish tyranny had goaded the seventeen provinces of the Netherlands into organized rebellion; and by the Pacification of Ghent of that year William was recognized as leader of the "common fatherland" against Spain.

By 1579, however, the new Spanish regent Parma succeeded in winning back the ten southern provinces to the Spanish allegiance. In that year the seven northern provinces (Holland, Zealand, Utrecht, Gelderland, Groningen, Friesland and Overijssel) organized for independence on their own. In 1580 Philip offered a reward to anyone who would rid the world of the Dutch leader. To this William replied in a dignified *Apology* (1581) in which he justified his rebellion against Spain; but in 1584 he was assassinated at Delft by Balthasar Gerard. Though he did not live to see the outcome of the struggle, under the leadership of his son Maurice the independence of the Netherlands was recognized in 1609. N. V. HOPE

WILLIAM III (OF ORANGE) (1650–1702)

Governor (Stadtholder) of the Netherlands, 1672–1702; King of Great Britain and Ireland, 1689–1702

William III (the only son of William II of Orange) was born at The Hague (of the Netherlands) and educated at Leyden University. In 1672, when Holland was invaded by the French king Louis XIV, William was made stadtholder, captain general, and admiral. In 1678 he was able to negotiate the Treaty of Nymegen, under which the Dutch territory was left intact. In 1677 he married his cousin Mary, daughter of the British King James II. James, a strong Roman Catholic, sought to favor his coreligionists, a policy highly unpalatable to his Protestant subjects. When a son was born to James and his wife in 1688, William accepted an invitation from James's opponents to come to their help. When he landed with an army at Torbay in 1688, James fled; thereafter, William and his wife were jointly proclaimed sovereigns of Great Britain. Though there was some opposition to the new monarchs in Scotland and Ireland, it was overcome by 1690.

Domestically, the reign of William was significant. It witnessed the foundation of the Bank of England in 1694 and the passage of the Bill of Rights and the Act of Settlement in 1702. William, however, was interested mainly in foreign policy, where his chief aim was to cement a European alliance that would curb the power of his arch-foe Louis XIV. At the head of a Grand Alliance, William took the field in the Belgian Netherlands, but he was defeated by the French Marshal Luxembourg at Steinkirk in 1692 and at Neerwinden in 1693. The tide turned in William's favor with the defeat of the

French fleet by the Dutch at the Battle of La Hogue in 1693 and the recapture of Namur in 1695. By the Treaty of Ryswick Louis formally acknowledged William's title to the British throne.

The death of King Charles II of Spain in 1700, and his bequest of his kingdom to Philip of Anjou, grandson of Louis XIV, touched off the War of the Spanish Succession, in which much of Europe was united against France. William, however, did not live to fight this war, since he was killed by a fall from his horse in 1702. But his associate John Churchill, later Duke of Marlborough, was ready to take command of the allied armies and lead them to victory. So of William it may be said that he "practically insured the success of his life's work, though he did not live to complete it." N. V. HOPE

WILLIAM OF MALMESBURY
(c. 1090–1143)
English historian and monk

Of both Norman and Anglo-Saxon ancestry, William became a Benedictine monk at Malmesbury. The seventh-century monastery was notable for its library, a fine one for the time. In the main William was a self-taught person, employing the library to his advantage and advancement in scholarship. By virtue of his study, especially of the Venerable Bede, he devoted himself to historical writing. From his pen came three significant works of that genre. His *Gesta regum Anglorum* (*Deeds of the Kings of the English*) was an account of kings from the time of the Anglo-Saxon states to the Norman state of his own day. Written in readable Latin, it did not spare its subjects from criticism. The *Gesta pontificum Anglorum* (*Deeds of the Bishops*, c. 1125) was a similar compilation dealing with the church. His *Gesta novella* (*Recent History*) was planned as an account of the civil wars waged by King Stephen and Queen Matilda, both claimants to the throne as successors of Henry I. It was, however, not completed before William died. He also wrote devotional treatises and compiled collections of lay and canon laws. But his fame rests on his historical narratives. Of his own

life little is otherwise known, except as he revealed it in his writings. A. CABANISS

WILLIAM OF OCKHAM
(c. 1280–c. 1349)
English philosopher and theologian

William of Ockham was an English Scholastic philosopher and the most influential theologian of his time. Born at Ockham near London, he studied at Oxford and later taught at Merton College there. As a member of the Franciscan Order, William became involved in a Franciscan dispute with Pope John XXII, who called him from Oxford to Avignon to answer for his views. William supported the teachings of the Spiritual Franciscans, which John had condemned as heretical. Imprisoned and excommunicated, William escaped in 1328 to the court of Holy Roman Emperor Louis IV (Ludwig) of Bavaria. There he became Louis's principal advisor and supported him in his contest with John. He probably spent the rest of his life in Munich and may have died there of the Black Death in 1349. During his later years he tried to effect reconciliation with the church, but it is not known whether he was successful.

In political matters, William taught that the papacy and empire were both founded by God and neither was superior to the other; each had its own sphere. In his *Dialogues* (1343) he laid the foundation of the modern theory of independence of civil rule from the church and proposed that the pope abandon all temporal power.

Philosophically, William was a nominalist—that is, he believed the real is always individual, not universal. General truths or ideas or universals have no real existence outside the mind and are only abstract terms developed by the mind as a result of the observation of particular things. He denied the synthesis of Aristotle and Christian doctrine worked out by Thomas Aquinas and others and thus contributed to the disentegration of Scholasticism.

William's religious views were closely related to his philosophical beliefs. In opposing Aquinas's synthesis of reason and revelation, he taught that theological dogma was not rationally demonstrable and must be accepted on the authority of the Church. But since he was in conflict with what he deemed to be a moribund papacy, he taught that the Bible alone was the only infallible source of authority, that the pope was not infallible, that a general council was the highest ruling power in the Church, and that the laity should be given a greater voice in the affairs of the Church. Moreover, he argued that God was above all knowledge and could not be apprehended by reason but only by faith. Thus he greatly influenced John Wycliffe and Martin Luther.

As his attacks on Aquinas's synthesis contributed to the demise of Scholasticism, many turned to mysticism or returned to Augustinianism for religious comfort during the fourteenth and fifteenth centuries. And with philosophy no longer tied to a defense of theology, it tended to become an enemy of theology. Furthermore, rationally-oriented individuals questioned the validity of some Christian doctrines.

William was also significant in the rise of modern science. His nominalism, his emphasis on direct experience of individual things, suggested that natural phenomena could be investigated rationally; thus, he paved the way for Francis Bacon and his scientific efforts. His nominalism was a medieval forerunner of the empiricism of the seventeenth and eighteenth centuries.
H. F. Vos

WILLIAMS, CHARLES WALTER STANSBY (1886–1945)
English writer

Charles Williams is, among other things, a splendid example of what one can accomplish in his spare time, for, though he was fully employed by the Oxford University Press, he managed to produce over thirty-five books, including poems, novels, dramas, literary criticism, biographies, Christian apologetics, and in addition countless essays, lectures, and book reviews.

Among his directly Christian works are *The Descent of the Dove* (1939) and *The Forgiveness of Sins* (1942), the former being, as

its subtitle indicates, "A short history of the Holy Spirit in the Church." His novels are the most popular of his works and they also are Christian in import. They do not lend themselves to quick reading but pay excellent dividends to anyone who spends time with them. His novel *Descent into Hell,* for instance, tells of a woman on her way to becoming a Christian and of a prominent military historian who chooses hell and goes there.

Charles Williams is well known for certain doctrines peculiar to his works. Of greatest significance are those of coinherence and substitution. Coinherence is simply the conception that men have their humanity in common, a "union of existences" that obtains from one generation to another. As John Donne said, "Every man's death diminishes me." Because we are thus dependent upon one another there is the need for exchange. Even nature possesses coinherence. A tree requires rain and rain requires the sun to return it to the skies. All life is interlocked and interdependent. Each person has a circle of friends with whom joys and sorrows are shared. Such coinherence naturally leads to exchange and the doctrine of substitution. Love, said Williams, is not simply beautiful—it is useful. The Scriptural teachings to bear one another's burdens is not just a pious maxim but a practical and necessary way of conduct. We are quite literally to substitute for one another, bearing the other's burden and, just as important, allowing the other to bear our burden. C. KILBY

WILLIAMS, SIR GEORGE (1821–1905)
Evangelist; founder of the Young Men's Christian Association (YMCA)

Born at Dulverton, England, and apprenticed to a draper, Williams was converted through reading the works of C. G. Finney. In 1841 he joined a London drapery firm and rose to become a partner. A meeting in 1844 in his home with twelve young men is usually regarded as the birth of the London YMCA. It was originally planned to benefit young tradesmen, but soon broadened its scope, subsequently expanding not only to various parts of Europe, but also to Australia, India, and South Africa. The first international conference for the YMCA was held in Paris in 1855. Its jubilee meetings in 1894 brought two thousand delegates from all continents. Williams was also known throughout the British Isles as an evangelist who appealed to all ages and classes. A contemporary publication said, "At no time perhaps is he more rousing than when addressing the formalist and the moralist." He was a staunch promoter of the temperance movement.

Williams's leadership also benefited many Christian organizations including the Bible Society, the London City Mission, and the Church Missionary Society. A man of great wisdom and of irenic spirit, he was made a freeman of London and in 1894 was knighted by Queen Victoria. J. D. DOUGLAS

WILLIAMS, ISAAC (1802–1865)

English tractarian and poet

Isaac Williams, whose long friendship with Thomas and John Keble led him to friendship with John Henry Newman and to membership in the Oxford Movement, was educated at Harrow and at Trinity College, Oxford. He became lecturer of philosophy at Trinity College in 1832, dean of the college in 1833, and vice-president from 1840 to 1842. While in Oxford, he also served as a curate under Newman at St. Mary's. After leaving Oxford, Williams served as an obscure country parson in Bisby (1842–1848) and in Stinchcombe (1848–1865).

His best-known poetical writings include *The Cathedral* (1838), which interprets Gothic architecture as a symbol of Christian doctrine; *The Baptistry* (1842), which is an attack on the Roman Catholic Church; and several hymns that appeared in *Hymns on the Catechism* (1842).

He contributed three tracts (80, 86, and 87) to "Tracts for the Times" (1842). His tract number 80, "Reserve in Communicating Religious Knowledge," was an attack against the Dissenters for preaching a "cheap grace." This tract caused an uproar,

which eventually lost him his rightful election to the chair of poetry at Oxford in 1842.

Some of Williams's other prose writings include *Harmony of the Four Evangelists* (1850) and *Devotional Commentary on the Gospel Narrative* (eight volumes, 1869–1870). His *Autobiography*, edited by Sir G. Provost, appeared in 1892.

D. ROETHLESBERGER

WILLIAMS, JOHN (1796–1839)

Known as the "Apostle of Polynesia"

Born in London, John Williams was an ironmonger's apprentice when in 1816 (two years after his conversion) he offered for missionary service and was sent by the London Missionary Society to the Society Islands. He not only evangelized, he also trained the natives in trade and economics. In 1821 he bought a schooner, and two years later discovered the island of Rarotonga, where he eventually translated the Scriptures and other books into the native language. Every significant island within a two-thousand-mile radius had been visited by the time he returned to England (in 1834). When he went back to the South Seas it was with sixteen missionaries, a newly equipped ship, and funds for his work. On a pioneering venture to the New Hebrides he was killed by natives who evidently had suffered at the hands of visiting sailors some years earlier. His death promoted a fresh wave of enthusiasm for missions. Williams wrote *A Narrative of Missionary Enterprises in the South Sea Islands* (1837), a most important and informed work. J. D. DOUGLAS

WILLIAMS, ROGER (c. 1603–1683)

Founder of Rhode Island; early advocate for the separation of church and state

Roger Williams was one of the most controversial men of America's colonial period. He was born in London and studied at Pembroke College, Cambridge. Soon after his graduation from Cambridge he was ordained in the Church of England (1629). Williams served briefly as a private chaplain, during which time he married. In 1631 he migrated to Boston because of his separatist views with respect to Puritan elements in the Church of England. Upon arrival in New England, Williams was offered the pulpit in Boston's only church, but he declined because of its ties with the Church of England. Early in his colonial experience, Williams spoke out against the practice of taking land from the native Indian population without fair payment. His concern over the treatment of Indians, however, was only one of the criticisms he brought against the Puritan establishment. Williams was also concerned about the relationship between the civil and church authorities in New England. Williams believed that the existing government, which set the civil authorities over the church, was fundamentally wrong. He believed that the civil government was responsible to preserve law and order, but that it had no authority to influence or interfere with religious belief and practice. Williams wrote, "It has been to England's shame to fashion and change garments and religions with wondrous ease, as a higher power or a stronger sword has prevailed." He further reflected that some of England's bloodiest chapters had been written by a tyrant's enforcement of one brand of religious belief or another. He had left England, in part, because the government had the Church of England under its thumb; he had no desire to face this same problem in the colonies.

Williams's criticism of the existing authorities, coupled with his outspoken demeanor, resulted in his banishment from New England in 1635. He fled southward in January of the following year, where he bought land from the Indians and founded the colony of Rhode Island. He named its first settlement Providence in recognition of God's help and guidance. Soon after this time he founded America's first Baptist church (1639). He went to England in 1642 and secured a charter for the colony. A pamphlet war with John Cotton drove him to write a number of well-known tracts in defense of religious liberty, including *The Bloody Tenent of Persecution* (1644) and *The Bloody Tenent Yet More Bloody* (1652). During a second stay in England (1651–1654) he was able to safeguard the colony's charter and defend the religious liberty enjoyed

there. Upon his return to Rhode Island, he became the colony's first president and served in that capacity until 1657. In 1683 Roger Williams died in poverty; the actual date of his death was never recorded. He could never have known that his views concerning the separation of church and state would become one of the enduring facets of American experience. M. R. NORTON

WILLIAMS, SAMUEL WELLS (1812–1884)

American missionary and diplomat to China; noted sinologue

Born at Utica, New York, Samuel Wells Williams graduated from Utica High School and Rensselaer Polytechnic Institute. The American Board of Commissioners for Foreign Missions sent him to Canton in 1833 as printer to the mission. He became an expert linguist and published a tonic dictionary of Cantonese, a vocabulary of the Court dialect, a syllabic dictionary of the Chinese language, and a course of lessons for foreigners. Williams published in 1848 his two-volume work, *The Middle Kingdom*, which was to be the standard history in English well into the twentieth century.

When he had learned Japanese and translated the Gospel according to Matthew, Admiral Perry took him to Japan in 1853 and 1854 as interpreter. In 1856 he became secretary and interpreter to the American legation to China. He and W. A. P. Martin were responsible for the insertion of the section on Christianity into the treaty of 1858. Williams resided at Peking beginning in 1863, sometimes being the American Minister. From 1877 until 1884 (the year of his death), he was professor of Chinese language and literature at Yale University. He was also president of the American Bible Society and of the American Oriental Society. P. BEAVER

WILLIAMS, WILLIAM (1781–1840)

Welsh Congregational preacher; generally known as "Williams of Wern"

Born in the parish of Llanfachreth, Merioneth County, at age thirteen Williams

heard a sermon from Rhys Davies that marked such an epoch in his religious life as to constitute his conversion. He attended the Pen-y-Stryd Independent (Congregational) Chapel, where he was received into full-communicant membership at the unusually early age of fifteen. For some time he worked with his father as a carpenter, but before he was nineteen he began to preach. From 1803 to 1807 he was enrolled as a ministerial student at Wrexham Academy in North Wales; and in 1808 he was ordained to the Congregational ministry as pastor of the Yoked Parishes of Wern and Harwood, near Wrexham. During his ministry there he not only built up these churches but also established three new congregations in the surrounding area. In 1834 he became one of the leaders in the Welsh "General Union," an organization whose object was to pay off chapel debts. In 1836 he accepted a call to the Welsh Tabernacle, Great Crosshall Street, Liverpool; but sickness and family difficulties induced him to return in 1839 to Wern, where he died the following year. He is frequently ranked as one of the three greatest Welsh pulpiteers, the other two being John Elias and Christmas Evans.
N. V. HOPE

WILLIBALD (c. 700–785)
Missionary bishop to southern Germany

Probably born in England, Willibald was a (maternal) relative of Boniface, the eminent pioneer missionary to continental Europe. He was educated largely under Egwald at the Abbey of Waltham in Hampshire. Accompanied by his father, Richard, and his brother Winnebald, Willibald's first notable activity was a pilgrimage to Rome in 722. The three also continued to travel in the Eastern empire for several years. Returning to Rome in 730, Willibald spent the next ten years at Monte Cassino (south of Rome), the famous Benedictine monastic complex.

Gregory III commissioned Willibald in 740 as a missionary worker for southern Germany. In 741, immediately on his arrival in Germany, Willibald was given priestly ordination by Boniface and sent to Eichstatt.

Later that year Boniface also consecrated him as bishop for the Eichstatt region. Spending his last forty-five years here, Willibald saw his labors for the gospel and church life bear much fruit. He deserves recognition as the earliest (and most outstanding) pioneer missionary to southern Germany. Among many other important events, Willibald witnessed the completion of large monastic facilities in Heidenheim (west of Eichstatt), a project pursued jointly with Winnebald and also their sister, Walburga. K. J. BRYER

WILLIBRORD (658–739)
Missionary bishop to Frisia

A native of Northumbria, Willibrord was educated first under Wilfrid at the monastery of Ripon (near York). He spent the years 678 to 690 in Ireland, primarily in the monastery at Rathmelsigi. Here under Egbert, the great abbot who strove to connect Irish Christianity with Rome, Willibrord was ordained as priest and began various church ministries. Most important, he became deeply infected with his era's potent Irish missionary spirit.

Willibrord and eleven companions left Ireland in 690 to spread the gospel in the Frisian Islands (the Netherlands and northern Germany). A recent conqueror of Frisia, Pepin II gave his full support to Willibrord and his plans for the gospel in Europe. Thus began the alliance between English Christianity and Europe's early medieval kings—a very critical connection especially during Charlemagne's reign. In 692, Willibrord traveled to Rome and returned with official papal approval for his mission. Another trip to Rome in 695 obtained Sergius I's consecration of Willibrord as bishop of the Frisians. Confirming such papal confidence, Willibrord and his group saw conversions by the thousands and increasing acceptance of Christianity in all northwestern Europe. Dozens of monastic facilities and church buildings sprang up very quickly. The rudiments of Church organization also now came into existence. The monastery and cathedral Willibrord erected at Utrecht became his bishop's residence and center for the Frisian work. Still another important site was the monastic retreat built by the mission at Echternach (eventually Luxembourg).

Beginning in 716, Pepin II's authority collapsed in most parts of Frisia. Radbod and his invaders began a rampage, killing many missionaries and leaders and destroying church buildings and other structures over a wide territory. Escaping to the north, Willibrord spent the next years preaching and organizing the church in Scandinavia and Germany. Finally in 719, Frankish rule regained control in Frisia, and Willibrord returned to scenes of great devastation. Yet a core of believers remained, and with characteristic energy Willibrord proceeded with the spiritual and material rebuilding of the Frisian church. And significantly, that same year, Boniface arrived in Frisia for the second time. Thus this great missionary's powerful labors began with assisting Willibrord in his Frisian rebuilding efforts. Conversions now once again began to multiply, and church life developed even faster than before.

Willibrord's last twenty years witnessed a remarkable growth in northwestern European Christianity. He deserves recognition as one of the continent's most effective early missionary leaders. Willibrord's work should be noted especially for its emphasis on training native church leaders. He also began employment of suffragan (assistant) bishops, a valuable asset to the mission in Frisia. None of Willibrord's writings are still extant except perhaps for a last testament. K. J. BRYER

WILSON, JOHN (1804–1875)
Missionary to India; orientalist

Born in the Scottish border county of Berwick, Wilson was educated at Edinburgh University, was ordained in 1828, and sailed for India under the Scottish Missionary Society. Within six months he was preaching in Marathi. He and his wife established schools, and a college was founded in Bombay (1832) that still bears his name. From 1835 he worked under Church of Scotland

auspices, but (like the majority of evangelicals) joined the Free Church of Scotland in 1843. Such was Wilson's grasp of oriental languages and literature that he greatly impressed the Hindu, Muslim, and Parsi leaders with whom he held public discussions. His work on *The Parsi Religion . . . Contrasted with Christianity* (1843) won him election as Fellow of the Royal Society, London. He declined offers of prestigious governmental posts lest they hinder his missionary usefulness. He traveled widely and was the first missionary to cross Sind. When the University of Bombay was founded in 1857, he became dean of arts and examiner in no fewer than six Eastern languages. His fame and influence extended throughout India and were acknowledged at home by his appointment in 1871 to his church's moderatorial chair. His other books include *The Evangelisation of India* (1849) and *Indian Caste* (1877), as well as other books on Hinduism. J. D. DOUGLAS

WILSON, ROBERT DICK (1856–1930)
Old Testament scholar and philologist

Born in Indiana, Pennsylvania, Wilson was educated at the College of New Jersey (Princeton University), where he eventually earned a Ph.D. in 1886. He studied theology at the Western Theological Seminary (Allegheny) in 1880 and 1881 and at the University of Berlin, Germany, in 1881 through 1883. In 1883 he was appointed instructor in Old Testament at Western Theological Seminary and in 1885 was promoted to a full professorship. In 1900 he became professor of Semitic philology and introduction to the Old Testament at Princeton Theological Seminary. In 1929 he left Princeton Seminary with J. Gresham Machen when the latter founded Westminster Seminary in Philadelphia. Wilson was appointed professor of Semitic philology and Old Testament criticism at Westminster Seminary, but he died the next year. Besides manuals of Hebrew and Syriac grammar, his published works include *Studies in the Book of Daniel* (1916), *Is the Higher Criticism Scholarly?*

(1922), and *Scientific Investigation of the Old Testament* (1923). N. V. HOPE

WINCKLER, HUGO (1863–1913)
Archaeologist and historian

Born in Berlin and educated in its university, in 1891 Winckler became a privatdozent in Semitic philology and in 1904 was appointed professor of Oriental languages. He wrote extensively on ancient history, as in his *History of Babylonia and Assyria* (1891) and his *History of Israel* (two volumes, 1895–1900). Under the auspices of the German Orient Society he began in 1906 excavations at Bogazkoy in Turkey, where he met with great success. In ruined storage chambers he found thousands of hardened clay tablets, most of them in an unknown language that turned out to be Hittite. Collaborating with the Turkish archeologist Theodore Makridi Bey, Winckler continued his excavations until 1912. In the course of his labors he unearthed the remains of a city whose temples, palaces, gateways, and fortifications showed that it must have been the site of an important metropolis. It was proved to be Hattusa, the capital of the Hittites, an ancient people who established a powerful empire in Anatolia and north Syria in the second millennium B.C. On the basis of his findings, Winckler was able to construct an outline of the history of the Hittite empire in the fourteenth and thirteenth centuries B.C. N. V. HOPE

WINDISCH, HANS (1881–1935)
New Testament scholar

Born in Leipzig and educated at Leipzig, Marburg, and Berlin, Windisch began his teaching career as a privatdozent in Leipzig in 1908. In 1914 he became professor of the New Testament and Early Christianity at Leyden, in the Netherlands. In 1929 he moved to Kiel, and in 1935 he succeeded Ernst von Dobschutz at Halle-Wittenberg, where he died. Windisch was an adherent of the Religionsgeschichtlicheschule of New Testament scholars, a group whose members contended that Christianity can best be un-derstood not in isolation but as one among the many religious phenomena in the Mediterranean world of the first century. He wrote monographs on early Christian thought—for example, *Baptism and Sin in Early Christianity to Origen* (1908) and *The Piety of Philo and Its Importance for Christianity* (1909). He also wrote commentaries on New Testament books—for example, on the Catholic Epistles (1911) and Hebrews (1913) in Leitzmann's *Handbuch zum Neuen Testament*, and on 2 Corinthians in H. A. W. Meyer's *Critical-Exegetical Commentary on the New Testament*. In addition, Windisch wrote books on particular New Testament subjects—for example, *Der Sinn der Bergpredigt* (*The Meaning of the Sermon on the Mount*, 1929). N. V. HOPE

WINKWORTH, CATHERINE (1819–1878)
Hymn translator; educationist

It is one of the ironies of church history that Calvin's rejection of "hymns of human composure" denied to English-speaking Christians the riches of New Testament–based congregational song for two hundred years. It was not until the nineteenth century that the riches of Lutheran hymnody began to become known in England. Catherine Winkworth was not the first English translator of German hymns, but she was the most voluminous and the best. She had published two collections: *Lyra Germanica I* and *II* (in 1835 and 1858). These volumes contained no music, however. In 1863, she published *A Chorale Book for England*, which presented a collection of her translations together with their proper tunes in four-part harmony. Then in 1869 there followed her illuminating volume *The Christian Singers of Germany*, which contained a readable account of the lives and work of many of the greatest German hymn writers, with examples of their poems in her apt English paraphrases. No one else did more to arouse interest in the "hymns from the land of Luther." Probably her best-known translations appear in the hymn "Now

Thank We All Our God," from the German of Martin Rinckart (1586-1649).
J. B. MacMillan

WINSLOW, EDWARD (1595–1655)
American pilgrim leader

Edward Winslow was born at Droitwich, Worcestershire, England, but little is known of his early life. While traveling on the Continent in 1617, the young man made contact with the Pilgrims in Holland. He became an active member of the group, earning his living as a printer. Three years later he joined those who took passage on the *Mayflower* for America.

Winslow's abilities soon brought him into prominence, and he became one of the leading figures in the early years of Plymouth Colony. His marriage to Mrs. Susanna White was the first marriage among the English in America, and their child Peregrine was the first white child born in New England. He served as an assistant to the governor nearly every year from 1624 to 1646 and as governor in 1633, 1636, and 1644. He seems to have had marked success in dealing with the Indians.

In the course of his service to Plymouth Colony, Winslow returned to England on a number of occasions. In 1624 he persuasively presented the Pilgrims' cause in negotiating with the Merchant Adventurers, who had financed the *Mayflower* voyage. During his stay he published *Good News from New England,* a narrative of the years 1621 to 1623. On another trip in 1634, Archbishop William Laud accused Winslow of "teaching" in the Pilgrim church and performing marriages. Since it was against the law for a layman to perform these functions, Winslow spent four months in the Fleet prison. On his last trip to England in 1646 he published *The Glorious Progress of the Gospel among the Indians in New England.* The following year he was one of the founders of the Society for the Propagation of the Gospel in New England.

In 1654 Oliver Cromwell appointed Winslow chairman of three commissioners charged with the task of capturing the Span-ish West Indies. Although failing in this objective, the British fleet did succeed in seizing Jamaica. On the return voyage, Winslow died of fever on May 8, 1655, and was buried at sea. His portrait, the only genuine likeness of any *Mayflower* Pilgrim, is preserved in the gallery of the Pilgrim Society in Plymouth, Massachusetts. R. L. Troutman

WINTHROP, JOHN (1588–1649)
English lawyer who became the first governor of Massachusetts

Born in Suffolk, Winthrop briefly attended Trinty College, Cambridge, and then studied law at Gray's Inn. He and his family were Puritans, and as King Charles I sought to establish high Anglicanism as the standard for English worship, like so many Puritans of his day Winthrop lost what little hope he still had for the Church of England. He looked into the opportunity of joining the Massachusetts Bay Company's venture to colonize America and decided to join. Before setting sail on the *Arabella* (1630), Winthrop was elected governor of the migrating Puritans. He settled in Boston and served as governor of Massachusetts numerous times before his death nineteen years later. In 1643, Winthrop helped to organize the New England Confederation and served as its first president.

The colonists' reasons for migration were varied, but Winthrop's leadership gave the movement a unified vision and a sense of Christian mission. As the *Arabella* neared Massachusetts Bay, Winthrop enunciated his vision in his famous lay sermon "A Modell of Christian Charity." He compared the Puritan journey from England with Israel's exodus from Egypt. They were escaping a land where a godless state governed the church and where the sins of centuries dominated the people's thinking and way of life. They would build a new England in the New World—the Promised Land. Their success or failure would depend upon whether they were faithful to God's covenant. Winthrop saw the Puritan migration to the New World as a chance to build a society governed by God's true people and God's principles for holy living. Might not New England become the very kingdom of God?

In support of Winthrop's vision, the civil magistrates attempted to maintain both moral purity and theological conformity among the people. This led to the civil government's domination of the New England church, one of the very reasons they had left England. The demand for theological conformity also led to the exiling of a number of well-known figures, including Anne Hutchinson and Roger Williams. Despite the eventual failure of Winthrop's "kingdom experiment," his belief that America had a moral and spiritual mission to the world endures to this day in American political thought. M. R. NORTON

WISEMAN, NICHOLAS PATRICK STEPHEN (1802–1865)
First Roman Catholic archbishop of Westminster

Born in Seville, Spain, where his Irish merchant father had settled, Wiseman was educated at St. Cuthbert's College, Durham, and the English College, Rome. Ordained in 1825, he taught oriental languages (in which discipline he was highly regarded) and was rector of the English College, Rome (1828–1840). He returned to England as bishop and president of St. Mary's College, Oscott, Birmingham, in 1840, and by the time he was transferred to the London district in 1846 he had won considerable fame as a preacher. He became vicar-apostolic in 1849, and when Pius IX announced the restoration of the hierarchy in England in 1850 Wiseman became archbishop of Westminster and cardinal. The restoration, however, had caused much indignation and uneasiness in the country. Protestants were furious, and Parliament prohibited Roman Catholics from assuming the title of bishop, but this was repealed in 1872.

Wiseman's numerous publications, apart from orientalist works, include *On the Connection between Science and Revealed Religion* (1828), *Twelve Lectures . . . on the Roman Catholic Church* (1836), *Recollections of the Last Four Popes* (1858), and *Sermons on Our Lord Jesus Christ* (1864). He established the *Dublin Review* in 1835. Such was Wiseman's linguistic ability that he said he could talk his way from East Asia to Europe's Atlantic coast. Westminster Cathedral, the focal point of Roman Catholicism in London, was built in his memory. J. D. DOUGLAS

WISHART, GEORGE (c. 1513–1546)
Scottish reformer and martyr

George Wishart was related to the lairds of Pitarrow, Aberdeenshire, Scotland, and may have been a brother of the justice clerk of James V. In 1532 he graduated from the University of Louvain, first out of 118 determinants. He then returned to Scotland, where he taught Greek in Erskine of Dun's school in Montrose, but as his religious views, vigorously expressed, aroused the opposition of the ecclesiastical authorities, he left for England, where he was soon in trouble again for preaching in Bristol against various Roman Catholic doctrines and practices. Having apparently recanted, he then went to Germany and Switzerland, where he translated the *First Helvetic Confession* into English. In 1543 he returned to England as a member of Corpus Christi College, Cambridge.

Shortly afterwards he returned to Scotland with the English ambassadors who had come to arrange a marriage between Queen Mary and Prince Edward, later Edward VI. At that point he may also have become involved in a plot to kidnap and murder Cardinal David Beaton, but nothing came of it. He now began to preach vigorously around Dundee against Roman Catholicism. The ecclesiastical authorities again went into action, forcing the city council to expel him. He therefore left for the southwest of Scotland, where he gained a large following among both the nobility and lay people. The earl of Glencairn was one of his principal supporters.

While in the southwest he heard that the plague had broken out in Dundee, so immediately he returned in order to comfort the dying. While he was doing so, the lairds from the southwest suggested that he should meet them at the end of the summer in Lothian, near Edinburgh, to which he agreed. When he arrived in Lothian, however, the lairds did not appear, and he was befriended by some of the local gentry and by a certain John Knox, who acted as his bodyguard, carrying a two-handed sword.

Notwithstanding this support, Cardinal Beaton persuaded the earl of Bothwell that Wishart should be arrested. Therefore, Wishart was seized at Ormiston shortly after he had told Knox to return to his tutoring duties. Bothwell pretended that he was taking Wishart into protective custody, but once he had him secure, he turned him over to Cardinal Beaton, who had him carried to St. Andrews, where he was tried, convicted of heresy, strangled, and burned, while Beaton watched from a window of his castle. Wishart's martyrdom had a great impact on Scotland. It not only stirred Knox to take up the leadership of the Protestant cause, but it also aroused the Protestant hatred of Beaton and all that he stood for and helped to bring about the murder of Beaton himself.

W. S. REID

WITHERSPOON, JOHN (1723–1794)

Presbyterian minister and educator

Born in the village of Gifford, eastern Scotland, Witherspoon matriculated to the University of Edinburgh at the age of thirteen. He received his M.A. degree in 1739 and in 1743 graduated in divinity. He was licensed to preach in the same year and served as parish minister in Beith (1745–1757) and Paisley (1757–1768). As a minister in Scotland, Witherspoon was part of the Popular Party, a conservative group that advocated purity of doctrine and the rights of local parishioners to choose the minister of their choice. They opposed the liberalizing tendencies of the Moderates, who did not favor lay patronage and emphasized morality over doctrine and politeness in learning, speech, taste, religion, and deportment. In 1754 Witherspoon published his famous *Ecclesiastical Characteristics*, a blistering attack against Moderate ministers whom he characterized as "paganized Christian di-

vines." He became the moderator of the Synod of Glasgow and Ayr in 1758, published three volumes entitled *Essays On Important Subjects* in 1764, and received the degree of D.D. from the University of St. Andrews the same year. After turning down calls to Rotterdam, Dublin, and Dundee, he accepted a call to the presidency of the College of New Jersey (later known as Princeton) in 1768.

Although Witherspoon was the choice of the New Side party of the Presbyterian Church in America, his views proved acceptable to the Old Side and allowed him to exercise a wide influence over the whole Presbyterian organization. His forceful personality and popular teaching made him a leader in both political and religious affairs. Through his leadership the Presbyterian Church was strengthened and divisions were healed, closer ties were achieved with the Congregationalists, and Presbyterian influence was extended. Under his presidency the number of college faculty increased, student enrollment grew, and the college financial status was improved. He introduced into the curriculum philosophy, French, Hebrew, history, and the art of public speaking. More important, he promoted the Scottish Common Sense school of thinking developed by Thomas Reid, which dominated American thinking for nearly a century.

Witherspoon's political career began slowly, being limited at first to local concerns. In 1776 he was chosen to be a delegate to the Continental Congress and arrived in Philadelphia in time to support the acceptance of the Declaration of Independence, becoming the only clergyman to put his signature to it. He served in the Congress almost continuously from 1776 to 1782 and participated in the debates over the Articles of Confederation. In later years he turned his energies toward rebuilding the college, which had suffered a severe setback during the Revolution, and to consolidating the gains within Presbyterianism. During this time he helped to reorganize the Presbyterian Church, doing a large share of the work on catechisms, confessions of faith, directory of worship, and the plan of government and discipline. He also was the leading figure in the establishment of the first General Assembly (1789) and became its first moderator. The last few years of his life were troubled with financial hardships both at the college and in his personal life, the death of his wife, and blindness (during his last two years). He died November 15, 1794, on his farm in Tusculum at the age of seventy-one and was buried in the "President's Lot" in Princeton. C. MITCHELL

WOOLLEY, SIR CHARLES LEONARD (1880–1960)
English archaeologist

Born in London and educated at New College, Oxford University, in 1905 Woolley became assistant keeper of the Ashmolean Museum in Oxford. His archaeological work began that same year, when he excavated in Nubia in partnership with Dr. Randall Maciver. In 1912 he was appointed leader of the British Museum expedition to Carchemish, in northern Syria. This excavation was interrupted by World War I, in which Woolley spent two years (1916–1918) in a Turkish prison camp, but was completed in 1919. In 1922 he began his major excavations at Ur of the Chaldees, in southern Iraq, tracing the history of the site back to its first settlement in 3700 B.C. This continued for thirteen years and yielded highly important documentary evidence concerning Sumerian civilization, particularly the royal cemetery of the first dynasty of Ur (c. 2750–2500 B.C.). From 1937 to 1939, and again from 1946 to 1949, he conducted excavations at Tell Atchana (ancient Alalakh) in southeastern Turkey north of Antioch and unearthed materials of significance for the relationship between the civilizations of Mesopotamia and those of ancient Greece and the Aegean. Woolley, who was knighted in 1935, published his findings in such works as *Ur of the Chaldees* (1929) and *Digging Up the Past* (1930). He is generally regarded as one of the most successful diggers ever to engage in field archaeology because of his flair for choosing the most promising sites and the most productive areas in them. N. V. HOPE

WOOLMAN, JOHN (1720–1772)
Colonial American Quaker who advocated the abolition of slavery

Born in Northampton, New Jersey, Woolman was raised on the family farm. His grandfather had been among the first settlers in Quaker West Jersey, just across the Delaware from the land destined to become the center for Quaker settlement in America—Pennsylvania. As a young man, Woolman moved to Mount Holly, where he worked as a tailor. This trade would support him at times throughout his life. He owned his own tailor shop for a time, but his desire for a deeper spiritual life led him to simplify his life. Deeply pious, he became a recorded minister of the Society of Friends (1743) and for thirty-seven years served as chairman for the quarterly business meeting in Burlington County. He began to travel extensively—thirty-nine trips in twenty-five years—ministering to Quaker communities throughout the Thirteen Colonies. Woolman died of smallpox on a visit to Friends in England, and was buried at York.

His *Journal* reveals a man who desired to follow the "pure leading" of God, undistorted by natural human self-interest. He was conspicuous, even among Quakers, for his intense mystical piety. Woolman's America was a world of economic growth and agricultural expansion. The need for labor brought slaves from Africa. The need for land resulted in war with the Indians. In this world of slavery, Indian abuse, and war, Woolman desired to bring reform. He was concerned that Friends not take part in the injustices that seemed to pervade colonial America. He believed that most, if not all, of society's problems could be traced to the pervasive principle of selfish pragmatism. In remedy, he called his fellow Quakers to live according to the principle of selfless love.

Woolman preached and wrote against slavery during a time when the practice was little questioned, and his testimony caused Quakers of the Philadelphia yearly meeting (1776) to denounce the practice. As a result of his efforts, many Friends, even some in the southern colonies, chose to free their slaves. Woolman also preached and wrote against the abuse of Indians, the ill-treatment of the poor, and conscription and taxation to support the war effort. He was a prophetic voice to Colonial America, but his influence was only significantly felt among the small population of Friends. Yet a century after his death, his writings (*Some Considerations on the Keeping of Negroes* and his *Journal*) made a significant impact upon the abolitionist movement in the nineteenth century. Woolman's call to the deeper spiritual life, the defense of the helpless, and the denunciation of selfishness is for Christians of all centuries. M. R. NORTON

WORDSWORTH, WILLIAM
(1770–1850)
English poet

Wordsworth was born in the beautiful Lake District of northwest England—a setting that deeply affected his personality, his ideas, and his art. By the time he was thirteen he had lost both of his parents and thus came to depend strongly on other family members, especially his sister Dorothy. In 1791 he graduated from Cambridge, though he won no distinctions there. The following year he went to France, where he made friends with the moderate revolutionaries and fell in love with Annette Vallon, a French girl with a Royalist heritage. In the winter of 1792 and 1793 Wordsworth returned to England, hoping to earn money to marry Annette and claim their daughter, Caroline. But it was ten years before they met again, by which time they had grown far apart. Disenchanted with the French Revolution as it grew more and more violent, Wordsworth fell into despair, from which he was healed by the companionship of Dorothy, the friendship with Samuel Taylor Coleridge, and his love of nature and poetry. Wordsworth and Coleridge collaborated on a slender volume of poems, a landmark in English poetry, published in 1798 and titled *Lyrical Ballads*. The poems were clearly romantic in tone, contrasting with the rational spirit of the late eighteenth century. Wordsworth lived a long life and was a prolific writer, but his best poetry was written between 1797 and 1808.

Wordsworth's verse reveals a strong reliance on feeling and emotion, a faith in the simple wisdom of children, a consciousness of mystical insights, a fervent devotion to nature, a love of solitude, and a rejection of materialism. Several early poems give evidences of pantheism, but he was an orthodox member of the Church of England. Some of his best poems are "Tintern Abbey," "Intimations of Immorality," "The Solitary Reaper," "Expostulation and Reply," "The Lucy Poems," "Michael," "The Prelude," and many sonnets. In 1842 he was granted an annual pension by the crown, and from 1843 until his death he was poet laureate. P. M. BECHTEL

WREDE, WILHELM (1859–1906)
New Testament scholar

Born at Buchen, near Bremen, Wrede was educated at the Universities of Leipzig and Göttingen and the Theological Seminary at Loccum. After a pastorate at Langenholzen (1887–1889), he began his teaching career as a privatdozent at Göttingen in 1889. In 1893 he accepted a call to Breslau, serving first as associate, then from 1895 as full professor. He wrote several volumes on New Testament literary and critical problems—for example, *Die Echtheit des Zweiten Thessalonischerbriefe* (*The Genuineness of the Second Epistle to the Thessalonians,* 1903). But his major contributions to the interpretation of the New Testament were two in number. The first is expressed in *Das Messiasgeheimnis in den Evangelien* (*The Messianic Secret in the Gospels,* 1901). In this he maintained that during his lifetime Jesus never claimed to be Messiah. It was only his resurrection that convinced his disciples of his messiahship, which they proceeded to read back into his earlier life. The second contribution is expressed in *Paulus* (1905; English translation, 1907). In this book Wrede argued that Christianity received its essential form largely from Paul's radical transformation of the teaching of Jesus. Both

of Wrede's viewpoints provoked much debate among New Testament scholars.
N. V. HOPE

WRIGHT, GEORGE ERNEST
(1907–1974)
Archaeologist; Old Testament scholar

Born in Zanesville, Ohio, Wright was educated at the College of Wooster (A.B., 1931), McCormick Seminary (B.D., 1934), and Johns Hopkins University (Ph.D., 1937). He taught Old Testament at McCormick Seminary from 1939 to 1958, when he became Parkman Professor of Divinity at Harvard University. Founder and editor of *The Biblical Archaeologist* for twenty-five years, he was president of the American School of Oriental Research from 1966 until his death. Trained in archaeology by W. F. Albright, Wright specialized in the chronological analysis of pottery. The expedition that he conducted in 1956 to biblical Shechem has been described as "the watershed of American expeditions to the Near East"—its methodology becoming the model for future excavations. Wright was also deeply interested in biblical theology, asserting that "biblical theology and biblical archaeology must go hand in hand if we are to comprehend the Bible's meaning." His published works covered both of his fields of interest—for example, *Biblical Archaeology* (1957) and *The Rule of God: Essays in Biblical Theology* (1961). N. V. HOPE

WYCLIFFE, JOHN (c. 1329–1384)
English reformer; Bible translator

A native of Yorkshire, Wycliffe attended Oxford University, where he received a doctorate of theology in 1372. Wycliffe, the most eminent Oxford theologian of his day, and his associates, were the first to translate the entire Bible from Latin into English.

Wycliffe has been called the "Morning Star of the Reformation" because he boldly questioned papal authority, criticized the sale of indulgences (which were supposed to release a person from punishment in purgatory), denied the reality of transubstantia-

tion (the doctrine that the bread and wine are changed into Jesus Christ's actual body and blood during Communion), and spoke out against church hierarchies. The pope reproved Wycliffe for his heretical teachings and asked that Oxford University dismiss him. But Oxford and many government leaders stood with Wycliffe, so he was able to survive the pope's assaults.

Wycliffe believed that the way to prevail in his struggle with the church's abusive authority was to make the Bible available to the people in their own language. Then they could read for themselves how each one of them could have a personal relationship with God through Jesus Christ—apart from any ecclesiastical authority. Wycliffe, with his associates, completed the New Testament around 1380 and the Old Testament in 1382. Wycliffe concentrated his labors on the New Testament, while an associate, Nicholas of Hereford, did a major part of the Old Testament. Wycliffe and his coworkers, unfamiliar with the original Hebrew and Greek, translated the Latin text into English.

After Wycliffe finished the translation work, he organized a group of poor parishioners, known as Lollards, to go throughout England preaching Christian truths and reading the Scriptures in their mother tongue to all who would hear God's word. As a result the Word of God, through Wycliffe's translation, became available to many Englishmen.

Wycliffe was loved and yet hated. His ecclesiastical enemies did not forget his opposition to their power or his successful efforts in making the Scriptures available to all. Several decades after he died. they condemned him for heresy, dug up his body, burned it, and threw his ashes into the Swift River.

One of Wycliffe's close associates, John Purvey (c. 1353–1428), continued Wycliffe's work by producing a revision of his translation in 1388. Purvey was an excellent scholar; his work was very well received by his generation and following generations. Within less than a century, Purvey's revision had replaced the original Wycliffe Bible.
P. M. BECHTEL & P. W. COMFORT

XAVIER, FRANCIS (1506–1552)

A member of the Society of Jesus who
evangelized in the East Indies and Japan

Born in the Spanish part of Navarre, Francis Xavier was the youngest son of a Basque high official, Juan de Yasu (and Juan's wife, Maria). During border struggles between France and Spain, the Xavier family was ruined. Forced to leave the family castle in 1524, Xavier studied law and theology at the University of Paris.

During his eleven years there, Xavier met Ignatius of Loyola, the founder of the Jesuits. Ordained in Venice (1537), Xavier spent his next two years in Italy, serving the poor and helping compile the Jesuit charter to submit to the pope.

Xavier's missionary endeavors began in 1542 at the Portuguese settlement of Goa (India)—source of the lucrative spice trade. He founded a missionary college and aided the native Indians, who were being exploited by unscrupulous merchants. From Goa he proceeded to southeast India, preaching in poor fishing villages, especially among the poor pearl fishers called the Paravars. In 1545 he traveled to Malacca in the Malay peninsula and the Molucca Islands (now part of Indonesia).

At this point, attracted by reports of the sophisticated Japanese culture, Xavier prepared to visit that largely Buddhist country. After returning to Goa in 1548, Xavier set out in 1549 for Japan, and after two years established a Christian community of about two thousand.

Appointed provincial of the flourishing Indian Jesuit society, he returned to Goa in 1552. The huge Chinese empire, however, was the missionary frontier Xavier longed to explore. He left for China but failed to gain admittance to the mainland and died on Shangchuan Island (off the southern coast of mainland China).

Xavier's missionary methods have been criticized for several reasons: his intolerance of the oriental religions; his urging Portuguese King John III to establish the Inquisition in Goa; and his use of government pressure as a proselytizing agency. He is credited, nevertheless, with 700,000 converts—the fruit of methodical mission work and efforts to preach in the vernacular. His unwearied missionary diligence has earned him the reputation of being a great Christian missionary. He was canonized in 1622.

N. V. HOPE

XAVIER, JEROME (1549–1617)

Jesuit missionary

Born at Beire, Navarre, a relative of Francis

Xavier (a famous missionary who was one of the charter members of the Society of Jesus), Jerome Xavier entered the Jesuit order at Alcala, Spain in 1568. In 1581 he embarked on a missionary career in the Orient, serving as rector of the Jesuit house first at Bassein, then at Cochin, and finally at Goa. Two Jesuit missions had been sent to the court of the Mogul emperor Akbar in 1580 and 1591. But when this emperor requested another in 1594, Xavier was appointed to head a delegation of three Jesuit fathers, who arrived the next year at the emperor's court at Lahore, subsequently following him to Agra. For over twenty years Xavier and his colleagues maintained close contact with Akbar, even accompanying him on extensive tours to Kashmir and the Deccan. And they took an equal interest in Jahangir, Akbar's son, who succeeded to the throne in 1605. Though both monarchs expressed an interest in Christianity, neither was willing to convert to it. In 1614 Xavier left the royal court and returned to Goa, where he died in June 1617 as archbishop-designate of Cranganore. He wrote several books that were translated into Persian—such as *The Fountain of Life,* a defense of Christianity against Islam, and *The Mirror of Purity,* a life of Christ. N. V. HOPE

Y

YOUNG, BRIGHAM (1801-1877)

Successor to Joseph Smith as leader of the Mormon church

Born in Whitingham, Vermont, Young had little schooling. He was working as a carpenter in Mendon, New York, when he was given the Book of Mormon. Two years later, he abandoned Methodism for the new sect and joined the movement as a workman at the Kirtland, Ohio, temple site. In 1835 Young became an apostle and rose to chief of the twelve apostles by 1838. He organized the Mormon move from Ohio to Independence, Missouri. Then, following the death of his first wife, he undertook a fifteen-month missionary tour of England. There he composed the first Mormon hymnal, established a church in London, and laid groundwork for his later program of mass emigration.

Young's leadership abilities came to the fore after Joseph Smith was killed in 1844. Upon learning of the "Prophet's" death, Young hurried from New England to Illinois and declared himself Smith's successor, a power grab still considered illegitimate by the Reorganized Latter-Day Saints. Young knew that the Mormons must flee Illinois, a move catalyzed by his arrest in 1846 for harboring counterfeiters. Upon his release, Young led a group to Winter Quarters (near Omaha), and from there launched westward, convinced by a vision that he would recognize the "land of promise" when he saw it. In July 1847 as the caravan of Mormons began their descent into the Great Salt Valley, Young announced, "This is the place."

Young's leadership in Utah was stormy, yet successful. He set up a Perpetual Emigration Fund to bring European converts to Utah, and a General Tithing Office as a kind of internal revenue and banking bureau. Attempts to develop an iron industry failed, as did his Brigham Young Express and Carrying Company, a precursor of the Pony Express. (The company folded when a United States mail contract was suddenly canceled.) When President Buchanan sent twenty-five hundred soldiers to tame the Utah territory, Young raised a three-thousand-man militia to harass the troops and maintain Mormon autonomy. He supervised the temple construction (1863–1867), established the University of Deseret (Utah), and supervised the last leg of the transcontinental railroad in 1869. Young's household numbered twenty-seven wives and fifty-six children. The Mormon church had grown to 140,000 at the time of his death. M. FACKLER

YOUNG, ROBERT (1822–1888)

Scottish biblical scholar; orientalist

Born in Edinburgh, Young found his early prospects dimmed by the loss of his father. As a Free Church of Scotland member, Young was actively associated with Thomas Chalmers's outreach to the working classes of Edinburgh. He was apprenticed to a printer and showed such diligence that by 1847 he had his own printing and bookselling business. He took naturally to oriental languages and published study aids to the Old Testament. For five years from 1856 he was in India as superintendent of the mission press at Surat. He also visited the United States, but most of his life was spent in the Scottish capital. His linguistic erudition was immense (he even spoke Finnish), and the precision of his mind is reflected in his monumental work, *Analytical Concordance to the Holy Bible* (1879). Generations of Bible students have benefited immeasurably from this work, which was many years in preparation. Its aim, in Young's words: that "readers . . . may give themselves more to the study of the original Scriptures, which have 'God for their Author, Truth without mixture of Error for their Matter, and Salvation for their End.'"

J. D. DOUGLAS

YUN, BARON TCHI-HO (1865–1945)

Korean nobleman; "father of the Southern Methodist mission in Korea"

As son of Korea's War Minister, Yun was born to power, but political upheaval forced his father into exile, and in 1885 Yun escaped to Shanghai, China. He entered the Anglo-Chinese College, where he became a Christian in 1887. From 1888 to 1893 he studied in America at Emory and Vanderbilt. Before returning to China he gave $250 to rouse Southern Methodists to start a mission to Korea. He became vice-minister of education, provincial governor, and briefly editor of the reform-minded newspaper the *Independent*.

When Japan invaded Korea in 1905 he left politics to found the Anglo-Korean School (1906) and join the Southern Methodist mission. He was imprisoned by the Japanese (1912–1915) on trumped-up charges. He then served as General-Secretary of the Korean YMCA (1915–1920). In 1930 he helped to unite the Northern and Southern Methodist missions and found the independent Korean Methodist Church. He died not long after he had been called from retirement to be the first Korean president (1941–1944) of Chosen Christian College (now Yonsei University). S. H. MOFFETT

Z

ZACHARIAS (died 752)

Last of the Greek popes, 741–752

A native of Calabria, Zacharias gained literary fame by translating the *Dialogues* of Pope Gregory I (590–604) into Greek in a version that was widely read in the Christian East. He also engaged in vigorous diplomacy designed to strengthen the ecclesiastical and political authority of the papacy. In the controversy over image-worship, in two important letters to the Eastern emperor Constantine V (Copronymos), Zacharias denounced the imperial iconoclastic policy and urged the restoration of the sacred images that the emperor had banned. In Italy Zacharias persuaded Liutprand, the powerful Lombard king (712–744), to return the four cities that he had taken from the Duchy of Rome and to desist from attacking Ravenna; thus he achieved peace with the Lombards. With the Frankish realm Zacharias enjoyed cordial relations, principally through Boniface (680–754), whose missionary activity in Frankland he ardently supported. In 751 Zacharias agreed to the deposition of the figurehead Merovingian king Childeric III, and he commissioned Boniface to crown as the legitimate successor the majordomo Pepin III, thus inaugurating the Carolingian dynasty and creating the Carolingian-papacy alliance. N. V. HOPE

ZAHN, THEODOR (1838–1933)

New Testament and patristic scholar

Born at Mors, near Essen, and educated at Erlangen, Basle, and Berlin (1854–1858), Zahn began his teaching career in 1868 as privatdozent at Göttingen, where he was promoted to an associate professorship in 1871. In 1877 he accepted a chair at Kiel, but a year later he transferred to Erlangen. In 1888 he went to Leipzig, but he returned in 1892 as professor of pedagogics and New Testament exegesis at Erlangen, where he remained until his retirement in 1909. Zahn contributed to almost every aspect of New Testament scholarship. He edited a New Testament commentary for which he wrote on seven books (Matthew, 1909; Luke, 1913; John, 1908; Acts, two volumes, 1919–1921; Romans, 1910; Galatians, 1905; and Revelation, two volumes, 1924–1926). He published twelve volumes embodying his studies on the New Testament canon: *History of the New Testament Canon* (two volumes, 1888–1892) and monographs in the series *Investigations into the History of the New Testament Canon* (ten volumes, 1881–1920), which contained much original work. In the patristic field he authored *Marcellus von Ancyra* (1867) and *Ignatius von Antiochen* (1873); and along with Adolf Harnack and Otto von Gebhardt he edited

the works of the apostolic fathers (Major, 1875–1878, and Minor, 1877). Very learned and thorough in scholarship, Zahn was conservative in his critical viewpoint; for example, he maintained that the fourth Gospel was the work of the beloved disciple, and he contended for the Pauline authorship of such disputed epistles as 1 and 2 Timothy and Titus. Zahn authored a two-volume *Introduction to the New Testament* (1897–1899; English translation, three volumes, 1909).
N. V. HOPE

ZEISBERGER, DAVID (1721–1808)
Moravian missionary to American Indians

Born at Zauchental in Moravia and reared at Herrnhut, Zeisberger went to Georgia in 1738 and then on to the new Moravian base in Pennsylvania. While studying the Iroquoian languages with the Onondagas, he was imprisoned by the New York officials. He spent more than ten years with the Iroquois between 1746 and 1763, but his principal ministry was to the Delawares. Zeisberger was one of the most prolific authors and translators of Christian literature for the Indians, producing numerous works in the Iroquoian dialects and Delaware. He led the Christian Delawares and Mohegan refugees in the building of Friedenhutten on the Wyalusing in 1763, and then as white-settler aggression grew intense he led them by stages across Pennsylvania and finally in 1772 into the Muskingum country of Ohio, then thought to be far beyond white contact. Half a dozen Christian villages prospered, but the British troops took the missionaries captive to Detroit, and during their absence American militia slaughtered all the Christians they could round up. Zeisberger shepherded the remaining Christians at various locations in northern Ohio and Ontario. After the Revolution the Moravian authorities sent him back to eastern Ohio to reestablish a town, but it was far too late. P. BEAVER

ZIEGENBALG, BARTHOLOMEUS (1682–1719)
Missionary to India

Ziegenbalg of Pulsnitz, Saxony, was the founder of the Danish-Halle Mission at Tranquebar, India, in 1706. Trained at Halle by August Hermann Francke, he was sent by King Frederick IV to the Danish colony. Opposed by the commandant, he was even imprisoned for four months. Ziegenbalg gained mastery of Tamil in eight months. He translated Luther's Small Catechism, the New Testament (1715), the Old Testament through Ruth, and other literature into Tamil. He also established a Tamil press. He set hymns to Tamil lyrics and German chorales, and he introduced the singing of Psalms. He began Portuguese, Danish, and Tamil day schools, a girls' school, and a Tamil "free charity" boarding school (1715). A seminary for catechists was also opened in 1716. As new personnel arrived the mission expanded, and the king appointed Ziegenbalg provost. Most unusual at that time of intense European narrowness, he came to a deep appreciation of Tamil culture. He did research into Tamil philosophy and religion and wrote a number of books of high quality. Support came from the British Society for the Promotion of Christian Knowledge, the king, and the German pietists. P. BEAVER

ZINZENDORF, NICHOLAUS LUDWIG COUNT VON (1700–1760)
Catalyst in the formation of the modern Moravian Church; pioneer of both ecumenism and mission work

Born in Dresden (Germany) into Austrian nobility, Zinzendorf was raised by his grandmother, who was a strong supporter of the Pietist movement. At the age of six Zinzendorf became aware of Christ's love and devoted his life to the Savior. He began his formal education at the Halle Pädagogium, a Pietist center (1710–1716). He delivered a valedictory there on the unity of Christian believers. Continuing his education at Wittenberg University (1716–1719), he desired to study theology but was pressed by family to study law for a governmental career. At Wittenberg he unsuccessfully attempted a reconciliation between the centers of Pietism and Lutheranism. Zinzendorf finished his education with foreign travel. From 1719 to 1720 his grand tour took him through Germany, Holland, and France, where he was introduced to nobility. He took the opportunity to meet with religious leaders of Reformed theology and Roman Catholicism, as well as with groups of Christians outside the established churches.

In 1721 he became the king's judicial counselor at Dresden. It was here that he opened his home for meetings to provide spiritual edification for those seeking it. He also published *The Dresden Socrates* to reach those outside the formal church. This publication drew great opposition from authorities. In 1722 Zinzendorf married the Countess Erdmuth Dorothea Von Reuss, a union that produced twelve children, although eight died in infancy. In the same year Zinzendorf purchased a large estate, which included the village of Berthelsdorf near the Bohemian frontier in Saxony. He invited persecuted believers to settle on his land. Soon Christians from different countries and religious backgrounds, among whom were descendants of the ancient Unitas Fratum of the Bohemian Brethren, sought refuge here. A colony was established and named "Herrnhut" (the Lord's Watch). Discord arose in Herrnhut due to disagreements over doctrinal and cultural matters. Zinzendorf intervened in 1727 and established common regulations by which all could live, and thus peace was restored. He also resigned his governmental post that year and moved to Herrnhut in the summer.

During this time Zinzendorf came upon a copy of the last meeting of the ancient Bohemian Brethren and was stirred by their vision of Christian love and unity. He then read the document to those at Herrnhut. The descendants of that ancient church along with Zinzendorf vowed to restore and preserve what existed among the Bohemian Brethren. They held a Christianity of the heart, proclaiming that the experience of faith and love toward the Savior was common to all who believed and was indeed the basis of unity.

Zinzendorf wanted the community to be members of the Lutheran church, but they were against it. In order to avoid friction, Zinzendorf became an ordained Lutheran minister so that the community was acknowledged to be part of the Lutheran church. The members of Herrnhut nevertheless also held their own meetings. The community life and the spiritual life were blended into a single unit at Herrnhut. Singing was incorporated into all facets of community life, as was Scripture reading. Zinzendorf was instrumental in providing devotional material and writing hymns as well as forming small groups for the mutual care of the believers. Prayer around the clock was started at Herrnhut and continued for one hundred years.

In 1731, while visiting the King of Denmark, Zinzendorf met a slave named Anthony from the Danish West Indies. Anthony was invited to Herrnhut, and there he spoke of the condition of the slaves in the West Indies. Some in Herrnhut were moved to visit the slaves and work among them to both help them and bring them the gospel. This was the start of the Moravian mission work.

The community, and especially Zinzendorf, attracted attention and also opposition. In 1732 a political investigation was undertaken to determine whether inhabitants of Herrnhut had been enticed by Zinzendorf to leave Moravia. The authorities also tried to determine what doctrine or practice caused so much opposition to Herrnhut. All was found to be in order. In 1734 Zinzendorf underwent a theological examination and was given a certificate of Lutheran Orthodoxy and later formally recognized as a minister by the theology faculty in Tübingen. Finally in 1736, because he was accused of stealing tenants from other landlords and because of intolerance towards nontraditional forms of Christianity, Zinzendorf was banished from Saxony. This action prompted Zinzendorf to travel for nearly ten years, many times on foot, visiting Germany, Switzerland, Holland, England, and America among other places. He was accompanied by the Pilgrim Congregation, a band of believers who participated in the establishment of new settlements after the pattern of Herrnhut.

One such settlement, called Herrnhaug, was visited in 1738 by John Wesley, who remarked, "Oh when shall this Christianity cover the earth, as waters cover the sea." Zinzendorf trained people to go out as an evangelical and ecumenical witness. Most of the expenses incurred by this work were met by him. In 1737 he was ordained as a bishop of the Moravian church by Daniel Jablonsky, the Court preacher in Berlin and the only surviving bishop of the ancient Bohemian Brethren. Another aspect of Zinzendorf's work was dubbed "Diaspora," a term borrowed from 1 Peter 1:1. Believers would go out in pairs to find those within and without the established churches who were longing for deeper spiritual fellowship.

Societies were then formed that read Moravian literature and held services along the Moravian pattern, but no formal connection was ever promoted with the church. Communion was taken in the denomination to which the society members belonged. Zinzendorf's idea was to revitalize those within the established churches by providing them with fresh spiritual food and promoting a oneness based upon a common faith. He realized that membership in institutional churches did not make one a Christian and that the true church had its members everywhere, within and without the organized churches. The Diaspora was to bring together those who belonged to this invisible true church and create a visible expression for the world to see. Zinzendorf wanted to see "ecclesiolas" (little true churches) living a life of Christian service and worship based upon a common faith and heartfelt experience. Zinzendorf drew inspiration from John 11:52, where the Lord stated his purpose of gathering together into one the children of God who were scattered abroad. Zinzendorf did not advocate either a union or a dissolution of the established churches, nor the start of a new denomination to effect this purpose. He felt that each congregation had some treasure to offer and that believers should draw from whatever good each denomination had. The "ecclesiolas" would exist alongside, and not in competition with, the established churches and, in theory, would serve to benefit them.

Evangelistic work went hand-in-hand with the settlements, and the Moravians in practice became a missionary church. As believers went to foreign lands they were expected to work to pay their own travel expenses and support themselves in the field. Zinzendorf always thought people should learn the dignity of laboring with their hands. He visited St. Thomas from 1738 to 1739 and was in America from 1741 to 1743 in hopes that he might carry out his work without interference from the established churches. He relinquished his rank and title and traveled as a Lutheran pastor under one of his other legitimate names, Herr Von Thurnstein. Unfortunately this move aroused suspicion. He worked among several tribes of Indians and preached in Reformed and Lutheran churches in Pennsylvania, as well as holding services in his home in Philadelphia. He held several conferences to promote unity, but they failed to produce the effect he hoped they would.

In 1746 Zinzendorf went to England to clarify the position of the Moravian Church as it pertained to the Church of England. They were not to be a new denomination but a spiritual influence with the established church. Zinzendorf was allowed to return to Saxony in 1747 but returned to England again for an extended period (1749–1755), where he propagated his ecumenical vision. An act of Parliament in 1749 recognized the Moravian Episcopal Church.

During the 1740s Zinzendorf passed through the most controversial period of his life. Always an original thinker, he incorporated nonconventional terms into his preaching and hymns that many considered unsuitable. The settlements too at times displayed a great deal of emotionalism and mysticism that was unsavory to some. In 1755 he returned to Herrnhut to spend the remainder of his days occupied with pastoral care.

During his lifetime Zinzendorf strove to bring Christians of all persuasions together on the ground of a common saving faith as a visible expression of Christian love to the world. Although his vision was not embraced by the traditional churches, many believers did live and spread this ecumenical gospel through the Moravian settlements, the Diaspora, and the Pilgrims' congregations. To feed the flock Zinzendorf wrote two thousand hymns as well as devotionals for all aspects of the church and mission life. He also produced a children's Bible, a modern language Bible, and a Bible with prefaces and summaries at a price affordable to the very poor. His stress upon the believers' direct experience of Christ gave vitality to all they were involved in. Zinzendorf's practice of ecumenism, mission work, and heartfelt Christian experience are his major contributions to the Church. His works, written and spoken, are chiefly in German. One volume in English, *Nine Public Lectures on Important Subjects in Religion* (1746), edited and translated by G. W. Forell (1973), provides a good representation of Zinzendorf's views. T. FIRAK

ZWEMER, SAMUEL MARINUS (1867–1952)
Apostle to Islam

Born in Vriesland, Michigan, Zwemer was educated at Hope College, Michigan (A.B., 1887), and New Brunswick Seminary (B.D., 1890). Ordained as a missionary by the Classis of Iowa of the Reformed Church in America, in 1890, along with James Cantine, he founded the Arabian Mission, making his headquarters first in Basra and then on the island of Bahrein. In 1894 this mission was taken over by the Mission Board of the Reformed Church in America. In 1913, at the request of the United Presbyterian Mission in Egypt, Zwemer accepted a call to move to Cairo (Egypt) and became an itinerant missionary to Muslims, not on a local but on a world scale. Between then and 1929 he visited many Christian missions across the Muslim world, making valuable contributions in South Africa and the Netherlands East Indies (now Indonesia). In 1929 he became professor of missions and the his-

tory of religion at Princeton Theological Seminary, retiring in 1936. Zwemer founded the quarterly *Moslem World* in 1911 and edited it until 1947. He was the author of fifty books, dealing with various aspects of Christian truth and with Christian-Muslim relations.

Zwemer was a most unusual person. He had the mind of a scholar and the heart of an evangelist, and to the end he maintained a perfect balance of the two. He was without doubt the greatest missionary statesman to the Muslim world during his sixty-year ministry. N. V. HOPE

ZWINGLI, HULDRYCH (1484–1531)
Swiss reformer

Born at Wildhaus in the mountainous Toggenburg, Zwingli was the son of the village mayor. He studied at Basel, Bern, Vienna, and then at Basel again, where he graduated with a B.A. in 1504 and an M.A. in 1506. At Basel he absorbed the teaching of Thomas Wyttenbach on Scripture and justification and also became the friend of the humanist Glareanus and his future supporter Leo Jud. Erasmus was his great hero at this period.

Ordained in 1506, Zwingli served for ten years in the parish of Glarus. Here he proved to be a good pastor and an able preacher. He continued his humanist studies, keeping up his Greek and trying to teach himself Hebrew. In 1513 and 1515 he served in the papal armies as chaplain to the Glarus mercenaries. His experiences led him to oppose the mercenary system; he was especially in opposition to French recruiting. Due to the resultant uproar, he accepted a new post at Einsiedeln in 1516.

The brief stay at Einsiedeln was important for two reasons. First, Zwingli had the chance to reach a wider audience when he preached to the many pilgrims to the shrine. Second, he was able to immerse himself in the Greek New Testament, from which he gained not only a personal understanding of justification but also a strong sense of the supremacy of Scripture over its human interpretation.

The turning point for Zwingli came in 1518, when he was called to Zurich as "people's priest." After being at the point of death in a severe outbreak of plague, he started his reforming program by persuading the city council to judge religious issues only by Scripture. Based on Zwingli's expository preaching on the New Testament, radical changes came rapidly between 1522 and 1525: a translation of the Bible began, the Lenten fast and celibacy of the clergy ended, and the city council broke with the diocese of Constance and adopted Zwingli's provocative Sixty-Seven Articles (1523). Next came the dissolving of the monasteries, the removal of images, the translating and simplifying of the church services, the destruction of the minster organ, and the reorganization of the minster school. The climax was reached in 1525, when a plain Communion, or Thanksgiving, replaced the Latin Mass.

Expansion and conflict followed the reconstruction in Zurich. By means of reforming friends and through the use of disputations, Zwingli was able to extend his theological and practical reforms to the important cities of Bern, Basel, and Schaffhausen, to the lesser centers of St. Gall and Glarus, and also to the city of Constance. At home, however, his more zealous supporters, who wanted even more radical reformation, brought about a break in 1525 when they set up their own "gathered" church and the council took steps to suppress the movement. In 1525 an unfortunate rift also developed between Zwingli and Luther over the nature of Christ's presence at the Lord's Supper. Literary debate merely widened the gap, and although Prince Philip of Hesse, in the interests of unity, tried to bring about agreement at the Colloquy of Marburg (1529), no solution could be reached.

Failure to achieve an alliance with the Lutherans left Zwingli concerned about the political security of Zurich and its Swiss associates. To counter the immediate threat of the Forest Cantons that were rejecting reform, he advocated a preventative strike, the First War of Cappel, which achieved its objective without bloodshed. He then looked abroad to France and Venice for religious and political support. When these overtures failed, he pressed for further action against the Forest Cantons, but lack of support for Zwingli gave these the initiative, and in the Second War of Cappel Zurich suffered defeat and Zwingli himself was killed (1531).

Although constantly engaged in practical business, Zwingli still snatched time for hastily composed but vigorous and original writing. Along with his Articles, the *Commentary on True and False Religion* (1525) constituted his most comprehensive statement. Other works that call for notice are his *Clarity and Certainty of Scripture* (1522), *Baptism* (1525), *Eucharist* (1525), *Divine and Human Righteousness*, and *Providence*. He summarized his teaching in the *Fidei Ratio* of 1530, prepared for the Diet of Augsburg, and his *Exposition of the Faith* (1531), written in an attempt to win over Francis I to the Reformation.

Zwingli has often been portrayed as little more than a reforming humanist in his thinking. He certainly had an intellectual bent and favored a rational style of argument, but his works are marked by increasing theological profundity as they come under biblical and Augustinian influence. Thus he moved away from his original suspicions of infant baptism as he considered the implications of the divine covenant and election and examined the New Testament meaning of baptism in relation to water, teaching, and the Holy Spirit. His original view of the Lord's Supper also underwent modifications, which prepared the way for the teaching of his successor Heinrich Bullinger and the later accord with John Calvin in the Zurich Consensus of 1548. Furthermore, Zwingli found in holy Scripture not a mere textbook of divine truth, but the powerful work of God that accomplishes what God wills and by which the Holy Spirit brings light and life to those who read it with humility and prayer.

Although he worked in the shadow of Luther and his sphere of action was only a small city-state, Zwingli made a contribution to the Reformation that should not be disparaged. He undoubtedly shared many of the deepest concerns of Luther, but he offered an alternative style of reform that was much more radical in both thought and practice. He also succeeded in extending the Reformation in this form to a good part of German-speaking Switzerland, and by way of Bern it was then taken up by Calvin in Geneva, received by a new impress, and thus acheived international status. Apart from his contribution in his own immediate area, Zwingli was in fact the pioneer without whom Reformed and Presbyterian theology and order could not have developed in the way they did. G. BROMILEY